METAL
THE DEFINITIVE GUIDE

METAL

THE DEFINITIVE GUIDE

HEAVY·NWOBH·PROGRESSI
THRASH·DEATH·BLAC
GOTHIC·DOOM·N

Garry Sharpe-Young

METAL
THE DEFINITIVE GUIDE

Garry Sharpe-Young

A Jawbone Book

First Edition 2007

Published in the UK and the USA by Jawbone Press

2a Union Court

20-22 Union Road

London SW4 6JP

England

www.jawbonepress.com

ISBN: 978-1-906002-01-5

EDITOR Joel McIver

CONSULTANT Bernard Doe

DESIGN Paul Cooper Design

JACKET Balley Design Ltd

Printed by Colorprint Offset Ltd (Hong Kong)

1 2 3 4 5 11 10 09 08 07

CONTENTS

continued over

CONTENTS continued

FOREWORD
BY ROB HALFORD OF JUDAS PRIEST

Almost four decades after its beginnings in Birmingham, England, in the late 1960s, the great journey of heavy metal continues!

Garry Sharpe-Young's book takes you on that journey. Here you will experience all the bands that have taken part and played significant roles in the growth and endurance of metal.

When Judas Priest formed and began to explore and experiment with metal, the world was a very different place. We had the pleasure and the challenge of introducing our unique style of music to the uninitiated – and all these years later it's a thrill and a pleasure to see and hear where those early adventures have led us all.

The variety and scope of heavy metal in today's scene is quite remarkable. Whatever your particular choice might be in the bands you enjoy, they are covered in depth throughout this comprehensive book.

One of the many things I love about metal is the way it has been able to cover so many territories in lyrical expression – and as a lyricist, it is fascinating for me to witness the contents and approaches writers seek to display. As it should be, there are no limits to what can and must be said – from diabolic extremes to direct observations about society on a simple statement: all topics are screamed out with passion and conviction in words and music.

Every band that's here carries that virtue – we are all connected by our love and fervent attitude towards all things metal!
So there you have it. Whether you were part of this tremendous story at its conception or you got on board along the way, to those of you who are now about to go 'freewheel burning', the worldwide metal community welcomes you.

So, heads down, start reading and banging – and see you at the end of the journey – whenever that might be!

Rob Halford
'The Metal God' 2007

INTRODUCTION

This is the bit you would normally skip. You're into heavy metal – *real* heavy metal – and so its roots and origins are common knowledge to you. Ingrained, accepted, dogmatically drilled in.

You're thinking: just get me to the music. I don't want to hear all that again. We all know that heavy metal came from the blues, we know that Willie Dixon, Muddy Waters, and B.B. King kicked the whole thing off, that white guys amped it a bit louder, that Jimi Hendrix twisted it into new shapes, and then Jimmy Page added malevolence to the mix and ... eureka! Heavy metal.

The trouble is, not only are you bored of the predictable old yarn but, secretly, deep in your ironclad heart, you know it to be wrong. All the books, all the potted histories, all the websites, regurgitate this tired, hoary mantra as a stock introduction.

Wake up. Smell the glove. It's leather and studded.

Music, like any creative force, evolves faster than any business or media constrictions can ever hope to place upon it. Heavy metal is about as close to the blues as you are to the first mud-skipping fish that crawled out of a cretaceous bog. You can map the DNA and prove the path, but you have to acknowledge that some rather mind-blowing changes took place along the way. The blues is a proud standalone musical force. It has its roots firmly planted in slavery and historical oppression. All of this is quite alien to heavy metal, a product of its age that inhabits realms far removed from reality.

In the 1960s, Britain was awash with blues devotees, and their enthusiasm spawned some of the mightiest names in the rock business. Jazz, too, had its ardent followers, while skiffle and folk played an important role. Bands such as The Yardbirds, Cream, The Who, and Fleetwood Mac took a precious and purist approach to playing blues. On both sides of the Atlantic, with Blue Cheer, Iron Butterfly, and Steppenwolf pitching in, white men amplified the blues. Turning a dial was hardly the greatest of innovations.

Two key figures pushed the blues near to breaking point – James Patrick Page and James Marshall Hendrix. 'Little' Jimmy Page, as he was known, had soaked up every conceivable musical influence on the London session scene. Having absorbed all possible styles, Page embellished his influences with grandeur and mysticism. It didn't take long from Led Zeppelin's first album of purloined blues workouts to the majesty of the fourth to see the guitarist straining the blues bubble to its maximum yield.

Jimi Hendrix, too, had sucked in every facet of blues, rock'n'roll, and R&B with his formative tryouts in clubs, where he went along as Jimmy James. When the cosmic axis aligned, Hendrix took his stockpile of sound scripture and moulded it into a completely new art form. Guitarists marvelled at the extraordinary noises he was able to wring out of his guitar. This was blues at its absolute limit.

Through different routes, Page and Hendrix took the blues to the very edge of the abyss and stared down – but didn't jump. Out there was the unknown. It was cold, uninviting and dangerous. Out there it was black.

"Black Sabbath absolutely invented heavy metal. I've read lots of essays and suchlike about tracing it all back further and further. It's as though these writers want to claim the source, a bit like Dr. Livingstone and the source of the Nile. But, as a purist metal musician, I can tell you – it's Black Sabbath." **ROB HALFORD**

"We didn't really know what we were doing. We had been through the pop, the blues, and everything else, but when we started putting our own music together as the four of us, something else just happened. I think, looking back, it might have been the fact that we had no notions about making our music popular. It was all very natural. Geezer coming up with the name Black Sabbath just put the icing on the cake." **TONY IOMMI**

Recorded history is a product of its age. In the 1970s, writers' own experiences swayed them into falling back a few decades in order to justify the presence of metal. Successive tracts have somewhat lazily repeated this, ad infinitum.

We're now living in a generation when bands throw out a dizzying range of influences. As diverse as the genre is, metal needs to be recognised as its own entity, not the by-product of another strain.

While we're at it, recognise that this book is about Metal with a capital M. Ask AC/DC, Aerosmith, Kiss, Bon Jovi, Rush, or Def Leppard if they are metal – you'll get a resounding "No!" Believe me, I've asked them all. Motörhead? Well, Lemmy is right about most things – except one.

Garry Sharpe-Young, JANUARY 2007
www.rockdetector.com

WHEN YOU USE THIS BOOK...

... please bear in mind that in compiling the discographies, we concentrated on listing the key albums and important singles. (In the discography listings, album titles are in CAPITAL LETTERS; all other releases are in Title Case.)

Where a compilation is essential, it has been included, but the majority of such releases had to be omitted. In the interests of sanity, we have focused on US and UK catalogue numbers and did not have space for worldwide data.

In a few instances where catalogue numbers in discographies could not be determined, we have indicated this with 'cnu', which means catalogue number unknown. Some releases that at press time were forthcoming have been marked as 'catalogue number tba', which means to be announced. Please be aware that all these proposed releases are subject to cancellations or delays. That's about it.

HEAVY
METAL

ROCK in the 1970s was the preserve of the elite, with students pontificating on the merits of overblown and self-aggrandising bastions of art-rock such as Emerson Lake & Palmer, Yes, Pink Floyd and Genesis. At the more rustic end of the spectrum, bands like Nazareth, Uriah Heep, Led Zeppelin, Thin Lizzy, UFO and Deep Purple played loud and hard – but steadfastly refused to extract themselves from the blues. Many of these artists also openly pursued progressive and even pop audiences. In terms of sheer power, AC/DC took rock to the very edge, without once hinting at metal. The 1970s were akin to a Jurassic era for rock music and, while the likes of Zep, Purple, Grand Funk, Kiss and Aerosmith paraded their platinum wares, with heavy metal a dirty word for much of the decade, one band – Black Sabbath – wallowed in the fetid swamps of cultdom.

By the middle of the decade, acts such as Germany's Scorpions were starting to make their presence felt. There were many unsung pioneers – bands that failed to capitalise on cult albums, or acts such as Budgie who put out a stream of punishing proto-metal riffology that the world failed to register. Motörhead, too, had their opening output ignored, until the NWOBHM movement (see Chapter Two) sucked them into its current.

At the very epicentre of heavy metal, Birmingham's own Judas Priest shook off a dodgy debut in 1974's Rocka Rolla to relaunch themselves as a full-blown heavy metal machine. A triptych of malevolence wrought into music – Sad Wings Of Destiny, Sin After Sin and Stained Class –preceded the earth-shaking Killing Machine. Singer Rob Halford stole into the secretive S&M world and emerged clad in the leather and studs that would visually define an entire epoch.

As the 1970s headbutted the 1980s, metal suffered a near-cataclysmic blow as Black Sabbath went into a tailspin. Two dodgy albums would push Ozzy Osbourne into self-doubt and ultimately exile. Thankfully, Ozzy returned with another innovator, Randy Rhoads, while Sabbath themselves breathed new life into tired lungs with the promotion of one of the greatest singers of the age, Ronnie James Dio.

These, then, were the acts that defined the blueprint for heavy metal. What followed were, in truth, variations on the same, lent character by individual talents and obsessions. Like a mighty oak, the genre weathered every storm, every fad and every fashion. Today, heavy metal stands prouder than ever.

BLACK SABBATH
THE PIONEERS OF HEAVY METAL

REGARDED BY MOST AS *the* original heavy metal band, Black Sabbath have an overbearing presence on the international metal scene that cannot be overestimated. Much more than amassing a platinum and gold disc collection that equates to over 100 million records sold, this unassuming Aston quartet pioneered an entirely new branch of the rock evolutionary tree, achieving nothing less than mutating rock music into heavy metal.

Before Black Sabbath, "heavy" music was merely blues amped just that bit louder and, in truth, most high status bands offered a really rather polite, even timid inkling of what was to come. Jimi Hendrix, Cream, Blue Cheer, Iron Butterfly and Led Zeppelin had taken their craft to its "progressive" outer limits. However, these acts held on steadfastly to the blues, not daring to take a leap into the void. Black Sabbath, by combination of unique talent, accident and blind ignorance, severed all the safety lines, took a flying leap of imagination, and in doing so ushered in a brave new age.

With their chosen doom/occult themes initially steered by bassist and songwriter Geezer Butler, the band's first crop of albums, the "famous five", impose an enormous legacy upon the heavy metal scene. Within these monumental slabs of metal perfection, guitarist Tony Iommi laid down riffs with the same authority and gravitas as Moses laying down commandments. Iommi's blues tradition, still redolent in his supremely fluid solo work, is starkly absent in riffs that are almost mechanically

charged. If there are seven wonders of the metal world, five of them belong to Black Sabbath: 1970's *Black Sabbath* and *Paranoid*, issued in February and September respectively, 1971's *Master Of Reality*, 1972's *Volume 4*, and *Sabbath Bloody Sabbath* in 1973. There is also a persuasive argument for adding a sixth to that list in 1980's resurrective *Heaven And Hell*.

While many musicians of the day manufactured sanitised tunes aimed at the heart and the charts, Iommi's spartan riffs only appealed to the deepest, loneliest recesses of the soul. In a world where the hippy ideals of peace and love had recently and spectacularly failed, Black Sabbath found a teenage audience numbed by disillusion and duly shepherded an entire generation into willing oblivion.

Black Sabbath – initially the core quartet of vocalist Ozzy Osbourne, guitarist Tony Iommi, bassist Geezer Butler and drummer Bill Ward – would incorporate over 30 musicians during the band's career. Chapter one closed in early 1979 as the band effectively splintered and became the sole property of Iommi. (He legally gained the full title in 1985). From here, American singer Ronnie James Dio pulled the group out of a creative nadir and back into platinum territory with 1980's *Heaven And Hell*. Sadly, this second phase only produced two sterling studio albums and one haphazard live outing before Iommi was left alone to face a period of flux and confusion, eventually given some stability by singer Tony Martin but seeing an ever-fluid ebb and flow of players in and out of the ranks. Finally, the original four reunited to reclaim their status by topping the roving, and all-conquering, Ozzfest events.

Until early 1979, Black Sabbath was fronted by the irrepressible figure of Ozzy Osbourne, equal parts self-styled 'Prince of Darkness/Daftness'.

A BIT OF FINGER

When the four musicians got together for the first time in August 1968, Tony Iommi was still coming to terms with an accident that very nearly put paid not only to the guitarist's career but possibly heavy metal as we know it. The tragic slip had, rather ironically, occurred on the very last day of his employment, with the next day being his scheduled big step into a career as a full-time professional musician: a tour of Germany had even been lined up. Just prior to this incident, his first real band unit had been The Rockin' Chevrolets, a sharp-suited rock'n'roll quintet with the guitarist playing alongside vocalist Neil Cressin, second guitarist Alan Meredith, bass player Dave Whaddley and drummer Pat Pegg.

"I was working a guillotine and sliced off the tops of two of my fingers. My fingers got caught in a machine and I lost the ends of the ring and middle finger on my fretboard hand [his right – Tony is left-handed]. I guess I lost concentration, as it was my last day at the job too. It was severe, because the doctors I saw told me that there was nothing they could do and I would not be able to play the guitar again. It really was devastating, because I had already made up my mind that I was going to become a full-time musician. I saw a lot of doctors and they all said the same thing. It was very depressing. I really didn't want to do anything else."

It was here that Iommi's perseverance with hand-made plastic fingertips, ingeniously crafted from a melted detergent bottle, gave him hope that he could perform once again. Heavy metal's most inspirational guitarist drew his own fortitude from the acclaimed gypsy jazz guitarist Django Reinhardt, a deft and innovative musician who had suffered a similar fate to that of Iommi.

"A friend of mine at work persuaded me to carry on, actually. I had basically tried and given up, but one day he played me this record by Django Reinhardt. I'd never heard him before but people called him the Jimi Hendrix of jazz guitar. I thought my friend was being quite cruel, because here he was, playing me this amazing guitar playing to someone whose career as a guitarist was over! Then he told me that I was going to play again, that everything was going to be OK. I was actually quite angry with him, but that's when he told me about Django's accident. He had crippled his hand when he was just 18. I couldn't believe he could play like that when his injuries were actually far worse than mine. He only had two fingers left – and if he could do that with his handicap, I really had no excuse."

Django Reinhardt's injuries resulted from a fire in his gypsy caravan home on November 2nd 1928. The heat from the blaze destroyed the function of his tendons, curling his fingers inwards and leaving him with just two operational digits. Resourcefully, the young Belgian re-learned the basic principles and invented an entirely new style of playing, soloing with just two fingers, using his damaged digits for dragging and barring, and employing thumb octaves and singular phrasings. In similar fashion, Iommi went back to the drawing board.

"At first I tried to swap around and play right-handed, but all my instincts were wrong, so that just didn't work at all. I then thought about playing with three fingers, just like Django played with two, so I taped my ring and middle fingers together and tried that for a bit. After that I started to make the plastic tips. I tried to make them like thimbles so they would sit on the ends comfortably. They took quite a bit of work – lots of sculpting and sanding down to get them just the right shape and size. Well, that was OK, but there was no grip really – so that was my next problem to get solved. I thought leather would fix that. That took some time too, because the leather strips needed shaping and I had to oil them so they would grip the strings."

Iommi's custom-made fingertips went through various prototype stages: his home-made melted-bottle devices acting as a blueprint for hospital-made tips. "I had to change my whole style of playing because I couldn't feel the strings any more. It was all a bit clumsy to start with, but I could see that it would work. I had to work out new ways of playing chords that most guitarists can do naturally but I couldn't do any more. It really was learning from scratch again. It took a long time, but each step got me closer. Because I couldn't feel the strings I had to guess where the ends of my fingers were, so listening to what I was playing became much more important."

Now renowned as one of the true legends of metal, thanks to his Black Sabbath years and his subsequent, massively successful solo career, Osbourne's trademark vocal style – in the early years an almost lycanthropic wail – allied to his fabled outrageous behaviour both on and off stage, have gained the Brummie true rock-idol status.

Black Sabbath was conceived in the heart of industrial Birmingham. Applying forensic profiling and cultural pre-determination to the origins of the four musicians would inevitably lead any analyst to one frightening conclusion – heavy metal. Birmingham, with its disproportionate influence on the genre, possesses some of the UK's bleakest areas. In the late 1960s and early '70s its industry was heavy and dirty, its canals were choked with oil and filth, and its chimneys and factories were blackened by grime and neglect. From the air, Aston's infamous spaghetti junction interchange resembles the contents of a rather vicious puncture wound, the city spilling out its steel and concrete guts for all to see. It was this unforgiving environment that produced Messrs. Osbourne, Iommi, Butler and Ward.

The band was assembled by a skinhead vocalist then known as Ozzy Zig (aka John Michael Osbourne), guitarist Anthony Frank 'Tony' Iommi, bass player Terry 'Geezer' Butler and drummer Bill Ward – who were first united, albeit briefly, under the name Polka Tulk Blues Band. The name Polka Tulk held no hidden meanings; Ozzy merely liked the sound of a shop's name in Handsworth, appropriating it for his own uses.

Osbourne's first attempts at singing came just after leaving school when, together with guitarist Jimmy Phillips, he founded the shortlived act The Prospectors. Before this, Iommi and Ward had been part of The Rest, a band fronted by a local celebrity, ex-Method Five frontman Chris Smith. The group later changed its name to Mythology.

Osbourne and Butler, the latter a rhythm guitarist at this point, were members of Rare Breed, an act that lasted a mere two gigs. Previously, Osbourne had performed with local bands The Black Panthers and Approach as well as having served six weeks of a three-month sentence in the Winson Green prison for burglary. Having been caught robbing stockings from the Sarah Clarke clothing shop in Aston, Ozzy was given a fine, which he couldn't afford to pay. When his father refused to help, he was jailed. It was during his incarceration at Her Majesty's pleasure that the singer gave his knees and knuckles their now-famous 'Ozzy' and smiley-face tattoos by rubbing blue floor-cleaning paste into his broken skin.

The quartet joined forces when Mythology lost both their singer and drummer. With the recruitment of Osbourne and Ward, Mythology changed its title to Music Machine, adding saxophonist Alan 'Aker' Clark and Jimmy Phillips on slide guitar. Before long Music Machine became The Polka Tulk Blues Band and trimmed down to a quartet, with Butler adopting a new role as bass player by taking two strings off his Fender guitar.

The band splintered when the quartet's interests in a distinctly heavier style of music began to show: Phillips opted out and would go on to become a keyboard player with exotically-titled club acts such as Purple Onion, Frog and Magic Roundabout. Meantime, The Polka Tulk Blues

Band conducted their debut gig on August 24th 1968 at the County Ballroom in Carlisle, supported by Creeque. Their next gig, at the Workington Banklands Youth Club, would be the last under that title.

CHANGES

Geezer Butler: "Most of our stuff goes back to 12-bar blues, really. Our younger fans sometimes find that surprising. When we were kids we started out playing along to those old records in just the same way people like Jimmy Page did. Back in those days that's how you learnt to play. We taught ourselves. All our early gigs were blues songs and that is what we were – a blues band. I suppose the transition to heavy metal was through Tony and I developing these very simple three-chord blues riffs into something of our own. It was like: OK, where can we go with this?

"Alvin Lee of Ten Years After had a big effect on us too. Alvin was doing the same thing, taking the blues but turning it around into something different. It's the same for Led Zeppelin, Jethro Tull and Deep Purple too, all those bands of that period just expressed the blues differently. It's all a tradition of the blues, so give us half the chance and we'll spend all day playing Willie Dixon. People seem surprised by that, but I tell them heavy metal would not exist without the blues. Black Sabbath would not exist without the blues."

Tony Iommi: "When we started, both Geezer and I were playing guitar and we learned everything we knew from the blues. Anyone who was serious about an instrument was either learning blues or jazz. The blues is a great place to start, to build on and find your own style. I would recommend it to anyone. Don't pick up a guitar and try to play my riffs. Get hold of some old Howlin' Wolf or Willie Dixon records first. That's the way to start. Ask Jimmy Page, Brian May, Rory Gallagher, Gary Moore, or any of those guys. There weren't that many bands around, and it was very creative because everyone was trying to find something different. Everything was based on the blues, though – everything.

"It really was inspiring, listening to what Jethro Tull, Taste, Cream, Traffic, or Ten Years After were all doing. There wasn't the huge numbers of bands around then, either, so if somebody made a really good record everybody picked up on it really quickly. You were very conscious about trying not to sound like anybody else, too. That was OK if you wanted to be a pop star, but if you thought you were serious you had to do your own thing. That doesn't seem to happen so much any more.

"I don't actually listen to much heavy metal at all, which might sound a bit strange. Americans in particular find it amazing that I don't spend all my time listening to Black Sabbath albums. Instinctively, if you put most bands of a certain age into a rehearsal situation the first thing they will play will be the blues. When I'm at home I'll still listen to my old blues records, Hank Marvin, or Frank Sinatra."

Geezer Butler: "Somehow what we came up with was no longer blues. I don't know what happened but we took it somewhere else. Tony's riffs were just so out there. I think that was the main thing, and with Ozzy on top singing my lyrics and Bill bashing away, it just became a completely new thing. We really didn't know what to call it. That's why we changed the band name, because we weren't a blues band anymore.

"A lot of bands back then had 'blues' in the title but we wanted to call ourselves something different, because we were different. For a long time people called us hippies but then we got called heavy metal, which was a lot better. The funny thing is, it seems that to make good heavy metal the best thing to do is to listen to something else entirely. There's quite a bit more to it than turning your amp up and waffling on about the devil."

Alvin Lee: "Tony did something quite original with the guitar. I mean, he's rooted in the blues, just like most of us, but I don't know what goes on between his head and his fingers, man, because that's sure not the blues any more!"

Within a short space of time the revised band had altered their moniker to the shortened Polka Tulk before another name change was enforced, the foursome becoming The Earth Blues Band before a subsequent truncation to simply Earth. Earth rehearsed at Newtown Community Centre in Aston and once again the band debuted in Carlisle, appearing at the Gretna Tavern in late September 1968. Gigs would be conducted squeezed onto minuscule stages, headed up by Ozzy sporting a spectacularly curly mop of hair and shod in sandals with a water tap (faucet) for a pendant. However, following an Earth support slot to Jethro Tull in Stafford-on-Trent, Iommi was poached by the headlining act: he actually left to join Tull for all of two weeks, replacing the departed Mick Abrahams.

Although the guitarist's tenure in Jethro Tull proved fleeting, he did appear with the band at The Rolling Stones' legendary *Rock'n'Roll Circus* filming session, recorded at Internel Studios in Stonebridge Park, Wembley during December. Iommi and Anderson did not gel and on completing the rehearsals for *Circus* Iommi quit. The guitarist returned for the day of filming, but when he asked to be reinstated, discovered that he had already been replaced. After a short liaison with The Nice guitarist David O'List, Jethro Tull found a permanent replacement in Martin Barre. With Iommi back in the ranks, Earth got back to gigging, returning to Carlisle's County Ballroom on December 21st.

The band signed over their business affairs to Jim Simpson's Big Bear Management during 1969. An industrious local entrepreneur, Simpson owned the legendary Birmingham haunt Henry's Blues House and managed nationally known acts such as Bakerloo, Tea & Symphony, his own Locomotive band, and – in later years – fellow Brummie heavyweights Judas Priest.

BEHIND THE WALLS OF SLEEP

Ozzy Osbourne: "A lot of those well-known songs came from the Star-Club in Hamburg, Germany. Because we had so much time to fill up, Tony, Geezer and Bill just had to fuckin' go for it and hope for the best! We had to play six 45-minute shows every day and only had one day off. Can you imagine doing that now?

"Tony would start, then Bill would kick in, then Geezer, and somewhere along the way I had to start singing. Sometimes Tony would put some really weird tempos in and somehow we'd make it into a song. We'd have musical arguments while these punters looked on with a beer in their hand. Quite a few songs on the first album started from those jams. 'War Pigs' used to go on forever."

Geezer Butler: "It started with the song 'Black Sabbath'. There was no grand plan. I had a dream where I woke up to see Satan standing at the end of my bed – only I was still dreaming. It scared the shit out of me, so I thought it might make a good subject for a song. If you read the words, 'What is this that stands before me?' it's all from that nightmare."

Earth put in an appearance in London with a batch of gigs at the legendary Marquee club, commencing in January 1969 as support to Jon Hiseman's Colosseum. Unfortunately their first appearance was nearly their last, as they were banned by the management. Fortunately, Ten Years After guitarist Alvin Lee, an influential fan, scored a reprieve for the band. Their first taste of European audiences came when Simpson booked a tour of Germany. The shows included a ten-date residency at Hamburg's infamous Star-Club, the once famous haunt of The Beatles, before a return for more UK gigs – including a date at the prestigious London Speakeasy.

That August, Earth travelled back to Germany for a second stint at the Star-Club. Although they were still operating under the Earth banner, the group's live set already included future Sabbath staples such as 'N.I.B.', 'Warning', 'The Wizard', 'Fairies Wear Boots' and 'Rat Salad'. Just before this second continental trip, the group had been presented with a problem when, arriving for a concert in Manchester, they discovered that the confused promoter had in fact thought he was booking a Tamla Motown-style R&B band of the same name. The presence of two acts bearing the same title was solved while in Hamburg: by the time the band was back on British soil they had taken on the title Black Sabbath. The new brand had been adopted after the 1963 Boris Karloff movie and a newly penned song of the same name, inspired by a particularly sinister 'sleep paralysis' nightmare that had befallen Geezer Butler. An attempt by Jim Simpson for them to consider his suggestion of Fred Karno's Army fortunately fell on deaf ears.

Simpson upped the ante by getting the band and producer Gus Dudgeon, an ex-member of Tea & Symphony, into the 8-track Trident Studios in Soho, London, to craft Black Sabbath's inaugural demo on August 22nd 1969. Engineer Rodger Bain would steer the sessions. The two tracks, 'Song For Jim' and 'The Rebel' (the latter featuring Locomotive keyboard player Norman Haines), became Sabbath's debut recordings. The group would also cut a version of Haines's 'When I Come Down', mis-titled 'When I Came Down' for the Sabbath version, and a prototype take of 'The Wizard'.

Performing at Banklands Youth Club in Workington once again on August 26th (Cumbria had been a focus of fan support from the band's inception), Earth announced from the stage that they had now become Black Sabbath. Their very first gig under the new name came on August 30th 1969 at the Winter Gardens venue in Malvern. To mark the transition, the global 'Earth' logo on Bill Ward's bass drums was covered by a hastily patched-together 'Black Sabbath'. As such, the very first Black Sabbath logo was fashioned in the most trusted piece of equipment in any roadie's toolbox – black gaffa tape.

With momentum gathering, subsequent gigs included showcase performances for major labels. Black Sabbath then engaged in a third round of shows at the Hamburg Star-Club. This groundswell of support enabled the band to gain a deal with the newly-established 'progressive rock' label Vertigo, an arm of Fontana. Recording sessions for Sabbath's eponymous debut album commenced in October. The band gained some valuable exposure the following month with an appearance on DJ John Peel's *Top Gear* radio show. Sabbath had performed an expenses-only gig at Wolverhampton's Lafayette Club earlier in September for Peel's benefit, and duly secured the influential DJ's enthusiastic support. Their session, which saw 'Sleeping Village' still going by the formative title of 'Devil's Island', was recorded at the BBC's Maida Vale Studios.

According to popular legend, Black Sabbath recorded their first Rodger Bain-produced album for a miserly £600 of Jim Simpson's money on a 4-track machine. An aspiring engineer on the project, laid down in London's Tottenham Court Road, would be none other than 'Colonel' Tom Allom, later to find fame as a platinum-status producer for Judas Priest. As an investment on Vertigo's part it was indeed a shrewd one: not only did the *Black Sabbath* album define a whole genre of music, it would go on to sell millions of copies for decades to come.

Early signs were not encouraging, however: the band's opening release as Black Sabbath barely raised a murmur in the media. A 7-inch single, 'Evil Woman (Don't Play Your Evil Games With Me)', a cover of a song originally penned by Minnesota act Crow, had seen a release in January 1970 through the Fontana label, re-released on the Vertigo label a few months later. Both releases sank without trace.

On Friday February 13th, *Black Sabbath* emerged ominously upon an unsuspecting world, laden with songs now regarded as all-time classics –

such as 'Black Sabbath', 'The Wizard' and 'N.I.B.' The last-named was thought at the time to be an acronym for 'Nativity In Black' but was in fact a reference to the shape of Bill Ward's "nibby" beard. (The punctuation was added by Ozzy to make it more "interesting".)

THE RIFFMEISTER

K.K. Downing: "I don't believe there is a heavy metal guitar player around that hasn't benefited from either being a fan or being subjected to the riffs and guitar playing of Tony Iommi. I think it goes without saying that everyone considers Tony to be the Number One supreme riff maker that there has ever been and probably will ever be. Needless to say, his influences have covered the planet since the beginning of anything pertaining to rock music as we know it."

Alvin Lee: "Tony is undoubtedly unique in his field. I know he has said some nice things about my playing, but I can't really hear anything I've done in his style. Tony just came up with his own thing, and that is such a rarity. Only a handful of guitarists have ever done anything unique and he's one of them. He has a very jazz approach and the fact that he can do what he does in spite of his false fingertips is pretty amazing."

Glenn Hughes: "The man is a giant on the guitar. The thing with Tony Iommi is that the passage of time has concealed a lot of what he did back in the early days. He invented a certain style of playing on those first two records. Nobody really got it back then, but he had developed something new. The way he constructs his riffs, the notes he uses, is actually pretty unusual. It has been a bit lost, unfortunately, because everyone from that point on copied him."

Graham Oliver (Saxon): "Tony is actually a very unorthodox player. He flicks from strings to accommodate his handicap. In fact it goes beyond him being just a great guitar player, because obviously he has to pull something extra special out from his boots too. The other thing that makes him quite amazing in my eyes is that he is on his own up there: everything rests on him.

If you just think about the riffs that he has come up with. I don't think any other guitar player, even Jimmy Page or Ritchie Blackmore, has that many classic heavy metal riffs to his name. Tony is certainly a one-off."

Dave Spitz: "Most rock people don't have a clue how amazing Tony actually is. Let me be perfectly clear: Tony Iommi absolutely invented heavy metal."

Ozzy Osbourne: "Tony doesn't think like other guitarists; he actually thinks more like a bass player. Geezer used to play the guitar too, so when they start working on something they really know how to make things work. It's always been a huge struggle for me to find a guitarist for my band because, with Tony, I was used to having something original every time. When I auditioned guitar players for my band I would just sit there and watch hundreds go through who just had nothing unique about them at all. People say I'm good at finding guitar players. I bloody have to be because I've got Tony bloody Iommi looking over my shoulder all the time."

Bearing an eerie sleeve – photographed at Mapledurham in Oxfordshire and depicting an ethereal female figure holding a black cat – with an inverted crucifix on the inner gatefold, *Black Sabbath* made an immediate visual impact. Musically, the album's almost Neanderthal bludgeoning heaviness and thick, industrial riffing took rock fans by storm. Quite simply, the band had delivered a unique brand of hard rock: nothing of its like had been heard before and Black Sabbath's profile was elevated rapidly due to that strongest of marketing devices, a polarisation of opinion. The debut swiftly reached Number 8 in the British charts with virtually no assistance from radio airplay.

Concert promotion to push the album saw the band opening up proceedings in Cardiff on February 5th at the Arts Centre Project at Sophia Gardens with Pink Floyd, Quintessence and Tea & Symphony. The British tour would include such salubrious venues as the East Ham Duke's Head, Salisbury's Alexis Disco and the Croydon Greyhound. Also on the agenda were more familiar residencies such as Mothers Club in Erdington and Jim Simpson's own Henry's Blues House.

Black Sabbath would also venture into Germany, appearing at the Essen Grugahalle Song Days festival, the band undoubtedly the heaviest proposition on an eclectic billing alongside Rhinoceros, Taj Mahal, The Groundhogs, Renaissance and The Keef Hartley Band. Returning to the UK, Black Sabbath appeared at the Whitsun May Bank Holiday weekend event at Plumpton Racecourse with Ginger Baker's Air Force and Chicken Shack on May 23rd: this gig was captured on a widely-circulated bootleg. The group put in a second gig that same day at Ewell Technical College supporting Caravan. En route to a gig the next day, at the Hollywood Music festival in Leycett, Newcastle-under-Lyme, Staffordshire, on a billing with Colosseum, Free, Traffic, Quintessence and headliners The Grateful Dead, Black Sabbath's van crashed into another vehicle on the motorway. As fate would have it, there were no injuries: coincidence revealed that the occupants of the other vehicle were all fans travelling to the very same gig.

Further German festivals had the group appearing alongside Rory Gallagher, Deep Purple, Free, Status Quo and Black Widow. It was already evident that, wherever they played and whoever they shared a billing with, no-one was heavier than Black Sabbath.

The year 1970 proved hectic but highly productive, as in June the band wrapped up recording for their second album, *Paranoid*. Initially the project, once again assembled with Rodger Bain's expertise, adopted the *War Pigs* title. However, the record company objected to 'War Pigs' due to the prevailing Vietnam War and also because there was a feeling that the song 'Paranoid' could be a possible hit. The 'War Pigs' title itself had been changed: the original composition was entitled 'Walpurgis'.

The group then returned to Germany for a further round of shows in August. It was at this juncture that Black Sabbath opted to switch management from Jim Simpson to Patrick Meehan, also responsible for handling the business career of Black Widow. However, the four musicians nearly hooked up with another local band as their high-flying friends in Led Zeppelin expressed an interest in managing their affairs.

An American tour had been set in place for July of 1970 but then cancelled, the group members concerned that the recent Charles Manson 'family' murders might generate adverse publicity. More UK gigs were scheduled as – quite incredibly – the *Black Sabbath* album was still tenaciously lodged in the charts some 42 weeks after its release. On August 8th, Black Sabbath played the 10th National Jazz & Blues Festival in Plumpton alongside Humble Pie and Yes.

The 'Paranoid' single peaked at Number 4, and remains Black Sabbath's biggest chart hit to date. Later admissions from the band revealed that this landmark metal milestone had been directly rooted in a jam based on the groove of Led Zeppelin's 'Communication Breakdown'. In Germany the band fared even better, as the 'Paranoid' single reached Number 1 on the singles listings and the album sold in huge quantities. The fickle finger of fate once again played mischievously here – as 'Paranoid' was an afterthought, initiated when management realised the album was falling short of its expected duration.

PARANOID

Geezer Butler: "We had actually wrapped the album up and were ready to go home when someone pointed out the record was too short. We had to get all the gear out again, set up, and then write a song from scratch. I suppose that's why 'Paranoid' sounds so instant – because it was! We looked at each other and said, 'What shall we do then?' We had nothing at all so we just jammed and hoped for the best. It's a reason why some people find the lyrics very cryptic. They're not; they just had no time to be put together properly."

IRON MAN

Geezer Butler: "That's from a kid's comic, actually. I liked the concept, which was basically about technology having the means to save the world but not actually doing it. 'Iron Man' has a strong green anti-pollution theme, too, but a lot of people missed that and thought it was just about a daft robot. I suppose Ozzy didn't help, because he would often make a joke of it onstage. It's quite a wacky story but I've got quite a thing for good science fiction. The funny thing was that Ozzy used to walk around wearing a T-shirt with a burnt iron mark on the back and nobody seemed to get it."

WAR PIGS

Geoff Nicholls: "That song always reminds me of Bill Ward. Whenever we would audition new drummers, Tony always tried them on 'War Pigs' because very few drummers could play it. They would come in with a big name and everything and make a complete balls-up of it. Why? Because it's a 3/4 waltz. Bill did the bloody thing in swing time."

The album scaled the charts all the way to the top, unceremoniously booting the classic Simon & Garfunkel LP *Bridge Over Troubled Water* from the top spot. *Paranoid*, hosting yet another crop of renowned classics – such as 'Hand Of Doom', the alarmingly clumsy 'Fairies Wear Boots' and the malevolent machinations of 'Iron Man' – had Black Sabbath exploring a much more varied spectrum of interests than its predecessor's simple predilection for the occult.

There would be little respite for the quartet, as live commitments plugging the sophomore outing saw the band back on the road in the UK during September, starting off in Wales again – this time at the Swansea Brangwyn Hall. Three shows in Switzerland were undertaken prior to a short burst of live activity in the Low Countries. By October Black Sabbath were putting in their first performance in the icy climes of Scandinavia: like Germany, these territories were soon to grant the band a further bastion of loyal support. The close of the month witnessed another first - the inception of a long trail of roadwork in the United States. It would be here that the realisation dawned upon the band that they were undoubtedly the heaviest act on the planet.

In North America the second album had reached Number 12 and settled in for a dogged chart tenure, eventually clocking up a staggering 65-week residency. The band's inaugural American shows also took place, with Black Sabbath first hitting American soil at JFK airport on October 28th 1970. The band's first shows, at Glassboro State College on October 30th before a University of Miami gig supporting prog-fusion act Canned Heat the next day, proved a huge success. A prestigious New York gig on November 10th, at Bill Graham's Fillmore East, saw Black Sabbath awkwardly opening for Rod Stewart & The Faces. Sabbath's first American trip would extend into a run of three San Francisco Fillmore West gigs, opening up for Arthur Lee's Love and Joe Walsh's James Gang.

Label and management, keen to capitalise quickly on these solid achievements, quickly scheduled the band's calendar for the following year. The first task for 1971 was the initial recordings for the *Master Of Reality* album, conducted at Island Studios in Notting Hill Gate, London. Only three songs were laid down before Sabbath were out on the road once again. The tour had been scheduled to start at the Royal Albert Hall on January 5th but the venue's management banned the group, fearing that fans would damage the fixtures. Nevertheless, the remaining shows, with guests Curved Air and Freedom, had sold out. The UK gigs closed at Leeds University on January 23rd and a week later Black Sabbath was putting in another first with a lightning dash to Australia, performing at Adelaide's Myponga Pop festival.

With their opening foray deemed a resounding success, Black Sabbath returned to North America with a gig at New Jersey's Sunshine Inn, Asbury Park, on February 17th 1971. Already the group was headlining major arena venues with acts such as Yes and even Fleetwood Mac in support, while for other dates they acted as the openers to bands such as Mountain. It would be on this tour that a man lunged at Tony Iommi with a knife. Racing across the stage at a gig in Memphis, Tennessee, on March 1st, the would-be assailant was thankfully bowled over and disarmed by a quick-witted roadie, David Hemmings.

August 1971 saw the release of the last of the Rodger Bain-produced triumvirate, *Master Of Reality*. The record peaked at Number 5 in the British charts, but provided the band with a strong 'out of the box' seller in America, being certified gold even before its release. Chock-full of classics once again, the set opened with an obvious ode to the green in 'Sweet Leaf', the song that surely inspired the stoner generation, before avalanching into environmental harbinger 'Children Of The Grave'. Commentators picked up on Butler's pseudo-Christian lyrical standpoint in 'After Forever', despite its inflammatory line "Would you like to see the Pope on the end of a rope?" Recorded in a blitzkrieg session of just over a week, *Master Of Reality* was the third slab of the Sabbath commandments. By now, some of the class snobbery had begun to crumble in the face of the band's success, evidenced by a further performance at London's prestigious Royal Albert Hall.

Even as *Master Of Reality* was hitting the stores, the band were confined in Rockfield Studios in Monmouthshire, working up songs for its successor. With the band redoubling their efforts, another North American tour then ensued, exhausting them to such a degree that UK gigs projected for November were rescheduled for the next year.

In early 1972 Black Sabbath entered Marquee Studios in London, breaking tradition by opting to self-produce along with manager Patrick Meehan. Mid-session, the group broke out of the studio confines to undertake their rescheduled UK tour, including a return to the Royal Albert Hall on February 17th 1972, with Wild Turkey as guests. Hardly pausing for breath, the band duly engaged immediately in a month-long round of US dates, the 'Iron Man' trek bolstered by a mis-matched Yes, with Wild Turkey in tow once again. A burst of European gigs finalised the schedule.

Volume 4, originally to be titled *Snowblind*, gave the band another Top 10 British album and featured the delicate ballad 'Changes' alongside the more brutal 'Snowblind'. The record had been manifested during May of 1972 at the world-famous Record Plant complex in California and completed at Island Studios in London in June. Just days later, Sabbath were back on the road in the USA but the unrelenting work took its toll – as Ozzy continually lost his voice. Gigs would be cancelled and, following a show at the Hollywood Bowl in September, Tony Iommi collapsed due to exhaustion. Bill Ward and Geezer Butler followed suit, the drummer contracting hepatitis whilst the bass player was hospitalised with a kidney complaint.

Iommi squeezed in time to record a session for Freedom vocalist Bobby Harrison's (unfortunately obscure) solo album *The Funkist*. Freedom were also part of Patrick Meehan's management stable and the band had opened for Black Sabbath on numerous occasions. The album saw a low-key release in America on the Capitol label in 1975.

The foursome recuperated throughout the winter of 1972 but opened the New Year with their most distant gig to date at the Great Ngaruawahia Music Festival Of Peace on New Zealand's North Island. A quick sojourn to Fiji preceded a run of Australian gigs before yet more European concerts: these were caught on tape by the Rolling Stones mobile studio. UK shows in March were backed up by Badger and a Cumbrian band whom Tony Iommi was mentoring, billed as Necromandus. Strangely, the Iommi-produced Necromandus album *Orexis Of Death*, recorded for Vertigo, was shelved. It would take a full two decades for its importance to be recognised.

The band returned to America to work on *Volume 4*'s follow-up, but

---

BLACK SABBATH discography

BLACK SABBATH, Vertigo VO 6 (UK), Warner Bros. WS 1871 (USA) (1970) **8 UK, 23 USA**

PARANOID, Vertigo 6360 011 (UK), Warner Bros. WS 1887 (USA) (1970) **1 UK, 12 USA**

MASTER OF REALITY, Vertigo 6360 050 (UK), Warner Bros. BS 2562 (USA) (1971) **5 UK, 8 USA**

VOLUME 4, Vertigo 6360 071 (UK), Warner Bros. BS 2602 (USA) (1972) **8 UK, 13 USA**

SABBATH BLOODY SABBATH, Vertigo 6360 115 (UK) (1973), Warner Bros. BS 2695 (USA) (1974) **4 UK, 11 USA**

SABOTAGE, NEMS 9119 001 (UK), Warner Bros. BS 2822 (USA) (1975) **7 UK, 28 USA**

WE SOLD OUR SOUL FOR ROCK'N'ROLL, NEMS 6641 335 (UK) (1975), Warner Bros. 2BS 2923 (USA) (1976) **35 UK, 48 USA**

TECHNICAL ECSTASY, Vertigo 9102 750 (UK), Warner Bros. BS 2969 (USA) (1976) **13 UK, 51 USA**

NEVER SAY DIE!, Vertigo 9102 751 (UK), Warner Bros. BSK 3186 (USA) (1978) **12 UK, 69 USA**

LIVE AT LAST, NEMS BS 001 (UK) (1980) **5 UK**

HEAVEN AND HELL, Vertigo 9102 752 (UK), Warner Bros. BSK 3372 (USA) (1980) **9 UK, 28 USA**

MOB RULES, Vertigo 6302 119 (UK), Warner Bros. BSK 3605 (USA) (1981) **12 UK, 29 USA**

LIVE EVIL, Vertigo SAB 10 (UK), Warner Bros. BSK 23742-1 (USA) (1983) **13 UK, 37 USA**

BORN AGAIN, Vertigo VERL 8 (UK), Warner Bros. 1-23978 (USA) (1983) **4 UK, 39 USA**

SEVENTH STAR, Vertigo VERH 29 (UK), Warner Bros. 1-25337 (USA) (1986) **27 UK, 78 USA**

THE ETERNAL IDOL, Vertigo VERH 51 (UK), Warner Bros. 9 25548-2 (USA) (1987) **66 UK, 168 USA**

HEADLESS CROSS, IRS EIRSACD 1002 (UK), IRSCD-82002 (USA) (1989) **31 UK, 115 USA**

TYR, IRS EIRSACD 1038 (UK), IRS X213049 (USA) (1990) **24 UK**

DEHUMANIZER, IRS EIRSCD 1064 (UK), Warner Bros. 9 26965-2 (USA) (1992) **28 UK, 44 USA**

CROSS PURPOSES, IRS EIRSCD 1067 (UK), IRS 72435-30413-2-8 (USA) (1994) **41 UK, 122 USA**

CROSS PURPOSES – LIVE, IRS 7243 8 30069 2 2 (UK), IRS 7243 8 300 69 2 2 (USA) (1995)

FORBIDDEN, IRS 7243 8 30620 2 7 (UK), IRS 724 8 30620 27 (USA) (1995) **71 UK**

REUNION, Epic EPC 491954-2 (UK), Epic E2K 69688 (USA) (1998) **41 UK, 11 USA**

PAST LIVES, Sanctuary SANDP18 (UK), Sanctuary 06076 84561-2 (USA) (2002) **114 USA**

BLACK BOX: THE COMPLETE ORIGINAL BLACK SABBATH (1970-1978), Warner Bros./Rhino R2-73923 (USA) (2004

found for the first time that their flow of ideas had ebbed. Relocating to rehearse in the suitably spooky setting of the dungeon of Clearwell Castle in Wales, Iommi came up with the classic riff for the track 'Sabbath Bloody Sabbath' and the creative juices started to flow once more. In November 1973 they released the renowned *Sabbath Bloody Sabbath* album to worldwide critical acclaim. Yes keyboardist Rick Wakeman gained another credit, providing the atmosphere on 'Sabbra Cadabra', while 'Spiral Architect' witnessed a spreading of creative wings with the inclusion of an orchestra.

For live work, keyboard player Gerry Woodruffe was added to the entourage. US road work saw an alliance with British band Bedlam, which featured future Sabbs drummer Cozy Powell. Demand in their home country would be satisfied with gigs in March before Black Sabbath put in one of their most important American appearances at the California Jam festival in April 1974, alongside Emerson Lake & Palmer and Deep Purple, playing to a staggering audience of over quarter of a million people. Returning home for a further set of gigs, Sabbath brought along Black Oak Arkansas to kick off the shows, notable for another drummer to weave his way into the Ozzy tapestry at a later date – Tommy Aldridge.

Touring excesses and managerial nightmares had taken the band to breaking point, with Iommi and Osbourne becoming ever more confrontational. The band duly wrestled their business affairs away from the clutches of Patrick Meehan. *Sabotage*, released in 1975, was the first offering to be produced by Iommi, and the record kept the flame alive. It was crafted at Morgan Studios in Willesden, London, during February and March, and the album's title was a direct reference to the group's financial woes. Famously, although unfortunately not captured on tape, these sessions were punctuated by jam sessions with the Led Zeppelin trio of Robert Plant, John Paul Jones and John Bonham.

The band put in another enormous American tour, supported by the larger-than-life Kiss. Bill Ward was by now employing a Botticelli-sized clam device to embellish his drum riser, and the band's extravagant stage garb included lengthy frills for Ozzy, ballooning silver flares on the part of Butler and jester-styled sleeves for Iommi, which dragged along the stage as they were so long. However, despite the extrovert visuals, the band had reached a creative crossroads musically, *Sabotage* witnessing a deliberate change of lyrical tack away from the previous occult themes that had served the band so well. Alarmingly, the album sleeve sported a photograph of the band in which Ozzy was clad in a Japanese kimono and Ward was disturbingly transparent in his girlfriend's red tights. Apparently the group had no idea the shoot was for the record cover.

Sabotage, peaking at Number 7 in the UK and Number 28 in the USA, still hosted some fine moments, with tracks such as the supreme tour de force that was 'Symptom Of The Universe', 'Am I Going Insane (Radio)', 'Hole In The Sky' and 'Supertzar'. Adventurously, Tony Iommi drafted in the English Chamber Choir for the latter track. Their fiscal affairs even made it onto song with 'The Writ', no doubt prompted by being served with legal documents while in the process of recording. Initial copies of the *Sabotage* album included a rare unaccredited track – 'Blow On A Jug'. This was actually Bill Ward singing the Nitty Gritty Dirt Band track, captured unawares by a studio engineer. Later pressings do not include this moment.

SABOTAGE

Ozzy Osbourne: "It all started to go wrong with Sabotage. We'd decided to ditch the occult stuff and start singing about something else, but it just didn't work. Our fans wanted the black magic, and the way they told us was by not buying the records. It took a while for us to see, because we were all so doped up and people kept coming to the shows. We'd also figured out that a hell of a lot of money was missing somewhere, so that's where the arguing and the suspicion

came in. The band was on such a ride with the touring that we'd be happy if we got bunged a grand now and again. What we didn't work out for far too long was that someone else was bunging themselves a million now and again.

"We figured if we got rid of the black magic we'd be happier, but it wasn't the fucking devil that made us unhappy, it was the fact we were junkies and we were broke. Sabbath Bloody Sabbath – that was the last real Black Sabbath album. It was downhill from there for me."

A compilation, *We Sold Our Souls For Rock'N'Roll*, charted well, but many thought the 1976 experimental effort *Technical Ecstasy*, making heavy use of string and synths, to be way below par. The album included a first for the band, as Ward took lead vocals for the first time ever on the track 'It's Alright'. Gerry Woodruffe was employed on keyboards once again. The band recorded at Criteria Studios in Florida with Robin Black behind the desk; The Eagles were cutting *Hotel California* in the same complex.

An inkling of what was to come was delivered in the unlikely form of a T-shirt. During the *Technical Ecstasy* sessions, Osbourne took to wearing a shirt sporting the legend 'Blizzard Of Ozz', a band title suggested by his father. Upon his return to the UK, Ozzy's external ambitions led to the surreptitious creation of a fresh band in union with Necromandus guitarist Barry Dunnery, bassist Dennis McCarten and drummer Frank Hall. Brief rehearsals were undertaken at Osbourne's home studio in Staffordshire, but due to the chaotic circumstances prevailing at the time, this project floundered.

Upon its release on September 25th 1976 in the US and October 8th in the UK, *Technical Ecstasy* marked a return to the Vertigo label for the band, the previous two records having been issued through NEMS. North American dates, commencing on October 22nd in Tulsa, Oklahoma, saw the band on the road supported by the unlikely duo of sugary-sweet AOR giants REO Speedwagon and up-and-coming NYC punks The Ramones. For these dates Bill Ward employed a grandiose, throne-like drum riser, sculpted from stained glass, bedecked by torches, packed with strobe lighting and dry ice pumps, and topped by a gothic chandelier. Other US shows found the likes of Boston, Ted Nugent and Bob Seger as openers. Although Black Sabbath drew in the expected numbers on the live front, *Technical Ecstasy* stalled in the charts, not even breaking into the US Top 50. The band's live standing remained high, as evidenced by a triumphant performance at New York's famed Madison Square Garden on December 6th.

The 'Technical Ecstasy' tour hit Europe in April with strong backing from a fiery support band named AC/DC. The tensions resulted in Geezer Butler actually being fired from the band in 1977. Bill Ward gave him the bad news at home. However, Butler was rapidly re-inducted. The fragile nature of the unit was tested further when Ozzy quit in September 1977.

That same year Iommi gave a hand to his local protégés Quartz, producing their first, self-titled album for Jet Records. Comprising longstanding friends of the Sabbath camp, Quartz was ably handled by Black Sabbath tour manager Albert Chapman. The resulting record was also of significance for its inclusion of band member Geoff Nicholls, later to become a staunch ally of Iommi. Naturally the guitarist also snuck in a couple of guitar solos, and even a rare flute passage on the song 'Sugar Rain', but would remain unaccredited due to contractual reasons.

A further stab at building a solo band found Ozzy in league with former Dirty Tricks personnel – guitarist John Fraser-Binnie, bass player Terry Horbury and drummer Andy Bierne – but just as this group readied themselves for rehearsals in London, Osbourne received a phone call to rejoin Black Sabbath.

In the interim, Black Sabbath had endeavoured to fill the void with ex-Idle Race, Fleetwood Mac and Savoy Brown vocalist Dave Walker. Recordings were made with Walker for the next album, but the liaison was shortlived and, scrapping the previous songs, Osbourne was enticed back for one last album, *Never Say Die*. The only track to surface from the Walker era was a version of 'Junior's Eyes' on the bootleg *Archangel Rides Again*. Walker was subsequently to re-join Savoy Brown.

QUARTZ

Geoff Nicholls: "Tony had produced the record and he was obviously going to play on it too. It's just that we couldn't say that at the time, for legal reasons. He did quite a bit on the record actually, a couple of solos. Ozzy sang on 'Sugar Rain' too. Again, we weren't allowed to credit him."

Black Sabbath ensconced themselves at Sounds Interchange Studios in Toronto, Canada, for the recording of *Never Say Die* in January 1978. Opening their world tour on May 16th in Sheffield, Sabbath appeared tired and uninspired, a state of affairs put sharply into focus by having as guests the youthful Van Halen, who stole the honours from the headliners throughout the tour. A welcome point of high-profile exposure for fans came with an appearance from the band on TV chart show *Top Of The Pops*, performing the title track from the album. Still with Van Halen, the band then embarked upon US dates, commencing in Chicago on August 14th prior to traversing the Midwest and closing East Coast shows in Seattle during September. Sabbath and Van Halen then engaged in German gigs before returning to North America for a second leg.

The album was issued in October and, despite entering the UK charts at Number 12, fared badly in the USA, where, issued a month later, it scraped to a lowly Number 69. The band was still a solid draw on the live circuit, though, as amply demonstrated by their well-attended November US dates. Black Sabbath's final gig with Ozzy Osbourne at the helm (aside from latter reunions) would be in Albuquerque, New Mexico, on December 11th.

In January 1979, Black Sabbath contracted their business affairs to Don Arden of Jet Records, noted for his pivotal role in making fellow Brummies the Electric Light Orchestra a worldwide success story. The band relocated to Bel Air in Los Angeles to commence work on a new studio record, mooted as a tenth anniversary career rejuvenator, but, despite laying down initial demos such as prototypes of 'Children Of The Sea' and 'Lady Evil', the band would fragment.

Ozzy Osbourne quit for the final time in late April, eventually resurfacing as a solo artist under the initial band handle of Blizzard Of Ozz. He would go on to an immensely successful post-Black Sabbath career – which would, ironically, overshadow that of Sabbath itself. Joining Osbourne would be erstwhile Uriah Heep drummer Lee Kerslake, former Quiet Riot guitar protegé Randy Rhoads and the experienced figure of ex-Chicken Shack, Widowmaker and Rainbow bassist Bob Daisley.

Tony Iommi, Geezer Butler and Bill Ward set about re-building their band. The guitarist pulled in his friend Geoff Nicholls from fellow Birmingham heavy metal band Quartz as an intended second guitarist while they searched for a singer. Iommi even approached former Deep Purple man David Coverdale to fill the vacancy, but this idea never got beyond the discussion stage.

Tony Iommi: "Yes, we did ask David Coverdale. There was a conflict of schedules, I think. He was up for it, but the timing was wrong. I've asked David a couple of times, actually, and each time he had only just signed up for something else."

Still targeting sometime Deep Purple frontmen, next in line on Iommi's wish list would be Glenn Hughes – but despite the singer being available and even attending some studio jam sessions, no proposal was formerly brokered.

Eventually, Sabbath announced that former Elf and Rainbow vocalist Ronnie James Dio had been secured – the first non-British musician to join the fold. Significantly, Dio would also be the only singer besides Ozzy Osbourne to front a platinum version of Black Sabbath. Blessed with Olympian vocal chords, Ronald Padova (to give him his real name) had brought his talents to bear on school outfits, including Ronnie & The Red Caps (who actually went so far as to release a single, 'Lover'/'Conquest', in 1958). The 1960s saw Dio heading up Ronnie Dio & The Prophets, a band in which he not only sang but juggled piano, bass and trumpet. Re-billed The Prophets in 1967, the act was to release a string of singles and one album, *Dio At Domino's*, on the Lawn label in 1963. Next in line would be The Electric Elves – latterly Elf – who were assembled with Dio's guitarist cousin and latter-day Rods mentor David 'Rock' Feinstein.

With the somewhat whimsical Elf, Dio began to force his name onto the world circuit, supporting Deep Purple and issuing consistently better albums. He would, along with his band, minus their redundant guitarist, be plucked from Elf and groomed for stardom by Ritchie Blackmore. The Dio-era Rainbow, which saw the singer's sense of majesty and grandeur coming to the fore, would provide a reliable barometer of what was to come for Black Sabbath. Dio had always imbued his projects with Gothic kitsch, mediaeval romanticism and familiar imagery such as dragons and rainbows.

Post-Rainbow, Dio quickly began assembling a new band unit in Connecticut with former Elf comrades, keyboard player Mickey Lee Soule and drummer Gary Driscoll. It was at this point that telephone communication with Tony Iommi began – at first rather enthusiastically, but subsequently dying down into silence. Endeavouring to forge ahead with his own proto-band, Dio, together with Lee Soule and Driscoll, relocated to Los Angeles. Another opportunity presented itself when Dio was invited to ally himself with a combo involving Blood Sweat & Tears guitarist Al Kooper, the highly respected Doobie Brothers and Steely Dan guitarist Jeff 'Skunk' Baxter and Little Feat drummer Richie Hayward. This star-studded liaison managed one rehearsal before Dio and Iommi crossed paths once again at the Rainbow Bar & Grill. Invited to check out the band's Bel Air studio, the singer found himself tactfully coerced into a jam. Within minutes, 'Children Of The Sea' had been brought to fruition. The next day Iommi phoned Dio to tell him Ozzy was out and the job was his.

CHILDREN OF THE SEA

Ronnie James Dio: "I hadn't been asked to become involved or anything; I was there to look at a studio, as far as I was concerned. Before I knew it the instruments had been strapped on and they started to play this song. Tony says, 'Do you think you can do anything with that?' No problem, I thought. I put myself in the corner for five minutes and then we jammed through 'Children Of The Sea'. We pretty much got it nailed first time. I think they were quite stunned."

However, Geezer Butler, believing the group could not persevere under the Black Sabbath name, quit – necessitating Geoff Nicholls and sometimes Dio himself to take on bass duties. The band nearly took another shape, however, as Nicholls initially assumed the role of second guitar player. In keeping with Iommi's original concept for the new group, Nicholls then shifted over to keyboards, a role he has occupied ever since. However, in his fleeting role as bassist, Nicholls unwittingly initiated one of the greatest heavy metal songs of all time – as some idle bass doodlings gave both Iommi and Dio the spark to forge the mighty title track 'Heaven And Hell'.

HEAVEN AND HELL

Ronnie James Dio: "Ideas and creativity were just flowing out of all of us at that point. We never got tired of it and we would play it for hours and hours. I think we were maybe thinking, 'Is it really this good?' I had the lyrics, the mood and melody for that, and I had a very firm concept of how I wanted the song to end up. Tony's riff was just great. We had to keep pruning the song back, too, because it was really growing."

Geoff Nicholls: "We had to cut it down from the eight and a half minutes and change the arrangement a bit, but it still ended up a bloody epic. Afterwards Geezer told me he would never have played that riff on the bass because it was so simple."

With an album in the works, the musicians had to decide upon a name for the project. At first Black Sabbath was not on the agenda, as Iommi and co believed Ozzy's new band was to be titled Sons Of Sabbath – and detractors in the opposite camp were labelling the Dio/Iommi alliance 'Black Rainbow'. Such uncertainties even moved Dio to suggest that they re-record the 'Black Sabbath' anthem to cement their claim. Behind the scenes, matters were also fragile, as the group were in the midst of switching management from Don Arden to Blue Öyster Cult mentor Sandy Pearlman.

Former Boston bassist Fran Sheehan was tried out for the role before, at Dio's suggestion, ex-Rainbow bassist Craig Gruber took up the position. Apparently at this juncture the band was to be given the truncated brand Sabbath; however, Gruber's tenure proved brief and Geezer Butler made a return in time to record their comeback album –with the full band name.

Heaven And Hell was demoed and rehearsed in Los Angeles, but the band opted to record at Miami's Criteria Recording Studios, ensconcing themselves in the home of The Bee Gees' Barry Gibb for the duration. It was here that Butler threw in his lot with the group once again. Delegated for the production role was Martin Birch.

On the cusp of the 1980s, Black Sabbath thought that they had wound up recording what was to be an undoubted renaissance for the band. However, one last track, the barnstorming 'Neon Knights', Geezer's only songwriting contribution to the record, was recorded in early 1980 as a last-minute addition at the Ferber Complex in Paris, France.

Despite the many adversities they had endured, Black Sabbath came up trumps with a massively successful album in *Heaven And Hell*. The record spawned many classics, including 'Children Of The Sea', the title track and even a hit single in 'Neon Knights', which saw Black Sabbath return to *Top Of The Pops*. Dio stamped his epic touch of majesty on the record, with the authority Iommi needed as a foil for his increasingly monolithic riffing. *Heaven And Hell* soon racked up over a million sales in America.

Live promotion for the album kicked off in Europe, opening with a show on April 17th in Aurich in north-western Germany. Intended purely to break the band in while out of the spotlight, the tour wove its way through provincial townships such as Oldenburg, Kaunitz, Fallingbostel and Rendsburg before diving into the Austrian capital of Vienna and closing at the Landshut Sporthalle in Germany. A higher-profile UK tour, bolstered by a four-night sell-out run at London's Hammersmith Odeon, saw Girlschool as support act. In June, the band, complete with a gargantuan crucifix-shaped lighting truss that burst into flames, returned to larger German venues, with Shakin' Street as openers. Gigs were notable due to the inclusion of an instrumental 'Sabbath Bloody Sabbath' and Dio's theatrical oratory during 'Heaven And Hell'.

Geoff Nicholls: "Ronnie delivered this big speech midway through 'Heaven And Hell'. Sometimes this 'speech' just went on and on and on. It started to get a bit bloody presidential. He would come with all of this stuff like: "Can you feel the power of the cross? Feel the force of the cross!" When Ronnie gave a cue the big cross at the back of the stage burst into flames.

"This one time Ronnie was really playing up on his speech and it was really dragging out. We were all looking at each other, wondering when he was going to end. He got his just deserts, though, because when he pointed to the cross it didn't explode into fire but just gave this farty little fizzle. We all burst out laughing and so did the entire audience. Ronnie was furious! He went absolutely ape-shit afterwards."

Black Sabbath then put on a monstrous tour of North America allied with co-headliners Blue Öyster Cult – billed as the 'Black and Blue' tour. Support along the way came from Molly Hatchet, Saxon and Riot. With *Heaven And Hell* selling in large numbers, gig attendances were healthy and the band performed at major Californian festivals such as the Oakland Day On The Green #2 (alongside Journey, in front of 80,000 people) and the Summer Blowout. However, shortly after the dates began, Bill Ward – who was travelling by road separately from the rest of the band – announced at a show in Denver that he was quitting. The years on the road had finally taken their toll on his health and sense of purpose with the band; he bowed out on August 19th following a gig at Bloomington Metropolitan Sports Center in Minnesota.

Members of Molly Hatchet were later to claim that such was the magnitude of ill luck Black Sabbath were dragging around with them, at one open-air show a solitary cloud deluged rain onto Black Sabbath on stage – leaving the audience completely dry.

The famed Cozy Powell was invited to fill the vacancy left by Ward but declined, apparently unwilling to share another band with Dio after his experiences in Rainbow. Black Sabbath rapidly drafted in ex-Axis, Bruzer and Derringer drummer Vinnie Appice – who, incidentally, was asked to join Ozzy Osbourne's new band at the same time but declined. The new man put in his Black Sabbath debut in Honolulu, Hawaii.

The *Heaven And Hell* expedition closed with a five-night stand in November 1980 in Tokyo, with the group forced to include additional matinee performances to cope with demand for tickets. Four shows in Sydney, Australia, brought the world tour to a conclusion.

MILWAUKEE MECCA ARENA, OCTOBER 1980

Fuelled by the flames of an Ozzy-versus-Dio debate in the media, bitter words spilled over into very real danger at Black Sabbath's Milwaukee Mecca Arena show in October 1980. The group first realised they had a situation brewing when Geezer's expected bass intro to 'N.I.B.' was absent.

Ronnie James Dio: "In between the songs the lights dimmed and at that precise moment Geezer had been hit on the head by something from the stage. I walked over to his side of the stage and he was there, concussed, with his hand up to his forehead – blood everywhere."

Geoff Nicholls: "Some nutter had thrown a brass cross at him! It had come very close to hitting him in the eye. They chucked it just as the lights went down so nobody saw it coming. Geezer was in a bad way. It had been an odd day. The audience was very into the whole Ozzy-versus-Ronnie thing, I remember, and there had been a lot of local media rubbish about the old devil worship too. A bit more than the regular crap we had to put up with. Just as we were trying to deal with Geezer, one of our road crew, Fergie, got hit by a bottle. It was like a bloody battleground."

Ronnie James Dio: "Unfortunately the tour manager took it upon himself to take this out on the audience. Of course, they hadn't seen what had happened, so when they heard this guy calling them 'assholes' and saying we were pulling the show, they went crazy."

Geoff Nicholls: "That crowd just tore the venue to pieces. The chairs were all made of old cast iron and wood and they ripped these things to pieces and were chucking them at us. We suffered a lot of damaged equipment. I remember looking out and seeing all these thousands of chairs flying through the air. There was not a lot we could do, because even the security was being attacked. We looked at each other and Tony said, 'Fuck this – let's get out of here!' They got Geezer and Fergie to hospital, but only just."

Maintaining their momentum, Black Sabbath swiftly turned out another spectacular album in *Mob Rules* which, if anything, saw them getting even heavier. However, the harmony that had governed the *Heaven And Hell* sessions was lacking, and internally the group was already starting to drift apart.

The title song, utilised in the animated *Heavy Metal* movie, was separately recorded as a precursor to the main album at Startling Studios, Tittenhurst Park, the former residence of John Lennon and Yoko Ono. Once the movie work was fulfilled, Black Sabbath launched into yet another UK tour, supported by AIIZ, which took the band through January of 1981. Demand for tickets for the prior *Heaven And Hell* dates had been so strong that a further sojourn across home turf was warranted. Once again Sabbath filled the hallowed portals of Hammersmith Odeon four times over.

Black Sabbath retired to the USA to record the album, investing the majority of their advance into a home-built studio and recording desk, which unfortunately failed to deliver a decent sound: the group completely re-cut everything again at the Record Plant. Strangely, the album artwork by artist Greg Hildebrandt sparked rumours that amid the rubble strewn about in the foreground of the painting was the barely disguised legend 'Kill Ozzy'.

Fans were unaware that *Heaven And Hell* was Black Sabbath's last album under contract to the Warner Bros. label and that internal company expectations, due to the last brace of poor-selling Ozzy-fronted records, were that this record was also doomed. When it unexpectedly started to sell, the label quickly exercised their option for further product. Dio was offered a solo deal at the same juncture.

Mob Rules gave the Sabbs faithful another dose of class and pedigree. Black Sabbath would make their mark on the British singles charts once again with the title track: Dio had proved that *Heaven And Hell* was no one-off and delivered yet another quality clutch of songs. In North America the album fell short of the platinum sales mark but still bolstered the band's reputation.

The band then embarked upon another gargantuan world tour in

Black Sabbath's Tony Iommi and Ozzy Osbourne: heavy metal pioneers

Canada, with Quebec's Coliseum being treated to the opening blast of *Mob Rules*-era Sabbath on November 15th 1981. A special guest – by way of a kind payback – would be Alvin Lee, the man who had so inspired Iommi and Butler in their formative years. Lee had put together his Ten Years Later band, which incorporated former Rolling Stones guitarist Mick Taylor.

LIGHTS OUT

Alvin Lee: "They had this huge bloody great cross that stood at the back of the stage with a million bloody lights on it. It looked amazing, but one night they switched it on and they blew out the electricity sub-station in the city. All the power and the lights in the venue went out. Of course, the crowd started to get a bit rowdy because everything stopped. The doors of the arena were electric too, so everyone was stuck there. When they got the power up again someone explained they had blown the sub-station and everyone cheered. They thought that was bloody great."

Sabbs lighting designer Martin Nicholas, an affable chap whose skin hosts a veritable aquarium of Japanese tattooed fish, had earlier fitted the cross light rig with a larger fuse to prevent the device blowing out. Unfortunately, when it did eventually give up the ghost it had juiced itself up to such a degree it took half the city with it.

Black Sabbath's festivities for the dawning of the new year in 1982 were played out in style, as New Year's Eve signalled the inception of a celebratory four-night run at London's Hammersmith Odeon venue to kick off another triumphant British tour. Such was the band's lofty standing in their home country that the bastion of heavy metal gigs, Newcastle's City Hall, welcomed the band for a three-night stand. For the British shows Sabbath had trimmed their set considerably, disappointingly omitting 'Turn Up The Night', 'Voodoo' and 'Falling Off The Edge Of The World'.

With the conclusion of British dates, and eager to sink their teeth back into the American pie once again, the band then launched into a second round of shows to promote the album. Hooking up with Sabbath at Greensboro, North Carolina, on February 16th was the high-energy Southern rock'n'roll band Doc Holliday, who would take on the mantle of opening act as the tour wound its way through Florida and Georgia. The *Mob Rules* tour's final gasp came at the Hoffman Estates Poplar Creek Music Theatre, Illinois on August 31st 1982.

Just prior to the release of a proposed double live album, *Live Evil*, culled from taped shows in Texas at San Antonio and Dallas along with Seattle, Washington, Dio exited amid a cloud of insults and accusations. Bizarrely, Black Sabbath accused the singer of sneaking into the studio after the rest of the band had gone, to push up the vocal levels on *Live Evil*. The group had divided into two creatively opposed camps, with engineer Lou DeCarlo caught in the middle.

LIVE EVIL

Geoff Nicholls: "The stories that got into the press were pretty accurate. What we didn't know at the time was that Ronnie was writing up his solo record at the time too. It got a bit comical really, because this thing of them creeping in at night went on for quite some time. Basically, Ronnie was pushing his vocals up. What he forgets, though, is if the vocals go up, the rest of it loses the heaviness and starts to sound small in comparison. The engineer was put in an impossible position because he was trying to please everybody."

Ronnie James Dio: "Vinnie and I would go into the studio and wait for Tony and Geezer. This is where it started. They simply didn't turn up, but this is where all the rumours of sneaky sessions came from. There was no sneakiness – we were there on time; they weren't.

Because they wouldn't turn up, obviously we got on with working in the meantime. Studio time is expensive and I'm not about to sit there and waste those dollars. If they're not there, what did they expect?"

Geoff Nicholls: "This whole farce went on for about ten days until, finally, Tony Iommi said to the engineer, 'Look Lee, tell me what the fucking hell is going on here.' Lee then threw his arms up and blurted it all out. Tony was livid and shouted back at him, 'I'm the one who's fucking in charge here!' That's when Tony found out and that's when he fired Ronnie."

Ronnie James Dio: "I called Vinnie and said, 'I'm out of Sabbath. I've been given the elbow. Do you want to be in a band with me?' Vinnie says, 'Absolutely!' No hesitation. So then we had the start of Dio."

In the increasingly bitter war for the fans' loyalty towards the two Black Sabbath camps, estranged singer Ozzy scored a major coup. In a simple manoeuvre – designed both to fulfil a recording contract he was eager to sever and to deliver a thundering statement of intent – Osbourne conjured up a double live album all of his own. Sabbath were given a sound drubbing, caught in a classic blitzkrieg pincer movement. In sales terms, Ozzy's *Speak Of The Devil* live record – titled *Talk Of The Devil* outside America, and recorded on September 26th and 27th at the Ritz in New York – would trounce *Live Evil*. Recorded with the late Randy Rhoads' second tour replacement Brad Gillis from Night Ranger, the record consisted solely of Black Sabbath tunes. Gillis, often sorely overlooked in the annals of Ozzdom, rampaged through the Sabbath classics – and most fans saw it as exactly what it was, a challenge to Iommi and Butler for the legitimacy of their claim to the name Black Sabbath.

Offered up in November 1982, *Speak Of The Devil* strode defiantly into the Billboard Top 20 with ease, leaving *Live Evil* neutered before it even hit the store racks in January 1983. As a newly shaven-headed Ozzy took to the live circuit once again, *Live Evil* stalled at Number 37 in North America. In short, Ozzy's makeshift, last-minute cobbling-together of a live album had won the day.

Auditioning new singers, Black Sabbath put both Samson's Nicky Moore and Lone Star's John Sloman through their paces. Even crooner Michael Bolton submitted a demo tape. A meeting at the familiar haunt of the Rainbow Bar & Grill to entice onboard the Whitesnake pairing of David Coverdale and Cozy Powell failed to yield solid results.

The band's next move took the rock world by total surprise, as it was announced that Black Sabbath's new singer would be none other than former Deep Purple man Ian Gillan alongside a reinstated Bill Ward. Many Gillan fans felt betrayed, as Gillan had – only weeks before – quit a British tour, claiming to be severely affected with a throat infection that would put him out of action for months. Gillan band-members also leaked the news that an abortive attempt at putting Deep Purple back together again had prompted the singer's move. When this proposed union faltered, Gillan got the welcome call from Black Sabbath.

Bill Ward was reinstated for recording, having been pulled from his latest venture Max Havoc, although Iommi called in his old Quartz ally Malcolm Cope to lay down drums for the album's demo tracks, prior to Ward taking up his position. With Ward in place, the band cut the finished tracks, with only one cut not making the final running order. Entitled 'The Falling' (often misnamed 'The Fallen' by bootleggers), the track was left off purely to maintain the desired 45 minutes of running time.

The ensuing album, *Born Again* – featuring an incredibly garish sleeve, designed by *Kerrang!* art director Steve 'Krusher' Joule – was slated by critics. Indeed, it soon emerged that the album cover was a photocopied, re-touched version of a photo used for a Depeche Mode single sleeve ('New Life', issued in 1981), simply coloured in and with added claws and horns. As it transpired, the picture was third-hand, originally credited to 'Rizzoli Press' on the front cover of a 1968 issue of *Man Alive* magazine.

TO BE OR NOT TO BE

Geezer Butler: "That Born Again album with Ian Gillan: that wasn't supposed to be Black Sabbath. That was the manager and the record company insisting we use the name, and I was opposed to it but they are the ones who can turn the tap off when it comes to paying for everything, so it became a Black Sabbath album. It wouldn't be the last time that happened, either."

Geoff Nicholls: "That album was designed as a new 'supergroup'. They didn't want to call it Black Sabbath at all because, well, it was Ian Gillan, wasn't it. How could that be Black Sabbath? Well, anyway, the record company got their way again, and so Black Sabbath it was. It's all about selling albums at the end of the day, and that is, as an artist, an argument you will always lose with a record company."

Ronnie James Dio: "I was expecting them to try and patch things up with Ozzy or go for a certain type of singer, but never in a million years would I have guessed Ian Gillan. The guy's voice is just too distinctively un-Sabbath. Ian Gillan has an amazing voice for Deep Purple. That fact is beyond question. It was never going to work with Sabbath, and I remember thinking some clown in a record company who knows nothing about music is responsible for this. Everyone knew there was no way in hell it could last."

The artistic combination of Gillan and Black Sabbath certainly jarred with many fans. Regardless, an equal number praised this strange alliance. The record still achieved an exceptionally high British chart placing and good international sales. Shortly after recording *Born Again*, Ward was forced to quit due to recurring health problems. He re-forged ties with Max Havoc on the production front, and was quickly replaced by a longstanding friend of Iommi's, Electric Light Orchestra drummer Bev Bevan.

BORN AGAIN

Born Again would be noted for its almost primitive production values. However, apparently this final result was not what was originally intended. Ian Gillan's famous Kerrang! magazine quote, "I saw the cover then puked; then I heard the record, then puked," has gone down in heavy metal folklore.

Ian Gillan: "It's crap. There is no other word to describe it. When we finished the album I stood behind the desk at The Manor in Oxford and gave it one final listen and it was fucking great. It wasn't just great, it was monstrous. I remember the smiles in the room.

"I took a cassette of that mix, which I thought was final. That's what I was told. The next thing I hear is that Geezer is unhappy because he thought the bass wasn't loud enough. So, he took it down to London, remixed the whole thing, and from that point on, radio refused to play it. It was bloody awful, plain and simple – a total fucking disaster. The band was great, the record was great, but it was issued to the public in a form that was wrong. It was crap and you have to lay the responsibility for that firmly on Geezer's doorstep.

"When I saw the cover I just thought, this has to be a joke. C'mon, somebody tell me this is a joke, right? But it wasn't. It was the real thing. I can remember looking at this thing. A bright red baby with fangs, two horns and long fingernails, and I'm just thinking to myself that this about summed the whole thing up. It was just so Black Sabbath. I would have been happier if Don had put a lump of cheese with two horns on it for the cover because at least they would have been honest. It was just so un-classy. In a way it didn't matter what the songs were like, how good I was onstage, or anything,

because it all just boiled down to that baby. That's all people would remember. Everywhere I went promoting that record, all I saw was that fucking baby.

"Strangely though, over the years, that cover has become almost as famous as some of the well-known Sabbath album covers because it was just so awfully bad. What was absolute rubbish 20 years ago is now an ironic classic. I've come to accept the baby in my life now. It's been a struggle."

This most controversial of Black Sabbath formations tested the water in Scandinavia, opening up the proceedings in Oslo at the Drammenshallen on August 18th supported by up-and-coming Danish band Pretty Maids. Sabbath ambitiously concocted a set-list covering all bases from both the Dio and Ozzy eras, including the welcome addition of 'Rock'n'Roll Doctor' and the quirky 'Supernaut' plus the highly unexpected addition of Deep Purple's 'Smoke On The Water'. There was even discussion, and rehearsal, of Electric Light Orchestra's 'Evil Woman' and Deep Purple's 'Black Night', although neither song made the final running order.

Headlining the 23rd National Jazz, Blues & Rock Festival at Reading that year, Black Sabbath rubbed salt in the wounds of a sneering British press, brazenly parading 'Smoke On The Water' as an encore. The festival organisers captured two of rock's most memorable moments, as co-headliners Thin Lizzy used the event to bow out.

Assailed by the press for Gillan's induction, the 'baby' album cover and the record's sound quality, Black Sabbath gave the media a fourth golden shot with the notorious Stonehenge stage-set. Constructed by Light & Sound Design in Birmingham, the fibreglass menhirs were constructed lifesize, far too big to fit into most venues. The spoof 'rockumentary' *This Is Spinal Tap* would rub salt into the wounds by duplicating the tale in reverse proportions.

Black Sabbath's tour then took them to Ireland, a festival at Dalymount Park Football Stadium in Dublin, before gigs across Spain, the Low Countries and Germany with fellow West Midlanders Diamond Head in support. Controversy continued to follow the latest incarnation of the band wherever they roamed: at a gig in Zwolle, Holland, one insulted fan even threw a wheelchair on stage in protest at the perceived sullying of the Black Sabbath legend.

The band limbered up for the big prize, North America, with rehearsals at the Maple Leaf ice hockey stadium in Toronto during October. Tragically, the debut show collapsed into farce with robed monks marching onstage, competing with a dwarf – dressed in a *Born Again* baby devil outfit atop Stonehenge. Thankfully, injuries sustained by the actor portraying the baby when he fell off the huge stage prop put an end to such nonsense.

CITY COLISEUM, QUEBEC, 20TH OCTOBER 1983

Ian Gillan: "I noticed this dwarf hanging around on the day of the show which obviously piqued my curiosity. When we got into the production rehearsal this dwarf was there again. What happened was so mind-boggling that we all had to pinch ourselves afterwards to make sure we had really seen it with our own eyes. The rehearsal involved an intro tape of a newborn baby, but distorted and flanged through the PA to sound utterly horrible. The dwarf then appeared dressed in red exactly like the baby on the album cover, complete with yellow horns and fingernails, and crawled about on top of Stonehenge before standing up and, with a scream, falling backwards onto a pile of safety mattresses.

"The baby's screaming stopped and an ominous bell began to toll and a line of roadies, dressed in monks' robes with cowls pulled down, sombrely shuffled onstage. I can imagine those roadies all having a good giggle under their cowls. This was the cue for the band to go on. All we needed at that point was a bearded lady, a couple of elephants and a high-wire act, and I think we could have got that down to perfection.

"Don Arden thought it was just wonderful, but Bev Bevan and I voiced our concerns that the whole thing was deeply disturbing and actually in very poor taste. Don basically told us it was show business and to shut up and get on with our jobs. When Don Arden tells you to shut up and get on with it, that is exactly what you do, so that was that."

Geoff Nicholls: "I bet Ronnie was fuming! First Ozzy had taken a dwarf out on the road with him and then Black Sabbath did the same. He was getting it from both ends. The dwarf was prancing along on top of Stonehenge, like he was supposed to. What was supposed to happen next was that the front-of-house lights would go off and he would take a dive. However, the back lights were supposed to stay on so he could see where to fall. The problem was that nobody had turned the back lights on in the first place, so that when the cue came all of the lights went off and he couldn't see a thing. It was pitch black, so of course he fell off in the wrong place. We all heard this tremendous screech of 'Aaaarrrgggh!' It wasn't part of the show. He had really hurt himself. but I don't think anybody cared because it was just so, so funny."

In spite of seemingly insurmountable odds, *Born Again* was selling strongly – Gillan's inclusion boosted interest internationally – and further US dates were planned. However, this line-up soon fell apart: on the surface this seemed due to them being harried by the press from all quarters, but in actuality Gillan had merely served out his contract for one album and one world tour while awaiting developments with Deep Purple. The timing was inopportune, however, as a further six weeks of scheduled US shows had to be cancelled. Gillan duly formed part of the classic Mk II Deep Purple line-up for their worthy comeback album, *Perfect Strangers*.

In 1984 Sabbath began consultations with producer Spencer Proffer about a possible collaboration on an album. Proffer was a hot ticket, having worked on the recent Number 1 Quiet Riot album *Metal Health*. The producer suggested that Black Sabbath hook up with former Steeler vocalist Ron Keel. The young American did not audition but instead cut a series of demos, produced by Slaughter's Dana Strum. These tapes consisted of a selection of tracks written by Canadian band Kick Axe and were suggested for use by Proffer for a forthcoming Black Sabbath product. However, Iommi was less than impressed with the producer's choice of material, and relations between Proffer and Black Sabbath were curtailed. Keel was also put out of the frame. But it wasn't long before news stories of his tenure with the band were leaked: Keel went on to major-label success with his own eponymous band, as Sabbath began the hunt once more for a singer. As for Proffer's rejected Kick Axe tracks, 'Running Wild In The Streets' would end up on the W.A.S.P. album *The Last Command* – deftly re-credited to Blackie Lawless – while the other two, 'Hunger' and 'Piece Of The Rock', would be covered by Carmine Appice's King Kobra.

ROCK BOTTOM
After dismissing any notion of working with Ron Keel and prior to enrolling David Donato, Black Sabbath tried out another singer.

Geoff Nicholls: "He was an American guy, funnily enough as short as Ronnie but he had this huge voice. The thing was, his name was David but he insisted on being called 'Da-Verd'. We were doing some songwriting up in my hotel room and he kept on correcting me every time I called him David.

"Anyhow, the tapes he submitted were great, but we needed to hear him sing live in rehearsal. What did it for us was that we were watching him from behind while he was singing, and he had this thing about wiggling his bottom while he sang. We were in hysterics, literally crying with laughter. Well, he knew something was up and kept looking around suspiciously and we would all rapidly adopt stony faces and look away. As soon as he turned to the front and started singing again, this little bum started to wiggle and we would all be rolling in tears again. Of course, when you're playing live you need to be concentrating on the show – not your singer's bum. Geezer stopped laughing, finally saw the serious side, and said, 'This is not very fucking heavy metal, is it?'"

Finally, Sabbath announced that Bill Ward had rejoined, and unveiled a new vocalist, the American David Donato, whose past credits listed various small-time Californian club bands such as Hero, Headshaker, Virgin and White Tiger (the last act alongside Kiss guitarist Mark St. John). The tape that secured Donato the job was recorded with ex-Deep Purple bassist Glenn Hughes and Mark Norton (aka Mark St. John) in a band named Dali.

With Donato fronting the band, Sabbath engaged in six months of rehearsals at the Rockhouse in Los Angeles. In early 1985 a now infamous Sabbath interview in *Kerrang!* mocked the new-look band. The heavily edited article was viewed by many as signalling the death knell for Donato's involvement – although, in reality, the singer maintained his position for many months afterward. The ongoing rehearsals culminated in a Bob Ezrin-produced demo. These sessions included the unreleased cuts 'No Way Out', 'Don't Beg The Master' and 'Dancing With The Devil'. The Donato incarnation of Black Sabbath then disbanded, with Geezer endeavouring to build a solo band in St. Louis.

Post-Sabbath, Donato's next shortlived project would be a brief union with guitarist Lanny Cordola and Barry Brandt (of Angel repute) dubbed The Void. Another call from the Sabbath camp had Donato cutting demos with Geezer Butler: subsequently, Donato re-emerged under the pseudonym Michael McDonald, fronting the shortlived outfit Keep in alliance with old colleague Mark St. John and Kiss co-founder Peter Criss.

Tony Iommi began demoing new material utilising the services of bassist Gordon Copley and ex-Icebreaker drummer Eric Singer, the rhythm section from the band of his then-girlfriend, Lita Ford. Demo sessions for what was originally planned as Iommi's solo album, *Seventh Star*, saw the inclusion of American TV evangelist Jeff Fenholt. The singer, a former frontman for Keith Relf's Armageddon, Bible Black and Joshua, claims to have been a member of the band between January and May 1985. However, this has been hotly disputed.

An unquestionable fact, however, is the existence of the demos themselves. These tracks, compiled on an unofficial album of pre-production material, reveal songs that eventually ended up on the *Seventh Star* album – recorded with different lyrics – such as 'Star Of India', 'Dark Side Of Love', 'In The Eye Of The Storm', 'Rock The World', 'Lock Myself Away', 'Don't Turn Away' and 'Love Has No Mercy'. Immediately after his Black Sabbath liaison, Fenholt embarked upon a series of solo Christian concerts in South America prior to returning to Los Angeles to front the hotly-tipped Driver for a brief period.

PHILADELPHIA JFK STADIUM, 13TH JULY 1985: LIVE AID
Tony Iommi: "It was something that I think nobody could have possibly said no to. It made our lives, our bands and our silly arguments all look as insignificant as they actually were. Nobody went into it thinking about a reformation. It was such a great pleasure to play with Ozzy, Bill and Geezer again. I don't think we played spectacularly well, but the day wasn't about that. The four of

us actually had a very good time. Being there was the important thing. You have to wonder, though, if we made any difference to the situation in Africa."

The Live Aid event on July 13th 1985 was the catalyst for an impromptu reunion of the original Black Sabbath. Ozzy, Iommi, Butler and Ward sprinted through just three numbers, 'Children Of The Grave', 'Iron Man' and 'Paranoid', but negotiations for a more permanent venture ultimately proved fruitless. Butler returned to Britain to set up a more AOR-orientated act that performed a handful of club shows.

With Sabbath having effectively fallen apart, Iommi got back to business with his solo album. The endeavour was originally projected to feature three vocalists: Ronnie James Dio, Judas Priest's Rob Halford and ex-Deep Purple and Trapeze star Glenn Hughes. As it turned out, Hughes cut all the songs. The singer delivered a majestic performance, but troubled times were ahead.

Apparently persuaded by manager Don Arden and the record company, this album was eventually to see the light of day in March 1986 under the rather unwieldy name of Black Sabbath Featuring Tony Iommi. Paradoxically, it was also to be one of the guitarist's brightest moments, despite much of the material on the finished album being original demos, some cut with Lita Ford bassist Gordon Copley.

A catastrophic chain of tribulation was to ensue. Produced by Jeff Glixman, *Seventh Star* was a highly polished album that gave Iommi freedom to explore the bluesier side of his nature and saw an awesome vocal display from Hughes. Much of the songwriting would be attributed to keyboard player Geoff Nicholls who, much to the relief of fans, finally took his rightful place in official band photos for this outing.

Iommi formed a new band around this album with Hughes, Nicholls, drummer Eric Singer and ex-White Lion bassist Dave 'The Beast' Spitz. Spitz had left White Lion to join Black Sabbath, but not before White Lion had in turn asked Singer to drum for them. Then without a record contract, the White Lion proposition did not seem too appealing to Singer or Spitz, who took up with Iommi.

GLENN HUGHES ON SEVENTH STAR

Recording: "We did the record really quickly, starting in July. The whole thing at Cherokee was completed in a matter of days, actually. I wrote a lot of stuff for Seventh Star, and so much stuff was put down, Tony wanted to use most of it. So I ended up doing the whole thing because Tony was really happy. I must stress that all the way through this I was being told this was Tony's solo record. The idea was to call it just Tony Iommi."

Black Sabbath: "When I learned that Don Arden and the record company had this wonderful idea of calling the album Black Sabbath I was really shocked. Even Tony was shocked and disappointed too, I think. I don't know what went on there, really, but it came out of the wash as some kind of awkward compromise as 'Black Sabbath featuring Tony Iommi'. I was horrified because the very first thing I can remember thinking was, 'Oh no, I have to go out on tour as the singer for Black Sabbath.' I was just thinking, 'How am I going to explain this to Ozzy?'"

The tour: "[My] eye socket had been badly damaged and a piece of bone had lodged in my sinuses. It was horrible. Consequently everything was blocked up with dried blood. It was pretty gruesome. So for the next three weeks I tried to sing with my vocal chords blocked. When I first tried to sing, it sound like a broken reed in a saxophone. A really strange, unnatural sound."

The end: "Do you know how they fired me? They shoved a goddamn note and a plane ticket under my door. I couldn't fucking believe it. They couldn't bear to tell me themselves face to face. I tried to find them but they refused to speak to me. It was all very school-boyish. Bye bye Black Sabbath."

The American tour started out in Cleveland, Ohio, on March 21st 1986 with support acts W.A.S.P. and Anthrax, but Hughes was struggling with well-documented and self-confessed drug-related problems. However, the day before the debut gig the vocalist was punched by a member of Black Sabbath's crew. With blood choking his throat, Hughes's performance suffered greatly, giving the band concern enough to secretly audition replacements. They would select Ray Gillen. Spitz had suggested the then unknown New Yorker after seeing him perform in the clubs fronting Rondinelli. Prior to joining Black Sabbath, Gillen had been considering a career move into the stage cast for the musical *Cats*.

Having joined Black Sabbath on the road as a standby, Gillen's real purpose was soon divulged. Hughes was formally notified that he was out of the band following a Connecticut show on March 29th, leaving Gillen to pick up the pieces for the remaining dates. The following UK tour, with ill-matched support act Zeno, played to half-empty houses despite the excellence of the new material, Gillen's superior vocals and the singer's magnetic presence. It seemed that the fans had simply had enough of constant line-up changes: one of the band's London Hammersmith Odeon gigs was filmed for commercial release, but due to the paltry crowd numbers on the day remained shelved.

Ray Gillen: "This is an uphill battle for us now – we are realistic. It just makes me fight harder. I want to sing better to make sure people leave believing that Sabbath is back on the rails again. And it is, it really is. I feel some confidence coming back, I really do.

"Tony tells people he is proud of this band and I believe it. I'm proud to be here. I view this like a God-given opportunity, because I was kind of plucked right out of the blue for this band. I love singing all these classic songs, but right now I'm just itching to sing in the studio. I want to have my name on a Black Sabbath record. I want to have my friends walk into a record store, pick up a Black Sabbath album and see my picture on there."

Black Sabbath then retired to Air Studios on the island of Montserrat, aided by producer Jeff Glixman. Unfortunately, Glixman upped and left midway through recording; his place was taken by Vic Coppersmith, brought in to assist Gillen with his vocals, but he hardly lasted any longer. As Dave Spitz bowed out with personal problems, former Rainbow and Ozzy Osbourne bassist Bob Daisley was enlisted to help the band out of a tight spot, as producer Chris Tsangarides finally topped and tailed the album in London. Daisley would end up recording all the bass parts as well as contributing lyrics to the record: he was later invited to join the band, and accepted. However, due to the chaotic nature of Black Sabbath at that juncture, the bassist subsequently took up an offer from Irish guitar maestro Gary Moore and invited Eric Singer to join him.

Further turmoil followed, as Gillen didn't stick around long enough to finish recording the next album, *Eternal Idol*. He opted instead to join ex-Thin Lizzy guitarist John Sykes and drum legend Cozy Powell in a formative version of Blue Murder. Gillen would also session for the second volume of the all-star Phenomena project album. When the proto-Blue Murder situation failed to gel for Gillen or Powell, the vocalist created another branch in the convoluted family tree by re-forging links with his former Sabbath drum partner Eric Singer, with Ozzy Osbourne guitarist Jake E. Lee's new blues-rock act Badlands. Gillen would die tragically young of an AIDS-related illness in early December 1993, but his legacy with Black Sabbath remains on a set of highly sought-after bootleg recordings of the original album sessions. Post-Badlands, Eric Singer enjoyed fame with Alice Cooper and Kiss.

Summoning up the energy to regroup yet again, Iommi pulled in Birmingham's Tony Martin, previously with The Alliance and Tobruk, to fill the vacant vocal spot. Ironically, Martin had unsuccessfully auditioned for the frontman position with Blue Murder, a spot subsequently given over to his Black Sabbath predecessor Ray Gillen. *The Eternal Idol* showcased Martin's vocal abilities, unfortunately tainted by a remarkable resemblance to Dio.

Lead single 'The Shining' had been in the works since the David Donato days. Initially billed 'No Way Out', it underwent a number of transitions, mutating in demo form through 'No Way Out' to 'Black Fire', then 'Power Of The Night' and 'Rise Up'. Despite the undoubted quality of the songs on the album – *Eternal Idol*, released in November 1987, is often hailed as an overlooked classic – this could do little to stem the tide and the record fared badly in the charts.

THE ETERNAL IDOL

Bob Daisley: "Montserrat was a beautiful place to work in. We would drink from warm coconuts straight off the tree, we had a cuisine chef on hand, and in the evening we would watch the sun sinking over the horizon. Not very fitting with the Black Sabbath image, I know, but that's how it was. There were plenty of goats about but I think we were all too relaxed to actually bother with sacrificing any."

Tony Martin: "I had to duplicate Ray's vocals exactly, whether I could hit the note or not. They really, really pushed me to get it exact, note for note. It was pretty gruelling. They wouldn't let me change anything, not the slightest thing. We also had to do it quick because the album had already cost them an arm and a leg."

Eric Singer: "There are some great songs on there. I never understood that credit for Bev Bevan for percussion, though. I know my drum patterns and I know what I did in the studio, and everything I hear is mine on the final thing. Percussion? What's that supposed to mean? Did he add a cowbell or a tambourine or something? I can't hear it if he did."

Black Sabbath then took to the road in Europe, with ex-Virginia Wolf bassist Jo Burt in the ranks along with drummer Terry Chimes, a veteran of an eclectic, non-metal range of acts such as The Clash, Generation X, Hanoi Rocks and Cherry Bombz. The band put in extensive road work throughout Germany and Italy, supported by Virgin Steele. A solitary London Hammersmith Odeon gig intended to round the year off was cancelled at short notice.

PANATHENAIKOS STADIUM, ATHENS, GREECE 20TH JULY 1987

Tony Martin: "God, that gig! They let the kids in during the soundcheck so we were all thinking, 'What the fuck is going on here?' It was mayhem. Tony was so furious he had the promoter up against a wall and was whacking him.

"When we started with 'Children Of The Grave' I went to the front of the stage as planned, the band was playing and ... I forgot the words. Of course, I had told Tony to keep playing, so he just kept on with the riff, giving me a strange look as if to say, 'What the fuck is he doing?' The words just escaped me completely, so I stood there for an eternity, but they just didn't come. I ran over to Geoff Nicholls and shouted, 'I've forgotten the words!' He tried to prompt me but of course it was just too loud. I couldn't hear him so I shouted back at him, 'Fuck!' and he shouted back at me, 'Fuck!'

"I then ran over to Tony Iommi and shouted, 'I've forgotten the words!' and he mouthed back at me, 'Fuck!' He solved it by going straight into the chorus, and from then on I was all right.

"Suddenly everybody rushed to the front and started trying to get onstage. These security guys just stood there ignoring the whole situation, so I had to resort to literally kicking people off the stage.

"Next thing I know is that the kids were scaling these lighting poles either side of the stage, and these things are starting to sway dangerously. There were kids hanging like monkeys in the rigging while we were playing."

Dave Spitz: "Tony Iommi looked at me and shouted, 'Let's get the fuck out of here!' I chucked my bass to my roadie and we just ran. This mob was after us, pulling at our clothes, and if they had pulled us down we would have been trampled. We just made it into the dressing room, where we got locked in."

In May 1988 Black Sabbath put in a surprise low-key appearance at a local nightclub, the Oldbury Top Spot, performing for charity. A lucky handful of fans witnessed one of the strangest ever band line-ups for this one-off gig, comprising Iommi, Martin, drummer Bev Bevan and keyboardist Geoff Nicholls handling bass duties. The event would prove to be the band's only non-Glenn Hughes live rendition of the *Seventh Star* track 'Heart Like A Wheel'.

An amusing Black Sabbath-related story emerged in April 1988 when *Kerrang!* ran an 'exclusive' story revealing plans for the top Welsh crooner Tom Jones to join the embattled band. The intention was to record a concept album and undertake a tour based upon the dual subjects of bullfighting and Welsh mining. The story was, of course, a well-conceived April Fool's Day hoax, fortunately enjoyed by both Iommi and Jones.

By this time, not only had the fans had enough, but Sabbath's record label's patience had worn thin. Vertigo dropped the band shortly after *Eternal Idol*'s release. Undaunted, Sabbath signed to Miles Copeland's IRS label and set about rebuilding their career with a clutch of strong album releases, kicking off with *Headless Cross* in April 1989, a record that re-kindled interest in mainland Europe and pulled in strong sales.

Meanwhile, another Black Sabbath player would be active on the live circuit. The Blue Thunder trio saw Bill Ward play alongside bassist Tim Bogert (a veteran high-profile member of Vanilla Fudge, Cactus, Marcus and Beck Bogert & Appice) and esteemed blues guitarist Walter Trout.

Sabbath's new album, *Headless Cross* – named after the medieval Worcestershire village where Tony Martin lived – naturally witnessed a further line-up shuffle, with Iommi and Martin drafting in ex-Rainbow, Whitesnake and MSG drummer Cozy Powell and little-known session bassist Laurence Cottle. The latter had made his mark behind the scenes on Gary Moore's *After The War* album and with sessions for Eric Clapton. Powell would be a valuable fit, with his name alone guaranteed to sell records.

For live work, Cottle was supplanted by former Whitesnake and Vow Wow bassist Neil Murray. Still, *Headless Cross* proved a welcome return to form and saw strong sales across Europe, particularly in Germany. The album, backed by a promotional video and strong promotion from IRS, rebuilt a great deal of the band's lost credibility.

The group took on North American dates in June 1989 supported by Metal Church, Silent Rage and Kingdom Come, but found enthusiasm thin on the ground and pulled out of the schedule before completion. *Headless Cross* had not crossed over into the USA, but elsewhere in the world the band's status was on the rise once again. Live action included shows in the UK, Europe, Mexico and Japan. A first came with a tour of Russia to huge audiences – sometimes upwards of 80,000 people a night – with matinee performances in Moscow's Olympic Hall and St. Petersburg's EKS Hall, performing ten back-to-back gigs in each city with British female rockers Girlschool.

Another superb album, *Tyr* in August 1990, was loosely based on Norse mythology – Tyr was the Viking war god. It found Black Sabbath solidifying their return in Europe. Stung by criticism directed at the lyrical content of *Headless Cross*, Tony Martin made no references to occult themes this time around. Unfortunately the band lost ground in the UK, where a September 1990 tour was pulled halfway through. Successful shows in Europe were opened by Circus Of Power. Unfortunately, in late 1991, the band suffered a serious setback when Powell was badly injured in a riding accident. The drummer's horse, Pip, suffered a heart attack and fell on Powell, fracturing his hip.

Although Sabbath had been continuously negotiating with Ozzy Osbourne for his return, in 1992 – following many false starts – Iommi and Butler finally opted for the next best thing by teaming up once more with Ronnie James Dio. Butler had jammed with the singer in North America on the *Lock Up The Wolves* tour, performing 'Neon Knights', after which the proposal to join forces once more was mooted. The idea was a necessary step for both parties, as Dio (the band) had suffered from less than capacity attendances on their American tour and Black Sabbath were in limbo following Ozzy's opt-out of reunion plans. With Dio rejoining, Tony Martin pursued a solo project, releasing a 1992 album *Back Where I Belong* for Vertigo in Germany that included a remake of Sabbath's 'Jerusalem' and studio aid from both Neil Murray and Cozy Powell. He would contribute lead vocals to two Misha Calvin albums, although these recordings had in fact been made much earlier, while the pre-Sabbath Martin was still with The Alliance.

With Cozy Powell still in recuperation from his horse-riding accident, his position was taken by Vinnie Appice. The resulting album was the Mack-produced *Dehumanizer*, which, despite being a heavyweight offering, failed to capture previous Dio-era glories, mainly due to a clutch of mediocre songs. Of the stronger material, it would transpire that 'Master Of Insanity', although uncredited, had been written by guitarist Jimi Bell for Geezer's earlier solo venture, The Geezer Butler Band.

Fans and Dio himself were unaware that another singer was back in the frame – Tony Martin. With old differences having resurfaced, Martin was called back into Rockfield Studios in Monmouthshire to re-record the *Dehumanizer* vocals. So productive were these clandestine sessions that a good portion of the following album was also put down on tape. When informed of the deception, Warner Bros., protecting their investment, insisted that the Dio version of the record be released in June 1992.

The band's *Dehumanizer* world tour opened in South America, with gigs in São Paulo, Porte Alegre and Rio de Janeiro, just before the album release. Unfortunately the projected resurrection failed to materialise and *Dehumanizer* opened at a disappointing Number 44 on the US charts. A first leg of American shows had Danzig opening, before British shows had Testament backing them up in September. Black Sabbath then toured Europe, followed by a stint of theatre gigs in North America supported by Californian thrashers Exodus and Germany's Skew Siskin.

In parallel, Ozzy was nailing the lid on his live work by performing his last two shows at Costa Mesa. The Oz invited Black Sabbath to play on the same bill and reunite for a few songs one last time following his performance. But the idea was anathema to Dio, who promptly announced that he was quitting once more, bowing out on the Sabbath stage on October 13th 1992 at the Henry J. Kaiser Convention Center in Oakland, California. This was not before another ugly war of words had ensued, including a fax to journalists from the Ozzy management camp detailing the paltry attendance figures that the Dio band had mustered the last time they played the Costa Mesa venue.

Remarkably, Black Sabbath did play at the Ozzy shows, with Judas Priest vocalist Rob Halford heading the band, the singer having learnt the entire set in two days. When it had first become clear that Dio was not going to perform, Tony Martin's services were requested, but then nixed by the Osbourne camp. With Martin out in the cold, Halford and Sabbath rehearsed at Vintage Studios in Phoenix and performed the next day in front of 20,000 fans. The next night Halford fronted the band again, before

handing over the microphone to Ozzy: the reunited band ripped through 'Black Sabbath', 'Fairies Wear Boots', 'Iron Man' and 'Paranoid'.

BLACK PRIEST?

Geoff Nicholls: "That was definitely the big plan, to get Rob into the band and sing on the next Black Sabbath album. Costa Mesa was like one big test, which the guy passed with flying colours. Discussions got to the point where he was going to be the next Black Sabbath singer and we all knew that could produce a monster of an album.

"Rob had everything. He could hit all those high notes, which meant that he could sing absolutely every song Tony Iommi had ever written; it was the first time that had ever happened. He had a reputation, he had his own fans, he was a Brummie, and his stage presence too was just awesome. What more could you ask? Both Tony Iommi and I really liked Rob's look then, too, with that whole Bela Lugosi 'Nosferatu' thing going on. I think Rob with Sabbath and the full show would have put us back on the map for sure."

During all this activity, ex-members Cozy Powell and Neil Murray re-founded one of Cozy's old acts, Cozy Powell's Hammer, with guitarist Mario Parga and singer Peter Oliver. This line-up only lasted one gig before the recruitment of another Black Sabbath face, Tony Martin. The band toured Europe, succinctly billed as Tony Martin & Friends. Powell and Murray would stick together to form Saints & Sinners.

Tragedy hit the Black Sabbath family on December 3rd 1993. Former singer Ray Gillen succumbed to AIDS, from which he had been suffering for many years, although he had kept this knowledge out of the public arena. Gillen's last recording sessions were with the New York Sun Red Sun project. Glenn Hughes organised a memorial concert at the Irving Plaza venue in New York the following February, reforming his classic Trapeze act for the occasion.

LINZ, AUSTRIA, 25TH MAY 1994

Tony Martin: "We suddenly encountered all this religious stuff down in Austria, which really felt weird. It seems they were upset about the fire on the angel's wings on the album cover. They really got quite upset about it and they banned all our gig posters in the town. They got some guy with a big stencil of a crocodile's mouth to go around town and paint this thing on top of all the posters. The crocodile covered up the flames. Apparently it was bad to set angels on fire, but it was quite all right to have large reptiles eating them.

"If you can believe this – because we didn't at first – the Bishop of Fulda sent an emissary down to check out the gig. This guy, in a long white trenchcoat, was there all night acting as an official observer in case we got up to anything naughty. In the audience was this lone guy with this placard, 'Save your souls – Turn to Jesus!' I asked the crew to turn a spotlight on him and said to the audience, 'Please give this guy a huge round of applause, because he's got the biggest bollocks of anyone here tonight.'"

The year 1994 saw another excellent if sadly overlooked Black Sabbath album, *Cross Purposes*. According to quotes from Geezer Butler, it was initially planned as an Iommi-Butler project album akin to Iommi's *Seventh Star*, but record company pressure saw its release under the Black Sabbath banner. The album boasted a heavyweight guest in the form of Eddie Van Halen, an (oddly) unaccredited co-writer of the track 'Evil Eye'. There is also speculation as to whether the famed guitarist actually performs on the track itself. A further oddity is that the jacket artwork (an angel with wings on fire) had already been used by the Scorpions for their 1991 single 'Send Me An Angel'. *Cross Purposes* spawned a poorly promoted live CD/video package, *Cross Purposes Live*.

Sabbath then toured North America once again with vocalist Tony Martin and new drummer Bobby Rondinelli, a veteran of Rainbow, this time in a heavyweight metal package with Motörhead and Morbid Angel, throughout February and March. There followed Japanese shows and a well received European jaunt with Coventry's own 1970s Sabbath-idolising support act Cathedral and American outfit Godspeed. However, in August 1994 Rondinelli was jettisoned prior to dates in South America for the 'Monsters Of Rock' shows partnered with Kiss: his place on the drum stool was once more in the hands of original member Bill Ward. The ousted New Yorker soon came back to the fore as a member of Blue Öyster Cult.

A Black Sabbath tribute album entitled *Nativity In Black* was then launched at the Los Angeles Foundations Forum. Essentially a selection of up-and-coming – and mainly American – acts such as Biohazard, White Zombie and Type O Negative playing in homage to their heroes, the album nonetheless featured some interesting combinations – such as Ozzy Osbourne and Therapy?'s rendition of 'Iron Man' and Megadeth performing 'Paranoid'. Also included was a track by The Bullring Brummies, a studio band consisting of Judas Priest and Fight vocalist Rob Halford, Geezer Butler, Fight guitarist Brian Tilse and The Obsessed guitarist Scott 'Wino' Weinrich.

As soon as an original Black Sabbath member was back in the line-up, another departed. Butler quit in September and went on to work on a solo album under the band handle of G//Z/R. The following month it was announced that the group had reinstated the *Headless Cross/Tyr*-era rhythm section of Neil Murray and Cozy Powell, alongside Iommi and Tony Martin.

Unfortunately the resulting album, *Forbidden* in June 1995, did not match the class of its predecessors, sounding rushed and lacking in overall sound quality. The somewhat pedestrian production was handled by Body Count guitarist Ernie C. and the album featured vocalist Ice-T guesting on the lead cut, 'The Illusion Of Power'. This awkward cobbling-together of styles was enforced by management, who believed Sabbath should try to emulate the success of Aerosmith/Run DMC, whose 1986 single 'Walk This Way' had been among the first rap-rock hits.

FORBIDDEN

Tony Martin: "The thing is, Forbidden was the last album under contract, so Tony wanted to get it away so he could get on with the reunion. There's no conviction or energy in those songs whatsoever. I can't stand to listen to the thing.

"When we learned about this rap guy [Ernie C] we just looked at each other and together we both said, 'This is bollocks!' That was probably the only light relief we got doing that record. Everybody was trying to put a brave face on it but we all knew it was the end."

Neil Murray: "Cozy wanted Headless Cross Part III but the record company were very resistant to that. Tony Iommi didn't want that either. He thought that that style was all a bit old hat and 1980s. Now we were faced with a rock industry that had since come to hail Black Sabbath as grunge godfathers. All that kind of thinking certainly played a part in the thinking behind the Forbidden album. I thought it was a mistake; Cozy thought it was a mistake. There were a lot of glum faces."

Cozy Powell: "I'm not ecstatic about the drum sound. If you listen to Headless Cross, the drums on there – that's my production. There is a big difference. I came in a bit late for this one, so basically just went in and did my thing, kept my mouth shut."

Tony Martin: "We hated the album and we all knew what was in store for us at the end of the tour. Tony was going to walk off into the sunset arm in arm with Ozzy and a big cheque and we were going to be out of a job. We were not happy one bit."

Still, Sabbath set out on tour in America once more, co-headlining with Motörhead for a second time. As these dates reached California, Powell was forced to leave to deal with personal problems and in came Bobby Rondinelli yet again to complete the schedule of a lengthy set of European dates, followed by Far Eastern and South Pacific concerts. With the *Forbidden* tour fulfilled, negotiations throughout much of the following year centred upon making a return for Ozzy Osbourne. Rondinelli would join Blue Öyster Cult in February 1997.

In mid 1996 it appeared that Iommi was working with vocalist Rob Halford once more for an album project, although the former Judas Priest vocalist still had commitments to his new industrial project Two. These proposals were subsequently put on ice and Iommi began recording solo material with his old ally Glenn Hughes, the veteran keyboard player Don Airey, longstanding colleague Geoff Nicholls and former Trapeze and Judas Priest drummer Dave Holland, for a projected solo album. Before this project was finalised – and from out of the blue – Sabbath relented to fan pressure and reunited their classic line-up.

Ozzy Osbourne headed up a touring extravaganza in North America, modestly titled 'Ozzfest'. The bill included his own band together with Pantera, Coal Chamber and Powerman 5000. The classic Black Sabbath were due to headline. Osbourne, Iommi and Butler forged the reunion, but Ward felt unable to commit himself – citing health reasons, both physical and mental.

Black Sabbath undertook the tour, which established itself as one of the biggest draws on the American touring circuit that year, aided by Ozzy Osbourne/Faith No More drummer Mike Bordin. While the American dates were under full steam, Butler put out his second and highly commendable solo affair with his band, now dubbed simply Geezer, in the form of *Black Science*. Enterprising bootleggers had also got hold of the Iommi-Hughes-Holland studio recordings and cheekily issued them as *Eighth Star.*

The Black Sabbath legend was kept alive by the release of Ozzy's compilation album, *The Ozzman Cometh*. Alongside more familiar solo Ozzy outings, the CD boasted four early unreleased Black Sabbath tracks, demo versions of 'Fairies Wear Boots', 'Behind The Wall Of Sleep', 'War Pigs' and 'Black Sabbath'.

The band, fronted by Ozzy, announced two shows at the Birmingham NEC in early December 1997, bringing Fear Factory as support. Both shows sold out, spawning a live album issued in 1998, *Reunion*. The record closed off with two brand new studio tracks, 'Psycho Man' and 'Selling My Soul'. Additional material was recorded, with lyrical input from Geoff Nicholls, but a planned full-length album never materialised. Nevertheless, upon its release *Reunion* gave Black Sabbath their first million-selling record since *Heaven And Hell.*

Progress was stalled on May 19th when Ward, who had been experiencing chest pains for some time, suffered what was later discovered to be a mild heart attack. With Ward's health still a subject of concern, Vinnie Appice was pulled from the ranks of Dio in 1998 to occupy the drum stool. Ward took most of the summer out, recuperating after health checks in order to resume his rightful position. The drummer did attend the Sabbath-headlined Ozzfest at Milton Keynes in June where, to everyone's amusement, Osbourne welcomed him on stage – and then pulled Ward's trousers down in front of 60,000 bemused onlookers.

Sabbath – rather prematurely as it happened – put in their "last ever" live gigs, dubbed The Last Supper, at Birmingham's NEC in late December 1999, with Ward back behind the kit. Appice then created his own act, Hunger Farm.

During 2000, Iommi took time out to perform with his less-than-serious club act Belch, a band that featured his ex-Sabbath friend Bev Bevan and comedian Jasper Carrott on vocals. Meanwhile, Osbourne was hard at work on a further solo album. After three decades, Iommi finally got around to issuing his first solo album proper – simply credited to Iommi. Both Osbourne and Ward were included on the track 'Who's Fooling Who'. The album featured a multitude of guest artists including Osbourne, Pantera's Phil Anselmo, Smashing Pumpkins mentor Billy Corgan, Foo Fighters leader Dave Grohl, Henry Rollins, Type O Negative's Pete Steele, ex-Soundgarden drummer Matt Cameron and former White Zombie drummer John Tempesta. Ward, meanwhile, was still endeavouring to complete his third solo album, provisionally titled *Beyond Aston*. A projected reissue of his first album, *Ward One: Along The Way*, was shelved when two songs that featured Ozzy on lead vocals created business complications.

Black Sabbath did reconvene for a summer 2000 show, although after the event they probably wished they hadn't. A surprise performance after an Ozzy Osbourne gig at the Anaheim Weenie Roast festival ended as a debacle when a revolving stage set snagged the band's gear, resulting in a long, embarrassing silence and lengthy delays. Undaunted, Sabbath would rise yet again during 2001, demonstrating renewed vigour as the main act at the California ESPN Action, Sports & Music Awards ceremony on April 7th.

This showing would provide a taster for another full-blown Ozzfest touring festival. Backing up the steadfast Brummies were contemporary acts such as Slipknot, Tool, Papa Roach, Amen, Soulfly, Disturbed and Black Label Society. Marilyn Manson would also figure, but only for the American dates. Even Geezer Butler's son got involved with his act Apartment 26. Also announced were Ozzy's plans for a solo album, apparently in stasis while a brand new Black Sabbath album was mooted.

A warm-up show just prior to the UK Ozzfest was held at the Birmingham Academy on May 22nd, with the band donating proceeds from the event to the homeless persons charity, St. Basils. Another display of nostalgia came in October with a long overdue, officially sanctioned release of archive live material. Divine Recordings, the label established by Ozzy's wife Sharon Osbourne, would announce the release of live tapes culled from the *Sabotage* world tour, suitably entitled *Live In '75*. However, just after a track listing and release had been set, the album was cancelled.

May 2001 witnessed a treat for fans when ex-Sabbath men Tony Martin and Neil Murray joined Bobby Rondinelli's self-titled band. Martin also found time to tour British clubs fronting Bailey's Comet as well as promote the *Cage 2* album, his second in league with Italian guitarist Dario Mollo. Meanwhile, Geoff Nicholls donated two of his compositions, 'Facing Hell' and 'Black Illusion', to Ozzy's 2001 album release *Down To Earth*.

SYMPTOMA MUNDI

In 2002, Rondellus, a group of classically trained Estonian medieval folk artists, transported an entire album of Sabs classics, Sabbatum, back to the 14th century. Sung in operatic style and played on original medieval instruments with lyrics translated into Latin, the record was a significant hit with the Sabbath faithful. Ozzy's trademark wails had become the Gregorian chants of Veikko Kiiver and the exquisite medieval harmonies of Maria Staak and Swedish singer Miriam Andersén, while Tony Iommi's crushing riffs had been transformed into delicate harp, bagpipe and fiddle passages.

Black Sabbath would hit music TV shows once again in the summer of 2002, courtesy of ex-member Ronnie James Dio and the video for his current single 'Push' from the Dio album *Killing The Dragon*. A lavish Bill Schacht-directed promo film would include appearances from the unlikely Tenacious D duo of Jack Black and Kyle Gass. Tenacious D had already signalled their respect for the band with the inclusion of the track 'Dio' on their current album. The video concept, in which a multitude of special effects would be employed, involved Tenacious D jamming Black Sabbath's 'Heaven And Hell' as an intro. The Dio-era Black Sabbath also gained media attention due to the announcement that artist Greg Hildebrandt's 'Mob Dream' (used as the cover art for the classic 1981 album *Mob Rules*) was up for sale at a cool $35,000.

The previously mooted live album reared its head again, retitled *Past Lives* and now set for release through the Sanctuary label. The album would comprise the *Live At Last* LP alongside further archive recordings. Following in the wake of medieval music act Rondellus, whose radical re-interpretations of Sabbath songs had enjoyed enormous underground success, the Czech String Quartet weighed in with a classical tribute in September. Yet another Black Sabbath tribute album gave a unique spin on the genre, with Killing Joke's Martin Atkins and his Opium Jukebox project publishing *Bhangra Bloody Bhangra*, giving classic tracks a distinct Indian slant, mixing traditional Eastern instrumentation with trance beats and electro. Meanwhile, Bill Ward returned to solo action, making available his new single 'Straws' in October.

As Ozzy unveiled for the summer of 2004 a somewhat more traditional-flavoured Ozzfest, including the reformed Judas Priest, the rumour mill began turning once more regarding a full-blown Black Sabbath reformation. By March, Iommi was in negotiation with Osbourne and, as the month closed, speculation arose that Geezer Butler had supplanted Rob Nicholson as bassist in Ozzy's band. On May 19th Black Sabbath announced the reformation of Osbourne, Iommi and Butler, seemingly once again to be joined by Mike Bordin on the drums. However, an outpouring of protest and some heartfelt words from Bill Ward soon saw the original drummer reinstated. In a further surprise move it was announced that keyboard player Geoff Nicholls was not being invited to play, thus ending his unbroken 24-year tenure with the band. In his place would be none other than Adam Wakeman, son of Yes keyboard player Rick.

Marking the return of Sabbath to the live stage, the Argentine label Blackstar C. Productions issued a tribute album, *Sabbath Crosses: Tribute To Black Sabbath*. Besides donations from major South American acts such as Nativo, Barilari, Sauron, Los Natas, Horcas and Beto Vazquez Infinity, this collection would be noted for a take on 'No Stranger To Love' from high-status Argentinian act Rata Blanca featuring Glenn Hughes on guest vocals.

Black Sabbath's opening show on the Ozzfest dates in Hartford, Connecticut, on July 10th witnessed an hour-long set of classics, controversially including a film backdrop for the track 'War Pigs' – which included president George W. Bush wearing a superimposed red clown nose cruelly juxtaposed on images of Adolf Hitler. Bill Ward was quick to distance himself from the film, stating that it did not represent his personal views towards President Bush and claiming the video was made without the drummer's "prior knowledge or consent". Once the initial burst of publicity had been garnered, the offending segment of film was soon dispensed with.

Meanwhile, Tony Iommi's shelved 1996 album was back in the news when earlier plans to release the Iommi-Hughes sessions as an internet download album were revised. Now scheduled as a regular album to be delivered through Sanctuary, the sessions had been somewhat re-worked under the Iommi handle. The guitarist had re-cut some of the main riffs and Dave Holland's drum work had been wiped and replaced by that of Jimmy Copley, who had worked with the Paul Rodgers band and M3. In addition, two songs had new bass guitar work added by Iommi's former Sabbath colleague Neil Murray.

Sensationally, Judas Priest's Rob Halford took over from Ozzy Osbourne for Black Sabbath's August 26th concert in Camden, New Jersey. Ozzy had been forced out of action by an attack of bronchitis but resumed his position to close out the remainder of the tour.

As the year closed, ex-Sabbath singer Tony Martin set *Scream* as the title of his solo record, revealing it was to include two archive tracks, 'Raising Hell' and 'Wings Of Thunder' – Sabbath out-takes from the *Tyr* and *Headless Cross* albums.

In 2005 a documentary film was launched to celebrate former Black Sabbath singer Ian Gillan's four decades of rock'n'roll. Among many other luminaries included in the movie, it featured contributions from Tony Iommi and Ronnie James Dio. Working with producer Nick Blagona, Gillan travelled to Toronto to cut an album during February that featured reworkings of tracks spanning his entire career, including some from Black Sabbath. Iommi featured on a remake of 'Trashed' from 1983's *Born Again*.

WHEELS OF CONFUSION
Taking the Black Sabbath tribute concept into previously uncharted realms would be the April 2005 offering Everything Comes & Goes. Constructed by names unfamiliar to the heavy metal world, the album included the likes of 'Reversible Sabbath', a composition from Japanese noisemongers Ruins, which involved a mesh of eight different Sabbath songs performed in reverse, while electronica duo Matmos re-rendered 'F/X' into a "barely audible jumble of electronic chirping".

The first signs of Black Sabbath activity for 2005 would be confirmation of an appearance at Denmark's Roskilde festival. As further gig announcements rolled in – including an appearance at the UK's Download festival (filmed for DVD release), German shows opened by Soulfly, and Scandinavian shows supported by Velvet Revolver – Osbourne dropped hints that another Black Sabbath album was probable. Meantime, the band, with Adam Wakeman once again installed on keyboards, headed up another series of US Ozzfest events, backed by Iron Maiden and a supporting cast including Velvet Revolver, Rob Zombie and Mudvayne.

Tony Iommi hooked up with Glenn Hughes once again to craft the *Fused* album. This highly commendable effort arrived shortly after Geezer Butler's latest GZR solo outing, *Ohmwork*, prompting rumours of a joint tour. In June, the Recording Industry Association of America (RIAA) revealed that Ozzy Osbourne as a solo artist had sold over 28 million albums in the USA – incredibly, a full 13 million albums more than Black Sabbath.

The Ozzfest ran without a hitch until the July 27th date at Holmdel, New Jersey, the PNC Arts Center, which saw Sabbath withdraw due to illness afflicting Ozzy. The band did perform an abbreviated set at Tweeter Center in Tinley Park, Illinois, on July 30th, but then pulled out of the Noblesville, Indiana, at Verizon Wireless Music Center, and a date at the Germain Theater in Columbus, Ohio. With Ozzy revealing he was suffering from acid reflux problems, the scheduled August 7th Ozzfest at Float Rite Park in Somerset, Wisconsin, was postponed to September 10th. At this juncture it was revealed that the singer was being coaxed through the shows by Ron Anderson, a retired opera singer, who monitored Ozzy's diet and lifestyle and even spoke directly to him on stage through an earpiece.

Black Sabbath's August 11th gig at White River Amphitheatre in Auburn, Washington, had fans witnessing the severity of Ozzy's ongoing vocal problems when his voice gave way in the midst of the track 'Dirty Women'. Ozzy threw his microphone down in disgust but was eventually coaxed out to struggle through the remainder of the set. The following day the singer made an official announcement: "After 10 years, the Ozzfest's name and reputation have been established. It's time for me to move on and do other things."

Ronnie James Dio stunned Black Sabbath fans in mid October with a casual remark during a BBC Radio 2 *Masters Of Rock* interview by stating: "Tony Iommi and I are going to write a couple of tracks together for a project that I think is called *Black Sabbath – The Dio Years*." The following month, at a ceremony held at London's Alexandra Palace, Black Sabbath was inducted into the UK Music Hall of Fame, joining the likes of Bob Dylan, Pink Floyd, Jimi Hendrix, The Who and The Kinks.

Of all the bands in this book, Black Sabbath's impact has arguably been the greatest. All metal fans owe them a huge debt.

BUDGIE
IN THE GRIP OF THE RIFF

AN ENDEARINGLY NAMED WELSH act hailing from Cardiff, Budgie have an influence on the heavy metal genre that has been tragically overlooked. Although the group attained a modicum of commercial success in the mid 1970s, with a steady output of quirky yet riff-heavy albums, they are often reduced to footnote status or casual mention. Always original in their approach, the group recorded tracks that were complex and way ahead of their time, but it would take the intervention of Metallica and their patronage of the 'Breadfan' anthem – long after Budgie's enthusiasm had been spent – to revitalise interest in their material.

Budgie spent most of the 1970s building a loyal cult following based on riff barrages married to songs with some of the most bizarre titles in metal, such as 'Hot As A Docker's Armpit', 'You're The Biggest Thing Since Powdered Milk', 'In The Grip Of A Tyrefitter's Hand' and 'Nude Disintegrating Parachutist Woman'.

The group was formed in 1967, putting in gigs in 1968 under the original name of Hills Contemporary Grass. They briefly took on the title Six Ton Budgie, with a line-up of the bespectacled vocalist-bassist Burke Shelley, guitarist Brian Goddard and the mysterious 'Kevin' on second guitar.

Truncating the band's name to Budgie, they debuted with a revised roster comprising Shelley, Goddard, guitarist Tony Bourge and drummer Ray Phillips. Their first demo was laid down in 1969 and by the following year Goddard had opted out, leaving Budgie as the classic power trio. Having built up a loyal following on the South Wales circuit, they struck out to London.

Budgie soon gained a reputation for distinctive songwriting and relentless riffs and signed to MCA in 1970. They engaged producer Rodger Bain, noted for his work with Black Sabbath, to craft their eponymous debut, which surfaced in June of that year. *Budgie* was a collection of drawn-out, proto-sludge progressivism, capped by Shelley's shrill nasal wail and constructed around some immense riffs delivered by Bourge. The album, spearheaded by the thunderous 'Guts', wasn't totally cohesive – as the odd fallback into boogie or the balladry of 'Everything In My Heart' and 'You And I' testified – but nonetheless invited the UK media to immediately pitch it against Black Sabbath. A barrage of club dates was capped by a performance at Barry Memorial Hall in December, where Budgie drew over 3,000 local fans.

Their second outing, *Squawk*, gained recognition for its distinctive Roger Dean artwork, which depicted a SR-71 Blackbird aircraft with a bird skull. *Squawk* is among the best lost underground metal classics and should really have broken the band into the major league. After all, Bourge's riffs topped the quality of previous efforts as Budgie delivered an awesome tour de force of metal. However, the album's muscular content was tempered by diversions into blues and even funk, which made for some confusing listening. It remained strictly of cult appeal.

Live work in 1971 included a brief spate of ill-matched dates opening for funk outfit Osibisa before forays into Europe. The following year saw little respite, with shows across France, Italy, Holland and Germany, and an intensive UK schedule that included opening slots for Thin Lizzy and Mott The Hoople. There was also a showcase performance on the 'Giants Of Tomorrow' stage in a marquee at the Great Western Express Spring Bank Holiday Festival in May, co-headlined by Nazareth and The Faces.

Never Turn Your Back On A Friend in 1973 opened with the accelerated brute force of 'Breadfan' but also included enigmas such as the grinding 'You're The Biggest Thing Since Powdered Milk' and 'In The Grip Of A Tyrefitter's Hand'. The group didn't stray far into progressive territory with this outing – but deliberately marched into those dangerous realms with gusto with the epic *Parents*. This third effort is widely recognised as Budgie's finest achievement.

Budgie then extended their reach into Europe with gigs in Switzerland, Spain – including a nine-night stand at the Double Zero Club in Barcelona – and Austria, followed by a mammoth series of shows in July and August supported by the up-and-coming Judas Priest.

The year 1974 opened with a further round of British concerts, with Priest once more in the opening spot. March and April saw the group playing in Germany before a rapid round of Norwegian gigs and May concerts in the UK, backed by Priest again.

Budgie's line-up remained stable throughout their first three major-label albums until Ray Phillips quit: the drummer would join ex-Sassafras vocalist Terry Bennett in Kracotoa and then surfaced in Ray Phillips's Woman, before much later joining Tredegar. Phillips was replaced by former Extreem and Bullion sticksman Pete Boot for 1974's *In For The Kill*. (Boot was superseded by ex-Quest member Steve Williams in December 1974 and went on to join Sweaty Betty and Possessed before forming Lion with ex-Priest vocalist Al Atkins.) Here, Budgie, apart from their strange interpolation of 'Bolero', simply delivered more of their winning formula – which, although it appeased their loyal fanbase, didn't manage to break the band into the wider market.

Bandolier was released in 1975 and recorded at Rockfield Studios in Monmouthshire. Williams's introduction into the fold had given the musicians more creative leeway to incorporate new textures into their sound, as evidenced on a slice of Latin Americana on the introduction to 'Slipaway'. The group used this record to penetrate deeper into European territories, including a live debut in Yugoslavia. In the usual Budgie fashion, the record contained some titular quirkiness with its closer, the suitably epic 'Napoleon Bona, Parts 1 & 2'. Fans lapped up the metronomic, heavyweight 'Breaking All The House Rules', but oddly the band still languished in cultdom.

The word games continued with 1976's hotchpotch *If I Were Britannia I'd Waive The Rules*. In that year the group also performed their first US dates, and although a projected tour launch in February was postponed, the trio finally made their live debut in front of an American audience at the Royal Oak Theater in Detroit on November 20th. Further US shows saw Budgie sharing stages with Sparks, Montrose and Captain Beyond. Budgie returned to the USA in the summer of 1977. Meanwhile, their success in the UK meant that they had risen to headlining status at London's Hammersmith Odeon.

John Thomas: "Budgie was in a strange place really, because they had built up this big set of fans who would buy the records and come out to the shows, but they were always in need of that big break. Lots of people had put a lot of money into the band, people who really believed in Budgie and loved the music. The trouble was, I think, that the band were nice guys, the managers were always nice guys – and that's not how you get on in this business. They even had members of the family writing lyrics to songs. Everyone knew that Budgie should have been huge. Maybe if the band had been called Vulture, or something, it might have worked."

Budgie's seventh album, *Impeckable*, recorded with Richard Manwaring behind the desk during a lengthy period in Canada, arrived on new label A&M in January 1978. The following month they played a well-attended clutch of UK theatre shows before embarking on their lengthiest US trek to date, which took the band right through the summer months. This Stateside foray produced the much-in-demand *Live At Atlantic Studios* live tapes, still much sought after by collectors. The band then briefly recruited another Quest member in second guitarist Myf Isaacs, who went on to various Welsh-language acts such as Bando, Crys and Eden.

Budgie then boosted their guitar arsenal with the recruitment of former Trapeze man Rob Kendrick. The year was seen out with a further successful run of UK concerts throughout October and November.

In February 1979 the group accompanied Nazareth for US gigs, the last shows to feature Kendrick. During this period the band recorded tracks in Dallas for a proposed album, but these were never issued.

Budgie then drafted in 'Big' John Thomas (previously a member of Bombshell and affectionately known as JT), debuting the new recruit at Stafford Bingley Hall on December 15th and recording the infamous Dave Charles-produced EP *If Swallowed Do Not Induce Vomiting*. The band set about promoting the record with a June 1980 headline trek in the UK. The full-length album *Power Supply*, again with Dave Charles producing, was Budgie at their most raucous yet, less refined and unafraid to stake their claim as a heavy metal band. Unfortunately, this alienated many of their long-standing fans. Further valuable exposure came when Budgie were hand-picked to open for Ozzy Osbourne's Blizzard Of Ozz shows, starting on December 9th at Glasgow's Apollo. For these gigs the group expanded their sound with keyboard player Lindsay Bridgwater, who also did duty for Ozzy Osbourne.

John Thomas: "Ozzy gave us a big favour with that tour. He chose Budgie for it and we made a great package. I'll never forget those gigs because we were playing to the Budgie diehards and introduced them to Ozzy's new band, plus of course all the Sabbath fans who were keen to see what Ozzy was up to now got introduced to Budgie. It was a perfect match and really set Budgie up with the next album."

BUDGIE discography

BUDGIE, MCA MKPS 2018 (UK), Kapp KS-3656 (USA) (1971)

SQUAWK, MCA MKPS 2023 (UK), Kapp KS-3669 (USA) (1972)

NEVER TURN YOUR BACK ON A FRIEND, MCA MDKS 8010 (UK), MCA MAPS 6624 (USA) (1973)

IN FOR THE KILL, MCA MCF 2546 (UK), MCA MCA-429 (USA) (1974) **29 UK**

BANDOLIER, MCA MCF 2723 (UK), A&M SP-4518 (USA) (1975) **36 UK**

IF I WERE BRITANNIA I'D WAIVE THE RULES, A&M AMLH 68377(UK), A&M SP-4593 (USA) (1976)

IMPECKABLE, A&M AMLH 64675 (UK), A&M SP-4675 (USA) (1978)

POWER SUPPLY, Active ACTLP 1 (UK) (1980)

NIGHTFLIGHT, RCA RCALP 6003 (UK) (1981) **68 UK**

DELIVER US FROM EVIL, RCA RCALP 6054 (UK) (1982) **62 UK**

WE CAME, WE SAW…, Pilot PILOT 14 (UK) (1998)

LIFE IN SAN ANTONIO, Noteworthy NP1 (UK) (2002)

THE LAST STAGE, Noteworthy NP12 (UK) (2004)

Budgie's cause was taken up by a new record label, RCA, for their 1981 album *Nightflight*, which – in contrast to *Power Supply*'s bludgeoning, NWOBHM-style riffs – visited calmer waters, even leaning towards cultured AOR on occasion.

In 1982 Budgie undertook a historic, massively attended tour of Poland. Performing in venues of up to 10,000 capacity, they sold out 12 shows plus matinee performances. This was followed by a sizeable set of shows in Yugoslavia. Western bands had for many years enjoyed a huge profile in the Eastern Bloc, mainly due to massive sales of counterfeit recordings, but Budgie would pioneer touring into these territories.

The *Deliver Us From Evil* album emerged in October 1982 but would only serve to backtrack on the progress made with *Nightflight*. Produced by Don Smith, *Deliver Us…* was awash with unnecessary keyboards, courtesy of ex-10cc and Camel man Duncan MacKay. Neutered by a lack of character, the record soon languished.

In the same year Budgie headlined the Reading Rock festival. A quite bizarre display bemused fans as the audience was bombarded with toy budgies and John Thomas performed on a monster 'Hooligan' guitar, suspended from the lighting rig. This surreal episode marked Budgie's first and last attempts at stage effects. The band then took up a further offer to support Ozzy Osbourne at his December arena concerts in the UK.

However, after a few October 1983 UK concerts supporting Diamond Head, the trio pulled out, and demos for a proposed new album were laid down but not used. Surprisingly, the band decided to suspend operations and officially bowed out with a UK tour in April and May 1984.

There was talk of a full-scale reunion, but other than a clutch of early 1985 concerts and one gig at Loughborough Town Hall in August 1986 supported by Grim Reaper, this amounted to nothing. A comeback tour was apparently curtailed due to a thumb injury sustained by Shelley, and another reunion attempt with ex-Magnum and UFO drummer Jim Simpson on board – the new sticksman debuted on September 26th 1987 at the Hammersmith Clarendon Hotel in London – saw the band putting in sporadic dates until the end of the year. However, the reunion petered out.

Shelley finally laid the band to rest the same year when he formed a low-key outfit dubbed The Superclerkes. Thomas, meanwhile, joined Bombshell while Simpson hooked up with Newcastle band Red Dogs. John Thomas appeared as a guest on the Phenomena concept albums *Phenomena* and *Phenomena – Dream Runner*.

Renewed interest in Budgie was fired up when one of the mightiest forces on the metal scene, San Francisco thrashers Metallica, covered 'Crash Course In Brain Surgery' in 1987 for *The $5.98 EP: Garage Days Re-Revisited*. The US act later went further in their appreciation for the Welsh trio by using as their show opener the seminal 'Breadfan', recorded as the B-side to the 'Harvester Of Sorrow' single. This quirky nugget of riff-driven madness would open Metallica's arena shows for many years to come, prompting legions of Metalli-fans to investigate the origins of this homage and replenish the Budgie royalty coffers.

Another premier American act to pay homage was Soundgarden, the Seattle grunge-mongers cutting a version of 'Homicidal Suicide'. Also getting in on the Budgie love-in would be no less a force than Iron Maiden, re-crafting 'I Can't See My Feelings' from *Bandolier* as the B-side of their 1992 single 'From Here To Eternity'.

Prompted by overseas curiosity and an unexpected boost in royalties, Budgie re-emerged in 1993 when drummer Ray Phillips was found to be touring the British clubs performing the band's standards under the band name Six Ton Budgie. More importantly for fans, in 1995 Shelley, Thomas and drummer Rob Jones played a festival in San Antonio, Texas, where Budgie were still major headliners, repeating the feat at the 1996 event for an audience of 25,000 fans.

John Thomas: "It's really quite strange that Texas really 'got' Budgie before anyone else, really. It's about the most un-English place you could ever be in, but for some reason the Budgie fans down there are totally into the band and ridiculously devoted. We play shows there and enormous numbers of people turn up just to see Budgie. They want to hear all the old classics and they keep asking when we're going back in the studio to do a new record. We could just keep playing in Texas forever."

Budgie, now comprising Shelley, Thomas and Steve Williams, returned to the now traditional San Antonio festival in 2000 on a bill with Dio and Legs Diamond. John Thomas was struck with a cerebral aneurysm that same year; fortunately, the guitarist made a full recovery in time to perform at the Legends Of Welsh Rock festival at the Cardiff International Arena on September 29th 2001, on a billing with Man, Sassafras, Kimla Taz and Racing Cars. Thomas then opted out of the band and Budgie drafted in Andy Hart in his stead.

The band was back at the Sunken Garden Theater in San Antonio in August 2002 on a billing with Judas Priest and Reverend, before Budgie put in their most extensive tour of the UK for a long time in September and October. That same year stoner band Federation X paid homage with a 7-inch single, covering 'Nude Disintegrating Parachutist Woman' in two parts.

Fans who were by now used to seeing two different versions of the band on the live circuit, Budgie and Six Ton Budgie, would see a third unit appear. Guitarist John Thomas announced his new band under the title of JT's Budgie; fronted by Matt Gillespie, the band included bassist Paul Gaskin and drummer Martyn Shaw.

Budgie introduced new guitarist Simon Lees in 2003, and for the band's San Antonio gig in March 2004 were partnered with The Michael Schenker Group and Moxy. A long overdue series of archive reissues was announced that year. In addition, the long-awaited tracks from the band's shelved third RCA album were also scheduled for release, billed as *The Last Stage*.

Budgie returned to the UK tour circuit in November and December 2004. To coincide, re-mastered reissues of the band's first two albums saw release. Budgie added extra tracks including 'Guts' and 'Nude Disintegrating Parachutist Woman' (recorded in late summer 2003 by Burke Shelley, Steve Williams and Simon Lees), as well as a previously unreleased alternative mix from 1971 of 'Crash Course In Brain Surgery'. Meantime, *Squawk* added a different mix of 'Stranded', 'Whiskey River' (recorded in 2003 by Shelley, Williams and Lees) and 'Rolling Home Again' (recorded by Shelley and Bourge in 2004).

A still proud Budgie headed out on a lengthy UK club tour in September 2005. Although the band generated a staunchly loyal fan base, Budgie's idiosyncrasies might well have significantly contributed to their downfall. By rights, the group's innovative approach to the genre and undoubted quality, not to mention dogged tenacity, should have seen them at the peak (beak?) of their profession. Thankfully, Metallica have gone some way to correcting the history books and spotlighting a talent that deserved so much more.

KK Downing (Judas Priest): "We used to play with Budgie a lot, which was fantastic for me because they were like my heroes for a long time. We supported them everywhere, all over the country. I remember the Radio Caroline DJ, Kid Jensen, used to play their album back to back, both sides from start to finish. I always thought they were underrated too: they were more the future, I thought. I thought stuff like 'Hot As A Docker's Armpit' had more going for it than a lot of stuff around at the time.

"I remember we used to all get together at the end of the night and have a big blues jam at the end of their show. It was like the Grateful Dead or something, with 122 musicians on stage. I hated it! Never liked that old blues thing. They were good times, though, and Budgie was a great band."

JUDAS PRIEST
HELL BENT FOR LEATHER

JUDAS PRIEST RATE AS ONE of the most successful of the pure metal acts to emerge from Great Britain. More than any other group, Judas Priest have steadfastly stuck to their guns, preaching the cause of heavy metal even in some of the toughest of times for the genre. Their uncompromising ethos has seen them sell over 30 million albums globally. Characterised by the superb interplay between guitarists KK Downing and Glenn Tipton, both of equal technical ability and each with an immediately identifiable trademark signature, Judas Priest have also benefited enormously from some of the most extreme vocal styles, courtesy of Rob Halford. Remarkably, the present-day line-up of this premier metal act features none of the original line-up, which first formed in early 1969 on the outskirts of Birmingham.

PRIEST BEFORE PRIEST
The familiar line-up of Judas Priest that fans know well actually features none of the original roll call, which first formed in early 1969 in the outskirts of Birmingham. However, it should be noted that in this early incarnation, the group then known as Judas Priest were firmly embroiled in the blues scene. The roots of the band trace back as far as 1967 and a collection of Birmingham blues-rock acts. An act named Blue Condition – consisting of ex-The Bitta Sweet members vocalist Al Atkins and bassist Bruno Stapenhill together with drummer Pete Boot – was the earliest outfit to hold a direct lineage. In 1968 Blue Condition folded, with Boot subsequently joining Extreem and Atkins and Stapenhill forming Halfbreed, a band also including guitarists Barry Civil and John Perry and ex-Jug drummer Jim Perry. Civil left to join Froot. With Jim Perry departing for blues band F.B.I. and later Stallion, Lion and Bodie & Jinx, the group opted for a re-think. Halfbreed changed titles to The Chapter Of Life, then

The Jug Blues Band, but would ultimately split.

Atkins and Stapenhill regrouped, titled Sugarstack, with guitarists Michael Reeves and Geoff Furnival, and John Partridge on drums. Sugarstack then split, with Reeves joining the high-profile Midlands act Possessed, reuniting with Boot in the process. Tragically, Reeves was killed in a road accident which put an end to the rise of Possessed. Furnival would join Extreem.

Atkins, Stapenhill and Partridge stuck together and took the name Judas Priest, from the Bob Dylan song 'The Ballad Of Frankie Lee And Judas Priest'. Pulling in guitarist John Perry and concentrating on a hard edged blues-rock direction, Priest set about gigging. Tragic circumstances intervened, when within days Perry was killed in a suicide-related car crash.

Alan Atkins: "John Perry was an incredibly gifted guitarist. The first version of Judas Priest really had something special with John, but his death really shook us up. That's when KK Downing auditioned for us –and we turned him down! He was very young then and full of enthusiasm. I have to say he looked great too, but when he plugged in and started to play it was just way too heavy for what we were looking for. Remember, Judas Priest was a blues band then. We then got in Ernie Chataway; he was only 17 but another dynamite player. Every band wanted Ernie but we got him. That's really when we started to build up a following."

KK Downing had been rejected simply because the members of the band at the time were unable to imagine their act with such a heavy guitar sound. The blond guitarist auditioned with an extreme variant on Cream riffs and wailing solos.

In 1970, after prolonged gigging of a set that often included covers by Spirit and Quicksilver Messenger Service, the band – Al Atkins on lead vocals, guitarist Ernie Chataway, bassist Bruno Stapenhill and drummer John Partridge – signed a management deal with Alan Eade and cut two songs in the studio, 'We'll Stay Together' and 'Good Time Woman'. The tape led to interest from Immediate, a newly established label conceived by Rolling Stones manager Andrew Loog Oldham. Judas Priest put in a successful showcase for the label at the George Hotel in Walsall (among the audience was Led Zeppelin frontman Robert Plant) and were duly contracted to a three-year deal. Work progressed towards a debut album, with the band recording the 'Holy Is The Man' and 'Mind Conception' acetate. But early hopes were dashed. Before any material could be laid down, the company went under. It was a heavy blow and a disheartened Judas Priest split in the summer of 1970.

Bassist Bruno Stapenhill formed Ram before teaming up with a soul act, The Ryegee Explosion. The bassman was subsequently to re-unite with ex-Blue Condition drummer Pete Boot and ex-Priest guitarist Ernie Chataway in Bullion, and then in Suicide.

Al Atkins stuck with Stapenhill and Boot to form Lion in 1974, an act that gigged solidly until their demise in 1978. Following Suicide, Stapenhill formed Warhead.

Following the break-up of the original Judas Priest, singer Al Atkins joined forces with an as yet unnamed trio comprising guitarist KK Downing, bassist Ian 'Skull' Hill and drummer John Ellis. Downing (real first name Kenneth) was born on October 27th 1951 in West Bromwich. The name Freight had been suggested by Downing and Hill, but at Atkins's prompting the name Judas Priest was resurrected. With Downing now in control, the group moved swiftly away from the blues and into territory which would later be defined as heavy metal.

KK Downing: "I really didn't have anything else in my life. Everyone else I knew had plans to do this or that, but all I ever wanted to do was play guitar. The prospect of failing and the band not working out was part of the big drive for me: I could never imagine it, so I just worked harder and practised more and more.

"There was much more pressure then to get a job, find a career, because to be in a band really meant you were going to have no money for a very long time. I do mean no money – absolutely nothing. We would play concerts and just make enough money to get home and maybe get some food to keep us going. There were times in the early days when it got very tough for all of us and it was a real test.

"It was purely the music that kept me going. I was so fired up by hearing what Cream or Jimi Hendrix or Black Sabbath were doing, I just knew that was it for me. Nothing else."

The band's set included covers by Quatermass and Jimi Hendrix alongside new original material such as 'Mind Conception', 'Holy Is The Man' and 'Whiskey Woman'.

The new-look Judas Priest played their debut concert on March 16th 1971 at Essington St. John's Hall, further engaging in supports to Trapeze, Strife and Thin Lizzy among others before John Ellis put in his final concert at the Derby Yeoman on October 6th. The band soldiered on, drafting former Glad Stallion and Tendency Jones drummer Alan Moore, inaugurating this version of the band on stage at the Newport Community Centre on the 15th of that month. The now obscure bands to which the fledgling Judas Priest lent support around the country included such names as Ace, Wild Angels, Dr. Ross, Burnt Oak, Danta and even Mahatma Kane Jeeves at the London Marquee. Moore stuck with the band until 1972, when he left to join Pendulum and Sundance. Moore was replaced by afro-topped drummer Chris 'Congo' Campbell.

The band had now signed a management deal with IMA, a Birmingham company run by Jim Simpson and Black Sabbath guitarist Tony Iommi. Also on their books was The Flying Hat Band, including in its ranks Glenn Tipton, along with Bullion, former Judas Priest bassist Bruno Stapenhill's new act and fellow Cumbrian heavyweights Necromandus.

Following the departure of Atkins and Campbell in May 1973, erstwhile Thark, Lord Lucifer, Athens Wood and Hiroshima vocalist extraordinaire Rob Halford enrolled, along with ex-Bakerloo and Hiroshima drummer John Hinch. The percussionist had missed out on Bakerloo's success, leaving Clem Clempson's highly touted blues trio just before their debut album in 1969. The group's new singer was born Robert John Arthur Halford on August 25th 1951 in Sutton Coldfield, Warwickshire, and was subsequently raised in Walsall.

The Downing-Halford-Hill-Hinch Judas Priest line-up cut their first proper demo recording of 'Ladies', 'Run Of The Mill' and 'Caviar And Meths' in 1974, landing them a deal with Gull Records, a new rock label set up by ex-MCA A&R man David Howells. The song 'Whiskey Woman' had by now evolved into 'Victim Of Changes' after Halford had made a marriage of the Atkins-penned song and his own 'Red Light Lady'. The song, alongside 'Run Of The Mill', would form part of a two-track demo recorded at Sarm Studios.

The band, now managed by colourful Midlands entrepreneur Dave Corke, who often used the pseudonym Eric Smith and whose office was a public telephone box, toured heavily, often supporting Budgie in the UK and even playing headline dates in Norway and Germany.

A crucial defining point in the band's evolution came with the acquisition of a second guitarist. Glenn Raymond Tipton, born on October 25th 1948 in Blackheath, was recruited just before the recording of the band's debut album, *Rocka Rolla*. Gull Records owner David Howells felt that in order to set the band apart from other rock acts they needed a unique angle. After proposals to introduce a saxophone into the equation

was rejected, a heavier version of Wishbone Ash was set to be the model. Tipton had made his name with fellow Birmingham outfit The Flying Hat Band, featuring Tipton on vocals and guitar, ex-Gnidrolog bassist Peter 'Mars' Cowling (later to join the Pat Travers Band), drummer Steve Palmer (younger brother of ELP's Carl Palmer) and occasionally singer Pete Hughes. Tipton's outfit had recorded an album for Vertigo but had been rejected by the label as "too heavy".

Despite this setback, The Flying Hat Band had been regular competitors of Judas Priest on the Midlands club circuit and had in fact just come off a European tour supporting Deep Purple when Tipton opted to join Priest. With his group disbanding due to Hughes's exit to join the military, the timing was perfect for Tipton. This union of two guitarists, each with a distinct sound, was to provide a twin guitar attack pushed to levels of ferocity beyond any Wishbone Ash comparisons.

KK Downing: "It wasn't our idea to bring in a second guitarist. The guy who signed us, David Howells, loved the songs, loved the band, but really wanted to set us apart from other bands. He was a big fan of Wishbone Ash and had worked with them at MCA. He thought that we should do something similar.

"I wasn't very keen at first but then we met Glenn in a music shop and got talking and thought: this is the guy. Once Glenn agreed to sign up we had to deal with it! Fortunately we got on great, as we both had similar backgrounds. Our styles really worked well together, too, and we really fed off each other. My playing got a lot better because Glenn was trying to compete with me, and vice versa. It was friendly competition but it worked for both of us and the band. At first we just sorted out who was going to play which solo, but it soon got to the point where we were working out songs to feature both guitars."

Producer Rodger Bain, who had made his name with Black Sabbath's early albums, apparently had a large say in the *Rocka Rolla* album's rushed, budget production. Bain cut the stage classic 'Caviar And Meths' from an eight-minute tour de force to a cameo instrumental, but decided to leave off the mighty quartet of 'Victim Of Changes', 'Genocide', 'Tyrant' and 'The Ripper', all of which had been thoroughly road-tested. Although unrepresentative of the band's true direction, the inaugural album, issued in September 1974, provided them with a useful launch platform, and despite lukewarm reviews the album jacket, rendered by John Pasche, landed a graphic design award that provided more valuable publicity.

John Hinch: "What most fans don't realise is that the Rocka Rolla album was never really finished. It was very rushed, and all the fancy drum stuff I had been planning on putting down was just left off because we ran out of time. I remember the finished thing sounding very tame, too. We all thought that what we recorded at the time sounded really big, but the album sounded really lightweight."
KK Downing: "The record sounded crap. We had recorded a heavy metal album and what we got was a pop record. All our performances were there, but everything was made to sound clean and nice. All the balls we had heard in the studio had just gone. Rodger Bain had done Black Sabbath before us, so that's really the kind of sound we were after. I remember Glenn and I listening to the guitars in the studio and thinking, 'Wow!' It was very, very heavy. Afterwards, it was really disheartening to go out and play and try and sell a record we really did not believe in. We got fed up of telling kids the album cover wasn't right, the sound wasn't right."

The band toured constantly, building up an impressive club following. Their British tour, supported by Jailbait, culminated in spectacular success at the 1975 15th National Jazz, Blues & Rock Festival. Incidentally, a bootleg of the Reading performance features the live favourite 'Mother Sun', which has never officially seen the light of day: Priest only recorded this song in an unfinished acoustic demo state for Gull. Once these dates were wrapped up, John Hinch exited.

John Hinch: "The song 'Mother Sun' was always our grand climax of the set. We played it every night and it always went down great. It was a big Queen type thing that really built. I was really surprised the band never recorded it on vinyl. We played it at the 1975 Reading festival and it went down a storm because we had been playing this song in hundreds of clubs all year long, so everyone knew it. Reading was a real turning point for Judas Priest because it was the first time the band had seen all their fans gathered in one place. The band just totally blew away every other band that day. Reading proved to everyone that Priest was really going places.

"I left Priest because I couldn't play the drums any more. When we were out on the road there was often a bit of argy-bargy with some locals, usually to do with girls. Once, Glenn and I got involved in a fight with this guy, I can't remember why, but Glenn was holding this guy so I could punch him. Anyway, I punched the guy in the face but he opened his mouth and bit down on my thumb and just wouldn't let go. He made a real mess of it, so that was that for my playing days, really."

By 1976 Judas Priest were carving out a niche as the most aggressive metal act on the circuit. Their next album, *Sad Wings Of Destiny*, was recorded with re-enlisted drummer Alan Moore. During his tenure with Sundance he had recorded two albums for Decca – 1973's *Rain Steam Speed* and 1974's *Chuffer*. On the production front, the band employed Max West (aka Geraint Hughes) and Jeffrey Calvert who, under the pseudonym of Typically Tropical, had recently scored a significant hit in the UK charts with 'Barbados'.

Sad Wings Of Destiny, majestically clad in an evocative Patrick Woodruffe artwork sleeve, would prove to be a groundbreaking album, and songs such as 'Genocide', 'Tyrant' and 'Island Of Domination' proved Judas Priest were on their way. Also included was 'Victim Of Changes', a seven-minute epic destined to be recognised as the band's all-time classic and still performed in concert some 25 years later. The song had originated in the earlier track 'Red Light Lady'.

Overall, the quality of material captured on *Sad Wings Of Destiny* revealed an enormous creative leap from *Rocka Rolla*. Oddly, the bulk of the songs had been available for the debut, the band having performed them live for many years previously.

The tour and general response to the album led before the end of the year to a worldwide deal with CBS, signed by Paul Atkinson and Robin Blanchflower. CBS gave Judas Priest an instant yes based on a single showcase set. Unfortunately this new business arrangement was made while the band were still under contract to Gull. Nevertheless, the group made the break and received a £60,000 advance to re-debut with the landmark *Sin After Sin* album, produced by Deep Purple bassist Roger Glover.

Sin After Sin, laid down with drums by renowned session man Simon Phillips, provided the momentum CBS were looking for, and with major label backing Priest were truly ready to take on the world. The band re-worked a much heavier cover of the Joan Baez track 'Diamonds And Rust' originally laid down for Gull. Pre-production for the record was conducted at Pinewood studios before a relocation to London's Ramport Studios (owned by The Who) in January 1977. *Sin After Sin* would prove to be an extension of the epic metal stylings of *Sad Wings Of Destiny* and hosted concert classics such as 'Starbreaker', 'Dissident Aggressor' and the

KK Downing showcase 'Sinner'. Also onboard, and missed by most observers, would be the track 'Raw Deal'. Halford quite openly broached his homosexuality in the lyrics, which made a direct reference to the infamous New York gay resort of Fire Island. However, for most of the band's fan base and the general public, the topic of these lyrics simply failed to register.

Although Phillips's services were requested on a full-time basis, the drummer, citing tour commitments with Jack Bruce's band, declined the invitation. To fill the vacancy the band settled on ex-Fancy drummer Les 'Feather Touch' Binks. *Sin After Sin* producer Roger Glover had previously used Binks on his 1974 concept album *Butterfly Ball*.

In March, Priest played Scandinavian gigs including the Oulu 'Kuusrock' festival in Finland, prior to a headline UK tour. Their first American shows in 1977, as guests for the somewhat mellower Foreigner and REO Speedwagon, climaxed with support slots to the mighty Led Zeppelin – at the personal invitation of Robert Plant – at San Francisco's 'Day On The Green' festival. The British tour, with fellow Brummies Magnum in support, ended with fans damaging the London Victoria Theatre venue as trouble flared up between the audience and heavy-handed bouncers. European shows in October provided Priest with valuable supports to AC/DC.

Stained Class, recorded at Chipping Norton Studios in the Oxfordshire Cotswolds, saw Priest deliberately distancing themselves from the ethereal themes of yore. The heavily sci-fi orientated album, although mostly produced rather thinly by Dennis Mackay, included the rip-roaring acceleration of 'Exciter' and the majestic stage classic 'Beyond The Realms Of Death'. With these sessions wrapped up, CBS requested an additional track for a single. Employing James Guthrie, noted for his Pink Floyd engineering credentials, the band crafted a version of Spooky Tooth's 'Better By You, Better Than Me' at Utopia Studios in London. *Stained Class*, surfacing in February 1978, would be Judas Priest's first album to break into the Billboard Top 200.

KK Downing: "Our drummer, Les Binks, actually started off 'Beyond The Realms Of Death'. It looks odd when you see the writing credits on the albums, because traditionally it's down to me, Glenn and Rob, but Les got his name on there almost by accident. Rob had this idea for a song but really had nowhere to put his lyrics.

"One day Les was messing about with this riff. He was playing a guitar upside down, because he's left-handed, and he came up with the opening riff to 'Beyond The Realms Of Death'. That kicked the whole thing off. He never played guitar again that I can remember."

As America beckoned, a rapid change in image occurred from the gothic and medieval to the menacing black leather that was to become Priest's trademark. Halford switched from flowing silks to a stark black outfit. Pushing *Stained Class* in the USA, Priest were mismatched with an ungrateful Foghat as headliners, but a rapturous reception came their way in July when they hit Japan for the first time.

The next album, *Killing Machine*, provided Priest's first hit singles in the shape of 'Take On The World' and 'Evening Star'. The album as a whole saw the band shift their lyrical slant to even more sci-fi lyrical themes.

Two successive sell-out British tours, the latter with Lea Hart as guest, bolstered their support. By this stage Halford's visual transformation had been completed, the singer now donning leather peaked cap and bullwhip and even taking to the stage riding on a Harley-Davidson motorcycle. When exaggerated reviews suggested Halford was actually whipping the audience, the group added 'I've been whipped by Rob Halford' pins to their merchandise. Halford's prescient sense of theatrics at this juncture in their career not only gave the group a globally identifiable stamp but also influenced the entire metal genre for many years to come.

Rob Halford: "Before Killing Machine, bands really just tried to keep up with the times. I know we did. Judas Priest just looked like all the other bands of the day, really. It's funny to look back at what we were wearing, all the scarves and robes and flowing sleeves, but it was commonplace if you look at what Sabbath or Uriah Heep or any of those guys were wearing.

"The band had undergone a big change on Stained Class and we leaped ahead even further with Killing Machine. I really wanted to take the image with us because, really, how can I sing those kind of songs wearing these gold high-heeled boots? It wasn't working.

"The whole S&M scene was very intriguing for me too. I knew about the whole sexual side of the image with the domination and everything, but one day I clicked that maybe this was what I needed to portray the music. I got fitted out at Mr. S Leathers in London: it's a quite notorious gay clothing store. I told them what I wanted and we just went from there. Once my first experiments with the leather and studs were accepted by the fans, I just went crazy with it and it really worked. KK was next to get himself sorted with the leather and then obviously the whole band had to fall in line too. The more extreme the image got – the whip, the bike, I even used a machine-gun onstage – the more the fans loved it."

KK Downing: "You have to credit Rob with inventing what is now regarded as the heavy metal uniform. Nobody else was doing that back then, and it gave our popularity a huge boost. I don't think anyone cared if it was gay or not, the image just fitted the power of the music so well. It was clever of Rob to do that, I think: he took the S&M thing and then made it into something of his own. It became Judas Priest and from then on every band was doing it.

"I first noticed it when we had Iron Maiden support us. Their guitar player looked like me and Paul the singer was just a bad copy of Rob. It's nice that we influenced them so much but they never acknowledged it. It created a lot of ill feeling and we almost chucked them off the tour."

Rob Halford: "There was this thing with Freddie from Queen. I had the whole leather thing going on with the bike, and then we see that Freddie Mercury is doing exactly the same thing. I wasn't having it, so, in a friendly way, I suggested we should duel for the image, so to speak, by challenging Freddie to a bike race – anywhere, any time. I never heard back. Freddie dropped the leather and the bike."

In North America, Priest had to rename the album *Hell Bent For Leather* as their record company felt the British title was too violent. The band used this opportunity to add an extra track to the US version, a cover of Fleetwood Mac's maudlin, Peter Green-penned 'Green Manalishi (With The Two Pronged Crown)'. During these same sessions the group cut renditions of The Rolling Stones' 'Play With Fire' and Gun's 'Race With The Devil', though both were passed over.

Rob Halford: "I don't know what happened with Ram It Down. There's some great tracks on there, some really strong material, but I think possibly the record was tainted by that fucking silly 'Johnny B Goode'. That really damaged us, and because there wasn't another single track to follow it up, it hurt. It's easy to say in hindsight, but we should not have done that. I guess we had in mind the missed opportunity we let go with Top Gun and Reckless, so we said yes without looking into it as much as we should have done.

"It's a bit like 'You've Got Another Thing Comin'' broke Screaming For Vengeance – but 'Johnny B. Goode' broke Ram It Down, in the other sense of the word. Overall, though, Ram It Down is actually a very heavy record, and Ken and Glenn really rip it up on a lot of those riffs. We did a version of The Rolling Stones' 'Play With Fire' for Ram It Down but it didn't get used. I always thought that was a shame."

The year 1979 opened in fine style as the chest-thumping tribal anthem 'Take On The World' gave the group its first hit single. Not only did Priest score radio exposure with the song but, following a *Top Of The Pops* TV performance, the track was adopted as a chant by soccer fans. In February the group returned to Japan for a sell-out tour prior to US roadwork, acting as support to UFO. With demand in their home country unsatisfied, another round of shows in May had Marseille as openers before a return across the Atlantic to act as special guests to Kiss throughout September.

Priest's next album proved to be the band's undoubted classic, September 1979's *Unleashed In The East*, the first of many to be produced by 'Colonel' Tom Allom. The band's new producer had made his mark as engineer on the first two Black Sabbath albums before producing Hudson-Ford and Pat Travers. Allom captured the band's live ferocity on stage in Japan, capturing two shows at Koseinenkin Hall, Tokyo on February 10th 1979 and Nakano Sun Plaza Hall, Tokyo on February 15th, as Priest truly became a world class act. As such, *Unleashed...* is generally regarded as one of the genre's landmark live albums. In the UK the LP landed at an impressive Number 10 on the album charts and scored a Number 70 placing in North America.

However, with rumours circulating that the finished product was far from the fully live album it purported to be, and dubbed by media as *Unleashed In The Studio*, Halford subsequently admitted that while the band played well on the Japanese dates he was suffering from a dose of laryngitis, necessitating a re-recording of the vocal tracks. The album cover 'live' shot too was from a studio shoot, photographer Fin Costello strategically placing the band members so as to obscure the drum kit, as drummer Les Binks had already vacated the band by this juncture.

The Japanese version, subtly re-titled *Priest In The East*, featured an extra four tracks, 'Rock Forever', 'Delivering The Goods', 'Hell Bent For Leather' and 'Starbreaker', spread over a 7-inch single, which would filter through to the UK market in the form of successive single B-sides. 'Beyond The Realms Of Death' featured on a three-track EP included on initial UK versions of the album, while 'Evil Fantasies', in an undubbed form, appeared as the B-side to the 12-inch single 'Living After Midnight' in 1980.

An incident the band might want to forget from that tour was when Rob Halford rode his Harley-Davidson onstage at St. Paul in Minneapolis and promptly drove straight into the orchestra pit. Fortunately for the singer, this potentially serious incident only resulted in cuts and bruises.

The Tom Allom-produced *British Steel* saw the arrival of drummer Dave Holland in favour of Binks, who went on to to work with Tytan and Lionheart before entering the world of session work. Holland, born on April 5th 1948 in Northampton, joined Priest in August 1979, having previously made his mark with Glenn Hughes's act Trapeze. He had also worked with Justin Hayward on his solo outings *Songwriter* and *Night Flight*.

The 1980s caught the quintet focusing on lengthy American tours. Nevertheless, a sell-out British tour in March maintained their following at home, with support coming from fast-rising Londoners Iron Maiden. With the New Wave Of British Heavy Metal at its peak, many fans attending the shows were more than mystified when it transpired that the support band looked remarkably similar to the headline act. Iron Maiden's guitarist Dave Murray was almost identical to Downing in stage wear and blond mane, while vocalist Paul Di'Anno matched Halford for studded belts and wristbands.

British Steel, which peaked at Number 4 on the British charts in April, gave the band three sizeable British hit singles and TV appearances promoting 'Living After Midnight', 'Breaking The Law' and the anthemic 'United'. In a surreal turn of events, the album's pre-publicity included a totally fabricated story conjured up by the McBrain PR company. Stories were given to the UK media stating that thieves had stolen the album's master tapes and had demanded a ransom of $100,000 for their return. In fact, every detail of the yarn was false, even down to claims that the album was recorded in France – the band had actually cut *British Steel* at Ringo Starr's Startling Studios.

The band's burgeoning status had CBS pre-empting single sales by marketing both 'Living After Midnight' and 'Breaking The Law' with Julien Temple-directed promotional shorts, the first such videos the band had created. The record also played host to a crop of uncompromisingly heavy tracks, with 'Metal Gods' and 'Grinder' remaining entrenched in the band's live set for many years to come. However, material such as 'Steeler' and the staccato 'Rapid Fire' were – oddly enough – not given regular live airings, despite being hailed as classics.

The album would be given a second wind in 2001 when a TV special prompted Scandinavian rock fans to put the album back into the Swedish charts at Number 17 – higher than its original 1980 chart placing.

Glenn Tipton: "Each album had given us more and more success up to that point and with British Steel we really felt we wanted to do something very stripped down and raw. We had done all the fantasy stuff and the science fiction, and it was about time we told the world who Judas Priest were. I can't think of a single song on the album I'm not happy with at all. We could have played all of it live.

"The album cover was perfect. It's a bit vague. I know some people can't bear to look at it because they think the razor blade is cutting into the fingers. The razor blade was also a punk thing too, so we decided to take it back. There was a real connection with Birmingham and its heavy industry. I even used to work for British Steel. At one time everything was made in Birmingham. All the old factories were closing down, there were a lot of industrial troubles going on, and people were having a hard time of it. We wanted an album title that was proud and was something we could tour across America and say: this is who we are."

In April the band put in an extensive run of German headline dates before heading off for a lengthy bout of North American touring with support from Def Leppard and co-headliners with the Scorpions. This live promotion and subsequent word of mouth would push *British Steel* to gold status, and steady sales eventually passed the platinum marker during 1989. Priest rammed the point home with what many regarded as a show-stealing performance at the first ever Castle Donington 'Monsters Of Rock' festival, headlined by Rainbow on August 16th.

February 1981's *Point Of Entry* album, recorded in Ibiza with Tom Allom once again at the controls, saw Priest mellow considerably, much to the distaste of British fans. The band had noticeably diluted the aggression of *British Steel* and presented an album laden with radio-friendly fillers. Even the unusually bland artwork came in for criticism and, unfortunately for the band, the American label's insistence that the sleeve be reworked for that territory resulted in an even worse compromise. Live promotion commenced in February with a trek through Europe with guests Saxon. A show at Amsterdam's Jaap Edenhal was then recorded for radio broadcast and to provide B-side tracks for singles. Oddly, fan favourite 'Steeler' would be originally slated for appearance as the flip to 'Hot Rockin'', making it onto acetates, but then swapped for a rather predictable 'Breaking The Law'.

Rob Halford: "We were really scratching our heads with Point Of Entry. The band wanted to do something different, but the record company had seen we could deliver three hit singles and wanted more of the same. We were not so sure, so I think Point Of Entry maybe suffers from too many people pulling in too many directions. It's a balance thing, really; I mean, you have songs like 'Hot Rockin' and 'Heading Out To The Highway', and then there's 'Desert Plains', which the fans have told us is one of our best tracks.

"It was all a bit confusing: the songs, the direction and the ridiculous story of the album covers. The funny thing was that the tour was our biggest yet, and when we played 'Solar Angels' and 'Desert Plains' they were super heavy. I think we maybe went a bit more over the top to compensate, but it worked."

The ensuing North American summer tour, on which Priest were again supported by Iron Maiden, The Joe Perry Project and Whitesnake, saw the band rise in stature with increasingly lavish stage shows featuring huge banks of lights and hydraulic risers, much of which was borrowed from Pink Floyd's production company. The band opened the shows impressively with 'Solar Angels', Tipton and Downing rising through clouds of dry ice. Pointedly, material from the new album was sparse. 'Troubleshooter' was quickly dropped, although 'Desert Plains' and 'Heading Out To The Highway' held a tenacious grip in the set for many years to come. Writing sessions for the band's next album were held in October before Priest returned for a successful British and European tour that November with the hard-hitting German act Accept in support.

It was the *Screaming For Vengeance* LP in 1982 that really cracked the States wide open for Judas Priest, providing the band with their first platinum album and hit single in the catchy 'You've Got Another Thing Comin''. (Such was the impact of this song that it was subsequently used in Burger King ads.) The album, sporting a robotic eagle dubbed The Hellion, contained a perfect mix of commerciality and aggression, for instance on the complex title track. *Screaming For Vengeance*, solidifying the band's production relationship with Tom Allom, was once again recorded in Ibiza.

A batch of original songs was scrapped in the early stages of recording as Judas Priest started from scratch. This process left the album short on material by the time they relocated to Florida for the mixing stage. It would be here that a quick-fire 'You've Got Another Thing Comin'' would be conceived and recorded in a matter of hours. The single, backed by a laser-fuelled Julien Temple video that included the enduring image of a council noise-pollution agent's head exploding, lodged itself on MTV's play lists and gave Priest their biggest US single hit to date. A point of curiosity for hardcore collectors would be the South Korean version of *Screaming For Vengeance*, which was pressed minus the title track.

Ian Hill: "We had a lot to prove after Point Of Entry, because a lot of our fans made it very clear they did not want us to go in that direction. Priest was still on the up, though, because the tour we had just finished was very successful, so now we had to focus ourselves totally on our more aggressive side again. With Screaming For Vengeance we said to ourselves: let's not listen to what other people think, let's just make the best, heaviest album we can. That's what we did."

KK Downing: "That was a real milestone for us. I think our honesty really showed there and the fans really welcomed us back. Screaming For Vengeance was really a pure heavy metal record. There was a bit of commercial material on there but nothing we thought would become as big as 'You've Got Another Thing Comin''. It was a very basic song we recorded right at the end in Florida. In fact, the finished track uses a lot of what was just supposed to be a studio demo, but it sounded so fresh we kept it.

"When it started to hit all over radio we were on tour and we got these reports that the album was still selling, so we changed our plans. It only took a few months to sell over a million copies. We just kept on playing and everywhere we went we could have gone back to again and again because the demand was there."

Rob Halford: "There was a lot of soul-searching going on with Screaming For Vengeance. We scrapped a lot of songs and started again. I think there was a real feeling that we wanted to give our fans exactly the album they really wanted, because Point Of Entry had missed the mark."

The tour saw the set stripped down to the basic Marshall cabinet walls following the lavish *Point Of Entry* stage set, and during the dates Priest broke off from their long-term management, Arnakata, and under the auspices of Secret Management Associates Inc handled business affairs for themselves. While still on the road, lengthy negotiations took place and Priest finally teamed up with Bill Curbishley, noted manager of Robert Plant and The Who. Once again Iron Maiden stepped in as opening act, later replaced by Uriah Heep and Coney Hatch before Australian act Heaven took over. Plans for dates in Europe were scrapped as sales of *Screaming For Vengeance* accelerated in the USA.

The tour was extended into the New Year, eventually totalling more than 100 American gigs, often with large arenas at full capacity for two-night bookings. At one of these shows a young drummer, Scott Travis, approached Glenn Tipton in a bar and inquired if he enjoyed playing with Dave Holland. Travis's naive enthusiasm in 1982 would pay dividends some seven years later.

Priest rounded off these dates with a showing at the prestigious 'US Festival' event laid on in San Bernardino by Apple Computers' mentor Steve Wozniak where the band, sandwiched oddly between Bryan Adams and Crosby Stills & Nash, played to an audience of over a quarter of a million people.

A matter of days later the band returned to Ibiza to craft the follow-up LP with Tom Allom and engineer Mark Dodson. The chest-thumping *Defenders Of The Faith* was released in January 1984, and Priest gave the public more of the same winning formula with another cover monster, The Metallian, and an outrageous stage set for their North American tour. The supremely over-the-top 'Eat Me Alive', a song initially billed as 'Bad Girls Wear Leather' with obvious references to oral sex, and the openly gay lyric to 'Jawbreaker', were quickly jumped on by the Tipper Gore-led PMRC as a prime example of metal's insidious influence upon America's youth.

In the UK the band opened proceedings with the January 1984 single 'Freewheel Burning', backed once again by a Julien Temple-directed promo video. Twelve-inch single versions of this lead track, originally given the working title of 'Fast And Furious', featured an extended guitar solo section that would not be featured on the album. One song that was recorded but didn't make the final album cut was 'Heart Of A Lion', later donated by Halford to Racer X.

Priest then took to the UK for a short burst of dates in December 1983 supported by Quiet Riot, during which they took time out to appear at the mammoth televised 'Dortmund Westfalenhalle Rock Pop' festival in Germany. This gargantuan event saw the band ranked alongside Iron

Maiden, Krokus, Def Leppard, Ozzy Osbourne, The Michael Schenker Group and the Scorpions.

January and February of 1984 found Priest traversing Europe with Ted Nugent and Raven in tow as guest artists. Their North American *Defenders* tour dates, running from mid March onwards and supported by Great White and Saxon, found the band in more ambitious mode, recreating the album cover in the stage set with a central Metallian head and jaws flanked by hydraulic claws which plucked Tipton and Downing from the stage. The US dates rolled on successfully until August before the world tour closed with a rash of Japanese dates the following month.

The group promoted the new opus with gusto, with the live set's opening number 'Love Bites' kick-starting the airing of no fewer than eight album cuts. Despite the quality of the album material, only the Bob Halligan Jr. penned 'Some Heads Are Gonna Roll' received much radio airplay. Nevertheless, by the close of this latest series of dates, *Defenders Of The Faith* attained platinum status in September 1988.

Priest's standing was further acknowledged by their billing on the Philadelphia stage of the global Live Aid event in 1985. That same year Halford would donate his services to the 'Stars' benefit record convened by Ronnie James Dio.

1986's *Turbo*, one of the first digitally-recorded metal albums, heralded a new age for the band. Recording again with Tom Allom, this time in the luxurious climes of Compass Point Studios in The Bahamas, once again the band had pushed the parameters of hard rock into controversial territory. While some believed that the ZZ Top-style synth guitars harked back to the poppier *Point Of Entry* days, the album actually succeeded in drawing in many new fans.

The record was originally intended as a double set, with a provisional title of *Twin Turbo* in homage to Glenn Tipton and KK Downing's recent purchases of Porsche 911 Turbos. Eighteen songs were cut for this proposed tenth anniversary release, from which recordings of only the more commercial tunes were finally chosen. Shelved material resurfaced on the 2002 remasters series as bonus tracks in the form of 'Red, White & Blue', 'Prisoner Of Your Eyes' and 'All Fired Up'.

While *Turbo* went platinum, bolstered by lavish videos for 'Turbo Lover' and 'Locked In', it would not achieve the target set for it by the band and label. It would transpire, however, that Judas Priest had missed out on a golden opportunity afforded them when the track 'Reckless' was requested by Warner Bros. for inclusion on the soundtrack to the blockbuster Tom Cruise movie *Top Gun*. The band turned the offer down and the soundtrack, fired by the Berlin smash 'Take My Breath Away', would subsequently go quintuple platinum.

Live work found Judas Priest opening up proceedings in Albuquerque, New Mexico, on May 2nd, this first US leg seeing Dokken as guests. While the band was packing the arenas, some unwelcome press came when *Kerrang!* reporter Derek Oliver leaked a story stating that Legs Diamond man Jonathon Valen was in reality providing the drum patterns from behind the stage. A belated explanation from the band explained Valen's presence as operating "electronic percussion".

A rash of July shows in Canada found Bon Jovi in the opening slot before the band tacked back into the USA for a round of dates with Krokus as support. The group's next destination, Europe, had hot German metal newcomers Warlock sharing the stages. UK gigs would be absent from the calendar but 1986 was capped by December dates in Japan.

The *Turbo* tour, which found Judas Priest playing to capacity arena audiences in the US, was recorded for the excellent *Priest Live* album and also spawned a Wayne Isham-directed live concert video. Strangely for such a landmark album, the record company promotion seemed at best apathetic. The group's original concept for *Priest Live* was to see the concert audio bolstered by studio tracks left over from the *Turbo* sessions, although this did not happen.

In 1988 Judas Priest took time out to record some experimental tracks, including a cover version of Diana Ross's 'You Are Everything' together with originals 'I Will Return' and 'Runaround', controversially with famed pop producers Stock, Aitken & Waterman. Ironically, the production team was at the time being managed by David Howells, the same man who gave the group their commercial start when he signed Judas Priest to his Gull label in the early 1970s. These sessions were never released, as the band deemed the eventual results inappropriate and instead fell back on their instincts, as successive albums would testify.

Ram It Down, featuring tracks left over from the original *Turbo* sessions, including 'Love You To Death', 'Hard As Iron', 'Monsters Of Rock' and the title track, plus a cover of Chuck Berry's 'Johnny B Goode', saw Judas Priest go back to basics. Unfortunately the overall quality of the record, bar the electro-epic 'Blood Red Skies', failed to appease the detractors from the *Turbo* era, and *Ram It Down* only scored gold status in the US. 'Johnny B Goode' and its associated movie, *Johnny Be Good*, had been pursued enthusiastically as the band hoped to reap the rewards they had missed with *Top Gun*. Unfortunately, the film bombed.

Global touring, dubbed 'The Mercenaries Of Metal' dates, commenced in Sweden during May with support from German melodic rockers Bonfire. Initially 'Johnny B Goode' featured in the set but would soon be dropped as it quickly became apparent that the accompanying movie had flopped. Most of Europe would be covered on this trek, including the by now customary lengthy haul through Germany, before long-overdue British shows. In their hometown of Birmingham, Judas Priest packed the small Powerhouse club. North American shows, featuring contemporary if ill-fitting name acts such as Cinderella and Slayer, who had recently covered 'Dissident Aggressor' from Priest's *Stained Class* album, kicked off in Canada during July, running right through until October.

For the renaissance *Painkiller* album, which saw the band back at their most ferocious, Judas Priest pulled in ex-Hawk and Racer X drummer Scott Travis. Holland had left due to "touring pressures", and the band's ex-drummer was later to attempt a series of Trapeze reformations. The incorporation of Travis was viewed by many as having injected new life into the band and the blistering drum solo that opened the album certainly gave no illusions as to the band's intent. Priest also closed their relationship with long-term producer Tom Allom in favour of Chris Tsangarides. The new face behind the desk had worked with the band before, having engineered the landmark *Sad Wings Of Destiny* LP. *Painkiller* would be Priest's first album to receive a Grammy nomination, and critics and fans hailed *Painkiller* as one of the band's finest achievements.

Rob Halford: "When Scott Travis came along we suddenly had this fantastic new drummer who was enabling us to do things musically we had never done before. We are now able to play stuff that Les Binks was playing previously and it's great. I've always been a fucking headbanger anyway, from day one. I love 'Exciter', 'Dissident Aggressor', 'Jawbreaker', 'Freewheel Burning' and all of that kind of breakneck stuff, that's where my heart's at."

Glenn Tipton: "Scott Travis made Painkiller a real drumming album and it's a long time since a record was so focused on the drums. I think metal fans really took notice, because right from the first second of Painkiller they know that Judas Priest is back, bigger and better than before. We were treading water a bit before, but now we have all these new fans coming to the gigs. It's a real word of mouth thing, which is the best form of advertising you can get. I think this is the hardest album we've ever done. There wasn't even any talk of a ballad or a slow track."

The *Painkiller* world tour proved hugely successful, with a long stint in America alongside support acts Pantera, Testamentm and Megadethm before the band played the gargantuan 'Rock In Rio' festival in Brazil. Then they hopped over to Europe with support act Annihilator, prior to shows in Japan and Hawaii. Priest would then hook up for another touring leg of America, co-headlining the 'Operation Rock'n'Roll' festivals with Alice Cooper atop an all-Sony billing of Motörhead, Metal Church and Dangerous Toys.

However, in Reno, Nevada – the scene of the soon-to-be-infamous 'subliminal messages' court case – Priest pulled in only 4,000 fans, despite donating profits from the show to local charities.

The band had been cited in a $3 million lawsuit by the parents of James Vance and Raymond Belknap, who alleged that hidden messages in Judas Priest songs directly incited a suicide attempt by the teenagers. The allegation was that the two had tried to kill themselves with a shotgun after listening to the track 'Better By You, Better Than Me' from the *Stained Class* album. It was probably one of the band's most innocuous songs – and a cover of a Spooky Tooth track at that. The assertions centred on Halford's breathing techniques during recording, with the victim's families claiming this audible noise on the track was a barely hidden message of 'do it'. The prosecution maintained that, having reverse-engineered the song, they found it to be "packed with subliminals in the lyrics".

Belknap had succeeded in killing himself instantly, while Vance survived, though horrifically mutilated. Having blown away the lower portion of his face, the teenager underwent more than 140 hours of surgery but would only live for three years. The families lost the legal issue. Vance died, apparently of a methadone overdose, just a few months before the court case.

The whole affair was documented in *Dream Deceivers* by filmmaker David Van Taylor, bringing the impact of the trial to an international TV audience. Once the case was settled, Judas Priest performed at the annual 'Foundations Forum' industry convention in California in September 1990, performing 'Better By You, Better Than Me' for the first time in ten years. Less tastefully, Priest's record label issued a radio promo single of the song – recorded backwards.

Rob Halford: "We thought it would be fun to do 'Better By You' again. It sounded great when we did it. When we were forced to listen to it in that silly fucking court case eight million times a day we got back into it again, and the thing was they kept playing it at 25rpm rather than 33rpm and it sounded really heavy. Ken said we should play it live at 25rpm, really slow and heavy."

KK Downing: "I think the most bizarre thing about that whole court case thing was that they picked the song 'Better By You', [even though] we didn't even write it. If they had done their homework they could easily have seen that there are songs on Stained Class that do deal with suicide and people dying. Of course we wrote them about the tragedy and waste of suicide, like 'Beyond The Realms Of Death' or the Jimi Hendrix thing with 'Heroes End', but they would have been easier targets.

"When they started on this whole breathing thing I just thought that these people were insane. They really needed to look much closer to home to see why those kids killed themselves. I didn't like the fact that suddenly Judas Priest was on the TV everywhere, all around the world, for all the wrong reasons. The whole thing was a complete world of madness to me because I've never met anybody stupid enough to try and get their fans to kill themselves."

The *Painkiller* world tour closed in Toronto in August 1991. For Halford it would not prove an ideal close of events as, riding onstage in customary fashion on his Harley-Davidson, he was concussed by a faulty drum riser, leaving the bemused band to rip through 'Hell Bent For Leather' minus vocals. After a temporary patch-up the singer finished the show but required hospital treatment afterwards.

All in all, the *Painkiller* album put Judas Priest back at the top of the heavy metal pile. With the album's promotion fulfilled, Halford announced his intentions to pursue a solo project, at first with the blessing of his band members. Giving some idea of the direction this project would take, Halford joined Pantera onstage in March 1992 for a gig at the Irvine Meadows Amphitheater venue in California performing 'Grinder' and 'Metal Gods'. This would provide the catalyst for the two forces to join together to contribute a track, 'Light Comes Out Of Black', for inclusion on the *Buffy The Vampire Slayer* movie soundtrack that July. Not known for working outside of Priest, Halford uncharacteristically turned up onstage with Skid Row for a rendition of 'Delivering The Goods' and also donated backing vocals to the track 'Goddamn Devil' on Ugly Kid Joe's album *America's Least Wanted.*

To the utter dismay of fans worldwide, Halford then left the band, taking his leave in September as inter-band arguments raged. With Priest inactive, he stole the limelight in mid-November 1992 in spectacular style, standing in as temporary vocalist for Black Sabbath at two now infamous gigs at the Pacific Amphitheater venue in Costa Mesa, California. Although Halford announced onstage that he would return with Judas Priest, he put all his energies into a new venture, the stripped-down Fight. This outfit, debuting with *War Of Words*, pursued a brand of metal that was too back-to-basics for many of the Priest faithful to appreciate.

Halford then busied himself with further Fight releases *Mutations* in 1994 and *A Small Deadly Space* during 1995, subsequently touring as guest to Anthrax and Metallica. In general, the media response was unforthcoming and sometimes even hostile, leading to poor sales. In 1996 he formed a new act, Halford, before discussions with Black Sabbath guitarist Tony Iommi. Although reports suggested that demos were laid down for this venture, unfortunately for fans of both Priest and Sabbath the collaboration never got beyond the talking stage. The singer, much to the chagrin of his fanbase, then went off in an industrial direction for a project in conjunction with Nine Inch Nails supremo Trent Reznor, entitled Two. The experiment was dogged by a now regretful yet famous quote in which Halford declared, "Metal is dead," and soon floundered.

During the lengthy lull, in February 1997 Glenn Tipton released his first solo album, *Baptism Of Fire*, on Atlantic. The guitarist had in fact recorded twice: he cut a first set of songs with The Who's John Entwistle on bass and the legendary former Black Sabbath, Rainbow and Whitesnake Cozy Powell on drums; the second time with younger players. The final LP found the guitarist working with old and new guns such as Mr. Big bassist Billy Sheehan, Suicidal Tendencies' Robert Trujillo, Ugly Kid Joe's Shannon Larkin, Bad 4 Good member Brooks Wackerman and C.J. De Villar.

The Tipton association with Powell prompted many rumours. However, Priest got back into gear with Scott Travis, who had been working with Halford's Fight but had remained loyal to the Priest camp.

Meanwhile, Priest were honoured by not one but two tribute albums. *Legends Of Metal: A Tribute To Judas Priest* – a Century Media two-volume set – featured Priest classics covered by Helloween, Saxon, U.D.O., Testament, Rage, Mercyful Fate, Iced Earth, Blind Guardian, Nevermore, Kreator, Angra and Stratovarius among others. Although a commercial success, it was readily pointed out by critics that none of these alternative versions matched the originals.

Rumours were by now in full force as to who would occupy the still vacant vocal position, with ex-Gamma Ray singer Ralf Scheepers constantly put in the frame (the German didn't exactly help matters by touring in a tribute band titled Just Priest). The former Accept vocalist David Reece would also audition. Another acknowledged close contender was Pennsylvania-born D.C. Cooper, later to join Danish rockers Royal Hunt.

Ripper Owens: "It was Scott Travis that tracked me down. He got hold of a video of me doing some Priest numbers and sent it to Glenn and KK, which was enough for them to get me over to the UK. I got off the plane and met them at the studio. First thing they said was that I needed a rest. God, I was tired, but this was Judas Priest, so there was no way I was going to sleep. We got into laying down some vocals and they told me there and then that I was the man."

Glenn Tipton: "The auditions we had were just exhausting. We thought that surely there must be a singer out there that can do what Rob does, but it took us hundreds of tapes to realise it was going to be a very tough job. At one point we thought it was going to be impossible. There were some really funny ones, too, like the guy who sent a tape in that just kept saying: 'Let's get this show on the road', or the guy who was so short his head was below the door handle. We had a lot of name singers apply, but vocally they just weren't there. Then out of the blue Scott sends this video and we seriously thought the guy was miming. That's how good it was. I knew then that we'd got our singer. Ripper sang 'Victim Of Changes' and it was note perfect."

In May 1996 Judas Priest finally announced their new vocalist, 28-year-old Ohio native Tim 'Ripper' Owens, previously with Winters Bane, Brainicide, Twist Of Fate and grunge tribute act Seattle. The singer had also been fronting a Priest tribute band, British Steel, a video tape of which had secured his place.

1997's *Jugulator* heralded the return of undiluted heavy metal from Priest in spectacular fashion – incredibly, Downing and Tipton had surpassed themselves with their most extreme music to date. Ripper Owens easily outstripped the recent accomplishments by Halford, a feat many longstanding Judas Priest fans had thought impossible.

Owens's inaugural live shows threw the newcomer straight in at the deep end with an ambitious tour of America, where healthy audience attendance verified the fact that Judas Priest fans had not drifted away in the seven-year hiatus. Later shows on this tour saw British perennials Motörhead as openers. After a string of very successful dates, Priest hit continental Europe again, this time with Dutch labelmates Gorefest as openers. The band were set to return to the stage in early 1998, although only two shows were arranged for the United Kingdom, in London and Wolverhampton.

The latter half of 1998 found the band basking in the glory of their awesome double live CD *Live Meltdown* and resuming dates in America and Mexico, including gigs with Megadeth. Meantime, the Ranch Life label pulled off a coup with the issue of the *Concert Classics* live album culled from a vintage 1980 Denver, Colorado, show on the *British Steel* tour. Although Priest fans were quick to snap up copies, the release was swiftly dropped due to objections from the band's management.

The return of Judas Priest had done much to reinvigorate the European metal scene, the impact creating a number of bizarre releases. Not only did Ralf Scheepers release the Priest soundalike Primal Fear album (including an album jacket that more than evokes memories of *Screaming For Vengeance*) but also ex-Priest men Al Atkins and Dave Holland resurfaced with the *Victim Of Changes* album, a record consisting of reworkings of ancient Judas Priest numbers.

With interest high, the band found themselves nominated for a prestigious Grammy award for the track 'Bullet Train'. In mid-1999 they were confirmed as special guests on the touring 'Ozzfest' extravaganza in America, but hopes for further dates were dashed when they announced the suspension of these shows, with the band in the throes of negotiating a new record contract, this time with Atlantic in America.

A further tribute album emerged in 1999 titled *Hell Bent For Metal*,

JUDAS PRIEST discography

ROCKA ROLLA, Gull GULP 1005 (UK) (1974)

SAD WINGS OF DESTINY, Gull GULP 1015 (UK), Janus JXS-7019 (USA) (1976)

SIN AFTER SIN, CBS 82008 (UK), Columbia PC 34787 (USA) (1977) **23 UK**

STAINED CLASS, CBS 82430 (UK), Columbia FC 35296 (USA) (1978) **27 UK, 173 USA**

KILLING MACHINE, CBS 83135 (UK) (1978) **32 UK**

HELL BENT FOR LEATHER, Columbia 35706 (USA) (1978) (US release of *Killing Machine*) **128 USA**

UNLEASHED IN THE EAST, CBS 83852 (UK), Columbia 36179 (USA) (1979) **10 UK, 70 USA**

PRIEST IN THE EAST - LIVE IN JAPAN, Epic 25.3P.145-6 (Japan) (1979)

BRITISH STEEL, CBS 84160 (UK), Columbia 36445 (USA) (1980) **4 UK, 34 USA**

POINT OF ENTRY, CBS 84834 (UK), Columbia 37052 (USA) (1981) **14 UK, 39 USA**

SCREAMING FOR VENGEANCE, CBS 85941 (UK), Columbia 38160 (USA) (1982) **11 UK, 17 USA**

DEFENDERS OF THE FAITH, CBS 25713 (UK), Columbia 39219 (USA) (1984) **19 UK, 18 USA**

TURBO, CBS 26641 (UK), Columbia 40158 (USA) (1986) **33 UK, 17 USA**

PRIEST... LIVE!, CBS 450 639-1 (UK), Columbia 40794 (USA) (1987) **47 UK, 38 USA**

RAM IT DOWN, CBS 461 108-2 (UK), Columbia CK 44244 (USA) (1988) **24 UK, 31 USA**

PAINKILLER, CBS 467 290-1 (UK), Columbia CK 46891 (USA) (1990) **24 UK, 26 USA**

JUGULATOR, Steamhammer SPV 085-18782 (Europe), CMC International 06076 86224-2 (USA) (1997) **82 USA**

MELTDOWN - '98 LIVE, Steamhammer SPV 089-18542 (Europe), CMC International 06076 86261-2 (USA) (1998) **74 UK**

DEMOLITION, Steamhammer SPV 085-72422 (Europe), Atlantic 83480-2 (USA) (2001) **165 USA**

LIVE IN LONDON, Steamhammer SPV 092-74262 (Europe / USA) (2003)

ANGEL OF RETRIBUTION, Epic 519300-2 (UK), Epic EK 92933 (USA) (2005) **39 UK, 13 USA**

comprising more extreme acts such as Agent Steel, Steel Prophet, Vital Remains and, ironically, Winters Bane.

Although out of the limelight themselves, Priest remained in the public eye due to the movie *Metal God*. The film was based on a 1997 *New York Times* article by journalist Andrew Revkin, titled 'Metal Head Becomes A Metal God', about Ripper's ascendancy to stardom. It was initially to star Brad Pitt and *Friends* actress Jennifer Aniston, and was to portray the rapid rise to fame of Ripper Owens from warehouse clerk to frontman for his all-time favourite band. However, both title and cast were tentative at this stage. (More on this shortly.)

Fans were kept in anticipation with a projected new Priest album scheduled for late 2000. An American summer tour was announced with an arena billing that combined forces with Nazareth and the Scorpions, but by April these proposed gigs would be pulled as the band maintained they needed further studio time. Meanwhile, the embers were stoked by the release on Century Media of *Heart Of A Killer*, a repackaged Winters Bane album featuring Ripper. Travis was also kept busy, having reformed Racer X as a side project for a fresh album.

By late 2000, with no new Priest album on the horizon, the rumour machine was in full flight suggesting in-fighting between Ripper and the rest of the band about the new material. Wilder allegations had Ripper ready to take the vocal position in Pantera, paving the way for Halford's return. Halford, meanwhile, was on the road in America guesting for Iron Maiden and including numerous Priest songs in his repertoire, including 'Running Wild', 'Electric Eye', 'Tyrant', 'Genocide' (a welcome rarity from *Stained Class*) and 'Riding On The Wind'.

The band was kept in the headlines throughout November 2000 when German metal band Iron Saviour gave a high-tech overhaul to 'Hellion/Electric Eye' and premier American band Iced Earth issued their take on 'The Ripper'. Priest were further honoured on the *Punk Goes Metal* tribute compilation when Divit covered 'Breaking The Law', and teen divas The Donnas spruced up 'Living After Midnight' on their *Turn 21* album. Another leftfield tribute witnessed an all-star cast of Los Angeles rockers participating on the Cleopatra tribute album *Breakin' The Law*, a record of industrial and electronic reworks of Priest staples. Perhaps the most enlightening track on the album was Electric Hellfire Club's radical interpretation of 'Green Manalishi'. In spite of all this related activity, frustratingly Priest appeared to be on a break throughout 2000.

Travis managed to squeeze in a solitary Racer X gig in support of their *Superheroes* album at the Hollywood Whiskey in May 2001 as Priest fans limbered themselves up for the release of the *Demolition* album.

That same month an indication of the band's future came with the start of a Sony reissue campaign of the Halford-era catalogue. The first set, *British Steel, Point Of Entry, Screaming For Vengeance* and *Defenders Of The Faith*, came with extra tracks. *British Steel* hosted a live track plus the previously unreleased Turbo song 'Red, White & Blue', and *Point Of Entry* added 'Thunder Road', another unheard track from the *Ram It Down* sessions. *Screaming For Vengeance*'s extra studio track 'Prisoner Of Your Eyes' was a further *Turbo* leftover, while *Defenders Of The Faith* was bolstered by 'Turn On Your Light', yet another *Turbo* outtake.

Touring in Europe would see a run of dates in Spain supported by Savatage as well as headlining slots on European festivals such as the German 'With Full Force' event.

Meantime in the USA the band's name was being kept in the spotlight by Boston pop-rockers American Hi-Fi, whose video for their hit single 'Flavor Of The Weak' had the band members reverting to their teenage years, waiting in the parking lot for a 1981 Priest gig.

Demolition finally arrived in July 2001 backed up by the single 'Machine Man'. Japanese fans would be treated to an extra track entitled 'What's My Name'. For such an important release the omens for *Demolition* did not look good: many critics savaged the album. However, as the dust settled the rock media in general began an about-turn, with many journalists claiming *Demolition* to be one of the band's finest works. Priest put in a sell-out London gig before the American tour dates due to commence on September 14th at Los Angeles's Universal Amphitheatre. Running mates for the first two-month leg were slated as Anthrax and Iced Earth.

Also arriving was the movie *Rock Star*. The film had seen many changes from its inception, and Priest fans were now in the quite surreal position of seeing a movie on public release about Owens but officially nothing to do with the band. The lead role had switched from Brad Pitt to Mark Wahlberg, who had previously made his name in the music world as teen rapper Marky Mark. The 'group' also boasted the talents of Ozzy Osbourne and Black Label Society guitarist Zakk Wylde, Dokken bassist Jeff Pilson and Jason Bonham, drummer with Bonham, Virginia Wolf and Airrace.

In the movie, echoing Ripper's tenure with Priest tribute band British Steel, Wahlberg heads a Steel Dragon tribute act, Blood Pollution. The real-life drummer for Blood Pollution is played by another bona fide rocker, Blas Elias of Slaughter. The movie was mooted in its original form to have the members of Judas Priest contributing music and acting as advisors, but strong disagreements over the direction of the storylines led to the formation of an all-new band and a revised title.

Promoting *Demolition*, Priest would state on the record that *Rock Star* was not in fact related to the Owens story and that if the film made any implications or statements to that effect, legal action would ensue. This was a quite bizarre situation for fans of the band and rock fans in general, who knew the behind-the-scenes story.

In light of the terrorist attacks on the USA of September 11th 2001, Priest – then performing in Mexico – cancelled their entire US tour, re-scheduling the dates for 2002.

The second round of remasters arrived in October, covering the group's late-1970s output. *Sin After Sin* added the unissued Gun cover 'Race With The Devil' plus a live 'Jawbreaker', *Stained Class* came with a *Ram It Down*-era 'Fire Burns Below' outtake and 1990 live version of 'Better By You, Better Than Me', *Killing Machine* offered a live 'Riding On The Wind' and *Defenders Of The Faith* demo for 'Fight For Your Life', whilst *Unleashed In The East* concluded with the extra four tracks originally included only on the Japanese pressing.

Closing out the year, the band put in a December 19th gig at London's Brixton Academy supported by Saxon. The event was filmed for a DVD release and was preceded the afternoon before the show with a video shoot for the ballad 'Lost And Found'.

Judas Priest, together with Anthrax, resumed their American tour in January 2002. In light of recent tribulations the tour was deemed a huge success, performing to capacity crowds. As well as including new *Demolition* material, the band would resurrect some rarely performed vintage tracks such as 'Desert Plains' and the 'United' anthem. Meantime the Columbia reissue campaign concluded in March with the last clutch of four albums, all with extra tracks. *Painkiller* added an unreleased studio take, 'Living Bad Dreams', plus a live version of 'Leather Rebel', *Ram It Down* offered live tracks 'Bloodstone' and 'Night Comes Down', *Live* added three further live cuts, 'Screaming For Vengeance', 'Rock Hard, Ride Free' and 'Hell Bent For Leather', while *Turbo* came with the unreleased 'All Fired Up' and live 'Locked In'. Despite the remasters campaign's commercial success, many diehard fans questioned the lack of care taken in the historical detail, as most of the extra studio tracks were given little contextual explanation and the live songs were given completely erroneous dates.

Judas Priest would announce another exhaustive set of US tour dates throughout the summer and fall of 2002, commencing in Toledo, Ohio, in early July. Longstanding fans would be pleased by the inclusion in the set of the rarely performed classic 'Exciter' as well as 'Devil's Child'. The tour saw an August date at the Sunken Garden Theater in San Antonio, Texas, backed up by Reverend and old comrades-in-arms Budgie.

A further heavyweight Judas Priest tribute album was delivered by the Nuclear Blast label in September. Among the inclusions were Annihilator's 'Hell Bent For Leather', Primal Fear's 'Metal Gods', Witchery's 'Riding On The Wind', Iced Earth's 'Screaming For Vengeance', Siebenburgen's 'Jawbreaker', Hammerfall's 'Breaking The Law', Benediction's 'Electric Eye', Death's 'Painkiller', Silent Force's 'All Guns Blazing', Steel Prophet's 'Dreamer, Deceiver', Armored Saint's 'Never Satisfied', Therion's 'Green Manalishi' and Thunderstone's 'Diamonds And Rust'.

The band's long established leather-clad image came under fire in August when PETA (People for the Ethical Treatment of Animals) sent an open letter to the band requesting that the lyrics to 'Hell Bent For Leather' be changed to 'Hell Bent For Pleather' (pleather being a hide substitute).

The group swiftly issued a response stating that they did not wear leather onstage, a statement somewhat at variance with reality. On a less surreal note the DVD *Live In London* topped the German national charts in its first week of release.

During downtime in October, Ripper Owens aided Ohio-based covers band The Sickness for a short burst of club dates, reuniting the singer with his erstwhile Winters Bane colleague bassist Dennis Hayes and drummer Tim Semelsberger (who had also played in an early Ripper-fronted act called US Metal).

As predicted throughout much of 2002 by media and fans and according to statements given by Scott Travis, Owens had seemingly exited the band. The report, published on the Canadian website Brave Words And Bloody Knuckles, apparently found the drummer hoping for the reinstatement of Rob Halford. However, within hours an official management statement quashed the report.

Priest then split from Atlantic following disappointing sales of *Demolition* (the record had barely sold 50,000 copies in the USA) and signed to the SPV Steamhammer label for North American territories for a double live album and the *Live In London* DVD in January 2003.

Early July 2003 brought the news that all Priest fans had been waiting for, with the reunion of band and Halford. Although rumours and conjecture had been in free flow for many years, apparently this decision was taken just weeks before the announcement. A new studio album was plotted for 2004 – the band's 30th anniversary. Also in July it was revealed that the new Iced Earth singer was none other than Tim Owens. However, Iced Earth's Jon Schaffer soon made it known that Owens had been hired to record vocals for *The Glorious Burden* album on a session basis, and before he had lost his position with Priest. As time progressed, Owens, who revealed that he had received the notification that he had lost his position in the band by email, would settle into the Iced Earth line-up for subsequent tour work. Owens was also known to be cutting material with 13 Faces guitarist John Comprix.

In early 2004 the disturbing news came that ex-Priest drummer Dave Holland had been convicted at Northampton Crown Court of trying to rape a special-needs youngster. The 55-year-old musician, sentenced to eight years in prison, denied all charges. The offences had occurred at the drummer's Stoke Buerne home between June and December 2002, when he was giving the 17-year-old drumming lessons.

As the reformed band unit settled down to write material for a new album, projected for 2004 release, Halford made time to participate in a VH1 TV documentary *AIDS: A Pop Culture History*. Meanwhile the band busied itself with the recording of a comeback album, with Halford subsequently revealing that enough material had been laid down for two albums.

The first concrete signs of Priest's return to the scene came with the announcement that the band were confirmed as headliners of the Sölvesborg 'Sweden Rock' festival in June 2004. Sony, with whom it was strongly rumoured the band were to re-sign, revealed plans for a lavish four-CD *Metalogy* box set for March. The 7-inch box came clad in leather and studded with 54 metal spikes.

European headline dates, with the debut show on June 2nd at the Stadionsporthalle in Hannover, Germany, saw Canadian thrashers Annihilator as support. A headlining performance at the Italian 'Gods Of Metal' festival would go ahead despite an earlier storm that had cancelled supporting acts UFO and Stratovarius.

Rob Halford: "We really didn't allow ourselves any time to get emotional about it or think too much because of the really tight schedule we set ourselves. From the day we decided we were going to do this, the pace has been just frightening. We were rehearsing right up to half an hour before our good friends in Annihilator hit the stage in Hanover. That's how tight it was.

"The show went like a dream. I looked to my right and there's KK, look to my left there's Glenn, glance back and see Ian and Scott, and it was such a rush. It just felt like coming home. It was truthfully just a great, great show. Nobody dropped any major bollocks, we just sailed right through it. In true British fashion we got off, grabbed a beer, and said, 'That was all right, wasn't it?'"

Priest would be announced as co-headliners, alongside Ozzy Osbourne, on the North American Ozzfest in July, topping the bill of Slayer, Slipknot, Dimmu Borgir, Superjoint Ritual and Black Sabbath. The band also scheduled 'Off-fest' headline dates with Slayer and Hatebreed along the way. On a rather lesser scale the band's original singer, Al Atkins, announced a band union with ex-Iron Maiden guitarist Dennis Stratton in a new unit dubbed The Denial. Also on the road was an addition to the burgeoning ranks of Priest tribute bands, Nudist Priest – who fostered publicity by performing onstage naked.

Sensationally, Rob Halford took over the lead vocal role from Ozzy Osbourne for Black Sabbath's August 26th concert in Camden, New Jersey, after Ozzy had been forced out of action by an attack of bronchitis. The 'Ozzfest', despite the cancellation of the last show in West Palm Beach, Florida, due to Hurricane Frances, was deemed an enormous success by much of the US media – and Judas Priest had consistently been the premier act.

Initially announced for a December 31st 2004 release, the reunion album, with a title of *Angel Of Retribution*, was pushed back to January 4th 2005, then to February 1st, and finally March 1st. A European and UK tour saw Judas Priest performing in many major venues and witnessed a strong union with the Scorpions, while In Flames supported in Europe. Notably the schedule included a stop at the Birmingham NEC, their hometown's biggest concert hall and a long-time ambition for the band. The show, replete with additional pyrotechnics and video screens, would be filmed for DVD release.

Despite much of 2005 being taken up with Judas Priest activities, Halford was keen to announce that a fresh Halford album was en route, retaining his last cast of musicians, guitarists Metal Mike Chlasciak and Roy Z with bassist Mike Davis and drummer Bobby Jarzombek. Even bassist Ian Hill got in on extracurricular activities, landing credits as producer of Cannock rockers The New Blacks' *Sound Of Loud* EP.

As the launch date for *Angel Of Retribution* drew nearer, Sony tempted fans who pre-ordered the album with a limited-edition bonus DVD featuring footage recorded in Barcelona and Valencia, Spain, during 2004, plus four 'collectable' Priest postcards. The band's first opportunity to perform material from the new album came on February 23rd at the Valbyhallen in Copenhagen, Denmark. *Angel Of Retribution* songs included in the set were 'Judas Rising', 'Revolution', 'Deal With The Devil' and 'Hellrider'. Surprise inclusions would be 'Hot Rockin'' from 1981 and 'I'm A Rocker' dating to 1988.

Angel Of Retribution's first chart impact came in Japan, where the album impressively landed at Number 4. The album debuted in the UK at a rather humble Number 39 but in the USA gave the band their highest ever chart placing at Number 12, selling over 58,000 copies in its first week and proving its strength by shifting a further 100,000 copies in the following two months. *Angel...* notably entered the national Greek charts at Number 1, giving the band their first ever career chart topper. North American arena gigs commenced in June with support from Queensryche.

Priest's first Polish gig, a sold out event scheduled for Katowice on April 6th, was cancelled due to the death of John Paul II and Poland's president declaring that all entertainment venues must cancel their shows for five days of official mourning. Spanish gigs in Madrid, Coruña, Zaragosa and Barcelona saw fellow veterans Baron Rojo as openers, while Japanese headline dates in May included a show at Tokyo's Budokan on the 18th. This gig, in front of 10,000 fans, was filmed for a DVD release, *Rising In The East*.

Following the US tour, which launched on May 30th at the Blossom Music Center in Cuyahoga Falls, Ohio, a second round of shows was projected for Europe, including headliners at Germany's 'Wacken Open Air' festival and the Spanish 'Metalway' event, but the band never played these gigs. As it turned out, a second US leg would be followed in September by South American gigs in Mexico, Brazil, Chile, Puerto Rico and Argentina, allied with Whitesnake. North American shows in October had Anthrax as openers.

KK Downing broke tradition with his first ever non-Judas Priest guest session on an album when he appeared on the tracks 'War No More' and 'Deceiver' on bassist Mick Cervino's self-titled Violent Storm album (Cervino had played with Yngwie Malmsteen and Blackmore's Night).

Judas Priest, Rob Zombie and Anthrax teamed up for a one-off 'Priest Feast' on October 30th at the Long Beach Arena. The band rounded off the year by hitting new territories, with shows in Ukraine, Moscow and St. Petersburg, and the Baltic states of Lithuania, Latvia and Estonia.

It has been a rollercoaster ride for Judas Priest followers, basking in the glory of such landmarks as *Stained Class*, *British Steel*, *Screaming For Vengeance* and *Painkiller*, and feeling the pain of damaging diversions such as *Point Of Entry* and *Turbo*. Thankfully, the classic team finally relented for the solid *Angel Of Retribution* with renewed enthusiasm and a promise of more metal to come.

MOTÖRHEAD
BORN TO WIN

IN JUNE 1975 Ian 'Lemmy' Kilmister, sometime Hawkwind, Rockin' Vicars and Opal Butterfly member, formed Motörhead, arguably the closest any band has ever come to epitomising the true essence of heavy metal – despite Lemmy's frequent insistence that his band is merely very loud rock'n'roll. The band's impact, Lemmy's lyrical themes, artist Joe Petagno's 'Warboar' iconography and their umlauted logo – not to mention a fanbase resolutely 'metal' in composition – all place Motörhead firmly in the heavy metal camp.

Lemmy was born in 1945 and was supposedly nicknamed thus because of his constant early habit of asking to borrow – "lend me" – money. Between 1963 and 1966 he played with Manchester-based outfits The Rainmakers and Motown Sect. He travelled to London on a mission inspired by the pre-Deep Purple Jon Lord, who had invited him to visit. When Lemmy turned up on his doorstep, Lord was on tour in Denmark, but Lord's mother offered Lemmy a place on the sofa.

After enrolling in The Rockin' Vicars, a band that dressed in Finnish national costume, Lemmy achieved a fair degree of popularity: the outfit issued two singles in the UK and even performed in the then-communist Yugoslavia. The band's efforts were rewarded by an invitation to an official state function in the presence of President Marshal Tito.

Lemmy opted out of The Rockin' Vicars to roadie for Jimi Hendrix for eight months before joining Sam Gopal as rhythm guitarist in 1968 and releasing *Escalator* in 1969. He then teamed up with the tail-end of another psychedelic rock outfit, Opal Butterfly.

The demise of Opal Butterfly in 1972 signalled a switch of instruments to the now familiar bass guitar and Lemmy's induction into the mightiest space-rock outfit of all – Hawkwind. He would play on four albums, and even fronted the band's biggest hit, the seminal 'Silver Machine'. His tenure with Hawkwind came to an abrupt close when, during the band's fourth North American tour, he was busted at the Canadian border for possession of cocaine and spent five days in

jail. Lemmy's stash turned out to be the lesser-graded amphetamine sulphate, and his band bailed him out for a final gig in Toronto – but it was to be his last with Dave Brock and co.

Lemmy then returned to Britain to assemble a new band, initially to be titled Bastard. He later opted for the more commercially acceptable Motörhead, an alternative 1960s slang term for a speed freak and the title of a song Lemmy had written for Hawkwind ('Motorhead' first appeared on the B-side of Hawkwind's 'Kings Of Speed' single in 1975). The first incarnation of the band signed to United Artists (as Lemmy was still under a "leaving member" clause in his contract from Hawkwind), with a line-up of Lemmy, guitarist Larry Wallis and drummer Lucas Fox, both recruited with the aid of Mick Farren from The Deviants. Wallis had quite a history before Motörhead, having been a member of The Entire Sioux Nation, Shagrat and Lancaster Bombers, as well as a stint with UFO and Pink Fairies. Also involved, albeit fleetingly, was guitarist Luther Grosvenor, better known as Ariel Bender of Mott The Hoople and Widowmaker.

The band debuted as support act to Greenslade on July 20th 1975 at London's Roundhouse, performing a shambolic set of cover songs by Hawkwind, Pink Fairies and others. Indicating the disrespect for musical convention that would follow over the next four decades, Lemmy's intro tape was a compilation of rants by Adolf Hitler. Ten equally chaotic concerts followed, finished off with a support gig to Blue Öyster Cult at London's Hammersmith Odeon.

Lemmy: "The first Motörhead was a fucking embarrassment. I don't know what we were thinking. It was me, Lucas Fox and Larry Wallis and it was dreadful. I had a human skull on my amp that I painted blue and that was, in hindsight, the best thing about the band. We just threw the band together. I didn't even know those guys, really, but at least it was enthusiastic.

"We played this gig with Greenslade – fucking Greenslade! I'm glad we played loud, because if anyone had managed to hear what we were actually doing they would have realised how awful it was. Honestly, we were the worst band you had ever seen."

The solitary album cut for United Artists was *On Parole*, recorded between December 1975 and February 1976 at Rockfield Studios in Monmouthshire, Wales, featured both Lemmy and Wallis on lead vocals. It was initially produced by Dave Edmunds before Fritz Fryer took over, and it featured the track 'City Kids', co-written by Wallis with Pink Fairies bassist Duncan Sanderson, which had first appeared on Pink Fairies' *Kings Of Oblivion* in 1973. Towards the end of the sessions the group drafted in new drummer 'Philthy Animal' Taylor, after Fox left (he was fired, according to Larry Wallis) in the middle of recording in order to join Warsaw Pact.

Unfortunately, the finished tapes were unceremoniously rejected by the label, effectively leaving the band high and dry. However, plans were still being made to perform the album live, and Wallis's studio overdubs indicated the need for a second guitarist. This position was filled by 'Fast' Eddie Clarke, formerly of Zeus and Blue Goose. The quartet's first rehearsal was followed by the sudden departure of Wallis, who departed for another Pink Fairies reunion.

The band then cut a single at Pebble Beach Studio in Worthing for Jake Riviera's Stiff label, a sign of their adoption of the emerging punk scene. The intention was to couple the inaugural Kilmister-Clarke-Taylor composition 'White Line Fever' with a rendition of the Tamla Motown classic 'Leavin' Here'. This had originally (spelled 'Leaving Here') been a hit in the US for Eddie Holland, of Holland-Dozier-Holland fame, on the Tamla Motown label in 1964, before becoming a UK hit for The Birds on the Decca label in 1965. However, its release

MOTÖRHEAD discography

MOTÖRHEAD, Chiswick WIK 2 (UK) (1977) **43 UK**
OVERKILL, Bronze BRON 515 (UK) (1979) **12 UK**
BOMBER, Bronze BRON 523 (UK) (1979) **24 UK**
ON PAROLE, Liberty LBR 1004 (UK) (1980) **65 UK**
ACE OF SPADES, Bronze BRON 531 (UK), Mercury SRM 1-4011 (USA) (1980) **4 UK**
NO SLEEP 'TIL HAMMERSMITH, Bronze BRON 535 (UK), Mercury SRM 1-4023 (USA) (1981) **1 UK**
IRON FIST, Bronze BRNA 539 (UK), Mercury SRM 1-4042 (USA) (1982) **6 UK, 174 USA**
ANOTHER PERFECT DAY, Bronze BRON 546 (UK), Mercury 811 365-1M-1 (USA) (1983) **20 UK, 153 USA**
NO REMORSE, Bronze PROLP5 823 300-1 (UK), Bronze/Island 90233-1-H (USA) (1984) **14 UK**
ORGASMATRON, GWR GWLP 1 (UK), Profile PAL 1223 (USA) (1986) **21 UK**
ROCK'N'ROLL, GWR GWLP 14 (UK), Profile PAL 1240 (USA) (1987) **34 UK**
NÖ SLEEP AT ALL, GWR GWCD 31 (UK), Enigma 7 75405-2 (USA) (1988) **79 UK**
THE BIRTHDAY PARTY, GWR GWCD 101 (UK), Enigma 7 73536-2 (USA) (1990)

1916, WTG/Epic 467481-2 (UK), WTG NK 46858 (USA) (1991) **24 UK**
MARCH OR DIE, WTG/Epic 471723-2 (UK), WTG NK 48997 (USA) (1992) **60 UK**
BASTARDS, ZYX Music 20263-2 (Europe) (1993)
SACRIFICE, Steamhammer SPV 085-76942 (Europe), CMC International CMC 7803 (USA) (1995)
OVERNIGHT SENSATION, Steamhammer SPV 085-18302 (Europe), CMC International 06076 86207-2 (USA) (1996)
SNAKE BITE LOVE, Steamhammer SPV 085-18892 (Europe), CMC International 06076 86238-2 (USA) (1998)
EVERYTHING LOUDER THAN EVERYONE ELSE, Steamhammer SPV 089-21142 (Europe), CMC International 06076 86268-2 (USA) (1999)
WE ARE MOTÖRHEAD, Steamhammer SPV 085-21822 (Europe), CMC International 06076 86292-2 (USA) (2000)
HAMMERED, Steamhammer SPV 085-74062 (Europe), Metal-Is 06076-85229-2 (USA) (2002)
LIVE AT BRIXTON ACADEMY, Steamhammer SPV 089-72622 (Europe) (2003)
INFERNO, Steamhammer SPV 085-69742 (Europe), Metal-Is 06076-85241-2 (USA) (2004) **95 UK**
KISS OF DEATH Steamhammer SPV 085-99912 (Europe), Sanctuary 06076-84784-2 (USA) (2006) **45 UK**

---

was stopped by an injunction from United Artists. Frustratingly, the band had no option but to sit it out and wait for the contract to expire. However, fans soon learned that the single had been bootlegged by French label Skydog, thus generating the first Motörhead collectable. When United Artists finally relented, Stiff included 'White Line Fever' on their 1977 compilation *A Bunch Of Stiffs*.

Motörhead then scored a deal with Chiswick, and before the band's album sessions, held in June 1977 at Escape Studios in Kent, conducted a brief flurry of UK dates in support of Hawkwind. The band also signed a management deal with Doug Smith at this juncture. A second attempt at an eponymous debut album, including Motörhead's take on 'Train Kept A-Rollin'' – originally recorded by Tiny Bradshaw in 1951 – charted at Number 43. The release was backed up by a London graffiti campaign mounted by ex-Moody Blues and Wizzard manager Tony Secunda, who at the time was managing the tastefully named Moors Murderers (featuring the pre-Pretenders Chrissie Hynde). Secunda's strategy included a UK tour in alliance with The Count Bishops, dubbed the 'Beyond The Threshold Of Pain' dates. However, just four gigs into this run Taylor broke his wrist in a fight with a crew member, and the gigs were cancelled.

Motörhead's next move was to lay down a raucous reworking of the rock'n'roll staple 'Louie Louie', originally a 1965 hit for The Kingsmen. In 1978 the band severed ties with Chiswick Records, switching to the Bronze organisation late that year, while Taylor and Clarke formed a side project called The Muggers with guitarist/vocalist John 'Speedy' Keen and bassist Billy Wrath for live gigs during gaps in Motörhead's schedule.

That October Motörhead got back into gear on the UK live circuit with support from The Lightning Raiders. To coincide with these gigs, Chiswick reissued the debut album in limited-edition white vinyl. During the latter part of these dates Motörhead were invited on to their first *Top Of The Pops* appearance with 'Louie Louie': the single peaked at Number 68 in the charts, leading Bronze to suggest recording a full album.

Lemmy: "WE'RE NOT A HEAVY METAL BAND! Look, we're not a heavy metal band. We're a loud, punk, rock'n'roll band, and that's that."

MTDG: But all your fans are heavy metal fans. How did you attract the wrong fanbase?

Lemmy: "I really don't know. I'm happy to have them, of course, but it's by default really. I came from Hawkwind, and when the band started we were in the middle of the whole punk thing. We played with punk bands, then one day I woke up and someone told me I was in a heavy metal band. Then everybody started to get a bit popular, like Saxon, Judas Priest and Iron Maiden, and our record happened to be out at the same time so there we were. Maybe I should have protested a bit more.

"A lot of it was timing. The press put us into this box and that was fine – at least someone was listening to us. Before that nobody gave a fuck about Motörhead."

MTDG: You look like a heavy metal band.

Lemmy: "Yeah … maybe if we'd been skinheads I would have been in a hardcore band for the past 20 years."

MTDG: Come on, though – the leather jackets, the long hair, the war-pig logo, the album covers, plus the fact you play very loud music to an audience of heavy metal fans. It must mean something to you?

Lemmy: "It means there are a lot of confused people in this world. The first gigs we did, we had all kinds of people turning up. Punks, hippies, rockers. That was just great, but now, I dunno, it's more one crowd. It's a great crowd of people, don't get me wrong. In America we still get quite a diverse audience."

MTDG: If I took polled the general population with a photo of you and asked them to tick a box to state if they thought you were heavy metal or rock'n'roll, which box do you think they would tick?

Lemmy: "They would tick the wrong box. They do it every time there's an election too. Have you noticed that?"

MTDG: But when you tour, you're not playing with The Damned or

The Exploited or Rancid. You're playing bills with Black Sabbath, Metallica, Megadeth and Saxon.

Lemmy: "Yeah ..."

MTDG: So you're a heavy metal band, then.

Lemmy: "No, we're still not a heavy metal band. We might look like one, sound like one, even smell like one, but we're a rock'n'roll band. Motörhead is closer to Johnny Thunders or The Damned than Judas Priest or Iron Maiden. We're a pretty simple animal under this sophisticated exterior. It's rock'n'roll, but we play it faster and louder."

MTDG: Why aren't you playing with rock'n'roll bands, then?

Lemmy: "They're all dead, my son."

The Jimmy Miller-produced *Overkill*, issued in March 1979, propelled Motörhead to the top of the heavy metal revival. With the success of the title track, the band scored a second *Top Of The Pops* performance. Motörhead's brash style, combined with melodic turns but almost always buried in an avalanche of aggression, coincided perfectly with the early-1980s heavy metal explosion.

Intense touring and many TV appearances saw Motörhead rise rapidly in stature, with each album topping its predecessor's performance. Their concerts were notorious for being loud, leading to a reputation that would become almost mythical. *Overkill* opened the floodgates, and there would be no looking back.

A UK tour with Girlschool in tow ensued, promoted by the issue of a limited-edition green vinyl version of *Overkill*. European dates followed, with the Scandinavian leg seeing the band incarcerated at Helsinki Airport after they were accused of wrecking the PA system at the 'Punkaroka Midnight Sun' festival. Maintaining the band's momentum in the UK, a further single was lifted from the album: 'No Class' was manufactured in three different sleeves, depicting Lemmy, Philthy and Eddie.

After playing a set at the Reading Rock Festival on August 24th, the group – working with Jimmy Miller behind the desk again – issued the quick-fire *Bomber*. Although it had been hastily recorded, *Bomber* reached Number 12 in the charts and provided Motörhead with their second classic. Although they had slowed the pace somewhat, their ferocity remained unparalleled, and the now famous album art – featuring Lemmy, Eddie and Philthy piloting a Heinkel He 111 bomber – would translate into one of the most recognisable stage sets ever devised. For touring in the UK with guests Saxon, the entire aluminium lighting rig would be transformed into an aircraft, complete with spinning lights for propellers. Predictably, United Artists opted to cash in on the band's success by releasing the 1975 *On Parole* album.

Motörhead then teamed up with punk frontrunners The Damned to create the Motördamn project, cutting two tracks – their own 'Over The Top' and a version of The Sweet's 'Ballroom Blitz'. The latter became the B-side of a Damned single, 'I Just Can't Be Happy Today', in 1979.

By the start of the 1980s, the band had scored their first Top 10 album, with the Vic Maile-produced *Ace Of Spades* peaking at Number 4 in October 1980, preceded by the Top 10-charting live EP *The Golden Years*. Chiswick Records weighed in on the band's profile, with four tracks cut during the *Motörhead* recordings released as the *Beer Drinkers* EP. On the live front, Motörhead took Weapon out as support band for a sold-out UK trek. However, the year closed on a sour note as Philthy broke his neck, apparently resulting from a well-intentioned grapple with a large fan of the band.

With Taylor in recovery, an enforced hiatus was filled with an amalgam of labelmates Girlschool and Motörhead, titled Headgirl. The resulting *St Valentine's Day Massacre* EP, which hit Number 5 based on the radio play of the Johnny Kidd & The Pirates track 'Please Don't Touch', saw the two bands combine for a memorable performance on

Top Of The Pops. Another collaboration came with Lemmy's involvement with The Young & Moody Band's 'Don't Do That'. These sessions also featured journeyman drummer Cozy Powell and, somewhat surreally, Irish pop sisters The Nolans.

Philthy got back behind the kit for a short round of French gigs alongside Girlschool in March 1981. This preceded a 'Short, Sharp, Pain In The Neck' UK set of three shows supported by Tank and Trust. The first Motörhead convention convened at Leeds Queens Hall, and two 'Motorbrat' shows were aimed at under-18s at Newcastle City Hall. A career highlight was to come when Motörhead unleashed what is probably the rawest live album of all time: *No Sleep 'Til Hammersmith*, recorded by Vic Maile on the Manor Mobile over a three-night stand. It deservedly crashed into the UK charts at Number 1.

Motörhead were now keen to crack North America. Lemmy's experiences there with Hawkwind had shown him the reality of pursuing the rock'n'roll lifestyle to the full. But back home, a high-profile show came on August 1st 1981 when Motörhead performed to 40,000 fans, headlining a bill of Ozzy Osbourne, Mahogany Rush, Triumph, Riot and Vardis at the 'Heavy Metal Holocaust' festival at Port Vale FC.

The next studio album, 1982's self-produced *Iron Fist*, reached Number 6 and was again backed by a lengthy sell-out tour, but some observers detected rumblings within the ranks and even a slight mellowing of direction. Following his intense dissatisfaction with a joint single between Motörhead and American act The Plasmatics – Lemmy and Wendy O. Williams's cover of Tammy Wynette's 'Stand By Your Man' – Eddie Clarke quit in May 1982, re-emerging in the Fastway project with ex-UFO bassist Pete Way.

His vacancy was filled almost immediately by ex-Thin Lizzy guitarist Brian Robertson, who joined Motörhead for their American tour and the band's first dates in Japan. The ensuing album, *Another Perfect Day*, was a fine body of work, but somehow the rough edges that had so attracted fans before were visibly lacking onstage – and Robertson was never truly accepted. The band toured Britain, but no longer to the expected full houses, and the new guitarist's clean-cut image and apparent unwillingness to learn older songs didn't endear him to the group's hardcore audience.

Lemmy : "We got Brian Robertson in the band because we thought we'd try to get someone of class involved, but he turned out to be worse than us. I think we did one good gig with him and the rest were dreadful. Everyone hated the album, and Robertson looked like a shop dummy. Next!"

The year 1984 proved make-or-break for the band. At one point Motörhead had only the stoic Lemmy left to carry on with the name. Robertson joined the Frankie Miller band and would later turn up in Statetrooper, Hellfire Club and The Clan. Lemmy auditioned a whole slew of guitarists and, unable to decide between the last two candidates, recruited them both, with Motörhead becoming a twin-guitar band for the first time.

The two were relative unknowns – Würzel (aka Michael Burston), who had just left the army, and Phil Campbell, previously of Welsh outfits Rocktopus and Persian Risk. Drummer Taylor stuck around long enough for a one-off TV performance on the *Bambi* episode of the cult comedy show *The Young Ones* before he too opted out for a short, non-recording liaison with Waysted. Motörhead duly drafted in the experienced former Saxon drummer Pete Gill.

The overhauled Motörhead debuted with the successful 'Killed By Death' single, penned by Lemmy, Würzel, Campbell and Gill. However, with both Campbell and Gill still bound by previous contracts, the song was only credited to Lemmy and Würzel. 'Killed By

Motörhead's Ian 'Lemmy' Kilmister: white line fever

Death' would feature on the leather-bound compilation album *No Remorse*, and Motörhead set out on a British tour in 1984, with Campbell repaying his erstwhile colleagues by granting Persian Risk a valuable support slot.

The Bill Laswell-produced *Orgasmatron*, released in 1986, vindicated the new blood. Motörhead undertook an extensive European tour with support acts Manowar and Exciter, including dates in eastern Europe: at one gig in Hungary they pulled in 27,000 people. The title track became another concert mainstay, and Brazilian thrashers Sepultura still cover it in their live set to this day.

Lemmy: "Orgasmatron is this idea that the three evils of the world – war, politics and *organised* religion – are all tied up in this thing. It's orgasmic because mankind lusts after destroying itself. You know, all politicians are the same – demonstrable swine. Whatever they say to get your vote, they all lie, cheat and abuse their position. It's the same with religion. It's blind obedience. People don't question it. Why do they want my vote? Why do they want my money?

"If I want to talk to God I'll retire to the toilet or go sit under a tree. Why do I need to go to a church or a mosque? Religion is the cause of most wars too. It's just disgusting. I thought it was so obscene that it seemed like some unseen power was at work behind the scenes, the Orgasmatron."

Lemmy and Würzel then took time out to produce and guest on Warfare's second album, *Metal Anarchy*, before a Motörhead US tour with Mercyful Fate and Exciter in support. A second American trek saw Cro-Mags and Megadeth as openers, but the latter were ousted after only two shows as accusations regarding bad treatment and insufficient soundchecks flew about in the press. Five years later, Megadeth mainman Dave Mustaine would publicly apologise for his behaviour.

A few songs from 1987's *Rock'n'Roll* album were included in the movie comedy, *Eat The Rich*, before Motörhead – with Taylor back on drums – again set about laying waste to Europe, this time with support act Savatage. UK dates in September and October 1987 came with Canadian act Sword as openers.

Motörhead in suave mode

The band undertook another successful British tour in 1989 with support act Thunderhead; however, the relentless grind of albums and heavy touring was hiding the fact that Motörhead were on a non-creative career plateau. The band took a long hard look at their predicament and decided to start from scratch. 1990 was a turning point for Motörhead as they finally shrugged off manager Doug Smith and GWR Records – to whom they had been signed since *Orgasmatron* – and secured new management with Phil Carson and a major deal with WTG/Epic in America. Lemmy relocated to Los Angeles and the band proceeded to record *1916* with producer and ex-Procol Harum member Pete Solley, with whom the band had been endeavouring to work since *Orgasmatron*.

While recording in California, Motörhead took a break to play a *Rip* magazine party. Other extra-curricular activities included Lemmy turning up in the sci-fi film *Hardware* playing a taxi driver. Once *1916* was released, the media cited it as a return to form: Motörhead returned to tour Britain with support act The Almighty before joining the American 'Operation Rock'n'Roll' tour with Judas Priest and Alice Cooper. Regrettably, they pulled out of the last dates due to Lemmy breaking a rib but got back on the road shortly after on a package tour with Ozzy Osbourne and Alice In Chains. The band was also given the well-deserved accolade of a Grammy nomination for *1916*.

Lemmy: "I don't know how that deal with Sony happened. I think we kind of got the sympathy vote because we had been around so long. It was all very weird. Nobody at the record company gave a fuck about the band and when we got nominated for a Grammy the bastards never even said thank you.

"It came at a good time for the band, though, because it allowed Motörhead to hit America properly again. At least we spent Sony's cash on something worthwhile. I dunno, you give yourself so much heartache trying to get a decent record deal, and when you get one it turns out to be the last thing you want."

Phil Taylor left for the second time in April 1992 amid rumours that his excessive lifestyle was affecting the band to unacceptable levels. A temporary replacement was announced in ex-Dokken, WWIII and King Diamond drummer Mikkey Dee (real name Michael Delaouglou), but not before the renowned journeyman drummer Tommy Aldridge, of Black Oak Arkansas and Ozzy Osbourne repute, had recorded drum parts for the new album, *March Or Die*. As recording wound up for the record, with Ozzy Osbourne and Guns N'Roses guitarist Slash guesting on 'I Ain't No Nice Guy', Dee's position within the band was confirmed, although the Swede only managed to lay down drum tracks for the track 'Hellraiser'.

With Slash on the record, Motörhead's connections with Guns N'Roses saw them play as special guests on the mammoth Metallica and Guns N'Roses co-headlining tour. After severing ties with Epic, the group's next outing would prove to be their most low-key. *Bastards*, released on the specialist German dance label ZYX in November 1993, saw only limited export distribution outside Germany. This would undoubtedly damage the band at a critical point in their career. Many die-hard fans believe *Bastards* to be a seminal work heard by too few.

Lemmy : "Mikkey is just what this band has needed. I never realised how bad Philthy was until Mikkey came into the band. We tried playing some of the older songs but they didn't sound right. You know why? Because we'd been playing them so sloppily for years. Mikkey can't do it. He's like a machine."

Unfortunately, tragedy was to strike the band when a fan was killed in a stage-diving incident at their London Forum show in June 1994 – an event that soured the year. Motörhead rounded off '94 with a US tour on a double bill with veterans Black Sabbath.

In early 1995 Motörhead hit the charts again with the single 'Born To Raise Hell', a collaboration with Ugly Kid Joe singer Whitfield Crane and Body Count's Ice-T. Lemmy appeared solo on the popular TV show *Don't Forget Your Toothbrush*. Würzel then announced his decision to quit the band in February, only revealing his intentions before a European tour, but his departure was delayed while the promotion for the new *Sacrifice* album was underway. Würzel wished Motörhead well and began to concentrate on his Gang Show project featuring Dogs D'Amour vocalist Tyla and former Thunder bassist Snake (Mark Luckhurst). This outfit put in a batch of London club gigs before folding.

Motörhead carried on as a trio, completing a successful European tour in 1995 with support act Grip Inc. Strangely, a short batch of well-attended British dates saw the pop-rock band Rub Ultra in support, but further American dates with Black Sabbath followed before another European tour and shows in South America.

Phil Campbell: "When Wurzel fucked off, we suddenly all looked a lot younger. We really were starting to look like three geezers and a dustman. We were going to get in another guitarist at first, but time was tight – we had this tour of Germany booked – so I said: let's try it with just the three of us. So we did the tour and at the end of it we all got pissed off that we hadn't got rid of him years ago. The band was just as loud, and not one person asked us where he was."

Lemmy: "Germany has always been good to Motörhead. There was a time when nobody gave a shit except in Germany, and I've never forgotten that. When the Germans told us we didn't need Wurzel any more, that was the vote I needed. Phil really started to shine too."

The year 1995 ended with Lemmy's 50th birthday in Los Angeles, celebrated at a party thrown by *Rip* magazine and an impromptu appearance by Metallica, billed as The Lemmys. Wearing Lemmy wigs, Metallica played a half-hour set comprising Motörhead songs: material from this session was later released as the B-side to a Metallica single, 'Hero Of The Day', in 1996.

Proving that you can never keep a good band down, Motörhead displayed their staying power with the ironically titled *Overnight Sensation* in 1997. The resulting American tour saw a Motörhead first when the band pulled out of co-headline shows with W.A.S.P. due to personal tensions between the two acts. Motörhead's persistence was to pay off when, later the same year, a British tour supported by Novocaine and DBH saw the band back in action with sell-out shows. As 1998 got into gear, Motörhead, promoting a fresh album in *Snake Bite Love*, were back on the touring circuit in North America, this time as openers to Judas Priest. The 1998 reissue of the *All The Aces* compilation (on Essential in the UK and Sanctuary in the US) included 1978 archive recordings of The Muggers on a bonus CD.

The band rounded off the decade with a series of European festival dates with Manowar, Dio and, in Scandinavia, Lion's Share. Back in Los Angeles, Lemmy put together an album paying homage to his 1950s rock'n'roll heroes with ex-Stray Cats drummer Slim Jim Phantom and Danny B Harvey of The Swing Cats. The album, *Lemmy, Slim Jim & Danny B.*, surfaced in 2000 and – rather disturbingly – featured Lemmy sporting a gold lamé suit.

The band's 25th anniversary shows in Britain were supported by American act Speedealer, and the London Brixton Academy gig saw the band joined onstage by Queen guitarist Brian May, German chanteuse Doro Pesch and guitarist Martin 'Ace' Kent of Skunk

Anansie. (The previous night, Lemmy had played on the same stage for another anniversary – Hawkwind's 30th.) Motörhead's 25th anniversary album, *We Are Motörhead*, arrived in May and included a raucous cover of the Sex Pistols anthem 'God Save The Queen'.

Predictably, the year 2000 found the band back on the road as headliners in America. Dee found himself unexpectedly in the news when, along with tour-bus driver David Smith, he was arrested for disturbing the peace while attempting to break down a hotel door. A scuffle with hotel security led to the arrival of the police and the two spent time in jail, Dee getting out just in time for the next gig in Oregon.

The Metal-Is label then issued yet another in a long line of Motörhead compilations, although thankfully for fans *The Best Of Motörhead* did include four previously unreleased live tracks. As well as the regular CD, a limited triple-vinyl-LP also emerged, with exclusive artwork from Joe Petagno and a bonus 7-inch EP.

The band's gruelling schedule would finally take its toll on the seemingly indestructible Lemmy in December. Motörhead put in Japanese dates before a London Brixton Academy gig, after which they immediately departed for gigs in Russia, Poland, Lithuania, Belarus, Finland, Sweden, Denmark, Norway and elsewhere. This intensive bout of touring – taking in 39 shows in 48 days – gave no chance for the singer to recover from influenza, and in Italy doctors finally called a halt. With Lemmy recuperating in hospital, Motörhead were forced to cancel shows.

Lemmy: "Touring is the lifeblood of the band. We make albums so we can go and play new music to the people. We're a working band and there are not too many left these days. I read a statistic once about people spending most of their lives in bed and watching television. That's not my life. I spend most of my life on the road.

"That's what it's about for me, getting onstage and doing our thing, seeing new people, seeing old friends. I don't like staying still for too long. There's no reason to stop, and no words in a magazine are going to make me question my lifestyle or the way I treat my body. When I die I hope it will be on the road somewhere."

Campbell would take time out to session on a 2001 UFO tribute album entitled *Only UFO Can Rock Me*, and Motörhead's headlining show at the 2001 German 'Open Air' festival in Wacken saw the nostalgic redeployment of the band's *Bomber* lighting rig. Touring in the UK in May saw support by Backyard Babies and Campbell's son Todd's band Psycho Squad. Lemmy would also turn up as a guest on German metal queen Doro's new album when she covered Motörhead's 'Love Me Forever' from *1916*. Another Lemmy appearance would be rather more low-key, as he added guest vocals to the title track of melodic rockers Boetz's *Call To Arms*.

The band's rendition of Twisted Sister's 'Shoot 'Em Down' would then feature on the Koch tribute album *Twisted And Strange*. The band themselves signed to the Sanctuary label Metal-Is for a new album and all their classic albums dusted down once more for a mass re-release: *Ace Of Spades*, *No Sleep 'Til Hammersmith*, *Bomber*, *Iron Fist*, *Overkill*, *Another Perfect Day*, *Orgasmatron*, *Rock'n'Roll* and *No Sleep At All*, plus the *All The Aces*, *No Remorse* and *The Chase Is Better Than The Catch* compilations.

On April 1st Motörhead performed a new single, 'The Game', live in the Houston Aerodrome for the WWF's 'Wrestlemania X-7' event. The single was also picked by wrestling star Triple H as his theme music, and band and wrestler appeared on the TV programme *Smackdown*.

In October the band put in another high-profile TV performance, this time on the popular comedy series *The Drew Carey Show*. Motörhead also managed to squeeze in a set of US headline shows from September 27th. It was then announced that Lemmy had formed a studio alliance with Kiss drummer Eric Singer and Def Leppard guitarist Vivian Campbell to record a version of Kiss's 'Shout It Out Loud' for the soundtrack of the 2002 movie *Ash Wednesday*. Motörhead's version of 'Shoot 'Em Down' was also included.

Promoting the new 2002 studio album *Hammered*, a pun on 'Mo-Hammered', produced by Bob Marlette and erstwhile Meat Loaf guitarist Bob Kulick, the band commenced a US tour in Dallas, Texas, on April 11th. Support bands for the trek were Morbid Angel and Today Is The Day. Other studio activity found Motörhead appearing among an all-star cast, donating their take of 'Rockaway Beach' to the 2002 Joey Ramone and Rob Zombie-assembled Ramones tribute album *We're A Happy Family*.

Castle Music in the UK and Sanctuary in the USA kept the unending stream of Motörhead releases well stoked with the issue of two double CD sets in May. *Tear Ya Down: The Rarities* consisted of the previously available *Dirty Love* and *Stone Dead Forever* collections, while *Keep Us On The Road: Live 1977* paired *Blitzkrieg On Birmingham* with *Lock Up Your Daughters*.

The band set out on European tour dates in October and November, performing with guests Anthrax in the biggest venues for some time: their London Wembley Arena gig added Hawkwind to the bill. A lengthy run of Scandinavian shows in much of November found Meldrum as support act. Some bonus publicity came when, quite bizarrely, a person purporting to be Lemmy apparently offered to surgically remove his trademark facial moles and sell them on the internet.

Mikkey Dee stepped in for recording sessions for German heavy metal act Helloween's new album in late 2002, as their regular drummer Mark Cross, afflicted with the Epstein-Barr virus, was too ill to perform in the studio. Dee also forged an alliance with Eurodance star E-Type (actually former Hexenhaus drummer Martin Eriksson) to perform club gigs in Sweden in January and February 2003. Motörhead were then confirmed as one of the headline attractions at the 'Big Beast Festival' in Japan in December 2002. Lemmy aligned himself with another rock'n'roll institution on March 14th 2003 when he stepped onstage at an MC5 reformation gig at London's 100 Club to take guest lead vocals alongside other high-profile stars.

Motörhead's headline US shows on the West Coast in April 2003 found Dwarves and High On Fire as support before the band hooked up with Anthrax in May for a batch of co-headliners. In the middle of this run, Campbell took a break due to the death of his mother; the band pulled in former Danzig guitarist Todd Schofield to cover gigs in Norfolk, Virginia, and Worcester, Massachusetts, until Campbell's return. Higher-profile US dates, commencing in July, saw the band co-headlining a strong package tour with Iron Maiden and Dio. UK headline shows for October saw The Wildhearts as support.

The band participated in the making of a mammoth 99-track, career-spanning box set entitled *Stone Deaf Forever!* released that same month by Sanctuary. To stem a glut of unsanctioned compilation releases, the group and the fan club assembled a definitive track listing, and the set included a 60-page booklet, newly commissioned artwork from longtime Motörhead artist Joe Petagno and no fewer than 19 previously unreleased tracks.

In November, Lemmy worked on his inaugural solo album at Berlin's Monongo studios, owned by the Kilmister-endorsed German rockers Skew Siskin. Lemmy had recently collaborated with Skew Siskin on 'Shake Me' from their *Album Of The Year* record: both bands then united for a tour of Germany and Switzerland, beginning on November 25th at Berlin's Columbiahalle.

Motörhead played the Royal Opera House in London's Covent Garden in February. The show, at the invitation-only Vilar Floral Hall at the home of classical opera, was part of a publicity campaign to boost tourism to the British capital. Shortly afterwards, Mikkey Dee put in a further performance in the backing band of Swedish pop act E-Type as part of the Scandinavian superstar's Swedish Eurovision entry. Lemmy then recorded a brace of songs with new act Young Heart Attack, one of which – a rendition of AC/DC's 'Get It Hot' – featured on the band's March single 'Tommy Shots'.

A new Motörhead album, initially given a working title of *Flames* but then confirmed as *Inferno*, appeared in June through the band's by now consistent partners Metal-Is in the USA and in Europe via SPV/Steamhammer. Guitar virtuoso Steve Vai contributed a guest solo to 'Terminal Show'. Motörhead recorded a version of Metallica's 'Whiplash', which they contributed to the Big Deal label's *Metallic Attack* tribute. *Inferno* fared well upon release across Europe, even making impressive headway into the national German Top 10.

Gigs in Europe in November and December were bolstered by heavyweight support from Sepultura and Swedish act The Ring. However, a batch of US dates was cancelled due to an aggravated foot injury sustained by Lemmy. A surprise guest at the band's November 27th gig at the Hammersmith Apollo was ex-guitarist Wurzel, joining them for an encore of 'Overkill'.

The band then took an unexpected diversion into the world of cult cartoons, re-recording their song 'You Better Run' under the new title 'You Better Swim' for inclusion on the *Sponge Bob Squarepants* movie soundtrack. In December the Motörhead cover of 'Whiplash' was nominated in the Best Metal Performance category for the 47th Annual Grammy Awards. Ironically, the track won the category.

Mikkey Dee then took an unexpected diversion by guesting on Christian band Liberty N'Justice's *Soundtrack Of A Soul*. Motörhead's US tour dates, commencing in March 2005, saw Corrosion Of Conformity and Brand New Sin as part of the road package, with West Coast dates adding Fozzy and 3 Inches Of Blood performing the honours in Canada.

Lemmy: "The rock bands of today are disgusting whiners. I think most of them bypassed being teenagers, because there is no rebellion in their soul, no rock'n'roll. They have failed their own generation by being bland bed-wetters. How dare they get on that stage and fake it with somebody else's sampled music? Where's the danger? Where's the fucking honesty gone today? The whole idea of rock'n'roll was you have a mouth, sing with it and pour whiskey into it; you have hands, play your guitar; you have a dick, get laid with it. Now they talk junk politics and wank themselves off in front of a computer. Excuse me?! Half of them can't even play their own instruments, and if you showed them a guitar solo they would shit their pants."

Motörhead's 30th Anniversary show, held on June 16th at the traditional stamping ground of the Hammersmith Apollo in London, saw a renewing of old ties with Girlschool as support. This collaboration, adding Swedish death metallers In Flames, toured the UK throughout October and December. Subsequent European and Scandinavian gigs featured Meldrum and Mondo Generator in support. To coincide, Sanctuary issued a deluxe two-disc version of the *Bomber* album, adding alternate versions and live tracks. A promotional video for the track 'Whorehouse Blues' notably featured Meldrum frontwoman Moa Holmsten.

Lemmy then appeared in the unlikely company of England soccer star Gary Lineker and model Lucy Pinder when the Motörhead frontman filmed a series of commercials for Walker's Crisps in late

June. Shortly afterwards, Motörhead's live schedule was interrupted when they were forced to withdraw from the 'With Full Force' festival, because Lemmy had been hospitalised in Germany with "circulation problems". A subsequent press release revealed that the singer was suffering from "extreme dehydration leading to exhaustion".

A 30th anniversary DVD entitled *Stage Fright* compiled footage from the band's December 7th 2004 show in Düsseldorf, Germany, alongside a second documentary disc. Yet another in a long line of tribute records came next. *Remember Me Now, I'm Motörhead*, through Scatboy, proved of interest as – among covers by the likes of The Orange Julians, Pale Horse, Empire Falls, Hammercocks and Ordained – it included Larry Wallis's original Motörhead demo for the track 'Old Enough To Know Better, But Much Too Young To Care'. Meanwhile, Phil Campbell made a guest appearance on *Bulletproof*, the major label debut from Detroit rapper Hush.

UK touring was punctuated by an unusual event when, on the day of a concert in Cardiff, Lemmy accepted an invitation by Conservative politician William Graham to address the Welsh assembly on the subject of drug abuse. Controversially, Lemmy, who revealed he had lost friends and acquaintances due to heroin abuse, used the speech to advocate legalising heroin in order to "wipe out dealers and stop criminalising young people".

The band closed out the year with a joint package tour of Australia allied with Mötley Crüe in December, while news came that Lemmy and the infamous Skullpig logo were to be rendered in 3D form by the Stevenson Entertainment Group.

As 2006 was ushered in, Motörhead delivered a familiar, if welcome, announcement, warning of another album and another tour. There is, quite simply, no other band like them.

Lemmy : "I didn't start Motörhead to get famous. Don't worship Motörhead; don't worship anyone. I don't care what you think as long as you're actually thinking for yourself. Y'know, I'm glad I never got fucking rich. I don't think I could stand all that pampering. I've always had everything I ever wanted and Motörhead gave me that. I started this band to play rock'n'roll and get laid. I succeeded!"

OZZY OSBOURNE
DIARY OF A MADMAN

WITHOUT DOUBT THE most familiar face in heavy metal, Ozzy Osbourne has a public profile that often overshadows his three-decade reign fronting the pioneering Black Sabbath and his own even more successful solo band. Offstage, Ozzy – born John Michael Osbourne in Aston, Birmingham on December 3rd 1948 – is humble, self-deprecating and filled with self-doubt, but the stage brings out his 'Prince of Darkness' alter ego, worshipped and revered by millions. Although he has racked up album sales into the many millions, he is often primarily associated with legendary outlandish behaviour such as biting the head off a dove, urinating on the Alamo and snorting ants.

Strip away these public excesses, however, and Ozzy's status as a true pioneer becomes obvious. Despite his many detractors, it is widely acknowledged that only his rustic, primal roar truly embodies the spirit of the original Black Sabbath. Since striking out solo, Ozzy's uncanny ability to recognise innovative genius in guitarists has seen his band spearheaded by such legends as Randy Rhoads, Jake E. Lee and Zakk Wylde.

Before going solo, Ozzy's star rose rapidly with Black Sabbath, and for much of the 1970s the group enjoyed both creative and commercial success with an historic quintet of albums. However, 1976's *Technical*

Ecstasy initiated a nosedive in sales and enthusiasm. With the inevitable disintegration of the band, Ozzy set about forging a fresh band with members of Cumbrian outfit Necromandus: guitarist Barry Dunnery, bass player Dennis McCarten and drummer Frank Hall. This line-up cut a set of rehearsal demos in 1977, apparently in a mellower, progressive rock style, for a proposed album, but then faltered and split.

Frank Hall: "Ozzy had a lot of offers on the table from a few record companies. The potential was just huge at that point because the press would jump on any new Ozzy album. He was really keen to show the world how good Baz was, too. The band was called Blizzard Of Ozz right from the start. There was one label in particular who were talking about very large advances, not just for Ozzy but for all of us."

Bob Daisley: "Ozzy's dad thought of Blizzard Of Ozz. Ozzy told him he was starting a new band before he left Black Sabbath the very first time, in 1977, and his dad suggested it then. Ozzy even got T-shirts made up with it on."

Later that same year, Ozzy formed another prototype solo act from the ranks of Polydor band Dirty Tricks with guitarist John Fraser-Binnie, bassist Terry Horbury and drummer Andy Bierne. This unit collapsed when Ozzy returned to Black Sabbath, ousting his temporary replacement, former Savoy Brown and Fleetwood Mac man Dave Walker. Ozzy then re-recorded Walker's intended vocals for the 1978 *Never Say Die* album and completed a lengthy tour, before retiring to California to commence work on an intended tenth anniversary opus. However, in mid-session Ozzy abruptly exited once more.

The dispirited Ozzy duly signed to Don Arden's Jet label and delegated his business management to Arden's daughter Sharon. After many months of shying away from the media, Ozzy assembled a new band with the assistance of bass player Dana Strum. A succession of guitarists would be auditioned, including latterday W.A.S.P. man Chris Holmes, before Strum convinced Osbourne that Quiet Riot's Randy Rhoads was the ideal candidate. The trio had intended to relocate to Britain but Strum, apparently through lack of a work permit, remained in Los Angeles. (He would subsequently find recognition with Vinnie Vincent's Invasion and Slaughter.) For a brief period Ozzy attempted to work up a further outfit with an unknown set of British musicians in his home studio, before inviting Rhoads to join him once again.

Rhoads was joined in England by Australian bassist Bob Daisley, a reliable veteran of Rainbow and Widowmaker. The position of drummer was harder to fill, and in the period of initial confusion ex-Skip Bifferty and Ten Years After drummer Dave Potts filled in for just over a week. A set of demos, which included 'Crazy Train', would also be put onto tape with Lone Star's Dixie Lee behind the drum kit. At this juncture, former Flying Hat Band and Bullion drummer Barry 'Spence' Scrannage managed to last the course of just one local pub gig. Eventually the group stabilised with the acquisition of the esteemed Uriah Heep drummer Lee Kerslake.

Lee Kerslake: "We had this little cassette player to play back the demo, so we gave it a quick listen then got on with it. Randy went into the 'Crazy Train' riff and I just put down what I thought would work. Bob looked at Ozzy and they gave each other a big smile, but Randy leapt about four foot in the air. 'We got one!' he shouted. It was really funny, he was so excited he simply couldn't contain himself. 'Oh man! At long last we got one!' he kept shouting. Ozzy and Bob looked relieved and happy that this was obviously going to work, but Randy was just over the top. I remember Ozzy had this big fox-fur coat on and he said to Bob and Randy: 'Are we happy now?' We were all grinning like little kids. Well, we all knew there and then.

Ozzy shook my hand and said to me, 'Here's my hand, here's my heart, 'til we're dead, 'til we part.' That was good enough for me. I was in."

Bob Daisley: "The best thing for Ozzy at that time was that myself, Randy, and Lee wrote him a bunch of songs that had practically no Black Sabbath influence whatsoever. I had never listened to a Black Sabbath album in my entire life. Honestly. That was probably a good thing. Especially with Randy Rhoads sounding absolutely nothing like Tony Iommi. Randy didn't like those old Sabbath albums at all. He couldn't bear to listen to them."

The group's Max Norman-produced debut album *Blizzard Of Ozz* contained future classics such as the careering 'Crazy Train' and the brooding 'Mr. Crowley', with sharper, more volatile and energetic music than Black Sabbath's later works, and it quickly provided Ozzy with the career impetus he needed. A single, 'Crazy Train', was released in August 1980 under the band title of Blizzard Of Ozz.

The single was followed by a brace of pseudonymous warm-up gigs under the name Law, followed by a full British theatre tour with support from Budgie. *Blizzard Of Ozz* proved an instant winner with metal fans and, in particular, acted as a showcase for the sparkling virtuoso guitar of Randy Rhoads. With his characteristic polka-dot Flying V and blistering solos, the fragile-looking Rhoads quickly gained living-legend status among fans. However, although British audiences quickly took to Ozzy's new band, the album was not initially granted a US release.

Ozzy capitalised on the European impact of the album with the quick-fire successor, 1981's *Diary Of A Madman*, again recorded with the Osbourne-Rhoads-Daisley-Kerslake line-up. Immediately after the release, Rudy Sarzo – a former Quiet Riot cohort of Rhoads – enrolled on bass guitar, while erstwhile Black Oak Arkansas drummer Tommy Aldridge and Rainbow keyboard player Don Airey were brought in to the fold for the touring band. Daisley and Kerslake had been unceremoniously dumped before the record's release, and it was with some degree of confusion that fans saw a photograph of the new line-up on the album cover.

Bob Daisley: "When Diary Of A Madman was released, Lee and I were bloody angry. It was no longer Blizzard Of Ozz, it was just Ozzy, and we were virtually erased. Our names are there but only in the smallest of fine print and only listed as songwriters. Rudy Sarzo and Tommy Aldridge were credited but never played a note on that record. Diary Of A Madman was recorded by Ozzy, Randy, Lee and myself, but anyone buying the album would never have been able to figure that out. It really was insulting. Even the production credits changed. Lee and I were left out there, too. I really could not see the point of that."

Tommy Aldridge: "Lee should be very proud of those records. I remember someone trying to get me to re-record the drums. I declined, saying I couldn't improve upon what he did. I didn't know it at the time but I was being approached not to 'improve' but only to 'replace' his performance. I didn't know why but can only imagine."

Concern from Ozzy's fans would be surpassed by outrage from his record company and the world at large when, in May 1981, during a marketing meeting with Epic Records, Ozzy casually bit the head off a dove. The repercussions of this publicity stunt would dog Osbourne for years to come, as his concerts were frequently besieged by animal-rights activists and religious protest groups.

With publicity at feverish heights, Ozzy engaged in a mammoth 14-month tour of North America, generating a hit album and a stream of sold-out, hysterical concerts that featured an elaborate, medieval castle stage-set and a bizarre dwarf named Ronnie. This diminutive human stage prop,

named John Allen, would be ritually hung each evening as a wicked barb aimed directly at Ozzy's replacement in Black Sabbath, the short-of-stature Ronnie James Dio. A brief respite from the American circuit came with the welcome slot alongside Motörhead at the Port Vale 'Heavy Metal Holocaust' festival when – ironically – Ozzy stepped in at the last minute to replace the promoter's first choice, Black Sabbath. Motörhead would then open for Ozzy in the States after Def Leppard and UFO had enjoyed support stints on the tour.

The *Diary Of A Madman* trek was notable for escapades from Ozzy that outranked even the infamous dove episode. A further encounter with wildlife saw Ozzy mistakenly biting off the head off a dead bat tossed onstage at a concert in Des Moines on January 20th 1982. What Ozzy believed to be a rubber toy hospitalised him, as the animal carried the risk of rabies infection. Ozzy surpassed even this by committing the most unpatriotic crime of urinating on the national shrine at Fort Alamo in San Antonio, Texas. The American media and evangelical clergy whipped up a storm of protest, which merely served to inflate the Ozzy legend.

Tragically, just as Ozzy appeared to have the world at his feet, everything crashed down to reality. After stopping over at the house of tour-bus driver Andrew Aycock in Leesburg, Florida, on March 19th – on the way to a festival in Orlando headlined by Foreigner – Aycock took Don Airey up in his light airplane. After a couple of circuits, Rhoads and make-up artist Rachel Youngblood boarded the plane. It is believed that Aycock misjudged his distance during the flight and clipped the tour bus in which Ozzy was sleeping, causing the plane to crash into the house. All three people on board were instantly killed.

RANDY RHOADS

Randall William Rhoads might just have been the last truly great guitar hero. He introduced a seismic change into the way metal guitar is played. Ironically, this slight figure's influence would be purely accidental, as Rhoads actually had very little interest in Black Sabbath. It was only when introduced into the Osbourne-Daisley-Kerslake axis that his eclectic arsenal of ecclesiastical Hypodorian and Mixolydian modes and breathtaking diversity began to shine. It is one of music's greatest tragedies that Randy's time on this earth was all too fleeting.

In the wake of such originality, Ozzy's task of matching his arch rival Tony Iommi proved doubly difficult. It was a quest that would only be satisfied by the very greatest in their field – Jake E. Lee and Zakk Wylde.

Kelly Garni (Quiet Riot): "Randy was a major, major Leslie West fan. Not enough is said about that. Mountain was a major influence on Randy. (He) also did a lot of Rolling Stones, stuff like 'Street Fighting Man' and 'Sympathy For The Devil'. Also at that time Alice Cooper was very big. Randy was especially taken with Glen Buxton's style of guitar playing. Randy loved to make weird noises on the guitar and he was fired up to do that by Buxton's Alice Cooper records. It's interesting that not many people have picked up on that, even the guitar magazines, which I think is because of the Ozzy/Sabbath association. Randy's inspiration really came from Leslie West, Glen Buxton and Mick Ronson.

"Randy came from a fairly religious background and had a big problem with all the black magic stuff. It was against everything he believed or had been taught. But Quiet Riot was going nowhere and Randy was sick of having no money."

Bob Daisley: "Randy, you could tell, was going to be a major talent. He would play an absolute blinder of a solo and then double it note for note exactly. Everything was completely worked out to the finest degree in his head. That's a rare talent. People came down from the record company on a pretty regular basis. When they heard Randy you could see they were thinking: what planet is this kid from? We were all very proud of the magic that we had. We had certainly stumbled onto something unique."

Lyndsey Bridgwater: "Songs such as 'Mr. Crowley' had a lot of classical influence. The way Randy could switch from lead to rhythm and vice versa really showed his virtuosity – in fact his ability knocked you flat. On the albums, there was an awful lot of guitar, sometimes seven or eight tracks with electric overlaid with acoustic and then lead too. When I first heard it I remember thinking, 'How the hell are we going to do that live?' but as soon as I heard Randy play, it became obvious. Randy could do it all. He was such a dynamo live. You wouldn't believe some of the things he could do."

John Thomas (Budgie): "He totally knocked me back. I can remember telling everyone: this guy is just brilliant. He looked an absolute star. He was an absolute magician on the guitar. His approach was just superb, he didn't play 'dark' like a lot of players then. Randy was very melodic. Absolutely perfect for Ozzy. I know Randy pretty much impressed the world. That's how good he was."

Don Airey: "The way Randy played, I needed a much different approach keyboard-wise compared to, say, working with someone like Ritchie Blackmore or Gary Moore. It had to be sparse, with sound effects and so on. Anything vaguely avant-garde, he really liked. He turned me on to a lot of diverse stuff – 18th-century guitar music, obscure film soundtracks, records by pianists Katia and Marielle Labèque, Ravel and Debussy. I remember his favourite chord, which was the one in the film *Carrie*, when the hand comes out of the grave – we'd play that bit of the video over and over again."

Paul Chapman (UFO): "Randy and I spent a good long time playing together. He showed me how to build complex chords from major scales, using triads and compounding third intervals. Consequently, the chord turned out to be an E7 (inversion) starting on the third (G-sharp) and not the root (E). That's when he showed me all about triads and chords, compound inserts, sevenths and ninths – his knowledge was quite unbelievable, really. His grasp of scales was way ahead of its time. I mean, the song 'Diary Of A Madman' is a Hungarian minor scale. Nobody did that back then. He was the first."

While this marked the loss of a pivotal player, Ozzy's band resolved to persevere with their touring commitments. Despite his enormous profile, Ozzy had difficulty in finding a replacement guitarist at first, although both Gary Moore and ex-UFO man Michael Schenker were rumoured to have been offered the position. Initially, Irishman Bernie Tormé, who had just left the Gillan band, filled Randy's shoes, but life on the road with Ozzy proved too much and after a handful of shows, which included New York's Madison Square Garden, Bernie departed. Fusion player Ray Gomez and ex-Bowie man Earl Slick were put through their paces, but it was Brad Gillis – formerly with Bay Area jazz-rock combo Rubicon and, at the time, bidding to get his new band Ranger a deal – who jumped on board and stayed the course to complete the dates. After the tour Sarzo quit to rejoin the imminent relaunch of Quiet Riot.

In 1982 Ozzy released a double live album called *Talk Of The Devil* (*Speak Of The Devil* in the USA and Japan). This record had initially been intended to contain studio-recorded Black Sabbath covers. However, after much deliberation Ozzy decided that its release was too close to the guitarist's death and issued a live recording of the Gillis line-up instead. Shrewd fans observed that *Talk Of The Devil*'s release was timed to appear just before Sabbath's own live outing, *Live Evil*, with Ozzy's pre-emptive strike stealing the thunder from his former comrades.

Bernie Tormé: "The first gig: everyone was under a great amount of stress. Looking at it in retrospect, it must have been the make-or-break as to whether it would carry on or not. Ozzy was very supportive, very helpful for the whole gig, took a lot of pressure off me. They probably really weren't that concerned with me, just so long as I didn't make a total balls of it.

"Tommy [Aldridge] said afterwards that I must have had the biggest balls in the world to do that gig, but the worst thing I could do was hit some bum notes. So fucking what? I hit a few, probably more than a few, but I got through it with no disasters. But what Ozzy and the band did that night really needed the biggest balls in the world. I am very proud of having helped them to get through that gig. I'm glad I had a chance to do that."

Ozzy then approached Y&T's Dave Meniketti with a view to replacing Gillis, but Meniketti declined. UFO and Fastway bassist 'Wild' Pete Way teamed up with Ozzy for the British shows, alongside a retained Gillis and keyboard player Lindsey Bridgewater. However, with the shows completed, this version of the band folded, with Way leaving to form Waysted and Gillis returning to America where, after a name change to Night Ranger, his own band would achieve great radio success. Ozzy's next guitarist could have been John Sykes from Tygers Of Pan Tang, but after being offered the position Sykes instead opted for Thin Lizzy.

Pete Way: "Out of the kindness of his heart, [Ozzy] simply said: 'Come and play bass with me.' So that's what I did. I didn't expect a salary or anything. I think Sharon was interested because I had proven writing skills with UFO, which may have come in handy later. I was just relieved. The god of rock'n'roll had taken pity on a poor destitute bass player.

"The very last thing Tommy Aldridge needed to deal with was me – not that he made it easy for me, though. In truth I didn't play the Ozzy songs very well. I guess he resented having a junkie for a bass player, and who can blame him. Onstage I would just be doing my best but I was struggling. I was totally addicted to heroin at the time."

Lengthy auditions in Los Angeles were held, once again with Dana Strum providing the contacts, which eventually turned up Dokken guitarist George Lynch and then Jake E. Lee (at first known as Jakey Lou), the Japanese-American ex-Ratt, Rough Cutt and Dio guitarist. Lynch was actually informed that he had secured the position – but Lee, arriving late for the audition, took the spot from him at the last minute. Also involved was the notorious bassist Don Costa, previously a shortlived member of Los Angeles shock-rockers W.A.S.P.

The Lee-Costa line-up debuted in Europe, playing Germany, Belgium, Switzerland and France as guests for Whitesnake. However, it took only a few gigs before Costa's outrageous antics – such as shredding his knuckles onstage with a cheese-grater – proved too much even for Ozzy, and the man was given his cards. The ousted bassist later formed the shortlived M80 with ex-Vendetta guitarist Niki Buzz. On the other hand, Jake E. Lee became an integral part of the Ozzy band, with a blend of superior stagemanship and exciting guitar playing, which was notable for his unique thumb techniques.

Dana Strum: "George Lynch was on fire. A great player. It was a good bit late and no one in the room was thinking other than George had got it. That included George and his then wife Christy, who was also there. Then Jake showed up. Ozzy and Sharon liked his image and vibe, the whole Crüe/Ratt type thing. Jake played very well and the night got very odd. I was told that George might not be the guy. Ozzy, Sharon, and Tommy kinda seemed to fancy Jake and his whole trip and vibe. George was shocked, very pissed and very upset. This was the worst thing for him."

Ozzy Osbourne: "Jake keeps himself to himself. He's very quiet offstage but he's fantastic in front of an audience. He's a real showman too. He nearly didn't make it. The bastard turned up an hour late for the audition so we nearly threw him out, but he looked a bit different and he had a good recommendation, so we gave him a shot. I had been listening to guitarists all day long, but as soon as Jake started playing I knew he was the man."

Daisley returned on bass to conduct a US tour, but Tommy Aldridge was fired soon into the trek and the drum position passed over to Carmine Appice, the well-known drummer with 1960s pioneers Vanilla Fudge. However, turmoil reigned as the forgiven Aldridge then usurped Appice. Bridgewater too packed his bags mid-tour, allowing Don Airey to rejoin on keyboards.

Ozzy's support acts for this American leg were melodic rock troupe Le Roux and Dutch rockers Vandenberg. Despite sold-out venues, the tour was blighted by religious fervour in the Bible Belt states, culminating in calls for Ozzy to be shot for his supposed blasphemy.

Lee's first vinyl outing with Ozzy was the Max Norman-produced *Bark At The Moon,* which emerged with an elaborate and very expensive jacket shot of Ozzy in full lycanthrope costume and special effects that was reported to have cost in excess of £50,000. Joining Lee on the record came Aldridge, Airey and Daisley, the latter contributing heavily on the lyrical front.

In 1984 many Ozzy fans paid high prices for a Japanese rarity, *The Other Side Of Ozzy Osbourne.* The LP, never released on CD, compiles B-sides with Randy Rhoads-era live material and a studio outtake of 'You, Looking At Me, Looking At You'.

Tragedy came later in 1984 with the death of 19-year-old fan John D. McCollum, who committed suicide with a .22 calibre handgun, apparently after spending a day listening to Ozzy's music. A year later, McCollum's parents filed suit against both Ozzy and CBS, alleging that the song 'Suicide Solution' from *Blizzard Of Ozz* had directly contributed to their son's death. As the song had been penned by Daisley about Ozzy's alcohol problems, the case was thrown out of court, but not before generating reams of negative press.

In July 1985, the world's largest rock event, Live Aid, was the catalyst for something fans had been hoping for since the 1970s – a full-blown original Black Sabbath reunion. Although it was a one-off event, the original quartet took to the stage in Philadelphia for a brief, three-song set – 'Children Of The Grave', 'Iron Man' and 'Paranoid' – before Ozzy returned to the studio to create the Ron Nevison-produced *Ultimate Sin,* an album that was to give him his highest chart placing yet in both North America and Britain.

True to form, yet another rhythm section was drafted in for the recording and subsequent tour, in this instance drummer Randy Castillo – a veteran of Stone Fury and Lita Ford's band – alongside the former Robin George band and Wildlife bassist Phil Soussan. This was the line-up the fans were presented with, but it is known that just before the new group was unveiled, bassists Greg Chaisson and Neil Murray plus drummers Fred Coury and Jimmy DeGrasso were briefly involved for rehearsals and demos. Also making an impression on the songwriting front would be new recruit Soussan, writing the single 'Shot In The Dark', Ozzy's biggest solo single success to date. However, controversy reigned when long-term cohort Daisley revealed that he had written all of Ozzy's previous lyrics but had not been credited for his contributions on *Ultimate Sin.*

To round off another highly successful world tour, Ozzy headlined the 1986 Castle Donington 'Monsters Of Rock' festival before embarking on a gargantuan American jaunt with support act Metallica. In Japan, Phil Soussan was sacked but rapidly re-instated, and in a gap between recording and touring Ozzy aided an old friend by guesting on Black Sabbath drummer Bill Ward's solo album *Ward One: Along The Way.*

As 1987 drew to a close, Jake E. Lee was fired – later turning up in the commendable Badlands – and the process of locating an able replacement was begun. Auditions whittled down hundreds of hopefuls

to a listing including Vinnie Moore, Chris Impellitteri, Mitch Perry, Nick Nolan, Terrif's Joe Holmes, Steve Fister of the Lita Ford band, and Rough Cutt's Amir Derakh. One of the very last guitarists to attend, recommended by noted rock photographer Mark Weiss, was the 21-year-old Zakk Wylde. The auditions would narrow down to just two candidates, with Wylde pitched against Hartford's Jimi Bell. When Zakk was chosen, Bell's consolation prize was to be diverted into another branch of the Black Sabbath family tree, joining bassist Geezer Butler's solo band.

Ozzy's gift for choosing exceptional guitarists hadn't waned, with Wylde as flamboyant and talented as any of his predecessors. Before achieving global notoriety with Ozzy, the guitarist (real name Jeffrey Weilandt) had paid his dues with New Jersey club acts Stonehenge and Zyris. In Zyris, Wylde went by the stage name Zakari Wyland. Zakk's official onstage debut with Ozzy came at a low-key New York gig at the Hard Rock Cafe in December.

Ozzy's band, now with Sabbath's Geezer Butler on bass, toured the UK in June and July 1988, supported by Jagged Edge. Phil Soussan had left to team up with Billy Idol for his *Charmed Life* album and would then unite with Mötley Crüe vocalist Vince Neil, writing songs for Neil's debut solo effort, *Exposed,* before forming Beggars & Thieves. Ozzy's new album, *No Rest For The Wicked,* was recorded with the reprieved Bob Daisley and also featured Saga singer Michael Sadler on backing vocals.

A stop-gap live mini-album, the contractual *Just Say Ozzy,* was culled from the world tour in 1990. Ozzy took time out in January 1991 to headline the London Wembley Arena 'Great British Music Weekend', topping a bill of Thunder, David Coverdale, The Quireboys and Magnum.

The next album was titled *No More Tears.* Geezer Butler was at first involved in the studio sessions alongside Wylde and Castillo, but then found himself substituted by former Killerwatt bassist Terry Nails. Another switch saw Daisley back in the studio alongside ex-Heavy Metal Kids and Lion keyboard player John Sinclair. With the *No More Tears* recording becoming protracted, Ozzy announced that his next live campaign would be the very last tour he would undertake. Years of well-documented alcohol and substance abuse had finally taken their toll, and Ozzy explained to fans that he simply wanted to concentrate on being a family man.

This so-called 'swan song' record was another strong effort, bolstered by a writing partnership with Lemmy of Motörhead. Reports suggested that more albums would follow, although not necessarily under the Ozzy Osbourne banner.

As the press speculated on a possible Black Sabbath reunion, it became known that Def Jam producer Rick Rubin had come close to getting Sabbath to reform. In the end, Ozzy chose to stay on the solo route and Tony Iommi re-recruited Ronnie James Dio for their 1992 *Dehumanizer* album.

Yet again another new face emerged in Ozzy's touring band as bassist Mike Inez was drafted. Ozzy headlined the prestigious Foundations Forum in Los Angeles, after picking up a Lifetime Achievement award, and embarked on a suitably mammoth tour.

The supposed end to Ozzy's touring career finally came with two historic shows at the Pacific Amphitheatre in Costa Mesa, California, in November 1992. Following a set by Black Sabbath fronted by Judas Priest vocalist Rob Halford (Dio had refused to perform), Ozzy was joined onstage after his own band's set by the original Sabbath line-up of Iommi, Butler and Ward for 'Black Sabbath', 'Iron Man', 'Fairies Wear Boots' and 'Paranoid'. There were negotiations for a money-spinning Sabbath reunion album and tour, including a projected Castle Donington headline appearance, but once shows had been announced the whole thing was pulled when business negotiations collapsed.

Ronnie James Dio: "Reuniting with Ozzy has always been like some kind of Holy Grail to Tony and Geezer: they follow it blindly. After every album and every tour they start talking about getting back with Ozzy, and of course Sharon and Ozzy just lap it up. Black Sabbath took a big step forward into a new generation, we sold a million albums, the concerts were great, and there was a lot of pride there. After that, after I went, the slide began. Their obsession since that day was in getting Ozzy back, and it showed in their decision making."

Ozzy's band splintered, with Wylde creating the Southern-tinged Pride & Glory and Randy Castillo teaming up with ex-Alien and Four Horsemen vocalist Frank Starr, bassist Terry Nails and guitarist John Lowery (aka Johnny 5) to create Bone Angel. With Lowery's departure for Rob Halford's Two project, Castillo, Nails and Starr morphed into Hard Luck alongside the Dio-credited guitarist Craig Goldy. Inez then joined Alice In Chains. During this period Ozzy also turned up on the Black Sabbath tribute album *Nativity In Black* performing a less than convincing 'Iron Man' with backing from the Irish alternative-rock band Therapy?.

Although he had promised retirement, Ozzy returned with a new album in 1995, *Ozzmosis*, written over a lengthy period and involving the talents of many songwriters and musicians. Initial recordings had been made with the superstar guitarist Steve Vai (of the David Lee Roth band and Whitesnake), a reinstated Bob Daisley and ex-Wild Dogs and Bad English drummer Deen Castronovo. This new quartet, billed as X Ray, worked up songs for a proposed album before Ozzy re-enlisted Zakk Wylde and hired former Whitesnake drummer Denny Carmassi, who had also played with Montrose, Gamma and Heart.

A whole host of songwriters was involved in the album, including Steve Dudas, Jim Vallance (who had worked with Bryan Adams) and Mark Hudson. Hudson would co-score a track with Ozzy entitled 'Rasputin' that, although it wasn't used for *Ozzmosis*, spurred ongoing work on a musical about the controversial Russian monk.

Steve Vai: "Everything was tuned down to C and I was using an octave divider on a lot of stuff. Very, very heavy. [Ozzy] is one of the most unique and interesting people I have ever met. Sort of like the godfather of metal. You would never believe how funny he is. Just the way he talks and explains things and the extraordinary stories he would tell constantly were historical delights. He's pure rock music and he's not in the least bit stupid or anybody's fool. He knows exactly what he wants and there is an honesty and realness to him that is undeniable. He has no circuit breaker between his head and his mouth and he speaks what he is feeling the moment he feels it. He acts the same around his musicians as he does with his family. He's very real. It was refreshing to have the opportunity to work with him for three months and it's an experience in this business I will cherish and remember for ever. After working with him, I know why his fans are so loyal and why they feel the way they do about him. They have good reason to."

White Lion bassist James Lomenzo cut the original *Ozzmosis* bass tracks, but he was replaced and his work overdubbed (Geezer Butler is credited on the album). Ozzy's friend Rick Wakeman also applied his talents to the keyboards. By the end of recording, Ozzy's band consisted of Wylde, a returning Geezer Butler and drummer Deen Castronovo. This rhythm section would also find the time to collaborate on Butler's own G//Z/R project, culminating in the *Plastic Planet* album.

In a typically offbeat move, Ozzy put in a cameo appearance in the movie *The Jerky Boys*, having previously appeared in the late-1980s movie *Trick Or Treat* as a preacher.

At the close of the *Ozzmosis* sessions, Wylde was reportedly sacked by Osbourne's management after the guitarist's much publicised liaisons with Guns N'Roses. Ozzy debuted his new guitarist Alex Skolnick – previously with Testament and Savatage – with a secret club gig at Nottingham Rock City in June. However, within days it had been announced that ex-Terrif, Lizzy Borden and David Lee Roth guitarist Joe Holmes had in fact secured the position. Skolnick returned to his Skol Patrol jazz-rock project.

Opening dates for the 1995 world tour started in Chile, but after just a handful of gigs Castronovo was out and Randy Castillo, pulled from Juice 13, was back on the drum stool. UK concerts in November would see Fear Factory in support.

Ozzmosis proved to be Osbourne's most successful outing for nearly a decade, debuting in the US *Billboard* album charts at Number 4 and selling over 127,000 copies in its first week of release. In early 1996 Ozzy was confirmed as a co-headliner with Kiss for the Castle Donington Festival. His ever-fluid band included Holmes, Faith No More drummer Mike Bordin and ex-Suicidal Tendencies bassist Rob Trujillo.

Ozzy successfully toured America the same year, supported by Slayer and Danzig, on outdoor dates billed as the 'Ozzfest'. These sell-out shows proved beyond all doubt that rock was far from waning in America and provided the catalyst for a much more ambitious live concept for the future.

This resurgence of support was backed by the compilation album *The Ozzman Cometh*, a CD that, along with more familiar Ozzy material, included four previously unreleased early Black Sabbath tracks and an unheard Ozzy track, 'Back On Earth', which had been originally recorded for the *Ozzmosis* album.

The 'Ozzfest' also gave Ozzy the opportunity to reunite with Black Sabbath, with Bordin supplying drums, and the reunion culminated in a pair of triumphant shows at the Birmingham NEC in Britain in early December. These dates saw original Black Sabbath drummer Bill Ward take his rightful place behind the skins once more.

With a lull in Osbourne's activities, he collaborated with the Wu Tang Clan on 'For Heaven's Sake' before finding himself back in the movies donating vocals to the song 'Walk On Water' for *Beavis & Butthead: Do America*. Ozzy also figured in the autobiographical hit *Private Parts*, based on the career of shock-jock Howard Stern – oddly, he supplied a version of Status Quo's twee 1960s pop hit 'Pictures Of Matchstick Men' with gothic metallers Type O Negative.

The extracurricular projects continued into 1998 with Ozzy lending guest vocals to the title track of Ringo Starr's *Vertical Man* opus and featuring on 'Nowhere To Run (Vapor Trail)' for inclusion in the *South Park* movie, in which an animated Ozzy famously got to bite off Kenny's head. The collaborations didn't end there: Ozzy teamed up with Coal Chamber (managed at the time by wife Sharon) for a rendition of Peter Gabriel's 'Shock The Monkey' on the band's 1999 album *Chamber Music*. Rapper Busta Rhymes got in on the act too, persuading Ozzy to grace his song 'This Means War!!' – actually a radically re-worked 'Iron Man'.

Ozzy and Sabbath would embark on another highly successful 'Ozzfest' jaunt across America in 1999. Although Mike Bordin was firmly entrenched on the drums, Shannon Larkin (of Wrathchild America, Ugly Kid Joe and Amen) would step in for one date at the close of the tour, playing drums for both Osbourne's band and Sabbath in the same day.

Ozzy then announced his drummer for 2000 as erstwhile Soulfly and Medication man Roy Mayorga. However, within a matter of weeks the Pride & Glory and Foreigner-credited sticksman Brian Tichy was on the drum stool. Osbourne then turned up in the movies again, putting in a cameo appearance in Adam Sandler's *Little Nicky*. On the musical front, he would repay a favour to Rick Wakeman, cutting lead vocals for the track 'Buried Alive' on the keyboard player's ambitious *Return To The Centre Of The Earth* album.

In November 2000 news of Ozzy's new band emerged, with Wylde and Butler making a return. The biggest surprise was the inclusion of Mötley Crüe drummer Tommy Lee. However, as soon as these reports leaked out they were swiftly and vehemently denied in typically colourful language. During April 2001 the usual Ozzy rhythm section of Bordin and Trujillo would back up erstwhile Alice In Chains guitarist Jerry Cantrell for live dates.

That summer Ozzy again topped the bill on the international 'Ozzfest', back in place with Black Sabbath. Zakk Wylde also featured his act, Black Label Society, promoting a live album that featured Zakk's version of 'No More Tears'.

Ozzy's new single, 'Gets Me Through', was announced for a September 2001 release but arrived in stores on October 1st. The accompanying album, *Down To Earth*, would also arrive in October, with Japanese copies boasting an extra track in 'No Place For Angels'.

Down To Earth debuted at Number 4 on the *Billboard* charts, shifting over 150,000 copies in its first week of sale. Notably, it would also give Ozzy his first Number 1 record in Sweden. Songwriting collaborators included Sabbath keyboard player Geoff Nicholls on 'Facing Hell' and 'Black Illusion', while 'Running Out Of Time' was co-penned by Foreigner guitarist Mick Jones.

The subsequent 'Merry Mayhem' tour, with support acts Rob Zombie, Mudvayne and Soil, didn't run smoothly. Ten dates, commencing on November 9th at the Compaq Center in Houston, were postponed when Ozzy suffered a stress fracture in his leg. The injury reportedly came about when Ozzy slipped in the shower prior to a gig in Tucson. The singer, apparently unaware of the severity of the damage to his leg, continued to perform until the pain became unbearable and doctors diagnosed the fracture. Ozzy recovered to resume action by November 29th in North Dakota.

Japanese shows in early 2002 were recorded for a live album and DVD entitled *Live At Budokan*. The UK leg of the 'Ozzfest' tour took place at Castle Donington on May 25th, with Ozzy heading the bill over Tool, System Of A Down, Slayer, Black Label Society and Cradle Of Filth. The American trek consisted of a revised billing with Ozzy adding P.O.D., Drowning Pool, Adema, Rob Zombie, Meshuggah and others to the cast. Robert Trujillo would double up duties with both Ozzy and Black Label Society. Sadly, former drummer Randy Castillo, who had enjoyed a term of duty with Mötley Crüe after his Ozzy adventures, lost a long battle against cancer on March 26th 2002.

Meanwhile, millions of TV viewers were tuning into *The Osbournes*, a hilarious peek at the private life of Ozzy and Sharon Osbourne at home. It rapidly climbed to the status of MTV's most successful show, and heralded the arrival of another member of the Osbourne clan into the music world when Ozzy's daughter Kelly cut a version of Madonna's 'Papa Don't Preach' backed by Californian nu-metallers Incubus. Longstanding fans felt the global impact of *The Osbournes* clouded Ozzy's musical achievements.

The long-running battle between Osbourne and his early-1980s rhythm section of bassist Bob Daisley and drummer Lee Kerslake was given new impetus when it was learned that, incredibly, the recent 'expanded' reissues of *Blizzard Of Ozz* and *Diary Of A Madman* had the original bass and drum parts excised and replaced by Robert Trujillo and Mike Bordin. Daisley and Kerslake eventually tried taking their claim to the Supreme Court, but the Court refused to hear the case.

With *The Osbournes* now the highest-rated MTV show, it came as no surprise that a further two series were secured, with the famous family netting a reported $20 million for the privilege. Ozzy also landed a cameo role in the latest movie from the Austin Powers series, *Goldmember*. Also released in June was a compilation album culled from *The Osbournes* and billed as *The Osbournes Family Album*, consisting of music from the show. Ozzy's own 'Crazy Train', 'Dreamer' and 'Mama, I'm Coming Home'

were included alongside crooner Pat Boone's take on 'Crazy Train', Kelly's 'Papa Don't Preach' and System Of A Down's cover of Sabbath's 'Snowblind'. The strength of the TV series was demonstrated when this record landed in the Top 20 of the *Billboard* charts. Yet more spin-offs from the TV show included a merchandise deal that not only saw the prospect of Ozzy figurines but Sharon, Jack and Kelly dolls too.

Back on the musical front, Ozzy pulled out of the Irish 'Ozzfest' on May 26th due to an undisclosed illness. Further troubles hit the European leg when Zakk Wylde reportedly fell ill, citing mental and physical exhaustion. This necessitated a rapid return to America, and gigs in Zurich, Copenhagen, Stockholm, Helsinki, St. Petersburg and Moscow were all cancelled. However, Ozzy was deemed by many critics to have stolen the show at the Buckingham Palace concert to celebrate Queen Elizabeth II's Golden Jubilee. He triumphed with a rendition of the perennial 'Paranoid' that included a guest appearance from Tony Iommi. The rhythm section for this one-off band was session bassist Pino Palladino and ex-Genesis drummer Phil Collins.

The first two US 'Ozzfest' dates on July 6th and 7th in Bristow, Virginia, and Pittsburgh, Pennsylvania, were rescheduled when it was learned that Sharon Osbourne was to undergo surgery for what was described as a 'treatable' cancer. Shortly after, Ozzy withdrew from ten 'Ozzfest' dates in order to be at his wife's side as she underwent chemotherapy, planning on a return for the Denver leg of the tour. In the interim, System Of A Down extended their set to cover his absence. However, Ozzy only missed two 'Ozzfest' dates.

The subsequent *Ozzfest 2002* album led off with Ozzy's own 'War Pigs'. Zakk Wylde provided his own Black Label Society's 'Berzerkers' and also guested for Soil. Even Kelly Osbourne got in on the action, duetting with Andrew W.K. on the final track, 'She Is Beautiful'.

By September it seemed that Kelly might be in line to rival her father in the future, as 'Papa Don't Preach' debuted in the UK singles charts at a healthy Number 3. Ozzy also put in a solo show with a marked difference on October 25th at the Palms Casino in Las Vegas, with promoters going as far as manufacturing $5, $25 and $100 Ozzy gambling chips. Ozzy was then the subject of rumours in late November, with talk of a Hollywood movie based on his life – Johnny Depp was mooted as the preferred candidate for the role.

Another Ozzfest was scheduled for the summer in North America, commencing on June 28th at the Verizon Wireless Amphitheatre in San Antonio, Texas. Various supporting acts included Korn, Marilyn Manson, Cradle Of Filth, Chevelle and Disturbed. Ozzy then laid down guest vocals on the song 'Stillborn' for Black Label Society's April 2003 album *The Blessed Hellride*, while Robert Trujillo joined forces with BLS for subsequent touring.

In an unexpected and curious turn of events, Trujillo joined Metallica in February while former Metallica and current Voivod bassist Jason Newsted teamed up with Ozzy's band a matter of days later. Trujillo's last performance with Ozzy's band came on March 14th at the Hard Rock Hotel in Las Vegas, Nevada. The new-look Ozzy band debuted with a run through four tracks – 'War Pigs', 'Believer', 'No More Tears' and 'Crazy Train' – on March 17th at a Los Angeles media showcase. Significantly closing a 23-year relationship, Ozzy severed ties with Sony in May.

The 'Ozzfest' did brisk business once again, defying trends in its usual fashion. However, Ozzy was forced to pull out of one gig at Marysville, California, when he contracted severe laryngitis. In July it was revealed that Ozzy had re-recorded the Black Sabbath ballad 'Changes' as a duet with daughter Kelly.

With Ozzy recovered from his laryngitis, the singer reclaimed his headlining slot on the 'Ozzfest' dates. Sad news arrived on July 4th when the singer's longstanding tour manager, Bobby Thompson, was found dead in his Detroit hotel room; Thompson had long been battling throat

Ozzy Osbourne in relatively sane mood

cancer. Ozzy led a mid-set silence and dedicated both 'Goodbye To Romance' and 'Mama, I'm Coming Home' to Thompson at his show in Independence Township, Michigan. He then pulled out of another show due to illness, with a non-appearance at the PNC Bank Arts Center in Holmdel, New Jersey, due to what was described as a mild case of pneumonia. Mid-tour, *Down To Earth* received a platinum award for one million US sales.

An interesting aside came when the former Blizzard Of Ozz rhythm section of bassist Bob Daisley and drummer Lee Kerslake formed a much vaunted supergroup billed as Living Loud with strong Deep Purple, Uriah Heep and Ozzy connections. Spending the summer recording in Florida, the duo joined Deep Purple guitarist Steve Morse, Australian vocalist Jimmy Barnes and the keyboard maestro Don Airey to cut an album of five new songs and no fewer than six re-workings of vintage Ozzy tracks.

Bob Daisley: "We did six Ozzy tracks on the Living Loud album because we were just disgusted at the way those first two albums had been castrated. There are thousands of fans out there who think that ... removing the original players from those records is one of the biggest crimes in music history. I can't believe it has made Ozzy a happy man. I knew Randy Rhoads well and I know exactly what he would have thought of it. I also know that, as a player, he would really get off on Steve Morse's versions."

Concern over Ozzy's health grew as UK and European tour dates were postponed, with the singer undergoing an operation on his foot. Although the gigs were re-scheduled to commence on October 22nd in Dublin and run through until December 5th in Munich, these shows too would be dropped, under doctor's advice. Reports emerged that Osbourne, who had shocked viewers with his physical appearance on *The Osbournes*, was suffering from a severe tremor which required medication. Successive statements in *The Los Angeles Times* revealed that a Beverley Hills physician, Dr. David A. Kipper, was under investigation for oversubscribing medicine to the star. Osbourne revealed he had been prescribed a cocktail of over 40 pills a day, including opiates, tranquillisers, amphetamines, antidepressants and an antipsychotic.

Meanwhile, Ozzy's band was undergoing further flux as Newsted stepped out of the group and the band rehearsed with Fear Factory's Christian Olde Wolbers for a period. European gigs, with Ozzy's band now joined by bassist Rob 'Blasko' Nicholson (ex-Cryptic Slaughter, Rob Zombie, Prong and Danzig), were announced for a third jaunt during 2004. These new dates included Ozzy's debut in Croatia at the Dom ?portova in Zagreb.

However, once more the live schedule would be put in jeopardy when Osbourne put himself out of action, crashing his quad bike at his Buckinghamshire home. The singer, who was apparently revived by his security guard Sam Ruston, broke eight ribs, a collarbone and a vertebra in his neck. Part of the singer's treatment included the fitting of a seven-inch internal steel device to strengthen his spine. At the same time as this setback, more positive news came with Ozzy's remake of Sabbath's 'Changes', which entered the UK singles charts at Number 1 – his first ever in his homeland. Osbourne, complete with neck brace, was released from intensive care just before Christmas.

Backing up the daily press onslaught in regard to Ozzy's accident and the success of 'Changes', press teasers were leaked to whet the appetite for the official *Osbournes* book. *Ordinary People* saw Sharon Osbourne apparently revealing indiscretions with the late Randy Rhoads. (Sharon said in the book: "When I talk about the early days of the love affair between Ozzy and me, I have to be honest – it wasn't just the two of us. Randy was a vital part of the tale. When Ozzy and I weren't speaking we turned to Randy, and when we were on loving terms he was there too.

On the road we often ended up in the back of the tour bus together, watching TV and dozing off without thinking anything of it. Not that we were having sex with each other. There was one time I was with Randy. Ozzy knows about it but has never wanted to discuss it. That's his way of dealing with it. But don't read any dissatisfaction into it. Ozzy knows the one-time occurrence was loving, not lustful. And he was just as in love with Randy as I was. He still cries when talking about Randy. So do I.")

Concrete facts came when *Billboard* delivered figures detailing that the 'Ozzfests' had racked up a staggering $146 million over 236 shows and had drawn in 3.8 million fans since their inception.

After announcing that he was to headline the 2004 'Ozzfest' over the reunited Judas Priest, Slayer, Slipknot, Dimmu Borgir, Superjoint Ritual and Black Label Society, Ozzy planned to have a team of doctors travel with him. As was traditional by now, the rumour mill sparked up once more in regard to a full-blown Black Sabbath reformation, and by March, Tony Iommi and Osbourne were in negotiation. As the month closed, speculation arose that Geezer Butler had supplanted Rob Nicholson as bassist in Ozzy's band: indeed, just hours later, Nicholson confirmed that he was out and intent on pursuing new music with his project The Death Riders. As predicted, Osbourne would indeed head up the 'Ozzfest' by fronting Black Sabbath once again.

Rob Halford: "Black Sabbath and Judas Priest – you can't get any heavier than that. It's the ultimate, history-making metal package. It's fantastic to have a bunch of daft Brummies onstage together putting on such a huge show. When I think of what we have both achieved, and where we all came from, it's just incredible. Just look at Ozzy. He walks onstage and he has the world at his feet. He is just this huge, huge star and yet he's one of the most down to earth people I've ever met. When I see Ozzy onstage and the way the fans hold him in respect, it's just incredible to behold."

Returning to studio work, Ozzy recorded a theme song for a new TV show, *Dog The Bounty Hunter*. MTV signed up Sharon and Ozzy for a new reality TV series, with *Battle For Ozzfest* based upon a band talent contest – the main prize being a slot on the 2005 bill, touring money, equipment and a possible record deal.

Former Alice In Chains guitarist Jerry Cantrell made public the fact that he was recording music for an Ozzy boxed set alongside Chris Wyse, bassist for Cantrell's jam band Cardboard Vampyres and The Cult. Manning the drums would be Mike Bordin, with Jim Cox on keyboards; additional guitar solos and steel guitar came courtesy of Robert Randolph. The collection, dubbed *Prince Of Darkness*, consisted of cover versions of The Beatles' 'In My Life', Buffalo Springfield's 'For What It's Worth', The Rolling Stones' 'Sympathy For The Devil', Arthur Brown's 'Fire' and King Crimson's '21st Century Schizoid Man'. Mountain's Leslie West appeared on a take of his band's 'Mississippi Queen'. Ozzy would share lead vocals with Ian Hunter on Mott The Hoople's 'All The Young Dudes'. The set landed at Number 36 on the *Billboard* charts.

October saw Ozzy back in the US *Billboard* charts in a fashion, as the single 'Let's Go' by Southern hip-hop pioneer Trick Daddy (aka Maurice Young) with a sample of 'Crazy Train' made the Top 5 in the rap charts and the Top 20 on the national singles charts.

Ozzy was thrust back into the international headlines in November when he bravely grappled with an intruder at his mansion in Chalfont St. Peter, Buckinghamshire. Although he caught the intruder in a headlock, the thief – who took an estimated $3.2 million-worth of Sharon Osbourne's jewellery – escaped by jumping out of a third-storey window. Both Osbournes were unhurt in the drama. Sharon subsequently appeared on the UK *Crimewatch* television programme in an effort to track down the jewels.

Ozzy's only UK live appearance of the year was planned for December 14th at the star-studded Royal Variety show at the London Coliseum in the presence of Prince Charles. However, he withdrew in order to undergo a further operation to ease pain caused by a metal plate that had been inserted after his quad bike accident.

Ozzy fronted up Black Sabbath yet again for the summer 2005 'Ozzfest' across North America. In June, the Recording Industry Association of America (RIAA) revealed that Ozzy Osbourne had sold over 28 million albums in the USA – incredibly, a full 13 million more than Sabbath.

The 'Ozzfest' ran without a hitch until July 27th, when Black Sabbath cancelled a show due to Ozzy's illness. The band did perform an abbreviated set at Tweeter Center in Tinley Park, Illinois, on July 30th but then pulled out of the Noblesville, Indiana, show and a date in Columbus, Ohio. With Ozzy suffering from acid reflux problems, the scheduled August 7th 'Ozzfest' at Somerset, Wisconsin, was postponed to September 10th. It was revealed that the singer was being coaxed through the shows by Ron Anderson, a retired opera singer, who monitored Ozzy's diet and lifestyle and even spoke directly to him on stage through an earpiece.

Sabbath's August 11th gig at White River Amphitheatre in Auburn, Washington, had fans witnessing the severity of Ozzy's ongoing vocal problems when his voice gave way in the midst of the track 'Dirty Women'. Ozzy threw his microphone down in disgust but was eventually coaxed out to struggle through the remainder of the set. The following day the singer made an official announcement: "After 10 years, the Ozzfest's name and reputation have been established. It's time for me to move on and do other things."

Ozzy, together with Wylde and Bordin, put in an unannounced performance of 'Crazy Train' in Foxboro, Massachusetts, for ABC's *NFL Kickoff* show leading into the season opener between the New England Patriots and Oakland Raiders at Gillette Stadium. Ozzy showed his allegiance by donning a Patriots jersey.

In November, both Ozzy and Sabbath were inducted into the UK Music Hall of Fame. During the band's live performance at the ceremony, held at Alexandra Palace in London, Ozzy typically made headlines by mooning the audience.

The year 2006 opened with news that, despite earlier press statements requesting audition tapes for guitarists, Ozzy was in fact to continue his relationship with Zakk Wylde. This move gave a welcome signal to fans that there would be a return to the harder-hitting style that had fostered legions of metal fans worldwide. The saga continues.

THE PRINCE OF DARKNESS
Ozzy Osbourne: "I can't tell you how I sing, there's no manual, it just comes out. I'm not one of those guys like Rob Halford or Glenn Hughes who can do all these amazing things, but I'm happy with what I did with Black Sabbath, because it really worked. I know a lot of people hate my voice, but I think it's unique, y'know?"

Ozzy Osbourne is much more than the comic anti-hero that today's generation have brought into their homes by way of *The Osbournes*. Before he was ever the king of comedy he had a three-decade reign as the Prince of Darkness. Quite simply, only the mercurial alliance of Ozzy, Iommi, Butler and Ward could have crafted the Sabbath commandments.

Ozzy's artistic achievements fronting Black Sabbath are all too often overlooked in the pursuit of outlandish stories and tabloid tales of terror and tomfoolery. Once the media gloss is stripped away, however, Ozzy's vocal performance on that illustrious first quartet of albums truly shines. During the early to mid 1970s, vocalists such as Led Zeppelin's Robert Plant, Uriah Heep's David Byron and Deep Purple's Ian Gillan may have been reaping the plaudits, but only Ozzy was able to holler that distinctive, rustic roar that entranced the masses on the darker fringes of life.

Ozzy Osbourne: "A lot of it was fear. If you grew up in Birmingham, then for a lot of people I knew, my mates at school, you would go to work in the factories and that's where you would stay until you dropped dead. It really was a shitty deal, because they worked you to the bone – and it was dangerous work, too. My dad tried to get me to learn a trade because he didn't want me in a factory either. I was just terrible at everything – plumbing, laying bricks. So I got scared. What was I going to do? Singing in a band gave me that chance, so I took it."

Rob Halford: "Ozzy has a voice. That might seem a very simple statement, but I mean it to say that nobody sounds like Ozzy. I don't think anyone will ever sound truly like Ozzy. With singers, you can have the hugest range but if your biological make-up is that bit special then you get this unique voice. And that's what Ozzy has. I just love those early Sabbath albums. It's what I grew up on, and it's what I still listen to today. I love those records as a fan of heavy metal but I also love them for Ozzy's vocals. There's a hell of a lot of power and a very special emotion there. Ozzy gets a raw deal because, well, he's Ozzy and he's always trying to get a smile on your face. But there's a huge talent there."

Glenn Hughes: "Ozzy is just the best. He's the man. I asked him personally if I could join Black Sabbath, because Ozzy has been such a friend to me over the years. He's a great, great singer. He gets a bad rap because of the whole legend that surrounds him, but the cat can really sing. He has a real passion for music. The whole thing is real with Ozzy."

Tony Martin: "Singing the Ozzy tracks with Black Sabbath was always very special for me because that's where I got it all from, really. It was the first Black Sabbath records that got me into heavy metal. It's only when you have to sing those songs that you realise just how much Ozzy put into them. I have to hand it to him, some of them are really difficult!"

Robert Plant: "The world would be a much duller place without Ozzy Osbourne."

SCORPIONS
GERMANY'S WORLDWIDE STING OPERATION

IN THE MID 1970S the rock world was given a valuable injection of colour courtesy of the Scorpions, whose German origin set them apart from the standard transatlantic formula. Initially, the focus was on the incredibly gifted guitarist Uli Jon Roth, but with his abrupt departure, Matthias Jabs, a hugely underrated player, took over lead work. Backing this up since the band's inception was rhythm guitarist Rudolf Schenker. This guitar team – Jabs with a customised white Explorer with black stripes and custom Jabocaster, and Schenker with an equally distinctive collection of Gibson Flying Vs – gave the world some of the classiest and most original riff patterns yet heard, a skill which the band pushed to mega-platinum international status.

While pursuing standard hard rock formulas (the Scorpions' reliance on balladry has proved itself commercially on countless occasions), it is the Schenker-Jabs combo that has given the band their status in the world of heavy metal, with the zenith of their aggression the superb *Blackout* album. While the group has operated in all musical spheres, they've always managed to include at least one metal nugget on each album.

The humble origins of Germany's biggest-grossing metal act date back to their formation in 1965 by guitarist Rudolf Schenker, who at first also handled lead vocals. Former Mushrooms vocalist Klaus Meine and guitarist Michael Schenker – younger brother of Rudolf – were in a band called Copernicus in their native Hannover with bassist Holger Twelve and drummer Mike Grimcke before joining Scorpions in December 1970. Before this, Michael played in his first act, The Innovates, in 1966, through Cry, later called Cry Express, in 1968, and from Copernicus to the Scorpions.

In 1972 the Scorpions released their debut album *Lonesome Crow* with a line-up featuring the Schenker brothers, Meine, bassist Lothar Heimberg and drummer Wolfgang Dziony. The album was the first of many in succession to be produced by Conny Plank. *Lonesome Crow* is an adventurous, jazzy effort, and markedly different in style to later works. Importantly, however, the Scorpions' ambitions were already evident at this early juncture: unusually for a German band of the time, Meine delivered his lyrics in English. Since the global rise of the band, *Lonesome Crow* has been reissued several times under different titles, including *Action*, *Gold Rock* and even *I'm Goin' Mad & Others*.

The band toured Germany heavily to promote the record, putting in support slots with Uriah Heep, Atomic Rooster and Rory Gallagher. Extra money was earned by writing the music to an anti-drugs film, *Das Kalte Paradies*, before hitting the road guesting for Chicken Shack and UFO to round off 1972. Interestingly, Harlis drummer Werner Löhr also claims early membership of the Scorpions. And American drummer Joe Wyman was a member of Scorpions during 1972-73 touring duties.

The opportunity to support UFO once more came in the summer of 1973. Michael Schenker, however, left the group and was persuaded to join UFO in bizarre circumstances. Arriving in Regensburg in June 1973 to support UFO, the Scorpions were dumbfounded when the headline act asked to borrow their gear and guitarist. Michael accepted the offer, appearing with both bands onstage for the gig until UFO's regular guitarist at the time, Bernie Marsden, arrived to complete the dates. The inevitable happened and after the tour Michael jumped ship to UFO. Shortly after, the Scorpions signed to RCA: Michael's replacement was ex-Dawn Road guitarist Uli Jon Roth (then known simply as Ulrich Roth).

Initially drafted in simply to fulfil a gig contract, Roth was persuaded to stay the course. Further changes followed for 1974's *Fly To The Rainbow*, with a new rhythm section of bassist Francis Buchholz and drummer Jürgen Rosenthal (Eloy, Dawn Road and Morrison Gulf). This line-up produced *Fly To The Rainbow* themselves, but for the ensuing *In Trance* record the Scorpions secured the services of ex-Jane keyboard player Dieter Dierks as producer. *In Trance* was the first of a succession of records in a lengthy production deal. For these sessions, Belgian drummer Rudy Lenners joined the band during Rosenthal's mandatory army service. Importantly, *In Trance* gave the band major sales in Japan.

Scorpions hit the autobahns once more in 1975 as support to The Sweet, with this tour also extending into Scandinavia, and first toured England in 1975 with their first gig at the famous Cavern club in Liverpool.

The group membership remained stable for 1977's *Virgin Killer*, the Scorpions' first gold-awarded record in Japan. The album jacket photo created quite a stir with its depiction of a young, naked girl with strategically-placed cracked glass. Many countries changed the cover artwork, deeming it obscene.

Lenners then opted out, turning up in the early 1980s in lower-key acts K-West and Steelover, and so for their final RCA studio album, *Taken By Force*, Scorpions pulled in drummer Herman Rarebell, who had been working with Procol Harum's Bobby Harrison. Rarebell afforded the band much-needed stability on the drum stool and gave the UK media much amusement with his alter ego, Herman ze German.

Taken By Force was a transitional outing for the group, a pull in artistic directions between Roth and the other band-members. Nevertheless, the quality remained high, with Roth's 'Sails Of Charon' – a mesmerising piece of work – juxtaposed against the blatant, primal motivation of 'He's A Woman, She's A Man', 'Steamrock Fever' and 'We'll Burn The Sky', all of which quickly became stage favourites. The band first toured Japan in April 1978, from which was drawn the double live album *Tokyo Tapes*, recorded in Tokyo Sun Plaza Hall on April 24th and 27th. However, despite Uli Jon Roth's inclusion in these gigs, an agreement with him was settled beforehand for his departure from the band.

Rudolf Schenker: "Uli plays guitar like a god. Really, his playing and the heart and soul he can put into a piece of music is just so inspiring, and it was just incredible for me to work with him in the studio and onstage. The trouble was that the band was naturally going in one way and this feeling wasn't in tune with what Uli wanted to do. He's very honest like that, and this resulted in the split. I guess you could say it really was musical differences.

"Then Michael came back, but it was difficult because he is my little brother and he had changed a lot. Too much success, too young. Michael was like a time-bomb back then. Everyone was telling him how great he was and that was not helping. He had some problems from his rock'n'roll lifestyle and that was affecting things, so he went."

Herman Rarebell: "Japan was a whole new world for the band. I remember when we first went there it was just so incredible to see the culture change. We just went crazy with the whole geisha thing. It really was like stepping onto a new planet and it made us realise that we really wanted the Scorpions to be a band that could conquer the world. That was fascinating for me, that we could write music that people in all these different countries loved. They might have nothing else in common, but they all owned the same Scorpions album."

Shortly after the Asian dates, Roth left to form Electric Sun and the band switched labels from RCA to Harvest EMI. That year the group inducted Scottish guitarist Billy Rankin (previously a member of Phaze) as a replacement. The union would be brief, however, with language difficulties being cited. Rankin would subsequently enjoy acclaim with Nazareth.

The first fruit of this new partnership was the groundbreaking *Lovedrive* in 1978, the first to feature new guitarist Matthias Jabs. A Hanover native, Jabs's past form included membership of local act Fargo and stint in Lady, Jane member Walter Nadolny's project, who released a single in Germany titled 'Feel The Fire'. With Roth hailed as a guitar guru, Jabs, despite his huge creative contribution both in terms of sensational soloing and riff production, found it difficult to attain the same appreciation.

Lovedrive also included the briefly returning Michael Schenker, who had temporarily bailed out of UFO, on three tracks. Former Skid Row and UFO guitarist Paul Chapman had been in the frame for the job but, after rehearsals with the band in June 1978, was re-enrolled into UFO.

Once again the LP jacket was controversial, with *Lovedrive*'s photograph of a bubblegum-enhanced breast-fondling session altered in the USA to obscure the offending mammary. The band's debut American appearance was in front of 70,000 fans in 1979 at the Cleveland 'World Series Of Rock' festival on a bill including Thin Lizzy, Aerosmith, Ted Nugent and AC/DC. Further touring on a package with AC/DC and Nugent followed.

Herman Rarebell: "We got a lot of good attention from our album covers: things like Lovedrive were really quite groundbreaking because they were sexually provocative, and even shocking, but the music inside was very sophisticated. We worked very closely with [fabled sleeve design agency] Hipgnosis to get the right feel for each record. I think that confusion really helped the band. Our songs were becoming the same way too, very sexually motivated like 'Another Piece Of Meat'. Actually that song is about kickboxing. Those guys really do get treated like pieces of meat, they're not human any more. I wrote the lyrics about that at first, but I could not resist adding a sexual twist, so I included some memories of a woman who treated me like a piece of meat."

Similar shock tactics were used on the subsequent *Animal Magnetism* album of 1980, which depicted a dog uncomfortably in heat. Nevertheless, the album delivered the grinding live classic 'The Zoo' and the sumptuous hit single 'Make It Real'.

Live action in the USA from May to July included special guest duties for Judas Priest, and in August the band played at the inaugural Castle Donington 'Monsters Of Rock' festival, which was headed up by Rainbow.

However, a serious blow to the Scorpions' career prospects came when Meine suffered a throat problem: so severe was his affliction that at one stage doctors advised him that his singing days were over. As Meine persevered with further treatments, the band hung on for over a year, awaiting his recovery. Fortunately, the much-delayed studio album *Blackout* captured Meine in superb vocal form and gave the fans the heaviest Scorpions LP to date. Indeed *Blackout*, released in 1982 and showing the Scorpions at their aggressive peak, was the album that truly broke them in America. The band then supported Rainbow on a US tour in 1982, plus two dates in Bangkok where both the delicate 'Holiday' and the soaring 'Always Somewhere' had been hit singles.

SCORPIONS discography

LONESOME CROW, Brain 1001 (Germany) (1972)
FLY TO THE RAINBOW, RCA PPL 1-4025 (UK), RCA cnu (USA) (1974)
IN TRANCE, RCA PPL 1-4128 (UK) RCA cnu (USA) (1975)
VIRGIN KILLER, RCA PPL 1-4225 (UK) RCA cnu (USA) (1976)
TAKEN BY FORCE, RCA PL 28309 (UK) RCA cnu (USA) (1977)
TOKYO TAPES, RCA PL 28331 (UK), RCA CPL2-3039 (USA) (1978)
LOVEDRIVE, Harvest SHSP 4097 (UK), Mercury SRM-1-3795 (USA) (1979) **36 UK, 55 USA**
ANIMAL MAGNETISM, Harvest SHSP 4113 (UK), Mercury SRM-1-3825 (USA) (1980) **23 UK, 52 USA**
BLACKOUT, Harvest SHVL 823 (UK), Mercury SRM-1-4039 (USA) (1982) **11 UK, 10 USA**
LOVE AT FIRST STING, Harvest SHSP 2400071 (UK), Mercury 814 981-1 M-1 (USA) (1984) **17 UK, 6 USA**
WORLD WIDE LIVE, Harvest SCORP 1 (UK), Mercury 824 344-1 (USA) (1985) **18 UK, 14 USA**
SAVAGE AMUSEMENT, Harvest CDSHSP 4125 (UK), Mercury 832 963-2 (USA) (1988) **18 UK, 5 USA**
CRAZY WORLD, Vertigo 846908-2 (UK), Mercury 846 908-2 (USA) (1990) **27 UK, 21 USA**
FACE THE HEAT, Mercury 518 280-2 (UK), Mercury 314 518 258-2 (USA) (1993) **51 UK, 24 USA**
LIVE BITES, Mercury 526 903-2 (UK), Mercury 314 526 889-2 (USA) (1995)
PURE INSTINCT, East West 0630-14524-2 (UK), Atlantic ATL 82913-2 (USA) (1996) **99 USA**
EYE II EYE, East West 3984-26830-2 (UK), Koch KOC-CD-8052 (USA) (1999)
MOMENT OF GLORY, EMI Classics CDC 7243 5 57019 2 3 (UK / USA) (2000)
ACOUSTICA, East West 8573-88246-2 (UK), Warner Bros. 8573-88249-2 (USA) (2001)
BAD FOR GOOD: THE VERY BEST OF SCORPIONS, Hip-O 314 548 118-2 (USA) (2002) **161 USA**
UNBREAKABLE, BMG 82876 60964-2 (UK), Sanctuary 06076-84700-2 (USA) (2004)

Matthias Jabs: "The Blackout album was important for me because my guitar playing really started to receive some attention there. For a long time I was just Uli's replacement, y'know? With Blackout the whole band was fired up. We had been through so much and even thinking the impossible when it looked like Klaus might lose his voice. Maybe that is why Blackout came out so good. We had everything to prove and nothing to lose. I have to say that I am very proud of my guitar playing and Rudolf's playing. As for Klaus' singing, what can you say? It is just an amazing record to listen to."

May 29th 1983 marked a spectacular milestone for the band, as they performed to their biggest audience to date. Estimated at almost half a million people, the San Bernardino 'US Festival' saw the band sharing a once-in-a-lifetime event with Van Halen, Judas Priest, Ozzy Osbourne, Triumph, Quiet Riot and Mötley Crüe.

Towards the end of 1983 there was much media speculation that Rarebell and Buchholz were out and Rainbow's rhythm section of drummer Bobby Rondinelli and bassist Jimmy Bain were in. Indeed, the band did admit that Bain and Rondinelli had recorded tracks for the new *Love At First Sting* album in Stockholm, Sweden, prior to switching back to Dierks's German studio with Herman and Francis. However, Rondinelli maintains that drum tracks on the album *Love At First Sting* are his. Bain later formed part of the highly successful inaugural Dio band, while Rondinelli would join Blue Öyster Cult and Black Sabbath.

Love At First Sting proved to be another hugely successful album for the band, breaking into the US *Billboard* Top 10 and soon attaining platinum status for one million albums sold. The record was issued in South America under the title *Amor A Primera Picadura*.

Preceding the album release was a pre-emptive single, 'Rock You Like A Hurricane'. This hook-laden anthemic monster latched onto US radio and hung on for a lengthy and rewarding tenure, giving the band a long-overdue commercial break into mainstream America. On the tour front, the Scorpions traversed North America throughout the summer months before a major series of Japanese shows in August, backed by Bon Jovi, MSG and Whitesnake. Back on European soil it would be Joan Jett & The Blackhearts who opened for gigs that took the band up to the close of the year.

The Germans truly stamped their authority on the international metal scene in 1985 with the release of their second live album, *World Wide Live*. Traditionally, live albums had proved to be lacklustre sellers in America, but *World Wide Live* soon passed the million sales mark, prompting a festival tour of America and a high billing on the 'Monsters Of Rock' shows in Europe. Defying all trends, *World Wide Live* was the second biggest selling live album in the USA that year. Following their appearance at the 1985 'Return Of The Knebworth Fayre', headlined by Deep Purple, the band undertook a further festival date in Malaysia.

Herman Rarebell: "We're over-perfectionists, which is a common fault in Germans. We were playing this kind of music before it was called heavy metal. Then someone came along in the 1970s and said: 'That's heavy metal!' and we thought: 'Oh, so that's what we've been doing.'"

In 1988 the Scorpions released the polished *Savage Amusement*. Although its riff content was high and the group clocked up yet more hits with 'Rhythm Of Love' and 'Passion Rules The Game', many fans criticised the sleek production and lack of spontaneity.

Scorpions rock the 1980s leather look

The year 1988 would prove historic not just for the Scorpions but also for rock in general, as the band was invited to perform in Russia. This groundbreaking trip resulted in the band performing no fewer than ten back-to-back sell-out performances at Leningrad's Sport And Culture Complex, supported by leading Russian band Gorky Park.

Live work in the USA, given impetus by sustained radio success, saw the group employing a gargantuan Flying V light rig. That summer the Scorpions joined the Van Halen-topped 'Monsters Of Rock' festivals, ranked alongside Metallica, Dokken and Kingdom Come, which pitched the band in front of audiences ranging from 50,000 to 90,000 every night.

On August 12th and 13th 1989 the band participated in the 'Make A Difference Peace Festival' in Moscow at the Lenin Stadium, appearing alongside the likes of Ozzy Osbourne, Mötley Crüe, Skid Row and Bon Jovi. The Scorpions would also contribute to the album *Stairway To Heaven – Highway To Hell* with a sterling cover of The Who's 'I Can't Explain'.

In 1990 the Scorpions switched record companies to align themselves with Phonogram. The move was a part of what seemed like a clean break for the band. The *Crazy World* album was the first in many years to feature a producer other than Dieter Dierks and the first on which the Scorpions had used outside songwriters. The production was initially handled by Bruce Fairbairn before the band opted for Keith Olsen, and the album included songs co-written with Bryan Adams's partner Jim Vallance. Behind the scenes, the band was embroiled in a lengthy legal wrangle with ex-producer Dierks.

The album sold well, hitting Number 1 in the band's homeland, and the Scorpions backed it up with the 'Crazy World' tour, starting in Europe with support act Winger. The album sales were further boosted when, on the back of perestroika, the single 'Wind Of Change' became an enormous international hit, topping the charts in no fewer than 14 countries.

Klaus Meine: "We could never predict what would happen with 'Wind Of Change'. Actually, it took quite a while for people to get it, but then it spread across the whole world really quickly. It became a hit everywhere. At first I wasn't too convinced with the song. I like the idea of world harmony and I really wanted to put my feelings about what was happening in the world into a song. When we first talked about the song I wasn't sure if it was strong enough; it was a little different. We even spoke about not including the whistling. It was unbelievable to see what 'Wind Of Change' did for us."

Crazy World went double platinum in Germany and clocked up combined international sales of over 14 million by the end of the tour. Initially failing to chart in Britain, it was reissued due to the international impact of 'Wind of Change' and duly charted. Although the Scorpions were at an all-time high, the band fractured as long-term band member Buchholz exited abruptly in May 1992 amid a cloud of rumour as the band also came under intense focus from the German tax authorities.

Klaus Meine: "Scorpions is like a family. I see this word used to describe other bands but it really is true. People have arguments and fights, they fall out, but there is a special bond after you have played onstage together, created music together. We have a great bond after all these years. We still talk to ex-band members, maybe not so often, but there are always possibilities. A lot of promoters want to get the guitarists back together, you know? Michael and Uli, for a special concert. I know the fans would love it. But Francis? No. Never again."

The Scorpions, amid the massive impact of grunge, found it hard to follow up the success of *Crazy World*, despite an extremely strong album

in 1993's *Face The Heat* – which was, if anything, a far more accomplished affair than its predecessor. Produced again by Bruce Fairbairn, *Face The Heat* relied more on traditional rockers than the traditional lightweight chart-stabbers and was the first album to feature new bassist Ralph Rieckermann. The band then put in a sterling headline performance at the Californian industry 'Foundations Forum' event to kick off their live campaign.

At this stage in their career the Scorpions had forged an international reputation of over 60 million album sales, 30 platinum albums and 78 gold records. Despite these achievements, for the first time they found it difficult to fill North American arenas.

Klaus Meine: "Grunge changed everything, that's for sure. For us, it was very interesting to see and hear what bands like Pearl Jam and Alice In Chains were doing. We understood it but it never affected us. I mean, with Face The Heat we actually got a bit harder, I think. It's probably our most heavy metal sounding album since Blackout, so you see there were no grunge influences there. It's one of the reasons we went with 'Alien Nation' as the single because it was really like saying to our fans: 'Don't worry – we're not gonna change.'"

Another surprise was the exit of the ever-reliable Rarebell, a heavy blow for the band as the drummer not only had provided a near two-decade backbone of stability but also had contributed greatly to the group's lyrics. Intriguingly, the ousted Rarebell bounced back in 1995 with his version of Glenn Miller's big-band classic 'In The Mood'.

For the recording of the 1996 album *Pure Instinct*, with the group on new label EastWest, the drum position was delegated to Curt Cress (Saga and Ochsenknecht). James Kottak (ex-Black Sheep, Kingdom Come, Wild Horses and Warrant) handled live work. The first single from the album, 'You And I', went straight into the German charts.

Unfortunately, 1999's Peter Wolf-produced *Eye To Eye* proved a major disappointment for the faithful. Bringing in outside songwriters, the band dispensed almost entirely with guitars on some tracks and offered electro-pop. The album did include an acoustic guest session from Foreigner guitarist Mick Jones, and even ex-drummer Rarebell was there on backing vocals. The band played as guests to Mötley Crüe for US dates in August.

Fortunately, the 2000 album *Moment Of Glory*, recorded with the Berlin Philharmonic and Ken Taylor on bass, went a long way to restoring the band's credibility. For this ambitious outing, classic Scorpions material had been rearranged by noted Austrian composer Christian Kolonovits. Klaus Meine would share vocals on this opus with a variety of singers, including the Genesis-credited Ray Wilson on 'Big City Nights', Lyn Liechty on 'Here In My Heart' and Zucchero on 'Send Me An Angel' and the title track, which featured the Vienna Children's Choir. *Moment Of Glory* recouped considerable success for the Scorpions, reaching Number 1 in Portugal.

Klaus Meine: "That album Eye To Eye, it really confused a lot of our fans, which surprised us. I mean, we're musicians, we need to find new ways of doing things, new ways of looking at our music, but maybe it was too much. For me, that album was not that different to a classic Scorpions record. There's some very deep, heavy stuff on there, plus the usual ballads our fans expect. I think it's because we put an experimental song as first track. A lot of people just couldn't get their heads around it. When we toured, our fans told us they thought the change was too big.

"The timing was in some ways bad for Moment Of Glory but the album itself was amazing for us. In actual fact the Berlin Philharmonic had put the idea to us about this during 1995, a long time before Metallica did their thing. As musicians, it opened up a whole new world for us. I think with Eye To Eye, Moment Of Glory and the acoustic record the band really started to go in some new areas, which made us appreciate our more traditional hard rock side even more."

The same year a collection of metal acts, including Helloween, Stratovarius, Rough Silk, Therion and Metalium, paid homage on the album *A Tribute To The Scorpions*, and American death metal band Six Feet Under covered 'Blackout' for their *Graveyard Classics* album.

Scorpions then geared up to present their orchestrated show in America but pulled the dates when Jabs injured his hand. The rescheduled American shows were followed by dates in Asia. Kottak then took time out to work further on his solo venture, Krunk, and appeared on Dokken bassist Jeff Pilson's solo album. The Scorpions bounced back in 2001 with the unplugged *Acoustica* album, which scored well on European charts: in Portugal it rapidly went double platinum, selling over 80,000 copies and staying at Number 1 for over 12 weeks.

In 2002 Scorpions maintained a hectic live schedule, undertaking a tour of North America with Deep Purple and Dio before orchestral shows in Europe during July. The latter gigs were performed with the Stuttgart Mercedes-Benz Orchestra, the Luxembourg Sinfonieorchester and the Berlin Symphoniker. The group's activities outside the rock sphere would also expand into a full-blown stage musical, *Wind Of Change*, performed at the Berlin Metropolis Theatre.

In May yet another Scorpions compilation album was announced in *Bad For Good – The Very Best Of The Scorpions*. Thankfully for fans, this collection did present something special with the inclusion of two previously unrecorded songs, 'Bad For Good' and 'Cause I Love You', both produced by Dieter Dierks (the group's first reunion with the producer in over 15 years). Tours included a mammoth two-month run of dates in Russia during October and November. The 21-show trek took the band further afield than ever before, taking in shows in the Ukraine, Belarus, Siberia and the Baltic states.

A North American tour for January through March 2003 came in alliance with the heavyweight combination of Dokken and the reformed Whitesnake. The band also put in some unique performances that August in the Opel car works in Rüsselsheim, and on Terceira Island and St. Miguel Island in the Azores.

The Scorpions, vowing to return to their heavier origins, set to work on a new studio album in December at Peppermint Park Studio in Hannover. Barry Sparks, noted for his work with Cosmosquad, Ted Nugent, Yngwie Malmsteen, Dokken, Uli Jon Roth and The Michael Schenker Group, laid down bass guitar on these sessions on the tracks 'Borderline' and 'Love 'Em And Leave 'Em'. In January the band revealed that Polish bassist Pawel Maciwoda, who could cite credits with Section 31 and Urbanator, had joined the ranks. The new man made his debut on January 12th on the German TV show *Twenty Years Of RTL*. Summer festival dates for the Scorpions included appearances at the Sölvesborg 'Sweden Rock' event and the Dutch 'Arrow Rock' show in Lichtenvoorde.

Matthias Jabs: "Russia has become so important in our lives. For a German band you have to remember that when we first played in Russia we were still banned from playing half of Germany in the DDR, so it was a very strange experience. We had already played some East European gigs, like Hungary, but Russia was just

something else for us. The love of the fans toward the band was mind-blowing. We did our first shows in Leningrad in 1988, then we did the Moscow Peace Festival, then more gigs in Moscow again and St. Petersburg.

"A good friend of ours then suggested that the rest of Russia needed to see the Scorpions too, so we played this crazy tour which went on forever and we played everywhere. We thought we had seen it all on the rock-tour scene but this was just amazing. Security was very heavy all the way. We played towns and cities that we never even knew existed and discovered that there are heavy metal fans everywhere in the world. Scorpions can play all over the world now. It's a great privilege for us."

Meantime, former drummer Rarebell launched a German tour with his new band R&R in late April. The group, which included former 7 Sins saxophonist and well-known actress Claudia Raab, released a debut album, *The Rhythm of Art*. The shows were far removed from a regular rock event, featuring a troupe of dancers as well as original paintings by Rolling Stones guitarist Ronnie Wood and Ronald Muri, founder of the pop-expressionist movement.

Back in more conventional realms with the Scorpions, *Unbreakable* placed the band high in the album charts across Europe but would struggle in North America. In Greece the album hit Number 1, pulling the *Best Of* compilation and *Acoustica* back into the charts too. The world tour found the band in Thailand, Malaysia, Indonesia, the United Arab Emirates and even Sinai in Egypt during October. Later that same month an extensive US headline tour was announced, with support from Tesla and Keith Emerson. Strangely, France, one of the band's most loyal territories, was neglected, prompting French fans to launch a petition to get the band to play.

In welcome news for fans of vintage Scorpions, former guitarist Uli Jon Roth revealed he had written a full, extended symphony-orchestra score for the classic track 'Sails Of Charon', featuring Liz Vandell of Sahara on vocals. A video of Vandell's performance was projected onto a screen as part of Roth's concerts in August, a US trek allied with another ex-Scorpions act, The Michael Schenker Group.

A European and UK tour in February and April, with Scorpions performing in many major venues, saw a strong union with Judas Priest. A notable event for longstanding fans came with the band's appearance at a September 10th concert in Colmar, France, where Uli Jon Roth and former drummer Rudy Lenners joined the band onstage, making this the first official reunion since the recording of the 1978 *Tokyo Tapes* concerts. Roth joined the Scorpions for live renditions of 'In Trance', 'Pictured Life', 'Kojo No Tsuki', 'We'll Burn The Sky' (dedicated to the song's lyric writer, Roth's late girlfriend Monika Danneman) and 'He's A Woman, She's A Man'. In keeping with the tradition of reaching into unfamiliar territories, the band hit Mexico and Brazil in October before a 'Peace For All' acoustic tour of Qatar, the United Arab Emirates and Egypt (where the band performed a concert at the Giza pyramids). Greek gigs in December for Uli Jon Roth saw the guitarist reunited with ex-Scorpions drummer Jorgen Rosenthal, the first time the pair had performed together since 1974.

Since becoming Germany's leading musical export in the late 1970s, the Scorpions have not only maintained that position but strengthened it in a career that has, to date, spanned four decades. Remarkably, age does not seem to be mellowing their determination to keep on cranking out those riffs.

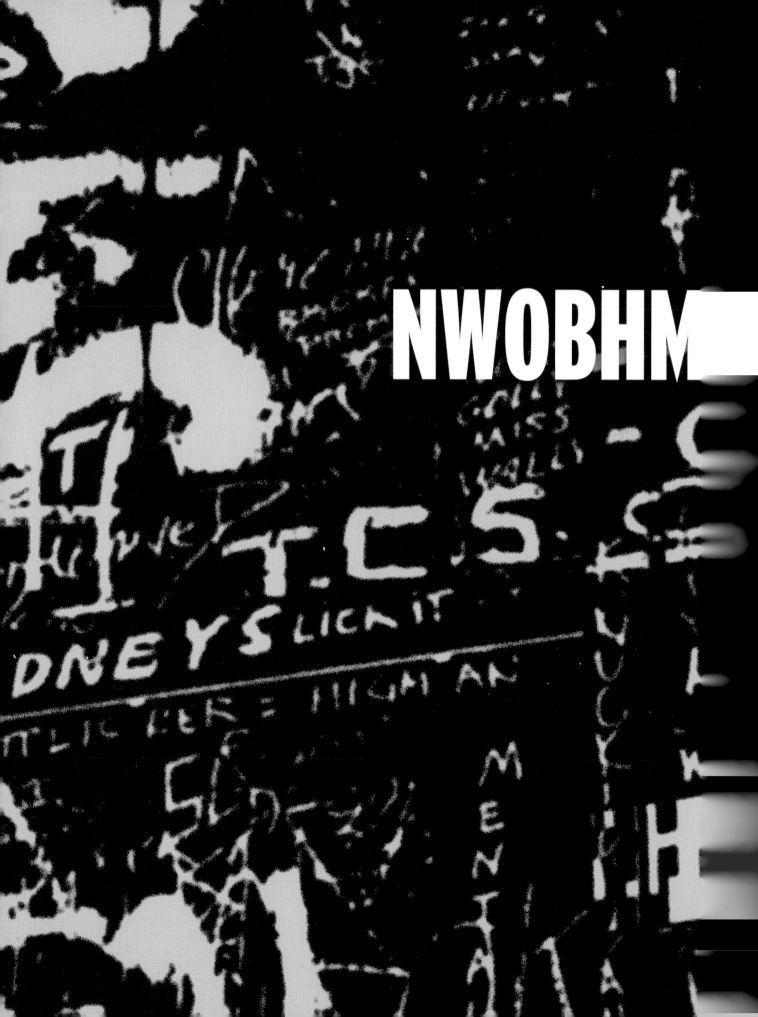

NWOBHM

NWOBHM

NWOBHM means the New Wave Of British Heavy Metal, which hit Great Britain during 1979. Although the term was invented by Alan Lewis, editor of music paper Sounds, the guts, heart and soul of the movement was very real, and its impact reverberates to the present day. Lewis might have concocted the unwieldy tag, first used by writer Geoff Barton on a sub-headline to a review of the historic metal meeting of Iron Maiden, Angel Witch and Samson at London's Music Machine on May 19th 1979, but the phenomenon to which it was attached was just too big to go unrecognised without some kind of historical flag-planting.

In 1979 the UK was tiring of punk and beginning to realise that the major rock acts that had been castigated, cursed and crucified in the pages of fanzines as "dinosaurs" were for the most part still alive and well and, paradoxically, selling even more records. Once punk had relinquished its hold, the musicians who had been lying low began to show their heads above the parapets once again. Fortunately for them, the punk DIY ethos had given them one valuable tool with which to work – the indie attitude.

As fast as bands sprang up, so did the labels to aid them on their way. Bullet Records, Terry Gavaghan's Guardian Records, Rondolet, Darryl Johnston's Ebony (in Hull), Paul Birch's Heavy Metal (in Sedgley) and David Wood at Neat in Newcastle – all nurtured the tide of amateur metal. Importantly, these labels were spread the length and breadth of the land, the NWOBHM springing up in England, Wales, Ireland and Scotland.

The new musicians had taken their cue from the second wave of major label acts such as Judas Priest, UFO, Rush, Blue Oyster Cult, AC/DC, Thin Lizzy and Van Halen. Inspiration came from such landmark recordings as Motörhead's Overkill, Bomber and Ace Of Spades, Judas Priest's Killing Machine and British Steel, AC/DC's Highway To Hell and Back In Black, Thin Lizzy's Black Rose and Chinatown, UFO's Strangers In The Night, and Black Sabbath's Heaven And Hell. These were truly monster years for great rock and a time of true heroes. With characters such as Rob Halford, Eddie Van Halen, Angus Young, Randy Rhoads and Ronnie James Dio peaking at the cusp of the decade, what self-respecting muso could fail to feel compelled to grab an axe and join in the fray?

London's pub and club scene fostered a host of bands, all parading the NWOBHM banner. A prime instigator in getting the music to the masses was DJ Neal Kay. His persistence in getting bands into clubs, on tour and on record was pivotal for their careers. Many a provincial band enjoyed their first taste of media exposure by inclusion in Kay's Soundhouse Top 10 metal charts in Sounds. Since 1975 Kay had been promoting the cause of metal at The Soundhouse, the capital's first heavy rock disco, based at The Bandwagon nightclub at the Prince Of Wales pub in Kingsbury, north-west London. Another champion was the late Tommy Vance, whose BBC Radio One Friday Rock Show delivered the riffs to the entire nation at the end of each week.

Only three groups really made it as far as international acclaim and commercial achievement – Iron Maiden from London, Barnsley-based Saxon and Def Leppard from Sheffield. Leppard's debut album, 1980's Tom Allom-produced On Through The Night, blends ambitious metal elements with the band's Bowie, Hoople and Lizzy influences.

Saxon had been slogging away since the early 1970s and issued their sensational 1980 Wheels Of Steel set with precision timing. Their motivation came from a similar arena to Def Leppard's, albeit a little gutsier in style by way of Free, Trapeze, Hendrix and Cream, However, their resolution in beefing up the guitar and Biff's determination to holler louder than anyone else on the planet easily placed Saxon on the metal side of the fence.

Iron Maiden tracked a chaotic course through the London pub circuit, wounded by membership changes but driven forward by the stalwart Steve Harris. This resolve put Maiden, then enhanced by Paul Dianno and Dave Murray, right in the zone when NWOBHM erupted. Of the entire pack, it would be Iron Maiden, backed up by a dedicated management team and very resourceful marketing that succeeded beyond the dreams of all others.

Ultimately, the NWOBHM gave an unprecedented boost to British rock, and to heavy metal on a global scale, not only putting many new names onto the map but also giving a second wind to already established bands. If you were there, if you spent every last penny you had feverishly snapping up 7-inch singles just because Witchfynde and Angel Witch sleeves looked cool, if your denim jacket was soaked in oil, adorned with patches and studs, then you'll know that the NWOBHM was much, much more than nostalgia.

ANGEL WITCH
THE WITCHING HOUR

ONE OF THE NWOBHM'S heaviest outfits, Angel Witch generated a cult following on the American West Coast based upon the occult overtones of their self-titled debut album, released in 1980. Once the NWOBHM began to wane, Angel Witch struggled to break out of cult status, consistently set back by fragile line-ups. Latterly, the band has found appreciation among the doom metal crowd for the Black Sabbath-like sounds of their debut LP.

Angel Witch were founded in 1977 by guitarist and band mentor Kevin Heybourne. Originally they were called Lucifer, but Heybourne switched to Angel Witch when he heard of another Lucifer doing the rounds. The band went through many musicians, including guitarist Rob Downing and drummer Steve Jones, before the classic power trio stabilised: Heybourne, bassist Kevin Riddles and drummer Dave Hogg.

The band's official debut on record was the song 'Baphomet' on EMI's now-legendary *Metal For Muthas* compilation in February 1980. Angel Witch also submitted a track called 'Extermination Day' to the 1980 BBC album *Metal Explosion*. EMI released a solitary single, 'Sweet Danger', which scored a minor impact on the national charts, peaking at Number 75. The label didn't take up an option to release an album, however, and Angel Witch switched to Bronze for their self-titled full-length album, produced by Martin Smith of the Electric Light Orchestra.

The album fared well, grazing the British charts at Number 75 for one week. The record's amalgam of classic metal and proto-doom found a keen audience. Tracks such as 'Gorgon', 'White Witch', 'Confused' and 'Atlantis' generated much appreciation among metal fans in both the UK and USA.

However, a series of damaging line-up shuffles hit the group in rapid succession. Hogg was diagnosed with leukaemia and was replaced by ex-E.F. Band drummer Dave Dufort soon after the album release. Dufort had been a member of 1965's The Voice, The Scenery and Paper Blitz Issue, all of which featured guitarist Miller Anderson. Dufort had then journeyed on to East Of Eden in the late 1960s (he appeared on the 1968 album *Mercator Projected*) as well as being a member of Kevin Ayers's band.

In the wake of *Angel Witch* the band ranked alongside Iron Maiden and Saxon at the forefront of the NWOBHM. Their tenure in the upper echelons of the scene was relatively shortlived, however, as gigs were few and far between. British shows were limited to London Marquee appearances and dates in the south-east of England in April and May of 1980, while the only date abroad was at the East German Erfurt Festival. A band-issued rarity, the *Give It Some Tickle* live cassette, saw limited release in 1981. This tape, released to fan cub members of the Angel Witch 'coven', was recorded at the Norbeck Castle, Blackpool on January 29th 1981 and closed with a cover of Black Sabbath's 'Paranoid'.

At one point Polydor were due to release a live album from a 1982 show, but this never surfaced and Angel Witch lost their deal. The group splintered, with Riddles and Dufort going on to form Tytan. As 1982 opened, Heybourne briefly flirted with Deep Machine, prior to playing the odd club gig as Angel Witch with a revised combo featuring bassist Jerry Cunningham and drummer Ricky Bruce.

The Angel Witch brand surfaced once again in 1985 when Heybourne and Gordelier severed ties with Blind Fury and duly enrolled original drummer Dave Hogg, together with vocalist Dave Tattum. This incarnation of the band laid down the commercial-edged *Screamin N' Bleedin'* album for the Killerwatt label. Media and fan reaction was far from enthusiastic and Hogg left the band once more after its release. He was replaced by former Dexys Midnight Runners drummer Spencer Hollman.

A third album, 1986's *Frontal Assault,* saw Angel Witch return to their former raw heaviness, but Tattum left on its completion, acquired by

melodic rock outfit Nightwing, leaving Heybourne to assume vocal duties. In 1989 the band added a second guitarist, Grant Dennison. A short tour of Holland followed with support act Satan, but Heybourne relocated to California, where nostalgia for the early Angel Witch reaped the reward of a live set of 'classics'. This emerged on Metal Blade in 1990 as *Live*. The band also recorded a demo at Prairie Sun Studios in San Francisco with guitarist Lee Altus of Heathen, Lääz Rockit bass player Jon Torres and Exodus drummer Tom Hunting, but failed to secure a new deal. Ex-bassist Peter Gordelier went on to join Driveshaft.

Although Angel Witch had failed to live up to their legend, the band remained an influence on groups that arrived on the scene in later years, with both Onslaught and Chicago doom act Trouble covering the classic 'Confused'.

Interest was renewed in 1996 by the release of a live album, *'82 Revisited*, on High Vaultage Records. Heybourne issued a compilation of various demos including the 1987 *Psychopathic* tapes and 1999's *Twist Of The Knife*. The resulting album, entitled *Resurrection*, was made available via the internet and then released through Crook'd Records in the USA and by Zoom Records in the UK in 2000.

Angel Witch were back in 2000 for live gigs and a projected new album. Alongside Heybourne the band consisted of guitarist Keith Herzberg, bass player Richie Wicks (a former lead vocalist of Sons Of Eden and Violently Funky) and drummer Scott Higham. The band bounced back in spectacular style with a performance at Wacken in Germany before setting to work on fresh studio material.

The list of bands who have covered 'Confused' increased in 2001 as American death metal act Six Feet Under cut a grindingly heavy take for *Graveyard Classics*, released in 2000. In August 2001 Higham decamped to join the highly regarded Shadow Keep. Ace Finchum, a former member of Welsh glam band Tigertailz, took his place. Unfortunately, in November the Angel Witch ranks fractured further with Wicks joining fellow NWOBHM resurrectees Tygers Of Pan Tang as their singer. During October 2002, Wicks, while maintaining his position with both Angel Witch and Tygers Of Pan Tang, enrolled as lead vocalist for power metal band Shadow Keep.

By January 2003 Angel Witch had been rebuilt once more, performing at the Bang Your Head festival in Germany. However, in a conflicting statement the trio of guitarist Keith Herzberg, bassist/vocalist Richie Wicks and drummer Scott Higham claimed that the band was, in fact, finished. The US Heybourne version of the band soon encountered line-up problems as Hunting decamped in order to concentrate on Exodus. Heathen and current Deconstruct drummer Darren Minter filled in.

Sadly, guitarist Myk Taylor, who appeared on three tracks on the *Resurrection* album, died from leukaemia on August 21st 2003. He was just 41 years old.

In spite of the band's chaotic family tree, it is certain that Angel Witch,

---

ANGEL WITCH discography

Sweet Danger, EMI 12 EMI 5064 (UK) (1980) **75 UK**
ANGEL WITCH, Bronze BRON 532 (UK) (1981)
SCREAMIN'N'BLEEDIN', Killerwatt KILP 4001 (UK) (1985)
FRONTAL ASSAULT, Killerwatt KILP 4003 (UK) (1986)
LIVE, Metal Blade CDZORRO 1 (UK), Metal Blade 7 73443-2 (USA) (1990)
'82 REVISITED, High Vaultage HV-1005 (Europe) (1996)
RESURRECTION, Angel Witch cnu (UK) (1998)
SINISTER HISTORY, Zoom Club ZCRCD 21 (UK) (1999)
2000: LIVE AT THE LA 2, Zoom Club ZCRCD 47 (UK) (2002)
ANGEL OF DEATH, Mausoleum 251061 (Europe) (2006)

in whatever guise, will continue into the future as long as their seminal debut album is remembered.

BLITZKRIEG
VICTIMS OF CHANGES

BLITZKRIEG'S ENTRY IN THE METAL history books comes thanks to just one song – their theme track 'Blitzkrieg'. The band were destined to be a minor footnote in the annals of the NWOBHM until Metallica covered the song on their November 1984 'Creeping Death' single. Despite the international press this generated, Blitzkrieg releases have been few and far between, mainly due to their fluid line-up. This lack of stability prevented them from maintaining a solid career.

Before Blitzkrieg, vocalist Brian Ross – the mainstay of the band – had auditioned with Tygers Of Pan Tang, was invited to join Samson and EF Band, and had briefly formed a band with ex-Whitesnake guitarist Bernie Marsden. He had also been involved with Kashmir and Anvil.

Although known as a Newcastle act, Blitzkrieg formed in Leicester in October 1980. The singer replied to an advert placed by local band Split Image, which consisted of guitarists Jim Sirotto and Ian Jones, bassist Steve English and drummer Steve Abbey. They were looking to replace their previous vocalist, Sarah Aldwinkle. Ross joined up and a new title of Blitzkrieg was suggested by Jez Gilman, although various club gigs were performed under the old name.

The band's inaugural product was a three-track demo cassette, which led to a 7-inch single for the Newcastle-based Neat label titled 'Buried Alive'. The same year Blitzkrieg contributed the track 'Inferno' to Neat's *Leadweight* compilation. In February 1981 the band underwent a line-up change, adding ex-Electric Savage guitarist John Antcliffe and bassist Mick Moore. Moore had previously played in the Leicester outfit Axe Victim with Ian Jones. He later recalled that the legendary 'Blitzkrieg', the B-side of the 'Buried Alive' single, had originally been conceived by his previous band Axe Victim under the title 'Bitch'. Jones had taken the nucleus of the song to Blitzkrieg with him: its riffs were an attempt to duplicate those of Dutch outfit Focus's 'Hocus Pocus' hit.

With a revised roster of players, Blitzkrieg garnered press coverage n the first issue of *Kerrang!* and went on to record a show supporting French metal band Trust in Newcastle for *Blitzed Alive*. However, the band spilt in December 1981, with Moore and Ross eventually forming the speed-orientated Avenger and Antcliffe joining Chrome Molly. Ross subsequently performed vocals with Satan for a tour of Holland, and Moore later exited Avenger, also to briefly associate with Satan. Ross kept in touch with Moore and, along with Jim Sirotto, teamed up again as Blitzkrieg to record the 1985 album *Blitzkrieg – A Time Of Changes* with Sean Taylor of Satan on drums and Tygers Of Pan Tang guitarist Mick Procter. The record consisted of archive tracks dating back as far as 1980, including 'Pull The Trigger' performed by Ross with Satan. At this point, Ross was also managing and singing for Lone Wolf, a position he would relinquish to reactivate Blitzkrieg.

The band underwent further reshuffling in June 1986, now leaving Ross as the sole surviving member as Procter teamed up with Spear Of Destiny. Blitzkrieg were duly reassembled with guitarists Chris Beard and J.D. Binnie, previously with Mandora, bassist Darren Parnaby and drummer Sean Wilkinson. This incarnation recorded a four-track demo in 1987, but the band split once more at the close of the year with Wilkinson, Parnaby, Binnie and Beard staying together in a glam-metal act called Liberty.

Ross, after a further re-think, started afresh in the summer of 1988. The singer gathered guitarists Glenn S. Howes – of doom band The Reign – and Steve Robertson, bassist Robbie Robertson and drummer Kyle Gibson, yet the only recorded product was a two-track demo before Blitzkrieg once more succumbed to another drastic membership shuffle.

By August 1989 only Ross and Howes remained, augmented by new guitarist Tony J. Liddle – previously with Saratoga, Predator and Violent Revolution – bassist Glen Carey and former Avenger drummer Gary Young. A video, *At The Kazbah*, was released and the long-awaited second mini-album *10 Years Of Blitzkrieg* arrived in 1991 on the Roadracer label. This collection saw re-recordings of the two 1981 7-inch single tracks with three new numbers.

Inevitably there were more departures. In early 1991 Carey, Young and Howes quit to form Hurricane. Ross then turned to his old comrade Moore together with ex-Satan drummer Sean Taylor and guitarist Paul Nesbitt. However, Moore soon decamped and Blitzkrieg trimmed down to a quartet of Ross, Liddle, Taylor and former Wheelbarrows From Hell bassist Dave Anderson. This line-up recorded *Unholy Trinity* in 1992 for Neat, but it languished in the vaults until 1995. The label, unaware of the NWOBHM renaissance in Europe and Japan, had no intention of issuing the record. When it finally saw the light of day, *Unholy Trinity* – despite Neat misspelling the band's name on the album – sold strongly in both territories and re-kindled interest in the band.

Blitzkrieg undertook a short tour of Greece in early 1996 with yet more new members – bassist Steve Ireland, ex-Marauder, and drummer Paul 'Sid' White. Liddle took his leave in January of 1997 for Tendahux, recording an as-yet-unreleased album. Further gigging found Blitzkrieg on tour in their strongest market, Germany, during the winter of that year. However, much to their amazement, the group found itself the centre of controversy when venues in Flensburg, Offenbach and Heidelberg refused to let them play due to the perceived historical connotations of the band name. Ireland was unable to fulfil the tour and a stand-in bassist, Gav Gray, was inducted. Gray subsequently made this position permanent. That same year the band intended to record a Japanese-language version of the track 'Blitzkrieg', but this did not occur.

In 1997 Neat issued *Ten*, essentially a reworking of *10 Years Of Blitzkrieg* but with further new material. Strangely, Blitzkrieg chose to re-record 'Blitzkrieg' yet again, taking this opportunity to alter the lyrics.

During 1998 Blitzkrieg worked on new material for Neat, although the band had evolved once more with Howes, fellow guitarist Martin Richardson and drummer Mark Hancock. The group returned with *The Mists Of Avalon*, a solid effort marred by an amateurish sleeve design. This line-up put in a rare appearance at the Wacken festival in Germany. Blitzkrieg personnel also formed part of a reunion Tygers Of Pan Tang show at the same event. Early 1999 found Blitzkrieg back in action, performing their first North American show, in New Jersey, with fellow NWOBHMers Sweet Savage and Raven. Subsequently, both Howes and Hancock decamped to concentrate on their priority act Earthrod in league with ex-Dead End guitarist Sean Jeffries.

BLITZKRIEG discography

Buried Alive, Neat NEAT 10 (UK) (1981)
A Time Of Changes, Neat NEAT 1023 (UK) (1985)
10 YEARS OF BLITZKRIEG, Roadracer RO 9302-2 (UK) (1991)
UNHOLY TRINITY, Neat Metal NM 002 (UK) (1995)
TEN, Neat Metal NM 010 (UK) (1997)
THE MISTS OF AVALON, Neat Metal NM 032 (UK) (1998)
ABSOLUTE POWER, Edgy EDGY 115 (UK) (2002)
A TIME OF CHANGES – PHASE 1, Castle CMDDD 523 (UK), Castle 72015 (USA) (2003)
ABSOLUTELY LIVE, Metal Nation MNR 001 (UK) (2004)
SINS AND GREED, Metal Nation MNR 004 (UK) (2005)

In 2002, Ross announced a projected album titled *Absolute Power* for Metal Nation Records, and another revised line-up. Liddle made a return, joined by second guitarist Paul Nesbitt, bassist Andy Galloway of Reign Of Erebus and Acolyte's Ruin, plus erstwhile Disposable Heroes drummer Phil Brewis. Blitzkrieg performed at the Motala Metal festival in Sweden and other events.

Predictably, 2003 ushered in a further new entrant for Blitzkrieg – guitarist Ken Johnson of Blast, Scream Dream and Meanstreak. A retrospective double-disc package, *A Time Of Changes – Phase 1*, arrived through Sanctuary, including unheard demos and rehearsal recordings.

Gigs in the north of England were taped for a projected live album bearing the title *Unleashed In The North East* (a reference appreciated by Judas Priest fans). However, it was delivered with the rather more predictable title of *Absolutely Live*. In late 2004 the band announced plans to record a new studio album, *Sins And Greed*, entering Trinity Heights Studios in Newcastle with Tygers Of Pan Tang guitarist Fred Purser as producer in March 2005. During these sessions the band cut a cover version of Priest's 'Hell Bent For Leather'. That same year, Howes joined another Newcastle NWOBHM reformation, Avenger. He also put together Judas Priest tribute band Judas Beast. In January 2006 Blitzkrieg parted ways with guitarist Nesbitt, drafting in Guy Laverick as replacement. This new recruit made his live debut in November as the band supported Doro on her UK dates.

Despite the line-up changes, the lack of finance and, most importantly, despite all the odds, it seems that while Brian Ross retains the NWOBHM spirit, Blitzkrieg will soldier on.

DIAMOND HEAD
WERE THEY EVIL?

DIAMOND HEAD ARE AMONG the most hallowed names in NWOBHM circles. Strangely, for a group tipped by many as most likely to succeed, they are better known today for their inspiration to many name acts – the most famous of which is Metallica, who retain the Diamond Head track

'Am I Evil?' in their live set to this day. Although Diamond Head attained a high profile, their two creative forces, singer Sean Harris and guitarist Brian Tatler, both shied away from the limelight for many years.

The band, named by Tatler after the 1975 Phil Manzanera album of the same title, formed in 1976 in Stourbridge, West Midlands while the individuals were still at school. Harris was auditioned in guitarist Tatler's bedroom in June 1976 after Tatler and drummer Duncan Scott had heard reports of Harris's vocal prowess during a school trip. The singer apparently signed a 'contract' with the group at school the next day. Bassist Colin Kimberley signed up a few months later.

Diamond Head put down their first demo songs at a Kidderminster studio in 1978. Impressively, the young group managed to score notable support slots, opening for both Iron Maiden and AC/DC. They then released their debut single, 'Shoot Out The Lights' backed with 'Helpless', in 1980 through the Happy Face label. The 7-inch single was sold through mail order ads in the weekly music paper *Sounds* and at concerts.

Diamond Head's next move was to finance a full-length album, a record again sold through mail order and at shows. The records were packaged in a plain white cardboard sleeve with each copy personally signed by a member of the band, although some are known to have been only partly signed by all four members – leading to a mysterious squiggle. The untitled album quickly sold out its first pressing of 1,000 copies and became a highly sought-after collectable. The first issue of the album with a plain white label is commonly known as *The White Album*, while a second run of 1,000 had the title *Lightning To The Nations* and track credits printed on the reverse. The album was later picked up by German independent label Woolfe, apparently unknown to the band, and released in Europe in 1981.

A second single followed, 'Sweet And Innocent', produced by Robin George – this time via the Wolverhampton-based Media Records. During 1981 Diamond Head capitalised on this progress with the 'Waited Too Long' single and the 'Diamond Lights' EP, all the time adding to their growing fanbase with a Radio One *Friday Rock Show* session and rave reviews for their live shows throughout the country.

Finally, their industry paid off and MCA took the bait, signing the

Diamond Head in a field of their own

quartet and releasing the *Four Cuts* EP in early 1982 and 'In The Heat Of The Night' later in the year. MCA issued the much anticipated *Borrowed Time* album in September.

Borrowed Time, clad in evocative Rodney Matthews artwork, entered the British charts to reach Number 24 and was critically acclaimed for its inventive riffing and passionate vocals woven around majestic themes. Diamond Head undertook a British tour to push the album; a degree of controversy surrounded the shows when Twisted Sister, announced as the support act, did not appear.

Borrowed Time elevated the group's status, but all was not well within the ranks. Indeed, the recording of the next album, *Canterbury* (originally titled *Makin' Music*), signalled the end of the road for Kimberley and Scott, both of whom parted company with Diamond Head before the Mike Shipley-produced record was completed. Replacements were swiftly recruited in former Samson bassist Merv Goldsworthy and drummer Robbie France.

Upon the release of the *Canterbury* album, fate struck a cruel blow when numerous pressing faults kept the album from attaining the chart status of its predecessor. Despite this setback, the album was a strong package, hosting such classics as the Eastern-flavoured 'Ishmael' and a grandiose 'The Kingmaker'. However, initial response by the hardcore following was muted, as the group had moved away from their classic metal influences in an attempt to be more adventurous.

This line-up, together with an added keyboard player, debuted at the 1983 Castle Donington 'Monsters Of Rock' festival as the opening act. Diamond Head supported Black Sabbath on their European tour of September 1983 and a UK headline trek took the band through October. However, their bad luck continued – a dodgy PA system resulted in a horrendous live sound and attendances in general were low. To top it all, a proposed single release of the grandiose 'Ishmael' was cancelled.

This streak of ill fortune continued as MCA dropped Diamond Head before the recording of a proposed fourth album, *Flight East*. This was the last straw as far as Tatler was concerned, the guitarist opting out to form Radio Moscow. France held a fleeting position on the UFO drum stool and briefly became a member of Skunk Anansie in the 1990s.

Sean Harris, on the other hand, lay low for quite a while before announcing the Notorious project alongside ex-Magnum guitarist Robin

George. Notorious cut one album at enormous expense, only to have it deleted almost immediately due to staff upheavals at the record company. Interestingly, Harris and Tatler were set to collaborate together under the pseudonym Magnetic AKA on 'Who's That Man' on the *Highlander II* movie soundtrack. Unfortunately, both Harris and Tatler's projects were far removed from the glory days of Diamond Head.

Whilst it seemed to outsiders that Harris and Tatler were struggling with the Diamond Head legacy, others were less reticent in acknowledging their former greatness. In 1984 Metallica showed their respect by covering a version of 'Am I Evil?' for inclusion on their 'Creeping Death' 12-inch single. This track was greeted with such enthusiasm that it became entrenched in the Metallica set list.

As Metallica's status rose, their allegiance to the NWOBHM, and in particular to Diamond Head, began to make its mark on record. The band had always performed Diamond Head tracks dating back to the early 1980s, but now they proceeded to immortalise these songs on disc. 'Am I Evil?' was followed by the inclusion of 'Helpless', cut in July 1987 for the *$5.98 EP: Garage Days Revisited* set, 'The Prince' bolstered the 1988 'Harvester Of Sorrow' single, and 'It's Electric' was used on 1998's *Garage Inc.* collection. This appreciation thrust Diamond Head's name back into the limelight in spectacular fashion.

Finally, at the instigation of mentor Pete Winkleman during 1990, Tatler and Harris gave Diamond Head fans the news they had been patiently waiting for and began writing songs again in earnest. They formed a new-look Diamond Head with bassist Eddie Chaos and former Requiem and Chase drummer Karl Wilcox: this line-up undertook a couple of anonymous gigs under the pseudonym Dead Reckoning before going back out on the road as Diamond Head for a short club tour.

The press reviews were ecstatic, and rightly so. Suddenly all that was lacking in the British rock scene became apparent as Diamond Head demonstrated with uncanny ease just what had made the band great the first time around. The group toured Britain again in November 1990 before entering the studio to record the comeback album, *Death And Progress*, for the Bronze label.

The album, eventually surfacing during 1993, featured contributions from Megadeth's Dave Mustaine and Black Sabbath's guitarist Tony Iommi, but was a less-than-spectacular release. Metallica then invited the band to appear with them as opening act at their outdoor Milton Keynes show, but Harris baffled the audience by arriving on stage dressed in Grim Reaper garb. Suddenly, the Diamond Head thread was unravelling again.

Sean Harris: "For a while the whole reunion thing was running along very smoothly. We did quite a few club shows and people were coming up to us and telling us they had seen nothing like it. I don't know what we were doing, because that's the way Brian and I had always approached a gig, but people were saying that it was the best gig ever.

"When we did Milton Keynes it was quite a historical day for Metallica, because they had both Diamond Head and Megadeth on the bill. We opened with 'Am I Evil' and you could see the faces on this enormous crowd just didn't get it. I think most of them thought we were being cheeky bastards by covering a Metallica song. No – we wrote it!"

The band split once again in 1994 and Harris continued under a new name of Easy, retaining all the band members minus Tatler, who teamed up with Thin Lizzy tribute band Dizzy Lizzy for a series of club gigs in 1995. A deal was offered by BMG, but the project fell apart. Diamond Head were then offered a slot on a 1999 Tokyo NWOBHM reunion gig alongside Praying Mantis and Tank, but turned the offer down. Tatler busied himself on the road with Celtic rock act Quill.

DIAMOND HEAD discography

Shoot Out The Lights, Happy Face MMDH 120 (UK) (1980)
LIGHTNING TO THE NATIONS, Happy Face MMDHLP 1015 (UK) (1980)
Sweet And Innocent, Media SCREEN 1 (UK) (1980)
Waited Too Long / Play It Loud, DHM DHM 004 (UK) (1981)
Diamond Lights, DHM DHM 005 (UK) (1981)
Four Cuts, MCA DHM 101 (UK) (1982)
In The Heat Of The Night, MCA DHM 102 (UK) (1982)
LIVING ON... BORROWED TIME, MCA DH 1001 (UK), MCA MCA-5382 (USA) (1982) **24 UK**
CANTERBURY, MCA DH 1002 (UK) (1983) **32 UK**
Rising Up, Bronze cnu (UK) (1991)
DEATH AND PROGRESS, Essential ESS CD 192 (UK) (1993)
EVIL LIVE, Essential ESD CD219 (UK) (1994)
LIVE IN THE HEAT OF THE NIGHT, Zoom Club ZCRCD 27 (UK) (2000)
Acoustic Four Cuts, cnu (UK) (2002)
ALL WILL BE REVEALED, Livewire LW 015-2 (UK) (2005)
IT'S ELECTRIC, Secret SMACD 941 (UK) (2006)

Diamond Head relented once again in 2001, heralding their resurrection with an acoustic show on November 21st at the Limelight Club in Hightown, Crewe. As the year drew to a close it was revealed that Tatler had apparently embarked on a studio project with Megadeth mainman Dave Mustaine.

The band were then announced as headliners of the April 6th 2002 'Metal Meltdown' festival in Asbury Park, New Jersey. For this show the band's line-up was Harris on vocals, Tatler and Floyd Brennan on guitars, Eddie Moohan (aka Eddie Chaos) on bass and Karl Wilcox on drums. A short burst of British club dates preceded the American event. The band also issued a limited run of 1,000 hand-numbered *Acoustic Four Cuts* EPs in March 2002. Performing at the Derby Bloodstock festival in August, Diamond Head set out on an extensive UK tour throughout September. Harris also found time in 2002 to guest on Gary Hughes's Arthurian concept album *Once And Future King*.

Although Diamond Head were announced as participants on the 2003 'Wacken Open Air' festival in Germany, the band were unable to commit due to recording schedules, laying down a new studio album with producer Andrew Scarth. Nevertheless, a band comprising members of Diamond Head and fellow NWOBHM legends Tygers Of Pan Tang plugged the gap with Jess Cox on vocals, guitarists Brian Tatler and Floyd Brennan, bassist Eddie Chaos and drummer Karl Wilcox.

After more than two decades fronting the band, Sean Harris stood down in August 2004, being swiftly replaced by Nick Tart, former singer of the Robin George band. Harris quickly countered, stating that that he was "shocked and dismayed" by the decision, which he had only learned about after the fact. The singer added: "As co-founder of the band, I am and will always be a member of Diamond Head and see no reason for this to change."

Nevertheless, the new Diamond Head, fronted by Tart, debuted at an invitation-only gig held at Dudley JB's club on December 1st. The band were then hand-picked by Dave Mustaine to support Megadeth on their February 2005 European dates, and a new album, *All Will Be Revealed*, was set for spring release.

Although Harris no longer heads the band, it seems that Diamond Head's future is assured thanks to the efforts of Brian Tatler, with a brand new album recorded for 2006 release.

GRIM REAPER
HEROES OF THE NWOBHM

HAILING FROM DROITWICH, just south of Birmingham, Grim Reaper secured a deal with Midlands based Heavy Metal Records in 1981, prompted by their inclusion of the track 'The Reaper' on the compilation album *Heavy Metal Heroes*. At this time the line-up consisted of vocalist Paul DeMercado (aka 'Woofer'), bassist Phil Matthews and drummer Angel Jacques alongside founder guitarist Nick Bowcott. Their *Bleed 'Em Dry* demo, famously recorded in a horse stable and seeing early member Dave Wanklin on bass, soon sold out its 500 copies. (Many NWOBHM collectors believe that the band released a 7-inch single, 'Can't Take Anymore', on Heavy Metal Records, but this was only a proposal and never actually saw the light of day.)

Steve Grimmett was drafted in to replace DeMercado in 1982 to put his vocals down on the demo cassette *For Demonstration Only*. Grimmett had come from local act Medusa. This band had also featured guitarist Lance Perkins and drummer Eddie Smith, later to adopt the respective noms de rock of 'Lance Rocket' and 'Eddie Starr' in glam titans Wrathchild. Another early Grim Reaper member was ex-Rough Justice drummer Brian 'Thunderburst' Parry, later to join Wrathchild and Original Sin. Grim Reaper also inducted drummer Lee Harris, a member of the band in the

early days, and signed to Ebony Records for their first album.

See You In Hell was recorded in just four days by producer Darryl Johnston in the living room of his terraced house in Hull. Grimmett also found time to perform lead vocal duties for Chateaux's debut album, *Chained And Desperate*, also on Ebony, as their Cheltenham-based labelmates unexpectedly found themselves in the studio minus a vocalist.

The debut 1983 Grim Reaper album, although hideously underproduced, fared exceptionally well in the US *Billboard* Top 100 through a licensing deal with major label RCA. Powered by heavy MTV rotation of a Jim Roseman-directed video for the title track, the album – issued in the USA on Friday July 13th 1984, went on to pass the 200,000 sales mark, peaking at Number 73 in the national charts. *See You In Hell* proved an apt title as the band explored dark themes within tracks such as 'Dead On Arrival' and 'Wrath Of The Ripper', wrapped around some classic British metal riffs and Grimmett's extraordinary vocals. The singer's immense range and depth of tone was often the focal point of reviews, setting the group apart from the pack.

Nick Bowcott: "America was a real eye-opener for us. Our first album was doing OK in Europe but when RCA took it on for the USA it just exploded. It just kept on selling, every week another 4,000 copies, another 4,000, another 4,000. MTV had us on four times a day every day. The fans were crazy. We went from playing in our local

Grim Reaper's Nick Bowcott with scythe-shaped axe

pub, to our mates and family, to thousands of people. People had the album cover tattooed on their backs. But when we got home nobody knew who we were."

Nick Bowcott: "RCA wanted us to fit in with everything they believed a rock band should be, so that meant custom-designed stage clothes and videos. It was all very uncomfortable because, to put it mildly, Grim Reaper is one of the ugliest bands you are ever going to see. They squeezed us into this tight leather and we were hanging out in all the wrong places. All those years of beer and chips had taken its toll."

Oddly, for a period in early 1983, the band experimented with keyboard player Andy Thomas, but soon reverted to the tried and tested four-piece formula. To promote their first offering, Grim Reaper played an American club tour alongside acts such as Exciter and Santers.

The second album, *Fear No Evil*, again suffered from a paper-thin production. With Johnston once again manning the desk, Grim Reaper crafted their follow-up in nine days. For this outing Lee Harris was superseded by Mark Simon. In spite of the budget production, the group still managed to gain success in the States, where they toured with Uriah Heep and played a show with Deep Purple at the gargantuan 'Texas Jam' festival. A promo clip was then shot for 'Fear No Evil' by Chris Gaberin. The video marked the introduction of the Grim Reaper mascot.

The third album saw Grim Reaper emerge after a lengthy legal battle with Ebony to sign with RCA in America. The band had originally recorded the album, then called *Night Of The Vampire*, at Ebony's new Hemingborough Hall studios during 1986, but when tapes were sent to RCA they were judged to be of such poor sound quality as to be unusable. While their career was being argued over by lawyers, Bowcott folded the band and found a job in a paper mill.

Steve Grimmett: "We originally recorded [Night Of The Vampire] at Ebony Studios with Darryl Johnston and it sounded like shit. The tapes were sent over to RCA America and rejected due to 'technical inadequacy'. I'll tell you how bad the Ebony recordings were – when our management asked for a master tape of the album to be sent over, they rang back and said: 'You've sent the wrong tape, these are rough demos.' It sounded fucking awful. RCA paid for us to re-record the entire thing with Max Norman, which gave us that professional touch we'd always lacked."

However, the group's management, Concrete, exercised a clause to free Grim Reaper of their shackles and the album was re-recorded. The end result was the excellent *Rock You To Hell*, produced by Max Norman, which finally showed the band in their true light. A cover of Blue Öyster Cult's seminal '(Don't Fear) The Reaper' was suggested by the record company to target radio play, and the band recorded the track but it did not make the final running order. Notably, the video for 'Rock You To Hell' saw Max Norman standing in on bass. Grim Reaper teamed up with Armored Saint and Helloween for the Hell On Wheels American tour to promote the album. At this juncture Wanklin was replaced with ex-Idol Rich bassist Geoff Curtis.

RCA were keen to build on Grim Reaper's profile and the proposed fourth album saw Bowcott writing more mainstream material with the likes of Surgin man Jack Ponti, a former associate of Jon Bon Jovi. The band performed a few low key British gigs with a new rhythm section of bassist Benje Brittain, previously a member of local act Health Warning, and drummer Mark Simon of Health Warning and Virgin Star. Unknown to fans, business wranglings with former label Ebony had damaged the group's financial standing to such an extent they could not continue.

Finance for a fourth record was stopped and Grim Reaper lost their

deal with RCA. Tragically, *Rock You To Hell*, the group's only real product with a professional sound, was never released in Europe.

In the wake of this disaster, former members Wanklin and Harris left the music business altogether. Grimmett's vocal prowess made him an immediate contender for a further post. Unfortunately, in a complete mismatch of styles, he went on to front the ill-fated Bristol thrash metal band Onslaught. Bowcott fared little better with a new act, Barfly, recording an album that never saw a release. The guitarist subsequently pursued a career in music journalism, writing for the US *Circus* publication among others. He also made a guest appearance on the Eyewitness album of 1995.

In 1994 Grim Reaper were back in America's living rooms through an unlikely source. MTV's latest cartoon sensation, the metal-loving *Beavis And Butthead*, mercilessly savaged a Grim Reaper video to such an extent that progress from that point on was halted. To the American public, the animated duo's attack became synonymous with the name Grim Reaper.

Grimmett pursued a new project, Lionsheart, a slick hard rock act which signed to Music For Nations and enjoyed considerable success in Japan, selling over 100,000 copies of their 1993 eponymous debut. This outfit lasted for three albums.

The year 2000 found Grimmett back in action forging a new act entitled Seven Deadly Sins. Against the band's wishes, this band found themselves billed as Grim Reaper for the Wacken festival the same year. The line-up for this one-off event included former Killers and The Shock drummer Pete Newdeck.

Meantime, interest in the Grim Reaper back catalogue saw the Spitfire label in America reissuing all three albums. During February 2002 the American band Seven Witches, led by Savatage guitarist Jack Frost, issued their *Xiled To Infinity And One* album, with a cover of Grim Reaper's 'See You In Hell'.

In 2005 the Majestic Rock label issued archive Medusa recordings, featuring Grimmett, under the billing *Clash Of The Titans*. That same year Grim Reaper would be thrust back onto TV screens, albeit in rather unexpected circumstances. Alt.rockers Weezer used footage from the band's 'Fear No Evil' video, lip-synching their own single 'We Are All On Drugs', over the top. Paradoxically, the very medium that killed the band's career first time around was now bringing the group's name back to a whole new generation – and a re-charged Grim Reaper announced a reformation gig for April 2006 at the 'Keep It True VI' festival in Germany.

No matter how hard Grimmett and Bowcott try to shake him off, it appears that the omnipresent figure of the Reaper always has them in his shadow. Fans are no doubt hoping for a long overdue fourth album.

HOLOCAUST
SMOKIN' SCOTS

HOLOCAUST WERE AN INVENTIVE Edinburgh metal act who scored a fair degree of coverage in the early 1980s due to their industrious approach and their impact on the NWOBHM scene with the classic song

'Death Or Glory'. Holocaust instigated a marketing and advertising campaign that made media in London take notice. Although sales of albums such as *The Nightcomers* and *Live: Hot Curry & Wine* were healthy, Holocaust had never been able to launch themselves onto the main UK market. The group fractured repeatedly, putting paid to any international prospects. However, they finally saw their just rewards when Metallica covered the track 'The Small Hours', originally featured on the May 1983 concert album *Live: Hot Curry & Wine*, on *The $5.98 EP: Garage Days Re-Revisited*, released in 1987. This homage by the thrash giants put Holocaust back on the map and prompted renewed recording activity.

Holocaust was formed in 1977, the group tracking their roots back to a pipedream school band. Buzzard, a band in name only with no musical instruments, duly evolved through various guises and different names, including Apollo and Preying Mantis. Hearing of the London-based Preying Mantis, the Scots switched their name to Holocaust.

The band's debut line-up included singer Gary Lettice, guitarist and songwriter John Mortimer, second guitar player Ed Dudley, bass player Robin Begg and drummer Niel Brockie. The fledgling Holocaust practised at their church hall as a favour from Brockie's father, the local minister. Two singles, 'Heavy Metal Mania' (July 1980) and 'Smokin' Valves' (December 1980), financed by the record shop owner for whom Lettice worked, created enough interest for a full-length album, *The Nightcomers*, in 1981.

According to a press release from their record company, Phoenix, the band played live with most of the NWOBHM frontrunners including Vardis, Tygers Of Pan Tang and Samson before any recorded product. However, this was all an elaborate fabrication: in fact Holocaust played with none of those acts. Fortunately, *The Nightcomers* generated positive press results and the ruse was never discovered.

Niel Brockie had left Holocaust by the time the album came to be recorded, his role being filled on a session basis by the drummer from pop act Pilot. Brockie's replacement was Paul Collins.

By 1982 guitarist John Mortimer had also quit, and Paul Collins found himself replaced by Ray Marciano (real surname Lafferty). A single, 'Coming Through', arrived in April 1982 and was the only Holocaust release not to feature Mortimer. The band disintegrated shortly afterwards, with Marciano and guitarist Ed Dudley forming Hologram. This new outfit proved to be a much mellower proposition than fans hoped for, and despite advertising which proclaimed "Holocaust is now Hologram", their record failed to sell.

In 1983 Phoenix released *Live: Hot Curry & Wine*, recorded in September 1981 and featuring new drummer Nicky Arkless. The group's unique Scottish slant came to bear on this record as reviewers struggled with the meaning of the song 'Jirmakenyerut', actually East Coast slang for a drunkard – "Does your ma know you're out?"

When Hologram fell apart, Marciano joined local act Mind's Eye. The Holocaust brand was relaunched in 1984 and a new album hit the racks in the form of *No Man's Land*. Another attempt to revive the band in 1988 saw John Mortimer teaming up with drummer Steve Cowan and ex-Just The Job bassist Graham Hall. In 1989 Metallica drummer Lars Ulrich, together with *Kerrang!* editor Geoff Barton, compiled a 10th anniversary of NWOBHM album for the Vertigo label featuring some of his favourite New Wave Of British Heavy Metal bands, and included Holocaust's 'Death Or Glory'.

Sadly, original bassist Robin Begg died in July 1990 after accidentally falling from a window ledge, and with Metallica having rekindled interest in the group, Holocaust persevered as a trio, mainly concentrating their efforts in Europe, releasing the progressive-tinged *Hypnosis Of Birds* in 1992 through Mortimer's own Taurus Moon Music imprint. This second chapter of Holocaust, financed directly by the Metallica royalties and punctuated by a further membership change (bass duties were handed

HOLOCAUST discography

Heavy Metal Mania, Phoenix PSP 1 (UK) (1980)

Smokin' Valves, Phoenix PSP 2 (UK) (1980)

Live - From The Raw Loud n' Live Tour, Phoenix PSP 3E (UK) (1981)

THE NIGHTCOMERS, Phoenix PSP LP 1 (UK) (1981)

Coming Through, Phoenix PSP 4 (UK) (1982)

LIVE (HOT CURRY & WINE), Phoenix PSP LP 4 (UK) (1983)

NO MANS LAND, Phoenix PSP LP 5 (UK) (1984)

The Sound Of Souls, Chrome CROM 301CD (UK) (1989)

HYPNOSIS OF BIRDS, Taurus Moon TRMCD 010 (UK) (1992)

Heavy Metal Mania '93, Taurus Moon TRMCDS 01 (UK) (1994)

SPIRITS FLY, Neat Moon NM 006 (UK) (1996)

COVENANT, Neat Moon NM 020 (UK) (1997)

THE COURAGE TO BE, Edgy EDGY 111 (UK) (2000)

PRIMAL, Edgy EDGY 114 (UK) (2003)

SMOKIN' VALVES: THE ANTHOLOGY, Castle CMDDD 653 (UK), Castle 72020 (USA) (2003)

LIVE - FROM THE RAW LOUD 'N' LIVE TOUR, Medium MTL001 CD (UK) (2004)

from Graham Hall to David Rosie), witnessed Mortimer, now with full creative control, pursuing a highly eclectic form of metal, winning favour from many quarters. The group's almost eccentric approach to metal structures, allied with Mortimer's lyrical stance – relaying both Christian and spiritual themes – set them apart: the band played second on the bill to Fates Warning at the 1993 'Wacken Open Air' festival in Germany and performed what was intended to be their last live show in Hamburg in May 1994.

Holocaust finally folded in June 1995, but were quickly resurrected as a tenacious interest in Germany was sustained. In particular, Kai Hansen's high-profile Gamma Ray covered the Holocaust track 'Heavy Metal Mania' on their *Live '95* album. The band then re-released 1992's *Hypnosis Of Birds* in new packaging with extra tracks, re-titled *Spirits Fly*. This collected the original album tracks and added Holocaust's payback to Metallica and Gamma Ray, with their renditions of 'Master Of Puppets' and a newly recorded 'Heavy Metal Mania'.

The group capitalised on this renewed momentum with brand new recordings in the following year. *Covenant* in 1997 saw Mortimer retaining Hall and Cowen and exploring the conceptual theme woven around the six-book literary series *The Chronicles Of Thomas Covenant The Unbeliever* by Stephen R. Donaldson.

A further outing, *The Courage To Be*, emerged in 2000 with new guitarist John McCullim, but the same year the band would start to fracture yet again. Meanwhile, the Holocaust name was kept in the public eye as American death metal band Six Feet Under covered 'Holocaust' as the lead track to their *Graveyard Classics* album.

Billed to perform at the Metal Meltdown III festival in New Jersey in April 2001, the band found itself without a rhythm section. Seattle native Bryan Bartley would become Holocaust's first American member while drummer Ron Levine, from Boston, Massachusetts (also the group's webmaster), joined for the gig as drummer. In 2001 this revised quartet cut the *Friday The 13th* promo EP, so named because all three tracks were recorded on that date.

Holocaust have rebuilt their fanbase across Europe and triggered cult appeal in the USA. In 2003 the Castle label assembled many of the group's harder-to-find tracks for the *Smokin' Valves* compilation, and a new album, *Primal*, was delivered in 2004. The band's future seems assured.

IRON MAIDEN
METAL PERSONIFIED AFTER THREE DECADES IN BUSINESS

MORE SO THAN ANY OTHER act, Iron Maiden exemplify the essence of British heavy metal. Propelled to the forefront of the NWOBHM movement, Iron Maiden astutely carved out a career backed by a supremely loyal fanbase. These devotees were served well as the group perfected the art of merchandising: their mascot Eddie, who graces all Iron Maiden artwork, became a household image on a staggering range of things. The group is centred on bassist Steve Harris, now the sole remaining founder member, who underpins many of the most recognisable songs in the Maiden catalogue with his trademark galloping bass runs.

Raised in the mid 1970s punk-ridden east end of London, Iron Maiden challenged the new-wave-infested charts by delivering highly-charged, no-compromise heavy metal. Formed by Harris in 1975, the band took their name from a medieval torture device and underwent a myriad of personnel changes following their initial line-up. Harris had started out as a member of Influence, which adopted the title of Gypsy's Kiss in time for their debut gig in 1973, in Poplar, east London: the band consisted of Harris, vocalist Bob Verschoyle, guitarist Dave Smith and drummer Paul Sears. Gypsy's Kiss gigs were centred on the London pub circuit, and the band featured many covers in their set from the likes of Deep Purple and Free.

After a handful of gigs, Harris decamped to join blues-boogie merchants Smiler, aligning himself with vocalist Dennis Wilcock, guitarists Mick and Tony Clee and Doug Sampson on drums. Harris opted out of this band in 1975 to form Iron Maiden, roping in vocalist Paul Day, the guitar pairing of Terry Rance and Dave Sullivan and drummer Ron 'Rebel' Matthews.

Almost immediately the fledgling Maiden hit membership problems: Day was ousted in favour of Smiler vocalist Dennis Wilcock, who added lurid stage theatrics to the show. Rance and Sullivan then lost their positions to guitarists Dave Murray, previously with Evil Ways, and Bob 'Angelo' Sawyer (aka Bob D'Angelo). Day later fronted More, The Sweet and Wildfire.

Sawyer was then cut out of the equation, and Murray's initial tenure was also shortlived. Within six months Murray had joined Urchin, and Iron Maiden became a single-guitar band, recruiting ex-Hooker musician Terry Wapram. The dynamics were filled out with the acquisition of keyboard player Tony Moore. However, Ron Matthews then left, later turning up in Tormé for the *Live* album released in 1984. In his stead came Barry Purkis, but this revised line-up only completed one gig.

With both Moore and Wapram leaving for pastures new, Murray was enticed back from Urchin, although the line-up ructions were far from over as Wilcock quit, followed in turn by Purkis. The latter adopted the stage name of Thunderstick and joined Samson, while Wilcock united with Wapram to form VI.

In 1978 Maiden drew in ex-Smiler drummer Doug Sampson and former Bird Of Prey vocalist Paul Dianno for a solid core alongside Harris and Murray. The group employed a variety of second guitarists from this point, including Paul Cairns, Paul Todd and Tony Parsons, although the main quartet were the men who cut the legendary EP *The Soundhouse Tapes*.

On the very last day of 1978, Maiden recorded *The Soundhouse Tapes*, taking the title from DJ Neal Kay's club at the Prince of Wales pub in Kingsbury, north-west London. The group recorded four tracks – 'Iron Maiden', 'Invasion', 'Prowler' and 'Strange World' – but time constraints prevented the latter track from being fully produced and the EP emerged as a three-track demo cassette. A 7-inch vinyl version was officially released on November 9th 1979. *The Soundhouse Tapes* EP sold well through mail order and at live gigs.

Dave Murray: "We paid for The Soundhouse Tapes ourselves but the original tapes, the master tapes, have gone now. It's a shame because we paid for the session but didn't think about paying for the actual master tape, so it just got recorded over by the next band that came into the studio. That's sad because that's where it really started for us. That was putting all that energy from the pubs onto tape. It's kind of odd to think how we were selling them ourselves back then, and now people pay crazy amounts of money for them."

Live shows at this point included a debut headliner at London's Marquee club on October 19th 1979, with Praying Mantis in support, plus a valuable support to Motörhead. EMI signed the band in December 1979 following a further batch of sold-out Marquee headliners, with the band championed by *Sounds* and DJ Kay. Iron Maiden immediately entered EMI's Manchester Square studios to cut 'Sanctuary' and 'Wrathchild' for the *Metal For Muthas* compilation. However, in early 1980 Parsons was asked to leave, and in came Dennis Stratton. A further change came when Sampson left to be replaced by ex-Samson drummer Clive Burr.

Stratton, pre-Iron Maiden, had been involved with United. This 1978 act, fronted by Stratton, consisted of Andy Pyle (of The Kinks, Savoy Brown, Alvin Lee and Juicy Lucy) on bass, John Gosling from The Kinks on keyboards and drummer Ron Berg (of Savoy Brown). Before United, Stratton had also played London clubs with Remus Down Boulevard. When Stratton quit United to join Maiden, Pyle, Berg and Gosling stuck together to create Network.

Iron Maiden began their live action for 1980 by headlining the 'Metal For Muthas' tour, which featured Praying Mantis among others. Their 'Running Free' debut single charted and Iron Maiden entered the history books by becoming the first band to perform live on *Top Of The Pops* since The Who in 1973.

Gaining further exposure, in March 1980 Maiden opened on Judas Priest's 'British Steel' UK tour. Opinion was sharply divided as to whether Iron Maiden were merely Judas Priest copyists or bona fide contenders, as Dianno and Murray in particular awkwardly emulated their counterparts Rob Halford and KK Downing with their leather stage garb. However, enough fans were impressed to boost the *Iron Maiden* debut album, produced by Will Malone at Kingsway Studios in London and released in April, reaching an impressive Number 4 in the British charts. American editions of the album came with an extra track, 'Sanctuary' (the band had re-recorded both *Metal For Muthas* tracks for the debut album, and this song featured a different guitar solo from Stratton and a police siren effect). However, the supposedly objectionable lyrics of 'Sanctuary' meant that it would not see the light of day in the UK until a 1990 CD reissue.

Flushed with success, the band undertook a well-attended 42-date headline British tour and put in a scorching performance at the annual Reading Festival (headlined by UFO) before setting off on a tour of Europe, opening for Kiss.

Stratton quit upon the Kiss tour's completion, to be replaced by ex-Urchin and Broadway Brats guitarist Adrian Smith, but this didn't stop crowds from filling out a British headline tour and supporting another single, a cover of 'Women In Uniform', a track from the Australian band Skyhooks. 'Women In Uniform' was the sole studio track on the Japanese import *Live!! + One* EP, the three live tracks – 'Sanctuary', 'Phantom Of The Opera' and 'Drifter' – having been recorded at a London Marquee show in July 1980.

With their second album, *Killers*, the group switched to Battery Studios and producer Martin Birch, renowned for his work with Deep Purple. *Killers* was issued in February 1981. North American editions came with an extra track, 'Twilight Zone'. Maiden powered through a mammoth world tour, kicking off with British headline dates supported by French veterans Trust. Further dates for most of the year included headline shows in Japan and an American tour supporting Priest once more.

Maiden finished their American tour with dates alongside a diverse range of acts including Whitesnake, Humble Pie and UFO and returned to Europe to perform festival dates with Kansas, Motörhead and Blue Öyster Cult. The incessant touring made *Killers* a gold album in Britain, France and Japan.

With momentum building rapidly, fans were stunned to learn that Dianno was quitting, apparently due to the strains of touring. Rumours quickly circulated about the identity of his replacement. It was alleged that Iron Maiden had secretly been auditioning singers while on tour in America.

Paul Dianno: "When I got sacked by Maiden I lost a lot of fans. They wanted me to play heavy metal but I'm a punk. I ended up doing something like fucking REO Speedwagon instead. It took a long time to realise that heavy metal was not something I could escape so I had better get back onto it. That was the Battlezone thing.

"They won't let me into the USA any more. Something to do with an Uzi machine gun I was carrying at the time. It's actually probably because I'm a Muslim. They don't like that at all. I read the

Koran years ago and it really touched me. I always believed but I just didn't know what I believed in. All I cared about was drinking as much as I could, taking as many drugs as I could and being violent. I lost a lot of friends, lost a lot of opportunities, because I was angry all the time. I was angry because of the way I was treated by Iron Maiden. I have a long way to go but Allah is the example for me. I can never be that perfect but I'm trying."

The smart money was on Samson vocalist Bruce Dickinson and, indeed, the man was announced as Iron Maiden's new recruitment shortly after Samson appeared at the Reading Festival. Dickinson made his live debut with Maiden in Bologna in early 1982.

The ousted Dianno created in rapid succession Lonewolf and then Dianno, releasing far mellower material than fans desired. His act toughened up considerably over the years with Battlezone and Killers, but he remained reliant on Iron Maiden material.

Iron Maiden's third album, *The Number Of The Beast*, released in March 1982, was a milestone, breaking the band internationally and providing numerous hit singles in Britain, including their first Top 10 smash with 'Run To The Hills'. Once again the band employed the winning formula of Birch and Battery Studios. Due to contractual

The classic Iron Maiden line-up

obligations with his previous management, Dickinson was unable to officially assist in the songwriting.

Another British tour was enormously successful, as were European dates with openers Blackfoot, and yet again the band supported Judas Priest in America. Other supports included stints with the Scorpions, .38 Special and Ritchie Blackmore's Rainbow. The world tour was rounded off by Australian and Japanese dates.

Prior to the recording of the group's fourth album, 1983's *Piece Of Mind*, drummer Clive Burr was replaced by former Pat Travers and Trust sticksman Nicko McBrain. Ironically, after a brief spell with Alcatraz, Burr joined Trust for a shortlived stay before forming the more melodically inclined Stratus and then joining Praying Mantis. McBrain had been a member of Axe earlier in his career, an outfit that included producer and Charlie guitarist Terry Thomas, and also appeared on albums by Streetwalkers and Stretch. Just prior to joining Maiden, McBrain had been involved with Informer, a band comprising erstwhile Stallion vocalist John Elstar, ex-Sidewinder and Stallion guitarist Stuart Smith and Whitesnake bassist Neil Murray.

Piece Of Mind was Martin Birch's third engagement at the desk for the band, although by now they were recording at Compass Point Studios, Nassau, in The Bahamas. Following the album's release, Iron Maiden launched into the by-now obligatory world tour, after *Piece Of Mind* entered the American *Billboard* charts at Number 127. The American tour got into gear with support acts Fastway and Saxon. Canadian band Coney Hatch (a particular favourite of Steve Harris) replaced Saxon and later guests were Quiet Riot.

In the latter part of 1983 the quintet travelled to Europe, where MSG opened, before appearing at one of the biggest metal festivals ever, a TV special in Dortmund as part of the *Rock Pop* televised concert series. The awe-inspiring two-day bill also included Scorpions, Judas Priest, Krokus, Def Leppard, Ozzy Osbourne, Quiet Riot and MSG.

With touring fulfilled, Maiden, with producer Birch in tow, again retired to Compass Point Studios to craft a fifth album. The band launched *Powerslave* in September 1984, and the ensuing world tour saw the quintet performing their first dates in Poland. In 1985, the band performed seven sold-out shows at the prestigious New York Radio City Music Hall with support act Queensrÿche. Further American supports were handled by W.A.S.P., Twisted Sister and Accept.

The 'World Slavery' tour caught Iron Maiden delivering the decibels to 26 countries over 200 shows and spawned a live video and album, *Live After Death*. The tracks were captured at a four-night stand held at the Hammersmith Odeon in London during October 1984 and Long Beach Arena in Long Beach, California, in March 1985. The Derek Riggs-created jacket art for this double album, featuring Eddie breaking out of a tomb, notably misquoted a passage from H. P. Lovecraft's *The Nameless City* on the gravestone.

By 1986 the band were ready for a more creative approach and, after recording in The Bahamas, Amsterdam and New York, released *Somewhere In Time*, which featured guitar-synths. *Seventh Son Of A Seventh Son* hosted more songs written by Smith than usual and was a success, marking the peak of the group's experimental phase, but the 1988 album was the closest the band ever came to a full-blown concept record. From this point, the band eschewed further moves towards experimentation and returned to the starker, stripped-down metal sounds of yore on later albums, often recording at Harris's home studio.

Bruce Dickinson: "It's not a formula thing, getting a sound that is all your own. You've either got it or you haven't. I've often thought that you could give a band all the same instruments, PA and gear as Iron Maiden, ask them to play the same song, and not many of them would sound special. I know none of them would sound like Iron Maiden. They might be better musicians but getting something to sound that bit special is about a whole lot more than that. Listen to those tribute albums. Not very good, are they? What makes Iron Maiden is the attitude, the soul and the passion. You can't stick that in a manual."

Steve Harris: "I don't think it's too healthy to analyse your sound because you'll end up disappearing up your own arse. Just play the music, is what I say. We all bring in different influences and colours to the music. A lot of my songs are kind of epic, I guess. I have a great love for 1970s progressive rock. I like that adventurous stuff that has no limitations, so you will see Iron Maiden doing things like that on Seventh Son Of A Seventh Son and some of our other big numbers, like 'Rime Of The Ancient Mariner'. Some of our songs are more gutsy, instinctive things and we can also go quite technical too. We have sets of fans who seem to like all the styles so it all works out."

The inevitable world tour shied away from a systematic, city-by-city tour schedule and Maiden blitzed their way through America and Europe by hopping from one major festival to another. The schedule's highlight was Iron Maiden headlining the 'Monsters Of Rock' festival above Kiss (Iron Maiden were the only band Kiss agreed to play beneath since 1974), David Lee Roth, Megadeth, Guns N'Roses and Helloween to a record-breaking crowd of over 100,000. Further dates in Europe led to an arena tour of Britain.

The year 1989 was a quiet one for the band but busy for the individual members. Both Smith and Dickinson released solo albums: Dickinson scored chart success with *Tattooed Millionaire* and a batch of singles. Smith found the going tougher with his more AOR-influenced project ASAP.

Birch and Maiden reassembled early in 1990 to record *No Prayer For The Dying* at Harris's own Barnyard Studios. For the first time in seven years the line-up changed, with Smith departing to concentrate on solo work. Ex-Gillan and White Spirit guitarist Janick Gers, who had toured with Dickinson as part of his solo band, soon landed the job.

Yet again the new album, debuting at Number 2 in the British charts, paved the way for a mammoth global tour. Opening with a low-key club gig at Milton Keynes, the tour – a stripped-down affair – sped through America before Gulf War I made dates in Australia and Japan unfeasible.

During 1990 Murray toyed with the idea of creating a solo project with American guitarist Nancy Chandler, and songs credited to the guitarist turned up on Chandler's 1993 album by the band Cheyenne.

Meanwhile, Harris paid homage to two of his influences by covering the Stray track 'All In Your Mind' and Golden Earring's 'Kill Me (Ce Soir)' as bonuses on the 'Holy Smoke' single. At Christmas that year Maiden leaped into the record books when their latest single, 'Bring Your Daughter To The Slaughter' became the first metal song to go straight into the British singles charts at Number 1. Much to the band's indignation, BBC Radio One still refused to playlist the single.

Fear Of The Dark, released in 1992, heralded another change for the band as, for the first time, jacket artist Derek Riggs was not used. In came noted sci-fi artist Melvyn Grant who lent the album cover a more up-to-date feel. Once more Maiden reached Number 1 in the British album charts.

In mid 1991 the band performed headlining dates in America with support act Anthrax and headlined the Roskilde Festival in Denmark, appearing with Winger, Primus and The Almighty. Throughout the tour, rumours abounded of Bruce Dickinson's discontent within the band. The vocalist had been strenuously pursuing his solo career, as well as his new-found activity as a comic novelist. Maiden performed their final gig with Dickinson at Pinewood Studios in front of an audience of members of the band's fan club. This turned out to be no ordinary gig, as magician Simon Drake – noted for his gory stunts – 'killed' members of the band prior to the finale of Dickinson being ritually 'slain' by Drake at the end of the televised show.

The Dickinson era was capped with the 1993 release of two live albums, *A Real Live One*, in March, and *A Real Dead One*, in October. The two sets, divided into old and new material, were recorded at a range of venues throughout 1992. The limited-edition *Live At Donington* arrived in November, clad in a plain white printed sleeve. It captured Dickinson's last major festival performance when Maiden headlined the 'Monsters Of Rock' festival on August 22nd 1992.

With Dickinson on the solo trail, Maiden fans faced uncertain times. Rumours followed that Helloween vocalist Michael Kiske had secured the position, and it was known that erstwhile La Paz, Midnight Blue and Praying Mantis singer Doogie White had been asked to audition twice. In the end, though, to many fans' amazement, Maiden recruited ex-Wolfsbane vocalist Blaze Bayley in 1994. The recording of the band's tenth studio album was slightly delayed when Bayley seriously injured his knee in a motorbike accident. During this lay-off Nicko McBrain took time out to gig with pub-rockers The Phil Hilborne Band.

Maiden lost their deal with EMI in North America during 1995, although they remained signed to the London office. For the USA, the group switched to the newly formed CMC International.

The new record, entitled *The X Factor*, was widely acknowledged as too radical a step for many Maiden fans to follow. The familiar epic romps had been replaced by darker, introspective themes, and Bayley's vocals came in for some vicious criticism. Swathes of hardcore fans lost faith. Interestingly, the 'Lord Of The Flies' single featured a cover of UFO's 'Doctor Doctor' as a B-side.

Blaze debuted onstage with Iron Maiden in Israel, with the new band's first test at Jerusalem's Sing Sing club on September 28th 1995. Maiden toured heavily throughout the end of 1995, although a planned Beirut show was cancelled by the authorities who insisted that it was likely to incite riots.

Maiden's British and European shows saw Yorkshire's doom metal act My Dying Bride in support. Harris et al were then able to perform a full-blown tour of the former Eastern Bloc, embracing Bulgaria, Slovenia, Hungary, Poland, Czech Republic and Rumania. However, for the first time the group were not selling out the venues, and touring was cut short. The official explanation was that Blaze had suffered an allergic reaction to certain substances used on the stages. In early 1996 the group played a one-off club show at Nottingham's Rock City, a date that saw Psycho Motel, the latest band featuring Adrian Smith, in support.

The *Best Of The Beast* compilation arrived in September 1996, the most impressive variant being a four-LP set with lavish gatefold artwork and a limited-edition book. A single, 'Virus', accompanied the album, various B-sides of which offered fans a chance to hear archive Iron Maiden recordings of 'Sanctuary' and 'Wrathchild' from the *Metal For Muthas* compilation and 'Prowler' and 'Invasion' from *The Soundhouse Tapes*.

Throughout 1997 Iron Maiden kept a low profile as they worked on a new album, although Harris did announce plans for his own label, Beast Records. Steve's first signings were Dirty Deeds, the London group fronted by ex-Chariot main man Pete Franklin.

Virtual XI, co-produced by Harris and Nigel Green, was more straightforward than the usual Maiden fare. Both 'The Angel And The Gambler' and 'Futureal' were released as singles, but sales were flagging.

Maiden set out on tour again during 1998, although attendance was not so good, with the band's loyal audience drifting away, apparently dissatisfied with Bayley's limitations. South American shows saw the band playing to capacity arena crowds, but with the political situation between

---

IRON MAIDEN discography

The Soundhouse Tapes, Rock Hard ROK 1 (UK) (1979)
IRON MAIDEN, EMI EMC 3330 (UK), Harvest ST-12094 (USA) (1980) **4 UK**
KILLERS, EMI EMC 3357 (UK), Harvest ST-12141 (USA) (1981) **12 UK, 78 USA**
THE NUMBER OF THE BEAST, EMI EMC 3400 (UK), Harvest ST-12202 (USA) (1982) **1 UK, 33 USA**
PIECE OF MIND, EMI EMA 800 (UK), Capitol ST-12274 (USA) (1983) **3 UK, 14 USA**
POWERSLAVE, EMI POWER 1 (UK), Capitol SJ-12321 (USA) (1984) **2 UK, 21 USA**
LIVE AFTER DEATH, EMI RIP 1 (UK), Capitol SABB-12441 (USA) (1985) **2 UK, 19 USA**
SOMEWHERE IN TIME, EMI EMC 3512 (UK), Capitol SJ-12524 (USA) (1986) **3 UK, 11 USA**
SEVENTH SON OF A SEVENTH SON, EMI CDEMD 1006 (UK), Capitol C2-90258 (USA) (1988) **1 UK, 12 USA**
NO PRAYER FOR THE DYING, EMI CDEMD 1017 (UK), Epic EK 46905 (USA) (1990) **2 UK, 17 USA**
FEAR OF THE DARK, EMI CDEMD 1032 (UK), Epic EK 48993 (USA) (1992) **1 UK, 12 USA**
A REAL LIVE ONE, EMI CDEMD 1042 (UK), Capitol CDP 7 81456 2 (USA) (1993) **3 UK, 106 USA**
A REAL DEAD ONE, EMI CDEMD 1048 (UK), Capitol CDP 7 89248 2 (USA) (1993) **12 UK, 140 USA**
LIVE AT DONINGTON, EMI CDDON 1 (UK) (1993) **23 UK**
THE X FACTOR 1995, EMI CDEMD 1087 (UK), CMC International 06076 86225-2 (USA) (1995) **9 UK, 147 USA**
VIRTUAL XI, EMI 7243 4 93915 2 9 (UK), CMC International 06076 86240-2 (USA) (1998) **16 UK, 124 USA**
BRAVE NEW WORLD, EMI 7243 5 26605 2 0 (UK), Colombia CK 62208 (USA) (2000) **7 UK, 39 USA**
ROCK IN RIO, EMI 7243 5 38543 0 9 (UK), Colombia C2K 86000 (USA) (2002) **186 USA**
DANCE OF DEATH, EMI 7243 5 93010 2 0 (UK), Colombia CK 89061 (USA) (2003) **2 UK, 18 USA**
DEATH ON THE ROAD, EMI 09463 36574 2 7 (UK), Sanctuary 96429 (USA) (2005) **22 UK**
A MATTER OF LIFE AND DEATH, EMI 09463 72321 2 5 (UK), Sanctuary 06076-84768-2 (USA) (2006) **4 UK. 9 USA**

Chile and Britain aggravated by the General Pinochet affair, Iron Maiden wisely pulled out of shows there.

In early 1999 the fans and press finally won the day as Bayley was ousted by the returning Dickinson. Adrian Smith also rejoined, lending Maiden an unexpected – but welcome – three-guitar assault. Bayley returned with his new act Blaze and the resulting *Silicon Messiah* album, retaining management links with Sanctuary.

The rejuvenated Maiden wowed North America with a sold-out 17-date tour before taking on European venues. An elaborate internet hoax branded the new Maiden product as *Majesty Of Gaia*, complete with fictitious track-listing. When the real product arrived in stores, *Brave New World* vindicated the return of Dickinson with a vengeance, despite the fact that 'Nomad', 'Dream Of Mirrors' and 'Mercenary' were re-worked versions of tracks originally demoed for *Virtual XI*. Maiden scored a Number 3 album in Germany, the 'Wicker Man' single went into the Top 10 in Britain, and *Brave New World* penetrated the upper reaches of the

European continent's national charts, marking a definitive renewal of fortunes.

Bruce Dickinson: "Why was Iron Maiden so successful? I've heard all the crap about the marketing and Eddie and all that and, yes, it's important, but ultimately it's about the music. It's hard to stand out as a heavy metal band but for those that can the rewards are there. I've never seen loyalty given to any band like Iron Maiden. Those people who knock us shouldn't be asking how many T-shirts we've sold, they should be asking why are those fans buying the T-shirts?

"It's strange, some people view Iron Maiden as a business, but the guys in the band only really care about getting up there on stage and putting on the best show we can. We love this music. You can't fake it."

A batch of European festival performances were cancelled when Gers sustained injuries after falling offstage in Mannheim. Iron Maiden were soon back in action, touring North America in the latter half of the year with support from Halford and Queensrÿche. The resurgence was marred by the stabbing of four fans at a Verizon Wireless Amphitheatre gig in Los Angeles.

Bizarrely, news emerged in 2000 that one of Maiden's earliest guitarists, Tony Parsons, had created a Maiden tribute band named Metalworks with ex-Alice Cooper and The Almighty guitarist Pete Friesin and ex-Judas Priest drummer Les Binks. Another ex-Maiden man, Paul Dianno, billed as Paul Dianno And The Beast, fanned the flames in early 2001 by issuing a live album consisting entirely of Iron Maiden songs.

Maiden themselves bounced back in spectacular style with *Rock In Rio* in March 2002. The same month they announced two benefit shows at the Brixton Academy in London in aid of former drummer Clive Burr, who had been diagnosed with multiple sclerosis. Demand was such that the run was extended to three sold-out nights. In a further move the band informed fans that all proceeds from the next single, 'Run To The Hills', would be devoted to the MS fund. The DVD version of *Rock In Rio* topped the UK music video charts on its first week of release. Later in the year Maiden pitched in further to aid the Clive Burr Trust by auctioning off a selection of band rarities, including a full drum kit, autographed guitars and even an Eddie stage prop from the *No Prayer For The Dying* tour.

On September 7th McBrain, Gers and Dickinson surprised Deep Purple fans by joining the rock veterans on stage during their London Hammersmith Apollo gig for a rendition of the classic 'Smoke On The Water'. A further treat came on October 21st when famed American progressive metal outfit Dream Theater performed the entire *The Number Of The Beast* album at the London Astoria. The band even rigged up a Dream Theater logo backdrop executed in the classic Maiden script.

In November the band launched the three-CD boxed set *Eddie's Archives*, a collection of rare live material issued through Columbia, dating from 1979 tracks until the band's headline show at Donington in 1988. This came in a limited-edition Eddie-embossed silver casket. Besides the music, the collection added an Eddie shot glass and a family tree on parchment scroll. A further single CD, *Edward The Great*, was released in North America the same day as *Eddie's Archives* on November 4th.

The band spent early 2003 producing a new album, *Dance Of Death*, with producer Kevin Shirley, the band's first studio effort to be mixed in 5:1 surround sound. A mammoth DVD package titled *Visions Of The Beast* emerged that July, chronicling over three hours of music and comprising more than 30 videos. Maiden were then confirmed as the headline act at the Donington Download festival in June, the only UK date on their 'Give Me Ed… 'Til I'm Dead' world tour. Oddly, the US band Murderdolls were the main support for the entire European leg.

When *Dance Of Death* was delivered to the public, the album gained

a slew of Number 1s in Iceland, Sweden, Greece and Italy. In the USA the record debuted at Number 18, selling over 40,000 copies in its first week of sale. By February, Iron Maiden had performed to over one and a half million people in 28 countries. In celebration the band issued a special release entitled *No More Lies: Dance Of Death Souvenir EP*. This included remixed versions of 'Journeyman' and the epic 'Paschendale' along with live video of the title track. *Dance Of Death* itself was given some very special treatment, issued in DVD-Audio format with high-definition 5:1 surround sound. The upgraded version of the album also added videos for 'Wildest Dreams' and 'Rainmaker'.

Subsequently, Dickinson provided some notable sounds on his BBC 6 Music *Rock Show* programme, guesting on a cover of Deep Purple's 'Black Night' with Therapy? and on a rendition of Black Sabbath's 'Black Sabbath' with emo band Funeral For A Friend. He also turned his hand to narration, providing the voice for the BBC World Service documentaries *Legends Of Rock*.

McBrain stepped out of Iron Maiden activities for a one-off show in South Florida to celebrate his 52nd birthday on June 5th. The drummer united with Deepset's Jonathan Murphy on vocals and Rick Baum on guitar, plus the Black Sabbath-credited Dave 'The Beast' Spitz on bass, to perform a set of covers, billed as Wrath Child. By July this band, adding Failsafe's Chris Proano on second guitar, had evolved into McBrain Damage, booking US shows throughout the summer.

In the absence of a new album, and delays in Dickinson's next solo outing, Maiden plugged the gap with a diverse array of merchandise including the *Powerslave* tin lunchbox, a *Somewhere In Time* 18-inch action figure with glowing red eyes, motion-activated lights and movement, and an official 2005 calendar. Further Iron Maiden product was delivered in October, with *The History Of Iron Maiden Part 1: The Early Days* DVD. This package consisted of the *Live At The Rainbow* and *The Beast Over Hammersmith* concert films, seven songs recorded at the 1983 Dortmund Rock And Pop festival, nine tracks captured at the Ruskin Arms in 1980, a previously unreleased *Live At Donington* shoot, a newly filmed history of the band, 1981 *Top Of The Pops* performances, and more. Also on the television front, Bruce Dickinson featured as presenter for a documentary, *Flying Heavy Metal*, charting the evolution of the passenger aeroplane, and guested on the Discovery channel's *Trainspotting*.

Iron Maiden announced plans for a huge live campaign throughout the summer of 2005 and then issued a special 25th anniversary single of 'The Number Of The Beast' in January. The band guested for Black Sabbath at the roving 'Ozzfest' events, but due to commitments in Europe, they missed the last seven 'Ozzfest' gigs, their position being taken by Velvet Revolver. A headline gig at Reykjavik in Iceland on June 7th was extra special as fans were flown to the event in a Boeing 757 piloted by Dickinson himself. These concerts marked the group's anniversary celebrations by drawing only on tracks from the first four albums.

June saw the range of official Iron Maiden merchandise expanding, with the National Entertainment Collectibles Association releasing *Somewhere In Time* and *Piece Of Mind* Eddie action figures. Maintaining momentum on the DVD front, a brand new release entitled *Death On The Road* was issued through EMI – a show originally filmed by German Viva TV at the Westfalenhalle Arena in Dortmund during the 'Dance Of Death' European tour in December 2003. The package also included a 70-minute documentary directed by Matthew Amos. Following Maiden's gig in Prague, no fewer than 11 albums re-charted in the national Czech charts.

To coincide with the band's headline appearances at the Reading and Leeds festivals in August, Maiden reissued their classic 'The Trooper' single, with various formats hosting live material recorded at the June 7th Icelandic gig in Reykjavik's Egishorllin Stadium. To coincide with this release Maiden permitted an exclusive download, a live version of 'The Trooper' recorded in Iceland.

Surreally, Maiden closed their 'Ozzfest' stint at the Hyundai Pavilion in Devore, San Bernardino, California, on August 20th with a show that would go down in history for all the wrong reasons. Throughout the band's set they were pelted with objects, including eggs, thrown by the crowd and had their power cut. To cap it all, during 'The Trooper' Dickinson's familiar onstage theatrics of waving a Union Jack flag was countered by an intruder waving an American Stars And Stripes, with the words "Don't fuck with Ozzy" painted on his back. These actions prompted Dickinson to launch into an anti-'Ozzfest' and Sharon Osbourne diatribe.

Iron Maiden put in another benefit concert for the Clive Burr Multiple Sclerosis Trust Fund at London's Hammersmith Apollo on September 2nd. In related news, keeping the rock tradition in the family, Steve Harris's 21-year-old daughter Lauren Harris launched her solo career with an album intended for release in 2006.

For a quarter of a century, Iron Maiden, bar one slight wobble in the mid 1990s, have reigned supreme as the biggest and the best that British heavy metal has to offer. Not only has Maiden's music spawned a multitude of imitators, but the band has served as an example for others to follow in the way they have nurtured their fanbase by personal interaction, merchandising, and the manufacture of a multitude of products across all formats. Add to this the fact that their autumn 2006 album *A Matter Of Life And Death* was hailed as their best in years, and the result is a unique entity.

RAVEN
ATHLETIC COULD-HAVE-BEENS

NEWCASTLE UPON TYNE'S "athletic rock" outfit Raven made a huge opening impact on the NWOBHM by way of their mandatory first three albums but sadly failed to live up to their initial promise. Their early efforts were manic metal sprints through excellent riffs and high-pitched, distinctive vocals. Success brought about a step up to a sustained US campaign, but, strangely, the group indulged themselves in a succession of poorly conceived albums. These wounded Raven almost irreparably. Despite their waning popularity in Britain, Raven fought back to command respect and a healthy fanbase across the world.

Raven, like many of their NWOBHM contemporaries, actually boasted a longer lineage than most fans imagined. The group dated as far back as 1974, with an initial line-up comprising brothers John and Mark Gallagher and Paul Bowden. However, at this stage Raven had only one classical guitar between them. Santa Claus came to the rescue and in December that year the band got electric guitars for Christmas.

Raven's first live date in December 1975 was memorable if only for the fact that both Gallagher brothers managed to fall offstage. By this point the band had added drummer Paul Sherrif, but within months he was out in favour of Mick Kenworthy. In this incarnation Raven opened for The Stranglers and The Motors. One of Raven's early headlining gigs included a Hell's Angels convention where the band were ordered to play 'Born To Be Wild' no fewer than ten times in the pouring rain. The band only stalled the show when Mark faked an electric shock.

Kenworthy drifted away in late 1977, replaced by Sean Taylor. Bowden departed in 1979, with his position filled by Pete Shore. Raven suffered another blow when Taylor quit, eventually enrolling in Satan.

Raven augmented the line-up once more with the addition of drummer Rob 'Wacko' Hunter, whose previous act Fastbreeder had included future Duran Duran guitarist Andy Taylor, and cut their first two-track demo, featuring 'She Don't Need Your Money' and 'Wiped Out'. Courtesy of Tygers Of Pan Tang manager Tom Noble, this tape secured the band a deal with local label Neat. Raven scored a track 'Let It Rip' on the *Brute Force* compilation.

Their debut 7-inch single, 'Don't Need Your Money', created interest in the band and lent enough impetus to the 1981 Steve Thompson-produced first album to push it into the album charts. *Rock Until You Drop* notably included a nod back to the 1970s with a Sweet medley, 'Hellraiser/Action'.

Wiped Out in 1982 saw the songs getting faster and the band, co-producing with Keith Nichol, honing their direction. Regrettably, the intended mixes for the album were not used, substituted by a mix unapproved by the band. However, the band's fans were still impressed. Raven's first American shows in 1982, alongside Riot and Anvil, were promoted by Jonny Zazula of the Rock'n'Roll Heaven record store in New Jersey.

Noted producer Michael Wagener, an early member of Accept alongside frontman Udo Dirkschneider, was drafted in for the 1983 follow-up *All For One* as Raven sought a more mature sound. It was also their first North American release for Zazula's Megaforce label. This affiliation led to Raven's first 36-date American tour with opening act Metallica, and further tours had Exodus and Anthrax in support.

At Raven's 1984 New York show the band headlined above Metallica and Anthrax. They have always maintained that an A&R representative for Elektra was impressed by Raven but on inquiring about the band's name was misinformed that it was Metallica.

Nevertheless, Megaforce's connection to Atlantic Records resulted in Raven stepping up a rung in 1984 to a major deal. However, Atlantic manoeuvred the band away from their speed-based attack towards a more mainstream approach, even requiring the band to wear bizarre spacesuit stage gear. Raven's audience were by now finding it hard to equate the

lyric writing. Metal fans and critics marvelled at the unprecedented rawness and ferocity of the guitar work, not realising that this sonic quality was more by chance than intention.

Chris Bradley: "We thought the album turned out a mess. We recorded it pretty much in one go in somebody's living room. We turned up expecting a recording studio and found this flea pit of a house instead. At the time we were gutted when we heard the finished thing, because we went in there intending to sound like Thin Lizzy but what we got was a bag of nails. We never saw the album cover until we got the finished thing. Then everyone started buying it all over the world and saying how much they loved the sound. We got huge piles of fan mail. It was bizarre."

Lacking any cohesive management, the band failed to capitalise on the album's enormous potential and rave reviews, despite appearing at many European festival dates, including the Dutch Aardschok event in February 1984 alongside Metallica and Venom, and French festivals with Sortilège. British club shows included many London Marquee dates. In fact, Savage lent direct support to Metallica's first ever UK concert at the Marquee on March 27th 1984.

Andy Dawson: "When we played the Marquee with Metallica, they were all over us. It was very weird because they wanted to know everything about us, like how did we get that guitar sound? It slowly dawned on us that they knew all of our songs and had every recording we had ever made – including demos. We met them again when we played Aardschok in Holland. They were nice guys but I never understood why they were so secretive about our influence on them, because they used to play our songs live and they recorded them too. If you listen to Loose 'n Lethal it all becomes very obvious."

Despite Ebony's inability to promote such a fine debut, the album racked up sales of about 25,000 in its first few months. The band duly fled for pastures new, hooking up with London's Zebra label. The first fruit of this liaison was the impressive 12-inch EP *We Got The Edge*.

The excellent reviews continued, quickly followed by the second album *Hyperactive*, which initially sold well. Serious backing was still lacking, however, and without solid finance the band could never break out of the club scene. They then recorded a somewhat pedestrian three-song demo, *This Means War*, before throwing in the towel.

Dawson, Renshaw and Brown went on to form Rebel with bassist Stuart Corden and ex-Nightvision vocalist Harry Harrison, cutting some very fine demos, but this outfit disbanded without a deal. Corden joined Glory Boys as Renshaw returned to his day job at the local factory.

A lengthy hiatus ensued, after which Bradley formed XL with guitarists Andy Wilson and Matthew Blick and drummer Dave Reynolds. XL recorded a BBC Radio One *Friday Rock Show* session with Dawson on guitar but never secured a record deal. Dawson and Harrison formed Red in 1992, a band also including XL's Blick, bassist Paul Cooper and ex-Valentine drummer Mark Allsop. The duo recorded again with Clownhouse, very much in the pop-rock mould, before forming the grunge-inspired Quango and then Husk. Both acts featured vocalist Harrison, who later joined the resurrected Witchfynde.

Bootleg versions of *Loose 'n Lethal* appeared in Europe during 1993 on the Reborn Classics label and, prompted by this, Dawson resurrected Savage in mid 1995 to record a new, self-produced album for Neat. This was *Holy Wars*, recorded with Bradley and Lindley. Japanese versions of the album, recorded at Bandwagon Studios in Mansfield, had two cover versions as extra tracks – UFO's 'Hot'n'Ready' and Thin Lizzy's 'Are You Ready'.

The group added ex-Storm Tribe and XL man Andy Wilson on second guitar in 1996 for live work and performed at the German 'Bang Your Head' festival alongside Tokyo Blade and Blind Guardian. Unfortunately, the band followed this up only with a show at a local Mansfield pub.

Lindley departed prior to the recording of 1996's *Babylon*, again cut at Bandwagon, and he later played live with The Luther Beltz Band. In came another erstwhile XL member on drums, Richard Kirk. Meantime, *Loose 'n Lethal* finally achieved an official CD re-release through Neat, with three unreleased demo tracks – 'No Cause To Kill' and 'The Devil Take You' from 1980, and 1979's 'Back On The Road'. The British Steel label also got in on the act, reissuing 1985's *Hyperactive* with extra material from *We Got The Edge*.

Savage recorded *Xtreme Machine* throughout 1998 and Dawson worked with Wilson, Harrison and drummer Paul Comeroy. When *Xtreme Machine* arrived in stores, it soon had Metallica fans talking as Savage had cheekily included the original Metallica demo of their song 'Let It Loose' as a bonus track.

SAXON
STEEL WHEELS – STILL ROLLING

BASED IN BARNSLEY, SAXON shot to the fore as part of the NWOBHM movement, and a succession of four high-quality albums put the band at the pinnacle of their profession with great speed. Once the embers of the NWOBHM had ceased to glow, Saxon battled their way through a mid-life crisis to emerge even stronger, concentrating their efforts on mainland Europe where they still maintain a sizeable following. During their major-label period the band suffered from a serious miscalculation in terms of direction, mellowing out significantly – but have more than made up for it in recent times with superb albums such as *Unleash The Beast* and *Lionheart*. Musically, Saxon are characterised by Biff Byford's distinctive, enormous vocal holler and an ability to craft some of the most memorable riffs in metal.

Although Saxon came to prominence in 1980 with the groundbreaking *Wheels Of Steel*, the origins of the Yorkshire band can be traced back a decade earlier, to the formation in 1970 of Blue Condition by guitarist Graham Oliver and bassist Steve 'Dobby' Dawson. A blues-orientated hard rock outfit, Blue Condition evolved into S.O.B. by 1974 (named after the Free album *Tons Of Sobs*) retaining the line-up of Oliver, Dawson, vocalist-guitarist Steve Furth and drummer John Walker.

The following year Furth departed to concentrate on a blues career, as S.O.B. began pursuing a heavier direction. Another local act, Coast (named after the Trapeze track 'Coast To Coast') were in the midst of disintegration, and the suggestion was made that bassist Peter 'Biff' Byford assume the role of S.O.B. vocalist. A deal was reached in which Coast guitarist Paul Quinn, formerly of Mighty Mouth and Pagan's Chorus, was also enrolled. During this early period S.O.B. gigged hard, the pressure telling as Walker quit. His position was taken briefly by Dave Cowell. After a matter of weeks former Glitter Band drummer Pete Gill made the position permanent and S.O.B. became Son Of A Bitch.

During this period Byford and Quinn joined The John Verity Band, with Byford on bass. When Verity became a member of Argent, Byford and Quinn kept gigging as the John Verity Band for a short time but eventually diverted their efforts back to Son Of A Bitch. With their new name, Son Of A Bitch debuted at Bradford's Talk Of The Town venue where an EMI executive, Pete Hinton, became convinced of their potential. The band were in turn referred to French label Carrere and a deal was signed in Paris.

However, as recording for the debut album ensued, the record company judged that there would be strong opposition in America from distributors for the name Son Of A Bitch and the band were persuaded to adopt the fresh title of Saxon. The band's self-titled debut album was cut at Livingstone Studios and produced by John Verity.

However, Saxon found themselves amidst the full force of the NWOBHM movement when they released the classic *Wheels Of Steel*, cut at Ramport Studios with Pete Hinton behind the desk, in February of the following year. This album, far more representative of Son Of A Bitch's live set than its predecessor, provided the band with the biker anthems for which Saxon would become renowned. Many believe that Saxon have never bettered tracks such as 'Wheels Of Steel', 'Motorcycle Man' and '747 (Strangers In The Night)'. In Britain the band toured heavily supporting Motörhead and Nazareth: *Wheels Of Steel* hit Number 5 in the UK and generated two major hit singles in '747 (Strangers In The Night)' and 'Wheels Of Steel'. The band also appeared at the inaugural 'Monsters Of Rock' event at Castle Donington in August 1980 alongside the headlining Rainbow, the Scorpions and Judas Priest, among others.

Graham Oliver: "Saxon were in the right place at the right time with the NWOBHM movement. Nobody really realised that the band had been going for a long time before that, and we didn't want to advertise the fact either. A lot of fans thought Wheels Of Steel was the first album, because our real debut was promoted so poorly. The truth was we had been slogging away for a bloody long time."

Biff Byford: "The thing about the NWOBHM was that everybody that made it in the end sounded different. That's why so many bands made it big. I mean, nobody sounded anything like Saxon – our riffs were different and my voice was too. Nobody else sounded like Iron Maiden. Once Def Leppard found their way, they sounded unique too. A lot of NWOBHM bands were actually bloody blues and pub-rock. Where are they now?"

American dates in support to Rush followed. Later in 1980 they capitalised on their popularity with *Strong Arm Of The Law*, once again employing both Ramport Studios and Pete Hinton as producer. Again Saxon produced a record with classics of the genre: the epic 'Dallas 1PM' about the assassination of John F. Kennedy, '20,000 Feet', 'Heavy Metal Thunder' and the title track all scored strongly with fans. With the album breaking into the UK charts at Number 11, the group toured Europe as support to Judas Priest before headlining Britain with Nottingham's Limelight in November and December 1980 as opening act. Saxon then landed the guest position to AC/DC's gigantic 'Back In Black' American tour before rounding off their US foray opening shows for Black Sabbath and Blue Öyster Cult.

Graham Oliver: "If you read the British press you thought Saxon was all about drinking tea, wigs and false teeth. They were merciless once they decided Saxon was an easy target. When we went to America, though, the whole world just seemed to open because we were playing to enormous crowds. It was so strange to see all these people coming just to see us. They didn't care about anything except the music, and it was really refreshing. Every album sold great, but we had no money. Then we signed to EMI and we got money, but the albums stopped selling. We couldn't win."

Denim And Leather bolstered Saxon's fanbase in 1981 with 'And The Bands Played On', written about their Donington festival appearance the previous year, and 'Never Surrender' keeping the band in the singles charts. The Nigel Thomas-produced record found Saxon recording outside the UK for the first time, utilising Aquarius Studios in Geneva, Switzerland, and Abba's Polar Studios in Stockholm, Sweden. However, by 1982 drummer Pete Gill was out. The official explanation was that Gill had damaged his hand, but other sources suggest that he was fired. The drummer would eventually join Motörhead in 1984 for their *Orgasmatron* album.

Saxon's replacement was Nigel Glockler, a former member of Krakatoa and Toyah's live band, who debuted on the live *The Eagle Has Landed* album. Initially Glockler was pulled in temporarily, but a mid-tour choice between Gill and Glockler went in his favour. Saxon performed a groundbreaking tour of North America in 1984 on the back of *Power And The Glory*, released in 1983. This record marked another first for the band as tracks were crafted at Axis Sound Studios in Atlanta, Georgia, with Jeff Glixman at the controls. Gigging saw a bout of co-headline shows across the USA with Mötley Crüe prior to support dates with Iron Maiden. The band returned to Europe for another lengthy tour with guests Accept.

The band maintained the momentum with the historically-themed *Crusader*, tracked at Sound City Studios in Los Angeles. Fortunately producer Kevin Beamish's past record with top AOR acts did not stifle the group's heaviness and the record found favour with fans, many of whom failed to notice that Saxon had included a cover version, a rendition of Sweet's 'Set Me Free'. For the *Crusader* tour the band employed a huge stage set based on castle battlements. They also became embroiled in a lengthy legal dispute with former label Carrere for alleged non-payment of royalties. This situation finally resolved itself in late 1985 when Parlophone gained rights to the band's back catalogue.

Biff Byford: "We were on a roll. Saxon hadn't put out a bad album. I mean, look back between Wheels Of Steel and Crusader. We kept the quality up all the way. That's what EMI wanted, of course, but as soon as we signed they changed their tune and started talking about radio songs and producers and cover versions. Why sign a band just to change them? I have to admit we did go along with it, probably because we thought they might know best. But they didn't. We should have stuck to our instincts."

Saxon's first album for Parlophone, *Innocence Is No Excuse*, produced by Simon Hanhart at Union Studios in Munich, Germany, was released while former label Carrere were still in court, claiming the band were still signed to them. The band toured Britain in 1985 supported by Denmark's Pretty Maids. *Innocence Is No Excuse* featured a tamer sound from Saxon but it nevertheless gave the band its highest US chart placing to date. Back at home, though, Saxon's support began to slide, *Innocence Is No Excuse* reaching only Number 36 in the charts. Longstanding Saxon fans watched as the band's new label steered Saxon's music into mellower territory for two more albums.

Saxon's next album, the Gary Lyons-produced *Rock The Nations*, recorded at Wisseloord Studios in Hilversum, Holland, saw the departure – apparently at the management's insistence – of a disillusioned Steve Dawson. He was replaced by former Heritage and Statetrooper man Paul 'Fasker' Johnson, although Byford had actually recorded all the bass parts for the album. A surprise inclusion was Elton John. The star had been recording in the same complex and was persuaded to put down piano on the tracks 'Party 'Til You Puke' and 'Northern Lady'.

Saxon toured Britain again in 1986, with their guests the Japanese act Loudness. North American shows found the band co-headlining with Yngwie Malmsteen. With their popularity on the wane, many felt that Parlophone did not regard Saxon as a priority act – and the subsequent Stephan Galfas-produced album, *Destiny*, with new drummer Nigel Durham, did little to revive the band's career or disprove this theory. However, their spirited cover of the Christopher Cross hit 'Ride Like The Wind' did temporarily revive their fortunes, as they garnered both radio and MTV exposure. It wasn't enough, however, and in 1988 EMI dropped the band.

SAXON discography

SAXON, Carrere CAL 110 (UK) (1979)
WHEELS OF STEEL, Carrere CAL 115 (UK), Capitol SQ-12502 (USA) 1980) **5 UK**
STRONG ARM OF THE LAW, Carrere CAL 120 (UK), Carrere 37679 (USA) (1980) **11 UK**
DENIM AND LEATHER, Carrere CAL 128 (UK), Carrere 37685 (USA) 1982
THE EAGLE HAS LANDED, Carrere CAL 137 (UK), Carrere cnu (USA) (1982) **5 UK**
POWER AND THE GLORY, Carrere CAL 147 (UK), Carrere 38719 (USA) (1983) **15 UK, 155 USA**
CRUSADER, Carrere CAL 200 (UK), Carrere 39284 (USA) (1984) **18 UK, 174 USA**
INNOCENCE IS NO EXCUSE, Parlophone SAXON 2 (UK), Capitol ST-12420 (USA) (1985) **36 UK, 133 USA**
ROCK THE NATIONS, EMI EMC 3515 (UK), Capitol ST-12519 (USA) (1986) **34 UK, 149 USA**
DESTINY, EMI CDEMC 3543 (UK), Enigma D2-73339 (USA) (1988) **49 UK**
ROCK'N'ROLL GYPSIES, Roadrunner RR 9416-2 (Europe) (UK), Enigma 7 73370-2 (USA) (1989)
SOLID BALL OF ROCK, Virgin cnu (UK), Charisma 91672-2 (USA) (1991)
FOREVER FREE, Warhammer WARCD 10 (UK) (1993)
DOGS OF WAR, Virgin 7243 839983 2 6 (Europe), Mayhem 11074-2 (USA) (1995)
THE EAGLE HAS LANDED PART II, Virgin 7243 841630 2 0 (Europe) (1996)
UNLEASH THE BEAST, Virgin 7243 844202 2 2 (Europe), CMC 06076 86221-2 (USA) (1997)
METALHEAD, Steamhammer SPV 085-21502 (Europe / USA) (1999)
KILLING GROUND, Steamhammer SPV 089-72560 DCD (Europe / USA) (2001)
HEAVY METAL THUNDER, Steamhammer SPV 085-74482 DCD (Europe / USA) (2002)
LIONHEART, Steamhammer SPV 085-69692 (Europe / USA) (2004)
THE EAGLE HAS LANDED III, Steamhammer SPV 99982 2CD (Europe / USA) (2006)

Biff Byford: "We came back with Solid Ball Of Rock. It didn't mean much in England or the USA, they were really slow on the uptake, but in Europe that was a massive album for us. It was just like Wheels Of Steel all over again. Ever since Solid Ball Of Rock we've had huge support in Germany. It's never wavered. When grunge killed everything else off, bands like us and Motörhead kept on going. Before that we were fucking broke. All our fans had buggered off because of EMI and we thought: what the hell do we do now? There was only one thing to do – play some heavy metal!"

With the end of the decade and their record deal, the group defiantly set about an enormous British tour to re-awaken interest, based on the live album *Rock'n'Roll Gypsies*, released through Roadrunner. Saxon's experimentation with a smoother sound had now closed and from this juncture the group returned to their natural raw stance. Paul Johnson left to join USI and was duly replaced by Tim 'Nibbs' Carter as another lengthy tour of Germany was undertaken, this time sharing the billing with Manowar. That same year Byford found time to session on the *Kaizoku* album by Japanese act Air Pavilion.

Saxon started 1991 by releasing the Kalle Trapp-produced *Solid Ball Of Rock*, committed to tape at Karo Studio in Brackel, and their first for new label Virgin. *Solid Ball Of Rock* witnessed a shift in the songwriting duties as new man Nibbs Carter scored credits throughout, composing five tracks. The ensuing world tour took them to territories such as Argentina, Brazil, Paraguay, Uruguay and even New Zealand.

The follow-up, *Forever Free*, was released in Germany with different sleeve artwork to that of the British version. Kloot executed the original jacket art, but interest in their homeland was still unsteady, and the gaming company Games Workshop – who put the album out through their custom Warhammer imprint – issued *Forever Free* with suitably lavish sci-fi artwork. Again Saxon took on a cover version, this time the Willie Dixon blues standard 'I Just Wanna Make Love To You'. *Forever Free's* uncharacteristically thin sound was handled by Herwig Ursin, the band constructing the record at Hey You Studios in Vienna, Austria and Gems Studios in Boston, Lincolnshire.

Saxon remained a strong draw in Germany and put in another highly successful European visit, co-headlining with Motörhead and dubbed the 'Bombers And Eagles' tour. The pair also put in a show at London's Hammersmith Odeon. Saxon later toured Britain as headliners with support act Frankenstein, but attendance was not good.

Enthusiasm for the band's output and concerts was still buoyant in mainland Europe, and the band's upward career turn commenced once again with 1995's *Dogs Of War*. The album saw co-production credits going to manager Rainer Hänsel. That same year Quinn contributed guitar parts to German act Sargent Fury's *Turn The Page*. In a shock move, his guitar partner Graham Oliver quit shortly after the release of *Dogs Of War*. Oliver's position was filled by Doug Scarratt on Saxon's subsequent British tour, where they were supported by Manchester's China Beach. *Dogs Of War*, although a fine album, found the band at a nadir of popularity in Britain. Released on Virgin in Germany, the record was issued in Britain by the independent HTD label.

Biff Byford: "The truth is we sacked Graham Oliver. There is no dispute over the name. We are Saxon and that's that. It's nothing to do with the name, because really it's all about money. It pisses me off, though, that kids in Spain are going to a gig because it has the name Saxon on the poster and a picture of me and they get to see a bunch of berks butchering our songs. They're scratching their heads and thinking, hang on a minute – that's not Biff. The law says there's one Saxon; the fans say there's one Saxon."

The group toured in Germany with Glenmore and played further dates in Texas. The year ended on a high as the band joined the December 'Blind Guardian Christmas Party' tour, headed up by Blind Guardian and also boasting Love/Hate, Skyclad, Rage and Yngwie Malmsteen. Some of these shows were recorded for what would become *The Eagle Has Landed Part II* live album.

Saxon cut a rare tribute in 1996 offering their version of 'You've Got Another Thing Comin'' to the Judas Priest tribute *Legends Of Metal*.

Confusion then reigned as the departed Oliver reunited with his erstwhile Saxon cohorts Pete Gill and Steve Dawson to form a new act and in the process issued a legal claim to the name Saxon. Eventually, after much public bickering, Oliver's new band titled themselves Son Of A Bitch, a throwback to pre-Saxon days. Further members were added to this new combo in ex-Thunderhead vocalist Ted Bullet and former Saracen guitarist Haydn Conway.

Saxon regrouped, pulling out all the stops for their next effort. The resulting album, 1997's *Unleash The Beast*, took many by surprise as they

delivered an album that ranked alongside *Wheels Of Steel* as one of their finest efforts. The Trapp-produced album included a touching tribute to their tour manager JJ (aka John Jones) who had passed away the year before.

Naturally, the band set out on the road in Europe, with support act Royal Hunt and ex-Victory and Eloy man Fritz Randow on the drum stool, but some of the dates were marred by poor attendances due to confusion over concert dates. Nevertheless, the strength of *Unleash The Beast* was not in doubt, and the band put in a batch of British concert dates in 1998.

The same year saw Saxon returning to America for a string of shows before an appearance at the Brazilian 'Monsters Of Rock' festival. The world tour ended in Holland as support to Deep Purple. Quinn put in some outside activity, laying down guitars on the Iron Maiden tribute *666 The Number One Beast.*

Saxon's future seemed unclear, however, as Son Of A Bitch performed as Saxon at a Dutch festival alongside Kingdom Come, at Spanish dates with Thunder and even at British shows. To confuse matters, *Destiny*-era drummer Nigel Durham replaced Gill in Son Of A Bitch, but not before being asked by Byford to replace Glockler in Saxon.

Oliver disbanded Son Of A Bitch in 1999 to form a Jimi Hendrix tribute band with his son on drums. However, by June the pair had teamed up with members of Stormwatch and Witchfynde to create The Luther Beltz Band. That same month the bona fide Byford-fronted Saxon

put in festival gigs in Germany with Böhse Onkelz, Rose Tattoo and Danzig.

Oliver and Dawson came back to the fore in early 2000 announcing an operating title of Oliver/Dawson Saxon. Joining them were drummer Durham, guitarist Haydn Conway and ex-Hurricane, Madam X and Shy vocalist John Ward.

Strangely for a British label – in this case Angel Air – the title of the welcome *Live At Donnington 1980* album was misspelled. *Diamonds And Nuggets* then appeared, featuring early unreleased material dating as far back as 1971.

The 2001 Saxon album *Killing Ground*, produced by Nikolo Kotzev of Brazen Abbott and Nostradamus, and mixed by erstwhile Accept guitarist Hermann Frank, saw the band embarking on a rare foray into cover versions, cutting a rendition of King Crimson's epic 'In The Court Of The Crimson King'. Initial copies of the album came with a bonus disc entitled *Classics Re-Recorded* comprising eight staples re-cut by the 2001 line-up.

Another lengthy bout of touring followed. The band would then support Judas Priest at their London Brixton Academy gig in December. During 2002 Saxon returned to the American touring circuit, opening with an appearance at the Asbury Park, New Jersey, 'Metal Meltdown' festival in early April.

Building on the successful *Classics Re-Recorded* project of the previous year, Saxon's 2002 album *Heavy Metal Thunder* was a set of reworked classics. Initial copies of the album also included a live video of 'Killing Ground' from the Wacken festival and five tracks recorded in San Antonio in April 2002.

A major victory for the band came in late February 2003 when the High Court in London ruled in favour of Byford over the legal right to use the name Saxon. Summer festivals found the band in a unique position by appearing at the Italian 'Gods Of Metal' festival and the German 'Rock Hard' event on the same day: they played in Italy at 5pm before being whisked on a plane to Dortmund for a show at 10. Saxon were soon back headlining on European soil, supported by Doro, Dionysus and Circle II Circle.

Saxon fans were intrigued to learn of former guitarist Graham Oliver's 2004 release, credited to Saxon and entitled *Alternative Innocence*. Released by the Majestic Rock label, the record consisted of alternative and unused versions of songs that made up the band's 1985 release *Innocence Is No Excuse*, along with three unreleased tracks.

Saxon rehearsed with the Paradise Lost, Kill II This and Blaze-credited Jeff Singer on drums, but by April were utilising Jörg Michael of Stratovarius in Gems Studio in Lincolnshire to record a new album, *Lionheart*. Besides his high-profile tenure with the flying Finns, Michael's credits read like a who's who of German metal, having played with Rage, Mekong Delta, Headhunter, Laos, Grave Digger, Axel Rudi Pell and Running Wild among others.

As *Lionheart* garnered praise and drew in a further set of fans, the new band kicked off a 25th anniversary tour in Scandinavia during September. Support came from Sweden's Dream Evil along with Germany's Metalium and Chinchilla. Alongside Doro, Bonfire, Edguy, Crystal Ball and In Extremo, they were among acts participating in the January 27th 2005 'Rock For Asia' festival held at the Saturn Arena in Ingolstadt, Germany to benefit the victims of the Asian tsunami.

Saxon then announced that they would celebrate 25 years of the NWOBHM movement with a themed tour of Germany during April. Their live show for these dates consisted solely of songs from the period, with writers from *Rock Hard* magazine working as DJs for the evening, spinning tracks from the NWOBHM era. However, these gigs, alongside an announced appearance at the Desert Rock festival in Dubai, were postponed after Biff Byford's house in Normandy burnt down. US tour dates, scheduled for May, would be pushed back into November.

Remedy Records weighed in with a double tribute album to Saxon billed *Eagleution*, and limited edition picture discs of *Saxon*, *Strong Arm Of The Law* and *Wheels Of Steel* appeared through the Back On Black label. Meantime, Byford put in a vocal appearance on German thrash act Destruction's *Inventor Of Evil*.

Following European live dates, Saxon welcomed back former drummer Nigel Glockler in August. However, the re-scheduled US tour dates, set for November, were pulled once again, apparently due to late delivery of visas. With dates re-established, the Saxon wheels of steel began to roll once again.

Saxon, like so many bands before them, were thrown off the tracks by the influence of a major label. The fact that they put their career back on the rails and then strengthened their position is a demonstration of the band's tenacity. Now into their third generation of fans, Saxon's output appears to be getting stronger with each release.

TANK
HEAVY METAL WEAPONRY

TANK, LIKE THEIR NAMESAKE, offered the loudest, ugliest and most lethal form of metal. Formed in Croydon in February 1980, the band

debuted as a trio of Algy Ward (Alasdair Mackie Ward), an established veteran of the punk scene with The Saints and The Damned, and the duo of guitarist Peter Brabbs and his brother, drummer Mark. Tank's brash approach made it inevitable that they would establish a reputation as a power trio in the Motörhead mould.

Two singles, 'Don't Walk Away' and 'Turn Your Head Around', were released in 1981 and '82, emerging the following year. Some felt that they sounded too similar to Lemmy and co for comfort, especially as the debut album, *Filth Hounds Of Hades*, was produced by Motörhead guitarist 'Fast' Eddie Clarke. Valuable press then came from a cover of The Osmonds' 'Crazy Horses'.

In spite of their detractors, Tank were quick to build a fanbase in Europe and Japan. Constant touring with Girlschool, Motörhead and Diamond Head over the next two years paved the way for a second album, *Power Of The Hunter*. This second chapter met with strong continental sales.

Changes were afoot by the time the group's conceptual third album emerged in June 1983, the group having aligned themselves with Music For Nations after the demise of former label Kamaflage. *This Means War* debuted Tank's new second guitarist Mick Tucker, previously with Axis and White Spirit. The John Verity-produced album also featured guest backing vocals by Jody Turner of Rock Goddess and Denise Dufort of Girlschool. However, after just one gig Peter Brabbs was sacked and Mark vacated his post to join Dumpy's Rusty Nuts.

Mark Brabbs created a shortlived band with erstwhile Ore members, bassist Dave Boyce and guitarist Dave Howard. In 1986 he was a member of Paul Samson's Empire, followed by a stint with Saviour. Tank very briefly inducted Michael Bettel as a replacement on guitar.

Meantime, Ward and Tucker enlisted ex-Chicken Shack and Headfirst guitarist Cliff Evans alongside former White Spirit drummer Graeme Crallan for a radical re-build of Tank. During late 1984 Tank famously supported Metallica on a European tour. Later shows included gigs in North America as openers to Raven prior to further headline shows of their own. Ward then produced Italian thrash band Bulldozer's *The Day Of Wrath* album for Roadracer in 1985. That same year the *Armour Plated* Tank compilation was delivered.

Having recorded a second album for Music For Nations, 1985's *Honour And Blood*, Tank replaced Graeme Crallan with Gary Taylor from Burnley's Streetfighter. The ousted Crallan joined London act Britton, and in 1987 Panama, where he reunited with White Spirit keyboard player Toby Sadler.

Following the *Tank* album, recorded in 1986 with Mick Tucker but only seeing a release in 1988, the band consisted of Ward, Evans and Gary Taylor (who was replaced by former Fastway drummer Steve Clarke in

1989). However, the band then folded, with Evans creating the shortlived Destroyer with ex-Ya Ya and Fastway frontman Lea Hart before working in the studio with Mask. Evans later joined Paul Dianno's Killers after Ward decided to bring Tank to a conclusion. Taylor travelled to America to form Shotgun Rationale with ex-Plasmatics man Chris Romanelli.

Although inactive, the Tank myth retained a cult following. German thrash act Sodom maintained the band's profile by covering 'Don't Walk Away' on their 1989 *Agent Orange* album and 'Turn Your Head Around' on the *Better Off Dead* set in 1990.

In 1993 there was talk of a reunion album, but nothing came of this. Ward spent time working with ex-Fastway and Destroyer drummer Steve Clarke and Asia guitarist Keith More, among others, before joining Clarke's jazz-rock act Network for the *Refusal To Comply* album. Ward later resurfaced in London club band Conspiracy during 1994 before joining Warhead, another power trio assembled by erstwhile Motörhead guitarist Würzel and Warfare mainman Evo.

During 1996 Ward rejoined The Damned, but before long the continental fascination for early-1980s metal acts had caught up with Tank and, offered a recording deal, the band duly reformed. Sodom once more got in one more shot of appreciation with their take on 'Shellshock' appearing on the *Ten Black Years – Best Of* album. The 1997 Tank line-up played the 'Wacken Open Air' festival in Germany and then undertook a tour of the country with Hammerfall and Raven. For most of the latter dates on this trek an injured Ward took to the stage with the aid of a walking stick. The *Necropolis* album saw a belated release through Neat in 1997.

The late-1990s incarnation of Tank – Ward, Evans, Tucker and ex-Battlezone drummer Steve Hopgood – issued the live album *The Return Of The Filth Hounds* for Rising Sun Records and put in a useful showing at the 1998 Bang Your Head festival in Balingen, southern Germany. The band also played in Japan during early 1999 on a NWOBHM billing including Praying Mantis, as Evans also began work on a fresh Killers project.

The Japanese Pony Canyon label then released *Metal Crusade '99*, a split album with NWOBHM era compatriots Samson, Praying Mantis and Trespass, recorded at the Hibiya Open Theatre, Tokyo that August. Archive concert recordings from a 1981 support to Motörhead in Dortmund during 1981 were released by the Zoom Club label in 2001 as *War Of Attrition – Live '81*.

Mid 2002 brought the prospect of a new studio album from Tank, entitled *Still At War*, set for release in Japan in early August through Spiritual Beast Records. The Tank crew for this outing had Algy Ward

joined by guitarists Cliff Evans and Mick Tucker with Bruce Bisland (of Praying Mantis, Sweet, Weapon and Statetrooper) on the drums. *Still At War* included re-recorded versions of 'And Then We Heard The Thunder' and 'In The Last Hours Before Dawn'.

In January 2004 Tank's schedule was interrupted when Ward was taken into hospital to have a tumour removed from his head. The singer had previously been suffering from hearing loss and headaches. Nevertheless, they completed the recording of a new studio album, *Sturmpanzer*, which included the Status Quo song 'Tune To The Music'.

German band Powergod, in alliance with Sodom's Tom Angelripper, cut a cover of 'The War Drags Ever On' for inclusion on *Long Live The Loud – That's Metal Lesson II* in July 2005. Maniacal Records announced the release of a limited run of 500 vinyl pressings of the live album *War Of Attrition – Live '81*. The LP version contained two tracks not available on the CD. Meanwhile, fans wait to see if the Tank will roll on.

WITCHFINDER GENERAL
CULT NWOBHM STALWARTS

THE STOURBRIDGE-BASED HEAVY metal band Witchfinder General were formed in 1979 by vocalist Zeeb Parkes, guitarist Phil Cope and drummer Steve Kinsell (credited as 'Kid Rimple'). They achieved little during their lifetime, with two albums given a generally poor media reception and infrequent live work. However, the latterday interest in the NWOBHM movement and then the resurgence of the doom metal scene have placed a renewed focus on the band.

Cope, Kinsell and bassist Rod Hawkes had all been colleagues in the school band Electrode, with Parkes their roadie. In the wake of this band, Kinsell forged Medway before reuniting with Parkes and Cope with Johnny Fisher on bass to forge Witchfinder General. The inaugural live performance took place at The Crown pub in Dudley.

Fisher was soon superseded by Kevin 'Toss' McCready, who was in turn replaced by Phil Cope. Cope also played bass on *Death Penalty* and was credited as 'Woolfy Trope'. McCready recorded the 'Burning A Sinner' and 'Soviet Invasion' singles and was eventually replaced by Rod Hawkes. During December 1980 Witchfinder General announced that they were to record a single, 'Invisible Hate', for release on the WFG label, but this never transpired. Instead, the band signed to Sedgley's Heavy Metal Records in 1980 and released the poorly-produced 'Burning A Sinner' 7-inch single.

The 1982 debut album *Death Penalty*, produced by Pete Hinton, attracted publicity as the cover featured glamour model Joanne Latham being ritually 'executed' on a Wednesbury cemetery gravestone. The second album, 1983's *Friends Of Hell*, saw the group split with their former rhythm section while in the studio, quickly adding bassist Rod Hawkes (aka 'Hawk Eye'). Drummer Graham Ditchfield replaced Kinsell in 1982 and played on both the *Death Penalty* and *Friends Of Hell* albums, but was replaced by 'Derm The Germ' (Dermot Redmond), who played

---

WITCHFINDER GENERAL discography

Burning A Sinner, Heavy Metal HEAVY 6 (UK) (1981)
Soviet Invasion, Heavy Metal 12HM 17 (UK) (1982)
DEATH PENALTY, Heavy Metal HMRLP 8 (UK) (1982)
Music, Heavy Metal HEAVY 21 (UK) (1983)
FRIENDS OF HELL, Heavy Metal HMRLP 13 (UK) (1983)
LIVE '83, Buried By Time And Dust / Nuclear War Now!
    Productions ANTI-GOTH 039 (UK / USA) (2006)

live with the band in 1983 and 1984. The group then fractured, with Ditchfield subsequently forming a reggae band, Chico In Cognito. The band officially ceased activities in November 1984.

Japanese label Teichiku reissed *Death Penalty* in 1990 in an inoffensive plain gold sleeve. That same year Metallica drummer Lars Ulrich included the track 'Witchfinder General' on his NWOBHM collection through Phonogram, *New Wave Of British Heavy Metal '79 Revisited*.

In recent times Witchfinder General have enjoyed posthumous respect from numerous death metal and doom bands. Despite the swell of interest in NWOBHM across Europe, it looked as though the Witchfinder General albums would never be reissued – as Heavy Metal label boss Paul Birch, a born-again Christian, objected to the band's lyrical stance. However, after much pressure, *Death Penalty* finally saw a 1996 CD release. *Friends Of Hell* was released on CD in 1998.

A rather oblique tribute was paid to the band when the Japanese grindcore band Bathtub Shitter's 2003 album *Lifetime Shitlist* found the band tackling 'No Stayer'. Coventry doom act Cathedral covered Witchfinder General's 'Rabies' on their 2004 archive collection *The Serpent's Gold*.

It would appear that the Witchfinder General legacy is secure, as US label Nuclear War Now! dug up archive concert recordings to issue as the *Live '83* album in 2006.

WITCHFYNDE
THE OTHER NWOBHM WITCH HUNTERS

FORMED IN 1976, North Nottinghamshire's Witchfynde stood for a time at the forefront of the NWOBHM movement. They were also one of the earliest forerunners of the occult/black metal genre.

The band signed to Round Records, releasing their first single 'Give 'Em Hell' in 1979 (the label reissued it in 1980 after renaming itself Rondelet) and supporting Def Leppard on tour. Although a deliberate air of mystery was cultivated thanks to the band's supposed 'dark practices', very real curiosity surrounded them after the release of their second album, 1981's *Stagefright*, when they apparently disappeared. During this period bassist Andro Coulton left, replaced by Pete Surgey. Witchfynde eventually re-emerged in 1983 with a new vocalist, Chalky White (aka Luther Beltz), replacing Steve Bridges, and released a successful single, 'I'd Rather Go Wild'. The ensuing concept album, *Cloak And Dagger*, was issued on Expulsion Records.

In the summer of 1984 Surgey was replaced by former Panza Division bassist Alan Edwards. There followed another lengthy absence before their next album on yet another label, the Belgian-based Mausoleum, with

---

WITCHFYNDE discography

GIVE 'EM HELL, Rondolet ABOUT 1 (UK) (1980)
STAGEFRIGHT, Rondolet ABOUT 2 (UK) (1981)
CLOAK AND DAGGER, Expulsion EXIT 15 (UK) (1983)
LORDS OF SIN, Mausoleum LORD 835354 (UK) (1984)
THE WITCHING HOUR, Edgy EDGY 113 (UK) (2001)

---

new member Edd Wolfe (Alan Edwards). The first 10,000 copies of *Lords Of Sin* came with a free four-track live EP titled *Anthems*, featuring 'Give 'Em Hell', Cloak And Dagger', 'Moon Magic' and 'I'd Rather Go Wild'. The band slunk back into the shadows in 1986, seemingly for good.

In 1995 Surgey and Beltz were reported to be playing in the blues covers band The Accelerators. However, in 1999 press announcements claimed that drummer Gra Scoresby (a founding member of Witchfynde), Beltz, guitarist Montalo (another original member) and Surgey were back together. These reports appeared to be spurious, however, as Beltz had been gigging with Stormwatch, with no intention of joining Witchfynde.

Beltz eventually founded The Luther Beltz Band alongside members of Stormwatch, briefly roping in former Saxon guitarist Graham Oliver. This outfit's first move was to cover a track for a low-budget European Demon tribute album.

The group evolved to incorporate Beltz and Montalo with Stormwatch bassist Dave Hewitt and ex-Savage and Dawntrader drummer Dave Lindley. However, by 2000 the Witchfynde story had become entangled in chaos as two bands were operating under the same name. Beltz and Hewitt were announced as playing at the prestigious German 'Wacken Open Air' festival as Witchfynde – as were Montalo, Scoresby and Surgey with fresh vocalist ex-Rebel and Clownhouse singer Harry Harrison, also billed as Witchfynde. However, with promoters as perplexed as the fans, neither band took to the stage.

The Beltz-led band took on the revised brand of Wytchfynde (note subtle spelling difference) and issued a new album for Demolition, *The Awakening*, during 2001. In parallel, the Harrison-led Witchfynde also recorded a new album, *The Witching Hour*, that same October. Beltz's outfit appeared to be in a state of disarray during early 2002. A new guitarist was inducted, Harris Nixon of The Carnival, although later Hewitt would team up with Tyrant, a new act founded by ex-Solstice guitarist Rich Walker.

Witchfynde, alongside Diamond Head, Jaguar, Praying Mantis and Bronz, united for the 25th Anniversary Of NWOBHM concert on November 4th 2005 at the Astoria in London. They retain a strong following.

AMERICAN THRASH METAL

AS HISTORY

has shown us, thrash metal was spawned by the New Wave Of British Heavy Metal. All the scene's major players had held affection for the USA's homegrown rock heroes throughout their school years, such as Van Halen, Kiss and Aerosmith, but at a pivotal juncture, just as these budding musicians had become old enough to strap on a guitar and decide on their own path to glory, they were hit by the underground and very cool concept of NWOBHM. With a natural teenage desire to make something of their own, the obvious choice was to play these songs faster, with more aggression, and with more determination. They had seen the logical progression from rock to metal and now it was their turn.

In truth, the leap wasn't so great. The more adrenalised elements of NWOBHM acts such as Def Leppard, Iron Maiden, the chugging Angel Witch, Blitzkrieg and the lightning-fast Savage bore remarkable similarities to the music that the young Americans were then crafting in their garages. Another huge influence was Motörhead. This new force opened the door to armies of teens armed with Flying Vs, bullet belts and a sense of purpose that would fuel genres such as thrashcore, crossover, technical speed metal and progressive metal.

There is an argument that upholds punk as another motivator for the budding thrashers. Certainly punk's street ethic played a part, but musically the thrash bands aspired towards technical proficiency, the antithesis of the punk approach. Furthermore, the precision of the riffing in thrash – executed with a machine-like picking-hand technique to ensure clarity at high speed – was always a point of discussion among fans when gauging the merits of bands and music. There was little room for punk's riffing sloppiness in these songs that relied on dizzying time signatures and complex, often lengthy structures built on riffs that alternated between chugging and shredding.

The focal point for the fledgling movement was California. In the Bay Area of San Francisco and Oakland, a collection of aspiring musicians had their thirst for speed satiated by a clutch of import record stores, such as Moby Disc and Oz Records, DJ Ron Quintana's KUSF *Rampage Radio* show, and in fanzines such as KJ Doughton's *Northwest Metal* and Metal Blade boss Brian Slagel's *New Heavy Metal Revue*. These outlets prompted the formation of school bands that morphed into Exodus, Anvil Chorus, Possessed, Blind Illusion, Vicious Rumors, Legacy, Control and Metal Church. Further down the coast, Los Angeles and its environs played host to Metallica, Abattoir, Agent Steel, Dark Angel and Slayer.

Surprisingly, the cultural centre of New York and New Jersey came in strictly second place, despite the presence of Anthrax and Overkill. Overkill staked an arguable claim to the very first thrash song with 1981's 'Unleash The Beast Within'. The only other real hot spot was Arizona, home to Flotsam And Jetsam and Sacred Reich.

Once instigated, thrash metal rose to ascendancy with suitable speed. Metal Church's instrumental demo *Red Skies* arrived in late 1981 and Metallica's *Power Metal* demo appeared in April 1982. Metallica's debut album, *Kill 'Em All*, hit the metal scene foursquare in July 1983. As the rock world reeled, the floodgates opened and thrash dominated throughout 1984 and into 1985 as Anthrax, Slayer, Exodus and Megadeth all debuted in style. By 1986 and 1987 thrash had taken its command of the metal media into the charts, and the genre proved beyond doubt that it was here to stay.

AGENT STEEL
MAD LOCUST METAL?

LOS ANGELES-BASED AGENT STEEL forged a reputation for precise, intense metal with a distinct, high-altitude vocal range and for their sci-fi, apocalyptic lyrical stance. The group made impressive headway in the UK and Europe, even attaining headlining status at London's Hammersmith Odeon, before imploding just as they seemed ready to step up into the big league.

Created by frontman John Camps, the roots of Agent Steel lay in Sanctuary, an act that dated back to 1980, when John Cyriis and drummer Chuck Profus co-founded a band under that name in November of that year, which folded during December 1981. Cyriis then formed a shortlived outfit dubbed Toxic Shok, initiated by ex-Deceiver guitarist Kurt 'Kilfelt'

Colfelt. When this project faltered, Camps was next to be found on the track 'Taken By Force' contributed by Sceptre to the Metal Blade Records 1983 compilation album *Metal Massacre IV*. As guitarist for Sceptre, the São Paulo-born, Guitar Institute of Technology-trained John Camps (aka João Campos) also featured as lead vocalist on the Abattoir track 'Screams From The Grave'. Camps, renaming himself John Syriis and later Cyriis, had auditioned for the position of lead vocalist with Abattoir. Demonstrating an impressive multi-octave range, he secured the position easily. However, within six months Cyriis was ousted and along with Chuck Profus engineered a new proposition billed as Agent Steel. During the interim, Profus was in a band called Abuser with bassist George Robb between October 1983 and July 1984.

Subsequently, the pair hooked up with George Robb in August to form Agent Steel, rounded out by guitarists Bill Simmons and Mark

Marshall. Strangely, John Cyriis issued a statement on September 17th 1984 claiming that Agent Steel had officially changed their name to Sanctuary. The line-up of the band at this time credited Cyriis, Mark Marshall, John Gott, George Robb and Chuck Profus. This was followed eight days later with a statement asking people to disregard the previous letter and stating that "the band is and always will be called Agent Steel". This inaugural line-up cut the four-song demo *144,000 Gone* in 1984.

As a portent of things to come, Agent Steel underwent a complete switch of guitarists when Marshall and Simmons were both removed. Marshall would go on to make his mark with Savage Grace. John Gott briefly occupied the six-string position before ex-Abattoir man Juan Garcia and former Toxik Shok colleague Kurt Colfelt were inducted as permanent members for the groundbreaking *Skeptics Apocalypse* album. This Jay Jones-produced LP, issued in August 1985 by Combat in the USA and Roadrunner Records in the UK, made an immediate global impact. Predictably, this band roster was also to prove fragile. Colfelt would bow out, later gaining recognition with the *Terror And Submission* album for his new act Holy Terror, and in his stead would come the teen protégé Bernie 'Versaille' Versye.

The leading thrash metal journal of the time, Britain's *Metal Forces*, would see editor Bernard Doe citing *Skeptics Apocalypse* as one of his favourite albums of the year, while readers voted Cyriis the fourth best metal vocalist.

The band made their first live appearance opening for Slayer in September 1984 at the Los Angeles Country Club. A brace of headliners later and Agent Steel were invited to open for British metallers Raven. To quicken the pace between albums and satisfy demand, the band released a highly praised 1985 EP titled *Mad Locust Rising*, which featured an extreme cover of Judas Priest's 'The Ripper'. Unfortunately, the internal ructions continued unabated, as Robb too made his exit in favour of bassist Michael Zaputil.

With thrash metal achieving an international high, Agent Steel put in a notable show at the infamous Dutch 'Aardschok Dag' festival and toured Europe as support to Overkill and Anthrax, billed the 'Speed Metal Attack' tour, during May of 1986. The band's media profile would be raised during this period with stories that Cyriis, dictating in interviews that he was convinced that a Mayan end-of-days theory signalled the end of the world, started to sign his autograph as '2011' – the supposed date of the impending apocalypse. This eccentricity only served to enhance Agent Steel's reputation.

The *Unstoppable Force* album, produced by Dan Johnson at Morrisound Studios, raised the band's reputation, although critics did note a mellowing of Cyriis' vocal delivery. Agent Steel were by now the subject of numerous major-label inquiries, and in November 1986 reports leaked out that Capitol were showing a serious desire to sign the band. Agent Steel showcased successfully for the label, but as negotiations dragged on, the proposed deal withered.

Unstoppable Force emerged in March 1987 but the band fractured once again. Garcia quit to form Evil Dead with his ex-Abattoir colleague bassist Mel Sanchez. Garcia, alongside future Testament and Slayer drummer John Dette, would also found the Spanish-language metal band Terror, later cutting the 1997 Mexican release *Hijos De Los Cometas*.

Cyriis and Profus, having relocated to Florida, conducted a European tour by drafting in hired hands, with guitarists James Murphy and Jay Weslord figuring among their number, as well as ex-Purgatory bassist Richard Bateman. This variant of Agent Steel put in their biggest concert to date, headlining at London Hammersmith Odeon supported by Nuclear Assault and Onslaught.

In December 1987 members of Agent Steel were arrested in Arizona on charges of aggravated assault on a youth. The bizarre allegations centred upon a 17-year-old male – actually a band roadie – whom the band had allegedly tied to a bed while urinating on him and exploding firecrackers on his chest. The charges were dropped, but another strange incident, in which Cyriis allegedly tried to force band members to get Agent Steel tattoos, also generated some unwelcome press attention. Whether the rumours of forced tattooing are true or not is unclear, but the fact remains that many of Cyriis's former associates sport Agent Steel tattoos.

In 1988 the troubled Agent Steel officially disbanded. While Cyriis, Garcia, Profus and guitar player Michael Hill assembled Pontius Prophet, issuing a two-track demo, *Rites Of Hatred*, that same year, guitarist James Murphy joined Hallows Eve, Death, Obituary and Cancer. He would also figure in the ever-fluid Testament line-up, record with the Danish band Konkhra, and release solo product.

Before the close of 1988 Cyriis declared his intention to retire. Profus would put his efforts into a new venture billed as Malfeitor, in union with ex-Pontius Prophet guitarist Michael Hill. Adding to the intrigue, it was soon revealed that Malfeitor's vocalist 'Max Kobol' was in truth none other than John Cyriis. Cyriis/Kobol then became frontman for Tampa, Florida, band Lemegeton, appearing on their *Evil Against Evil* demo. Cyriis re-emerged in 1990 fronting New York's Black Reign. None of his post-Agent Steel ventures got beyond the demo stage.

Ex-member Richard Bateman enrolled in Nasty Savage in 1989. A decade later Bateman founded After Death with ex-Morbid Angel, Nocturnus and Incubus man Mike Browning. Tragically, Bateman was later killed in a car accident.

Agent Steel reformed in 1999, prompted by an offer to perform at the annual German 'Wacken Open Air' festival. German label Century Media would aid their cause by reissuing their entire back catalogue, each record featuring bonus tracks. Agent Steel's reformation line-up consisted of ex-Sybil singer Bruce Hall, guitarists Juan Garcia and Bernie Versailles, erstwhile Evil Dead bassist Karl Medina and drummer Chuck Profus.

The industrious Versailles also contributed to the Engine project album, assembled by Armored Saint's Joey Vera and Fates Warning's Ray Alder, as well as standing in as live guitarist for Fates Warning.

Agent Steel cut the second Judas Priest track of their career with 'Beyond The Realms Of Death' for the Dwell label's tribute album *Hell Bent For Metal*. It would also be included as a bonus track on American-release versions issued by Metal Blade of the band's uncompromisingly intense comeback album *Omega Conspiracy*.

Solidifying the reunion, Agent Steel toured Germany in early 2000 on a package bill with Riot, Anvil and Domine. Meanwhile Cyriis, apparently now going under the name of Max Havlock, resurfaced again in 2000 with a fresh act titled Outer Gateways.

With Cyriis making a legal claim upon the band title, Agent Steel would rename themselves Order Of The Illuminati for new recording

---

AGENT STEEL discography

SKEPTICS APOCALYPSE, Roadrunner RR 9759 (Europe), Combat MX 8029 (USA) (1985)

Mad Locust Rising, Music For Nations 12KUT 124 (UK), Combat MX 8080 (USA) (1986)

UNSTOPPABLE FORCE, Music For Nations MFN 66 (UK), Combat 88561-8096-2 (USA) (1987)

OMEGA CONSPIRACY, Candlelight CANDLE038CD (UK) (1999), Metal Blade 3984-14333-2 (USA) (2000)

ORDER OF THE ILLUMINATI, Scarlet SC 063-2 (Europe), The End 538 (USA) (2003)

Earth Under Lucifer, Scarlet SC 075-2 (Europe) (2003)

projects in 2001. As such the band laid down a cover of Black Sabbath's 'Hole In The Sky' for donation to a tribute album, *Evil Lives: A True Metal Tribute To Black Sabbath*. The same year would witness the retirement of Profus, with Rigo Amezcua taking over the drum stool for the band's appearance at the Kalamazoo 'Metal' festival. Versailles also found time to act as producer for death metal band Sadistic Intent.

As 2002 dawned it appeared that the relationship between Cyriis and the ongoing band had defrosted somewhat, with a possibility that the next studio album might emerge under the Agent Steel banner after all. In March the band performed the second annual 'Hellfest' event in Whittier, California, alongside fellow vets Exodus. That December Cyriis resurfaced in yet another new band, Stellar Seed.

Agent Steel signed to the Italian Scarlet label and in May 2003 under the Agent Steel banner issued the *Order Of The Illuminati* album, recorded at Cameltoe Studios in Bellflower, California. UK and European dates in October, dubbed the 'Bonded By Metal' trek, found Agent Steel co-headlining a billing comprising Exodus, Nuclear Assault, God Dethroned, Mortician, Occult and Callenish Circle. However, the band removed themselves from this billing halfway through the trek due to disagreements with the booking agency.

Agent Steel announced a high-profile return to the live circuit with an appearance at the 'Keep It True IV' festival held in April 2005 at the Tauberfrankenhalle in Lauda-Koenigshofen, Germany. To celebrate the 20th anniversary of *Skeptics Apocalypse*, they performed the thrash classic in its entirety. Subsequent European gigs saw Belgian thrashers After All as support. That same month Bruce Hall was announced as new frontman for Steel Prophet.

On July 9th 2005 Agent Steel lined up at The Pound outdoor amphitheatre in San Francisco alongside Testament, Vicious Rumors, Lääz Rockit, Hirax, Dreams Of Damnation, Dekapitator, Mudface, Neil Turbin, Brocas Helm and Imagika for the 'Thrash Against Cancer' benefit. Working with producer Bill Metoyer, the band entered the studio on October 17th to craft a new album. Agent Steel announced a signing with Dutch label Mascot Records in July 2006. Their fans eagerly await the next step.

ANNIHILATOR
TECHNICALLY EXPERT POWER/THRASH METALLERS

THE VANCOUVER-BASED metal band Annihilator gained distinction as Canada's leading thrash metal outfit. Guitarist Jeff Waters, the only constant member in the band's history, is known for his inventive riffing style. Prior to founding Annihilator, Waters had been a member of Ottawa's Trojan Hammer. Featuring a line-up of Waters, vocalist John Perinbam, bass player Kevin Jung and drummer Mike Lane, Trojan Hammer managed only two gigs, at the Churchill Arms. Waters and Perinbam also assembled a recording outfit along with drummer Mike Farmer, dubbed The Jeff Waters Project, just before forming the first Annihilator line-up.

At its earliest stage Annihilator was a duo of vocalist-guitarist Waters and vocalist John Bates. This pair demoed the song 'Annihilator', with Waters handling all instrumentation, including the drums. Once this song had been put down on tape, bass player David Scott was then enrolled – but the trio's eagerness to present the act as a full-blown band unit meant that friend Rob Lange, who had just rendered the demo artwork, stood in as a pseudo-drummer for the first Annihilator 'band' photograph.

The outfit then located a real drummer, Paul Malek, and expanded their sound by employing second guitarists Myles Rourke and Joe Bongiorno in quick and equally fleeting succession. Malek offered the basement of his mother's clothing store as a rehearsal space and it was

---

here that the *Welcome To Your Death* sessions were conducted. However, Malek opted out and Québec native Richard Death manned the drums for a short period.

Reinstating Malek, this line-up produced a further demo, billed *Phantasmagoria*, with Waters assuming lead vocals, after which Annihilator again re-formed. Interest had been gained from a business manager in Vancouver, prompting a relocation from Ottawa for the guitarist in August 1987. Once established in British Columbia, Waters set about constructing an entirely fresh band, joined by second guitarist Casey Taeves and former Assault drummer Ray Hartmann. Singer Dennis Dubeau had been auditioned but Waters chose the peroxide-maned, hard-drinking ex-DOA and Iron Gypsy bassist Randy Rampage. DOA had been a renowned act that also provided the launch platform for Black Flag and Danzig drummer Chuck Biscuits. Pre-Annihilator, Rampage had even issued a solo 12-inch EP in 1982. The new-look Annihilator cut the two-song *Alison Hell* demo in 1988, this effort landing the band a deal with Roadrunner. Two further tracks, 'Wicked Mystic' and 'Word Salad', were also worked up during this period. Casey Taeves was to last a matter of days, enough to appear in one official photograph. Bassist Wayne Darley enrolled in 1989. Meanwhile, Paul Malek created Ivory Knight alongside Perinbam for the *Voices In Your Nightmare* demo.

Annihilator's traditional approach to metal gave them prominence toward the end of the thrash boom and their September 1989 debut album *Alice In Hell*, opening deceptively with the acoustic arpeggio of 'Crystal Ann' before launching into a barrage of technical thrash, won them many converts. Acknowledged as one of the very finest works of the genre, *Alice In Hell* – assembled at Fiasco Brothers Studios during the latter half of 1988 – was financed by a Canadian government grant. Although guitarist Anthony Greenham, bassist Darley and drummer Hartmann are credited on the debut Annihilator album they did not take part in the recording, as Waters himself laid down all the instrumentation except drums. Apparently in a similar way to the Casey Taeves situation, Greenham had auditioned for the band and even appeared in the photo shoot for the *Alice In Hell* album and is credited on the sleeve, but in later

years Waters maintained that Greenham was never a band member. He did however appear in a promotional video for the song 'Alison Hell'

Taking *Alison Hell* on the road, now with Dave Scott Davis installed on guitar, ultimately led to the dismissal of Rampage. Towards the close of a US-Canadian trek allied with Testament, the singer apparently voiced concerns over commitments to his day job. Fearing this would jeopardise touring plans, Rampage was let go – much to the chagrin of fans. Although Annihilator had come late in the day to the first thrash wave, the sheer quality and ferocity of the debut soon had many earmarking the group as a force to be reckoned with. The title track 'Alison Hell' made great inroads on the international metal scene, generating solid album sales.

For 1990's *Never, Neverland* album the Omen, Panther and Prisoner credited singer Coburn Pharr took the vocal position, as Annihilator seemed poised on the edge of becoming a major act. Some fans bemoaned the absence of Rampage's high-powered roar, despite Pharr's greater range, and many were bemused by the oddball 'Kraf Dinner', an ode to macaroni and cheese. The bulk of *Never, Neverland* stood up well, though, capitalising on the debut.

The band set out on a world tour as a single-guitar combo – Dave Scott Davis having lost his place – and played the prestigious European support slot on Judas Priest's 'Painkiller' tour. *Never, Neverland* doubled the sales of its illustrious predecessor, but Waters still had his eye on potential recognition outside the band, auditioning for Megadeth in 1990. According to Dave Mustaine, Waters came close to securing the position – but it was not to be. Once live work for *Never, Neverland* had been fulfilled, Pharr took his leave, only to return to the ranks shortly afterward as Annihilator pulled in second guitar player Neil Goldberg. However,

once again Pharr decamped, subsequently re-fronting Omen. The band fractured further still as Ray Hartmann relinquished his post.

Further line-up changes slowed progress, with August 1993's *Set The World On Fire* utilising singer Aaron Randall. While Hartmann had contributed percussive work to three tracks, drums on the song 'Phoenix Rising' were supplied by Rick Fedyk of Double Dealer and Mike Mangini. *Set The World On Fire* mellowed Annihilator's trademark sound somewhat, even succumbing to balladry, a factor picked up by both fans and critics. The single from the album was a nod to their former touring colleagues – a rework of Judas Priest's 'Hell Bent For Leather'. The line-up of Waters, Randall, Goldberg, Darley and drummer Mike Mangini took to European stages, after which the drummer bailed out to join Extreme in time for their 1994 Castle Donington festival appearance. Goldberg also exited and was replaced by former guitarist Dave Scott Davis for a headlining Canadian tour and US dates supporting Lillian Axe, but the beleaguered band stoically committed themselves to Japanese shows. Despite Darley being unable to participate on the Japanese dates, Annihilator soldiered on with former guitar player Dave Scott Davis covering the bass position. New man Randy Black took on drum duties, and this quartet also embarked on a short run of US shows .

In 1994, Annihilator – now minus their deal with Roadrunner – saw Waters tackling lead vocals alongside drummer Randy Black. This duo delivered the 1994 album *King Of The Kill* for Music For Nations. Subsequently, Dave Scott Davis was reinstated and Cam Dixon was drafted on bass. Roadrunner delivered a parting shot with the *Bag Of Tricks* compilation in October, this valuable collection pooling demos, live material and the previously unreleased songs 'Back To The Crypt', 'Gallery' and 'Fantastic Things'.

By 1996 Annihilator had effectively trimmed down to Waters, Scoot Davis and Black. Bassist Lou Bujdoso was drafted in to promote the *Refresh The Demon* album, a groove-themed affair arriving in March 1996. Label distribution for *Refresh The Demon* included CMC International for the USA, Music For Nations in the UK and FEMS in Japan. Just prior to European gigs, the outfit was dealt a heavy blow as Randy Black backed out. After drafting in new drummer Dave Machander, the band went ahead with the gigs. Waters also took time out from his main act to guest on rather more mellow outings, including Pokerface's 1996 album *Life's A Gamble* and the following year's self-titled effort from The Distance. Roadrunner raided their archives further to issue in November the live album *In Command (Live 1989-1990)*, comprising concerts fronted by the Rampage and Pharr line-ups and closing with a cover version of AC/DC's 'Live Wire'.

By December 1996's *Remains*, recorded at the guitarist's own Watersound Studios in Maple Ridge, Annihilator had effectively become Waters's solo project. The band had progressively retreated further from their thrash roots with every release, and *Remains* – to the abject horror of their devoted following – took an even greater leap into the realms of electro and even dance music, aided by guitarist John Bates and singer Dave Steele. The following year Roadrunner reissued the band's early albums in remastered form with additional demo tracks.

The year 1999 saw the band bowing to fan pressure and reinstating both Rampage and Hartmann for the much lauded *Criteria For A Black Widow*, a welcome return to the band's former spirit and heaviness that unashamedly utilised visual, lyrical and musical themes from *Alice In Hell*. Evolving yet again, the band pulled in new bass man Russell Bergquist. Randall and Hartmann, meanwhile, had founded Speeed with Seven Witches and Frostbite guitarist Jack Frost for their 1999 album *Powertrip Pigs*.

Ex-Liege Lord and Overkill man Joe Comeau joined the band in 2000 for *Carnival Diablos*, cementing the thrash revival. With riffs once more in abundance, the group offered up a latter day metal classic in the gargantuan 'Hunter Killer', but their quirky Canadian humour failed them at the last post with the unaccredited 'Chicken & Corn'. Comeau diverted himself in late 2000 with a one-off reunion with his erstwhile Liege Lord guitar partner Paul Nelson to cut a version of 'Too Scared To Run' for a Uriah Heep tribute album.

February 2001 found Annihilator on a headlining tour of Germany supported by a strong billing of Nevermore, Soilwork and Rawhead Rexx. Drummer Ray Hartmann would bow out in favour of the returning Randy Black. In his time away from the fold, the drummer had been busying himself with an ambitious German-based conceptual project band entitled Rebellion. Fronted by erstwhile Xiron and Black Destiny vocalist Michael Seifert, Rebellion had been established by ex-Grave Digger men guitarist Uwe Lulis and bassist Tomi Göttlich, Black as drummer, and with Warhead's Björn Eilen on second guitar. This unit issued their debut *Shakespeare's MacBeth - A Tragedy In Steel* in March 2002.

Throughout the latter half of 2001, Annihilator were preparing for a new studio album, billed *Waking The Fury* and slated for a March 2002 release through the German Steamhammer label. The European version came with a bonus live recording of 'Shallow Grave' and a radio edit of 'Nothing To Me' while Japanese variants added a live 'Refresh The Demon' recorded in Rumania. During November, guitarist Curran Murphy of Aggression Core and Nevermore joined the ranks. However, bassist David Scott Davis would be forced out of the band due to injury. Annihilator announced European tour dates for April and May 2002, commencing in Vienna, Austria and backed up with strong support from Seven Witches and Debase.

In an odd twist of events, Waters joined the veteran epic power metal band Savatage for their summer European 2002 dates. Al Pitrelli, Savatage's recently re-inducted six-stringer, was unable to make the tour due to prior commitments. Annihilator revealed in October that they had signed to the German AFM label for a double live album, suitably entitled *Double Live Annihilation* and set for early 2003 release. That same month it emerged that former Annihilator guitarist Neil Goldberg had assembled a rap-flavoured nu-metal project dubbed Redlist, working in league with Talisman and Yngwie Malmsteen veteran singer Jeff Scott Soto, keyboard player and programmer Dave Fraser and a rapper named Eric.

Guitarist Curran Murphy garnered production credits with San Francisco metal band Vengince, crafting their self-titled debut album at Smiley Studios in Seattle. Randy Black then deputised for German power metal band Primal Fear's summer 2003 US dates, joining them full-time during August. In May, vocalist Joe Comeau backed out and Annihilator duly replaced him with the Vancouver native Dave Padden. The band's European tour schedule throughout June and July saw appearances at the German 'Rock Harz' and 'Wacken Open Air' festivals, the Italian 'Summer Day In Hell' event, the Swiss 'Metal Dayz' gig and the 'Waldrock' Netherlands show.

With Randy Black firmly in position with Primal Fear, the band welcomed back former drummer Mike Mangini in October for recording of a new studio album entitled *All For You*, released through The End label in the USA and by the German AFM label. Bassist Russell Bergquist, pursuing a solo venture, exited the band in January 2004. A new rhythm section of bassist Sandor de Bretan, previously with Sudden Thunder, and drummer Rob Falzano was installed during March. *All For You* certainly presented a new sound for the band, observers picking up on Padden's vocal similarities to Duran Duran's Simon Le Bon and the music a good deal more diverse than before.

In other activity, Jeff Waters and Curran Murphy had their composition 'Forever Ends' included on the April 2004 *Cans Beyond The Gates* album, a solo effort from Hammerfall vocalist Joacim Cans. Also keeping himself active, Joe Comeau stepped in as temporary bassist for Painmuseum's performance at the New Jersey March 'Metal Meltdown VI'

festival. Annihilator gained a valuable round of support dates on Judas Priest's European dates in June.

In August it was revealed that Waters had been in talks with Megadeth's Dave Mustaine. Already holding a placing in Megadeth's history, Waters was in consideration for the live line-up of the band, but this union did not transpire. Waters was, however, engaged as engineer on a remix project for fellow Canadian veterans Exciter, remixing the band's first six albums for reissue by Megaforce. Another project under proposal was an all-new band unit with Dave Padden.

In October, Waters created some media waves by brazenly claiming that he was "the fastest/tightest-picking guitarist in the world". Pointedly, not too many people came forward to refute his claims. The year 2005 opened with the guitarist contributing to a conceptual track titled 'War Of Wars' on the Spanish thrash metal band Legen Beltza's *Dimension Of Pain* album. Waters and Curran also guested on the 2005 album *Repent Or Seal Your Fate* by Hannover thrashers Reckless Tide. Jeff also worked on 2005 solo album recordings by Greek keyboard player Bob Katsionis.

In March 2005 vocalist Randy Rampage and drummer Ray Hartmann teamed up with bassist Stu Carruthers of Grip Inc. and Just Cause, guitarist Ash Blue (ex-Strapping Young Lad) and guitarist-vocalist Kick from Vertical After to forge the 'urban punk/metal' band Stress Factor 9. Meanwhile, Curran Murphy announced his new project, Shatter Messiah. Fronting the band was Breaker and ex-Archetype singer Greg Wagner, with Annihilator's Rob Falzano on drums.

Annihilator returned in September 2005 with the *Schizo Deluxe* album, the band's eleventh studio opus, on which Waters and Padden were joined by Ottawa native Tony Chappelle on drums. *Schizo Deluxe* closed the circle in the group's steady musical journey back towards *Alice In Hell*: the reaction to the new record's unbridled retro-thrash was ecstatic, particularly in Europe. Annihilator were rejoined by bassist Russell Bergquist for European touring.

In early January 2006, Dave Padden announced the formation of heavy metal concept Silent Strain, a unit hailing from Canada, Denmark and Russia, comprising Mnemic guitar player Mircea Eftemie Gabriel, second guitarist Cory McBain of Cyanotic, bassist Rick Struve from God Awakens and Civil Ruin, and Igor Chiefot on the drums. The following month, ex-Annihilator man Joe Comeau joined Swedish metal band Tad Morose as their new frontman.

European gigs were announced for July but then postponed in order to complete album recordings. However, Annihilator did still play the Spanish 'Metalway' festivals, in Guernica and Jerez, as a quartet with Waters, Dave Padden handling both vocals and rhythm guitar, returning bassist Russ Bergquist and drummer Ryan Ahoff.

Waters remains one of the thrash metal scene's most gifted players.

ANTHRAX
WHEN THRASH MET SKATEWEAR – AND SURVIVED

ANTHRAX ARE THE EAST COAST cornerstone of the celebrated Big Four Of Thrash Metal who struck North America during the mid 1980s. While Metallica, Megadeth and Slayer were all Californian in origin, New Yorkers Anthrax rapidly developed their own distinct style, partly by avoiding the serious nature of their competitors' lyrical themes through topics such as social issues, Stephen King novels, comic-book heroes such as Judge Dredd, and plentiful cover versions. The group found an enthusiastic fanbase in Europe, which then transferred to North America when their then-radical fusion of metal and hip-hop broke the band into platinum status.

Along the way, Anthrax sparked a fleeting fashion wave of beach shorts, although unfortunately this perceived reliance on image over content provoked a backlash among fans that undoubtedly damaged the band's reputation at a pivotal point in their career. Their adoption of the NYHC 'Applecore' logo and a penchant for skateboard culture also drew critical ire. The group did bounce back from these aberrations, through sheer dogged persistence, and despite an increasingly fragile line-up has remained a solid force on the international metal scene. Anthrax were without question the most musically adventurous of the major players, their experimentation crossing musical boundaries that others had deemed uncrossable.

Band mentor ex-Four X guitarist Scott Ian (Scott Ian Rosenfeld) put the band together while attending Bayside High School in Queens, with fellow students Dan Lilker on guitar, a gangly mop-topped veteran of White Heat, and Ken Kushner on bass. Roadie John Connolly briefly tried out for the vocal position, and Dirk Kennedy of Hittman has also claimed an early association. The Anthrax title was suggested by Lilker.

Dan Lilker: "I came up with the name when it came up in hygiene class. The teacher was talking about diseases and I just thought the name had a great sound to it, great for a metal band. When I saw the word written on the board it looked cool too."

Kushner, who subsequently forged World Bang, soon lost his post to Paul Kahn who in turn was replaced on four-string by Dan Lilker; Greg Walls also joined as second guitarist. Connolly was first superseded by Scott Ian's 14-year-old brother Jason Ian before the role of frontman was stabilised in August 1982 with the acquisition of ex-Amra singer Neil Turbin, another Bayside student. The band's first drummer, Dave Weiss, was forced out when he was severely injured in a hit-and-run car accident. The position was duly filled by Greg D'Angelo. In later years Jason Ian re-emerged fronting Reverend.

Before enrolling Turbin, the budding Anthrax had performed a brace of 'pay to play' shows at the North Stage Dinner Theatre in Glen Cove and My Father's Place. A further switch in personnel saw Walls briefly replaced by Bob Berry, a blues player who had been recommended by Riot's Rhett Forrester. Berry's tenure was fleeting, and Dan Spitz, an employee at Rudi's Music on 48th Street and ex-member of another notable proto-thrash outfit – New Jersey's Overkill – was drawn into the fold. Anthrax's dedication was already paying dividends. Their refusal to perform only original material contributed to their popularity in New York among fans but did create practical problems.

Neil Turbin: "Scott was big on equipment, in fact the whole band was. When Anthrax played even back then we went out with the full backline: double-stacked Marshall cabs either side. Of course, having the Kiss logo on our road cases was also a talking point too. Getting Danny Spitz into the band was a good call. Scott had at least seven guitars and every pedal imaginable, and Danny had similar gear. It really helped that he could totally shred on the guitar too. Danny brought a lot of skill into the band. He was cocky, challenging, always in your face, but he and Scott clicked and it made for some great riffing."

Neil Turbin: "We refused to play covers. That was an easy way out and a lot of bands did it, but Anthrax was about total metal, total originality. I remember when we played our first gig to promote the album we did a headline slot at just under 40 minutes. The promoter went crazy! He wanted us to go and play some more, play some covers. Scott just said, 'No covers'. That was the way Anthrax was back then."

The band's first recording, at Sonic Recording Studios in Fremont, Long Island, was a three-song demo comprising 'Sin', 'Antichrist' and 'Hunting Dog'. Other recordings included 'Pestilence' and 'Satan's Wheels'. During a second round of recording D'Angelo decided to quit, opting to join Cities before subsequently enjoying a high profile with White Lion. He was duly replaced by Charlie Benante in September 1983.

The band captured the interest of Megaforce guru Jonny Zazula with the track 'Soldiers Of Metal' from a further demo. Zazula and his wife Marsha ran the famous import shop Rock'n'Roll Heaven on the New Jersey turnpike and was already involved in the career of another budding speed metal band – San Francisco's Metallica. In fact, Anthrax had first met Zazula at one of his live promotions featuring Raven, Riot and Anvil. The band then cut their first single, again at Sonic Studios. It was produced by none other than Manowar guitarist Ross Friedman, a.k.a. Ross 'The Boss' Funicello, and entitled 'Soldiers Of Metal', backed by 'Howling Furies'. Three thousand copies of the single were sold in a mere two weeks.

The role of the Zazulas as catalysts for thrash metal cannot be underestimated. Anthrax had yet to hear the term 'thrash metal' but their collective quest for new music and the arrival of Zazula's protégés Metallica provided the spark.

Neil Turbin: "The Zazulas used to run a stall on a flea market. They had all this stuff we had never seen before. Really cool, advanced stuff like Tank, Angel Witch, Warning from France, Venom, Loudness and Accept. Most of the metal we were absorbing came through Johnny Jonny.

"I guess Anthrax was a heavy metal band back then. When Metallica arrived, it certainly changed Scott's way of thinking too. Jonny played him a Metallica demo, I remember. We all had different influences: Scott with Cheap Trick and Iron Maiden; Danny Lilker with Angel Witch; mine was Judas Priest 'Hell Bent For Leather', Saxon and Accept. In fact the track 'Metal Thrashing Mad', which is where a lot of journalists picked up on the word 'thrash', was written by myself when I was trying to get that kind of groove metal sound Accept had on 'Flash Rockin' Man'. I used the word 'thrash' because I felt 'Metal Headbanging Mad' didn't sound right. It was in a British magazine called Kerrang!. It was in a review for Exciter but the journalist, Malcolm Dome, referred to us by name as a reference and called Anthrax a thrashing band. Up until then we called ourselves speed metal."

Scott Ian: "Punk and metal were the two influences on the early band. Iron Maiden and the NWOBHM scene was really important, and we bought any of those singles and albums that we could. In New York, punk was giving the band that extra edge, too, and we had that with the riffs and the speed we were picking up on from the European bands. It was very exciting then. It seemed like every single you bought by a new band was giving you something new. Anthrax was a really hungry band and we just devoured this stuff."

A variety of shows locally and as far afield as Boston, where they opened for Swiss act Krokus, gained the band an ever-increasing following and contributed to the initial success of their *Fistful Of Metal* debut album, produced by Carl Canedy of The Rods. Initially, Ross The Boss was projected to record the LP, but delays caused by out-of-commission studios in Rochester saw this plan scotched. Before a new location could be found, the band spent three nights sleeping in a hotel basement before travelling on to craft their record at Pyramid Recording in Ithaca. The recording of the album was not a smooth ride: with the *Fistful* sessions underway, tensions started to surface that would ultimately lead to Turbin's departure. Post-Anthrax, Turbin would work with Japanese guitar god Kuni on his 1986 album *Masque*. In 1988 he was fronting the Kurt James Band. After a relocation to California, Turbin involved himself in a myriad of successive projects, which failed to gel.

Neil Turbin: "We were supposed to record the album with Ross the Boss at the same studio Metallica had used to cut Kill 'Em All, but when we got there they were literally pulling all the gear out. The band slept for three nights in this hotel basement whilst we figured out what to do. Finally we went to Ithaca and stayed at the Rock N' Roll Hotel in Cortland. It wasn't a real hotel, just two sisters who put up bands. This is when Carl Canedy came onboard.

"Danny Lilker and I were not the best of friends. Nothing against him, we just never clicked. There was too much about him that was not working. He didn't rehearse, he didn't dress appropriately, and most importantly he didn't learn the songs. He spent all his time playing these Iron Maiden riffs, but when we came to put bass down for 'I'm Eighteen' he just couldn't do it. A very simple, straight-time riff took him a whole day. I was bummed out. It was expensive and things like that meant I had to squeeze all of my vocals into just two days."

Fistful Of Metal, including a rendition of Alice Cooper's 'I'm Eighteen', certainly made an impact. Although the less than subtle album cover (a fist punching out of a mouth) forced many critics to baulk, the music gave fans of the burgeoning thrash scene reason to celebrate. The record was raw and rushed, but the spirit and attitude eclipsed any technical misgivings. The band recognised their limitations but still remained proud of their first album achievement.

Anthrax then toured the American heartland for the first time on a 40-date trek with Raven. Following the release of *Fistful Of Metal* Dan Lilker left the band and was replaced by Charlie Benante's cousin and Scott Ian's roadie, Frank Bello. Lilker went on to form the thrash-hardcore act Nuclear Assault.

Scott Ian: "That record, y'know, it's very basic. I hate the mix, the guitar sound, everything. For a metal album, the guitars are quite tame for me. Somehow, though, it still works. We captured something there that took Anthrax to the rest of the world."

Anthrax operated minus a vocalist for some two months before the position was briefly filled by Matt Fallon. However, he too departed, causing a delay to recording a planned EP, *Raise Hell*, which was to include a live version of 'Metal Thrashing Mad' and a cover of The Sex Pistols' 'God Save The Queen'. Fallon teamed up with another high profile act, New Jersey's Skid Row, before being ousted from that band before their multi-platinum debut album.

A new vocalist was drafted into the band in November 1984, ex-Bible Black and Megaforce man Joey Belladonna (real name Joseph Bellardini), recruited at the suggestion of Carl Canedy. He debuted on the *Armed And Dangerous* mini-album, which arrived in February 1985. This stopgap release featured re-worked songs from *Fistful Of Metal* plus that Pistols cover.

Ian and Benante's side project with M.O.D.'s vocalist Billy Milano and erstwhile Anthrax member Dan Lilker was S.O.D. (short for Stormtroopers Of Death), and they released their debut album, *Speak English Or Die*, two months before the second Anthrax album, *Spreading The Disease*. Although strictly amateurish in both concept and design, S.O.D. became a surprise hit, selling large quantities of records worldwide, prompting tour work and conversely giving the next Anthrax album a welcome boost.

Road work in Europe during May 1985 saw Anthrax billed on the 'Metal Hammer Road Shows' alongside Agent Steel and Spitz's former comrades Overkill. The self-produced *Spreading The Disease*, issued in October 1985, carved out a distinctive niche for the band. Firmly in the thrash metal camp, it was possibly their toughest release and set them

apart from other contenders with a unique edge. Joey Belladonna's refined approach to the vocals and the inventive riffing of Ian and Spitz put *Spreading The Disease* ahead of the pack.

Meanwhile, Anthrax's ascendancy had been duly noted by the major labels and Island took on the band for future product. Released in March 1987, *Among The Living*, produced by industry veteran Eddie Kramer, grossed sales of over 400,000. Anthrax's subject matter widened as they delved into Stephen King's horror fiction for the title track. 'Efilnikufesin (N.F.L.)' concerned actor John Belushi's drug tragedy, the plight of native Americans inspired 'Indians', and Judge Dredd comics supplied subject matter for 'I Am The Law'. 'Indians' and 'I Am The Law' were issued as singles and made valuable impressions on the charts, and both became crowd favourites, with 'Indians' often performed onstage by Belladonna in full feathered chieftain head-dress.

February 1987 saw Anthrax traversing mainland Europe with support acts Celtic Frost and Florida's Crimson Glory. The band then toured North America supporting Kiss during 1987 and also appeared at the British Castle Donington 'Monsters Of Rock' festival. Anthrax would guest for Metallica on European dates, too, although these shows were curtailed with the tragic death of Metallica bassist Cliff Burton in Sweden. Further British shows saw Testament in support, while a nationwide tour of America, supported by Exodus and Celtic Frost, rounded off the year.

In 1987 the band's increasing popularity in Japan led to the reissue of *Fistful Of Metal* in new packaging with the addition of a couple of live tracks featuring Joey Belladonna singing 'Panic' and 'Raise Hell'.

Anthrax activated huge crossover appeal with their rap-metal single 'I'm The Man', which was swiftly certified gold in America for 500,000 sales. Truly a cross-cultural piece of work, 'I'm The Man' was co-produced by Eddie Kramer, with a guitar run inspired by the traditional Jewish folk song 'Hava Nagila'. It reached Number 53 on the singles charts, remained lodged on radio and bridged the divide between rap and metal, providing opportunities for other acts in their wake. The EP also included two live cuts and a rendition of Black Sabbath's 'Sabbath Bloody Sabbath'. Strong radio action for 'I'm The Man' rewarded Anthrax with their first platinum award.

The September 1988 album *State Of Euphoria*, co-produced by the band and Alex Perialis, included a version of Trust's 'Antisocial'. *State* continued the upward trend in sales, peaking at Number 30 on the US charts and 12 in the UK, their career best. Touring was once again intensive, as Anthrax opened arena shows for Ozzy Osbourne in late 1988. Dates in Britain with guests Living Color followed before a lengthy headlining jaunt sponsored by MTV and supported by Exodus once more and Germans Helloween. Live work did not end there, though, and Anthrax returned to Britain with fellow Megaforce labelmates King's X as guests. The Anthrax musicians also featured as guests on a rap single by New Yorkers U.F.T.O. in 1988.

Joey Belladonna: "It's interesting how the band is being dissected right now. It's as though people want to know just what makes Anthrax tick, and they're trying to find cracks too: OK, they made it this far, let's start to pull them down before they get a bit too big for those boots. I've started to see that in the magazines now. They just invent stuff and ask the opinion of some guy in a band that we've never met.

"I'm a singer in a successful thrash metal band but I like Steve Perry. So what? I think if you listen to my vocals you can tell there is a lot of passion and craft being put into what I do, at least I hope so, and that comes from listening to all kinds of music. Before Anthrax I was in a heavily Rainbow and Black Sabbath-orientated band so I was scoring all that great stuff from Dio. We all bring our own colour to the music with Anthrax, and I think that is part of what gives the

band its edge. Anthrax is not predictable, album by album, we're not going to give you what you expect, even if it's a cover version. There's a lot in the mix here: there's old style heavy metal, there's New York hardcore, there's punk, there's hip-hop. We're not restricted; there are no barriers."

Anthrax recorded various cover versions during the *State Of Euphoria* sessions for use as B-sides, including The Sex Pistols' 'Friggin' In The Riggin', Kiss's 'Parasite' and The Ventures' 'Pipeline'. These tracks emerged in August of 1989 as the *Penikufesin* EP ('nice fuckin' EP' backwards). This set, bolstered by a French-language version of 'Antisocial', gave Anthrax another gold sales certification in the USA.

The band opened for Iron Maiden on a European tour at the close of 1990 but returned to America to find that their label, Island, had been radically reshaped following its purchase by Polygram, which effectively severed the ties between label and band. In spite of this struggle, the Mark Dodson-produced *Persistence Of Time* album went on to achieve gold status, shifting more than 600,000 copies as Island and Anthrax parted company. Undoubtedly inspired by criticism aimed at the group's light-hearted manner, questionable apparel and a glut of gimmickry, *Persistence Of Time* showed a darker side to Anthrax, bordering on the progressive, with tracks not only longer but deadly serious in nature. An offbeat cover version came with a take on Joe Jackson's 'Got The Time', another hit for the band.

To promote the record, Anthrax undertook a bold move on the live front, touring as part of the 'Clash Of The Titans' arena package in 1991, sharing a co-headlining bill with Megadeth, Slayer and opening act Alice In Chains. The original intention of this touring project was to present an awesome combination of the Big Four Of Thrash including Metallica. Hetfield and co passed on the offer, but nevertheless the assembled bill drew in sizeable crowds. Anthrax employed the clock artwork from the album jacket in their stage set, the hands of time spinning wildly out of control during the title number. For the European leg, Alice In Chains were replaced by Suicidal Tendencies and Anthrax by Testament, but shows were sell-outs almost throughout.

In June 1991 the band compiled the album *Attack Of The Killer B's*, a novel approach that garnered Anthrax yet another gold record. The album contained 'Bring The Noise', B-sides, live tracks and previously unreleased material. A brace of live numbers, 'Keep It In The Family' and 'Belly Of The Beast', had been recorded in 1990 on the 'Persistence Of Time' tour.

'Bring The Noise', recorded first by rappers Public Enemy and originally part of the *Attack Of The Killer B's* album, found its way onto mainstream radio, giving Anthrax an airing to fans outside hard rock. With such exposure, Anthrax and Public Enemy teamed up to tour America as a unique pairing, with support act Young Black Teenagers, a band for whom Benante had provided drumming services on their debut album. The groundbreaking tour encountered problems from reluctant promoters, but in the end over 20 highly successful shows were performed in America. British dates saw Prong as third band on the bill.

Despite riding on an undoubted high, Belladonna shocked fans by leaving. For many years the rumour machine had suggested differences of musical taste between the singer and the core of the band. Anthrax drafted in John Bush, a man who had carved his reputation with Californian metal act Armored Saint and had famously rejected an offer to join Metallica in 1982.

Bush's impressive debut with Anthrax, the Dave Jerden-produced *Sound Of White Noise*, entered the *Billboard* Top 10 in May 1993 and broke the million sales mark in America. Limited-edition variants hosted cover versions of Cheap Trick's 'Auf Wiedersehn', Thin Lizzy's 'Cowboy Song', The Smiths' 'London', Beastie Boys' 'Looking Down The Barrel Of A Gun', Kiss's 'Love Her All I Can', and a Strings Mix of 'Black Lodge'. The Japanese version of the album also had an Al Jourgensen remix of 'Potters Field'. In April 1994, Anthrax's former label Island issued a live album simply dubbed *The Island Years*, mixed by Michael Barbiero and Steve Thompson and taped at Irvine Meadows, California, on October 19th 1991 and at Electric Lady Studios on January 28th 1992.

Although *Sound Of White Noise* performed beyond expectation, the band's fall from grace came remarkably swiftly when, in 1995, they hit an all-time low. The band had switched to work with the Butcher Brothers production team on the *Stomp 442* album. Spitz left the band before recording and, although it was a fine album, *Stomp 442* proved to be the low sales point for the band, only scoring a Number 47 position in *Billboard* that October. Elektra Records and Anthrax duly severed relations; undaunted, the determined band teamed up with horror punks The Misfits for yet another successful tour of America.

With Anthrax in hiatus, Ian and Benante resurrected the original line-up of S.O.D. for a 1997 American tour, culminating in a slot at the Milwaukee 'Metalfest'. Other offbeat endeavours included the convening of Doom Squad, one of the more interesting interpretations lent to the Judas Priest tribute album *Legends Of Metal*. Doom Squad was a one-off band convened for a very much tongue-in-cheek rendition of 'Burnin' Up' and included Scott Ian and John Bush, Armored Saint bassist Joey Vera and drummer Gonzo, with Accept's Jörg Fischer on guitar.

Strangely, a full two years after Danny Spitz had quit Anthrax, his guitar tech Paul Crook was still temping on a live basis. Anthrax found a new stable at Ignition for their next studio outing. Lead guitar duties on the *Volume 8: The Threat Is Real* album, delivered in July 1998, were shared by Ian, Benante and Crook. Pantera's 'Dimebag' Darrell Abbott performed on 'Inside Out' and 'Born Again Idiot' while his bandmate, vocalist Phil Anselmo, guested on 'Killing Box'. Frank Bello sang lead vocals on the 'hidden' bonus track 'Pieces', which closed the record. Outside the metal sphere, Ian sessioned on Tricky's *Angels With Dirty Faces* album. Unfortunately, the slide in appreciation continued downward, with *Volume 8* only making Number 118.

Anthrax returned to Britain for a one-off show in London in October 1998 and bounced back the following year with a best-of album, *Return Of The Killer A's*. The CD had both Belladonna and Bush uniting to record a cover of The Temptations' 'Ball Of Confusion' and remixes by Al Jourgensen of Ministry. In the family spirit, former bassist Dan Lilker also put in an appearance.

With Anthrax's career path now less rigid, John Bush made time to temporarily reunite with Armored Saint during 1999 for their much lauded *Revelation* album but maintained his position with Anthrax. Bush also guested on a version of the Scorpions' 'Blackout' on death metal combo Six Feet Under's *Graveyard Classics* album.

The band's 2000 American tour found Skid Row guitarist Snake filling in. Anthrax went out as guests to Mötley Crüe but, with the tour drawing less than the anticipated numbers, they were unable to fulfil all of the shows and bailed out before the tour's completion. In summer 2001 a

Twisted Sister tribute album, *Twisted And Strange*, would witness Anthrax offering up their take on the glamsters' 'Destroyer'.

Bush's focus in mid 2001 was on an Armored Saint archive collection before recording a new album with Anthrax. Later in the year Anthrax, with new guitarist Rob Caggiano of New York's Boiler Room and producer of acts such as Primer 55, Dry Kill Logic and 36 Crazyfists, were all set to jump on the high-profile 2001 American tour of metal legends Judas Priest for the late summer. The act also announced a new deal with Beyond Records, a subsidiary of BMG. The first fruits of this liaison were the reissued *Stomp 442* and *Sound Of White Noise*, both with rare foreign B-sides added.

However, just before the Judas Priest tour, the terrorist attacks on the USA of September 11th forced the cancellation of all shows. The attacks not only disrupted tour plans but put the very nature of Anthrax's existence into jeopardy: with America assailed by fears of biological and chemical warfare, an anthrax virus scare in October put the spotlight firmly on the band. In a *Washington Post* article, Scott Ian confessed to having stocked up on supplies of the anthrax virus antidote Cipro, vowing: "I will not die an ironic death." Meanwhile, fans were asked to consider if the band should change its name.

As the anthrax terror campaign worsened, the group ironically found themselves afforded the kind of heavyweight press exposure on TV, radio and newsprint they had been lacking for so long. Indeed, the band's official website scored a massive three million hits in just under two weeks.

Anthrax, billed alongside Ace Frehley, Overkill, Sebastian Bach and a reunited Twisted Sister, put in a live appearance on November 28th at New York's Hammerstein Ballroom 'New York Steel' event, a benefit event for families of the New York police and fire officers who had lost their lives at the World Trade Center attacks. The whole event was organised by Eddie Trunk, the esteemed host of WNEW FM's *Saturday Night Rocks!*. Pointedly, the band wore matching boiler suits bearing the legend 'We're Not Changing Our Name'.

Amid all this publicity, former vocalist Neil Turbin announced his comeback with the *Threat Con Delta* album. Amsterdam's Ronnie Borchert, Mitch Perry (erstwhile Michael Schenker Group, Heaven and Talas guitarist) and Kurt James of Steeler and Dr. Mastermind were involved in the studio sessions.

Anthrax finally got to tour with Judas Priest in January 2002 as the re-scheduled dates got underway. An early incident on the sold-out tour came when Caggiano was arrested and jailed for throwing a hot dog at a taxi driver in Denver.

Among the traditional cover versions laid down by the band for the new album, *We've Come For You All*, were takes on 'Next To You' by The Police, The Ramones' 'We're A Happy Family' and U2's 'Exit'. Longtime supporter 'Dimebag' Darrell put in a guest appearance on the tracks 'Cadillac Rock Box' and 'Strap It On'. Incredibly, the band also managed to draft Roger Daltrey of The Who into the studio to lay down vocals on the song 'Taking The Music Back'.

Anthrax would head up a thrash bill of Machine Head, Testament and Exodus in Sao Paolo, Brazil on April 20th. Paul Crook, now a member of Sebastian Bach's live band, debuted his new group Gotham (he joined Meat Loaf's touring band in early 2003), while rumours surfaced that Dan Spitz had recently united with Iron Maiden drummer Nicko McBrain for an undisclosed project. This revelation came unexpectedly, as Spitz had been out of the limelight for many years, becoming a vocal Christian since his departure from the band and devoting himself to gaining qualifications in the precision art of watch-making. Subsequently it was revealed that Spitz was working up new material with his bassist brother, erstwhile Black Sabbath, Great White and Nuclear Assault man Dave 'The Beast' Spitz, with none other than white rap artist Vanilla Ice contributing vocals.

Anthrax's *We've Come For You All*, originally slated for a September issue, was postponed, first pushed back to a February 2003 release and then extended to April. This disappointing news was tempered by word that the band would hook up with Motörhead for European tour dates throughout October. That same month a new Anthrax track, 'Love Siege', was made available as an internet download. The song had been cut for the soundtrack for director John Carpenter's *Ghost Of Mars* movie and included Guns N'Roses guitarist Buckethead on guest lead solos.

Although the group had originally opted to sign with another label for the North American release of *We've Come For You All*, this relationship dissolved and Anthrax signed with Sanctuary for this territory. Nuclear Blast handled the album for Europe. *We've Come For You All* was generally regarded as a return to form, but only grazed *Billboard* at Number 122, an indicator of the long, upward struggle to come.

US versions of the album came with exclusive live video footage of 'Got The Time' in addition to the rare 'Among The Living / I'm The Man / Caught In A Mosh' medley. A promotional video for the album track 'Safe Home' scored a coup by including not only a cameo appearance from nu-punks Sum 41 but also one by *Matrix* movie star Keanu Reeves. European headline dates in March saw Belgians After All as support. Anthrax then reprised the union with Motörhead for US gigs in May.

To coincide with European shows in June, Anthrax released a special two-disc version of *We've Come For You All*, the second disc comprising eight rare tracks. The band would be back out on the road in the USA, commencing on July 29th in San Diego for their ambitious 'Taking The Music Back' 2003 trek. Support for the first leg of shows was lent by Lamb Of God and E. Town Concrete while dates from mid-August onward had Lacuna Coil added as guests. The group also found itself on the television screens of the nation, characterised as the fictional band Titannica in the DVD movie *Run Ronnie Run*.

The year 2004 opened on a happy note for Scott Ian, the guitarist announcing his engagement to longtime girlfriend Pearl Aday, none other than the eldest daughter of Meat Loaf. Fortune continued to smile on Paul Crook as he was subsequently hand picked as lead guitarist for the Queen stage musical *We Will Rock You*. Current guitarist Rob Caggiano kept busy outside Anthrax by producing the *Nymphetamine* album for the renowned British black metal band Cradle Of Filth.

In a surprise move, bassist Frank Bello, after two decades of service to Anthrax, quit in February 2004, relocating to Los Angeles in order to work with a new band being assembled by Page Hamilton of Helmet. The Helmet connection would be strengthened as Scott Ian forged a temporary union with Hamilton to cut a version of 'Motorbreath' for a Metallica tribute album through Big Deal Records entitled *Metallic Assault*.

The band reacted to Bello's defection by pulling in Armored Saint and Fates Warning man Joey Vera as a temporary substitute. Getting back to the road, Anthrax toured Japan and Australia, with support coming from Killswitch Engage and Soilwork in April of 2004, before European festival performances.

That same month saw the arrival of Anthrax's second live album, *Music Of Mass Destruction*, recorded during performances at Chicago's Metro in December 2003. Unfortunately the promotional video for the track 'What Doesn't Die' was rejected by MTV after it had originally been accepted by the *Headbangers Ball* programme. Apparently MTV's watchdogs deemed scenes depicting zombies on fire and Scott Ian knocking the head off a zombie too graphic.

Maintaining the momentum, a collection of Joey Belladonna/Neil Turbin-era songs performed by the band's present line-up, initially dubbed *Metallum Maximum Aeturnum* but then switched to *The Greater Of Two Evils*, arrived in November. The songs had been recorded 'live' in the Avatar studios in New York City over the course of two days and the track list had been voted by fans through the band's website. Before this

release, Anthrax launched their own range of limited-edition vintage-shaped skateboards. The record was promoted by a promotional video for the track 'Deathrider', filmed at the Snitch nightclub in New York City. A US tour, allied with Dio and Fireball Ministry, commenced in September.

That December, a remark from Shadows Fall frontman Brian Fair ignited rumours of a full-blown 'classic' Anthrax reunion of Joey Belladonna, Dan Spitz, Scott Ian, Frank Bello and Charlie Benante. The conjecture gathered pace when this proposed reformation was alleged to be in discussion for a position at the 'Ozzfest' event. By February these rumours would be confirmed, with the classic Anthrax apparently set to take up position on the 'Ozzfest' alongside Iron Maiden and Black Sabbath. Strangely, as momentum for this union gathered, the offer was seemingly withdrawn, certainly damaging the reformation's prospects.

In January 2005 Anthrax's appearance at Holland's 'Dynamo Open Air' festival in May and the French 'Fury Fest', Sweden 'Rock' and Italian 'Gods Of Metal' events in June was confirmed as featuring both Joey Belladonna and Dan Spitz, reuniting the pre-1987 line-up. The band's South American shows of February were affected by the Argentine club fire tragedy of the previous year and new government restrictions forced cancellations in Buenos Aires, Argentina, and Bogata, Colombia.

An all-Brazilian tribute album would be unveiled with *Indians... NOT!*, released by Sao Paulo's Collision label and featuring artists such as Arena Age, Rhestus, Still Life, Hell Trucker, Blakk Market and Dynahead.

On February 23rd, a special show at Chicago's Aragon Ballroom featuring Anthrax, Disturbed, Drowning Pool and Soil was organised to

ANTHRAX discography

Soldiers Of Metal, Megaforce MRS-01 (USA) (1983)

FISTFUL OF METAL, Music For Nations MFN 14 (UK), Megaforce MRI 469 (USA) (1984)

Armed And Dangerous, Megaforce MRS 05 (USA) (1985)

SPREADING THE DISEASE, Music For Nations MFN 62 (UK), Megaforce/Island 7 90480-2 (USA) (1986) **113 USA**

AMONG THE LIVING, Megaforce/Island CID 9865 (UK), Megaforce/Island 7 90584-2 (USA) (1987) **18 UK, 62 USA**

I'm The Man, Megaforce/Island 12IS 338 (UK), Megaforce/Island 7 90685-2 (USA) (1987) **53 USA**

STATE OF EUPHORIA, Megaforce/Island CID 9916 (UK), Megaforce/Island 7 91004-2 (USA) (1988) **12 UK, 30 USA**

PERSISTENCE OF TIME, Megaforce/Island CID 9967 (UK), Megaforce/Island 422-846480-2 (USA) (1990) **13 UK, 24 USA**

ATTACK OF THE KILLER B's, Megaforce/Island CID 9980 (UK), Megaforce/Island 422-848804-2 (USA) (1991) **13 UK, 27 USA**

SOUND OF WHITE NOISE, Elektra 7559-61430-2 (UK / USA) (1993) **14 UK, 7 USA**

STOMP 442, Elektra 7559-61856-2 (UK / USA) (1995) **47 USA**

VOLUME 8: THE THREAT IS REAL, Ignition IGN 740343 (UK / USA), (1998) **73 UK, 118 USA**

RETURN OF THE KILLER A's, Beyond 63985-78067-2 (Europe / USA) (1999)

WE'VE COME FOR YOU ALL, Nuclear Blast NB 0699-2 (Europe), Sanctuary 06076-84609-2 (USA) (2003) **102 UK, 122 USA**

MUSIC OF MASS DESTRUCTION, Nuclear Blast NB 1297-2 (Europe), Sanctuary 06076-84688-2 (USA) (2004)

THE GREATER OF TWO EVILS, Nuclear Blast NB 1274-2 (Europe), Sanctuary 06076-84709-2 (USA) (2004)

ALIVE 2, Nuclear Blast NB 1582-2 (Europe), Sanctuary 06076-84764-2 (USA) (2005)

cover bereavement costs for the family of Damageplan security guard Jeffrey 'Mayhem' Thompson and medical expenses for injured Damageplan crew members John 'Kat' Brooks and Chris Paluska. Anthrax opened their show with Pantera's 'Fucking Hostile' before delivering a version of 'A New Level' with Vinnie Paul and Pat Lachman. Grim Reaper's Nick Bowcott guested on lead guitar in the Anthrax set.

Although it was common knowledge, Anthrax made the classic reunion official on April 1st with a global press conference held at Sirius Satellite Radio in New York City. The band also used the occasion to announce their participation in the Slave To The Metal Foundation, created to 'bring public awareness to the dangers of the anthrax vaccine'.

Australian gigs in May found fellow veteran thrashers Mortal Sin as support. The band stopped in London in June to perform a short set at the *Metal Hammer* magazine awards, delivering 'Got The Time', 'Caught In A Mosh' and 'Indians', and with Brian Fair of Shadows Fall guesting on a set-closing rendition of Pantera's 'A New Level'. US and Canadian shows in September had Anthrax replacing Dream Theater as co-headliners of the Megadeth-led Gigantour dates. On the release front, a two-disc compilation entitled *Anthrology: No Hit Wonders (1985-1991)* was accompanied by a live album culled from the reunion shows dubbed simply *Alive 2*. Maintaining the pace on the road, Anthrax opened for Judas Priest once again in September and October.

At the time of writing, anticipation centres on the prospect of a new Joey Belladonna-fronted Anthrax album. With the band's track record of diversity and disregard for convention, just what direction Anthrax might take in the future is unforeseeable. The only surefire predictions are that the band's recent 20th anniversary will surely be eclipsed by a 25th and that there will be some mosh-tastic music in the interim.

ANVIL
AS HEAVY AS IT SOUNDS

ORIGINALLY KNOWN AS LIPS on their formation, this no-frills metal combo out of Toronto even pre-dated Canadian rock institution Rush. The main protagonists, frontman Steve Kudlow (aka 'Lips') and drummer Robb Reiner, had been operational earlier still with the band Gravestone, formed back in April 1973. The band were active on the live scene throughout the decade and solidified in 1978 with the acquisition of rhythm guitarist Dave Allison and bassist Ian Dickson, and the first Anvil

Anvil

product was originally issued under the Lips name. The debut 1981 album, entitled *Hard 'N' Heavy*, was in fact intended to be purely demo material. But as an enterprising unit eager to recoup their recording costs, the band issued 1,000 vinyl copies on their own Splash label. Gradually Lips graduated from an S&M bondage-themed shock-rock show into raw heavy metal. However, many of the early onstage appendages, such as Lips' notorious dildo holster, made the transition into later years. Still as Lips, the outfit's initiative came to the attention of Attic Records, who quickly re-released the album under the band name of Anvil due to protestations from disco act Lipps Inc.

Hard 'N' Heavy retained a large degree of the Lips rock'n'roll routine but, along with their lyrical obsession with sex, did hint at much heavier things to come. Tracks such as 'Bondage' and 'School Love' pointed at familiar output throughout the band's future catalogue. *Hard 'N' Heavy* also boasted a beefed-up take on the Rolling Stones classic 'Paint It Black'.

Anvil made their first foray onto the live scene in Canada with a bunch of club shows leading to a nationwide support slot to Girlschool, although Lips did take time out to produce a demo for Kraken.

1982's *Metal On Metal*, produced by Chris Tsangarides, boasted the unique honour of having the track 'Mothra' recorded by Lips (Steve Kudlow) using a vibrator on his guitar rather than the more usual plectrum, a technique that had already gained press coverage when he deployed it during live shows.

An uncompromising slab of heaviness, *Metal On Metal* was the first album to demonstrate the band's adherence to full-on metal, powered by the frenetic double-bass-drum work from the engine room of Reiner. Taking the songs to the people, Anvil conducted a world tour that took in a high-profile gig at Castle Donington's August 1982 'Monsters Of Rock' festival in the UK.

The follow-up, 1983's *Forged In Fire*, was an equally heavyweight offering, again with Tsangarides in charge of the faders. Strangely, the LP became the focus of a media backlash in previously robust bastions of support such as the UK and Europe. Anvil's road work spanned the entire globe to promote the record, including a slot on the Black Sabbath-headlined UK Reading festival in August, supports to Whitesnake in Europe, and Japanese dates in September 1983.

Many major acts took direct inspiration from *Forged In Fire*, and it is recognised today as the band's creative high point. However, Anvil reeled from savage reviews, and as album sales levelled out they found themselves without a record deal. Nevertheless, Attic capitalised on the group's standing with the 1985 *Backwaxed* collection, a semi-compilation comprising previously unreleased outtakes, the B-side 'Steamin'' from the 1982 *Anvil* UK EP, and songs taken from the previous three records. Lips surprised many when he revealed that the title track, recorded during the *Forged In Fire* sessions, was originally deemed too offensive for public consumption.

Anvil then performed in Japan again, playing the 'Super Rock' festival at Seibu Stadium in Tokyo in August 1985. The band went into the studio that same year to cut demos with producer Ric Browde, a somewhat strange choice for Anvil as his credits included lighter acts such as Poison. Songs recorded were 'Rockin'', 'Mad Dog', 'Worlds Apart' and 'Straight Between The Eyes'. Finding a new stable with Metal Blade, Anvil bounced back with 1987's *Strength Of Steel*, featuring a cover version of The Stampeders' 'Wild Eyes'.

After the *Pound For Pound* and live *Past And Present – Live In Concert* albums, both co-produced by the band and Paul LaChapelle, Dave Allison quit in 1989, ditching the music business entirely to find a new vocation in stereotypical Canadian tradition as a lumberjack. This defection prompted a period of inactivity for the band, broken finally by press statements indicating a forthcoming album, first titled *Tools Of Torture*, then *Evoke The Evil*. They finally bounced back with the Belgian

ANVIL discography

HARD 'N' HEAVY, Attic LAT 1100 (Europe / Canada) (1981)

METAL ON METAL, Attic LAT 1130 (Europe / Canada) (1982)

FORGED IN FIRE, Attic LAT 1170 (Europe / Canada) (1983)

BACKWAXED, Roadrunner RR 9776 (Europe), Viper VPR 106 (Canada) (1985)

STRENGTH OF STEEL, Roadrunner RR 9618 (Europe), Metal Blade CDE-73267 (USA) (1987)

POUND FOR POUND, Metal Blade 7 73336-2 (USA) (1988), ZYX Metallic ZMCD1011 (Europe) (1989)

PAST AND PRESENT: LIVE IN CONCERT, Roadracer RO 9453-2 (Europe), Metal Blade 7 73412-2 (USA) (1989)

WORTH THE WEIGHT, Maximum 7323-11000-2 (Canada) (1991), Mausoleum 904.004.2 (Europe) (1992)

PLUGGED IN PERMANENT, Massacre MASS CD098 (Europe), Metal Blade 3894-14122-2 (USA) (1996)

ABSOLUTELY NO ALTERNATIVE, Massacre MAS CD0134 (Europe), Hypnotic HYP 1059 (Canada) (1997)

SPEED OF SOUND, Massacre MAS CD0173 (Europe), Hypnotic HYP 1070 (Canada) (1998)

PLENTY OF POWER, Massacre MAS CD0256 (Europe), Hypnotic HYP 1079 (Canada) (2001)

STILL GOING STRONG, Massacre MAS CD0330 (Europe), Hypnotic HYP 1082 (Canada) (2002)

BACK TO BASICS, Massacre MAS CD0410 (Europe), Screaming Ferret Wreckords NMS011 (USA) (2004)

label Mausoleum and Canadian label Maximum, a newly founded concern of Helix manager William Seip, for the 1991 *Worth The Weight* album with new guitarist Sebastian Marino in tow (as a New Yorker, Marino was Anvil's only non-Canadian member). Following the album release, Anvil pulled in bassist Mike Duncan. Meanwhile, English metal crew Benediction had covered 'Forged In Fire' for their 1992 EP *Dark Is The Season*. Tungsten paid tribute to the same song on their 1993 album *183.85*.

Guitarist Marino made himself busy with Ramrod, cutting two demos in 1994 with Liege Lord singer Joseph Comeau and drummer Bill Mount before teaming up with cult New York speed metal merchants Overkill for their 1997 effort *From The Underground And Below*. Marino also found time to produce a 1996 album by Devastator.

Anvil had been away from the public eye for the longest period so far, but got back into action with an all-new cast involving bassist Michael Duncan and guitarist Ivan Hurd for 1996's de-tuned *Plugged In Permanent*, released by Hypnotic in Canada and Massacre in Germany. Japanese versions added an exclusive track, 'Stolen'. Anvil now included the linchpin of Lips, mainstay drummer Robb Reiner, and two new faces: guitarist Ivan Hurd and former Edge Unknown bassist Glenn Five (real name Gyorffy).

Quickly back into the fray, Anvil followed up with *Absolutely No Alternative* in 1997, boasting a completely re-recorded take on 'March Of The Crabs'. Song titles such as 'Piss Test', 'Hair Pie' and 'Show Me Your Tits' gave ample evidence that the Canadians' humour had remained intact. They were back again in 1998 with *Speed Of Sound*, issued across the globe by way of Massacre for Europe, Rock Brigade in Brazil, Avalon Marquee in Japan and Hypnotic in their homeland. *Speed Of Sound* displayed an Anvil aware of the present metal climate, Robb Reiner even introducing blastbeats. A curious distinction in the artwork, depicting an anvil-aircraft, saw only the German version firing a missile. Japanese

variants hosted two extra studio tracks, 'Kick Some Ass' and 'Vengeance To Kill'.

With Germany's fascination in the late 1990s for early-'80s cult metal acts, Anvil made a return to the touring circuit, undertaking a nostalgic series of dates with Flotsam And Jetsam and fellow Canadians Exciter. The band rounded off 1998 by performing at the long-established 'Wacken Open Air' festival in Germany.

Anvil toured Germany in early 2000, sharing a package bill with Riot, Agent Steel and Domine. The year 2000 also saw an *Anthology Of Anvil* compilation released, with extensive liner notes by the esteemed Canadian metal journalist Martin Popoff.

German Massacre-label variants of 2001's Pierre Rémillard-produced album *Plenty Of Power* differed to Canadian-distributed CDs in having the final exclusive track as 'Dirty Dorothy'. The Hypnotic Canadian label replaced this song with 'Left Behind', actually a tune dating back to the Lips/Reiner Gravestone days. Sebastian Marino and his colleagues in the Ramrod rhythm section took to the stage at the German 'Wacken Open Air' festival the same year as part of a reunion line-up of Liege Lord.

Anvil scheduled a new album, *Still Going Strong*, for release through Massacre in Europe and Hypnotic in Canada in June 2002. The band headlined the Montreal 'Powerpack' festival on November 8th, topping a bill over Hanker, Heaven's Cry and Soulforge.

The March 2004 album, *Back To Basics*, was recorded with Rémillard in Quebec. As a bonus, digipacks of the album included a DVD of the band's August 1998 Wacken performance. The band's profile was momentarily heightened in the US when Screaming Ferret Wreckords undertook a campaign to release no fewer than seven back-catalogue albums. Although announced, the albums failed to appear in stores.

Unfortunately Ivan Hurd fell from a ladder in May, breaking four ribs and his left wrist and suffering a cracked tailbone. As a result he was unable to perform with the band at the July 24th 'Gates Of Hell' festival at the FunHaus in Toronto, Ontario. His replacement was George Vee.

German heavy metal band Powergod cut a cover version of 'Motormount' for inclusion on their *Long Live The Loud – That's Metal Lesson II* album, released through Massacre in July 2005. Lips guested on this version, as did Rough Silk's Ferdy Doernberg on pedal steel guitar. Anvil scheduled European dates for November in a road alliance with Phantom-X.

In early 2006 Anvil re-forged links with producer Chris Tsangarides for a new album, and the future looks positive for this most persistent of bands.

DARK ANGEL
THRASH PIONEERS EXTRAORDINAIRE

FROM LONG BEACH, CALIFORNIA, Dark Angel were seen by many as spearheading the second round of the thrash metal wave to break out of America, although in truth the group had been active far earlier. Their influence would be telling on Slayer in particular, guitarists Jeff Hanneman and Kerry King often running through Dark Angel riffs in soundchecks. Critically, though, Dark Angel's tour de force, the 1986 *Darkness Descends* album, would be completely overshadowed by Slayer's *Reign In Blood*, released just weeks beforehand. Dark Angel were unable to attain adequate promotion and failed to build up a European following, belatedly arriving on the continent in 1989.

The group was formed during 1981 as Shell Shock with founding members Don Dotty, Jimmy Durkin and Robbie Yahn at Downey High School, the teens' ambitions extending to recording a demo. To differentiate themselves from the rising speed metal flock, Dark Angel adopted the tag 'caffeine metal'. A second demo, laid down in 1982 and entitled *We Have Arrived*, secured the interest of two parties: the local Metalstorm/Azra label; and the French Axekiller company. In 1984 contracts were signed.

Dark Angel's inaugural 1985 LP, a Bill Metoyer-produced re-working of the demo tracks from *We Have Arrived*, featured the line-up of vocalist Don Doty, guitarists Eric Meyer and Jimmy Durkin, bassist Robbie Yahn and drummer Jack Schwartz. An earlier Dark Angel drummer, Bob Gourley, had graduated from a fleeting appearance in the fledgling Slayer, and then upon his departure from Dark Angel formed Powerlord, releasing the 1988 album *The Awakening*.

Without financial backing, the band's ability to plug *We Have Arrived* was restricted to local Los Angeles shows, where they supported the likes of Slayer, Agent Steel and Savage Grace. However, they benefited from a unique promo release to back up 1986's *Darkness Descends* album: the accompanying single track 'Merciless Death', released by Azra, came in a variety of bizarre shapes such as a skull, a wheel, a square, a black heart and even, quite surreally, a Christmas tree.

The band had lost the services of Schwartz, the drummer joining Holy Terror, and in his stead came Lee Rausch, a former member of Megadeth. However, Rausch's place was soon taken briefly by a returning Jack Schwartz before Carnage and Wargod man Gene Hoglan stabilised the position. Besides his band activities, Hoglan was well known on the local metal scene as lighting technician for Slayer, Omen and Savage Grace and a journalist for *The Headbanger* fanzine. By coincidence, the drummer had also briefly been a member of another Dark Angel, a completely different set of musicians who later became Carnage. With Wargod, Hoglan had featured on two demos, *Into The Abyss* and *Day Of Atonement*.

In a straight swap, as Hoglan teamed up with Dark Angel in December 1984, Lee Rausch hopped over to join Wargod. There was almost a further connection with Megadeth when Dave Mustaine requested the services of both Jimmy Durkin and Eric Meyer, but both guitarists declined the offer. The revised Dark Angel debuted on December 31st 1984, sharing a bill with Hirax at Radio City in Anaheim. Reissues of the first album, *We Have Arrived*, included Hoglan's picture rather than that of Schwartz.

Darkness Descends, with production handled by Randy Burns, witnessed a switch in labels – to Combat for the US and Music For Nations subsidiary Under One Flag in the UK. *Darkness* further improved the

band's standing as Dark Angel began to carve out their own niche: Hoglan had taken over in the lyrics department, and fans relished the group's unexpected song themes.

With sessions completed, Rob Yahn took his leave, handing the bass position to Mike Gonzalez. Tours to push the record, which had garnered enthusiastic reviews on a global scale, had Dark Angel scoring supports with Motörhead and Cro-Mags in New York, and Megadeth and Slayer, before embarking on the nationwide 'Gates Of Darkness' tour in January 1987 with co-headliners Possessed. These dates saw the inclusion of vocalist Jim Drabos from Death Force. Reports emerged claiming Doty had been involved in a car accident. Doty couldn't go on tour because, without insurance, he had to work to reimburse the damage he had caused in the collision. Doty came back into the fold as Dark Angel gained the guest slot at the Hollywood Palladium date for Slayer's finale of their *Reign In Blood* world tour. There was a headline run in Texas that July, after which Doty was asked to leave. The singer had failed to show up for the first night's performance in San Antonio.

With Doty's exit, the group initially requested the services of Watchtower singer Jason McMaster, but although McMaster performed as guest bassist for dates in Texas, this union never transpired. The group also approached Wrathchild America's Brad Divens, who turned them down, and Stephan Taylor from Sacrilege B.C., who also declined.

Soldiering on, the band eventually recruited Ron Rinehart (previously with Messiah) in September 1987, for January 1989's *Leave Scars* album. Although Michael Monarch, veteran guitarist with Steppenwolf, was officially given production credits, the band themselves put most of the record together. The album took Hoglan's lyrical observations to further extremes, tackling subjects such as suicide and sexual abuse. The first-person characterisation of child molestation on the track 'Death Of Innocence' was deemed too graphic by Combat, who initially omitted the words of this song from the lyric sheet. On a lighter note, *Leave Scars* also featured cover versions of Led Zeppelin's 'Immigrant Song' and Fear's 'Action' and 'I Don't Care About You'. Also involved was Viking vocalist Ron Daniels (aka Eriksen), duetting with Rinehart on the track 'Promise Of Agony'.

Leave Scars was promoted with the tempestuous 'Ultimate Revenge' tour in 1989, partnered with Death. Mid-tour, in Boston, Massachusetts, Dark Angel suffered a major blow when Durkin quit, the band citing "personal problems and marriage problems". Dark Angel persevered, playing shows as a four-piece before drafting Viking axeman Brett Eriksen on a stand-in basis. In spite of the chaos, and the severe criticism levelled at the production of *Leave Scars*, the album still entered the national charts.

European shows in October 1989 saw the band hooked up with Nuclear Assault and Acid Reign. While in Nuremburg, Germany the line-up unexpectedly changed when bassist Mike Gonzalez was jailed for

LA thrashers Dark Angel

vandalising cars. Nuclear Assault's Dan Lilker substituted in order to get the band through the tour. A notable UK concert – a three-way billing at London's Hammersmith Odeon with Swedish doom act Candlemass and UK thrashers D.A.M. – was filmed and issued as the video *Three Way Thrash*. A full-blown US tour saw Overkill play alongside Dark Angel before a short burst of gigs allied with Savatage and Testament wrapped up the world tour. To maintain momentum, a radio broadcast was put out as the in-concert album *Live Scars*.

Dark Angel's next album, *Time Does Not Heal*, increased the crunch factor courtesy of some skilful production tactics by Terry Date. The album boasted a much more technical approach: press releases boasted that *Time Does Not Heal* included no fewer than 246 riffs. Despite great reviews, European gigs with Re-Animator as opening act, and their biggest-selling record to date, Dark Angel were set to implode. In late 1991 Brett Eriksen was replaced by former Silent Scream guitarist Chris McCarthy, but the band collapsed when Ron Rinehart bowed out in September 1992.

After announcing a new-found Christian faith, Rinehart founded Hunger alongside colleague Eric Meyer, bassist Greg Rowe and drummer R.D. Davis. This outfit issued a three-song 1994 demo before calling it a day. Subsequently Rinehart formed Oil with former Deceiver, Desire and Captain Black guitarist Blake Nelson, and the band issued the *Refine* album for Kaluboné Records. Meyer made a name for himself as a producer, working with Transmetal and Recipients Of Death.

Gene Hoglan joined Death in 1994 for their *Individual Thought Patterns* album. Rumours circulated in 1999 that Dark Angel were set to reform, and a European tour schedule was announced in collaboration with Ancient Rites for that September. Sadly, it didn't come to pass. Hoglan later re-emerged as part of the 2001 death metal combo Tenet, led by erstwhile Sacrifice and Interzone vocalist Rob Urbinati and including Strapping Young Lad guitarist Jed Simon along with Grip Inc. bassist Stuart Carruthers.

Jim Durkin arrived on the scene again with his new act Dreams Of Damnation and their *Let The Violence Begin* album. By September of 2001 the guitarist had joined the reformed Hirax. Rumours emerged in mid 2002 that a full-blown Dark Angel reformation, comprising Ron Rinehart, Eric Meyer, Jim Durkin and Gene Hoglan, was set to take place. It soon transpired, though, that the rhythm section for the revamped band was in fact ex-Morgion bassist Jeremy Peto and drummer Al 'Mayhem' Mendez of Dreams Of Damnation – although within a matter of days of the announcement Hoglan took up his rightful place.

Back in action, Dark Angel took on a North American tour during December with Into Eternity acting as support. However, the 'new' line-up debuted live in early October with an unannounced appearance at the conclusion of Dreams Of Damnation's opening set at the Galaxy Theater in Santa Ana, California, where Durkin's current act was supporting Kreator and Destruction. Al Mendez took on the drum role for this brief outing.

In December, bassist Danyael Williams was enrolled and Strapping Young Lad guitarist Jed Simon was announced as taking Durkin's place for West Coast and European gigs. However, within days Simon had scotched the proposed union. Durkin was kept active alongside Abattoir frontman Steve Gaines, Mastaba six-stringer guitarist Marcelo Lima and drummer Al Mendez in the project band Pagan War Machine.

Dark Angel's proposed summer 2003 comeback tour was scuppered when Ron Rinehart suffered a major injury to the cervical region of his spine as well as several herniated discs in his neck. Nevertheless, the group got back to work in September, cutting a version of Metallica's 'Creeping Death' for the Big Deal label's tribute album *Metallic Assault*. The international fanbase waits to see if the band can resurrect themselves once more.

DEATH ANGEL
THE TRIUMPH OF THRASH OVER ADVERSITY

DEATH ANGEL EXCITED thrash metal fans with their arrival in 1987 as the latest export from the rapidly expanding Bay Area metal scene. The group was known for straying from thrash conventions, first impacting with the quirky radio hit 'Bored' and employing a distinctly technical approach to their playing. Regrettably, their ascendancy was thwarted by a horrific accident at a critical juncture.

The Filipino act, originally formed by teenage cousins – guitarist Rob Cavestany, bassist Dennis Pepa and drummer Andy Galeon – soon carved out a niche fanbase in San Francisco. Although the band came together in 1982, briefly billed as Dark Theory before taking the Death Angel name from a book cover, it would be five years before their first album – the widely admired *The Ultra-Violence* – was released.

The youngsters initially performed in clubs as a standard heavy metal covers act, tackling tracks by artists such as Judas Priest, Ozzy Osbourne, Scorpions, Kiss, Tygers Of Pan Tang and Iron Maiden. The trio became a quartet after introducing Dennis Pepa's brother Gus on second guitar. Death Angel's recording debut came in 1983 with the four-song *Heavy Metal Insanity* demo, produced by Matt Wallace. Remarkably, drummer Galeon was a mere 11 years old at the time of recording. At this juncture Rob Cavestany handled lead vocals. The band took on Kat Sirdorfsky as their manager and began a shift towards thrash metal, admitting new-found influences from Exodus, Mercyful Fate and Metallica, whom the group supported at San Francisco's Kabuki Theatre in 1985. Inducting new frontman Mark Osegueda, another family member, the new-look Death Angel debuted as support to Megadeth at The Stone in San Francisco on November 24th 1984. The 1985 demo *Kill As One* was produced by Metallica guitarist Kirk Hammett: this fact alone provoked curiosity among the labels, and Death Angel received offers from the Enigma, Combat and French Black Dragon labels.

Death Angel put their signatures down with Enigma to cut *The Ultra-Violence*, working with Davy Vain of Vain as co-producer in June 1986.

Death Angel: kill as one

the bass role to John Ricci for studio purposes, was to re-record early material for a retrospective compilation. This set, comprising revisited material from 1983's *Heavy Metal Maniac*, 1984's *Violence And Force*, 1985's *Long Live The Loud*, 1992's *Kill After Kill*, 1997's *The Dark Command* and 2000's *Blood Of Tyrants*, emerged with the title *New Testament – Coven Of Re-Recorded Classics*. Exciter added new bass man Rob 'Clammy' Cohen to the ranks in April 2004. A further round of archive releases in late 2004 came courtesy of Megaforce, with the band's first six albums remixed by none other than Annihilator's Jeff Waters.

A European tour beginning in early October saw Swedish power metal merchants Steel Attack and Germany's Black Abyss as support acts. German heavy metal band Powergod cut a cover version of 'Fall Out/Long Live The Loud' for inclusion on their *Long Live The Loud – That's Metal Lesson II* released through Massacre in July 2005. In September Dan Beehler disbanded his Bëehler project and once again set to work on new Exciter material with former guitarist Paul Champagne. Jacques Bélanger quit Exciter again in April 2006, citing "differences of opinion". The band, despite the tribulations they have endured, are obviously still a force to be reckoned with.

EXODUS
BONDED BY THRASH

A SAN FRANCISCAN speed metal band formed in early 1980, Exodus only just missed out on stardom, despite appearing with almost perfect timing atop the crest of the first thrash wave. Primarily because the band weren't swept along in the first big wave, Exodus wallowed around in the resulting flotsam for far too long. Ultimately, this resulted in dysfunction, label changes and membership shuffles that would dog the group throughout their career.

Before the major labels wised up to thrash metal, and certainly prior to Metallica gaining a foothold, it was probably Exodus who had the most die-hard set of fans on the scene. Ultimately, the fragile state of the band membership and a lack of real focus saw Exodus squeezed out of the Big Four Of Thrash. While commercial rewards never came their way, artistic recognition did – legions of extreme metal outfits are quick to pinpoint Exodus as a direct influence.

As countless history books record, Exodus featured Metallica guitarist Kirk Hammett in their original line-up. The founding Exodus incarnation saw Hammett joined by second guitarist Tim Magnello, bassist Carlton Nelson and drummer Tom Hunting, the latter also handling lead vocals. Initially, the band operated in NWOBHM-worshipping territory, performing covers by the likes of Def Leppard and UFO before adopting their more familiar thrash stance. The proto-Exodus crumbled, with Nelson going on to join Blizzard, Outrage and Fuhrer. Jeff Andrews, fleetingly a member of Possessed, took the bass position, but further changes saw Tim Magnello opting out, being substituted by Gary Holt, a former guitar tech of Hammett's. Exodus evolved further when Paul Baloff assumed the role of frontman for a 1982 demo comprising the tracks 'Whipping Queen', 'Death And Domination' and 'Warlords'. The band rapidly made its presence felt on the live scene, performing with the likes of Anvil Chorus, Lääz Rockit and Vicious Rumors. This live activity and the rabid underground trading of the demo marked out Exodus as the leading speed metal band of its day.

David Wayne (Metal Church): "The Bay Area scene was just buzzing. It was electric. It was just kids playing metal, all styles of metal. Exodus was king of the heap. Everyone had the demo and their shows were just totally insane. I mean, it was positively dangerous to go to an Exodus gig because of all the moshing and all

the fighting and shit. I've never seen a crowd like it. They whipped them up into a frenzy. I know Metallica saw that too and they just had never seen anything like it. Y'know, Metal Church and Exodus kind of had similar problems behind the scenes, but Metallica got the breaks, they got organised, and look where they are. Ask anybody about Exodus, though, back in the day, and that was the Number 1 band until they took Kirk."

Fate dealt the band's exalted standing a heavy blow in early 1983 when Hammett's services were urgently requested by Metallica. Upon the recommendation of Metallica soundman Mark Whitaker, also involved with Exodus's business affairs, Hammett had been earmarked as successor to the errant genius Dave Mustaine. On tour on the East Coast, Metallica had finally decided to ditch Mustaine and required Hammett to complete the tour. The Exodus man flew out to New York to join up with Metallica on April 11th and put in his inaugural gig with his new act on the 16th at the Showplace in Dover, New Jersey. At this same juncture, the deeply wounded Exodus discarded Jeff Andrews and recruited Rob McKillop in his stead.

Mike Maung was briefly employed on guitar before joining disco combo Freaky Executive, and he was replaced by Evan McCasky. This latest candidate lasted just one gig. Potential guitarists in line for recruitment included Jon Torres of Thunderhead, Iron Assault and Warning, along with Rick Hunolt. The latter secured the position and a second demo session, the two-track *Die By His Hand* set, emerged in 1983, as did a rehearsal recording that same July. At this juncture, the Exodus name was still revered among the burgeoning thrash scene in California. The group nurtured its growing legion of dedicated fans, opening for Metallica, Raven, Metal Church, Motörhead, Heaven, Suicidal Tendencies and Loudness while playing a profusion of headline gigs.

Exodus continued demoing into 1984 with the promotional recordings *A Lesson In Violence*. Further tracks were laid down at Turk Street Studios by Anvil Chorus and Control's Doug Piercy, famously recorded minus many of the vocal tracks due to the band running out of funds. Back on the club scene, Exodus strengthened their reputation with gigs with Death Angel, Vermin, Anthrax, Slayer and Possessed.

Exodus belatedly debuted on vinyl in 1985 with the *Bonded By Blood* album, recorded for the New York-based Torrid label in July 1984 at Prairie Sun Studios with Mark Whitaker as producer. Although the album languished due to business problems, gigs in 1984 saw the band sharing stages with Hirax, Death Angel, Mercyful Fate and Megadeth.

Initial promo copies of *Bonded By Blood* supplied to journalists bore the originally planned title of *A Lesson In Violence*. In response to its controversial if somewhat amateurish artwork – depicting demonic Siamese twins – many countries chose to change the jacket art to a simple band logo. This first Exodus LP, licensed to Music For Nations for the UK, saw a line-up of vocalist Paul Baloff, guitarists Rick Hunolt and Gary Holt, bassist Rob McKillop and drummer Tom Hunting. *Bonded By Blood* sold strongly across Europe in particular, but the critical delay in its release may well have cost Exodus their position at the head of the pack, as Metallica and the rest had already put out their own high-impact debuts. (A subsequent CD version of *Bonded By Blood*, issued by Century Media in 1999, came with the bonus live tracks 'And Then There Were None' and 'A Lesson In Violence'.)

With their debut finally out, Exodus were to catapult themselves into the thrash major league, although a minor spat developed when it was learned that lyrics from the Exodus track 'Hell's Breath' had been re-used in Metallica's 'Creeping Death'. Unfortunately, the band could not extend the promising start driven by *Bonded By Blood* and they steadily lost ground with each successive release, despite no let-ups in quality.

Exodus partnered Venom and Slayer for national tours in April, with tracks from a show at the notorious Studio 54 in New York City included on the VHS video *The Ultimate Revenge*, which surfaced in April 1985 through Combat. In August the group scheduled US and Canadian dates with Exciter, but the Canadian act dropped off the tour after just three gigs, leaving Exodus to persevere, culminating in Montreal on August 17th at the 'Banzai' festival alongside Slayer, Metal Church, Hallow's Eve and Agent Steel. The following month witnessed the first Exodus gig on European soil, guesting for Venom across the UK, Denmark, France, Switzerland, Italy, Holland and Germany. The Eindhoven gig was bootlegged for the *And Then There Were... 300* and *Strike Of The Beast* albums.

Upon their return to the USA, Baloff and Holt forged the ad hoc side project Spastik Children in alliance with Heathen's Doug Piercy on bass and Fred 'Rotten' Cotton on drums. This notorious and nebulous band would famously incorporate figures such as Metallica's James Hetfield and Cliff Burton, James McDaniels, Piranha's Al Voltage and Faith No More's Jim Martin. The year closed out for Exodus in style: in late December 1985 the band journeyed to Brooklyn, New York, to perform a one-off date at the L'Amour club supported by Agnostic Front and Lethal Aggression, before returning to the West Coast for a New Year's Eve gig alongside Metallica, Metal Church and Anthrax.

After completing pre-production demos for a second album, and a June 14th 1986 gig with Anthrax at the New York Ritz, Paul Baloff left, initially to team up with Hirax for a brief liaison and turning down an offer

from German thrashers Destruction, as Exodus struggled to extricate themselves from their American deal with Torrid. During the hiatus, Holt busied himself producing a demo for erstwhile Exodus bassist Carlton Nelson's Fuhrer.

Exodus announced their new frontman as Steve 'Zetro' Souza of Legacy (who later evolved into Testament). Souza debuted with his new band at two gigs at The Farm in San Francisco on July 17th and 18th. For the latter concert Baloff would join Souza on stage during the encore to sing 'Bonded By Blood'. The group then recorded the *Pleasures Of The Flesh* LP, released by Combat in 1987. The album would be swiftly re-released a few years later when the band scored a major deal with Capitol. Some versions of *Pleasures Of The Flesh* included a cover version of AC/DC's 'Overdose'. November of that year found Exodus traversing the West Coast and into Texas with Celtic Frost as co-headliners, before hooking up with Anthrax in December.

With 1988 drawing in, ex-member Paul Baloff announced his new act Piranha, comprising guitarists Ron Shipes and former Execution man Chuck Sedlak, bassist Bob Eggleston and drummer Fred Cotton. There were great expectations for this band from the Exodus faithful, but Piranha soon splintered and Baloff joined Heathen.

Tom Hunting was forced to leave the band in the midst of tour duties alongside Anthrax and Helloween, reportedly due to a mysterious stomach virus, and was temporarily replaced by Vio-lence's Perry

A rejuvenated Exodus for the 21st century

EXODUS discography

BONDED BY BLOOD, Music For Nations MFN 44 (UK), Combat/Torrid MX 8019 (USA) (1985)

PLEASURES OF THE FLESH, Music For Nations MFN 77 (UK), Combat 88561-8169-2 (USA) (1987) **82 USA**

FABULOUS DISASTER, Music For Nations MFN 90 (UK), Combat 88561-2001-2 (USA) (1989) **82 USA**

IMPACT IS IMMINENT, Capitol CDEST 2125 (UK), Capitol C2-90379 (USA) (1990) **137 USA**

GOOD FRIENDLY VIOLENT FUN, Roadracer RO 9235-2 (UK), Relativity 88561-2026-2 (USA) (1991)

FORCE OF HABIT, Capitol CDEST 2179 (UK), Capitol C2-96676 (USA) (1992)

LESSONS IN VIOLENCE, Music For Nations MFN 138 (UK), Relativity 88561-1117-2 (USA) (1992)

ANOTHER LESSON IN VIOLENCE, Century Media 77173-2 (Europe / USA) (1997)

TEMPO OF THE DAMNED, Nuclear Blast NB 1218-2 (Europe), Nuclear Blast America 1218 (USA) (2004)

SHOVEL HEADED KILL MACHINE, Nuclear Blast NB 1376-2 (Europe), Nuclear Blast America 1376 (USA) (2005)

Strickland. On a headlining American tour in 1989 the group wound up using Anthrax drum tech John Tempesta, who would take over full-time as Hunting opted out. Hunting was later involved in IR8, a demo project put together by Metallica's Jason Newsted. Former bassist Mike Butler re-emerged with The Flexapleasers and punk glam act American Heartbreak. A notable Exodus release in 1989 was the *Objection Overruled* EP, a three-track effort that included a rendition of Ted Nugent's 'Free For All'. Capitol issued the *Impact Is Imminent* album in June 1990 but the group struggled to achieve the sales their label had anticipated. Exodus shifted to Relativity for the 1991 live album *Good Friendly Violent Fun*, which once again included an AC/DC cover in 'Dirty Deeds Done Dirt Cheap'.

The band adopted a new style and direction in 1992, bringing in well known British producer Chris Tsangarides to craft the *Force Of Habit* album, released that August. But many longstanding fans failed to appreciate the shift away from pure thrash. The adventurous set, despite supremely heavy epics such as 'Architect Of Pain', even included covers of Elvis Costello's 'Pump It Up' and The Rolling Stones' 'Bitch'. Japanese variants added two extra tracks in 'Crawl Before You Walk' and 'Telepathetic'.

Gary Holt: 'We did Force Of Habit, which was kind of a change in pace for us, but things within the band were not good. Nearly all of us had some major issues with drugs – if they want to individually admit it or not. That had caught up with us. I made some space in my head to finally look at the whole thing from another perspective and realised that the fun had gone a long, long time ago. We were not thinking about the music any more because there was just so much other shit to deal with. Personally, I wanted to just get back in the studio, record the fastest, nastiest, thrashiest album ever, then tour until I dropped, but we just weren't thinking like that any more.

"There was a lot of tension between everybody. We never got into feuds or any of that shit, but money was a worry. Capitol Records turned into one big fucking nightmare. Throw speed into that mix and it was just too much. I didn't get into Exodus to have all this shit going on so I said fuck it, see ya."

Unfortunately, Exodus folded, a victim of the disdain of longstanding fans for their latest effort and the onset of grunge and post-thrash apathy.

The group – Baloff, Hunolt, Holt and Hunting along with new bassist Jack Gibson – reformed for 1997's *Another Lesson In Violence*, a collection of live recordings of the band's 'classics', which included the Kirk Hammett co-written 'Impaler', never previously available on record. Holt had been working with Jack Gibson and Tom Hunting in Wardance before the reunited Exodus, and Souza was operating his act Dogface with ex-Rexxen and Heathen guitarist Ira Black, later of Vicious Rumors. *Another Lesson In Violence* was notably produced by ex-Sabbat guitarist Andy Sneap.

The band soldiered on, appearing at the 'Dynamo' festival in Holland in the early summer of 1997, but with internal strife mounting, they split again shortly after. Death metal band Six Feet Under covered 'Piranha' on their *Graveyard Classics* album in 2000.

Exodus buried the hatchet in August 2001, reuniting for a one-off gig at the 'Thrash Of The Titans' festival in aid of Testament frontman Chuck Billy's cancer treatment fund.

Sadly, Paul Baloff died after a stroke in late January 2002, which had left him comatose with irreparable brain damage. The singer was just 41. Despite this huge loss, Exodus persevered, pulling in old colleague Steve 'Zetro' Souza in order to fulfil February engagements in Anaheim and an appearance at the 'Whittier Hellfest' in March. The band continued the momentum by stretching out dates into the summer, including a show at the Milwaukee 'Metalfest' in July and the German 'Wacken Open Air' event in early August. December dates had Exodus performing in Greece with The Haunted and Tankard, and then playing in the UK, Holland, France and Belgium. The group united with Six Feet Under, Marduk, Immolation and Kataklysm for Xmas Festivals shows in Holland to close off the year.

Gary Holt: "Paul's death was just so tragic. I'll remember him as such as enthusiast for the music. He was just so into Exodus. The thing was, we knew the score, and with Paul going like that we then had to take a good, long hard look at ourselves, which was not easy. In fact it was ugly because there was a lot of shit to admit to. We were all on speed. That's the way Exodus functioned. Exodus was its own worst enemy. The fans saw the music and kept saying: 'Hey, why aren't you guys putting out more music? What's the delay?' They were frustrated. The people who worked with us could see the deal. Exodus was fucked. It was all about drugs.

"Only Jack Gibson was clean, but obviously that meant he had to deal with us being fucked up all the time, so the whole band was just rotten to the core. Our mistakes were ours alone, and with Paul dying that was the big wake-up call. It took a long time, nearly a year, but myself, Rick Hunholt and Tom Hunting cleaned up our act. Suddenly things started to look like they might be fun again!"

Exodus were projected to record a new studio album, once again using the services of Andy Sneap as producer, on a new label set up by two Exodus enthusiasts, their former manager Toni Isabella and erstwhile Capitol A&R executive Rachel Matthews, who had been responsible for signing them to the major label back in the 1980s. The band stirred up controversy and generated some press when courier giants FedEx objected to the band selling T-shirts at shows bearing the legend 'FedExodus – Total Destruction Guaranteed Overnight'.

The band put in a one-off show in Las Vegas opening for Halford and a short burst of December dates along with Testament and Vio-lence, but these gigs were cancelled due to Rob Halford's visa problems. Exodus then parted ways with Souza in mid January. Their search for a new singer ended within weeks, as he rejoined in February. Hunting announced extracurricular activity by forming part of a new-look Angel Witch, but the drummer quickly pulled out, stating that his Exodus commitments took priority.

The band would sign their comeback album *Tempo Of The Damned* to German label Nuclear Blast in August 2004. UK and European dates spread into October, dubbed the 'Bonded By Metal' trek, and found Exodus topping a bill comprising Nuclear Assault, Agent Steel, Mortician, God Dethroned, Occult and Callenish Circle. A limited-edition tour single, 'War Is My Shepherd', was available at these shows. The band filmed video clips for 'War Is My Shepherd' and 'Throwing Down' in late November with director Maurice Swinkels.

Gary Holt: "We made Tempo Of The Damned clean and we made it with Andy Sneap. That was the turning point for us, those two factors. We had a blast making the record and I cannot remember the last time I felt that way about an album. Andy as a producer was just incredible. Unbelievable talent. He's an old Exodus fan so he knew the history, he knew our way of making music, plus he's a great guitar player too, so the chemistry was just instant. There was none of this compromise and fighting with Andy, because he wanted to make exactly the same record we did. Before, if a producer said, 'Not good enough,' we would be thinking, 'What the fuck do you know about Exodus?' But with Andy, he says: 'It's shit – do it again,' and it's yes sir, because the guy knows Exodus even better than we do.

We tried to capture some of that 1980s crunch but keep it right up to date too. The record has some huge balls and a lot of that is not the guitar, it's Jack. All our records before swallowed the bass. Where is it? This time around Andy said: 'Let's push that bass right in your face.' It works great."

The Exodus live schedule extended into 2004 with European dates, including an appearance at the Sölvesborg 'Sweden Rock' event, slated for the summer. As an adjunct to Exodus activities, guitarist Gary Holt and band manager Steve Warner forged the Drug Pig project, cutting tracks at Tsunami Studio in Northern California.

September witnessed Japanese shows, followed up by Central and South American gigs in Mexico, Brazil, Chile and Argentina. However, Steve 'Zetro' Souza was forced to sit out these dates after falling ill during the group's Japanese trek. Filling in for him would be Exhumed frontman Matt Harvey. However, the position became clearer within hours of the first gig in Mexico when band manager Steven Warner told the Blabbermouth network that Souza was out. "He did not quit, he was fired!" said Warner. The separation would prove far from amicable, Gary Holt labelling Souza a "fat motherfuckin' shit brick" on the band's official forums and claiming that the singer withdrew from the tour less than 24 hours before the first gig.

Wardance singer John Miller was set to join Exodus to complete the dates. However, in a bizarre turn of events Gary Holt then publicly slammed Miller, claiming the singer was an "insane idiot and had one of his mental breakdowns the day before we were to leave". These gigs were then re-scheduled for October, seeing Skinlab and Re:Ignition singer Steev Esquivel as new frontman. Meanwhile, aggrieved Brazilian fans promptly convened the 'Fuck Off Zetro' festival in Belo Horizonte featuring local acts Drowned, Absolute Disgrace, Helltrucker, Betrayer and Perpetual Dusk. The Esquivel-fronted Exodus toured the West Coast of America in October as support to Megadeth.

Unfortunately, the band's bad luck continued: Esquivel's eyes were contaminated with "unknown chemicals" at the San Diego gig on October 26th. With the singer under medication, Exodus drafted in Testament's Chuck Billy as stand-in for the following San Francisco Warfield gig. The band announced Rob Dukes, guitarist with East Coast outfit Cheatin'

Soccer Moms, as their new singer in January 2005. That same month bassist Jack Gibson, retaining his ties to Exodus, joined Vile to record their album *The New Age Of Chaos*.

The Exodus line-up was re-vamped once more in May after Tom Hunting was hospitalised due to illness. Stepping into the breach would be the Slayer, Testament, Systematic and Forbidden-credited Paul Bostaph. As the band set to work on a new album at Trident Studios in Pacheco, California, reports emerged in June suggesting that Rick Hunolt had departed. Rumours soon placed Heathen's Lee Altus in the frame, this appointment being confirmed in late July. *Shovel Headed Kill Machine*, a grand return to form, emerged in October 2005.

November headline dates in Europe saw Hypocrisy and Keep Of Kalessin as support. The band announced a touring partnership as part of the December 2005 'X-Mas' festivals in Europe ranked alongside the recently resurrected UK thrashers Onslaught, Occult, Kataklysm, Unleashed, Behemoth, and Primordial. That same month, leading Spanish death metal band Avulsed covered 'Piranha' on their EP *Reanimations*.

The group participated in the 'Extreme The Dojo Vol. 15' shows in Japan with The Haunted and Nile in late February 2006. US touring resumed with Cryptopsy and Immolation in April, following with shows into May bolstered by The Classic Struggle and Full Blown Chaos. The group hit the US touring circuit again in September, forming a strong billing alongside Hatebreed, Napalm Death, The Black Dahlia Murder, Despised Icon and First Blood.

Now cleaner and certainly meaner, Exodus seem to be a revitalised force. Having recently issued two of their finest albums to date, and with the enthusiasm and organisation to back up the music with regular touring, it seems that the band has turned a corner.

FLOTSAM AND JETSAM
STILL SWIMMING AGAINST THE METAL TIDE

FLOTSAM AND JETSAM WERE founded in 1981 in Phoenix, Arizona, and their tenacity and fortitude has been tested to a far greater degree than most bands. Despite their impressive albums, they have been dogged by line-up problems (particularly in the bass department), label switches and business tribulations. Unfortunately they are better known as the first successful band to feature Metallica's Jason Newsted, and despite major-label backup they have struggled to rid themselves of that stigma. Nevertheless, Flotsam And Jetsam stuck to their guns, releasing a string of commendable metal albums and conducting some punishing tours.

Jason Newsted originally hailed from Battle Creek, Michigan. His first band was the 1977 high school combo Diamond, which was followed by Gangster. This unit evolved into Paradox in 1980 with the addition of drummer Kelly David-Smith, and then into Scottsdale-based Dogz with the recruitment of guitarists Mark Vasquez and Mark Horton. Dogz added vocalist Eric A.K. (Knutson) in 1983, and Horton made way for Ed Carlson as the band renamed itself Flotsam And Jetsam. Carlson's early inspiration had come from Kiss, whose classic *Alive* album had prompted him to pick up the guitar. The band started by playing local support gigs to the likes of Malice, Autograph, Armored Saint, Megadeth and Alcatraz.

Flotsam And Jetsam's demo tapes, starting with August 1985's *Metal Shock* (comprising 'Hammerhead', 'The Evil Sheikh', 'I Live You Die' and 'The Beast Within') and followed by *1985 Bootleg*, attracted the attention of several independent metal labels, leading to tracks on the compilation albums *Speed Metal Hell II* and *Metal Massacre IV*. The latter led to a deal with Metal Blade. The band's first album, *Doomsday For The Deceiver*, produced by Brian Slagel at Music Grinders in Eldorado and Track Recording Studios in Hollywood, was chock full of quality, aggressive metal. Roadrunner licensed the record for Europe.

FLOTSAM AND JETSAM discography

DOOMSDAY FOR THE DECEIVER, Roadrunner RR 9683-1 (UK),
Metal Blade MBR 1063 (USA) (1986)
NO PLACE FOR DISGRACE, Roadrunner RR 9549-2 (UK), Elektra
60777-2 (USA) (1988) **143 USA**
WHEN THE STORM COMES DOWN, MCA DMCG 6084 (UK), MCA
MCAD-6382 (USA) (1990) **174 USA**
CUATRO, MCA MCD 10678 (Europe), MCA MCAD-10678 (USA)
(1992)
DRIFT, MCA MCD 11212 (Europe), MCA MCAD-11212 (USA) (1995)
HIGH, Metal Blade 3984-14126-2 (Europe / USA) (1997)
UNNATURAL SELECTION, Metal Blade 3984-14184-2 (Europe /
USA) (1999)
MY GOD, Metal Blade 3984-14370-2 (Europe / USA) (2001)
DREAMS OF DEATH, Crash Music CMU61150 (Europe / USA)
(2005)
LIVE IN PHOENIX, Mausoleum 251077 (Europe) (2006)

Doomsday For The Deceiver ignited a wave of global interest in the band. Flotsam And Jetsam stood apart not only because of their location – most thrash metal bands came from California and New York – but also due to the diverse nature of their material. The album included the Hitler-themed 'Der Führer', accounts of notorious murders such as 'She Took An Axe', and the introduction of the heroic Flotzilla character. The group was also not afraid to inject some humour, as in 'U.L.S.W.' (Ugly Little Slimy Wench).

Newsted's departure to Metallica occurred in late October 1986 on the recommendation of Brian Slagel. He honoured his final Flotsam And Jetsam gig commitment on October 31st and by November 8th was performing onstage with Metallica at the Country Club in Reseda.

This burst of publicity dramatically boosted sales of *Doomsday For The Deceiver* as curious Metallica fans snapped up the album. The band carried out live commitments with the temporary services of Sacred Reich's Phil Rind. Following these early post-Newsted live dates, ex-Sentinel Beast bassist Mike Spencer was hired. Flotsam And Jetsam were then picked up by Metallica's label Elektra and the group gained the valuable support slot on a European tour with Megadeth in 1987.

Spencer lost his position in early 1988 to Troy Gregory. The 1988 album *No Place For Disgrace* was produced by Bill Metoyer and mixed by Michael Wagener at no fewer than four Californian recording locations,

the band hopping between Music Grinder and Track Records once again, plus Pacific Studios in Chatsworth and Preferred Sound in Woodland Hills, taking them from December 1987 until February 1988. The album scored extra press attention for its rip-roaring version of the Elton John hit 'Saturday Night's Alright For Fighting'. Although the band fared well opening for King Diamond in America during 1988, by the end of the tour their deal with Elektra had been lost.

Some 15 months later the group bagged a new deal with MCA and began recording their third album, *When The Storm Comes Down*, with producer Alex Perialas in New York. The album, clad in a regrettably amateurish jacket design, appeared in 1990. Troy Gregory gave notice mid-term into a US tour, forcing the band to curtail projected European dates. Eventually, an auditioning process located Chicago native Jason Ward to fill the vacancy left by Gregory.

The adventurous *Cuatro*, released in 1992 and produced by Neil Kernon at Dotch City Sound in Glendale, was a solid record but did little to improve their status. Lyric writing had been Jason Newsted's job and then Gregory's, but *Cuatro* saw the task handed to manager Eric Braverman. On an international scale, Flotsam And Jetsam's sales hovered frustratingly around the quarter of a million mark for each album release, a trend that would continue.

The band recorded a track co-written with Dave Ellefson of Megadeth, 'Date With Hate', although strangely this did not make the running order for the album and only saw a release as the B-side of the 'Swatting At Flies' single.

Drift appeared in 1995 and had been committed to tape in a home-built studio on a friend's pecan farm outside El Paso, Texas, once again produced by Kernon with a final mix handled by Michael Barbiero. Expanding their sound, the group used keyboards for the first time on the tracks 'Blindside' and 'Missing'. *Drift* was dedicated to the late Nine Inch Nails guitarist Jeff Ward, Jason's brother, who had died following heroin addiction. The band then toured in America supporting Megadeth and Korn in July but, despite radio impact with the track 'Smoked Out', MCA let the band go.

Flotsam And Jetsam returned to the scene after a lengthy absence, reuniting with both their former record company Metal Blade and producer Bill Metoyer. The resulting album, *High*, crafted at Vintage Records in Phoenix, proudly stated the band's intentions towards true metal with song titles mimicking band logos such as those of Judas Priest, Kiss and AC/DC. The album also includes a version of Lard's 'Fork Boy'.

The band returned to live action with a new drummer, Craig Neilson, at the 'Bang Your Head' festival in southern Germany, headlined by Blind Guardian, before a lengthy bout of touring alongside Anvil and Exciter.

Upon their return, the band drafted in a further new member, guitarist Mark Simpson, who made his debut on January 1999's *Unnatural Selection*, which co-produced by James Lockyer. Simpson actually left the band to join George Lynch's Lynch Mob, but had returned to the fold by the summer of 2000 as Flotsam And Jetsam set to work on another album. With the band gearing up for release of a May 2001 album, *My God*, (discarding a previously announced title of *Obsessive Repulsive*), again using Bill Metoyer behind the desk, it was revealed that Eric A.K. was doing the club circuit with a country & western band, The A.K. Corral.

Flotsam And Jetsam commenced a short burst of American club dates, kicking off with a Los Angeles Troubadour gig on July 28th. As August drew to a close it was reported that Eric A.K., the band's vocalist for more than 20 years, had departed. His replacement for the tour was James Rivera of Destiny's End and Helstar. With the tour wrapped up, Rivera would then team up with Seven Witches, debuting with the band at their July appearance at the 'Classic Metal Fest II' in Cleveland, Ohio.

Flotsam And Jetsam were offered a support tour with Swiss rockers Krokus toward the close of 2002 but found themselves in the awkward

Flotsam And Jetsam (Jason Newsted at far right)

position of lacking a lead singer. Bassist Jason Ward was then scheduled to deputise for Halford's Ray Riendeau for New Year shows: the regular Halford bassist had suffered a family tragedy just beforehand. However, the gigs were cancelled when Rob Halford himself was denied entry to the USA with visa difficulties.

James Rivera forged an all-new act, Distant Thunder, in August 2003 with ex-Destiny's End guitarist Eric Halpern and Symphony X bassist Mike Lepond. This trio soon scored a deal with Massacre.

Flotsam And Jetsam – now with returned vocalist Eric A.K., guitarists Ed Carlson and Mark Simpson, bassist Jason Ward and drummer Craig Nielsen – signed a two-album deal with Crash Music in May 2004. Surprisingly, the band laid down a version of Metallica's 'Damage Inc.', for the Big Deal tribute *Metallic Attack*.

The band then allied with contemporaries Overkill and Death Angel for the September 'Thrash Domination' tour of Japan, footage from these concerts being used for the *Live In Japan* DVD. The A.K. Corral, the country & western side-project of Eric A.K., issued *A Different Brand Of Country* in November through their own label, Stillwest. Flotsam And Jetsam resumed live work in 2005, appearing at the 'Deep Freeze Winter Metal' festival in Westminster, Colorado. The band, with Tom Giatron and Mark Simpson as their production team, spent the early part of the year at Genesis Studios in Phoenix, Arizona, recording a new record, *Dreams Of Death*. Craig Nielsen guested on the album *Modes Of Alienation* by the Boston-based instrumental prog-metal project The Alien Blakk. A reissue of *Doomsday For The Deceiver* was scheduled for late 2006. After two decades in business, Flotsam And Jetsam may never have overcome the stigma of losing a member to Metallica – but their place in metal history is assured.

INFERNÄL MÄJESTY
TROUBLED THRASH B-LEAGUERS

THE FIRST RECORDING FROM TORONTO thrash metal combo Infernäl Mäjesty was their four-track *Infernäl Mäjesty* demo cassette in 1986, cut at Triumph's Metal Works studios. The band consisted of singer Chris Bailey, guitarists Kenny Hallman and Steve Terror, bass player Psycopath and Rick Nemes on drums. Both Hallman and Terror had previously operated with Laced, the guitarist also having conducted live operations with The Astrid Young Band. After a brief flirtation with the name Overlord, the group switched to Infernäl Mäjesty.

Infernäl Mäjesty's debut 1987 album *None Shall Defy* was released through Roadrunner, the New York office having received a demo from a European fan, and gained glowing reviews. A near-flawless execution of pure thrash, *None Shall Defy* blazed brightly – but unfortunately a lack of marketing meant its merits were largely overlooked. The alliance with Roadrunner soon came to a halt.

The band subsequently released the demos *Nigresent Dissolution*, recorded at Wellesley Studios in 1988, and the Brian Taylor-produced

---

INFERNAL MAJESTY discography

NONE SHALL DEFY, Roadrunner RR 9609 (Europe), Banzai BRC-2002 (Canada) (1987)
UNHOLIER THAN THOU, Hypnotic HYP 1062 (Canada) (1998)
CHAOS IN COPENHAGEN, Infernal Majesty cnu (Canada) (2000)
ONE WHO POINTS TO DEATH, Black Lotus BLRCD066 (Europe), Galy GALY-018 (USA) (2004)
SYSTEMATICAL EXECUTION, label tba (2007)

Creation Of Chaos, during 1992. This second session marked a shift in band personnel: the new man on vocals was simply named Vince, with bassist Psycopath replaced by Bob Quelch and Kevin Harrison on drums (Rick Nemes had joined Inner Thought). Bizarrely, Infernäl Mäjesty found themselves the subject of mainstream media attention when Vince was jailed, charged with vampiric activity. Apparently the vocalist had slashed his girlfriend's wrist and sucked her blood. Vince, who went on to front Bloodwurm, died of a heroin overdose on October 14th 2001.

Dutch label Displeased reissued *None Shall Defy* in 1997, adding the *Nigresent Dissolution* demo tracks as bonus material. With interest renewed, Infernäl Mäjesty resurrected itself with original vocalist Chris Bailey for live work across Europe. In March 1997 a brace of brand new songs, 'Where Is Your God?' and 'Gone The Way Of All Flesh', was donated to the *Kanada* compilation album. The group, signing to domestic label Hypnotic and with Chay McMullen now installed on bass, returned to the studio for August 1998's *Unholier Than Thou*. The band then blasted Europe, touring alongside Cannibal Corpse and Dark Funeral that September. An April 2000 live album, *Chaos In Copenhagen*, recorded on October 14th 1998 at the Loppen Club in the Danish capital, added two cover versions of Infernäl Mäjesty tracks by other acts, namely Dawn's 'Night Of The Living Dead' and Christ Denied's take on 'Overlord'.

The 2002 line-up – lead vocalist Chris Bailey, guitarists Steve Terror and Kenny Hallman, bassist Kiel Wilson, and ex-Grudge drummer Kris DeBoer – cut a four-track demo. Eric Dubreuil was incorporated on bass in October for recording at Profile Sound Studios in Vancouver of a new album, *One Who Points To Death*. The record, produced by Sho Murray and mastered by Obliveon's Pierre Rémillard at Wild Studios in St-Zenon, Québec, was slated for April 2004 issue through the Greek Black Lotus label in Europe, while North American release was handled by Canada's Galy Records. On a temporary basis, Cradle To Grave's singer Greg Cavanagh filled in for a batch of live shows.

The band had located new singer Brian Langley (previously of Mecha Messiah) and undertook a six-week Canadian tour with support act Dead Jesus. The kick-off show came as a support to Metal Church at the Cobalt in Vancouver on June 20th. According to the band, they lost out on support gigs to W.A.S.P. in August because the headline act deemed Infernäl Mäjesty "too heavy for the bill". European shows scheduled for September were cancelled due to work visa problems.

The band were soon back on the road, acting as support alongside fellow Canadians 3 Inches Of Blood for Norwegian black metal act Satyricon's US dates, commencing on December 2nd in San Francisco. However, Infernäl Mäjesty, citing "personal reasons", abruptly dropped from these dates just prior to commencement. The band announced touring plans for Europe in early 2005 in partnership with Californian thrash veterans Hirax. A new album was then readied. *Systematical Extermination* was recorded in December and produced by Kataklysm's Jean-François Dagenais, marking Brian Langley's recording debut with the band. Infernäl Mäjesty continue to plough their own unique furrow.

MEGADETH
REVENGE SELLS ... AND BUSINESS IS GOOD

MEGADETH ARE THE VEHICLE with which Metallica refugee Dave Mustaine – a guitarist and composer of unquestionable if erratic genius – has made his mark upon the world. Initially fuelled by anger, resentment and an out-of-control lifestyle driven by drug and alcohol addiction, the band has been through many incarnations (although bassist Dave Ellefson remained a core linchpin until recent years), with their most stable and commercially successful guise comprising Mustaine, Ellefson, guitarist Marty Friedman and drummer Nick Menza.

Exorcising his demons, Mustaine has recently cleansed himself in full public view, taking Megadeth to the top echelons of the genre as part of the much vaunted Big Four Of Thrash. By the late 1980s the band's uncompromising and challenging musical output, characterised by Mustaine's vocal venom and an uncanny ability to craft hooks of immense magnitude, gave credibility to their claim of being the world's "state of the art speed metal band". For much of Megadeth's career, the media have portrayed the band's very existence as an act of revenge aimed squarely at Metallica. This unfortunate perception masks Mustaine's very real achievements.

The teenage Mustaine's very first band was Panic, in California, but it came to a tragic end when a car crash – in which Mustaine was involved – killed the driver and band's drummer. He fell in with the fledgling Metallica, but a simmering power struggle resulted in Mustaine's ejection in April 1983, at his own admission for drunkenness. The guitarist was dispatched mid-tour from New York to California on a Greyhound bus. Megadeth came together almost immediately after Mustaine's dismissal, just four months before Metallica were to record their debut, *Kill 'Em All*.

Local fanzines presumed the new band to be Fallen Angel, although in reality no hard and fast name was chosen. 'Fallen Angel' fell by the wayside and Megadeth came into being with Mustaine, bassist Matt Kisselstein and drummer Lee Rausch.

This unit broke up after rehearsals, and a fresh combo was assembled, including bassist Dave Ellefson, his room-mate, Minnesota native Greg Handevidt, and Rausch and Mustaine. Megadeth's debut live performance came with a show at San Francisco's Ruthie's club. At this juncture Mustaine announced the recruitment of vocalist Lor Kain and Richard Girod on drums. However, the group soon dispensed with Kain and Girod. Further turmoil saw Handevidt next in line for dismissal, Mustaine citing the main as a lack of hair. Handevidt, after a spell in a job washing turkeys, resurfaced in 1987 with the band Kublai Khan, releasing a solitary album *Annihilation*. He then opted out of the music business, choosing a new career as a military mortician. When Rausch opted out (he later enjoyed a brief tenure with Dark Angel), the band drafted in another drummer, Dijon Carruthers, but he too was to depart.

Dave Mustaine: "Carruthers had persuaded us, possibly motivated by fear of any racial prejudice, that he was Mexican-Spanish. He was a fairly light-skinned guy, but I was never interested what colour he was. It wasn't like the thing with Metallica and Lloyd Grant. I discovered he was in fact black when his much darker brother, Kane Carruthers, who was in this band The Untouchables, was introduced to me at a party. I fired the freak there and then. Not because he was black, which didn't matter, but because he had lied to us."

Dave Ellefson: "I remember in the Bay Area everyone going: 'Man, these guys are so fast, they're so cool.' Now they're all drunk and burned out. It was all so mindless! The Bay scene was happening, but some of it was just shit. It's no good playing as fast as you possibly can or thrashing as hard as possible, that's just shit. It's great for neckaches, and that's it."

The first Megadeth recordings came in a three-track demo that included 'Love You To Death', 'Skull Beneath The Skin' and 'Mechanix'. The band's first gigs on the club circuit, now including former jazz drummer Gar Samuelson, utilised Slayer's Kerry King as stand-in second guitarist for a total of five shows before Chris Poland was enrolled. The latter had played with Welkin and a female-fronted pop act called No Questions, whose image involved jumpsuits and make-up, and had appeared on a 7-inch single entitled 'Videobrat'. (In a surreal twist of fate, the man who introduced both Samuelson and Poland to the band, Jay Jones, died in 1997, stabbed to death with a butter knife in a fight with his brother-in-law over a baloney sandwich.)

Megadeth still intended to have a lead vocalist at this point, and Mustaine wondered about Diamond Head frontman Sean Harris, but this never got beyond the talking stage.

Dave Mustaine: "There was this singer. I can't remember if we were even Megadeth at that point or why and how this dude got involved, but suddenly we had a singer. The dickhead that came to sing for us turned up wearing eyeliner and carrying a six-pack. I showed him the door straight away, but only after we had drunk his beer. What was his name? I could not tell you. I'm surprised there is not some dude all over the internet claiming to be Megadeth's first singer, but there isn't yet."

Megadeth's first album, May 1985's *Killing Is My Business... And Business Is Good*, was recorded at Indigo Ranch Studios, Malibu and at Crystal Sound Labs, Hollywood on a shoestring budget, but still packed enough intensity to make the world's rock media sit up and take notice when issued by Combat in America and Music For Nations in Europe. The reported budget of $8,000 was alleged to have been used mainly to feed addictions: whatever the reality, Mustaine dispensed with allotted producer Karat Faye midway through proceedings and completed the engineering process himself.

The album included the Mustaine-penned track 'Mechanix', re-titled 'The Four Horsemen' for Metallica's *Kill 'Em All*, and a twisted cover of the Nancy Sinatra hit 'These Boots Are Made For Walking', subsequently removed from later pressings due to objections by the copyright holder, songwriter Lee Hazlewood, who expressed horror at Mustaine's "perversion" of the original lyrics.

The *Killing Is My Business...* jacket introduced the Vic Rattlehead character, a skull adorned with metal visor, stapled jaw and chains that would adorn most future Megadeth products. Although marred by its thin production, the debut was chock-full of the trademark style of intense riffing that made Megadeth a unique entity.

Poland departed, and Megadeth drafted the former Captain Beefheart musician Mike Albert on guitar. The band undertook American dates with Canadians Exciter, but within three months the situation was reversed, with Poland reassuming his role in time for the second leg of the 'American Killing For A Living' tour. A New Year's show in San Francisco featured the band on a bill that included Exodus, Metal Church and, somewhat awkwardly, Metallica.

The band's second album, produced by Mustaine and Randy Burns, was recorded before the band secured a major deal but would emerge in remixed form in 1986 on Capitol as *Peace Sells... But Who's Buying?*. The album had, in its original mix, been pressed up in a test batch by Music For Nations, who anticipated gaining the rights to release it, before Megadeth announced that they had signed to Capitol. Thus, white-label copies do exist as one of the rarer Megadeth collectables.

Peace Sells... But Who's Buying? was clad in an Ed Repka-rendered jacket depicting Vic Rattlehead attempting to sell a devastated United Nations headquarters. It marked a shift in Mustaine's lyrical focus, now pursuing themes of global politics and the occult. The significance of Mustaine's most renowned lyric (the title song's "What do you mean, I don't believe in God? I talk to him every day") only became clear in later years.

The resulting tour – at first in support of Motörhead (before friction between the two bands prompted Megadeth to opt out) and then Alice Cooper – saw a rift developing between the two Daves and Samuelson and Poland. This came to a head at Megadeth's debut British gig, headlining at London's Hammersmith Odeon. The show, supported by Metal Church, highlighted the band's paper-thin division between genius and chaos. With the news that their gear had been impounded at customs and released only hours before the show, combined with the band's onstage resentment, Megadeth's show had many wondering whether they had been in the presence of the next metal sensation or a bunch of sorry burn-outs.

During a break between road dates, Mustaine earned production credits on the debut album from Sanctuary, *Refuge Denied*, before the gig schedule resumed. Dates in North America saw King Diamond and Mayhem as support. By the tour's close in Hawaii, Samuelson was asked to leave following numerous on-the-road disappearances and occasions when he would fall asleep at inopportune moments. Poland persevered but would lose his position when recording for a third album began.

Chris Poland: "I was a drug addict and I would substitute alcohol when I couldn't get my drug of choice. When I drank, it would keep me from shaking and having the chills, withdrawals and stuff. So when I was onstage I was very often just insane. Really pissed off. It's a weird place to be; it's disgusting. There were a few times when we blew it totally.

"I think a lot of the decadence and partying clouded our heads. Y'know, I love [Dave Mustaine] like a brother, and you know how you fight like brother? You push each other then laugh and say 'you stupid jerk' and it's OK, but eventually we couldn't do that any more. We started getting into fist fights and it was getting pretty ugly.

"We were insane for a very long time. I mean really wrecked. For a while it was extreme fun but … I don't know, it got really fucked. I mean, when you play with a band for five years only to end it in violence, all you have is the violence that you leave with. I didn't play guitar for a year after Megadeth. I just hung around and became decadent again."

It was many years before Samuelson re-emerged, on the 1997 Fatal Opera album *The Eleventh Hour*. Poland would eventually shed his addictions and put in a touring stint with The Circle Jerks in the bass role. He then issued the solo album *Return To Metalopolis* before creating Damn The Machine, then Mumbo's Brain. A further solo album, *Chasing The Sun*, followed in 1999.

Megadeth confirmed their revised line-up in November 1987. Alongside Mustaine and Ellefson were ex-Broken Silence guitarist Jeff Young and, from Detroit, Meanies drummer Chuck Behler (who had been Samuelson's drum technician). The noted Slayer drummer Dave Lombardo had been offered the vacant drum position before Behler but reportedly turned the gig down because of Mustaine and co's acknowledged drug problems.

Jeff Young had gained the position after he had coached ex-Malice guitarist Jay Reynolds for the job. Although Reynolds briefly gained a place in Megadeth, Young ousted him midway through recording of *So Far, So Good… So What?*.

With this fresh roster of players, Megadeth performed their second British show as headliners of the 'Christmas On Earth' festival atop a bevy of thrash acts including Nuclear Assault, Overkill, Lääz Rockit, Voivod and Cro-Mags, before American dates with Dio. By the tail end of these gigs with the former Rainbow and Black Sabbath singer, and their album nestling in the American top 30, Megadeth had turned the tour (initially with slow ticket sales) into their own vehicle. A brief rest period was quickly curtailed by more headline shows, this time with Germans Warlock as openers.

So Far, So Good… So What?, delivered in January 1988, featured a cover version of The Sex Pistols' 'Anarchy In The UK', which charted in Britain and boasted guest guitar from Pistols man Steve Jones. Other material included a reworking of a track debuted at Megadeth's first ever concert: originally entitled 'Megadeth', it evolved into 'Burnt Offerings' before winding up on the band's third album as 'Set The World On Fire'.

MEGADETH discography

KILLING IS MY BUSINESS… AND BUSINESS IS GOOD, Music For Nations MFN 46 (UK), Combat MX 8015 (USA) (1985)

PEACE SELLS… BUT WHO'S BUYING?, Capitol CDEST 2022 (UK), Capitol CDP 7 46370 2 (USA) (1986) **76 USA**

SO FAR, SO GOOD… SO WHAT!, Capitol CDEST 2053 (UK), Capitol CDP 7 48148 2 (USA) (1988) **18 UK, 28 USA**

RUST IN PEACE, Capitol CDEST 2132 (UK), Capitol CDP 7 91935 2 (USA) (1990) **8 UK, 23 USA**

COUNTDOWN TO EXTINCTION, Capitol CDEST 2175 (UK), Capitol CDP 7 98531 2 (USA) (1992) **5 UK, 2 USA**

YOUTHANASIA, Capitol CDEST 2244 (UK), Capitol 7243 8 29004 2 9 (USA) (1994) **6 UK, 4 USA**

HIDDEN TREASURES, Capitol 33670 (UK), Capitol 7243 8 33670 2 3 (USA) (1995) **28 UK, 90 USA**

CRYPTIC WRITINGS, Capitol CDEST 2297 (UK), Capitol 7243 8 38262 2 3 (USA) (1997) **38 UK, 10 USA**

RISK, Capitol 499134 (UK), Capitol 7243 4 99134 0 0 (USA) (1999) **29 UK, 16 USA**

CAPITOL PUNISHMENT: THE MEGADETH YEARS, Capitol 5259162 (UK), Capitol 7243 5 25916 2 6 (USA) (2000) **66 USA**

THE WORLD NEEDS A HERO, Metal-Is MISCD006 (UK), Sanctuary 06076-84503-2 (USA) (2001) **16 USA**

RUDE AWAKENING, Metal-Is MISDD019 (UK), Sanctuary 06076-84544-2 (USA) (2002) **115 USA**

THE SYSTEM HAS FAILED, Sanctuary SANCD 297 (UK), Sanctuary 06076-84708-2 (USA) (2004) **60 UK, 18 USA**

GREATEST HITS: BACK TO THE START, Capitol 8739292 (UK), Capitol 73929 (USA) (2005) **65 USA**

UNITED ABOMINATIONS, Roadrunner catalogue number tba (Europe / USA) (2007)

The brooding 'In My Darkest Hour' was an autobiographical piece voicing Mustaine's thoughts at the moment when he had learned of the death of Metallica's Cliff Burton's. A rather more vicious song was targeted at ex-guitarist Chris Poland as Mustaine dedicating 'Liar' to his former colleague. Expectations were high as the thrash movement reached its zenith and Megadeth's third album clocked up advance North American sales of over 450,000.

However, the year could not go by without controversy. With the press continually fanning the embers through numerous Metallica-versus-Megadeth articles, it was alleged that Mustaine claimed that Metallica's 'Leper Messiah' from their *Master Of Puppets* album was a thinly disguised version of an early track he had written titled 'The Hills Ran Red'. Metallica hit back with strong denials.

Back in business the same year, Megadeth went into the studio to re-record a fresh version of 'These Boots Are Made For Walking' for inclusion on the *Dudes* film soundtrack. They then returned to Europe for a headline tour with support from Seattle's Sanctuary, with whom Mustaine had worked on the production front. Although many dates were sold out, Mustaine threw the band straight into controversy when he made positive remarks about the IRA while onstage in Northern Ireland. The audience was far from appreciative and began spitting at the frontman.

The troubled times were far from over. After an impressive appearance at the Castle Donington 'Monsters Of Rock' festival, Megadeth once more split down the middle with Young and Behler out, the drummer joining Black & White. Young unsuccessfully auditioned for melodic rockers Danger Danger.

An embittered Mustaine launched into a very personal and vitriolic stream of abuse about his former guitar partner, even going so far as to suggest that Young was in love with Warlock chanteuse Doro Pesch and could not handle the fact that Pesch was supposedly writing love letters to Mustaine.

Jeff Young: "The next Megadeth album is gonna be scary. I can see the direction the riffs Dave and I are working out, and the collaboration next time around will throw away the rule books. It'll make the first three Megadeth albums look like they belong in the crib."

Jeff Young: "Doro Pesch and I will be working on a project some time in the future, an EP or something. We'll just write some songs that we really like to play. Billy Sheehan will play bass and Tommy Lee from Mötley Crüe will play drums. Megadeth are also changing management, we'll be going with the same management that has Bon Jovi and Mötley Crüe."

Dave Mustaine: "That guy Jeff Young. He had to go. I mean, everything that came out that guy's mouth was just the highest grade of pure horseshit. It was embarrassing."

Later in 1988, Megadeth celebrated a Top 20 British singles chart hit with their version of Alice Cooper's 'No More Mr Nice Guy' from the soundtrack to Wes Craven's *Shocker* movie. This track featured the first contributions from ex-Rhoads drummer Nick Menza. Coincidentally, the new drummer had been Behler's drum technician, just as Behler had been Samuelson's. It took Menza three stabs to land the job: after he had failed two auditions, Mustaine himself taught Menza the songs. It transpired that Menza's ability had been there all along, but the prospect of joining Megadeth had reduced him to a bag of nerves at auditions.

The vacancy for a lead guitarist fuelled rumours concerning Heathen's Lee Altus, Savatage's Criss Oliva, Pantera's Diamond Darrell and Annihilator's Jeff Waters. Waters nearly got the gig, but Darrell was offered the position. The Pantera guitarist insisted, however, that his brother, Pantera drummer Vinnie, also be given a job, and negotiations broke down.

Mustaine resorted to pulling in erstwhile ally Chris Poland to conduct demo recordings for a new album, but it was to be former Deuce, Vixen, Hawaii and Cacophony man Marty Friedman who landed the permanent position. The result of this union was the Mike Clink-produced *Rust In Peace*, released in September 1990. Recording took place as Mustaine simultaneously underwent drug rehabilitation treatment, but the final collection of tracks was to be their most mature effort to date, giving them a further hit.

Marty Friedman: "This album is just so precise, it's like a clock. If you listen to a lot of the early thrash records they are sloppy as fuck. I mean, the playing is really bad. Rust In Peace has that kind of military precision to it, and when you get that, everything just locks into place and you start to get that groove that really makes a song work. Dave Mustaine is just amazing at that, getting that rhythm guitar to sit in the groove and really drive it along. Some of his chord threads are mind-blowing. He's totally underrated because he's a loudmouth and you have to deal with a lot of crap with Dave before you get down to the raw essence of the man. He's a master musician. The guy's a fucking genius too, though, so be prepared to deal with everything that goes with that."

Rust In Peace, viewed by many fans as the pinnacle of Megadeth's artistic achievement, provided Mustaine with a wide canvas in which he put down his observations on the Irish conflict, the war in the Middle East, nuclear weapons and aliens.

British touring in March 1991 saw strong support from both The Almighty and Alice In Chains. Megadeth's ambitions took an upward swing on the touring front as they forged part of the immense 'Clash Of The Titans' touring bill. Originally mooted to comprise the Big Four, including Metallica, the eventual trio of Megadeth, Slayer and Anthrax still proved a major draw, and the North American dates, with openers Alice In Chains, proved a huge success with sell-out attendances. The band then dropped in a couple of San Francisco club shows billed as Vic & The Rattleheads, and by October 'Clash Of The Titans', now Megadeth and Slayer with support from Testament and Suicidal Tendencies, slammed into Britain and Europe. On returning to America the band hooked up with British metal legends Judas Priest for their 'Painkiller' tour.

July 1992's *Countdown To Extinction*, cut at Enterprise Studios in Burbank, California, would propel Megadeth into the major league with the momentum gained from their previously strong releases. It just missed out on the US Number 1 position and propelled Megadeth past the two million sales mark for the first time. The album, produced by Dave Mustaine and Max Norman, proved transitional in merging thrash with a more formatted hard rock approach, featuring strong tracks such as the title number, 'Skin O' My Teeth', 'Sweating Bullets' and the near mantric 'Symphony Of Destruction'.

Despite this heady success, in 1993 Mustaine was, by his own later admission, still teetering on the edge. Megadeth performed as Vic & The Rattleheads once again at Nottingham's Rock City on June 3rd before playing as special guests for none other than Metallica at the Milton Keynes Bowl two days later, sharing the bill with Diamond Head and The Almighty. Mustaine optimistically announced from the stage, "The ten years of bullshit between Metallica and Megadeth is over."

A 1993 support tour of North America to Aerosmith was curtailed when, in Houston, Texas, Megadeth were forced out, Mustaine apparently unable to perform. Aerosmith themselves were none too pleased at remarks Mustaine made about their age. The vocalist entered into another round of detoxification treatment, and in the lull Ellefson busied himself with production for Texan metal act Helstar on their *Multiples Of Black* album.

Megadeth reunited for two interim projects: the 'Angry Again' track for the *Last Action Hero* movie soundtrack; and '99 Ways To Die' submitted for the *Beavis And Butthead* compilation album on Geffen. Marty Friedman also found time for a solo album.

Megadeth then relocated to Phoenix, Arizona, constructing a brand new studio for themselves dubbed Fat Planet, to work with Max Norman once again on the *Youthanasia* album. The album, issued in October 1994, broke into the American Top 5 and went double platinum as Megadeth embarked on an almost year-long world tour. The album artwork was banned in Thailand, Malaysia and Singapore for depicting an old woman hanging babies on a clothes line – and the babies depicted in the video for the album track 'Train Of Consequences' were censored by MTV worldwide.

Mustaine's continual battle against his addictions brought about a much publicised and harsh regime that prohibited backstage alcohol, duly put into force for all Megadeth shows. Megadeth toured South America in 1994 with support from British rockers The Almighty and the USA the following year with Fear Factory as openers. A welcome first for the band saw a one-off show in Tel Aviv, Israel.

Punctuating this road work in July, the retrospective *Hidden Treasures* arrived in stores, collecting some of Megadeth's rarer output and non-album tracks. To cap a gruelling 11 months on the road, Megadeth made another foray into South America in September 1995 as part of the Monsters Of Rock bill alongside Ozzy Osbourne, Alice Cooper, Faith No More and Paradise Lost. With the close of the tour Mustaine busied himself with the MD45 project, a punk industrial album in collaboration with Fear's Lee Ving.

Megadeth made a respectable return in June 1997 with *Cryptic Writings*, which entered the US charts at Number 10, selling 75,000 units in its first week of release. The album was crafted in Nashville at the Tracking Room studios and, surprisingly, produced by ex-Giant man Dann Huff. Used to unforgiving recording schedules, Mustaine was somewhat taken aback when Huff, a committed Christian, explained he could not work on Sundays as he had to take his family to church. This potential problem was solved when Mustaine attended church with his family too – a decision that would have consequences for the band further down the line.

Dave Mustaine: "It was funny. I read these horror stories about Megadeth working with Dan Huff and this confusion and anger related to that. You know what? Poor Dan was getting it much tougher on the other side. All his friends were saying to him: 'Why are you working with Megadeth? Don't you know about them?' He was getting shit for getting involved with us and our fans were giving us shit for working with Dan. All I can tell you is the guy knows what he's doing and is an amazing musician. It works. Get over it."

Behind the scenes, Megadeth had switched the management of its business affairs from Ron Laffitte to Bud Prager, an industry veteran best known for his successes with AOR giants Foreigner. *Cryptic Writings* would display a much more radio-orientated direction than any previous product, a trend that continued with ensuing releases. Fans voiced concern not only at Megadeth's shift in musical values but also at their new short haircuts and snappy clothes – a far cry from the band's thrash roots.

The band toured Britain in June 1997, supported by Kill II This, still comfortably selling out venues. Returning to the USA, where *Cryptic Writings* remained firmly lodged in the album charts, Megadeth, with guests Life Of Agony, busily set about touring to push the album past the gold sales mark. Dates in Mexico had Judas Priest as special guests. In spite of its shortcomings, *Cryptic Writings* still managed to surpass a million sales in the USA. The first 500,000 copies were printed on a silver background, with subsequent manufacturing runs on black. In 1998 the EP *Cryptic Death* featured instrumental reworkings of five tracks from the album.

Nick Menza took a leave of absence in 1998: it was later revealed that he had been let go due to health concerns. Menza turned up in 1999 on the Fireball Ministry album *Ou Est La Rock?*, working with ex-Obsessed and Goatsnake bassist Guy Pinhas. Without a regular percussionist, Brian Howe stood in on drums for Megadeth's contribution of 'I'll Get Even' to the soundtrack of the animated movie *Songs Of The Witchblade* in 1998. That same year guitarist Jeff Young resurfaced in a somewhat unlikely form, contributing to Brazilian flamenco artist Badi Assad's *Chameleon* album.

Eventually a permanent replacement was located in the Y&T, Suicidal Tendencies and White Lion-credited drummer Jimmy DeGrasso. The resulting album, *Risk*, found Megadeth ploughing deeper into commercial territory. Lead track 'Crush 'Em' garnered publicity when it was used by WCW professional wrestler Bill Goldberg as his entrance theme; it was also included on the soundtrack to Belgian action star Jean-Claude Van Damme's movie *Universal Soldier: The Return*.

Dave Ellefson: "We had this whole new behind-the-scenes team for Cryptic Writings and Risk that were totally geared towards hits. They had this big success with Foreigner and convinced us they could do the same with Megadeth. I don't know what we were thinking! They wanted a complete change. We had to wear these clothes to fit in, we had our hair styled, they even interfered with the songs and the lyrics. It was like: 'Hey, you can't say that because radio won't play it.'

There were lots of other things too. We lost Vic, our mascot, because they didn't like it. Lots of stupid things, even trying to tell Dave how to speak, what to say and what not to say. We kept having fans saying to us saying: 'What the fuck are you doing? I hate you now!'

"They were strange times though. Nirvana, grunge, all that shit – and the record companies were running scared because all they had were heavy metal bands, which overnight became an embarrassment. The way I look at it, the musicians did themselves no favours because, like Megadeth, they listened to the wrong people. Suddenly every band changed the way they looked and sounded. We were guilty. Megadeth should have been braver. It was probably the dumbest thing we've ever done."

Risk drew an outcry from fans and struggled to manage 350,000 sales in the USA. Nevertheless, the band put in a series of well attended American dates in 2000 as part of the 'Maximum Rock' tour alongside Mötley Crüe and Anthrax. Unfortunately, the tour did not prove to be the ideal package the band had hoped for as the headliners struggled to pull in anticipated audiences and Anthrax quickly dropped off the billing.

The year 2000 saw Al Pitrelli replacing Friedman. Pitrelli, although highly respected as a musician, was acknowledged by many as a 'guitar for hire', having been involved with Danger Danger, Alice Cooper, Asia, Widowmaker, Savatage, Blue Öyster Cult and the Stephen Pearcy Band as well as non-rock acts such as Kool & The Gang, Celine Dion and Michael Bolton.

Megadeth donated a rendition of 'Never Say Die' for the Black Sabbath tribute album *Nativity In Black II* before writing 'The Day The Music Died' for the *Get To You* album from Jeannine St. Clair.

Risk had seriously wounded Megadeth's standing and Capitol let the band go, putting out a compilation – *Capitol Punishment* – in 2000 as a parting shot. The record boasted the inclusion of two fresh tracks recorded with Pitrelli, 'Kill The King', and 'Dread And The Fugitive Mind', plus a closing Megadeth medley mix.

For their May 2001 release, *The World Needs A Hero*, Megadeth would switch labels to Sanctuary, which was led by Iron Maiden manager Rod Smallwood. The album had been recorded earlier for Capitol but was handed back to the band upon the split. Fans were pleased as Mustaine promised a return to the heavier form of the past and the lead single 'Motor Psycho' rocketed straight in at the Number 1 position for American rock radio plays in its first week of release. The album duly debuted high at Number 16 in the American charts, selling over 60,000 copies in its first week.

Meanwhile, it was revealed that the singer now part-owned a restaurant in Phoenix along with Alice Cooper and a number of sports celebrities. The menu naturally included Megadeth meatloaf. In the UK Megadeth toured with support by the Finnish 'thrash cello' quartet Apocalyptica.

A projected Malaysian date as part of their 2001 Far Eastern dates at the Warp Club on August 2nd in Kuala Lumpur was cancelled when the Malaysian government objected to the band's imagery, deeming it "unsuitable for the youth of Malaysia". The band were warned off in the strongest terms and threatened with arrest if they attempted to play the concert.

A subsequent North American bout of touring suffered no such problems, commencing at the Saltair in Magna, Utah, on September 7th and running through to a close in New York at the Irving Plaza on October 16th. The headliners' set fluctuated throughout as fans had been invited to vote for their favourite tracks. Meanwhile, Marty Friedman re-emerged with his new project Red Dye #2; the guitarist would also work with UFO guitarist Michael Schenker on an all-instrumental studio project.

Megadeth were riding on a renewed commercial high, and were the subject of strong rumours hinting at a joint Metallica-Megadeth tour in the future – possibly even involving a bipartisan unit, dubbed Meta-Mega by Mustaine. However, this never came to pass.

With the close of US dates, Mustaine headed back into the studio along with producer Bill Kennedy for a remix of the band's debut album *Killing Is My Business… And Business Is Good*. The revised version would include tracks from earlier demos, but initially not their take on 'These Boots Are Made For Walking', permission still denied from the original lyric writer following Megadeth's less than subtle change of words on their original session. As it transpired, 'Boots…' did make the final running order, as did bonus demo versions of 'Last Rites (Loved To Death)', 'Mechanix' and 'The Skull Beneath The Skin'.

As the year drew to a close, with Megadeth now proudly sitting on 15 million album sales to date, it was revealed that Mustaine had embarked upon a studio project with Diamond Head guitarist Brian Tatler. Also in the works was Megadeth's first live offering, a double CD and DVD affair entitled *Rude Awakening* and issued in March.

On April 3rd 2002 fans were shocked to learn that Mustaine had suffered a severe nerve-damage injury to his left arm. He subsequently announced his departure from the band – which to all intents and purposes folded Megadeth. The singer had lapsed from a lengthy period of sobriety and cut off the circulation to the radial ulnar nerve in his arm while falling asleep in an awkward position in the La Hacienda Rehabilitation Center in Hunt, Texas. The announcement came only hours after conjecture that Mustaine was likely to pull out of the band after he had reportedly found God.

The fallout from Mustaine's shock news was almost immediate, with rumours indicating that Dave Ellefson was about to join Metallica (who had lost their long-time bassist Jason Newsted in 2001). Ellefson was keen

to get back to work, writing songs for Dry Kill Logic's second album and acting as co-producer for the Canadian band Warmachine.

Meanwhile, Al Pitrelli's next career move was so sudden that it did not have time to generate any speculation: the guitarist announced on April 7th that he was rejoining Savatage, ousting the previous incumbent, Jack Frost. However, before taking up this post, Pitrelli would undertake live work with former Skid Row vocalist Sebastian Bach. Within days, further rumours had it that Ellefson was coming onboard to supply bass, although these would prove to be unfounded.

Marty Friedman and Ellefson then put in a surprise showing on Steve Richards's *Southbound Train* album, performing on the Buddy Holly track 'That Makes It Tough'. Ellefson would also act as producer on demos for Phoenix-based Twist Dead Fable.

Jimmy DeGrasso joined Stone Sour on a temporary basis for their October US dates, filling in for Joel Ekman who had fractured his wrist. The Friedman-Ellefson-DeGrasso axis united for road work in early 2003 in support of the guitarist Ekman's *Music For Speeding* solo album.

Megadeth fans were pleased when word arrived of the September 2003 'Guitarevolution' tour of North America, fronted up by Marty Friedman, along with Chris Poland and his fusion band Ohm, and ex-Testament guitarist Alex Skolnick's eponymous jazz-fusion Trio.

Al Pitrelli engaged in a left-field project dubbed O'2L in alliance with keyboard player Jane Mangini, and Dave Ellefson also stayed in the public eye, laying down bass for four tracks on the new Soulfly album. Jimmy De Grasso was then confirmed as part of the much-vaunted White Lion reformation.

Dave Mustaine was back in the studio in early 2004, co-writing a track for Christian rock band Pillar. He issued a press release confirming that new Megadeth material was on the horizon. Work had begun on bringing unused songs from the archive up to full strength and compiling new material written after October 2003. Although the classic *Rust In Peace* line-up had been mooted, Mustaine assembled a studio band comprising Chris Poland plus a rhythm section of bassist Jimmy Sloas from Christian bands Dogs Of Peace and The Imperials, and the Frank Zappa, Sting and Duran Duran-credited jazz drummer Vinnie Colaiuta.

Capitol planned a full reissue schedule of the remastered catalogue albums to coincide with fresh product, and among the reworkings would be the MD45 project, boasting newly recorded vocals from Mustaine. All the archive Megadeth albums boasted extra tracks in the form of rare B-sides and previously unheard demos. *Rust In Peace* saw the inclusion of demos featuring lead guitar by Chris Poland, but unfortunately what was intended by Mustaine as an acknowledgement of Poland's contributions backfired when the ex-guitarist sued him for their presence on the remaster. The case was settled out of court.

A new release, *The System Has Failed*, set for September issue through Sanctuary, was recorded at Phase Four studios in Tempe, Arizona. The album was originally set to feature jacket artwork by Ed Repka, the artist who had crafted many of Megadeth's classic sleeves, but this idea was scotched when cost became an issue. The album, strongly hinted by Mustaine to be Megadeth's last before he launched into a solo career, would be preceded by the single 'Die Dead Enough'.

David Ellefson announced the formation of his new act F5, actually founded back in 2002. For this venture he would be joined by guitarists Steve Conley and John Davis, drummer David Small, and singer Dale Steele. F5 worked on recordings with producer Ryan Greene for an album release.

Fans welcomed the reinstatement of Nick Menza to the Megadeth drum stool in July. That same month Mustaine took some uncharacteristic verbal swings at his former longstanding ally Ellefson. Within days of this broadside, Ellefson filed an $18.5 million lawsuit against Mustaine in the Manhattan Federal Court, alleging that the singer shortchanged him on profits and backed out of a deal to turn Megadeth Inc. over to him when the band broke up in 2002. Mustaine swiftly counter-sued, alleging that in May 2004 Ellefson executed a settlement agreement in which he gave up his 20 per cent interest in Megadeth. Unfortunately for the ex-bassist, his case was thrown out of court. Subsequently, a further legal agreement put restrictions on Ellefson's right to use the Megadeth name in interviews or articles.

Annihilator guitarist Jeff Waters, a man who already had a place in Megadeth's history, began talks with Mustaine for the live line-up of the band. However, it was Glen Drover, a veteran of Eidolon and King Diamond, who secured the position. Shortly afterward, Iced Earth bassist James MacDonough was confirmed too. MacDonough's early career had seen terms of duty with Florida outfits Mad Axe, Delta 9, Invader, Oracle and Brutal Assault.

A promotional clip for the track 'Die Dead Enough' launched the marketing for the comeback album *The System Has Failed*. The album sold 45,935 copies in the United States in its first week of release, to debut at Number 18 on the *Billboard* 200 chart. In Canada the album sold 5,046 units on its debut at Number 10, setting a new high in the band's career by debuting in the highest chart position in that territory. Meanwhile, the recently-issued Capitol remasters series was also released as a box set entitled *Hell Wasn't Built In A Day: The Complete Remasters*.

With days to go before the tour, commencing on October 23rd in Reno, Nevada, it would be revealed that Nick Menza, apparently not up to full physical strength, had vacated the drum stool in favour of Eidolon's Shawn Drover. Capping the year, Mustaine would also find himself on screen as part of the 2005 *Rock School* documentary chronicling the pioneering work of Paul Green's School Of Rock Music in Philadelphia. The singer fronted a version of 'Peace Sells…' backed by musicians from the school.

Mainland shows in Europe throughout February saw NWOBHM veterans Diamond Head as support act before Megadeth put in Japanese and Australian headliners, the latter with opening act Dungeon, in April. Mustaine's newfound Christian faith put the band back into the news when Greek concerts, on June 17th and 18th in Athens and Thessaloniki, saw the ousting of domestic black metal band Rotting Christ. Objecting to their presence, Mustaine stated as part of a lengthy explanation that he "would prefer not to play on concerts with Satanic bands". Apparently Mustaine claimed that Rotting Christ could play, but in that event Megadeth would withdraw.

The band unveiled the 'Gigantour' festival trek for US action in late July, heading a bill comprising Dream Theater, Fear Factory, The Dillinger Escape Plan, Symphony X, Nevermore, Dry Kill Logic and West Virginians Bobaflex. Dream Theater fulfilled these dates until September, when their position was taken by Anthrax. Apparently Mustaine was not only instrumental in personally picking the bands for this bill but also insisting on a "fan-friendly" ticket price of $35. Megadeth scheduled its second ever performance in Israel, on June 22nd at the Tel Aviv 'Metalist' festival. Unfortunately Megadeth's performance was stopped by police just four songs into their set due to the collapse of safety barriers.

In parallel with this intensive live activity, a Megadeth retrospective album emerged, *Greatest Hits: Back To The Start*, boasting a tracklist voted by fans, as well as a two-disc DVD, *Arsenal Of Megadeth*. The album shifted just over 17,000 copies in its first week of US sales to debut at Number 65 on the national *Billboard* charts.

The August 2nd 'Gigantour' stop proved memorable when Dream Theater's set at the Nokia Live venue in Dallas saw the inclusion of an encore tribute to fallen guitar hero 'Dimebag' Darrell Abbott of Pantera and Damageplan. The band performed a rendition of Pantera's 'Cemetery Gates' with Dave Mustaine alongside Burton C. Bell of Fear Factory and Russell Allen of Symphony X.

Mustaine intriguingly announced that he would declare his intentions about the future of Megadeth following the band's October 9th concert in Buenos Aires, Argentina. The frontman duly announced from the stage: "I told you earlier tonight that I was gonna let all of you know first before the rest of the world what our decision was – whether or not we were gonna continue with Megadeth," before a rendition of 'Coming Home'. Once the song was complete, Mustaine stated matter-of-factly: "Yes."

As February opened, Megadeth revealed that they had parted ways with bassist James MacDonough, prompting rumours of a reunion with Ellefson. However, within days, former Black Label Society bassist James Lomenzo had been drafted in.

Mustaine has proved to both fans and industry that Megadeth are in demand and that this appetite is far from being fulfilled. Most significantly, the last Megadeth album and world tour proved to Mustaine himself that the band has lost none of its competitive edge and reason for being. So far, so good… so more?

Dave Mustaine: "Spirituality is something that catches up with you. You go through certain things: for me it was revenge, anger, addiction. I hit the bottom, the very dregs of life. All these things I dealt with. It took a long, long time but I turned everything around to a positive. I started Megadeth out of pure revenge, burning revenge. Everything I did was motivated towards that end. I would come up with better riffs, record better songs, make better albums, have a better drummer, a better bass player. It's all wrong, but you have to learn the hard way. To learn something you have to go through some adversity. It's painful.

"My journey has been with Megadeth. It's not the Hallelujah trip. I've turned something negative into a big positive. I'm still learning. Every day. But now I can appreciate why things happened the way they did. If you're a real fan you'll see that spirituality all the way through Megadeth. Sometimes I wasn't sure of it myself at the time, but it's there.

"I'm not going to go Stryper or anything like that. One of the lessons I have learned is to have strength in my own beliefs. I don't need to tell other people what to do or how to think. I'm not going to tell you how to live. All you're going to get from me is heavy metal."

METAL CHURCH
BOW TO THE FIRST CHURCH OF METAL

SEATTLE'S METAL CHURCH WERE one of the true founders of the early 1980s North American thrash metal scene. Although they arrived in the teeth of the thrash gale, Metal Church always had much more to offer, their brand of metal being forward-thinking enough to indicate what was to come. With Metal Church, a punk attitude met 1970s epic rock head on and, probably because the band was too big for the narrow confines of thrash, their recording history was erratic. Metal Church's first three albums are rightfully held up as near-masterpieces, so it's ironic that, following a mid-term slump, their attempted comeback, *Masterpeace*, fell short of such recognition.

Guitarist Kurdt Vanderhoof created the band upon his departure from punk act The Lewd, titling it after the nickname of his San Francisco apartment. As his previous band steered away from punk and into a hardcore thrash direction, Vanderhoof found himself more and more intrigued by the metal scene. A post-gig conversation at a 1980 concert proved decisive when Leviathan guitarist Rick Condran and drummer Aaron Zimpel convinced Vanderhoof that they should unite in the 'ultimate' metal band. Vanderhoof, Condran, bassist Steve Haat and drummer Aaron Zimpel (aka Aaron Whymer) then created Anvil Chorus – The Church Of Metal. Meanwhile, the remnants of Leviathan – Zimpel, who switched to vocals, bassist Bill Skinner and drummer Kenny Feragen – trod their own path to become progressive rock trio Vienna.

Kurdt Vanderhoof: "I got musically bored with the punk scene. I mean, the first-generation punk scene was great and a lot of fun, but it got very limiting, not only musically but also in terms of any kind of success. OK, that is great because that was what the punk scene was all about, but I wanted to try and achieve more. Then the New Wave Of British Heavy Metal vibe started creeping in here and I was like, wow, here we are … this is what I was waiting for!

"We were taking from the punk scene as far as the energy was concerned … and beefing it up a bit. It was an all-for-one, one-for-all kind of vibe, which I really miss now. It's not just here in Seattle but throughout America. There is not really a scene of any kind … it is so fragmented. It was great back then that, from just a crappy-sounding cassette, people became fans of your band all over the country and all over the world."

Upon his return to Aberdeen, Washington, in 1981, Vanderhoof made his first all-instrumental demo, consisting of the Leviathan track 'Red Skies', 'Heads Will Roll' and 'Merciless Onslaught'. A pair of local musicians, guitarists Thaen Rasmussen (ex-Vy-King) and Doug Piercy (ex-Cobra and Delta) liked the name Anvil Chorus so much that they took it for themselves. They did however offer acknowledgement with their track 'Bow To The Church Of Metal'. Vanderhoof trimmed the name of his act down to Metal Church. The new band went through numerous drummers, at one stage even inviting the pre-Metallica Lars Ulrich to enrol.

Kurdt Vanderhoof: "[Lars] had just come over from Denmark, and was staying in San Francisco visiting some relatives, and he hooked up with myself and Ron Quintana [Metal Mania fanzine editor] and got involved in the scene down there. He was going to do it and he had heard our demos, but he was on the way to Los Angeles to live with his dad, so he wasn't gonna stay."
Lars Ulrich (Metallica): "I love what Kurdt was doing with the

Church Of Metal. Back then that's what they were called. Actually, they had a ton of names so it got confusing. I was impressed by their heaviness, it was very old school in a strange kind of way, and David was a hell of a singer. As soon as we had the chance we took them out on the road with us. They had just been signed so the opportunity was there. It worked out neat for everyone."

Sinister Savage man Billy McKay fronted Metal Church for a spell before founding Griffin. Singer Ed Bull was invited to join the band, but Condran objected. When the guitarist quit, Bull was on the mike-stand the very next day. Abandoning Vienna, Zimpel also joined on drums. With this line-up Metal Church cut their second demo, which included a reworking of 'Heads Will Roll' titled 'Put The Chains On', an Anvil Chorus number, 'Arab Nations', 'Wake Up And Die' and 'The Trap Is Set'. The last track displayed the enmity between Bull and Condran, with a chorus of "Die Ricky, die!".

Despite fervent interest in the band and intensive tape trading by fans, this early incarnation of Metal Church folded, with Haat going on to a temporary stint with Griffin and local glam-metal act Jetboy. Bull founded Control with guitarists Dino Scarposi and Bill Tuder: a later version of Control featured ex-Anvil Chorus guitarist Doug Piercy, later of Heathen. Zimpel, meanwhile, joined Anvil Chorus. Vanderhoof journeyed back to Auburney, Seattle, to create Shrapnel. By 1983 this act had evolved into a second incarnation of Metal Church, with a line-up of Vanderhoof, vocalist David Wayne, guitarist Craig Wells, bassist Duke Erikson and drummer Kirk Arrington. An earlier Shrapnel vocalist, Mike Murphy, opened up the vacancy for Wayne by bailing out to join Rogues Gallery. The band debuted on May 4th 1984, performing at the D&R Theater in Aberdeen with Rogues Gallery and the Melvins as opening acts. Before long, Metal Church's uncompromising approach had placed the band alongside Queensryche at the head of the Seattle scene. Early devotees included soon-to-be influential figures such as Kurt Cobain and Layne Staley.

In 1984, after contributing the track 'Deathwish' to the Seattle-based Ground Zero label's *Northwest Metalfest* compilation LP, Metal Church signed to the same label and, allowed just ten days to cut the tracks, released their critically acclaimed, self-titled debut. This ignited an electrifying response through the global metal underground and shifted significant copies on expensive import. Fans found the heavy price more than justified by one of the heaviest albums ever to find its way onto vinyl. Capped with an irreverent rendition of Deep Purple's 'Highway Star', *Metal Church* ranged from punishingly heavy rustic metal to state-of-the-art thrash.

The debut album was reissued by Elektra in 1985 after a major deal that propelled the group to the forefront of the mid-1980s thrash metal boom. The band closed the year as part of one of the ultimate thrash concerts, alongside Metallica, Megadeth and Exodus at a New Year's Eve bash at the San Francisco Civic Center.

In 1986, Metal Church released their second album, *The Dark*, probably their finest moment to date. Committed to tape by producer Mark Dodson and engineer Terry Date, *The Dark* blended high-octane thrash with monumental heavy metal and caught the band expanding into epic territory with songs such as 'Watch The Children Pray' and 'Burial At Sea'. *The Dark* broke into the *Billboard* Top 100 at Number 92. On November 8th 1986 the band's headline show at the Country Club in Reseda went down in thrash history as Metallica took on the opening spot to break in their new bassist, Jason Newsted. Major exposure was guaranteed by a support tour with Metallica in Europe and Canada.

Metal Church

David Wayne: "We learned a lot with The Dark. I think that as a follow-up to the first album it was valid, and I know a lot of kids got off on it. Part of the confusion was to do with the fact that, although

METAL CHURCH discography

METAL CHURCH, Steamhammer SH 0023 (Europe), Ground Zero GZ 002 (USA) (1984)

THE DARK, Elektra 960 493-1 (UK), Elektra 60493-2 (USA) (1986) **92 USA**

BLESSING IN DISGUISE, Elektra K 960817-2 (UK), Elektra 60817-2 (USA) (1989) **75 USA**

THE HUMAN FACTOR, Epic 4678162 (UK), Epic EK-47000 (USA) (1991)

HANGING IN THE BALANCE, Rising Sun SPV 084-62170 (Europe), Blackheart BH 1001 (USA) (1994)

LIVE, Steamhammer SPV 085-18562 (Europe) (1998)

MASTERPEACE, Steamhammer SPV 085-18702 (Europe), Nuclear Blast America 64072 (USA) (1999)

THE WEIGHT OF THE WORLD, Steamhammer SPV 085-69862 (Europe), Steamhammer SPV 69862 (USA) (2004)

A LIGHT IN THE DARK, Steamhammer SPV 085-99872 (Europe), Steamhammer SPV 99872 (USA) (2006)

we had some very fast songs, we were never really a thrash metal band. Of course, every interview and everything the record company put out labelled us thrash. That wasn't a problem in some ways because we could do that for sure. There was a lot more to Metal Church though. If you listen to that record, there's shit there that Metallica was doing later on."

However, after a band bust-up, Wayne was ejected. In later years he revealed that band problems with drugs had forced him out of the picture. His first attempt at putting a new band together involved ex-W.A.S.P. guitarist Randy Piper but only got as far as songwriting sessions before the singer moved on. The frontman then worked with ex-Lizzy Borden guitarist Gene Allen, Reverend and later Intrinsic. The singer also had a brief tenure with Heathen.

David Wayne: "It was shitty timing, that's for sure. We had a great, high-profile record and we had just spent most of the year touring with Metallica, but the drugs were getting out of control. It wasn't just my problem, so I had to walk. It was the toughest thing because we were brothers, we were family, and we had achieved all this together, but if I had stayed I was going to go down. I knew that. I took advice and they basically said whatever situation you are in, whoever your friends are – walk away. I tried to put a band together with Randy Piper from W.A.S.P. but it was back to square one, so that was another situation I had to say goodbye to."

Kurdt Vanderhoof: "Well, he would say that, but he was definitely sacked. There was a lot of in-fighting going on due to drugs, egos and all that kind of stuff. We just weren't getting on with David and he had to go. It was a tough decision because that was the time when Metal Church were just peaking."

The group entered the studio in August 1988 to work on the *Deadly Blessing* album, with Terry Date promoted from engineer to producer. The band were now fronted by ex-Heretic singer Mike Howe and had added former Blind Illusion guitarist John Marshall. Howe had been suggested to the band by Vanderhoof, the guitarist having produced the debut Heretic album. In 1992 Howe appeared on the second Bootsauce album, *Bull*, guesting on the track 'Touching Cloth'.

Deadly Blessing arrived in 1989, attaining Number 75 on the US album

charts, but also signalled the withdrawal of Vanderhoof, whose dislike of touring prompted him to opt out. However, he remained a central character in Metal Church, penning all but two of the *Deadly Blessing* numbers. He later formed Hall Aflame and released an album through IRS.

After switching labels to Epic, Metal Church put out the 1991 album *The Human Factor* with production credits going once again to Mark Dodson. Although it was a solid effort, the record failed to provide upward momentum. Marshall, meanwhile, boosted the band's profile in an unusual manner when he was drafted into Metallica on a temporary basis. Their singer James Hetfield had burnt his hand in an on-stage pyrotechnics accident and handed his guitar duties over to Marshall for much of their American tour. This was the second time Marshall had depped for Hetfield – the first occasion was in 1987 when the frontman had broken his wrist while skateboarding.

October 1993's *Hanging In The Balance*, released on Joan Jett's Blackheart label, a subsidiary of Epic, saw the inclusion of Jerry Cantrell from Alice In Chains on the opening song, 'Gods Of Second Chance'. Unfortunately, promotion for the album was poor and the use of a garish cartoon on the jacket also put off many fans. The group toured Europe again, heading up the heavyweight yet eclectic October 1995 Zodiac Mindwarp, Vicious Rumors and Killers package. During this period the band took on Joan Jett's manager, Kenny Laguna, to handle their business affairs. The union soured when Laguna sold unauthorised live tapes to a Japanese label for release. With touring commitments fulfilled, Metal Church duly collapsed.

In 1997 Kurdt Vanderhoof made his recording comeback with the modestly titled Vanderhoof, a band that also included old Metal Church colleague Kirk Arrington. Although the Vanderhoof album surprised many with its quality, the classic *Dark*-era Metal Church reunited in mid 1998 with a live album of tapes recorded in the mid 1980s. The band then came back with a fresh studio album, *Masterpeace*, somewhat confusingly released with the track titles in the wrong order. Reviews ranged from disappointed to middling, and *Masterpeace* was generally viewed as a backward step for the band: Vanderhoof himself re-dubbed the record *Disasterpeace*. Nevertheless, the group toured Europe with Thunderhead in October and November 1999. By 2000 Metal Church had a new rhythm section of bassist Brian Lake and drummer Jeff Wade, both performing parallel duties with Vanderhoof.

The story took a further twist when it emerged that Wayne had set up a new act titled David Wayne's Metal Church. The band featured ex-Warrior guitarist Joe Floyd, former Joint Forces, Geezer Butler Band and Thunderhead guitarist Jimi Bell and drummer B.J. Zampa – a veteran of Yngwie Malmsteen, MVP, the Tony MacAlpine band and Thunderhead.

Vanderhoof made a return in 2002 with *A Blur In Time*, featuring new vocalist Drew Hart and the reinstated Kirk Arrington on drums. David Wayne was back in the news in July 2003 after joining Bastardsun, the British metal band assembled by former Cradle Of Filth guitarist Stuart Anstis. Metal Church themselves regrouped the same year, with original members Vanderhoof and Arrington bringing on board vocalist Ronny Munroe from Seattle metal band Rottweiler. Local gigs were conducted under the pseudonym of Mental Search. The following year the revamped band, having cut a new album called *Weight Of The World*, included former Malice guitarist Jay Reynolds. Winter 2004 dates in the US saw Canadians 3 Inches Of Blood as support act.

Although Vanderhoof prioritised *Weight Of The World*, he also fired up a progressive rock project entitled Presto Ballet with vocalist Damon Albright, bassist Brian Lake and keyboard player Brian Cokeley alongside former Church member Jeff Wade on drums.

In 2005 live dates for Metal Church in Europe were cancelled, including a headline slot at the Dutch 'Raise Your Fist' festival. The band did play on the American 'Metal Blast' tour with W.A.S.P., L.A. Guns and Stephen Pearcy. However, with Vanderhoof already having agreed to engineer material for Trans-Siberian Orchestra, his place on these dates would be filled by Vicious Rumors and Emerald Triangle man Ira Black.

The Metal Church family was dealt a huge blow on May 10th with the death of David Wayne. Just 47 years old, the singer died of complications from injuries he had sustained in a head-on automobile accident some months before.

Early February 2006 saw a line-up change. An official announcement read: "Due to health complications from years of struggling with diabetes, Kirk Arrington has stepped down as Metal Church's drummer. He will be missed and we wish him only the best." Jeff Plate of The Savatage, Chris Caffery and Trans-Siberian Orchestra took his place. Resolving to keep the congregation placated, Metal Church were supported by German acts Victory and Gorilla Monsoon on their European tour dates in June. Metal Church remain as one of thrash metal's most important bands.

METALLICA
FROM EARLY GARAGE DAYS TO GROUP THERAPY AND BEYOND

ARGUABLY THE WORLD'S BIGGEST metal band, Metallica was essentially the brainchild of Danish emigré Lars Ulrich (born December 26th 1965), a self-confessed fan of New Wave Of British Heavy Metal. Ulrich relinquished a potential career as a tennis professional in order to beat the living daylights out of the drums, and the vision he created became the leading light of the thrash metal scene. As well as being genre originators, Metallica also completed an astounding transition into the mainstream. In fact they now stand at the head of metal as a whole.

Heading the thrash charge from San Francisco to the East Coast, into the UK and Europe, and then out to the world, Metallica's status as frontrunners has never been eclipsed. Their success in the general metal arena has been so enormous that one of the most radical about-turns in music, with the *Load* and *Reload* albums, did little to harm their overall popularity.

Although they are profiled as a San Francisco-based group, Metallica were actually formed by Ulrich in Los Angeles. While Ulrich can take much of the credit for the rise of Metallica, the band's inception took place after one Ron McGovney and the Aerosmith-fixated James Hetfield (born August 3rd 1963) met at Los Angeles East Middle School in 1977.

In 1979, Hetfield's first band was Obsession, covering classic rock acts such as UFO – hence the band name – Black Sabbath and Led Zeppelin. Obsession consisted of Hetfield on vocals and guitar, Jim Arnold on lead guitar, bassist Ron Veloz and drummer Rick Veloz. Hetfield's classmate Ron McGovney roadied for the band. Still learning from their early idols, Hetfield and Arnold teamed up in 1980 with Jim's brother Chris on drums to form the Rush covers band Syrinx. This trio soon splintered, and downtime was filled by Hetfield and McGovney jamming with drummer Dave Marrs.

The duo's next attempt was a more serious venture, Phantom Lord, involving guitarist Hugh Tanner. This act segued into Leather Charm, with Hetfield on vocals and Troy James on guitar, with the rhythm section comprising McGovney on bass and Jim Mulligan on drums. Leather Charm saw the very first attempts by Hetfield at composing original material, some of which eventually found their way into Metallica's repertoire. 'Hit The Lights' was born out of these sessions, and two other Leather Charm songs, 'Let's Go Rock'n'Roll' and 'Handsome Ransom', would later be combined to become 'No Remorse'. However, the band was still heavily reliant on covers, including Iron Maiden tracks and 'Hollywood Teaze' by Girl.

With the band gradually adopting a heavier stance, a parting of the ways with Jim Mulligan occurred. Responding to an advert pitched in the Los Angeles paper *Recycler* in April 1981, Leather Charm invited one respondent, Lars Ulrich – previously a member of Hellcastle – for a meeting in Newport Beach. However, they dismissed him quickly: apparently the little Danish kid with an obsession for the New Wave Of British Heavy Metal was not the candidate they were seeking. The drummer duly returned to Europe, where he would spend a few months following Diamond Head and Motörhead's Lemmy around the gig circuit – he was actually taken in by DH vocalist Sean Harris and guitarist Brian Tatler at one point – before flying back to Los Angeles intent on finally assembling the band of his dreams.

Ulrich's enthusiasm and powers of persuasion scored an inclusion on a compilation album, *Metal Massacre*, issued through the newly-formed Metal Blade Records, headed up by his friend Brian Slagel, owner of the *New Heavy Metal Revue* fanzine. Slagel's commitment to include a song from Lars – he was unaware that Ulrich didn't have a band at the time – gained the drummer valuable leverage in gaining favour with Leather Charm.

Lars Ulrich: "I've seen all this shit, that I couldn't play the drums. Does it affect me? No – because when I started the band I couldn't play. All I had was the thirst to make the band happen. Everything just rocketed though and our learning period, my learning period, just evaporated. We did the Metal Massacre song, we did demos, we were playing gigs. Everything just went so fast so we were learning on the hoof. It was raw energy that got us through. Later, when we got the chance, we all took lessons to improve our game."

Despite not being a particularly good drummer at the time, Ulrich convinced Hetfield and McGovney to recruit him, eventually leading to the formation of Metallica. The Metallica name won out over Red Vette and Blitzer, and had been suggested by Ron Quintana, a dedicated metal activist and DJ at KUSF Rampage Radio. Quintana was all set to fire up his own highly influential fanzine and was deciding between two names he had come up with, *Metallica* and *Metal Mania*. Ulrich suggested that the latter would be more suitable for a fanzine and took Quintana's first option for his own use.

Guitarist Lloyd Grant completed the new band after replying to an advert in *Recycler*. It was this line-up that featured on the first *Metal Massacre* compilation album. Unfortunately, the group was miscredited as Mettallica on the first pressing, and McGovney and Grant's names were also misspelled as Mcgouney and Llyod. However, the album included a whole host of names that would become commercial forces in the future, such as Ratt, Ron Keel's Steeler, Bitch, Malice, Florida's Avatar (Savatage) and Cirith Ungol.

Grant's tenure with the group was temporary, and another guitarist subsequently answered the very same *Recycler* ad, which the band had left running. Ex-Panic guitarist Dave Mustaine was snapped up after an audition, but Grant would be kept on in the sidelines.

Despite the Hetfield-Grant-McGovney-Ulrich team receiving credits on *Metal Massacre*, the actual recording line-up was different. 'Hit The Lights' was cut by Hetfield and Ulrich on a Tascam 4-track the day before Slagel's deadline for inclusion, Hetfield also contributing bass guitar, and both Grant and Mustaine donating lead guitar solos. Grant's was chosen for the final product.

With Mustaine on board, 'Hit The Lights' was re-recorded for the second pressing of *Metal Massacre*, complete with Mustaine's solo and McGovney added on bass. This version featured the correct spelling of the band name. Post-Metallica, Grant reappeared in the mid 1980s with a new act, Defcon, and contributed the track 'Red Light' to a 1986 compilation album, *Thrash Metal Attack* released by New Renaissance Records.

Hetfield was still wary of his vocal talents so the band pulled in Ruthless vocalist Sammy Dijon in early 1982. The union was brief – a matter of weeks – and no gigs were performed with this line-up. Still fronted by a reluctant James Hetfield, Metallica had their first gig on March 14th 1982 at the Radio City venue in Anaheim. With little in the way of original material, they performed a clutch of NWOBHM songs, pointedly neglecting to mention that these were in fact covers. At that first concert, Metallica performed their own numbers 'Hit The Lights' and 'Jump In The Fire' plus Diamond Head's 'Helpless', 'Sucking My Love', 'Am I Evil?' and 'The Prince', plus 'Killing Time' – originally by Irish band Sweet Savage – and the frantic, pre-thrash 'Let It Loose' by premier British band Savage. At this formative stage – long before the thrash tag was conceived – Metallica were content to identify themselves as the 'Young Metal Attack'.

Lars Ulrich: "Back then, there was no plan except make music. We didn't know we were 'thrash metal'. What made us fast? I don't know. I think the energy of it all, the desire to take what we loved and build on that. Sometimes we played faster live than how we originally intended too because we were scared to death up there, y'know? We were just kids. Those first gigs were just an amazing thrill, tons of adrenaline, which makes you go faster. Once one of us had taken the pace up we would all follow. When we started, not too many bands had that kind of speed – Exodus, I think, but bands like Slayer came later, quite a bit later."

Lars Ulrich: "It was difficult to think too far ahead. We took each step up one at a time. Now we have a full agenda where someone gives us a plan of what Metallica will be doing for the next 18 months. When we started, we could not tell you what was happening after next week. We took anything given to us: playing with Ratt, playing with Stryper. If it put us in front of people, we would take it. The future never meant too much to us so long as the future was making music. We knew where we wanted to go but we had no map. Now that is all done for us, but the band still handles the details. We're an extreme band, but we're extreme in many directions. Extreme to me means unpredictable. That's what makes us who we are."

The band then set to work recording their first demo, which featured 'Hit The Lights', Sweet Savage's 'Killing Time' and Savage's 'Let It Loose'. Oddly, Savage would be excised from Metallica's history, with only a bootleg single, originally released on the 'Bongwater' label in 1987, bearing testament to the influence of the Mansfield metal act.

The tape gained them the valuable support slot to Saxon at the Whiskey A Go-Go club in Los Angeles. The Barnsley big teasers were playing two shows back to back, and originally Mötley Crüe were scheduled to play; however, Crüe's status had exceeded the support position and Tommy Lee suggested that Metallica fill the March 27th slot instead, with Ratt opening up the first night. The band's two sets were still sustained by NWOBHM covers but notably saw the addition of the Dave Mustaine-composed 'Metal Militia'.

Unfortunately, Metallica didn't get to meet their heroes, as Saxon's dressing room was closed to visitors – harbouring as it did an inconsolable Ozzy Osbourne, still reeling from the death of Randy Rhoads.

Metallica enlisted another guitarist, Damien C. Phillips (real name Brad Parker), for a gig at the Concert Factory in Costa Mesa on April 23rd. The show, despite debuting another new track, 'Mechanix', was so bad that he was fired on the spot. Undaunted, Parker returned to the scene with Odin.

Metallica then cut the four-track *Power Metal* demo, which contained 'Hit The Lights', 'Mechanix', 'Jump In The Fire' and 'Motorbreath', before deciding to secure the services of a lead vocalist who could do a better job of fronting the group than Hetfield. Until such a person could be found, Hetfield sang and played rhythm guitar, first adopting this combination on May 25th, when Metallica put in a gig at Ulrich's school, Backbay High in Costa Mesa.

Metallica then performed as a five-piece on May 28th at the Concert Factory in Los Angeles with vocalist-guitarist Jeff Warner. The gig, at which Metallica opened for Roxy Rollers, Leatherwolf and August Redmoon, was apparently such a disaster that the singer was immediately sacked. Back to a quartet, the group played Radio City in Anaheim once again on June 5th, just before *Metal Massacre*'s release on June 14th.

The band then considered requesting the services of Jess Cox, previously of Newcastle's Tygers Of Pan Tang. However, once they had seen pictures of Cox, this proposal was swiftly nixed. To compound their frustration, the sole vocalist actually asked to fill the post, John Bush of Armored Saint (and later Anthrax), turned the request down.

John Bush: "Metallica did ask me to join, but I said no for all the right reasons. People must think that's crazy, but you have to remember the scene then. Metallica was nobody. Armored Saint was hot, you have to remember that. Also, I was very tight with the guys, back to elementary school in fact. Armored Saint was getting interest from all kinds of places, and we had a lot of people starting to turn up at shows.

"Metallica came to see Saint at a gig in Anaheim, at The Woodstock in 1982. I heard they were interested in asking me to join, which they did later. The thing was that Metallica was this new kind of thing, and nobody back then – I don't care what they say now – nobody could have predicted what would happen. I didn't know the guys either, so there was no real interest. It was great to be asked, in fact a lot of people asked, but Armored Saint was really strong.

"Some time after Kill 'Em All had come out I heard the same thing again, but I never understood that because James was singing great then and he was doing a great job. I understood the lack of confidence back in '82 but not for Ride The Lightning. James owns that record."

Lars Ulrich: "Only a couple of days ago we were actually sitting around talking about how it would be now if John Bush had joined the band. Obviously it's impossible to know how different it would have been, but I can't imagine Metallica without James Hetfield up there growling into the microphone, fucking curved over and everything. It's really weird to think about it. I mean, nothing against John Bush, I think he's a great vocalist, but ... well, thank God it didn't happen!"

[Bernard Doe, Metal Forces issue 41, 1989]

The summer months of 1982 gave Metallica another taste of recording, as Kenny Kane at Rocshire Records subsidiary High Velocity persuaded the band to go into Chateau East Studios in Tustin to record a proposed EP. However, the label was shocked to discover that the finished tapes were not the songs they had hoped for: Kane had believed that the Diamond Head and Savage tracks were originals. As they didn't have the songs they had anticipated, Rocshire shelved the deal; the tapes, cut in June, were soon to surface on the underground tape-trading scene as the *No Life 'Til Leather* demo.

The demo, apparently published by Metallus Maximus Music, had several tracks that would become legendary – 'Hit The Lights', 'Mechanix', 'Motorbreath', 'Seek And Destroy', 'Metal Militia', 'Jump In The Fire' and 'Phantom Lord'. With *Metal Massacre* the focal point for US recognition of Metallica, the *No Life 'Til Leather* cassette succeeded in spreading the name internationally. Figures such as Ron Quintana in California, Bernard Doe in the UK, and *Aardschok*'s Metal Mike in Holland would prove instrumental in igniting worldwide fervour for the band. Meantime, Metallica honed their live craft back in Los Angeles, supporting the likes of Steeler, Ratt and Stryper, and playing at private parties.

By now, Metallica had relocated to San Francisco, as they did not wish to be associated with the rising Los Angeles metal scene, which was awash with image-conscious bands such as Mötley Crüe. The group had been garnering more favour in 'Frisco, not least because of the support offered on a thriving underground level by the now influential *Metal Militia* fanzine run by Ron Quintana. Metallica's first gig in the city was as part of the Brian Slagel-organised 'Metal Massacre Night' at the Berkeley Keystone on September 18th, on the same billing as Bitch and Hans Naughty, filling in for a non-appearance by Cirith Ungol.

However, increasing friction and the relocation resulted in a split with McGovney. Prior to his eviction, McGovney performed with Metallica at further concerts, including opening slots with Lääz Rockit and Y&T, plus a November 29th concert backed up by Exodus at the San Francisco Old Waldorf. This gig – the first to incorporate the frenetic 'Whiplash' – was saved for posterity by a live desk recording, *Live Metal Up Your Ass*. The following night Metallica played the Mabuhay Gardens, Ron McGovney's final gig. The bassist resurfaced in 1986 as part of Phantasm, the act assembled by ex-Hirax frontman Katon DePena.

Taking Brian Slagel's advice, Metallica added former Trauma bassist Cliff Burton (born February 10th 1962) in McGovney's place during late December 1982. Importantly, Burton brought with him much more than the four strings on his bass and his infamous anti-fashion bell-bottomed jeans. Before Burton's arrival, Metallica's demos used bass guitar as a predictably solid backbone, but the new bassist introduced the concept of 'lead bass', not only anchoring the group's tunes but also embellishing them. Burton expanded the group's range of influences, too, introducing American and UK punk and early-1970s progressive rock.

The band officially became residents of the El Cerrito district of San Francisco on February 12th 1983. The city not only had a set of fans who were more receptive to metal but also quickened the pace of development as Metallica rubbed shoulder to shoulder with the likes of Anvil Chorus, Possessed, Metal Church and Exodus. Metallica's debut with Cliff Burton came on March 5th at The Stone venue. Immediately displaying his talents, Burton featured his solo spot, '(Anesthesia) Pulling Teeth', at this first gig.

Lars Ulrich: "We never really got on with the Los Angeles audiences too well. We had a loyal 200 or so people, but it never really got beyond that. In the early days, Los Angeles was still very much poser and glam, and we were really the first band to do something different from all the Mötley Crüe, Ratt and Steeler-sounding bands, because me and James were interested in all the British metal, and that's how we were naturally playing. We first started going up the coast to San Francisco in the fall of '82 to play a few gigs just to get the hell away from Los Angeles. It was great up there, we were drawing something like 600 or so at every gig and making money out of it, which is something we had never done in Los Angeles. So we thought: maybe we should look into relocating up there?

"Another thing that played a big role in Metallica moving to San Francisco was getting Cliff Burton, who lived there, to join the band. We had wanted Cliff in the band ever since we saw him playing in Trauma. At first he was a little hesitant, but he finally decided to join us in December 1982, although a part of the agreement was that we moved up to San Francisco, since he wanted nothing to do with Los Angeles. So, after we had kicked out Ron (McGovney) and spent five weeks or so getting our stuff together, off we went."

[Bernard Doe, Metal Forces issue 3, 1983]

Metallica were soon deep in discussions with Firesign Records, Shrapnel and Metal Blade. Unfortunately for Brian Slagel, Metal Blade was short of funds and so the chance went begging. A neat example of serendipity would see Lars Ulrich's efforts to reach Jonny Zazula – a New Jersey-based Anthrax manager and Rock'N'Roll Heaven record store owner – coincide with the arrival on Zazula's desk of *Live Metal Up Your Ass*. Blown away by what he recognised as supercharged NWOBHM, Zazula contacted journalist KJ Doughton in order to offer Metallica his assistance. Ulrich returned the call the very next day.

Zazula then financed an East Coast trip, wiring $1,500 to get the band and its rented truck across the country to New Jersey. However, after a brace of shows with The Rods and Dutch outfit Vandenberg, Dave Mustaine was unceremoniously fired after a showdown over his alcohol-fuelled behaviour. Mustaine completed one further gig with the band, on April 9th at L'Amour in Brooklyn, New York, supporting The Rods, before he was sent packing. The ex-guitarist soon busied himself with creating a new act – Megadeth.

Lars Ulrich: "After we had left San Francisco to join Jonny Z on the East Coast we encountered a lot of problems with what we like to refer to now as 'the road test'. We had to fire a few roadies who couldn't take life on the road, and neither could Dave [Mustaine]. After about a week and a half we wanted to kick him out, but we had such a heavy schedule with gigs and recording the album that we didn't know when to send him home. Jonny Z suggested we did it as quickly as possible. So, we played a gig on the Saturday night with The Rods and, after spending all day Sunday sobering up, Dave left on the Monday morning. That same afternoon Kirk [Hammett] came in, and on that Friday of the same week he was on stage with us, which shows how much ability he's got … he learnt the whole set in just four days."

[Bernard Doe, Metal Forces issue 3, 1983]

A replacement was swiftly found from burgeoning Bay Area outfit Exodus, who also happened to be managed by Metallica sound engineer Mark Whitaker. Exodus six-stringer Kirk Hammett (born November 18th 1962) was duly enrolled. As it transpired, Mustaine's increasingly erratic conduct had triggered clandestine approaches to Hammett some time before the East Coast tour. Hammett slotted in smoothly and first stepped onstage with Metallica on April 16th at The Showplace in Dover, New Jersey, a gig that preceded a batch of guest slots with Newcastle proto-black metallers Venom.

After futile attempts by Zazula to attract record company interest, the *Kill 'Em All* album was recorded in Rochester, New York, and released on Zazula's specially-established Megaforce label (named as such by Cliff Burton) with distribution from Relativity. The album was licensed to ex-Secret Records boss Martin Hooker's new Music For Nations company for release in the UK, while Roadrunner took the album for Holland, Banzai for Canada, RGE for Brazil, King for Japan, and Bernett for France. Amusingly, the record had been intended to be titled *Metal Up Your Ass*, with its jacket depicting an arm emerging from a lavatory bowl and wielding a large knife. Relativity persuaded the band that this wasn't a good choice. However, the eventual choice of *Kill 'Em All* – and its accompanying jacket – were no less subtle. T-shirts featuring a depiction of the album's original title and cover art would be produced some time later.

Kill 'Em All presented the metal world with an enigma. In truth, metal had been performed as fast and aggressively before – witness Judas Priest's 'Exciter' in 1978 – but never had a band contemplated, let alone recorded, a whole album's worth. Playing fast was obviously not an interesting diversion for Metallica: it was the essence of their approach,

James Hetfield of Metallica in his prime

and it was this ethos that engendered thrash. The quartet's unbridled ambition was captured on the album's jacket, with its now-familiar barbed logo, a hammer and blood image, and four mean-looking teens – three with acne and one sporting a feeble attempt at stubble far beyond his years.

No fewer than five songs had been co-penned by ousted genius Dave Mustaine, hinting at a glorious alternative universe of metal had he stayed the course. In later years, every song on *Kill 'Em All* would be covered at least ten times over by other bands. Thousands of bands were kick-started in garages across North America after just one spin. The album's influence was simply enormous, but at the time of release both band and supporters found it tough going.

In early 1984 Music For Nations issued 'Jump In The Fire' as a 12-inch single, backing it with supposedly live versions of 'Seek And Destroy' and 'Phantom Lord'. Both were actually re-recorded in the studio, MFN dubbing on applause from a London Marquee Club performance by British progressive rock band Twelfth Night.

The group set out on tour to support the *Kill 'Em All* album, eventually making it over to Britain. Originally they had been booked to play through Europe between March 21st to April 3rd on a three-band bill dubbed the 'Hell On Earth' tour with Canadian power trio Exciter and fellow American outfit The Rods. Unfortunately, ticket sales were mysteriously poor and the tour was scrapped. Nevertheless, the group arrived in London and put in two headlining stints at the Marquee in late March: their very first UK gig on March 27th was supported by Savage. They had previously made an appearance at the Aardschok festival in Holland on February 11th while on a tour of the continent with Venom again. In June, further European gigs followed as guests to Twisted Sister. After these shows, Metallica travelled to Ulrich's native Denmark to begin work on their second album with producer Flemming Rasmussen, who had engineered Rainbow's *Difficult To Cure* album in 1983. The band had specifically wanted to record in Europe and had been impressed with Rasmussen's work on the Rainbow album.

A brand new Metallica album, *Ride The Lightning*, was recorded in a month and a half at Sweet Silence Studios in Copenhagen. Rasmussen later recalled in a magazine interview that the band were earnestly shopping for a major deal while in the throes of recording. At one point it looked highly likely that Bronze Records would sign the group, until the label insisted that they should scrap what they were doing and re-record the album in Britain. Needless to say, Metallica refused.

Thrash metal was still in its infancy when the vital *Ride The Lightning* opus arrived. If *Kill 'Em All* had proved a revolutionary inceptor, it was to be *Ride* that took the genre into the wider public arena. Where the record scored over its predecessor was in the maturity of the material, the band's most persuasive use of hooky melodies to date, and their first professional production job, courtesy of Rasmussen. Metallica presented a far more solid front, despite carrying over two Mustaine co-penned tracks in the title cut and 'The Call Of Ktulu'. Lyrically, the entire record is a homage to death, each track exploring various paths to demise – suicide, drowning, pestilence, nuclear war and electrocution.

The album switched effortlessly between jagged riffing, tranquil pseudo-classical intros and instinctive groove. Opening with a very Randy Rhoads baroque acoustic passage, Metallica hurtled into a helter-skelter 'Fight Fire With Fire' before slowing the pace a few notches with 'Ride The Lightning' – thunderingly heavy throughout. A rather obvious but still ominous bell chime bolsters 'For Whom The Bell Tolls'. 'Fade To Black' follows, two-thirds of which is a beautiful, acoustic trap upon which to spring one of the weightiest pieces of music Metallica had yet to write. (The record's clear Black Sabbath influence was lost on reviewers at the time: the layered riffing and solo arrangements of 'Fade To Black' are not a far stretch from some of Iommi & co's 1970s output.)

'Trapped Under Ice' increases the speed yet again and the biblical 'Creeping Death' tips the scales once more into true classic territory. With the possible exception of a slightly under-mature 'Escape' (hated by Hetfield, apparently, and sporting the obligatory heavy metal siren sound effect) and the slightly jittery 'Trapped Under Ice', every song scored an easy ten.

Ride The Lightning was released in July 1984. Initial copies – issued by Music For Nations in the UK, Megaforce in the US and Banzai in Canada – saw the track 'For Whom The Bell Tolls' incorrectly spelled as 'For Whom The Bells Toll'.

Without any compromise in Metallica's trademark ferocity, the songs were more accessible than previous efforts, and the album was the first real step in taking Metallica's sound to the mainstream rock audience. The accompanying 'Creeping Death' single was bolstered with two caustic cover versions of Blitzkrieg's 'Blitzkrieg' and Diamond Head's 'Am I Evil?'. Such was the impact of these songs that they would stay in the band's live set for many years.

Metallica's 1984 European tour was dealt a hammer blow that nearly ended it. While waiting for shipment, equipment worth $40,000 was stolen in Boston, necessitating hasty negotiations to hire replacement gear.

With the band's burgeoning cult following spilling over rapidly into mainstream success, major label Elektra was quick to buy out the Megaforce contract – this despite Megaforce having already shipped albums to American stores, selling in sufficient quantities to crack the *Billboard* Top 200. Elektra pulled out all the stops in promoting *Ride The Lightning*, maintaining sales levels even after it was revealed that Metallica had severed connections both with Megaforce and Zazula as manager. From now on, the experienced Q-Prime organisation of Peter Mensch and Cliff Burnstein, noted for success with AC/DC and Def Leppard, would handle their affairs.

Although Metallica's ascendancy to greater things seemed assured, in early 1985 the media momentarily focused its attention on Dave Mustaine, back in the ring with his debut album for Megadeth. The album included the track 'Mechanix', a revised version of which had appeared on Metallica's debut as 'The Four Horsemen'. The world's rock press, and Mustaine, would be keen from then on to devote acres of print to the acrimonious split between the two parties.

In August 1985 thrash metal arrived in Donington thanks to Metallica's inaugural appearance at the infamous 'Monsters Of Rock' festival held at the Donington Park racing circuit in Leicestershire, England. Playing a creditable fourth on the bill above Brit pomp-rock outfit Magnum and San Diego glamsters Ratt, and just below Bon Jovi, Marillion, and the headlining ZZ Top, Metallica played a set lasting around 55 minutes. They topped off 1985 with a crushingly heavy New Year's Eve gig in San Francisco: joining Metallica on the bill were Exodus, Metal Church and, one suspects somewhat awkwardly, Megadeth.

In their downtime, Hetfield and Burton assembled the kickabout band Spastic Children: with Hetfield on drums, Spastic Children undertook club gigs with vocalist Fred Cotton and guitarist James McDaniel.

Metallica had originally planned to record their third album in America, retaining Flemming Rasmussen's services. However, a fruitless search for the perfect environment in Los Angeles led to the band returning to Sweet Silence in Copenhagen. The resulting *Master Of Puppets* album, taking a full three months to record and finally released in March, proved to be a huge stride forward.

Despite the undoubted impact of *Master Of Puppets*, the glory was marred by Dave Mustaine, who put in a claim that the song 'Leper Messiah' was in fact a reworked version of a cut titled 'The Hills Run Red'. Metallica flatly refuted the suggestion, admitting the song was based on an old riff but not one that Mustaine delivered. The American teen metal press lapped it up, offering regular Metallica versus Megadeth articles.

Musically, *Master Of Puppets* didn't stretch the quite stupefying leap that had existed between *Kill 'Em All* and *Ride The Lightning*, but it did still push forward on all levels. Bearing in mind that its predecessor was close to being as perfect as a heavy metal record could be, *Puppets* saw the confident Metallica draw the song lengths out to near epic proportions. Oddly, for a band by now on a guaranteed rocket ride to international stardom, the entire lyrical content of this album is shrouded with a morose, foreboding introspection. When prospects never looked brighter, Metallica could be found grubbing around in the dark for something ugly to moan about. Tracks such as the title cut, 'Disposable Heroes', 'Welcome Home (Sanitarium)' and 'Leper Messiah' all deal with an inability to control destiny.

Metallica laid two monolithic menhirs of thrash metal at either end of the proceedings – 'Battery' and 'Damage Inc.' – and used the remainder of the album to experiment. They played another neat trick to kick things off, a Latino acoustic prelude interrupted rudely by the crushing 'Battery'. The forceful instrumental 'Orion' is an enthralling whirlwind of sound, making the listener wonder why they later discarded this route if they could generate such successful non-lyrical pieces.

Once again, Kirk Hammett excelled throughout. His personal star has often been dulled by the sheer enormity of Metallica, but as an innovator he truly deserves more recognition. Hetfield stamps his authority too, with this record seeing him make some real achievements.

Master Of Puppets was perhaps most noteworthy due to its strength of individual will. The two preceding outings bore their influences proudly, but here the band had broken the chains and truly come into its own: any traces of NWOBHM, Sabbath or Priest are gone. This is 100 per cent unadulterated Metallica from start to finish.

Cliff Burton: "With bass, it's difficult to find heroes. Not too many bass players look cool. I like a lot of guitar, like Thin Lizzy and Tony Iommi. Lots of melody but some exciting things. Uli Jon Roth from the Scorpions is an amazing player. Schenker too. That early Scorpions shit. Bass, it's Geezer Butler and Lemmy. I like the way they both do things differently with the bass. You can't beat Black Sabbath. It's a trip to think I'm playing here [tonight at Birmingham Odeon] and this is where Geezer Butler stood on the same stage. And Rush. Yeah, Rush. Geddy Lee. Progressive shit, really."

Puppets hit the gold mark in America in 1986 and became the first thrash-era album to break the *Billboard* Top 100, surely aided by Metallica's exposure on the road in America opening for Ozzy Osbourne. The band's UK tour began at St. David's Hall in Cardiff on September 10th. Opening the shows across Europe would be Anthrax, this mighty pairing making the dates the strongest thrash package to date. John Marshall was deputising on rhythm guitar for Hetfield, still nursing his skateboard-damaged arm, sustained during the tail-end of the Ozzy tour. Metallica wrapped up British dates with a London Hammersmith Odeon show on the 21st prior to crossing over to mainland Europe.

Riding at an all-time high, Metallica's exalted position was to be dealt a tragic blow when a road accident took the life of Cliff Burton on the morning of Saturday September 27th 1986. En route from Stockholm to Copenhagen, Metallica's tour bus skidded off an icy road near the Swedish town of Ljungby, throwing the bassist out of the window near his bunk. The musician was flung into a ditch and the bus tipped over on top of him. Burton, just 24, was killed instantly.

Metallica received encouragement from Burton's parents to press on in the aftermath of the accident. Auditions were held with Armored Saint's Joey Vera, who had also been considered as a replacement for McGovney in 1982, Lääz Rockit's Willy Lange, Watchtower man Doug Keyser, and the pre-Primus bassist Les Claypool. Eventually they recruited the Phoenix,

Arizona-based Flotsam And Jetsam bass player Jason Newsted (born March 4th 1963). The band committed themselves to a previously scheduled Japanese tour, which opened on November 15th at Shibuya Kokaido in Tokyo, a little over a month since the accident.

Metallica wound up their European tour in January and February 1987, having played dates in Switzerland, France, Belgium, Holland and Poland, before completing Scandinavian dates. The last of these shows, in Gothenburg, Sweden on February 13th, would witness a live cover of Mercyful Fate's 'Return Of The Vampire'. The year 1987 would prove trying for Hetfield as he broke his wrist skateboarding in May. (The guitarist vowed to give up the sport.)

Metallica then went back into the studio to cut a covers EP, *The $5.98 EP: Garage Days Re-Revisited*. A novel homage to their inspirations and influences, it fitted in well with the Metallica ethos: included were Diamond Head's 'Helpless', Holocaust's 'The Small Hours', Budgie's 'Crash Course In Brain Surgery' and a Misfits medley 'Last Caress/Green Hell'. The international version also featured Killing Joke's 'The Wait'. The EP, a previously untested commercial move, was a solid success, lodging itself in the American charts for eight weeks.

On August 22nd 1987 Metallica made a triumphant return to a rain-sodden Castle Donington to appear third on a Bon Jovi-topped 'Monsters Of Rock' bill. They then joined the European leg of the festivals, which were topped by Deep Purple.

Newsted took time out in late 1987 to briefly re-unite with his old act Flotsam And Jetsam in Arizona when he performed an impromptu jam at a Sacred Reich show with his old band-mates and Slayer guitarist Kerry King. Metallica rounded off the year with a tribute video to their late bass player. The $19.99 home video *Cliff 'Em All* would include live material as well as home video recordings.

Recording a successor to *Master Of Puppets* began with Guns N' Roses studio man Mike Clink, but within months longstanding ally Flemming Rasmussen had supplanted the big-name producer and Metallica, ensconced in Los Angeles' One On One Studios, started the album again from scratch in early 1988. That April the group announced the album title as an echo from the closing line of the Declaration Of Independence, *…And Justice For All*. It would be the first product for Vertigo (owned by PolyGram), Metallica's new label for the world outside the US, which was still handled by Elektra.

Despite the problems in the studio, Metallica retained fan awareness in 1988 by clambering aboard the touring extravaganza that was the American 'Monsters Of Rock' package. Based upon the tried and tested British formula of the same name, the American version, featuring a heavyweight package of Van Halen, Scorpions, Metallica, Dokken and Kingdom Come, looked a winner – but was to eventually flounder due to high ticket prices. Metallica themselves fared well, even though the first month of the tour had them flying back to Bearsville, New York, in a desperate race to finish mixing *Justice* (on which Newsted was to gain his first writing credit with the band for the lead track, 'Blackened').

The album was aired secretly in Los Angeles as the band, dubbed Frayed Ends, jammed out new material to a select few. A single, 'Harvester Of Sorrow', was released, backed by another clutch of covers. Dating to the Mike Clink sessions, Metallica tackled Budgie's 'Breadfan', an old warhorse that they opened their live show with for many, many years, and yet another Diamond Head homage, 'The Prince'.

Following on from three albums that had seen the band catapult to the absolute pinnacle of the heavy metal elite, their fourth outing, wheeled out in September 1988, should have been an out-and-out killer, but it failed to match the expectation. The biggest bugbear amongst the Metallica faithful was that such strong material had been bleached arid-dry by a soul-sucking production. Guitars scratched along like loathsome insects and the bass pinged like an annoying video game.

Thankfully, song-wise …*And Justice For All* was hugely impressive, Metallica's fourth effort in a line that contained zero filler. The album's tour de force is 'One', a horrifying cameo of despair built on Dalton Trumbo's pacifist treatise 'Johnny Got His Gun'. Everything about this song – its complexity, its lyrical rawness, the leering Pushead artwork and the unnerving video – simply define the essence of Metallica, pushing heavy metal to the very brink.

Metallica really did push it, too, with two tracks close to ten minutes in length – 'To Live Is To Die' which contained prose from the late Cliff Burton, and the title track (which finally weighed in after a two-and-a-half minute intro) – while most hover well over the six-minute mark. The buzz-saw *Kill 'Em All*-style short, sharp, shock tactics had been fully supplanted as Metallica became almost dangerously progressive – Hammett in particular made the most of the space by drenching the entire record with some exquisite soloing. It would be their last excursion into stretching the metal landscape.

James Hetfield's growth as a songwriter is a strong element of the record. His previous fascination with different methods of death and paranoia gave way to something close to social commentary. Wisely, he steered clear of posturing, but his observations were none the less harrowing for this: there is a tangible determination and passion in his vocal delivery throughout.

Putting the parchment-like production to one side, …*And Justice For All*, from the reversed intro to 'Blackened' through to the juddering finale of the lightning-fast 'Dyer's Eve', is recognised by many as Metallica's last truly great album.

Lars Ulrich: "I must admit that listening to Justice now, I do wonder why we put three-minute intros onto some of that stuff. Obviously that is what we were into at the time. And out of all of the Metallica albums to date, it's no secret that Justice is by far the less accessible of them all. I just find it funny that it's sold better than the others by over three to one."

[Bernard Doe, Metal Forces issue 51, 1990]

James Hetfield: "With Justice I think we went for something we didn't really achieve. We wanted a really up-front, in-your-face album and it didn't really work out. The drums are fucking awful, there's no depth to it. I don't know what the fuck we were doing, but back then we liked it for some reason."

[Bernard Doe, Metal Forces issue 64, 1991]

On the album's release, Metallica hit Europe, starting with a show in Budapest, Hungary before a headlining American tour with strong support from Queensrÿche. The trek marked Metallica's first real use of a stage prop, a monumental statue that dramatically collapsed at the peak of the album's title track.

February 1989 found the band invited to perform at the Grammy awards. Metallica didn't win (they, along with the world, watched incredulously as the award went to Jethro Tull), but this inaugural foot in the door at the Grammys was a portent of what was to come. Another first for the group came with the issue of the starkly uncommercial 'One' as a single in April 1989. Not only did this song succeed on radio against all logic, but it also came backed by Metallica's first promotional video. For this film, they visualised the 'Johnny Got His Gun' story in numbing horror.

The band completed their …*And Justice For All* world tour in South America in October 1989. Lars Ulrich, together with *Kerrang!* editor Geoff Barton, then compiled an album, *New Wave Of British Heavy Metal '79 Revisited*, featuring some of his favourite New Wave Of British Heavy Metal bands for the Vertigo label to celebrate the tenth anniversary of the movement.

In February 1990, Metallica returned to the Grammy awards. This time …*And Justice For All* won. A subsequent European tour beginning in May saw strong support from the veteran Dio, before the band ensconced themselves in the studio to begin the writing process for their next album. Utilising One On One Studios once again, they chose to break ties with Flemming Rasmussen and work with Canadian hit-maker Bob Rock. The band picked up a further Grammy in February 1991 for their take on Queen's 'Stone Cold Crazy' recorded for Elektra's 40th anniversary compilation album, *Rubaiyat*.

By the start of the summer, the rock world was holding its breath for the new album and, when the simply titled *Metallica* was launched, it was apparent from the off that this was the record to propel them into the major league. Hitting the American Number 1 position, the album, racking up in excess of 598,000 in its first week of sales, would doggedly retain its grip in the *Billboard* charts for a staggering 85 weeks.

The album's upfront marketing did not bode well – simplistic blacker than black, with an advertising campaign that didn't really work, because the image of a black snake on a black background defeated most print adverts. With only Spinal Tap's *Smell The Glove* to compare with such a graphic exercise, fans were rightly concerned.

Metallica was a far cry from *Master* and *Justice*. The band stripped songs down to the marrow – no frills, no engaging riff duelling. The artistic leap was a major one as Metallica, unbelievably, became radio-friendly. With commerciality and heavy metal making for uneasy bedfellows, the impact of the music here, and its unquestionable importance in the international history of metal, is all the greater. Metallica found melody, and importantly they realised how to truly harness it. Bob Rock had made his reputation by generating multi-platinum arena rock and, married to Metallica's latest set of songs, it could only be a win-win formula.

Lars Ulrich: "Bob Rock came when we needed a change. We were getting very progressive. I mean, the songs were just getting longer and more complex and we were getting worried about playing them, too. The Justice album took a long time, we were getting very protective over the songs, and maybe we needed to loosen up. I think all we could have done if the band had carried on that way was some huge, horrible concept album, two songs, 45 minutes each – and then where do we go?

"We started to think about the way the fans reacted to our songs, and it was the early songs, the ones that lasted three, four minutes, that were getting the biggest cheers. So, OK, that's what we'll do. We know we can do that.

"With Bob, we wanted a good mix. We wanted that big sound at the bottom end, and I don't care if that sound is on a Bon Jovi record, The Cult or a Metallica record. The sound is the sound and we needed that."

The song 'Enter Sandman' blew away all the opposition in 1991. An immediately striking song – simplistic, riff based, sinister and grooving – it was Metallica's bravest step and took them straight into mainstream rock clubs alongside Crüe, Poison et al. It garnered a new legion of fans, sucking in an entirely fresh generation as a counterfoil to the seismic shock of Nirvana's *Nevermind*: 'Enter Sandman' and 'Smells Like Teen Spirit' defined 1991.

Fortunately, the album was far from a one-trick pony as 'Wherever I May Roam' and 'Sad But True' also pulled in honours for songsmithery. Resolutely traditional in emphasis, these tracks were both broodingly heavy and accessible. The harder material – 'Through The Never', 'Don't Tread On Me', 'Of Wolf And Man' and Jason Newsted's baby 'My Friend Of Misery' – kept the hardcore faithful happy yet still stuck to the new blueprint. A point of celebration for the Metallica faithful would be that, for the first time, the bass guitar actually had a presence and that Kirk Hammett had just about perfected his soloing. Indeed, two major strengths of *Metallica* are Hammett's superb cameo pieces and Newsted's engine-room grunt.

Lars Ulrich: "I really think on this album Kirk has hit a stride in his playing in terms of feel and attitude. With Jason, I guess we misfired on Justice, but this time around I didn't want to make the same mistake again, so very early on we steered the bass more towards the drum kit, to shy away from the guitar a little. To me the whole thing makes the album sound fuller, something we've always wanted to achieve but had failed to do so before."

[Bernard Doe, Metal Forces issue 64, 1991]3

Further radio penetration was afforded by the string-driven 'Nothing Else Matters'. This track was something of a landmark for the group as, undetected by most at the time, Hetfield's country & western influences were beginning to play hard in Metallica's repertoire. Nashville would never admit it, but Hetfield gave the city a vital shot in the arm from the most unexpected of quarters.

Although it was a massive personal success for the band, the record also set them up for life financially. *Metallica*'s staggering sales triggered an army of pretenders to switch from hack-and-slash riffing to more subdued, pastoral moods: this didn't work, of course, but it did tip the metal world on its axis.

In August, Metallica undertook the European 'Monsters Of Rock' festivals as special guests to AC/DC before an appearance in Moscow at the Tushino Airfield on September 28th to a monstrous crowd of over half a million. The band returned home to headline the San Francisco 'Day On The Green' festival before kicking off their suitably Alexandrian-scaled 'Wherever I May Roam' world tour.

The year 1992 was beckoned in with Metallica winning another in a long line of Grammy awards. In April the band performed 'Stone Cold Crazy' at Wembley with Queen guitarist Brian May as part of the Freddie Mercury tribute concert. With both 'Nothing Else Matters' and 'Wherever I May Roam' extending their presence in the charts, Metallica geared up for a leviathan American arena tour, sharing the headline slot with Guns N' Roses for a set of 'Monsters Of Rock' dates that many critics viewed as a complete mismatch. Support came from Motörhead and Faith No More.

During these shows Hetfield was badly burned by a stage flare in Montreal. With their frontman unable to play guitar, Metallica drafted Metal Church's John Marshall to fill in the guitar parts to finish off the tour. The 'Monsters Of Rock' extravaganza wound up in October but there was little respite as the band headed for Europe for further shows until the end of the year.

They accumulated further awards in 1993 at the American Music event and were back on tour in March in the more far flung territories of Asia, Australia and South America, before the 'Nowhere Else To Roam' dates in Europe. Some of these shows including Megadeth as guests.

In November they launched their most ambitious release to date with the *Live Shit: Binge & Purge* box set. Retailing at $60, the 'flight case' pseudo-tin box included three live CDs and a trio of three-hour concert videos. The concert film was taken from Seattle, culled from two *...And Justice For All* gigs in August 1989, and San Diego, from two shows in January 1992 and the 'Wherever I May Roam' dates. Audio was spread across Mexico City Sports Palace tapes. UK editions were restricted to 10,000 units and demand was so high that these sold out almost immediately.

May 1994 had the road-hungry Metallica on the loose yet again. This time the shows were known collectively as the 'Live Shit' tour, with

support coming from Danzig and Candlebox. The band also appeared as one of the main attractions at the resurrection of the famous Woodstock festival during August 13th before winding up the tour in Florida. Notably, on August 21st Metallica invited Judas Priest vocalist Rob Halford on stage at the Bicentennial Park venue in Miami to rip through a full version of 'Rapid Fire'.

The winter months were spent writing for a new album, which would herald a radical new era for the band and test the loyalty of hardened metal fans. The bulk of 1995 then found Metallica in the studio, while interim activities included a performance at the Castle Donington 'Monsters Of Rock' festival on August 26th and a gig inside the Arctic circle with Hole, the 'Molson Polar Beach Party' in Tuktoyaktuk, Canada on September 3rd. The Donington show would provide a treat for fans and keep bootleggers happy when the band ripped out a version of Iron Maiden's 'Remember Tomorrow'.

Jason Newsted indulged in a further extra-curricular project IR8 in 1995: recorded at his home studio with ex-Steve Vai and Frontline Assembly man Devin Townsend, and former Exodus drummer Tom Hunting, tapes were laid down but the project went no further. Nevertheless, these recordings made it onto the radio airwaves, apparently much to the chagrin of Hetfield and his colleagues.

With the impact of the *Metallica* album still ringing in the industry's ears (it had clocked up a staggering 12 million sales in America alone), anticipation was high for the new record – *Load*. So eager were fans for new material that the album shifted 680,000 copies in its first week on sale.

What devotees got with *Load* was a far cry from the Metallica of yore. Band photographs issued for promotion shocked traditional metal fans to the core. Gone was the none-more-black dress code and de rigueur long hair: Metallica now came across as a newly shorn set of people with a distinct identity crisis. Not only had Hammett taken to adopting a look more in keeping with an early-1970s pimp, complete with batwing-collared gaudy shirts and fur coats, but Ulrich had taken to sporting eyeliner. With Metallica visually aping U2's drag-pop look, both bands using monochrome pictures by Anton Corbijn, fans who had force-fed themselves a diet of 'Metal Militia' and 'Whiplash' scratched their heads in amazement – especially when Ulrich declared in an interview, albeit apparently tongue in cheek, that "we're a pop band". Newsted stayed out of the controversy while Hetfield, more and more acknowledged as the leader, appeared to be more intent on hunting wild animals than involving himself in the press furore.

With *Load*, Metallica and their fan base clashed head on. *Metallica* in 1991 had ushered in a whole new generation of fans for the band, but they had kept the music heavy enough to pull their existing die-hard followers with them; with *Load*, Metallica only seemed to succeed in drubbing both camps.

In truth, much of *Load* was not that far removed from the previous outing, despite the five-year gap. Ultimately though, with no 'Enter Sandman', 'Wherever I May Roam' or 'Nothing Else Matters', the album simply fell flat based on song quality. *Load* ambled along for a full 80 minutes of near-torpor, punctuated all too briefly by a few bright sparks.

'Until It Sleeps' and 'Hero Of The Day', by far the best songs on offer and both quasi-ballads, alongside the only other strong track, the straight-outta-Nashville 'Mama Said', demonstrated that Metallica had obviously wanted to make a creative jump with this record. In searching for an elusive groove, the truly great songs for which the band was renowned fell by the wayside. Starkly simplistic and doggedly narrow in tempo, they delivered a heavy swing album – without the swing.

Fortunately for Metallica, the industry and radio was sympathetic to *Load*. The new music served to alienate many longstanding fans, and the band seemed to be pushing themselves out onto the margins in other areas, as in various interviews little secret was made of their drug-taking. Nonetheless, Metallica's status as proper rock giants was assured when the *Load* American tour was announced as being the third biggest tour of the year for that territory, grossing some $37 million dollars and only surpassed by The Rolling Stones and U2.

The album was released in June and bolted straight to US Number 1, staying high in the charts for a tenacious 40 weeks. The band's touring also bore witness to their new approach as Metallica headlined the touring 'Lollapalooza' festival with support from Soundgarden and The Ramones. They then won another award at the MTV Video Music celebrations but were eager to get back out on the road again, beginning a lengthy series of dates dubbed 'Poor Touring Me' in Europe in September.

The band's roguish intentions were still intact, though, in spite of their newfound pop sensibilities. Pulling off rip-roaring versions of The Anti-Nowhere League's expletive-laden 'So What' and The Misfits' 'Last Caress' at the MTV awards got Metallica banned from future events. As the year closed, their touring plans merely rolled on, as December ushered in the North American leg of 'Poor Touring Me'.

The year 1997 started with a bang with a performance at the American Music Awards, the band also walking off with the 'best metal/hard rock album' award. February saw the release of the 'King Nothing' single and Metallica finally wound down their 'Poor Touring Me' schedule the following month with a final show in Edmonton in Alberta, Canada. One gig of particular note on this trek came on February 22nd at the Palace of Auburn Hills, Michigan, when no less a figure than Ted Nugent strode onstage to blast through a version of 'Stranglehold' with them.

Metallica were soon back in action, returning to the studio to add closure to the *Load* follow-up *Reload*, only taking a break for European festival performances and for Hetfield's wedding in August. As the band wound up work on *Reload* in October they put in an unusually low-key showing by playing an acoustic benefit gig for the Bridge School in San Francisco.

In an attempt to get back to their roots, they hosted a series of fan gatherings throughout Europe in November 1997. These events enabled the hardcore following not only to listen to a playback of the *Reload* album but also to catch the band playing a live set in an intimate club. The same month saw the conclusion of a quite bizarre legal wrangle in which a fan, Todd Miller, claimed he had lost his sense of smell after attending a Metallica gig in Iowa during 1993. Miller's sensory deprivation reportedly came after he suffered a head injury at the gig. The case was settled but the verdict undisclosed.

Metallica then announced their intentions for a free gig to launch the *Reload* promotion campaign. Initially, though, venues under consideration were unforthcoming with offers and eventually the band put in a performance in front of 50,000 non-paying fans in the car park of Philadelphia's Core States Arena, the show coming a matter of days after an impromptu blast at London's Ministry Of Sound club on November 13th. This gig was captured on tape, with tracks such as Queen's 'Stone Cold Crazy' and Killing Joke's 'The Wait' turning up on variants of the later 'Turn The Page' single.

The debut single from *Reload*, the melodramatic 'The Memory Remains', shot straight into the British and American charts – and straight into fan debate, too. Female backing vocals were provided by Marianne Faithfull, the band having stopped off in Dublin especially to record her. The album, selling over 435,000 copies in its first week of sale, shot straight to Number 1 in America as the band performed 'Fuel' and 'The Memory Remains' on *Saturday Night Live*.

Serving up *Reload*, Metallica were sticking to their guns despite the negative reaction given to *Load* and promptly received a double whiplash from their fans. Notably, all hints of eyeliner had been dispensed with, the album packaging awash with live-performance photos, seeing the band in strictly 'back to black' mode. *Reload*'s jacket, again rendered by Andres Serrano, was pretty much a whole load of nothing. Even the famous jagged logo had been sharply pruned to corporate blandness. Visually, *Reload* reeked of a quick fix. What mystified fans, with the barbs of criticism aimed at *Load* still stinging their hides, was the band's desire to issue this material at all – and much criticism at the time indicated their stature had risen to such an exalted level that they had effectively divorced themselves from reality.

Nevertheless, the year ended on a high with a performance at the *Billboard* awards and the addition of another award to their collection, this time in the 'Best Hard Rock Band' category.

Lars Ulrich: "Garage Inc. was a bit of an exorcism for us, all four of us. Load and Reload were intense pieces of work, and we needed to do something to lighten the atmosphere a little bit. Our fans know our history because we've been very open about where we come from and the bands that gave us the urge to play. This time we could put together some new ideas, because we're not just about Saxon and Diamond Head and Angel Witch and Blitzkrieg. There are all these creative influences coming into play. Choosing was difficult because you have to say: did this song influence me or do I just like it as a song? I mean, I could have put Oasis on there, but do you really want to hear that?"

Metallica got back into gear during 1998 with a fresh batch of cover versions assembled together with previous efforts under the title *Garage Inc.*, essentially a massively expanded reissue of their cult 1987 EP. *Garage Inc.* not only catered to the wearying fans, vocal in their objection to the band's sharp change in direction with *Load* and *Reload*, but also threatened a thriving bootleg industry. The fascination with Metallica's roots and influences had spawned a clandestine catalogue of bootlegs, which the ever more fiscally-minded Metallica sought to cap.

The first disc collected newly recorded covers, taking in a wide ranging array of artists from rock stalwarts such as Blue Öyster Cult, Black Sabbath and Thin Lizzy to minor metal icons such as Mercyful Fate. Metallica's slant toward middle America is recognised with a take on Bob Seger's 'Turn The Page' and Lynyrd Skynyrd's 'Tuesday's Gone', while Nick Cave's 'Lover Man' is probably the most unexpected inclusion. Notably, Metallica still clung on to Diamond Head, revisiting 'It's Electric'. Perhaps launching into Thin Lizzy's 'Whiskey In The Jar' was enough to satisfy Hetfield's obvious cravings to explore more traditional avenues. It worked for Phil Lynott, and radio was kind to Hetfield's take too.

Disc two consisted of the original 1987 sessions and former B-sides –unpolished forays though rustic Diamond Head, Sweet Savage, Holocaust and Blitzkrieg tracks, much more in tune with the band's origins. Diamond Head had no fewer than four tracks devoted to them. Curiously, however, Savage were neglected yet again.

Budgie's 'Crash Course In Brain Surgery' was a welcome reminder that the band's artistic roots lay strictly in the 1970s, the underrated Welsh trio's highly inventive trait of weaving complicated riffs finding an obvious echo with Metallica. As an offbeat closer, The Misfits 'Last Caress/Green Hell' had by this time been established as an undisputed party staple.

Garage Inc. closed with four live tracks culled from Lemmy's 50th birthday party when the band surprised the old warhorse by muscling their way onstage to play an impromptu set of Motörhead covers, adorned in Lemmy wigs. If that wasn't respect enough, the band funnelled some rather large royalty cheques Mr. Kilmister's way. On the road, the group also put in an unexpected cover version, performing AC/DC's 'Let There Be Rock' to a rapturous reception in Sydney, Australia on April 4th.

In 1998 both Hetfield and Ulrich became fathers – Cali Tee Hetfield was born in June and Myles Ulrich in August – before fans had their appetite for rarities satisfied with the Australian DJ live album *Poor Touring Me*. Only issued to radio stations, the promotional album had eight tracks recorded live in Texas during May 1997 with audio taken from the *Cunning Stunts* video.

On October 18th, Metallica performed a one-off show at the unlikeliest of venues, Hugh Hefner's Playboy Mansion, for the *Orgazmo* movie premiere. *Garage Inc.* was pushed live with a short round of key-market nationwide gigs lasting just a week during November.

Metallica won a prestigious Grammy award for 'Better Than You' in the 'Best Metal Performance' category in 1999. In April the band undertook an ambitious venture by performing two concerts with the San Francisco Symphony Orchestra. These shows would be collated for a double album release, *S&M*, later in the year. In the meantime the band set out on tour once more to promote *Garage Inc.*.

The year 2000 was spent in production for *S&M* and the album was released in November. Opinion was sharply divided as to the merits of the record but, needless to say, worldwide sales were high. Metallica had always serviced their hardcore fans with a welcome glut of live material on B-sides and special fan club releases, so a traditional live album would have proved unadventurous to say the least. With *S&M* the band took matters to the opposite extreme. This experiment could easily have tipped into the utterly pompous, daring to mix heavy metal with classical music but, as Lars Ulrich's expensive tastes in high art revealed, Metallica was a band of individuals not willing to pay too much credence to tradition.

As expected, the band's more restrained moments, 'Nothing Else Matters', 'One' and 'Until It Sleeps', worked best of all. Indeed, 'Until It Sleeps' was without question given a far more superior air than the original. Notably, much of the *Load* and *Reload* material suffered from being simply ordinary when pitched against their more illustrious predecessors. 'Fuel', complete with slide-guitar intro, probably fared the best but was still no competition for a grandiose 'Master Of Puppets' or a near eight-minute romp through 'Enter Sandman'.

The two worlds blended well and Metallica's sonics worked with the combined and substantial forces of Michael Kamen's orchestra. An electric-driven show throughout, a great deal of the strings were employed in the same manner as large-scale keyboard washes. Where the orchestra was allowed to dictate a new direction on songs, it was often placed into the realms of a blockbuster movie soundtrack – exemplified by a song such as 'For Whom The Bell Tolls', with Hetfield adding a quirky "Absolutely!" in favour of the more traditional "Yeah".

A point of curiosity was the single release 'No Leaf Clover', a strong track that would have injected some much needed zest into *Reload* – another mystery as to why this song was a hangover from those sessions. Overall, Metallica's grand experiment came close to a total triumph.

The band rounded off the year by performing 'Until It Sleeps' with full orchestra at the *Billboard* awards in December. Metallica had also beaten another major act at their own game: German veterans the Scorpions had been planning their own similar venture for some time beforehand.

Besides *S&M*, a rather special album also emerged in 2000. The limited edition *The Garage Remains The Same*, with both title and artwork punning Led Zeppelin, was released to platinum card-carrying members of the Metallica fan club. The album consisted of six live tracks recorded in Santiago, Chile during 1999.

Needless to say, the band had something special planned for the turn of the century, headlining New York's Madison Square Garden with support acts Ted Nugent and Kid Rock. The new millennium started off well for Metallica as they won another Grammy award for 'Best Metal Performance' for their rendition of 'Whiskey In The Jar'.

Outside activity saw Hetfield appearing alongside Jim Martin on the track 'Eclectic Electric' on Primus's 2000 album *Antipop*. Metallica music came with their contribution of a new composition, 'I Disappear', also

released as a single, for the movie soundtrack to *Mission: Impossible 2*.

The band was kept in the press the same year with a legal action they brought against internet company Napster, accusing the writers of the file-sharing program of depriving them of royalties by allowing the download of Metallica tracks. Apparently the group had first been made aware of this practice when unfinished studio demos of 'I Disappear' began to surface online. Napster replied by posting an animated cartoon on their site featuring a Neanderthal Hetfield who could only mouth "Money good!, Napster bad! Beer good!" Vocal fans, still smarting from *Load* and *Reload*, found Metallica's stance on the issue to be antiquated at best. The Napster issue alienated Lars Ulrich from many of his fans in the gathering download debate. A more complimentary tribute was made when Gregorian, a collection of choral chanters, covered 'Nothing Else Matters' on their *Masters Of Chant* album.

The band certainly wasn't hurting when it came to live campaigning. They spent the summer months of 2000 on the road in North America with their 'Summer Sanatorium' arena tour, bolstered by Kid Rock, Korn and Powerman 5000. By the close of the year it was announced that Metallica had grossed over $40 million in tour receipts.

The band's long-established stability was rocked in February 2001 when Newsted announced his departure. The bassist's reasoning for his abrupt exit lay in his frustrated attempts to explore musical projects outside the confines of Metallica. Hetfield, Hammett and Ulrich resolved to record the band's next album as a trio, although increased speculation put the spotlight firmly onto ex-Ozzy Osbourne and Alice In Chains man Mike Inez as a potential new recruit. Another name prompting conjecture would be that of the original bass wildman, Pete Way of UFO. As it transpired, Inez would join Black Label Society and Way resumed UFO activity.

METALLICA discography

KILL 'EM ALL, Music For Nations MFN 7 (UK), Megaforce MRI 069 (USA) (1983)

Whiplash, Megaforce MRS-04 (USA) (1983)

Jump In The Fire, Music For Nations 12KUT 105 (UK) (1984)

RIDE THE LIGHTNING, Music For Nations MFN 27 (UK), Megaforce MRI 769 (USA) (1984) **87 UK, 173 USA**

Creeping Death, Music For Nations 12KUT 112 (UK) (1984)

MASTER OF PUPPETS, Music For Nations MFN 60 (UK), Elektra 60439-1 (USA) (1986) **41 UK, 29 USA**

The $5.98 EP: Garage Days Re-Revisited, Vertigo METAL 112 (UK), Elektra 60757-1 (USA) (1987) **27 UK, 28 USA**

...AND JUSTICE FOR ALL, Vertigo 836 062-2 (UK), Elektra 60812-2 (USA) (1988) **4 UK, 6 USA**

METALLICA, Vertigo 510 022-2 (UK), Elektra 61113-2 (USA) (1991) **1 UK, 1 USA**

LIVE SHIT: BINGE & PURGE, Vertigo 518 726-2 (UK), Elektra 61594-2 (USA) (1993) **56 UK, 26 USA**

LOAD, Vertigo 532 618-2 (UK), Elektra 61923-2 (USA) (1996) **1 UK, 1 USA**

RELOAD, Vertigo 536 409-2 (UK), Elektra 62126-2 (USA) (1997) **4 UK, 1 USA**

GARAGE INC., Vertigo 538 351-2 (UK), Elektra 62323-2 (USA) (1998) **29 UK, 2 USA**

S&M, Vertigo 546 797-2 (UK), Elektra 62463-2 (USA) (1999) **33 UK, 2 USA**

ST. ANGER, Mercury 0602498653388 [(UK), Elektra 62853-2 (USA) (2003) **3 UK, 1 USA**

Metallica ensconced themselves at Presidio Studios – actually a rented barracks at the San Francisco army base – in an effort to craft a new album. Although a batch of fresh tracks would be hammered out to completion, the band opted to keep the material in the vaults.

The band, in typically unorthodox fashion, employed a novel method of auditioning potential bassists. Playing a website re-launch party in San Francisco on July 29th, they would draw upon members of their official fan club to perform onstage with the band, and the reaction of the audience would determine if the candidates got beyond the opening song. The victor was treated to a day out and dinner with the band, but ultimately this PR exercise did not produce the desired candidate.

Metallica got to grips with more personal internal affairs during the layoff before a new album, as their website announced that Hetfield was receiving treatment for "alcoholism and other addictions". For a man seen on stage for years playing a guitar emblazoned with "More beer!" and fronting a band with the alter ego of Alcoholica, Hetfield's problem appeared somewhat inevitable. He did receive the unanimous backing of fans, however, and duly emerged having conquered his demons.

Newsted, after a one-off concert with The Moss Brothers in San Francisco supporting celluloid spoof outfit Spinal Tap, re-emerged with two school friends – vocalist-guitarist Dylan Donkin and drummer Brian Sagrafena – as Echobrain, a band that had actually been a going concern for many years behind the scenes. Newsted also revealed plans to release material he had assembled over the years in alliance with such artists as Andreas Kisser of Sepultura, drummer Tom Hunting of Exodus, with Devin Townsend on *IR8 vs Sexoturica* and Machine Head's Robert Flynn.

Echobrain put in their debut live showing on August 19th 2001 as part of the 'Nadine's Wild Weekend' events in San Francisco. By September it had emerged that the bassist was working in the studio with a re-united Voivod, acting as producer, bassist and, for his own Chophouse imprint, label head. Meanwhile, with Metallica on hold minus a bass player, the band received an offer from Megadeth's Dave Mustaine and bassist Dave Ellefson to found an interim live act to be dubbed Meta-Mega. No public response was forthcoming and the idea withered.

For the fourth year running, Metallica fan club members would be rewarded with another 'Fan Can' release. *...And All This For You* included a live CD culled from a Dallas, Texas, gig in 1989, a live video originally broadcast on German TV, and various other goodies locked away in the by now obligatory tin can. Metallica had earlier treated fans to lavishly stocked Fan Cans in 1996, 1997 and 1998.

During January 2002, as rumours spread of involvement between Lars Ulrich and Kirk Hammett and former Van Halen star David Lee Roth, it was also learned that the Metallica pair had collaborated with rapper Ja Rule for 'We Did It Again', included as part of a compilation album *Ghetto Stories*. James Hetfield would get in on the action outside Metallica too, adding guest vocals on Govt. Mule's 'Drivin' Rain' contribution to the all-star NASCAR compilation album *Crank It Up*.

The high profile progressive rock act Dream Theater added a rather novel twist to their touring activities in 2002. When booked for a two night consecutive venue run, the band would perform the entirety of *Masters Of Puppets*.

When in April Dave Mustaine made his announcement that Megadeth was to fold due to the severe nerve injury that the ex-Metallica man had suffered to his left arm, the rumour mill sprang into action, placing Mustaine's long-serving bassist Dave Ellefson as a prospect for the still vacant position in Metallica. While the rock media concentrated on these developments, other parties would be keeping an eye on Lars Ulrich's domestic position, the drummer putting his San Francisco abode on the market for $11 million and auctioning off some paintings – including much sought-after Basquiat works – at Sotheby's in London for a record $5.5 million. Both Ulrich and Hammett would unexpectedly take to the

stage for famed 'Red Rocker' Sammy Hagar's last night of three gigs at the famous Bay Area Fillmore venue. The choice of material was a surprise, too, as Hagar and the Metallica duo, alongside guesting Van Halen bassist Michael Anthony, ripped through a set of Montrose songs.

Metallica then recorded a Ramones track for a 2002 tribute album before appearing surreptitiously as Spun, playing a surprise set at Club Kimo's in San Francisco in early June. Hetfield, Ulrich and Hammett were joined by their producer Bob Rock, who played bass for the show – which included no fewer than four Ramones covers: 'Commando', 'Today Your Love, Tomorrow The World', '53rd And 3rd' (their contribution to the *We're A Happy Family* tribute) and 'Now I Wanna Sniff Some Glue'. Also on hand was standard Metallica fare: the rarely performed 'Hit The Lights' as well as a workout of a brand new song. Hetfield remained seated throughout the show, in recuperation for surgery on his neck.

The singer's well documented passion for country & western reared its head again when it was revealed that the Metallica frontman had laid down guitar tracks on a remix of country singer Carolyn Dawn Johnson's single 'Complicated'. It later emerged that Hetfield had also completed an entirely solo rendition of Waylon Jennings's 'Don't You Think This Outlaw Bit's Done Got Out Of Hand' for a 2003 tribute album *I've Always Been Crazy*. Hetfield not only sang on this track but also performed guitar, bass and drums.

Still minus a permanent bassist, Metallica threw a live party gig in San Francisco to celebrate the launch of their new-look official website. Two contest winners would be given the opportunity of a lifetime as the band performed 'Creeping Death' with fan Andrew Boyer and 'Seek And Destroy' with another competition entrant, Elena Repetto of the thrash act Imagika. Bob Rock then took over four-string duties for the Ramones cover 'Commando' and the remainder of the set.

Work continued apace on the album, witnessed by one lucky fan who was prepared to pay a whopping $48,000 to the TJ Martell Foundation charity for the privilege of a day in the studio with the band, winning an eBay auction for the prize. Meanwhile, the release of a mammoth Metal Blade 20th Anniversary box set brought good news for Metallica fans as it included a rare version of 'Hit The Lights' featuring Lloyd Grant.

With seven tracks of their new album already fully recorded, Metallica started auditioning bassists, by invitation only, during December. They also revealed plans to perform on the summer 2003 European festival circuit with appearances at Denmark's Roskilde festival and the German events 'Rock Am Ring' on the Nurburgring and 'Rock Im Park' in Nürnberg.

The former Kyuss and then current Unida bassist Scott Reeder took part in auditions for the bass vacancy during early January: other candidates put through their paces included former Suicidal Tendencies and current Ozzy Osbourne bassist Robert Trujillo, Danny Lohner of Nine Inch Nails, Eric Avery of Jane's Addiction, and erstwhile Marilyn Manson man Twiggy Ramirez.

Outside internal activities, the band were riding a wave of unwelcome – albeit forced – press coverage when a cheeky punk band from Edmonton brazenly entitled themselves Metallica. Needless to say the Californian giants' lawyers soon swung into action, delighting the publicity-seeking Canadians. The real Metallica, including Bob Rock on bass, grabbed the headlines back by performing an impromptu set on a flatbed truck in the car park of the Network Coliseum in Oakland, California, the venue for a Raiders-Titans game. Metallica, revealing the title of their highly anticipated new album as *St. Anger*, announced a summer stadium tour of the USA allied with Linkin Park and Limp Bizkit with support from Deftones and Mudvayne.

In late February, Metallica revealed that Robert Trujillo was to be their new bass player. In a curious turn of events, Jason Newsted then promptly joined the Ozzy Osbourne band.

Metallica's first show with Trujillo would be as part of an MTV special on the band. This lavish spectacle, dubbed *MTV Icon*, included bands such as Sum 41 performing 'For Whom the Bell Tolls' and 'Enter Sandman' and Staind with a rendition of 'Nothing Else Matters'. Pop teen-diva Avril Lavigne covered 'Fuel', rapper Snoop Dogg took on 'Sad But True', Korn covered 'One' and Limp Bizkit 'Sanitarium'. The evening closed, after an introduction by actor Sean Penn, with a set by Metallica themselves.

As part of the promotion for *St. Anger*, the band announced a run of four back-to-back gigs for fan club members at the Fillmore Theater in San Francisco from May 18th to 22nd. The group also revealed three consecutive shows in Paris on June 11th, performing at La Boule Noire, Le Trabendo and finally the 1,500-capacity Bataclan. Despite official denials that the band was to perform at the Iron Maiden-headlined 'Download' festival in Britain, the band, after shooting a *Top Of The Pops* television appearance, did in fact put in an impromptu ten-song set for unsuspecting fans.

Such was upfront demand for *St. Anger* that the official release date was pulled forward in an effort to stem bootlegging attempts. Initial copies of the record came with a DVD documenting the band performing the entire set from the album live in the studio but, for lucky fans in Australia and New Zealand, there was also a free 14-track assemblage of archive tracks. Fulfilling predictions, *St. Anger* bowed in on the *Billboard* charts at Number 1, having shifted over 416,000 albums in the process. European showings were less grand, the record debuting at Number 3 in the UK, although *St. Anger* took a clean sweep of Number 1s across Scandinavia. Unfortunately for Metallica, the opening burst of expectation was near nullified by an almost universal swathe of bad reviews. By the time these had hit print, *St. Anger* had already moved over three million copies. The band's stripped-down attitude, and the annoying detail of Ulrich's snare drum in particular – a tinny abomination that scars the album deeply – came in for the harshest criticism.

St. Anger was the subject of apologist remarks from Bob Rock even before a note had been heard, the producer explaining the sound as an attempt to achieve a raw 'garage' sound and feel. What the public got was a record that, although over-lavishly packaged, had all the finesse of a demo. Hetfield's vocals came across as first-take, lazy guide efforts with none of the expected spit, bile and phlegm. Riffing was sub-par at best and, most offensive to fans, *St. Anger* possessed not a single guitar solo.

Feelings ran so high over the musical merits of *St. Anger* that one band, Scumgrief, even organised an 'Anti-Metallica' live event. Festival attendees could trade in copies of *St. Anger* in exchange for a CD featuring unreleased and demo material from each of the bands on the bill. An unfazed Metallica got to grips with their 'Summer Sanitarium' arena dates, still pulling in many capacity audiences. South American shows in Brazil and Chile were scheduled for September.

Brushing off the damning criticism of *St. Anger*, the band's label went into overdrive to promote the album, and a second single came in September. 'Frantic' came backed with a variety of differing coloured single covers and track selections for various territories, cleverly guaranteeing collectability and chart placings. Metallica then cancelled shows in Japan and South America, their record label citing "band members' exhaustion" as the cause.

The January 2004 single 'The Unnamed Feeling' featured a whole crop of classic tracks recorded in Paris the year before. The band, unveiling a lengthy second run of North American dates, won a prestigious Grammy Award in the 'Best Metal Performance' category for *St. Anger* at the 46th annual show held at the Staples Center in Los Angeles. Meantime, *Rolling Stone* magazine placed Metallica as the fifth highest rock'n'roll earner in North America for 2003, reckoning their 'Summer Sanitarium' tour had grossed close to $50 million. Behind the scenes, the band would benefit from a shake-up of the Warner Brothers recording stable, shifting from long-term imprint Elektra over to Warners for future product.

North American touring in the first half of 2004 had the band packaged with support band Godsmack: these dates grossed a cool $22 million. As the world tour rolled into Europe and Scandinavia, the band not only sustained but strengthened their appeal: their concert at the Olympic Stadium in Helsinki, Finland on May 28th was attended by 46,000 people, an astonishing figure bearing in mind the country's 5.5 million population. This huge wave of support was translated to the national Finnish album charts, where no fewer than six Metallica albums occupied the Top 40. They fared even better in Sweden where their gig in Gothenburg on May 30th propelled most of their back catalogue into the charts. The group's June 4th 'Rock In Rio' festival performance in Lisbon, Portugal was broadcast live to more than 45 countries via several television channels.

Lars Ulrich was hospitalised just before the band's headlining slot at the 'Download' festival in England on June 6th. Apparently the drummer had been taken ill while travelling in a private plane between Lisbon in Portugal and the UK, the decision being made to divert to Germany where an ambulance took him to hospital. Quickfire replacements were sought in the backstage area of the show with Hetfield, Hammett and Trujillo jamming with Machine Head's Dave McClain, Hatebreed's Matt Byrne and Life Of Agony's Sal Abruscato among others. However, for a truncated nine-song set, Metallica employed Dave Lombardo of Slayer on 'Battery' and 'The Four Horsemen', while Joey Jordison of Slipknot covered 'For Whom The Bell Tolls', 'Creeping Death' and 'Seek And Destroy', whilst drum tech Flemming Larsen took on 'Fade To Black'. Jordison returned for 'Wherever I May Roam', 'Last Caress', 'Sad But True', 'Nothing Else Matters' and 'Enter Sandman'. Ulrich was back in his rightful place for the band's next gig, in Ludwigshafen, Germany.

Meantime, further acknowledgement of the band's standing poured in as Hammett was honoured with the 'Outstanding Guitarist' award at the California Music Awards on June 6th, and the following day Metallica scooped the 'Best International Act' award at the second annual *Metal Hammer* awards in London.

A new single, 'Some Kind Of Monster', was released in July to capitalise on the release of the Joe Berlinger and Bruce Sinofsky directed documentary movie of the same name. This EP – limited editions of which came with a free T-shirt – contained live renditions of 'The Four Horsemen', 'Damage, Inc.', 'Leper Messiah', 'Motorbreath', 'Ride The Lightning' and 'Hit The Lights', recorded in Paris on June 11th 2003. Selling just shy of 30,000 copies in its debut week, 'Some Kind Of Monster' hit Number 37 on the US *Billboard* charts.

One setback came in Croatia when a June 27th appearance at Gradski Stadion in Zagreb was cancelled due to "insurmountable technical difficulties". Metallica's show at Prague's T-Mobile Park on July 1st proved unusual, the group taking to the stage an hour early to allow fans to watch their national soccer team play against Greece in the Euro 2004 semi-final.

On the Metallica covers front, acts such as Motörhead, Flotsam And Jetsam, Death Angel and Dark Angel all contributed to the latest tribute album *Metallic Assault*. Fittingly, Motörhead's take on 'Whiplash' landed Lemmy and his cohorts with a surprise Grammy win.

Metallica's North American 'Madly In Anger With The World' campaign recommenced in St. Paul, Minnesota, on August 16th. This show also marked the launch of Metallica's official biography, *So What: The Good, The Mad, And The Ugly*, through Broadway Books. Fans pre-purchasing the 1,000-page tome and picking up a special wristband would be eligible for a meet-and-greet with the band on the day of the concert. Subsequent concerts saw a shift in song content as 'Some Kind Of Monster' was debuted in Peoria, Illinois, on the 24th. During this show the band also performed 'Trapped Under Ice', an exceptionally rare outing for this song. Metallica closed out the first leg with a show in Lubbock, Texas, notable for a set containing the first ever live rendition of 'Sweet Amber'.

The second leg of the tour maintained the momentum of the first, illustrated by the fact that the Montreal Bell Centre concert on October 4th sold out its 19,000 tickets in less than three hours. A further night was duly added to the itinerary. Canada also scored with the addition of a second Québec City 'Colisée Pepsi' concert, this show added as a fundraiser for CHOI 98.1 FM radio station, threatened by closure by the CRTC. The first Québec show sold all 13,000 tickets in under three hours.

In October, Metallica provided more fodder for die-hard US collectors with the issue of *Vinyl Box*, which contained special editions of its first four studio albums, as well as *The $5.98 EP: Garage Days Re-Revisited* EP and the European 'Creeping Death' picture disc. Restricted to just 5,000 hand-numbered copies, *Vinyl Box* saw *Kill 'Em All*, *Ride The Lightning*, *Master Of Puppets* and *...And Justice For All* expanded to double-vinyl sets on 180-gramme audiophile vinyl with new gatefold jackets.

James Hetfield performed a "metal version" of Waylon Jennings's 'Don't You Think This Outlaw Bit's Done Got Out of Hand' during the 'CMT Outlaws' concert taping at Nashville's Gaylord Entertainment Center on September 7th. Meanwhile, back on the Metallica tour, the band maintained their interest in keeping the live set fluid by performing 'Wasting My Hate', breaking a seven-year hiatus for that song in Québec, and then performing 'The God That Failed' for the first time in ten years at the Washington, D.C., MCI Center gig on October 17th. By the time the band had wrapped up the 'Madly In Anger With The World' tour, it had grossed a reported $53.8 million in box office receipts.

In December the Metallica track 'Some Kind Of Monster' would be nominated in the 'Best Hard Rock Performance' category for the 47th annual Grammy Awards.

May 2005 saw the announcement that Kirk Hammett had contributed guest guitar to Santana's *All That I Am* album. The same month, the Recording Industry Association of America revealed that Metallica had sold over 57 million albums in the USA, with only Led Zeppelin, AC/DC and Aerosmith ranking above them in terms of rock sales.

Having kept a relatively low profile since completing their world tour, the band entered the studios on September 20th 2004 ... not to record music, however, but to voice parts for their character inclusions in *The Simpsons*. They returned to the live stage playing two shows opening up for The Rolling Stones in their home city of San Francisco at the SBC Pacbell Park on November 13th and 15th.

Metallica's first announced live work for 2006 broke new territory as the group headlined three festivals in South Africa during March, their first visit to the continent. The group put in shows in Centurion, Durban and Cape Town, topping the 'Coca-Cola Colab Massive Mix' bill that also included Simple Plan, The Rasmus, Seether, Fatboy Slim and Collective Soul. The group then revealed plans to break off from cutting a new album in order to hit the summer festival circuit, confirming headline gigs at Germany's Nurburgring 'Rock Am Ring' and Nürnberg 'Rock Im Park' festivals and the 'Download' events at Castle Donington in the UK and Dublin in Ireland.

As this book goes to press in 2006, Metallica possess an almost unassailable position of strength. Their status is such that three savagely criticised studio albums in a row have not dampened the fanaticism of millions of fans, who continue to purchase tickets and albums. Far lesser errors of artistry have killed the careers of other major acts stone dead, illustrating just how powerful Metallica have become.

Anticipation, curiosity and even dread will precede a new album. Can Metallica right the wrongs they have committed, or are the groundbreaking days of *Ride The Lightning* and *Master Of Puppets* never to be repeated?

NUCLEAR ASSAULT
NOT QUITE GAME OVER YET

AS PART OF THE MID-1980S thrash explosion, New York's Nuclear Assault leapt to the fore due to the motivating force of bassist Dan Lilker. Although the gangly, mop-topped bassist had been a co-founder of Anthrax, naming the band and being pivotal in the recording of their debut album *Fistful Of Metal*, he severed ties with them in 1983 due to disagreements with then-vocalist Neil Turbin. Nuclear Assault were formed in 1984 and turned out to be a much rawer proposition than his previous outfit, paving the way for Lilker's even more brutal musical endeavours later on. In the interim, he had instigated the commercially successful spoof metal of S.O.D. (Stormtroopers Of Death) alongside Anthrax guitarist Scott Ian and M.O.D. vocalist Billy Milano.

Nuclear Assault's line-up for the inaugural *Brain Death* EP of 1986 was Lilker, vocalist John Connelly (also an early member of Anthrax), guitarist Anthony Bramante and ex-Harter Attack and TT Quick drummer Glenn Evans. A still earlier version of the band had included Mike Bogush on guitar and Scott Duboys on drums; Duboys would later resurface as a member of Warrior Soul.

The group's first full-length set, the Alex Perialas-produced *Game Over*, was recorded at Pyramid Sound Studios in Ithaca, New York, in May 1986 and was released the same year. The album displayed Lilker's love of hardcore, aiming Nuclear Assault towards wider acceptance than the thrash crowd, and courted controversy with the track 'Hang The Pope'. With the band's rapidly growing profile on the crossover scene, drummer Evans found time to invest in a new label, Arena. The first release on Arena was the 'Salt In The Wound' single by his previous outfit Harter Attack.

Mini-album *The Plague*, released in 1987, was a collection of old and new material cut at The Music Grinder, Los Angeles with Randy Burns behind the desk, included the infamous 'Buttfuck', a song lyrically targeted at Mötley Crüe vocalist Vince Neil, retitled more tamely on later represses as 'You Figure It Out'. *The Plague* was originally to be titled *Cross Of Iron* with a cross on the jacket; however, the Combat label feared possible objections from religious organisations. Nuclear Assault's first foray into Europe came the same year, with dates alongside Agent Steel.

Nuclear Assault quickened the pace with 1988's *Survive*, another Randy Burns production: this album made Number 145 on the US charts. A return to Europe in 1988 as guests to Slayer gave Nuclear Assault access to far larger crowds and, fuelled by the audience reaction, the band returned for further dates as headliners, supported by Acid Reign and Re-Animator. They then opened for Sepultura in South America.

The British label Music For Nations' imprint Under One Flag kept product flowing in 1989 with a brace of EPs, *Fight To Be Free* and *Good Times, Bad Times*, the latter headed up by the titular Led Zeppelin cover and featuring another wry stage favourite in 'Lesbians'. The next album, *Handle With Care*, delivered in 1989, brought the band to its artistic peak, hitting the US charts at Number 126. The live act was caught on the later *Live At Hammersmith Odeon* album.

When Lilker announced details of his new side project, Brutal Truth, which had signed with the Earache label, it appeared to fans that Nuclear Assault was losing priority. The 1991 IRS album *Out Of Order* was a less than enthusiastically received release – featuring an odd cover of the Sweet's 'Ballroom Blitz' – and seemed to confirm this view. Torn between Brutal Truth and a lacklustre Nuclear Assault, Lilker opted for the former. Just as he had pioneered crossover thrash with Nuclear Assault's debut, the bassist spearheaded grindcore with Brutal Truth's 1992 debut album, *Extreme Conditions Demand Extreme Responses*.

Glenn Evans and John Connelly rebuilt Nuclear Assault by pulling in former Ace Frehley bassist Karl Cochran on guitar and erstwhile White Lion, Black Sabbath and Great White bassist Dave Spitz. Cochrane soon lost his place to a returning Anthony Bramante, and East Coast touring followed. The band set about another American tour in 1992, bolstering their live sound with former TT Quick guitarist Dave DiPietro and ex-Prophet guitarist Scott Metaxas. The last effort under the banner Nuclear Assault came with 1993's *Something Wicked*, with the band now comprising Connelly, DiPietro, Metaxas and Evans. Headline shows across Europe to promote the album in June saw Depressive Age as support act. Meanwhile, Dan Lilker contributed bass to the Holy Moses 1994 album *No Matter What's The Cause*.

Following a lengthy run of commendable and influential albums, Lilker disbanded Brutal Truth after an Australian tour in September 1998. Lilker resumed activity with S.O.D. for their *Bigger Than The Devil* album, the bassist also operating black metal band Hemlock as a side endeavour. Yet another venture found Lilker assembling The Ravenous in 2000 for the *Assembled In Blasphemy* album with Necrophagia frontman Killjoy and drummer-vocalist Chris Reifert of Autopsy.

Lilker unexpectedly announced the reformation of the classic Nuclear Assault line-up of John Connelly, Anthony Bramante and Glenn Evans for an appearance at the 2002 'Wacken Open Air' festival in Germany and the New Jersey 'Metal Meltdown IV' event. Shortly after, a live album, recorded by Screaming Ferret Wreckords at the band's May 11th performance in Attleboro, would be confirmed as the band's new release. Anthony Bramante bowed out in August and Erik Burke, a scene veteran with Valpurgia, Kalibas, Lethargy, Sulaco, Mungbeandemon and Blatant Crap Taste connections, took over on guitar. Nuclear Assault then got back into touring mode, kicking off a gig in Springfield, Virginia, on December 29th before more shows in January 2003.

Connelly would also guest for Candy Striper Death Orgy, contributing guest lead vocals and guitar to their debut album. Scott Metaxas would be announced for co-production duties on Billy Milano's 2002 M.O.D. album *The Rebel You Love To Hate,* released in 2003.

The band's resurgence progressed as Nuclear Assault were confirmed as participants in the April 2003 European No Mercy festivals. The group formed part of a heavyweight billing comprising Testament, Marduk, Death Angel, Pro-Pain, Malevolent Creation, Darkane and Callenish Circle. In May the band inducted the Minus, Nuclear Theory, Rite Bastards, Denythefallout and Aimed Aggression-credited guitarist Scott Harrington to replace Bramante. UK and European dates projected into October, dubbed the 'Bonded By Metal Over Europe' trek, with the band co-headlining a thrash/death metal bill of Exodus, Agent Steel, Mortician, God Dethroned, Occult and Callenish Circle.

A brand new Nuclear Assault album, *Third World Genocide,* featuring a guest appearance from former guitarist Eric Burke, was recorded for Screaming Ferret Wreckords in spring 2004. Studio guests included Eric Paone of Candy Striper Death Orgy on backing vocals, while Travis Horton of Red Right Hand and Distrust added vocals and banjo to the track 'Long Haired Asshole'. Unfortunately for the band, *Third World Genocide* met with scathing reviews.

Nuclear Assault opened 2005 with a burst of South American shows with fellow thrash veterans Death Angel. European dates saw the band

NUCLEAR ASSAULT discography

GAME OVER, Under One Flag FLAG 5 (UK), Combat 88561-8118-1 (USA) (1986)

Brain Death, Under One Flag 12 FLAG 105 (UK), Combat 88561 8119-1 (USA) (1986)

The Plague, Under One Flag MFLAG 13 (UK), Combat 88561-8155-1 (USA) (1987)

SURVIVE, Under One Flag CD FLAG 21 (UK), IRS IRSD-42195 (USA) (1988) **145 USA**

Fight To Be Free, Under One Flag 12 FLAG 105 (UK) (1989)

Good Times, Bad Times, Under One Flag 12 FLAG 107 (UK) (1989)

HANDLE WITH CARE, Under One Flag CD FLAG 35 (UK), In-Effect 88561-3010-2 (USA) (1989) **126 USA**

OUT OF ORDER, Under One Flag CD FLAG 64 (UK), IRS X2-13107 (USA) (1991)

LIVE AT HAMMERSMITH ODEON, Roadracer RO 9167-2 (Europe), Relativity 88561-1100-2 (USA) (1992)

SOMETHING WICKED, Alter Ego ALTGOCD 003 (UK), IRS X2-13172 (USA) (1993)

ASSAULT AND BATTERY, Receiver RRCD 244 (UK) (1997)

ALIVE AGAIN, Steamhammer SPV 085-74962 (UK), Steamhammer SPV 74962 (USA) (2003)

THIRD WORLD GENOCIDE, Steamhammer SPV 085-69722 (UK), Steamhammer SPV 69722 (USA) (2005)

joined by guitarist Karl Cochran, a veteran of the Ace Frehley and Joe Lynn Turner bands. US shows in August with Testament prefaced the US 'Metal Crusaders' tour, set to take place in May and June 2006 alongside Kataklysm, Graveworm, Vader, Speed Kill Hate and The Absence. However, due to what was described as an "urgent immediate family situation", the band dropped off this tour to be replaced by Germany's Destruction. It remains to be seen if Nuclear Assault can return to credibility.

OBLIVEON
B-LEAGUE CANADIAN THRASHERS

THE TECHNICAL THRASH metal act Obliveon emerged in Montréal, Québec, in January 1987, when their name was originally spelt Oblivion. Although the group's precision approach to the genre won many plaudits and praiseworthy reviews, they struggled to break onto the world market and remained consigned to cult status. They recorded two demos – *Oblivion* and *Whimsical Uproar*. The band's line-up at this stage consisted of vocalist-bassist Stéphane Picard, guitarist Martin Gagné and drummer Francis Giguère. A further demo effort issued in 1989, *Fiction Of Veracity*, seeing the departure of Giguère and the enlistment of drummer Alain Demers and guitarist Pierre Rémillard, led in turn to the 1990 debut album, *From This Day Forward*, for the UK-based Active label. Initially the record only saw European distribution but was later picked up for Canada by Press Play.

The sophomore effort *Nemesis* arrived in 1993 as a self-financed effort. A video clip of the live favourite 'Dynamo' was played on a regular basis on the Canadian Much Music and Musique Plus television channels. The following year Bruno Bernier, previously with Sarkasm, was added as lead vocalist, and this incarnation of Obliveon cut the 1995 *Cybervoid* album for the ASA label. In mid 1997 the Soundscape Music label reissued

OBLIVEON discography

FROM THIS DAY FORWARD, Active CD ATV 14 (UK) (1990)
NEMESIS, Obliveon OBL-102 (Canada) (1993)
CYBERVOID, ASA ASACD01 (Canada) (1995)
Whimsical Uproar, Soundscape Music SSM001CD (Canada) (1997)
Planet Claire, Obliveon promo only release; no catalogue number (Canada) (1998)
CARNIVORE MOTHERMOUTH, Hypnotic HYP 1072 (Canada) (1999)
GREATEST PITS, Great White North GWN 009 (Canada) (2002)

Whimsical Uproar, although they only offered three tracks of the original four, released on CD to mark Obliveon's tenth anniversary. The band also donated their version of Ozzy Osbourne's 'Suicide Solution' for the Olympic Records tribute *Legend Of A Madman*. Curiously, Obliveon issued as a promotion sampler a version of The B-52s' 'Planet Claire' in 1998. A further full-length album, *Carnivore Mothermouth*, was released in 1999.

Obliveon split in March 2002, although Great White North Records put out the compilation *Greatest Pits* that same May. Rémillard was soon touting a fresh thrash act, Black Cloud. This band saw the six-stringer allied with Ghoulunatics frontman Patrick Mireault, former Voivod man Jean-Yves 'Blacky' Thériault on bass, Daniel Mongrain of Martyr on second guitar and Flo Mounier from Cryptopsy on drums. He then carved out an esteemed career as a producer, scoring credits with Voivod, Cryptopsy, Gorguts, Neuraxis, Ion Dissonance and Krisiun among many others. Also, he briefly joined the ranks of A Perfect Murder in 2005.

Obliveon

OVERKILL
BLOODY BUT UNBOWED

ONE OF THE MOST STOIC and uncompromising metal bands on the circuit, Overkill have stubbornly refused to acknowledge trends. So dedicated were the band that they were the very first of the thrash legions to break the ten album barrier, with 1999's *Necroshine*. Their New York heritage burns bright on each and every album as riffs clash with punk ethos and street hardcore. Visually, too, Overkill set themselves apart by way of a winged skull mascot and garish green logo, apparently adopted simply to make the group's gig posters stand out among the uniform black and red of other acts.

Overkill were formed in New Providence, New Jersey, in 1981 by drummer Rat Skates (aka Lee Kundrat) and bassist Carlos 'D.D.' Verni after the pair had dropped out of the hardcore punk outfit Lubricunts. Overkill's early incarnation was completed by ex-D.O.A. vocalist Bobby 'Blitz' Ellsworth and guitarist Dan Spitz. With Skates taking on the mantle of band spokesman, Verni provided the songwriting. A second guitarist, Rich Conte, was inducted and the newly established quintet began gigging locally with a cover-dominated set, tackling metal standards by the likes of Judas Priest, Black Sabbath and Iron Maiden.

Spitz took his leave in order to join Anthrax, and in 1983 the former member of The Dropouts Bobby Gustafson joined the existing trio of Ellsworth, Verni and Skates in time to lay down the *Power In Black* demo. A five-track blast of undiluted metal, the tape contained 'Overkill', 'The Beast Within', 'There's No Tomorrow', 'Death Riders' and 'Raise The Dead'. As a statement of intent, Overkill's dedication made their purpose clear: "To all the false faggot poser wimps of the clubs. Stick this tape up your ass."

By 1984 exposure generated by the demo led to an appearance of 'Feel The Fire' on Metal Blade's *Metal Massacre V* compilation and 'Death Rider' was included on the *New York Metal '84* collection. Ever the opportunists, Azra Records signed the group for the July 1985 release of the four-track *Overkill* EP, actually the same material as November 1984's *Rotten To The Core* demo. However, it was to be Jon and Marsha Zazula's Megaforce label that snapped Overkill up for a full blown debut album, 1985's *Feel The Fire*, produced by Rods drummer Carl Canedy and released towards the end of the year. German label Noise International took the record on for European issue.

Jonny Zazula had been a fan of Overkill since the *Power In Black* demo and had sold 1,500 copies through his New Jersey record store Rock'n'Roll Heaven. The band were contracted after the Zazulas had seen them open for Anvil at L'Amours club in Brooklyn, New York. Now with an album behind them, Overkill set about breaking out of the New York circuit, conducting nationwide concerts with Megadeth.

Thrash fans revelled in Overkill's approach to the genre, especially Ellsworth's rasp-ridden growl, which would dominate proceedings for the next 20 years and more. As with the late arrival of product from their Californian counterparts Exodus, *Feel The Fire*'s belated release put Overkill into the unenviable ranks of the second wave of thrash. As such, most international audiences had no knowledge that many of their songs dated back years. Undaunted, the quartet arrived in Europe during the first half of 1986 opening for labelmates Anthrax – although they weren't on the bill of the show Anthrax performed at London's Hammersmith Palais, having already gone home to the States. Overkill did, however, return to Europe later in the year as guests to Slayer.

The group's status rose sharply in the United States with 1987's Alex Perialis-produced *Taking Over* album, as Megaforce product was now marketed and distributed through Atlantic Records. They even managed to force their way onto MTV courtesy of a video clip for the track 'In

Union We Stand'. Back on European soil, Overkill provided backing for Helloween. Their presence was maintained on the market with an EP release – less than subtly titled *!!!Fuck You!!!* – headed up by a D.O.A. cover version and bolstered by live tracks captured on tape at the Phantasy Theatre in Cleveland that June. The foursome was dealt a heavy blow, however, when Rat Skates, a prime driving force, relinquished his position. Overkill persevered, drawing in substitute Mark Archibole for a few gigs before locating Sid Falck, previously of Paul Dianno's Battlezone, as a permanent addition.

Although Alex Perialis reprised his role at the desk, Michael Wagener took on the mixing job for 1988's *Under The Influence*. Still very much in the New York tradition, the album – highlighted by 'Hello From The Gutter' – blended thrash and hardcore with buzz-breaks akin to their Big Apple comrades Anthrax and Nuclear Assault.

Terry Date would handle the sonics on 1989's *The Years Of Decay*. Musically, this record was marked by an almost epic nine-minute title track, while the punchy 'Elimination' was chosen for video treatment. US touring, billed the 'Dawn Of The Decade', had Overkill packaged with Testament.

1991's *Horrorscope*, produced again by Terry Date, included a radical reworking of Edgar Winter's 'Frankenstein' and saw the band in a new guise. Internal disputes had prompted Gustafson's departure prior to recording, and to plug the gap Overkill pulled in former Faith Or Fear man Merritt Gant and their erstwhile guitar technician Rob Cannavino. Meanwhile, Gustafson joined up with ex-Slayer drummer Dave Lombardo in a new act entitled Grip Inc. but his tenure would be brief. The ex-guitarist also turned up as a session player on the solitary Cycle Sluts From Hell album.

In the midst of touring to push *Horrorscope*, Sid Falck left the band and was superseded by M.O.D. drummer Tim Mallare. Overkill returned in 1993 with *I Hear Black*, produced by Alex Perialis and engineered by Raven drummer Rob Hunter. The album provided the band with room to experiment, and 'Spiritual Void' was picked for a video: concerts across Europe had Overkill sharing stages with Savatage and Non-Fiction.

W.F.O. (Wide Fuckin' Open), recorded at the Ambient Recording Company in Stamford, Connecticut, in spring 1994, was Overkill's final output for Atlantic. With this set of tracks the group reverted to their formative years and pumped out acerbic, unrelenting thrash. *W.F.O.* included an uncredited track entitled 'Gasoline Dream' toward its end. The record was given weight by a video clip for 'Fast Junkie' and North American road work backed by Jag Panzer and Massacra.

As the major labels rushed headlong into grunge, an astute Overkill swiftly jumped ship to Tom Lipsky's CMC International label. A live double album, *10 Years Of Wrecking Your Neck – Live*, taken from a show in Cleveland, usefully documented the band's career to date. Initial copies included material from the long out of print *Overkill* EP.

Overkill endured a further structural challenge in 1995 as Gant withdrew into family life, later forging Blood Audio, and Cannavino swapped his guitar for the lure of motorbike racing. By the 1996 album *The Killing Kind*, Overkill had found themselves with a huge cult following in Germany, due to a combination of tenacity and dogged refusal to compromise musically. The band now consisted of Blitz, Verni and Mallare joined by guitarists Sebastian Marino and Joe Comeau. While the former had six-string experience with Canadian heavyweights Anvil, Comeau was more of a surprise, known previously not for his guitar work but as lead singer with Liege Lord.

The Killing Kind, mixed by Chris Tsangarides, garnered numerous 'album of the month' credits, selling well enough for the band to undertake extensive headlining German tours, firstly in February backed by Accuşer and Megora and again in November with Anvil and Stahlhammer as running mates. Ellsworth also found time in 1996 to produce a promo CD for New Jersey act Dirt Church, while another outside excursion had Overkill putting their distinctive stamp onto a take of Judas Priest's 'Tyrant' for the Century Media tribute collection *Legends Of Metal – A Tribute To Judas Priest*.

Archive tracks from the highly sought-after *Overkill* and *!!!Fuck You!!!* EPs plus additional 1990 tracks tided fans over in 1997 when released as *!!!Fuck You!!! And Then Some*. September 1997's *From The Underground And Below* caught the band shifting gear and delivering the most ferocious record of their catalogue to date. In May 1998 they united with Nevermore, Jag Panzer and Angel Dust for a trek across continental Europe.

With a high-impact album to promote in the USA, Overkill were forced to break their hectic schedule when it was learned that Blitz was suffering from a strain of facial cancer, squamous cell carcinoma. Thankfully, the singer made a full recovery and used this enforced period of introspection to flavour the lyrics of the band's next studio opus, *Necroshine*, issued in February 1999. Marino backed out to have his position taken by Dave Linsk (aka David Polinski) of New Jersey's Anger On Anger. *Necroshine* was taken to the road with a short burst of German dates and appearances at the 'Full Force' festival and Dutch 'Dynamo' events.

Later that same year Overkill trod a well-worn path with an album of covers, *Coverkill*. The band offered their interpretations of tracks by Black Sabbath, Judas Priest, Kiss, Deep Purple, Jethro Tull, The Ramones and, naturally, Motörhead's 'Overkill'. It would come as a surprise to those familiar with their music that no fewer than three Black Sabbath songs were covered – 'Changes', 'Never Say Die' and 'Cornucopia'. Many of these tracks had been stored over an expanse of time, allowing the group to build an album-length product.

In February 2000 they set about laying waste to Europe once again with Canadian thrashers Annihilator and Germany's Dew-Scented. Joe Comeau subsequently exited and joined former tour mates Annihilator. Two ex-Overkill men, Comeau and guitarist Sebastian Marino, would make their presence felt at the August 2000 'Wacken Open Air' festival, participating in a one-off Liege Lord reunion.

The quartet of Ellsworth, guitarist Dave Linsk, bassist D.D. Verni and drummer Tim Mallare then self-produced 2000's *Bloodletting* album at Carriage House Studios in Stamford that summer. Overkill toured Germany in November, with Joe Comeau assuming his former position as

Overkill

OVERKILL discography

Overkill EP, Metalstorm MS 2851 (USA) (1985)
FEEL THE FIRE, Megaforce MRI 1469 (USA) (1985), Noise N 0035 (Europe) (1986)
TAKING OVER, Megaforce/Atlantic 781 735-1 (UK), Megaforce/Atlantic 7 81735-1 (USA) (1987) **191 USA**
!!!Fuck You!!! EP, Under One Flag 12 FLAG 104 (UK), Megaforce/Caroline CAROL 1345 (USA) (1987)
UNDER THE INFLUENCE, Megaforce/Atlantic 781 865-2 (UK), Megaforce/Atlantic 7 81865-2 (USA) (1988) **142 USA**
THE YEARS OF DECAY, Megaforce/Atlantic K7 82045-2 (UK), Megaforce/Atlantic 7 82045-2 (USA) (1989) **155 USA**
HORRORSCOPE, Megaforce/Atlantic 7567-82283-2 (UK), Megaforce/Atlantic 7 82283-2 (USA) (1991)
I HEAR BLACK, Atlantic 7567-82476-2 (UK), Atlantic 7 82476-2 (USA) (1993) **122 USA**
W.F.O., Atlantic 7567-82630-2 (UK), Atlantic 7 82630-2 (USA) (1994)
10 YEARS: WRECKING YOUR NECK – LIVE, Edel 0086132RAD (Europe), CMC International 06076-87603-2 (USA) (1995)
THE KILLING KIND, Edel 0086502CTR (Europe), CMC International 06076-87604-2 (USA) (1996)
!!!FUCK YOU!!! AND THEN SOME, Steamhammer SPV 085-18722 (Europe), Megaforce 1974-2 (USA) (1997)
FROM THE UNDERGROUND AND BELOW, Steamhammer SPV 085-18772 (Europe), CMC International 06076-86219-2 (USA) (1997)
NECROSHINE, Steamhammer SPV 085-18882 (Europe), CMC International 06076-86267-2 (USA) (1999)
COVERKILL, Steamhammer SPV 085-21542 (Europe), CMC International 06076-86279-2 (USA) (1999)
BLOODLETTING, Sanctuary SANCD 051 (UK), Metal-Is 06076-85202-2 (USA) (2000)
WRECKING EVERYTHING – LIVE, Spitfire SPITCD223 (UK), Spitfire SPT 15223-2 (USA) (2002)
KILLBOX 13, Spitfire SPITCD224 (UK), Spitfire SPT 15224-2 (USA) (2003)
RELIXIV, Regain RR 058 (Europe), Spitfire SPT 15159-2 (2005)

a fill-in, supporting Halford. The unit shifted shape again towards the close of this tour as Verni was attending his pregnant wife; his replacement was Derek 'Skull' Tailer of Dee Snider's Sickmuthafuckers. The band would put in a short burst of dates in America in late November 2001 with Nevermore.

The 2002 line-up of Overkill consisted of Ellsworth, Verni, Derek Tailer (now on guitar), second guitarist Dave Linsk and drummer Tim Mallare. This combo cut recordings for a live DVD and album project, *Wrecking Everything – Live*, at New Jersey's Asbury Park in March. Overkill-headlined shows in Europe during June 2002 would see Blaze and Wicked Mystic as opening acts. However, Ellsworth collapsed onstage during the band's set in Nürnberg, Germany on June 27th. The singer had suffered a minor stroke but would soon make a full recovery.

In January 2003 Overkill guitarists Linsk and Tailer and drummer Tim Mallare, together with Anger On Anger singer Mario, combined their talents in a brand new 'old school' thrash project called Speed Kill Hate. Meanwhile, former Overkill guitarist Bobby Gustafson resurfaced in the South Florida-based Response Negative.

The band's March 2003 album *Killbox 13* was notable for its delegation of desk duties to Colin Richardson, breaking a long tradition of self-production. Minus Tailer, they toured Europe in November 2003 with support from Seven Witches and Belgian hardcore act After All. The band allied themselves with Testament, Flotsam And Jetsam and Death Angel for a 'Thrash Domination 04' Japanese tour in September 2004. Blitz also made time to guest on former Hades man Dan Lorenzo's solo album of that year, *Nice Being Alone*.

Overkill signed with Sweden's Regain label in October to record *ReliXIV*, their 14th full-length album. On the 29th of that month the band, with the noteworthy inclusion of Dream Theater man Mike Portnoy on drums, put on a special show for DJ Eddie Trunk's annual Halloween party at the Hard Rock Café in New York City.

For the group's European gigs in May, Overkill drafted former Hades and Havochate drummer Ron Lipnicki. The band's set at the major 'Sweden Rock' festival in June included Portnoy once again for the song 'Elimination'. Overkill then engaged in US touring, although September shows in Houston and Corpus Christi were cancelled due to Hurricane Rita.

Coming up to their 15th album, Overkill have weathered everything a fickle industry could throw at them, including line-up changes, and – in Ellsworth's case at least – even human frailty. Today, Overkill seem stronger than ever, built on a bedrock of European support and a renewed appreciation in their homeland.

POSSESSED
THRASH/DEATH PIONEERS

THE SAN FRANCISCO BAND Possessed, one of the prime instigators of the Bay Area thrash scene, would have an influence far more widely across the extreme metal scene, particularly the death and black metal genres, long after they had disbanded. Indeed, Possessed are generally acknowledged to be among the very earliest groups to brand their style of music as 'death metal'.

Founded in 1983, Possessed were originally fronted (under a different name) by singer Barry Fisk. The band also included the Exodus-credited Jeff Andrews on bass. Tragically, ill-fortune struck the band early in their career when Fisk committed suicide, shooting himself in the mouth and blowing out his windpipe.

With Jeff Becerra, previously of Marauder and Blizzard, replacing Fisk, the band, which included guitarists Mike Torrao and Brian Montana with Mike Sus on drums, cut a four-song demo in 1984 billed simply (and presciently) *Death Metal*. This tape, recorded in just ten hours, excited the interest of Metal Blade Records. The label included 'Swing Of The Axe' by Possessed on the *Metal Massacre VI* compilation in 1985. The song was culled from a second demo, recorded at Dangerous Rhythm Studio in Oakland with engineer Matt Wallace. Montana was then fired, apparently in a disagreement over the band's image. Larry Lalonde, another Blizzard recruit, took his place for the Randy Burns-produced debut album *Seven Churches*. Still attending high school, the Possessed members used their Easter holiday to record the LP.

Seven Churches emerged in October 1985, although not in the packaging originally intended. The band had at first conceived a jacket with gravestones bearing the individual members' names plus a nun hanging from a tree. Opening with a lift from Mike Oldfield's 'Tubular Bells Part 1', *Seven Churches* vented forth a far blacker and Luddite brand of thrash metal than had been heard before. However, Becerra's primal roar and the harsh music polarised opinions.

Seven Churches was issued through Combat in the USA with Roadrunner taking on the European licence. Possessed's first international concert came with an appearance at the 'World War III' festival in Montreal, Canada, alongside Nasty Savage, Celtic Frost, Voivod and Destruction in November 1985.

POSSESSED discography

SEVEN CHURCHES, Roadrunner RR 9757 (Europe), Combat MX
  8024 (USA) (1985)
BEYOND THE GATES, Under One Flag FLAG 3 (UK), Combat
  88561-8097-1 (USA) (1986)
The Eyes Of Horror, Under One Flag MFLAG 16 (UK), Combat
  88561-8168-1 (USA) (1987)
Resurrection, Agonia ARMLP001 (Europe) (2003) 10-inch vinyl,
  limited to 500 copies
AGONY IN PARADISE, Agonia ARCD010 (Europe) (2004)

The follow-up, *Beyond The Gates*, produced by Rods drummer Carl Candey, came in a lavish foldout jacket, a rare extravagance for a thrash act. Fittingly, *Beyond* was delivered to the public on Halloween 1986. Promoting the record across the Atlantic (where Music For Nations' Under One Flag imprint had issued it), Possessed toured Europe in November 1986 with Voivod and Deathrow (with a solitary London date adding English Dogs to the bill). Subsequent US shows saw Possessed out on the road with Dark Angel.

Possessed's third outing was the 1987 mini-album *The Eyes Of Horror*, produced by none other than guitar guru Joe Satriani, Lalonde's guitar tutor. It found the group mellowing slightly. After this release, Possessed fractured, leaving Torrao to carry on the name. Lalonde would join veteran speed metal combo Blind Illusion for a period, after which he created the offbeat but commercially successful Primus. Becerra's post-Possessed fate was less happy, as he suffered the misfortune of being shot by two drug addicts in 1989, leaving him paralysed from the waist down.

Possessed resurfaced in late 1991, demoing with a line-up comprising Torrao, guitarist Mark Strausberg, erstwhile Desecration bassist Bob Yost and drummer Walter Ryan. The band supported Machine Head the same year and cut a further two-song demo at Razor's Edge Studios in October 1991. Possessed's last incarnation came in 1993. Former guitarist Mike Hollman joined hardcore merchants Pro-Pain in 1994. Ryan joined Machine Head, then hardcore band Madball before a stint with Oakland's Powerhouse.

Although their career was short, the band's music is now held in high regard – in particular by today's black and death metal legions. Indeed, a Possessed tribute album surfaced in 2000, and Los Angeles band Sadistic Intent's contribution featured none other than Jeff Becerra on vocals. Cannibal Corpse cut versions of 'The Exorcist' and 'Confessions' as exclusive tracks for Japanese editions of their albums.

The Polish Agonia Promotions label appeased Possessed fans in 2003 by issuing a limited edition 10-inch vinyl mini-LP, *Resurrection*. This outing, restricted to 500 copies, and a 10-inch vinyl picture disc version restricted to 200 copies, consisted of tracks from the band's debut demo tape *Death Metal*, previously unreleased cuts 'Pentagram', 'Twisted Minds' and 'Fallen Angel', and a brand-new studio song from Becerra's new project Side Effect, which featured Ken Bertoncini, Ed Varni and Rick Durocher, all ex-Torqus.

The Dutch Karmageddon Media label issued a further Possessed tribute in 2004 entitled *Tribute To Possessed... Seven Gates Of Horror*. Bands paying homage included Absu, Amon Amarth, Angel Corpse, Cannibal Corpse, Impious, Diabolic, God Dethroned, Houwitser, Krabathor, Pentacle, Sinister and Vader. That same year Agonia unearthed a soundboard tape from a January 1987 show in Ohio and released these tracks as the *Agony In Paradise* album.

Florida black metal band Kult Ov Azazel revealed in January 2006 that Jeff Becerra was contributing lyrics and guest vocals to a new album, on which he also headed up a cover rendition of Possessed's 'Holy Hell'. His band remains deeply respected by extreme metal fans worldwide.

RAZOR
SHARP BUT UNDERRATED

A PROLIFIC THRASH OUTFIT known for their low-budget yet aggressive releases, Razor would develop quite a cult following. Unfortunately the group is often overlooked outside their homeland due to the amateurish artwork of their early output and the European licensing on Roadrunner, a label that rushed out lots of low-quality metal with little promotion during the 1980s. These factors resulted in Razor's caustic brand of lethal thrash being overshadowed by many lesser acts.

Razor, hailing from Guelph, Ontario in Canada, first issued a five-song demo in 1984. The quartet made their commercial debut for Voice Records with the self-funded *Armed And Dangerous* mini-album, produced by Terry Marostega at Waxworks Studios in St. Jacobs and released in May 1984. The band consisted of vocalist Stace 'Sheepdog' McClaren, guitarist Dave Carlo, bassist Mike Campagnolo and drummer M-Bro (aka Mike Embro). Only 1,200 copies of the original 12-inch vinyl pressing were manufactured.

Attic Records took the band on for the April 1985 follow-up, *Executioner's Song*, released on the label's Viper imprint, these sessions being laid down at Future Sound in Toronto with Marostega manning the production desk once more. This outing also found a European and UK audience through a licensing deal with Roadrunner, but although the Dutch concern would put out a string of Razor albums, the band never made it out of the USA and Canada to promote the records onstage. *Evil Invaders*, crafted at Phase One Studios in Toronto with Walter Zwol now handling production, offered a quick-fire third album that same October. Razor made a small slice of music history by shooting a promotional video for the 'Evil Invaders' title song, a rarity for an indie metal band at the time. The clip helped the album to become the group's most commercially successful. *Malicious Intent*, their last for the Attic Music Group, was hot on its heels in April 1986.

Razor's next effort, *Custom Killing* – again produced by Terry Marostega at Waxworks Studios – only received a Canadian release on the band's own Fist Fight imprint, in July 1987. *Custom Killing* broke away from the short-sharp-shock thrash tactics that had served Razor so well up to then and instead focused on lengthier, more involved material.

For 1988's *Violent Restitution*, a vicious revival of no-holds-barred

RAZOR discography

Armed And Dangerous, Voice M 26957 (Canada) (1984)
EXECUTIONER'S SONG, Roadrunner RR 9778 (Europe), Viper VPR
  103 (Canada) (1985)
EVIL INVADERS, Roadrunner RR 9732 (Europe), Viper VPR 112
  (Canada) (1985)
MALICIOUS INTENT, Roadrunner RR 9698 (Europe), Viper VPR
  116 (Canada) (1986)
CUSTOM KILLING, Fist Fight FPL 3042 (Canada) (1987)
VIOLENT RESTITUTION, Steamhammer SPV 85-7571 (Europe),
  Roadracer RCD-9486 (USA) (1988)
SHOTGUN JUSTICE, Fringe FPD 3094 (Canada) (1990)
OPEN HOSTILITY, Fringe FPD 3114 (Canada) (1991)
EXHUMED, Fringe FPD 3133 (Canada) (1994)
DECIBELS, Hypnotic HYP 1058 (Canada) (1997)

speed metal, only Carlo and McLaren remained, with some new faces: bassist Adam Carlo, Dave's brother, and drummer Rob Mills. *Violent Restitution* gained a German licence on Steamhammer but, although the album saw a release in Japan through Teichiku Records, this was as part of a strange double package with Australian act Hobbs' Angel Of Death.

McLaren was sacked before the album was released and Bob Reid, previously a member of London's SFH (SamFuckingHain) was quickly pulled in to fill the gap for 1990's *Shotgun Justice*. Canadian touring saw Razor packaged with Sacrifice and Disciples Of Power. Unfortunately Rob Mills suffered a car accident which put him in a leg brace.

The group bowed out in 1991 with the *Open Hostility* album, cut at Umbrella Sound in Toronto, the band at this juncture comprising Bob Reid on vocals, Dave Carlo on guitar, SFH bassist Jon Armstrong – and a drum machine in place of the injured Mills. Razor performed what was intended to be a final concert on October 2nd 1992. Reid and Armstrong resumed their positions with SFH for a brace of albums, *One Of Those Days* in 1992 and *All You Can Eat* in 1994.

A double best-of set, *Exhumed*, arrived in 1994 through Steamhammer in Europe and Fringe in Canada, paving the way for a full-blown Razor reformation. In 1997 the self-produced *Decibels* record was released by Hypnotic Records. By this stage Rich Oosterbosch of SFH was manning the drums. Leading Swedish death metal act Hypocrisy weighed in too, paying homage with a rendition of 'Evil Invaders' on their album *The Final Chapter* that same year.

Razor were still active in 2006, composing songs for another album.

SACRED REICH
WAR PIGS OF THRASH

SACRED REICH WERE FORMED at Coronado High School in Scottsdale, Arizona, in 1985, and their first stable line-up was vocalist-bassist Phil Rind, guitarists Jeff Martinek and Jason Rainey, and drummer Greg Hall. The group debuted late that year with a four-track cassette demo, *Draining You Of Life*. It was intended that an early singer, Dan, would put down vocals – but illness prevented his participation, requiring Rind to step up for singing duties.

At this juncture, Martinek had a change of heart and opted out for a military career. This vacancy was plugged by Wiley Arnett. The songs 'Sacred Reich' and 'Ignorance' were given the benefit of re-recording and, with strong support from Flotsam And Jetsam's Jason Newsted, 'Ignorance' found inclusion on the Metal Blade compilation album *Metal Massacre VII*. From here, the group soon snagged a full-blown album deal with Metal Blade. The debut, *Ignorance*, was released in October 1987. From this point, Sacred Reich – managed by Gloria Bujnowski, who would later look after Sepultura and Soulfly – launched into a relentless touring schedule.

The stopgap *Surf Nicaragua* mini-album, which included 'Draining You Of Life' from the first demo and a version of Black Sabbath's 'War Pigs', was the release that pushed Sacred Reich onto the world market. Such was the positive response to this record that Sacred Reich would find themselves on a previously unplanned world tour. North American dates kicked in during 1988 with Atrophy and Forbidden before European shows with Motörhead. The band then hooked up once more with Forbidden through Europe in 1989. Sacred Reich's appearance at the 'Dynamo Open Air' festival in Eindhoven, Holland was caught on tape for the mini-album *Alive At The Dynamo*, released through Roadracer in Europe and Metal Blade in the USA.

Sacred Reich returned with the politically-charged *The American Way* in 1990, a collection unexpectedly boasting a hybrid thrash-funk workout '31 Flavors' that extolled the merits of other musical strains. Although '31

Flavors' was unrepresentative of the album, Metal Blade chose it for the radio promotion song. US touring included a high-profile support slot to Pantera's 'Vulgar Display Of Power' tour, while gigs in Europe found Venom as opening act.

The 1993 Dave Jerden-produced *Independent* album was carved out at Eldorado Studios in North Hollywood (appropriately, as it was made for the new Disney-owned Hollywood label). The record boasted a new Sacred Reich line-up of Rind, guitarists Wiley Arnett and Jason Rainey, and drummer Dave McClain, a veteran of San Antonio Slayer. The accompanying three-song EP, *A Question*, saw the band covering Fear's 'Let's Have A War'. Unfortunately the gap between the two albums resulted in diminished support.

Following a request by Columbia Records, in 1994 Sacred Reich intended to donate their rendition of Black Sabbath's 'War Pigs' to the *Nativity In Black* tribute album, but while the track featured on pre-release promotional EPs issued to radio stations, it failed to appear on the finished album.

The band remained relatively quiet in 1995, but another of their Sabbath covers, 'Sweet Leaf', surfaced on the *Hempilation 96: Freedom Is NORML* album. They also cut a version of Judas Priest's 'Rapid Fire' with a guest vocal from Rob Halford, but it remains unreleased. Earlier that year, Dave McLain had been offered a position with Machine Head, which he declined, but he would eventually join the high profile Californian neo-thrashers in December.

Shortly after 1996's *Heal* album, produced by Bill Metoyer, Greg Hall rejoined the fold but Chuck Fitzgerald took the drum stool for the band's world tour. That same year esteemed Swedish death metal band Dark Tranquillity honoured the band with a cover of the 'Sacred Reich' anthem as a bonus track for their album *The Gallery*.

Hall was back in the band by 1997 as Fitzgerald journeyed on to Tongue-n-Groove and then Gypsycho. Sacred Reich discovered that *Heal*'s enthusiastic reception in Europe was not mirrored in their homeland, where the dissipation of thrash meant a struggle for recognition. Forced to disband, Sacred Reich bowed out with November 1997's live album *Still Ignorant (1987–1997)*.

In a 2001 alliance with former St. Madness vocalist Patrick Flannery, Wiley Arnett formed a band entitled The Human Condition. However, his plans were put on hold on August 2nd when he rolled his car while driving to Phoenix. The guitarist suffered several cracked ribs, bruising of his spleen, bruises and abrasions.

Meantime, Hall joined Soulfly in October 2001. This act obligingly paid homage to Sacred Reich by covering 'One Nation' for their 2002 album, simply billed *3*, the track also featuring Arnett on guitar. In early 2003 the recovered Arnett came back to the fore with The Human

Condition, an alliance now also featuring Scott Twitty of Bludgeon. Today, Sacred Reich are remembered with great respect by 1980s thrash fans.

SACRIFICE
ON THE ALTAR OF METAL

OVER FOUR ALBUMS OF CORROSIVE thrash, Toronto's Sacrifice left an indelible legacy in the extreme metal arena, directly galvanising legions of North American acts. The teenage vocalist-guitarist Rob Urbinati and guitarist Joe Rico formed the band in 1983, hiring vocalist John Baldy, bassist Scott Watts and drummer Andrew Banks. This formation started out by tackling Black Sabbath, Exciter, Metallica and Judas Priest covers before advancing to their own brand of speed metal. Drummers came and went in quick succession, Banks being succeeded by Craig Boyle who in turn lost his post to Ernst Flach. A series of rehearsal tapes saw local distribution: one three-track affair that made it onto the underground tape-trading market consisted of a Metallica cover version, 'The Four Horsemen', plus 'Turn In Your Grave' and 'Warriors Of Death'. Aiding local thrash comrades, both Rob Urbinati and Joe Rico guested on the 1984 Slaughter demo *Bloody Karnage*.

Sacrifice debuted live in support of local glam-rock outfit Herrenvolk, fronted by a pre-Skid Row Sebastian Bach, on January 12th 1985 at Larry's Hideaway in Toronto. The set consisted of Exciter, Slayer and Metallica covers and proved to be the last with Baldy, who was fired shortly afterward. Boyle also decamped, joining Lethal Presence, leaving Gus Pynn to stabilise the percussion department. Sacrifice recorded a demo, *The Exorcism*, funded by Brian Taylor of local record store the Record Peddler at Accusonic Studios in June 1985.

Signing to the Diabolic Force imprint of Fringe Records, Sacrifice delivered the Brian Taylor-produced album *Torment In Fire*. Although horrifically under-produced, the record – delivered in June 1986 – did generate a strong response on the burgeoning thrash scene. Just as *Torment In Fire* was issued, the group was back in the studio preparing more new material, including a demo of a version of Discharge's 'The Possibility Of Life's Destruction'. On the live front, the band built up a loyal following in the city by opening for bands such as Slayer, Exodus, Megadeth and King Diamond. In October 1986 they shared the billing of the Montreal Spectrum 'No Speed Limit' festival alongside Possessed, D.R.I., Aggression and Agnostic Front among others.

In early 1987 Sacrifice made their first foray into the USA, conducting Midwest shows backing Straw Dogs and Corrosion Of Conformity, these gigs preceding the recording of second album *Forward To Termination*. Introducing near-progressive elements, they benefited hugely from an improved production and Canadian sales were boosted by regular television airing of the promotional video 'Re-Animation'. *Forward To Termination* gained licences worldwide with Metal Blade in the United States and Roadrunner in Europe. Performances in the USA saw Sacrifice alongside King Diamond, Trouble, Nuclear Assault, Death, Death Angel

and Hallows Eve, at the inaugural Milwaukee 'Metalfest'. However, projected tours with Blood Feast and Death Angel fell through due to lack of finances, although a short run of shows with Nuclear Assault took them back into the Midwest. Another scheduled set of gigs with Hirax and At War was also pulled. Hooking up with Nuclear Assault once more, Sacrifice embarked on Canadian dates in July 1988 and put themselves back into recording mode for a three-song demo that December, just before East Coast concerts with Motörhead.

The third offering, *Soldiers Of Misfortune*, was to emerge via Diabolic Force in October 1990. Although Metal Blade took the record for the USA, no European licence was forthcoming. Canadian gigs in September 1990 witnessed a road union with labelmates Razor.

In early 1991 drummer Gus Pynn made way for former Dark Legion man Mike Rosenthal, himself quickly superseded by ex-Herrick pounder Darren Foster. However, Foster's tenure was fleeting and Michael Rosenthal took up the drum position. On July 27th 1991, Sacrifice played the Milwaukee 'Metalfest' again, the billing including artists such as Cyclone Temple, Deicide, Massacre, Napalm Death and Sepultura. US touring then ensued that October together with Christians Believer and Birmingham's Bolt Thrower.

With Razor guitarist Dave Carlo as producer, the band recorded a fourth album, *Apocalypse Inside*, for Metal Blade. However, the line-up then fractured: once the sessions were completed Scott Watts was ousted in favour of Interzone's Kevin Wimberley to tour the record in July 1993 across the USA with Gorefest and Death. It wasn't enough to buck the downward trend in thrash sales, though; dropped by Metal Blade, Sacrifice folded.

Frontman Rob Urbinati later created Interzone for the 1999 *Cydonia* album. By late 2002 he was touting a fresh act entitled Tenet comprising veteran drummer Gene Hoglan of Dark Angel and Death fame, Strapping Young Lad guitarist Jed Simon, erstwhile Grip Inc. bassist Stuart Carruthers, plus ex-Forbidden and Testament guitarist Glen Alvelais.

In late 2004 the Brazilian label Marquee announced that they were set to reissue 1986's *Torment In Fire*, 1987's *Forward To Termination* and 1990's *Soldiers Of Misfortune*. In addition, a live album was proposed, culled from 1989 concert recordings. The *Torment In Fire* release came as a double limited-edition CD with hand-numbered slipcase, adding extra tracks culled from *The Exorcism* demo plus no fewer than 22 live tracks

---

SACRIFICE discography

TORMENT IN FIRE, Roadrunner RR 9697 (Europe), Restless 7 72159-1 (USA) (1986)

FORWARD TO TERMINATION, Roadrunner RR 9595 (Europe), Restless 7 72223-1 (USA) (1987)

SOLDIERS OF MISFORTUNE, Metal Blade 9 26538-2 (USA) (1991)

APOCALYPSE INSIDE, Metal Blade CDZORRO 62 (UK), Metal Blade 9 45235-2 (USA) (1993)

Sacrifice

recorded at Larry's Hideaway, Toronto in 1984 and from 1986 gigs in Toronto and Quebec. The reissue of *Forward To Termination* added album demos plus live tracks recorded in Kitchener, Ontario in 1986, Toronto in 1987 and Rochester, New York, in 1988.

In early 2005 Urbinati fired up a side project, War Amp, a blues-based retro-doom outfit involving former Jaww and Soulstorm members. The following year, Sacrifice reunited, comprising Urbinati, guitarist Joe Rico, bassist Scott Watts and drummer Gus Pynn. The band put in a one-off headline appearance at the September 23rd 'Day Of The Equinox II' festival held at the Opera House in Toronto.

SLAUGHTER
CANADIAN METAL GURUS

SLAUGHTER, A REVERED NAME on the thrash and death metal scene, suffered in the same manner as many Canadian acts when searching for recognition outside the tape-trading network. The band, raised in Scarborough, Ontario, were created in August 1984. Co-founder Terry Sadler, handling vocals and bass guitar, was already a seasoned veteran of the local Toronto scene, having served terms with Blind Ambition, Blissmass, Lizzy Borden, Megolith, Metal Fatigue, Nazz, and The Halo Of Flies. Along with vocalist-guitarist Dave Hewson and drummer Ron Sumners, Sadler forged Slaughterhouse, soon truncating the title to Slaughter.

The group made their mark with the opening demo sessions *Meatcleaver* and *Bloody Karnage*, the latter featuring Joe Rico and Rob Urbinati of Sacrifice as guest players. The third set, *Surrender Or Die*, followed in 1985 and rapidly spread throughout the underground tape trading grapevine, even impacting on the demo Top 10 charts in the UK magazine *Metal Forces*. Their live debut came with the 'Live Karnage' event alongside Sacrifice on March 25th 1985 at Toronto's Larry's Hideaway venue, their set being distributed straight from the soundboard as the *Live Karnage* demo, brazenly sporting their influences with covers of Hellhammer's 'Massacra' and Venom's 'Witching Hour'. That same May another gig opening for Sacrifice at Gilmore's in Toronto was recorded for the *Live Bedlam* demo.

Local radio DJ Brian Taylor secured the rights to the *Surrender Or Die* demo, releasing this commercially as the first from Attic Records' subsidiary Diabolic Force. Slaughter capitalised on this with the debut album *Strappado*, recorded in a lightning 24 hours – again for Diabolic Force – at Future Sound in Toronto, with Taylor behind the board. Although it had been cut in February 1986, *Strappado* remained in the vault for a lengthy period due to financial constraints. Before this, a promotional three-track single titled 'Nocturnal Hell' emerged, limited to 1,000 copies.

Earlier the same year Slaughter had been joined by Death frontman Chuck Schuldiner, who had relocated from Florida. However, Schuldiner's

tenure lasted a matter of weeks before he journeyed back home to re-activate Death. Live work would be restricted to a grand total of just 15 concerts, the largest of which was held in July 1986 as support to Celtic Frost and Voivod at the Toronto Concert House.

Sumners made his exit during September 1986. After fleetingly employing Storm and Death Adder drummer Scott Day, the group re-structured with former Lethal Presence guitarist Bobby Sadzak and, in May 1987, drummer Brian Lourie. In mid 1987, the much delayed *Strappado* was delivered, immediately drawing ecstatic reviews. Slaughter cut a further album, *Paranormal*, in July 1988, but these tapes never saw the light of day during the group's career. Metal Blade then showed interest, prompted by the band's December 1988 demo *The Dark*, and 'The Fourth Dimension' taken from the *Paranormal* demo was duly included on the *Metal Massacre Ten* compilation, released in 1990.

Further ructions hit the band in 1992 when Sadler bade farewell, having initially quit in 1988, then returning in 1989, before quitting again in 1990. Hewson then formed an alliance with guitarist Bobby Sadzak, bassist Mike Dalton and drummer Brian Lourie in Strappado, this move away from the Slaughter title prompted by the chart success of the Las Vegas hair band of the same name. The new unit only issued two sessions, *Fatal Judgement* and *Not Dead Yet*, before splitting. However, the Headache label encouraged the burgeoning Slaughter legend by issuing a bootleg CD, *Strappado*.

Slaughter was resurrected in order to donate a version of 'Dethroned Emperor' to a 1996 Celtic Frost tribute album put out through Dwell Records. This revised version of the band would collapse once again, although Sadzak, together with singer Kelly Montico, had created the industrial outfit Inner Thought, releasing *Worldly Separation* in 1993 and the 1995 follow-up *Perspectives*.

In 1999, pioneering UK grindcore act Napalm Death paid homage to Slaughter by rendering their version of 'Incinerator' on their EP *Leaders Not Followers* – and Utopian Vision Music released the *Surrender Or Die* demos on CD, complete with additional tracks recorded at the time but left off the demo.

A slew of Slaughter re-releases arrived during 2000, including the shelved *Paranormal*, live cuts, and demos. The German Nuclear Blast label reissued *Strappado* with an extra CD of live recordings from Slaughter's inaugural March 1985 gig and rehearsal tapes. The band's legacy was given further prominence during 2004 when Hell's Headbangers Records released *Fuck Of Death*, a compilation of the January 23rd 1986 rehearsal recordings conducted with Schuldiner (who had died in 2001). This vinyl-only outing was restricted to 1,000 copies, the first 100 pressed on grey splatter vinyl with 500 manufactured as picture discs. Further tracks arrived in the form of a split 7-inch single on Horror Records of Denmark in collusion with Nunslaughter. The infamous Pittsburgh death metal band also paid tribute on their side of the vinyl with a cover of Slaughter's 'Nocturnal Hell'.

SLAUGHTER discography

Nocturnal Hell, Fringe FPS 1725 (Canada) (1986)
STRAPPADO, Fringe FPL 3028 (Canada) (1987)
SURRENDER OR DIE, Utopian Vision Music, cnu (Canada) (1999)
NOT DEAD YET / PARANORMAL, Nuclear Blast NB 0663-2 (Europe/ USA) (2001)
FUCK OF DEATH, Hell's Headbangers HELLS 003 (USA) (2004)
Sadist, Horror HOR 011 (Europe) (2004) split single with NunSlaughter

---

SLAYER
STILL REIGNING IN BLOOD AFTER ALL THESE YEARS

SLAYER ARE WITHOUT QUESTION the most dedicated of the acts to break out onto the world stage from the American thrash phenomenon. With their unwillingness to compromise, they have apparently defied all the odds to place themselves in the position of regular chart entrants, despite little radio airplay.

The band's music is unrelentingly intense, fuelled by drummer Dave Lombardo (who is often voted the world's best drummer in many metal magazines), the lethal guitars of Kerry King and Jeff Hanneman, and the almost inhuman vocals of sometime respiratory therapist Tom Araya. This combination made Slayer not only mould-breakers but an act plagiarised by countless lesser bands. Lyrically, they are unafraid to venture into overtly controversial realms, with satanism, murder and Nazism familiar territory.

Slayer's early recordings, put out through Metal Blade, were marred by inadequate production and almost universally dismissed by the rock media. Many thrash fans also found Slayer's inaugural bursts of speed difficult to stomach when compared with the precise riffage of rising stars such as Megadeth, Anthrax and Metallica. However, as time passed, Slayer amassed a dedicated hardcore fanbase, which is among the most loyal in metal.

Hailing from Huntington Park, California, Slayer was founded in 1981, by uniting former Sabotage drummer Lombardo, King and Araya from Quits, and Hanneman. The band was originally titled Dragonslayer, apparently inspired by the 1981 movie of the same title. Early photographs betray the fact that the proto-Slayer indulged themselves in some garish eye make-up, but this was thankfully abandoned. At first they pursued a traditional heavy metal stance, their sets including Judas Priest and Iron Maiden covers, but were persuaded to accelerate to thrash tempos upon listening to Brian Slagel's first *Metal Massacre* compilation.

Slayer debuted their first fast track, 'Aggressive Perfector', on *Metal Massacre IV*. A three-track rehearsal demo followed in August 1983, comprising 'Fight 'Til Death', 'Black Magic' and 'The Antichrist', which rapidly became a much-traded item on the underground metal scene. That August, Slayer demoed again, putting down 'Evil Has No Boundaries' and 'Crionics'.

King then teamed up with fellow Los Angeles speed metal band Megadeth, performing a handful of gigs on a temporary basis. During this period of flux, Lombardo was briefly supplanted by drummer Bob Gourley, later to join Dark Angel and then Powerlord.

Metal Blade's owner Brian Slagel had noted the reaction to Slayer's inclusion on his compilation and duly signed the band, putting them in the studio to record *Show No Mercy* during night-time sessions in November 1983 while Lombardo graduated from high school. The record was rush-released a matter of weeks after completion. The mainstream rock press hated the record, proclaiming it an unintelligible mess, but to their dismay it sold in droves.

The band then went out on the road, putting in a UK appearance at London's Marquee club before setting off on the 'Haunting North America' tour. This trek was backed by the issue of the EP *Haunting The Chapel* in August 1984. Slayer's no-compromise image – based initially on satanism – saw them using inverted crosses onstage and King wearing a leather armband studded with supersized nails.

The first product of 1985 was a VHS video dubbed *Combat Tour – The Ultimate Revenge* with live footage of four tracks filmed on Slayer's US trek alongside Venom and Exodus, captured at New York's Studio 54 club. Their second album, *Hell Awaits*, produced by the band and engineered by Bill Metoyer, arrived in September 1985, and Slayer defied their detractors: the new music was easily equal in ferocity to the debut album's songs. A readers' poll in the British rock magazine *Metal Forces* saw Slayer sweeping the board, gaining honours for best band, best live band, best album and best drummer.

However, Slayer only began to make serious headway when Rick Rubin, owner and producer of Def Jam Records, signed the band in 1986. With this move the band broke away from the expected path pursued by so many thrash acts: Def Jam was an imprint better known for an eclectic range of artists including the likes of The Black Crowes, Beastie Boys and Run DMC.

The first fruit of this liaison was the 28-minute, Rubin-produced *Reign In Blood*, a pure thrash album that took the genre to new levels of extremity, as exemplified by Lombardo's 248bpm drumming on the third track, 'Necrophobic'. Incredibly, the album broke into the *Billboard* album charts, the first of many Slayer albums to do so.

Reign In Blood attracted immediate condemnation thanks to the lyrics of the opening track, 'Angel Of Death'. The song dealt with the Auschwitz camp doctor Josef Mengele, leading many observers to accuse Slayer of fascist sympathies. Def Jam's distributors in the USA, the mighty CBS, refused to handle the album. The band retorted that the lyrics of 'Angel Of Death' were merely observations rather than endorsements, reminding critics that Araya, a Chilean, was hardly an all-American white boy. Unfortunately, the blonde, blue-eyed Hanneman compounded the problem by wearing SS collar patches, iron crosses and Nazi insignia in photos; he even adorned one of his guitars with cuff titles of notorious SS Panzer divisions such as Totenkopf and Das Reich. Slayer's tour T-shirts of the time bore the statement 'Slaytanic Wehrmacht' (the title applied to their fan club) and featured a skull encased in a World War II German helmet.

The band provoked further adverse reaction with a new logo, a Nazi-style eagle with the swastika replaced with the Slayer logo and pentagram. The furore over 'Angel Of Death' was so great that their British distributor, Geffen Records, owned by the Jewish entrepreneur David Geffen, dropped the album from its schedules. Ironically, Geffen had been quick to capitalise earlier on Slayer's dumping by CBS. Eventually London Records took on *Reign In Blood* for the UK.

Slayer then embarked on the 'Reign In Pain' tour (enjoying the comforts of a tour bus for the first time), crossing America with Overkill before European dates with openers Malice. Such was the fans' extreme loyalty that Malice were very often the subject of ugly scenes, having to endure booing and spitting.

Kerry King unexpectedly found himself all over the radio in 1986, although not with Slayer. Fellow Def Jam signing the Beastie Boys, whose album *Licensed To Ill* had been a Number 1 hit, had asked the guitarist to donate a suitably manic solo to the track 'No Sleep 'Til Brooklyn'.

With Slayer's burgeoning popularity, former label Metal Blade were quick to capitalise, releasing *Live Undead*, a picture disc semi-live EP of tracks culled from 1984 American shows.

In December 1986, in the midst of an American tour, Lombardo announced that he was quitting. Rumours circulated that the cause of the split was an argument over Lombardo's wife being on the road with the band. Slayer duly continued with substitute T.J. Scaglione of Whiplash. As the tour rolled on, Slayer hooked up with W.A.S.P., an ill-fated union that witnessed a bitter war of words between the two bands about which of them was selling more tickets.

Slayer were back in the headlines in 1987 when at the 11th hour they pulled out of a headlining slot at the prestigious Aardschok festival in Holland. A great degree of ill-feeling was generated, until the band explained that with the cancellation of Metallica due to the death of Cliff Burton, Slayer had no intention of performing – but that their agency had neglected to inform the relevant parties.

Lombardo, who during his sabbatical had turned down the opportunity to join Megadeth, was enticed back into the band in April 1987 in time to record the next album. The reinstated drummer did, however, nearly miss a batch of British dates when a work permit was refused. Slayer plugged the gap between albums by covering Iron Butterfly's 'In A Gadda Da Vida' for the movie soundtrack *Less Than Zero*.

July 1988's *South Of Heaven*, which saw Slayer slowing the pace, included a cover of Judas Priest's 1977 classic 'Dissident Aggressor' and gave the band a further increase in sales. Although they were attempting to extricate themselves from black metal lyrical themes, Rubin insisted that the word 'Satan' appear on the record: at the last minute Araya reworked the lyrics for 'Read Between The Lies' to include a reference to Old Nick.

American dates kicked off with support from Nuclear Assault. Slayer finally got the opportunity to play major American arenas at the end of 1988 when they were invited to join as guests on Judas Priest's 'Ram It Down' tour.

Slayer then took a two-year break, during which time they severed ties with their British record company London. They had been far from amused when the single 'Mandatory Suicide' was released on the very last date of the British tour.

Slayer returned in 1990 on the 'Clash Of The Titans' tour alongside two other members of the Big Four Of Thrash, Megadeth and Anthrax, for a series of monumental arena shows across America and Europe. For the first 18 European shows, co-headliners Slayer and Megadeth were joined by Suicidal Tendencies and Testament. For the Stateside dates, with Anthrax now hopping onboard, the then relatively unknown Alice In Chains opened. One result of this alliance was that Araya was invited to guest on Alice In Chains's *Dirt* album. His contribution comes in the form of a Slayer-esque scream on an untitled track.

Seasons In The Abyss arrived in October 1990, breaking into the US *Billboard* charts at Number 40 and giving the band a Top 20 record in the UK. A video for the title track was filmed in Egypt. Musically, *Seasons* was the group's most caustic outing to date. The track 'Dead Skin Mask', concerning serial killer Ed Gein, complete with the whimpers of a young child for added effect, provoked particular disgust.

A double live album, *Decade Of Aggression*, followed in 1991 and entered the US charts at Number 55. It was proudly issued in a raw state, incorporating none of the usual live album clean-ups or overdubs. Disc one consisted of a July 13th 1991 gig at the Lakeland Coliseum, Lakeland, Florida, while the second hosted material recorded at Wembley Arena in London on October 14th 1990 and Orange Pavilion in San Bernardino, California, on March 8th 1991. A limited edition of 10,000 metal-box collectables added two extra tracks, 'Skeletons Of Society' and 'At Dawn They Sleep'.

In May 1992, Lombardo quit again, his first post-Slayer project being Voodoo Cult. He then formed Grip Inc. with Voodoo Cult guitarist Waldemar Sorychta, a band who have released two albums to date. Lombardo's substitute was ex-Forbidden man Paul Bostaph. Slayer broke him in with gigs across California, Arizona, and Baja, Mexico, prior to an appearance at the Iron Maiden-headlined Donington 'Monsters Of Rock' festival in August 1992.

During 1994 Slayer teamed up with gangsta rapper Ice-T to cut a track for the soundtrack to the movie *Judgement Night*, a cover of British punk act The Exploited's 'Disorder'. They then shot back to their previous status with *Divine Intervention* in October 1994. The album blasted into the *Billboard* Top 100 at an incredible Number 8. The record continued the band's custom for dealing with beyond-the-pale subject matter as Hanneman's penchant for Nazi history re-surfaced with 'SS-3', the licence plate of the staff car of Reynard Heydrich, governor of Bohemia and Moravia. Meanwhile, '213' dealt with another serial killer, Jeffrey Dahmer: the number was that of his notorious apartment.

Divine Intervention was quick to achieve gold status and Slayer's longevity was confirmed when *Reign In Blood*, *South Of Heaven* and *Seasons In The Abyss* were all confirmed gold. Naturally the band generated controversy once again, this time by using a photograph on the inner sleeve of dedicated fan Mike Meyer's rendition of the Slayer logo – carved with a razor into his own arm.

The band geared up for a world tour with openers Biohazard and Machine Head prior to a showing at the 'Monsters of Rock' festival headlined by Metallica. Subsequent touring saw Slayer appearing on a 'Monsters Of Rock' bill in South America alongside Kiss and Black Sabbath. An accompanying video, *Live Intrusion*, filmed at the Mesa Amphitheater in Mesa, Arizona, on March 12th 1995 and including a cover

of Venom's 'Witching Hour', was released through American Recordings.

Slayer paid homage to their musical heroes in 1996 by cutting the *Undisputed Attitude* album (originally titled *Selected And Exhumed*) made up of their favourite punk tunes and three original compositions, including the uncharacteristically brooding 'Gemini', which boasted Kerry's first use of a seven-string guitar, and 'D.D.A.M.M.'. Covers included songs by T.S.O.L., England's G.B.H., and no fewer than three Minor Threat tracks. The Japanese version added Suicidal Tendencies' 'Memories Of Tomorrow'. The event was marred for the band when Bostaph made his exit after recording to concentrate on a jazz career. Drummerless, Slayer were forced to cancel South American and European tours.

While Slayer were offering tributes to their mentors, a series of Swedish compilation albums entitled *Slaytanic Slaughter* were released on which various Scandinavian acts covered their favourite Slayer song. Slayer resumed activity with the addition of erstwhile Testament drummer John Dette, but his tenure was fleeting as Bostaph was duly reinstated, with Dette returning to the Testament camp. In his time away from the band Bostaph had formed the oddball outfit The Truth About Seafood.

Slayer were pushed unwittingly back into the public arena again in 1986 when their music was cited in a lawsuit as a direct influence on the 1995 murder of a 15-year-old girl, Elyse Marie Pahler. The teenager had been kidnapped, tortured and killed by three members of a black metal band, Hatred. Pahler had been butchered with a hunting knife and her corpse then subjected to necrophilia. The prosecution alleged that the band members were influenced and inspired by lyrics from the track 'Necrophiliac'. The court cleared the band in 2001.

Slayer, still maintaining their studio relationship with producer Rick Rubin, came up with new product in 1998, with *Diabolus In Musica*. Japanese variants added the usual extra track, 'Unguarded Instinct'. Live activity to promote the record had Slayer appearing in June on the bill of the 'Ozzfest' at Milton Keynes, England. The group had been scheduled to appear on the American dates, but the spot on the bill eventually went to Megadeth.

In 1999 the band teamed up with Berlin techno-punks Atari Teenage Riot to mould the track 'No Remorse (I Wanna Die)' for the *Godzilla* movie soundtrack. The following year they contributed a take on 'Hand Of Doom' for the Black Sabbath tribute album *Nativity In Black 2*. Araya had also been writing material with Max Cavalera of Soulfly, the track 'Terrorist' being featured on Soulfly's 2000 album *Primitive*. Not to be outdone, King provided a guest guitar solo on the cut 'Goddamned Electric' from Pantera's 2000 album *Reinventing The Steel*.

Slayer supplied a new track, 'Bloodline', to the movie soundtrack album *Dracula 2000* and the song 'Here Comes The Pain' for the wrestling compilation album *WCW Mayhem* in 1999.

Next they were in the studio in Vancouver, laying down a new Matt Hyde-produced album prior to hooking up with Pantera, Morbid Angel, Static-X and Skrape for the 'Extreme Steel' American tour.

Early rumours that the album was to be titled *Soundtrack To The Apocalypse* proved false (this title would be used later), and the succinct *God Hates Us All* was duly chosen. The album's artwork, a blood-soaked Bible punctured by nails, was deemed unacceptable for display in many retail outlets and many copies had the original concept disguised by a false cover depicting four gold crosses on a white background. Remarkably, *God Hates Us All* was released on September 11th 2001. This horrific coincidence resulted in many stores pulling the album from the shelves for fear of protest at the title and songs such as 'God Send Death', 'Warzone' and 'Payback'.

European festival shows, dubbed the 'Tattoo The Planet' dates, originally in alliance with Pantera, Biohazard, Vision Of Disorder and Static X, were far from trouble-free. Following the terrorist attacks, Pantera pulled out of the tour, leaving Slayer as headliners.

King then guested on the track 'Final Prayer For The Human Race' on the 2002 Hatebreed album *Perseverance*. Less welcome news for Paul Bostaph was an aggravating wrist condition that had apparently forced his exit from the band. This statement from the band was strongly refuted by the ex-drummer. Bostaph subsequently enrolled in Systematic and later re-joined Testament. Slayer kept it in the family by re-inducting their illustrious former colleague Dave Lombardo, albeit announcing this as a temporary measure.

It soon emerged that the hot contender to secure the job was Proscriptor McGovern (also known as Emperor Proscriptor Magikus; real name Russ Givens), the leader of ancestral black metal band Absu. Other close candidates were erstwhile Soulfly member Joe Nunez, whose family reportedly baulked at the idea of his joining Slayer, as well as Dying Fetus and Misery Index man Kevin Talley. Another surprise candidate was Blink-182's Travis Barker.

Slayer, with Lombardo manning the drum kit, donated a cover version to the NASCAR-sponsored *Crank It Up* compilation in the summer of 2002. Deep Purple's 'Highway Star' was apparently the first choice, but the group switched to the Alice Cooper classic 'Under My Wheels' and then to Steppenwolf's 'Born To Be Wild' (Type O Negative recorded 'Highway Star'). Araya made his presence felt on the Henry Rollins-assembled West Memphis Three benefit album *Rise Above*, lending vocals to a version of Black Flag's 'Revenge'.

The band were announced as headliners of the American 'H82K2' festivals alongside In Flames and Soulfly. They were also confirmed as one of the headline attractions at the mammoth 'Beast Fest' event in Japan during December 2002. Lombardo, still maintaining membership of Slayer, revealed plans to record a solo album consisting entirely of drum solos.

In 2003 the band put out a concert DVD entitled *War At The Warfield*, directed by Jon Bon Jovi's cousin Anthony Bongiovi at the Warfield Theater in San Francisco, Californial, on December 7th 2001. A lengthy string of US Jägermeister-sponsored headline dates, commencing on October 9th 2003 and running through until mid December, saw Hatebreed and Arch Enemy as support acts. Regional guests included E-Town Concrete, Hemlock, Lazy American Workers, Sworn Enemy, Skinlab, Five Feet Thick and Dry Kill Logic.

In the midst of this live activity the band issued a lavish three-CD and single DVD box set entitled *Soundtrack To The Apocalypse* and including back-catalogue material. Songs were included that had previously only been available as Japanese bonus cuts and live DVD material. A limited edition deluxe version, housed in a fake-blood and floating-skulls ammo box package came with an extra CD of a full-length concert from a 2002 show in Anaheim, California, as well as a wall banner and a replica backstage laminate.

In early 2004 Lombardo put in a recording session for the soundtrack of the remake of the classic splatter film *Dawn Of The Dead*. The drummer also issued the *Incorporated* album from his other act Grip Inc. and received unexpected exposure when he acted as a stand-in for Lars Ulrich for Metallica's Castle Donington 'Download' festival performance in June. Lombardo played 'Battery' and 'The Four Horsemen' before Slipknot's Joey Jordison and Metallica drum tech Flemming Larsen tackled the remainder of the set.

Slayer were confirmed for the US 'Ozzfest' that summer with Ozzy Osbourne, Judas Priest, Dimmu Borgir, Hatebreed, Slipknot and Black Label Society. The band also scheduled 'Off-fest' headline dates with Priest and Hatebreed along the way. A brief burst of Canadian dates in June saw the band hooked up with Damageplan and Otep.

A special show in Augusta, Georgia, on July 11th was filmed for the Dean Karr-directed DVD *Reign In Blood Live: Still Reigning*, the band running through the entire tracklisting of the landmark *Reign In Blood*. The band's 1980s eagle backdrops and inverted crucifix lighting rig were

specially reinstated for these dates. They promised something extra special for fans as an encore, and delivered by raining fake blood from the lighting rig during 'Raining Blood', soaking the band and their gear.

Slayer's September 1st gig at Myrtle Beach in South Carolina was cancelled when Araya was rushed to hospital suffering from kidney stones. Returning to Europe, they acted as co-headliners with Slipknot, with support act Hatebreed for the October tour, dubbed 'The Unholy Alliance'. Araya had more problems in Europe, though, completely losing his voice mid-set during a show in Munich, Germany on September 27th. Although Hatebreed's Jamey Jasta took on lead vocals for 'Raining Blood' the band was forced to cut their show short.

A rapid return to the US saw the band invited back to headline a further run of the Jägermeister Music tour over Killswitch Engage and Mastodon, kicking off on October 29th in Springfield, Missouri. Touring across Europe with Slayer, Lombardo also made time to put in individual drum-clinic solo performances en route. Intriguingly, Lombardo, in collaboration with DJ Spooky, was assembling a studio project entitled Drums Of Death, described as an "homage to Def Jam's pioneering rock-rap fusions of the 80s", with Meat Beat Manifesto's Jack Dangers as producer and guitarist Vernon Reid of Living Colour guesting. The drummer guested on Finnish classical metal act Apocalyptica's eponymous 2005 album, too, featuring on the track 'Betrayal/Forgiveness'.

The quartet, together with engineer Josh Abraham, entered studios in Los Angeles on February 28th to cut a new record. Upfront promotion was novel, coming in the shape of an EP release, *Eternal Pyre*, and featuring album track 'Cult', only available through Hot Topic stores in the USA. Summer 2006 US headliners commenced in June, dubbed the 'Unholy Alliance – Preaching To The Perverted' tour, with Mastodon, Lamb Of

SLAYER discography

SHOW NO MERCY, Metal Blade E1034 (USA) (1983), Roadrunner RR 9868 (Europe) (1985)

Haunting The Chapel, Metal Blade MBR 1024 (USA), Roadrunner RR 125508 (Europe) (1984)

LIVE UNDEAD, Metal Blade MBR 1037 (USA), Roadrunner RR 125500 (Europe) (1985)

HELL AWAITS, Metal Blade MX 8020 (USA), Roadrunner RR 9795 (Europe) (1985)

REIGN IN BLOOD, London LONLP 34 (UK), Def Jam GHS 24131 (USA) (1986) **47 UK, 94 USA**

SOUTH OF HEAVEN, London LONLP 63 (UK), Def Jam GHS 24203 (USA) (1988) **25 UK, 57 USA**

SEASONS IN THE ABYSS, Def American 846 871-2 (UK), Def American 9 24307-2 (USA) (1990) **18 UK, 40 USA**

DECADE OF AGGRESSION: LIVE, Def American 510 605-2 (UK), Def American 9 26748-2 (USA) (1991) **29 UK, 55 USA**

DIVINE INTERVENTION, Def American 74321 23677 2 (UK), Def American 9 45522-2 (USA) (1994) **15 UK, 8 USA**

UNDISPUTED ATTITUDE, American 74321 35759 2 (UK), American 9 43072-2 (USA) (1996) **31 UK, 34 USA**

DIABOLUS IN MUSICA, American 491302 2 (UK), American CK 69192 (USA) (1998) **27 UK, 31 USA**

GOD HATES US ALL, American 586 331-2 (UK), American 314 586 332-2 (USA) (2001) **31 UK, 28 USA**

SOUNDTRACK TO THE APOCALYPSE, American B0001519-02 (USA) (2003)

CHRIST ILLUSION, American 9362-44300-2 (UK), American 44300-2 (USA) (2006) **23 UK, 5 USA**

God, Children Of Bodom and Thine Eyes Bleed as support. Early dates were re-scheduled after Tom Araya underwent gallbladder surgery and needed time to recuperate.

Christ Illusion sold over 62,000 copies in its first week of release to land at Number 5 on the US album charts, the band's highest ever domestic position. The album also landed in the Top 10 in Australia and just missed out on the top spot in both Germany and Finland. Notably, Slayer were set to co-headline what was billed as 'Hell And Heaven United' alongside Christian rockers Stryper for the Monterrey 'Metal Fest' on September 23rd at the Coca Cola Auditorium in Monterrey, Nuevo Leon, Mexico. However, Slayer pulled out, quoting "personal reasons". The band are still among the most intense experiences any metalhead can have.

SUICIDAL TENDENCIES
WHEN HARDCORE MET THRASH METAL

SUICIDAL TENDENCIES ALWAYS stood out from the thrash metal pack because of their hardcore punk influences and their 'gang' image: vocalist Mike Muir and his cohorts often appeared in photographs dressed as if they had emerged from Los Angeles gang culture, their eyes hidden behind bandanas and Pendleton check shirts held only by the neck button. The band also penetrated skateboard culture thanks to songs such as 'Possessed To Skate'.

The Suicidals, as they became known, were established in Venice, California, in 1980 and endured numerous line-up changes before stabilising in 1982. They rapidly built up a rabid local following, despite famously annoying *Flipside* magazine to such an extent that they won readers' polls in the 'Biggest Asshole' and 'Worst Band' category. However, this negative press only heightened awareness of the group.

They contracted with independent label Frontier for an eponymous 1983 debut, produced by Glen E. Friedman and engineered by Randy Burns. The album marked Muir out as an articulate commentator on the hypocrisy of state religion, youth decay, corporate greed and US national politics. The frontman highlighted more serious concerns by employing spoken-word passages to dramatic effect. Muir was backed by guitarist Grant Estes, bassist Louiche Mayorga and drummer Amery 'AWOL' Smith, and the band made a point of placing a large advert for the record in *Flipside*.

They signed to major label Virgin in 1986 after support from MTV for the video to 'Institutionalized' and a spot in the cult 1984 movie *Repo Man* considerably raised the band's profile. They even put in a cameo appearance in an episode of *Miami Vice*, which also used the song. 'Institutionalized' pulled them clear of their indie hardcore roots and broke into the charts on both sides of the Atlantic. Blind Illusion bassist Les Claypool was brought in as producer for *Join The Army*, recorded at the Record Plant in Hollywood in January 1987.

Although it was relatively successful for a thrash album, peaking at Number 100 on the US national charts, *Join The Army* alienated a large quota of early fans who felt the band had strayed too far from their roots. This period also witnessed the first fracture in the ranks, with Estes and Smith bowing out: the band debuted guitarist Rocky George and drummer R.J. Herrera.

Bassist Louiche Mayorga joined his erstwhile bandmates Estes and Smith to form Uncle Slam, debuting the new act with the *Say Uncle* album on Caroline Records in 1988.

The Suicidals then signed to Epic in the USA and, utilising Cherokee Studios in Hollywood in April 1988, crafted the Mark Dodson-produced *How Will I Laugh Tomorrow When I Can't Even Smile Today*. This album, released in September 1988, saw the band enlarged with the addition of ex-No Mercy rhythm guitarist Mike Clark and bassist Bob Heathcote. However, just as Suicidal Tendencies were seemingly entering the big league, their controversial name made them ripe targets for the moral majority. California's police department, fearing that Muir's crew was merely a front for a Los Angeles gang, even went so far as to ban them from performing in their hometown. The notorious pressure group the PMRC kept up a campaign against the band, claiming that a number of teenage suicides were directly attributable to them. Longstanding fans who appreciated the group's mix of humour and politics were both bemused and angry.

In 1990 Suicidal Tendencies brought in bassist Robert Trujillo for *Lights... Camera... Revolution*. This album, again produced by Dodson and recorded at Rumbo Recorders and Amigo Studios, saw a shift towards more straightforward metal. The track 'Send Me Your Money', a forthright attack on American TV evangelists, proved a huge hit with the fans and quickly became a staple of live shows. The band's morbid sense of humour was amply displayed on 'Disco's Out, Murder's In'.

The band stepped onto the international touring circuit that September alongside Testament, Slayer and Megadeth on the European 'Clash Of The Titans' extravaganza. Both Muir and Trujillo captured more than their fair share of the limelight at this juncture with their funked up side project act Infectious Grooves together with erstwhile Jane's Addiction drummer Stephen Perkins. They would release two well-received albums and test the duo's stamina, as Infectious Grooves often opened for Suicidal Tendencies.

The Suicidals' next album, *Still Cyco After All These Years*, was actually a re-recording of their debut, adding a further two remakes from *Join The Army*. As the first album was now long out of print, and Frontier were showing little inclination to re-press it, the band – together with producer Mark Dodson – chose the practical option of simply re-cutting the entire record from scratch. Their efforts were rewarded with a Grammy nomination for 'Institutionalized' but, in the main, their fanbase preferred the rawness of the original.

June 1992's *The Art Of Rebellion* was the band's best-selling record, reaching Number 52 in the *Billboard* charts, produced by Peter Collins.

Hardcore specialists Suicidal Tendencies

SUICIDAL TENDENCIES discography

SUICIDAL TENDENCIES, Frontier FLP 1011 (USA) (1983)
JOIN THE ARMY, Virgin CDV 2424 (UK), Caroline CAROL CD 1336 (USA) (1987) **81 UK, 100 USA**
HOW WILL I LAUGH TOMORROW WHEN I CAN'T EVEN SMILE TODAY?, Virgin CDV 2551 (UK), Epic EK-44288 (USA) (1988) **111 USA**
CONTROLLED BY HATRED – FEEL LIKE SHIT... DÉJÀ VU, Epic 465399-2 (UK), Epic EK-45244 (USA) (1989) **150 USA**
LIGHTS... CAMERA... REVOLUTION, Epic 466569-2 (UK), Epic EK-45389 (USA) (1990) **59 UK, 101 USA**
THE ART OF REBELLION, Epic 471885-2 (UK), Epic EK-48864 (USA) (1992) **52 USA**
STILL CYCO AFTER ALL THESE YEARS, Epic 473749-2 (UK), Epic EK-46230 (USA) (1993) **117 USA**
SUICIDAL FOR LIFE, Epic 476885-2 (UK), Epic EK-57774 (USA) (1994) **82 USA**
FRIENDS & FAMILY, Suicidal 13 (USA) (1997)
Six The Hard Way, Suicidal 14 (USA) (1998)
FREEDUMB, Nuclear Blast NB 0368-2 (Europe), Suicidal 71215 (USA) (1999)
FREE YOUR SOUL... AND SAVE MY MIND, Nuclear Blast NB 0528-2 (Europe), Suicidal 18 (USA) (2000)
FRIENDS AND FAMILY 2, XIII Bis 05072 (Europe) (2001)

They announced a new recruit in Vandals drummer Josh Freese, who also took over the drum stool in Infectious Grooves. The band opened up on Megadeth's hugely successful headline dates in both 1992 and 1993, and in October 1993 they backed Alice In Chains in Australia.

The Paul Northfield-produced *Suicidal For Life* in 1994 had Suicidal Tendencies recording without a permanent drummer at Groove Masters in Santa Monica and Ocean Way Studios in Hollywood. Many fans voiced their displeasure at the lack of subtlety on the album: having gained respect for his insight and lyrical wit, Muir blasted listeners with four songs in a row with the dumbed down 'Don't Give A Fuck', 'No Fuck'n Problem', 'Suicyco Muthafucka' and 'Fucked Up Just Right'. He admitted later that these caustic diatribes were deliberate, due to the band's awareness during recording that *Suicidal For Life* would be the closing chapter with Epic. In spite of this, they still engaged in high-profile touring, supporting Metallica in the USA and performing in South America on festival bills with Kiss, Slayer and Black Sabbath.

Freese joined the studio-bound Guns N' Roses, then Pearl Jam and A Perfect Circle. White Lion and Y&T man Jimmy DeGrasso deputised for the album sessions before he joined Megadeth.

Dropped by Epic, Suicidal Tendencies folded. Rocky George created Samsara with Cro-Mags members Harley Flanagan and Parris Mayhew. Trujillo found himself part of the Ozzy Osbourne band after an interim stint with Pale Demon. Muir assembled a studio band, including Sex Pistols guitarist Steve Jones, for the recording of a 1995 album under the name Cyco Myko, titled *Lost My Brains (Once Again!)*.

In 1996 Slayer covered the Suicidals' 'Memories Of Tomorrow' on their *Undisputed Attitude* covers album. However, the track only made it onto the Japanese pressing. Meantime, the Suicidal Tendencies brand was maintained with compilation albums *Friends And Family* and *Prime Cuts*. The latter effort sported fresh tracks recorded by Muir, with guitarist Dean Pleasants, bass player Josh Paul and drummer Brooks Wackerman.

The band returned in November 1998 with a six track-EP produced by Michael Vail Blum and Paul Northfield and titled *Six The Hard Way*.

The resurrected outfit then put out a full-length album, *Freedumb*, in May 1999 through the Side One Dummy label. Wackerman opted out, focusing on his Hot Potty band. Essentially promoting themselves, the group found valuable exposure as part of the mammoth 'Warped' US tour. Suicidal Tendencies signed to Germany's Nuclear Blast label for the European release of *Freedumb*, and the self-produced *Free Your Soul And Save My Mind* followed in August 2000.

By early 2002 Rocky George had re-emerged, touting a fresh act, Harley's War, with ex-Cro-Mags frontman Harley Flanagan and former Warzone guitarist Jay Vento. Meantime, ex-Suicidals guitarist Anthony Gallo returned as part of ex-Megadeth drummer Nick Menza's new band.

The 2002 Suicidal Tendencies line-up consisted of Muir, Mike Clark on guitar, Dean Pleasants on second guitar, bassist Steve Brunner and Ron Brunner Jr. on drums. The Brunner brothers' commitment to rapper Snoop Dogg would see the band without their services for one gig, for which they enrolled Josh Paul and drummer Dave Hidalgo Jr.

In early 2003 ex-member Robert Trujillo became Metallica's new bass player, this appointment putting a renewed focus on his former band. An extensive round of touring in Europe in the latter half of 2003 proved arduous for Muir. After these dates the frontman entered hospital for two operations on his back, and a series of South and Central American tour dates for February 2004 was curtailed. That year also found Rocky George uniting with Ugly Kid Joe and Medication man Whitfield Crane to cut a version of Metallica's 'Master Of Puppets' for the *Metallic Assault* tribute album through Big Deal Records.

Gigs announced in Europe for the summer of 2005 were cancelled when it was announced that Muir was suffering "serious health problems". Festival dates for Brazil would be announced but then withdrawn when it was revealed that Muir was to undergo another round of back surgery.

Working with producer Paul Northfield, Suicidal Tendencies commenced work on a new studio album in January 2006. Their fanbase remains as solid as ever.

TESTAMENT
ALWAYS PRACTISING WHAT THEY PREACH, AGAINST ALL ODDS

TESTAMENT HAVE ALWAYS BEEN staunch campaigners of the thrash cause and came tantalisingly close to achieving major success despite a succession of damaging membership changes. The band was founded in 1983 as Legacy in the San Francisco Bay Area, a fertile home of thrash metal. As Legacy, the Oakland-based band consisted of high-school-student guitarists Eric Peterson and his cousin Derrick Ramirez, bassist Greg Christian, and drummer Louis Clemente. A 1984 four-song demo saw Ramirez handling lead vocals, after which Steve 'Zetro' Souza was recruited as frontman. Recruiting guitarist Alex Skolnick, tutored by none other than Joe Satriani, a second demo session arrived in 1985, the track 'Reign Of Terror' gaining exposure from inclusion on the *Eastern Front Vol. 2* compilation album. These tracks were produced by Doug Piercy, a noted scene guitarist with credentials stretching through Control, Cobra, Anvil Chorus and Delta. However, Souza then bailed out to join another local up-and-coming thrash outfit, Exodus.

Jonny Zazula's Megaforce label took the band on, this arrangement securing major distribution through Atlantic Records. To avoid legal clashes with another band also titled Legacy, they switched names to Testament, the intended title of their first album. A valuable acquisition was former Guilt and Rampage vocalist Chuck Billy, who would become the focal point and lynchpin of the band, drafted in for the Alex Perialas-produced debut *The Legacy*. Such was the undisputed quality of this album, recorded at Pyramid Sound Studio, Ithaca in New York and issued

TESTAMENT discography

THE LEGACY, Megaforce/Atlantic 781 741-1 (UK), Megaforce/Atlantic 7 81741-2 (USA) (1987)

Live At Eindhoven, Megaforce/Atlantic 780 226-1 (UK) (1987)

THE NEW ORDER, Megaforce/Atlantic 781 849-2 (UK), Megaforce/Atlantic 7 81849-2 (USA) (1988) **81 UK, 136 USA**

PRACTICE WHAT YOU PREACH, Megaforce/Atlantic 782 009-2 (UK), Megaforce/Atlantic 7 82009-2 (USA) (1989) **40 UK, 77 USA**

SOULS OF BLACK, Megaforce/Atlantic 7567-82143-2 (UK), Megaforce/Atlantic 7 82143-2 (USA) (1990) **35 UK, 73 USA**

THE RITUAL, Megaforce/Atlantic 7567-82392-2 (UK), Megaforce/Atlantic 7 82392-2 (USA) (1992) **48 UK, 55 USA**

Return To The Apocalyptic City, Megaforce/Atlantic 7567-82487-2 (UK), Megaforce/Atlantic 7 82487-2 (USA) (1993)

LOW, Megaforce/Atlantic 7567 82645-2 (UK), Megaforce/Atlantic 7 82645-2 (USA) (1994) **122 USA**

LIVE AT THE FILLMORE, Music For Nations CD MFN 186 (UK), Burnt Offerings 86264-2 (USA) (1995)

DEMONIC, Music For Nations CD MFN 221 (UK), Burnt Offerings cnu (USA) (1997)

THE GATHERING, USG 1033-2 (Europe), Fierce 11157 (USA) (1999)

FIRST STRIKE STILL DEADLY, Spitfire SPITCD083 (UK), Spitfire SP 15083-2 (USA) (2001)

LIVE IN LONDON, Spitfire SPITCD262 (UK), Spitfire SP 15516-2 (USA) (2005)

in June 1987, that many predicted that Testament would join thrash metal frontrunners Metallica, Megadeth, Slayer and Anthrax. The group capitalised on favourable press and fan reaction by touring across the USA and Europe as support to Anthrax.

Megaforce maintained the momentum by combining a studio out-take, 'Reign Of Terror', with live tracks culled from the band's showing at the famed Dynamo festival in Holland as the December 1987 European release *Live In Eindhoven*, oddly not released in the band's homeland until 1990. The studio follow-up, May 1988's *The New Order*, maintained and indeed boosted the quality levels. Cut again at Pyramid in Ithaca, New York, and produced again by Perialas, engineering credits went to Raven drummer Rob 'Wacko' Hunter. The record, which landed the band at Number 136 on the *Billboard* charts, included a brave take on Aerosmith's 'Nobody's Fault' among the expected riffage.

The band's fortunes rose with August 1989's *Practice What You Preach*. Employing Perialas yet again, but at the new location of Fantasy Studios in Berkeley, California, this album even cracked the *Billboard* Top 100. It saw Testament shifting their lyrical focus away from their previously esoteric musings and onto more realistic concerns such as politics and the environment.

In 1990 the band promoted the *Souls Of Black* album – their first to break tradition with Perialas by pulling in Michael Rosen for desk duties – and found themselves in the opening spot on the mammoth 'Clash Of The Titans' European tour with Megadeth, Suicidal Tendencies and Slayer. Despite this global exposure, they appeared to have plateau'd commercially, the album only gaining slightly in sales on its predecessor.

The Tony Platt-produced *The Ritual* in 1992 was recorded at One On One Studios in Los Angeles and gave Testament their highest US chart position to date, at Number 55. They had polished up their sound and slowed the pace for *The Ritual*, going for a more anthemic feel. In particular the uncharacteristic ballad 'Return To Serenity' came in for

heavy praise and brought in a new set of fans. At this high point, Skolnick opted out to join Savatage. By 1995 he had received a better offer to join Ozzy Osbourne. However, the guitarist only lasted for one gig, a secret bash at Nottingham's Rock City. Skolnick followed his passion and founded the jazz-rock band Attention Deficit with Primus drummer Tim Alexander for a 1998 album.

Meanwhile, Testament failed to maintain a stable line-up for 1993's *Return To Apocalyptic City*, a six-track stopgap mini-album. Unfortunately for the band, fragile membership would plague them for the rest of the decade and into the next. The new man on the drum stool was the highly respected ex-Forbidden and Slayer drummer Paul Bostaph, while ex-Forbidden guitarist Glen Alvelais also came on board.

Low in 1994 featured death metal journeyman guitarist James Murphy, whose credits include Agent Steel, Death, Obituary, Disincarnate and Cancer, and Exodus drummer John Tempesta. The album, recorded at A&M Studios in Los Angeles, was issued in the midst of the grunge and alternative rock revolution, and the band, in spite of cannily employing noted alt.rock producer Garth Richardson and veteran mixer Michael Wagener, struggled to get noticed. Although fans and critics were unanimous in their praise for *Low* and its return to form, the record was swamped by grunge and a marked lack of enthusiasm from Atlantic. Shortly after recording, Tempesta teamed up with White Zombie, and Atlantic – a staunch ally since the debut – let the band go.

The line-up for the *Live At The Fillmore* album, recorded at a sell-out show at the famous Haight-Ashbury venue, consisted of Chuck Billy, guitarists Eric Peterson and James Murphy, bassist Greg Christian and former Evil Dead drummer John Dette. Down to a duo of Billy and Peterson, the band folded for a short period as the original pairing announced a new group, Dog Faced God. These sessions would ultimately emerge as the new Testament album.

The exceptionally dark *Demonic*, released in 1997 and produced by Doug Hall, was Testament's first for new label Spitfire via the band's Burnt Offerings imprint. It featured Billy, Alvelais and Peterson, plus Ramirez on bass and ex-Death drummer Gene Hoglan. Prior to recording, Dette had vacated his position, making a high-profile career move to Slayer. Subsequently, bass was handled by the erstwhile Death and Sadus man Steve DiGiorgio. Sadly, *Demonic*'s profile suffered heavily when the distribution company went into bankruptcy. Fortunately, 1997 also found the newly formed Mayhem Records issuing a compilation album, *Signs Of Chaos: The Best Of Testament*, covering the group's finest moments.

Another quick change ensued on the drum stool after *Demonic*'s release as Hoglan took up an offer to fulfil live work with Strapping Young Lad, leaving a gap for the reinstatement of Dette – whose tenure in Slayer had only lasted a matter of weeks. Billy, meanwhile, put in an appearance on Murphy's 1999 solo album *Feeding The Machine*.

Testament underwent another dramatic line-up change as Alvelais was given his marching orders again. Murphy stepped in once more and former Slayer drummer Dave Lombardo played on 1999's *The Gathering*. Dette then regained and lost his position in favour of Steve Jacobs, while Murphy was replaced by Vicious Rumors guitarist Steve Smyth.

Murphy's removal signalled the beginning of a run of bad luck for the band's health. Apparently the guitarist had been acting out of character for some time, prompting his dismissal: only later, after extensive surgery to remove a brain tumour, was the cause of Murphy's behavioural problems revealed.

Smyth, DiGiorgio and Peterson launched a black/thrash side project named Dragonheart with Sadus drummer Jon Allen. DiGiorgio later joined Iced Earth. This band later switched titles to Dragonlord. Smyth doubled duties, appearing as Randy Zakk Iommi in the Black Sabbath tribute band Sweet Leaf in union with Skitzo frontman Lance Ozanix. He also contributed guitar to Skitzo's 2000 album *Got Sick*. By 2000 Alvelais was

fronting LD/50, a band including bassist Oddie McLaughlin, drummer Jeremy Colson and G/Z//R vocalist Clark Brown.

On the Testament front, news emerged in early 2001 that Chuck Billy had been diagnosed with cancer. The singer got stuck straight into a regime of treatment to defeat the disease and was aided in spirit by the announcement of a benefit concert in his name, dubbed 'Thrash Of The Titans'. The highly anticipated concert, held on August 11th at the San Francisco Maritime Hall, pulled together a stellar cast of thrash bands such as Heathen, Flotsam And Jetsam, S.O.D., Anthrax, Forbidden Evil, reformations of Exodus, Vio-lence and Death Angel, and even a reformation of Legacy. A retrospective studio album of Testament classics, *First Strike Still Deadly*, was also begun in earnest with former vocalist Steve Souza committed to guest on tracks.

Derrick Ramirez was the latest Testament member to join Dragonlord, in March 2002. Guitarist Glen Alvelais, besides his activities with Bizarro and LD/50, also involved himself with F-Bomb, a union with Souza, guitarist Jason Brown, bassist Kevin Moore and LD/50 drummer Jeremy Colson. Meanwhile other ex-Testament members, drummer John Dette and bassist Greg Christian, debuted their new band Pushed, in July.

Yet another endeavour with strong Testament connections was unveiled during the summer of 2002 with the Sadus pairing of frontman Darren Travis and bassist Steve DiGiorgio embarking on an all-star union billed as Suicide Shift. The project included Billy, drummer Per Moller Jensen of The Haunted, and Murphy. Meanwhile, ex-drummer Chris Kontos was preparing an album for his new act The Servants.

Testament then put in a one-off show in Las Vegas supporting Halford and a short burst of December 2002 dates with support acts Exodus and Vio-lence. Rob Zombie drummer John Tempesta filled in for the group's West Coast tour after regular drummer Jon Allen was forced to bow out due to a family emergency. Spiral Architect and Borknagar drummer Asgeir Mickelson was a temporary stand-in for Allen.

April 2003 found Testament on the road in Europe as part of the roving 'No Mercy' festivals. Returning to the USA, the group partnered with Halford and Immortal for the ill-fated 'Metal Gods' tour, this trek unfortunately collapsing within a few dates. DiGiorgio then took time out to lay down bass on Painmuseum's *Metal Forever* album before Testament engaged his services once again for European festival gigs, including the 'Wacken Open Air' and 'Earthshaker' events in Germany.

Steve Smyth temporarily joined Seattle's Nevermore for their European and US gig schedule from September 2003. Testament spent the latter months of the year and into the New Year recording a new studio album. Summer 2004 dates had them touring Europe, including appearances at the Budapest 'Summer Rocks' festival and the Dutch 'Waldrock' event. During early 2004 both Chuck Billy and Eric Peterson donated their services to a tribute album, *Within The Mind*, assembled by James Murphy in honour of the late Death pioneer Chuck Schuldiner.

Paul Bostaph rejoined Testament in February 2004, and guitarist Steve Smyth left the band on the eve of a European summer tour. Smyth duly joined Nevermore on a full-time basis, confirming this appointment with an appearance in the video for the track 'I, Voyager' in April. Halford guitarist 'Metal' Mike Chlasciak filled the vacancy.

Throughout June 2004, Testament hit the continental festival circuit, putting in appearances at the 'Gods Of Metal' in Italy, 'Sweden Rock', 'Summer Rock' in Budapest, Hungary, 'Provinssirock' in Finland, 'Fury Fest' in France, 'Bang Your Head' in Germany, and 'Graspop' in Belgium. These European dates were struck by bad luck, though, when Peterson fractured his leg falling down a flight of stairs at the Kozel Pub Club venue in Martin, Slovakia. Hospitalised in Vienna, Peterson learned he had sustained three separate breaks, putting him out of contention for the tour. Chlasciak covered until former guitarist Steve Smyth flew in to complete the dates.

Meanwhile the erstwhile Testament rhythm section of bass player Greg Christian and drummer John Dette were back in the news, enrolling in New York's Havochate.

Testament were set to ally themselves with Death Angel, Flotsam And Jetsam, and Overkill for a 'Thrash Domination 04' Japanese tour in September. However, the group pulled out due to Peterson's injury. Chuck Billy briefly fronted Exodus for their October date at San Francisco's Warfield Theater, standing in for frontman Steev Esquivel, whose eyes had been contaminated with "unknown chemicals" during the previous gig.

Chuck Billy and Eric Peterson then announced that original guitar player Alex Skolnick, original bassist Greg Christian and drummer John Tempesta would reunite for a brief burst of European gigs in May 2005. In this formation, Testament scheduled an appearance at the 'Dynamo Open Air' festival on May 7th 2005 in Hellendoorn, Holland, by coincidence sharing the stage with reformed 1980s-era line-ups for both Anthrax and Lääz Rockit. Further European dates saw Austrian thrash act Demolition in support.

The band's profile on the North American gig circuit rose considerably throughout the year, commencing with a July 2nd support to Judas Priest at the Mountain View Shoreline Amphitheater. On July 9th they lined up at The Pound outdoor amphitheatre in San Francisco alongside Vicious Rumors, Lääz Rockit, Hirax, Agent Steel, Dekapitator, Mudface, Neil Turbin, Brocas Helm, Dreams Of Damnation and Imagika for the 'Thrash Against Cancer' benefit. US shows in August witnessed a road partnership with Nuclear Assault before Japanese gigs in September. South American festival dates in October in Mexico, Brazil and Chile saw an unavailable Alex Skolnick substituted by a returning Mike Chlasciak. Gigs in March 2006 saw Jon Allen of Sadus and Dragonlord manning the drums. Louie Clemente was forced out of July shows too, citing "medical reasons", necessitating the recruitment of Exodus, Slayer, Forbidden and Systematic adept Paul Bostaph.

Two decades on, and with only Eric Peterson and Chuck Billy surviving the course, Testament's loyalty to the thrash creed has served them well. Throughout that period the band have never pandered to the mainstream or inflicted their dedicated fans with anything close to commercialism. Fine testament indeed.

WHIPLASH
THE THREE TONYS IN FULL SWING

WHIPLASH IS A FEROCIOUS trio from Passaic, New Jersey, founded in 1984. Although the act's membership has changed several times over the years, it is the classic "treble Tony" trio format for which Whiplash is remembered: ex-Toxin guitarist Tony Portaro, bassist Tony Bono and drummer Tony 'T.J.' Scaglione. The group's early offerings of raw, minimalist thrash found favour among die-hard thrashers, but with virtually no touring or promotion the group were destined to remain forever in the underground. Whiplash collapsed after three albums but were summoned back for a second round in the mid 1990s by German label Massacre.

The group was formed from the amalgamation of two previous acts –Jackhammer, which issued the *Fire Away* demo in March 1984, and Toxin – to form a fresh act, later fronted by vocalist Mike Orosz. As a statement of intent, the band was titled after the landmark Metallica song 'Whiplash'. The quartet unveiled themselves with the *Full Force* demo prior to Orosz and Harding leaving the ranks. The remaining duo, with Portaro handling bass and vocals, kept the momentum going with a further cassette, the mis-spelt *Thunderstruk*, delivered that same August.

For the next session in 1985 the band drafted in bassist Tony Bono and, after unsuccessful attempts to locate a lead vocalist, settled on the trio format with Portaro reluctantly taking on singing duties for their third, five-track tape, *Looking Death In The Face*. Remarkably, Portaro recorded these cuts with his arm in plaster, having suffered a broken arm in a car accident. Nonetheless, the combination of these two tapes secured Whiplash a deal with Roadracer (as the first band signed directly to the US office of the Roadrunner subsidiary) for their commercial debut, *Power And Pain*. The record undoubtedly had its faults, with a garish jacket depicting a cartoon head being squeezed by a less than believable robotic arm, and production values at best enthusiastic, but *Power And Pain* thrashed hard to the last minute. The Metallica influences dominated, but the group's strengths lay in the cyclonic drumming abilities of Scaglione, the nimble agility of Bono, and Portaro's rustic vocal delivery.

In 1986 the 18-year-old Scaglione received an offer he could not refuse from thrash masters Slayer. Scaglione's skills would be put to the test in the full public gaze, as he was replacing Dave Lombardo, renowned as one of the very finest drummers of the genre. Whiplash duly drafted in Joe Cangelosi on the drum stool for the 1987 follow-up album *Ticket To Mayhem*, another untempered thrash workout. Scaglione's tenure in Slayer would prove brief, as Lombardo returned, and in 1987 he forged Zero Hour, a collaboration with vocalist Joe Haggerty, ex-Deathrash bassist Pat Burns and the guitar pairing of the Massacre-

Whiplash

credited Robbie Goodwin and NYC Mayhem and Agnostic Front man Gordon Ancis. The drummer subsequently journeyed on to Ludichrist.

In late 1988 Whiplash, taking advice from their label, added vocalist Glenn Hansen and, retaining Cangelosi on drums, began to gather together material for a third album titled *Insult To Injury*. In keeping with the amateurish nature of previous album covers, *Insult To Injury*'s jacket depicted a wheelchair-bound rocker about to be hit by a locomotive. Whiplash then ground to a halt, explaining later that they had never received any royalties and simply ran out of steam.

Scaglione was announced as the new drummer in Southern-infused retro-rockers Raging Slab around the same period. He later joined hardcore units Cause For Alarm and Sheer Terror.

Meanwhile, Cangelosi united with German thrash veterans Kreator for their *Cause For Conflict* album. Bono joined the hardcore band Into Another, fronted by ex-Youth Of Today vocalist Richie Birkenhead, for their eponymous 1992 album. Scaglione and Portaro would find themselves as members of the same band in 1993 when the duo acted as touring musicians for Billy Milano's M.O.D. European dates.

German label Massacre then persuaded Whiplash to cut another album for the European market, and Portaro and Scaglione pulled in Burn singer Rob Gonzo and bassist Jimmy Preziosa to construct the 1996 *Cult Of One* album. The record drew ecstatic reviews. Whiplash joined with Riot and labelmates Skyclad for a 1996 European tour and, although Whiplash's intense brand of retro thrash seemed an uneasy bedfellow for Skyclad's whimsical folk metal, the tour served both acts well. Drums were now in the hands of Rob Candella.

Upon the tour's completion, Gonzo was unceremoniously fired and Whiplash manoeuvred guitarist Warren Conditi into the lead vocal position. Massacre put out the Steve Evetts-produced *Sit, Stand, Kneel, Prey* offering in 1997.

The band issued the *Thrashback* album in 1998, a collection of re-recorded archive material – some of which dated back as far as 1984. One of these early tracks, 'Chained Up, Strapped Down', was retitled 'Nails In Me Deep'. Some critics took issue with the alteration of songs which they regarded as classics – and especially vilified the band's cleaner vocal sound – but overall the return of Whiplash was welcomed.

In 1999 the Dutch label Displeased repackaged the first two albums as a double CD and released a collection of demos and rarities entitled *Messages In Blood – The Early Years*. Another reissue CD, *Insult To Injury*, consisted of live tracks recorded in 1986 at the legendary CBGBs club in New York City.

Scaglione later played with hardcore acts The North Side Kings, Zero SRI, and Mantra, a band led by Channel Zero guitarist Peter Iterbeke that included Scaglione's erstwhile Whiplash colleague bassist Jimmy Preziosa. Sadly, ex-Whiplash member Tony Bono, at the age of just 38, died of a heart attack in May 2002. His band's legacy remains strong.

WHIPLASH discography

POWER AND PAIN, Roadrunner RR 9718 (Europe / USA) (1985)
TICKET TO MAYHEM, Roadrunner RR 9596-2 (Europe / USA) (1987)
INSULT TO INJURY, Roadracer RO 9482-2 (Europe / USA) (1989)
CULT OF ONE, Massacre MASS CD087 (Europe) (1996)
SIT, STAND, KNEEL, PREY, Massacre MAS CD0129 (Europe) (1997)
THRASHBACK, Massacre MAS CD0148 (Europe) (1998)
MESSAGES IN BLOOD – THE EARLY YEARS, Displeased D-00067 (Europe) (1999)

UK
THRASH
METAL

GREAT BRITAIN

GREAT BRITAIN, for so long a leader in the field of rock and metal, was caught uncharacteristically napping with the advent of thrash metal. Just as the NWOBHM-era bands were finding their feet on the US touring circuit, America responded with its own invasion of the UK and Europe. In time, perhaps, another wave of British bands might have risen to meet the challenge, but they had no chance. The American invasion of Metallica, Megadeth, Slayer, Anthrax and more utterly dominated the scene. Across the Channel, Germany was rising once again with Kreator, Sodom and Helloween.

American thrash was so big, and rose so quickly, that the scene in the UK could not respond. Labels struggled vainly in an attempt to snap up domestic thrashers but were faced with an absence of bands, or at least acts with sufficient talent. This sad fact dominated the British thrash scene as the majors rushed desperately to get bands into studios before their time.

There were exceptions. The prescient Music For Nations label grabbed the cream of the crop – Onslaught, Acid Reign and Reanimator all started out there. Unfortunately all three acts later lost their nerve. Neat Records, the home of Venom, never really got a grip on thrash, with quality acts such as Avenger, Warfare and Atomkraft neutered by pathetic budgets. The majors were left to an embarrassing tug of war over the likes of Slammer and Toranaga. The end products proved dull, generic and – crucially – inferior to the work of the US Big Four.

The brightest hopes for UK thrash came with Xentrix, Pariah and Sabbat. Xentrix benefited hugely from a deal with Roadrunner, who had at least picked a band with some degree of originality. Granted, the band's early work was decidedly Metallica-influenced, but they grew up fast – a ferocious live act cut down in their prime by the novelty factor. Who you gonna call? Not Xentrix, apparently.

Pariah (or was it Satan?) made solid inroads into Europe, but a string of crunch-laden albums were marred by a schizophrenic campaign that ultimately caused their demise. With some consistency, Pariah could have made it.

The other contender was Nottingham's Sabbat. They bypassed the majors and the London clique to sign with Germany's Noise Records. They were the only act with real originality, due to a combination of Andy Sneap's muscular riffing and Martin Walkyier's legendary aptitude for pagan prose. Sabbat issued two albums of distinction, sold vast amounts of records and then gutted themselves in full public view. This spectacular act of hara-kiri spawned two forces of note: Sneap, as a producer of high repute; and Walkyier, fronting Skyclad, as an artisan for our times and creator of yet another sub-genre.

UK thrash metal was unable to compete with America and dwarfed by the tidal tonnage coming out of Germany, and its death throes resorted to hopeless tactics, indulging in offbeat, decidedly unfunny humour. Fans deserted the scene in droves; Lawnmower Deth provided the coup de grâce.

ATOMKRAFT
NUCLEAR RIFFAGE

ATOMKRAFT FROM WERE ONE of the first speed metal bands, forming in Newcastle Upon Tyne, England in 1979. The band was rooted in the late-1970s punk act Moral Fibre, which consisted of bassist Tony 'Demolition' Dolan, drummer Paul Spillett and guitarists Ian Legg and Chris Taylor. With Legg decamping, Ian Drew took over the vacant six-string position, but he too would soon leave. At this juncture Taylor made a trip to Germany and came back sporting a badge with the environmental message "Atomkraft – Nein Danke!" (Nuclear power – no thanks!).

Suitably inspired, the band re-christened themselves Atomkraft, believing this to be more in keeping with their new metal sound. The band, now minus Taylor, drafted in guitarist Steve White and bassist Mark Irvine alongside Dolan and Spillett. However, after their inaugural gig, Irvine's parents persuaded him that he had no future with the act and he left.

Atomkraft then demoed two four-song demos, opening with 1981's Keith Nichol-produced *Demon* set before entering the Wallsend based

Neat Records' Impulse studio for the 'Total Metal' / 'Death Valley' session in 1983. Although the tape attracted interest on the American underground metal scene, the band broke up, with Dolan relocating to Canada to try his luck.

He soon returned and set about reforming Atomkraft with drummer Ged Wolf, ex-Tysondog and brother of Venom manager Eric Cook, and 16-year-old guitarist Rob Matthew. A further demo, *Pour The Metal In*, secured a deal with the Neat stable for the *Future Warriors* album, again with production credits going to Keith Nichol. As revealed in later years, Atomkraft were famously contracted for a three-album deal, including publishing, for a total advance payment of £1 (about $1.50).

The band secured their first European shows opening for Venom and supported Slayer at the Marquee. This inaugural London show did not go without incident, though, as equipment breakages forced the band to cut their set to a mere three songs. Further shows in Europe had Atomkraft supporting Exodus and Venom.

Trouble struck when Dolan left the band midway through the recording of a proposed EP to be titled *Your Mentor*, leaving Wolf and Matthew to pick up the pieces. A new line-up was quickly assembled, with new additions Ian Davison-Swift, former Avenger and Satan vocalist,

Atomkraft, with frontman Tony Dolan (who later acted in Hollywood blockbusters) in the foreground

what they were doing. Looking back, I think they made a mistake, because when I was learning the early songs I realised the band was about being very raw, that kind of Kill 'Em All thing. They had terrible problems with their former singer in the studio, so they went to the opposite end to get someone like me. The record came out fine but live it wasn't comfortable. London Records signed one band and then straight away tried to turn it into something else. The fans saw through it all and it didn't look good. There were a few thrash metal bands all snapped up at the same time and not one of them worked out because the labels just didn't have a clue."

Keeler departed to form Mirror Mirror with erstwhile Preyer drummer Lloyd Coates. Former Grim Reaper singer Steve Grimmett, who had made his mark in North America with three chart albums, joined the band to re-record the vocals on the album, injecting a much needed dose of class to the band. *In Search Of Sanity*, mixed at Atlantic Studios in New York City, found the group tackling AC/DC's 'Let There Be Rock' once again, backing this as a single with a promotional video. A further single, the power ballad 'Welcome To Dying', was backed by a further brace of covers: Van Halen's 'Atomic Punk' and the Stranglers' 'Nice N'Sleazy'. Regrettably, it was a hideous mismatch, and after a low-key European tour in alliance with Annihilator and UK dates with Horse, Grimmett decamped.

The band drafted in Canadian-born vocalist Tony O'Hora, previously with the much mellower Larrakin and Torino. An album was announced for release, billed *When Reason Sleeps*, but was never issued. Onslaught's proposed material for this record witnessed a radical swing away from their thrash roots and, in the midst of these sessions, London dropped the band. The independent FM Revolver announced that they would release *When Reason Sleeps*, although this never happened. The group undertook an extensive UK headline tour throughout November and December 1990, supported by New Yorkers Dead On and Keeler's Mirror Mirror, but both Hinder and Trotman then quit.

The best days of the group were behind them and Onslaught split, with Grice and Rockett forming the funk-rock outfit Frankenstein, managed by producer Pete Hinton. Frankenstein consisted of the two ex-Onslaught men plus former Rhode Island Red vocalist Tony Bryan, ex-Tokyo Rose bassist Bod Presley and ex-Mirror Mirror guitarist Alan Jordan. Frankenstein achieved little beyond supporting Saxon on their poorly-attended 1993 British tour.

Steve Grimmett, on the other hand, found a great deal of success in Japan with the more traditional hard rock delivered by his new group, Lionsheart. Following a run of three Lionsheart albums, the singer fronted Pride and Seven Deadly Sins.

In 1999 Rockett turned up on the Hora-Kane album *Eternal Infinity*, fronted by O'Hora. The vocalist fronted Praying Mantis between 1998 and 2002. During 2003 he was fronting the fabled 1970s glamsters Sweet and in September 2004 joined Statetrooper, not as a singer but as a bassist. Greek black metal band Thou Art Lord included a cover version of 'Power From Hell' on their May 2005 album *Orgia Daemonicum*.

Surprisingly, Onslaught resurrected themselves in 2005, announcing a touring partnership as part of the December 2005 'X-Mass' festivals in Europe alongside Exodus, Occult, Kataklysm, Unleashed, Behemoth and Primordial. Joining guitarist Nige Rockett, drummer Steve Grice, vocalist Sy Keeler and bassist Jim Hinder was guitarist Alan Jordan (ex-Mirror Mirror, Rhode Island Red and Frankenstein). A debut gig for the rejuvenated act took place on November 25th at their old Bristol haunt, the Fleece And Firkin, where they debuted a new, very fast song.

Meanwhile, Tony O'Hora issued his debut album, *Escape Into The Sun*, through the Italian Frontiers label in January 2006. Acting as guitarist and producer for the project would be Magnus Karlsson, the Swede of

Starbreaker repute. On the live front, Onslaught acted as support to Venom in the UK during March. It seemed as if the band now had a more promising outlook than during their first attack on the scene.

RE-ANIMATOR
STILL NOT REBORN

YORKSHIRE THRASHERS RE-ANIMATOR managed to cruise the shortlived UK thrash wave on the back of their debut six-track mini-album, 1989's *Deny Reality*, issued through the Music For Nations subsidiary Under One Flag. The group, having scored their deal with a two-song demo cut at Animal Tracks Studios in Hull in March 1988, consisted of vocalist-rhythm guitarist Kev Ingleson, guitarist Mike 'Dis-Able' Abel, bassist John Hanson and drummer Mark Mitchell. The tracks were laid down with a session singer, Tony Calvert of Welsh thrashers Tortoise Corpse.

On the live front, Re-Animator toured as support to Exodus, Acid Reign, Dark Angel and Nuclear Assault. The band was managed initially by Music For Nations owner Martin Hooker, then Nuclear Assault manager Paul Loasby. 1990's *Condemned To Reality* bolstered their reputation, but Re-Animator undertook a severe left turn in their brand of music, adopting the in-vogue funk approach for their third album, 1991's *Laughing*. Having gathered fans with their previous two albums, Re-Animator's liberal use of horn sections, odes to Laurel & Hardy, an unaccredited a cappella stab at Monty Python's 'Always Look On The Bright Side Of Life', and even a dash of reggae did not serve them well.

RE-ANIMATOR discography

Deny Reality, Under One Flag MFLAG 32 (UK) (1989)
CONDEMNED TO ETERNITY, Under One Flag CDFLAG 37 (UK) (1990)
LAUGHING, Under One Flag CDFLAG 53 (UK) (1991)
THAT WAS THEN... THIS IS NOW, Under One Flag CDFLAG 67 (UK) (1992)

Re-Animator

Line-up changes affected the band, with Ingleson and Abel superseded by singer Lee Robinson and guitarist Adam Clarke, as Grahame Dixon was enrolled on rhythm guitar. The final outing, 1992's *That Was Then... This Is Now*, included a cover version of Thin Lizzy's 'Cold Sweat'. John Wilson resurfaced in ska band Badness and Mark Mitchell journeyed through punk band The Happy Durals before enrolling in a Hawkwind covers band as Denbo Drumwind. A CD reissue of *Condemned To Eternity* added the *Deny Reality* material.

SABBAT
THE BEST OF THE BUNCH?

SABBAT, A NOTTINGHAM-BASED 'satanic opera' styled quartet, formed from a previous school act, Hydra, whose line-up included vocalist Martin Walkyier, guitarist Adam Ferman, bassist Frazer Craske and drummer Mark Daley. They soon added second guitarist Andy Sneap, discovered in attendance at a Hell concert in February 1985, but Ferman and Daley quit and a name change to Sabbat was agreed. Simon Negus, previously of local glam band Brazzen Huzzy, then enrolled.

Sabbat's direct inspiration, Hell, were local heroes way before their time and had issued a self-financed single, 1983's 'Save Us From Those Who Would Save Us', recorded at Ebony Records studios in Hull. This offering sold well but was slated in the UK media, who simply failed to comprehend the band's direction. Hell had contracted to Belgian label Mausoleum, but two weeks before recording a proposed album the label collapsed. Disillusioned, Hell split and, sadly, singer Dave G. Halliday later committed suicide by gassing himself with exhaust fumes in a car in 1987.

Taking Hell's over-the-top approach as their cue, Sabbat were noted for their onstage theatrics as well as the supremely creative lyrical talents of Walkyier. The act's first recordings came in the shape of the May 1986 *Magik In Theory And Practice* demo, recorded in their rehearsal ballroom for the princely sum of £10 (about $15). The first enthusiastic review of the band came with this author's demo spotlight in US magazine *Aardschok America*. Sabbat debuted live at a young offenders' institute in Doncaster before recording their *Fragments Of A Faith Forgotten* demo, gaining the band much critical praise and ultimately leading to a deal with Germany's Noise label. Once they had the offer from the Berlin stable, Sabbat had to wait for Sneap to turn 18 before they could sign the contracts.

However, the first commercially available Sabbat record was a flexidisc for Games Workshop's November 1986 *White Dwarf* magazine entitled 'Blood For The Blood God'. This non-album track was produced by ex-Hell and Paralex guitarist Kev Bower. Sabbat's debut album *History Of A Time To Come*, recorded in Hannover, Germany during September 1987 with producer Roy Rowland, launched the band to the forefront of the British thrash metal scene, with Walkyier's distinct pagan and historical themes interwoven into its impressive epic songs. For such a young group of musicians, *History Of A Time To Come* portrayed a remarkable maturity, immediately placing Sabbat at the spearhead of thrash in their homeland. Lyrical matter ranged from uncompromising critiques of organised religion, such as 'For Those Who Died' and 'The Church Bizarre', to equally barbed attacks on fascism with 'Behind The Crooked Cross', all embellished with Walkyier's novel command of language. Impressively, the album went on to sell in excess of 60,000 copies within its opening year.

Andy Sneap: "At first they said there would be no compact disc, but after about two weeks of its release it did around 20,000. Lo and behold a CD popped through my letterbox. It did a lot better than everyone anticipated."

SABBAT discography

Blood For The Blood God, Games Workshop (UK) (1988) flexidisc
HISTORY OF A TIME TO COME, Noise N 0098 (Europe), Noise FW-44263 (USA) (1988)
DREAMWEAVER: REFLECTIONS OF OUR YESTERDAYS, Noise N 0132-2 (Europe), Noise WK 45180 (USA) (1989)
MOURNING HAS BROKEN, Noise N 0162-2 (Europe), Noise 4837-2-U (USA) (1991)

Roy Rowland (producer): "It's very rare that I come across something that is entirely different. A lot of musicians, in some respects, try to put something in their music that you've heard once or twice before. Sabbat were a completely original sentiment. I found it very creative working with them."

Martin Walkyier: "It didn't take us long to realise we were selling a huge amount of records. It was completely staggering, but what made us really angry was that we had signed to this small German label and were selling truckloads of albums and getting no money, and all these crappy little bands were being given crazy album budgets by the big companies and were selling next to nothing. Sabbat was the only original thing out there for a long time and people really appreciated that. The whole thing got fucked up because of money, of course. Looking back, we should have been stronger. Who knows what could have happened?"

Sabbat played the 'Dynamo' and 'Eindhoven' festivals in 1988 as part of a very successful European tour. Shortly afterward, Sabbat acquired second guitarist Simon Jones, previously known as Jack Hammer from Holosade, to replace touring guitarist Richard Scott, on loan from London band No Excuse, who accompanied the band on the European tour.

The group's second album, *Dreamweaver: Reflections Of Our Yesterdays*, produced by Roy Rowland, was an opportunity for Walkyier to really let his imagination fly as Sabbat launched the crucial release in the form of a concept based on the Brian Bates book *The Way Of Wyrd*. They subsequently toured Europe, including British shows backed by Xentrix and support dates to Manowar in Spain. This same touring combination hit the UK in December 1989. Surprisingly, Walkyier and

Sabbat

Craske then quit after internal disputes: the vocalist went on to form the highly successful and industrious folk-rock act Skyclad. Craske opted out of the music business, returning to a printing career.

Andy Sneap: "When Martin went, so did the swords and bones. Martin's doing all that pagan thing now and I still have the greatest respect for him for all that; he's an incredible lyric writer. But I really don't think Sabbat would work now if we'd continued along that pagan path."

Martin Walkyier: "I would like to carry on with that image Sabbat had. I can't see why I should change. As far as I'm concerned all of Sabbat's image was my contribution anyway. So I'll take that into Skyclad as well as my musical contribution."

Dani Filth (Cradle Of Filth): "Sabbat was very inspirational. I really enjoyed the fact that everything about the band was done to perfection: the words, the artwork, the complexity of the songs. They put out a total package, and the first two albums are great pieces of heavy metal art. Martin's stories were utterly enthralling because he is such a poet. There is a lot of the Sabbat spirit in Cradle Of Filth, a lot."

American vocalist Richie Desmond, who had previously auditioned as guitarist for Celtic Frost, joined Sabbat in 1990. The band's line-up at this point consisted of Sneap, Desmond, guitarist Neil Watson and bassist Wayne Banks. However, neither record company nor fans were impressed with the resulting album, *Mourning Has Broken*, which sorely lacked Walkyier's innovative input.

Noise dropped the band and, after two disastrous British dates, the last one in Derby, Sneap pulled the plug on both the tour and the band. Negus joined local act Glory Boys, while Sneap and Banks went on to form Godsend. When Godsend dissolved after a batch of demos, Sneap began carving out a niche as a producer, making a name for himself with high-profile bands such as Stuck Mojo, Exodus and Machine Head among many others.

In 1995 there were rumours of a Sabbat reformation with Walkyier and Sneap, but this came to nothing. Sabbat reared its head again in 2000 when Britain's leading black metal exponents Cradle Of Filth covered 'For Those Who Died' with Walkyier providing guest vocals.

As 2001 dawned, an announcement was made that a band entitled Return To The Sabbat (the name Sabbat had since 1983 rested with a Japanese band) was planned for a one-off live show comprising Walkyier, Craske and Jones in alliance with former Talion guitarist Pete Wadeson along with Skyclad and Undergroove drummer Jay Graham. However, Wadeson would decamp even before the group's debut gig, a warm-up for the Derby 'Bloodstock' festival. Walkyier put in his last show with Skyclad the same evening.

As the situation developed it became clear that Return To The Sabbat was indeed a long-term proposition. Graham parted ways with Skyclad as Return To The Sabbat announced their intentions for further live dates. In early 2002 Jones also left the band due to family commitments, his replacement being Andy Newby. Return To The Sabbat put in a valuable support slot to Cradle Of Filth at a low-key club gig at the Oxford Zodiac club, the night before the headliners' 'Ozzfest' appearance. Return To The Sabbat acted as special guests to the newly reformed Swedish doom legends Candlemass at their long-overdue UK performance at the London Mean Fiddler in mid July. Meanwhile, besides his ever-growing list of production credits, Sneap was reported to have joined Fozzy, the then spoof 1980s metal band convened by WWF championship wrestler Chris Jericho and various members of Stuck Mojo.

Swedish black metal act In Aeternum weighed in with their appreciation of Sabbat by recording their rendition of 'By Thy Command'

culled from the original demo *Magik In Theory And Practice*. Walkyier himself spent early 2003 formulating his new venture The Clan Destined, an ill-fated pagan collective involving erstwhile Immortal bassist Iscariah. The singer guested on the track 'Blood And Sand' on Bradford metal band Bloodstream's debut album *Black Storm Harvest*.

Ex-Sabbat bassist Wayne Banks joined Blaze as well as the touring line-up of Brazen Abbott in 2003. With The Clan Destined fragmenting in acrimonious circumstances, Martin Walkyier broke a lengthy silence in April 2006 announcing that he was permanently withdrawing from making music.

SACRILEGE
EARLY THRASH NEARLY-WERES

INFLUENCED HEAVILY BY the punk movement, Birmingham thrash metal band Sacrilege were formed in 1984, fronted by female vocalist Tam (aka Lynda Simpson). The group's opening 1984 line-up saw Tam ranked alongside guitarist Damian Thompson, bassist Tony May and drummer Liam Pickering, this unit cutting a brace of demos that same year. Sacrilege also featured on the Mortarhate compilation *We Won't Be Your Fucking Poor*, with the song 'Dig Your Own Grave', and on the Angelican Scrape Attic flexidisc shared with Execute, Hirax, Concrete Sox and Lipcream. The latter release bore no label details, but the architect behind this hardcore assemblage, Digby Pearson, formed the Earache label soon afterwards.

The group's debut commercial product, *Behind The Realms Of Madness*, a six-track mini-album released in 1985, shifted a respectable 7,000 copies. Former Warhammer man Mitch Dickinson was brought in as second guitarist, although soon after recording Dickinson left the band to pursue more hardcore projects with Heresy and, much later, Unseen Terror. Sacrilege were then approached by FM Revolver, but this ultimately led nowhere.

The band recorded again, this time with the assistance of Rob Bruce at Birmingham's famous Rich Bitch studios. Recording was completed for *Within The Prophecy* with producer Mike Ivory in January 1987, when Music For Nations subsidary Under One Flag stepped in with a deal. At this juncture the band recruited new bassist Paul Morrisey and second guitarist Frank Healy, although in late 1987 drummer Andy Baker was replaced by Paul Brookes.

The third album, *Turn Back Trilobite*, issued in April 1989, saw Sacrilege move away from mainstream thrash and explore slower, more doom-orientated material with a bit of folk thrown in for good measure. At this point the band's line-up consisted of Tam, a returned Damien Thompson, Frank Healy on bass and Spikey T. Smith on drums. Regrettably, the band turned in very few live appearances, which resulted in a fairly stagnant career, despite the increasing sales of successive albums.

SACRILEGE discography

Angelican Scrape Attic, no label (UK) (1985) split flexidisc with Hirax, Lipcream, Execute & Concrete Sox
Behind The Realms Of Madness, Children Of The Revolution GURT 4 (UK) (1985), Pusmort 0012-09 (USA) (1986)
WITHIN THE PROPHECY, Under One Flag FLAG 15 (UK), Metal Blade 72229-1 (USA) (1987)
TURN BACK TRILOBITE, Under One Flag CDFLAG 29 (UK), Metal Blade 72405-2 (USA) (1989)

Ian Davison-Swift in November 1982. He in turn was usurped by erstwhile Raven man Sean Taylor. McCormack would later turn up in Huddersfield band Battleaxe. Reed, meanwhile, remained with the band as a roadie.

This paved the way for the debut single, 'Kiss Of Death', comprising two tracks taken from the first four-song demo, while another two songs from that demo appeared on the *Roxcalibur* compilation album on the Guardian label in 1982.

Davison-Swift stuck with the group until just prior to the recording of *Caught In The Act*, his position being taken by Blitzkrieg and Avenger vocalist Brian Ross for recording, as Swift filled Ross's boots in Avenger. Following the recording of *Court In The Act*, Brian Ross was quickly replaced by Lou Taylor after Tysondog's Alan Hunter temporarily filled in for live commitments following Ross's departure, the band claiming that his lack of onstage charisma was the main reason that Ross was asked to leave. During this period of confusion, drummer Sean Taylor also manned the kit for Warrior as a sideline.

Shortly after this carousel of vocalists, in 1985 the band attempted to lose the occult associations and open up a wider audience, and renamed themselves after Lou Taylor's previous band, Blind Fury. The original Blind Fury had been initiated in London by Angel Witch veteran Kevin Heybourne with Taylor and a rhythm section comprising Marquis De Sade bassist Peter Gordelier and drummer Steve Coleman. They debuted live on May 21st 1983 at the Catford Saxon Tavern. However, this union soon fell apart, Heybourne resurrecting Angel Witch and taking Gordelier with him. Taylor relocated northwards, taking the band name with him.

In this guise, the new-look Blind Fury put out the more commercial *Out Of Reach* album, but the attempt failed. Satan fans rejected the softer stance and at the same time *Court In The Act* was fast becoming a cult classic on the West Coast of America. In an about turn, the band promptly kicked out Lou Taylor and reverted to the Satan name, also changing back to a more metallic approach. During this transition the group recruited vocalist Michael Jackson, previously with Rough Edge. A new Satan album followed, 1987's *Suspended Sentence*, promoted by German touring in support of Running Wild for two tours, the first in April and the second in October 1987. Following his final departure, Lou Taylor went on to front Tour De Force and was briefly with Welsh act Persian Risk. He later became known on the London club scene as a rock DJ.

Pariah then formed as a direct descendent from Satan. Once again a name change was thought to be appropriate due to the connotations of

Post-Sacrilege, Healy and Baker joined Cerebral Fix, and Healy later went on to Benediction. Baker would also be involved with Arbitrater. Brookes also joined Benediction and then the power metal band Marshall Law in 1999. In early 2005 it was reported that Sacrilege's 'Lifeline' had been covered by Benediction, featuring the Bolt Thrower duo of vocalist Karl Willetts and guitarist Barry Thompson.

SATAN (aka Blind Fury and Pariah)
VICTIM OF CHANGES

METAL ACT SATAN BEGAN life in Newcastle Upon Tyne in 1979 and created a huge cult interest in Europe and the West Coast of America with their first album, 1983's *Court In The Act*. They clawed out a significant market for themselves in Europe but would rarely perform live in the UK. Tragically, for a band so obviously ahead of their time when it came to precision speed metal, Satan inflicted upon themselves a bewildering series of changes both in personnel and in name. Buckling under record company pressure, the musicians issued product under three names: Satan; Blind Fury; and Pariah. This lack of cohesion would prove to be their undoing.

The original Satan line-up included guitarist Russ Tippins and Steve Ramsey, vocalist Andrew Frepp, bassist Steven Bee and drummer Andy Reed. Frepp was soon replaced by Paul Smith. At this stage Satan was still a school act. Bee was superseded on bass by Graeme 'Bean' English and Steve Allsop took over on vocals. The group's first four-song demo surfaced in November 1981. They then pulled in another frontman, Trevor Robinson, for a brief tenure.

Reed's position behind the drum stool was relinquished to Ian McCormack, who played on the *Into The Fire* demo, recorded with singer

Satan

SATAN / BLIND FURY / PARIAH discography

As SATAN
Kiss Of Death, Guardian GRC 145 (UK) (1982)
COURT IN THE ACT, Neat NEAT 1012 (UK), Metal Blade 70666-1 (USA) (1983)

As BLIND FURY
OUT OF REACH, Roadrunner RR 9814 (Europe) (1985)

As SATAN
Into The Future, Steamhammer SPV 60-1898 (Europe), Steamhammer SHE 4002 (USA) (1986)
SUSPENDED SENTENCE, Steamhammer SPV 08-1837 (Europe), Steamhammer SHLP 7003 (USA) (1987)

As PARIAH
THE KINDRED, Steamhammer SPV 76-7528 (Europe) (1988)
BLAZE OF OBSCURITY, Steamhammer SPV 85-7595 (Europe) (1989)
UNITY, Aartee Music cnu (Europe) (1997)

As SATAN
LIVE IN THE ACT: DYNAMO CLUB 1983, Metal Nation MNR 003 (UK) (2004)

the old moniker. The first album was recorded with producer Roy Rowland. Unfortunately *The Kindred*, released in 1988, was never given a British release as Pariah concentrated on the lucrative European market.

The second album, 1989's *Blaze Of Obscurity* – recorded at Horus Studios and produced by the band – built upon the success of the debut and proved that the name change had been the correct move, as Pariah albums sold in greater numbers than previous Satan records. In 1991 the leading German metal band Blind Guardian paid due reverence by rendering their version of Satan's 'Trial By Fire' for their *Somewhere Far Beyond* record.

However, Pariah folded amid financial wranglings with their record company, even though sessions intended for a third album, recorded by guitarists Steve Ramsey and Russ Tippins, bassist Graeme English, ex-Satan and Battleaxe drummer Ian McCormack and former Tysondog vocalist Alan Hunter, was recorded at Links Studios in Newcastle during 1993. With interest in the NWOBHM at a high in mainland Europe during the mid 1990s, unreleased Pariah recordings from 1990 were unearthed as the *Unity* album in 1998.

Once the group had called it a day, English and Ramsey partnered erstwhile Sabbat frontman Martin Walkyier, enjoying European success with the innovative Skyclad, debuting in 1991 with *Wayward Sons Of Mother Earth*. Tippins, forsaking the harder end of the musical spectrum, became a regular on the north-eastern club circuit with folk band McAllum and an Abba covers troupe.

During the mid 1990s, a Ross-Tippins-Ramsey-English-Taylor Satan reunion album was on the cards at one point, but this project was allegedly shelved by domestic interference. A further stab at a reformation came when Brian Ross attempted to resurrect the band for a one-off appearance at the German 'Wacken Open Air' festival, but it was to no avail. Further reports came in September 2003, suggesting the *Court In The Act* line-up was set to reform for a one-off performance at the German 'Keep It True II' festival, to be held in April 2004. However, just weeks after this announcement the band were forced off the billing. Satan fans

were appeased somewhat by the issue of archive live recordings from the 1983 'Dynamo' festival, entitled *Live In The Act*.

The band subsequently announced a reformation of Brian Ross, Graeme English and Steve Ramsey for a one-off performance at the 'Wacken Open Air' festival that August. Satan then announced a further high-profile appearance at the April 2005 'Keep It True IV' festival held in the Tauberfrankenhalle in Lauda-Koenigshofen, Germany. It seems that the Satan chapters are yet to be concluded.

SLAMMER
HARDWORKING BUT UNSUCCESSFUL

THIS BRADFORD THRASH METAL band was fronted by vocalist Paul Tunnicliffe, who had been through a variety of acts including Excalibur, Staffordshire's Steel and Rough Justice. Slammer, centred on lead guitarists Milo Zivanovic and Enzo Annecchini with Andy Gagic on drums, debuted with the *Controlled Kaos* demo in 1988. The following year they recorded a Radio One *Friday Rock Show* session with newly recruited ex-Deadline bassist Russell Burton.

During the American thrash explosion, which saw the Big Four break worldwide, British record companies fell over themselves to sign homegrown thrash acts – little realising that the scene had already peaked. In the melée, Polygram picked up Onslaught, Chrysalis took on Toranaga, and Warners opted for Slammer. It seemed like a dream come true for the fledgling thrashers but it soon turned into a nightmare as the rock media universally rounded on them.

The Mark Dodson-produced debut album, 1989's *The Work Of Idle Hands*, was hammered by the critics, who saw Slammer as nothing more than bandwagon-jumpers. Undaunted, they toured hard with plenty of record company support, playing with Onslaught, American hardcore act Sacrilege BC, and The Crumbsuckers.

March 1990 saw the band opening across Britain for Motörhead, and in May they hooked up with Celtic Frost for shows across the Low

Slammer

Countries and the UK. The same year Burton split to form Bitter And Twisted with ex-Acid Reign and future Cathedral guitarist Adam Lehan.

Warners were quick to discard the band, and New Model Army bassist Stuart Morrow joined as they signed to Wolverhampton-based indie Heavy Metal Records for the 1990 *Insanity Addicts* EP and the *Nightmare Scenario* album of 1991. Without Dodson's guiding hand, both outings fell below par. Slammer put in a notable support to Pantera at the London Marquee in March 1991 but Morrow left for Leeds alt.rockers Loud the following year.

Slammer guitarist Milo Zivanovic returned to the scene in early 2002 touting a Metallica tribute band, Damage Inc., for a tour of Holland.

TORANAGA
TOO LITTLE, TOO LATE

BRADFORD-BASED THRASHERS Toranaga, named after a fictitious shogun warrior, formed in 1985 and benefited hugely from the late-1980s British thrash upsurge. The line-up included ex-Rival bassist Andy Burton and erstwhile Charger drummer Steve Todd. Vocalist Mark Duffy joined in February 1988 from the ranks of Millennium.

The band's first product was the Kevin Ridley-produced mini-album *Bastard Ballads*, but the band's progress was stifled by Peaceville's distributor Red Rhino going bust just as it was released. Nevertheless, the record secured the band enough attention to warrant a Radio One *Friday*

Toranaga

Rock Show session and serious interest from Chrysalis A&R man Alistair Cunningham.

Confusion arose when Duffy under the pseudonym of Dark Murphy lent his vocals to Major Threat for their 1988 demo. Peaceville were none too pleased and Toranaga had to issue a statement to the effect that Duffy was still a full-time member of the band and had not joined Major Threat. Other side activities saw guitarist Andy Mitchell acting as producer on local colleagues Amnesia's album *Unknown Entity*. In 1989 Toranaga performed in Europe, opening for Venom in Holland and later hooking up with the joint Sabbat and Manowar winter expedition. Chrysalis issued the somewhat formulaic album *God's Gift* in 1990 to middling reviews. An EP, *Eden – Beauty And The Beast*, including a cover version of Fleetwood Mac's 'Oh Well', saw promotional issue in 1991. Notable gigs included supports to Uriah Heep at London's Astoria and to Annihilator at the Marquee.

However, the band soon ran out of steam and called it a day. In 1993 Duffy formed the more industrial flavoured The Seed, releasing a demo in 1995. This act would subsequently evolve into X-Seed, issuing the 1996 *Desolation* album through the Bleeding Hearts label.

XENTRIX
WHO YOU GONNA CALL?

XENTRIX WERE A SPEED metal act from Leyland, England formed in 1986. They displayed a good deal of character and individuality but, unfortunately, the spectre of their 1990 'Ghostbusters' single haunted the band throughout their career as they endeavoured to be taken seriously. Although valuable media coverage was generated, especially when Columbia Pictures demanded that the single jacket be reprinted due to its depiction of the *Ghostbusters* logo (a ghost flipping a middle finger), the band found themselves lumped in with novelty thrash acts.

The group was founded at school in Preston, Lancashire, and known as Sweet Vengeance. Members came and went, including singers Dacaw Hough and Sean Owens, bass player Peter Hiller and drummers John Brennan and Dave Catchpole, but the core remained guitarist Chris Astley, son of the Fylde Guitars maker, guitarist Kristian Harvard and drummer Dennis Gasser.

Under the early name the group recorded various demos and contributed 'Black Mail' to an Ebony Records compilation album, *Full Force*, before releasing the demo *Hunger For Death*, cut at Amazon Studios in Liverpool. Tracks included 'Blackmail', 'Hunger for Death', 'Nobody's Perfect' and the quirky instrumental 'G.A.A.F.' ('Grand As A Frog'). Bassist Ste Hodgson was let go and Melvin Gasser, brother of Dennis, handled bass before Paul MacKenzie took over.

The group scored a deal with Mark Palmer at Roadrunner on the strength of a bullish *Metal Forces* review and a showcase gig in early 1989 as the British thrash explosion peaked. The label's first move would be to suggest a name switch from the rather dated Sweet Vengeance to Xentrix. Xentrix toured with Sabbat in Britain during 1989 to promote their *Shattered Existence* album, released that September on Roadrunner's Roadracer label, produced by John Cuniberti at Gas Street Studios in Birmingham. This first exposure to national touring nearly turned into a disaster when, just prior to the dates, Astley suffered an accident to his hand, drilling through it while assembling flight cases. Consequently, the guitarist wore a special glove in order to play. Xentrix scored a valuable opening slot to Testament at London's Hammersmith Odeon.

They were invited to record a *Friday Rock Show* session for Tommy Vance at the BBC Maida Vale Studios, during which they laid down an impromptu take on Ray Parker Jr.'s 'Ghostbusters' movie theme. The follow-up single certainly heightened Xentrix's profile but soon became a

XENTRIX discography

SHATTERED EXISTENCE, Roadracer RO 9444-2 (UK), Roadracer RCD 9444 (USA) (1989)
Ghostbusters, Roadracer RO 2435-2 (UK), Roadracer RD 2435 (USA) (1990)
FOR WHOSE ADVANTAGE?, Roadracer RO 9366-2 (UK), Roadracer RCD 9366 (USA) (1990)
Dilute To Taste, Roadracer RO 9320 (UK), Roadracer RD 9320 (USA) (1991)
KIN, Roadracer RO 9196-2 (UK) (1992)
SCOURGE, Heavy Metal HMR XD 198 (UK) (1996)

with the same band and Megalomaniacs, before a run of UK headliners with guests Skyclad. Switching producers, the band drafted Mark Flannery to cut 1991's *Dilute To Taste* EP, featuring new studio material and four live tracks recorded at a hometown gig at Preston Polytechnic. Performing opening honours at the Hammersmith Odeon once again, Xentrix undertook support for Sepultura.

The band's third full-length offering, *Kin*, witnessed a subdued aggression and slower pace from the expected all-out thrash attack and the introduction of Nobody's Fool keyboard player Carl Arnfeld. Xentrix's 1992 single 'The Order Of Chaos' featured a B-side rendition of The Teardrop Explodes' 'Reward'. A short burst of UK dates was undertaken before the band requested that the Roadrunner contract be terminated. A three-song demo was then produced, aimed at securing a new deal with a larger company, but it only generated one offer, from the small Heavy Metal Records. At this juncture the band, accepting the deal, split with Chris Astley.

Xentrix pulled in new singer Simon Gordon, previously with Rawhead, and guitarist Andy Rudd, and were still doing the rounds of club gigs in late 1994. They returned in 1995 for the low-key comeback album *Scourge*, delivered through Heavy Metal Records, but folded soon after.

Xentrix put in a one-off reunion gig at the Fox Lane Cricket Club in Preston in 2001. Simon Gordon returned to the scene in 2005 fronting the high-profile City Of God, a band assembled with former Kill II This guitarist Mark Mynett.

In a surprise move, Xentrix reformed in 2006 to conduct two gigs, at the Bitter Suite in Preston on February 25th, to celebrate Paul MacKenzie's birthday, and at the Engineers' Club in Barrow-in-Furness on March 17th, before returning to their day jobs. Is this one thrash metal ghost that won't be laid to rest?

burden. Tiring of the attention given to 'Ghostbusters', the band substituted it in the live set with a rendition of the Beastie Boys' 'Fight For Your Right (To Party)', although this song would never be issued commercially.

The 1990 album, *For Whose Advantage*, cut at Loco Studios in South Wales with John Cuniberti once again handling production, was a strong offering, but was overlooked. For this outing Xentrix tackled another unconventional cover version, Gillan's 'Running White Faced City Boy', featured on the CD version of the album. The band's first foray into Europe came with support dates to Annihilator. Further live work saw UK shows with support from Tankard followed by German dates packaged

US DEATH METAL AND GRINDCORE

AS THRASH

metal peaked, it was as if a sector of its audience smelt the advent of mainstream pressures and was already on the search for something harder, faster and more satisfying. Just as James Hetfield and his colleagues had created thrash by souping up NWOBHM-style riffing in order to satiate their hunger for more aggression and speed, so a fresh generation of guitarists took thrash apart piecemeal to reconstruct it into an even more dangerous beast. If the rock world had at first been horrified by thrash's apparently ignorant approach to melody, death metal didn't even cite ignorance as an excuse. Melody was beaten to death and thrown in the trash in pursuit of sheer speed and heaviness.

Naturally, there is much debate as to the first usage of the term 'death metal'. Prime contenders include Bay Area satanic thrashers Possessed, who labelled themselves a death metal band in 1984, and the late Thomas 'Quorthon' Forsberg of black metal titans Bathory, who claimed to have invented the term even if his band didn't pursue the same direction. One instigator for the genre was undoubtedly Slayer, a band that stood at the very harshest borderlines of thrash. The aggression of the most radical thrash outfits and a desire to get back to the punk ethos spawned death metal.

With guitars increasing in velocity, so the rhythm section was forced to accelerate to maintain parity. This sprint approach produced what is now recognised as one of the deadliest weapons in the death metal arsenal – the blastbeat. The concept of this deadly device, a 200bpm-plus staccato barrage of kick and snare-drum, was first employed by D.R.I. drummer Eric Brecht on his band's debut 1983 album. Although it had almost certainly been employed by the Texan crossover act merely as a novelty, percussionists soon realised that the technique could form a framework upon which to build a new edifice of sound.

Vocally, a simple gruff texture was no longer appropriate. If the music was bordering on the fringes of extremity, then so must its narrative style, and thus a growling, grunting, for the most part unintelligible 'cookie monster' style was invented by Massacre's Kam Lee. Lyrically, early death metal themes were predictable, focusing on the darker side of life, but gradually matured into more philosophical realms. This ripening of talents was paralleled by the advent of technical death metal, the first major example of which was Death's 1991 opus *Human*.

Driving the death metal machine came a promulgation of plague-bearing indie labels, such as JL America, Red Stream, Moribund, Olympic, Grindcore International and Wild Rags. The most aggressive US company was probably Relapse, force-feeding the devoted by way of intensive, gore-soaked ad campaigning for such influential forces as Suffocation and Incantation. Importantly, Relapse also paved the way for Nuclear Blast's entry into the US marketplace.

To the outside world, Florida – and more specifically the engineer's chair located behind the board at Morrisound Studios in Tampa – was genesis ground zero for death metal. The sheer weight of high-quality, groundbreaking product that can be directly traced to this studio is staggering. Initially, Morrisound produced a stream of hackneyed local bands of varying quality, but once death metal was born, it seemed that all roads led to Morrisound.

In truth, death metal got its start further up the coast, almost certainly with Killjoy's Necrophagia, Blood Feast, Necrovore and Illinois goregrinders Impetigo. Chicago's Master, and their widely-leaked but unreleased 1985 album, also proved pivotal. Rabid and incestuous tape-trading between bands marked out Necrophagia as scene originators and leaders, but by the time the marketing machines had got into gear their worth was largely ignored. It is only with the insistence towards honesty from the Florida musicians themselves that Necrophagia's legacy has been realised.

Nevertheless, it was Florida that provided the source for the majority of artists who gained an international footing – with Obituary, Death, Massacre, Atheist, Morbid Angel, Cynic, Deicide, Malevolent Creation and Cannibal Corpse all tracing back to the same well of inspiration. Arbiters of taste and decency could at least resign themselves to the fact that the movement was a strictly underground one – that is, until Earache Records announced that Morbid Angel had sold over a million albums.

Perversely, as death metal's energies on one front were directed at these extremes, on the other side the manufacture of more accessible, melodic death metal saved its neck commercially. Gothenburg became the new Tampa and the genre received a new lease of life. Crucial in bridging this geographic gap was Hypocrisy's Peter Tägtgren, who took the seed from Florida to Scandinavia, where other key figures – such as Edge Of Sanity's Dan Swanö – turned it into something entirely new. And in the UK and Europe, legions of acts were swiftly triggered into action.

ATHEIST
LEGENDARY FUSION PIONEERS

REGRETTABLY, THE SARASOTA, FLORIDA-based 'jazz-death' outfit Atheist issued just three albums, which excelled with highly complex innovation and took metal into previously uncharted realms. Although they were held in awe by their peers, Atheist found it tough going on the commercial circuit.

In 1984, singer-guitarist Kelly Shaefer formed Oblivion, this act featuring Steve Flynn on drums. The following year the band – now fronted by singer Scrappy and with Roger Patterson on bass – evolved into R.A.V.A.G.E. The group, minus Scrappy, recorded the five-track demo *Rotting In Hell* in August 1985, later commonly known as *Kill Or Be Killed*. The band was augmented by second guitarist Mark Schwartzberg for a second demo, *On We Slay*.

The band then contributed 'Brain Damage' and 'On They Slay' to the 1987 *Raging Death* compilation album released on the Godly Records label. Renaming themselves Atheist, their first undertaking was the 1987 demo *Hell Hath No Mercy*. The group issued another demo the following year, *Beyond*, featuring 'No Truth', 'Choose Your Death', 'Beyond', 'On They Slay' and 'Brain Damage', and supported the likes of Testament, S.N.F.U., Death Angel and Obituary before signing to British label Active Records. The band had originally signed a deal with the US label Mean Machine Records, a subsidiary of Three Cherries Records, but the label was on the verge of bankruptcy, so an arrangement was made with Active to take the band.

The Scott Burns-produced debut album *Piece Of Time*, worked up at Morrisound in Tampa, was issued in February 1990. Bizarrely, guitarist Rand Burkey not only played his instrument left-handed, but he performed this feat on a regular, upside-down guitar with the strings aligned for a right-handed player.

On February 12th 1991 Atheist suffered a huge blow. A major auto accident involving the entire band tragically resulted in the death of Roger Patterson. Persevering, the band added ex-Cynic bassist Tony Choy to record *Unquestionable Presence*, released in October 1991. Flynn opted out after the completion of dates with Cannibal Corpse. Choy exited too, accompanying Dutch death metal crew Pestilence for their 1991 world tour. He later found an alternative, and more sedate, career as a jazz musician on a cruise boat.

The May 1993 *Elements* album was, by the band's own admission, thrown together in haste in order to fulfil their label contract, but it still proved to be a worthy effort. Josh Greenbaum handled drums in the studio. European dates ensued alongside Benediction, with Shaefer joined by guitarist Frank Emmi and drummer Marcel DeSantos. Atheist then bowed out of public view. With the albums deleted, no official product would be forthcoming for over a decade. Emmi later figured in Gentlemen Death, while Burkey hooked up with erstwhile Crimson Glory vocalist Midnight.

Shaefer's Neurotica side project became a full-time venture. The ex-Atheist man was still at it in 2001, launching the *Living In Dry Years* album – produced by none other than Brian Johnson of AC/DC. Schaefer has recently acquired the rights to all Atheist material for a round of long-overdue CD re-releases. During 2001 Shaefer, Burkey, Emmi and Flynn announced the reformation of Atheist.

However, in October 2002 it was revealed that Shaefer would be involved in a project of the highest magnitude, fronting the new band of the erstwhile Guns N'Roses triumvirate of guitarist Slash, bassist Duff McKagan and drummer Matt Sorum. However, his tenure was shortlived as the band pulled in ex-Stone Temple Pilots frontman Scott Weiland and evolved into Velvet Revolver.

Shaefer then launched a fresh band project, Starrfactory, with ex-E3 and Seraphine man Donny Jaurols, Noah Thompson of Megablatta and erstwhile Sanctuary drummer Dave Budbill. The singer also featured as a guest artist on the 2003 *Moments Of Clarity* progressive rock album by

---

ATHEIST discography

PIECE OF TIME, Active CD ATV 8 (UK), Death CAROL CD 2201 (USA) (1990)
UNQUESTIONABLE PRESENCE, Active CD ATV 20 (UK), Death 9 26717-2 (USA) (1991)
ELEMENTS, Music For Nations CDMFN 150 (UK), Metal Blade 9 45370-2 (USA) (1993)

Cryptic Vision. Meanwhile, word arrived in late 2003 that Rand Burkey was preparing a new band, Random Xaos.

In September 2004 Shaefer, switching to the guitar role, teamed up with ex-Burial frontman Mike Callahan in a southern-Florida based project called Unheard. However, in early 2005 it was reported that Shaefer, alongside Unheard guitarist Donny Jaurols, was plugging a brand new band, Big Machine, sponsored by AC/DC's Brian Johnson.

Steve Flynn resurfaced in 2005 with a new band, Gnostic, with Caustic Thought vocalist Kevin Freeman, Corpseworm and Severed guitarist Sonny Carson, and Corpseworm and Caustic Thought bassist Stephen Morley.

The entire Atheist catalogue was reissued by Relapse in 2005. The collection commenced in July with a foil-stamped box set, limited to 1,000 copies, comprising vinyl versions of each Atheist LP plus the R.A.V.A.G.E. *On They Slay* 7-inch EP. Atheist announced a reformation in January 2006 to perform at the Italian 'Evolution' festival and Germany's 'Wacken Open Air' event. A line-up was announced of Shaefer, Burkey, Choy and Flynn. However, Burkey was forced out due to "legal problems" and Gnostic's Chris Baker substituted. The band also pulled in second guitarist Sonny Carson of Gnostic to cover for Shaefer, the frontman's abilities hampered by tendonitis and carpal tunnel syndrome.

During Atheist's European run of dates Tony Choy suffered a sizable accident when he fell through an unsecured part of the large outdoor stage at Italy's 'Evolution' festival on July 16th. Fortunately the musician was uninjured but, having broken all his bass strings, had to borrow another instrument to finish the set. It seems Atheist's adventures are not over yet.

AUTOPSY
GORE BLIMEY

THE TRULY HORRIFIC AUTOPSY, originally known as The Aborted, were formed in San Francisco during 1987 when drummer Chris Reifert left the volatile ranks of Death, following their *Scream Bloody Gore* album. The new combo debuted in December that year with a four-track demo, executed at ATR Studios in Lafayette, comprising 'Human Genocide', 'Embalmed', 'Stillborn' and 'Mauled To Death'. These sessions featured Eric Eigard on bass. Guitarist Eric Cutler sang lead vocals on 'Mauled To Death' whilst Reifert handled lead vocals on the other three tracks. A second demo, *Critical Madness* issued in July 1988, featured guitarist Danny Coralles and Ken Sorvari on bass. Autopsy made their mark on the scene by incorporating proto-sludge, using choking sluggishness as a counterfoil to death metal's usual speed.

The highly influential British label Peaceville then signed the group, and the debut 1989 album, *Severed Survival*, came adorned in a sickening jacket – depicting an unfortunate individual being ripped to pieces, with the band logo rendered in lumps of flesh. This first edition rapidly became a collector's item after it was replaced by the more generally known 'doctors' cover. Demand was heightened by blood-red vinyl editions and, naturally, a picture disc.

The group had utilised Sadus bassist Steve DiGiorgio for *Severed Survival*, conducted under the production guidance of Metal Church guitarist John Marshall at Starlight Studios, but the band soon found a re-enlisted substitute Ken Sorvari in time for European live work with Bolt Thrower and Pestilence.

In 1990, prior to a European tour, Sorvari left, to be replaced by Eric's bother Steve Cutler. The band then executed dates in Holland throughout February, again with Pestilence and Bolt Thrower, on the 'Bloodbrothers' tour. Suffocation bassist Josh Barohn also featured as a member the same year: he later formed Welt and Iron Lung.

A stopgap EP, *Retribution For The Dead*, emerged in 1991. Steve Cutler departed after 1991's *Mental Funeral*, the self-produced tracks for which were laid down in just six days at Different Fur Studios in San Francisco. Autopsy then played a 1992 festival in Detroit (with Mortician, Vital Remains and Repulsion), appearing as a trio because Eric Butler had broken his hand.

Autopsy re-enlisted the services of DiGiorgio for the March 1992 *Fiend For Blood* EP before adding Barohn on a permanent basis. The spasmic thrash/doom collision *Acts Of The Unspeakable*, released that October, was hyped as Autopsy's "sickest fuckin' album ever" – that is, until July 1995's scatological comeback *Shitfun*. This outing, clad in one of the grossest sleeves to adorn a metal album to date, saw a guesting Clint Bower of Hexx on bass guitar. *Shitfun* deliberately explored previously uncharted depths of repellence with faecal-themed material such as 'I Shit On Your Grave', 'I Sodomise Your Corpse' and 'Shiteater'. The album's sleeve, and its change in direction towards primitive grind-punk, alienated a large sector of the band's audience.

Although *Shitfun* had made an undeniable mark, Autopsy split.

AUTOPSY discography

SEVERED SURVIVAL, Peaceville VILE 12 (UK) (1989)
Retribution For The Dead, Peaceville VILE24TCD (UK) (1991)
MENTAL FUNERAL, Peaceville VILE25CD (UK), Peaceville VILE 25-2 (USA) (1991)
Fiend For Blood, Peaceville VILE29TCD (UK), Caroline VILE 29-2 (USA) (1992)
ACTS OF THE UNSPEAKABLE, Peaceville VILE33CD (UK), Caroline VILE 33CD (USA) (1992)
SHITFUN, Peaceville CDVILE49 (UK) (1995)
Tortured Moans Of Agony, Necroharmonic Productions cnu (USA) (1998)
RIDDEN WITH DISEASE, Necroharmonic Productions SLEAZY 001 (USA) (2000)
TORN FROM THE GRAVE, Peaceville CDVILE 84 (UK) (2001)
DEAD AS FUCK, Necroharmonic Productions SLEAZY 006 (USA) (2004)

Reifert then created Abscess and then in 2000 The Ravenous, with Anthrax, S.O.D. and Nuclear Assault bassist Dan Lilker and Necrophagia's Killjoy. In early 2002 Reifert guested on the *Murderous, Ravenous* record by Murder Squad, the Swedish death metal project made up of Dismember and Entombed members.

The specialist death metal label Necroharmonic Productions issued a nine-track double 7-inch coloured vinyl live EP, *Tortured Moans Of Agony*, during 1998. The same label combined Autopsy's early demos plus two 1990 live tracks for 2000's *Ridden With Disease*. Reifert continued on the path of the extreme the following year, announcing the formation of a fresh project subtly titled EatMyFuk.

A retrospective DVD, *Dark Crusades*, appeared in 2006. Clocking in at three hours, the set included numerous concert films including the band's last ever live show on July 29th 1994 at Ruthie's Inn, San Francisco. Necroharmonic Productions added to the archives with vintage live tapes issued as the 2004 *Dead As Fuck* album. Today, Autopsy's legacy remains clear in the burgeoning goregrind scene.

BRUJERIA
US-MEXICAN DEATH METAL CRIMINALS – SUPPOSEDLY

ALTHOUGH THEY STARTED LIFE as a supposedly anonymous Mexican death metal band, Brujeria ('witchcraft') were led by Fear Factory guitarist Dino Cazares and drummer Raymond Herrera in collusion with Napalm Death members and Faith No More's Billy Gould. Brujeria's unique marketing ploy was to adopt the personae of anonymous Mexican drug barons and, for a while, they fooled the metal world – until their identities were leaked.

The initial 1989 band consisted of guitarist El Asesino (Cazares) and bassist Güero Sin Fe (Gould), this pair cutting the singles '¡Demoniaco!' for Nemesis in 1990 and 'Machetazos' through Jello Biafra's Alternative Tentacles imprint the following year.

The band shifted shape in 1993 as new members were inducted: singer El Brujo (Juan Brujo), drummer Greñudo (Fear Factory's Raymond Herrera) and bass player Fantasma (Pat Hoed of Down By Law). This unit cut the *Matando Güeros* album for Roadrunner, released in July 1993. With artwork featuring a photograph of a charred, severed head and the music a brutally unrefined grindcore, the album caused controversy from the outset. A sick sense of humour prevailed over the entire affair, as evidenced by songs such as 'Matando Güeros' ('Killing White Boys'), 'Molestando Ninos Muertos' ('Molesting Dead Children') and 'Chinga Tu Madre' ('Fuck Your Mother').

The band's second slice of depravity, *Raza Odiada*, arrived in August 1995. The jacket was more refined this time around – a heroic portrait of the Zapatista Army of National Liberation guerilla leader Insurgente Marcos. The record opened with a satirical speech by Dead Kennedys leader Jello Biafra, pouring diatribe against "brown skinned" immigrants choking California. Brujeria's response, a hail of gunfire, acted as an inceptor into a deluge of grind.

Drummer Nick Barker, ex-Cradle Of Filth, Dimmu Borgir and Lockup, contributed to the November 2000 album *Brujerizmo*; the same year, Brujeria's *Marijuana* EP, released through Gould's Kool Arrow label, commendably spoofed the pop hit 'The Macarena' in death metal style.

A Brujeria offshoot sprang up in late 2001: the *Corridos de Muerte* album, released via Kool Arrow/Demoniaco, was credited to Asesino ('Assassin'), which featured Cazares and Herrera alongside Static-X bassist Tony Campos.

The break-up of Fear Factory in 2002 seemed to have repercussions for Brujeria – Sadistic Intent drummer Emilio Márquez was reported to

BRUJERIA Discography

Demoniaco!, Nemesis NEM-026 (USA) (1990)
Machetazos!, Alternative Tentacles VIRUS 113 (USA) (1992)
MATANDO GÜEROS, Roadrunner RR 9061-2 (UK / USA) (1993)
El Patron, Alternative Tentacles VIRUS 142 (USA) (1994)
RAZA ODIADA, Roadrunner RR 8923-2 (UK / USA) (1995)
Marijuana, Tee Pee TP011CD (USA) (2000)
BRUJERIZMO, Roadrunner RR 8504-2 (UK / USA) (2000)
MEXTREMIST! GREATEST HITS, Koolarrow KACD010 (UK / USA) (2001)

have supplanted Herrera in both Brujeria and Asesino. These rumours were quickly denied, but in fact Márquez (El Sadístico) did join Asesino. The official line-up of Brujeria in July 2003 stood at vocalist El Brujo, guitarist El Asesino (Cazares) and drummer Hongo Jr. (Nick Barker).

Brujeria united with Soulfly for the September 'Aztlan Fest '03' US tour, dates that also included Delinquent Habits and Mexican ska-punks Cabrito Vudu and were designed to showcase international Latin artists.

A July 2004 Brujeria gig in McAllen, Texas, was cancelled after Cazares was reportedly bitten on the leg by a brown recluse spider, causing a massive infection. Suffering from fevers and hallucinations, the guitarist was hospitalised for two days. Nevertheless, Brujeria still performed two sold-out shows in Los Angeles at the Key Club that same month, the group's debut shows in the city after a 14-year ban. Every other attempt by the band to play Los Angeles had previously been blocked by protest. In January 2005 Cazares announced his decision to quit.

Asesino released *Cristo Satanico* in 2006. Back on the road in 2006, Brujeria – with a new rhythm section of Angelito (Tony Laureano of Malevolent Creation and Nile) on drums and El Cynico (Carcass man Jeff Walker) on bass, announced shows in Chile, Argentina and Mexico for January and then partnered with Cephalic Carnage for US shows in February. The band remain a hard-hitting force.

BRUTAL TRUTH
GRINDCORE TO THE LIMIT

BRUTAL TRUTH, NEW YORK grindcore exponents with a thirst for speed, were created during a lull in Nuclear Assault's activities in 1990 when the distinctive figure of lanky, mop-topped bassist Dan Lilker – previously with Anthrax and S.O.D. – assembled the band in order to indulge his love of extreme hardcore. Eventually, Lilker dropped out of Nuclear Assault to focus on the new band, which consisted of guitarist Brent McCarty, drummer Scott Lewis and, later, vocalist Kevin Sharp.

Early demo recordings made by the band while still a trio were issued on the bootleg EP *The Birth Of Ignorance* on Liberated Records. With Lilker's pedigree, a deal was quickly signed with grindcore exponents Earache for a Colin Richardson-produced album, *Extreme Conditions Demand Extreme Responses*. Opening with the 33-second burst of 'P.S.P.I.', the album careered through the most ferocious grindcore yet committed to tape, all punctuated by anti-capitalist vitriol, disturbing narrative and industrial sound samples from an array of construction tools. A 1992 7-inch single, 'Ill Neglect', featured a raucous cover of The Butthole Surfers' 'The Shah Sleeps In Lee Harvey's Grave'.

Brutal Truth paid their live dues in America opening for Cathedral, Carcass and Napalm Death before guesting for Fear Factory in Europe. During the tour, Lewis departed and was replaced by former Ninefinger man Rich Hoak.

BRUTAL TRUTH discography

EXTREME CONDITIONS DEMAND EXTREME RESPONSES, Earache MOSH069CD (UK), Relativity/Earache 88561-1142-2 (USA) (1992)

Ill Neglect, Earache MOSH 80 (UK) (1992)

Perpetual Conversion, Earache MOSH084CD (UK), Relativity/Earache 88561-1188-2 (USA) (1993)

NEED TO CONTROL, Earache MOSH110CD (UK / USA) (USA) (1994)

Brutal Truth / Spazz, Rhetoric RH 32 (USA) (1996) split EP with Spazz

Machine Parts + 4, Deaf American DA-02000 (USA) (1996)

KILL TREND SUICIDE, Relapse RR 6948-2 (Europe / USA) (1996)

In These Black Days: Volume 2, Hydra Head HH666-13 (USA) (1997) split single with Converge

Brutal Truth / Rupture, Rhetoric RH 40 (USA) (1997) split EP with Rupture

SOUNDS OF THE ANIMAL KINGDOM, Relapse RR 6968-2 (Europe / USA) (1997)

GOODBYE CRUEL WORLD!: LIVE FROM PLANET EARTH + 13, Relapse RR 6425-2 (Europe / USA) (1999)

For Drug Crazed Grindfreaks Only!: Live From Noctum Studios + 1 , Solardisk SOLD-005 (Europe) (2000)

Pushing the boundaries even further, Brutal Truth forged a liaison with Coventry techno act Larceny to record the February 1993 'Perpetual Conversion' 7-inch, the B-side of which featured a version of Black Sabbath's 'Lord Of This World'.

The October 1994 album *Need To Control*, again overseen by Richardson and hosting a take on The Germs' 'Media Blitz', was uniquely formatted as a box set of 5-inch, 6-inch, 7-inch, 8-inch and 9-inch singles. Bonus cuts included radical reworkings of Celtic Frost's 'Dethroned Emperor' and Pink Floyd's seminal 'Wish You Were Here'. As this album was released, Lilker was dabbling in another project, Exit 13, together with

Lewis, and guesting on the *No Matter What The Cause* album by German band Holy Moses. A Brutal Truth tour of Australia, Japan and America followed, before European dates in summer 1994 saw the band packaged with Macabre and Pungent Stench.

The band, feeling that Earache lacked the necessary commitment, broke away from the label. It was two years before Brutal Truth signed up with American label Relapse. In the interim the quartet were far from inactive, contributing tracks to the *Nothing's Quiet On The Western Front* compilation and issuing split EPs with Spazz, featuring 'Rumours', originally by Die Kreuzen, and the Melvins song 'Zodiac'. Another 1996 EP, *Machine Parts*, involved five different live recordings of 'Collateral Damage' fronted by Exit 13's Bill Yurkiewicz and Napalm Death's Barney Greenaway.

Brutal Truth's third album, *Kill Trend Suicide*, issued in October 1996, was laid down at the Cutting Room in New York and produced by Billy Anderson. Successive releases included a brace of split EPs, shared with Converge (another Hydra Head 7-inch featuring Black Sabbath's 'Cornucopia') and Rupture.

In 1997 Hoak teamed up with Corrosion Of Conformity's Mike Dean to record an album under the resurrected name of Ninefinger. Brutal Truth musicians then embarked on less-than-conventional side activity when they made an appearance in a porn movie, *Studio X*. The band played two songs live and even took a part in the acting, although not in the explicit scenes. Lilker then took time out to resurrect S.O.D. as the original line-up toured America.

The September 1997 album *Sounds Of The Animal Kingdom*, recorded that June at Baby Monster Studios in New York, gave Brutal Truth fresh audiences and included an unlikely cover of jazz maestro Sun Ra's 'It's After The End Of The World'. Exit 13's Bill Yurkiewicz was the producer: he also featured as guest vocalist on the track 'Postulate Then Liberate'. The Japanese release added bonus cover versions in Agathocles' 'Hippie Cult', Nausea's 'Cybergod' and Black Sabbath's 'Cornucopia'. Brutal Truth then undertook a demanding 90-date tour of America to wind up 1997 on a tour with Cannibal Corpse, Immolation and Oppressor.

Despite steady progress and increased sales, the band split after an Australian tour in September 1998. Lilker resumed activity with S.O.D. for their *Bigger Than The Devil* album and played with black metal band Hemlock and death metallers The Ravenous alongside Necrophagia's Killjoy and Chris Reifert of Autopsy.

Hoak re-emerged in 2000 with his subtly-titled new band, Total Fucking Destruction. Meanwhile, Brutal Truth received a posthumous honour from *The Guinness Book Of Records*, awarded the title for Shortest Music Video Ever for the 1994 'Collateral Damage' clip – 48 images blurred in rapid succession over 2.18 seconds.

Lilker announced the reformation of the classic Nuclear Assault line-up for an appearance at the 2002 'Wacken' festival in Germany. Kevin Sharp made waves in late 2003 with his induction into the grind supergroup Venomous Concept with guitarist Buzz Osbourne of Melvins and Fantomas and the Napalm Death rhythm section of bassist Shane Embury and drummer Danny Herrera.

Lilker was also in the driving seat for Overlord Exterminator in early 2004, a black metal combo featuring Adam Bonacci from Withered Earth on vocals and Commit Suicide's Lee on bass guitar. This band's presence was first announced by internet demos posted in February. That same autumn the bassist forged Crucifist, a death/black metal band featuring singer Ron Blackwell, Orodruin and Night Conquers Day guitarist John Gallo, and Mike Waske of Orodruin on drums.

Brutal Truth reunited in May 2006 in order to record a version of 'Sister Fucker' for a benefit album, *For The Sick – A Tribute To Eyehategod*, released on Emetic Records. The band remain one of the heaviest ever to emerge from America.

Brutal Truth (Dan Lilker third from left)

CANNIBAL CORPSE
DEATH METAL'S MOST CONSISTENT BAND?

BUFFALO, NEW YORK DEATH METAL scene-leaders Cannibal Corpse have stayed the course over an impressive stream of uncompromising records since their debut album in 1990, *Eaten Back To Life*. Their album artwork has always remained deliberately provocative, with many releases being issued in tamer variants of the originals – indeed, certain releases are completely banned in specific territories. Despite this, by 2000 the band, now based in Tampa, Florida, had shifted half a million records.

They were conceived during 1988 in the wake of the breakdown of two acts, Tirant Sin and Beyond Death. Recorded in Niagara Falls, the band's eponymous five song-demo – which opened with 'A Skull Full Of Maggots' – soon secured a recording contract with Metal Blade. The line-up on the hard-hitting Scott Burns-produced *Eaten Back To Life* – delivered in August 1990 – consisted of vocalist Chris Barnes, guitarists Bob Rusay and Jack Owen, bassist Alex Webster and drummer Paul Mazurkiewicz. Unfortunately for protectors of society's morality, material such as 'Rotting Head', 'Shredded Humans' and 'Edible Autopsy' merely provided a hint of what was to come. Two notable studio guests included Deicide's Glen Benton and Opprobrium's Francis Howard on backing vocals for the songs 'Mangled' and 'A Skull Full Of Maggots'.

Scott Burns also manned the board for July 1991's *Butchered At Birth*. Once again Glen Benton appeared as backing vocalist, making his presence felt on 'Vomit The Soul'. By this juncture the band's gore-soaked imagery and uncompromising song titles were beginning to make sharp inroads into the mainstream media. The record jacket, with a dismembered female corpse presided over by a pair of zombies and baby corpses hanging in the background, caused *Butchered At Birth* to be banned from sale in Germany. In America many stores carried the album in a plain white sleeve.

Tomb Of The Mutilated, yielded up for public consumption in September 1992 and once more crafted by Burns at Morrisound, maintained the momentum. Cannibal Corpse put in extensive road work in North America, Europe and Russia. *Tomb* provided no respite in either the ferocity of the band's music or the hideous nature of the album's jacket, with the artwork depicting two decomposing corpses engaged in oral sex. A March 1993 EP, *Hammer Smashed Face*, included a cover of Possessed's 'The Exorcist' and a surprise rendition of Black Sabbath's 'Zero The Hero', both originally included as exclusive Japanese bonus tracks on *Tomb Of The Mutilated*. European variants were boosted with up to five songs, including 'Meat Hook Sodomy' and 'Shredded Humans'. The track 'Hammer Smashed Face' was thrust into the public limelight when comic actor Jim Carrey insisted that both the track and the band be included in the soundtrack to his hit movie *Ace Ventura: Pet Detective*.

The Bleeding, laid down at Morrisound during late 1993, was issued in April 1994 and sold over 100,000 units in the USA alone. This outing found Rusay ejected in favour of Rob Barrett, a veteran of Dark Deception, Solstice and Malevolent Creation. Lyrically, the band plumbed new depths of depravity, illustrated with beyond-the-pale song titles 'Stripped, Raped And Strangled', 'She Was Asking For It' and 'Fucked With A Knife'. Naturally the original album art, a tapestry of corpses, was censored. The band added dates in Australia and South America to a three-month stint in the USA that summer with Cynic as openers. *The Bleeding* was the last Cannibal Corpse album to feature Chris Barnes, the vocalist opting out to concentrate on his side project Six Feet Under during the recording of the next studio record, which at that stage had the working title of *Created To Kill*.

The 1996 line-up for the now re-titled album, *Vile*, involved Owen, Barrett, Webster, Mazurkiewicz and ex-Monstrosity vocalist George

CANNIBAL CORPSE discography

EATEN BACK TO LIFE, Metal Blade CDZORRO 12 (UK), Death CAROL CD 1900 (USA) (1990)

BUTCHERED AT BIRTH, Metal Blade CDZORRO 26 (UK), Death CAROL CD 2204 (USA) (1991)

TOMB OF THE MUTILATED, Metal Blade CDZORRO 49 (UK), Metal Blade 3984-14003-2 (USA) (1992)

Hammer Smashed Face, Metal Blade MZORRO 57 (UK), Metal Blade 3984-14014-2 (USA) (1993)

BLEEDING, Metal Blade CDZORRO 67 (UK), Metal Blade 3984-14037-2 (USA) (1994)

VILE, Metal Blade 3984-14204-2 (Europe / USA) (1996) **151 USA**

GALLERY OF SUICIDE, Metal Blade 3984-14251-2 (Europe / USA) (1998)

BLOODTHIRST, Metal Blade 3984-14277-2 (Europe / USA) (1999)

LIVE CANNIBALISM, Metal Blade 3984-14302-2 (Europe / USA) (2000)

GORE OBSESSED, Metal Blade 3984-14390-2 (Europe / USA) (2002)

Worm Infested, Metal Blade 3984-14432-2 (Europe / USA) (2002)

15 YEAR KILLING SPREE, Metal Blade 3984-14449-2 (Europe / USA) (2003)

THE WRETCHED SPAWN, Metal Blade 3984-14475-2 (Europe / USA) (2004)

KILL, Metal Blade 3984-14560-2 (Europe / USA) (2006) **170 USA**

'Corpsegrinder' Fisher. Japanese copies added 'The Undead Will Feast' and a video of 'Devoured By Vermin' to the running order. *Vile* gave the band their only *Billboard* chart position to date, peaking at Number 151 in May – the first death metal record to break into *Billboard*. Cannibal Corpse made it into the households of North America in an unexpected fashion when Republican vice-presidential candidate Bob Dole branded the group as practitioners of a "numbing exposure to graphic violence and loveless sex". Democrat senator Joseph Lieberman also weighed in on this moral crusade.

Touring for *Vile* was exhaustive and saw Cannibal Corpse performing

The early line-up of Cannibal Corpse

for nearly a full year, including guest spots in the USA to both Anthrax and the Misfits. European gigs in the spring were bolstered by Immolation and Vader, while a headlining round of US dates saw backing from Brutal Truth, Immolation and Oppressor. Japanese touring that year saw Defiled as opening act. The intensity of the band's live set during this period was captured on the concert video *Monolith Of Death*. Once again Cannibal Corpse broke records when *Monolith*'s sales made it the highest-selling death metal video ever.

The band added former Nevermore guitarist Pat O'Brien for *Gallery Of Suicide*, these sessions in April 1998 utilising producer Jim Morris. Once more the Japanese edition boasted extra material in a cover of Sacrifice's anthem 'Sacrifice'. A change of producer to Colin Richardson did not sway the band from their course for the follow-up, *Bloodthirst*, recorded at Village Studios in El Paso, Texas. This time the lucky Japanese were treated to a take on Possessed's 'Confessions' as their bonus incentive. The world campaign that followed consisted of two North American treks and no fewer than three separate European tours. September 1998 gigs in Europe had Infernal Majesty and Dark Funeral as running-mates. Promoting *Bloodthirst*, the band were back on the road in Europe during October 1999, heading a billing of Marduk, Angel Corpse, Aeternus and Defleshed.

Cannibal Corpse's inaugural live album, *Live Cannibalism*, was culled from February 2000 shows at the Rave in Milwaukee and the Emerson Theatre in Indianapolis, arriving in September. A full six tracks were excised from the German edition – songs from the band's first three albums were and remain illegal in that territory.

Ex-member Barrett founded Hateplow with Phil Fasciana of Malevolent Creation to issue the 2000 album *The Only Law Is Survival*. Guitarist Pat O'Brien announced his death metal combo Ceremony, centred on Morbid Angel vocalist-bassist Steve Tucker and Disastronaut guitarist Greg Reed. Trym, erstwhile Emperor drummer, was recruited into Ceremony during 2002. Renowned Spanish death metal act Avulsed honoured Cannibal Corpse with a cover version of 'Edible Autopsy' on their March 2001 *Bloodcovered* mini-album.

The group enjoyed something of a renaissance with *Gore Obsessed* and embarked on a further round of American dates alongside Incantation, Dark Funeral and Pissing Razors, commencing on April 24th in Los Angeles. *Gore Obsessed* was their eighth studio album and marked a slight shift in emphasis with the employment of Neil Kernon as producer. Initial variants of the record hosted a 'secret' bonus track – a cover of Metallica's 'No Remorse'. Japanese editions hosted a live cut of 'Compelled To Lacerate'. European headline dates commenced on September 19th 2002 in Eindhoven, Holland with a month's worth of dates supported by Dew-Scented and Severe Torture.

The band announced the release of a DVD version of *Monolith Of Death* and a six-track limited and numbered EP – *Worm Infested* – for mid-2002. The EP contained three *Gore Obsessed* outtakes, a cover of Accept's 'Demon's Night', and exclusive Japanese and European tracks. Cannibal Corpse were back on European soil in September for an extensive run of dates over Dew-Scented, Severe Torture and Viu Drakh. They returned to the road in the USA in November, allied with touring compatriots Hate Eternal, Macabre and Cattle Decapitation, and Southern gigs in December found Malevolent Creation as support. The band scheduled a headline run of dates throughout Europe in April 2003. Meanwhile, Owen united with the Epitaph and Resurrection-credited drummer Kevin Astl and female guitarist Analia Pizzaro in a brand new 'aggro hard rock' band called Adrift, in November.

They promoted a four-disc retrospective box set, *15-Year Killing Spree* – comprising three audio CDs and a DVD – and put in a run of headline gigs commencing February 12th in Houston, Texas, traversing North America in league with Exhumed, Hypocrisy and Vile. The band then

formed up part of the 2004 European 'No Mercy' festivals from March 29th, sharing the bill with Spawn Of Possession, Hypocrisy, Kataklysm, Carpathian Forest, Vomitory, Prejudice and Exhumed. US shows in July and August featured The Black Dahlia Murder and Polish act Decapitated as openers.

In 2004, Cannibal Corpse donated their rendition of 'Confessions' to the *Seven Gates Of Horror* tribute album to Possessed. Just before a US tour in July, partnered with The Black Dahlia Murder and Severed Savior, Owen quit the band in order to prioritise his Adrift venture. He closed his 15-year tenure with the explanation that his "heart just wasn't in it any more". Despite this, Owen promptly joined Deicide. Rumours soon put Origin's Jeremy Turner in the frame to fill the vacancy for the tour's duration, and he duly completed the remaining scheduled dates.

Cannibal Corpse's North American road campaign continued into the winter, packaged with Napalm Death, Macabre, Kataklysm and Goatwhore. George Fisher missed the band's November 16th show at The World in Pittsburgh, hospitalised due to a sudden illness caused by a viral lung infection. The band proceeded to run through an instrumental set, capped with a guest vocal appearance from Kataklysm frontman Maurizo Iacono.

In side activity, Alex Webster founded Machinations Of Dementia, a technical extreme metal project co-masterminded by guitarist Ron Jarzombek of Watchtower and Spastic Ink. Initially this band included Lamb Of God drummer Chris Adler. but he bowed out in December 2005 due to other commitments.

Cannibal Corpse then drafted in former guitarist Rob Barrett, whose previous tenure lasted between 1993 and 1997, for the 'Northwest Death Fest' in Seattle on April 3rd. Following a one-off August 13th performance at the Party.San Open Air festival in Germany, the band scheduled recordings for a new album at Mana Studios in Tampa, Florida, in October with producer Erik Rutan. The result was *Kill*, released in early 2006.

The band then joined the European 'No Mercy' festival package for dates across Germany, Austria, France, Switzerland, Belgium and Holland in April, ranked alongside Finntroll, Kataklysm, Grimfist and Legion Of The Damned. They subsequently engaged in a gigantic roving festival billing with the US 'Sounds Of The Underground' tour throughout the summer, commencing in Cleveland, Ohio, on July 8th. Australian gigs in October saw Plague and Psycroptic as support, with New Zealand gigs being backed by Ulcerate. November saw US dates backed by Necrophagist, Unmerciful and Dying Fetus. Cannibal Corpse look set to dominate the US death metal scene for years to come.

CATTLE DECAPITATION
VEGETARIANS WITH A MANIFESTO

SAN DIEGO DEATH METAL BAND Cattle Decapitation were founded in 1996. They push a militant vegetarian message backed up by suitably horrific graphics. Eschewing the standard fare of demons and monsters, the group have successfully employed the cow motif throughout much of their product, using this docile bovine supplier of meat uniquely as a figure of horror.

Drummer Dave Astor was known for his work with sci-fi 'horrorcore' act The Locust, which featured former Cattle Decapitation guitarist Gabe Serbian as drummer. As Cattle Decapitation, they bowed in with a 7-inch single – 'Ten Torments Of The Damned' – that same year. Only 4,000 singles were produced. The artwork – a cow awaiting execution from the decapitating blow of an axe – was an understated portent of what was to come. However, shortly afterwards, their frontman suddenly decamped without warning. The group was brought back up to strength with the enrolment of erstwhile Strangulation drummer Travis Ryan, the Cattle Decapitation duo impressed by his vocal performance on a session with

The band announced touring plans for the USA in November 2003, playing with Hate Eternal, Deicide and Krisiun. Recording sessions for a new album billed as *Humanure* were curtailed in January 2004 after bassist Troy Oftedal broke his wrist. The Bill Metoyer-produced album immediately stoked controversy and was banned once again in Germany, with its gut-wrenching sleeve artwork depicting a cow excreting human remains. However, before the close of August the band admitted defeat – claiming that they had "received too many complaints that people are unable to find the album" – and the album was re-pressed with an inoffensive wasteland cover.

US shows in September saw the band play with Deicide, Goatwhore and Jungle Rot. They announced plans for a split release in collaboration with Caninus for 2005 through Wartorn Records.

Cattle Decapitation returned in summer 2006 with the new studio album *Karma.Bloody.Karma*, continuing the anti-meat-trade theme with an album cover depicting a cow as the war goddess Kali. Produced by Billy Anderson, the album included guest appearances from Joey Karam of The Locust and John Wiese of Sunn 0))) and Bastard Noise. Shortly after recording, the band parted ways with Michael Laughlin, citing "personal reasons" and drafted in ex-Unholy Ghost and Royal Anguish man J.R. Daniels. Subsequent live dates saw alliances with Necrophagist and From A Second Story Window. US dates for September and October 2006 were cancelled, the band claiming their fill-in drummer was not cut out for touring. Cattle Decapitation remain one of the few metal bands whose message hits as hard as their music.

CRYPTOPSY
CANADIAN DEATH PIONEERS

MONTRÉAL'S CRYPTOPSY WERE created in 1992 by erstwhile Necrosis personnel – vocalist Lord Worm (aka Dan Greening), guitarist Steve Thibault and renowned speed drummer Flo Mounier – together with former Reactor guitarist Dave Galea. Necrosis, formed in 1988, issued two demos, *Realms Of Pathogenia* in 1991 and *Necrosis* in 1992, prior to the name change. Cryptopsy was rounded off by bassist Kevin Weagle for the opening four-song demo session *Ungentle Exhumation*. The early incarnation of Cryptopsy was quite theatrical, with many shows beginning with Lord Worm rising from a dirt-filled coffin and actually eating large white worms.

Formative line-up changes would see Galea breaking ranks, to be superseded by Jon Levasseur, whilst Weagle also left the fold, and Cryptopsy pulled in replacement Martin Fergusson.

Cryptopsy's debut album, *Blasphemy Made Flesh*, was produced by Rod Shearer. Recorded in April 1994 for the independent label Gore Productions and released later in the same year, the album was licensed in Europe to Invasion Records, who released it with a different cover.

Further line-up shuffles saw the exit of both Fergusson and Thibault. The band signed to the Swedish Wrong Again company for the follow-up, *None So Vile*, co-produced by Obliveon guitarist Pierre Rémillard. *None So Vile* was reissued in Europe in 1999 by the Dutch label Displeased.

Eric Langlois was enrolled as bassist for Cryptopsy's third album, *Whisper Supremacy*, released in September 1998, this time for Germany's Century Media label. Guitarist Miguel Roy was added following the recording. After the band signed to Century Media the lyrical content and image were toned down considerably, causing some critics to call for a return to the gore-metal stylings of the first two releases instead of this kinetic death metal.

Cryptopsy suffered another major blow when Lord Worm decided to retire from the band, finding a somewhat more sedate career path as an English teacher. His move was on good terms: the previous incumbent

his other act, Anal Flatulence. With Ryan's induction, Astor and Serbian switched roles, with Serbian now the band's guitarist.

Under this incarnation the group released their debut 1999 album, *Human Jerky*, through the Reno, Nevada-based Satan's Pimp label. Issued on 'urinary tract infection'-coloured vinyl, the first pressing of 1,000 copies sold out in its first week. Establishing a precedent for album covers designed to shock, *Human Jerky* was emblazoned with a severed cow's head against a background of pulped meat.

A follow-up arrived remarkably quickly, as Cattle Decapitation were keen to prove they were far from a one-off – and *Homovore*, issued on 'cow'-coloured vinyl, emerged before the end of the year. Three tracks from this outing were re-cut with Spanish vocals for the '¡Decapitacion!' 7-inch green vinyl single released by Accident Prone Records. These three songs formed part of the three-way split EP, *The Science Of Crisis*, shared with Ticwar and Nebraska's Armitron, and released by the Toyo label.

The band, adding Troy Oftedal on bass, included a demo version of 'The Regurgitation Of Corpses' to a Metal Blade compilation *Uncorrupted Steel*, prompting a deal with the label for a 2002 album, *To Serve Man*. Again the band caused consternation with their choice of artwork, a human divided in the manner of butcher's meat cuts, spilling his intestines onto a plate.

After this session, Cattle Decapitation recruited guitar player Josh Elmore and gave their rendition of the Carcass track 'Burnt To A Crisp' to the Necropolis tribute compilation, *Requiems Of Revulsion*.

The Metal Blade debut ran into immediate controversy in Germany, where distribution company SPV reportedly refused to handle the album due to the unnerving artwork by Wes Benscoter. November 2002 shows found the band on the road in North America with Cannibal Corpse, Hate Eternal and Macabre.

The group severed ties with Dave Astor in May 2003, pulling in former Creation Is Crucifixion man Michael Laughlin. Laughlin's first task with the band was to lay down the track 'Cloacula: Anthropophagic Copromantik' for the *Uncorrupted Steel II* compilation. Meanwhile, Miller took time out from the schedule to work with Los Angeles based 'power-noise-industrial' metal band Pro Death.

even introduced the band to his replacement, ex-Infestation vocalist Mike DiSalvo. Promoting *Whisper Supremacy*, which featured Lord Worm on backing vocals, Cryptopsy undertook their inaugural American tour, with Nile, Oppressor and Gorguts. Further shows in 1999 saw Roy out of the picture, replaced by former Seisme six-stringer Alex Auburn as the band hit the road in the States, this time with Poles Vader. The group also put in a European showing at the Dutch 'Dynamo' festival as well as dates in Japan. For their fourth album, *And Then You'll Beg*, the band set out on the 'Pain Cometh' tour with support from Candiria.

Mike DiSalvo decided to leave the band: his last live performance was at the August 4th 2001 'Wacken Open Air' festival in Germany. Despite this blow, Cryptopsy's future seemed assured as Century Media USA showed faith by licensing for re-release the band's first two albums, *Blasphemy Made Flesh* and *None So Vile*. The label used the original artwork for *Blasphemy Made Flesh* with a few minor changes. In August the band announced Martin Lacroix, previously with Spasme, as their new vocalist.

Cryptopsy recorded their June 1st appearance in front of 1,800 fans at the Medley in Montreal for a live album, *None So Live*, released in 2003. The band headlined the Detroit, Michigan, 'Xtreme Benefest' in November, a two-day death metal extravaganza aimed at raising funds for cancer-stricken scene veteran James Murphy.

In August 2002, Flo Mounier forged part of a new thrash covers act, Black Cloud, for a one-off appearance at the 'Thrashback' festival in Montréal on November 9th 2002. This band boasted the prodigious talents of B.A.R.F. frontman Marc Vaillancourt and bassist Jean-Yves 'Blacky' Thériault of Voivod, alongside Ghoulunatics frontman Patrick Mireault, Pierre Rémillard of Obliveon on guitar and Daniel Mongrain of Martyr on second guitar. Cryptopsy's Alex Auburn substituted temporarily for Quo Vardis in March 2003. The band parted ways with vocalist Lacroix in October that year. Original vocalist Lord Worm rejoined Cryptopsy in December 2003.

Flo Mounier acted as stand-in drummer for Ghoulunatics during May 2004 when their regular sticksman Brian Craig was out of action with a sprained ankle. Meanwhile, Emetic Records reissued *Blasphemy Made Flesh* and *None So Vile* as a double-vinyl gatefold package, limited to 1,000 copies worldwide.

Cryptopsy put in an impressive swathe of dates across Canada during September and October 2004 culminating with an appearance at the Trois-Rivières Metalfest. For the first set of shows, former guitarist Miguel Roy acted as stand-in for Jon Levasseur. For the second portion, beginning in Québec City, Dan Mongrain of Martyr and Gorguts took over. These gigs

CRYPTOPSY discography

BLASPHEMY MADE FLESH, Invasion I.R. 011 (Europe) (1994)
NONE SO VILE, Wrong Again WAR 009 CD (Europe) (1996)
WHISPER SUPREMACY, Century Media CM 77242-2 (Europe), Century Media CM 7886-2 (USA) (1998)
AND THEN YOU'LL BEG, Century Media CM 77309-2 (Europe), Century Media CM 8009-2 (USA) (2000)
NONE SO LIVE, Century Media CM 77442-2 (Europe), Century Media CM 8142-2 (USA) (2003)
ONCE WAS NOT, Century Media CM 77542-2 (Europe), Century Media CM 8242-2 (USA) (2005)

produced the live DVD *Trois-Rivières MetalFest IV*.

Stand in guitarist Daniel Mongrain exited in May 2005 in order to prioritise Martyr. That same month the band entered Studio Vortex in Saint-Constant, Québec with producer Sébastien Marsan to work on a new album. The album arrived that October, with a special 'deluxe' edition, limited to 10,000 copies, clad in an embossed, foil-stamped digipak. Road work continued in late 2005, with shows in October and November with Suffocation, Cephalic Carnage, Aborted and With Passion. For these gigs Cryptopsy recruited Christian Donaldson from Mythosis to fill in on second guitar.

The band returned to Europe in January 2006, backed by a supporting cast of Grave, Aborted, Dew-Scented, Vesania and Hurtlocker. That same month Martin Lacroix joined Covenance, a band assembled by Misery Index members Matt Byers on drums and guitarist Bruce Greig.

US touring was set to resume with Exodus and Immolation in April, but these shows were cancelled due to immigration problems. Scandinavian gigs were announced for August and September in collaboration with Aborted, Visceral Bleeding and Vesania, with the band also hooking up with She Said Destroy, Gorerotted and Sylosis for a UK run of dates that same month. This trek included a one-off support to Celtic Frost in London, and the band would no doubt be welcome to return whenever they choose.

DEATH
LEGENDS CUT DOWN BY TRAGEDY

TRUE PIONEERS OF THEIR GENRE, Death were centred upon frontman Chuck Schuldiner and were one of the prime instigators of death metal. Of the six studio albums issued in the band's heyday, three are acknowledged as undisputed classics. Their leader's sense of purpose and honesty forced the Florida band along at a pace which his musicians often failed to match as he strove towards musical excellence.

After forming in 1984, their early demos were recorded under the name of Mantas by the teenage trio of guitarist Schuldiner, former Thatcher guitarist Rick Rozz (real name Frederick DiLillo), and drummer-vocalist Barney 'Kam' Lee. The first demo, *Emotional*, was issued in the spring of that year.

By the summer a second session, recorded within the confines of Schuldiner's garage, resulted in the *Death By Metal* demo. Mantas was then dismantled but the same triumvirate regrouped as Death, re-releasing *Death By Metal* in September complete with new Death branding, artwork depicting a crude inverted crucifix and two grinning skulls, and the addition of the song 'Zombie'. That same month the group distributed *Death Live 11/9/84*, a Mantas live recording of 13 tracks incorporating a rendition of Venom's 'Poison'.

Cryptopsy

A third studio attempt, the five-track *Reign Of Terror* tape, was laid down in October 1984, with various versions sporting fluid track listings – including a subsequently discarded instrumental 'Zombie Attack' – before an inaugural New Year's Eve gig in Tampa as openers to Nasty Savage. This gig was committed to tape, dubbed *Infernal Live* and sold to fans through *Guillotine* magazine.

In March 1985 Rozz made his exit. As a duo, Schuldiner and Lee came up with a further demo, the single-track *Rigor Mortis*. Later, guitarist Matt Olivio and bassist Scott Carlson from the Michigan-based Genocide briefly brought Death up to strength, but Lee then departed. Schuldiner journeyed to San Francisco to form a new band with drummer Eric Brecht, but this venture soon faltered, dispensing just one studio demo session, *Back From The Dead*, in October, and the concert set *Live At Ruthie's Inn* during December. As Schuldiner returned to Florida, his former band-mates Rozz and Lee were gearing up for the arrival on the scene of their new act, the influential Massacre.

Once again Schuldiner relocated in an attempt to kickstart his career, in January 1986 travelling to Toronto where he briefly joined Canadian band Slaughter. His Slaughter collusion was fleeting, resulting in just one track – 'Fuck Of Death'. Back in Florida, Schuldiner resurrected Death with drummer Chris Reifert and distributed rehearsal tapes, including a three-song cassette in March 1986 that featured the Slaughter song. More recording resulted in the April *Mutilation* demo – and this tape finally landed the band a deal, with Combat Records.

Initially, Death convened at the Hollywood Music Grinder studios with producer Randy Burns and the newly-enrolled second guitarist John Hand. However, Hand was reportedly unable to keep pace with Death's material and had his services excused before recording a note. The first album, *Scream Bloody Gore*, released in March 1987 in North America by Combat and licensed to Music For Nations's subsidiary Under One Flag imprint for European issue in June, was a somewhat pedestrian and predictable death metal outing, proving an unreliable marker for what was to come. Death, firmly centred on the erratic talent of Schuldiner, were to develop into a finely honed and technically proficient band and the leader of the genre over successive releases.

Reifert departed in 1987 to form Autopsy, releasing a four-track demo in 1988 and a string of notoriously sickening albums thereafter. Schuldiner reconstituted Death by enlisting the bulk of Massacre – Rick Rozz on guitar, Terry Butler on bass and Bill Andrews on drums. This line-up undertook Death's first North American tour, including a performance at the Milwaukee 'Metalfest'.

The November 1988 album *Leprosy*, produced by Dan Johnson at Morrisound in April 1988, solidified the band's burgeoning reputation. Although Terry Butler was credited with bass on the album jacket, it was in reality Chuck Schuldiner who performed these duties. *Leprosy* was a staging post, marking the first move away from the familiar gore-soaked subject matter with tentative steps into more philosophical realms, laid out over songs of longer duration – a pattern that would develop with each successive release. Death, alongside Forbidden, Raven and Faith Or Fear, then featured on the live video *The Ultimate Revenge* recorded in October at the Trocadero Theatre in Philadelphia.

Death toured Europe in 1989 alongside Gang Green and support act Despair prior to American dates with Dark Angel. However, before recording the third album, Rozz returned to his act Massacre. For the *Spiritual Healing* album, committed to tape at Morrisound with Scott Burns and issued in March 1990, Death consisted of Schuldiner, bassist Terry Butler and drummer Bill Andrews. Rehearsals were held with guitarist Mark Carter before erstwhile Agent Steel and Hallows Eve man James Murphy was drafted in. Murphy greatly enhanced the cutting-edge guitar element of the band. *Spiritual Healing* gave a platform for Schuldiner to expand upon political and social themes such as human

cloning, vigilantism, evangelism and capital punishment, and although he was not yet in possession of the musicians to fully implement his ambitions, he was even able to experiment with progressive leanings.

Following the album's release, Murphy was unceremoniously fired, later joining Obituary before enjoying terms with British thrash act Cancer, Testament and Danes Konkhra, as well as issuing solo albums. Death initially set about touring as a trio before adding Cynic's Paul Masvidal on a temporary basis. This inclusion was significant as it provided the first clue towards the next stage of evolution for the band.

North American dates in 1990 with Carcass and Pestilence were completed using the services of ex-Evildead guitarist Albert Gonzalez. Death then enlisted former Rotting Corpse guitarist Walter Trachsler for the remaining dates of their American tour with Kreator.

Somewhat bizarrely, Death then toured Britain (with Kreator) minus Schuldiner, who was reportedly advised to stay in America for health reasons. Ex-Devastation and Rotting Christ drummer Louie Carrisalez filled in on vocals, while Trachsler substituted on guitar. The fans refused to accept a touring line-up minus Schuldiner – in spite of a series of bizarre allegations that he had renounced extreme music and was pursuing a glam-metal path – and the dates were far from a success. Upon their return to America, both Butler and Andrews joined Massacre.

Schuldiner was quick to resurrect the band, finally managing to attain the services of Cynic's Paul Masvidal full-time. Masvidal had guested on the 1991 Master album *On The Seventh Day God Created Master* between stints with Death. Alongside Schuldiner and Masvidal were former Sadus bassist Steve DiGiorgio and Cynic drummer Sean Reinert, and this line-up recorded the *Human* album, released that October. Japanese editions hosted an uncharacteristic cover version of 'God Of Thunder', originally by Kiss. *Human*, despite its unfocused production, went down in musical history as one of the quintessential death metal releases. With Schuldiner clearly in possession of the requisite skills, heading a gifted set of musicians and realising his own talents on the lyrical and songwriting front, his aspirations for technical yet intense metal had been fulfilled.

For Death's 1991 touring line-up Schuldiner was joined by Masvidal, Reinert and bassist Scott Carino. After US and Canadian dates, the band toured Europe as part of a Christmas package in alliance with Napalm Death, Dismember and Cannibal Corpse before playing in Britain in February 1992 with support from Viogression. A useful promotional aid came with a video clip for the track 'Lack Of Comprehension'. Later that year Relativity Records issued the compilation album *Fate*.

Paul Masvidal and Sean Reinert returned to Cynic in 1993, releasing their debut album *Focus*. Carino went to Fester and in 2000 was a member of Lowbrow. The revised version of Death now saw the inclusion of King Diamond guitarist Andy LaRocque and Dark Angel's Gene Hoglan on drums. For the recording of June 1993's *Individual Thought Patterns*, DiGiorgio stepped in once more. The album was backed up by the filming of a second video, for the song 'The Philosopher', and while many predicted that it would be inferior to its predecessor, reviewers and fans alike agreed that it fell only slightly short.

Commitments with King Diamond prevented LaRocque from involving himself in live work. Death soldiered on, enlisting Craig Locicero of Forbidden for European shows and Ralph Santolla of Eyewitness for American dates, supported by Dutch act Gorefest, and for subsequent European festivals. Santolla later came to the fore in the melodic rock community with acts such as Millenium and Monarch.

The *Symbolic* album, the first for new label Roadrunner, emerged in March 1995 and was to have been recorded with LaRocque and former Watchtower and Retarded Elf bassist Doug Keyser – but the guitarist was obliged to record the King Diamond album *The Spider's Lullaby* and no fee could be agreed for the bassist. DiGiorgio and LaRocque departed in early 1995, replaced by ex-Pain Principle bassist Kelly Conlon and guitarist

Bobby Koelble. Death toured America with Nevermore the same year. Kelly Conlon would team up with Monstrosity and later Vital Remains.

Surrounded by this confusion, Schuldiner still somehow managed to pull off another near-perfect example of the death metal genre. *Symbolic* is recognised as the closing chapter of Death's triptych of genius. The fractious nature of the band's existence had taken its toll, however.

Schuldiner changed tack completely later the same year, putting Death on ice and generating a new project, Control Denied, very much in the power metal mould. The plan had been for Schuldiner to work with the original Winters Bane vocalist, but he was lured away for a more permanent liaison with Wicked Ways. Control Denied was now down to Schuldiner, bassist Brian Benson and drummer Chris Williams.

Another version of the band saw Schuldiner and Williams joined by guitarist Shannon Hamm and Scott Clendenin on bass, both of Talonzfury. Although Control Denied had recorded an album's worth of material and received offers from various labels, Williams departed, replaced by ex-Burning Inside and Acheron drummer Richard Christy.

The outcome was inevitable, and Death announced their reformation in October with a line-up of Schuldiner, guitarist Hamm, drummer Christy and a returning DiGiorgio on bass. DiGiorgio nonetheless retained his full-time participation in Sadus and also reunited with another ex-Death guitarist, James Murphy, for one of his side projects, Disincarnate.

Death duly returned to the scene in April 1997, back on European soil and heading up the 'Full Of Hate Easter' festivals alongside Obituary, Entombed, Samael, Neurosis, Crowbar, Killing Culture and Strapping Young Lad. The group signed to Nuclear Blast for 1998's *The Sound Of Perseverance*, an album that saw a further progression towards straight heavy metal. Schuldiner was aided in this effort by Hamm, Christy and bassist Scott Clendenin. The album included a stab at Judas Priest's supercharged 'Painkiller'.

Ex-Death drummer Gene Hoglan would turn up on the drums for the 1998 album *Ill-Natured Spiritual Invasion* by Norwegian outfit Old Man's Child. Meanwhile, Death played in Europe with Benediction and in America with Hammerfall.

Although 1999 heralded the welcome release of Schuldiner's Control Denied album, *The Fragile Art Of Existence*, fate dealt a cruel blow when the frontman was diagnosed with a brain tumour. Schuldiner, who had learnt of the disease on his 31st birthday, had an operation in January and spent the bulk of the year in recuperation. The same year, Century Media

DEATH discography

SCREAM BLOODY GORE, Under One Flag CD FLAG 12 (UK), Combat 88561-8146-2 (USA) (1987)

LEPROSY, Under One Flag CD FLAG 24 (UK), Combat 88561-8248-2 (USA) (1988)

SPIRITUAL HEALING, Under One Flag CD FLAG 38 (UK), Combat 88561-2011-2 (USA) (1990)

HUMAN, R/C RC 9238-2 (Europe), Relativity 88561-2036-2 (USA) (1991)

INDIVIDUAL THOUGHT PATTERNS, Roadrunner RR 9079-2 (Europe), Relativity 88561-1168-2 (USA) (1993)

SYMBOLIC, Roadrunner RR 8957-2 (Europe / USA) (1995)

THE SOUND OF PERSEVERANCE, Nuclear Blast NB 0337-2 (Europe), Nuclear Blast America 6337 (USA) (1998)

LIVE IN L.A. (DEATH & RAW), Nuclear Blast NB 0554-2 (Europe), Nuclear Blast America 6554 (USA) (2001)

LIVE IN EINDHOVEN '98, Nuclear Blast NB 0679-2 (Europe), Nuclear Blast America 6679 (USA) (2001)

CHUCK SCHULDINER: ZERO TOLERANCE, Karmageddon Media KARMA021 (Europe) (2004)

CHUCK SCHULDINER: ZERO TOLERANCE II, Karmageddon Media KARMA056 (Europe) (2004)

CHUCK SCHULDINER: ZERO TOLERANCE, Candlelight USA CD CDL 182 (USA) (2005) US 2-disc version of European releases

would unveil an impressive five-album vinyl boxed set.

The year 2000 found Christy back on the drum stool aiding fellow death metallers Incantation for live commitments before touring with Iced Earth. DiGiorgio, meanwhile, played in the Dragonlord project of Testament guitarist Eric Peterson. Napalm Death paid homage in their own oblique way by including a Death cover on their *Leaders Not Followers* album, although the song in question was from an early demo and does not appear on any official Death release.

Schuldiner, now receiving the experimental drug Vincristine, was still very ill by mid 2001, and the Hammerheart America label organised an online auction to raise funds for a second operation. Among the items auctioned off was one of Schuldiner's own guitars and a Steve DiGiorgio custom bass. Nuclear Blast pitched in by releasing the *Live In LA (Death & Raw)* album. Issued on both CD and double-LP formats, the recordings were taken direct from the soundboard at the band's Whiskey A Go-Go show on the 'Sound Of Perseverance' dates. Across America and Europe the extreme metal community rallied to the cause, putting on numerous benefit shows. Sadly, Chuck Schuldiner died on December 13th 2001. Metal fans and the metal media were stricken, having lost one of their most talented members.

In 2002, ex-Death musicians were active on the scene. Bassist Kelly Conlon joined the Boston-based progressive metal act Infinity Minus One, and Gene Hoglan, beside his work with Strapping Young Lad, formed part of the reconstituted Dark Angel line-up. As 2003 drew in, plans were announced for a Death tribute album involving James Murphy, ex-Malevolent Creation vocalist Brett Hoffmann, ex-Malevolent Creation and Suffocation drummer Dave Culross, and CKY guitarist Deron Miller. The album, by early 2004 dubbed *Within The Mind – In Homage To The Musical Legacy Of Chuck Schuldiner*, later added the Slipknot pairing of Mick Thompson and Paul Gray, Mudvayne's Ryan Martinie and Chad Gray, Iced Earth drummer Richard Christy, Testament's Chuck Billy and Eric Peterson, the Painmuseum and Halford-credited Mike Chlasciak, Jean-François Dagenais of Kataklysm, Patrick Mameli from Pestilence, Luc

Death

Lemay of Gorguts, and Peter Tägtgren of Hypocrisy. In June, guitarist Matt Bachand and drummer Jason Bittner of Shadows Fall also contributed sessions. Darkest Hour guitarist Kris Norris's contributions were recorded backstage at the 'Ozzfest' Tampa Amphitheater concert.

Karmageddon Media releases for 2004 included the *Zero Tolerance* archive sets of demo and live material. The first album consisted of Death's 1985 *Infernal Death* and 1986 *Mutilation* demos alongside previously unreleased demo recordings by Control Denied. *Zero Tolerance II* was made up of the first Mantas demo, *Death By Metal*, from 1984, the *Reign Of Terror* session from the same year, and a Death live show recorded at the After Dark club in Texas during the *Spiritual Healing* tour in 1990. Although as recordings these sets were welcome additions to the Schuldiner legacy, the manner of their release was unfortunately overcast with controversy, with very public legal spats between Chuck's mother and the Dutch label. This bitterness resulted in the final product being sadly sub-par in presentation and backed by almost non-existent promotion.

Former band members continued to be active throughout the scene. Paul Masvidal and Sean Reinert re-emerged that year in prog-rock outfit Aeon Spoke, touting the album *Above The Buried Cry*. In April 2006, Death vocalist Kam Lee and bassist Terry Butler were revealed to have formed retro thrash/death metal combo Denial Fiend. Whatever the future holds, Chuck Schuldiner will be present in spirit for many years to come on the metal scene he helped to create.

DEICIDE
IN HOMAGE TO SATAN

DEICIDE WERE THE FIRST AMERICAN satanic death metal band to push the novelty factor into the realms of the dangerous. Early shows saw vocalist-bassist Glen Benton drenched in the blood of a pig, bedecked in studded body armour (which he called 'God armour') and sporting on his forehead a burned-in upside-down cross. Remarkably for a metal band operating in such extremes, Deicide maintained a rock-solid line-up for 15 years of Benton plus brothers Eric Hoffman and Brian Hoffman on guitars and Steve Asheim on drums. The band continues to maintain a strong fanbase.

Deicide emerged from the cult band Amon, founded in 1987, who released two demos – August 1987's eight-track garage recording *Feasting The Beast* and *Sacrificial* in December 1989. This second session scored a deal with Roadrunner. The new name Deicide arrived in June 1990 with an eponymous album recorded in February that year by Scott Burns at the spiritual home of US death metal, Tampa's Morrisound Recording studio. All six *Sacrificial* tracks were re-crafted for this opus. This winning formula of studio and producer was cemented for the next three albums.

The *Deicide* album broke little if any new ground in musical terms, but Benton's skill at manipulating the media was matched by a half-hour burst of savage blasphemy, driven by Asheim's impressive percussive abilities. The lyrical content was entirely devoted to the practices of Lucifer and his minions, with the exception of opener 'Lunatic Of God's Creation' and 'Carnage In The Temple Of The Damned', which referred respectively to Charles Manson and Guyana occultist Jim Jones.

That same year Benton featured as a backing vocalist on another groundbreaking recording, Cannibal Corpse's *Eaten Back To Life*. Further controversy was whipped up after the second album, June 1992's *Legion*, when two New Jersey teenagers tortured and killed a dog, leaving its carcass hanging in a tree. When questioned by authorities, the youngsters claimed inspiration from Deicide.

Legion, intended as a quick-fire response to the furore engendered by the debut, was so rushed that the original sessions clocked in at just over 20 minutes, requiring the band to return to the studio to record extra material. With this early notoriety, the band built up a fanbase with surprising speed: Roadrunner later reissued the Amon demos in 1993, re-credited to Deicide and marketed as *Amon: Feasting The Beast*. Benton then aided leading Mexican thrash act Transmetal with backing vocals on the same year's *Dante's Inferno*.

Although Glen's style was undoubtedly death metal in delivery, the singer's vocal appreciation of a satanic belief system, his willingness to engage in media-sponsored set discussions on good and evil with church members – including a debate with the late former Twelfth Night vocalist and vicar Geoff Mann – and the apparently witnessed shooting of squirrels in his garden, put Deicide firmly in the black metal camp. So vociferous were the media against Deicide that the band's notoriety spread into areas not normally troubled by black metal. Benton's comments regarding his supposed treatment of animals led to bomb threats that blighted a winter 1992 European tour. A more pointed message left with the media, allegedly from the Animal Militia organisation, informed Benton that he would be killed if he stepped on English soil. Deicide's British and European shows went according to plan until the Scandinavian leg when a bomb exploded at the Fryshuset club in Stockholm, Sweden. The device actually detonated during touring partners Therion's set, although it had been timed to go off in the middle of Deicide's scheduled stage time. Nobody was seriously hurt, although the bomb caused several minor injuries and blew apart part of a wall and roofing. However, the object of the assault was unclear as support band Gorefest had also received death threats from another source. A fake bomb constructed from a clock and wires was thrown onstage in Manchester, temporarily halting the show. The band finished the remainder of the European tour without major incident.

Benton, whose first son was tactfully named Daemon, rather intriguingly voiced premonitions that he would die aged 33. Needless to say, his 33rd birthday passed without such an event.

Deicide's third album arrived in April 1995. *Once Upon The Cross* immediately provoked outrage, with its cover art depicting a slaughtered Jesus. In the USA large stickers were placed over the offending image. However, upon opening the CD case, purchasers were confronted by even more graphic artwork, portraying an eviscerated Messiah. Once the shock value had been overcome, the record was given enough impetus to land at a suitable Number 66 in the national British charts. *Once Upon The Cross* was widely regarded as the last great Deicide album.

Serpents Of The Light slithered out in October 1997, replete once again with provocative artwork – this time showing Jesus with a forked serpent tongue. The album hosted a fourth round of zero tolerance toward Christianity and included concert favourite 'Blame It On God'. A live album, *When Satan Lives*, emerged a year later.

The band's July 2000 release, the wryly titled *Insineratehymn*, was as uncompromising as ever, the unrelenting river of blasphemy triggered by another stage staple, 'Bible Basher'. Rumblings of discontent were boiling to the surface, though, as the band began voicing dissatisfaction with their label, complaining of an unfavourable degree of promotion and budgeting.

They toured as headliners in America during May 2001, topping a bill comprising Marduk, Gorguts and All Out War. *In Torment, In Hell* was delivered that September, but obviously all was not well in the Deicide camp. When reviews pointed towards the album's roughshod finish, the group claimed that Roadrunner had released an uncompleted product.

During early 2002, Glen Benton cut session lead vocals for Vital Remains' *Dechristianize* album, leading to speculation as to the future of Deicide. However, the band themselves were soon afterwards in the recording studio cutting a 2002 album. European tour dates slated for November saw them heading up a proposed six-band bill, but this roster was subsequently slashed to Deicide, Mystic Circle and Centinex.

Terminating their long relationship with Roadrunner, the band signed

of the *Stop At Nothing* album, topping a bill of Skinless, Divine Empire and Misery Index. Many more 2003 shows followed.

Following September 2004 gigs in Mexico, a further US tour, 'Mock The Vote', came in support of Gwar. However, just before this Dying Fetus parted ways with Vince Matthews, stating: "This action was taken due to a number of musical, professional, and personal reasons that we feel do not need elaboration at this time." Yet more changes for these gigs saw the addition of session drummer John Longstreth, of Origin, Skinless, The Red Chord and Exhumed, replacing a temporarily unavailable Erik Sayenga.

Meanwhile, Sayenga fired up side project Warthrone, a union with ex-Witch-Hunt, Necropsy and Sanguinary singer Richard Johnson and ex-Witch-Hunt, Warfair and Dark Purity keyboard player-bassist Kristel. In February 2005 Vince Matthews and Bruce Greig allied with Misery Index drummer Matt Byers for a new project, Covenance.

Meanwhile, Dying Fetus toured with Six Feet Under, Dark Funeral, Disbelief, Nile, Wykked Wytch and Cataract for the 2005 'No Mercy' festivals, beginning in early March. Drummer Erik Sayenga left the band "due to circumstances beyond his control" in early May and was replaced by Duane Timlin. Kevin Talley acted as fill-in for The Black Dahlia Murder in February 2006 and joined Hate Eternal in March.

Dying Fetus entered Hit & Run Studios in Rockville, Maryland, during late September to cut fresh album tracks. November saw US dates for Dying Fetus backing Cannibal Corpse, Unmerciful and Germany's Necrophagist.

HATE ETERNAL
EXPERT DEATH METAL GRIND

HATE ETERNAL ARE ONE OF TWO bands led by ex-Ripping Corpse and Morbid Angel guitarist Erik Rutan, who also operates a female-fronted symphonic metal project, Alas. These two bands shared equal space on a 1997 industry promo release, *Engulfed In Grief*.

The Tampa Bay-based Hate Eternal signed up with Wicked World, a death metal subsidiary of UK label Earache Records. For the recording of the *Conquering The Throne* album, which emerged in October 1999, Rutan pulled in ex-Intercine bassist Jared Anderson, drummer Tim Yeung and Suffocation and Welt guitarist Doug Cerrito. At the time, Rutan was still assisting Morbid Angel as live guitarist and establishing a reputation as a producer, having handled Brazilian act Krisiun's *Conquerors Of Armegeddon* album of 2000 among many others.

Hate Eternal toured as support to Cannibal Corpse and Dethroned, with the band's line-up now including former Malevolent Creation drummer Derek Roddy. Anderson was drafted into the ranks of Morbid Angel for their 2001 UK dates when their regular frontman Steve Tucker was forced to bow out. However, Hate Eternal went beyond the status of a side project when a new album, *King Of All Kings*, was announced for September 2002. Gigs to promote the release included a run of shows in Brazil the same month.

Erstwhile Hate Eternal drummer Tim Yeung would be employed as session drummer for the 2002 Aurora Borealis album *Time, Unveiled*. Coincidentally, Roddy had sat in with Aurora Borealis on earlier albums. November 2002 found Hate Eternal on the road in North America on a billing with Cannibal Corpse, Cattle Decapitation and Macabre. They then toured the UK in December with support from Kataklysm and Deranged.

The band then brought in Randy Piro for Jared Anderson, at first only as a temporary replacement, and united with Dying Fetus, Kataklysm and Into Eternity for North American dates in February and March 2003. Rutan suffered a cracked vertebra when the band's van went off the road in Wisconsin on March 8th, but the singer was released from hospital and persevered with the tour. He soon recovered enough to mix the album

Total Death from leading Colombian death metal band Masacre. Meanwhile, Anderson backed out of band activities to commit himself to a drug rehabilitation programme.

Hate Eternal allied with Arch Enemy, Evergrey and The Black Dahlia Murder for a short but intensive run of US dates in August before hooking up with Hatebreed, Madball, Terror and Cephalic Carnage for September shows. The band announced further touring plans for the USA in November 2003, playing alongside Deicide, Krisiun and Cattle Decapitation. In January 2004 they headlined over Dying Fetus, Deeds Of Flesh and Prejudice in Europe. Rutan then gained mixing credits for Swedish act In Battle's 2004 album *Welcome To The Battlefield*, the guitarist also donating a solo to the track 'Serpent'.

The band announced the addition of second guitarist Eric Hersemann of Lord Blasphemer and Diabolic to their ranks in May 2005. They headed up a summer package comprising Krisiun, Incantation, Into Eternity and All Shall Perish for US gigs in June. However, with Incantation forced out of the Canadian leg due to "legal issues", Jungle Rot took over the vacant support slot for those gigs. This tour preceded a batch of Australian shows.

A new album, *I, Monarch*, preceded by a Shane Drake-directed video for the title track, arrived on June 28th through Earache. *I, Monarch* came in three formats – a regular CD, a limited-edition slipcase CD with different cover art, and a vinyl picture disc restricted to 1,000 copies.

Erik Rutan spent December 2005 producing Cellador's *Enter Deception* album. As 2006 opened, drummer Roddy teamed up with Blotted Science, a technical metal project masterminded by guitarist Ron Jarzombek of Watchtower and Spastic Ink alongside Cannibal Corpse bassist Alex Webster, also a member of Hate Eternal.

Hate Eternal announced European gigs for April 2006 but cancelled these, also losing the services of Roddy. A new set of shows resulted in an April US trek alongside Arch Enemy, Chimaira, Nevermore and God Forbid, and later adding Temple Of Brutality. Kevin Talley of Chimaira, Dying Fetus and Misery Index stepped in as substitute drummer. The band then hooked up with Spawn Of Possession and Shadows Land for

HATE ETERNAL discography

CONQUERING THE THRONE, Wicked World WICK 006 CD (UK / USA) (1999)
KING OF ALL KINGS, Earache MOSH 260 CD (UK / USA) (2002)
I, MONARCH, Earache MOSH 286 CD (UK / USA) (2005)

European touring in May. Standing in on drums was Reno Kiilerich, who had credits with Dimmu Borgir, Dew-Scented, Vile, Old Man's Child and Panzerchrist. (Former vocalist Jared Anderson died in his sleep on October 14th 2006 at the age of 30.) The band remain in the US death metal vanguard.

IMMOLATION
BURNING IN THE FIRES OF DEATH METAL

THE FERVENTLY ANTI-CHRISTIAN metal band Immolation were formed in Yonkers, New York, in February 1988 by frontman Ross Dolan, drummer Neal Boback and two erstwhile Rigor Mortis guitarists, Robert Vigna and Thomas Wilkinson. Two demos, in July 1988 and June 1989, were recorded prior to the July 1991 *Dawn Of Possession* album and the recruitment of drummer Craig Smilowski. These tracks were constructed under the guidance of Harris Johns at Musiclab Studios in Berlin for Roadrunner. *Dawn Of Possession* quickly found appreciation on a crowded market, mainly due to its convoluted unorthodoxy, pinch harmonics, atonal riffing and the abundance of minor keys – all forming a disturbing avalanche of unpredictability.

In January 1995 Repulse Records collected the band's earlier demos and Rigor Mortis sessions, plus live tapes from New Rochelle, New York, in December 1988 and Belle Vernon, Pennsylvania, in June 1989, releasing them as the *Stepping On Angels... Before Dawn* compilation.

Immolation switched labels to Metal Blade and issued the February 1996 *Here In After* album. Former Fallen Christ and Disassociate drummer Alex Hernández joined upon completion of the *Here In After* sessions. Touring saw shows in Europe with Cannibal Corpse. In July 1998 the group entered Millbrook Sound Studios to forge *Failures For Gods* with producer Paul Orofino, and Metal Blade released this set a full year later. An exercise in near-indecipherable technicality, the album's subtleties were regretfully lost in a muddy mix.

The band toured America in 2000, sharing a bill with Six Feet Under. A fourth album, *Close To A World Below*, appeared in November, rectifying many of the sound problems of its predecessor.

John McEntee of Incantation deputised for Vigna on later tours, and with the latter returning to action, former Angel Corpse man Bill Taylor took over from Wilkinson in 2001. Tours in Europe in May found Immolation headlining over Deranged, Destroyer 666, Decapitated and Soul Demise. The band signed to Olympic Records for North America and the French Listenable label for Europe, issuing the October 2002 *Unholy Cult* effort, again produced by Paul Orofino.

IMMOLATION discography

DAWN OF POSSESSION, Roadracer RC 9310-2 (Europe / USA) (1991)
STEPPING ON ANGELS... BEFORE DAWN, Repulse RPS 004 CD (Europe) (1995)
HERE IN AFTER, Metal Blade 3984-14102-2 (Europe / USA) (1996)
FAILURES FOR GODS, Metal Blade 3984-14197-2 (Europe / USA) (1999)
CLOSE TO A WORLD BELOW, Metal Blade 3984-14349-2 (Europe / USA) (2000)
UNHOLY CULT, Listenable POSH 042 (Europe), Olympic Recordings OLY 0227-2 (USA) (2002)
HARNESSING RUIN, Listenable POSH 065 (Europe), Olympic Recordings OLY 0244-2 (USA) (2005)

The band also scheduled a European headlining tour in December in alliance with Deranged, backed by German black metal act Mystic Circle and Sweden's Insision. Further concerts witnessed the band forming part of an impressive cast for European 'Xmass' festivals in December alongside Six Feet Under, Marduk, Kataklysm, Dying Fetus and Hate. Later gigs in Holland added veteran thrashers Exodus to the bill. There was no let-up on the live front in 2003, Immolation teaming up with Cradle Of Filth for European gigs in March and April and then Grave and Goatwhore for US shows in June. Hernández was forced to drop off the US tour in June when he developed a hernia. He was replaced by Steve Shalaty who has since become a permanent member.

During early 2004 Dolan donated his services to a tribute album, *Within The Mind*, assembled by guitarist James Murphy in honour of the late Death mentor Chuck Schuldiner. Former Immolation drummer Hernández joined Uruguayan death metal band Requiem Aeternum for their album *The Philosopher* in May 2004. Meanwhile, Immolation entered the studio in July with producer Paul Orofino for their seventh studio album, *Harnessing Ruin*, set for February 2005 release through Listenable and for March in the USA through Olympic Recordings. The band collaborated with Deicide, With Passion, Skinless and Misery Index for US dates in May 2005. North American touring resumed with Exodus and Cryptopsy in April 2006.

Immolation cut new album tracks with producer Paul Oforino at Millbrook Sound Studios in New York during November. Their fanbase remains loyal.

INCANTATION
BLACK/DEATH FUSION EXPERTS

INCANTATION, FROM JOHNSTOWN, Pennsylvania, straddle the border between black and death metal and are cited by many of today's acts as a direct inspiration. A clutch of highly regarded modern bands stem directly from Incantation: many musicians have passed through their ranks. The band first came together in August 1989 with erstwhile Bloodthirsty Death guitarist Brett Makowski and bassist Aragon Amori plus ex-Revenant men John McEntee and Paul Ledney (Ledney had previously played with G.G. Allin's infamous Connecticut Cocksuckers).

In January 1990 this line-up cut a rehearsal demo, which included a cover version of Hellhammer's 'Third Of The Storm'. A major fallout occurred, however, when McEntee was left alone as Makowski, Amori and Ledney decamped en masse to found the notorious black metal act Profanatica, releasing a string of highly controversial EPs.

Immolation

At this juncture McEntee was also the substitute guitarist for death metal unit Mortician, whose frontman Will Rahmer provided guest vocals for the 'Entrantment Of Evil' 7-inch single. That March, Incantation featured a line-up of McEntee, bassist Ronnie Deo and the ex-Decay pairing of guitarist Sal Seijo and drummer Peter Barnevic. Seijo and Barnevic had been recruited from an ad posted in a local music store, while Deo had responded to a musicians-wanted posting in the *East Coast Rocker*. In June another set of demos was laid down. However, both Seijo and Barnevic would part ways with the band.

In August the same year, Incantation were back up to strength, having enrolled Bill Venner on guitar and Jim Roe on drums, again located through the *East Coast Rocker*. Unfortunately, Venner's tenure was fleeting, although he did provide a worthy service by executing Incantation's now familiar logo. As a quartet of Rahmer, McEntee, Deo and Roe, Incantation performed at the October 'Day Of Death' festival in Buffalo. Meanwhile, 'Entrantment Of Evil' emerged as a violet vinyl 7-inch in September on the Seraphic Decay label.

November 1990 saw the induction of former Putrefact guitarist Craig Pillard. The new guitar man had issued a series of solo demos accredited to Nocturnal Crypt, including a self-titled 1987 effort as well as *Recrudescence Of…* in 1988 and a rehearsal tape the following year.

With Rahmer's commitments to Mortician increasing, his position was made vacant and Pillard subsequently stepped into the vocal role. This line-up released the single 'Deliverance Of Horrific Prophecies', originally intended as a split shared with Amorphis. This November 1991 outing was the band's inaugural product for Relapse Records. The group then undertook its first North American tour, alongside Anal Cunt and Phlegm. With the dates completed in November 1992, Deo opted out.

Incantation brought in ex-Crucifier man Dan Kamp on bass for the recording of 'Emaciated Holy Figure', donated to Nuclear Blast's *Death Is Just The Beginning Volume II* compilation. Further touring saw the band out on the road with Autopsy, Vital Remains and Morgue. Roe and Kamp broke ranks after these shows.

In August 1993 the band announced the recruitment of a new rhythm section – Necrosion bassist Dave Niedrist and Deteriorot drummer John Brody. With a tour waiting in the wings and recording of the debut album, *Onward To Golgotha*, to be completed, they solved matters by re-employing Roe to handle drums in the studio while Brody learned the material for the live show.

Onward To Golgotha, produced by Steve Evetts at Trax East Studios, provided a fresh perspective to the US death metal scene, being one of the first high-profile albums not stamped with the Morrisound/Florida trademarks. Instead, Incantation went for a swarming set of riffs and low-register growls corralled by a thick, choking production. Although the

record was by no means a genre cornerstone, it did possess enough individuality to set the band on its way.

Mortal Throne Of Nazarene was the title of their second album, a self-produced effort engineered by Garris Shipon at Excello Recording Studios in March 1994. However, following this second set and European dates in conjunction with Sinister and Deadhead, frontman Craig Pillard broke away from the group. Before long bassist Ronnie Reo and drummer Jim Roe joined him to found Womb, an act that evolved into Disciples Of Mockery.

Competition between Disciples Of Mockery and Incantation was so fierce that at the 1994 'Deathstock' festival in New York, Pillard's band played a full set of Incantation numbers just before Incantation themselves took the stage. Confusion reigned in death metal circles when an alternative mix of *Mortal Throne Of Nazarene*, issued that November, was re-released under the new title of *Upon The Throne Of Apocalypse*, with a reversed track order and a sticker proclaiming 'Pagan Disciples Of Mockery'. Later, Pillard's band became Womb again, although they reverted to Disciples Of Mockery for a 1999 three-track promotion CD.

Amid all this, Incantation regrouped, enlisting Duane Morris on vocals and guitar for a tour in alliance with Morgue, Afterlife, Anal Cunt and Morpheus Descends. Malevolent Creation were originally scheduled to headline, but with their cancellation Incantation were elevated to headline status. With the tour rolled up, the band fractured yet again: this time it was Brody and Niedrist who said their farewells.

Incantation then relocated to Ohio, with lone founder member John McEntee creating a completely revised roster. Morris was retained as frontman, with ex-Blood Of Christ bassist Randy Scott and Escalation Angel man Kyle Severn recruited on drums.

An American tour with Fear Of God and Swedes Grave was nearly curtailed when Scott decided not to go along for the ride. However, the band carried on without bass as a trio of McEntee, guitarist Duane Morris and drummer Severn. In March 1995, Mike Donnelly of Disgorged teamed up with the band as they performed a short tour of Mexico in 1995, sharing a bill with Immolation and Acid Bath. Further confusion followed as Morris bailed out, only to return shortly after. The problem recurred halfway through touring as Morris upped and left again. Daniel Corchado of Mexican acts Cenotaph and The Chasm was hastily drafted in to complete the dates.

Donnelly was the next to leave and Incantation took on yet another guise by pulling in bassist Mary Ciullo, Mortician and Deathrune man Mike Saez on guitar, and a re-enlisted Will Rahmer on vocals. This unit demoed and put in three shows in New York, Pennsylvania and Cleveland.

During March 1996, McEntee and Severn were joined by Malignancy bassist Kevin Hughes and vocalist-guitarist Nathan Rossi of Rottrevore for American dates with Mortician and Anal Cunt. Rossi then bowed out and Pillard became frontman once again for *The Forsaken Mourning Of Angelic Anguish*. Mike Saez was also involved in this line-up on a session basis.

Hughes then took his leave, and once more Incantation called on Daniel Corchado, this time for the bass role. Tragically that same year former bassist Aragon Amori died.

The October 1997 *Forsaken Mourning* mini-album, produced by Bill Korecky, featured a cover of Death's 'Scream Bloody Gore'. Corchado occupied the frontman spot for a burst of touring, and Saez was invited on board for American gigs with Vital Remains and European dates with Avulsed, Adramelech and Deeds Of Flesh. Saez was unable to commit to later gigs and so, switching Corchado to guitar, Incantation performed as a trio minus bass again. Despite this ebb and flow of members, the *Diabolical Conquest* album was released in April 1998.

Bob Yench, a veteran of Morpheus Descends and Brimstone, filled the bass position in April 1998. Incantation set about touring with Morbid Angel and Vader, but Corchado was obliged to leave midway through these dates. With an appearance at the Milwaukee 'Metalfest' already

Incantation

booked, the band took on Tom Stevens as vocalist-guitarist. Stevens had previous credits with Savage Death, Exile, Brimstone, Nokturnel and Morpheus Descends. This line-up undertook further shows in Canada with Morbid Angel, but Severn was ineligible to cross the Canadian border. Chris Dora of Integrity, Soulless and Decrepit quickly stepped in to save the day.

The band then suffered a major blow when, returning home from a gig in Dallas, Texas, their van overturned. Both McEntee and Severn were badly injured, and following the accident Severn decided to retire from the band. Clay Lytle of Fatal Aggression occupied the drum stool for Incantation's appearance at the 1998 Chilean Metalfest. Ranked alongside Death and Cannibal Corpse, the band performed to over 7,000 South American fans in one night. After the gig, Lytle dropped out.

Incantation moved bases to Pennsylvania, recruiting a new sticksman, Rick Boast of Necrotomie. The band then hooked up with Angel Corpse and Brazilians Krisiun for the nationwide 'American Diabolical Extermination' tour before Boast also left. Chris Dora stood in again for the band's 'Metal March Meltdown' set in New Jersey's Asbury Park in March 1999. In April, Mark Perry (aka Tophetareth) of Texan act Death Of Millions became the latest in a long line of Incantation drummers. A headline tour of Canada ensued, after which Perry opted out. In July 1999 Stevens also took his leave in order to resurrect Nokturnel.

For a batch of dates in Argentina, the ever-reliable Chris Dora came in on drums and Mike Saez rejoined as frontman. A 2000 album, *The Infernal Storm*, was recorded with session drummer Dave Culross of Malevolent Creation and for tour work the band pulled in Richard Christy (Death, Control Denied and Iced Earth).

Kyle Severn was back in the fold by August 2000 for American gigs with Nile and Impaled. Severn involved himself with the high-profile Wolfen Society, featuring Acheron's Vincent Crowley, Vital Remains singer Jeff Gruslin, and Dark Funeral guitarist Lord Ahriman. Severn also performed gigs with Acheron and committed to studio sessions for a single.

Incantation then geared up for a month-long tour of the States in early 2001 with Immolation and Goatwhore. However, the dates were abruptly curtailed at a gig in Queens, New York: the band's van was broken into outside the Voodoo Lounge venue before the show, and then various band-members and friends became involved in a vicious fight. Saez had stepped in to prevent a fracas involving his former Deathrune band mate Chris Shaw, who was stabbed seven times in the back and face. Saez also received major wounds to his arm. Another friend, Pete Schulz, received deep lacerations to the arm. The attacker fled from the venue but was chased and caught by Kyle Severn who apprehended the man and held him until police arrived. The injuries to Saez were so severe that the tour was cancelled. He was rushed into hospital at a later date with stomach pains but would make a full recovery.

Incantation switched labels from Relapse to Necropolis and put in a series of hugely successful Brazilian shows with Rebaellion in May 2001, after which Yench decided to relinquish his position. The Sao Paulo gig was recorded, albeit only from the soundboard, for a live album, *Live - Blasphemy In Brazil Tour 2001*. Released by Mutilation Records, it was limited to 2,000 copies, all of which quickly sold out. Joe Lombard took over bass for a set of German dates in August.

A tour in Europe for February 2002, backed up by Infernal Poetry and Iniquity, was postponed when Severn suffered a back injury. The group then embarked on a further round of American dates, headlined by Cannibal Corpse and billed alongside Dark Funeral and Pissing Razors, commencing on April 24th in Los Angeles. A new studio album, *Blasphemy*, produced by Bill Korecky, arrived in June before a headline North American trek billed as the 'Summer Of Blasphemy' tour with Impaled, Decapitated and Fall To Dead. These dates kicked off on July 25th at the Al Rosa Villa venue in Columbus, Ohio, with later shows on

INCANTATION discography

Entrantment Of Evil, Seraphic Decay SCAM 003 (USA) (1990)
Deliverance Of Horrific Prophecies, Relapse RR 012 (USA) (1991)
ONWARD TO GOLGOTHA, Relapse RR 6037-2 (Europe / USA) (1992)
MORTAL THRONE OF NAZARENE, Relapse RR 6905-2 (Europe / USA) (1994)
UPON THE THRONE OF APOCALYPSE, Relapse RR 6922-2 (USA) (1996) limited edition 1,000 copies
The Forsaken Mourning Of Angelic Anguish, Repulse RPS 020 CD (Europe) (1997), Relapse RR 6974-2 (USA) (1998)
TRIBUTE TO THE GOAT, Elegy ER02 (USA) (1997)
DIABOLICAL CONQUEST, Relapse RR 6982-2 (Europe / USA) (1998)
THE INFERNAL STORM, Relapse RR 6442-2 (Europe / USA) (2000)
LIVE – BLASPHEMY IN BRAZIL TOUR 200, Mutilation MUT 013 (Brazil) (2001) limited edition 2,000 copies
BLASPHEMY, Candlelight CANDLE070CD (UK), Necropolis NR073IC (USA) (2002)
Relapse Singles Series Vol. 3, Relapse RR 6588-2 (Europe / USA) (2004) split release with Rottrevore, Repulsion and Monstrosity
DECIMATE CHRISTENDOM, Listenable POSH 060 (Europe), Olympic Recordings OLY 0241-2 (USA) (2004)
Thieves Of The Cloth, Ibex Moon cnu (USA) (2006)
PRIMORDIAL DOMINATION, Listenable POSH 087 (Europe), Ibex Moon MRI2087 (USA) (2006)

the schedule adding Dragonlord to the bill. The news arrived shortly after the confirmation of these dates that Vincent Crowley of Acheron and Wolfen Society had joined the band. Further gigs saw the band headlining throughout Europe in August with support from Pandemia.

In February 2003 the band inducted new guitarist Lou 'Sonny' Lombardozzi, as John McEntee took over vocals. Lombardozzi was noted for playing both left- and right-handed on a unique, double-neck guitar.

In this formation the group undertook the 'Rotting With Your Christ' US tour that month, partnered with Pungent Stench, Beyond The Embrace and Rune. Incantation played in New Zealand and Australia in June but were involved in a high-speed car crash on their way to a gig in Bexley, Australia. Severn, McEntee and Lombardozzi were all injured, but not seriously. However, Severn's chest injuries forced him out of an appearance at the 'Bloodlust' festival in Sydney. Local bands were added so that Incantation could perform a shortened set with Psycroptic's Dave Haley standing in on three songs. Meanwhile, Astriaal man Gryphon took on 'Ibex Moon', a song his band had been performing live as a cover.

Incantation recovered and embarked on US dates with Funerus and Disgorge. Both McEntee and Severn doubled live duties with Funerus, a band mentored by McEntee's wife and bass player Jill. South American gigs in November saw Incantation shifting shape once more, inducting Thomas Pioli of Hemlock, Ceremonium and Obliteration repute. This was a re-recruitment for Pioli, who had earlier played bass for Incantation's 1992 'Onward To Golgotha' dates. Incantation then signed with France's Listenable Records for European licensing and inked a deal with Olympic Records for the USA in early 2004.

The band entered the Mars Recording Compound in Cleveland, Ohio, with the faithful Bill Korecky on March 5th to track their eighth album, *Decimate Christendom*, scheduled for early-July release. European shows that November, dubbed the 'Clash Of Demigods', saw the band forming up a package with Krisiun, Ragnarok and Behemoth. However, Kyle Severn was forced to withdraw from these gigs due to the death of his mother. Ilmar Uibo of the French black metal band Bloody Sign filled in on drums for the tour.

In early 2005 the band hooked up with The Chasm, Mortician and Arsis for the 'Winter Migration Broootality' US tour. The band's next tour, suitably dubbed 'European Decimation', took in April gigs throughout Italy, Portugal, the UK, Holland and Germany in partnership with Catastrophic, Funerus, Jungle Rot and Hexenhammer. Incantation then played with Hate Eternal, Krisiun, Into Eternity and All Shall Perish at US gigs in June. However, due to "legal issues" the band were forced to skip the Canadian dates of this trek, instead filling the gap with East Coast shows supported by Circle Of Dead Children and Estuary. Lombardozzi subsequently worked with Fleshtized and Castration.

Gigs in Poland during September saw support from Gortal and Sphere, before concerts in Mexico in February 2006 featuring Roberto Lizárraga of Infinitum Obscure on bass. Korecky and the band cut a new album, *Primordial Domination*, at Mars Recording Compound during April and May. US shows commencing in late May saw Incantation hooked up with Vital Remains, Sin Of Angels and New Zealanders Dawn Of Azazel. The group then announced the 'Decimate Spain' shows in July with Irredemption, after which further sessions were conducted on the new album, *Primordial Domination*.

Relapse Records reissued the classic *Onward To Golgotha* in October, adding a DVD comprising three full live sets from the 1992 line-up. Today, the band's influence is readily acknowledged.

KATAKLYSM
HYPERBLASTING CANADIANS

QUEBEC CITY DEATH METAL ACT Kataklysm debuted with the February 1992 demo tape *The Death Gate Cycle Of Reincarnation*, and this wicked slice of extreme audio more than justified their self-styled tag of "Northern hyper-blast metal". Kataklysm differentiated themselves by adding an avant-garde slant to their technical death metal and eschewing tired lyrical themes.

The initial line-up was vocalist Aquarius Sylvain Mars Venus (Sylvain Houde), guitarists Jean-François Dagenais and Stéphane Côté, bassist Maurizio Iacono and drummer Ariel Saïed. The band signed to the German Nuclear Blast label for a 1993 EP, *The Mystical Gate Of Reincarnation*, comprising the original demo tracks plus an additional song, 'The Orb Of Uncreation'. A further round of studio pre-production resulted in the *Vortex Of Resurrection* demo. By this juncture the band was down to a quartet, having lost the services of Côté (who formed Obscene Crisis) and introducing Max Duhamel on drums for 'Vision The Chaos', a 1994 7-inch single issued by the Boundless label.

Promoting the February 1995 *Sorcery* album, Kataklysm put in European shows including dates with Deicide and became the first Canadian band to tour Mexico. Duhamel was then forced to leave the band in late 1995 due to cartilage damage to his right knee. His replacement was an American, Nick Miller. This line-up laid down the June 1996 album *Temple Of Knowledge (Kataklysm Part III)*. Unfortunately, their next product, the in-concert *Northern Hyperblast Live*, was a barely-treated soundboard recording, damaging their ascent somewhat.

By 1998 Duhamel had returned and the band welcomed new bassist Stéphane Barbe. However, this was followed by the exit of Sylvain Houde, and Iacono took over the vocals. This marked a change of pace toward a more commercial orientation. The band switched to the Canadian Hypnotic label for the experimental *Victims Of The Fallen World* album in October 1998, but this record saw limited distribution, not even gaining a US release.

KATAKLYSM discography

The Mystical Gate Of Reincarnation, Nuclear Blast NB 0093-2 (Europe), Nuclear Blast America 6090 (USA) (1993)

Vision The Chaos, Boundless TG 002 (Europe) (1994)

SORCERY, Nuclear Blast NB 0108-2 (Europe), Nuclear Blast America 6877 (USA) (1995)

TEMPLE OF KNOWLEDGE (KATAKLYSM PART III), Nuclear Blast NB 0157-2 (Europe), Nuclear Blast America 6157 (USA) (1996)

VICTIMS OF THIS FALLEN WORLD, Hypnotic HYP 1064 (Canada) (1998)

NORTHERN HYPERBLAST LIVE, Hypnotic HYP 1069 (Canada) (1998)

THE PROPHECY (STIGMATA OF THE IMMACULATE), Nuclear Blast NB 0470-2 (Europe), Nuclear Blast America 6470 (USA) (2000)

EPIC: THE POETRY OF WAR, Nuclear Blast NB 0621-2 (Europe), Nuclear Blast America 6621 (USA) (2001)

SHADOWS & DUST, Nuclear Blast NB 1032-2 (Europe), Nuclear Blast America 1032 (USA) (2002)

SERENITY IN FIRE, Nuclear Blast NB 1227-2 (Europe), Nuclear Blast America 1227 (USA) (2004)

IN THE ARMS OF DEVASTATION, Nuclear Blast NB 1527-2 (Europe), Nuclear Blast America 1527 (USA) (2006)

Re-signing with Nuclear Blast, Kataklysm cut *The Prophecy (Stigmata Of The Immaculate)* in April 2000 at Montreal's Victor Studios. Guests included Rob the Witch of Necronomicon and Mike DiSalvo of Cryptopsy. A place on the European 'Nuclear Blast' festivals with Hypocrisy, Raise Hell, Destruction and Crematory followed, and three tracks from these concerts were later used on a DVD.

Touring to promote September 2001's *Epic (The Poetry Of War)* – a concept album tackling the Roman Empire – Kataklysm put in a run of Canadian dates commencing in Quebec on August 4th. American dates were scheduled with Marduk, but the band later backed down from these shows.

Kataklysm then announced the recording of a fresh album, *Shadows And Dust*, for September 2002. The Roman motif was still at the forefront – opening track 'In Shadows And Dust' used the *Gladiator* movie theme as its intro. Dagenais then produced Malevolent Creation's excellent *The Will To Kill* album.

The band headlined the summer 2002 'Death Across America' dates, backed up by Beyond The Embrace, Misery Index and Divine Empire. Canadian gigs saw strong support from Montreal's Necromonicon and Toronto's Blood Of Christ. The band put in a short batch of UK dates packaged with Hate Eternal and Deranged before forming part of an impressive cast for European 'Xmass Festivals' in December with Six Feet Under, Immolation, Marduk and Hate. Later gigs in Holland added veteran thrashers Exodus to the bill. Meantime, Iacono's solo project L.O.S.T., having now switched names to Stamina, was being courted by various major labels.

The band united with Hate Eternal, Dying Fetus, and Into Eternity for North American dates in February and March 2003. Drummer Duhamel retired from the band in late January and J.F. Richard of Ion Dissonance filled in at short notice. Martin Maurais was enrolled as a permanent replacement in March.

Kataklysm united with The Haunted, Shai Hulud and Skinless for extensive US dates throughout the summer. In August the group was back on the festival circuit in Europe with appearances at the German Wacken

Open Air and Partysan events with a headliner at the Czech Brutal Assault meeting. Canadian headline gigs preceded a showing at the Las Vegas Metalfest before the recording of a new album. The band also revealed that they had been commissioned to record the theme song to the horror movie *Female Flesh Eaters*. This renewed flush of success for the band saw them securing a further long-term album deal with Nuclear Blast in July.

A run of US headline dates was cut short in late September as they headed into the studio to commence work on *Serenity In Fire*, for which Hypocrisy's Peter Tägtgren donated a guest vocal on the track 'For All Our Sins'. Dagenais made time in early 2004 to donate his services to the Death tribute album, *Within The Mind*, assembled by James Murphy.

The band then formed part of the 'No More Serenity' headline tour, presented by *Metal Maniacs* magazine in March 2004, alongside Misery Index, Cannae and Through The Discipline. Further promotion came with a video for the track 'As I Slither'. European dates alongside Crowbar and an appearance at the 'With Full Force' open air festival in Germany were cancelled when the estimated birth-date of Iacono's baby was brought forward.

The band spent the summer re-recording their debut album, *Victims Of This Fallen World*. Believing that the demise of the Hypnotic label had consigned the record to the vaults forever, the group decided to re-craft the entire record from scratch to make it available again. However, they were less than pleased when in August the original version, alongside *Northern Hyperblast Live*, was licensed for a re-release through Linus Entertainment. Kataklysm asked fans to boycott this release.

After European gigs with Mystic Circle, Into Eternity and Graveworm, US tours in October saw the band flanking Napalm Death and Goatwhore, with off-days from this trek plugged by gigs with Macabre. Opening up 2005, the band toured the USA in February partnered with Danzig and Trivium. Working up songs for a new album, *In The Arms Of Devastation*, the band parted ways with drummer Martin Maurais due to "personal and professional reasons" and brought back Max Duhamel. The same month,

official recognition came the band's way when they won the Best Metal Group category at the Canadian Indie Music Awards.

European headline gigs in June came with support from Graveworm and Eminence. The band entered the studio on July 10th to record *In The Arms Of Devastation*, featuring a guest vocal from Kittie's Morgan Lander and contributions from Tim Roth and Rob Doherty of Into Eternity.

The band then toured as part of the December 2005 'X-Mass' festivals in Europe alongside resurrected UK thrashers Onslaught, Exodus, Occult, Unleashed, Behemoth, and Primordial. The group also formed part of the European 'No Mercy' package for dates across Germany, Austria, France, Switzerland, Belgium and Holland in April, alongside Cannibal Corpse, Grimfist and Legion Of The Damned. These shows were swiftly followed up by dates supporting Bolt Thrower. However, Kataklysm pulled out of the dates at the end of the tour for "reasons beyond the band's control". They were included on the 'Metal Crusaders' North American tour in May and June 2006 alongside Vader, Graveworm, Nuclear Assault, Speed\Kill/Hate and The Absence.

Still retaining an appetite for the road, Kataklysm teamed up with Neaera, Fear My Thoughts and fellow Canadians Quo Vadis for the 'Road To Devastation' European tour in January 2007, where they were set to receive more support from their fanbase.

MACABRE
MURDEROUS MUSIC

CHICAGO'S MACABRE ARE noted for their ultra-extreme music, dubbed by the band as 'murder metal' and based on an almost obsessive theme of serial murderers. Frontman C.D. ('Corporate Death') owns several paintings by the serial killer John Wayne Gacy, given to him personally by the murderer, who was executed in 1994. C.D. even attended the trial of

MACABRE discography

Grim Reality, Decomposed M-1 (USA) (1987)
Shit List, Gore GORE 001 (Europe) (1988)
GLOOM, Vinyl Solution SOL 020 (UK) (1989)
Nightstalker, Relapse RR 021 (USA) (1993)
SINISTER SLAUGHTER, Nuclear Blast NB 070 (Europe), Nuclear Blast America 6060 (USA) (1993)
Behind The Wall Of Sleep, Nuclear Blast NB 109-3 (Europe), Nuclear Blast America 6891 (USA) (1994)
Unabomber, Hammerheart HHR 030 (Europe), Decomposed DR-003 (USA) (1999)
DAHMER, Hammerheart HHR 071 (Europe), Olympic Recordings OLY 0213-2 (USA) (2000)
Macabre, D.B.D. DBD-001 (USA) (2001) split EP with Capitalist Casualties
Morbid Campfire Songs, Decomposed cnu (USA) (2002)
Drill Bit Lobotomy, Hater Of God HOG-19 (USA) (2003)
MURDER METAL, Season Of Mist SOM 076 (Europe), Season Of Mist America 76 (USA) (2003)

Jeffrey Dahmer for inspiration. The singer employs a lunatic, histrionic vocal style guaranteed to give any listener the chills. Macabre is rounded out by bassist Nefarious and Dennis The Menace on drums.

The band opened their own perverse Little Shop Of Horrors in 1987 with the Decomposed label EP *Grim Reality*, by which early stage their serial-killer fetish was already much in evidence, with odes to Ed Gein, Albert Fish and the Son Of Sam set to a blizzard of punk and grindcore. Ingeniously, the track 'Mass Murder' was in fact a triptych of instrumentals – 'Sulphuric Acid' being a guitar solo, 'Morbid Curiosity' a bass solo and, naturally, 'Lethal Injection' a closing drum solo.

Some 1987 demos, titled *Shit List*, were released as a 7-inch single in 1988, subsequently reissued by Gore Records in 1990 in a limited run of 777 copies on white vinyl. Meanwhile, UK label Vinyl Solutions issued the full-length *Gloom* album. Macabre's appreciation for the world's most loathsome examples of humanity now extended to expressions of admiration for Harvey Glatman, David Brom, Patrick Purdy, Fritz Haarman and the elusive Green River murderer.

Macabre switched to the then-fledgling Nuclear Blast label for the April 1993 *Sinister Slaughter* outing, a veritable bloodbath in homage to 20 of their preferred mass murderers. Jacket artwork cleverly spoofed The Beatles' *Sgt. Pepper* montage, substituting celebrities with individuals of a much more malevolent nature. A July 1994 follow-up EP, *Behind The Wall Of Sleep*, included the band's first cover version, a remake of the Black Sabbath title track.

Macabre slunk back into the shadows until 1999, re-emerging with the *Unabomber* mini-album. The *Dahmer* album of 2000, produced by Neil Kernon, was a concept based around the twisted life of the cannibalistic mass murderer Jeffrey Dahmer and probably the first death metal album to include a twisted remake of a song from *Charlie And The Chocolate Factory*. The long out of print *Grim Reality* was remixed by Neil Kernon for release in 2002 on Decomposed. A further outing, *Morbid Campfire Songs*, provided an unexpected slant on the formula, as a clutch of acoustic renditions credited to the Macabre Minstrels duo of Corporate Death and Nefarious.

The band confirmed a string of dates in Holland and an appearance at the German 'Wacken Open Air' festival, before November 2002 shows saw the group on the road in North America on a package with Cannibal Corpse, Cattle Decapitation and Hate Eternal. Macabre released the

Murder Metal album in 2003 through French label Season Of Mist.

A run of European gigs in January and February 2004 had Macabre allied with Polterchrist, Cephalic Carnage and Brutus. These shows included the band's first UK performance for more than a decade, at London's Camden Underworld. US shows into March hooked the group up with Premonitions Of War, The End and Rune.

Macabre teamed up with Dutch death metallers The Monolith Deathcult and British act Screamin' Demon for UK shows in August and September 2005. Their August 26th show at the Bibelot in Dordrecht, Holland was filmed for the DVD release *Live in Holland – True Tales of Slaughter And Slaying*, issued in July 2006. The murder metal saga continues.

MALEVOLENT CREATION
THE WILL TO KILL CONTINUES

A FEROCIOUS AND UNCOMPROMISING death metal act founded in Buffalo, New York, Malevolent Creation centred on former Resthaven guitarist Phil Fasciana and vocalist Brett Hoffmann. The initial line-up, created in 1987, also featured second guitarist John Rubin, bass player Mark Van Erp and drummer Mark Simpson. A demo in 1989 with three tracks – 'Injected Sufferage', 'Epileptic Seizure' and 'Violent Offspring' – saw restricted distribution of just 100 cassettes. Another three-song set followed, simply dubbed *Demo 1990*, clinching a contract with Roadrunner.

Roadrunner installed the band in their Florida death metal hit factory Morrisound to cut tracks under the guidance of Scott Burns. Malevolent Creation's commercial debut, *The Ten Commandments*, was delivered in September 1990, although the band had shifted shape, with Jeff Juszkiewicz taking Rubin's post and Jason Blachowicz substituting for Van

Erp. The album highlighted Malevolent Creation's obvious affection for Bay Area thrash metal, with the band often coming across like an accelerated Slayer. Hoffmann's glass-cutting screeches offered an alternative to the by-now-commonplace death metal growls.

Guitarist Juszkiewicz parted ways with the band in 1991. Swede Peter Tägtgren also played in Malevolent Creation, as well as Meltdown, but returned to his home country to found Hypocrisy (initially named Seditious). In order to complete a planned American tour with Devastation and Demolition Hammer, the band temporarily pulled in the services of Monstrosity guitarist, and former Malevolent Creation member, John Rubin. For April 1992's *Retribution*, again hacked out at Morrisound with Burns at the board, the band utilised the services of the Solstice and Abysmal-credited guitarist Rob Barrett and drummer Alex Marquez.

Stillborn, retaining a stable line-up plus the addition of Rubin, but now engineered by Mark Pinske, followed in October 1993. Reviews were unkind for a meandering record that lacked the enthusiastic bite of its forerunners and battled a muddy, reverb-drenched production. Naturally, Malevolent Creation hit the live circuit to promote the record, including a stop at the Milwaukee 'Metalfest', three tracks from which surfaced on a four-way split album, *Live Death*, issued via Restless Records in collaboration with Cancer, Exhorder and Suffocation. In 1994 both Fasciana and Barrett ensconced themselves in the studio with drummer 'Crazy' Larry Hawke in a side project, Hateplow. Tragically, Hawke perished in May 1997, killed while attempting to save his dog in a house fire.

By 1995 Malevolent Creation had parted ways with both Roadrunner (to hook up with the Pavement label) and vocalist Hoffmann (who subsequently busied himself with Swiss act Silent Death). Demos were recorded with bassist Jason Blachowicz handling lead vocals and ex-Disgorged, Suffocation and R.I.P. drummer Dave Culross: this formation then put down tracks for the August 1996 offering *Eternal*. After a switch of bases, this self-produced album was executed at Criteria and Inner Face Studios. The 1997 compilation album *Joe Black*, a retrospective of rare tracks, demos and a take on Slayer's 'Raining Blood', then appeared as a limited edition release.

Malevolent Creation's subsequent line-up, which now included drummer Derek Roddy, saw the band trimmed down, with only Blaschowicz and Fasciana remaining. Roddy also sessioned for Aurora Borealis and later Nile. The Paingod and Creature-credited John Paul Soars was installed on guitar for a new Malevolent Creation studio album, *In Cold Blood*, released in 1997.

Hoffmann returned for 1998's *The Fine Art Of Murder* alongside Fasciana, Barrett, bassist Gordon Simms and drummer Dave Culross. Blachowicz, Soars and Roddy then united to forge Divine Empire, releasing two albums – *Redemption* and *Doomed To Inherit*. Soars also operated with Solstice, Burner and Wynjara.

In 2000, Dave Culross aided Incantation, laying down session drums for their *Infernal Storm* album. The same year found Culross in collusion with Fasciana and Barrett for the Hateplow album *The Only Law Is Survival*. Malevolent Creation released the *Envenomed* album in 2000.

In a display of brotherhood, Hateplow supported Malevolent Creation on their February 2001 headlining shows across Europe. On his return, Hoffmann was arrested upon entry into the United States and imprisoned for parole violation dating back to 1995. The incarceration of their vocalist forced Malevolent Creation to withdraw from a series of American dates with Monstrosity. This latest incident involving Hoffmann eventually triggered his removal from the band for a second time, Hateplow's Kyle Symons taking over vocals in January 2002. In late 2001 Blachowicz, newly freed from jail after an assault charge, created the female-fronted Wykked Wytch.

The band were part of the European 'No Mercy' touring festival in March and April 2002 with Vader, Catastrophic, Destroyer 666, Hypocrisy,

Disbelief, Immortal and Obscenity. Jean-François Dagenais of Canadian act Kataklysm was confirmed as producer for 2002's *The Will To Kill*, and a Polish tour in October saw the band playing with Vomitory and Septic Flesh. Although Justin DiPinto had handled drums in the studio, Ariel Alvarado subsequently assumed the role.

Meanwhile, Dave Culross was making news with two extreme metal ventures, one an alliance with guitarists Jason Brennan and Frank Maggio (previously with Iron Lung, Evil Eye and Social Disease) and a separate venture with Slipknot guitarist Mick Thompson.

Breaking a five-year hiatus, the band toured the Southern states of the USA as support to Cannibal Corpse in December. Malevolent Creation

Malevolent Creation

continued this run of shows throughout January and February 2003, supported at various stages by Bloodlet, Reflux, Dead To Fall, Between The Buried And Me and Deeds Of Flesh.

Their resurgence progressed as the band, now with Nile drummer Tony Laureano on board, were confirmed as participants in the April 2003 European 'No Mercy' festivals with Testament, Marduk, Death Angel, Pro-Pain, Nuclear Assault, Darkane and Callenish Circle. Meanwhile Hoffmann and Culross participated in the Death tribute album assembled by James Murphy.

The band embarked on their first Brazilian tour since 1991 during July, recording shows for future DVD and live-album use and re-signing with Nuclear Blast for a 2004 studio album. Dave Culross then returned to the fold and Jeff Juszkiewicz made a return with his Atlanta-based sludge trio Tualatin. Scandinavian shows in June saw the band partnered with Dying Fetus.

Two ex-Malevolent Creation drummers were in the news, with Alex Marquez linking up with his former Solstice bandmate Dennis Munoz in a 1980s-style thrash outfit with a working title of Apocalypse Rising. The quartet was completed by second guitarist Willy Medina and bass player Mike Marabell. Meanwhile, Culross's band Pummel, working with ex-Iron Lung and Social Disease guitarist Frank Maggio, saw vocalist Tom Bush, bassist Mark Astrin and second guitarist Steve Seigerman completing the line-up.

Malevolent Creation's July 2004 *Warkult* album, recorded at Liquid Ghost Studio in Boca Raton, Florida, included a cover rendition of 'Jack The Ripper' by cult Australian band Hobbs' Angel Of Death. Summer festival appearances in Europe included 'Rock Hard', 'With Full Force' and 'Up From The Ground' in Germany, 'Skeleton Bash' in Austria, 'Fury Fest' in France, 'Graspop Metal Meeting' in Belgium and 'Rock The Nations' in Istanbul. The band cancelled the latter show when the promoter failed to supply enough travel tickets for the band to get to the venue.

Further misfortune struck when a planned London Underworld headlining show was cancelled as violent storms in the English channel prevented ferry crossings from France. Returning to the USA, Malevolent Creation commenced live work with a *Warkult* release party on July 24th at Fort Lauderdale's Culture Room. Meanwhile, a live album, *Conquering South America*, recorded during the band's 2001 tour of Brazil and engineered by Jean-François Dagenais, surfaced in September.

In October 2004, Apocalypse Rising's Alex Marquez and Dennis Munoz allied with Fasciana and former Malevolent Creation drummer Gus Rios in a new band. Brett Hoffmann also resurfaced in January 2005, touting a demo from his new band Down The Drain. Summer 2005 dates, commencing in Florida in early July, had Malevolent Creation packaged with Origin, Divine Empire and Animosity. In September the band made a concert return to Puerto Rico at the Mayaguez University Plaza, supported by Inflammatory and Sepulchral, this being the first time in over a decade that the band had played on the island. The following month there were more changes as they lost guitarist Rob Barrett to Cannibal Corpse and bassist Gordon Simms, swiftly replacing them with returning members John Rubin on guitar and Jason Blachowicz on bass.

European shows in January and February 2006 witnessed strong backing from Bolt Thrower, Nightrage and Necrophagist. For these gigs the group welcomed back original vocalist Brett Hoffmann. Malevolent Creation are now one of the most reliable death metal bands on the planet.

MASSACRE
INFLUENTIAL DEATH METAL PIONEERS

DEATH METAL ACT MASSACRE were created by some ex-Death members: vocalist Kam Lee (aka Barney Lee), guitarist Rick Rozz (Frederick DeLillo), bassist Terry Butler and drummer Bill Andrews. In common with their previous band, Massacre relied on precision riffing

MASSACRE discography

FROM BEYOND, Earache MOSH027CD (UK), Relativity/Earache 88561-2038-2 (USA) (1991)
Inhuman Conditions, Earache MOSH060CD (UK), Relativity/Earache 88561-1110-2 (USA) (1992)
PROMISE, Earache, MOSH096CD (UK / USA) (1996)

and the trademark Florida crunch, but Lee was also something of a catalyst as one of the originators of the death metal growl (along with Possessed's Jeff Becerra). Despite their importance, Massacre's reputation rests merely on one album and one EP.

Massacre were first assembled as a covers band, comprising singer Mark Brents, Allen West and the Obituary-credited JP Chartier on guitar, bassist Scott Blackwood and drummer Andrews. Brents and Blackwood were dispensed with and Michael Borders took over the bass. Border's formative acts included Cyanide, alongside the pre-Six Feet Under Allen West and Greg Gall. Pre-Death, Rozz had operated with Thatcher

This line-up debuted live with two back-to-back gigs: the first supported by Executioner (who later, via Xecutioner, became known as Obituary); the second as openers to Morbid Angel. Hawaiian native Lee was pulled in as frontman in early 1985. This version of Massacre recorded an inaugural March 1986 demo cassette, featuring 'Aggressive Tyrant', 'Mutilated' and 'Death In Hell'. Chartier then exited and Trevor Peres from Obituary was auditioned but not asked to join the band.

Massacre's second demo, *Chamber Of Ages*, was recorded that November and marked the introduction of Death and Genitorturers guitarist Rick Rozz. In addition, a six-song live cassette was recorded at Streets Club in April 1986, the group's first gig with Kam Lee and Rick Rozz. Interestingly, Massacre's live set at this time included the Death song 'Corpse Grinder'. The band were also experimenting once again with a twin guitar sound, with the vacancy briefly filled by Robbie Goodwin. Rumours that they had signed to Cobra Records for an album titled *From Beyond* proved premature.

Borders was superseded by Butler, and Goodwin departed. In 1987 the band were put on hold while Rozz, Butler and Andrews sessioned on Death's *Leprosy* album. Lee then formed Abhorrent Existence with Pete Slate of Acheron and Mark Lavenia from Incubus and Equinox.

Within the year Massacre got back into gear, with Lee and Rozz flanked by new members Butch Gonzales on bass and former Whiplash man Joey Cangelosi on drums. However, both Terry Butler and Bill Andrews were soon back in the fold. Massacre got back into the studio on November 9th 1990 to put down six songs for the *Second Coming* demo. Distributed to a variety of labels, this session met with an offer from UK label Earache.

Massacre's first and only album, *From Beyond*, appeared in July 1991, comprising nine tracks, with the first pressing boosted by a single-track 7-inch single of 'Provoked Accurser'. Now afforded international exposure, the band were set apart by their unique qualities: Lee's inhuman roar and Rozz's mechanical riffing. Constructed at Morrisound in Tampa and helmed by British producer Colin Richardson, *From Beyond* bridged the gap between thrash and what was rapidly being recognised as a whole new species – death metal.

The band's first European tour, now with second guitarist Steve Swanson, saw Texans Devastation and German act Morgoth in support. The 1992 EP *Inhuman Condition* featured a version of Venom's 'Warhead' with that band's singer Cronos on vocals. Massacre toured Europe in 1993 on a package bill with Grave and Demolition Hammer. Upon their return the band folded, with Rozz creating Mindsweep.

Massacre: death metal pioneers

MISERY INDEX discography

Overthrow, Anarchos ANA 001 (USA) (2001), Fadeless FAD 008 CD (Europe) (2002)

Created To Kill, Bones Brigade BB 014 CD (Europe) (2002) split release with Drowning, Brodequin and Aborted

Misery Index / Commit Suicide, Willowtip WT-015 (USA) (2002) split single with Commit Suicide

Misery Index / Structure Of Lies, Deep Six DS-48 (USA) (2003) split single with Structure Of Lies

RETALIATE, Nuclear Blast NB 1122-2 (Europe), Nuclear Blast America 1122 (USA) (2003)

Dissent, Anarchos ANA 003 (USA) (2004)

Misery Index / Bathtub Shitter, Emetic cnu (USA) (2006) split single with Bathtub Shitter

DISCORDIA, Relapse RR 6675-2 (Europe / USA) (2006)

For July 1996's *Promise* reformation album, actually recorded at Wolf's Head Studio some two years earlier, Massacre drafted in two new members – bassist Pete Sison and drummer Syrus Peters. Unfortunately the record, a lethargic sub-gothic affair complete with a curious rendering of Concrete Blonde's 'Bloodletting' with guest vocals from Christine Whitten, signalled a radical shift away from the band's former glories and was savaged by fans and media alike. The band struggled on, however, pulling in vocalist-guitarist Kenny Goodwin, but soon collapsed.

Lee continued to work on the Florida metal scene, and by 2000 the frontman had created a swathe of acts including Kauldron, Cadaverizer, Urizen and Soul Skinner.

In April 2006, Lee and Butler were reported to have formed retro thrash/death metal combo Denial Fiend, co-assembled by an elite cast comprising guitarist Sam Williams, previously with Down By Law, and erstwhile Nasty Savage drummer Curt Beeson. The Massacre legend remains intact.

MISERY INDEX
GLOOMCORE PIONEERS?

MISERY INDEX WERE FORMED in Baltimore by sometime Dying Fetus/Suffocation drummer Kevin Talley, Dying Fetus bassist-vocalist Jason Netherton and guitarist Mike Harrison, a veteran of acts such as Mainframe, Cadaver Symposium, Pessimist, Autumn Dawn and Sadistic Torment.

For the 2001 *Overthrow* EP, released on their own Anarcho label, the new band were rounded off by second guitarist Sparky Voyles of M.O.D., Dying Fetus, Fear Of God and Sadistic Torment. Both Voyles and Talley were involved in a fleeting M.O.D. reunion in summer 2001 but soon returned to action with Misery Index.

During December 2001 Voyles instigated two side projects – a black metal unit entitled True Unholy Death in league with Pessimist drummer John Gordon, and a grindcore act named Criminal Element working with Dying Fetus vocalist Vince Matthews.

In early 2002 the band cut two new tracks plus a cover version of Disrupt's 'Reality Distortion' for a split EP in union with Commit Suicide. Voyles then left the True Unholy Death project. The *Overthrow* mini-album was then reissued as a limited-edition 12-inch vinyl LP through Good Life Recordings. The special edition included the full *Overthrow* roster of tracks on the A-side while the flip featured recordings from an 88.9 WERS Emerson College Radio live session cut in April.

Kevin Talley auditioned for the drummer vacancy in Slayer during spring 2002, apparently coming close to securing the job. Misery Index then formed part of the fifth annual 'Death Across America' dates in summer 2002 headlined by Kataklysm and backed up by Beyond The Embrace and Divine Empire.

In September the band announced a deal with the German Nuclear Blast label for a new album. *Retaliate* was recorded at Wild Studios in St. Zenon, Quebec with Kataklysm's Jean-François Dagenais as producer. With the departure of Mike Harrison and Kevin Talley, the latter going on to session on Daath's *Futility* album, a new cast was unveiled including second guitarist Bruce Greig, previously with Dying Fetus, Together We Fall and Next Step Up, alongside drummer Matt Byers. Talley had exited to pursue a more rock-orientated project billed Grayson Manor. The revamped Misery Index's first move was to plot a split single release in league with Arizona's Structure Of Lies.

Misery Index then co-headlined a North American tour in May 2003, completing a bill of Skinless, Divine Empire and Dying Fetus. The band were confirmed for the 2003 'X-Mass Festivals' European tour commencing in London on December 7th, alongside Destruction, Amon Amarth, Nile, Deicide, Dew-Scented, Graveworm and Disbelief.

During November, former Misery Index guitarist-vocalist Mike Harrison made a return, announcing his new outfit Kommissar. Drummer Matt Byers parted ways with Misery Index in March 2004, and former drummer Kevin Talley filled in while a replacement was found. By June, Talley was inducted back into the fold as a full-time member. The band hit further line-up problems the following month, when guitarist Greig exited. Misery Index duly re-inducted former member Mike Harrison for the remaining dates, the new band debuting at a July 21st date in Buffalo, New York. Unfortunately the band's problems in the drum department would continue as Talley bailed out to join Chimaira before the close of the month. A swift replacement was located in Adam Jarvis from St. Louis band All Will Fall.

The band put together a limited 10-inch vinyl and CD EP, *Dissent*, released through the group's own Anarchos Records. Besides the epic 13-

minute title track, the EP also featured Quicktime movies of live and studio footage. *Misery Index DVD Volume 1* was also on its way, featuring a live set recorded in Athens in 2003. Back on the road, Misery Index teamed up with Neuraxis for a short Canadian tour in late October.

The year 2005 saw more intensive touring, commencing with a round of February concerts with Suffocation, Behemoth and Cattle Decapitation before an announced collaboration with Immolation, Skinless, With Passion and Deicide for US dates in May. To boost their sound, the band drafted in touring guitarist Mark Kloeppel of Cast The Stone. However, in their own words, they were "booted" from the Deicide tour in early April and duly set about a short burst of headliners with Magrudergrind and Rotten Sound.

Byers and Greig bounced back onto the scene with Covenance, a collaboration with ex-Dying Fetus singer Vince Matthews. Meanwhile, Misery Index ended their business relationship with Nuclear Blast in September.

Japanese gigs in March 2006 had the band paired with Montreal's Neuraxis. That same month they put in their live debut in Puerto Rico with a brace of shows in Quebradillas and Catano, while Kevin Talley joined the ranks of Hate Eternal. In May, Misery Index released a new album, *Discordia*. Both vinyl versions and the Japanese release had an extra track, a cover version of Nasum's 'Digging In'.

Misery Index lent support to Fear Factory's extensive round of European and UK dates beginning at the end of March. The US road campaign throughout the summer was unrelenting: in mid May the band played with Disfear, Phobia and Strong Intention before uniting on June 10th with From A Second Story Window, Cattle Decapitation, Animosity and Job For A Cowboy for a run of gigs into mid July. Concerts in November were backed by Intronaut and Swarm Of The Lotus. The band seem set for new adventures in the near future.

MONSTROSITY
BRUTAL DEATH SCENE-LEADERS

MONSTROSITY ARE A BRUTAL TAMPA death metal band who, despite the fluid nature of the rest of their line-up, remain centred upon drummer Lee Harrison. Regarded as among the very finest practitioners of the genre, Monstrosity have focused their efforts on precision rather than quantity of output.

The group were created during August 1990 in Fort Lauderdale with George 'Corpsegrinder' Fisher handling lead vocals, nicknamed after one

Monstrosity

MONSTROSITY discography

Darkest Dream, Nuclear Blast NB 055 (Europe) (1992)
IMPERIAL DOOM, Nuclear Blast NB 055-2 (Europe), Nuclear Blast America 6032 (USA) (1992)
Burden Of Evil, Relapse RR 011 (USA) (1992)
MILLENNIUM, Nuclear Blast NB 0208-2 (Europe), Conquest Music CM 9301 (USA) (1996)
IN DARK PURITY, Metal Age Recordings 300108-2 (Europe), Slipdisc 008 638 002-2 (USA) (1999)
ENSLAVING THE MASSES, Hammerheart HHR 088 (Europe), Conquest Music CM 43434 (USA) (2001)
LIVE EXTREME BRAZILIAN - TOUR 2002, Mutilation 027 (Brazil) (2002)
RISE TO POWER, Metal Blade 3984-14481-2 (Europe), Conquest Music CM 2 5124 (USA) (2003)
Relapse Singles Series Vol. 3, Relapse RR 6588-2 (Europe / USA) (2004) split release with Rottrevore, Repulsion and Incantation

of his early bands. They debuted in 1991 with the *Horror Infinity* demo, laying down four tracks at Miami's Natural Sound Studios.

That same summer the group relocated to Tampa. Monstrosity guitarist Jon Rubin stood in for Malevolent Creation on a temporary basis for their 1991 North American tour and teamed up with that band on a frequent ad hoc basis before finally joining the band full-time.

Cynic guitarist Jason Gobel guested on Monstrosity's *Imperial Doom* album, their debut for German label Nuclear Blast, recorded at the familiar Morrisound Studios. He also acted as live fill-in for a solitary date opening for Pestilence and Death. Gobel was subsequently replaced by Mark English for their European tour with Pestilence in 1992. The undeniable quality of *Imperial Doom* helped it permeate the metal underground, generating sales in excess of 50,000.

Monstrosity bassist Mark Van Erp was then busted on a drugs charge, caught in possession of two ounces of cocaine, and was unable to travel outside America. The band swiftly hired Cannibal Corpse guitarist Rob Barrett to handle bass, including shows in Lima, Peru and Canada in 1995. Touring in Europe saw the band utilising Death's Kelly Conlon on bass.

For the 1996 *Millennium* album, issued via Conquest Music in the USA and Nuclear Blast in Europe, Monstrosity drafted in guitarist Jason Morgan. Lead vocals were recorded by Fisher but after his defection to Cannibal Corpse the band pulled in former Eulogy man Jason Avery for live work. During this time the band hired former Nevermore and Chastain guitarist Pat O'Brien to conduct a 1997 tour with Vader and Broken Hope. However, once these dates were fulfilled O'Brien also decamped to Cannibal Corpse.

Following 1999's *In Dark Purity*, which closed with a cover of Slayer's 'Angel Of Death', Morgan departed to join Morbid Angel and Hate Eternal guitarist Erik Rutan's Alas project. Initially, Monstrosity worked with Brutality's Jay Fernandez in the studio, but then they drafted in one-time Eternal guitarist Tony Norman. After the album sessions, the band fired Conlon and substituted him with Mike Poggione of Execration, Scab Maggot and Capharnum.

The band headed out on a US headline trek throughout September and October 1999, backed by Dimmu Borgir, Samael and Epoch Of Unlight. Meanwhile, Morgan created Wynjara for a 2000 album, while Conlon briefly joined Vital Remains in 2001.

Monstrosity's December 2000 US tour included Newport death metal act Desecration in support. After crafting the 2001 live album *Enslaving The Masses*, which also hosted archive demo material, Avery quit to concentrate on his career as a tattooist. The band then hired Sam Molina, known as guitarist with Fort Meyers act Calibos, to take on lead vocals.

During July and August 2001, Monstrosity led the 'Bloodletting North America Part 2' tour alongside Deeds Of Flesh, Dutchmen Pyaemia, Odious Sanction and Sabbatic Feast. The band joined forces with Dying Fetus, Vader and Krisiun and Houwitser for the 'Intervalle Bizarre' European tour during September and October.

October 2002 saw the band heading up a ten-date tour of Poland backed by a cast of Vomitory, Trauma, Sceptic, Lost Soul, Dissenter and Contempt. Conlon joined Boston-based progressive metal act Infinity Minus One the same month.

Guitarist Tony Norman undertook tour work with gothic black metal outfit Lover Of Sin in Europe during March 2003. Meanwhile, Monstrosity welcomed Jason Avery back to the fold that same month. His replacement, Sam Molina, stayed on as second guitarist. This revised line-up were due to break themselves in with a show in Puerto Rico in May. Monstrosity's latest album, *Rise To Power*, arrived in September. Norman once more subbed himself out that year, joining forces with Morbid Angel for November US dates.

Still promoting *Rise To Power*, the band geared up for a run of 2004 European dates, beginning on May 1st in Zwickau, Germany, partnered with Dark Disciple. Unfortunately the tour was cancelled on May 4th with only a handful of dates completed. In a rare admission, a statement confirmed that "turnouts have been too bad; losing money day by day is no fun for the bands". Avery quit Monstrosity after the tour. He was later replaced by Brian Werner.

Bassist Mike Poggione, retaining his Monstrosity links, also teamed up with Lecherous Nocturne and toured with Trivium as a session bassist in 2004. Tony Norman joined the reunited Terrorizer in late 2005. Monstrosity lined up with Deeds Of Flesh, Vile and Impaled for the 'Gutting Europe 4: Triumph In Black' European tour beginning in Poland during late March 2006. Despite the fractious nature of their existence, Monstrosity have a spirit that seems impervious to all adversity.

MORBID ANGEL
ECCENTRIC BUT TALENTED GENRE PIONEERS

DEATH METAL ACT MORBID ANGEL, founded in Tampa during 1984, broke down the barriers between extreme music and commercial success. They later blew their chances of entering the big league after a series of alleged remarks by frontman David Vincent, which were said to be fascist in nature. The world's rock media, in spite of the band's denials, erupted in an outcry against these supposedly rightwing tendencies. Despite the controversy, Morbid Angel racked up combined sales of over a million albums by 1998.

The band came together at high school under the name Ice, with Trey Azagthoth (real name George Emmanuel III), Dallas Ward and Mike Browning. They subsequently adopted the title Heretic before discovering another band of the same name. At this juncture Azagthoth suggested Morbid Angel. The band's inaugural gigs found them honing their skills with cover versions of songs by Angel Witch, Slayer and Mercyful Fate.

Having performed initially as a trio, the group then brought in singer Kenny Bamber to record a 1985 two-song demo of 'Demon Seed' and 'Welcome To Hell'. Bamber exited and Morbid Angel persevered as an instrumental act before Ward took on the vocals. In August 1985 a demo billed *The Beginning* consisted of a hotch-potch of tracks, featuring vocals from both Bamber and Ward. Next in line for the frontman role was vocalist-guitarist Richard Brunelle.

Unfortunately, Ward was then convicted of a drugs offence and incarcerated. This measure forced the band to re-think and, pulling in

John Ortega as second guitarist, Brunelle was given the vocal role. At one stage Morbid Angel fleetingly rehearsed with a female singer named Evilynn. This proposed band did not come up to standard, though, and before long Mike Browning tried his hand at the vocal role.

With record company interest rising, Morbid Angel cut a 1986 four-song demo, *Scream Forth Blasphemies*, comprising 'Hellspawn', 'Chapel Of Ghouls', 'Angel Of Disease' and 'Abominations'. This tape soon found its way onto the underground trading market, spreading the band's reputation. What was to be the band's debut album, *Abominations Of Desolation*, recorded in North Carolina in May 1986, was shelved due to the line-up disintegrating into a fight over Browning's girlfriend. After these recordings, Browning opted out and John Ortega too departed, later to found Matricide. Georgia native Sterling Von Scarborough, previously fronting his own act Incubus, was drafted in that summer as vocalist-bassist.

Scarborough, leaving to forge a new Incubus with ex-Morbid Angel drummer Mike Browning and Terror guitarist Gino Marino, was supplanted by David Vincent (aka David Stuppnig). The bassist, having led his own act Buried In Cemetery, had been an acquaintance of the band for some time, having financed and produced the *Abominations Of Desolation* sessions. The new line-up, comprising Vincent, Azagthoth, lead vocalist Michael Manson and drummer Wayne Hartshell, relocated to North Carolina to cut new demos. Manson soon dropped out, leaving Vincent to take on the frontman role for Morbid Angel's commercial debut, a 1988 7-inch single titled 'Thy Kingdom Come', released on Switzerland's Splattermaniac label. With this more solid unit, sales began to accelerate, as did the band's worldwide recognition.

The first album, *Altars Of Madness*, cut at Tampa's fabled Morrisound studios, surfaced through the leading extreme metal label Earache in May 1989. CD versions added an extra track, 'Lord Of All Fevers And Plagues', plus alternative remixes of album tracks with outtake guitar solos. The world's first dose of Morbid Angel was stunning: Azagthoth and Brunelle had summoned up a snake's nest of riffs that deliberately defied convention, hammering and sliding outside accepted templates. This almost surreal approach provided a platform for even greater experimentation to come. *Altars Of Madness*, although it was undeniably a classic, did have its faults: the muddy production masked much of the

---

MORBID ANGEL discography

Thy Kingdom Come, Splattermaniac SMR 1-66 (Europe) (1988)
ALTARS OF MADNESS, Earache MOSH011CD (UK),
    Combat/Earache 88561-2022-2 (USA) (1989)
BLESSED ARE THE SICK, Earache MOSH031CD (UK),
    Relativity/Earache 88561-2032-2 (USA) (1991)
ABOMINATIONS OF DESOLATION, Earache MOSH048CD (UK) (1991)
COVENANT, Earache MOSH081CD (UK), Giant 9 24504-2 (USA) (1993)
Laibach Remixes, Earache MOSH112CD (UK) (1994)
DOMINATION, Earache MOSH134CD (UK), Giant 9 24612-2 (USA) (1995)
ENTANGLED IN CHAOS, Earache MOSH167CD (UK) (1996)
FORMULAS FATAL TO THE FLESH, Earache MOSH180CD (UK / USA) (1998)
LOVE OF LAVA, Earache MOSH180CDL (UK / USA) (1999)
GATEWAYS TO ANNIHILATION, Earache MOSH235CD (UK / USA) (2000)
HERETIC, Earache MOSH272CD (UK / USA) (2003)

bass and Vincent's vocals and lyrics were almost lost. On the live front, the group participated in the Earache-organised 'Grindcrusher' tour of Europe that winter with Bolt Thrower, Carcass and Napalm Death.

Blessed Are The Sick appeared in July 1991. Self-produced at Morrisound, the album corrected many of its predecessor's flaws. Its cover art, a dark but elegant J. Delville painting, *Les Tresors De Satan*, was an intelligent departure from the death metal norm. The album, despite being a more deliberate and considered body of work, was soon one of the most revered albums in extreme metal history. As an introduction to the savagery, the album opened with a delicate slice of ambience, the first hints of the more adventurous approach to come in later years. Notably, although Morbid Angel were targeted as Satanists for the entire decade, their second album largely dropped the anti-Christian rhetoric of *Altars Of Madness*.

In September 1991, just before a lengthy American tour, *Abominations Of Desolation* finally saw a release through Earache. The album had been bootlegged relentlessly after the band's ascendancy into the upper echelons of extreme metal.

Guitarist Richard Brunelle drifted away in mid 1992. Morbid Angel filled his shoes briefly with former Incubus man Gino Marino, but before long Brunelle was back. However, he decamped again in autumn 1992 to found Eon's Dead. The trio of Vincent, Azagthoth and Sandoval crafted the *Covenant* album, utilising the familiar Morrisound facilities but enlisting Metallica producer Flemming Rasmussen to handle the board. The final tapes were mixed down at Rasmussen's Sweet Silence studio in Copenhagen.

June 1993 saw Morbid Angel reach such a stature that their *Covenant* album was signed over to the massive Warner Bros. corporation, and in the USA albums would be released on the label's Giant imprint. Backed by a promo video for 'God Of Emptiness', the album was the band's biggest commercial success to date, shifting over 130,000 copies in the USA alone. With tour support now guaranteed, the band closed the membership gap with ex-Ripping Corpse and Eulogy guitarist Eric Rutan, drafted for European dates. However, for support dates to Motörhead and Black Sabbath in America, commencing in Connecticut on February 8th 1994, Richard Brunelle made a temporary return.

Meanwhile, an EP of remixes by the cult industrial act Laibach surfaced, a groundbreaking move for an extreme metal act. The *Laibach Remixes* EP came delivered in CD format with black artwork, as well as a silver 12-inch variant. Meanwhile, ex-member Sterling Von Scarborough, under the pseudonym Nocticula, released a demo, restricted to just 66 copies, under the banner *Liba Nocticula*.

May 1995's *Domination* showed the band with a stronger grip on their premier-league status. Their first recorded output to include Erik Rutan, the album drew some criticism from longstanding followers due to its occasional diversion into slow, sludge metal, specifically on 'Where The Slime Lives', soon a live favourite. Vinyl variants came in differing artwork to the CD versions and the record saw limited-edition releases in a metal tin, restricted to 1,000 copies. A planned slime-filled green jewel case sleeve was shelved after claims of leaking toxic substances.

Domination soon surpassed the 80,000 sales mark in the USA and Morbid Angel undertook an enormous touring schedule throughout 1995 and into 1996. Dates began in their home state of Florida for an American tour before extensively covering Europe: February 1996 saw the band back in America prior to a return trip to Europe. These shows yielded the live album, *Entangled In Chaos*.

The band suffered a double blow in 1997 with the departure of Vincent and the collapse of their deal with Warners Bros. However, Azagthoth picked up the pieces and renegotiated a revised deal with their former label, Earache, and pulled in ex-Merciless Onslaught and Ceremony man Steve Tucker to plug the gap left by Vincent. In 1998

Vincent joined the S&M-themed Genitorturers alongside his wife, their frontwoman Geni.

Although Erik Rutan appeared as main songwriter and contributor to the *Formulas Fatal To The Flesh* album, the band pulled in guitarist Richard Brunelle for live work as Rutan decamped to concentrate on his other two acts Alas, in union with Therion's Martina Hornbacher-Astner, and Hate Eternal. The first 5,000 copies of *Formulas* came with a free bonus CD entitled *Love Of Lava*, comprising the guitar solos from the main body of work. Sales exceeded 45,000 copies in North America.

Rehearsals for the tour to promote the record did not go well and Burnelle was let go; Rutan got the call for assistance. Following the *Formulas* tour Rutan decamped yet again and produced the *Conquerors Of Armageddon* album for Brazilian death metallers Krisiun in 2000. Rutan returned to the fold later in 2000 for *Gateways To Annihilation*, a record that kicked off with an introduction of a genuine swamp-frog chorus.

Morbid Angel toured Europe in December 2000, headlining an almighty death metal package that included Enslaved, The Crown, Behemoth, Hypnos and Dying Fetus. US sales of *Gateways* fell just short of 40,000 copies.

Before the band's 2001 UK dates it was announced that Tucker would be standing down for personal reasons and to concentrate on his death metal combo Ceremony with Cannibal Corpse guitarist Pat O'Brien and Disastronaut guitarist Greg Reed. Erstwhile Emperor drummer Trym Torson was recruited into Ceremony during 2002. However, this proposed band never materialised. Hate Eternal's Jared Anderson took over vocals and bass.

American shows saw the band supporting Pantera before their own winter run of headline dates, dubbed the 'Extreme Music For Extreme People' tour, with Deicide, Soilent Green, Zyklon and Exhumed.

Rutan busied himself towards the close of 2001 as producer for his erstwhile Ripping Corpse colleagues for their sophomore Dim Mak release, *Intercepting Fist*. Morbid Angel then joined Motörhead's 'Hammered' summer 2002 tour of America as guests. Shortly afterwards, Rutan announced his departure from the band in order to concentrate his efforts on Hate Eternal. Meanwhile, Brunelle resurfaced touting his new act Paths Of Possession.

A Morbid Angel tribute album, *Tyrants From The Abyss*, was delivered by Necropolis Records in September 2002 featuring artists such as Zyklon, Vader, Behemoth, Krisiun, Angel Corpse, In Aeternum, Infernal and Diabolic.

Although various press reports suggested that the band were in discussion with former vocalist David Vincent, Steve Tucker stepped back as Morbid Angel frontman for a 2003 studio album, *Heretic*. Meanwhile, drummer Mike Browning was demoing with the Florida-based Lisa The Wolf, with Erik Rutan handling production chores.

Heretic, released in September, was issued in a slew of variations including a German-only boxed set with a complimentary 18-track bonus disc, *Bonus Levels*. There was also a double-CD version and a picture disc LP. US dates with Superjoint Ritual saw the band recruiting Tony Norman of Monstrosity to handle second guitar. A lengthy round of European shows commencing on February 20th in Hardenberg, Holland saw Brazilians Krisiun in support. A promo video for 'Enshrined By Grace', directed by Pete Bridgewater, depicted the band "performing in an infernal ring of fire while the unenlightened masses stare at a mind-numbing screen".

As *Heretic* exceeded 20,000 sales in the USA, the group continued touring across North America into April 2004 with support coming from Suffocation, Satyricon and Premonitions Of War. Confusingly, Morbid Angel's management issued a statement that the band had severed ties with long-term label Earache in July. Within 24 hours Earache fired back with a press release of their own, claiming that in fact the band's option still had a further two weeks to run.

Morbid Angel's classic line-up, with frontman (and future Genitorturers bassist) David Vincent at far left

Scheduled South American gigs, due to commence in Monterrey, Mexico on August 7th, were cancelled as reports emerged that Steve Tucker had suffered a "massive anxiety attack and had to be hospitalised". The frontman soon responded, stating that he had contracted a lung infection "due to my excessive travel and the variety of weather and environments that I endure in these travels".

David Vincent, retaining his role with the Genitorturers, duly rejoined Morbid Angel for their rescheduled South American dates. Now with their classic line-up back in place, Morbid Angel announced co-headline US dates in union with Soulfly for February 2005 followed by a run of European and Scandinavian shows supported by Danes Hatesphere, to take them into April.

Meanwhile, Tucker was announced as back on the tour circuit, apparently as stand-in bassist for Nile's March European festival dates, but this union never transpired. A scheduled showing at a Portuguese festival in June was put in jeopardy when rhythm guitarist Tony Norman apparently went missing. Although the guitarist eventually turned up alive and well, Morbid Angel persevered without him, scheduling South American gigs in Brazil, Chile, El Salvador, Guatemala and Mexico for September. The band was announced as engaged in the 'X-Mass Fest Part II' European tour, set to begin in early December with Enthroned, Unleashed, Primordial and Ensiferum. However, these dates were pulled after Unleashed withdrew.

Jared Anderson and Steve Tucker revealed that they were collaborating in February 2006 on a new death metal venture. Meanwhile, Morbid Angel announced April US tour dates with Canadian band Despised Icon, Poles Behemoth and Brazilian band Krisiun. August European festival dates saw a welcome return to the *Domination* line-up as guitarist Erik Rutan rejoined the fold. (Former vocalist Jared Anderson died in his sleep on October 14th 2006 at the age of 30.) Morbid Angel, despite their uneven work in the last few years, remain among the very finest practitioners of their genre.

NECROPHAGIA
MASTERS OF HORROR

THE PROTO-DEATH METAL act Necrophagia, from Wellsville, Ohio, bowed in with the November 1984 cassette *Rise From The Crypt*. The group had formed a year earlier, with singer Killjoy (aka Frank Pucci), guitarist Larry Madison, bass player Bill James and drummer Joe Blazer, claiming joint rights to inventing death metal along with their close allies and enthusiastic tape-trading partners, Florida's Death. *Rise From The Crypt* was a crudely hacked-out rehearsal recording but perfectly captured the group's ferocity and horror worship, the latter becoming their best-known feature.

More demos included *Autopsy On The Living Dead* in 1985 and two cassettes recorded the following year, *Death Is Fun* and *Power Through Darkness*. *The Nightmare Continues*, cut at Peppermint Studios, arrived in 1987. That same year the group signed to Californian label New Renaissance Records, operated by Hellion singer Ann Boleyn, and *Season Of The Dead* followed swiftly. The record was a truly sinister collection of malevolent curses uttered by Killjoy atop laboured, drudging metal satiated in reverb, and it pulled in exemplary reviews. However, Necrophagia split in 1989, torn by conflicts of opinion and not fully realising the impact that their limited output had made upon the extreme metal scene. As the years passed, this legacy grew in importance.

Killjoy then formed an eponymous band, signing a new deal with New Renaissance for the *Compelled By Fear* album. He reformed Necrophagia in the late 1990s with a fresh line-up of bass player Dustin Havnen, drummer Wayne Fabra and guitarist Anton Crowley. News rapidly spread throughout the metal world that 'Anton Crowley', named after occult practitioners Anton LaVey and Aleister Crowley, was none other than Pantera vocalist Phil Anselmo, and that a guest on the track 'The Cross Burns Black' was singer Maniac of Mayhem.

This band re-debuted with *Holocausto De La Morte* for Red Stream Records. Maintaining the momentum, an EP entitled *Black Blood Vomitorium* surfaced in February 2000. This release proudly sported the proclamation "Banned in 31 countries!" Other product emerging that year included the *Ready For Death* bootleg and the official *Legacy Of Horror, Gore And Sickness* compilation of 1980s demos.

Killjoy also made time for other endeavours, including his involvement in the 2000 black metal project Eibon. With a solitary track on the *Moonfog 2000* compilation album, Eibon consisted of Killjoy, Mayhem's Maniac, Satyricon's Satyr Wongraven, Darkthrone's Fenriz and Anselmo.

The same year found Killjoy fronting Viking Crown, with 'Crowley' again, as well as yet another extreme metal supergroup, The Ravenous, with S.O.D. bassist Dan Lilker and Autopsy/Abscess guitarist Chris Reifert.

A further Anselmo/Killjoy band came in November 2001, Enoch, which also boasted the inclusion of Mirai Kawashima from cult Japanese black metal band Sigh. As it transpired, Anselmo never participated. In mid 2002 Necrophagia announced a complete overhaul of the band, with Anselmo no longer involved. The band now featured Killjoy, drummer Wayne Fabra, Frediablo (the former Immortal bassist Iscariah, Gorelord and Wurdulak man) on guitars, Fug of Wurdulak on guitars and Kawashima handling keyboards. The band planned a new album, *The Divine Art Of Torture*, for release through the Season Of Mist label. By August it was revealed that Daemonia's Titta Tani, also lead vocalist for prog-metal band DGM, had taken the drumming role. Necrophagia were now crediting themselves individually as: Killjoy "Black blood vomiting and corpse shrieks"; Frediablo "Morguefiend masturbator of hellstrings"; Fug "Nekromantic six string suicide"; Iscariah "Desecrator of goat's blood and cloven hooves"; Mirai "Grand inquisitor of pain, torture and hauntings"; and Tani "Tombstones and witchfyre".

Killjoy's stamina was further tested with the introduction in the summer of 2002 of black metal band Hellpig, a collaboration with Slipknot

NECROPHAGIA discography

SEASON OF THE DEAD, New Renaissance NRR 15 (USA) (1987)

DEATH IS FUN, Red Stream RSR-0106 (USA) (1997)

HOLOCAUSTO DE LA MORTE, The Plague PLAGUE 001 (Europe), Red Stream RSR-0126 (USA) (1998)

Black Blood Vomitorium, Red Stream RSR-0131 (USA) (1999)

LEGACY OF HORROR, GORE AND SICKNESS, Vinyl Collectors VC 006 (Europe), Baphomet 2114 (USA) (2000)

Devil Eyes, Red Stream RSR-0145 (USA) (2001) split picture disc 7-inch single with Anteaus

Cannibal Holocaust, Season Of Mist SOM 044 (Europe), Renegade 7014 (USA) (2001)

Kindred Of A Dying Kind, Red Stream RSR-0163 (USA) (2003) split single with Sigh, limited edition 1,000 copies

THE DIVINE ART OF TORTURE, Season Of Mist SOM 069 (Europe), Season Of Mist America 69 (USA) (2003)

Goblins Be Thine, Red Stream RSR-0170 (USA) (2004)

HARVEST RITUAL VOLUME 1, Season Of Mist SOM 101 (Europe), Red Stream RSR-0181 (USA) (2005)

SLIT WRISTS AND CASKET ROT, Red Stream RSR-0190 (USA) (2006)

drummer and Murderdolls guitarist Joey Jordison and Watchtower and Dangerous Toys singer Jason McMaster. Also mooted was a collaboration billed as Amicuss, involving Anselmo, Killjoy, Jordison and Amen's Casey Chaos.

The 2003 Necrophagia 7-inch single 'Kindred Of A Dying Kind', limited to 1,000 copies, gave fans a collectable item as the A-side was an unreleased track from 1998, while Japanese act Sigh covered Necrophagia's own 'Young Burial'. Iscariah also became the bassist for Amok, the grind-thrash venture fronted by Aeternus and Taake vocalist-guitarist Radek (aka Larva), and worked alongside ex-Skyclad singer Martin Walkyier in The Clan Destined.

Necrophagia readied a new studio album, *Harvest Ritual Vol 1: Penance*, for 2004 issue. The track 'Stitch Her Further' was co-written by Slipknot's Joey Jordison, who also contributed guest vocals. The *Goblins Be Thine* EP was also released in 2004, through Red Stream. Two DVDs were in the works, *Nightmare Scenarios* and *NecroTorture/Sickcess*, the latter a combination of a live performance filmed in Valencia, Spain with a "gore filled road movie" directed by Fred Vogel and Killjoy.

In August, Killjoy joined the Danish ambient band Forlis as vocalist. Simultaneously, Frediablo's black metal undertaking Hemnur released the *Ravnsvart* demo in October, also crafting a debut album, *Untamed Norwegian Black Metal*, for early 2005 issue through Baphomet. The guitarist readied a third Gorelord album, *Norwegian Chainsaw Massacre*, released in May 2005 via Coffin Records.

In summer 2005 Necrophagia toured the USA for the first time in many years, heading up a billing supported by Engorge, Typhus and Sumeria. These shows included appearances at the 'Return Of Darkness And Evil' and Milwaukee 'Metalfest' events. That August, Frediablo relinquished his associations with Necrophagia, Gorelord, Wurdulak and Chamber Of Strength to prioritise Grimfist, although he would later quit this band.

Predictably, Necrophagia returned to the fore once again, issuing a limited edition live album, *Slit Wrists And Casket Rot*, before touting the *Deathtrip 69* album in September. The group also announced an EP, *Satan's Skin*, and Diabolos and ex-Nokturne guitarist Undead Torment was added to the ranks in July 2006. Like one of the undead characters in their songs, it seems that Necrophagia will never die.

NILE
A UNIQUE DEATH METAL FORCE

DEATH METAL BAND NILE, from Greenville, South Carolina, have been justifiably hailed as the next major-league contender on the scene. Infusing their work with ancient Egyptian themes, the quartet, led by Karl Sanders, have forged a reputation for precise attention to detail in the execution of their music, the accuracy of their translated texts, and the expansive explanatory annotations that embellish each CD booklet.

The initial quartet of frontman Karl Sanders, bassist Chief Spires, and drummer Pete Hammoura issued two demos on their own Anubis label. In 1995 the five-track demo *Festivals Of Atonement* was issued, after which guitarist John Elhers augmented the band roster. In 1996 they followed up with the three-track *Ramses – Bringer Of War*, the title cut inspired by Holst's classical work *Mars – Bringer Of War*. These demos led them to a very brief relationship with Visceral Productions, which reissued the latter demo in 1997. However, Visceral collapsed before anything could be arranged, and Nile were soon snapped up by Relapse. The band augmented their sound with the addition of second guitarist Dallas Toler-Wade after the departure of Elhers.

In April 1998 they released their debut album, *Among The Catacombs Of Nephren-Ka*. An air of mystique came from choir chants apparently by

NILE discography

Ramses Bringer Of War, Visceral Productions VP-007-CD-S (USA) (1997)
AMONGST THE CATACOMBS OF NEPHREN-KA, Relapse RR 6983-2 (Europe / USA) (1998)
BLACK SEEDS OF VENGEANCE, Relapse RR 6448-2 (Europe / USA) (2000)
IN THE BEGINNING, Hammerheart HHR 068 (Europe), Relapse RR 6449-2 (USA) (2000)
IN THEIR DARKENED SHRINES, Relapse RR 6542-2 (Europe / USA) (2002)
ANNIHILATION OF THE WICKED, Relapse RR 6630-2 (Europe / USA) (2005)

the Gyuto Drupka Tibetan monks, as well as Damaru human skull drums attributed to Mahala Kapala and thigh bone flutes and Turkish gongs played by Drilbu Dungkar. This exoticism masked what was, in fact, a supremely brutal death metal album, with one high point the pulsating 'Die Rache Krieg Lied Der Assyriche' ('The Vengeance War-Song Of The Assyrians'), on which Sanders' Egyptian obsession manifested itself to full effect.

Extensive touring followed and, eager to capitalise on the success of this innovative and respected band, Relapse remastered and reissued the first two demos in early 2000 as *In The Beginning*.

Nile then toured America in 2000 supported by Incantation and Impaled. Hammoura damaged his shoulder and was unable to perform on that September's breathtaking *Black Seeds Of Vengeance* album. Derek Roddy of Malevolent Creation and Aurora Borealis stepped in for studio duties while Tony Laureano took over for live work.

Black Seeds Of Vengeance elevated Nile from the cult underground into the death metal mainstream, putting the focus on the band as long-term contenders. The album, which had taken over a year to compose and arrange, featured a vast array of instrumentation as diverse as tablas, African choirs, Tibetan doom drums, gongs and sitars.

Following European touring in early 2001, longstanding bassist Chief Spires decamped, superseded by the Demonic Christ and Darkmoon player Jon Vesano. A new studio album, *In Their Darkened Shrines*, was scheduled for September 2002 release through Relapse. American headline dates were announced with Arch Enemy, Hate Eternal and Origin slated to support. Nile journeyed to Japan to appear at the Tokyo 'Beast Fest' extreme music festival in December. The band's status had risen to such a level that US dates were being projected into January 2003 with Nile headlining a full metal package of Napalm Death, Dark Tranquillity, Strapping Young Lad and Australians The Berzerker.

Drummer Tony Laureano joined Malevolent Creation's live line-up in March for their appearances at the April 2003 European 'No Mercy' festivals. Nile's live schedule intensified, with September North American dates dubbed 'The Art Of Noise 2'. This run of shows saw the band allied with Kreator, Vader, Amon Amarth and Goatwhore. The band were then confirmed as headliners for the 'X-Mass Festivals' European tour, commencing in London on December 7th, heading up a strong billing incorporating Destruction, Amon Amarth, Deicide, Graveworm, Dew-Scented, Misery Index and Disbelief.

In September 2003 Spires and Ehlers joined forces in a new band called Shaitan Mazar. In mid 2004 Sanders donated a guitar solo to the track 'Xul' on the *Demigod* album from Polish death metal veterans Behemoth. Drummer Laureano joined Norwegian black metal act Dimmu Borgir on a session basis for the duration of their Ozzfest dates because regular sticksman Reno Killerich had been unable to obtain a US work visa.

During downtime for Nile in mid 2004, Toler-Wade was the stand-in drummer for Greenville, South Carolina band Lecherous Nocturne. Meanwhile, Sanders, working with singer Mike Breazeale, made an ambient textured solo album, *Saurian Meditation*, for October issue.

Nile then drafted in Greek drummer George Kollias, a veteran of Nightfall, The Circle Of Zaphyan and Sickening Horror, to record *Annihilation Of The Wicked*. Limited-edition variants came packaged with a serpent-ankh pendant, colour album poster, vinyl sticker, and embroidered patch.

In February 2005 Nile severed ties with Vesano, inducting the Morbid Angel-credited Steve Tucker for live work. However, Tucker's union with the band never transpired and 19-year-old Joe Payne took up bass duties. In addition, Toler-Wade assumed lead vocals. The band then forged a road alliance with Six Feet Under, Dark Funeral, Disbelief, Dying Fetus, Wykked Wytch and Cataract for the 'No Mercy' festivals 2005 European tour, beginning in early March. The group then scheduled US tour dates for April 2005 in partnership with headliners King Diamond, Poles Behemoth and The Black Dahlia Murder. This batch of gigs saw Krieshloff of Dominion and Lecherous Nocturne occupying the bass role. *Annihilation Of The Wicked* debuted on the national Swedish charts in June at Number 27. A video for the track 'Sacrifice Unto Sebek' was shot in Atlanta, Georgia, with director Chad Rullman.

Further gigs announced for the USA with Chimaira, All That Remains and 3 Inches Of Blood were announced, but the band withdrew, citing "scheduling conflicts". Meanwhile, ex-Nile drummer Tony Laureano was still performing live on the European festival circuit with Dimmu Borgir, subsequently joining another Norwegian black metal band, 1349.

Live work in 2006 saw the band teaming up with Hypocrisy, Soilent Green, Raging Speedhorn, Decapitated and With Passion for a North American tour commencing in early January. The group then participated in the 'Extreme The Dojo Volume 15' shows in Japan with The Haunted and Exodus, in late February. Nile signed to the Nuclear Blast label in May, and their epic saga looks set to continue.

OBITUARY
FLORIDIAN SWAMP RESIDENTS

HAILING FROM BRANDON, the same Florida town as Nasty Savage, Obituary play brutal death metal with gore themes. The band, one of the first of the Sunshine State's death metal pioneers, started life in 1985 at high school and were originally known as Executioner before the subtle name change to Xecutioner. Guitarist Trevor Peres and the Tardy brothers, vocalist John, and drummer Donald issued a self-financed single, 'Metal Up Your Ass' / 'Syco-Pathic Mind', under the original Executioner name, with 100 copies on 7-inch vinyl and 500 copies on cassette on their own Xecution Music Productions label. Further recordings came in the form of a two-song demo, 'Find The Arise' and 'Like The Dead', which eventually surfaced on Godly Records' *Raging Death* compilation.

Adopting the new title of Obituary to avoid confusion with Boston contemporaries Executioner, the band began recording a full-length album for the Godly label but signed the tapes over to Roadrunner before their completion. The *Slowly We Rot* sessions had been conducted at Morrisound in Tampa on a primitive 8-track machine, with Scott Burns as producer. Although this combination of studio and producer would soon become synonymous with the entire death metal genre, *Slowly We Rot* was Burns' first ever commercial undertaking.

Slowly We Rot crawled out into an unsuspecting world in April 1989. Although acts such as Death had pre-empted them, Obituary took death metal beyond established extremity, the ferocity and primal nature of John

OBITUARY discography

SLOWLY WE ROT, Roadracer RO 9489-2 (Europe), R/C RCD 9489 (USA) (1989)
CAUSE OF DEATH, Roadracer RO 9370-2 (Europe), R/C RCD 9370 (USA) (1990)
THE END COMPLETE, Roadrunner RR 9201-2 (Europe), R/C RCD 9201 (USA) (1992)
WORLD DEMISE, Roadrunner RR 8995-2 (Europe / USA) (1994)
BACK FROM THE DEAD, Roadrunner RR 8831-2 (Europe / USA) (1997)
DEAD, Roadrunner RR 8755-2 (Europe / USA) (1998)
FROZEN IN TIME, Roadrunner RR 8156-2 (Europe / USA) (2005)

Tardy's vocal delivery being the most violent ever delivered so far. Meanwhile, guitarists Allen West and Trevor Peres carved out fresh musical terrain, opening the floodgates for Floridians such as Malevolent Creation, Deicide, Morbid Angel and Cannibal Corpse. Shunned by the mainstream, and with its juvenile cartoon-style artwork not aiding exposure, *Slowly We Rot* found hallowed status in metal's gutter regions.

The group suffered a setback when bassist Daniel Tucker was officially listed as missing in Florida after disappearing on May 1st. He was found in September, seemingly having suffered injury and partial amnesia in a car crash. After recovering he chose not to pursue a "heavy metal lifestyle".

West quit in 1990 just as the group had added Frank Watkins to replace Tucker. The guitarist, who subsequently joined Six Feet Under and Lowbrow, was replaced by ex-Agent Steel, Hallows Eve and Death guitarist James Murphy in time to record the *Cause Of Death* album, which included a cover of Swiss avant-garde band Celtic Frost's 'Circle Of The Tyrants'. *Cause Of Death*, a more convoluted and at times close to progressive outing, emerged in September 1990.

The band debuted their revised line-up with UK dates in May 1991, supported by Cerebral Fix. The following year Murphy departed to join British death metallers Cancer, and West was reinstated, as the band set out touring America opening for Sacred Reich.

The third album, *The End Complete*, again produced by Scott Burns, was issued in April 1992. The band's standing was now such that the album intruded into the UK and German national charts. A fourth opus,

Obituary: hanging out

the supremely tight *World Demise* of 1994, found Obituary slotting in a short European co-headlining tour towards the end of the year, sharing the billing with Brazilians Sepultura; support came from The Rollins Band and Voodoo Cult. Obituary toured Europe in 1995 headlining over Eyehategod and Pitchshifter.

Back From The Dead was out in 1997, and that April saw Obituary back on European soil, heading up the 'Full Of Hate Easter' festivals alongside Entombed, Death, Samael, Neurosis, Crowbar, Killing Culture and Strapping Young Lad.

Obituary's run had come to a halt, however, and shortly afterwards the band splintered. In late 1997 Roadrunner reissued the first two albums in remastered form with the addition of bonus tracks. Fans were kept guessing into the next year with a live album, suitably titled *Dead*, recorded at the Axis in Boston, Massachusetts, on September 10th 1997.

Nearly three years of inactivity ensued before fans learned that the group had ceased operations. Peres created a side project titled Catastrophic in 2000. Roadrunner laid a fitting tombstone on Obituary's career with the 2001 *Anthology* release. This collection compiled tracks from the four albums to date as well as previously unheard demos, including a cover of Venom's 'Buried Alive' from the *World Demise* sessions. Noteworthy inclusions came from Massacre guitarist J.P. Chartier and bassist Jerome Grable on the demo track 'Find The Arise'.

In 2002 it emerged that erstwhile drummer Donald Tardy had joined the backing band for the briefly much-vaunted rock artist Andrew WK. Three-fifths of the classic Obituary line up – the Tardy brothers and bassist Frank Watkins – reunited on stage at Andrew WK's July 27th 'Ozzfest' gig in West Palm Beach, Florida, to perform Obituary tracks, fuelling rumours of a reformation. The band members finally revealed plans for a new album, billed as *Frozen In Time*, in January 2004. They persuaded producer Scott Burns to come out of retirement and revisited Morrisound studios to capture the old authenticity. A concession to the modern world came with the employment of producer Mark Prator, utilising his Tampa ProTools studio, Red Room Recorders. Meanwhile, Trevor Peres allied himself with an unlikely collaborator, donating his skills as studio guest to rapper Necro's album *The Pre-Fix For Death*. Obituary, Master and Visceral Bleeding teamed up for the Legends Are Back European tour, commencing in early October.

Frozen In Time emerged in July 2005, charting in Germany. Obituary then headed up European touring in January and February 2006 with support from Samael and German hardcore band Maroon. The band played a gig in Barcelona, Spain on January 27th as a quartet when Peres was unable to fly out of Italy due to severe weather conditions. Obituary played just two UK shows, plus one in Ireland, as part of their European tour in June 2006. The band hooked up with Gojira and Gorerotted for a run of UK dates in August. Their August 24th concert at the Stodola Club in Warsaw, Poland was captured on film for release as a DVD, entitled *Frozen Alive*, through Metal Mind Productions. After such a long career, the band's legacy seems secure at last.

SIX FEET UNDER
HIGH-QUALITY US DEATH METAL

TAMPA, FLORIDA, DEATH METAL combo Six Feet Under were initially created as a side project by Cannibal Corpse frontman Chris Barnes, Obituary guitarist Allen West and erstwhile Massacre and Death bassist Terry Butler. Greg Gall of Last Rite assumed command of the drums. Barnes had fronted Cannibal Corpse for their most notorious slash-fests, 1990's *Eaten Back To Life*, 1991's *Butchered At Birth*, 1992's *Tomb Of The Mutilated* and *The Bleeding* in 1994. Six Feet Under had already been instigated before the recording of his swansong Cannibal Corpse opus.

This lineage alone guaranteed an immediate profile and swift acquisition by Metal Blade.

The debut album, *Haunted* – produced by Brian Slagel and Scott Burns at Morrisound Studios and issued in September 1995 – predictably kept up the gore factor of the various band-members' previous acts, and consistent touring pushed the release past the 35,000 sales mark. *Haunted* took on a rumbling, groove-laden path as opposed to the musicians' prior endeavours, its catchiness triggering debate as to whether Six Feet Under had strayed too far from death metal norms. However, the European audience latched onto the fresh formula from the start, providing the group with a stable platform of operations for the future.

With Barnes obviously placing his priorities with Six Feet Under, the unit subsequently evolved into a fully-fledged band when the singer was ejected from his previous act. Six Feet Under grasped the opportunity and hit Europe foursquare in the summer of 1996.

A live mini-album, October 1996's *Alive And Dead*, consisted of cuts recorded during the previous bout of European touring at Pratteln in Switzerland and Hengelo in Holland, two fresh studio recordings, and a version of Judas Priest's 'Grinder' – these last three tracks laid down at Criteria Studios in Miami. The release plugged a gap between bouts of recording while West was committed to the latest Obituary album.

Six Feet Under's sophomore outing, *Warpath* – sporting a rendition of NWOBHM act Holocaust's 'Death Or Glory' and housed in a striking neon-green jewel case – arrived in September 1997. However, the group suffered an unexpected blow when West opted out.

The band returned to action with *Maximum Violence* in July 1999, a record that garnered healthy reviews and included a Kiss cover, 'War Machine'. The group had drawn in Massacre and Last Rite-credited second guitarist Steve Swanson to supersede West. *Maximum Violence* surpassed the 100,000 sales mark, a rarity for a death metal record in those times. As momentum gathered, Metal Blade reissued the album as a two-disc set, adding a crop of live tracks. Japanese versions came with extra material, namely takes on Iron Maiden's 'Wrathchild' and Thin Lizzy's 'Jailbreak'.

By 2000, West had created his own act, Lowbrow, with Nasty Savage men Ben Meyer and Curt Beeson and Death bassist Scott Carino. Matt Cohen briefly joined the Six Feet Under ranks, and Six Feet Under's *Graveyard Classics* album, out in October 2000, was a compilation of covers of songs by AC/DC, Black Sabbath, The Sex Pistols, Dead Kennedys, Exodus, Savatage, Venom and Jimi Hendrix. John Bush of

Six Feet Under

METAL

Anthrax and Armored Saint guested on vocals for a version of the Scorpions' 'Blackout'.

The band resumed action in August 2001 with *True Carnage*. The album included Body Count vocalist and rapper Ice-T as guest vocalist on 'One Bullet Left' and Karyn Crisis of Crisis duetting with Barnes on 'Sick and Twisted'. The latter was trumpeted as the first ever death metal male-female duet. Japanese editions added a bonus track, a live version of 'Torture Killers'.

True Carnage gave Six Feet Under valuable commercial success in Europe, charting in both Germany and Austria. However, the video for 'The Day The Dead Walked' was turned down by both MTV and MTV2 due to its supposedly extreme nature.

Six Feet Under undertook a lengthy bout of American touring in the summer of 2002, commencing in Houston, Texas, on May 31st supported by Skinless and Sworn Enemy. The band's June 14th Minnesota gig was recorded for a DVD and a live album. September 2002 tour plans for North America had the band paired up with Hatebreed, and they then headed up an impressive cast for the European 'Xmass Festivals' in December, strongly supported by Marduk, Immolation, Kataklysm, Dying Fetus and Hate. Later gigs in Holland added Exodus to the bill.

The group maintained the momentum for September 2003's *Bringer Of Blood*, the album giving Six Feet Under their highest advance sales figures to date, landing at Number 36 on the German charts. Six Feet Under set Kings Of The Roadkill as the title of their January US shows, these gigs seeing support from Full Blown Chaos and Bile. The group teamed up with labelmates Criminal and Fleshcrawl for a two-week European tour throughout February and March 2004. Headline shows in the USA throughout April saw a variety of support acts at various stages, including The Red Chord, The Black Dahlia Murder, On Broken Wings, Misery Signals, Bury Your Dead and The Heavils.

In readiness for *Graveyard Classics II*, promoted by a video for a cover of AC/DC's 'Rock'n'Roll Ain't Noise Pollution', a further round of North American shows throughout August and September were bolstered by opening acts Misery Bleeding, Internal Bleeding and Premonitions Of War. With teaser press releases stating that *Graveyard Classics II* was a "unique" album, it was apparent that the band had stuck to their word – by covering an entire album, namely AC/DC's seminal *Back In Black*.

Losing no momentum, by October 1st SFU were back in Morrisound recording a new album, *13*, for 2005 issue. In January the band filmed a video for 'Shadow Of The Reaper', directed by Gary Smithson and featuring actors Meagan Crawford and Aaron Kinser. Six Feet Under then

played with Nile, Dark Funeral, Disbelief, Dying Fetus, Wykked Wytch and Cataract for the 'No Mercy Festivals' European tour in early March.

A four-CD boxed set, *A Decade In The Grave*, was released in late November, comprising two discs of archive album tracks, a 21-track live DVD, and rare sessions from demos dating back to 1985, plus rehearsal recordings. The band put in an extensive European tour in October 2005 with Kat, Born From Pain and Debauchery across France, Austria, Switzerland, Denmark, Holland, Belgium and Germany.

In November, Barnes announced that he was to session lead vocals on the *Swarm!* album for Finnish death metal band Torture Killer. US dates for September and October 2006 saw the band hooking up with Krisiun, Decapitated and Abysmal Dawn, and live work in December across Europe saw them lined up with Darzamat, Gorefest, Belphegor and Krisiun for the 'X-Mass' festivals. SFU remain one of the more successful American death metal acts.

SUFFOCATION
LEGENDS IN THEIR OWN LIFETIME

NOW REGARDED AS ONE of the most influential original death metal bands, New York's Suffocation led the way in deconstructing their art down to the finest, microscopic components, building songs of great complexity. Very often their tracks compressed enough riffage to fuel an entire album, this obsessive devotion to their craft firing up a new branch of the death metal family tree.

Suffocation were initially founded as Social Disease in 1986. The band debuted with a line-up of vocalist Frank Mullen, guitarists Doug Cerrito and Terrance Hobbs, bassist Josh Barohn and drummer Mike Smith. This unit arrived with the three-track demo tape *Reincremation* in April 1990.

Suffocation's inaugural release, the *Human Waste* EP, emerged in May 1991, issued by Nuclear Blast in Europe. In America, it marked the influential Relapse label's first ever release. The title track had been lifted straight from the previous demo, but the newly recorded tracks barely surpassed it in terms of production quality. However, Suffocation scored with the bewildering welter of riffs.

The band then switched labels to Roadrunner, turning around *Effigy Of The Forgotten* in October the same year. This release included re-recorded versions of the 1990 demo tracks 'Involuntary Slaughter' and 'Reincremation' (featuring guest vocals from singer George 'Corpsegrinder' Fisher) alongside 'Mass Obliteration'. Again Suffocation focused on their now trademark extreme attention to detail, with massed 'nano-thrash' riffing, Mullen's inhuman bellow, and unrelenting blastbeats. Chris Richards replaced Barohn soon after the recording.

The May 1993 opus *Breeding The Spawn* saw Terrance Hobbs and Paul Bagin acting as producers. In 1994 Suffocation donated 'Infecting The Crypts' to the *Live Death* compilation album, though by this time Doug Bohn filled in behind the drum kit.

Bohn joined goremongers Autopsy prior to founding Welt with his Suffocation colleague Doug Cerrito on guitar for the 1994 *Paranoid Delusion* EP; Welt changed names in 1996 to Iron Lung, releasing the *Chasing Salvation* album on Diehard Records.

Touring after their May 1995 album *Pierced From Within* – again produced by Scott Burns – Suffocation replaced drummer Bohn with Disgorged and Malevolent Creation man Dave Culross to record the *Despise The Sun* EP, distributed via the band's management company Vulture Records during 1998. This outing, with a reworked 'Catatonia' from the *Human Waste* EP, unfortunately languished in obscurity with minimal promotion.

The exalted position that Suffocation had achieved after a decade of output could not sustain them, however, and the group ceased activities.

During 1998 guitarist Cerrito joined Hate Eternal (the act founded by Ripping Corpse and Morbid Angel guitarist Erik Rutan) for their *Conquering The Throne* album. Culross duly rejoined Malevolent Creation.

Highlighting the impact Suffocation had made upon the scene, Greek label Repulsive Echo compiled a 2001 tribute album with an international cast. Homages were made by Prophecy, Devourment, Putrilage, Severed Savior, Internal Bleeding and Detrimental as well as Canadian band Rotting, Australians Miscreant, Finns Deep Red, Spain's Wormed, Japan's Vomit Remnants, Greek band Inveracity, Dutch bands Pyaemia and Disavowal, Germans Harmony Dies, and Beheaded from Malta.

Reports surfaced in August 2002 that Suffocation were set to reunite, citing a line-up of vocalist Frank Mullens, guitar players Terrance Hobbs and the Pyrexia and Internal Bleeding-credited Guy Marchais, bassist Josh Barohn and drummer Mike Smith. To complement this news, Relapse picked up the neglected *Despise The Sun* EP for re-release. By late 2003 the band had set *Souls To Deny*, released in April 2004, as a title for a new album. A video for the track 'Surgery of Impalement' was filmed at Philadelphia's infamous Eastern State Penitentiary, notable for having once held gangster Al Capone.

The group, after switching bassists once again and bringing on board former Decrepit Birth man Derek Boyer, intensified their live industry, touring across North America into April 2004 as part of Morbid Angel's 'Heretic' dates with Satyricon and Premonitions Of War. Extending live work into May, the band hooked up with Dying Fetus and Malamor. Dates in January 2005 saw Suffocation playing with Behemoth and Soilent Green. As this trek extended into February, the band retained Behemoth as road partners but added Cattle Decapitation and Minneapolis outfit Devilinside. Road work continued throughout 2005, witnessing October and November shows with Cryptopsy, Cephalic Carnage, Aborted and

Suffocation

With Passion. Mike Smith made time for a track on the October-released Roadrunner United 25th anniversary album, *The All-Star Sessions*, helming the kit for the Matt Heafy-compiled 'Dawn Of A Golden Age'.

Suffocation announced touring plans for the summer of 2006, kicking off the Sthress tour in July alongside Poison The Well, It Dies Today, Himsa, Darkest Hour, Bury Your Dead, Shadows Fall, Throwdown and Still Remains. A new self-titled Suffocation album was released in September 2006. The band united with headliners Fear Factory, Sweden's Hypocrisy and Polish act Decapitated for US shows in November 2006. Suffocation's fanbase remains utterly loyal and the future looks bright.

TERRORIZER
GRIND PIONEERS

AN ILLUSTRIOUS NAME ON THE extreme metal underground circuit, Terrorizer had a career that was short, sharp and utterly brutal. And had it not been for an influential fan, Napalm Death's Shane Embury, the band would have been lost to obscurity.

The Los Angeles-based Terrorizer consisted of Nausea singer Oscar Garcia and guitarist Jesse Pintado – subsequently of Napalm Death – alongside bassist Alfred 'Garvey' Estrada and Morbid Angel drummer Pete Sandoval. Terrorizer often performed Master's 'Funeral Bitch' at live shows and had reputedly taken their name from another Master song, 'Terrorizer'. The band had actually gone their separate ways before Earache requested the *World Downfall* album, released in November 1989 at the insistence of Embury. Morbid Angel's David Vincent stood in on bass for the sessions, completed in just eight hours.

Polish death metal act Vader covered Terrorizer's 'Fear Of Napalm' and 'Storm Of Stress' on their 1996 *Future Of The Past* album. New York's Exit 13 also covered 'Storm Of Stress' that same year. Terrorizer stopped working when Pintado joined Napalm Death, although there were persistent rumours of a reformation. By 2003 both Garcia and Estrada were fronting Nausea.

Terrorizer finally relented in late 2005 and reunited, swiftly signing to Century Media Records. Joining guitarist Pintado and drummer Sandoval

Terrorizer

SUFFOCATION discography

Human Waste, Nuclear Blast NB 051 (Europe), Relapse RR 6015-2 (USA) (1991)

EFFIGY OF THE FORGOTTEN, R/C RC 9275-2 (Europe), R/C RCD 9275 (USA) (1991)

BREEDING THE SPAWN, Roadrunner RR 9113-2 (Europe / USA) (1993)

PIERCED FROM WITHIN, Roadrunner RR 8948-2 (Europe / USA) (1995)

Despise The Sun, Vulture Entertainment 0002-2 (USA) (1998)

SOULS TO DENY, Relapse RR 6586-2 (Europe / USA) (2004)

THE CLOSE OF A CHAPTER: QUEBEC CITY – LIVE 2005, Suffocation cnu (USA) (2006) only available through the band's online store

SUFFOCATION, Relapse RR 6584-2 (Europe / USA) (2006)

TERRORIZER discography

WORLD DOWNFALL, Earache MOSH016CD (UK),
   Relativity/Earache 88561-2035-2 (USA) (1989)
DARKER DAYS AHEAD, Century Media CM 77540-2 (Europe),
   Century Media CM 8420-2 (USA) (2006)

in the new roster were Resistant Culture vocalist Tony Militia (aka Anthony Rezhawk) and the Eternal, Morbid Angel and Monstrosity-credited guitarist Tony Norman. Their comeback album, *Darker Days Ahead*, recorded at Juan 'Punchy' Gonzalez's Diet of Worms Studios, emerged in August 2006.

Sad news came on August 27th with the death of Jesse Pintado. The guitarist had died from liver failure at the Erasmus MC hospital in Holland. It remains to be seen if Terrorizer have a future without him, although any further activity seems unlikely.

VITAL REMAINS
DECHRISTIANIZED DEATH METALLERS

AN ILLUSTRIOUS NAME IN DEATH metal circles, Rhode Island's Vital Remains infuse their music with blasphemous, black metal-style content. The band's first line-up for the *Reduced To Ashes* demo in 1989 consisted of vocalist Jeff Gruslin, guitarists Paul Flynn and Tony Lazaro, bass player Tom Supkow and drummer Chris Dupont. There was a further tape, *Excruciating Pain*, with new drummer 'Ace' Alonzo, and a 7-inch single, 'The Black Mass', for the French label Thrash. Recorded in November 1990, the single shifted over 1,500 copies in two weeks. This first commercial outing bolstered the band's reputation and led to a deal with Deaf Records, a subsidiary of British label Peaceville. Vital Remains released the *Let Us Pray* album in August 1992, issued through Grind Core International in the USA. Peaceville had also issued a 1993 split clear vinyl 7-inch single, 'Amulet Of The Conquering', in collaboration with Morta Skuld, as part of their exclusive and now exceptionally sought after Collectors Club series.

A three-month US road alliance across the country with Autopsy, kicking off in May 1993, led to sessions for a second album, *Into Cold Darkness*, which was released in March 1995. The album closed with a cover version of Celtic Frost's 'Dethroned Emperor'. The band also cut a rendition of Venom's 'Countess Bathory', this song only included on Peaceville's 1996 compilation *Under The Sign Of The Sacred Star*.

By the recording of March 1997's *Forever Underground*, the group's first offering for French label Osmose Productions, they had trimmed

down to a trio of Lazaro, bassist Joseph Lewis and drummer David Suzuki. Taking a brief diversion, they were included on the 1999 Judas Priest tribute album *Hell Bent For Metal*, covering 'You've Got Another Thing Comin''. Another cover executed that same year was their interpretation of Mercyful Fate's 'To One Far Away / Come To The Sabbath', featured on *The Unholy Sounds Of The Demon Bells – A Tribute To Mercyful Fate*, a collection issued through Poland's Still Dead Productions.

Vocalist Jeff Gruslin was replaced by Thorn, and the band released the *Dawn Of The Apocalypse* album in November 1999. The following year Vital Remains sacked Thorn, as the remaining band-members cited alleged drug abuse. They rehired Gruslin in time for European dates as part of the 'No Mercy' festival alongside Poland's Vader, Brazil's Rebaelliun and Germany's Fleshcrawl.

Late 2000 found Gruslin back on the scene as part of the prominent Wolfen Society project, which included erstwhile Acheron man Vincent Crowley, Incantation's Kyle Severn and Lord Ahriman of Dark Funeral. The Dutch label Cryonics then reissued the debut demo *Reduced To Ashes* on CD.

The band enlisted ex-Monstrosity and Death bassist Kelly Conlon, but he soon bailed out, requiring lead guitarist Ron Greene to play bass for the interim. In April 2002 vocalist Jake Raymond and lead guitarist Ron Greene parted ways with the band, founding a new project, Cast Of Vengeance, in league with former Vital Remains bassist and frontman Joe Lewis. Greene also joined Leukorrhea.

In a major coup, the band pulled in none other than Glen Benton of Deicide to record lead vocals for their *Dechristianize* album, which marked a renaissance for the band. The album was recorded at Morrisound by Lazaro on guitars, and David Suzuki on guitars, bass and drums. Vital Remains' debut gig with Benton was the 2003 Milwaukee 'Metalfest'.

The band hooked up with Vehemence for a week at the end of August 2004. Suzuki enrolled in Deicide for their October and November dates with Nominon and Germany's Hidden In The Fog as support acts.

In early 2006, ex-Vital Remains drummer Marco Pitruzella joined US death metal band Vile to conduct their 'Gutting Europe' tour in March and April. Vital Remains themselves conducted West Coast 'God Killers' shows alongside Deicide (with Glen Benton doing double frontman duty each night), Crematorium and Oregon's Desolation, and shows commencing in late May had them hooking up with Incantation, Sin Of Angels and New Zealanders Dawn Of Azazel. The band then teamed with Dismember, Grave, Demiricous and Withered for a North American tour, starting in September. They remain a much-respected band.

VITAL REMAINS discography

The Black Mass, Thrash THR008 (Europe) (1991)
LET US PRAY, Deaf DEAF 009 (UK), Grind Core 89812-2 (USA) (1992)
Amulet Of The Conquering, Peaceville Collectors CC 4 (UK) (1993) split single with Morta Skuld
Excruciating Pain, Wild Rags WRR-045 (USA) (1995)
INTO COLD DARKNESS, Peaceville CDVILE 48 (UK) (1995)
FOREVER UNDERGROUND, Osmose Productions OPCD 050 (Europe / USA) (1997)
Reduced To Ashes, Cryonics CRY 02 (Europe) (1999)
DAWN OF THE APOCALYPSE, Osmose Productions OPCD 077 (Europe / USA) (2000)
DECHRISTIANIZE, Century Media CM 77431-2 (Europe), Olympic OLY 0229-2 (USA) (2003)
HORRORS OF HELL, Century Media CM 8254-2 (USA) (2006) limited edition 5,000 copies

Vital Remains, with Glen Benton centre

NORWEGIAN BLACK METAL

NORWAY

NORWAY is synonymous with black metal, an extreme branch of the metal tree with such entrenched and historically unarguable roots that, in musical terms, the country's culture will be forever blighted by its indelible stain. Sinister names such as Darkthrone, Enslaved, Burzum, Satyricon, Mayhem, Gorgoroth, Immortal, Dimmu Borgir and Emperor have come to eclipse those of Henrik Ibsen, Edvard Grieg and the country's greatest contribution to the international music scene, A-Ha. Not since the Viking longboats set out from the fjords has Norwegian culture imposed itself so harshly on the world.

Once thrash and death metal had reached the ears of impressionable youth, a profusion of bands suddenly took up arms. It is a mystery why so many chose to move from standard death and gore lyrics, which is where all the major names started out, and switch to reverence of Satan and his minions. Once Mayhem had made the switch, other acts simply fell into line. The catalyst for this was undoubtedly Mayhem singer Oystein 'Euronymous' Aarseth, whose teenage fascination with Soviet Russia and traditional metal then focused on what until then was seen merely as some kind of bogeyman. Heavy metal's treatment of Satan, even with the comical interpretations of Venom, had only been used until then to enhance a bad-boy image. Norway's youth looked beyond the imagery and took the next step towards becoming practitioners.

This was the greatest difference between the Norwegian bands and those who had gone before them. Music became a sideshow for the action. In this surreal timeframe, tragedy became the norm as teen violence and vandalism escalated into suicide, church burning and ultimately murder. The media coverage surrounding these events gave the bands a notoriety upon which they thrived and spurred many thousands of followers in their wake.

The Norwegian black metal scene basked briefly in the international spotlight, with Carpathian Forest, Ancient and Borknagar rising in a second wave, before it became incapable of sustaining itself. The major name acts invariably reacted to market forces and their own maturity by developing into new realms, exploring ancestral folk, gothic, ambient and industrial landscapes. The braver of these artists, such as Ulver and Deathstars, have carved out new fanbases in these areas. Another dilution came when key personnel were lost. Mouthpieces such as Euronymous and Burzum's Varg Vikernes were either dead or behind bars, and inter-band intolerances affected stability.

Black metal in Norway threw up another new phenomenon: multi-tasking. Previous tradition had dictated that an artist remain loyal to one single band before gaining recognition and striking out solo. Almost from the outset, though, Norwegian musicians ignored this rule and operated in numerous bands and solo projects, covering a wide range of styles. It is not uncommon for an individual to adopt a multitude of pseudonyms, perform numerous roles, and be a member of many acts – all in parallel. Ironically, some of the best known names drifted so far from their roots that they then found themselves forced to conjure up "true kvlt" side projects.

It is a paradox that the band most often vilified for not having remained 'true' to the cause, Dimmu Borgir, is without question the leading artist in their field in terms of sales. Dimmu Borgir took the essence of black metal and forged for themselves a successful formula and significant sales, where the sometime scene-leaders Mayhem, Emperor and Immortal have floundered following ill-thought-out experimentation. Having endured their growing pains, it seems that the bands who once led the scene are now reverting back to the rawness at which they once excelled.

ANCIENT
INDIVIDUAL BLACK METAL THINKERS

ANCIENT WERE INITIALLY formed in Eidsvaagneset, Bergen as a solo project by Aphazel (aka Magnus Garset), an erstwhile member of death metal act Putrefaction, in late 1992. The group's prominence rose steadily due to their inclusion of two significant female contributors, Kimberley Goss and Deadly Kristin, and their relocation to the USA, but were elevated still further in 1999 when the band's album *The Cainian Chronicle* was linked to one of Finland's most notorious murders.

Aphazel's solo undertakings expanded into the beginnings of a band in 1993 when drummer-vocalist Thorg (Henrik) joined. The project then performed a handful of Norwegian gigs, with Molested's bass player Kenneth Lian on loan. Ancient's first official three-track demo appeared that September, featuring 'Eerily Howling Winds', 'Triumphs Of An Arc-Angel' and 'Det Glemte Riket'. The last song was also featured on the Metal Blade compilation *Metal Massacre XII*. The tape sold over 700 copies and gained the band a deal with Listenable Records in France. At this juncture Thorg changed his stage name to Grimm. An EP, *Det Glemte Riket*, was laid down at Hindu Lydstudio in February 1994: 2,000 copies were pressed in 7-inch format, of which a collectable 500 were manufactured in blue vinyl. Meantime, the album *Svartalvheim*, cut during the same sessions, emerged in December.

Further gigs followed, this time utilising the services of Asmodeus's bassist Qyasyar Archant. In August 1995 Devilish Entertainment issued a limited-edition 1,000-piece run of *Svartalvheim* on vinyl with different jacket art. Ancient's next offering, the *Trolltaar* EP, was constructed at Warlust Studios with producer Michael Omlid in April 1995. Studio players included Lise-Kari Haavardstun Stalheim and, somewhat experimentally, euphonium player Knut Arne Kringstad. With the release of the 1,000-only *Trolltaar* in November, Grimm left the band.

Aphazel then relocated the band from Bergen to the USA, and into the Ancient ranks came Lord Kaiaphas, previously known as Lord Vlad Luciferion while a member of Thokk and Grand Belial's Key. The band, signing to Metal Blade, also added drummer Kjetil. Ancient's second album, *The Cainian Chronicle*, recorded at Unisound by Dan Swanö in January 1996, emerged in June, notably featuring guest female vocals from 17-year-old Kimberley Goss of Chicago's Avernus. The band had now become almost entirely American. Ancient's evolution was made apparent by the semi-conceptual nature of *The Cainian Chronicle*, much of its content drawn from the Biblical saga of Cain's temptation by Lilith, with the remaining passages pursuing mythological, pagan themes. An unintentionally funny video for the song 'Lilith's Embrace' depicted the band obliviously headbanging while Kiaphas drew blood from Goss.

European touring elevated the band's status. However, Goss was unceremoniously fired, and duly joined Dimmu Borgir, at first on loan for their European tour but with a permanent relationship later the same year. Goss would also put in live showings with Therion and subsequently founded power metal band Sinergy.

October 1997's *Mad Grandiose Bloodfiends*, recorded at Cue Recording Studios, in Falls Church in Virginia, included a cover of Mercyful Fate's 'Black Funeral', and Japanese versions hosted an extra track, 'Morte El Potere'. By now, Ancient were effectively a duo of Aphazel and Kiaphas, but recorded with New Orleans native Erichte (aka Saelok) of Spiritual Darkness (later Spiritus Tenebrae) on female vocals, Akrabu and Crimson Moon bass player Vampir Scorpios, and a musician called 'Jesus Christ' on guitar and other stringed instruments. For touring purposes Ancient pulled in Bloodstained Dusk drummer Profana.

Confusion followed the band into 1998 as they imploded yet again. Out went Kaiaphas and Erichte and in came bassist Tony, while Christ moved over to keyboards. Erichte soon came back onto the scene with her Spiritus Tenebrae project, while Kaiaphas poured his energies into Oroboros. Aphazel uprooted the band once more, this time for its second trans-global shift, to Italy.

By 1999, Ancient's line-up for the album *The Halls Of Eternity*, executed at Flying Studios in Gravellona Toce, consisted of Aphazel on lead vocals and guitar, vocalist Deadly Kristen, keyboard player Jesus Christ and drummer Krigse. Dhilorz was recruited on bass to finalise the membership shortly after the recordings, and Iblis guitarist Thidra was recruited for live work. World touring then ensued, including the band's inaugural push through Scandinavia.

Ancient's album *The Cainian Chronicles* was back at the forefront of media attention in August 1999 when Finnish black metal devotees Jarno Sebastian Elg, Terhi Johanna Tervashonka and Mika Kristian Riska were sentenced by a court in Hyvinkää for what was described by the media as a Satanic, ritualistic murder. The grisly crime had first come to light in October 1998 when a severed leg had been found on a rubbish tip.

Although the details of the case were deemed so horrific as to be held under Finnish secrecy laws for a 40 year period, newspapers claimed that the unnamed victim "suffered prolonged torture and eventually was strangled to death", after which the murderers partook in "ingesting some of the body parts". Unfortunately for Ancient, this

ANCIENT discography

Det Glemte Riket, Ancient, no catalogue number (Europe) (1994)

SVARTALVHEIM, Listenable POSH 006 (Europe) (1994)

Trolltaar, Damnation DAMNATION3 (Europe) (1995)

THE CAINIAN CHRONICLE, Metal Blade 3984-14110-2 (Europe / USA) (1996)

MAD GRANDIOSE BLOODFIENDS, Metal Blade 3984-14143-2 (Europe / USA) (1997)

DET GLEMTE RIKET, Hammerheart HHR 042 (Europe) (1999)

THE HALLS OF ETERNITY, Metal Blade 3984-14201-2 (Europe / USA) (1999)

TRUE KINGS OF NORWAY, Spikefarm NAULA 006 (Europe) (2000) split album with Emperor, Immortal, Dimmu Borgir and Arcturus

God Loves The Dead, Metal Blade 3984-14352-2 (Europe / USA) (2001)

PROXIMA CENTAURI, Metal Blade 3984-14361-2 (Europe / USA) (2001)

NIGHT VISIT, Metal Blade 3984-14483-2 (Europe / USA) (2004)

EERILY HOWLING WINDS – THE ANTEDILUVIAN TAPES, Sleaszy Rider SR-0036 (Europe) (2005)

unsavoury episode took place while the three killers were listening to their 1996 album.

The group put in a landmark performance at the 2000 'Wacken Open Air' festival in Germany. After these dates, Aphazel and Deadly Kristen busied themselves with the Gothic ambient project Dreamlike Horror.

In 2000, Ancient welcomed ex-Bedeviled and Bloodstorm drummer Diego 'Grom' Meraviglia on board for the EP *God Loves The Dead*. Not to be outdone with other members' side ventures, Grom played with Doomsword, appearing on the Italian doom band's *Resound The Horn* album, Dhilorz played with Infliction, and Jesus Christ put his energies outside the band into Fullmoon Shadow.

In February 2001 Ancient issued the mini-album *God Loves The Dead*, featuring a cover of Iron Maiden's 'Powerslave', remixes, and two videos. The full-blown *Proxima Centauri*, arguably the band's most accomplished work to date, arrived in October the same year. Their line-up for this effort consisted of Aphazel on "burning guitars, lead vocals and bestial rage", Deadly Kristin on "female vocals and seductive black arts", Grom on "drums of destruction", Jesus Christ on "infernal keyboards and blasphemy", Dhilorz on "apocalyptic bass guitar", and session guitarist Thidra. For live work Ancient employed the services of another Italian, Aleister Demon of Faust repute.

In mid 2002 Hammerheart announced a re-release of *Det Glemte Riket*, adding the *Trolltaar* release plus the 'Det Glemte Riket' 7-inch and unreleased material. August had Deadly Kristin announcing a new band, Frozen Soul, in league with Tom Sibrän Van Iersel as main composer on guitars and 'growl' vocals and Björn Jonsson on bass.

Drummer Grom made headway with his 'prog-black' project band Hortus Animae, signing to the Black Lotus label for a debut album, *Waltzing Mephisto*. Deadly Kristin, converting to Islam, joined up with the technical Seattle-based progressive death metal band Byaxis. Meanwhile, Ancient got to work on a new album in late 2003, recording *Night Visit* at the Mirage and Alpha-Omega studios with producer Fredrik Nordström. Former Ancient singer Kaiaphas made a guest appearance on one track on the album.

Germany's Supreme Chaos label announced a CD containing

Ancient's original *Eerily Howling Winds* demo from 1993 along with other unreleased tapes from the beginning of the band's career. Scheduled for March 2005 issue, the set was titled *Eerily Howling Winds – The Antediluvian Tapes*. Aphazel and Deadly Kristen's Dreamlike Horror project signed to the Greek Sleaszy Rider label for their March 2005 debut *Delightful Suicides*. The same label re-released *Det Glemte Riket*, *Trolltaar* and the *Eerily Howling Winds – The Antediluvian Tapes* sessions, all including extra bonus tracks.

The band then toured with Denmark's Illdisposed and German act Final Breath for European dates throughout March 2005. April found Grom rehearsing with Fire Trails, the new act assembled by Vanadium leader Pino Scotto, and in early September the drummer announced that he was to close his five-year tenure with Ancient. Deadly Kristin partnered with DJ Celt Islam and sitar player Dawoud Kringle in the UK on the Sufi-electro project Analogue Fakir. During late 2005 Grom enrolled into the ranks of Andark as a live session drummer.

ARCTURUS
SIDE PROJECT EXTRAORDINAIRE

ALTHOUGH THEY ARE NOW widely recognised as a cardinal force, Arcturus was originally put together in Oslo as a side project in 1989 by members of death metal band Mortem. After demo cassette that year, *Slow Death*, Mortem took on the new name of Arcturus.

The first product was a 1990 demo, *My Angel*. A 1991 7-inch EP, also entitled *My Angel*, featured Mayhem's Hellhammer (Jan Axel Blomberg) on drums, keyboard player-guitarist Steinar Sverd Johnsen, and Marius Vold on vocals and bass. Issued through French label Putrefaction, *My Angel* was pressed in 1,100 copies and made all the more collectable by having three different-coloured sleeves – yellow, blue or green. Shortly afterwards Arcturus was put on ice as both Sverd and Hellhammer busied themselves with Emperor, but the band evolved to comprise Borknagar and Ulver's Garm (aka Kristoffer Rygg, naming himself after the Norse dog guardian of hell) on vocals and Samoth (Tomas Thormodsæter Haugen) from Emperor on guitar. The 1995 symphonic doom-imbued *Constellation* EP, issued through Samoth's Nocturnal Art label, came in a limited edition of 500 copies. Taking an unorthodox spin on the normally rigid black metal template, *Constellation* employed clean vocals and a palette of keyboards to temper the ferocity of the guitars.

In 1994, Samoth was imprisoned for arson after setting fire to churches and was replaced by Carl August Tidemann of Tritonus. Arcturus added a second guitarist in the form of Skoll (Hugh Mingay) who had played with Fimbulwinter, Ulver and Ved Buens Ende. *Aspera Hiems Symfonia* (Latin for 'harsh winter symphony') arrived in June 1996 as the sophomore release, through Ancient Lore Creations. This full-length album reprised the *Constellation* material, retitling 'Icebound Streams And Vapours Grey' as 'Wintry Grey' and enhanced with fresher cuts.

The October 1997 album *La Masquerade Infernale* saw Ved Buens Ende and Borknagar man Simen Hestnæs contributing alongside Garm, as well as Knut Magne Valle on guitar. Recording for this endeavour commenced in December 1996 into May of the following year, conducted at Garm's own Jester Studios. Carl August Tidemann again donated his skills to two tracks – the seven-minute instrumental 'Ad Astra' and 'Of Nails And Sinners' – while Ulver's Erik Olivier Lancelot (aka AiwarikiaR) performed flute. An exercise in despondency, *La Masquerade Infernale* was positively pastoral when compared to previous output. From the renditions of Edgar Allan Poe's 'Alone' and Joen Hernik Svaeren's 'Throne Of Tragedy', via Garm's searing castrati

ARCTURUS discography

My Angel, Putrefaction PUT 006 (Europe) (1991)
Constellation, Nocturnal Art Productions ECLIPSE 003 (Europe) (1995)
ASPERA HIEMS SYMFONIA, Ancient Lore Creations ALC 002 (Europe) (1995), Century Black 7835-2 (USA) (1996)
LA MASQUERADE INFERNALE, Music For Nations CDMFN 230 (UK) (1997)
DISGUISED MASTERS, Jester TRICK003 (Europe) (1999)
TRUE KINGS OF NORWAY, Spikefarm NAULA 006 (Europe) (2000) split album with Emperor, Immortal, Dimmu Borgir and Ancient
ASPERA HIEMS SYMFONIA / CONSTELLATION / MY ANGEL, Candlelight CANDLE 067 CD (UK), Candlelight USA CANUSCD0029CD (USA) (2002)
THE SHAM MIRRORS, Prophecy Productions PRO 049 (Europe), The End TE026 (USA) (2002)
SIDESHOW SYMPHONIES, Season Of Mist SOM 100 (Europe), Season Of Mist America 100 (USA) (2005)

and subterranean bellows, to the reliance on vocal-less bridges, the album placed Arcturus firmly in avant-garde territory. Originally intended for release by the elite Misanthropy label, that imprint's financial woes necessitated a license through Music For Nations.

In 1999 Arcturus released the remix album *Disguised Masters*, which included contributions from When's Lars Pedersen, and Garm made his presence felt on Ulver's sprawling *Themes From William Blake's The Marriage Of Heaven And Hell*. During 2000, Hestnæs joined Dimmu Borgir as bassist. The same year found Sverd guesting on Fleurety's *Department Of Apocalyptic Affairs*.

The 1996 *Aspera Hiems Symfonia* album was given a lavish re-release through the British Candlelight label in 2002. Remixed by Garm, the record added the complete track listings from the highly collectable *Constellation* and *My Angel* EPs.

Garm was now seeking recognition for "voices of ghosts and monkeys and general manipulation" and relabelled himself Trickster G. Rex as Arcturus returned in April with *The Sham Mirrors*. Once again the group – wryly dubbing themselves 'The Institute Of Common Oblivion' – plundered historical prose, lifting from Samuel Beckett for the closing track 'For To End Yet Again'. Dag F. Gravem was installed on bass and Emperor frontman Ihsahn contributed "spitting voice" on 'Radical Cut'. Incessant in their desire for experimentation, Arcturus gave the album soothing qualities, if paradoxically dominated by Hellhammer's drum flurries.

Garm bowed out of Arcturus in early 2003 to prioritise Ulver, and was replaced by Spiral Architect singer Øyvind Hægeland. They got off to a difficult start in 2005 with the departure of Hægeland in early January, and he was swiftly replaced by Hestnæs again. The revised band, having contracted to Season of Mist for a new album, *Sideshow Symphonies*, debuted on January 27th at the London 'Inferno' festival. Mainly composed by Sverd, *Sideshow Symphonies* was recorded at the band's own Mølla studios and featured a guest female singer, Silje Wergeland of Octavia Speranti. Alter egos abounded once again – Sverd as "Ship Captain", Hestnæs as "Alien Translator", Knut Valle as "Space Navigator", Hugh Mingay as "Warcraft Engineer", and Hellhammer delegated as "Turret Gunner". Guitarist Tore Moren also sessioned.

There were shows in Europe and Scandinavia and the band headlined a one-off package comprising Confessor, Nattefrost, Red

Harvest and Tsjuder at the Season Of Mist-promoted 'Sonic Solstice' festival in Oslo on September 24th 2005. European touring. commencing in October. saw the band in alliance with Red Harvest and Kill The Thrill for the 'Shipwrecked In Europe' dates. Arcturus are now one of the scene's most respected acts.

BORKNAGAR
BLACK METAL SUPERGROUP

BERGEN'S BORKNAGAR, created during 1995, are made up of various members of the death metal elite. Molested's Øystein Garnes Brun (aka Panzerschwanz) had composed an album's worth of music and lyrics, and gathered Ivar Bjørnson of Enslaved as keyboard player, drummer Grim (Erik Brødreskift) of Immortal and Gorgoroth, bass player Infernus (Roger Tiegs) of Gorgoroth, and Ulver's Garm (Kristoffer Rygg) as lead vocalist.

Over a series of innovative albums, the band maintained their status – despite ongoing line-up tribulations and members' commitments to other high profile groups. At first they delved into melodic black metal but then drifted successively into progressive Viking-edged metal with philosophical and pagan content.

Following two demos, *Stalk The Dead* and *Unborn Woods In Doom*, Brun's previous group Molested ploughed a stereotypical death metal furrow, putting out a 1995 album *Blod-Draum* on the Effigy label and an EP, *Stormvold*, in 1997. Molested, existing in parallel to Borknagar for some time, scored a deal for a proposed second album, but Brun opted to close off this avenue to fully prioritise Borknagar.

Unusually, the new band chose not to demo material and launched straight into their debut album with the Norwegian-language *Borknagar*, recorded at Bergen's Grieghallen Studios and released through Malicious in February 1996. A thoroughbred manifestation of bombastic black metal, *Borknagar* held true to a formulaic combination of growled vocals, buzz guitars, sweeping synths and blastbeat drumming, with only the respite of the acoustic punctuated 'Ved Steingard' and 'Tanker Mot Tind' giving any hint of future direction.

Switching to Century Media, the band – having dropped Infernus in favour of new four-stringer Kai K. Lie and with Garm now working as 'Fiery G. Maelstrom' – followed up with *The Olden Domain*, crafted at Woodhouse studios in Dortmund and issued in August 1997. With Grip Inc. guitarist Waldemar Sorychta as producer, Borknagar took a daring leap forward with *The Olden Domain*, stretching the confines of the genre into unexplored areas. While the guitar power base

remained cruelly triumphant, the essence of Borknagar swelled into epic magnificence. Black metal elements remained, with bursts of blastbeats and guttural vocals – now significantly in English – but highly mature works such as the rousing 'A Tale Of Pagan Tongue', the monolithic instrumental 'Ascension Of Our Fathers' and the piano piece 'Om Hundredeaar Er Alting Glemt' showed that the band had charted a new course.

Borknagar undertook a European tour that September alongside Hecate Enthroned, Rotting Christ and Old Man's Child. All did not run smoothly, however, as vocalist Garm unexpectedly withdrew his services on the eve of the tour. Borknagar rapidly supplanted Garm with erstwhile Lamented Souls and Arcturus man I.C.S. Vortex (Simen Hestnæs) and bolstered their live sound with a second guitarist, Jens F. Ryland of Dødheimsgard. Their third album, *The Archaic Course*, emerging in October 1998, was also laid down at Woodhouse Studios. Here Borknagar opened themselves up in order to fully explore the Nordic myths, their technical ability and range of expression manifesting a near-prog masterpiece in the process.

They put in a tour of America during 1999 as part of a bill including Emperor, Witchery, Peccatum and Divine Empire – and this despite the band playing as an understrength trio of Brun, Hestnæs and Ryland. Grim had died from a drug overdose on October 4th, deemed as suicide, and bassist Kai K. Lee had quit. They quickly recruited Lazare (Lars A. Nedland) of Solefald on keyboards and guest drummer Nick Barker of Cradle Of Filth and Dimmu Borgir.

The 2000 album *Quintessence*, produced by Hypocrisy's Peter Tägtgren at Abyss Studios that January, was recorded with new drummer Asgeir Mickelson of progressive rock act Spiral Architect and Anesthesia. Lazare's contribution in the studio was to replace the architectural keyboard structures with expansive and detailed playing. As such, *Quintessence* marked a shift away from the epic and into the truly progressive. However, in August the band had to pull out of a projected tour with Mayhem after Hestnæs, who had been a part-time bassist in Dimmu Borgir under his pseudonym of I.C.S. Vortex, decided to concentrate solely on that act.

The same month Borknagar enrolled erstwhile Morpheus Web, Satyricon and Emperor bassist Tyr (Jan-Erik Torgersen). By November the vocal position had been filled by Vintersorg (aka Andreas Hedlund), who had played in his own act Vintersorg and the folk metal combo Otyg. The newly stabilised Borknagar then put in a valuable

Borknagar

BORKNAGAR discography

BORKNAGAR, Malicious MR012CD (Europe) (1996)
THE OLDEN DOMAIN, Century Media CM 77175-2 (Europe), Century Black 7895-2 (USA) (1997)
THE ARCHAIC COURSE, Century Media CM 77236-2 (Europe), Century Media CM 7936-2 (USA) (1998)
QUINTESSENCE, Century Media CM 77289-2 (Europe), Century Media CM 7989-2 (USA) (2000)
EMPIRICISM, Century Media CM 77399-2 (Europe), Century Media CM 8099-2 (USA) (2001)
EPIC, Century Media CM 77499-2 (Europe), Century Media CM 8199-2 (USA) (2004)
ORIGIN, Century Media CM 77599-2 (Europe), Century Media CM 8299-2 (USA) (2004)

appearance at the Norwegian 'Quart' festival in early July as support to Cradle Of Filth.

The October 2001 *Empiricism* album, released in North America in January the following year, featured vocalist Vintersorg, guitarists Øystein G. Brun and Jens F. Ryland, bassist Tyr, keyboard player Lazare and Mickelson on drums. Working with studio engineer Børge Finstad, the band tracked this album at Fagerborg Studio and Toproom Studios. Brun and Vintersorg founded an adjunct to Borknagar in late 2002 entitled Íon; guitarist Jens F. Ryland left the band in mid February 2003; and drummer Mickelson became a temporary stand-in with Bay Area thrash adepts Testament that same month.

Borknagar set about recording their sixth album, *Epic*, in early 2004, recording at Toproom and Fagerborg Studios with co-producer Finstad. For these sessions Mickelson also handled bass guitar as they had parted ways with Tyr.

Borknagar's touring plans were put on hold due to a profusion of newborns in the camp, with three band members – Brun, Vintersorg and Mickelson – becoming fathers. In January 2005, Hestnæs rejoined as the band's new frontman. Brun indicated in early 2006 that forthcoming Borknagar enterprises would be acoustic in nature.

More side activities culminated in the announcement of the Íon project of Vintersorg and Øystein G. Brun, soon re-titled Cronian, and a further Hedlund solo concern, the 1970s-style prog-rock concept Waterfield for a debut album *The Astral Factor*. Borknagar themselves returned in October with the *Origin* album. Their place in the pantheon of Norwegian black metal is assured.

BURZUM
THE MOST NOTORIOUS BLACK METAL BAND OF ALL?

THE INFAMOUS BERGEN black metal band Burzum, originally known as Kalashnikov, formed in 1988 as Uruk-Hai. Burzum's history is embroiled in controversy and, with the band's sole member imprisoned, the music has developed a true underground following.

In the early days the group were steeped in JRR Tolkien's fictional lore, with the names Uruk-Hai, Grishnackh and Burzum ('darkness' in Orcish) all lifted from Orc titles and languages. Uruk-Hai included drummer Erik Lancelot (aka AiwarikiaR), subsequently a member of Ulver.

Band leader Varg Vikernes, whose stage name was Count Grishnackh after an Orc, was born Kristian Vikernes. His new forename, Varg, means 'wolf'. The band split in 1990 and Vikernes formed Satanel with Immortal members Demonaz and Abbath. He also dabbled in a death metal side project, Old Funeral. Satanel disintegrated in 1991 with Vikernes resurrecting Uruk-Hai under the new name of Burzum.

A demo of instrumental rehearsal recordings was put together with a cassette cover adorned by a concentration camp photograph. The demo consisted of 'Lost Wisdom', 'Spell Of Destruction' and 'Channeling The Power Of Souls Into A New God' plus an unaccredited outro, recorded on May 17th 1991. Often travelling the seven-hour plus journey from the West Coast of Bergen to Oslo, Vikernes would stay for extended periods in the capital with members of Mayhem. This connection solidified itself into a working relationship with Mayhem frontman Euronymous (real name Øystein Aarseth), who offered to release Burzum's first album on his Deathlike Silence Productions label. DSP also produced two-track promo cassettes before the album release, and a more comprehensive 12-track demo tape surfaced.

Burzum was released in March 1992, recorded at Bergen's

Grieghallen Studios with both 'Mr. Pytten' (aka Eirik Hundvin) and Euronymous receiving production credits. Euronymous later donated a solo to the song 'War'. The original vinyl was divided into "Side Hate" and "Side Winter". A misprint on the original pressing had 'Ea, Lord Of The Depths' mistakenly listed as 'Ea, Lord Of The Deeps'.

Although the album was released through Deathlike Silence, the manufacturing had, according to Vikernes, been financed out of his own pocket by way of a loan to Euronymous. When the album sold out of its first pressing and the money had not been returned by the Mayhem leader, the seeds of resentment were sown.

Burzum was a remarkably mature piece of work, particularly when compared to the other product spewing out of Norway at the time. Varg's lone genius constructed songs of complex, atonal structures and accentuated riffing, often switching schizophrenically between blastbeats and drawn-out, dirge-like manipulations. As black metal endured its birth pangs, Vikernes was already looking toward the future of the genre by placing emphasis on atmospherics.

Essentially still a solo project, Burzum did feature Emperor guitarist Samoth on bass on the *Aske* ('Ashes') mini-album, released in 1992. Poignantly, *Aske*'s cover depicted a photograph of the burned-out ruin of Fantoft stave church. This historic building, one of only 32 remaining in Norway at that time, was torched on June 6th 1992 – the first of many.

Burzum's fourth album, *Hvis Lyset Tar Oss* ('If The Light Takes Us') was recorded in September 1992. In January 1993 Vikernes gave an interview in the Helvete record store owned by Euronymous, in which the machinations of the burgeoning Inner Circle (see Mayhem entry) were greatly exaggerated, apparently in order to gain exposure for the shop and Deathlike Silence. The journalist reported his findings to the police, who promptly had the interviewee jailed when he admitted involvement in church burnings. Upon his release, Vikernes was angered by Euronymous when he learned that while he had been incarcerated for a publicity stunt, the Helvete premises had been closed.

The feud between Euronymous and Vikernes festered. The Burzum man later claimed to have learned of a plot concocted by Euronymous to trick him into a meeting to sign a new contract, knock him out with a stun gun, take him into the woods, and torture him until he died, capturing the entire affair on video. With memories still fresh of Mayhem singer Dead's untimely demise and documentation on camera by Euronymous, perhaps the premise seemed reasonable.

Vikernes was then implicated in a number of church burnings along with other members of the Norwegian black metal scene. The story reached its nadir on August 10th 1993, when Vikernes murdered Euronymous by stabbing him to death. He had driven from Bergen with Mayhem guitar player Snorre Ruch (aka Blackthorn) as a companion, arriving in Oslo in the early hours of the morning. According to Vikernes, an argument rapidly escalated into violence in which Euronymous was stabbed in his apartment and then chased outside, with Vikernes stabbing him in the back. The final blow came when Vikernes stabbed Euronymous through the forehead, and the body fell downstairs. Vacating the scene, Vikernes disposed of his bloodied clothes in a lake and then journeyed home. His prepared alibis broke down, and on August 19th he was arrested. Despite all of this, the *Det Som Engang Var* album was released in 1993.

Before his arrest, Vikernes, when asked by *Kerrang!* magazine journalist Kee Barrett to comment on Euryonymous's death, offered to "dance and piss on his grave". This quote was later denied by Vikernes. Charged with first-degree murder, as well as arson charges in relation to Åsane church, Skjold church in Vindafjord and Holmenkollen chapel, as well as possession of stolen explosives, Vikernes was given a maximum sentence of 21 years.

Hvis Lyset Tar Oss was finally released in May 1994 via Misanthropy, the record enclosed in a traditional monochrome line drawing, this time *Fattigmannen* ('The Pauper') by traditional Norwegian landscape-naïve-folk artist Theodor Kittelsen. Four lengthy songs were intended by Varg to take the listener on a journey, inducing trance with the subtle shifts of 'Det Som En Gang Var', bludgeoning with the ferocious 'Hvis Lyset Tar Oss' and 'Inn I Slottet Fra Droemmen' before lulling us back into the real world with the soothing keyboard ambience of 'Tomhet' ('Emptiness'). Burzum returned in 1996 with *Filosofem*, again issued through Misanthropy.

Vikernes once more provoked headlines in early 1997 when a T-shirt he had designed for Burzum while in jail caused outrage and was banned. Featuring the SS death's-head logo on the chest and the slogan 'Support your local Einsatzkommando', Vikernes proved that his controversial philosophies could still make an impression from the prison cell.

Vikernes completed work on the *Dauði Baldrs* (Death Of Baldur) album in 1997. The music was a conceptual piece based on the Norse God Baldur, son of Odin and Frigga, the deity of innocence and light, and had been recorded on the keyboards he was allowed to keep in his cell. Somewhat disturbingly, the album cover featured Viking warriors – one in a cloak bearing the distinctive insignia of the Scandinavian SS division 'Wiking' and another cradling a baby and sword.

Vikernes' anti-hero status was partly revealed when his mother, Lena Bore, was jailed for helping to finance an attempt by the right-wing organisation Einsatzgruppe to spring her son from jail. The intended destination for Burzum's leader was apparently South Africa.

The *Hliðskjálf* record was assembled in the confines of Vikernes' prison cell on a computer and a keyboard, and released in April 1999. Titled after the throne of Odin, the album featured printed lyrics, but

BURZUM discography

BURZUM, Deathlike Silence Productions ANTI-MOSH 002 (Europe) (1992)

Aske, Deathlike Silence Productions ANTI-MOSH 005 (Europe) (1993)

DET SOM ENGANG VAR, Cymophane Productions EYE 001 (Europe) (1993)

Hvis Lyset Tar Oss, Misanthropy AMAZON 001 (UK) (1994)

FILOSOFEM, Misanthropy AMAZON 009 (UK) (1996), Feral House 66602 (USA) (1997)

DAUDI BALDRS, Misanthropy AMAZON 013 (UK) (1997)

HLIDSKJÁLF, Misanthropy AMAZON 021 (UK) (1999)

DRAUGEN – RARITIES, Back On Black BOB037CD (UK) (2005)

none of these were actually suing on the record, which was purely instrumental.

A Burzum tribute album, *Visions*, was released in 2002 on the Cymophane label featuring the likes of Starchamber, Ewigkeit, Nokturnal Mortum and Schizoid. As the myth of Burzum showed little sign of disappearing, in 2003 the Dead Ringer label granted both *Dauði Baldrs* and *Hliðskjálf* their first US release. Further releases, such as Vargsmal, followed.

Vikernes made headlines on October 25th 2003 when, aided by accomplices, he escaped from prison. He had recently been transferred to the low security Tønsberg jail but had expressed fears for his personal safety. Norwegian newspapers reported that he held a family at gunpoint in order to hijack their car and was then pursued by several police vehicles until brought to a halt. Apparently as part of his escape kit, Vikernes was in possession of a gas mask, knives, camouflage clothing, a portable GPS navigator, maps, a compass, a mobile phone, a headset and a laptop computer. His lawyer, John Christian Elden, claimed that his intention was to flee Norway and join the French Foreign Legion. In April 2004 Vikernes learnt that his attempt to flee had added a further 14 months to his sentence.

In February 2006, Candlelight Records prepared on their website a new artist page for Burzum, apparently in anticipation of Vikernes' release from prison. However, the prisoner's parole hearing in June did not go in his favour, due in part to a retroactively enforced change in legislation, the Norwegian government having increased parole hearings in 21-year sentences from 12 years to 14. Vikernes' eventual emergence from prison will be of great interest to black metal fans, although no one knows exactly where his career will go from there.

CARPATHIAN FOREST
IN THE WOODS

THIS UNWAVERINGLY RAW act, with their disturbing catchphrase of "Carpathian Forest wants you dead!", adhere to "anti-human, anti-life" black metal. They hail from Sandnes and consist of Nordavind and Nattefrost, assisted by Green Carnation bassist Tchort (aka Terje Vik Schei) and drummer Anders Kobro (ex-In The Woods..., Scariot and Green Carnation). Initially Nattefrost was named Lord Nosferatu, while Nordavind took on the pseudonym Lord Karnstein.

The group's first appeared as Enthrone, recording a 1991 demo *Black Winds*. After the name change, the *Bloodlust And Perversion* demo followed. A rehearsal session was also distributed, incorporating renditions of Bathory's 'Call From The Grave' and Venom's 'Warhead'.

CARPATHIAN FOREST discography

In These Trees Are My Gallows, Carpathian Forest cnu
(Europe) (1993)

Through Chasm, Caves And Titan Woods, Avantgarde Music
AV 011 (Europe) (1995)

BLOODLUST AND PERVERSION, NYX NYX-01 (Europe) (1997)

BLACK SHINING LEATHER, Avantgarde Music AV 031 (Europe)
(1998)

He's Turning Blue, Avantgarde Music AV 048 (Europe) (1999)
7-inch picture disc

STRANGE OLD BREW, Avantgarde Music AV 051 (Europe)
(2000), Mercenary Musik CD-71252 (USA) (2001)

MORBID FASCINATION OF DEATH, Avantgarde Music AV 061
(Europe), Mercenary Musik cnu (USA) (2001)

**WE'RE GOING TO HELL FOR THIS – OVER A DECADE OF
PERVERSIONS**, Avantgarde Music AV 067 (Europe) (2002)

DEFENDING THE THRONE OF EVIL, Season Of Mist SOM 068
(Europe), Season Of Mist America 68 (USA) (2003)

SKJEND HANS LIK, Season Of Mist SOM 077 (Europe), Season
Of Mist America 77 (USA) (2004)

FUCK YOU ALL!!!!, Season Of Mist SOM 114 (Europe), Season
Of Mist America 114 (USA) (2006)

The rhythm section for these tracks consisted of bassist Grimm's Damnatus with Lord Blackmangler on the drums. Two demos in 1993, *In These Trees Are My Gallows* and *Journey Through The Cold Moors Of Svarttjern*, solidified the band's reputation.

The band debuted in 1995 for the Italian label Avantgarde with the mini-album *Through Chasms, Caves And Titan Woods*. A session rhythm team was drafted in from Sea Of Dreams in the form of bass player John Martin Haarr and Svein Harald Kleppe on the drums. The second commercial release, *Bloodlust And Perversion*, arrived in 1997, collecting the band's three demos.

The third album, *Black Shining Leather*, was released in August 1998, recorded by Nattefrost, Nordavind and drummer Lazare (aka Lars Nedlund) of Solefald and Borknagar. The album, although a blazing, unrelenting black metal maelstrom for most of its duration, closed with an unexpected take on The Cure's 'A Forest'. A 1999 picture disc 7-inch single, 'He's Turning Blue', was backed by a cover of Mayhem's 'Ghoul'.

Nordavind quit the band before the release of the 2000 album *Strange Old Brew*. This release evoked film noir atmospherics, drenching its tracks in reverb and even featuring a saxophone on the piano-driven 'House Of The Whipcord'. Nattefrost was also operational with side project World Destroyer.

Morbid Fascination Of Death in 2001 increased the emphasis on rhythm and standard rock riffing, the beginnings of the group's distinct brand of 'hell rock'. Studio guests included C. Alucard and Hatepulse's Eivind Kulde on backing vocals alongside singer Nina Hex and saxophonist Motorsen. Carpathian Forest toured Europe that autumn on a package billing with Behemoth and Norway's Khold. A compilation album, *We're Going To Hell For This – Over A Decade Of Perversions*, featured three new tracks and a slew of live material, arriving in October 2002. It included a blackened interpretation of Discharge's 'The Possibilities of Life's Destruction' and faithful tributes to Darkthrone's 'In The Shadow Of The Horns' and Venom's 'In League With Satan'.

Nattefrost pursued activities with The Bloodline (alongside Mysteriis of Diabolicum) and Setherial (with Sethlans Larva Shaytan

from Aborym). His connection to the Italian black metal band was strengthened with a guest appearance on Aborym's 2002 album *With No Human Intervention*.

A new studio album, *Defending The Throne Of Evil*, produced by Terje Refsnes, was set for issue in March 2003 but delayed into September. The record juxtaposed technical black thrash, groove, Norwegian and English lyrics, saxophone, and the quirky cameo 'The Old House On The Hill'. *Defending The Throne Of Evil* was subsequently issued in limited-edition double vinyl format, adding an extra track 'Humiliation Chant'.

The band formed part of the 2004 European 'No Mercy' festival with Spawn Of Possession, Hypocrisy, Kataklysm, Cannibal Corpse, Vomitory, Prejudice and Exhumed. However, vocalist Nattefrost sustained injuries in an accident, suffering torn muscles and a fractured collarbone. Doctors advised the singer to withdraw from the shows in order to recuperate, and the band duly performed an instrumental set for the opening shows. Nattefrost was scheduled to rejoin them for the April 3rd Vienna show.

The 2004 album *Skjend Hans Lik*, released through Season Of Mist, consisted of new tracks alongside demo recordings from *Bloodlust And Perversion* dating back to 1992. In September, Nattefrost was revealed to be participating in Helvete, a black metal supergroup with Darkthrone frontman Nocturno Culto, guitarist General K of Disiplin and drummer Bård 'Faust' Eithun, sometime of Emperor, Aborym and Dissection.

An extensive round of European headline shows in February 2005, dubbed 'The Art Of Provocation', found Carpathian Forest supported by Tsjuder, Wykked Wytch and E-Force. The new bassist was Vrangsinn of Hatepulse and World Destroyer. The band then toured throughout Central and South America. A new album, *Fuck You All!!!! Caput Tuum In Ano Est*, arrived in June 2006. Secondary guitar duties were now handled by Bloodperverter (aka Goran Boman) of Neon God and Opus Forgotten.

Early 2006 brought news that Vrangsinn, Nattefrost and Nordavind had participated in Secht, a black metal collective involving drummer Dirge Rep of Gorgoroth and Neetzach, Nocturno Culto of Darkthrone, Nag of Tsjuder, Gaahl of Gorgoroth and Trelldom, Apollyon of Aura Noir, and Høst from Ragnarok and Taake, among others. The band continue to go from strength to strength.

DARKTHRONE
UNCHANGING BLACK METAL GRIMNESS

SELF-PROCLAIMED "true Norwegian black metal" band Darkthrone have courted a great deal of controversy over a string of brutally stark albums. They proved themselves to be capable musicians with their death metal debut album *Soulside Journey* but then performed a complete artistic U-turn, dispensing with precision and technical dexterity and playing black metal in its rawest state.

The band, formatively entitled Black Death, convened in Kolbotn, Ski during 1987 with vocalist-drummer Gylve Nagell and guitarist Anders Risberget. Their first demo came in 1987 with the *Trash Core* cassette, hosting tracks such as 'Black Death's Nuke War' and 'Pizzabreath'. *Trash Core*, with artwork depicting a wandering troll armed with a rake drawn by Nagell, was recorded in the attic of Risberget's parents' house. Black Death put down more tracks that October, dubbed *Black Is Beautiful*, by which time they had been joined by Ivar Enger on bass. Their repertoire now featured songs such as 'Pizza Monsters' and 'Nasty Sausage'.

Resolving to take a more serious approach to their art, they conceived a new name, Darkthrone, inspired by a lyric in Celtic Frost's song 'Jewel Throne'. Nagell adopted the stage name Fenriz, after the Nordic wolf god, and Enger – switching to guitar – became Zephyrous. The new band recorded the five-track *Land Of Frost* demo in March 1988. Anders Risberget was still a member, and Dag Nilsen contributed bass.

The single-track July 1988 tape *A New Dimension* included the intro 'Twilight Dimension', leading into 'Snowfall'. Darkthrone had evolved further by this stage, introducing guitarist Ted Skjellum (Nocturno Culto).

March 1989's *Thulcandra* followed before *Cromlech* appeared in December, the latter recorded live. Meantime, Fenriz's side project Isengard issued their debut demo *Spectres Over Gorgoroth*. The *Cromlech* session, the first product to bear the now-familiar Darkthrone logo, was reissued the following year packaged with the *Thulcandra* sessions.

Darkthrone made their way to the fledgling Peaceville label in Yorkshire, England, where label boss Hammy was swiftly building a roster incorporating some of the most influential metal acts of the next decade, such as My Dying Bride, Anathema, Paradise Lost and At The Gates. The extreme nature of *Cromlech* positioned the band in this elite pack of pioneers.

Darkthrone then travelled to Sweden to record the Tomas Skogsberg-produced *Soulside Journey* album in 1990. For this outing, Nagell took on the new alter ego of Hank Amarillo. *Soulside Journey* was an evocative slice of thundering death metal, bordering on the fabled Gothenburg sound. Replete with unorthodox riffing, high speeds on songs such as 'Sempiternal Sepulchrality', two technical instrumentals in 'Accumulation Of Generalization' and 'Eon', and even keyboard details, *Soulside Journey* contained no black metal elements whatsoever.

In May 1991 a short burst of Finnish shows was conducted with speed metal act Prestige. This would turn out to be the last time the band appeared on stage for over a decade. Instead, they underwent a profound transformation shortly afterwards, foregoing their earlier influences and plunging headlong into the rawest form of black metal. The band actually recorded an album's worth of material, but scrapped these tracks as redundant.

The image of the trio – now Fenriz, Zephyrous and Nocturno Culto, with Nilsen in a session role – was completed by corpsepaint, and there was a deliberately primitive regression across all areas of operation, stripping their music down to the bone and even reducing their visuals to roughly-assembled monochrome photocopies set to maximum contrast and annihilate all detail. This was the new, anti-aesthetic Darkthrone who constructed *A Blaze In The Northern Sky*.

Despite lining up a British tour in 1992, they manipulated a canny piece of anti-publicity and cancelled the dates, wishing to disassociate themselves from the black metal 'trend'. They then closed ranks, refusing all press interviews and vowing never to play live again.

Under A Funeral Moon arrived in early 1993, just before the spate of Satanic church burnings in Norway. Those who had believed that Darkthrone had fully explored the concept of minimalism on *A Blaze In The Northern Sky* were shocked by the album's harsh content. In taking black metal to the absolute limit, Darkthrone delivered an album of horrific sonic value, gloriously grim and brazenly nihilistic, with the thinnest of productions that exposed a bleached, skeletal sound. Refusing to perform any interviews, Darkthrone remained resolutely silent about the whole affair.

A 1994 solo album arrived from Fenriz, titled *Vinterskugge*, a collection of archive demos, released under the band name Isengard, but Darkthrone too remained industrious and *Transilvanian Hunger*

emerged in February. Its hideous non-production, the deliberate misspelling in the album title, the sudden, unexplained departure of Enger, the involvement of one of Norway's most controversial figures, and one of the very worst attempts at promotion by exploiting an untouchable taboo – all this made the album a grim landmark.

Unfortunately, the record – bearing the legend 'Norsk Arisk Black Metal' (Norwegian Aryan Black Metal) – was preceded by a notorious press release that resulted in many distributors refusing to handle it. The band had demanded Peaceville include the sentence: "We would like to state that *Transilvanian Hunger* stands beyond any criticism. If any man should attempt to criticize this LP, he should be thoroughly patronized for his obvious Jewish behaviour." Peaceville issued both this statement and their own response, acknowledging that they could not censor their artists but also taking the opportunity to damn the sentiment. An embarrassing fudge then ensued, Fenriz claiming that the word "Jewish" was often used in Norway as a substitute for "stupid", adding that the whole debacle was a "cultural misunderstanding".

Further awkward focus was placed on the contribution to the album of convicted murderer Varg Vikernes. The Burzum leader had supplied lyrics to 'Graven Takeheimens Saler', 'I En Hall Med Flesk Og Mjød', 'As Flittermice As Satans Spys' and 'En As I Dype Skogen' from his prison cell. An often overlooked fact in historical context is that *Transilvanian Hunger* was almost totally sung in Norwegian, almost

cover not to carry a photograph of the band. Instead, they adorned the record in an elaborate fantasy design. Abbath switched to guitar to cover for the absent Demonaz, in doing so enhancing the familiar Immortal assault with a precision that led critics to hail the album as "technical black thrash". The group also donated a rendition of 'To Walk The Infernal Fields' to a Darkthrone tribute album, *Darkthrone Holy Darkthrone*. For touring, they introduced Enchanted bassist Iscariah (Stian Smorholm).

The April 2000 album *Damned In Black* provided evidence that recent tribulations had not altered Immortal's onward pursuit, as the record sold over 40,000 pre-sale copies and made an impression on the national German charts. With Iscariah's bass mixed high – his BC Rich Ironbird giving the first real distinction to the low end on any Immortal record – the band furthered their immersion into full-on thrash. They undertook a tour of America alongside Angel Corpse and Krisiun before headlining Mexican shows.

Immortal left longstanding label Osmose for Nuclear Blast by February 2002's *Sons Of Northern Darkness*. Variants included a vinyl edition, put out by former label Osmose, a limited edition 'quadfolded' digipack, and a metal box – the last of which, restricted to 1,000 copies, sold out before official release.

The band then headlined the gargantuan European 'No Mercy' festival in March and April 2002 with Vader, Catastrophic, Destroyer 666, Hypocrisy, Disbelief, Malevolent Creation and Obscenity. American support dates to the mighty Manowar were also projected. However, these were without Iscariah who, after a three-year term, left the band in late March to concentrate on Necrophagia. Immortal regrouped in May with Pain bassist Saroth taking the vacant guitar role. The following month Abbath took time out to act as guest musician on Dimmu Borgir's album *Death Cult Armageddon*.

In July 2003, as drummer Horgh and ex-Immortal bassist Iscariah unveiled Grimfist and their Peter Tägtgren-produced album *Ghouls Of Grandeur*, word leaked that Immortal had folded. Official statements from Nuclear Blast shortly afterwards put forward the case that the band's career was not in fact over – and that they were taking a lengthy break from activity. Within 24 hours, however, Immortal themselves confirmed that they had indeed called it a day. Townsend Avalanche Music duly compiled an Immortal tribute album, *Epimythion – Tribute to Immortal*.

Iscariah cut demos in Bradford, UK with his Dead To This World

project in April 2005. Meanwhile, Abbath joined forces with original Immortal drummer Armagedda, Enslaved and Malignant Eternal guitarist Arve Isdal (going by the name of Ice Dale), and Gorgoroth bassist King Ov Hell (as TC King), in a project simply entitled I. Former Immortal guitarist Demonaz contributed lyrics.

In June 2006, Abbath indicated in an interview for Germany's *Rock Hard* magazine that Immortal members were in discussions for a reunion. Shortly afterwards, live appearances were confirmed for 2007, and the fanbase breathed a sigh of relief.

MAYHEM
GODFATHERS OF NORWEGIAN BLACK METAL

MAYHEM ARE THE PRIMARY instigators of the monumental Norwegian black metal scene and of the second wave of global black metal in general. The Oslo and Langhus-based band have inspired a myriad of imitators, with their personal heritage woven with tragedy and controversy, befitting the undisputed pioneers of the genre. Their late leader Euronymous (Øystein Aarseth) has been hailed as the godfather of the scene, thanks to his pioneering record label Deathlike Silence and his record shop, Helvete ('Hell'), which was a focal point for the movement in its early days.

Aarseth's first musical steps in learning the guitar were taken with vocalist Nils Svensson from Ski-based band Hell Rats. The Mayhem concept was born around 1983, with Aarseth spotting the name in a news item on Venom's *Welcome To Hell* debut album and in particular the song 'Mayhem With Mercy'. The very first Mayhem consisted of Aarseth on guitar, singer Truls, bassist Glenn Larsen and Hell Rats drummer Espen Mortensen. Performing cover versions, this proto-unit, which lasted into mid 1984, performed a solitary gig at a high school party.

The 16-year-old Aarseth, now dubbing himself Destructor, forged a union with Musta bassist Necrobutcher (aka Jørn Stubberud) and drummer Kjetil Mannheim. Rehearsals in Langhus saw Aarseth's former colleague Nils Svensson handling vocals for a period. Following Svensson, Mayhem briefly employed singer Stele. Even though Mayhem were still covering songs at this stage by the likes of Celtic Frost, Bathory and Venom, Aarseth – now calling himself Euronymous – was already experimenting with corpsepaint, a staple accessory of the black metal legions for years to come.

Having released a demo in 1986 titled *Voice Of A Tortured Skull*, Mayhem – now comprising vocalist Messiah, Euronymous, Necrobutcher and Mannheim – were proud to announce that this tape featured "the worst possible sound quality". Few could disagree. The four-song effort included a cover version of Venom's 'Black Metal'. Messiah's place was then taken by Maniac (real name Sven Erik Kristiansen). Another demo was titled *Pure Fucking Armageddon*. The same year Posercorpse Music issued a further cassette, also titled *Pure Fucking Armageddon*, but featuring the *Voice Of A Tortured Skull* tracks on the 'Fuck' side and rehearsal recordings on the 'Off' side.

In December 1986, an unlikely collaboration took place when Mayhem were on a trip to Germany to market *Pure Fucking Armageddon*. As well as Euronymous and Necrobutcher, this impromptu yet notorious diversion – named Checker Patrol – featured vocalist Robert Gonnella, guitarist Michael Hoffman and bass player Markus Ludwig of the German band Assassin. The music was described on the cassette cover as "Evil fucking noise and drunken screams." Inebriation may have caused the misspelling of the band's name on the front cover as Cheker Patrol.

A rehearsal session, recorded on January 17th and 18th 1987, was also issued. This cassette featured covers of Venom's 'Witching Hour' and the Dead Kennedys' 'California Über Alles'.

Mayhem's debut March 1987 album, *Deathcrush* – pressed by Posercorpse Music – was more of the same. The original manufacturing run was 1,000 vinyl albums and the same quota of cassettes, but only the LPs had the closing outro track. *Deathcrush*, sporting a grim photographic sleeve of two severed, gibbeted hands, is widely acknowledged as the first true black metal album.

Introduced by the Conrad Schnitzer-composed militaristic yet overly ambitious march of 'Silvester Anfang', the album then launched into the breakneck 'Deathcrush'. The most primitive of production values only served to enhance the ferocity of *Deathcrush*, highlighted by 'Necrolust', 'Chainsaw Gutsfuck' and the cover of 'Witching Hour', performed even faster than the original. The musicianship was amateur at best but the intent shone through, and Maniac's vocal performance – hugely emotive screeching for the most part – inspired many bands to follow in their wake. So influential was this album that it was almost a staple requirement for thousands of budding black metal disciples.

Mayhem evolved as both Maniac and Mannheim quit the band. For a brief period in the summer of 1988, Mayhem employed vocalist Kittel Kittilsen and drummer Torben Grue from death metal combo Vomit. However, the same year the band acquired drummer Hellhammer (Jan Axel Blomberg) and Swedish vocalist Dead (Per Yngve Ohlin). Dead had previously fronted Morbid, a band which also included in its ranks the pre-Entombed duo of Lars Göran Petrov and guitarist Ulf Cederlund. With this new blood, Mayhem's music evolved into ever bleaker and starker territory than before, fuelled by Dead's lyrics.

The opening of the Helvete record store in Oslo's old quarter at Schweigaardsgate 56 in mid 1991 was pivotal to the rise of Mayhem. Euronymous's latest venture was established in order to generate funds for the next Mayhem release and provide a focal point for the burgeoning black metal scene. Associates of the Mayhem leader at this time included Immortal, Darkthrone, Enslaved, Thorns, Emperor,

Burzum and Arcturus. Although he was a grand self-publicist, Euronymous is generally acknowledged as the prime mover in persuading these acts to switch their allegiance from death metal to black metal. He had also issued Merciless's *The Awakening*, the first release by his Deathlike Silence label, which he had named after the first track on Sodom's 1986 album *Obsessed By Cruelty*.

Despite the limited nature of their releases, Mayhem were beginning to create international waves by now. Their extreme theatrics often found pigs' heads scattered about the stage, and Dead once hospitalised himself after his penchant for cutting himself on stage led to severe blood loss.

It was to be six years before a follow-up to *Deathcrush* appeared, although constant demand led Euronymous to issue it on CD through Deathlike Silence in 1993. During this time Mayhem conducted only a smattering of live gigs, one of which – on November 26th 1990 – was recorded for *Live In Leipzig* for the Italian Avantgarde label's Obscure Plasma subsidiary. This was the only recorded product to feature Dead. Once more the production quality was roughshod: the concert recordings on the finished product even suffered from tape skip during the intro. Thankfully, Hellhammer's drumming discipline held the show together, but *Live In Leipzig* accentuated the band's ill-rehearsed nature with mis-cued intros, forgotten riffs and general sloppiness. All this was superfluous, however, when Dead's inhuman wails and the harsh crudity of Euronymous's playing were considered. Myths soon gathered around these tapes, with some claiming that the band doused their audience with festering meat and positioned bags of crow carrion onstage in order to revel in the odour of death while they performed. What is known is that, in a practice that was to become tradition, Mayhem impaled pigs' head on poles for the shows.

The 21-year-old Dead apparently committed suicide in his residence on Sørumvein Road in the Kråkstad district on April 8th 1991. It seems the singer was jocular on the day of his suicide, an act he carried out by slashing his wrists and shooting himself in the head with a shotgun, using ammunition given to him as a present by Varg 'Count Grishnackh' Vikernes of Burzum, a close associate of Euronymous. Dead's somewhat strange suicide note simply read: "Excuse all the blood." Euronymous and Hellhammer found the body and, before calling the authorities, they decided to take some photographs of it as a memento. Hellhammer himself made a necklace from pieces of Dead's skull as a gory keepsake. According to the drummer, Euronymous collected up his deceased bandmate's brain tissue to concoct a cannibalistic stew.

Dead had died wearing a T-shirt bearing the legend "I Love Transilvania". This motif, combined with Euronymous's post-mortem culinary exploits, allegedly inspired the title of Darkthrone's later album *Transilvanian Hunger*.

Euronymous's shocking photo of Dead, pictured slumped over his bed with his brain emerging from his shattered skull, was later used as the front cover of a live bootleg, *Dawn Of The Black Hearts* – Dead's final Mayhem concert, recorded in Sarpsborg. Although the official explanation for Dead's death was that he had sliced his wrists with a large kitchen knife and then shot himself, the *Dawn Of The Black Hearts* cover raised questions, as it clearly shows the knife on top of the shotgun.

Necrobutcher then bailed out of Mayhem, seemingly at odds with Euronymous's attempts to position himself as a black metal figurehead. Mayhem recruited ex-Thy Abhorrent vocalist-bassist Occultus (real name Stian Johannsen) and Thorns guitarist Blackthorn (real name Snorre Ruch) in an attempt to move forward. Occultus happened to be the editor of the *Sepulchral Noize* fanzine and an employee of Euronymous at Helvete. Meanwhile, Deathlike Silence Productions was

---

MAYHEM discography

DEATHCRUSH, Posercorpse Music FRANK 001 (Europe) (1987)

LIVE IN LEIPZIG, Obscure Plasma 92007 (Europe) (1993)

DE MYSTERIIS DOM SATHANAS, Deathlike Silence ANTI-
MOSH 006 (Europe), Century Black 7767-2 (USA) (1994)

Out From The Dark, Black Metal BMR 001 (Europe) (1996)
limited edition picture disc: 800 red, 1,000 gold

Freezing Moon, Black Metal BMR 002 (Europe) (1996) limited
edition picture disc of 1,000 copies

Wolf's Lair Abyss, Misanthropy AMAZON 012 (UK) (1997)

Ancient Skin, Misanthropy cnu (UK) (1997)

Necrolust, Vinyl Collector VC002 (Europe) (1996) split 7-inch
single with Zyklon-B, limited edition of 1,000 copies

MEDIOLANUM CAPTA EST, Avantgarde Music AV039 (Europe)
(1999)

GRAND DECLARATION OF WAR, Season Of Mist SOM 027
(Europe), Necropolis NR054 (USA) (2000)

LIVE IN MARSEILLE 2000, Season Of Mist SOM 042 (Europe)
(2001)

EUROPEAN LEGIONS, Season Of Mist SOM 049 (Europe) (2001)

U.S. LEGIONS, Renegade 7001 (USA) (2001)

LEGIONS OF WAR, Season Of Mist America 73 (USA) (2003)

CHIMERA, Season Of Mist SOM 084 (Europe), Season Of Mist
America 84 (USA) (2004)

growing, with Euronymous issuing the *Obscuritatem Advoco Amplectere Me* album from Swedish act Abruptum and *Scorn Defeat* from Japan's Sigh.

Occultus only lasted a matter of weeks, exiting to found Perdition Hearse and later gothic rock act Shadow Dancers. Lacking a vocalist and bassist, Mayhem pulled in guest vocalist Attila Csihar of Hungary's Tormentor for their masterpiece, the *De Mysteriis Dom Sathanas* album. Bass was supplied by Varg Vikernes of Burzum. Euronymous had other problems bearing down on him, with an impending court appearance for allegedly attacking two people with a broken bottle.

The relationship between Euronymous and Vikernes was less jovial than it appeared, however, exacerbated by an outstanding loan owed to Vikernes by Euronymous for the manufacturing costs of Burzum's debut album. Mayhem and Burzum began to compete for the title of Norwegian black metal leaders and a war of words erupted between Euronymous and Vikernes. In a turn of events still shocking after many years, this culminated in Vikernes stabbing Euronymous to death.

In the early hours of August 10th 1993, Vikernes and Blackthorn arrived at Euronymous's apartment in Oslo after a seven-hour drive from Bergen. When the Mayhem guitarist answered his knock on the door, Vikernes stabbed Euronymous with a knife, inflicting over 20 separate wounds, finally dispatching him with a puncture to the forehead.

An autopsy revealed that Euronymous had suffered two wounds to the head, five to the neck and 16 in his back. Initially, authorities believed that an ongoing verbal feud between Norwegian and Swedish bands was to blame, but Vikernes was implicated when a bloodied contract left at the scene was found to carry his fingerprints. When Blackthorn and other associates came under police pressure, their testimonies resulted in the arrest of Vikernes. He received a jail sentence of 21 years – and the myth of Euronymous began to grow.

Hellhammer teamed up with Mysticum during this period but then concentrated his efforts on Mayhem once more. Mysticum, unable to find a human equivalent with the desired skills, promptly replaced him with a drum machine.

The Mayhem album *De Mysteriis Dom Sathanas* (a Latin mistranslation of 'Lord Satan's Secret Rites') arrived in May 1994. Despite a request by Euronymous's parents to have Vikernes's bass parts removed, they remained on the finished disc.

Hellhammer vowed to continue with Mayhem, re-recruiting Maniac and Necrobutcher with guitarist Blasphemer (aka Rune Ericksen) of Aura Noir. He involved himself in the side project Arcturus with Ulver vocalist Kristoffer Rygg, (aka Garm) and Samoth Tomas 'Samoth' Haugen of Emperor, and briefly joined Emperor for their debut album. He also appeared on the 1998 *Nexus Polaris* album by Covenant, yet another project put together by members of Dimmu Borgir, Cradle Of Filth and Arcturus.

Towards the end of 1995, *Dawn Of The Black Hearts* was released as a bootleg, gory cover shot and all. The album was made up of early tracks and live cuts dating back to 1986, including two Celtic Frost and two Venom tracks. Black Metal Records weighed in with a 1996 picture disc, *Out From The Dark*, comprising tracks from Dead's last rehearsal. A further release, *A Tribute To The Black Emperors*, collated Mayhem's demo songs with tracks from Dead's band Morbid. A 1997 Mayhem single release was culled from two studio tracks, 'Carnage' and 'Freezing Moon', originally laid down for the Swedish label CBR in 1991.

The band returned with the 1997 *Wolf's Lair Abyss* EP, released through the new British imprint Misanthropy. Mayhem surprised many fans when they actually took to the stage in late 1997 for a whirlwind of live performances that re-established the veracity of their claim as black metal leaders. The touring line-up found Hellhammer alongside Maniac, Blasphemer, Necrobutcher and stand-in guitarist Alexander, on

loan from Fleurety. A further live album, *Mediolanum Capta Est*, surfaced in 1999 via Avantgarde.

The now-stable Mayhem switched labels again to the French company Season Of Mist for the highly experimental and semi-conceptual June 2000 album *Grand Declaration Of War*. This work finally broke the group free from its past, incorporating clean vocals from Maniac, discordant song structures, and industrial sounds. Spiral Architect singer Øyvind guested in the studio. Hardened fans baulked at uncharacteristic mellow passages, and the near-trance techno of 'A Bloodsword And A Colder Sun' came in for outright condemnation in some quarters.

Maniac appeared alongside Pantera's Phil Anselmo, Satyricon's Satyr Wongraven, Necrophagia's Killjoy and Darkthrone's Fenriz for the Eibon project, which issued one track on the *Moonfog 2000* compilation, and guested on Fleurety's 2000 album *Department Of Apocalyptic Affairs*.

Hellhammer guested on the Troll 2000 album *The Last Predators*, a project of The Kovenant and ex-Dimmu Borgir man Nagash. In keeping with black metal tradition, Necrobutcher was active with a side project, Kvikksølvguttene. He also turned up as a guest on the Bloodthorn album *Under The Reign Of Terror*, contributing to a cover of Mayhem's own 'Deathcrush'.

During October 2001, rumours circulated that Maniac was about to decamp and that Mayhem would fold. Later statements confirmed that Maniac had indeed considered leaving but had revised his opinion following an enthusiastic tour response.

More guest appearances followed, with Hellhammer operating under his real name of Jan Axel for melodic rock outfit Jorn and for Swedish 'suicidal' black metal act Shining. Meanwhile, Maniac donated his services to the *Ceremony In Flames* album from Wurdulak, assembled by Killjoy of Necrophagia. Blasphemer also kept busy with his Mezzerschmitt venture and session guitar work on the 2002 Gehenna album *Murder*. Mezzerschmitt, with Blasphemer as 'Herr Schmitt', also included Hellhammer ('Hauptmann Hammer') and Red Harvest keyboardist Lrz, arriving with the EP *Weltherrschaft*.

During 2002, Season Of Mist released a boxed set, *The Studio Experience*, containing Mayhem's entire official catalogue on vinyl LPs. Limited to 2,000 copies, the set also included a 7-inch single comprising two ultra-rare previously unreleased tracks recorded with Dead on lead vocals.

Mayhem came in for unwelcome attention in March when a sheep's head thrown from the stage in Bergen on March 6th fractured the skull of a 25-year-old audience member, Per Kristian Hagen. More practical matters saw the band retreating to the mountains of Norway with a mobile studio to cut a new album, *Chimera*. Hellhammer was also drumming for trad-metal band Carnivora, the brainchild of former Jorn Lande band guitarist Tore Moren.

Issued in April 2004, *Chimera* came in a first run that included 1,000 coloured vinyl albums and 500 picture discs. The album landed at Number 28 in the national Norwegian charts. Mayhem united with Poland's Decapitated, Estonian band Manatark and Japanese act Defiled for a European tour commencing early April. They announced plans to celebrate their 20th anniversary with a special show at the Rockefeller in Oslo, to be recorded for DVD.

Rumours circulating in June suggested that Maniac had been expelled from the ranks and former singer Attila Csihar had been re-installed. Within hours, this conjecture was officially denied.

'Freezing Moon' was chosen for a compilation assembled by Darkthrone drummer Fenriz, released through Peaceville and titled *Fenriz Presents: The Best Of Old School Black Metal*.

Mayhem began the process of assembling a new album in August.

The first new material was the track 'Anno Vampir' on a Season Of Mist compilation released in September. In mid November the earlier rumours citing Maniac's departure and the re-recruitment of Csihar were officially confirmed. On November 17th, Csihar stepped onstage with Dissection for renditions of two old school black metal classics – 'Elizabeth Bathory' by Tormentor and Mayhem's 'Freezing Moon' – during the band's appearance at Kultiplex in Budapest, Hungary.

In early 2005, Maniac announced a punk project, Bomberos, in union with ex-Emperor and Thorns drummer Bård 'Faust' Eithun. Meanwhile, Hellhammer sessioned on recordings for Dimmu Borgir. Mayhem's first performance with the reinstated Csihar came on December 10th at Budapest's Petofi Hall. Shows in late January and February saw stops in Indonesia, Taiwan, Thailand, Singapore and Malaysia. The last date was banned by the authorities, and shortly afterwards the show scheduled for Jakarta, Indonesia was also cancelled.

Re-signing with Season Of Mist in May 2006, Mayhem revealed the title of a new album: *Ordo Ab Chao*. The band proved they are still able to stir up controversy when their 'traditional' use of pigs' heads onstage during their headline performance at the 'Gates Of Metal' festival in Hultsfred, Sweden broke local laws. They continue undeterred.

SATYRICON
GENIUS IN BLACK METAL FORM

SATYRICON PERFORM BLACK METAL with some unique twists. They were founded in Oslo in September 1991 by frontman Satyr (aka Sigurd Wongraven), Lemarchand (Håvard Sørensen), bassist Wargod (Vegard Blomberg) and drummer Exhurtum (Carl Michael Eide). The group were rooted in a proto-death grind band, Eczema, established in 1990 by Eide and Blomberg and subsequently featuring Jørgensen. When frontman Satyr joined Eczema – just as they were moving to a black metal and changing their name to Satyricon – he was a mere 15 years old.

The group debuted with a demo, commonly known as *All Evil*, recorded with engineer S.K. Sunde on June 21st and 22nd 1991. Lemarchand and Eide were ejected after these sessions, the drummer going to Ulver before founding Ved Buens Ende in 1993, debuting with a 1994 demo *Those Who Caress The Pale*. Eide, re-billed as Aggressor, became an industrious figure on the black metal scene, contributing to Aura Noir and Inferno. Satyricon's subsequent 1994 demo, *The Forest Is My Throne*, recorded as a duo of Satyr handling vocals, guitar and bass with Frost (Kjetil Haraldstad) on drums, was later issued as a split CD with Haugesund Viking metal act Enslaved. Satyr also constructed and later issued a solo album, *Fjelltronen*, under the title Wongraven.

Satyricon's opening full-length album, *Dark Medieval Times*, was set to be recorded during August 1993 at Skoklefald Studios. The album was put in jeopardy midway through when the band's label, Sweden's No Fashion Records, were unable to fund the entire session. Satyr and Frost raised the finances themselves to complete the tracks in September. At first an attempt to mix the tapes was conducted at Grieghallen Studios in Bergen but Satyr then returned to Skoklefald for a final remix. Upon release by Moonfog Records (a subsidiary of avant-garde label Tatra Productions), the album, purposely rustic in sound quality, lacked all text – album credits, names of those participating and lyrics – in order to project an air of mystery.

The Shadowthrone album of 1994, laid down at Waterfall Studios, featured Samoth (Tomas Haugen) from Emperor on bass, but he was incarcerated shortly afterwards for church-burning and was replaced by Kveldulv (actually Ted Skjellum, aka Nocturno Culto, from Darkthrone). The Emperor, Arcturus and Ulver-credited SS (Sverd

Steinar Johnsen) sessioned on keyboards. The following year found Frost involved with Zyklon-B's *Blood Must Be Shed* album alongside Draug Aldrahn of Dødheimsgard and Emperor men Ihsahn and Samoth.

Satyricon's next album, *Nemesis Divina*, cut in January and February 1996 and emerging that April through Moonfog, notably included Nebelhexe (Andrea Meyer-Haugen) of Hagalaz' Runedance as guest narrator on the track 'The Dawn Of A New Age'. Lyrics to 'Du Som Hater Gud' were donated by Fenriz. *Nemesis Divina* accelerated Satyricon's profile in mainland Europe through a licence to Century Media.

Satyricon pulled in Død (Daniel Olaisen) of Trioxin and Cobalt 60 for live guitar work and toured Europe alongside Dissection and Gorgoroth in 1996. The 1997 EP *Megiddo – Mother North In The Dawn Of A New Age* gave fans a diverse view of Satyricon and enhanced the group's status significantly with a new licence to Nuclear Blast. 'The Dawn Of A New Age', was given an industrial remix by Apoptygma Berzerk, while 'Forkhekset' was a live version recorded in Germany; 'Night Of Divine Power' was a re-recording of 'The Dark Castle In The Deep Forest'; and further industrial treatment was given to a cover version of Motörhead's 'Orgasmatron'. Additional musicians on the EP included guitarist Anders Odden and keyboard player Grothesk (Stephan Groth) of Apoptygma Berzerk.

Ensuing concert dates in 1997 witnessed a revamped Satyricon, with Død joined by Svartalv of Aeternus and Gehenna on second guitar. Word arrived that erstwhile Dismember man Daemon (Richard Cabeza) had enrolled, but this union was fleeting. Olaisen assembled side project Scariot in 1997 for the album *Deathforlorn*.

Another transitional outing, the May 1999 *Intermezzo II* EP, furthered this brave new direction. Boasting a rendition of legendary Brazilian black metal band Sarcofago's 'INRI', the set was convened by Satyr and Frost in collusion with guitarist Sanrabb, Crest Of Darkness bassist Ingar Amlien and Vegard Blomberg handling samples.

Having established themselves in the upper ranks of the Norwegian hierarchy, Satyricon chose not to solidify this success but to challenge it in a daring move. In September 1999 they branched out into ever more radical and experimental areas with the *Rebel Extravaganza* album. Confusingly, it opened with an uncredited track,

Satyricon

actually entitled 'Down South, Up North', with a reprise later in the running order. Featured guests at the Ambience Studios sessions were as diverse as Darkthrone's Fenriz (who supplied a simple tambourine beat), Anders Odden, Snorre Ruch of Thorns (as S.W. Krupp), session musicians Bjørn Boge on bass and Lasse Hafreager on Hammond organ, Norwegian trance artist Ra, and actress Trine Svensson. Icily executed, *Rebel Extravaganza* cast off any vestiges of ancestral or folk orientation, adopted standard rock verse-chorus structures, and wallowed in post-industrialism.

Olaisen decamped from the line-up to found the retro death metal act Blood Red Throne, later issuing *Monument Of Death*. In 2000, Wongraven was involved in the black metal side project Eibon alongside Mayhem's Maniac, Darkthrone's Fenriz, Necrophagia's Killjoy and Pantera frontman Phil Anselmo.

Following headline shows in Europe with guests Behemoth and Hecate Enthroned, the band moved out of the familiar black metal field to support Pantera on their 2000 European dates. For touring duties Satyricon included former Emperor bassist Tyr (Jan-Erik Torgersen), Spiral Architect's Steinar Gundersen and Old Man's Child's Cyrus (Terje Andersen) on guitar. Frost made a return to the scene with 1349 and did some session work in 2002 for Gehenna.

Satyricon then became one of the very first black metal acts to sign to a major label, hooking up with Capitol for the 2002 *Vulcano* (later changed to *Volcano*) album in Scandinavia, but remaining with Nuclear Blast for the rest of the world. A video for the track 'Fuel Is My Hatred' was directed by the acclaimed Swedish film maker Jonas Åkerlund. Preceding the new album was a compilation, *Ten Horns – Ten Diadems*, which included an exclusive cut titled 'Serpent's Rise'. The band now included Gundersen's Spiral Architect and Lunaris colleague Lars Norberg on bass. For live work, Satyricon added Arnt Ove Grønbech (aka Obsidian C) of Keep Of Kalessin on rhythm guitar and Enslaved keyboard player Ivar Peersen (aka Ivar Bjørnson). *Volcano* reached Number 4 on the Norwegian album charts. Drummer Frost took a further diversion by joining Keep Of Kalessin for an mini-CD, *Reclaim*, issued in December 2003, featuring Obsidian C. and Attila Csihar (Mayhem, Aborym and Tormentor) on vocals.

A somewhat unexpected diversion for Wongraven came in February 2004 with Black Diamond Brigade, a one-off Kiss tribute act with Amulet vocalist Torgny Amdam, Knut 'Euroboy' Schreiner of Turbonegro on guitar, Faith No More's Billy Gould on bass and Tarjei Strøm on the drums. Their rendition of 'Black Diamond', included on the compilation album of the same name issued in February by Universal, peaked at Number 6 on the Norwegian singles charts. The band played a one-off TV performance at the Alarm awards in Bergen, teasing the audience with the intro to Black Sabbath's 'War Pigs' before launching into 'Black Diamond'.

Satyricon were set to continue touring across North America into April 2004 as part of Morbid Angel's American 'Heretic' dates partnered with Suffocation and Premonitions Of War. However, just weeks before, the band's participation seemed in jeopardy when drummer Frost was refused a work visa. According to Norwegian newspaper reports, this stemmed from a prior conviction for violence. The situation was saved when the Enslaved, Emperor, Disiplin and Zyklon-credited Trym Torson stepped in as replacement. Unfortunately the band's woes did not end there: the night before Satyricon was to travel, guitarist Arnt Grønbech was assaulted and received cuts to the face from a beer bottle. The musician required stitches but made the tour. Subsequently, Grønbech was awarded 130,000 Norwegian kroner (about $18,500) in compensation and his attacker was found guilty of first-degree assault and sentenced to four months in jail.

Frost announced that he had joined another major force on the Norwegian black metal scene – Gorgoroth. However, within weeks of this news the drummer backed out, citing conflicting priorities with Satyricon.

Volcano finally surfaced in the USA on Sony imprint EatUrMusic (the label run by System Of A Down guitarist Daron Malakian) a full 18 months after its European release. Satyricon's August 2004 appearance at the 'Wacken Open Air' festival in Germany proved a landmark event as, following a regular live set, Nocturno Culto stepped up to front four Darkthrone songs with the band: 'Kaatharian Life Code', 'The Hordes Of Nebulah', 'Transilvanian Hunger' and 'Under A Funeral Moon'.

With Frost still denied access to the USA, Satyricon employed the high-profile figure of Slipknot drummer Joey Jordison for the 'Return Of The Antichrist' headlining dates commencing on December 2nd in San Francisco. Support for these gigs came from two Canadian acts, Infernal Majesty and 3 Inches Of Blood.

However, the tour came to a jarring halt after a little over a week's worth of dates. An ominous silence was broken a few days later when it was revealed that guitarists Steinar Gundersen and Arnt Ove Grønbech had been arrested after the December 14th performance at the Fun Haus in Toronto. Both were charged with drugging and raping a woman on Satyricon's tour bus after the concert. The guitarists, claiming innocence, were bailed for $50,000 each. The case was continuing at the time of writing.

January 2005 found Satyr acting as co-producer on new material for Thorns. Meanwhile, Satyricon entered Puk Studio in Denmark with producer Mike Frasier on October 17th to commence work on a new album, *Now, Diabolical*. In January 2006 the group announced they had signed to Roadrunner for territories outside Norway and the USA. Released in April 2006, vinyl versions of *Now, Diabolical* added an extra track, 'Storm (Of The Destroyer)'. The album crashed into the Norwegian charts at Number 2. A diversion from the norm, brass sections appeared on three tracks, arranged by Øivind Westby.

As the band expanded still further beyond the black metal template, a notable live date at the Sentrum Scene in Oslo on November 4th saw Satyricon joined onstage by the Norwegian Broadcasting Orchestra and Oslo Philharmonic Orchestra. Whatever their next step, it is sure to be epic.

WORLDWIDE BLACK METAL

BLACK metal is the ugliest branch of the heavy metal tree, a mutated, misshapen aberration, a true "thing that should not be". Rock music had always flirted with Satan in his theatrical role as ol' Nick, but it was almost always exclusively tongue in cheek. Black metal recognised that the lord of the deep was deadly serious in his intent and needed to be afforded due respect with a whole new musical style. This, importantly, is the structural difference: not only did this crop of new artists lyrically treat Lucifer with adoration, but also they manufactured a new form of metal with which to do so. It is a factor often overlooked by casual commentators: black metal is much, much more than its visual aesthetic.

Quite perversely, the style that became black metal was borne out of ignorance. Venom from Newcastle Upon Tyne, England, Bathory from Sweden, Denmark's Mercyful Fate, and Swiss avant-garde pioneers Celtic Frost kickstarted the genre, but their punk-meets-metal doodlings could hardly be called accomplished. Where this triumvirate succeeded, though, was to outweigh their lack of proficiency with extreme enthusiasm in other areas. Naturally this rebellious reverence for Satan and his minions drew an easy appeal, and with the music being so basic, it also meant that legions of impressionable young teens could quickly follow in their footsteps with immediately satisfying results. Once this goal had been achieved, these bands could then apply themselves to perfecting the art: the choking, mid-frequency guitars; the rasping, inhuman vocal style; bone-dry, blastbeating drums; and hugely distorted sound quality. What was previously lambasted as underproduction became the desired effect – anti-music.

Image, previously utilised as an embellishment, was to hold equal status to the accompanying audio terror. Venom, Bathory and Celtic Frost all adopted pseudonyms, making this the norm and allowing for an even greater range of blasphemy under the protection of anonymity.

While black clothing was a prerequisite – preferably leather, preferably adorned with pseudo armour by way of studs and spikes – the other trademark of the genre came from Mercyful Fate leader King Diamond. Inspired by Alice Cooper and Kiss, Diamond had taken to monochrome face paint for horrific effect. This makeup, given the name 'corpsepaint', would become de rigueur. A multitude of variations on the pattern ensued, somewhat unfortunately lending ammunition to outside detractors as many latter-day acts' attempts at ghoulishness led to an army of pandas, badgers and penguins.

Traditionally, heavy metal was produced by a select clutch of countries, firmly centred on the UK and North America. Now the power base shifted, Scandinavia elevating itself rapidly to a position of prominence (see chapter 6 on Norwegian black metal). Europe has proved to be more receptive. France, Italy, Greece and Germany boast healthy black metal scenes. France in particular is a hotbed of authentic pseudo-Norwegian bands determined never to bow to fashion. In Germany, both Mystic Circle and Agathodaimon have achieved prominence. Greece is a staunch supporter of all metal genres and has used acts such as Rotting Christ and Septic Flesh to break down barriers.

Eastern Europe has been a fertile breeding ground for Beelzebub's battalions. Poland's Behemoth now engage in sustained global campaigning, but few other acts have broken internationally. Nevertheless, Poland, Hungary, Rumania, Bulgaria, the Czech Republic and particularly the Russian states host an ever increasing tidal wave of bands. Unfortunately, the politics of prominent bands such as Graveland and Nokturnal Mortum put them beyond the pale.

In another example of tradition being overthrown, those bands that dared rise out of cultdom were viciously savaged. Strangely for a country with such a strong metal tradition, in Britain only Cradle Of Filth really achieved mainstream recognition. They sit at the top of a very steep pyramid with virtually no competition. It is strange that the UK's sense of innovation, apart from an early burst of genius that was Sabbat, has so completely failed in the area of black metal. Cradle Of Filth's success, which continues to this day, was met by vilification of the highest order.

In a clear reversal of roles, it was the USA that struggled to break acts through. Bands such as Grand Belial's Key, Judas Iscariot, Acheron, Kult Ov Azazel, Abazagorath, Demonic Christ and Krieg gained cult recognition but, with the exception of Absu, failed to exploit this into commerciality in the same manner as their European and Scandinavian counterparts. Satan has enjoyed higher prominence in the death metal field, courtesy of blasphemous acts such as Slayer, Deicide, Nunslaughter, Morbid Angel and Incantation.

ABIGOR
MUCH-RESPECTED BLACK METAL AUSTRIANS

ABIGOR WERE MENTORED by avowed Satanist Peter K and have released a steady stream of uncompromising albums since their debut. The band take their name from the goetic demon commander (also known as Eligor) and bellowed forth a bewildering pantheon of works, juxtaposing primitive black metal with extravagant experimentation.

Abigor originated in Dobermannsdorf, Austria with a line-up of drummer T.T. (aka Thomas Tannenberger), guitarist Virus666 P.K. (aka Peter Kubik) and vocalist Rune, the latter switching his stage name to Tharen. Kubik and Tannenberger had a musical history back to childhood, both performing during 1990 with outfits such as To Mega Therion and In Sin. In this first incarnation, Abigor – falling in with the familiar corpsepaint, cowls and medieval weaponry – headed up the Austrian Black Metal Syndicate alongside the likes of Summoning, Gromm and Pazuzu.

The group cut four demos starting with autumn 1993's four-track *Ash Nazg...*, comprising 'Dance Of The Dead', 'In Sin' and 'Shadowlord', the December follow-up *Lux Devicta Est*, an eponymous February 1994 effort, and then *Moonrise* in March of the same year.

Tharen departed, and the band utilised the services of Silenius (aka Michael Gregor) from Summoning for a further 1994 tape billed as *In Hate & Sin*, which, although not available for public consumption, secured the band a deal with the Napalm label. The inaugural album, *Verwüstung: Invoke The Dark Age*, set the scene for further releases. Indeed, its lyrical stance and the deliberately inflammatory remarks against Christianity in interviews by band-members created tribulation even before its release. The Austrian authorities' objections caused a delay to its issue of several months. Originally slated for a summer 1994 arrival, *Verwüstung* finally hit the market that November. The initial run of 5,000 came in a monochrome sleeve before a coloured variant arrived.

During the spring of 1995, Abigor re-recorded an earlier demo track, 'Shadowlord', for inclusion on the Napalm compilation *With Us Or Against Us Volume 1*. That same year, Kubik, billed as December Fog, released the demo *In The Realm Of Ancient Shadows*.

Abigor's *Orkblut: The Retaliation: Storming Onwards On Pagan Paths*, a 25-minute saga relating the lifespan of a pagan warrior – recorded in November and December 1994 – introduced ambient passages, making for a harsh division of sound between the militaristic metal and sedate segues, opening with a spoken narrative and closing with a poignant flute finale titled 'Langsam Verhallte Des Lebens Schmerz'.

Nachthymnen (From The Twilight Kingdom), cut at Tonstudion Hörnix with co-producer Georg Hrauda in late May 1994, brought a new focus to the Austrian black metal scene. The record secured attention for its inclusion of female singer Elisabeth Toriser, of Antichrisis and Dominion, marking Abigor out as one of the pioneers in this combination of ambient and black metal. During November 1995 the band recorded the first instalment of the grandiose *Opus IV* record, *Horns Lurk Beyond The Stars*, and then crafted the second chapter, *Blut Aus Aeonen Pt.2*, in May 1996. The group's intention was to put out a brace of EPs, but Napalm combined the two sessions for *Opus IV*. A mini-album, *Apokalypse*, recorded in just two days, followed. None of these records revealed any leanings towards commercialism.

Abigor and Amestigon members founded Heidenreich during 1998. The same year the band issued two limited editions, the instrumental 'Structures Of Immortality' 7-inch EP in September, restricted to 500 copies, and a compilation of early demos titled *Origo Regium 1993-1994*, limited to 1,000 and swiftly selling out.

The full-length *Supreme Immortal Art* marked a creative transition for

Abigor, employing a greater use of keyboards, courtesy of Kubik's wife, Lucia Mariam Faroutan. While recording, Tannenberger was arrested on narcotics-related charges, leaving Kubik to finish the album. Although symphonic in design, the final mix complemented the synthesisers to the detriment of the percussion, resulting in a greater swing away from the band's trademark rawness than they had intended.

As Abigor set to work on 1999's *Channeling The Quintessence Of Satan*, Silenius opted to decamp, voicing concern over the group's new direction. The erstwhile frontman swiftly forged Kreuzweg Ost, an industrial-styled concept in league with Martin Schrienk of Pungent Stench. Meanwhile, *Channeling The Quintessence Of Satan*, with its cover graced by Albrecht Dürer's 1514 woodcut *The Knight, Death And The Devil*, was completed with Thurisaz of Heidenreich as the band's new vocalist. In May 2000, Abigor lost another founder member as T.T. made his exit. Moritz Neuner, a veteran of Angry Angels, Korova, Evenfall and Dornenreich among many other acts, filled the vacancy.

The 2000 *In Memory...* EP featured covers of Slayer's 'Crionics' and Kreator's 'Terrible Certainty', originally cut for Dwell Records tribute albums. The cover art, a graphic representation of an evisceration, was banned, affording the band plenty of press coverage. The EP was reissued with new cover artwork and two extra songs. The *Satanized (A Journey Through Cosmic Infinity)* album was released in March 2001.

The group spent much of 2001 recording a new album provisionally titled *Warmachine (Angels Fall)*. The band enrolled Stefan Fiori of Italian gothic black metal band Graveworm as their new singer in April 2002. It seemed that a rare live outing for Abigor would occur in July when the band scheduled a performance at the 'Skeleton Bash' festival in Innsbruck, Austria. However, an injury suffered by guitarist Kubik curtailed this event. In the aftermath, Abigor put out an official statement claiming they would never play live.

Although by mid 2002 *Warmachine (Angels Fall)* had still not surfaced, reports emerged of a further Abigor release to be titled *The Dead White Moonlight Songs*. The group then signalled the imminent delivery of a split 7-inch single, a re-recorded 'Dawn Of Human Dust', in collaboration with Belphegor. None of these mooted releases transpired, however, and the only material to surface, belatedly in 2004, was a 7-inch single through Dark Horizon Records titled 'Shockwave 666'. The unexpectedly experimental nature of one of these tracks, 'Repulsor (Pulsar 2003)', revealed Abigor's new unorthodox vision.

Kubik dissolved Abigor in June 2003, explaining his decision with the statement: "I simply can't identify myself, nor Abigor, with today's black metal genre any more." Silenius, Kubik and Neuner founded St. Lucifer in late 2003. Neuner joined Graveworm in early 2004 and as that year closed joined veteran German act Atrocity.

In March 2006, Kubik placed both his Hellbound and St. Lucifer projects on hold and reformed Abigor. With Lukas Lindenberger on drums, Kubik extended an offer of reformation to former band personnel T.T., Thurisaz and Silenius. Drawing in Sethnacht Eligor (aka Alexander Hornung) as new vocalist, a fresh Abigor album was projected to be titled *Fractal Possession*. Sethacht's tradition included studio association with Dominus Satanas, Hellbound, Eschaton and Blood Stained plus live activity with Ewig Frost, Incineration and In Slumber. The band seem poised to make their next move.

ABRUPTUM
EVIL INCARNATE

FOR THE MOST PART, Abruptum are a duo – Ophtalamia founder It (aka Tony Särkkä) and Marduk member Evil (Morgan Håkansson). The Satanic black metal band from Stockholm, Sweden are of such extreme nature that their self-description as "the essence of pure audio evil" has gone unchallenged even by those immersed in the most radical quarters of the scene. What Abruptum lack in song structure they make up for with unnerving screams and avant-garde rhythms.

Before Abruptum, It fronted the Finspång-based crossover act Brejn Dedd, releasing three demos, *Brejn Dedd* and *The Ugly Tape* in 1988 and 1989's *Born Ugly*: all featured none other than Dan Swanö on drums.

Early Abruptum works included the February 1990 demo *Hextum Galaem Zelog*, after which bassist Ext was discarded, and an August 1990 session, *The Satanist Tunes*. The latter was dedicated to "The superior, unholy ancient one – Thy one without name or shape", with a warning to potentially parsimonious purchasers: "No used stamps OK!" These early recordings already displayed Abruptum's trademark 'black noise' sound – proto-sludge riffing laden with reverb and heavily reliant on keyboard atmospherics.

The two-track 'Evil' 7-inch single emerged the following year on the Psychoslaughter label, after which founding member All (aka Jim Berger)

ABRUPTUM discography

Evil, PS PS-003 (USA) (1991)
OBSCURITATEM ADVOCO AMPLECTÉRE ME, Deathlike Silence ANTI-MOSH 004 (Europe) (1993)
IN UMBRA MALITIAE AMBULABO, IN AETERNUM IN TRIUMPHO TENEBRAUM, Deathlike Silence ANTI-MOSH 009 (Europe) (1994)
EVIL GENIUS, Hellspawn HELL 002 (Europe) (1995)
VI SONUS VERIS NIGRAE MALITIAES, Full Moon Productions FMP 009 (USA) (1996)
De Profundis Mors Vas Cousumet, Blooddawn Productions BLOOD 006 (Europe) (2001)
CASUS LUCIFERI, Blooddawn Productions BLOOD 014 (Europe) (2004)

---

left the band. A third demo was then issued, the exceptionally rare October 1992 session *Orchestra Of Dark*. The Deathlike Silence label, owned by Mayhem leader Euronymous, put out their inaugural full-length album, *Obscuritatem Advoco Amplectere Me*, in 1993. Abruptum's second album, 1994's *In Umbra Malitiae Ambulabo, In Aeternum In Triumpho Tenebraum*, consisted of one hour-long song. As word began to spread among the metal fraternity, Abruptum's exercises in laboriously slow 'audio hell' began to attract followers. These megalithic slabs of noise with no patterned riffs or rhythms in evidence were overlaid with screams and wails – which were convincing enough to foster a myth suggesting that the band-members actually tortured themselves during the recording process in order to capture genuine anguish on tape.

Abruptum's It created a side project, Vondur ('Evil'), in 1993: an album, *Stridsyfirlysing*, featuring former Abruptum vocalist All, was released in 1995. The first 666 copies of the CD came with a free (and genuine) razorblade, the artwork proclaiming "Kill yourself."

An album of early Abruptum demos, plus solo material from the 'Evil' single, was released in 1995 on Hellspawn records as *Evil Genius*. Their 1996 album, recorded at Abyss Studios with Hypocrisy's Peter Tägtgren as engineer and released through Full Moon Productions, was titled *Vi Sonus Veris Nigrae Malitiaes*, which translates as The Aural Essence Of Pure Black Evil.

Side projects Ophthalamia and Vondur were now running in parallel. Särkkä, having relinquished his post in Abruptum in 1996 following alleged death threats, activated a new thrash metal/traditional rock venture with Michael Bohlin titled 8thSin during 2000, signing to Black Lodge Records. Evil soldiered on with Abruptum, releasing the March 2004 album *Casus Luciferi* through Swedish label Blooddawn Productions. This outing witnessed the band toning down their aggression considerably in favour of monotonous, ambient dirges.

ABSU
CELTIC-AMERICAN BLACK METAL?

SELF-STYLED "ANCESTRAL OCCULT METAL" act Absu are titled after the ancient Sumerian word for the abyss and feature vocalist-drummer Proscriptor McGovern (Emperor Proscriptor Magikus, aka Russell Randell Givens), who claims direct lineage to the Scottish clans and frequently wears a kilt to bolster his assertions. Although firmly in the black metal marketplace, the Plano, Texas-based group have successfully attempted to brand themselves as a "dark occult metal" band. Lyrically, Absu blend Sumerian and Mesopotamian folklore and mythology with ceremonial magic, the rites of the cabbala, Gnosticism, and Celtic mythology. They derive other dominant themes from Scottish, Irish and Germanic histories.

The unit began life as the 1989 band Dolmen, founded by Shaftiel (aka Michael) and Lord Equitant Infernian (aka Ray). In 1990, the band changed their name to Azathoth and by 1991 this act had evolved into Absu, releasing a demo, 'Immortal Sorcery', in May and a further four-song demo, *Return To The Ancients*.

The Temples Of Offal EP, comprising earlier demo tracks, was released in late 1991, and a further set of demos, *Infinite And Profane Thrones*, arrived the following year. However, guitarist Gary Lindholm and drummer Daniel Benbow opted out. Fresh blood was found from the disintegration of the band Magus, and Emperor Proscriptor McGovern and Daviel Athron Mystica duly joined the fold in time for the debut 1993 album *Barathrum: V.I.T.R.I.O.L.*, the subtitle a Latin acronym for "visiting the insides of the earth". Gothic Records put out the original version of *Barathrum* and a later European edition, manufactured by French label Osmose, was issued in different artwork. A second guitarist, Black Massith, was added after earlier contributing keyboards. Mystica then left the fold, requiring Equitant to cover both bass and guitar. Absu pulled in erstwhile Goreaphobia vocalist Mezzadurus (Chris Gamble) for touring purposes.

Pre-Absu archive Dolmen tracks were issued as *On The Eve Of War* through the Black Montana Productions label, but the success of the band's debut resulted in a lengthier contract signed with Osmose, who released *The Sun Of Tiphareth* in March 1995, recorded by Proscriptor on vocals and drums, Shaftiel on guitar and Equitant on bass. Notably, Absu re-worked Morbid Scream's 'The Coming Of War' for this set. Collectors soon snapped up a blue vinyl rarity, restricted to just 300 units. A limited edition EP *...And Shineth Unto The Cold Cometh* also arrived in 1995. Only 500 copies were pressed.

Further product to appease Absu devotees was issued in 1995 with Proscriptor's solo debut, *The Venus Bellona*, released through Cruel Moon International. Adventurously, this eclectic set, self-described as "Allaxitonian/Glenorchy Fantasy Musick", included A Flock Of Seagulls cover version 'I Ran (So Far Away)'. The album title is a metaphor for Proscriptor himself – the planet Venus is associated with his zodiacal sign, Gemini, and Bellona means war god. Studio sessions came from Absu's own Equitant on bass with Ellisile contributing acoustic guitar. *The Venus Bellona* was released in varying formats. The North American version, on Dark Age Productions, was issued as a double vinyl album with unique artwork. Swedish imprint Cruel Moon International's vinyl version was restricted to 726 copies.

Absu's *The Third Storm Of Cythräul*, including Morbid Scream's self-titled anthem, was out in January 1997. Limited digipacks closed with an extra track, 'Akhera Goiti – Akhera Beiti (One Black Opalith For Tomorrow)'. Despite the ascendancy of Absu, the musicians engaged themselves in a swathe of extracurricular activities. Mezzadurus convened a side project titled Blood Storm, releasing – among others – the 1997 album *The Atlantean Wardragon*. Equitant was also operating an eponymous electronic solo project, having issued the 1994 demo *Great Lands Of Minas Ithil (City Of Isildur)*, while Proscriptor had a side act called Melechesh.

Proscriptor also performed live drums for Judas Iscariot and found time to engage his talents in mediaeval act Moonroot alongside Mike Riddick of The Soil Bleeds Black. The core membership of Absu also occupied themselves in Equimanthorn, releasing albums via the Greek Unisound label: *Nindinugga Nimshimshargal Enlillara* in 1994 and 1999's *Lectionum Antiquarum*, which was compiled from early demo and live recordings.

Absu marked a return to action with an interim EP in September 1998, *In The Eyes Of Ioldanach*, preceding what many devotees regard as the band's masterpiece, the May 2001 album *Tara*. So involved and intricate were Proscriptor's Celtic storylines that a lyric sheet with a full-blown explanatory glossary was deemed necessary. Although Absu's songwriting, musical precision and narrative certainly peaked with *Tara*, it was Proscriptor's breathtaking dexterity on the drums that stole the show.

Guitarist-vocalist Alex Colin Tocquaine from the French act Agressor teamed up with Absu on a session basis during mid 2001. The band enrolled Kashshaptu on guitar during October. McGovern made time in January 2002 to perform drums on the new Demonic Christ studio album. He was also linked to premier thrashers Slayer, with word arriving that McGovern had auditioned for the band and was at one time among the favourites for the position. That same year marked the arrival of Proscriptor's second solo collection, *The Serpentine Has Risen*, released through Dark Age Productions. Another unusual choice of cover interpretations was provided with renditions of 'Castle Walls', originally by Styx, and Cliff Richard's 1970s Pop hit 'Devil Woman'.

The band announced the departure of Equitant Ifernain in June, and

ABSU discography

The Temples Of Offal, Gothic THIK 003 (1992)
BARATHRUM: V.I.T.R.I.O.L., Gothic 001 (USA) (1993), Osmose Productions OPCD 020 (Europe) (1994)
...And Shineth Unto The Cold Cometh..., Osmose Productions OPEP 005 (Europe) (1995) limited edition 7-inch vinyl 500 copies
THE SUN OF TIPHARETH, Osmose Productions OPCD 029 (Europe / USA) (1995)
THE THIRD STORM OF CYTHRAUL, Osmose Productions OPCD 045 (Europe / USA) (1997)
In The Eyes Of Ioldánach, Osmose Productions OPCD 070 (Europe / USA) (1998)
TARA, Osmose Productions OPCD 098 (Europe) (2001), Olympic Recordings OLY 0226-2 (USA) (2002)
MYTHOLOGICAL OCCULT METAL: 1991-2001, Osmose Productions OPCD 173 (Europe), Osmose Productions OPCD 2173 (USA) (2005)

the run of setbacks culminated in August when McGovern was forced out of action. While not fronting Absu, Givens operated a gardening business and had jumped from a ladder after a falling branch nearly hit him. The resulting injury to his wrist completely shattered the scaphoid bone, requiring reconstructive surgery and an enforced lay-off for many months.

The archive Dolmen tracks, *On The Eve Of War*, were reissued in 2003 in a limited run of 666 vinyl albums through the Iron Pegasus label. During 2004, Absu donated their rendition of 'Swing Of The Axe' to the *Seven Gates Of Horror* tribute album to Possessed.

Proscriptor launched a new label venture in June entitled Tarot Productions. The first product would be a solo undertaking by Proscriptor's *Thoth Music(k)* for a limited-edition EP. Proscriptor released his third solo opus, *726: The Sign Of My Number*, on Tarot Productions during 2004.

Planned future releases included archive Absu material as well as rare recordings from related artists Equimanthorn, Heaven's Devils, Equitant, Divine Eve and Starchaser Network.

In 2005 Osmose Productions announced the arrival of a double-CD set, *Mythological Occult Metal: 1991-2001*. This collection consisted of alternative versions, rehearsal recordings, live tracks taken from shows between 1993 and 1997, and material only previously available on 7-inch singles.

May 2006 saw Poland's Agonia label re-releasing *The Sun Of Tiphareth*, *The Third Storm Of Cythräul* and *Tara* on collector's edition picture discs. Agonia also issued a live EP, *L'Attaque Du Tyran: Toulouse, Le 28 Avril 1997*, comprising performances recorded by the band while on tour in France in 1997.

Although Absu's career has been erratic and fragmented, the band stands alone amongst the international black metal fraternity. With artists such as Krieg, Judas Iscariot, Kult Ov Azazel, Demonic Christ and Black Witchery all chosing a determinedly underground position, Absu are the only US act to have achieved significant commercial success.

BATHORY
BLACK AND VIKING METAL PIONEERS

BATHORY WERE AN EXTREME metal band based around the enigmatic Quorthon (who was previously nicknamed Ace Shot). Although the fact was denied officially throughout the band's lifespan, it was understood by

BATHORY discography

BATHORY, Black Mark Production BMLP 666-1 (Europe) (1984)
THE RETURN......, Black Mark Production BMLP 666-2 (Europe), Combat MX 8041 (USA) (1985)
UNDER THE SIGN OF THE BLACK MARK..., Under One Flag FLAG 11 (UK), New Renaissance NRR33 (USA) (1987)
BLOOD FIRE DEATH, Under One Flag FLAG 26 (UK) (1988), Maze MCD 1063 (USA) (1990)
HAMMERHEART, Noise International NUK 153 (UK), Noise International 4827-2-U (USA) (1990)
TWILIGHT OF THE GODS, Black Mark Production BMCD 666-6 (Europe / USA) (1991)
JUBILEUM VOLUME I, Black Mark Production BMCD 666-7 (Europe / USA) (1992)
JUBILEUM VOLUME II, Black Mark Production BMCD 666-8 (Europe / USA) (1993)

REQUIEM, Black Mark Production BMCD 666-10 (Europe / USA) (1994)
OCTAGON, Black Mark Production BMCD 666-11 (Europe /USA) (1995)
BLOOD ON ICE, Black Mark Production BMCD 666-12 (Europe / USA) (1996)
JUBILEUM VOLUME III, Black Mark Production BMCD 666-16 (Europe / USA) (1998)
DESTROYER OF WORLDS, Black Mark Production BMCD 666-15 (Europe / USA) (2001)
KATALOG, Black Mark Production BMCD 666-17 (Europe / USA) (2002)
NORDLAND I, Black Mark Production BMCD 666-18 (Europe / USA) (2002)
NORDLAND II, Black Mark Production BMCD 666-20 (Europe / USA) (2003)
IN MEMORY OF QUORTHON, Black Mark Production BMBOX666-27 (Europe / USA) (2006)

industry insiders that Tomas Börje 'Quorthon' Forsberg was the son of Black Mark Records owner Börje Forsberg. This fact was staunchly denied, and journalists were often given deliberately erroneous "inside information" – including lavish usage of Swedish profanities as fictitious names. Quorthon's real identity was only confirmed after his tragically early death.

With Bathory, Quorthon prided himself on overblown, epic chunks of metal that attracted a staunchly loyal fanbase among both fans and bands. Although Bathory enhanced their mystique by staying away from the stage, this was not by design but because of the simple fact that there was never a line-up stable enough to put on a show. Bathory's early take on black metal is an essential bedrock to the genre, as illustrated by the profusion of major acts eager to deliver cover versions. These have included Dark Funeral, Dimmu Borgir, Dissection, Emperor, Marduk, Mystic Circle, Satyricon and The Crown among many others. Bathory also provided a catalyst for the ancestral Viking metal movement.

Before founding Bathory, Quorthon, billed as Ace the Spunky Black Spade, had made his mark on the Finnish metal scene by designing the 1982 covers for Oz's *Fire In The Brain* LP and the *Turn The Cross Upside Down* EP. His yearning to pursue music as a vocation was inspired by a love of Motörhead, Black Sabbath and the second wave of UK punk acts such as The Exploited, GBH and Discharge.

Bathory were founded in Stockholm, Sweden and came to attention of the masses through the tracks 'The Return Of Darkness And Evil' and 'Sacrifice', both featured on the Tyfon Grammofon *Scandinavian Metal Attack* compilation of 1984. Bathory were created a year before, on March 16th 1983, comprising Black Spade on vocals and guitar (he'd had previous experience with Agnosticum and punk outfit Stridskuk), bassist Fredrick Hanoi, and drummer Vans McBurger (real name Jonas Åkerlund). The rhythm section had just vacated their posts in heavy metal band Die Cast. These tongue-in-cheek pseudonyms were adopted by the trio, each just 18 years old, in reaction to the common practice among Swedish career musicians to re-brand themselves with false, Americanised stage names. Åkerlund took his cue from Vans sneakers and McDonalds fast food, and Quorthon's brief use of Ace Shoot, later Ace Shot, came from two Motörhead song titles, 'Ace Of Spades' and 'Straight Shooter'.

Quorthon laid down the very first Bathory demos in June 1983, featuring 'Sacrifice', 'Live In Sin', 'Die In Fire' and 'You Don't Move Me (I Don't Give a Fuck)', utilising bass player Rickard Bergman and drummer Johan Elvén, friends from his Stridskuk days. The musicians deliberated over various band names, including Nosferatu, Mephisto, Elizabeth Bathory, and Countess Bathory, before settling on Quorthon's first choice of Bathory. For the *Scandinavian Metal Attack* album, Black Spade re-titled himself Ace Shoot before finalising his identity as the alter ego Quorthon, this one discovered in a list of demons. Bathory's inclusion on *Scandinavian Metal Attack* came down to pure chance, as a late withdrawal by a Finnish act opened up a space for two songs. The group put down their tracks at Elektra Studios in Stockholm on January 23rd 1984, later adding sound effects, backwards narrative and guitar solos.

Scandinavian Metal Attack sold in large numbers, particularly through export into Europe and the USA. With Bathory often pinpointed in magazine reviews, the Tyfon label requested a full album. In May, Bathory demoed two further songs, 'Satan My Master' and 'Witchcraft', Quorthon once again drafting in Bergman and pulling in Obsklass drummer Stefan Larsson.

The three then entered the 8-track Heavenshore Studios on June 14th to cut their first album: they would use this studio, actually a converted garage at the back of a private residence, for the bulk of their recording career. *Bathory* was a makeshift affair, with much of the material written in the studio. The demo track 'Witchcraft' was re-written as 'Reaper'. The low budget that governed the sessions, totalling just 56 hours, extended to the album graphics, the front jacket a collage of photocopied images, while the song 'Necromancy' became 'Necromansy' on the cover credits because the band ran out of Letraset letters. The entire monochrome presentation was dictated by lack of finances. However, band and label did go to the expense of producing a gold first pressing, which unfortunately turned out lemon yellow. Only 1,000 of these yellow versions made it to distribution.

By the record's release in October 1984, *Bathory*, forsaking traditional vinyl A and B sides for a 'Darkness' side and an 'Evil' side, found a ready audience with the thrash metal end of the metal market. Alongside Venom's debut, the LP is universally pinpointed as the catalyst for the entire black metal movement. Visually, *Bathory* made an impression with its now infamous black-and-white goat motif and Quorthon's penchants for bone jewellery, pentagram backdrops and blood gargling.

In November 1984, Bathory crafted four songs for a projected EP: 'Children Of The Beast', 'Crown Of Thorns On The Golden Throne', 'Crucifix' and 'Necronomicon'. However, the EP never saw the light of day. Despite the first record selling strongly, Quorthon was still without a backing band. In February 1985, the second album, originally *Revelation Of Doom* but switched to *The Return Of Darkness And Evil*, was committed to tape at Elektra Studios by Quorthon, bass player Andreas

Johansson and drummer Stefan Larsson. Johansson was given his marching orders midway through the session and Quorthon recorded the remaining bass tracks. *The Return Of Darkness And Evil* emerged that May.

Soon back in Heavenshore once again, Quorthon and Larssen cut six more songs – 'Black Leather Wings', 'Hellfire', 'Majestica Satanica', 'Circle Of Blood', 'Wicca', 'The Call From The Grave' and 'Undead' – for a project given the title *Okkulta*. These tracks too never surfaced commercially.

In an attempt to assemble a permanent band during 1985, Quorthon offered a position in Bathory to Carsten Nielsen, the drummer for Danes Artillery, but he declined. Chris Witchhunter of Sodom travelled from his German home base to Sweden to rehearse with the band, but he also departed. The band almost relented on their resolve not to perform in 1986, when a European tour with Celtic Frost and Destruction was mooted, but without a solid band structure this fell through.

Bathory's third album found Paul Pålle Lundberg of local acts Salamander and Destitute manning the drums. Christer Sandström was recruited on bass but was soon dispensed with, and Quorthon resumed four-string duties again for recording that September. A working title of *Nocturnal Obeisance* was dropped in favour of *Under The Sign Of The Black Mark*. The album cover was ambitious, with a demon atop a cliff face – actually a photograph shot at the Royal Swedish Opera House with bodybuilder Leif Ehrnborg brandishing an ox bone, made up as the devil figure. *Under The Sign Of The Black Mark* was released in May 1987, the first Bathory product to benefit from licensing deals with Combat in the USA and Music For Nations in the UK.

Somewhat exhausted by the original Bathory concept, Quorthon next made a set of demos that took the band into the folklore inhabited by Vikings and their gods. An album's worth of material was discarded as too radical a departure from the successful formula. The group structure remained fluid, with Cliff of Driller Killer another early bass player.

A rhythm section of Kothaar and Vvornth was credited on October 1988's *Blood Fire Death*, although Quorthon later revealed that these names were given to a succession of musicians who had passed through the ranks. *Blood Fire Death* for the first presented a band photograph of Bathory, a now classic depiction of three warriors clad in leather chaps wielding swords. Quorthon also scored an impact in print with the distribution of promo photographs depicting himself in spectacular fire-breathing poses. Meanwhile, as Bathory's star rose, co-founder Jonas Åkerlund went on to a highly successful career post-Bathory as a video director, earning awards for stars such as Metallica, Madonna and U2.

April 1990's *Hammerheart* removed Bathory from the Satanic arena and shifted the concept squarely to Viking mythology. Bathory's music took a further major change of direction on June 1991's *Twilight Of The Gods*, the raw edge dropped in favour of sombre sophistication, even going so far as to remould Holst's *Planets* suite. This found favour with some fans but prompted scorn from others.

Quorthon issued a solo album on Black Mark in 1993, simply titled *Album*, but it distanced the man even further from his early trademark sound. Indeed, so vicious was the backlash that Bathory's next records, November 1994's *Requiem* and February 1995's follow-up *Octagon*, plunged back into primal punk metal of the most basic order. *Octagon* suffered a setback at the last minute before release when it was decided that the lyrics to two tracks – 'Resolution Greed' and 'Genocide' – were too extreme, and a cover version of the Kiss classic 'Deuce' was included instead. The missing two tracks were later issued on the *Jubileum Volume III* compilation. It is generally acknowledged that the horrifically underproduced *Octagon* forced the punk ethos to unwelcome levels: reviews were savage in their condemnation, highlighting Quorthon's juvenile display of scatological lyrics.

Blood On Ice appeared in May 1996. For this outing, opening with the deceptively delicate sounds of Scandinavian fauna and closing with a

crushing ten-minute epic, 'The Revenge Of The Blood On Ice', Quorthon had plundered the archives, re-recording Norse-themed material from the group's post-*Under The Sign Of The Black Mark* days.

In 1997, Bathory paid homage to Motörhead with a rip through the classic 'Ace Of Spades', donated to the tribute album *Black Mark Tribute Vol. 1*. That same year various Greek black metal acts including Kawir, Exhumation and Deviser contributed to the *Hellas Salutes The Vikings* tribute. A more substantial album came the following year featuring heavyweight names such as Marduk, Gehenna, Dark Funeral, Emperor, Necrophobic and Satyricon, titled *In Conspiracy With Satan*. Bathory kept up with the covers, providing a take on Black Sabbath's 'Sabbath Bloody Sabbath' to *Black Mark Tribute Vol. 2*. They also laid down 'Detroit Rock City' by Kiss, but this never left the vaults. Another solo Quorthon album, the 23-track double disc *Purity Of Essence*, was released in 1997. Displaying a very different side to the man's persona, this body of work was more in line with traditional rock'n'roll, even including an unashamed love song.

A lengthy hiatus was broken with October 2001's *Destroyer Of Worlds*, a blend of Viking-inspired tunes and outright thrash tunes. Another Bathory product, albeit unofficial, arrived in early 2002. Issued by the British Imperial Creations label, a split album with Dark Funeral consisted of six early Bathory demos from the early 1980s coupled with Dark Funeral live tracks.

The band flouted convention with their next release, splitting recent recordings into two separate full-blown albums. On November 18th 2002 *Nordland Part I* was issued and in January 2003 *Nordland Part II*. During these sessions Bathory cut a version of Kiss's 'Black Diamond' for inclusion on the Nuclear Blast tribute *Creatures Of The Night*. In early 2004, Quorthon and Lake Of Tears session vocalist Jennie Tebler commenced recordings for a project dubbed Silverwing.

The 39-year-old Tomas Börje 'Quorthon' Forsberg was found dead in his apartment in Stockholm, Sweden on June 7th 2004. The apparent cause of death was heart failure. Media and fans were quick to pay tribute. Leading Irish band Primordial's appearance at the 'Irish Day Of Darkness' festival on June 12th was marked with a special performance assembled by Nemtheanga in honour of the late Bathory leader. Running through several Bathory numbers, including 'Woman Of Dark Desires', 'Raise The Dead' and 'A Fine Day To Die', Nemtheanga fronted up a unit comprising Sol Axis members guitarist Joey and drummer Necrohammer, Gaesa bassist Phil, and Brian O'Connor of Kingdom.

In Norway, a gathering of elite black metal musicians revealed that they were to perform a special set of classic Bathory songs during August's 'Hole In The Sky' festival. Those committing to the tribute included Satyr of Satyricon, Abbath of Immortal, Apollyon of Aura Noir, Bård 'Faust' Eithun (sometime of Emperor), Gaahl of Gorgoroth, Ivar from Enslaved, Nocturno Culto of Darkthrone, and Samoth of Zyklon and Emperor. The UK black metal act Cradle Of Filth added a cover of Bathory's 'Bestial Lust' to Japanese variants of their *Nymphetamine* album.

Also in 2004, Bathory's classic cut 'Dies Irae' was chosen for *Fenriz Presents: The Best Of Old School Black Metal*. The posthumous Jennie Tebler 'Silverwing' single emerged through Black Mark Records in April 2005. A comprehensive Bathory boxed set, *In Memory Of Quorthon*, containing three CDs, a DVD, a 174-page book and the infamous fire-breathing poster, was released in June 2006.

BEHEMOTH
SUCCESSFUL POLISH EXTREMISTS

POLISH BLACK/DEATH METAL act Behemoth, based in Gdańsk, sustained global touring and an album output that have elevated them to international status. Their seemingly inexhaustible appetite for live work has put them on a par with fellow Poles Vader in terms of their work ethic and worldwide coverage.

The group arrived with the December 1992 demo *Endless Damnation*. Further tapes included *The Return Of The Northern Moon*, issued in 1993 with Graveland's Rob Darken on keyboards, and *...From The Pagan Vastlands*, closing with a cover of Mayhem's 'Deathcrush'. These were initially released by Pagan Records but later in Europe on the German labels Last Epitaph and Nazgûl's Eyrie, and in the USA on Wild Rags. Behemoth's line-up for these sessions consisted of Nergal ("war summonings, mayhemic rhythm guitar, acoustic guitar, witching bass and sword pagan whispers"), Frost (aka Rafa Bauer, "chainsaw and electric lead guitar"), Baal ("drums of war and hellhammers, backing voices") with session bassist S.K. and keyboard player Czarek Morawski. Darken was in evidence again, supplying "evil winds".

Behemoth then signed to Entropy Productions for a 1994 EP, the utterly grim *And The Forests Dream Eternally*. Down to a duo of Nergal ("Black Emperor of Behemoth") and Baal Ravenlock ("Lord of Iron Thorns"), with Czarek Morawski on keyboards, the combo signed to domestic label Pagan, recording *Sventevith (Storming Near The Baltic)* in December 1994. Demonious provided two instrumental fillers, 'Ancient' and 'Hell Dwells In Ice'.

January 1996's *Grom* saw Les (aka Leszek Dziegielewski) delegated to bass duties. Behemoth's Les and Nergal also formed part of Damnation, which released the *Rebel Souls* album in 1996 on Malicious Records. Drummer Ravenlock forged Hell-Born as a side project with Damnation and Behemoth guitarist Les, issuing an eponymous album in 1996.

Behemoth then drafted in new drummer Inferno, debuting the new sticksman with the EP *Bewitching The Pomerania*. Another full-length offering followed through Solistitium: *Pandemonic Incantations* was delivered in March 1998 with Nergal, Inferno, bassist Mefisto and Piotr Weltrowski on keyboards. Domestic Polish versions included the song 'Chwala Mordercom Wojciecha (997-1997 Dziesiêæ Wieków Hańby)', replaced by 'With Spell Of Inferno' on international variants.

The group, pulling in guitarist Havok, moved to another new label, Italy's Avantgarde Music, for the next phase of their career as they morphed into a more streamlined death metal sound on October 1999's *Satanica*. Significantly, Behemoth were now employing poet Krzysztof Azarewicz to add depth to their lyrical content. *Thelema.6*, emerging in November 2000, pursued a path of speed and technicality similar to its predecessor: Devilyn's Marcin Nowak (aka Novy) provided studio bass

with Maciej Niedzielski contributing keyboards. Digipacks added a further four tracks, including a take on David Bowie's 'Hello Space Boy'.

Behemoth then toured Europe in December 2000 as part of an almighty death metal package including Enslaved, Morbid Angel, The Crown, Hypnos and Dying Fetus.

The Polish Metal Mind label issued a lavish two-CD retrospective set in 2001, *Chaotica – The Essence Of The Underworld*. Besides archive material and demo cuts, the collection included previously unreleased covers of Mayhem's 'Freezing Moon' and Destruction's 'Total Disaster', recorded during the *Grom* sessions. A further release, *Antichristian Phenomenon*, collected together Behemoth's cover versions of 'Sathanas' by Sarcofago, 'Hello Space Boy' from David Bowie, 'Day Of Suffering' by

Behemoth

Morbid Angel, and Mayhem's 'Carnage', plus a video shoot for 'Christians To The Lions'. Behemoth were out on the road again in Europe during the autumn of 2001 with Carpathian Forest and Norway's Khold.

The Russian Irond label reissued *Satanica* in February 2002, adding a slew of extra tracks. Meanwhile, Metal Mind released the *Metal Box* three-CD set comprising the two *Chaotica* albums plus a disc of Behemoth live in Toulouse during 1999.

European dates slated for November 2002 saw the band promoting the album *Zos Kia Cultus (Here And Beyond)* on a bill including headliners Deicide alongside Centinex, Destroyer 666, Diabolic and Antaeus. However, Behemoth and many of the other bands were subsequently dropped from these shows. During December they undertook headline shows in Poland supported by Darkane. Former bassist Rafa 'Frost' Bauer joined Immemorial in early 2003.

The band's live schedule increased during 2003 as they undertook their debut US dates in April as part of the 'Coalition For Muzikal Armageddon' tour with Deicide, Amon Amarth, Vehemence and Revenge. The group then tagged on to the first three shows of the April 'Metal Gods' trek alongside Halford, Testament and Primal Fear before joining the 'Un-Natural Born Killers' tour with Six Feet Under, Skinless and The Black Dahlia Murder.

Bassist Novy then joined Vader. After pulling in Orion as replacement, Behemoth reverted to a session bassist, Istvan from California black metal band Rise. However, they suffered a further casualty as guitarist Havok was let go, but soon got back to work with UK and European dates before shows in the US and Mexico.

Promoting a limited edition EP, *Conjuration*, which featured covers of Venom's 'Welcome To Hell' and the unexpected 'Wish' by Nine Inch Nails, the band put in a burst of Baltic-state gigs in September. Nergal took time out to add vocals to the track 'Revenge' on stoner band Corruption's 2003 *Orgasmusica* album. He also joined the Israeli black metal band Salem during their national Independence Day gig at the City Hall Club in Haifa on May 24th 2004 for a set that included both Salem and Behemoth songs. European shows that November dubbed the 'Clash Of Demigods' saw the band playing with Krisiun, Ragnarok and Incantation.

A new album, *Demigod*, recorded at Hendrix Studios, included a guest guitar solo on the track 'Xul' by Karl Sanders of Nile. The choral intro to the song 'Sculpting The Throne Ov Seth' was provided by the Academic Male Choir from Lublin. The album, which debuted at a highly impressive Number 15 on the Polish album charts, was accompanied by a video for the track 'Conquer All' from director Joanna Rechnio. A DVD, *Crush.Fukk Create: Requiem For Generation Armageddon*, was set for September issue via Regain. It included footage of two complete shows from 2003's 'Party San' festival and 2001's 'Mystic Festival', backed up with documentary footage and videos.

North American dates in January 2005 saw the band partnering with Suffocation and Soilent Green. As this trek extended into February the band retained Suffocation and added Cattle Decapitation and Minneapolis outfit Devilinside. Headline dates in Poland during March saw the band heading a billing of Pandemonium and Frontiside, with the 'Hate Means Hate' European tour seeing Swedes In Battle as openers. The summer found the band engaged in a round of North American dates with King Diamond, Nile and The Black Dahlia Murder. A video for the track 'Slaves Shall Serve', directed by Rechnio again, appeared alongside a six-track EP. The band then joined forces with the Danzig-headlined 'Blackest Of The Black' US dates with Chimaira, Mortiis, Himsa and The Agony Scene. A run of Canadian dates preceded two gigs in Turkey.

The group announced a tour as part of the December 2005 'X-Mass' festival in Europe and April 2006 US tour dates with Morbid Angel, Canadian band Despised Icon and Brazilian group Krisiun. This was followed by the 'Sounds Of The Underground' tour throughout the summer. With such an admirable work ethic, it seems that the band will maintain their place at the forefront of European death metal.

CRADLE OF FILTH
UNLIKELY LEADERS OF THE BLACK METAL SCENE

CRADLE OF FILTH ARE THE world's biggest-selling black metal band, and their prominence and mainstream status leads to the most vitriolic of divisions among fans. They have successively strengthened their eminence on each album, battling both criticism and internal division. Remarkably, the group's progress has even swept aside a bewildering series of line-up changes.

Since their first album, they have been assailed by accusations from black metal elitists, vilifying their association with the genre. In fact, the band raised themselves above the stereotypes soon after the launch of their debut record, exploring an ever-diversifying range of bohemian and neo-Gothic topics, often rooted in the clandestine eroticism of 19th century literature and imbued with Dani Filth's contagious sarcasm.

They have built their reputation on hard gigging and inventive albums, all aided by an impressive merchandising campaign with a vast range of deliberately provocative but still highly creative T-shirt slogans. One particular design, bearing the title "Jesus Is A Cunt", landed several fans in jail on blasphemy charges.

Cradle Of Filth were created in Suffolk, England during 1991 with vocalist Dani Filth (aka Daniel Lloyd Davey), whose previous acts apparently included PDA and Feast On Excrement, guitarist Paul Ryan, bassist Jon Richard and drummer Darren Garden. Filth had also been involved with The Lemon Grove Kids, a band titled after the Ray Dennis Steckler horror movie. At first the new band went by the title Burial but, upon discovering the Liverpool act of the same name, adopted Cradle Of Filth. Fired by exposure to Celtic Frost, early Gathering and Paradise Lost, Dani – the lynchpin of the band – cut short a journalistic career at the *East Anglian Daily Times* to embroil himself in the murky world of extreme metal.

This inaugural line-up cut the death metal-styled demo cassette *Invoking The Unclean* in 1992, shortly after which they added second guitarist Robin Graves (Robin Mark Eaglestone), previously with Malicious Intent and Nightbreed. Further rehearsal recordings were made: *The Black Goddess Rises* included a cover version of the US death metal classic 'Dawn Of Eternity' by Massacre. A split cassette, *A Pungent And Sexual Miasma*, also surfaced, shared with Middlesbrough's Malediction. Early live work in the UK included supports to visiting Scandinavian acts Cadaver and Red Harvest.

Another 1992 demo followed, the seven-track *Orgiastic Pleasures Foul*, after which Richard took his leave to create Hecate Enthroned. The band shifted Graves to bass to plug the vacancy and took the opportunity to bring in Paul Allender on second guitar and Benjamin Ryan on keyboards. Cradle Of Filth contracted to the low-budget Tombstone label and recorded an intended debut album, *Goetia*. When it became clear to the studio owners that Tombstone could not finance the sessions, the tapes were erased.

The group persevered: their third demo, *Total Fucking Darkness*, issued in December 1993, set the mould for future works and scored a deal with London-based Cacophonous Records. Former Solemn drummer Will 'Was' Sarginson joined at this juncture but lasted a handful of gigs. Cacophonous's strategy was to introduce the band with a single, but the musicians took it upon themselves to deliver a full-blown album. February 1994's *The Principle Of Evil Made Flesh* found them with yet another new face, as Nicholas Barker took over the drum stool. Now fully launched into the public eye, Cradle Of Filth had a deliberately provocative approach that elevated them to the status of scene leaders. Extreme metal fans were intrigued by the inflammatory band title and the attention to detail, ranging from the lesbian erotica of the album cover art through to Dani Filth's obsessively-wrought lyrics. Notably, Darren White of Anathema guested on the track 'A Dream Of Wolves In The Snow', with other embellishments courtesy of singer Andrea Meyer Haugen, known as Nebelhexe of Hagalaz's Runedance, and cellist Soror Proselenos. The closing track, 'Imperium Tenebraum', was credited to Frater Nihil (aka Neil Harding), reputed to be head priest of The Order Of The Absu.

European touring in January 1994 found Cradle Of Filth opening for At The Gates and Anathema as well as providing the opening honours for Emperor's first set of UK dates. Rishi Mehta was also a guitarist for Cradle Of Filth during 1994 before uniting with Benjamin Ryan and Zakk Bajjon to create Crowfoot and then Rainmaker 888.

Paul Ryan, Benjamin Ryan and Paul Allender all bailed out to form The Blood Divine with ex-Anathema vocalist Darren White in late 1995. Vowing to carry on, Dani quickly filled the ranks with guitarists Stuart Anstis and, apparently, Jared Demeter with Damien Gregori on keyboards. However, rumours abounded that 'Jared Demeter' was an entirely ficticious character. The band's second album, *Vempire... Or Dark Faerytales In Phallustein*, was produced by Zakk Bajjon, sometime bassist for Witchfinder General and Lionsheart. Cementing a trend that continues to this day, these sessions found the band utilising two female backing vocalists, Sarah Jezebel Deva (Sarah Jane Ferridge) and Danielle Cneajna Cottington. The band acknowledged that this 36-minute outing was hastily conceived as a means of fulfilling their contractual obligations to Cacophonous, enabling a move onto greater things. The record included a reworked version of 'The Forest Whispers My Name'.

Dani Filth: "Those really were shit years. It was a time when we were getting out of the deal with Crapophonous. We were totally to blame because we had a contract but we didn't want to be part of that any more. It was a shit deal and was doing nothing for the band. There was so much pressure on us to really deliver, and we knew that if we stayed there it was all going to go horribly wrong.

"We were losing money, we were losing band members. So then all the bitching started and then I see this other band that really was just a poor imitation of Cradle. It was pitiful. It seemed to go on forever, and at one point it looked like there was no solution except to shut everything down. Ultimately we couldn't do it. We actually held onto the master tapes because we knew that giving them away would be a waste. In the end we gave them the EP, Vempire, so we could close the deal and end the contract. We kept the tapes for Dusk And Her Embrace and used those as the next album. We were talking to quite a few labels ... while all this was going on, so we knew there was a good future there."

Just as media interest peaked in the black metal scene, Cradle Of Filth found themselves embroiled for most of 1995 in legal proceedings against their record company. On a more optimistic note, they engaged in negotiations with numerous labels, including Earache. Once legally free, they signed up to Music For Nations for Europe and Fierce Recordings in the USA, in the process replacing Demeter with former Solstice and Ship Of Fools man Gian Pyres (real name John Piras).

The August 1996 album *Dusk And Her Embrace – Litanies Of Damnation, Death And The Darkly Erotic*, was produced over a full 72 recording tracks by Kit Woolven, better known for his mellower work with the likes of Thin Lizzy and Magnum. The band's abilities had now begun to catch up with their ambition and this third album witnessed a blooming of character. Not only did they diversify into intriguing complexity, complete with orchestration, but the songs accelerated in

CRADLE OF FILTH discography

THE PRINCIPLE OF EVIL MADE FLESH, Cacophonous NIHIL 1CD (UK) (1994)

V EMPIRE... OR DARK FAERYTALES IN PHALLUSTEIN, Cacophonous NIHIL 6CD (UK) (1996)

DUSK AND HER EMBRACE – LITANIES OF DAMNATION, DEATH AND THE DARKLY EROTIC, Music For Nations CDMFN208 (UK), Fierce Recordings FIERCE 11096-2 (USA) (1996)

CRUELTY AND THE BEAST, Music For Nations CDMFN242 (UK), Fierce Recordings FIERCE 11128-2 (USA) (1998) **48 UK**

From The Cradle To Enslave, Music For Nations CDMFNX254 (UK), Metal Blade 3894-14301-2 (USA) (1999)

MIDIAN, Music For Nations CDMFN666 (UK), Koch KOC-CD-8219 (USA) (2000) **63 UK**

BITTER SUITES TO SUCCUBI, AbraCadaver COF001CD (UK), Spitfire SPT-15207-2 (USA) (2001) **63 UK**

LOVECRAFT & WITCH HEARTS, Music For Nations CDMFN285 (UK), Koch KOC-CD-8412 (USA) (2002) **95 UK**

LIVE BAIT FOR THE DEAD, AbraCadaver COF006DD (UK) (2002) **175 UK**

DAMNATION AND A DAY, Sony Music 510963-2 (UK), Epic EK71423 (USA) (2003) **44 UK, 140 USA**

NYMPHETAMINE, Roadrunner RR 8282-2 (UK), Roadrunner 168 618 282-2 (USA) (2004) **89 USA**

THORNOGRAPHY, Roadrunner RR 8113-2 (UK), Roadrunner 168 618 113-2 (USA) (2006) **46 UK, 66 USA**

pace and Dani Filth's prose, loosely based upon the works of Sheridan Le Fanu, came to the fore.

CD digipack versions added an extra bonus track in a re-recorded 'Nocturnal Supremacy', while Music For Nations released a limited-edition coffin-shaped variant of the album, enhanced by a take on Slayer's 'Hell Awaits', the instrumental 'Carmilla's Masque' and a revised version of 'Nocturnal Supremacy'. Sarah Jezebel Deva featured once again; other vocal contributions came from Danielle Cneajna Cottington and Cronos of Venom, the latter credited with a "war cry" on the song 'Haunted Shores'. *Dusk And Her Embrace* gave Cradle Of Filth their first chart placing, with a humble Number 107 in their homeland. The keener Finns put the record into their Top 30.

The band acquired ex-Brutality guitarist Brian Hipp for live work in 1996. They toured Europe in 1997 with dates in Austria supported by doom merchants Jack Frost. Shortly after the band's appearance at the 1997 Milwaukee 'Metalfest' they announced their new keyboard player as Anathema and Ship Of Fools member Les 'Lecter' Smith. Meanwhile, London fan Rob Kenyon was found guilty at Bow Street Magistrates Court of committing "profane representation under the 1839 Act" for wearing the "Jesus Is A Cunt" T-shirt. He was fined £150 (about $240), a fee the band paid on his behalf.

In 1998 *Cruelty And The Beast* saw Cradle Of Filth reaching a peak of public awareness. Conceptual in theme, the record hung on the grisly tale of the blood-drinking countess Erzebeth Bathory (1560-1613). They scored a significant coup in persuading actress Ingrid Pitt, who had portrayed Bathory in the 1971 Hammer horror movie *Countess Dracula*, to narrate passages. Their ploy of depicting the naked female form on album covers extended here to Erzebeth, as described in legend, bathing in virgins' blood. Unfortunately, *Cruelty And The Beast* was marred by inadequate production, the band having opted to self-produce in collaboration with Jan Peter Genkel. The final results severely hampered Barker's normally bombastic percussive work, noted by many reviewers.

Limited double-CD versions came in new artwork and included covers of Venom's ubiquitous 'Black Metal', Iron Maiden's 'Hallowed Be Thy Name' and Sodom's 'Sodomy And Lust' alongside 'Lustmord And Wargasm (The Relicking Of Cadaverous Wounds)' and 'Twisting Further Nails (The Cruci-Fiction Mix)'. Another restricted release was the 'gravestone' edition, again including extra tracks and portraits of the band members as victims of mock killings. Comments from Dani Filth suggested an attempt at recording Manowar's 'Kill With Power', although this has yet to surface.

Dani Filth: "I think what sets us apart is the fact that we're true to ourselves. I know a lot of bands who always have their eye on what is going on around them, to see where to jump next, and that to me was shocking. I can talk to you all day about Manowar, Iron Maiden and Judas Priest. The part of Cradle Of Filth that really excites me is not knowing where this whole thing is going. Every album is totally different to the last one and as every year passes I discover more outrageous things to occupy my mind with.

"It's a very English band too, I think. I have a deep interest in gothic literature, Byron, Shelley, the way forbidden topics, like eroticism, were hidden in so many ways. A lot of that comes through in our music and lyrics. There are always layers to peel away with each listen. There is also a lot of classic English tongue-in-cheek humour, too. Irony and sarcasm are two things Britain really excels in. For the first-time listener there is a lot to deal with, but it's worth it."

Barker departed in acrimonious circumstances in early 1999, going on to another high-profile black metal outfit Dimmu Borgir, as well as Lockup with Hypocrisy's Peter Tägtgren, Napalm Death's Shane Embury and Jesse Pintado. The drummer also appeared on the 'Mexican' death metal band Brujeria's *Brujerizmo*.

Cradle Of Filth set to work on their next album, *From the Cradle To Enslave*, and an accompanying video directed by Alex Chandon of *Pervirella* fame, with the temporary employment of The Blood Divine and December Moon sticksman Wes Sargison. Another temporary drummer was Dave Hirschheimer of Infestation.

During the summer of 1999 the band fractured once again, with both Pyres and Hirschheimer departing, the drum stool now being occupied by former At The Gates man Adrian Erlandsson. Cradle undertook American festival dates with a session guitarist.

Allender was brought back into the ranks in late 1999 from his post-Blood Divine act Primary Slave, and Pyres returned to the fold. The turbulence was far from complete, however, as keyboard player Smith and guitarist Anstis were both given their marching orders. The only new material to emerge were two tracks on the *From The Cradle To Enslave* EP, the title track and 'Of Dark Blood And Fucking' (the EP was completed with covers of the Misfits' 'Death Comes Ripping' and Anathema's 'Sleepless'). Former keyboard player Damien rejoined the band for these sessions. Predictably his tenure was brief, only appearing on the American Metal Blade-released version of the EP and the track 'Pervert's Church'.

The band pulled in former My Dying Bride keyboard player Mark De Sade (real name Mark Newby-Robson), but after a handful of gigs his place was taken by another erstwhile My Dying Bride man, Martin 'Foul' Powell. The Cradle line-up for the John Fryer-produced *Midian*, released on Halloween 2000, stood at Filth, Pyres, Allender, Graves, Powell and Erlandsson. Also involved in the project was actor Doug Bradley, famed for his role as the malevolent Pinhead in the *Hellraiser* movies, donating

narrative parts. For their fourth full-length work, they tackled another ambitious concept, stimulated by Clive Barker's novel *Cabal* and the subsequent celluloid version *Nightbreed*.

Limited editions of *Midian* included a cover of Sabbat's 'For Those Who Died' with a guest vocal from Sabbat and Skyclad singer Martin Walkyier. The band toured Europe in late 2000 with veterans Christian Death as guests. There was a huge degree of fraternisation between the two bands, as members of Cradle Of Filth including ex-drummer Was Sarginson appeared on Christian Death's 2000 album *Born Again Anti-Christian*. Pyres also guested on the Extreme Noise Terror album *Being And Nothing*. European touring took the band through November and December. In the summer of 2001, they offered their take on Twisted Sister's 'The Fire Still Burns' to the Koch International tribute album *Twisted And Strange*.

In readiness for the next upward step, Cradle Of Filth created their own label, AbraCadaver, for the release of June 2001's *Bitter Suites To Succubi* mini-album. This interim offering saw new material, including a sequel to 'The Black Goddess Rises', alongside re-workings of vintage cuts 'The Principle Of Evil Made Flesh' and 'Summer Dying Fast'. Also onboard were two instrumentals and a rendition of the Sisters Of Mercy track 'No Time To Cry'. Produced by Doug Cook, *Bitter Suites To Succubi*'s place in the band's canon was highlighted by the fact that it was the only recording crafted by the same line-up as the previous release.

Robin 'Graves' Eaglestone's position was relinquished to former Dreamweaver and Anathema bassist Dave Pybus in June for the North American leg of the tour. Eaglestone joined the expatriated Chilean death metal combo Criminal. Another round of US shows for Cradle saw rising death metal band Nile alongside God Forbid in support.

Stepping into the breach left by the withdrawal of American acts after the 9/11 terrorist attacks, the band appeared as last-minute substitutes on the massive 'Tattoo The Planet' European tour. Shortly afterwards, it was announced that they had signed to major label Sony for future product.

Concluding their dealings with the band, Music For Nations weighed in with a lavish compilation, *Lovecraft & Witch Hearts*, comprising MFN catalogue tracks and a second disc of archive material, cover versions and remixes. Also released was a DVD, *Heavy, Left-Handed & Candid*, centred on concert footage from a Nottingham Rock City gig.

The band then appeared at the famous Castle Donington as part of the May 2002 'Ozzfest' event. As a warm-up the night before the 'Ozzfest', Cradle put in a low-key club gig at the Oxford Zodiac, supported by Martin Walkyier's Return To The Sabbat,.

In July the band unveiled details of their first official live album, *Live Bait For The Dead*, set for August 2002. The bulk of the material was recorded live at Nottingham Rock City in April 2001. The double-CD also included two more live tracks, recorded during soundchecks, alongside studio remixes of tracks from *Bitter Suites To Succubi*, covers, a previously unavailable remix of 'From The Cradle To Enslave', and a studio demo of 'Scorched Earth Erotica'.

Bringing the full weight of Sony's budget to bear, Cradle Of Filth entered Parkgate Studios in August 2002 with Doug Cook manning the production board to record *Damnation And A Day*, a 17-track affair utilising the 40-piece Budapest Film Orchestra and the 32-piece Budapest Film Choir. It was divided into four separate chapters – 'Fantasia Down', 'Paradise Lost', 'Sewer Side Up' and 'The Scented Garden'. Narration came from David McEwen, who had scored notoriety as the serial killer Kemper in 2001's *Cradle Of Fear*, in which Dani appeared as The Man. McEwen also appeared in the video for 'Her Ghost in the Fog', lip-synching Doug Bradley's original vocal parts. Longstanding member Pyres, one of the few points of stability, made a break from the band before the end of the month, apparently in an amicable split over musical differences. The guitarist subsequently joined Christian Death.

Cronos (Venom): "Cradle Of Filth take a lot of shit from these so-called black metal elitists, but they haven't got a clue. Look, here's how it is: Venom invented black metal, OK? So I know what I'm talking about. You've got to give Cradle the respect they deserve. They are totally for real but they don't do what Venom do, they do their own thing – and the work they put into that is just fucking incredible, man. To me, a poser is someone who is using a scene, but Cradle Of Filth invented their own scene. Yeah, they use black metal, death metal, heavy metal and all that weird old shit that Dani puts into it as well, and it comes out as Cradle Of Filth."

Dani Filth: "I couldn't give a fuck what people say or think, outside of the people that come to our shows and buy the records. I'm too involved in what I'm doing to bother with all that. Look, whatever you do, if you make music, you paint a picture, or you write a book – you can expect the criticism. There is absolutely no way of avoiding it, so you had better steel yourself for it. With the whole black metal thing, it boils down to jealousy. I'm not ashamed because the band is selling a lot of records. They can wrap it up however they want, but that's what we're dealing with. Cradle Of Filth is on a major label, we're in the magazines, we're the charts – so fucking what? These people are worms."

A short run of December UK dates was cancelled when Dani was diagnosed with a respiratory condition. The gigs were re-scheduled for April 2003. European touring found veteran US death metal act Immolation as openers. The band scored a major coup with their rather uncharacteristic daylight inclusion on the North American 'Ozzfest' and broke new ground for the genre by being the first black metal band to break into the *Billboard* Top 200 – *Damnation And A Day* entered at number 140. A bout of co-headlining November US shows then saw the band partnered with Type O Negative, Portuguese act Moonspell and Sweden's Soilwork. In an unexpected diversion, Dani made news as he was chosen as the voice of the lead character in the cartoon movie *Dominator*.

Cradle Of Filth's collaboration with Sony ended in December by mutual consent, and the band signed to the major independent Roadrunner, projecting a new studio album dubbed *Nymphetamine* to be produced by Anthrax guitarist Rob Caggiano. Second guitarist James McIlroy was introduced during these sessions. Final keyboard and vocal parts, including those of Sarah Jezebel Deva once again, were crafted for a final mix by Colin Richardson. The featured artist on the title track, 'Nymphetamine (Overdose)', was former Theatre Of Tragedy and current Leaves' Eyes singer Liv Kristine. The Norwegian singer also graced the Dani Jacobs-directed promotional video for this song, filmed in an underground vault near the London Dungeon. Japanese variants of *Nymphetamine* added a cover version of Bathory's 'Bestial Lust'. The album shifted 13,818 copies in its first week of US sales to debut at Number 89 on the *Billboard* charts.

South American gigs in Mexico, Ecuador, Colombia, Chile and Brazil were unveiled for September. Allender suffered a serious hand injury before the tour, necessitating the swift recruitment of Dan Turner, the band's sound engineer, as temporary replacement.

Cradle Of Filth's merchandise gave another fan, Norwich's Dale Wilson, a taste of the law when he was arrested by two police officers, suitably on Halloween. Pleading guilty to "religiously aggravated offensive conduct", he was discharged after the judge ordered the garment to be destroyed. Wilson paid £150 costs (about $270) and was advised to "grow up".

Cradle's November 'Headbanger's Ball III' US touring partners were Arch Enemy, Bleeding Through and Himsa. An interruption came on November 8th when the Cincinnati, Ohio, show was cancelled after a man was stabbed during a fight before the concert began.

In an echo from the past, the band's proposed design for the first T-shirt to promote the single 'Gilded Cunt' was set to feature the image of a bare-breasted woman bleeding from her crotch and adorned with the words "You Gilded Cunt" on the reverse. This time the garment did not reach public sale, with reports that workers at the merchandise company Blue Grape "downed tools in disgust".

An expanded version of *Nymphetamine* arrived in March 2005 with a second disc of exclusive tracks including a remake of Cliff Richard's 1976 hit 'Devil Woman' with guest vocals by King Diamond. The band created an animated video for the track based upon the characters in the *Dominator* movie and comic series. In December the track 'Nymphetamine' was nominated in the Best Metal Performance category at the 47th annual Grammy Awards.

Moonspell and The Haunted were the special guests to Cradle Of Filth for an extensive European 2005 tour from February through to April. However, longstanding bassist Pybus relinquished his position in January, citing "personal reasons". For touring purposes the band pulled in Charles Hedger.

October found the infamous "Jesus…" T-shirt back in the news when fan Adam Shepherd was convicted under new anti-hatred laws, designed to ban people from displaying religiously insulting signs. He was given 80 hours' community service and told to pay £40 costs (about $70).

The band announced in November that album sessions were set to include a number of cover versions, including Samhain's 'Halloween II' for inclusion on the soundtrack to the film *Underworld: Evolution*, Shakespear's Sister's 'Stay', once again featuring Leaves' Eyes singer Liv Kristine, and Heaven 17's 'Temptation' as a duet with Harry from Dirty Harry. The band announced UK headline dates for December supported by Cathedral and Octavia Sperati. To coincide, a DVD entitled *Peace Through Superior Firepower* emerged, chronicling two sold-out gigs in Paris that April, a historical documentary, and videos.

Dani Filth contributed vocals to the Roadrunner United 25th anniversary album *The All-Stars Sessions*, featuring on the track 'The Dawn Of A Golden Age' composed by Matt Heafy of Trivium. Touring bassist Hedger replaced McIlroy on guitar and Pybus returned on bass. Ushering in 2006, the band went to Lincolnshire's Chapel Studios with producer Rob Caggiano to cut a new album, *Thornography*. Sarah Jezebel Deva added her vocal contributions in mid March, as did Ville Valo of H.I.M. on the song 'The Byronic Man'. In mid May the group announced that their original proposal for *Thornography*'s album cover had been rejected by Roadrunner. The artwork that arrived in stores depicted a maiden cradling the decapitated head of a crucifixion victim.

The band put in a significant appearance at the Guns N'Roses-headlined 'Download' festival at Castle Donington, England on June 11th. The following month Adrian Erlandsson announced that his side act Nemhain, a union with his wife, fetish model Morrigan Hel (aka Amber England), was to debut live on August 27th at Bar Monsta in London.

December UK tour dates were set to be supported by the reunited Sabbat, the revered British occult metal institution reforming after direct encouragement from Cradle Of Filth. Cradle remain at the top of their game, although how long they can maintain a truly extreme approach is open to speculation.

DARK FUNERAL
RAW BLACK METAL

DARK FUNERAL PERFORM BLACK metal in its purest form, never pandering to any form of experimentation. The band were assembled in Stockholm, Sweden during 1993 by ex-Necrophobic guitarist Blackmoon (David Parland) and Lord Ahriman (Micke Svanberg). The line-up was

The band made every effort to lay on a terrifying spectacle, with displays of fire-breathing and pigs' heads on spikes flanked by inverted crosses. These dates, the first leg of what would become the 'Satanic War' tour, were so successful that Dark Funeral toured Europe again in February 1997. For this batch of shows Bal-Sagoth and Ancient opened. By September they were back with Tägtgren, laying down the much-anticipated *Vobiscum Satanas* album. The group's reach extended into debut American shows throughout November, commencing in Chicago at the 'Expo Of The Extreme' festival and a short East Coast tour with Chicago's Usurper.

In 1998 they embarked on the 'Ineffable Kings Of Darkness' tour with Enthroned and Liar Of Golgotha. These dates featured Dominion as session bassist. Following their second major festival appearance at the Swedish Hultsfreds event, Typhos was removed and Dominion, originally a guitarist, took over the role, with Caligula reverting to both vocals and bass. Further line-up flux included Alzazmon making his exit. The band then inducted long-term friend Gaahnfaust (Robert Lundin), who had briefly been a member in 1996. Dark Funeral then formed part of the 'Blood For Satan' European package, sharing stages with Cannibal Corpse and Infernal Majesty.

In March 2000, they paid homage to their mentors by cutting covers of Mayhem's 'Pagan Fears', King Diamond's 'The Trial', Sodom's 'Remember The Dead' and Slayer's 'Dead Skin Mask' for the inflammatory *Teach Children To Worship Satan* EP. This included the new track 'An Apprentice Of Satan', for which a live video was shot and broadcast globally. Live dates ranked the band alongside Deicide, Immortal and Cannibal Corpse for the 'No Mercy' festivals.

Fervour for the band was now riding at such a high that Necropolis in North America, Hellspawn in Sweden and Hammerheart in Europe reissued the band's first mini-album, re-titled *In The Sign...* and repackaged with the 1996 Bathory covers, rare photographs and histories. During 2000, Caligula and guitarist Dominion (Matti Mäkelä) united with erstwhile Dark Funeral drummer Gaahnfaust to found side project Dominion Caligula, releasing the album *A New Era Rises* in 2000. Not to be outdone, Lord Ahriman created a transatlantic collaboration, Wolfen Society, with ex-Acheron leader Vincent Crowley, Kyle Severn of Incantation and erstwhile Vital Remains man Jeff Gruslins.

Dark Funeral themselves added former Defleshed drummer Matte Modin to the ranks in late 2000, debuting their new member at the 'Full Force' and 'Wacken' festivals. The band got back into action with the well-received Tägtgren-produced album *Diabolus Interium*. An appropriate 6,666 digipacks were bound in fake leather.

Another Dark Funeral product arrived in early 2002, albeit a bootleg, from the British Imperial Creations label. *Live Hultsfreds, Sweden* consisted of live tracks recorded at the Scandinavian festival paired with six early Bathory-cover demo tracks from the early 1980s. The group embarked on a further round of American dates, headlined by Cannibal Corpse and billed alongside Incantation and Pissing Razors. Richard Cabeza of Dismember, Unanimated, Born Of Fire and Murder Squad played bass.

Just as Australian dates together with Astriaal were projected for October, Dominion vacated the guitar spot. As it transpired, the Australian concerts were curtailed but Dark Funeral did put in a run of dates in Japan, Taiwan and Singapore that month. Support for most of these shows came from Taiwanese act Chthonic.

The band pulled in Mordichrist and Skellington guitarist Chaq Mol (aka Bo Karlsson) and returned to live action in mid 2003 at 'Wacken'. South American gigs were set for September with support from Averse Safira, Valhalla and Avec Tristesse. Recordings from these dates were compiled as the live album *De Profundis Clamavi Ad Te Domine*. Later that year Emperor Magus Caligula joined the elite death metal side project of retro act God Among Insects, featuring guitarist Lord K (aka Kenth

completed by vocalist and bassist Themgoroth and drummer Draugen and the band issued the four-track *Dark Funeral* EP, recorded at Dan Swanö's Unisound Studios and released on Hellspawn on May 4th 1994, when Dark Funeral also played their inaugural gig at the Luse Lottes pub in Oslo. The record was also released on cassette in Poland on Carrion Records, retitled *Open The Gates*. Following the EP's release, Draugen departed, eventually turning up as a member of Svartsyn; he was succeeded by Equimanthorn.

Dark Funeral attempted to record an album, *The Secrets Of The Black Arts*, at Unisound with Swanö but were dissatisfied with the results and the tapes were scrapped. The band subsequently relocated to Abyss Studio in June 1995, re-recording the entire album with a new track 'When Angels Forever Die' with Hypocrisy's Peter Tägtgren as engineer. *The Secrets Of The Black Arts* took an unconventional spin on the black metal formula, with the band entrenching themselves in repetitive riffs and mantra-like choruses. The album included a cover of Von's 'Satanic Blood' and was boosted by a video for the title track. Licences were secured with Metal Blade in North America and Mystic Productions in Poland.

Just before *The Secrets Of The Black Arts* appeared in January 1996, the band underwent a roster change with the addition of vocalist-bassist Emperor Magus Caligula (aka Masse Broberg), the original vocalist of Hypocrisy, and drummer Alzazmon (aka Tomas Asklund) of Dawn and Infernal. This new unit debuted at Dark Funeral's first festival, 'Under The Black Sun' in Berlin.

Dark Funeral took on covers of Bathory's 'Call From The Grave' and 'Equimanthorn' in 1996 for the tribute album *In Conspiracy With Satan*. Further ructions hit the band as Blackmoon quit to concentrate on a self-titled solo project: his place was taken by Typhos, previously a member of Stockholm's Funeral Mist.

Touring in Europe had the band supported by Italians Necromass.

Dark Funeral, Hellspawn HELL 001 (Europe) (1994)
THE SECRETS OF THE BLACK ARTS, No Fashion NFR 011
(Europe) (1996), Death 3984-14121-2 (USA) (1997)
VOBISCUM SATANAS, No Fashion NFR 027 (Europe), Metal Blade
3984-14173-2 (USA) (1998)
In The Sign..., Hellspawn HELL 006 (Europe) (2000), Necropolis
NR 065 (USA) (2001)
Teach Children To Worship Satan, No Fashion NFR 039
(Europe) (2000)
DIABOLIS INTERIUM, No Fashion NFR 066 (Europe), Necropolis
NR 070 (USA) (2001)
UNDER WINGS OF HELL, Hammerheart HHR 092 (Europe)
(2001) split album with Infernal
DEVIL PIGS, Karmageddon Media KARMA 057 (Europe),
Candlelight USA CDL0132CD (USA) (2004) split album with Von
**DE PROFUNDIS CLAMAVI AD TE DOMINE: LIVE IN SOUTH
AMERICA 2003**, Regain RR 0403-051 (Europe) (2004),
Candlelight USA CDL0216CD (USA) (2005)
ATTERA TOTUS SANCTUS, Regain RR 070 (Europe), Candlelight
USA CDL0249CD (USA) (2005)

Philipson) of Leukemia and The Project Hate, bassist Tomas Elofsson from Sanctification and Vomitory drummer Tobias Gustafsson.

Dark Funeral partnered with Goatwhore and Zyklon for the 'Extreme The Dojo Volume 9' Japanese gigs in January 2004. They then resumed touring with a spate of Mexican dates in February before hooking up with Defleshed for a short burst of Italian dates. The band's Israeli debut came with a gig in Tel Aviv during November, supported by local bands Lehavoth, Winterhorde and Armilos. Ex-drummer Tomas Asklund came back to the fore by joining the resurrected Dissection.

Signing to Regain, the band toured with Six Feet Under, Nile, Disbelief, Dying Fetus, Wykked Wytch and Cataract for the 'No Mercy Festivals' 2005 European tour in early March. However, the group pulled out on March 19th, claiming that they had been forced out by influenza. The band entered Dug Out studios in Uppsala during late May with producer Daniel Bergstrand to cut a new album. That same month, drummer Modin acted as fill-in for Scaar and performed festival dates with Defleshed.

Album recordings in July for *Attera Totus Sanctus* saw ex-Meshuggah man Gustaf Hielm on bass. The album entered the Swedish charts at Number 35 in November. *Attera Totus Sanctus* was licensed to Icarus Music in Argentina and Sylphorium Records in Colombia.

Dates in Europe during February and March saw the band sharing stages with Amoral, Naglfar, Asmodeus and Endstille. The French leg of the tour saw additional support from Otargos. Festival appearances in the summer included 'Metalliga Open Air' and 'Kaltenbach Open Air', both in Austria, the Gernika 'Metalway' festival in Spain and September's 'Braincrusher' event in Anröchte, Germany. Dark Funeral remain among the most dedicated practitioners of their art.

ENTHRONED
SECOND-TIER BLACK METALLERS

BELGIAN BAND ENTHRONED, hailing from the Namur and Ghent region, found unintended infamy with the suicide of their drummer Cernunnos (aka Dan Vandenplas). The sticksman had been a founder member of the group in late 1993 when he united with Lord Sabathan (Franck Lorent) of Dying Corpse and Blaspherion and erstwhile Mystica and Hybrid Viscery guitarist Tsebaoth (Vincent). Before this, Cernunnos, Lord Sabathan and Fabrice Depireux (aka Namroth Blackthorn) had issued three demos in the late 1980s as Morbid Death. Tsebaoth and Sabathan also issued a self-titled 1993 demo as Slanesh.

Enthroned released an August 1994 demo, *Blackwinds*, and a September split EP with Ancient Rites, *Scared By Darkwinds*, before signing with Osmose Productions' subsidiary label Evil Omen. The band inducted ex-Infected, Magia Posthuma and Heresia guitarist Nornagest following the self-produced debut album *Prophecies Of Pagan Fire*, released in October 1995. Half of this material was lifted directly from the *Blackwinds* demo. Enthroned would tour with the likes of Blood, Ancient Rites, Enslaved and Marduk. However, Tsebaoth quit in favour of Nebiros, another erstwhile Magia Posthuma man.

The group manoeuvred to British label Blackend for a second album, *Towards The Skullthrone Of Satan*, with a licence for North America granted to Metal Blade. Just as the musicians were preparing to enter the Hautregard studio with engineer André Gielen, Cernunnos – suffering from severe depression – hanged himself on April 19th 1997. With no pause in operations, the group pulled in Asphyxia's Da Cardoen as session drummer. *Towards The Skullthrone Of Satan* was released in 1997 and included Venom frontman Cronos as guest on the track 'Satan's Realm'.

Enthroned recorded a tribute to their late drummer in 1998, *Regie Sathanas*, the EP including material written by Cernunnos while in Morbid Death and a cover of Sodom's 'The Conqueror'. Drums were now in the hands of Namroth Blackthorn. Touring in Europe found the band as guests to Dark Funeral prior to a second bout with Hecate Enthroned and Usurper.

The band's fourth album, *The Apocalypse Manifesto*, was co-produced by Hypocrisy's Peter Tägtgren. Here Enthroned took a major step up in terms of quality, expanding their audience considerably. Unfortunately a mistake in the manufacturing process resulted in the first pressing being devoid of the fifth track, 'Post-Mortem Penetrations (Messe Des Saintes Mortes)'. Enthroned supported Marduk on their epic European tour in late 1999. The debut album was then reissued by Blackend with extra demo tracks, live tracks and the out-take 'Post Mortem Penetration'.

During 2000, the band lost the services of guitarist Nebiros, and Nerath Daemon, also a member of Emptiness, was announced as replacement in time for a short German tour. Following these dates, they entered the studio to record the *Armoured Bestial Hell* album. Another line-up change found Namroth Blackthorn ousted in favour of Alsvid from the notorious French act Seth. Issued in April 2001 and packaged in cover artwork from the hand of Rok of Sadistik Exekution, *Armoured Bestial Hell* prompted another run of European shows and a month-long stint in America.

The band announced a switch to the Austrian Napalm label in 2002. A European tour with Aeternus, Hecate Enthroned, Agathodaimon, Mörk Gryning and Infernal Poetry ensued during spring 2002. They then headlined a European trek with Greek veterans Rotting Christ and Ireland's Primordial. Under the banner 'Days Of Suffering' the band allied themselves with Agathodaimon, Seth and Destinity for European dates in April and May.

Enthroned set about recording their next album, *XES Haereticum*, in April 2004 at Spiderhouse Studios with veteran thrash producer Harris Johns. In June, the band added new guitarist Nguaroth from Wapenspraak En Drinkgelag and Aguynguerran, the new line-up debuting on July 25th at the 'Frontline' venue in Ghent. Following a string of South American shows, drummer Glaurung enrolled in October.

In a surreal turn of events, the group's erstwhile label Blackend issued

ENTHRONED discography

Scared By Darkwinds, Afterdark no number (Europe) (1994) split 7-inch vinyl picture disc with Ancient Rites

PROPHECIES OF PAGAN FIRE, Evil Omen EOR 004 (Europe / USA) (1995)

TOWARDS THE SKULLTHRONE OF SATAN, Blackend BLACK008CD (UK) (1997), Metal Blade 3984-14164-2 (USA) (1998)

Regie Sathanas: A Tribute To Cernunnos, Blackend BLACK011CD (UK) (1998), Metal Blade 3984-14261-2 (USA) (1999)

THE APOCALYPSE MANIFESTO, Blackend BLACK018CD (UK) (1999), Cleopatra 1112 (USA) (2001)

ARMOURED BESTIAL HELL, Blackend BLACK031CD (UK), Cleopatra 1148 (USA) (2001)

CARNAGE IN WORLDS BEYOND, Napalm NPR 113 (Europe / USA) (2002)

Goatlust, Painkiller PKR-021 (Europe) (2003) limited edition 7-inch vinyl single 1,000 copies

XES HAERETICUM, Napalm NPR 149 (Europe / USA) (2004)

BLACK GOAT RITUAL: LIVE IN THY FLESH, Napalm NPR 165 (Europe / USA) (2005)

a four-CD compilation entitled *The Blackend Collection*. Enthroned were vicious in their condemnation of this set, as song listings were wrongly ordered, credited tracks excised and – for some bizarre reason – the song 'The Scourge Of God' was printed on the cover as 'Scourge Of Anal Lust'. In more positive news, Enthroned announced the release of their first live album, entitled *Black Goat Ritual: Live In Thy Flesh*, for issue in 2005 through Napalm Records.

In early 2005 the band contributed to the Townsend Avalanche Music Immortal tribute album entitled *Epimythion – Tribute to Immortal* with their rendition of 'Eternal Years On The Path To The Cemetery Gates'. That June Glaurung joined Emptiness while Sabathan sessioned for US act Demonic Christ.

Devotees were delivered vinyl reissues of the first two albums in 2006 through Painkiller Rex Records, the first 100 of which were pressed on red vinyl. The band got back into live action in June, appearing at the 'Graspop Metal Meeting' event. Their perseverance has seen them gain considerable ground in recent years.

MARDUK
DEDICATED TO BLASPHEMY

MARDUK ARE A BLACK metal band from Norrköping, Sweden. Initially called God, they switched names to that of the Sumerian deity in 1990, rapidly elevated themselves into the genre's premier league with a stream of unrelentingly raw albums.

The band were created in 1990 by sometime punk guitarist Morgan 'Mr. Evil' Håkansson and ex-Lucy Seven vocalist Andreas Axelsson. Other musicians on the first demo included guitarist Joakim 'Grave' Göthberg, previously a member of Grimorium, and bassist Rickard Kalm.

Marduk's notorious *Fuck Me Jesus* EP of June 1991 – actually their first demo, at first a cassette tamely branded *Demo#1* and pressed onto vinyl – was graced with a jacket depicting a naked woman inserting a crucifix between her legs from behind; it was subsequently banned across Europe. This same unit cut tracks for an intended EP, the thoroughly brutal *Here's*

No Peace, in December 1991, at Hellspawn Studios, but these tapes did not make it to commercial release. Instead, the tracks were disseminated in demo form.

The band then signed to No Fashion Records, but by the time the debut, *Dark Endless*, arrived in June 1992, Marduk's line-up had shifted to Håkansson, Axelsson, Göthberg, guitarist Magnus 'Devo' Andersson and ex-Chained and Allegiance bassist Roger 'Bogge' Svensson (aka B.War). Despite its ferocity, *Dark Endless* – self-produced but mixed by Dan Swanö – involved some degree of experimentation, with riffs ratcheted down to doom metal weight, as well as some near-melodic passages. However, these aberrations were soon resigned to history as Marduk honed their craft.

The band switched to the French label Osmose Productions, a union that would serve them for a lengthy and productive period. Prior to *Those Of The Unlight*, released in October 1993, Göthberg assumed the lead vocal role as Axelsson had left to join Edge Of Sanity. Andersson also left to concentrate on Allegiance, Overflash and Cardinal Sin. Göthberg joined Andersson as the drummer in Cardinal Sin before founding Darkified.

On *Those Of The Unlight*, Marduk captured a sound that married raw black metal with an underlying groove and a crystal clarity not normally associated with the genre. This formula gave the band an identity on the somewhat faceless black metal scene.

With their third album, December 1994's *Opus Nocturne*, they toured Europe supporting Immortal on their 'Sons Of Northern Darkness' tour. In June 1996 the *Heaven Shall Burn... When We Are Gathered* album, noticeably devoid of keyboards, was issued. Here the band presented two distinct new variations to their sound, as the album was the first to employ new vocalist Legion (aka Erik Hagstedt) of Black Goat and Ophthalamia, and was greatly accelerated in velocity. Marduk released the *Glorification* EP that November, which featured cover versions: Piledriver's 'Sex With Satan' and 'Sodomize The Dead', Destruction's 'Total Desaster' and Bathory's seminal 'The Return Of Darkness And Evil'. The limited vinyl variants also included a take on Venom's 'Hellchild'.

Marduk's line-up now consisted of Håkansson (also an active member of Abruptum), vocalist Legion, Overflash guitarist Kim Osara, bassist B.War and drummer Fredrik Andersson. Göthberg had decamped to found Dimension Zero, a high-profile union with In Flames guitarist Jesper Strömblad, ex-In Flames six-stringer Glenn Ljungström and Luciferion and Diabolique drummer Hasse Nilsson.

For their 1996 European tour, the band drafted in their producer and

Marduk

MARDUK discography

DARK ENDLESS, No Fashion NFR 003 (Europe) (1992), Necropolis NR 005 (USA) (1993)

THOSE OF THE UNLIGHT, Osmose Productions OPCD 015 (Europe / USA) (1993)

OPUS NOCTURNE, Osmose Productions OPCD 028 (Europe / USA) (1994)

Fuck Me Jesus, Osmose Productions OPCD 030 (Europe / USA) (1995)

HEAVEN SHALL BURN... WHEN WE ARE GATHERED, Osmose Productions OPCD 040 (Europe / USA) (1996)

Glorification, Osmose Productions OPMCD 043 (Europe / USA) (1996)

LIVE IN GERMANIA, Osmose Productions OPCD 054 (Europe / USA) (1997)

Here's No Peace, Shadow SHADOW 002 (Europe) (1997)

NIGHTWING, Osmose Productions OPCD 064 (Europe / USA) (1998)

PANZER DIVISION MARDUK, Osmose Productions OPCD 080 (Europe / USA) (1999)

Obedience, Blooddawn Productions BLOOD 003 (Europe) (2000), Century Media CM 8034-2 (USA) (2001)

INFERNAL ETERNAL, Blooddawn Productions BLOOD 007 (Europe) (2000), Century Media CM 8035-2 (USA) (2001)

LA GRANDE DANSE MACABRE, Blooddawn Productions BLOOD 008 (Europe), Century Media CM 8036-2 (USA) (2001)

BLACKCROWNED, Blooddawn Productions BLOOD 011 (Europe), Century Media CM 7984-2 (USA) (2003) limited edition boxed set 10,000 copies

Hearse, Blooddawn Productions BLOOD 013 (Europe) (2003)

WORLD FUNERAL, Blooddawn Productions BLOOD 014 (Europe) (2003)

PLAGUE ANGEL, Blooddawn Productions BLOOD 018 (Europe) (2004), Candlelight USA CDL0167CD (USA) (2005)

Deathmarch, Blooddawn Productions BLOOD 020 (Europe) (2004)

WARSCHAU, Blooddawn Productions BLOOD 032 (Europe) (2005)

Hypocrisy/Abyss guitarist Peter Tägtgren as a stand-in member, although plans were also laid to convene ex-Necrophobic and Dark Funeral member David 'Blackmoon' Parland into the fold. These dates produced the concert recording *Live In Germania*.

In 1997 the group's 1991 *Here's No Peace* sessions were finally released as an EP by Shadow Records. Their choice of accompanying artwork, a German WWII Panzer IV tank bordered with the EP title in the style of an SS cuffband, strongly moulded public perception of the band.

That October, Marduk utilised Tägtgren's Abyss Studios for the *Nightwing* album, released in April 1998. *Nightwing*, loosely themed on the exploits of Vlad The Impaler – by way of the closing 'Dracul Wayda', 'Kaziklu Bey (The Lord Impaler)', 'Deme Quaden Thyrane' and the triumphal 'Anno Domini 1476' – opened up a wider international audience for the band.

Various members then collaborated with Swedish punk act Wolfpack to create Moment Maniacs. The recordings resulted in 1999's *Two Fuckin' Pieces* album. Also arriving in March that year, and continuing the band's war theme, was the *Panzer Division Marduk* opus. With such World War II German imagery the band were obviously flirting with Nazi ideology, but while they kept the album title, they put a British tank on the cover to ward off further associations. However, track titles such as 'Christraping Black Metal' and 'Fistfucking God's Planet' showed there had been little room for compromise on the religious front. Once again Marduk had changed tack musically: the album was so witheringly fast that a new term, Norsecore, was applied to describe the point where black metal is performed so fast that it meets grindcore head-on. On the road in Europe during October 1999, the group joined a heavyweight bill of Defleshed, Angel Corpse, Aeternus and Cannibal Corpse.

The year 2000 saw the issue of a mini-CD, *Obedience*, featuring Marduk's rendition of Celtic Frost's 'Into The Crypt Of Rays'. US editions put out by Century Media dropped the original bondage sleeve but added live tracks. Marduk members also contributed to the 2000 album *The Howling* by Devil's Whorehouse.

The band celebrated their 10th anniversary with the issue of a double live album. *Infernal Eternal* consisted of live tapes collected from the French leg of their 1999 world tour. The now-rare *Here's No Peace* EP was reissued once again, this time by Blooddawn Productions in 5,000 numbered copies, adding two Bathory covers 'In Conspiracy With Satan' and 'Woman Of Dark Desires'.

A new studio album, *La Grande Danse Macabre*, arrived in March 2001. Century Media released it, as well as *Obedience* and *Infernal Eternal*, in North and South America. *La Grande Danse Macabre* found Marduk at their most schizophrenic, pitching Norsecore against sluggish doom metal like some psychotic pendulum.

Touring in America found the band supporting Deicide for a run of dates with Gorguts and All Out War during May. They returned to Europe for a month of headline shows before rounding things off on July 23rd with an appearance at the Belgian 'Graspop Metal Meeting' headlined by Motörhead and Judas Priest. However, gigs in Eastern Europe and Russia were cancelled at the last minute. The band were advised these shows were no longer part of the schedule and curtailed the tour, only to find that their tour manager had stolen the entire tour income. He was later arrested.

Marduk then donated a song to a video for American motocross star Brian Deegan. Entitled 'Deathride', the track was in fact *Panzer Division Marduk* material compiled into a medley and recorded with new lyrics.

An autumn 2001 US tour with Amon Amarth, Kataklysm and Diabolic was postponed when the band ran into difficulties due to various members' criminal records. Ironically, American officials had earlier written to the band to congratulate them for not postponing the tour in the wake of the 9/11 attacks. The tour was re-set for January 2002, but once again they suffered setbacks on trying to enter the USA: Amon Amarth and Diabolic began the tour minus the headline act.

The new year ushered in a limited-edition boxed set, *Blackcrowned*, comprising two CDs of rare and unreleased material, vintage rehearsals, re-recorded archive tracks, a Misfits cover version, and a video. Marduk parted ways with drummer Andersson in March 2002. His replacement was announced as Emil Dragutinovic, who had played with Nominon, Legion and was occasional lead vocalist with Spawn Of Possession.

Marduk looked finally set to tour America throughout the summer of 2002 as special guests to Danzig. However, literally within hours of the announcement it seemed the Swedes' age-old problems with US immigration had curtailed these plans. The band then co-headlined an impressive cast for European 'X-Mass' festivals in December, supported by Six Feet Under, Immolation, Kataklysm, Dying Fetus and Hate. Later gigs in Holland added veteran thrashers Exodus to the bill.

The band's next album was provisionally titled *Funeral War* (later switched to *World Funeral*), slated for February 2003. They revealed that a cover of Possessed's 'Phantasm' had been laid down in these sessions: this duly turned up as part of a teaser EP entitled *Hearse*. *World Funeral* itself also came as a picture disc, limited to just 1,500 pressings.

Marduk were confirmed as participants in the April 2003 European 'No Mercy' festivals with Testament, Darkane, Nuclear Assault, Pro-Pain, Malevolent Creation, Death Angel and Callenish Circle. Fans were in for a surprise at the 'Party.San Open Air' festival in Germany that August as former vocalist Göthberg took to the stage to guest on 'The Black'. This performance was filmed for inclusion in a DVD, *Funeral Marches And Warsongs*.

The band embarked on an extensive South American trek during October and November, but vocalist Legion suddenly quit in mid November. Projected appearances in Greece and the 'Blackest Of The Black' festival in London were cancelled. Marduk announced their new vocalist in February as Mortuus, previously known as Arioch in Funeral Mist and Triumphator. Recordings for a 2004 album included a collaboration between Marduk and the industrial percussion project Arditi, a venture of Henry Möller from Puissance and Mårten Björkman. In May bassist B.War was superseded by Magnus Devo Andersson, former second guitar player on the first two albums *Dark Endless* and *Those Of The Unlight*, who had recently pursued his own project Laid To Rest.

In August, Legion and B.War united with guitarist Jim Durkin of Dreams Of Damnation and Dark Angel repute in a new Los Angeles-based death metal project. Meanwhile, Marduk cut a new album, *Plague Angel*, at Endarker Studios in Norrköping. This was also issued as a limited edition vinyl LP in 1,000 hand-numbered copies, while another restricted run of CD digipacks added the video for 'Steel Inferno'.

The band commended their Deathmarch world tour and were announced as one of the main attractions on the 'X-Mass Fest' with Napalm Death, Finntroll, Vader, The Black Dahlia Murder and Belphegor. A special EP, *Deathmarch*, was made available for release at these shows. However, on February 12th drummer Emil Dragutinovic had his arm broken in a baseball bat attack, forcing the band to cancel their UK dates. *Plague Angel* was finally granted a belated US release in March 2005 through Candlelight.

Marduk toured Europe and Scandinavia throughout September 2005 with support from Mystic Circle. However, the last three scheduled shows in Denmark and Sweden were cancelled when the band's bus broke down in Germany. They closed the year with the live album *Warschau*, a double concert set recorded on Polish 'Deathmarch' dates during 2004. A vinyl pressing was restricted to just 500 copies.

European headline dates in May 2006 saw support from Italian act Necrodeath before headliners in Mexico and preparation for another slice of blasphemy in the form of the *Blood Puke Salvation* DVD. Marduk remain at the vanguard of Swedish black metal.

MERCYFUL FATE
BLACK METAL DIAMOND GEEZERS

WHEN HEAVY METAL CAME to the fore once again on the back of the NWOBHM, fans began to turn their attention outside the UK and USA to focus on Europe and Scandinavia. Many acts were championed but only a handful proved to have any tenacity. However, Denmark's Mercyful Fate endured thanks to a number of distinguishing factors – singer King Diamond's unique falsetto vocals, his onstage persona and the band's Satanically charged lyrical content. While it was commonplace for metal bands to flirt with Lucifer and his minions on occasion, Mercyful Fate made it their trademark. Fortunately for the Danes, they had the musical muscle to back up this novel approach.

Mercyful Fate evolved from Copenhagen punk/heavy rock outfit Brats, formed in the late 1970s by guitarist Hank Shermann (aka Rene Krolmark or Hank De Wank). In 1979 Michael Denner enrolled alongside vocalist Yenz (later to front Geisha and Y) and drummer Monroe. The Brats recorded one track for a 1979 compilation LP, *Pair Punk*, and released one full album on CBS, *1980 Brats*, which made quite an impact in Europe, selling particularly well in France. It even led to 'Zombie People' picking up British airplay courtesy of Capital Radio's Alan Freeman.

1980 Brats was basically a proto-metal album with punk overtones, although it also included a quirky folk song sung in Russian by Denner. However, the group disbanded and Shermann linked up again with Denner, who had formed Danger Zone with frontman King Diamond (aka Kim Bendix Petersen), a veteran of Brainstorm and Black Rose, along with Timi Grabber and drummer Nick Smith, later replaced by Kim Ruzz. Diamond, forgoing a promising career as a professional footballer, had already made a name for himself in Europe with the Black Rose stage show, which thrived on bloody theatrics. This trait spilled over heavily into his new band.

Still named Brats, this fresh band recorded a demo featuring the tracks 'Some Day', 'Death Kiss', 'Love Criminals' and 'Combat Zone'. Diamond immediately stamped his distinctive seal on the proceedings with his high-range vocals. His eardrum-shattering falsetto was to become the band's trademark. While the shrill operatics put off many metal fans, it did identify the singer and inspired a dedicated group of fans. Shortly after the demo, the band switched names to Mercyful Fate (there is conjecture that the group briefly operated as Back To Hell) and the song 'Love Criminals' began to pick up heavy airplay on Dutch radio thanks to the underground tape trading scene.

Mercyful Fate demoed again in March 1981, recording at The Rocktape Studios in Copenhagen. Three songs were laid down by Diamond, Shermann, Carsten Van Der Volsing on both guitar and bass, and stand-in drummer Jan Musen. A further promo recording involved Danger Zone songs 'Killed For Love' rebranded as 'Running Free' and 'Not Amusing' morphed into 'Hard Rocker'. Also onboard were 'Love Criminals', an evolution of a track from the Brats days. That autumn the group, having fleetingly employed Benny Petersen, utilised Karma Studios to put down another batch of songs.

On the strength of the final tape, the band were invited to Hull, England by Darryl Johnstone at Ebony Records to record a track, 'Black Funeral', for the *Metallic Storm* compilation. They also recorded 'Walkin' Back To Hell' during the Ebony session, but this song was not released. It later surfaced as 'A Dangerous Meeting' in 1984.

As a live act, Mercyful Fate were an extremely heavy proposition, with the twin guitar work of Shermann and Denner added to the distinctive wail of Diamond. The singer developed a second focus of attention with chilling monochrome face-paint inspired by Alice Cooper. Along with his penchant for microphone stands made of fake human femurs and a theatrical stage show imbued with liberal pseudo-Satanic overtones, Mercyful Fate were certainly out to be noticed.

With interest in Holland outpacing the rest of Europe, the band signed to Dutch company Rave On in September 1982, cutting tracks over three days at Stone Sound Studios in Holland. This resulted in a four-track mini-album, often referred to as *Nuns Have No Fun* due to its schlocky artwork featuring a crucified nun. Beyond the visuals, the music was equally lurid, with the chorus of 'Nuns Have No Fun' exclaiming "C.U.N.T. – that's what you are!" In later years it was revealed that the track 'A Corpse Without A Soul', despite being held in great esteem by the metal masses, was in fact a truncated edit. The original lasted ten minutes but the engineer's tape ran out before the band wound up – hence its 6:52 duration on the EP.

The EP's impact on the underground scene was huge, and Ron Quintana's San Francisco magazine *Metal Mania* voted it EP Of The Year. While in England on a short tour in March 1983, which included a memorable show at the Clarendon Hotel in London's Hammersmith, the band recorded a session for BBC Radio One's *Friday Rock Show* featuring the tracks 'Evil', 'Satan's Fall' and 'Curse Of The Pharaohs'.

MERCYFUL FATE discography

Mercyful Fate, Rave-On RMLP-002 (Europe) (1982)
Black Funeral, Music For Nations 12KUT 106 (UK) (1983)
Black Funeral, Megaforce IOM-2 (USA) (1983) limited edition
 7-inch vinyl picture disc 2,500 copies
MELISSA, Music For Nations MFN 10 (UK), Megaforce MRI-369
 (USA) (1983)
DON'T BREAK THE OATH, Music For Nations MFN 28 (UK),
 Combat MX 8011 (USA) (1984)
THE BEGINNING, Roadrunner RR 9603 (Europe / USA) (1987)
A DANGEROUS MEETING, Roadrunner RR 9117-2 (Europe),
 Roadrunner RRD 9117 (USA) (1992) split album with King
 Diamond
RETURN OF THE VAMPIRE: THE RARE AND UNRELEASED,
 Roadrunner RR 9184-2 (Europe), Roadrunner RRD 9184 (USA)
 (1992)
IN THE SHADOWS, Metal Blade CDMZORRO 61 (UK), Metal Blade
 9 45318-2 (USA) (1993)
The Bell Witch, Metal Blade CDMZORRO 78 (UK), Metal Blade
 PCDS 53911 (USA) (1994)
TIME, Metal Blade CDMZORRO 80 (UK), Metal Blade P2 53942
 (USA) (1994)
INTO THE UNKNOWN, Metal Blade 3984-17026-2 (Europe), Metal
 Blade P2 50586 (USA) (1996)
DEAD AGAIN, Metal Blade 3984-14159-2 (Europe / USA) (1998)
9, Metal Blade 3984-14242-2 (Europe / USA) (1999)

As momentum gathered, Mercyful Fate split with Rave On and signed to Roadrunner in Europe and Music For Nations in Britain in early 1983. That July, with producer Henrik Lund at Easy Sound Recording in Copenhagen, they recorded their debut album, *Melissa*, titled in honour of a medieval Danish witch whose skull Diamond claimed to own. US versions, manufactured by Megaforce, provided extra incentive for collectors, as the first pressing featured a different take of the title track. A single, 'Black Masses'/'Black Funeral', was also issued.

The band promoted *Melissa* album heavily, opening for the likes of Uriah Heep, Gillan and Girlschool. Regrettably, Diamond claimed responsibility for invoking the "evil presence" that electrocuted Girlschool vocalist Kim McAuliffe at a show in Copenhagen. The band also courted controversy when they pulled out of a British tour supporting Manowar after just one date at St. Albans City Hall. Mercyful Fate claimed that as they had contributed financially to the costs of the tour they were being treated unfairly by the headliners in terms of set-up times and soundchecking. Manowar denied the allegations and Mercyful Fate were promptly ditched in favour of Birmingham band Crazy Angel.

In May 1984, the band recorded their second album, *Don't Break The Oath*, again with Lund in charge of the faders, and embarked on their first American dates, both as headliners and as openers for Motörhead. The album was another success, scoring many European chart positions.

The Danes were hit with the departure of Shermann in December 1984 as the guitarist opted to form the much more commercial Fate. This group achieved critical acclaim but little else before Shermann reunited with Michael Denner to forge Zoser Mez in a more traditional metal mould at the start of the new decade. Ruzz famously opted out of the music business and took up a more sedate profession as a postman.

With Shermann out of the group it wasn't long before King Diamond opted to break up the band in order to pursue his self-titled solo band (see separate entry in chapter 9, Power Metal). However, the line-up was always fragile and, combined with a dispute with their record label, Diamond's band ceased operations at the turn of the decade.

Mercyful Fate's legend was continually stoked with the emergence of archive collections *The Beginning* and *Return Of The Vampire*, both in 1992. After hearing material by Zoser Mez, King felt that the time was right to reform Mercyful Fate with Shermann, Denner, and Grabber. Original drummer Ruzz could not be torn away from his day job in the postal service, and Morten Nielsen, previously with Apocalypse and Force Majeure, laid down the drums for the comeback album. The band shared a stage with Metallica for their reuninon show in May 1993. They then appeared at the legendary 'Dynamo' festival in Eindhoven, Holland during June. The *In The Shadows* album, offered up in August, featured guest drummer Lars Ulrich of Metallica on a revamped version of the 1982 demo track 'Return Of The Vampire'. Once touring duties were fulfilled, Grabber made the decision to return to family life.

The Bellwitch was a 1994 mini-album comprising three live numbers and two new songs, 'The Bell Witch' and 'Is That You Melissa?'. October 1994's *Time* witnessed the group on full throttle once more, and they toured North America in early 1995 supported by Solitude Aeturnus. *Time* included the track 'Castillo Del Mortes', originally laid down as a 1992 Zoser Mez demo instrumental entitled 'Land Of Goshen'.

In early 1996 the band received a request to record a Judas Priest cover version. Their suitably spine-tingling interpretation of 'The Ripper' was included on Century Media's *Legends Of Metal: A Tribute To Judas Priest*. They added drummer Bjarne T. Holm to the line-up that same year for the complex *Into The Unknown*, which featured bassist Sharlee D'Angelo (Charles Andreason), former sessioneer for Facelift and ex-King Diamond member. Subsequent live work found Denner's position taken by Mike Wead (Mikael Wikström) of Memento Mori for the closing dates. In late 1997, Roadrunner reissued the early titles in remastered form and featuring bonus tracks. Outside Mercyful Fate, the band-members occupied themselves with a slew of ventures.

In January 2002, the band split from Metal Blade. Two years later their classic cut 'Evil' was chosen as a pioneering piece of music for a compilation assembled by Darkthrone drummer Fenriz, released through Peaceville and titled *Fenriz Presents: The Best Of Old School Black Metal*. Also paying homage were Canadian power metal band Eidolon, cutting a cover of 'The Oath' with Denner playing guest solos. Both Shermann and Denner repaid the favour, donating guitar solos to Eidolon album recordings in 2005. Mercyful Fate are assured of a place in metal history: respect is due.

MYSTIC CIRCLE
RELIABLY METALLIC GERMANS

LEADING BLACK METALLERS Mystic Circle from Ludwigshafen, Germany were founded in 1992 as a duo of vocalist-bassist Graf von Beelzebub (aka Marc Zimmer), previously a member of Mannheim's Crematory, and drummer Aaarrrgon. Adding guitarist Mephisto, the band recorded the demo *Dark Passion* in 1994. Rhythm guitarist Agamidion bolstered the band's sound as they switched from death metal to black metal, proving this point with a further tape in 1995 titled *Von Kriegen Und Helden*. The following year saw a further demo in the form of *Die Götter Der Urväter*. The 7-inch EP *Kriegsgötter – Der Weg Nach Wallhall* followed before a debut album, *Morgenröte – Die Schrei Nach Finsternis*, recorded at the Soundbunkerstudio in Ludwigshafen with Giants Causeway bassist Guido Holzmann as producer, arrived through Last Episode Records. After these sessions, guitarists Mephisto and Excess man Agamidion made their exit. Two tracks were delivered as the interim 'Schwarze Magie' 7-inch split single in 1997, a self-financed collusion with grind protagonists Blood.

In early 1998, the band recorded *Drachenblut*, based on the German legend of the Nibelungen. The rebuilt band were now bolstered by guitarists Isternos and Ezpharess, with Baalsulgorr handling keyboards. *Drachenblut* was promoted to the masses that October at shows with Cannibal Corpse, Deicide and Infernal Majesty. The reaction was such that a second tour was executed in February 1999 with Eisregen, Old Man's Child, Runemagick and Sacramentum.

Infernal Satanic Verses was released in December 1999. Notable studio guests included the Cradle Of Filth soprano Sarah Jezebel Deva, Ina Heiden, and Giants Causeway man Kalle Friedrich.

Further live dates, including a valuable appearance at the 'Wacken' festival, witnessed the temporary employment of second guitarist Xeron. October 1999 saw the band engaging in the 'Infernal Gods Of War' European tour alongside Graveworm, Suidakra and Stormlord. Co-founder Aaarrrgon opted out at this juncture. The drummer, switching his pseudonym to Blackwar, joined Donsdorf-based Zorn as guitarist. The band's January 2000 shows, supported by Limbonic Art and Brazil's Rebaelliun, featured Graveworm's drummer Martin Innerbichler aiding on a session basis.

The 2000 EP release *Kriegsgötter II* featured demos and covers of Celtic Frost's 'Circle Of The Tyrants', recorded live, Acheron's eponymous theme, and Bathory's 'On The Road To Asa Bay'. They conducted these recordings as a quartet of Graf von Beelzebub, Ezpharess, Baalsulgorr and drummer Blizzard. Unfortunately, touring obligations found Mystic Circle

MYSTIC CIRCLE discography

Kriegsgötter – Der Weg Nach Wallhall, Last Episode cnu (Europe) (1996)

MORGENRÖTE – DER SCHREI NACH FINSTERNIS, Last Episode LEP 007 CD (Europe) (1996)

Schwarze Magie, Last Episode cnu (Europe) (1997) split 7-inch vinyl single with Blood

DRACHENBLUT, Last Episode LEP 018 CD (Europe) (1998), Pavement Music 76962-32301-2 (USA) (1999)

INFERNAL SATANIC VERSES, Last Episode LEP 048 CD (Europe) (1999)

Kriegsgötter II, Last Episode LEP 061 CD (Europe) (2000)

THE GREAT BEAST, Massacre MAS CD0257 (Europe) (2001)

DAMIEN, Massacre MAS CD0329 (Europe) (2002)

OPEN THE GATES OF HELL, Massacre MAS CD0391 (Europe) (2003)

UNHOLY CHRONICLES 1992-2004, Massacre MAS CD0451 (Europe) (2004)

THE BLOODY PATH OF GOD, Dockyard 1 DY 100012 (Europe) (2006)

in the unusual position of performing live with a drum machine. The drum stool was subsequently occupied by Raziel and swiftly thereafter by Abyss (aka Marc Reign) of Gunjah and Orth.

Promoting 2001's *The Great Beast*, their first for new label Massacre and featuring female vocals from Ophelia (Ruth Knepel), the band put in more European touring. The year was closed in December with a tour backed by Ancient Rites and Abortus. Baalsulgorr closed his tenure in 2002 and Abyss also left, hooking up with Destruction.

The *Damien* album surfaced in September 2002, with digipack versions hosting their interpretation of the *Lost Boys* movie theme 'Cry Little Sister'. They pursued further touring into 2002, uniting in November with Deicide, Centinex and Antaeus. Their 2003 album was *Open The Gates Of Hell*: Australian dates in October saw Abortus acting as support before German headliners.

The band undertook European tour dates with Kataklysm, Graveworm and Into Eternity in October 2004, and a compilation album, *Mystic Circle Unholy Chronicles 1992–2004*, was issued to coincide. Alongside studio tracks, this double album included the video clip for 'Awaken By Blood', live material culled from the 2004 'Wave-Gotik-Treffen' festival, and a Romanian television interview. The same year, drummer Alex Necrodemon sessioned for Australian act Herratik, previously known as Abortus. In February 2005, Mystic Circle signed to the newly established Dockyard 1 label, co-owned by Iron Savior's Piet Sielck, for the album *The Bloody Path Of God*.

Mystic Circle parted ways with Necrodemon in July, although they maintained a relationship with their ex-member, utilising him as producer at his newly-built recording studio for their next album. A replacement drummer was soon announced in Dementum, and the band entered State Of The Art Studios on October 5th to cut *The Bloody Path Of God*, featuring a cover of Celtic Frost's seminal 'Circle Of The Tyrants'. Gigs outlined for November and December were scratched, the band citing "drummer problems": they finally installed new sticksman Astaroth in May 2006.

Mystic Circle announced a lengthy run of shows throughout Mexico, Honduras and El Salvador during September and October. Plans for 2007 included 'The Domination Tour' alongside Rotting Christ, Carpathian Forest, Malevolent Creation, Incantation and Neuraxis.

ROTTING CHRIST
HELLENIC BLACK METALLERS

ROTTING CHRIST, FOUNDED in Athens in 1987, are the foremost Greek black metal act. Even though the group are one of the most blasphemously-named acts of their ilk, in their earliest incarnation the band were very much a grindcore act. This was apparent on a 1988 rehearsal demo *Decline's Return*, replete with such morsels as 'Embryonic Necrocannibalism', 'Syringo Myelial Chemical Neurosurgery' and 'Thyrotoxicosis'. This was followed by the studio demo *Leprosy Of Death*.

A split single, 'The Other Side Of Life', was shared with Sound Pollution in January 1989. Shortly afterwards, a dramatic shift to the darker side took place. The band consisted of vocalist-guitarist Necromayhem (aka Sakis Tolis), bassist Mutilator (Jim), also active with Varathron, and drummer Necrosauron (Themis Tolis).

Following the June 1989 *Satanas Tedeum* demo, the band secured a deal with Norwegian label Deathlike Silence Productions, but this venture was curtailed when label boss Euronymous was murdered by Burzum's Varg Vikernes. Rotting Christ were now a quartet with the addition of keyboard player Morbid (aka George Zaharopoulos). A further split single shared with Italy's Monumentum was issued through Obscure Plasma Records in 1991.

Undaunted by the collapse of Deathlike Silence, Rotting Christ self-financed a mini-album, *Passage To Arcturo*, and used a 1992 demo titled *Ade's Winds* to sign to French label Osmose, which released the *Thy Mighty Contract* album. For this outing, Morbid adopted a new pseudonym of Magus Wampyr Daoloth. The band employed two session players to tour with Blasphemy and Immortal on the quaintly dubbed 'Fuck Christ' tour.

Rotting Christ split from Osmose in an ugly war of words before signing to Greek label Unisound. So bitter was this dispute that their former label took the unusual step of vowing never to reissue their product in the future. As well as recording a new album, Unisound also pressed Rotting Christ's 1989 demo *Satanas Tedeum* onto vinyl. Unfortunately, the *Non Serviam* album suffered greatly from a minimal promotional campaign.

The band toured Mexico in April 1995. They were reduced to a trio with the departure of Daoloth, who later joined Necromantia, Diablos Rising, Raism and Thou Art Lord, working alongside guitarist Necromayhem among others. The band's debut for Century Media, April

Rotting Christ

ROTTING CHRIST discography

The Other Side Of Life, TNT cnu (Europe) (1987) split 7-inch vinyl EP with Sound Pollution

Rotting Christ, Obscure Plasma cnu (Europe) (1991) split 7-inch vinyl EP with Monumentum

Passage To Arcturo, Decapitated DEC 003 (Europe) (1991)

Dawn Of The Iconoclast, Decapitated cnu (Europe) (1991)

Apokathelosis, Osmose Productions OPEP 04 (Europe) (1993)

THY MIGHTY CONTRACT, Osmose Productions OPCD 012 (Europe / USA) (1993)

NON SERVIAM, Unisound USR 012 (Europe) (1994)

Satanas Tedeum, Unisound USR 015 (Europe) (1994)

THE MYSTICAL MEETING, Unisound UNIFORCE 002 (Europe) (1995)

TRIARCHY OF THE LOST LOVERS, Century Media CM 77128-2 (Europe), Century Black 7828-2 (USA) (1996)

The Mystical Meeting, Century Media CM 77181-1-P (Europe) (1997) limited edition 10-inch vinyl picture disc 500 copies

A DEAD POEM, Century Media CM 77166-2 (Europe), Century Media CM 7866-2 (USA) (1997)

Der Perfekte Traum, Century Media CM 77247-3 (Europe) (1999)

SLEEP OF THE ANGELS, Century Media CM 77248-2 (Europe), Century Media CM 7948-2 (USA) (1999)

KHRONOS, Century Media CM 77294-2 (Europe), Century Media CM 79946-2 (USA) (2000)

GENESIS, Century Media CM 77414-2 (Europe), Century Media CM 8114-2 (USA) (2002)

SANCTUS DIAVOLOS, Century Media CM 77514-2 (Europe), Century Media CM 8214-2 (USA) (2004)

1996's *Triarchy Of The Lost Lovers*, was produced by ex-Holy Moses guitarist Andy Classen and included Themis Sauron (aka Necrosauron) as drummer. Previously, percussion had come from a drum machine. The digipack version included no fewer than three Kreator cover versions, 'Tormentor', 'Flag Of Hate' and 'Pleasure To Kill'.

An important concert came in mid 1997 with an appearance at the Megadeth-headlined 'Rockwave' festival at the Apollon Stadium in Athens. The band brought in two new recruits for the 1997 album *A Dead Poem*: ex-Nightstalker man Andreas on bass and Payanotis on keyboards. The record was produced at Woodhouse Studios in Hagen, Germany by Samael keyboard player Xy and featured Moonspell vocalist Fernando Ribeiro on the track 'Among Two Storms'. Touring in Europe found the band sharing a bill with Old Man's Child and Sacramentum before a brief foray into Turkey and another European run in October sharing the stage with Tiamat.

Century Media re-released *Thy Mighty Contract* in 1997 with two rare single cuts, 'Visions Of The Dead Lover' and 'The Mystical Meeting'. A January 1998 album, *Sleep Of The Angels*, had production credits going out to both Xy and Grip Inc's Waldemar Sorychta. The group opted for experimentation, toning down in order to accommodate electronics, keyboards and a cleaner vocal style. Needless to say, the backlash from devotees of their early works was harsh. A monumental tour of Europe with Deicide, Ancient Rites, Aeternus and Behemoth followed before North American, Brazilian and Mexican gigs. Themis Sauron was injured in a Mexican earthquake, although not seriously.

A 1999 Rotting Christ EP, *Der Perfekte Traum*, hosted four live tracks culled from the '96 European dates. *Khronos* followed in August 2000, according to the sleevenotes recorded while "buried under ice" at producer Peter Tägtgren's Abyss Studios in Sweden. They opted to avoid the expected path of most black metal acts and deliberately took a retrograde step for their 2002 album *Genesis*, produced by Classen once again. The resurrection of the old Rotting Christ logo symbolised their return to raw, primitive metal.

The band hooked up with Enthroned and Primordial for a European tour in January 2003. Parting ways with keyboard player George, apparently to "re-emphasise the band's desire to reconnect with their early 90s philosophy and sound", in February 2004 the band played alongside Decapitated, Anata and Thus Defiled.

A new album, *Sanctus Diavolos*, appeared in May, produced by Sakis Tolis at SCA Studios in Athens and mixed by Fredrik Nordström at Studio Fredman in Gothenburg. Meanwhile, a Brazilian tribute album, entitled *An Evil Existence For Rotting Christ*, was issued in June via Recordshop Productions. Participants included Sanctifier, Malefactor, Folk Lord, Sower, Insanity, Mystifier, Lord Blasphemate, Morcrof, Raven Land, Caifaz, Malkuth, Aguares, Blessed In Fire and Miasthenia.

The band announced that they were to lose the services of longstanding guitarist Kostas in July. His last show with the band was at the Uriah Heep-headlined 'Masters Open Air' festival in São Paulo, Brazil on July 24th. Gigs in December were played with Swedish veterans Grave.

Projected concerts on June 17th and 18th in Athens and Thessaloniki on a festival headlined by Megadeth were lost when the main band's outspoken frontman objected to their presence, stating that he "would prefer not to play on concerts with Satanic bands". Apparently Mustaine claimed that Rotting Christ could play, but in that event Megadeth would withdraw. Naturally the Greek act were forced off the bill.

Rotting Christ, joined by Nightfall guitarist George Bokos, marked their first Irish performance by headlining the July Day of Darkness Metalfest in Ballylinan, County Laois. The European 'Blitzkrieg III' tour of September and October 2005 saw the band packaged with Vader, Anorexia Nervosa and Lost Soul.

In January 2006 *Passage To Arcturo* and *Non Serviam* were reissued with bonus tracks through Unruly Sounds in North America, a subsidiary of The End Records, and Season Of Mist in Europe. At two shows in Larissa during February the group performed tracks solely from their early classic albums (1989's *Passage To Arcturo*, 1992's *Thy Mighty Contract* and the 1994 set *Non Serviam*) for a live album recording. Rotting Christ remain in a unique position at the head of their country's metal scene.

VENOM
IT'S ALL THEIR FAULT

VERY FEW OBSERVERS WOULD dare dispute Venom's claim to having invented black metal. As a result, they are among the most influential acts in this book. Typically, the early albums by this trio from Newcastle Upon Tyne, England were largely dismissed by the rock media, although they were later declared classics, in spite of their deliberately primitive approach. The group eschewed rock stardom for a punk metal ethos and in doing so rapidly propagated a loyal global fanbase.

Venom's roots lay in the late-1970s acts Guillotine, Album Gracia, Oberon and Dwarfstar. In 1978, Conrad Lant was a guitarist with Album Gracia: members of this band, including vocalist Keith Ballard and drummer Kevin Robson, decamped to found a new act the same year, Dwarfstar. At the same juncture, another local band, Guillotine – featuring guitarist Jeffrey Dunn – retitled themselves Venom in 1979. The inaugural line-up of this group was Dunn, vocalist Dave Blackman, second guitarist Dave Rutherford, bassist Dean Hewitt and drummer Chris McPeters. Both Blackman and McPeters lost their places in August that year to Oberon members Tony Bray on drums and singer Clive Archer. Oberon played a

part in Venom's later career when guitarist Eric Cook became manager of the band.

Venom, with bassist Alan Winston, pulled in Lant as replacement for Rutherford in November. Days before the band's debut gig in Wallsend, Winston bailed out, forcing Lant to take over bass, which he did in punkish fashion – plugging a bass into a guitar amp.

By 1980, Venom had decided upon a satanic image, "de-christening" the band members in suitable fashion. Archer became Jesus Christ, Lant was Mr. Cronos, Bray Abaddon, and Dunn Mantas. A three-song demo was cut in April featuring early versions of 'Angel Dust', 'Raise The Dead' and 'Red Light Fever'. At a second session, recorded for a miserly £50 (about $120), they laid down six more tracks, with Lant taking lead vocals for 'Live Like An Angel'. Archer packed his bags soon after and the classic Cronos-Mantas-Abaddon line-up of Venom was born.

The band's approach combined Lant's punk persuasions with direct inspiration from the global rock giants. In early interviews, the band professed a desire to blend the energy of Judas Priest with the theatrics of Kiss. Signed to Neat Records, Venom debuted in 1980 with a single, 'In League With Satan'/'Live Like An Angel', and immediately came to the attention of *Sounds* journalist Geoff Barton. His championing of the group brought Venom to the attention of the metal-loving public, although the trio had yet to play a gig. The single was recorded at Impulse Studios in Wallsend, above an old cinema complex, and produced by Steve Thompson and Mickey Sweeney.

The group's first album, *Welcome To Hell*, was produced at Impulse once again, this time with Keith Nichol behind the board. It was issued in 1981 in a variety of formats including picture disc, regular black, white, grey, or purple vinyl. The record was deliberately unrefined and, while its rawness caused consternation among a rock audience raised on finesse, the group found a keen set of fans eager to embrace such lack of pretension. The crudely-drawn Lucifer character on the album jacket appeared to hide his secrets behind a malevolent Mona Lisa-style smirk.

In 1982, Venom again employed Impulse Studios and Keith Nichol for the equally ugly *Black Metal* set. A preceding single coupled the non-album tracks 'Bloodlust' and 'In Nomine Satanas'. While *Welcome To Hell* had incited curiosity, it was *Black Metal* that triggered the global Venom phenomenon. Neat handled UK versions while Roadrunner licensed the album for European territories. Once again, limited editions saw the album pressed on a variety of coloured vinyl including white, grey, purple, green, red, brown, or 'swirled'. A green marbled version is now worth over $550. Notably, a young teenager in the Norwegian town of Ski, Øystein Aarseth, took the song title 'Mayhem With Mercy' to name his new act – Mayhem.

The same year, the band conducted their first BBC Radio One *Friday Rock Show* session, laying down 'Black Metal', 'Nightmare' and 'Bloodlust'. These tracks also made an appearance on the sought-after *French Assault* import EP.

Venom's third album, 1983's *At War With Satan*, found the Geordie triumvirate taking huge strides forward, especially abroad, where the semi-conceptual LP greatly increased the band's following. Europe took to the band in dedicated fashion, and this appreciation would remain steadfast long after the UK had tired of the trio's antics.

Venom's initial live performance almost ensured that they never played a club again, with the event marked by a handmade stage prop falling over and firing pyrotechnics into the audience. The band's first European live date came in Belgium, where they headlined above Picture and Acid. On the continent, they were able to translate their mystique into material success with a series of major festival appearances and tours, including a trek through Europe in 1984 with Metallica as the support act. They were virtually shunned by the UK audience, where a succession of announced tours were scrapped – although the *The 7th Date Of Hell* video did arise after the group's spectacular debut at London's Hammersmith Odeon on the 'At War With Satan' tour.

Cronos: "I can remember reading a headline that said fans were fleeing from Hammersmith Odeon holding their ears because it was too loud. Fucking great! That's exactly what we wanted to do. We didn't want Venom to be something you could see night after night. It had to be something you experienced in a whole new way. We wanted to shock the audience physically with all the noise, the flames, and so much smoke you couldn't breathe. We wanted people to know they had been to a Venom gig because a week later their ears would still be ringing and they'd still be choking."

Before going in to record *Possessed*, Cronos produced fellow Neat label act Tysondog's first album, *Beware Of The Dog*, although – somewhat bizarrely – he then announced to the world that it was "shit". The year 1985 began disastrously for the band. Although Combat gave earlier Venom product an official US release for the first time, adding revised artwork and extra tracks in the process, the new *Possessed* album was roundly mocked and a planned Canadian and North American tour was thrown into turmoil when Mantas succumbed to glandular fever. The dates were put back and, as his health worsened, the band recruited Avenger guitarist Les Cheetham and Fist guitarist Dave Irwin to fill his shoes. Their New York Studio 54 show with Exodus and Slayer was less than successful as Mantas, now with restored health, was denied access to America due to passport problems.

Mantas left in 1986 following American dates with support act Hirax. Demos were conducted for a proposed album entitled *Deadline*, but with the guitarist's exit this project was shelved. A live album surfaced, *Eine Kleine Nachtmusik*, recorded at the band's now legendary October 8th 1985 London Hammersmith Odeon appearance and a 1986 gig at The Ritz, New York. Mantas resurfaced shortly after with his own self-titled project, which issued one album, 1988's *Winds Of Change*. He soon retired to concentrate on establishing a martial arts centre. Meanwhile, Cronos busied himself producing the 1986 album from Warfare, *Mayhem Fucking Mayhem*.

Mantas was replaced by two guitarists, Jimmy C. (Jim Clare) and Mike H. (Mike Hickey), who performed their first live shows with Venom in Brazil, with support act Exciter, as well as on Japanese dates. Before joining Venom, Clare had operated with Newcastle acts Hardline and Hellfire. The initial concept of nicknaming Clare 'The Mighty Horn' and Hickey as 'King Incubus' was thankfully abandoned.

This new line-up recorded the lukewarm *Calm Before The Storm* for RCA subsidiary Filmtrax. The album, featuring some of the aborted *Deadline* material, saw the band endeavouring to pursue a more mature approach than the bludgeoning ferocity of yore, but merely succeeded in alienating fans, who were unaware that the tracks used for *Calm Before The Storm* were not intended as finished product. They were originally intended as demos, recorded at Neat's Impulse Studios and subsequently remixed in London.

Following live dates, the band set to work on a new studio album, but internal friction resulted in a parting of ways. Cronos and Clare broke away, relocating to America and resurfacing in a band simply known as Cronos, releasing 1990's *Dancing In The Fire*. Cronos also included Mike Hickey and drummer Chris Patterson.

In 1988, Mantas appeared again, this time as guest guitarist on Warfare's *A Conflict Of Hatred*. Venom regrouped in 1989, enticing Mantas back into the fold alongside Abbadon, bassist-vocalist Tony Dolan and rhythm guitarist Al Barnes. Barnes had previously worked with Mantas on his solo album while Dolan was an ex-Atomkraft member. This line-up debuted with *Prime Evil*, released in 1989. The same year the band cut a

version of Black Sabbath's 'Megalomania', which subsequently surfaced on the *Witching Hour* compilation.

They took to UK stages again in late 1989, billed under the pseudonym Sons Of Satan. This included a 'secret' London Marquee gig – which attracted only a handful of followers, giving ample indication of the public apathy towards the band. The 1990 mini-album *Tear Your Soul Apart* featured Mantas, Abaddon and Dolan and included a bizarre cover of Judas Priest's 'Hell Bent For Leather'.

Venom released the *Temples Of Ice* album in 1991. Produced by Abaddon and Kevin Ridley at Lynx studios in Newcastle Upon Tyne, the album hosted a rendition of Deep Purple's 'Speed King' and, perhaps

---

VENOM Discography

WELCOME TO HELL, Neat NEAT 1002 (UK) (1981)

In League With Satan, Neat NEAT 08 (UK) (1982)

BLACK METAL, Neat NEAT 1005 (UK) (1982)

Bloodlust, Neat NEAT 13 (UK) (1982)

Die Hard, Neat NEAT 27 (UK) (1983)

Die Hard, Megaforce IOM-1 (USA) (1983) limited edition 7-inch vinyl picture disc 1,000 copies

Warhead, Neat NEAT 38 (UK) (1983)

Manitou, Neat NEAT 43 (UK) (1984)

AT WAR WITH SATAN, Neat NEAT 1015 (UK) (1984) **64 UK**

Nightmare, Neat NEAT 47 (UK) (1985)

POSSESSED, Neat NEAT 1024 (UK), Combat MX 8022 (USA) (1985) **99 UK**

LIVE – OFFICIAL BOOTLEG, American Phonograph APK 12 (UK) (1985)

American Assault, Combat MX 8034 (USA) (1985)

Canadian Assault, Banzai BAM 1002 (Canada) (1985)

French Assault, New NW2317 (France) (1985)

Hell At Hammersmith, Neat NEAT 53-12 (UK) (1985)

JAPANESE ASSAULT, VAP 35177-25 (Japan) (1986)

Scandinavian Assault, Sonom AB SON XS-100 (Sweden) (1986)

EINE KLEINE NACHTMUSIK, Neat NEAT 1032 (UK) (1986)

LIVE IN CONCERT: EINE KLEINE NACHTMUSIK (A LITTLE LIGHT NIGHT MUSIC), Qwil TU 7900 (USA) (1987)

German Assault, Roadrunner RR 9659 (Germany) (1987)

CALM BEFORE THE STORM, Filmtrax MOMENT 115 (UK), K-Tel International NU 632-1 (USA) (1987)

PRIME EVIL, Under One Flag CDFLAG 36 (UK), Kraze 1064 (USA) (1989)

Tear Your Soul Apart, Under One Flag CDMFLAG 50 (UK) (1990)

TEMPLES OF ICE, Under One Flag CDFLAG 56 (UK) (1991)

IN MEMORIUM, Music Collection International VNM CD 1 (UK) (1991)

THE WASTE LANDS, Under One Flag CDFLAG 72 (UK) (1992)

SKELETONS IN THE CLOSET, Castle Communications CCSCD 367 (UK) (1993), Griffin Music GCDVE-172 (USA) (1994)

THE SECOND COMING, Warhead CMA 001 (UK) (1996)

CAST IN STONE, Steamhammer SPV 088-18812 (Europe), Deadline Music CLP 0247-2 (USA) (1997)

RESURRECTION, Steamhammer SPV 085-21752 (Europe), Steamhammer SPV 21752 (USA) (2000)

MMV, Castle Music CMXBX 743 (UK), Castle Music 36231 (USA) (2005)

METAL BLACK, Castle Music CMFCD 1282 (UK), Sanctuary 34112 (USA) (2006)

Venom, the most influential band in this book alongside Black Sabbath

more prominently, a tribute song, 'In Memory Of (Paul Miller 1964-90)', to the late journalist, a staunch champion of underground British acts. *The Waste Lands*, released in 1992, had an expanded recording roster comprising Dolan, Mantas, Abaddon, Al Barnes, former Atomkraft man Steve White (aka 'War Machine') on second guitar and V.X.S. (actually two separate people) on keyboards. Both albums sank quickly from public view.

Nevertheless, enthusiasm outside the UK was still strong, and Venom's first show promoting *The Waste Lands* was on a festival billing at the Winter Palace in St. Petersburg, Russia ranked alongside UFO, Magnum, Sweet, Girlschool and Asia. The success of this event, televised to over four million Russians, prompted a request for the new line-up to record classic tracks for a special Russian release. The group duly laid down these tracks, but no release was forthcoming. The songs later re-surfaced on the *Kissing The Beast* collection. However, Music For Nations opted against continuing with the band and Dolan, achieving success in his parallel career with the Royal Shakespeare Company, decided to quit, citing Abaddon's claims in the press linking Venom with Satanism as the main reason.

In 1994, a Venom tribute album, *In The Name Of Satan*, featured a high-profile collection of artists paying homage. Tracks included Kreator's interpretation of 'Witching Hour', Anathema's 'Welcome To Hell', Voivod's 'In League with Satan', Nuclear Assault's 'Die Hard', Skyclad's 'Prime Evil', Sodom's apt '1000 Days In Sodom', Candlemass with 'Countess Bathory', Paradise Lost with 'In Nomine Satanas' and Venom themselves donating an industrial mix of 'Warhead' and 'Holy Man'.

Japanese black metal outfit Sigh marked their own form of recognition with an entire album of Venom tracks, *To Hell and Back*. Meanwhile, Mike Hickey teamed up with Carcass in 1994. Cronos also came out of the shadows, lending backing vocals to Cradle Of Filth's *Dusk And Her Embrace*.

A protracted three years of negotiations finally resulted in the original band reforming in 1995 to ecstatic European media response. Venom returned in bombastic style by headlining the Burgum 'Waldrock' and Eindhoven 'Dynamo' festivals. At Eindhoven, the band used vast amounts of pyro, with one particular blast so powerful that their backdrop came to rest over the drum kit halfway through the set. An edited form of this show was released as the video/CD package *The Second Coming*.

Cronos: "When we had the re-resurrection of the band in 1995, I quickly discovered that I was the only one interested in recreating what the original band was all about. You might call that a lack of progress, but for me, I just hadn't changed my philosophies towards the music, what Venom stood for, or the kind of metal I wanted to record and play live. The other guys had moved on. If you listen to Abaddon's solo record, that's where he was at – electro industrial shit. If you listen to what Mantas is doing now, that's where his heart is, in that nu-metal stuff. That was the problem, y'see. It looked like Venom, but in reality there was only one of us really into it. For all the will in the world, and all the fans' expectations of us, it just wasn't going to work. It wasn't black metal, because the original feeling was gone. A lot of the album Cast In Stone I really like, but some of it, like 'Domus Mundi' – what's that shit?"

Venom spent a large chunk of 1997 recording their ninth studio album, *Cast In Stone*, only interrupting proceedings to headline the 'Metal Invader' festival in Athens, Greece. The recording was drawn out even further when, as it neared completion, the band scrapped the previous efforts, opting to re-record the entire body of work. Initial copies of *Cast In Stone* came with re-recordings of Venom classics.

They made a return to America in 1997, headlining the Milwaukee 'Metalfest', but European dates supported by Swedes Hammerfall were cancelled due to Cronos undergoing surgery for vocal nodes. A wealth of Swedish bands paid tribute the same year by way of the *Promoters Of The Third World War* set.

The 2000 Venom album *Resurrection* saw Abbadon replaced by Def-Con-One member, Cronos's brother Antton. The former skinsman issued a somewhat bizarre solo album, *I Am Legion*, which was duly slated by fans and media alike. Cronos contributed guest vocals to Dave Grohl's Probot project of 2001. Unfortunately, in March 2002 Cronos sustained a severe injury in a climbing accident. Some consolation for the frontman lay in Sanctuary Records' reissues of the first three Venom albums, all with extra tracks and extensive liner notes.

During the summer of 2002, former Venom and Cronos guitarist Jim Clare united with Tygers Of Pan Tang drummer Craig Ellis and bass player Willie Angus in a new band, Passion Play. By August this project had adopted the revised name of Tribal Core.

In October, Drummer Antton, while maintaining his membership of Venom, teamed up with Newcastle act Nu-Future Cowboys. He was also an active member of Def-Con-One. Venom themselves got back into action in early 2004, gearing up for a new studio album. American guitarist Mykus, actually former member Mike Hickey, was announced as the latest recruit to the fold in March. Meanwhile, Mantas was active in a project titled Zero Tolerance.

Venom returned with a new studio album, *Metal Black*, recorded for Sanctuary, in March 2006. This album, crafted by Cronos, guitarist Mike Hickey and drummer Antton, witnessed a deliberate return to their original 1980s sound. That December, Cronos guested on album recordings by leading Italian extreme metal band Necrodeath.

Venom's live strategy to push *Metal Black* opened with UK headliners backed by Onslaught. That same month the group recorded a four-song session for the BBC at London's Maida Vale studios. Summer festival appearances followed at the Italian 'Gods Of Metal', Finnish 'Tuska', German 'Earthshaker' and 'Sweden Rock' festivals.

Cronos: "We have amazing hardcore fans right across Europe. The only thing right now is the pyro situation. Venom is notorious for its explosive live show, lots of explosions, fire and shit, but that's looking difficult because of all the terrorist restrictions. We can't travel around hauling a trailer full of pyro any more because, basically, if it fell into the wrong hands it's a boatload of boom."

Unfortunately, campaigning for *Metal Black* did not run smoothly. The band announced a two-day 'Thrash Domination' stint at Tokyo's famed Club Citta on September 16th and 17th alongside Death Angel, Sodom, Dragonlord and Onslaught. However, they pulled out, stating that Cronos had been taken ill.

US shows for August, to be supported by Devildriver, were cancelled due to "immigration problems". The band rescheduled these dates, commencing later that same month, now with Goatwhore as support act. Venom remain much respected for their pioneering work on the metal scene – and rightly so.

DOOM
METAL

DOOM

DOOM is the most antiquated subgenre of heavy metal, the only strain able to trace its DNA right back to the Big Bang of Black Sabbath. When Sabbath invented heavy metal, they also sired doom. Sabbath, their close followers, and the American outfit Pentagram all purveyed a similar brand of music, but the first use of the 'doom' appellation did not come until the early 1980s, with a second wave of devotees such as Witchfinder General, Trouble, Saint Vitus and The Obsessed. As the name implies, doom provided a counterfoil to spine-cracking thrash and death metal, focusing squarely on the power of chord delivery as opposed to sheer speed.

Whereas other styles of metal can claim diverse lineage, doom is rooted solely to Black Sabbath. The band was to be the subject of unceasing tides of appreciation: early-1980s doom, the bastard child that was grunge, and then a fresh wave of doomsters. This last, traditionalist generation, personified by Lee Dorrian's purists Cathedral, Solitude Aeternus, Electric Wizard and the truly heavyweight Candlemass, aimed for authenticity above everything else.

A fourth stream of bands then took the genre into exciting new directions, with the north of England spawning Paradise Lost, My Dying Bride and Anathema. These innovative bands prompted the formation of further branches: gothic metal and doom death. In the latter category, Katatonia and Opeth wallowed in supreme melancholy.

The next chapter – stoner rock and metal – featured groups such as Kyuss, Monster Magnet, Fu Manchu and Queens Of The Stone Age, which aimed for more laidback, semi-commercial territory. Then came sludge, a murky and primitive amalgam of varying styles. At the opposite end of the scale, tentacles of doom slithered their slug trails outwards into the nether regions of drone, employing ambient and industrial elements to produce an anaesthetising numbness.

Doom metal expands to this day, with Thergothon, Funeral, Shape Of Despair and Skepticism inspiring near suicidal, sub-ambient funeral doom – with the hardcore field injecting their angst to engender sludge and a plethora of Satanically-charged outfits forging black/doom side-projects.

ANATHEMA
WHEN DOOM METAL MET INDIE-ROCK

DOOM METAL BAND Anathema formed in Liverpool, England in 1990 as Pagan Angel, recording a demo, *An Iliad Of Woes*, in November and releasing it in January 1991. The band consisted of singer Darren White, guitarists Vincent and Daniel Cavanagh, bassist Duncan Patterson and John Douglas on drums. They then recorded the *All Faith Is Lost* demo and a 7-inch single, 'They Die', for Swiss label Witchhunt; Duncan Patterson played bass on the latter. This provoked the interest of Peaceville Records, who signed the band in January 1992.

The band contributed the track 'Lovelorn Rhapsody' to Peaceville's *Volume 4* compilation before releasing their acclaimed *Crestfallen* EP. Cut at Academy Studios in Bradford by the band and label boss Paul 'Hammy' Halmshaw, *Crestfallen*'s engaging cover photograph – reviving pre-Raphaelite imagery taken up by swathes of artists since then – drew in listeners who were entranced by the group's engaging twist on the doom genre. A keen fanbase was attracted by Anathema's juxtaposition of ferocious riffage with the fragile, exemplified by their prose and guest singer Ruth Wilson on 'Everwake'.

The band's first full-length album, February 1993's *Serenades*, also received excellent reviews and intrigued audiences with its cover art, this time depicting a disturbing bandaged female form with a horse's skull. The record's blend of primitive doom with highbrow lyrical art, such as 'Lovelorn Rhapsody', 'Under A Veil (Of Black Lace)' and 'J'ai Fait Une Promesse' again featuring Wilson, by now placed Anathema on equal par with their labelmates My Dying Bride. This enabled the band to tour Europe with support acts Cradle Of Filth and Sweden's At The Gates before performing shows with Germany's Pyogenesis and Finland's God Forsaken.

The band contributed a cover of 'Welcome To Hell' to a Venom tribute album before playing the 'Waldrock' festival in Belgium and the 'Vosselaar' festival in Holland. After headlining the 'Manic Depression' festival in Rumania to 5,000 fans, they performed dates in Brazil, headlining the 'Independent Rock' festival as well as playing shows in Sao Paulo and Belo Horizonte.

During 1994, the rare 'We Are The Bible' single, only issued to members of the Peaceville label collectors' club, was pressed on "spiritual" purple vinyl. In May, Anathema revisited Academy Studios to record *Pentecost III* before tours through Russia, Lithuania, Sweden, Spain and Portugal.

In March 1995, the band trimmed down to a quartet as frontman White was forced out and Vincent Cavanagh assumed the role of lead vocalist. White promptly formed a new act, The Blood Divine, with three ex-Cradle Of Filth members – guitarists Paul Allender and Paul Ryan together with keyboard player Benjamin Ryan. Meanwhile, *Pentecost III* emerged in May through a new distribution deal between Peaceville and Music For Nations. Anathema had chosen not to deviate from their chosen path, with the album weighed down by three leviathan enterprises in 'Kingdom', 'We, The Gods' and 'Memento Mori' (12 minutes long, including the instrumental 'Pentecost III' as an introduction), as well as the uncredited 'Nailed To The Cross/666'.

The re-shaped band chose a fresh venue for their next work, travelling to Lynx Studios in Newcastle Upno Tyne for *The Silent Enigma*. Originally to be titled *Rise Pantheon Dreams*, this album, issued in August 1995, marked a turning point in the band's sound, a brave transition that brought new appreciation from a more mainstream band of listeners. Reviewers often quoted Pink Floyd references: this also caused a withdrawal of support from hardened doom fanatics.

Experimenting further, Anathema took up the services of producer Tony Platt for the *Eternity* album at The Windings Studios in Wales during the autumn of 1996. The progressive hints displayed on *The Silent Enigma* now took full flight, paving the way for successive outings. Guests in the studio included the Cradle Of Filth-credited keyboard player Les 'Lecter' Smith and Dominion's Michelle Richfield. Surprisingly, noted folk singer Roy Harper put in an appearance, gracing 'Hope' with his distinctive narration. This song's origins passed many critics by, despite its pedigree. 'Hope' had been composed but shelved by Pink Floyd frontman David Gilmour for a once-mooted project with Led Zeppelin guitarist Jimmy Page.

In side activity, Daniel Cavanagh linked up with Trouble frontman Eric Wagner in Lid, releasing an album called *In The Mushroom*. In late 1997 former Solstice drummer Shaun Steels was enrolled into Anathema: Smith migrated to Cradle Of Filth.

The band laid down two obscure cover versions for Peaceville's 1998 *X* compilation – Pink Floyd's 'Goodbye Cruel World' and Bad Religion's 'Better Off Dead'. The pursuit of the extraordinary continued with the piano-driven *Alternative 4*, overseen by Kit Woolven and arriving in June 1998 with My Dying Bride's Martin Powell's violin skills. The introspective record garnered reviews ranging from middling to downright confused. UK gigs in September of 1998 saw the band packaged with Moonspell and Therion. Patterson departed midway through the tour to be temporarily replaced with ex-Dreamweaver bassist Dave Pybus. Patterson used his time away to initiate Antimatter, a pure ambient endeavour involving Michael Moss.

Steels was replaced by John Douglas in early 1999, completing a line-up comprising the Cavanagh brothers and Pybus, now a full-time member. The *Judgement* album, recorded with Kit Woolven at Damage Inc. Studios in Ventimiglia, Italy, took Anathema into an all-embracing atmospheric musical landscape. European dates in November 1999 saw Anathema in support to Tiamat.

Powell joined Cradle Of Filth in 2000 and by the summer of the following year Pybus had also been lured into the same black legion. An Anathema career retrospective, *Resonance*, was issued in September 2001, pre-empting the group's next original set of tracks, *A Fine Day To Exit*. This suicide-themed slab of melancholy, produced by Nick Griffith, closed with 'Temporary Peace' – which, despite officially clocking in at 18:46, in fact segued out after six minutes with the remainder made up of sounds of waves crashing on a beach and idle banter. A video was filmed for 'Pressure' but a projected single release was cancelled. Concerts commencing in November saw the inclusion of George Roberts on bass.

The band made a return in November 2003 with the album *A Natural Disaster*, enhanced by the tones of female singers Anna Livingstone and Lee Douglas. They performed a special acoustic gig with a string quartet on February 27th 2004 at The Picket club in Liverpool to benefit the city's Quiggins alternative shopping centre. An earlier gig, conducted at the Krzemionki TV studio in Kracow, Poland on January 31st, was captured on film for the *Were You There?* DVD.

Danny Cavanagh took time out to guest for the Celtic acoustic band Leafblade for Low Countries gigs in early May. He also recorded a set of cover songs in tribute to the cult songwriter Nick Drake, released as a limited edition of 1,000 through Strangelight Records. Anathema then geared up for a full scale European tour. Their June 2nd show at Copérnico in Spain was filmed for the national TV programme *Los Conciertos De Radio 3*. The band also donated a rendition of 'How Fortunate Is The Man With None' to the 2004 Dead Can Dance tribute album *The Lotus Eaters*.

On September 10th Anathema, temporarily label-less after Music For Nations was acquired by the Zomba Records Group, put in a special acoustic show at London's Mean Fiddler as special guests to Blackfield, a

Doom legends Anathema

ANATHEMA discography

ANATHEMA discography

The Crestfallen EP, Peaceville VILE36TCD (UK) (1992)

They Die, Witchhunt 9205 (Europe) (1992)

SERENADES, Peaceville VILE34CD (UK) (1993), Futurist 11037-2 (USA) (1994)

We Are The Bible, Peaceville CC6 (UK) (1994) Peaceville Collectors Club 7-inch vinyl single

Pentecost III, Peaceville CDMVILE51 (UK), Mayhem/Fierce Recordings 11087-2 (USA) (1995)

THE SILENT ENIGMA, Peaceville CDVILE52 (UK) (1995), Mayhem/Fierce Recordings 11109-2 (USA) (1997)

ETERNITY, Peaceville CDVILE64 (UK) (1996), Mayhem/Fierce Recordings 11100-2 (USA) (1997)

ALTERNATIVE 4, Peaceville CDVILE73 (UK), Mayhem/Fierce Recordings 11112-2 (USA) (1998)

JUDGEMENT, Music For Nations CDMFN250 (UK), Koch KOC-CD-8225 (USA) (1999)

RESONANCE, Peaceville CDVILE82 (UK), Peaceville 61082 (USA) (2001)

A FINE DAY TO EXIT, Music For Nations CDMFN260 (UK), Koch KOC-CD-8245 (USA) (2001)

A NATURAL DISASTER, Music For Nations CDMFNX298 (UK) (2003), Koch KOC-CD-9539 (USA) (2004)

RESONANCE 2, Peaceville CDVILED99 (UK), Peaceville 61099 (USA) (2004)

project featuring Steven Wilson of Porcupine Tree and Aviv Geffen. Danny Cavanagh extended this concept further with a solo semi-acoustic tour in September with Sean Jude of Leafblade as support.

A further acoustic concert, held on March 1st 2004 in Shepherds Bush in London, saw the band performing with cello player Dave Wesling, the Japan and Porcupine Tree-credited Richard Barbieri, Tim Bowness of No-Man and Markus Reuter of Centrozoon, and the Europa String Choir. During April, the band acted as support to Porcupine Tree's European dates. Danny Cavanagh undertook solo concert dates throughout Scandinavia during March 2006.

The first sign of renewed Anathema activity was an announcement of supports to H.I.M. in April, with the band also releasing three new tracks as downloads – 'One Day', 'Everything' and 'Angels Walk Among Us'. A brief Turkish tour was scheduled for May. Anathema remain one of the more accomplished metal bands of the genre.

CANDLEMASS
HEAVYWEIGHT DOOM METAL

A HALLOWED NAME IN metal circles, Candlemass were probably the first band to reshape the doom genre in the wake of Black Sabbath in the 1970s. Based in Stockholm, Sweden, they arose from an earlier band, Nemesis, featuring Leif Edling (vocals, bass) and guitarist Christian Weberyd, along with second guitarist Anders Wallin and drummer Anders Waltersson. Prior to the dissolution of the group, Nemesis had released the highly-praised *The Day Of Retribution* album in 1984.

Candlemass debuted on the tape-trading circuit with the four-song *Witchcraft* demo in 1984, featuring a line-up of Edling, Weberyd and drummer Mats Ekström. A second guitarist, Kjell Svensson, also appeared on the demo. After a second demo that November, the band signed to the French Black Dragon label. Having added former A.T.C. guitarist Mats

Björkman (aka Mappe), they began recording their debut album *Epicus Doomicus Metallicus* at Thunderload Studios with Ragne Wahlquist, frontman for Heavy Load, manning the board.

During the recording of the album Weberyd opted to leave: by the time it was released, the group's vocalist Johan Langquist and drummer Ekström had also departed. Nonetheless, the album, which emerged in June 1986, raised the band's profile considerably and impressed many critics with its grandiose and utterly compelling doom metal dirges – hideously depressing and exceptionally heavy. With doom metal scarce on the landscape in 1986, many reviewers simply tagged the band as Black Sabbath clones, but record buyers soon shrugged these assumptions aside, recognising the band as an original force.

Edling and Björkman took well over a year to put a new line-up together, and were obliged as a result to pass on the offer of a tour with Black Dragon labelmates Heir Apparent and Savage Grace. They settled on new drummer Jan Lindh, after which erstwhile Mercy vocalist Eddie 'Messiah' Marcolin (real name Jan Alfredo Marcolin) was recruited. Marcolin, a rather portly chap, cut a strange figure on stage, choosing to wear a monk's habit, but his remarkable near-operatic vocal style quickly became the band's trademark. In March 1987 this fresh line-up demoed two tracks, 'Bewitched' and 'Battle Cry'. Guitarist Lars Johansson joined Candlemass in the summer of 1987, replacing an earlier recruit, Mike Wead.

Having split from Black Dragon, Candlemass enrolled the help of former Shades Records man Dave Constable as manager, and by the end of 1987 had recorded a new album, *Nightfall*, issued that November through the newly-established Axis label, co-owned by Constable.

Unfortunately, the band had to postpone their debut show in Britain, pulling out of a scheduled support slot to King Diamond at London's Hammersmith Odeon in November 1987 because Johansson had broken his arm. They finally appeared on British shores at the end of March the following year, with two London Marquee shows and a gig in Birmingham. They had created quite a buzz with *Nightfall*, both in Britain and Europe, and – following their successful appearance at the Dutch 'Dynamo' festival later that year – several record companies put in bids. However, the band remained loyal to Axis (who changed their name to Active for legal reasons), with the albums issued in North America through Metal Blade. They rounded off a magnificent year by supporting Slayer in Norway and Sweden after original openers Nuclear Assault pulled out.

The band's third album, November 1988's *Ancient Dreams*, was even more successful, even denting the North American national *Billboard* charts. Regrettably underproduced, with its guitar punch particularly diluted, *Ancient Dreams* nonetheless hosted such monolithic menhirs of metal as 'The Bells Of Acheron' and 'Mirror Mirror'. CD variants included an additional track, a Black Sabbath medley of 'Symptom Of The Universe', 'Sweet Leaf', 'Sabbath Bloody Sabbath', 'Into The Void', 'Electric Funeral', 'Supernaut' and 'Black Sabbath'. A live show in Stockholm was recorded and released as *Live* in 1990. Its studio follow-up, *Tales Of Creation*, was released in 1989 and followed by a European tour as headliners before hitching up with King Diamond to tour Europe once more.

The archive Nemesis album *The Day Of Retribution* was re-released through Active at the height of Candlemass's fame during 1990, with the addition of bonus tracks 'Blackstone Wielder' and 'Demons Gate'. These songs had featured on the very first Candlemass demo with a line-up of leader Edling, guitarist Mats Björkman, second guitarist Klas Bergwall and drummer Mats Ekström.

The band's progress was hindered somewhat by the departure of Marcolin, and the singer himself was never quite able to match his profile in Candlemass on a journey through two albums with Memento Mori and then his band Stillborn. Initially, the band pulled in Johan Lanquist, the singer from *Epicus Doomicus Metallicus*, but this lasted for just one rehearsal. After lengthy auditions throughout 1992, ex-Talk Of The Town and Speedy Gonzales singer Thomas Vikström landed the job to record *Chapter VI*. Unfortunately, despite Vikström's quality as a vocalist, fans only seemed to accept the band with Marcolin at the helm. Candlemass fragmented soon afterwards, with Edling forming the experimental Abstrakt Algebra with former Treat and Swedish Erotika vocalist Mats Levén.

Johansson teamed up with Veni Domine vocalist Fredrik Olsson to form a metal project titled Zoic in 1995, which resulted in an album, *Total Level Of Destruction*, the following year. Vikström, meanwhile, featured as guest vocalist on the 1996 album by Brazen Abbott, *Live And Learn*.

Candlemass chose to return to the fray in 1997 in rather odd circumstances. It transpired that Edling had gone into the studio to record a projected second effort for Abstrakt Algebra, but as recording progressed a name switch to Candlemass was felt to be more appropriate for the style of the music. The 1997 line-up of the band thus consisted of Edling alongside erstwhile Gone vocalist Björn Flodquist, former Carcass and Arch Enemy guitarist Mike Amott (who also played with Armageddon and Spiritual Beggars), ex-Brick guitarist Patrik Instedt, and Abstrakt Algebra's drummer Jejo Percovich. Europe's Ian Haugland guested on drums.

The band returned with the primitive-sounding *Dactylis Glomerata* in April 1998 and then pulled in guitarist Mats Ståhl. The band delved even further back into the primeval 1970s rock soup for 1999's *From The 13th Sun*, with the album even including a drum solo.

The classic Candlemass line-up were tempted into a reunion for the 2002 'Sweden Rock' festival. The reunited band, which featured vocalist Marcolin, bassist Edling, guitarists Björkman and Lars Johansson with drummer Lindh, debuted at the Black Lucia Christmas party held by *Close-Up* magazine in Stockholm on December 13th 2001. Meanwhile, the newly created Powerline label reissued the first four classic Candlemass albums. A collection of demos titled *The Black Heart Of Candlemass* also appeared, credited to Edling.

The band put in a long overdue UK performance at the London Mean Fiddler venue in mid July, sponsored by the *Total Rock* radio show. The Swedes were supported by a strong cast including Martin Walkyier's Return To The Sabbat, Devolved, The Dukes Of Nothing, and expatriated Chileans Criminal. The return of Candlemass was also marked with the launch of the *Documents Of Doom* DVD, issued in November and comprising live footage from a gig in Fryhuset during 1990. A further release was signalled with news of a double live album *Doomed For Live – Reunion 2002* through the GRM Music Group.

It was then reported that, behind the scenes, Edling had formed another band in league with his former Abstrakt Algebra colleague, Mats Levén. Krux, which laid down a debut album for 2002 release through the Mascot label, saw contributions from the Entombed rhythm section of drummer Peter Stjärnvind and bassist Jörgen Sandström, although the latter would switch to guitar. Other guitarists involved in the sessions included Nicko Elgstrand of Terra Firma and Fredrik Åkesson from Talisman.

Yet another Candlemass spin-off, C.R.A.N.K., featured guitarist Mats Björkman with the Lion's Share rhythm section of bassist Pontus Egberg and drummer Johan Koleberg, as well as singer Alex Swerdh and guitarist Ulf Larsson of the Kiss cover band Kyss.

It emerged in March 2004 that Candlemass guitarist Lars Johansson and drummer Jan Lindh had forged a new band, Creozoth, with X-Plode vocalist Michael Storck and the Oz and Red Fun-credited bassist Tobbe Moen.

Candlemass recorded a two-song demo of 'Witch' and 'Born In A Tank' in August 2003 and put in a live show at the Cologne 'Popkomm' industry convention that same month. However, a post on the band's website in May 2004 announced: "We are truly sorry to inform you that Candlemass have disbanded!" Despite this, good news came with an impending tribute album set to feature Opeth, The Hellacopters, The Haunted, Cathedral, Grand Magus, Krux and Satyricon.

GMR Music announced a compilation entitled *Essential Doom* for 2005

CANDLEMASS discography

EPICUS DOOMICUS METALLICUS, Black Dragon BD 013 (Europe) (1986)

NIGHTFALL, Axis AXIS LP3 (UK), Metal Blade 72241-1 (USA) (1987)

ANCIENT DREAMS, Active ACT CD7 (UK), Metal Blade 73340-2 (USA) (1988)

TALES OF CREATION, Music For Nations CDMFN95 (UK), Metal Blade 73417-2 (USA) (1989)

LIVE, Music For Nations CDMFN109 (UK), Metal Blade 26444-2 (USA) (1990)

CHAPTER VI, Music For Nations CDMFN128 (UK) (1992)

Sjunger Sigge Fürst, Megarock MRRCDS003 (Europe) (1993)

THE BEST OF CANDLEMASS: AS IT IS, AS IT WAS, Music For Nations CDMFN166 (UK) (1992)

DACTYLIS GLOMERATA, Music For Nations CDMFN237 (UK) (1998)

Wiz, Froghouse FROG 001 (Europe) (1998) 10-inch vinyl EP

FROM THE 13TH SUN, Music For Nations CDMFN253 (UK) (1999)

Candlemass, Trust No One Recordings TRUSTNO14 (Europe) (2001) limited edition 7-inch vinyl single 1,000 copies

THE BLACK HEART OF CANDLEMASS: LEIF EDLING DEMOS & OUTTAKES '83-'99, Powerline PLRCD008 (Europe) (2002)

DOOMED FOR LIVE – REUNION 2002, Powerline PLRCD009 (Europe) (2003)

DIAMONDS OF DOOM, Powerline PLRLP010 (Europe) (2003)

ESSENTIAL DOOM, Powerline PLRCD014 (Europe) (2004)

CANDLEMASS, Nuclear Blast NB 1448-2 (Europe), Nuclear Blast America 1448 (USA) (2005)

featuring the unreleased 'Witches' from the August 2003 demo as well as a bonus DVD featuring video footage of the band's performance at the 'Rock Hard' festival in Germany in 2003.

Despite the announcement of the group's split in May, Candlemass issued another press statement in early November stating that they were to enter Stockholm's Polar Studios that same month in order to record a 20th anniversary album. Apparently this rapid resurrection had been

Candlemass

sparked by the musicians jamming through 'Samarithan' and 'Solitude' at Mats Björkman's wedding in August, prompting the compilation of a three-track demo of 'Black Dwarf', 'Spellbreaker' and 'Witches'. Candlemass had tested the waters with former Black Sabbath singer Tony Martin on some demo recordings, although this had not worked out.

The band announced their signature to Nuclear Blast in January 2005. A new album was accompanied by a slew of limited edition 7-inch singles released through the Vinyl Maniacs label, including 'Solitude'/'Crystal Ball' and 'At The Gallow's End'/'Samarithan'. That same month a notable Finnish reinterpretation of the classic 'Solitude' was released by Swallow The Sun, featuring Reverend Bizarre vocalist Albert Magus.

On its release in May 2005, *Candlemass* entered the Swedish album charts at Number 7. In outside activity, Marcolin put in a guest appearance on German thrash act Destruction's *Inventor Of Evil* album. Further product came with *Curse Of Candlemass*, a DVD issued through Escapi Music documenting the band's Stockholm Klubben gig in November 2003.

Candlemass's summer festival dates included appearances at the Sölvesborg 'Sweden Rock' show, Spain's 'Vega Rock' event, Norway's 'Inferno' festival, Germany's 'Wacken Open Air' and 'Bang Your Head' festivals and the Italian 'Iron Fest'. The band then revealed plans to tour with Destruction and Finland's Deathchain in December. The first leg of dates was opened by Belgians After All, with the latter half supported by German act Personal War. However, Björkman missed gigs in Gothenburg, Malmö and Osnabrück, forced out due to "family reasons", leaving Candlemass to persevere as a quartet.

In late April 2006 Marcolin quit, declaring that he had no intentions of returning. However, shortly afterwards the other band members put up an official post stating that they were confident Marcolin, who they believed was suffering from "severe pre-recording psychosis", would record the album tracks. Candlemass remain one of the most respected bands in the doom genre.

CATHEDRAL
WHAT LEE DORRIAN DID NEXT

A FAMOUSLY ECCENTRIC BAND formed in Coventry, England by ex-Napalm Death frontman and Rise Above label owner Lee Dorrian, Cathedral were initially rounded out by guitarist Garry Jennings – previously with Yorkshire thrash act Acid Reign – and bassist Mark 'Griff' Griffiths, a former roadie for Carcass and editor of doom fanzine *Under The Oak*.

The band's first rehearsals took place in March 1990 at Selly Oak's

famous Rich Bitch Studios, also home to genre godfathers Black Sabbath. With Griff initially handling rhythm guitar, the budding Cathedral formation found its footing by way of some Saint Vitus jams to set the mood. The first drummer was ex-Varukers and Sacrilege man Andy Baker, replaced after a handful of rehearsals by former Filthkick member Ben Mochrie. Unable to locate a suitable bassist, Griff adopted the four-string, while second guitarist Adam Lehan, also of Acid Reign, completed the contingent. This eclectic gathering of players, pooling prior traditions ranging from grindcore, thrash and death metal, were duly funneled into Dorrian's grandiose doom vision.

Lee Dorrian: "Cathedral was quite a challenge because, after experiencing the extremes of Napalm death – and before that, punk – it really left a big question about where I wanted to go next. I could see all the copycat stuff going on with Napalm, and that to me was no longer extreme, because I define extreme as something that pushes boundaries, not just follows blindly what someone else has done.

"So the whole Cathedral thing came about because I had always had this secret affection for old doom. Actually, the whole doom scene had been neglected. I mean, obviously there was Black Sabbath, but I thought the whole grunge thing had completely missed the point there. You had underground bands like Pentagram, Candlemass, Revelation, Count Raven and Trouble, but there were very few people who knew about them. I had no idea about forming a band at first, it was just a laugh, maybe a demo – just some jamming with friends, really. Cathedral became an opposite extreme to Napalm Death, which was great, because people were thinking that there was no audience for this kind of music. We proved there was."

The group recorded its first demo, *In Memorium*, issued in October 1990 with a cover of Pentagram's 'All Your Sins', and then found themselves invited to contribute the track 'Ebony Tears' to the *Dark Passages* compilation the same year. A second demo followed in 1991. They then toured Britain with S.O.D. and Saint Vitus before more domestic touring with Sadus and Morbid Angel in March and Paradise Lost in Holland during April. In October, they found themselves once more on the road in Britain on a somewhat mismatched bill with Young Gods, Silverfish and New Cranes.

Mike Smail of Penance and Dream Death performed on the debut *Forests Of Equilibrium* album, recorded at Workshop Studios in Redditch between July and August 1991, but soon afterwards the band recruited a permanent drummer in Mark Ramsey Wharton, another Acid Reign veteran. *Forest Of Equilibrium* came wrapped in a sumptuous Dave Patchett-designed gatefold jacket. Evoking the bizarre landscapes of Hieronymous Bosch, this artwork provided the perfect foil for the capricious music. Cathedral's sluglike pace and near-painful bottom end launched headlong into an extreme metal world dominated by speed and brittle harshness. As such, Dorrian's gut instincts in re-forging a forgotten art form put doom metal fairly and squarely back into the spotlight.

The year 1992 began with an EP, *Soul Sacrifice*, backed by British dates alongside Anathema and My Dying Bride, before the band toured Europe with labelmates Carcass, Entombed and Confessor as part of the 'Gods Of Grind' tour. These shows were rounded off by more European dates with Saint Vitus.

The Earache package theme developed with Cathedral teaming-up of with Napalm Death, Carcass and Brutal Truth for the American 'Campaign For Musical Destruction' tour, before they returned to Europe to round off the year in Germany with Napalm Death, Crowbar and Trouble. They also committed two tracks, 'Shock Waves' and 'Solitude', to Earache's Black Sabbath tribute album, *Masters Of Misery*.

In 1993 the band toured extensively before Griffiths departed to form

Cathedral

Year Zero, later joining Blackstar with ex-Carcass members. A temporary replacement was found in Mike Hickey of Cronos and Venom. In early 1994, Cathedral suffered another line-up shuffle when both Lehan and Wharton left.

To promote *The Ethereal Mirror* album – the Japanese version of which boasted two extra tracks, 'Skylifter' and 'Funeral Request (Rebirth)' – the band toured during 1994 with guitarist Victor Griffin and drummer Joe Hasselvander, both on loan from cult American metallists Pentagram. The band by now sported some very 1970s stage garb. The degree to which they were prepared to mock convention was matched only by the width of Dorrian's flares.

Lee Dorrian: "The mainstream scared the hell out of me. I thought we got dangerously close to that when we did The Ethereal Mirror because that was this big production thing, that really caused us to lose focus. That whole time dealing with Columbia was just so disillusioning and gave us a good reminder about what we really ought to be doing. That's why it got a bit surreal with the Statik Magik EP. I think we needed to make the point that we were still loonies at heart.

"I find that with the running of the Rise Above label, too. People have this misconception that I'm a doom purist, but nothing could be further from the truth. I take in everything, and what really excites me is total musical freedom."

Cathedral's status rose considerably throughout Europe during the year, a highlight of which was a prestigious opening slot for their heroes Black Sabbath. Acrimony arose, however, when Griffin quit before the end of the tour, quickly followed by Hasselvander, resulting in cancellation of British shows. The tour was eventually rescheduled with ex-Trouble drummer Barry Stern stepping into the breach.

Lee Dorrian: "It was heartbreaking to see the original band break up, because you always have these romantic notions that it's going to be a 'brotherhood against the world' type of crusade. It was the major label pressure, really. We did a long American tour with Mercyful Fate and Flotsam And Jetsam that was very deflating for us. It's no fun being in the middle of nowhere when you're not enjoying it and you start wondering why you're even there. Being onstage made up for all that, but then you had to deal with all the shit the next day. It got too much for both Griff and Adam. I was very sad to see them go. Cathedral became a refuge for some of my favourite musicians after that. We used Columbia's cheque book to bring in all my musical heroes until they wised up and dropped us into a load of debt."

The band got back on the road for some pre-Christmas shows with guests Electric Wizard and Mourn, lining up now as Dorrian, Jennings, ex-Repulsion bassist Scott Carlson and former Shades Of Grey drummer Dave Hornyak.

Beginning 1995 with European dates alongside Deicide and Brutal Truth, the band again shifted personnel, with Hornyak and Carlson departing due to the financial constraints imposed upon them after the band had been dropped in America by Columbia. No sooner had their fans got used to this latest incarnation than Cathedral brought in former Trespass bassist Leo Smee and ex-Torino drummer Brian Dixon in May 1995.

They then released *The Carnival Bizarre*, produced by Kit Woolven. The track 'Utopian Blaster' featured guest guitar from none other than Black Sabbath guitarist Tony Iommi. In order to promote the new album, Cathedral scheduled British headline shows with support from Anathema and Mourn prior to a Euro-Scandinavian tour with Motörhead.

Dorrian was reported to have contributed lyrics and guest vocals to ex-Death SS guitarist Paul Chain's solo album *Alkahest*, which surfaced in

CATHEDRAL discography

Soul Sacrifice, Earache MOSH40CD (UK), Columbia CK 53149 (USA) (1992)

FORESTS OF EQUILIBRIUM, Earache MOSH43CD (UK), Relativity/Earache 88561-1093-2 (USA) (1991)

THE ETHEREAL MIRROR, Earache MOSH77CD (UK), Columbia CK 53633 (USA) (1993)

Twylight Songs, Ultimatum BRILL01 (USA) (1993) 7-inch blood red vinyl single

In Memorium, Rise Above RISE 008 (UK) (1994)

Statik Magik, Earache MOSH106CD (UK) (1994)

Cosmic Requiem, Columbia CK 64326 (USA) (1994)

THE CARNIVAL BIZARRE, Earache MOSH130CD (UK /USA) (1995)

Hopkins (The Witchfinder General), Earache MOSH152CD (UK / USA) (1996)

SUPERNATURAL BIRTH MACHINE, Earache MOSH156CDM (UK / USA) (1996)

CARAVAN BEYOND REDEMPTION, Earache MOSH211CD (UK /USA) (1998)

IN MEMORIAM, Rise Above CDRISE 21 (UK) (1999), The Music Cartel 31 (USA) (2000)

ENDTYME, Earache MOSH236CD (UK / USA) (2001)

Gargoylian, Southern Lord SUNN09.5 (UK / USA) (2001) 7-inch vinyl EP

THE VIIITH COMING, Dream Catcher CRIDE 49 (UK), Spitfire SPT 15144-2 (USA) (2002)

THE SERPENT'S GOLD, Earache MOSH233CD (UK / USA) (2004)

THE GARDEN OF UNEARTHLY DELIGHTS, Nuclear Blast NB 1199-2 (Europe) (2005), Nuclear Blast America 1199 (USA) (2006)

1996. The same year, Cathedral issued the 'Hopkins (Witchfinder General)' single, which featured a cover of the Crazy World Of Arthur Brown hit 'Fire'. The album *Supernatural Birth Machine* fared well, and the Australian market was treated to a gatefold edition complete with comic strip, while Japanese variants added an exclusive track, 'Tucker's Luck'.

Dorrian busied himself in mid 1996 on the *Dark Passages Vol. II* compilation issued by his Rise Above label, which featured acts such as Orange Goblin, Pentagram, Trouble and Electric Wizard besides Cathedral themselves.

Cathedral re-emerged in 1997 by performing a set at Whitby's 100th anniversary festival of Bram Stoker's *Dracula* novel. The *Masters Of Misery* Black Sabbath tribute was issued in North America for the first time, of note because Cathedral had replaced their previous opening cut, 'Shock Waves', with 'Wheels Of Confusion'. The *Caravan Beyond Redemption* album was released in 1998, and the following year's *In Memorium* was a reissue of the band's 1990 demo with live recordings from 1991.

The year 2000 had Smee founding side project Firebird with ex-Carcass guitarist Bill Steer and Spiritual Beggars' Ludwig Witt. Meanwhile, Dorrian contributed guest vocals to Dave Grohl's *Probot* album of 2001. He also founded Teeth Of Lion Rule Divine with Burning Witch's Steve O'Malley, Goatsnake's Greg Anderson and erstwhile Iron Monkey member Justin Greaves. Cathedral released *Endtyme* in 2001.

The band's *The VIIth Coming* was scheduled for an October 2002 release. Japanese editions on the Toy's Factory label added an exclusive track, 'Golconda'. A UK headline tour in November found Electric Wizard as support act. As 2003 broke, the band headed up a lengthy trek throughout Europe during January and February with guests Samael and

Hungarian newcomers Without Face. Cathedral subsequently united with Strapping Young Lad and Samael for September North American dates dubbed the Redemption Tour.

The band signed to Nuclear Blast in mid 2003, working on a new album with a provisional title of *Seeds Of Decay*. Meanwhile, former label Earache compiled the double album set *The Serpent's Gold*, including unreleased material including a cover version of Witchfinder General's 'Rabies'. A short round of UK dates preceded an appearance at 'Wacken' in Germany. In October the band lent support to H.I.M.'s UK shows.

In 2004, ex-Cathedral guitarist Victor Griffin released a solo album, *Late For An Early Grave*, through Outlaw Recordings. Issued as a vinyl pressing, only 525 copies were manufactured. Former Cathedral drummer Barry Stern died in early 2005.

The band, working with producer Warren Ryker, entered New Rising Studios in May to record their eighth album, entitled *The Garden Of Unearthly Delights*. European touring scheduled for October was to witness a grand doom union of Candlemass and Grand Magus. However, these dates fell through. Nevertheless, UK touring in December had the band packaged with Cradle Of Filth and Octavia Sperati. It seems that Cathedral will continue to attract devotees for some time to come.

ELECTRIC WIZARD
KINGS OF THE DOPETHRONE

ELECTRIC WIZARD OFFER A quintessentially English slant to the doom/stoner genre. The band, established in Bournemouth, Dorset, started life as Thy Grief Eternal, recording a 1992 demo *...On Blackened Wings* before shortening their name to Eternal. Ex-Lords Of Putrefaction vocalist Justin Oborn fronted the band at this point, also comprising Lords bassist Dave Pedge and drummer James Evans. However, after the British pop charts had been hit by the female R&B quartet of the same name, Eternal executed a name-change to Electric Wizard.

Signing to Rise Above Records, the custom label owned by Cathedral's Lee Dorrian, their first full-length opus, *Electric Wizard*, arrived in 1995, giving a solid display of blatant yet unashamed Sabbath worship. The same year the group donated the track 'Demon Lung' to a split 7-inch single with the pre-Orange Goblin outfit Our Haunted Kingdom. The cult US stoner imprint Man's Ruin debuted the band to American audiences with the limited edition *Chrono.naut* EP.

January 1997's *Come My Fanatics...*, recorded at Red Dog Studios in July the previous year, saw a Japanese release adding the extra track 'Return To The Sun Of Nothingness'. Electric Wizard truly found their identity with this record, whose listening pleasure could be likened to that of drowning in a vat of engine oil. With no thought given towards variation, bar an excursion into tribalism on the instrumental 'Ivixor B/Phase Inducer', Electric Wizard lumbered through a set of numbing zombie sounds choked out by Oborn's Les Paul. This unique guitar sound gave Electric Wizard its trademark. The 1998 mini-album *Supercoven*, a dismal post-psychedelic exercise featuring drummer Mark 'Groaning' Greening, was released by mail order in a limited edition. A snapshot of curios, the EP hosted one live track captured in Holland and a cut from a 1994 demo session.

The first two Electric Wizard records were re-packaged as a single set for re-release in 1999 before the third outing, *Dopethrone*, appeared, recorded as a trio of Oborn, Bagshaw and Greening. Plummeting further into 1970s psych-acidity, the band broadened their approach, hinged on the 16-minute epic 'Weird Tales'.

Recording for their fourth album, *Let Us Prey*, was severely delayed when Greening fell off a bicycle and damaged his arm. A further setback came when Oborn was hospitalised with alcohol poisoning. Rise Above finally put out *Let Us Prey* in March 2002.

After North American touring in the summer, headlining over Sons Of Otis and Unearthly Trance, the band released a press statement stating that the final gig, at Philadelphia's Khyber Pass venue on June 27th, would be their last show. However, the band were back in action during November acting as support for Cathedral's UK tour. Former Iron Monkey guitarist Justin Greaves joined the band late that same month.

April 2003 saw their longstanding rhythm section of bassist Tim Bagshaw and drummer Mark Greening severing ties in order to found Ramesses with former Spirmyard bassist/vocalist Adam Richardson. Oborn relocated to North America to rebuild the band from scratch, pulling in second guitarist Liz Buckingham of 13 and Sourvein repute plus bassist Rob Al-Issa for a revamped line-up. The *We Live* album was released in 2004.

The band partnered with Pod People for Australian dates in October and November of 2005. Rise Above issued the Thy Grief Eternal *...On Blackened Wings* tracks as a limited edition EP in 2005. With a complete album reissue series during 2006, the Electric Wizard industry is still going strong.

ELECTRIC WIZARD discography

ELECTRIC WIZARD, Rise Above RISE 009 (UK) (1995)

Demon Lung, Rise Above RISE 011 (UK) (1995) split 7-inch vinyl single with Our Haunted Kingdom

COME MY FANATICS...., Rise Above CDRISE 14 (UK) (1997)

Electric Wizard / Orange Goblin, Man's Ruin MR-071 (USA) (1997) split CD single with Orange Goblin

Chrono.Naut, Man's Ruin MR-083 (USA) (1997) 10-inch vinyl single

Supercoven, Southern Lord SUNN04 (UK / USA) (1998)

DOPETHRONE, Rise Above CDRISE 27 (UK) (2000), The Music Cartel 44 (USA) (2001)

LET US PREY, Rise Above RISECD 36 (UK), The Music Cartel 60 (USA) (2002)

WE LIVE, Rise Above RISECD 48 (UK), The Music Cartel 81 (USA) (2004)

PRE-ELECTRIC WIZARD 1989-1994, Rise Above RISECD 61 (UK), Candlelight USA CDL0270CD (USA) (2006)

MY DYING BRIDE
THE LIGHT AT THE END OF DOOM METAL?

MY DYING BRIDE ARE AT THE forefront of the British doom metal movement alongside Anathema and Paradise Lost. Of this fabled trio, My Dying Bride have – apart from one infamous aberration – stuck resolutely to their trademark scheme of relentlessly slow, heavy chords with morose lyrics.

The group, from Halifax in northern England, were rooted in Abiosis, which issued a three-track demo, *Noxious Emanation*, in 1990. The initial line-up was vocalist Aaron Stainthorpe, guitarists Andrew Craighan and Calvin Robertshaw plus drummer Rick Miah. Re-formed as My Dying Bride that June, the band released the *Towards The Sinister* demo, noted for its complete absence of bass, recorded over two days in late November at Revolver Studios with Tim Walker manning the production board. They followed this with the 'God Is Alone' 7-inch single, restricted to 1,000 copies, on the French Listenable label, again utilising both Walker and Revolver Studios in May 1991. The band signed to budding Peaceville to release the *Symphonaire Infernus Et Spera Empyrum* EP in 1992, debuting new bassist Ade Jackson in the process.

MY DYING BRIDE discography

God Is Alone, Listenable POSH001 (Europe) (1991) 7-inch vinyl single

Symphonaire Infernus Et Spera Empyrium, Peaceville VILE27TCD (UK) (1992)

AS THE FLOWER WITHERS, Peaceville VILE32CD (UK) (1992)

Unreleased Bitterness, Unbridled Voyage WW1 (UK) (1993) 7-inch flexi-disc

The Thrash Of Naked Limbs, Peaceville VILE37TCD (UK) (1993)

TURN LOOSE THE SWANS, Peaceville VILE39CD (UK) (1993), Futurist 11046-2 (USA) (1994)

Sexuality Of Bereavement, Peaceville CC5 (UK) (1994) Peaceville Collectors Club 7-inch vinyl single

I Am The Bloody Earth, Peaceville VILE44TCD (UK) (1994)

THE STORIES, Peaceville VILE45 (UK) (1994) limited edition boxed set 3,000 copies

TRINITY, Peaceville CDVILE46 (UK), Fierce Recordings 11067-2 (USA) (1995)

THE ANGEL AND THE DARK RIVER, Peaceville CDVILE50 (UK) (1995), Mayhem/Fierce Recordings 11092-2 (USA) (1996)

LIKE GODS OF THE SUN, Peaceville CDVILE65 (UK) (1996), Mayhem/Fierce Recordings 11103-2 (USA) (1997)

34.788%... COMPLETE, Peaceville CDVILE74 (UK), Mayhem/Fierce Recordings 11127-2 (USA) (1998)

THE LIGHT AT THE END OF THE WORLD, Peaceville CDVILE79 (1999) (UK), Peaceville 61079 (USA) (2001)

MEISTERWERK 1, Peaceville CDVILE81 (UK) (2000), Peaceville 61081 (USA) (2001)

MEISTERWERK 2, Peaceville CDVILE85 (UK), Peaceville 61085 (USA) (2001)

THE DREADFUL HOURS, Peaceville CDVILE90 (UK), Peaceville 61090 (USA) (2001)

THE VOICE OF THE WRETCHED, Peaceville CDVILED117 (UK), Peaceville 61117 (USA) (2002)

SONGS OF DARKNESS, WORDS OF LIGHT, Peaceville CDVILED110 (UK), Peaceville 110 (USA) (2004)

ANTI-DILUVIAN CHRONICLES, Peaceville CDVILEB130 (UK) (2005) boxed set

Deeper Down, Peaceville CDVILES158 (UK) (2006)

A LINE OF DEATHLESS KINGS, Peaceville CDVILEF150 (UK), Peaceville 150 (USA) (2006)

My Dying Bride's first full length album, *As The Flower Withers*, arriving in May 1992, established them among press and fans alike. Jointly produced by label owner Paul 'Hammy' Halmshaw and the band, the record stunned many critics, who struggled to find suitable descriptions for the radical nature of this work. In the midst of this confusion, few would disagree that My Dying Bride had, in one fell swoop, turned the doom metal genre on its head.

The group had driven deep into the core essence of doom, drastically overhauling every aspect of its composition. Songs were drawn out into near-unbearable dirges, capped by the violin-imbued colossi of 'The Bitterness And The Bereavement' and 'The Return Of The Beautiful'. Stainthorpe's approach was closer to the great British poets than to that of standard rock'n'roll writers, and MDB's deliberately infantile logo challenged convention.

As The Flower Withers provided the opportunity for their first tour of Europe. The progress gained by another EP, 1993's *The Thrash Of Naked Limbs*, was marred by drummer Miah damaging his hand, leading to the cancellation of a projected tour with labelmates G.G.F.H. Prior to the groundbreaking 1993 *Turn Loose The Swans*, which came in three different covers, the band added violinist-keyboardist Martin Powell to the band and toured Europe once more. *Turn Loose The Swans*, beginning with the piano and violin lament of 'Sear Me MCMXC III' and hinged on the utterly woeful 'The Crown Of Sympathy', slowed the pace even further and plunged deeper into sombre, sluglike doom. Another set of EPs, *Sexuality Of Bereavement* and *I Am The Bloody Earth*, kept the momentum going during 1994.

The Angel And The Dark River was delivered during May 1995 and, in a rare high-profile moment of mainstream activity, My Dying Bride gigged as support to Iron Maiden across Europe. The album contained six more slabs of morose melancholy, marking a shift in the band's strategy as for the first time they dropped the death metal growl of Stainthorpe in favour of a clean vocal delivery. Fans were quick to hail the opener 'Cry Of Mankind' as a classic, even though the mind-numbing keyboard outro dragged on for a full five minutes. Limited editions of this record included a second disc of live material recorded at the 'Dynamo Open Air' festival in Holland.

My Dying Bride's fourth full-length endeavour, *Like Gods Of The Sun*,

hit home in October 1996 in similar bleak fashion to its predecessor. Touring in Europe during March 1997, the band were on a bill with Therion, Sentenced, Orphanage and Dark for the 'Out Of The Dark III' festivals. Drummer Rick Miah departed and for their 1998 album sessions the band pulled in the services of Year Zero and Valle Crusis drummer Mike Unsworth. Yasmine Ahmid of Ebony Lake played keyboards.

October 1998 saw My Dying Bride issuing the experimental *34.788%... Complete*, cut with yet another new drummer, ex-Dominion man Bill Law. The record witnessed a break from the gothic imagery associated with the band. A sharp division of opinion branded the album either as a self indulgent failure or a richly rewarding diversion. Stainthorpe's vocals on the record took on a heavily distorted air, keyboards and samples usurped guitars, and songs ebbed and flowed without formal structure. Undoubtedly the most adventurous song of the band's entire catalogue was 'Heroin Chic', a mechanical, expletive-infested duet with Michelle Richfield of Dominion. The band remained

My Dying Bride

strangely inactive on the touring front, though, and guitarist Calvin Robertshaw departed. He was swiftly replaced by erstwhile Solstice, Serenity and Khang member Lee Baines.

The Light At The End Of The World was viewed not just as a welcome return to form, including a reprise for Stainthorpe's early growling, after the sidestep of *34.788%*, but as one of the finest outings of the doom genre. For touring in 1999, the band pulled in Bal Sagoth's Jonny Maudling for keyboards. Their line-up was completed with the addition of erstwhile Anathema and Solstice drummer Shaun Taylor-Steels and former Solstice guitarist Hamish Glencross. Meantime, ex-My Dying Bride keyboard player Mark Newby Robson joined Cradle Of Filth, rebilling himself Mark De Sade.

The November 2001 offering *The Dreadful Hours* included a remake of 'The Return Of The Beautiful' from the debut record, now billed as 'Return To The Beautiful'. My Dying Bride witnessed a change of keyboard players in April 2002 when Sarah Stanton took over from Ahmed. They also announced the release of their first live album, *The Voice Of The Wretched*, the same month. Hamish Glencross and Andrew Craighan launched their BlackDoom label in 2003. The band then put in a short burst of European dates in October 2003, supported by UK act The Prophecy, the first signing to BlackDoom.

They returned in March 2004 with the album *Songs Of Darkness, Words Of Light*, warning fans in advance that change was in the air and that the track 'My Wine In Silence' was their most commercial effort to date. In late December, Taylor-Steels injured his ankle in a canoeing accident and the band drafted in John Bennett from The Prophecy while he recovered.

Releases announced in early 2005 included the retrospective boxed set *Anti-Diluvian Chronicles*, which included new remixes of 'The Wreckage Of My Flesh', 'My Wine In Silence' and 'The Raven And The Rose', plus the live DVD *Sinamorata*, recorded in Antwerp, Belgium during October 2003. *Sinamorata* also featured two video shorts made by fans for 'Hope The Destroyer' and 'My Wine In Silence'.

In September 2005 it was reported that erstwhile keyboard player Martin Powell and his ex-Cradle Of Filth colleague guitarist James McIlroy had united with ex-Himsa guitarist Matt Wicklund in a brand new band called Prey. Meanwhile, My Dying Bride returned to live action in the UK during November. The *A Line Of Deathless Kings* album was set to be released in October 2006.

PENTAGRAM
OBSCURE BUT INFLUENTIAL DOOM METAL PIONEERS

ONE OF THE FORERUNNERS of doom metal, Pentagram remained an obscure cult act for many years but were brought to public attention by the new wave of doom bands, such as Cathedral, many of which cited Pentagram as a direct influence. The band, dating back to 1971, have been through numerous line-ups and many break-ups. Despite this, they have built up a dedicated following.

The group, at first named Pentagram and then Macabre, were based in Arlington, Virginia, and released their first single, 'Be Forewarned'/'Lazy Lady', in July 1972 as a limited run of 1,000 copies. Some copies had the band name misspelled as Macbre. At this time they included mainman Bobby Liebling, guitarist Vince McAllister, bassist Greg Mayne and drummer Geof O'Keefe. Earlier participants had included guitarist John Jennings and drummer Steve Martin.

Pre-Pentagram, both O'Keefe and Mayne had been in the band Space Meat, which enrolled Liebling as lead vocalist and re-billed themselves Stone Bunny. With Liebling's departure, the band reverted to Space Meat;

PENTAGRAM discography

Be Forewarned, Intermedia Productions TBSM 003 (USA) (1972) 7-inch vinyl single released under the name Macabre

Hurricane, Boffo Socko RI3859 (USA) (1973) limited edition 7-inch vinyl single 200 copies

Under My Thumb, Gemini Productions 002 (USA) (1974) limited edition 7-inch vinyl test pressing 100 promotional copies

Livin' In A Ram's Head, High Voltage 666 (USA) (1979) limited edition 7-inch vinyl single 500 copies

PENTAGRAM, Pentagram DEVIL4 (USA) (1985)

DAY OF RECKONING, Napalm FLAME 006 (USA) (1987)

Relentless, Peaceville CC1 (UK) (1992) Peaceville Collectors Club 7-inch white marbled vinyl single

RELENTLESS, Peaceville VILE38CD (UK) (1993) UK issue of the 1985 *Pentagram* album

BE FOREWARNED, Peaceville VILE42CD (UK), Fierce Recordings 11069-2 (USA) (1994)

HUMAN HURRICANE, Downtime Recordings DTR 001 (Canada) (1998)

REVIEW YOUR CHOICES, Black Widow BWRCD 031-2 (Europe) (1999)

SUB-BASEMENT, Black Widow BWRCD 055-2 (Europe) (2001)

TURN TO STONE, Peaceville CDVILED112 (UK) (2002)

FIRST DAZE HERE: THE VINTAGE COLLECTION, Relapse RR 6521-2 (Europe / USA) (2002)

A KEG FULL OF DYNAMITE, Black Widow BWRCD 065-2 (Europe) (2003)

SHOW 'EM HOW, Black Widow BWRCD 078-2 (Europe) (2004)

FIRST DAZE HERE TOO, Relapse RR 6522-2 (Europe / USA) (2006)

other names included Virgin Death and Wicked Angel before they reverted to Pentagram in 1973.

This inaugural line-up cut the Skip Groff-produced 'Hurricane'/'Earth Flight' single in 1973 for Boffo Socko Records, adding second guitarist Randy Palmer in time to cut a promo single, issued in 1974, featuring a cover of The Rolling Stones' 'Under My Thumb' and an original track, 'When The Screams Come'. Having made an impression on vinyl, Pentagram debuted live at the Junior College in Montgomery, Maryland, on December 8th 1973.

Before Palmer officially joined the ranks of Pentagram in 1974 he committed compositions to tape with O'Keefe, Liebling and mutual friend Mike Matthews. The project was billed as Bedemon after a mispronunciation of two earlier suggestions, 'Behemoth' and 'Demon'. These initial sessions resulted in a three-song demo comprising 'Child Of Darkness', 'Serpent Venom' and 'Frozen Fear'. The enthusiasm engendered by these tracks culminated in a whole album's worth of material. Two of these Bedemon songs, 'Starlady' and 'Touch The Sky', were subsequently utilised by Pentagram.

According to Liebling, Kiss main-men Gene Simmons and Paul Stanley attended a Pentagram rehearsal and offered to buy two compositions, 'Hurricane' and 'Starlady', for $10,000 each – provided that they could be re-credited to Simmons/Stanley. Liebling apparently turned the offer down. Randy Palmer, the chief writer of 'Starlady', has said that he was never approached to sell the song.

Pentagram split at the end of 1976, but a new version of the band materialised in 1978 and released the 'Livin' In A Ram's Head'/'When The Screams Come' single. With this record they underwent a drastic change, with Liebling joined by guitarists Richard Kueht and Paul Trowbridge, bassist Martin Swaney and drummer Joe Hasselvander. However, they split following the release of the single, although the band were active again in 1981 – by pure coincidence, on Halloween – when Liebling teamed up with Hasselvander in Death Row, a band featuring guitarist Victor Griffin and erstwhile Pentagram bassist Martin Swaney, who had joined Death Row a week after Liebling was recruited. By 1984, under pressure from fans, Death Row became Pentagram.

This line-up recorded the band's first full-length album, *Pentagram*, but Hasselvander, who recorded a solo album entitled *Lady-Killer* for the Pentagram label in 1985, departed before its release and the same year joined Simmonds, the band assembled by Savoy Brown man Kim Simmonds. The drummer sessioned for Burning Starr and then teamed up with British athletic rockers Raven. Hasselvander – also as a member of Armageddon – appeared under the pseudonym of Matthew Hopkins on the thrash album by Devil Childe, which included Jack Starr of Virgin Steele.

Undeterred, the band pulled in drummer Stuart Rose for the recording of a second album, *Day Of Reckoning*. After a series of live dates, Pentagram folded yet again in the summer of 1988. The band did resurface in 1989 but predictably split shortly afterwards. However, interest was renewed when English label Peaceville re-released both albums in 1993. The Peaceville reissue of *Pentagram* was re-titled *Relentless* and featured different artwork from the original.

Griffin had relocated to California, founding Pistonhead with the illustrious Wino of The Obsessed. Hasselvander was persuaded to opt out of Raven, and Griffin and Swaney also returned.

Griffin and Hasselvander joined for a European tour with Cathedral, lending a degree of credibility to the British band, but returned to resurrect Pentagram for the *Be Forewarned* album, released in 1994. This featured a reworking of Pistonhead's 'Too Late'. Dates in America saw headliners and supports to Ace Frehley. Hasselvander and Swaney left Pentagram in 1996 and were replaced by drummer Gary Isom and bassist Greg Turley. The band then broke up again due to drug problems.

During 1998, the Canadian label Downtime Recordings issued a compilation of rare and unreleased Pentagram material from the 1970s, *Human Hurricane*, including tracks recorded with Marty Iverson on guitar. Griffin broke ranks again, indulging in a drink and drugs binge brought on by the deaths of family members. When he emerged from the other side of this purgatory, Griffin had become a Christian, later creating the spiritually-based doom act Place Of Skulls with ex-Death Row bassist Lee Abney.

The band returned in 1999 for the *Review Your Choices* album on the Italian Black Widow label. In renewed activity, the band – now featuring Dale Russell as live drummer – laid down tracks for Blue Cheer and Captain Beyond tribute albums. They undertook reunion dates with Liebling, Griffin, Hasselvander and Lee Abney of Place On Skulls on bass.

Upon hearing of doom act Pale Divine's plans to cut a cover of '20 Buck Spin' for their 2001 debut album *Thunder Perfect Mind*, Liebling was impressed enough to guest on the track. He also scored lyric credits and vocals on the previously instrumental closing track 'Dark Knight'. Pentagram then released the 2001 album *Sub-Basement* via Black Widow, while Relapse released the compilation *First Daze Here – The Vintage Collection* in 2002. Former Pentagram guitarist Randy Palmer died on August 8th 2002 from injuries sustained in a car accident on July 31st.

Continuing interest in Pentagram during 2002 resulted in the release of Peaceville's *Turn To Stone* compilation and the 1978 live performance *A Keg Full Of Dynamite* through Black Widow. A new Pentagram surfaced during September 2003, comprising Liebling alongside the Internal Void duo of guitarist Kelly Carmichael and bassist Adam S. Heinzmann, with Mike Smail of Penance on drums. This line-up released the 2004 album *Show 'Em How* through Black Widow.

February 2004 found Liebling adding guest vocals to 'On The Slab' on

Falcon's self-titled debut album. That same year, Californian gore metal band Exhumed included a rendition of the Pentagram song 'The Ghoul' on their covers album, *Regurgitated Requiems: Garbage Daze Re-Regurgitated*.

Unfortunately, a planned comeback gig in Washington DC in January 2005, alongside Alabama Thunderpussy and The Hidden Hand, was marred when Liebling was taken ill and hospitalised just before the show. Members of Internal Void substituted with a mainly instrumental set of Pentagram covers: Hasselvander sang '20 Buck Spin'.

On May 26th 2006 Vincent McAllister, guitarist and a founding member, died of cancer at the age of 51. Relapse Records released the compilation *First Daze Here Too* in March 2006. Even after such a long and turbulent career, Pentagram remain a relatively obscure band. Perhaps their true influence will be acknowledged as the years pass.

REVEREND BIZARRE
FINNS OF DOOM?

DEALING IN AN ALL-ENVELOPING quagmire of doom metal, Reverend Bizarre didn't so much burst as dragged themselves onto the metal scene with their debut album, *In The Rectory Of The Bizarre Reverend*. The band hold a unique record for the genre, having scored a major hit single in their homeland.

Reverend Bizarre originally convened in the small Southern Finnish town of Lohja during 1994 with a line-up of vocalist-bassist Magister 'Witchfinder' Albert (aka Albert Magus, sometime of Herven Agal, Werwolf Lodge, Threshold Of Your Womb and many other bands), guitarist Peter Vicar and drummer Juippi. Early demos comprising four instrumental tracks were recorded in 1996 – without microphones and straight onto a cassette recorder. With Vicar's relocation to Turku in 1997, the band folded.

In 1998, Albert also moved to Turku and the group was resurrected with drummer Earl Of Void (aka Jay Lovely), who had just been released from prison. This trio weighed in with 1999's *Dr. Who*-themed demo *Slice Of Doom*, recorded in three days that August. This session soon sold out and another version was released, minus the track 'Pyramids Of Mars' and with different intro and outro sequences.

The same year, Vicar activated Mesmer, a bleak, progressive metal venture with drummer Earl of Void. Initially, this side band was fronted by Magus. After two demos, 1998's *Mesmer* and 2000's *A Beginning*, the group took on the name Orne for 2002's *Root Of All* session. Both Earl Of Void and Albert were operational with doom-noisecore endeavour KLV (Kehitysvammaisen Lapsen Vanhemmat, Finnish for "parents of a deficient child").

Reverend Bizarre figured on the Saint Vitus tribute *A Timeless Tale* issued by Raven Moon Records and on the compilations *Not Of This Earth*, released by Black Widow, and Myskatonic's *At The Mountains Of Madness Vol. II*. Their debut album, 2002's *In The Rectory Of The Bizarre Reverend* – released by the Mastervox subsidiary Sinister Figure – was so enormously heavy as to almost defy description. The closing track, 'Cirith Ungol', weighed in at a gargantuan 21 minutes. *Harbinger Of Metal* followed in September 2003, classified as an EP although it clocked in at over an hour in length; it included a cover of Burzum's 'Dunkelheit'.

In February 2004 the US label Hellride paired Reverend Bizarre with Orodruin for a split EP. It was only issued as a 12-inch vinyl single restricted to 500 copies; the Finns' contribution was the 15-minute 'Demons Annoying Me'. *Metal Coven* added to the split-release tally; this shared effort with Minotauri featured the track 'Apocalyptic Riders', which featured a guesting Patrick Walker of San Francisco's Warning.

The band's first compilation was delivered by PsycheDOOMelic Records, *Slice Of Doom*, and collected demos and rehearsals. Reverend Bizarre's underground appeal had by now crossed over into the

mainstream metal market, and the leading Spinefarm label reissued *In The Rectory Of The Bizarre Reverend*. This new version added a bonus disc, *Return To The Rectory*, which had a video and eight audio tracks, including a cover of Barathrum's 'Dark Sorceress (Autumn Siege)'.

REVEREND BIZARRE discography

IN THE RECTORY OF THE BIZARRE REVEREND, Sinister Figure SFGCD10 (Europe) (2002)

Harbinger Of Metal, Spikefarm NAULA042 (Europe) (2003)

Blood On Satan's Claw, Metal Coven MCR-003 (Europe) (2003) limited edition split 7-inch vinyl single with Ritual Steel 500 copies

Reverend Bizarre / Orodruin, Hellride Music HRM-1 (USA) (2004) limited edition split 12-inch vinyl EP with Orodruin 500 copies

Apocalyptic Riders, Metal Coven MCR-004 (Europe) (2004) limited edition split 7-inch vinyl single with Minotauri 500 copies

SLICE OF DOOM 1999-2002, PsycheDOOMelic PSY 012 (Europe) (2004)

Slave Of Satan, Spikefarm NAULA064 (Europe) (2005)

II: CRUSH THE INSECTS, Spikefarm NAULA 066 (Europe), Season Of Mist America 119 (USA) (2005)

Thulsa Doom, Aftermath Music cnu (Europe) (2006) limited edition 7-inch vinyl single 500 copies

Under The Sign Of The Wolf, The Church Within CW002 (Europe) (2006) limited edition split 7-inch vinyl single with Mannhai 1,000 copies

Following the band's appearance at the September 'Autumn Of Doom' festival in Schweinfurt, Reverend Bizarre united with Officium Triste and Well Of Souls for a round of German dates. Meanwhile Orne's debut album, *The Conjuration By The Fire* – once more with Witchfinder manning the microphone – was set for release by Black Widow Records.

In January 2005, Magus featured as guest vocalist on Swallow The Sun's interpretation of the Candlemass classic 'Solitude'. Incredibly, Reverend Bizarre's May single, 'Slave Of Satan' – comprising one 12-minute track, including a recitation of the Black Liturgy by Daniel Nyman of Oak – entered the Finnish charts at Number 2. A new full-length album, *II: Crush The Insects*, arrived in June.

The band announced their first US dates for July, partnering with Indiana's The Gates Of Slumber and Houston's Well Of Souls for the Pilgrimage Of Doom trek. A further 2004 EP, *Thulsa Doom* – delivered through Aftermath Music and limited to 500 'blood red' vinyl copies – featured two new recordings in homage to Conan The Barbarian. Doom metal can never be said to be mainstream when bands such as Reverend Bizarre continue to fly its flag.

SAINT VITUS
CRIMINALLY OVERLOOKED DOOM LEGENDS

ALTHOUGH CALIFORNIAN DOOM outfit Saint Vitus are now hailed as a pioneering and influential act, the band battled apathy for much of their career. The Los Angeles-based group originally formed as Tyrant in 1978, stabilising – after trying out two temporary frontmen – as vocalist Scott Reagers, guitarist Dave Chandler, bassist Mark Adams and drummer Armando Acosta. Dispensing a quagmire of subterranean doom metal, they left many critics reeling with their eponymous 1984 debut record,

SAINT VITUS discography

SAINT VITUS, Noise N 009 (Europe), SST SST 022 (USA) (1984)
The Walking Dead, SST SST 042 (USA) (1985)
HALLOW'S VICTIM, SST SST 052 (USA) (1985)
BORN TOO LATE, SST SST 082 (USA) (1986)
Thirsty And Miserable, SST SST 119 (USA) (1987)
MOURNFUL CRIES, SST SST 161 (USA) (1988)
V, Hellhound H 0005-2 (Europe) (1989)
LIVE, Hellhound H 0010-2 (Europe) (1990)
HEAVIER THAN THOU, SST SST 266 (USA) (1991)
C.O.D., Hellhound H 0017-2 (Europe), Nuclear Blast America 6069 (USA) (1992)
DIE HEALING, Hellhound H 0035-2 (Europe) (1995)

released on S.S.T. Records – the punk label owned by Black Flag guitarist Greg Ginn.

Reagers left the fold at the end of 1985 after recording *Hallow's Victim* (although he returned in the mid 1990s). An EP, *The Walking Dead* (featuring Reagers) emerged that same October. Saint Vitus were next fronted by The Obsessed's Scott 'Wino' Weinrich for 1986's *Born Too Late*, cut at Total Access Studios in Redondo Beach. Vocal takes laid down by Reager were re-recorded by Wino. September 1987's EP *Thirsty And Miserable* was headed up by a cover of Black Flag's title track.

Promoting *Mournful Cries*, recorded at Music Grinder Studios in Hollywood in March 1988, Saint Vitus toured Europe extensively, putting in a rare UK show with Agnostic Front. Wino also aided Lost Breed for demo recordings at this point.

The following year, the group signed with German doom specialists Hellhound Records for the *V* album. The 1990 *Live* album was recorded at Gammelsdorf in Germany during 1989. Touring Europe once more in 1990, they were supported by Swedish band Count Raven. Wino then opted out to reform The Obsessed. After that band came to grief in 1995, Wino re-established himself with Shine and Spirit Caravan.

After Wino's departure and 1991's *Heavier Than Thou*, a compilation of material from the band's first four albums, Christian Lindersson of former opening act Count Raven joined the band as 'Lord Chritus'. Somewhat surprisingly, the mainstream metal star Don Dokken was chosen to produce 1992's *C.O.D.* (Children Of Doom) album; afterwards the band folded. Saint Vitus reformed with Reagers for May 1995's *Die Healing*, recorded in Berlin and produced by Harris Johns for the Noise label, but soon fractured yet again.

Lindersson re-emerged with a new act, Terra Firma, created with ex-Unleashed guitarist Fredrik Lindgren. Guitarist Dave Chandler created Debris Inc. with another esteemed doom veteran, Ron Holzner of Trouble.

News emerged that a Wino-fronted Saint Vitus were due to reform for an appearance at Germany's 'With Full Force' festival in July 2003. Indeed, the classic *Born Too Late* line-up of Wino, guitarist Dave Chandler, bassist Mark Adams and drummer Armando Acosta broke a decade of silence with a reunion gig on July 1st at the Double Door in Chicago, Illinois. Southern Lord Records weighed in with a re-release of *V* complete with a DVD of Wino's first ever show with the band. In fitting tribute, Swedish act Grave cut a version of 'Burial At Sea' for their 2004 album *Fiendish Regression*.

A heavyweight Saint Vitus tribute album, *A Timeless Tale*, was announced through Ravenmoon Records in 2004, including contributions from Internal Void, Northwinds, Goatsnake, Ogre, Abdullah, Rwake, Paul Chain, Volume, Black Manta, The Black, Dreaming and Earthride. Few bands have had such an influence with such a short active career.

SAMAEL
DOOM METAL WITH DARK TOUCHES

PROUD TO BE RECOGNISED as one of the gloomiest bands in Europe, the Swiss band Samael have built up an enviable reputation for quality metal with a unique touch over a series of finely crafted albums. *Eternal* from 1999 is widely acknowledged as a classic of the doom genre.

Samael heralded their arrival with the 1987 demo *Into The Infernal Storm Of Evil*. This session, crafted by vocalist-guitarist Vorphalack and Pat Charvet on drums, showed a band bursting with ambition but not yet in possession of the technical ability or experience to get their message across. Nevertheless, the chamber-like echo applied to the vocals hinted at a greater majesty to come. A second demo, *Macabre Operetta*, was issued the following year, after which Charvet bowed out to join Misery.

The group's 1989 three-track EP *Medieval Prophecy* – recorded as a duo of Vorphalack (credited with "vociferations") and his drumming brother Xytraguptor – featured a cover of Hellhammer's 'The Third Of The Storms', while demo track 'Into The Dark' was re-worked to add five minutes and renamed 'Into The Pentagram'. The EP was issued through Necrosound Records, with two cover variations adding to its collectability. Samael's next release in 1990 was the *From Dark To Black* demo.

Signing to Osmose Productions, the band released *Worship Him* in June 1990, the very first release on Osmose. For this album, recorded in Taurus Studios that March, the band was enhanced with the addition of bassist Masmiseîm (aka Christophe Mermod). *Worship Him* generated unexpectedly substantial sales, eventually surpassing 100,000 in Europe alone.

Blood Ritual arrived in December 1992 for Century Media. The record was cut at T&T Studios in Gelsenkirchen, Germany with production credits going to Grip Inc. guitarist Waldemar Sorychta.

A 7-inch picture-disc EP, *After The Sepulture* emerged in 1993 with a re-recorded variant of the title track and a cover of Venom's 'Manitou', and was limited to just 500 copies. Samael's next full-length offering, *Ceremony Of Opposites* – with Sorychta once again manning the board – was released in February 1994. With the band's profile rising, Century Media issued a compilation of the *Worship Him* and *Blood Ritual* material in November 1994 as *1987-1992*. The May 1995 *Rebellion* mini-album, laid down at Woodhouse Studio at Hagen in Germany, boasted a cover of Alice Cooper's 'I Love The Dead' and an unlisted, hidden track – 'Static Journey'.

The group added keyboard player Rudolphe H. for live dates in 1995 with Sentenced. For the recording of August 1996's *Passage* all drum parts were programmed, and Xytraguptor (later 'Xytra', then simply 'Xy') assumed a new role as keyboard player. *Passage* marked a new phase in the group's career, introducing heavily industrial elements. Initial copies of *Passage* came with a bonus disc, *Xytra's Passage*, with instrumental remixes of the album tracks by Xytra plus reworked archive material, 'Wintersonnenwende' and 'Der Stamm Kains'. A second guitarist, Kaos from French death metallers Gorgon, was brought in for the recording and live dates.

Samael's relationship with Sentenced was strengthened as Vorphalack added backing vocals to the Finns' *Down* outing. Xytra's skills in the studio were now recognised outside Samael, with production credits on two albums by Greek black metal veterans Rotting Christ, *Sleep Of The Angels* and *A Dead Poem*. He also operated his own label, Parallel Union, in collaboration with War D. of Alastis.

April 1997 found the band back on European soil and heading up the 'Full Of Hate Easter' festivals alongside Obituary, Death, Entombed, Neurosis, Crowbar, Killing Culture and Strapping Young Lad. The mini-album *Exodus* was issued in June 1998. Promoting the *Eternal* album, released in July 1999, the band headed out on a US trek through September and October with Monstrosity, Dimmu Borgir and Epoch Of Unlight.

Before 2002 European festival performances, guitarist Kaos announced his departure. In early 2003, the band acted as special guests to UK veteran doom act Cathedral and Hungarian newcomers Without Face on a lengthy trek through Europe. Samael then united with Strapping Young Lad and Cathedral for September North American dates, dubbed the 'Redemption' tour. Product that year came in the form of an elaborate DVD, *Black Trip*, filmed at three concerts. Century Media also collected the entire output for the boxed set *Since The Creation* in December.

In 2004, the band, having fulfilled their contract to Century Media, signed a new deal with Sweden's Regain for Europe and Asia but established their own Galactical Recordings for the rest of the world. A new album, *Reign Of Light* – co-produced by Sorychta – was set to arrive in the summer. A listening session for the media took place on August 10th at the HR Giger museum in Switzerland. *Reign Of Light* was subsequently picked up by Nuclear Blast for a December US release, and that same month the band conducted European dates with electro-metal act Oomph! and Marseilles' Dagoba.

Also in 2004, the band had their classic cut 'Into The Pentagram' chosen for the compilation *Fenriz Presents: The Best Of Old School Black Metal*. An EP, *On Earth* – released in June 2005 – included a cover of Depeche Mode's 'I Feel You'. Xy fractured his wrist in a snowboard accident during December, forcing him out of live work for a time.

Nevertheless, Samael lined up European touring in January and February 2006 with Obituary and Maroon as the archive collection *Era One & Lesson In Magic #1* hit the shelves. This double disc involved electro material originally put down on tape in 2002 and further ambient tracks recorded in 2003.

Vorphalack, who had been using the shortened name of Vorph for some years, guested on Tristania's 2006 album *Illumination*. The band continue to reap critical and commercial rewards for their work.

SLEEP
LEGENDARY DOOM/STONER PIONEERS

SLEEP, FROM SAN JOSE, CALIFORNIA, were a celebrated doom-rock act who, since their demise, have entered the annals of stoner folklore. The band emerged with the 1991 *Volume One* album for Tupelo, recorded by vocalist-bassist Al Cisneros, guitarists Matt Pike and Justin Marler and drummer Chris Hakius. Sleep had evolved from a punk-inclined band, Asbestosdeath, established by Cisneros, Hakius and guitarist Tom Choi. Asbestosdeath graduated to a quartet with the introduction of Pike on guitar and, as their music became more doom-laden with the singles 'Dejection' for Profane Existence and the self released 'Unclean', Choi departed, eventually founding Operator Generator. Asbestosdeath then recruited Justin Marler as replacement and switched their title to Sleep.

After Sleep's debut, exposure in Europe came with a signing to the British label Earache for *Sleep's Holy Mountain* in 1992. By this stage Marler had vacated the picture: by his own confession, the guitarist had been near to suicide and had succumbed to self-mutilation. Marler's response to his illness was to enter a Russian Orthodox monastery to live the life of a monk for several years.

The impact made by *Sleep's Holy Mountain* on the underground scene caught the interest of major labels and Sleep duly signed to London for a follow-up. Announced in the press as *Dopesmoker*, the album – recorded before the London deal – only emerged on Tee Pee Records in 2003. In fact, the band had opted to completely rewrite and re-record the lyrics. The project, scheduled for a 1995 release, emerged as a mammoth 52-minute leviathan of a track, dubbed *Jerusalem*. London balked and dropped the band, and Sleep dissolved in 1997.

With *Jerusalem* now the stuff of legend, trading on the bootleg market was rampant. Eventually, Lee Dorrian's Rise Above label secured official rights to the album for UK licence, while in North America a release was negotiated through the Music Cartel.

Pike set about formulating a fresh act, emerging with High On Fire in 1999 and issuing a three-track eponymous EP followed by *Art Of Self Defense* in 2000. Marler, no longer residing in a monastery, surfaced with a new project, The Sabians, with Hakius. This band, including guitarist Patrick Huerta and bass player Rachel Fisher, put out the *Empty Your Heart* demo before releasing *Beauty For Ashes*, produced by Fudge

---

SAMAEL discography

Medieval Prophecy, Necrosound cnu (Europe) (1989) 7-inch vinyl EP
WORSHIP HIM, Osmose Productions OPCD 001 (Europe), JL America/Osmose Productions OS-41080-2 (USA) (1991)
BLOOD RITUAL, Century Media CM 9737-2 (Europe), Century Media CM 7737-2 (USA) (1992)
After The Sepulture, no label or catalogue number (Europe) (1993) limited edition 7-inch vinyl picture disc single 500 copies
CEREMONY OF OPPOSITES, Century Media CM 77064-2 (Europe), Century Media CM 7764-2 (USA) (1994)
Rebellion, Century Media CM 77099-2 (Europe), Century Media CM 7799-2 (USA) (1995)
PASSAGE, Century Media CM 77127-2 (Europe), Century Media CM 7827-2 (USA) (1996)
Exodus, Century Media CM 77210-2 (Europe), Century Media CM 7910-2 (USA) (1998)
ETERNAL, Century Media CM 77185-2 (Europe), Century Media CM 7885-2 (USA) (1999)
Since The Creation..., Century Media CM 77545-0 (Europe) limited edition 12-inch vinyl picture disc boxed set 2,000 copies
Telepath, Regain RR 057 (Europe) (2004),
REIGN OF LIGHT, Regain RR 055 (Europe) (2004), Nuclear Blast America 1405 (USA) (2005)
On Earth, Regain RR 061 (Europe) (2005)
ERA ONE / LESSON IN MAGIC #1, Century Media CM 77625-2 (Europe), Century Media CM 8325-2 (USA) (2006)

SLEEP discography

VOLUME ONE, Tupelo/Very Small 34 (USA) (1991)
Vol 2, Off The Disk OTD-15 (USA) (1992) limited edition 7-inch vinyl EP 1,000 copies
SLEEP'S HOLY MOUNTAIN, Earache MOSH79CD (UK) (1992), Earache MOSH79CD (USA) (1993)
JERUSALEM, Rise Above CDRISE 19 (UK), The Music Cartel 12 (USA) (1999)
DOPESMOKER, Tee Pee TPE-049 (Europe / USA) (2003)

Tunnel man Alex Newport in 2002, followed by *Shiver* in 2003. During April 2004, Al Cisneros founded Om with Chris Haikus.

Sleep's legacy cannot be overstated when it comes to the doom and stoner scenes, and fans of those genres owe them a considerable debt.

SOLITUDE AETERNUS
OLD-SCHOOL DOOM FOR ALL

THE ULTRA-HEAVY DOOM metal act Solitude Aeturnus were created in Arlington, Texas, in 1987 by erstwhile Rotting Corpse guitarist John Perez. Initially titled Solitude, the band put out the 1987 *And Justice For All* demo before altering their name to avoid confusion with the Delaware act of the same name. The band's line-up at this juncture was Perez, vocalist Kris Gabehardt, guitarist Tom Martinez, bassist Chris Hardin and drummer Brad Kane.

The band, with only Perez remaining from the original incarnation, soon separated themselves from the thrash metal pack with the launch of *Into The Depths Of Sorrow* in 1991: this displayed the band's obvious homage to Black Sabbath in epic, sluggish workouts. Perez was joined by singer Robert Lowe, guitarist Edgar Rivera, bass player Lyle Steadham and drummer John Covington.

The group originally signed to King Classic Records, with the album ready for release in 1990, but due to problems with the label it didn't see the light of day until the following year. By this time the group had been snapped up by Roadrunner, which released *Beyond The Crimson Horizon* in 1992.

After touring in America with Killers, they switched to Pavement Records for 1994's *Through The Darkest Hour*, issued in Britain on Bulletproof. Supporting its release, the group hit the road with American tours opening for Mercyful Fate and European dates with Revelation.

They were disappointed with 1996's *Downfall* album from a production angle and, more to the point, by the fact that it was not pushed in America or Europe. The cover was changed for the European version without the band's knowledge, because the record company deemed it "too dark". Nevertheless, the Texan group picked up some dates with Morgana Lefay in 1997 and gained a new deal with the German Massacre label. Bassist Steadham departed, replaced by Steve Moseley.

Adagio, released in 1998, was recorded at Rhythm Studios in Bidford, England and co-produced by the band and Paul Johnston. A bonus track, a cover of Black Sabbath's 'Heaven And Hell', was included for good measure. They also covered Ozzy Osbourne's 'No More Tears' for the *Legend Of A Madman* tribute album.

Solitude Aeturnus then readied a re-release of *Into The Depths Of Sorrow* for January 2004. This revised version added demo versions of

'Opaque Divinity' and 'Mirror Of Sorrow' plus an unreleased track, 'City Of Armageddon' taken from a rehearsal recording. The band then projected a new studio album, with the provisional title of *Alone*, for release through Massacre in Europe in November 2006.

Lowe underwent surgery to remove his gall-bladder and correct a lower abdominal hernia. Once back on the scene, the band set to work on *Alone* with a line-up of Lowe, Perez, Moseley (now on guitar) and new members James Martin on bass and Steve Nichols on drums. They embarked on a run of concerts in Greece during April 2006 and remain at the forefront of the doom movement.

THE OBSESSED
WINO'S CELEBRATED DOOM MONSTERS

THIS CULT WASHINGTON DC doom metal outfit, centred on the renowned figure of Wino (real name Scott Weinrich), were formed in 1977, originally as Warhorse. Early shows fronted by singer Vance Bockis – which featured the band in make-up and high heels – demonstrated their eclectic blend of influences, including covers of songs by The Beatles and The Sex Pistols.

As Wino was joined by bassist Mark Laue and drummer Ed Gulli (who replaced former sticksman Dave Williams, aka Dave Flood), the band released the now-rare *Sodden Jackal* EP in 1983. A further track, 'Concrete Cancer', emerged on the 1985 Metal Blade compilation album *Metal Massacre VI*. Wino then jumped ship to front California's Saint Vitus, replacing Scott Reagers, and also anonymously performed bass duties for the Mentors in 1987. With Wino on board, Saint Vitus released a series of classic doom efforts, such as *Born Too Late* and *Mournful Cries*, finally bowing out with 1990's *Live* album.

German doom label Hellhound issued in 1990 a collection of archive tracks – titled *The Obsessed* but commonly known as *The Purple Album* – prompting a reformation of the band with Wino, Acid Clown bass player Danny Hood and ex-Poison 13 and Acid Clown drummer Greg Rogers. *Lunar Womb* from 1992 was recorded with Scott Reeder on bass after Hood died in a motorbike accident.

Such was the impact of the *Lunar Womb* album that The Obsessed were now a recognised influence on the scene, and the band were signed up to major label Columbia. Reeder decamped to stoners Kyuss: his place was taken by former Beaver, Scream and B.A.L.L. man Guy Pinhas for the 1994 *The Church Within* album. Promotion was accelerated for this release with support dates to White Zombie, an appearance at the 'Dynamo Open Air' festival in Holland, and even video airings on MTV.

Wino then featured in the ad hoc Bullring Brummies act that included Black Sabbath bassist Geezer Butler and Judas Priest vocalist Rob Halford, and they contributed a track to the *Nativity In Black* Black Sabbath tribute album.

With Columbia dropping the band, The Obsessed struck out into indie territory once again, issuing the *Altamont Nation* EP through Bongload Custom Records. This included a rendition of Grand Funk Railroad's 'Inside Looking Out'. However, the band inevitably folded once again in 1995. Wino created Shine, an act that soon evolved into Spirit Caravan with ex-Wretched bassist Dave Sherman and former Iron Man and Pentagram drummer Gary Isom. Spirit Caravan debuted in 1999 with the *Dreamwheel* EP and the *Jug Fulla Sun* album. Shine had previously released a self-titled two-song 7-inch single featuring 'Lost Sun Dance' and 'Courage' on Tolotta Records in 1997.

Pinhas and Rogers forged Goatsnake with erstwhile Kid Engine guitarist Greg Anderson. Pinhas left this act (his temporary replacement being Scott Reeder) to join Acid King and Fireball Ministry, the latter act with former Megadeth drummer Nick Menza.

SOLITUDE AETERNUS discography

INTO THE DEPTHS OF SORROW, Roadracer RO 9265-2 (Europe), Roadracer RRD 9265 (USA) (1991)

BEYOND THE CRIMSON HORIZON, Roadracer RO 9168-2 (Europe), Roadracer RRD 9168 (USA) (1992)

THROUGH THE DARKEST HOUR, Bulletproof CDVEST 35 (UK), Pavement Music 76962-32214-2 (USA) (1994)

The New Wave Of American True Metal, BPR BP-02 (USA) (1996) split 7-inch vinyl single with Iron Rainbow

DOWNFALL, Hengest IRSCD993022 (UK), Pavement Music 76962-32252-2 (USA) (1996)

ADAGIO, Massacre MAS CD0161 (Europe) (1998), Olympic Recordings 008 638 001-2 (USA) (1999)

ALONE, Massacre MAS CD0530 (Europe) (2006)

The appropriately named Doom Records kept fans of the band happy during the mid to late 1990s with a series of re-releases and rare archive recordings. The *Incarnate* album of 1999, issued by Southern Lord, was a collection of early demos and rare material, including an unreleased lead track 'Yen Sleep' and cover versions of Grand Funk Railroad's 'Inside Looking Out' and Lynyrd Skynrd's 'On The Hunt', the latter featuring Dale Crover of Melvins on drums.

Paying tribute, Foo Fighters covered 'Iron & Stone' as a B-side to their 2000 single *Breakout*. Wino also appeared on Dave Grohl's Probot album, and his reputation as a doom legend remains intact.

TROUBLE
STONER LEGENDS

TROUBLE FORMED IN CHICAGO in 1979 and debuted with a self-titled album in 1984 on the Metal Blade label. The band remained a cult act throughout the greater portion of their career, and it was only with the stoner rock trend of the mid 1990s that their legacy was recognised.

The group first committed their Christian-themed brand of doom metal to tape in 1980 with a three-track demo recording. Two more studio sets ensued, capped by a live recording in 1983, comprising originals and takes on Accept's 'Son Of A Bitch', Angel Witch's 'Confused' and even Michael Winner's *Deathwish* movie theme. At this stage Trouble consisted of singer Eric Wagner, guitarists Bruce Franklin and Rick Wartell, former Witch Slayer bassist Sean McAllister and Jeff Olson on drums. Their ambitions reached the ears of California's Metal Blade label, who put out the March 1984 single 'Assassin'.

Trouble's opening album, titled simply *Trouble* but often referred to

as *Psalm 9*, came clad in a jacket depicting a weathered tree atop a skull-shaped hillock. The record, a collaborative production credited to the band, label boss Brian Slagel and engineer Bill Metoyer, was ground out at Track Studios in February 1984 for release just weeks later. The album's thick slabs of doom, culled from prior demos, closed with a crushing rendering of Cream's 'Tales Of Brave Ulysses'. Unfortunately, Metal Blade's then-limited promotional budget didn't do justice to the material, and although reviews were glowing, Trouble found it difficult to step up beyond local support.

The lyrics of the band's second album, *The Skull*, touched on some of their personal problems, including substance abuse and conflicts of character. Unsurprisingly, the group then fractured, with Jeff Olson quitting in late 1985 to enter the church and Ron Holzer usurping McAllister. With two creditable albums behind them, and rising international appreciation, Trouble's religious persuasions soon came under scrutiny. Questioned on their supposed Christian outlook, the band denied any such stance.

June 1987's *Run To The Light* saw them reform with a fresh rhythm section of Ron Holzner and drummer Dennis Lesh. Again reviews were positive, but still Trouble struggled. They then signed with Rick Rubin's Def American label for an eponymous album, released in early 1990. At this point the band had settled on a line-up comprising Wagner, Rick Wartell, Bruce Franklin, Holzner and ex-Zoetrope drummer Barry Stern. Rubin took the production chair for this record, encouraging Trouble's experiments with psychedelia.

Following 1992's *Manic Frustration*, their last for Def American, the band welcomed Olson back into the fold for their swansong, *Plastic Green Head*. This record, a Vincent Wojno-produced set, delved deeper into 1960s-style acidity to such a degree that it boasted covers of The Beatles' 'Tomorrow Never Knows' and The Monkees' 'Porpoise Song'.

Later shows saw Trouble fronted by former Exhorder vocalist Kyle Thomas. The band also operated for a short period with Crowbar drummer Craig Nunebacher before Stern's return. They eventually added former Shades Of Grey and Cathedral drummer Dave Hornyak as replacement for Stern.

After various individual projects, Trouble reformed in October 2002, reconvening a line-up of Wagner, Wartell, Franklin, Holzner and Olson. However, Holzner soon broke away and was replaced by former This Tortured Soul bassist Chuck Robinson. The combo set to work on a new album, *Simple Mind Condition*, comprising five classic Trouble numbers along with two new songs.

Probot, fronted by Eric Wagner, put in a one-off live performance of 'My Tortured Soul' on January 28th 2004 at the MTV studios in New York City. Joining the Trouble frontman for the occasion were project mentor Dave Grohl, doom legend Wino, Greg Anderson of Southern Lord Records and Foo Fighters mixer Nick Raskulinecz. Sadly, Barry Stern died in early 2005.

British dark ambient act Antimatter included a cover of Trouble's 'Mr. White' on their July 2005 *Planetary Confinement* album. Meanwhile, Trouble completed work on *Simple Mind Condition* in November. The release of *Simple Mind Condition* was set for 2007, leaving fans anticipating more doom-laden greatness to come.

Trouble

POWER
METAL

POWER

POWER metal is, many believe, a perfected form of heavy metal, focused on technically challenging riffing and traditional, often fantasy-based lyrics. The finest power metal bands aim towards the vocal excellence of Judas Priest's Rob Halford, Iron Maiden's Bruce Dickinson, or Queensryche's Geoff Tate combined with extreme guitar proficiency, such as that of Yngwie Malmsteen. A reliance on finely crafted riffs is a prerequisite.

The movement rose during the early 1990s, given momentum by Germany's unrelenting appreciation for '80s metal. Germany had always had a power metal contingent – Blind Guardian, Helloween, Gamma Ray, Running Wild, Angel Dust, and so on – but these bands were confined almost exclusively within the country's borders for many years.

When it became clear that the USA and UK had temporarily exhausted their supply of metal in the wake of grunge, German musicians and industry movers reactivated the careers of second- and third-tier US bands – such as Vicious Rumors, Lizzy Borden, Tyrant, Anvil, Armored Saint, Cirith Ungol, Crimson Glory, Fates Warning, Metal Church, and Manilla Road – and formed their own homegrown equivalent. Often ignored in the USA, these bands reformed due to fan pressure and performed in front of major crowds at festivals such as the famous Wacken Open Air event.

Another significant player was Manowar (see chapter 11), a band whose image and idealism had placed them firmly in cultdom in America and Britain. Europe had no such prejudices, and the group maintained a robust base of fans across the continent. Other US bands who had held true to the cause, such as Savatage, Virgin Steele, Iced Earth, and Nevermore, also all saw a rapid rise in popularity.

While this movement was gathering, a Swedish band caused power metal to explode into the mainstream. Hammerfall (see chapter 13) were formed as a kickabout jam band by a fluid cast of death metal players who held traditional metal bands in close affection. Much to their surprise, this party act found a keen audience and their debut album – at first released on a minor Dutch imprint – was soon snapped up by Nuclear Blast. Much to everybody's surprise, Hammerfall's first record not only sold in large quantities but prompted a whole new generation across Europe to strap on leather studded wristbands and raise their fists in triumph. Hammerfall were the first of a new wave of power metal bands, breaking the genre worldwide and into the teen market.

Hammerfall's success gave a second wind to the likes of Saxon and Manowar, who proceeded to sell in greater quantities than ever before. German bands such as Brainstorm, Sacred Steel, Primal Fear, and Majesty also gained recognition.

Branches soon spun off, with the likes of Rhapsody and Stratovarius pursuing symphonic, epic themes; progressive metal was engendered by the likes of Kamelot and Threshold; and even "happy" power metal was evolved by Edguy. Power metal is still very much a vital force on the scene, with newer acts such as Dragonforce gaining a rapid foothold.

DRAGONFORCE
THE BRAND NEW HOPE OF 'EXTREME POWER METAL'

LONDON-BASED POWER METAL band Dragonforce were known as Dragonheart for much of their early career, issuing a demo titled *Valley Of The Damned* under this name. Founded in 1999, the group took the spirit of the European mid-1990s power metal resurgence to new heights, simply quadrupling the intensity of the riffs and solos. Within a few short years, not only did they find themselves heading the pack, they also cracked the US charts with their third album. Before signing to the Sanctuary label, the band switched names to Dragonforce due to the number of acts with similar titles.

For the band's first rehearsals in October 1999, Dragonheart employed Z.P. Theart on vocals, guitarists Herman 'Shred' Li and Sam 'Heimdall' Totman (both members of the uprooted New Zealand black metal act Demoniac), New Zealand-born bass player Steve Scott, and Slovenian-born Matej Setinc (also of Demoniac) on drums.

Demoniac, promoting their second album, *Stormblade*, had relocated to England during 1997 to take part in the World Domination tour of Europe headlined by Dark Tranquillity and Enslaved. After one more album, 1999's *The Fire And The Wind*, Demoniac collapsed, paving the way for Dragonheart.

With Setinc's early departure, Peter Hunt briefly occupied the drum stool, and the group also enrolled former Dog Day Sunrise keyboard player Steve Williams. A demo entitled *Valley Of The Damned* surfaced in June 2000. These recordings were produced by Karl Groom of Threshold, with Clive Nolan of Pendragon adding keyboard touches. Dragonheart bassist Steve Scott joined competitors Shadow Keep during 2000, while Diccon Harper, previously a member of Phoenix, filled the vacancy that November. Williams also made his exit.

The band, still called Dragonheart at this point, supported Halford and Stratovarius in December 2000. Vadim Pruzhanov came in as the new keyboard player for the Halford gigs, with just two days' notice. At this juncture, Steve Williams forged the symphonic metal act Power Quest, pulling in Scott and Totman, the guitarist maintaining a foot in both

DRAGONFORCE discography

VALLEY OF THE DAMNED, Noise N 0373-2 (Europe), Noise 74084
(USA) (2003)
SONIC FIRESTORM, Noise N 0385-2 (Europe), Noise 74142 (USA)
(2004)
INHUMAN RAMPAGE, Roadrunner RR 8070-2 (UK), Roadrunner
168 618 034-2 (USA) (2006) **103 USA**

camps, and personnel from Italian metal band Arthemis. The name
change from Dragonheart to Dragonforce was announced on December
6th 2001.

The line-up remained fluid and Harper decamped in March 2002. As
the debut album, *Valley Of The Damned*, emerged in January 2003, the
Dragonforce line-up consisted of vocalist Theart, guitarists Li and Totman,
keyboard player Pruzhanov, drummer Didier Almouzni, and stand-in
bassist Adrian Lambert. Almounzi exited that June just before an
appearance at the Sweden Rock festival. Christian Wirtl of Swedish act
Soul Source was a temporary replacement.

Dragonforce started recording a new studio album in November 2003,
enrolling the Bal-Sagoth credited Dave Mackintosh on drums. Japanese
dates in January 2004 had the band supporting veteran German act
Helloween. An album-release show at London's Underworld on February
13th saw French labelmates Heavenly as opening act. The band set *Sonic
Firestorm* as the title of their new record, slated for April. European dates
in May saw the band opening for W.A.S.P.. Mackintosh dislocated his
elbow en route from Paris to the UK, putting him out of action for six
weeks, and the band completed the rest of the tour with a drum machine.
A further mishap came at the band's Gates Of Metal festival appearance
in Hultsfred, Sweden on July 31st when Li missed his plane, requiring the
band to perform with Totman as sole guitarist. Dragonforce then
scheduled a headlining UK tour for October.

The band's 2005 live campaign opened with support shows to Angra
in Greece during February. Dragonforce then landed a major coup on the
live front when they were selected as opening act for Iron Maiden's
European summer festival dates in Poland, Italy, and Greece. A headline
UK tour, dubbed 'Meet The Sonic Firestorm', was announced for September.

The band parted ways with bassist Lambert in October, pulling in
Frédéric Leclercq of Heavenly and Maladaptive as substitute. Dragonforce
were set to make their US live debut on November 22nd with a headlining
show at the legendary CBGBs club in New York, but cancelled this gig
due to "unforeseen circumstances" which prevented the whole band
gaining entry into the USA. Instead, a listening party for the *Inhuman
Rampage* album was held at the venue on the same date, attended by
Totman and Theart. That same month the band revealed a new deal with
Roadrunner.

In early 2006, Peter Hunt joined Marshall Law. European touring in
February 2006 across Switzerland, Spain, Portugal, France, Sweden, and
Germany found Dragonforce supporting Edguy. For shows in the UK, the
roles were reversed, with Edguy as the opening act. These gigs once again
found Leclercq occupying the bass role: by February 2006 he had been
confirmed as a permanent replacement for Lambert. Dragonforce then hit
Canada and the USA in April and May supported by Protest The Hero and
Sanctity. The band then put in a significant appearance at the Guns N'
Roses-headlined 'Download' festival in the UK on June 11th.

The 'Ozzfest' loomed for the US 2006 summer season, and the group
shared the stage with Ozzy Osbourne, Disturbed, System Of A Down,
Black Label Society, and Lacuna Coil. Just before these concerts, the
Inhuman Rampage album entered the US charts at Number 103.

In the packed metal scene of 2006, it takes a special band to stand
out: experts agree that Dragonforce, with their incredibly speedy
approach, may be that very band.

EDGUY
EUROPEAN POWER HOPEFULS

EDGUY ARE A YOUNG POWER metal outfit hailing from Fulda in
Hessen, Germany, who have elevated themselves into the major league in
Europe through a succession of strong albums blessed with inventive
riffing, some supreme Euro-melodies, and, on occasion, frontman Tobias
Sammet's unique brand of oddball humour. The group, taking their name
from a school tutor named Edgar, were formed in 1992 and at first
operated as a covers act. By 1994, the fledgling band had enough original
material for a brace of demos, *Evil Minded* and *Children Of Steel*.
However, with no real label interest forthcoming, the band members
funded their debut album, *Savage Poetry*.

It made a keen impression on the German media, and the AFM label
stepped in to pick up Edguy and craft a quick-fire follow-up, *Kingdom Of
Madness*. Naturally, AFM promptly reissued *Savage Poetry*, albeit in new
jacket art, making the original an instant collectable.

After the re-release of the debut, drummer Dominik Storch departed,
and sessions for the 1998 album, *Vain Glory Opera*, were fulfilled by Blues
Power man Frank Lindenhall. A permanent drummer was found in Felix
Bohnke, a former member of Exiled and Merciless Gnom. For *Vain Glory
Opera*, Stratovarius's Timo Tolkki guested on guitar while Blind
Guardian's Hansi Kürsch and Warrior's Ralf Zdiarstek also put in an
appearance – these high-profile inclusions demonstrated the regard that
Edguy had already achieved in a short space of time.

In side activity, Edguy frontman Tobias Sammet guested on Squealer's
1998 album *The Prophecy*: the same year, this connection was
strengthened when Squealer bassist Tobias Exxel jumped ship to join Edguy.

Theater Of Salvation maintained the momentum in 1999, scoring chart
entries in Germany and Sweden. In a novel move, Edguy gave *Savage*

EDGUY discography

SAVAGE POETRY, Edguy cnu (Europe) (1995)
KINGDOM OF MADNESS, AFM 37585-422 (Europe) (1997)
VAIN GLORY OPERA, AFM 38760-422 (Europe) (1998)
THEATER OF SALVATION, AFM 0046522 (Europe) (1999), Metal
   Blade 3984-14312-2 (USA) (2000)
Painting On The Wall, AFM AFM 0505 (Europe) (2001)
MANDRAKE, AFM AFM 050-2 (Europe) (2001)
BURNING DOWN THE OPERA – LIVE, AFM AFM 068-9 (Europe)
   (2003)
King Of Fools, Nuclear Blast NB 1240-2 (Europe), Nuclear Blast
   America 1240 (USA) (2004)
HELLFIRE CLUB, Nuclear Blast NB 1244-2 (Europe), Nuclear Blast
   America 1244 (USA) (2004)
HALL OF FLAMES, AFM AFM 088-9 (Europe) (2004), Locomotive
   Music 176 (USA) (2005)
Lavatory Love Machine, Nuclear Blast NB 1302-2 (Europe),
   Nuclear Blast America 1302 (USA) (2004)
Superheroes, Nuclear Blast NB 1504-2 (Europe), Nuclear Blast
   America 1504 (USA) (2005)
ROCKET RIDE, Nuclear Blast NB 1600-2 (Europe), Nuclear Blast
   America 1600 (USA) (2006)

Poetry a third lease of life by re-recording all the original songs. It was released as a special-edition double CD: one disc had the revised versions; the other the 1995 originals. The new-look *Savage Poetry*, subtly re-titled *The Savage Poetry*, broke into the charts across Europe in 2000. With Edguy rapidly going from strength to strength in Europe, Tobias Sammet made space to assemble a mammoth cast of players for his ambitious Avantasia project of 2000. The eponymous album, which also featured Edguy guitarist Jens Ludwig, saw guests from acts as diverse as Gamma Ray, Helloween, Rhapsody, Stratovarius, At Vance, Within Temptation, and Virgin Steele.

Not to be outdone, bass guitarist Exxel conceived a solo project, Taraxacum. The resulting *Spirit Of Freedom* album, released by MTM Metal, found Exxel drawing in the talents of Steel Prophet vocalist Rick Mythiasin, Rough Silk keyboard player Ferdy Doernberg, his Edguy colleague Felix Bohnke on drums, and erstwhile Squealer man Frank Wolf also on drums.

A new album, *Mandrake*, was recorded at Rhön Studios in Fulda, engineered by Norman Meiritz and mixed and mastered at Finnvox Studios by Mikko Karmila and Mikka Jussila. The record, boasting a guest vocal spot from Rob Rock, was launched in September, preceded by a taster CD single, 'Painting On The Wall'. The release confirmed the still-ascendant status of the band with national chart action in Germany, Sweden, and France. Edguy got into the spirit of live action with an anonymous appearance at the Paris Dunois venue on October 7th. The band, cheekily billed as Mandrake, opened the show for Heavenly (who were using the event as a release party for their *Sign Of The Winner* album).

The band shifted from the AFM label to Nuclear Blast in mid 2003, marking this manoeuvre with a 2004 EP, *King Of Fools*. A new full-length album, the Norman Meiritz and Sascha Paeth-produced *Hellfire Club*, included collaborations with the Babelsberg film orchestra. Initial editions of the album added two exclusive bonus tracks in a re-worked 'Children

Of Steel', originally included on the band's 1994 demo, and another version of 'Mysteria', featuring Kreator vocalist Mille Petrozza on vocals. This new material was debuted to a national audience in January when a private concert at the 250-capacity Underground club in Cologne was aired live on the prestigious *Rockpalast* WDR TV show. Bowing in at Number 89 on the national charts in Brazil, *Hellfire Club* marked the first time a Nuclear Blast artist had appeared on the Brazilian chart. It made Number 26 in their homeland and a worthy Number 6 in Sweden.

The band united with Brainstorm for a lengthy run of German shows commencing in April 2004 before partnering with Nocturnal Rites and Tad Morose for Scandinavian dates in May. The single and video to back these shows, 'Lavatory Love Machine' – concerning Sammet's induction into the mile-high club – amply illustrated the band's unique sense of humour. An extra track on the CD single was a surprising acoustic workout of Europe's 'I'll Cry For You'. Rounding off the year, Edguy issued a double compilation album entitled *Hall Of Flames*, a re-mastered set including previously unheard songs. Tobias Sammet then took time out of the Edguy schedule to lend guest vocals to Rob Rock's *Holy Hell* album.

The band, alongside Doro, Bonfire, Saxon, Crystal Ball, and In Extremo, were among acts participating in the January 27th 2005 'Rock For Asia' festival held at the Saturn Arena in Ingolstadt, Germany to benefit the victims of the December Indian Ocean tsunami disaster.

Working with Sascha Paeth as producer, Edguy entered Gate Studio in Wolfsburg to cut an EP, *Superheroes*, during May. It featured a cover version of Magnum's 'The Spirit'. Former Helloween frontman Michael Kiske guested; Edguy then partnered with Hammerfall and Canadians Into Eternity for US summer dates.

The album *Rocket Ride* emerged in January. Japanese versions on the Avalon Marquee label hosted an additional three tracks. European touring in February 2006 across Switzerland, Spain, Portugal, France, Sweden, and Germany found Dragonforce supporting. For shows in the UK, the roles

Edguy

were reversed, with Edguy as the opening act. Japanese gigs in March had Savage Circus as support. The band continue to head up the new wave of European power metal: watch this space.

HALFORD
THE METAL GOD GOES SOLO

DURING SOME 20 YEARS as frontman for Birmingham metal legends Judas Priest, vocalist Rob Halford came to epitomise the term 'heavy metal' – not only with his onstage regalia of studded leather but also a vocal range and expression that few could match. He was born Robert John Arthur Halford on August 25th 1951 in Sutton Coldfield near Birmingham, England, and raised in nearby Walsall.

After a 1991 world tour to promote Judas Priest's *Painkiller* album, Halford announced he wished to pursue solo work. After a guest slot with Black Sabbath, he performed at two shows in Costa Mesa, California, during November 1992 when Ronnie James Dio pulled out – and following a collaboration with Pantera he formed Fight (see chapter 18), then Halford. Signed to Nine Inch Nails guru Trent Reznor's Nothing Records, Halford became Gimp and then Two. By now adopting the Nosferatu look and proclaiming metal to be dead, Rob surprised nobody when in January 1998 he outed himself as a gay man during an MTV interview. Many of his fans were already aware of this fact, but it generated a great deal of media coverage.

It came as no great shock when the Two project – despite being an adventurous experiment – proved commercially disastrous, and by late 1999 Halford had returned to his metal roots. The singer announced his comeback with the downloadable track 'Silent Screams', a new management deal with Sanctuary (responsible for Iron Maiden at the time), and a new album, *Resurrection*, which many thought to be Halford's finest effort yet in his career. Meanwhile, rumours of a Priest reformation spread.

The *Resurrection* album, released in 2000, included a duet, 'The One You Love To Hate', sung with Iron Maiden vocalist Bruce Dickinson as well as a track co-written with Priest collaborator Bob Halligan Jr. Halford's pre-production had involved discussions with Attie Bauw and Tom Allom, both with clear Judas Priest connections.

The singer's live band included drummer Bobby Jarzombek, guitarist Patrick Lachman, previously with State Of The Art and also a member of Diesel Machine, and the Polish-born axeman Mike 'Metal Mike' Chlasciak, along with ex-Dirty Blonde and Two bass player Ray Riendeau.

Rob toured as support to Iron Maiden in the UK during November and included numerous Judas Priest numbers in his live set, including 'Electric Eye', 'Riding On The Wind', 'Tyrant', and 'Running Wild'. High-profile gigging included dates in Japan, where *Resurrection* made a huge impact, reaching Number 4 in the charts. Fans at these gigs were treated to rare live versions of Priest tracks such as 'Stained Class' and 'Genocide'. When the dust settled, *Resurrection* was regarded as an undisputed success. Rumours surfaced in late 2000 of a joint project with Rob Halford, Bruce Dickinson and Geoff Tate (of Queensryche), titled The Three Tremors.

Early 2001 witnessed the double live album *Live Insurrection*. Once again produced by Roy Z, the record also included reworked studio versions of Judas Priest out-takes 'Heart Of A Lion' and 'Prisoner Of Your Eyes'. Japanese versions of the album on JVC Victor also included a version of the Scorpions' 'Blackout' with a guesting Rudolf Schenker.

Halford readied a second studio album, *Crucible*, for release in mid 2002. A batch of European summer festivals followed. Halford were also confirmed as the headline act at the 'Soyorock' festival in Kyung Gi Do, Korea during August but made a public announcement stating that Rob was to withdraw from forthcoming gigs due to exhaustion. The singer had

HALFORD discography
RESURRECTION, Metal-Is MISCD001 (UK), Metal-Is 06076 85200-2 (USA) (2000)
LIVE INSURRECTION, Metal-Is MISDD007 (UK), Metal-Is 06076 85205-2 (USA) (USA) (2001)
CRUCIBLE, Metal-Is MISCD020 (UK), Metal-Is 06076 85233-2 (USA) (2002)
Fourging The Furnace, JVC Victor VICP-62225 (Japan) (2003)

taken the unusual step of apologising in print for recent lacklustre performances. More tellingly, he publicly expressed a desire to re-unite with Judas Priest.

Halford's proposed live activities in North America in support of *Crucible* were limited to a one-off show in Las Vegas with Testament and Vio-Lence. Three shows had been planned – in Las Vegas, San Diego, and Anaheim – but were postponed at the last minute due to problems with Halford's work visa. Eventually, three shows were announced in February at House Of Blues venues in Las Vegas, West Hollywood, and Anaheim. However, Lachman exited before these gigs to concentrate on Diesel Machine and later Damageplan: his departure was announced in December 2002.

Halford's much-vaunted 'Metal Gods' 2003 North American tour included Testament, Immortal, Painmuseum, Primal Fear, Amon Amarth, and Carnal Forge for dates commencing in late April. The first three gigs saw Polish black metal veterans Behemoth along for the ride. The band parted ways with Ray Riendeau before these gigs, replacing him with erstwhile Lizzy Borden, Terriff, and Branom man Mike Davis. Fans were delighted to see Halford including rare Judas Priest moments such as 'Never Satisfied' from the 1974 *Rocka Rolla* album, the first time the track had been aired live in over 25 years.

However, fans were shocked when the entire tour, bar the initial dates, was unceremoniously pulled at short notice due to "contractual difficulties". Halford quickly rescheduled a handful of West Coast shows, with only the gig at the House Of Blues in West Hollywood on June 7th remaining from the original itinerary, taking along Testament, Painmuseum, and Leatherwolf for fill-in dates. Even these hastily regrouped shows didn't go without a hitch, as dates dropped off and Painmuseum pulled out citing "economic" reasons. Skinlab filled in for two dates.

Early July brought the news that all Priest fans had been awaiting, with the reunion of band and Halford. Although rumours and conjecture had been spreading for many years, apparently this decision was only taken weeks before the announcement. A new studio album was plotted for 2004, the band's 30th anniversary. As the reformed band settled down to write material for the new record, Rob made time to participate in a VH1 television documentary, *AIDS: A Pop Culture History*.

Despite much of 2005 being taken up with the new Judas Priest album *Angel Of Retribution* and a world tour, Rob was keen to announce a fresh Halford album, retaining Chlasciak and Roy Z. with bassist Mike Davis and drummer Jarzombek. Although Judas Priest is now very much the focus for him, it appears that demand for both Halford and Fight material will see the issue of future solo material.

A flurry of Halford releases, available exclusively through Apple's iTunes, arrived in November 2006, including: a new song, 'Forgotten Generation'; reissues of earlier albums; an expanded EP titled *Silent Screams*; and a best-of album, *Halford: Metal God Essentials – Volume 1*, featuring two new songs from the current *Halford IV* writing sessions. A DVD, *Halford – Live At Rock In Rio III*, and a new studio album, *Halford IV*, were at the time of writing scheduled for 2007 release through Rob

Halford's own label, Metal God Entertainment (MGE). With such a packed schedule, despite the singer's ongoing commitment to Judas Priest, it's clear that the Halford story is not over yet.

HELSTAR
POWER/THRASH EXPERTISE FROM THE SOUTH

HIGH-OCTANE POWER-BASED metallers Helstar, created in Houston, Texas, during 1982, came to the fore on the underground tape-trading scene with their debut 1983 demo. An early line-up consisted of ex-Deathwish and Scorcher vocalist James Rivera, guitarists Larry Barragan and Tom Rogers, bassist Paul Medina, and drummer Hector Pavan.

The impact made by the demo landed Helstar a deal with Combat in November 1983 and the resulting debut album, 1984's *Burning Star*, was produced by drummer Carl Canedy of The Rods. Oddly, Rivera went by the pseudonym Bill Lionel for this set. The original version came in a cover depicting a red-cowled wizard, but this was subsequently changed to the more familiar science fiction-based artwork. Music For Nations took the record on for the UK market. Critical reactions from the metal community were swift and unanimously positive.

During 1985, Helstar inducted new members: guitarist Rob Treviño, bass player Jerry Abarca, and drummer Rene Luna.

Following the Randy Burns-produced *Remnants Of War*, issued in Europe in 1986 through Berlin's Noise label, Helstar split from Combat and, re-locating to Los Angeles, signed a fresh deal with Metal Blade. Ructions hit the band soon afterwards, though, and Treviño and Luna opted out to make way for guitarist Andre Corbin and drummer Frank Ferreira, while Barragan quit after a row with both the band's management and his colleagues. He intended to form a new band, Betrayer, but quickly rejoined Helstar.

November 1988's *A Distant Thunder* album saw Helstar covering the Scorpions classic 'He's A Woman, She's A Man'. The record received

HELSTAR discography

BURNING STAR, Music For Nations MFN 20 (UK), Combat MX 8007 (USA) (1984)

REMNANTS OF WAR, Noise N 0043 (Europe), Combat MX 8052 (USA) (1986)

A DISTANT THUNDER, Roadrunner RR 9524-2 (UK), Metal Blade 7 73403-2 (USA) (1988)

NOSFERATU, Roadracer RO 9438-2 (Europe), Metal Blade 7 73419-2 (USA) (1989)

MULTIPLES OF BLACK, Massacre MASS CD053 (Europe) (1995)

TWAS THE NIGHT OF A HELISH X-MAS, Metal Blade 3984-14306-2 (Europe / USA) (2000)

THE JAMES RIVERA LEGACY, Iron Glory IG 1018 (Europe) (2001)

positive reviews and Helstar proceeded to tour America and Europe, opening for Tankard and Yngwie Malmsteen. On their return, the band migrated back to their native Houston, and internal frictions caused Helstar to split again.

Following the September 1989 *Nosferatu* release, Helstar cut a further demo tape consisting of 'Social Circle', 'Scalpel In The Skin', 'Sirens Of The Sun', and 'Changeless Season'. The recordings involved Rivera, Abarca, Barragan, guitarist Aaron Garza, and drummer Russell DeLeon. Soon afterwards, Barragan totally withdrew from the metal scene, finding a new calling with a Tex-Mex bar band. Helstar struggled on, playing gigs on the local circuit under a new name, Vigilante.

As Vigilante, the band members began negotiations with Megadeth bassist Dave Ellefson with the intention of recording a four-track demo with Ellefson acting as producer. Although the deal with Ellefson fell through, Vigilante recorded and released a six-song EP. However, circumstances forced their hand as, with the return of Abarca and under pressure, they reverted back to their Helstar name. After Megadeth lost a support slot with Aerosmith, Ellefson found himself with more time to work with Helstar, and the planned demo evolved into the *Multiples Of Black* album, released in 1995 on German label Massacre.

By 1998, Rivera was fronting Destiny's End for their *Breathe Deep The Dark* album. The singer founded a new act in 2000, Project Rivera, which consisted of Z-Lot-Z guitarist Eric Halpern, Mystic Cross guitarist Don LaFon, Outworld bassist Brent Marches, Victim keyboard player Adam Rawlings, and drummer Rick Ward of Midnight Circus.

In May 2000, Metal Blade released a live Helstar album, *Twas The Night Of A Helish X-mas*, which was widely criticised as an inferior-quality bootleg from an old Christmas show. The band's legacy was not ready to die yet, however, as in 2001 the Iron Glory label issued a compilation of material under the Helstar name called *The James Rivera Legacy*. The first four tracks on the compilation were the unreleased post-*Nosferatu* demo, while the last six came from the rare *Vigilante* EP.

In August 2001, Rivera joined Flotsam And Jetsam, after their longstanding vocalist Eric A.K. departed, and then teamed up with Seven Witches, debuting with the band at the 'Classic Metal Fest II' in Cleveland, Ohio, in July.

An all-new act with strong Helstar ties was announced in August 2003 as James Rivera and Destiny's End guitarist Eric Halpern united with Symphony X bassist Mike Lepond in Distant Thunder. The resulting album in 2004, *Welcome The End*, included a re-working of Helstar's 'Run With The Pack'. Distant Thunder undertook an extensive round of European headline shows in December, although by the time the shows were booked they were under the Helstar name once again. Meanwhile, guitarists Larry Barragan and Rob Trevino alongside drummer Russell

Helstar

DeLeon founded Eternity Black. A five-song demo, recorded at Spyder Studios with producer Gregg Gill, emerged in early 2005.

In mid 2005 it was reported that James Rivera was contributing to the Dawnrider project assembled by Majesty mentor Tarek 'Metal Son' Maghary. The singer, keeping up his road miles with tribute band Sabbath Judas Sabbath, joined Vicious Rumors in September. Retaining this post, as well as his duties in Killing Machine, Rivera was seen fronting a Helstar reunion in May 2006. The singer was joined by the *Remnants Of War* roster: guitarists Larry Barragan and Rob Treviño, bassist Jerry Abarca, and drummer Russell DeLeon. And so Helstar soldier on.

ICED EARTH
MUSICALLY DEXTEROUS, FULLY-COMMITTED US METAL

THE INTENSE, NO-COMPROMISE METAL purveyed by Iced Earth has allowed the band to rise from an obscure mid-1980s indie act to a position of prestige in mainland Europe. Musically, Iced Earth have developed from their formative power/thrash to more refined, yet still heavy, melodic metal identified by Jon Schaffer's galloping rhythm guitar.

Iced Earth began life in Indiana in 1984 as Purgatory, with a teenage line-up of vocalist Gene Adam, guitarists Schaffer and Bill Owen, bassist Dave Abell, and drummer Greg Seymour. Schaffer, a native of Franklin, Indiana, built the project, and it was his resolution that provided stability in the coming years. Another ex-Purgatory man, bassist Richard Bateman, made a fleeting appearance at this early juncture: he later came to prominence in Agent Steel and Nasty Savage. As Purgatory, the band released two demo cassettes: the four-track *Burning Oasis* and *Psychotic Dreams*, comprising 'Jack' and 'In Jason's Mind'. Further recordings came in the form of the *Horror Show* demo in 1986, featuring a new composition, 'Dracula', and reworkings of 'Jack' and 'In Jason's Mind'. However, the band opted for a name change once they had been alerted to a Cleveland outfit also called Purgatory.

At this point, Iced Earth were a shock-rock outfit, wearing cassocks on stage and dousing their audience in liver and blood as part of the theatrics. Thankfully, these tactics were soon discarded as they concentrated on their music. Iced Earth's first official effort was the tape that secured their career and landed them a deal with Germany's Century Media label – the *Enter The Realm* demo, comprising 'Colors', 'Enter The Realm', 'Nightmares', To Curse The Sky', 'Solitude', and 'Iced Earth'. The band also made an appearance on the *Metal Mercenaries* compilation with a song produced by ex-Savatage bassist Keith Collins.

A Tom Morris-produced self-titled album arrived on the European market in November 1990 and was granted a US release some three months later. *Iced Earth* originally sported artwork depicting a falling angel, and these first pressings later became collector's pieces. While they garnered praise for their riffs and songwriting, the bulk of which was a collaboration between Schaffer and Randall Shawver, the band saw the record draw criticism for Adam's rasped vocal style and its below-par sound quality. Seymour was briefly replaced by Mike McGill for a European tour, after which McGill was unceremoniously fired and the band brought in Richie Sechiarri.

The second release, *Night Of The Stormrider* – cut at Fullersound Studios, once again with Tom Morris at the board – saw John Greely assuming the role of frontman, although predictably his tenure was short. The production of this firmly thrash-orientated second offering was a vast improvement over the debut, greatly improving the band's prospects. *Night Of The Stormrider* was issued in Europe in 1991, but once again US fans had to wait, this time until April 1992.

April 1995's *Burnt Offerings* featured Rodney Beasley on drums and new vocalist Matt Barlow, a man who gave Iced Earth a degree of stability as well as an instantly recognisable vocal and visual presence. Prior to joining them, Barlow had fronted the Florida act Cauldron, a band that included Pessimist guitarist Kelly McLauchlin. With *Burnt Offerings*, laid down at the famous Morrisound complex in Tampa, Schaffer took on co-production responsibilities alongside Tom Morris to craft another unrelenting thrash barrage with a more menacing stance than its predecessors. Iced Earth played in Germany in June 1995 as part of the 'Summer Metal Meetings' festivals alongside Running Wild, Gamma Ray, Grave Digger, Rage, and Glenmore.

For the groundbreaking *The Dark Saga* of 1996, Iced Earth shed their thrash leanings for a drop in pace and employed the services of studio engineer Mark Prator on drums. The album was based on a concept from Todd McFarlane's *Spawn* comic book, with vocal embellishments on 'A Question Of Heaven' by Barlow's sister Kate. Digipack versions added a bonus cut – a rendition of Judas Priest's 'The Ripper'. Abell quit soon after this release; Keith Menser featured in the accompanying photo, despite going no further with the band.

Days Of Purgatory, released in 1997, was a collection of reworked tracks from the band's *Enter The Realm* demo and cuts from the first two albums. Drums came courtesy of Oracle's Brent Smedley. In 1998 the band relocated from Florida to Indiana and put in a triumphant performance at the German 'Wacken Open Air' festival as the *Something Wicked This Way Comes* album, issued in June, cracked the German charts at Number 19. For this album, Prator once again manned the drums and the 19-year-old prodigy Larry Tarnowski replaced Shawver. James MacDonough – a Florida scene veteran of Delta 9, Invader, Oracle, and Brutal Assault – then arrived on bass guitar. Somewhat inconsistently, minus Shawver's songwriting contributions, the record jumped between the classic and the mundane. Undoubtedly it attracted a sizeable set of new fans, but also it confused the more loyal devotees.

ICED EARTH discography

ICED EARTH, Century Media 84 9714-2 (Europe) (1990), Century Media CM 7714-2 (USA) (1991)

NIGHT OF THE STORMRIDER, Century Media 84 9727-2 (Europe) (1991), Century Media CM 7727-2 (USA) (1992)

BURNT OFFERINGS, Century Media CM 77093-2 (Europe), Century Media CM 7793-2 (USA) (1995)

THE DARK SAGA, Century Media CM 77131-2 (Europe), Century Media CM 7831-2 (USA) (1996)

DAYS OF PURGATORY, Century Media CM 77165-2 (Europe), Century Media CM 7865-2 (USA) (1997)

SOMETHING WICKED THIS WAY COMES, Century Media CM 77214-2 (Europe), Century Media CM 7914-2 (USA) (1998)

ALIVE IN ATHENS, Century Media CM 77275-2 (Europe), Century Media CM 7975-2 (USA) (1999)

The Melancholy E.P., Century Media CM 77327-2 (Europe) (2000)

HORROR SHOW, Century Media CM 77305-2 (Europe), Century Media CM 8005-2 (USA) (2001)

TRIBUTE TO THE GODS, Century Media CM 77406-2 (Europe), Century Media CM 8106-2 (USA) (2002)

The Reckoning, Steamhammer SPV 056-74983 (Europe / USA) (2003)

THE GLORIOUS BURDEN, Steamhammer SPV 085-74972 (Europe), Hunter 74972 (USA) (2004) **145 USA**

THE BLESSED AND THE DAMNED, Century Media CM 77506-2 (Europe), Century Media CM 8206-2 (USA) (2004)

A stopgap 1999 release, the *Melancholy* mini-album, included cover versions of Bad Company's 'Shooting Star' and Black Sabbath's 'Electric Funeral'.

The triple album *Alive In Athens*, recorded in front of 120,000 fans, landed Iced Earth a Greek Number 1. The line-up for this opus consisted of Barlow, Schaffer, Tarnowski, Opposite Earth's Rick Risberg on keyboards, and the returning Brent Smedley. Schaffer's side project Demons & Wizards, a union with Blind Guardian's Hansi Kürsch, also blew the European charts wide open, giving the guitarist a second chart-topper in Greece. Demons & Wizards' success interrupted the Iced Earth schedule as Schaffer's new combo toured on the festival circuit with Control Denied/Death drummer Richard Christy.

By mid 2000, again without a permanent drummer as Smedley had opted out to form Tempest Reign, Iced Earth pulled in Christy for live commitments. Christy also found time to commit to his side-project band Burning Inside with Acheron's Michael Estes and Black Witchery's Steve Childers.

Iced Earth's June 2001 *Horror Show* album found Christy officially inducted into the ranks along with guest bassist Steve DiGiorgio, formerly of Death and Sadus. As its title suggests, *Horror Show* featured songs devoted to movie anti-heroes such as the Werewolf, Dracula, and Frankenstein and included a cover of the Iron Maiden instrumental 'Transylvania'. The album saw the band topping the Greek national charts yet again and gave them improved European chart positions in most territories. The *Melancholy* mini-album was expanded and reissued, adding a cover of Judas Priest's 'The Ripper'. MacDonough returned to the Iced Earth clan as touring bassist in mid 2001.

Touring possibilities in America stepped up significantly for the band when they were announced as openers to the Judas Priest and Anthrax tour. However, the terrorist attacks on the United States on September 11th resulted in the cancellation of the entire tour.

Rounding up the band's efforts to date, Century Media weighed in with the gargantuan *Dark Genesis* boxed set to close 2001. The lavish package contained remastered versions of early albums, the *Enter The Realm* demo, plus a bonus tribute disc, *Tribute To The Gods*.

The tribute disc was released separately during 2002 and saw Iced Earth taking on 'Creatures Of The Night' and 'God Of Thunder' by Kiss, 'Number Of The Beast' and 'Hallowed Be Thy Name' by Iron Maiden, 'Highway To Hell' and 'It's A Long Way To The Top' by AC/DC, 'Burnin' For You' and 'Cities On Flame (With Rock'n'Roll)' from Blue Oyster Cult, 'Screaming For Vengeance' by Judas Priest, 'Dead Babies' by Alice Cooper, and Black Sabbath's 'Black Sabbath'.

The band's headlining 'Feel The Horror' European tour commenced in Hardenberg, Holland on January 17th 2002. A run of US dates then kicked off on April 8th at the Everson Theater in Indianapolis. There was strong support on these shows from Colorado label mates Jag Panzer and Swedish melodic death metallers In Flames.

In late 2002, Richard Christy sessioned on demos for Wykked Wytch. The drummer was also a participant in a new side venture billed as Leash Law, an alliance with Wicked Ways and Rob Rock guitarist Rick Renstrom, bassist Steve Eldar, plus Crimson Glory and Seven Witches singer Wade Black. Meanwhile, Iced Earth, signing to SPV, set *The Glorious Burden* as the title of a forthcoming new studio album. Just before the recording, the band severed ties with guitarist Larry Tarnowski.

Iced Earth fans were shocked to learn that longstanding singer Matt Barlow had opted out of the band in June 2003, a decision apparently taken as far back as December the previous year. The vocalist left to pursue a bachelor's degree in Criminal Justice Administration. Press statements revealed that Barlow's vocals on *The Glorious Burden* would be wiped and a new vocalist found to complete the album. Meanwhile, the prolific Eyewitness, Millennium, and Monarch guitarist Ralph Santolla, having previously sessioned for the band, was announced as a new member.

By July, it was revealed that the new Iced Earth singer was none other than former Judas Priest frontman Tim 'Ripper' Owens. Although Schaffer initially sounded cautious about the exact status of Owens, a subsequent official release confirmed that the singer had joined the band. With the release of *Burden*, the general consensus among the global metal fraternity was that Owens had surpassed even his performances with Judas Priest, but opinion was sharply divided as to the merits of the themes threaded through the record – which involved the Declaration of Independence, the Revolutionary War, and the American Civil War. Overall, the concept succeeded: *The Glorious Burden* broke into the *Billboard* charts at Number 145, selling 8,626 copies in its first week of release and charting healthily across Europe.

Tim 'Ripper' Owens: "It took a lot for me to sing The Glorious Burden. Firstly, because I knew that Matt had sung it before, and Matt's a great singer, but also because the whole idea of the album was so heartfelt and emotional. It's not your regular comic-book heavy metal album; there is a lot on there that goes right to the very essence of what it is to be an American, so this was a huge undertaking. Also, of course, I knew that this was Jon Schaffer's biggest risk too, so absolutely everything about this had to be exactly right. I think I repaid the faith Jon showed in me because I really gave it my all and I'm damn proud of it. Is it better than what I did with Judas Priest? Yes it is!"

In outside activity, Santolla featured as guest soloist for 'Forgotten Demise' on Toronto Metal outfit Warmachine's 2004 debut *The Beginning Of The End*. European mainland gigs for Iced Earth in 2004 saw the group uniting with high profile acts Thunderstone and Primal Fear.

Unfortunately, these gigs were postponed when Schaffer had to undergo surgery for a lower back problem. An extensive North American trek throughout April and May had the band partnered with Children Of Bodom and Evergrey. Richard Christy bailed out mid-tour, and Iced Earth drafted in Bobby Jarzombek of San Antonio Slayer, Riot, Spastic Ink, and Halford. Japanese dates were set to follow but shows scheduled for late May in Tokyo and Osaka were pulled due to Christy's departure. The band returned for a second North American leg throughout the summer with Trivium and Beyond The Embrace.

In related news, the former Iced Earth team of vocalist Gene Adam, bassist Dave Abell, and Mark Prator on drums, along with guitarist Bill Owen of the pre-Iced Earth group Purgatory, forged a new band – tentatively and wryly dubbed Unearthed. The group cut a two-song demo comprising 'Fire In The Sky' and 'Unearthed'.

Santolla left Iced Earth in June, promptly joining Sebastian Bach's solo band alongside another erstwhile Iced Earth man, drummer Mark Prator. The guitarist revealed future plans for a concept album, Ex Cathedra, in a proposed alliance with bassist DiGiorgio, Gene Hoglan of Strapping Young Lad, Dark Angel, and Death, and Tom Englund from Evergrey.

Iced Earth's August 2004 compilation set, The Blessed And The Damned, featured two discs of remastered tracks clad in an elaborate piece of artwork from Russian artist Leo Hao, constructed to allow the purchaser to choose angels or demons for the front cover. In September, bassist James MacDonough opted out to join Megadeth. Meanwhile, the ex-Iced Earth quota of Sebastian Bach's band increased as Steve DiGiorgio joined the fold. Tim Owens used the Iced Earth demos to cut solo demo tracks with producer Jim Morris at Morrisound Studios in Florida.

In November, Santolla made a public statement revealing that he was suffering from a degenerative condition in the bones of his jaw. Costly treatment would include bone grafts and reconstructive surgery and, to offset some of the medical bills, a benefit concert in Tampa, Florida, headlined by Sebastian Bach was scheduled for January 2005.

That same month, Bobby Jarzombek laid down drums for a new Demons & Wizards album. Tim Owens used Jarzombek's services when he tracked solo material with 13 Faces and Spawn guitarist John Comprix, billed as Beyond Fear. The singer also lent vocals to a version of Black Sabbath's 'War Pigs' included on the Michael Schenker Heavy Hitters album. In May, Sebastian Bach's ties to Iced Earth were strengthened still further when he recruited Jarzombek onto the drum stool. Meantime, ex-Iced Earth man Ralph Santolla joined Deicide.

In mid 2005, Jon Schaffer was ready to reveal his ambitions for the next Iced Earth opus. Once again featuring Tim Owens on vocals, the guitarist's vision called for a conclusion to the saga of Something Wicked This Way Comes. Fans wait with bated breath.

KING DIAMOND
CORPSEPAINT AND THAT FEMUR MICROPHONE

IN APRIL 1985 THE CULT BLACK metal band Mercyful Fate split, and vocalist King Diamond (real name Kim Bendix Petersen) regrouped with Fate's guitarist Michael Denner and bassist Timi G. Hansen (formerly known as Timi Grabber) with a new self-titled band. The other original band members were ex-Nadir and Geisha drummer Mikkey Dee (real surname Delaoglou) and guitarist Floyd Konstantin, the latter superseded by former Trafalger and EF Band guitarist Andy LaRocque (Anders Allhage). This new recruit became Diamond's longstanding collaborator and the only point of stability alongside the singer throughout the band's history.

King Diamond's first release was the rather strange 12-inch single, 'No Presents For Christmas', launched on Christmas Day 1985. The US cover depicted him in full make-up with Rudolf the reindeer peering over his shoulder.

King concentrated his efforts mainly on North America, where Mercyful Fate had built a strong and loyal following. The debut album, Fatal Portrait, was produced by Rune Höyer and issued in February 1986 through Roadrunner. It echoed his former band, but had the Satanic element stripped out, replaced with overblown horror theatrics. Fatal Portrait hung on a story involving the return of a spirit named Molly, a young girl imprisoned in an attic. The lyrical shift was a wise one, as previously King had been exposed for his lack of understanding of Satanism and the occult themes of Mercyful Fate. The album landed impressively at Number 33 on the Swedish charts.

KING DIAMOND discography

No Presents For Christmas, Roadrunner RR 125485 (Europe), Roadracer RR 125485 (USA) (1985)

FATAL PORTRAIT, Roadrunner RR 9721 (Europe), Greenworld/Roadracer GWD90529 (USA) (1986)

Halloween, Roadrunner RR 65484 (Europe), Greenworld/Roadrunner GWP90559 (USA) (1986) 12-inch vinyl picture disc EP

The Family Ghost, Roadrunner RR 125476 (Europe), Roadracer RR 125476 (USA) (1987)

ABIGAIL, Roadrunner RR 9622 (Europe), Roadracer RRD 9622 (USA) (1987) **123 USA**

The Dark Sides, Roadrunner RR 2455-2 (Europe), Roadracer RRD 2455 (USA) (1988)

THEM, Roadrunner RR 9550-2 (Europe), Roadracer RRD 9550 (USA) (1988) **89 USA**

CONSPIRACY, Roadrunner RR 9461-2 (Europe), Roadracer RRD 9461 (USA) (1989) **111 USA**

THE EYE, Roadrunner RR 9346-2 (Europe), Roadracer RRD 9346 (USA) (1990) **179 USA**

IN CONCERT 1987 – ABIGAIL, Roadrunner RR 9287-2 (Europe), Roadracer RRD 9287 (USA) (1990)

A DANGEROUS MEETING, Roadrunner RR 9117-2 (Europe), Roadrunner RRD 9117 (USA) (1992) split album with Mercyful Fate

THE SPIDER'S LULLABYE, Massacre MASS CD0062 (Europe), Metal Blade P2 53965 (USA) (1995)

THE GRAVEYARD, Massacre MAS CD0103 (Europe), Metal Blade P2 50587 (USA) (1996)

VOODOO, Massacre MAS CD0155 (Europe), Metal Blade 3984-14149-2 (USA) (1998)

HOUSE OF GOD, Massacre MAS CD0233 (Europe), Metal Blade 3984-14308-2 (USA) (2000)

KING DIAMOND AND BLACK ROSE: 20 YEARS AGO – A NIGHT OF REHEARSAL, Metal Blade 3984-14359-2 (USA) (2001)

NIGHTMARES IN THE NINETIES – AN INTRODUCTION TO THE ARTIST, Massacre MAS CD0285 (Europe) (2001)

ABIGAIL II – THE REVENGE, Metal Blade 3984-14379-2 (Europe / USA) (2002)

THE PUPPET MASTER, Massacre MAS DP0400 (Europe), Metal Blade 3984-14445-2 (USA) (2003)

DEADLY LULLABYES – LIVE, Massacre MAS DP0415 (Europe), Metal Blade 3984-14499-2 (USA) (2004)

The second album, *Abigail*, released in June 1987, was self-produced and cut at Sound Track Studios in Copenhagen. The record was themed on the tale of Abigail, the ghost of a child murdered by Count de la Fey on July 7th 1777. After *Abigail*, Denner left due to the pressure of constant touring and was replaced by ex-Madison guitarist Michael 'Moon' Myllynen.

They toured the album in America with Chicago doom metal band Trouble before undertaking 15 shows in Germany opening for Motörhead as well as headlining shows. The hard graft of touring paid off and in North America *Abigail* reached Number 123 in the *Billboard* charts, selling over 150,000 copies.

Prior to recording the next album, *Them* – which referred to a malevolent body of spirits – Diamond relocated to Los Angeles in order to attempt success in the American market. The band replaced Myllynen and Timi Hansen with ex-Geisha guitarist Pete Blakk (Peter Jacobsson) and bassist Hal Patino.

Them, another conceptual affair, appeared in July 1988 and bolstered the success of King Diamond in America by charting in the Top 100. Touring plans were initially shelved to allow the band to contribute soundtrack music to the horror movie *Boggs*. An EP was issued in October, *The Dark Sides*, intended to keep King Diamond's name in the public eye. The EP also caught the attention of Kiss singer Gene Simmons, who objected to King's face-paint, claiming that it was too close to his patented design, known to millions across the world. An out-of-court settlement was reached and King was obliged to alter his design.

After the recording of *Them*, drummer Mikkey Dee quit, later to work with Don Dokken and WWIII before landing a permanent place in Motörhead. He was replaced with San Francisco musician Chris Whitemeier, previously a drum tech for Whitesnake's Tommy Aldridge. Dee played on August 1989's *Conspiracy*, which continued the plot of *Them*, but the subsequent tour featured Swedish drummer Snowy Shaw. With its production credits shared between Chris Tsangarides, Andy LaRocque and Roberto Falcao, the album scored respectably on the US charts.

More line-up changes befell the group during the recording of October 1990's *The Eye*. The story hinged on a time-transporting pendant worn by the executed witch Jeanne Dibasson. Although Shaw was in the studio, the band also used a drum machine. Once the album was finished, both Blakk and Patino were shown the door, with the ousted guitarist duly forging Totem Pole (later to become known as Blakk Totem). King Diamond drafted in guitar player Mike Wead, previously with Hexenhaus, Memento Mori, and Abstrakt Algebra, and bassist Sharlee D'Angelo (aka Charles Andreason).

The continuous flux in personnel and friction with their record company came to a head, and the singer ended his long-term association with Roadrunner with the *In Concert 1987 – Abigail* live album in 1991. Around the turn of the decade King chose to reform Mercyful Fate, bowing back in with an August 1993 album *In The Shadows*, followed by *Time* in October 1994. From this juncture onwards, Diamond led a public double life, alternating between King Diamond and Mercyful Fate albums and tours.

The singer switched back to King Diamond, adding a new complement of members for *The Spider's Lullabye* in June 1995. *Lullabye* found Diamond weaving a tale located in Devil Lake Sanitarium and involving treatment for insanity by spider-bite. An American rhythm section were delegated for these sessions – ex-Atrox and Mindstorm bassist Chris Estes and Mindstorm drummer Darrin Anthony. The album was a solid success, charting in Sweden, Denmark, and Finland, and was the first for new label Massacre.

Mercyful Fate released *Into The Unknown* in August 1996, with a further King Diamond record appearing just weeks later. *The Graveyard*

related the woes of a lunatic seeking sanctuary in a cemetery and was once again constructed at Sound Lab Studios in Dallas, Texas. Estes and Anthony were re-employed while Herb Simonsen handled guitar. In late 1997, Roadrunner reissued the King Diamond back catalogue in remastered form, with some albums featuring additional bonus tracks. Meanwhile, Shaw, D'Angelo, and La Rocque founded Illwill and released a 1998 album, *Evilution*.

February 1998's King Diamond album *Voodoo*, another horror conceptual effort, saw King and LaRocque – who had produced the debut album by Sweden's Midvinter during 1997 – joined by second guitarist Herb Simonsen, bassist Estes and Chastain drummer John Luke Herbert. The latter superseded Anthony, who had been put out of action after a serious car accident. *Voodoo* had started life with the working title *The Plague* but was steered towards the black magic of the US Southern states after research by Estes. Pantera guitarist 'Dimebag' Darrell lent a solo to the title track.

The band added Canadian guitarist Glen Drover from the highly rated Eidolon for tours across the USA in April and May 1998. King then diverted his attention to the next Mercyful Fate offering, *Dead Again*, launched in June. Mercyful Fate again captured King's attention into the following year with the *9* album.

Diamond put in a rare guest appearance for Chicago death metal combo Usurper, appearing on the title track of their album *Necronemesis*. Drover plus new bass player Dave Harbour subsequently appeared on the June 2000 King Diamond album *House Of God*, these tracks laid down at Nomad Recording Studio in Carrollton, Texas. Former bassist Hal Patino returned to the ranks in 2000, ousting David Harbour.

With King Diamond signing to Metal Blade for North America and Massacre for Europe in 2002, Massacre were quick to issue a compilation, *Nightmare In The Nineties*. The King then contributed vocals to Dave Grohl's *Probot* album of 2001, singing on 'Sweet Dreams'.

Metal Blade released *King Diamond And Black Rose 20 Years Ago (A Night Of Rehearsal)*, an archive collection of unedited live demo tracks from one of Diamond's earliest acts, Black Rose. With the inclusion of a Golden Earring cover, 'Radar Love', the album displayed King's early blues-rock roots, giving fans a rare chance to hear the singer in regular voice, minus his trademark falsetto.

The year 2002 proved an eventful one for King Diamond, with a rare admission that album sales were on the downturn, despite a well-received studio record, *Abigail II: The Revenge*, released in January 2002. The band placed the blame squarely on internet filesharing and advised fans that they would start recording a new album, *The Puppet Master*, at King's home studio to save on recording costs. The recording of the album also took place at Los Angered Recording in Gothenburg, Sweden, Nomad Recording Studios in Dallas, Texas, and Solna Sound Recording in Sweden. According to initial reports, *The Puppet Master* – a conceptual horror piece set against a background of Budapest – would be the most controversial King Diamond outing yet.

Before its release in 2003, King Diamond – with Matt Thompson of Autumn Silence, Shaolin Death Squad, and Bat Castle on the drums – returned to touring in North America with guests Entombed, Nocturne, and Single Bullet Theory. Meanwhile, Diamond prepared a long overdue live album, *Deadly Lullabyes Live*, mixed at LaRocque's Los Angered studio outside Gothenburg. September saw the announcement that ex-King Diamond guitarist Glen Drover had entered the big league by joining Megadeth.

King Diamond scheduled US tour dates for April 2005 with Nile, Poles Behemoth, and Detroit's Black Dahlia Murder. European gigs in Italy and Spain were planned for April and May 2006. The concert at the Kåren venue in Gothenburg on April 21st memorably featured Motörhead drummer Mikkey Dee, King Diamond's original skinsman, performing

'Halloween' during the encore. The King is now a legend in his own right: respect is due.

MASTERPLAN
POST-HELLOWEEN METAL DEXTERITY

MASTERPLAN IS THE HIGH-PROFILE post-Helloween endeavour of guitarist Roland Grapow and drummer Uli Kusch. The pair severed ties with Helloween in acrimonious circumstances in late 2001, at first calling their new venture Mr. Torture. The highly rated Norwegian singer Jørn Lande filled the vocalist position; Lande is a veteran of Yngwie Malmsteen, Ark, Millenium, and Mundanus Imperium. He was a session man for Beyond Twilight's 2001 opus *The Devil's Hall Of Fame*, and as a solo artist billed as Jorn had issued *Starfire* in 2000 and *Worldchanger* in October 2001. Iron Savior man Jan S. Eckert was on bass and the Finnish keyboard player Janne Warman (Children Of Bodom, Warmen) made up the ranks. This formidable collection of talents assured the band a weighty reception.

They debuted with an EP, *Enlighten Me*. Issued through Andy Allendörfer of Squealer's AFM label in November 2002, the single debuted on the German charts at a startling Number 15. The self-titled debut album, released in January 2003 through AFM and produced by Andy Sneap, included a cover of Led Zeppelin's 'Black Dog' and a duet between Lande and erstwhile Helloween vocalist Michael Kiske on 'Heroes'. Japanese versions, released by the Avalon Marquee label, differed from European issues by replacing 'Enlighten Me' and 'Bleeding Eyes' with 'Through Thick And Thin' and 'The Kid Rocks On'. Masterplan had their version of 'Black Dog' included on the Locomotive Music Led Zeppelin tribute album *The Metal Zeppelin – The Music Remains The Same*.

Grapow and Kusch took a sizable contingent of the Helloween fanbase with them and *Masterplan* was a robust opener, chock-full of high-quality material. From strong initial sales across Europe, the new band quickly built up a solid fanbase across the world, with particular appreciation in South America. Importantly, *Masterplan* placed Lande's vocal prowess, a heady blend of classic blues and thundering power, onto a larger world platform.

A sustained bout of European touring had Masterplan confirmed as support for Hammerfall's forthcoming January and February 2003 European trek. However, the band saw its first casualty before this when Janne Warman pulled out in September 2002, unable to participate due to commitments with Children Of Bodom. A replacement was swiftly found in Axel Mackenrott from Catch The Rainbow and Punch TV. Amid all this activity, Grapow made time to guest on the MVP album *The Altar*, released in 2003, and produce the debut album *Prism* from Hamburg act Arctic Fields. Kusch loaned himself out to Iron Savior for a one-off gig in August 2002 when their regular drummer Thomas Nack injured his hand before the group's appearance at the 'Wacken' festival.

Lande then signed a solo deal with AFM, recording a third solo outing (again billed as Jorn) titled *Out To Every Nation* in the summer of 2003. Musicians on this opus included bassist Magnus Rosén of Hammerfall alongside the Pagan's Mind pairing of guitarist Jörn Viggo Lofstad and

drummer Stian Kristoffersen. *Out To Every Nation*, released in 2004, charted in both Norway and Sweden.

As the members of Masterplan set to work on a second album, the band were honoured with a European Border Breakers Award – in recognition of the highest sales for a debut album across the European Union – at the January 2004 Midem convention in Cannes, France. That same year, Grapow would guest on the all-star *Execution* album in 2005, assembled by Renato Tribuzy, vocalist of Brazilian act Thoten. He appeared on two tracks, 'Absolution' and 'Web Of Life'.

Masterplan entered Crazy Cat Studios in Hamburg, Germany with producer Andy Sneap in July to cut their second album, *Aeronautics*. A preceding EP, *Back For My Life*, was released in November 2004 and included non-album tracks 'Killing In Time' and 'Love Is A Rock'. Fans of Brazilian band Shaman attending their November 20th show in Martin, Slovakia received a surprise when Grapow guested on stage, featuring on 'Pride' and a cover of Judas Priest's 'Breaking The Law'. Axel Mackenrott also got in on the sessions, performing on Nevermore's *This Godless Endeavour*.

European shows in 2005 saw Masterplan sharing stages with an 'Aces High' package featuring Rob Rock, Circle II Circle, and Pure Inc. Kusch then instigated a new band, Beautiful Sin; a debut album, *The Unexpected*, was set for May 2006 release through AFM. That same month, Masterplan fans received a shock when, in the midst of songwriting sessions, Lande quit, quoting "musical differences". After he left, Lande still performed live with Masterplan for touring commitments, making his final appearance with the band at the Lokersefeesten on August 8th 2006 in Belgium. He was eventually replaced in October 2006 by vocalist Mike DiMeo (previously with Riot and The Lizards).

Drummer Uli Kusch left Masterplan in October 2006 and was replaced by Mike Terrana, a man with a wealth of high-profile credentials with the likes of Yngwie Malmsteen, Axel Rudi Pell, Metalium, and Rage. Despite these recent line-up shuffles, the band remain hotly tipped for the future.

NEVERMORE
MUCH-PRAISED METAL STALWARTS

The Seattle-based technical metal outfit Nevermore were created in 1992 by ex-Sanctuary vocalist Warrel Dane, guitarist Jeff Loomis, bassist Jim Sheppard, and drummer Mark Arrington.

Sanctuary had come to prominence with the inclusion of two demo cuts on the *Northwest Metalfest* compilation. Immediately apparent was that vocalist Dane, a former member of Serpent's Knight, was in possession of one of the most powerful voices on the metal scene. Sheppard had previously been a member of local glam band Sleze, an outfit fronted by a pre-Alice In Chains Layne 'Candy' Staley, and Loomis had been with Experiment Fear.

Sanctuary's first made their mark with a 1986 demo, which scored them a deal with Epic. The debut album, 1987's *Refuge Denied* – produced by Megadeth main man Dave Mustaine – featured a weighty cover of Jefferson Airplane's acid classic 'White Rabbit', which featured Mustaine's guitar parts on the intro. Dane's prior act, Serpent's Knight, had covered the same track on a 1983 demo.

Sanctuary proceeded to tour Europe as support to Megadeth before recording the equally impressive Howard Benson-produced *Into The Mirror Black*, recorded at Sound City in Van Nuys, California, and issued in February 1990. The group had built an international reputation but fell foul of Epic's withdrawal of support, and they folded.

Nevermore's initial 1992 demos, *Utopia*, kindled the interest of renowned producer Neil Kernon, who offered his services for further recordings in 1994. The resulting tapes landed Nevermore a deal with Germany's Century Media. Kernon continued his relationship with the

---

MASTERPLAN discography

Enlighten Me, AFM/Painful Lust PLCD0075 (Europe) (2002)
MASTERPLAN, AFM AFM 061-2 (Europe) (2003)
Back For My Life, AFM AFM 0845 (Europe) (2004)
AERONAUTICS, AFM AFM 084-2 (Europe), Candlelight USA 128 (USA) (2005)

NEVERMORE discography

NEVERMORE, Century Media CM 77091-2 (Europe), Century Media CM 7791-2 (USA) (1995)

In Memory, Century Media CM 77121-2 (Europe), Century Media CM 7821-2 (USA) (1995)

THE POLITICS OF ECSTASY, Century Media CM 77132-2 (Europe), Century Media CM 7832-2 (USA) (1996)

DREAMING NEON BLACK, Century Media CM 77191-2 (Europe), Century Media CM 7891-2 (USA) (1999)

DEAD HEART IN A DEAD WORLD, Century Media CM 77310-2 (Europe), Century Media CM 8010-2 (USA) (2000)

Believe In Nothing, Century Media CM 773143 (Europe) (2000) limited edition CD EP 1,500 copies

ENEMIES OF REALITY, Century Media CM 77410-2 (Europe), Century Media CM 8110-2 (USA) (2003)

THIS GODLESS ENDEAVOR, Century Media CM 77510-2 (Europe), Century Media CM 8210-2 (USA) (2005)

band, producing extra tracks at Robert Lang Studios in Seattle to make up their eponymous February 1995 debut. Drums on this effort were shared between Mark Arrington and new member Van Williams. Rave reviews followed, and Nevermore, now augmenting their line-up with second guitarist Pat O'Brien, set out touring America alongside Death.

It was during this tour that Dane's famously long hair nearly proved to be his undoing. He fell drunkenly asleep next to the wheel of the band's truck, and a roadie drove off without realising that the singer was present. Dane's mane caught in the axle of the vehicle and it dragged him 30 yards down the road; for the rest of the dates the vocalist had to walk with the aid of sticks. Later dates, with Dane thankfully recovered, saw the band supporting Blind Guardian in Germany, winding up a world tour by appearing before 100,000 people at the prestigious 'Dynamo Festival' in Holland.

A limited-edition EP followed in July, *In Memory*, recorded by Neil Kernon at Village Productions in Tornillo, Texas. It included radical reworks of Bauhaus's 'Silent Hedges' segued with 'Double Dare'.

Nevermore's second full-length album, the compellingly cynical *The Politics Of Ecstasy* – named after the Timothy Leary book – arrived in July 1996. By this stage, Germany had succumbed to Nevermore's brand of technical thrash, although as yet their name meant little outside mainland Europe. In late 1997, following a European tour alongside fellow Americans Iced Earth, O'Brien joined goremongers Cannibal Corpse. His position was taken by former Forbidden axeman Tim Calvert. During 1998, Nevermore toured North America with Flotsam And Jetsam before further European shows with Overkill.

The third album, *Dreaming Neon Black*, was released in January 1999. Poignantly, the record's concept was based on the disappearance of Dane's girlfriend, who had been involved in a religious cult. The album story threads through a tortuous journey ending in suicide, although in reality Dane's erstwhile friend's fate remains unknown. The outpouring of emotion from Dane on this record had fans hailing *Dreaming Neon Black* as a classic. However, the band had merely set the stage: better was still to come.

Nevermore trimmed to a quartet after the loss of Calvert for *Dead Heart In A Dead World*. The album, produced by Andy Sneap, saw a return to Village Productions in Texas during July 2000 and included a twisted interpretation of Simon & Garfunkel's 'The Sound Of Silence'.

On its issue in September, *Dead Heart* became the first Nevermore record to make its mark on the charts, scoring a Number 57 entry in Germany. With sales sustained, a subsequent reissue added three extra tracks – 'All The Cowards Hide', 'Chances Three', and the band's take on

Judas Priest's 'Love Bites'. That Priest cover was generally regarded as the standout on a Century Media tribute album to Birmingham's finest.

The band, now with second guitar supplied by Aggression Core man Curran Murphy, toured America the same year, sharing a package bill with Fates Warning and Planet X. A September 2001 run of dates in America would find Nevermore as guests to Savatage. The band put in a further burst of dates as headliners, kicking off at the L'Amour venue in Brooklyn, New York City, on November 23rd. Guests for these dates were Overkill and Scar Culture.

During November, guitarist Curran Murphy bailed out to join Canadians Annihilator. In early 2002, drummer Van Williams unveiled details of his Pure Sweet Hell side endeavour: a six-track demo featured Williams joined by Christ Eichhorn on guitar, bass and keyboards. The pair strengthened the Nevermore connection by enlisting Loomis to lay down a solo on 'Faded', while Curran Murphy appeared on 'Shadow'.

Nevermore drafted in ex-Vicious Rumors, Testament, and Dragonlord guitarist Steve Smyth to fill the vacancy left by Murphy for European dates and selected gigs on the US 'Vans Warped' tour, a first for a metal act, as this festival is usually confined to punk and punk-related bands. However, the dates were subsequently cancelled. Meanwhile, the band provided two live tracks, 'Engines Of Hate' and 'Beyond Within' – recorded at the Hollywood Roxy in September of 2001 – as part of the Century Media tenth anniversary DVD. The band also cut a rendition of 'Ride The Lightning' for a Nuclear Blast Metallica tribute collection, *A Tribute To The Four Horsemen*.

Nevermore entered a Seattle studio in early 2003 with former Queensryche guitarist Kelly Gray as producer for the album *Enemies Of Reality*. Unfortunately, the end result was widely condemned for its muddy production. Live shows before this release saw the inclusion of Jag Panzer's Chris Broderick as stand-in second guitarist. In spite of the audio problems, the album went on to be Nevermore's biggest commercial success to date, entering the German charts at Number 34 and making impressions in Holland and Italy. Limited-edition double-CD sets of *Enemies* included videos for 'What Tomorrow Knows', 'Next In Line', and 'Believe In Nothing' as well as footage from Century Media's tenth anniversary show.

The band paired up with Arch Enemy for co-headlining European gigs throughout September and October, with Steve Smyth on second guitar. Smyth stayed onboard for subsequent US shows and joined Nevermore on a full-time basis in April 2004, splitting from Testament and appearing in the video for 'I, Voyager'.

The group took the almost unprecedented step of recording new parts for and remixing *Enemies Of Reality* in order to eliminate the sound deficiencies, drafting in Andy Sneap to give the album new life in January 2005. Fans who had already purchased the original version were offered the remake at just $5. The following month, Sneap tackled a new Nevermore album, *This Godless Endeavor*. These sessions featured Masterplan's Axel Mackenrott on keyboards and led to a cover of Ozzy Osbourne's 'Revelation (Mother Earth)'.

A notable contribution in 2005 was 'Tomorrow Turned Into Yesterday' for the compilation *Code Red*, given to US soldiers on duty in the Middle East. Nevermore then joined the 'Gigantour' festival, headlined by Megadeth and Dream Theater, for US action in late July 2005 to coincide with the entrance of *This Godless Endeavor*. The album surpassed all previous sales, impacting on charts in Germany, Italy, Switzerland, France, and Greece.

Festival and supporting dates took the band into 2006. With Sheppard undergoing a procedure for Crohn's disease, the former Megadeth and Iced Earth bassist James MacDonough stepped in to cover. The band suffered another medically-related blow when Smyth was diagnosed with end-stage kidney failure, the result of a congenital birth defect. Jag Panzer guitarist Chris Broderick filled in for the US dates. Yet another dose of bad

US power metal titans Nevermore: Warrel Dane is at forefront

luck hit the band – forcing cancellation of their May 13th show in Grand Rapids, Michigan – when Dane was taken ill. Smyth was due to resume his position for European shows commencing in June, but his kidney failure put paid to these plans. Initially, Nevermore performed in Italy as a quartet, prior to bringing in Broderick again to complete the run.

Word arrived in June that Dane was preparing for his first solo album, an intriguing collaboration with Peter Wichers of Soilwork. In October, the group united with a heavyweight billing consisting of Stratovarius, Black Label Society, Saxon, Sepultura, After Forever, Primal Fear, and Gotthard for the 'Live'n'Louder' festivals in Mexico, Argentina, and Brazil. Nevermore have built a huge fanbase and, assuming their music retains its high quality, they should be with us for a long to come.

NOCTURNAL RITES
EVER-EVOLVING SWEDISH VETERANS

FOUNDED AS NECRONOMIC IN 1990 by guitarist-vocalist Fredrik Mannberg in a more extreme death metal vein, Nocturnal Rites – from Umeå in northern Sweden – shifted their emphasis to a more streamlined traditional metal approach. The band cut *The Obscure* demo, with Mannberg handling vocals, in early 1991.

Although the demo attracted label interest, the band opted to play the waiting game, not least because of the rapid shift in their music to more melodic pastures. Around this time, drummer Tommy Eriksson, also involved with Shadowseeds, decamped and was substituted by Ulf Andersson, a former member of Naglfar. The band also added a second guitarist, Mikael Söderström. Their new direction called for a new style of singing, resulting in the recruitment of ex-Gotham City vocalist Anders Zackrisson. A further series of songs were put down on tape, prompting interest from the Dark Age label, which signed the band in 1994. Dark Age in turn licensed the album to Dave Constable's Megarock concern.

In A Time Of Blood And Fire (1995) garnered international praise, setting up the band for bigger and better things to come. Despite this positive step, Söderström decided to leave, and his vacancy was soon filled by former Auberon man Nils Norberg. During this time, both Mannberg (aka 'Psycho') and bassist Nils Eriksson ('Snake') were operational with thrash metal band Guillotine, issuing the 1997 album *Under The Guillotine*.

Nocturnal Rites' second album, *Tales Of Mystery And Imagination*, was issued in Japan in late 1997 and was picked up by Century Media for Europe the following year. The band benefited hugely from the renewed focus on traditional metal, as spotlighted by fellow Swedes Hammerfall, and 1998's *Tales Of Mystery And Imagination* sold well. The band put in extensive touring in Europe, opening for Overkill and playing alongside Nevermore and Angel Dust.

The Sacred Talisman capitalised on this progress during 1999 and introduced a new drummer, Owe Lingvall. Once more the band set out on a lengthy run of European shows with Nevermore and Lefay. However, Zackrisson decided that he wanted out at this critical juncture. Bringing in Jonny Lindqvist, the group returned to the studio to commit the *Afterlife* to tape – this record, issued in August 2000, also witnessed the introduction of Mattias Bernhardsson on keyboards.

The band toured Europe with Labyrinth and Iron Savior during April 2001. A new album, *Shadowland*, produced by Daniel Bergstrand, arrived in September, proving they were as unashamedly heavy as ever. The band supported Saxon throughout Europe in January 2003 and, in union with Hammerfall, lined up to co-headline shows in Japan in March before playing with Tad Morose and Edguy on Scandinavian dates in May.

Nocturnal Rites issued their sixth album, *New World Messiah*, produced by TT Oksala, in March 2004. Fredrik Mannberg made time to

guest on 6th Awakening's *Perfect War* demo. In October, bad luck befell the band when drummer Lingvall was involved in an accident at his summer house in which he almost lost an eye.

In February 2005, Century Media celebrated the band's tenth anniversary with the release of *Lost In Time: The Early Years Of Nocturnal Rites*, a double-CD set containing their first two albums, 1995's *In A Time Of Blood And Fire* and 1997's *Tales Of Mystery And Imagination*. The collection added rare bonus tracks and brand new re-recordings featuring vocalist Jonny Lindqvist. A new album, *Grand Illusion*, was prepared at Toontrack Studios in Umeå. Guests included Stefan Elmgren of Hammerfall, Jens Johansson of Stratovarius, Henrik Danhage from Evergrey, Kristoffer W. Olivius of Naglfar, and even the Swedish cross-country skiing world champion Per Elofsson.

On April 1st and 2nd 2005, Nocturnal Rites engaged in the 'Demons Of The Opera' concerts with the Hans Ek-conducted Philharmonic Orchestra at the Opera House in their native Umeå. The Swedmetal label then issued a split single with Falconer in 2005, a 7-inch limited to 500 copies and featuring the Nocturnal Rites track 'Okahoo', previously only available as a Japanese bonus on the 2000 *Afterlife* album. The band are now rightly regarded as having transcended their roots to become a beast with its own unique vision.

NOCTURNAL RITES discography

IN A TIME OF BLOOD AND FIRE, Dark Age/Megarock MRR CD 032 (Europe) (1995)

TALES OF MYSTERY AND IMAGINATION, Century Media CM 77208-2 (Europe), Century Media CM 7908-2 (USA) (1998)

THE SACRED TALISMAN, Century Media CM 77232-2 (Europe), Century Media CM 7932-2 (USA) (1999)

AFTERLIFE, Century Media CM 77292-2 (Europe), Century Media CM 7992-2 (USA) (2000)

SHADOWLAND, Century Media CM 77432-2 (Europe), Century Media CM 8132-2 (USA) (2002)

NEW WORLD MESSIAH, Century Media CM 77532-2 (Europe), Century Media CM 8223-2 (USA) (2004)

LOST IN TIME: THE EARLY YEARS OF NOCTURNAL RITES, Century Media CM 77623-2 (Europe) (2005)

Okahoo, Swedmetal SM-02-7 (Europe) (2005) limited edition split 7-inch vinyl single with Falconer 500 copies

GRAND ILLUSION, Century Media CM 77592-2 (Europe), Century Media CM 8292-2 (USA) (2005)

PROGRESSIVE GOTHIC AND SYMPHONIC METAL

GOTHIC

GOTHIC metal drew from a number of inspirations but was undoubtedly sourced in the bleak backyard of northern England. As fate would have it, three bands independently manifested themselves at one critical juncture and were all enterprisingly snapped up by the fledgling Peaceville label. Once Anathema, Paradise Lost, and My Dying Bride were launched on the world, things would never be the same again. These bands drew from a wide-ranging set of forward-thinking innovators such as Celtic Frost, Christian Death, and The Sisters Of Mercy, applying this dark sound to a Sabbath-influenced bedrock. While the new gothique soon blanketed Europe, the USA seemed strangely immune – with one noteworthy exception in Type O Negative.

With the drive towards the epic back on the agenda, Finland's Nightwish accelerated internationally, with enough momentum to foster another new wave in their wake. Nightwish pushed to the fore the idea of operatic female lead vocals, until then restricted to the avant-garde and experimental. Before long, every label had its female-fronted gothic metal band. Within Temptation soon strode out into a worthy second place, with After Forever, Epica, Elis, Flowing Tears, Autumn, Darzamat, and a multitude of others in their wake. Worthy bands who had been dodging just below the mainstream radar for many years, such as Theatre Of Tragedy, The Gathering, and Tristania, also used this opportunity to full advantage – while another outfit, Lacuna Coil, carved out their own sizeable niche.

AFTER FOREVER
PRECOCIOUSLY TALENTED GOTH-METALLERS

A GOTHIC DOOM ACT WITH A strong sense of the majestic, After Forever employed three vocalists – Floor Jansen on soprano, Mark Jansen on "screams", and death metal grunts courtesy of Sander Gommans. The group, in their mid-teens and based in Reuver, Netherlands, were conceived as Apocalyps during 1995 with guitarists Mark Jansen and Gommans, bassist Luuk van Gerven, keyboard player Jack Driessen, and drummer Joep Beckers. Floor Jansen enrolled in 1997. After Forever's recording debut came in 1999 with the *Ephemeral* and *Wings Of Illusion* demos.

Signing to Transmission Records and still with an average age of only 19, the band's commercial debut came with the 2000 single 'Follow In The Cry' and the album *Prison Of Desire*, produced by Hans Pieters and Dennis Leidelmeijer at Excess Studios in Rotterdam. Japanese versions of this record added the bonus track 'Wings Of Illusion'. Ambitiously, on *Prison Of Desire* the band used a vocal choir comprising bass Hans Cassa, tenor Caspar De Jonge, alto Yvonne Rooda, and sopranos Melissa 't Hart and Within Temptation's Sharon den Adel. After Forever's opening gambit made a serious impact upon the European metal scene, with Jansen's almost flawless soprano bringing the group particular attention. The singer made a further mark with the Ayreon project's conceptual *Universal Migrator Part I: The Dream Sequencer* album, duetting with Johan Edlund of Tiamat.

This momentum, afforded by favourable press and fan reaction to the debut, was maintained with the 2001 *Decipher* album. The single 'Emphasis' from the following year included two tracks, a cover of Queen's 'Who Wants To Live Forever' and 'Imperfect Senses', featuring Damien Wilson of British prog-rock act Threshold on guest lead vocals.

During April 2002, founder member Mark Jansen decamped to form Sahara Dust (they became known as Epica in 2003), with his replacement announced as Bas Maas. Floor Jansen had recently donated guest lead vocals to the Star One sci-fi concept album of Ayreon mentor Arjen Lucassen and toured with this project in September.

The October 2003 EP *Exordium* included a cover of Iron Maiden's 'The Evil That Men Do'. European package-tour dates for January 2004 found the group in league with Amaran, Dark Moor, and French veterans Nightmare. A full-length album, *Invisible Circles*, was released in March 2004. They followed this up with a round of Mexican dates with guests Arkhe before returning to the European mainland for shows in April and May with Flowing Tears. That month, the band dispensed with keyboard

player Lando van Gils, who had replaced Joep Beckers after *Prison Of Desire*. Joost van den Broek, formerly of Sun Caged, took his place.

In February 2005 the group commenced the recording of a new album, *Remagine*, laying down drums, bass, and guitars at Excess Studios in Rotterdam, with the vocals recorded and mixing conducted at producer Sascha Peath's Gate Studios in Wolfsburg, Germany. The band received a blow that same month when keyboard player André Borgman, who had replaced Jack Driessen after *Prison Of Desire*, was diagnosed with cancer. Following surgery, Borgman rejoined the ranks, although Ed Warby of Star One, Ayreon, and Gorefest acted as stand-in for the band's February 11th show at the Heineken Music Hall in Amsterdam. Koen Herfst of Xenobia was then recruited as temporary drummer.

October found the band appearing at the Belgian 'Metal Female Voices III' festival alongside a cast comprising Lacuna Coil, Leaves' Eyes, Epica, Elis, Midnattsol, Skeptical Minds, Mercury Rain, Asrai, Autumn, Diluvium, and The Legion Of Hetheria.

In early 2005, Joest van den Broek featured in the multi-national hard rock outfit The Cotton Soeterboek Band, comprising a veteran cast including Ayreon singer Robert Soeterboek, guitarist Alan Cotton, Mike Davis from Halford and Lizzy Borden on bass, and Driver man Reynold 'Butch' Carlson on drums. The keyboard player also guested on the *Ohm* album from Brazilian melodic metal band Sagitta. Meanwhile, both Jansen and Gommans put in session spots on the album *The Dominion Gate* by veteran French metal band Nightmare.

The group then played dates in South and Central America in July and August, taking in Mexico, Brazil, Argentina, and Chile. *Remagine* appeared in September. An October single, 'Being Everyone', featured a

---

AFTER FOREVER discography

PRISON OF DESIRE, Transmission TM-023 (Europe) (2000)
DECIPHER, Transmission TM-029 (Europe) (2001)
Exordium, Transmission TM-041 (Europe) (2003), Transmission TM-3041-2 (USA) (2004)
INVISIBLE CIRCLES, Transmission TM-045 (Europe), Transmission TM-3045-2 (USA) (2004)
REMAGINE, Transmission TM-055 (Europe) (2005)
MEA CULPA, Transmission TMD-067 (Europe) (2006)

non-album cut, 'Face Your Demons', with guest vocals by Marco Hietala from Nightwish. An After Forever concert at Tilburg's 013 venue on October 22nd was a special event as the band was accompanied by noted wind orchestra Orpheus. Drummer Borgman played a one-off show with fellow Dutch rock band Sustain on December 3rd.

After Forever's European 2006 tour was supported by French heavy metal band Nightmare and Rumanian symphonic metal act Magica. Transmission Records released the After Forever compilation album, *Mea Culpa*, in June 2006; in October, the band signed a new deal with Nuclear Blast. With such powerful backing, After Forever look set to improve their standing on the metal scene.

DREAM THEATER
DEXTEROUS PRO-METAL SCENE-LEADERS

WITHOUT DOUBT THE MOST important progressive rock act to emerge in recent years, Dream Theater have been rewarded with critical acclaim and hard album sales. The first of a second wave of progressively inclined acts, they were signed to MCA subsidiary Mechanic at a time when their style of music was relatively unpopular; however, the group swiftly fostered an enthusiastic degree of support, regularly cracking the charts and keeping pace with demand for product by releasing a series of exclusive fan-club releases.

In September 1985, bassist John Myung and guitarist John Petrucci – friends since childhood – met drummer Mike Portnoy at the famous Berklee School Of Music in Boston, Massachusetts. Kevin Moore was engaged on keyboards, having known Petrucci from elementary school, while the teenage Portnoy was recording tracks with guitarist S.A. Adams.

At first the fledgling band – known as Majesty – worked with vocalist Chris Collins, but they soon replaced him with Charlie Dominici, a former member of pop-rockers Frankie & The Knockouts, and recorded a four-track demo that sold out quickly, despite its poor production. Further sessions throughout 1985 and 1986 followed before the band were forced to change their name: Majesty was owned elsewhere. The new Dream Theater name was suggested by Portnoy's father, who had recently seen a movie in a cinema of that name.

After recording better-produced demos, Dream Theater signed with Mechanic and worked with producer Terry Date on the album *When Dream And Day Unite*. The record was reportedly completed with a three-and-a-half-week deadline hanging over the band's heads. Producer Terry Brown was drafted in to remix the album tracks for promotional copies. The track 'The Ytse Jam' was a reference to their former guise – 'Ytse Jam' being 'Majesty' backwards. *When Dream And Day Unite* was released in June 1989: reviews were positive but sales less than buoyant, due to the prevalence of glam and thrash metal.

After requesting a release from Mechanic Records – who, the band claimed, had offered no promotion for the first album – Dream Theater bought themselves out of their contract. Searching for a replacement for Dominici in 1989, they had begun work with another singer when they received a tape from James LaBrie, a native of Penetanguishene, Ontario, who was about to sign a solo deal with Aquarius Records. LaBrie had replaced vocalist Sebastian Bach of Skid Row fame in a band that became known as Winter Rose. The singer was invited down to New York to try out for Dream Theater and, after one jam session, the Canadian was offered the job.

The band were virtually guaranteed a deal with Atco if they found the right singer, and they duly signed to the label in 1991, entering BearTracks Studios in Suffern, New York, in October that year to record their second album, *Images And Words*. Derek Oliver, sometime music journalist, was instrumental in securing the band for Atco.

Dream Theater had now found the creative space in which to purvey their art. On its arrival in March 1992, *Images And Words* – produced by David Prater – turned the curiosity engendered by the debut into hard sales, the record reaching Number 61 on the US charts. The newly-acquired fans, relishing the band's lavish over-expression and musical ability, remained loyal for many years to come.

Appeasing the demand for live product, the group taped their April 23rd 1993 London Marquee show for an EP release. A gig three days later at the Nakano Sun Plaza in Tokyo was filmed for the *Images And Words: Live In Tokyo* video. European shows in November featured Damn The Machine in support.

For Dream Theater's next full-length record, *Awake* – produced by Duane Baron and John Purdell – the musicians took an unexpected diversion into darker, more introspective realms to produce their heaviest work to date. However, Moore quit without warning before the final mixdown, subsequently resurfacing in 1998 with Chroma Key. He was temporarily replaced for live work with Jordan Rudess of Speedway Boulevard before ex-Kiss associate Derek Sherinian took over for a full tour. Rudess duly joined the jazz-rock band Dixie Dregs.

The mini-album *A Change Of Seasons*, released in 1995, found the band in looser mode. The 23-minute title track, scored at BearTracks Studios, prefaced an eclectic selection of live cuts captured at the famous Ronnie Scott's Jazz Club in London on January 31st 1995. These included takes on Elton John's 'Funeral For A Friend' and 'Love Lies Bleeding', Deep Purple's 'Perfect Strangers', and a medley of Led Zeppelin's 'The Rover', 'Achilles Last Stand', and 'The Song Remains The Same'. The evening was capped by a jam on excerpts of Pink Floyd's 'In The Flesh', Kansas's 'Carry On My Wayward Son', Queen's 'Bohemian Rhapsody', Journey's 'Lovin', Touchin', Squeezin'', Dixie Dregs' 'Cruise Control', and 'Turn It On Again' by Genesis.

Fallen Into Infinity from 1997 was produced by Kevin Shirley and featured a guest vocal appearance from King's X man Doug Pinnick on the track 'Lines In The Sand' and a surprisingly impressive co-write with Desmond Child on 'You Not Me'. The record caused division among the fans, however, many of whom believed that Dream Theater had pandered to commercial pressures.

The band toured America in 1997 alongside Dixie Dregs. Portnoy and Petrucci were both involved in the side-project group Liquid Tension Experiment with respected sessioneers Tony Levin – of Peter Gabriel and King Crimson repute – and Rudess once again. Liquid Tension Experiment released an acclaimed self-titled album through Magna Carta in early 1998.

The *Once In A LIVEtime* album was released in 1998. The following

Dream Theater

year Sherinian left the band, and in came his obvious successor Rudess for 1999's *Metropolis Pt 2: Scenes From A Memory*. The album continued the theme of 'Metropolis Part 1', a track on *Images And Words*. The side projects continued, with Rudess pairing off with his ex-Dixie Dregs drumming colleague Rod Morgenstein for the Rudess/Morgenstein album, and his inclusion on the classical *Steinway To Heaven* album alongside Sherinian and Yes maestro Rick Wakeman. Myung re-united with Sherinian, Morgenstein, and King's X's Ty Tabor to forge the Platypus project. In 1999, Portnoy allied himself with Marillion bassist Pete Trewavas, Spock's Beard's Neal Morse, and The Flower Kings' Roine Stolt to create Transatlantic, releasing the *SMPTe* album in 2000 on Radiant Records in the USA and InsideOut Music in Europe. The working title for the project was originally Morse/Portnoy/Trewavas/Stolt, and it was announced in October 1999 that the band would be called Second Nature, but then in November 1999 their name was confirmed as Transatlantic.

In September 2001, a triple-CD emerged titled *Live Scenes From New York*, comprising a show recorded at the Roseland Ballroom in New York on August 30th 2000. However, due to a ghastly coincidence, the album was pulled from the shelves on the day of its release – September 11th – thanks to its sleeve artwork, which depicted New York City, including the World Trade Center, in flames. Needless to say, the artwork was hastily revised. In more encouraging news, Dream Theater's Brazilian fan club announced the assembly of a tribute album featuring artists such as Sigma 5, Evora, Last Rites, Operact, Longjam, and Abstrakt.

The 2002 album *Six Degrees Of Inner Turbulence* numbered only six songs, with one of them the marathon 40-minute title track. The band added a novel twist to their touring by performing the entirety of Metallica's *Master Of Puppets* album when booked for two consecutive nights at any venue. Fans who had not been made aware of their intention to do so were somewhat mystified. The band also played US dates with King's X and Joe Satriani.

Portnoy was revealed as the mentor behind a new prog-rock supergroup in May, having assembled an impressive line-up including keyboard player Kevin Moore, Fates Warning guitarist Jim Matheos, ex-Cynic and Gordian Knot bassist Sean Malone, and Pain Of Salvation vocalist Daniel Gildenlöw. Before long Gildenlöw was out of the frame and the project was being billed as OSI (Orchestra Of Strategic Influence).

Dream Theater then announced European tour dates for October, performing two sets with an intermission and no support act. On the 21st they performed the entirety of Iron Maiden's *Number Of The Beast* album at their second night at the London Astoria. The band faithfully represented the album – with the exception of a jazz-flavoured 'Gangland' – and even rigged up a backdrop with the Dream Theater logo executed in the classic Maiden script. They then co-headlined a US prog-metal extravaganza in June with Queensryche and Fates Warning.

With the band's unceasing success, demand for live material and early Majesty recordings prompted drummer Portnoy to establish his own Ytsejam label in order to beat the bootleggers. The first of these releases was 2003's *The Majesty Demos 1985-1986* and Dream Theater's *Live In Los Angeles, California 5/18/98*. The LA set featured Ray Adler of Fates Warning and Iron Maiden frontman Bruce Dickinson as guests.

A new studio album, *Train Of Thought*, produced by Petrucci and Portnoy, was readied for November issue with European tour dates announced for January. In the midst of this activity, LaBrie was also active with Frameshift, a collaboration with guitarist Henning Pauly of Chain that resulted in the 2004 album *Unweaving The Rainbow*.

Dream Theater established a ticket-ranking system for their spring US dates. Fans could choose to purchase upgrades into bronze, gold, or platinum tickets, the last of these granting privileges such as a seat in the first five rows, an exclusive T-shirt, tour laminate and autographed photograph, and a meet-and-greet opportunity with the band.

DREAM THEATER discography

The band have also released many fan-club albums. From 1996 until 2003 these were issued each Christmas, but since then their frequency and number have increased greatly.

WHEN DREAM AND DAY UNITE, Mechanic DMCF3445 (UK), Mechanic MCAD42259 (USA) (1989)

IMAGES AND WORDS, Atco 7567-92148-2 (Europe / USA) (1992) **61 USA**

LIVE AT THE MARQUEE, Atco 7567-92286-2 (Europe / USA) (1993)

AWAKE, EastWest 7567-90126-2 (Europe / USA) (1994) **65 UK, 32 USA**

A CHANGE OF SEASONS, EastWest 7559-61842-2 (Europe / USA) (1996) **58 USA**

FALLING INTO INFINITY, EastWest 7559-62060-2 (Europe / USA) (1997) **52 USA**

ONCE IN A LIVETIME, Elektra 7559-62308-2 (Europe / USA) (1998) **157 USA**

METROPOLIS PART 2: SCENES FROM A MEMORY, Elektra 7559-62448-2 (Europe / USA) (1999)

LIVE SCENES FROM NEW YORK, Elektra 7559-62661-2 (Europe / USA) (2001) **120 USA**

SIX DEGREES OF INNER TURBULENCE, Elektra 7559-62742-2 (Europe / USA) (2002) **46 USA**

TRAIN OF THOUGHT, Elektra 7559-62891-2 (Europe / USA) (2003) **53 USA**

LIVE AT BUDOKAN, Rhino 8122-76545-2 (Europe / USA) (2004)

OCTAVARIUM, Atlantic 7567-83793-2 (Europe / USA) (2005) **72 UK, 36 USA**

SCORE – 20th ANNIVERSARY WORLD TOUR, Rhino 8122-74062-2 (Europe / USA) (2006)

Celebrating their 15th anniversary, the group put on a special show on March 6th at the Pantages Theater in Los Angeles. Performing the *When Dream And Day Unite* album in its entirety, they were joined by original singer Charlie Dominici on the songs 'To Live Forever' and 'Metropolis Part 1', the latter also featuring Sherinian.

Fans were treated with a slew of 'official bootleg' releases through the Ytsejam label with the *When Day And Dream Unite Demos 1987-1989*, as well as *Tokyo, Japan 10/28/95* and *Master Of Puppets – Cover Series*. The band extended their 2004 tour schedule with prog-rock pioneers Yes for autumn US dates. On October 29th, Portnoy manned the drums for East Coast thrash veterans Overkill, performing at DJ Eddie Trunk's annual Halloween party at the Hard Rock Café in New York City. A live album and separate DVD, both titled *Live At Budokan*, were released in 2004.

A 2005 solo album from LaBrie, *Elements Of Persuasion*, included contributions in the studio from Italian guitar prodigy Marco Sfogli, Kim Mitchell, bassist Bryan Beller, Matt Guillory of Dali's Dilemma on keyboards, and Mangini on drums. Petrucci too put out solo product: his *Suspended Animation* album also emerged in 2005. Pointedly, Dream Theater's own album for 2005, *Octavarium*, gained the distinction of being the last album recorded at the famous Hit Factory Studios in New York.

During March, Rudess took time out to tour the East Coast with Blackfield, the project of Steven Wilson of Porcupine Tree and Israeli singer-songwriter Aviv Geffen. Another recording announcement took fans by surprise as early singer Dominici revealed plans for the release of a trilogy.

A G3 mini-tour of Japan in May found Petrucci in a band with Dave

LaRue on bass and Portnoy on drums, flanking Joe Satriani and Steve Vai. Portnoy also temped for Fates Warning, manning the drums for their appearance at the Headway festival in Amstelveen, Netherlands on April 3rd. In June, Portnoy acted as special guest for Overkill at the 'Sweden Rock' festival, performing on the song 'Elimination'.

Dream Theater co-headlined the 'Gigantour' festival alongside Megadeth for US action in late July, topping a bill comprising Fear Factory, The Dillinger Escape Plan, Symphony X, Nevermore, Dry Kill Logic, and Bobaflex. The August 2nd 'Gigantour' set in Dallas saw the inclusion of an encore tribute to the late 'Dimebag' Darrell Abbott of Pantera and Damageplan. The band performed a rendition of Pantera's 'Cemetery Gates' with guests Dave Mustaine from Megadeth, Burton C. Bell of Fear Factory, and Russell Allen of Symphony X. Dream Theater fulfilled the 'Gigantour' dates until September, when their position was taken by Anthrax.

Back on European soil, the band performed Pink Floyd's *Dark Side Of The Moon* in its entirety as their second set on October 11th at the Heineken Music Hall in Amsterdam. Gigs across South America in December wrapped up the year.

During the band's Japanese tour in January 2006, they used their second-night stands in Tokyo and Osaka to perform Deep Purple's *Made In Japan*. Mike Portnoy then assembled Amazing Journey, a one-off tribute band assembled to pay homage to The Who. Vocals came from Gary Cherone of Van Halen and Extreme, with Paul Gilbert of Mr. Big and Racer X on guitar, and Billy Sheehan from Mr. Big and Talas on bass. This impressive quartet undertook a brief burst of US shows in May 2006.

A new Dream Theater live album and separate DVD, both titled *Score*, were released in August 2006. By this stage the band were international heroes on the prog-metal scene, and they look set to extend their influence even further in the next few years.

EPICA
VISIONARY GOTH-METAL

CONTINUING IN THE POPULAR tradition of female-fronted gothic metal bands from the Low Countries, Epica were conceived by former After Forever guitarist Mark Jansen. The band's second guitarist Ad Sluijter was previously a member of Cassiopeia and also has After Forever connections, as does keyboard player Coen Janssen. Drummer Jeroen Simons is also ex-Cassiopeia, while bassist Yves Huts (aka Enuresor) has a tradition with Axamenta and black metal band Gurthang. Epica, based in Limburg, Netherlands, are led by the classically trained mezzo-soprano opera singer Simone Simons.

For a short period, the band went by the title Sahara Dust, including former Trail Of Tears vocalist Helena Iren Michaelsen and drummer Iwan Hendrikx of Silent Edge and Exivious. Ex-Within Temptation and Sun Caged drummer Dennis Leeflang stepped into the breach for the December 2002 two-song demo *Cry For The Moon*. However, with the enrolment of Simone Simons and Jeroen Simons (no relation), in 2003 the group adopted the Epica name in homage to the Kamelot album of the same name.

The debut Sascha Paeth-produced album *The Phantom Agony*, which offered gothic metal with choral vocals from Simon and death grunts from Jansen, gave the band immediate success by landing straight in the Dutch national charts. Extensive touring throughout Europe in April and May 2004 was backed by the single 'Cry For The Moon'. Subsequent festival dates saw Epica performing at the Leipzig 'Wave Gotik Treffen' event, 'Graspop' in Belgium and the Turkish 'Rock The Nations' meeting in Istanbul. Further product arrived in October in the form of the DVD *We Will Take You With Us/2 Meter Sessies*, coming with an additional bonus

CD containing material from the *2 Meter Sessies* TV programme.

Epica united with Austrian act Visions Of Atlantis for European touring in September. The band also put in an appearance at the Nightwish-headlined 'Metal Female Voices Fest II' event held in Brussels during November. The supporting cast included Flowing Tears, Sengir, Darkwell, Visions Of Atlantis, Ashes You Leave, and Syrens Call. Shows in Mexico were projected for December, but Simone Simons was rushed to hospital with appendicitis midway through these gigs. María Victoria Pérez of the support band The Legion Of Hetheria filled the vacancy to complete the tour.

New recordings completed in late 2004 featured Kamelot frontman Roy Khan. Returning the favour, Simone Simons appeared in the video for Kamelot's 'The Haunting'. The band, promoting the album *Consign To Oblivion*, announced a return to the European touring circuit in March 2005 with Kotipelto and Kamelot.

Epica struck out into new territory with the September 2005 album *The Score – An Epic Journey*, an entirely instrumental piece of work crafted as a soundtrack to the movie *Joyride*. October found the band appearing at the Belgian 'Metal Female Voices III' festival alongside Lacuna Coil, Leaves' Eyes, The Legion Of Hetheria, Elis, Midnattsol, Skeptical Minds, Mercury Rain, Asrai, Autumn, Diluvium, and After Forever. European dates that same month had French outfit The Old Dead Tree in support.

In November, Epica's South American status was recognised and given a higher profile still when they performed on the Brazilian TV show *Do Jô*, a programme attracting over 10 million viewers. The band united with Kamelot for US concerts in September and South American shows in December.

The Road To Paradiso, a book package featuring previously unreleased demo and live recordings, interviews, and photos, was released in May 2006. Drummer Jeroen Simons left Epica in October; meanwhile, Simone Simons is constantly being linked to the vacant vocalist position in Nightwish. However, Epica issued a statement in November 2006 stating that Simone would not be leaving the band, and their future remains bright.

EVERGREY
ATMOSPHERIC PROG ACT FROM SCANDINAVIA

THIS HIGHLY REGARDED PROGRESSIVE metal band from Helsingborg, Sweden – established during 1996 – specialise in maudlin yet intricate works of gravitas. Evergrey's 1998 album *The Dark Discovery*, released on the GNW (Gothenburg Noise Works) label, witnessed guest performances from King Diamond's Andy LaRocque, who also acted as producer, and Freak Kitchen's Mattias Eklundh. The recording band

EVERGREY DISCOGRAPHY

THE DARK DISCOVERY, GNW GNW02CD (Europe) (1998)

SOLITUDE, DOMINANCE, TRAGEDY, Hall Of Sermon HOS 7111 (Europe) (1999)

IN SEARCH OF TRUTH, InsideOut Music IOMCD 081 (Europe), InsideOut Music America IOMACD 2025-2 (USA) (2001)

RECREATION DAY, InsideOut Music IOMCD 117 (Europe), InsideOut Music America IOMACD 2051-2 (USA) (2003)

THE INNER CIRCLE, InsideOut Music IOMCD 165 (Europe), InsideOut Music America IOMACD 2079-2 (USA) (2004)

A NIGHT TO REMEMBER, InsideOut Music IOMCD 203 (Europe), InsideOut Music America INO-40847 (USA) (2005)

MONDAY MORNING APOCALYPSE, InsideOut Music IOMCD 240 (Europe), InsideOut Music America INO-48882 (USA) (2006)

consisted of singer Tom Englund, guitarist Dan Bronell, bassist Daniel Nöjd, keyboard player Will Chandra, and drummer Patrick Carlsson.

Evergrey switched to the Hall Of Sermon gothic rock specialists for May 1999's *Solitude – Dominance – Tragedy* outing. The album release party was held in Bochum, Germany at a gig with Rage. However, Nöjd decamped and Evergrey enlisted two new recruits, bassist Michael Håkansson and Soilwork keyboard player Sven Karlsson, both erstwhile members of black metal band Embraced. Håkansson also divided his duties with The Forsaken.

European dates saw the band opening the German 'Bang Your Head' festival and touring alongside Crimson Glory and Kamelot. They found time too to donate a rendition of 'Rising Force' to an Yngwie Malmsteen tribute album. Before the year was out, guitarist Dan Bronell departed, and the band drafted in Henrik Danhage. They signed to InsideOut Music for a third album, the September 2001 conceptual piece *In Search Of Truth*.

Keyboard player Sven Karlsson was let go later in the year, his replacement being Chris Rehn. By 2002, Evergrey had installed Rikard Zander in the keyboard role for a new album, *Recreation Day*, with producer LaRocque. Shortly after the release of the record, in March 2003, drummer Carlsson severed ties with the band and was superseded by Jonas Ekdahl. The band played with Hate Eternal, Arch Enemy, and The Black Dahlia Murder for a short run of US dates in August. More gigs followed *The Inner Circle*, released in April 2004 by InsideOut Music.

Håkansson, maintaining his commitment to Evergrey, resurrected his former act Embraced in June 2004. That summer, Englund and Arnold Linberg acted as the production team for the Dragonland album *Starfall*. Evergrey filmed an October 9th show in Gothenburg for a live DVD.

Danhage and Jonas Ekdahl then revealed a raw side project dubbed Death Destruction with ex-Hammerfall bassist Fredrik Larsson. Meanwhile, Håkansson played session bass on new recordings for The Project Hate. Evergrey, promoting March 2005's *A Night To Remember*, supported Dream Theater frontman James LaBrie's European solo dates in April. Impressively, the DVD of *A Night To Remember* topped the national Swedish charts. Danhage guested on the Nocturnal Rites album *Grand Illusion*.

The band entered the studio in late 2005 to craft an album with the production team of Sanken Sandqvist and Stefan Glaumann. *Monday Morning Apocalypse*, issued in March 2006, entered the Swedish album charts at Number 6. A brief run of homeland shows followed in April. Evergrey then drafted in former Crystal Age bassist Fredrik Larsson in July to replace Håkansson, and their fans await their next move with great anticipation.

FATES WARNING
VETERAN PROG-METAL PIONEERS

STOIC PROGRESSIVE METAL BAND Fates Warning have weathered nearly two decades of shifting musical trends thanks to a steadfast fanbase. Operating for many years below the radar, the group have nonetheless generated a commendable catalogue of work.

The band from Hartford, Connecticut, were initially named Misfit on their original formation in 1982 with a line-up of vocalist John Arch, guitarists Victor Arduini and Jim Matheos, bassist Joe DiBiase, and drummer Steve Zimmerman. Misfit cut 1983 demo sessions before renaming themselves Fates Warning. A series of demo recordings in 1984 led to a track on the *Metal Massacre V* compilation and the resulting appreciation resulted in a long-term deal with Metal Blade.

The September 1984 debut album *Night On Bröcken* was actually a barely brushed-up clutch of demos recorded by Doug Clark at The Gallery in East Hartford and remixed by Bill Metoyer. It established the band firmly in the traditional metal mould, with few hints of the future among its galloping, Maiden-esque arsenal of riffs. Two alternative covers used before widespread distribution – amateurish paintings of a burning witch and a fairytale scene – became highly sought after.

The band became more complex with October 1985's *The Spectre Within*, Arch in particular maturing enough to use his vocals in unexpected fashion. The group travelled to Hollywood, California, to put down these tracks with Metoyer at the El Dorado studio. They were still struggling against the tide, but word of mouth was building. Arduini then departed, and in came ex-Demonax guitarist Frank Aresti.

The November 1987 album *Awaken The Guardian*, a more diverse landscape punctuated by brooding acoustic passages, broke into the American Top 200. Despite this, Arch quit, unable to reconcile himself with the band's musical direction. He was superseded by Ray Alder.

This new line-up recorded *No Exit*, released in March 1988 and produced by Roger Probert and the much-in-demand Max Norman: it included the 22-minute epic 'The Ivory Gates Of Dreams' spread over eight chapters. Fates Warning scored valuable airplay with the track 'Silent Cries' and the album made it to Number 111 on the US charts. However, the band's stability suffered a further knock when Zimmerman opted out.

They added erstwhile Warlord drummer Mark Zonder (aka Thunder Child) for touring in Europe before recording the Terry Brown-produced *Perfect Symmetry* album for issue in August 1989. Dream Theater keyboard player Kevin Moore guested, and *Perfect Symmetry* gave a large contingent of the band's devotees a rude awakening, eschewing the

Fates Warning

FATES WARNING discography

NIGHT ON BRÖCKEN, Roadrunner RR 9823 (Europe), Metal Blade 71102 (USA) (1984)

THE SPECTRE WITHIN, Roadrunner RR 9737 (Europe), Metal Blade 72088 (USA) (1985)

AWAKEN THE GUARDIAN, Metal Blade 73231 (1986), Roadrunner RR 9660 (Europe) (1987) **191 USA**

NO EXIT, Roadrunner RR 9558-2 (Europe), Metal Blade D2-73330 (USA) (1988) **111 USA**

PERFECT SYMMETRY, Roadrunner RR 9451-2 (Europe), Metal Blade 7 73408-2 (USA) (1989) **141 USA**

PARALLELS, Metal Blade CDZORRO 31 (UK), Metal Blade 9 26698-2 (USA) (1991)

INSIDE OUT, Massacre MASS CD037 (Europe), Metal Blade P2-53915 (USA) (1994)

CHASING TIME, Metal Blade CDZORRO 84 (UK), Metal Blade 3984-14085-2 (USA) (1995)

A PLEASANT SHADE OF GREY, Massacre MASS CD125 (Europe), Metal Blade 3984-14129-2 (USA) (1997)

STILL LIFE, Massacre MASS CD147 (Europe), Metal Blade 3984-14188-2 (USA) (1998)

DISCONNECTED, Massacre MASS CD242 (Europe), Metal Blade 3984-14324-2 (USA) (2000)

FWX, Metal Blade 3984-14500-2 (Europe / USA) (2004)

---

expected riffage for a headlong plunge into progdom and shifting the emphasis in order to highlight Mark Zonder and Joe DiBiase's contributions.

Parallels, released in October 1991, was another fine effort in a similar vein and saw Fates Warning comfortably delving into more technical territory. Significantly, the group had crafted this opus with producer Brown at Metalworks Studios in Toronto, utilising Dream Theater's James LaBrie on the track 'Life In Still Water'. *Parallels* was constructed in unorthodox fashion, with interviews revealing that the individual musicians had mailed in taped contributions for Jim Matheos to assemble in the studio.

Fates Warning's burgeoning status in Europe resulted in a new deal with Germany's Massacre label for the July 1994 album *Inside Out*. This album, co-produced by Metoyer, featured credits for anonymous session musicians under the pseudonyms George Hideous, Fidel Horrendous, Sal Mortadelli, and Arthur Letsgoberg. (These names featured on numerous albums – also being credited for 'catering' and 'tour accounting' – and are widely believed to be the band members themselves.) A compilation, *Chasing Time*, was released in 1995. Guitarist Frank Aresti and bassist Joe DiBiase left the band the following year, with DiBiase replaced by longtime Armored Saint bass man Joey Vera.

A Pleasant Shade Of Grey, produced by Terry Brown at the Carriage House, Stamford, Connecticut, was Fates Warning's first foray into a full-blown concept, with a 55-minute, 12-instalment suite capped by a chorus of bell chimes. The double live set *Still Life*, emerging in October 1998 and hosting *A Pleasant Shade Of Grey* in its entirety on disc one, appeared (and in Japan featured a bonus rendition of the Scorpions' 'In Trance'). Agent Steel guitarist Bernie Versailles guested on the title track. Both Alder and Vera involved themselves in the Engine project with Versailles, producing a highly-rated eponymous 1999 album. Matheos took a left turn for an almost jazz-based solo album the same year, *Away With Words*.

Disconnected arrived in July 2000, and the band toured America with Savatage in 2001. Metal Blade reissued the *Night On Bröcken* and *The Spectre Within* albums in September 2002. *Night On Bröcken* was clad in its original cover art for its first release on CD and added four rarities in an original 1984 Misfit demo of 'Last Call', 1983 rehearsal tapes of 'The Calling' and 'Flight Of Icarus' by Iron Maiden, and a live take of 'Kiss Of Death' recorded at the L'Amour club. *The Spectre Within* reissue boasted a 1985 live version of 'Radio Underground', a rehearsal session of 'The Apparition', and two tracks from the *Dickie* demo, 'Kyrie Eleison' and 'Epitaph'. Many solo and side projects followed before Vera temporarily enrolled in Anthrax as stand-in for the departed Frank Bello. Zonder joined the legendary hard rock outfit Montrose for a gig at the Dallas Guitar Show.

Fates Warning's new album, *FWX* – recorded at Carriage House studios in Stamford – was released in October 2004. The band employed Dream Theater drummer Mike Portnoy for an appearance at the 'Headway' festival in Amstelveen, Netherlands on April 3rd 2005. Further European gigs saw Spock's Beard drummer Nick D'Virgilio taking the role.

Metal Blade issued an expanded, remastered edition of the band's 1986 classic *Awaken The Guardian* in June. This new three-disc version added a CD of live and demo tracks plus a DVD of live footage from 1986. InsideOut Music also issued a DVD, *Live In Athens*, filmed at the band's February 20th 2005 show in Greece. Fates Warning have earned their place at the head of the progressive metal scene and have influenced many other bands along the way. They remain a much-respected act.

KAMELOT
KNIGHTS OF THE METAL TABLE?

KAMELOT WERE CREATED during 1991 by guitarist Thomas Youngblood and drummer Richard Warner in Tampa, Florida, and have become a noted progressive metal band who've made headway into the European rock market with a series of ambitious releases, first breaking into the charts with 2003's *Epica*.

The early Kamelot were fronted by Mark Vanderbilt with Sean Christians on bass. The group recorded a three-song demo in 1991 and then debuted commercially four years later with the *Eternity* album, recorded at the famous Morrisound Studios in Tampa by Jim Morris. Alongside Youngblood, Warner, and Vanderbilt was new bassist Glenn Barry and keyboard player David Pavlicko. Millenium vocalist Todd Plant and keyboard player Howard Helm sessioned in the studio.

Kamelot followed up in 1997, retaining a stable line-up for *Dominion*. The albums drew attention to the uncanny resemblance of lead vocalist Mark Vanderbilt to Midnight, the singer with an earlier Florida export, Crimson Glory. Touring Europe to promote *Dominion*, Kamelot allied with Angra and Virgin Steele. A line-up change then saw Warner replaced by Casey Grillo.

Before the recording of a third album, July 1998's *Siege Perilous*, Kamelot recruited Roy Khan (aka Roy Sætre Khantatat) on vocals, previously with the highly-rated but now-defunct Norwegian prog-metal band Conception, and Crest Of Darkness. His Conception colleague Tore Østby donated a guest solo to the song 'Siege'. Pavlicko then exited, leaving the band to persevere as a quartet. Youngblood founded a side project, Monarque, in 1999 – fronted by none other than ex-Kamelot vocalist Mark Vanderbilt.

Kamelot made greater strides into the European market with *The Fourth Legacy*, produced by Sascha Paeth at Gate Studios in Wolfsburg, Germany. These tracks were constructed by Khan, Youngblood, Barry, and Grillo with additional drums supplied by Dirk Bruineberg of Elegy and Robert Hunecke-Rizzo of Heavens Gate. Expanding their horizons, Kamelot also drew from a diverse range of session artists, including the Fallersleben String Quartet, percussionist Farouk Asjadi, flautist Simon

McTavish, and female vocalists Rannveig Sif Sigurdardóttir and Cinzia Rizzo.

The band drew in Günter Werno from Vanden Plas on keyboards. The summer of 2000 witnessed the 'New Allegiance Tour', traversing Germany, Austria, Switzerland, the Netherlands, Belgium, Italy, Greece, and Spain, and during these dates recordings were made for Kamelot's first live album *The Expedition*. Arriving in October 2000, the album closed with three previously unheard studio tracks.

The band's 2001 album *Karma* was jeopardised when Khan was involved in a car crash. The singer emerged relatively unscathed, however, and sessions continued. The band then put in a series of European festival performances in summer 2001, appearing at Italy's 'Gods Of Metal', Germany's 'Bang Your Head' and Spain's 'Rock Machine' events. *Karma*, again produced by Paeth, became the band's debut chart entry in Germany, reaching Number 85. It was enhanced by a wide-ranging arsenal of vocalists, a string quartet, and the Rodenberg Symphony Orchestra. Youngblood contributed to the adventurous 2001 Consortium Project debut album.

Kamelot forged an alliance with Axxis for a run of European tour dates, with Axxis headlining on the German dates before switching to opening act for the rest of Europe. Rhapsody drummer Alex Holzwarth stood in for the first nine shows, but regular drummer Casey Grillo took back the reins for the Offenbach gig.

The band decided upon an even more adventurous undertaking for *Epica*, hinging the entire affair on Goethe's epic *Faust*. Guests abounded once more, with Rhapsody's Luca Turilli putting down a flurry of notes on 'Descent Of The Archangel', Elegy's Ian Parry donating vocals to 'Interlude VI – Dawn', and there's also a backing choir. Keyboard landscapes were given shape by Günter Werno and Jan P. Ringvold.

The record arrived in January 2003; for touring in support of the album, including debut shows in Japan, Kamelot drafted in former Yngwie Malmsteen keyboard player Mats Olausson. Mexican dates in early 2004 found the band employing Vanden Plas man Günter Werno on keyboards. New recordings throughout the summer were cut for the *Soul Society* album, but by September this project had taken on a new title, *The Black Halo*. Produced by Sascha Paeth and Miro at Gate Studio in Germany, the sessions featured guest appearances by keyboard player Jens Johansson of Stratovarius, Shagrath of Dimmu Borgir, Mari of Masqueraid, Herbie Langhans of Seventh Avenue, Thomas Rettke of Heaven's Gate, and Simone Simmons of Epica. The recording was punctuated by a live performance at the ProgPower event in Atlanta, Georgia, with the band joined on stage by Midnight and Ben Jackson, former members of Crimson Glory. That December, the band with director Patric Ullaeus shot two videos for 'The Haunting' (featuring a cameo appearance from Simone Simons) and 'March Of Mephisto'.

Kamelot introduced the veteran German keyboard player-guitarist

Oliver Palotai to the ranks and announced a return to the European circuit in March 2005, partnering with Kotipelto and Epica. Japanese dates were scheduled for April with support from Silent Force. The band then made their Canadian live debut on November 20th as the headliners of Quebec's 'International Metal Fest' at the Capitole Theater. US dates in November saw Seven Witches in support, and the band united with Epica for South American shows in December. A new Kamelot live album and separate DVD, *One Cold Winter's Night*, were released in November 2006, consolidating their position near the forefront of the American metal scene.

LABYRINTH
A DOSE OF MEDITERRANEAN DARKNESS

LABYRINTH, ESTABLISHED IN MASSA in Italy during 1991, went through many musicians in their early years, and at one stage in 1993 they were fronted by Relics singer Luca Cappellari, later of Drakkar and White Lilith. The first firm steps were taken when Labyrinth issued the 1995 *Midnight Resistance* demo, recorded by singer Joe Terry (Fabio Tordiglione), Olaf Thörsen (Carlo Andrea Magnani) and Anders Rain (Andrea Cantarelli) on guitars, Andrea Bartoletti on bass, and Frank Andiver on drums and keyboards. The demo secured a deal with Underground Symphony Records for the December 1995 EP *Piece Of Time*, recorded with Ken Taylor on keyboards and Chris Breeze (Cristiano Bertocchi) on bass.

A full-length album, *No Limits*, was released in 1996 by the Pick Up label, and they secured a valuable licence for Japan on the Teichiku imprint. *No Limits* fared well in the Far East, remaining in the charts of the influential *Burn* magazine for many months.

During 1997, Labyrinth replaced vocalist Lione with Dan Keying for live work. Keying was invited to join the band full-time but opted to create his own power metal act Cydonia. Ex-vocalist Joe Terry, now under the name of Fabio Lione, joined Athena and Rhapsody, the latter a highly successful union. Unknown to many, the singer also pursued an alternate 'Eurobeat' pop career under the pseudonym of Powerful T.

March 1998's *Return To Heaven Denied* album, their first for new label Metal Blade, was co-produced by Pat Scalabrino and Louis Stefanini at New Sin Audio and featured guitarists Olaf Thörsen and Anders Rain, Andrew McPauls (Andrea De Paoli) on keyboards, ex-Vanexa man Rob Tyrant (Roberto Tiranti) on vocals, Chris Breeze on bass, and Vision Divine man Mat Stancioiu on drums.

Return To Heaven Denied opened up Europe for the band, thanks to a focus on the in-vogue power metal genre and Metal Blade's effective distribution and marketing. Rob Tyrant (Roberto Tiranti) left the band in 1998 after the release of *Return To Heaven Denied* and was replaced by

Italy's Lacuna Coil, with singer Cristina Scabbia seated

Domine and ex-Sabotage singer Morby (Adolfo Morviducci). However, Tyrant/Tiranti returned to the band in 1999. Labyrinth reinforced their status by sharing the stage with Black Sabbath, Stratovarius, Blind Guardian, Iced Earth, and Helloween at the 1998 Italian 'Gods Of Metal' festival before engaging with Hammerfall for mainland dates in October.

The June 1999 mini-album *Timeless Crime* was a conceptual work based on the history of Venice and featured a collection of new and old material taken from the *Midnight Resistance* demo and the *No Limits* and *Return To Heaven Denied* albums (and gave fans a bonus in the form of an uncredited hidden track, a version of Sanctuary's cult thrash classic 'Die For My Sins'). In 1999, the band appeared again at 'Gods Of Metal' and performed at a swathe of other festival events.

Lione and Thörsen reunited in 2000 for the Vision Divine project and the eponymous album. Thörsen also guested on the 2000 Skylark album *Divine Gates*. Labyrinth then put out *Sons Of Thunder*, produced by Neil Kernon before, according to the jacket credits, it was "totally remixed" by Alfredo Cappello. However, Labyrinth were dealt a heavy blow when Olaf Thörsen quit the band in November 2002.

They regrouped, signing with Germany's Century Media to issue a self-titled album during July 2003. Guitarist Pier Gonella joined the band for touring duties to promote *Labyrinth*. Gonella was later announced as a permanent band member at the beginning of 2004. After more solo and side projects, the group switched to the Spanish Arise label for 2005's *Freeman*.

Cristiano Bertocchi left the band in April 2006 and joined Vision Divine: vocalist Roberto Tiranti now also plays bass. According to the band's website, the new Labyrinth album (due for release in 2007) will be titled *6 Days To Nowhere*, which their considerable fanbase awaits with great expectations.

LACUNA COIL
NOT JUST A PRETTY FACE

LACUNA COIL WERE FOUNDED in Milan, Italy in 1994 as Sleep Of Right. The band have steadily risen with a series of strong albums to become widely tipped for greater status. In recent years, blessed with the photogenic Cristina Scabbia, they have made serious headway into the European rock market and have transferred this interest successfully into the USA.

Scabbia had previously been employed as a session singer, first meeting male vocalist Andrea Ferro and bass player Marco Coti Zelati in Milan's Midnight club. The band operated under a revised name of Ethereal prior to adopting Lacuna Coil, which they adopted as a poetic synonym for 'empty spiral'. A two-track Ethereal demo in May 1996 led to a deal with Germany's Century Media.

On the release of the debut mini-album, produced by Grip Inc.'s Waldemar Sorychta, Lacuna Coil were unkindly tagged by a British journalist as "Gothic doom Bon Jovi with female vocals" while the band merely described their music as "darkly dreamy". Before the release, a December 1997 support tour in Europe to Portuguese act Moonspell was followed by the departure, three shows into the tour, of guitarist Raffaele Zagaria (who had joined the band in 1994), guitarist Claudio Leo, and Leonardo Forti (who replaced original drummer Michaelangelo). Undaunted, Lacuna Coil persevered, pulling in Anders Iwers from Tiamat and Cemetary on guitar and Markus Freiwald of Kreator on drums.

The band regrouped in January 1998, enlisting Thy Nature's Cristiano Migliore on guitar and Time Machine's Cristiano Mozzati on drums. This revised formation embarked on European touring throughout April with The Gathering and Siegmen. Shows featured Node's Steve Minelli on guitar and keyboard player Alice Chiarelli.

Lacuna Coil put in an inaugural set at the August 1998 'Wacken' festival before gearing up for the recording of *In A Reverie*. As 1999 opened, the band were brought up to strength with the addition of guitarist Marco Biazzi and soon after engaged in European mainland touring with England's Skyclad. On the back of these gigs, Lacuna Coil jumped on board the May 'Into The Darkness' package alongside Samael, My Insanity, and Grip Inc.. Returning to their homeland, the band played the 'Gods Of Metal' festival headlined by Metallica, and guested for Lacrimosa in Germany during October. The last three dates were cancelled when Biazzi broke a rib falling downstairs.

The new millennium witnessed Lacuna Coil back in action with the *Halflife* EP, including a cover of Dubstar's 'Stars'. They undertook a series of headline shows in Europe in April and performed in Mexico for the first time during December. A new studio album, *Unleashed Memories*, was released in January before more European dates and a place in the high-profile March 'Metal Odyssey' package of Dimmu Borgir, Nevermore, In Flames, and Susperia. In April, the band executed headline gigs in Italy, and in December they toured North America for the first time as support to Moonspell.

Lacuna Coil announced a month of North American dates commencing in San Francisco on September 16th 2002, backing up headliners In Flames and Sentenced with support from Killswitch Engage. However, with the release date for a new studio album, *Comalies*, pushed back, the band later withdrew from these shows. An extensive European tour scheduled as guests to Sentenced took the band through October. The arrival of *Comalies*, preceded by the single 'Heaven's A Lie', did much to establish the band as one of the leading lights on the post-gothic rock

---

LACUNA COIL discography

Lacuna Coil, Century Media CM 77201-2 (Europe), Century Media CM 7901-2 (USA) (1998)

IN A REVERIE, Century Media CM 77234-2 (Europe), Century Media CM 7934-2 (USA) (1999)

Halflife, Century Media CM 77239-2 (Europe) (2000)

UNLEASHED MEMORIES, Century Media CM 77360-2 (Europe), Century Media CM 8060-2 (USA) (2001)

COMALIES, Century Media CM 77560-2 (Europe), Century Media CM 8160-2 (USA) (2002) **194 USA**

KARMACODE, Century Media CM 77660-2 (Europe), Century Media CM 8360-2 (USA) (2006) **47 UK, 28 USA**

scene. The band announced North American tour dates for January 2003, billed as the '4 Absent Friends Tour', with Opeth, Paradise Lost, and Tapping The Vein. Unfortunately, the band were forced to drop out of these gigs due to visa difficulties. However, they did tour North America, supporting Opeth, in May 2003.

As the video for 'Heaven's A Lie' received major TV rotation in Germany, Lacuna Coil's European headline gigs in December saw them topping a bill comprising Moonspell, Passenger, and Poisonblack. The band then put in an extensive run of headline Italian dates in March and April 2004 as 'Heaven's A Lie' dominated Italian radio.

US sales of *Comalies* were now past the 60,000 mark and the band formed an American touring package alongside headliners P.O.D. and support acts Blindside and Hazen Street. A new single, 'Swamped', featured on the soundtrack to the movie *Resident Evil: Apocalypse*. Lacuna Coil then joined the ranks of the 'Ozzfest', sharing the second stage with headline act Slipknot and supports Unearth, Lamb Of God, Every Time I Die, Hatebreed, Atreyu, and Bleeding Through. The *Comalies* album was reissued as a special 'Ozzfest' two-disc set, adding acoustic renditions, live performances, radio edits, and videos for 'Heaven's A Lie' and 'Swamped'.

In July it was revealed that *Comalies* had passed the 100,000 sales mark in the USA and that Lacuna Coil had become Century Media's top-selling artist to date: with over 250,000 sales worldwide at this point, they were said to be the top-selling Italian rock act of all time. This momentum pushed the album into the *Billboard* charts in July, hitting Number 194 by selling 5,818 copies in one week and marking the debut *Billboard* placing for both band and label. With promotion for *Comalies* finally at a close, the band returned to Italy. Scabbia almost immediately found herself back in the studio, duetting with famous Italian singer Franco Battiato on the song 'I'm That' on his Sony album *Dieci Stratagemmi*.

November found the band in Milan working on pre-production with Waldemar Sorychta. The group closed the year with a special performance on December 27th at the Carling Apollo in London's Hammersmith alongside In Flames, Caliban, and Chimaira. Century Media capped 2004 by announcing that *Comalies* was the label's best-selling record to date, selling nearly 150,000 copies in the USA over the previous 12 months, and that the album had broken all sales records for the company. By March 2005 *Comalies* had surpassed 200,000 sales.

In 2005, 'Swamped' featured on the *Code Red* album, a collection given to US soldiers in the Middle East. October found the band headlining the Belgian 'Metal Female Voices III' festival alongside The Legion Of Hetheria, Leaves' Eyes, Epica, Elis, Midnattsol, Skeptical Minds, Mercury Rain, Asrai, Autumn, Diluvium, and After Forever.

The new album *Karmacode*, produced by Sorychta and released in April 2006, featured a cover of the Depeche Mode track 'Enjoy The Silence'. Upon release of the album, the band engaged in a series of major-city acoustic performances and in-store signings across the USA.

Lacuna Coil announced US touring plans supporting Rob Zombie in April to coincide with the new album, and the group shared the 'Ozzfest' stage with Ozzy Osbourne, System Of A Down, Hatebreed, Black Label Society, Disturbed, and supporting cast. The female-fronted metal trend set by Lacuna Coil and Finns Nightwish may have run its course, but the band clearly possess enough talent to warrant a place on the international metal scene for years to come.

MOONSPELL
GOTHIC ELEGANCE FROM IBERIA

Brandoa-based Moonspell are the band that put Portugal on the international metal map. They were founded in the 1989 as Morbid God and released the *Serpent Angel* demo in 1992 with former Bactherion

bassist Tetragrammaton (real name João Pedro). On January 24th 1993 the band, who had changed their name to Moonspell, released the original version of the *Anno Satanæ* demo, which was re-distributed through Lion Records in February. The same year, the group featured on the *Mortuary Vol. 1* split album issued by Skeleton Records, shared with Bowelrot, Silent Scream, Extreme Unction, and Thormentor. Both vocalist Langsuyar (Fernando Ribeiro) and guitarist Mantus sessioned in 1993 on Filii Nigrantium Infernalium's *Os Métodos Do Pentagrama* demo.

The Molon Lave label issued a 7-inch single, 'Goat On Fire' / 'Wolves From The Fog', in 1994. Citing Satan as a "source of inspiration", the cover listed the band as Langsuyar T.R. on lead vocals, Mantus H.G.D. on lead guitar, Malah L.L. on rhythm guitar, Tetragrammaton T.M. on bass, and Nisroch O.F. on the drums.

French label Adipocere then issued the EP *Under the Moonspell* in 1994. The members were listed as Langsuyar Tenebrarum Rex ("Dramatic, erudit vox and passioned metaphors"), Mantus Iberius Daemonium ("Six string occult citar"), Tanngrisnir Imperator Ignis ("Six string celtic harp"), Tetragrammaton Tremendae Majestatis ("Four string Arabic 'ud"), Neophytus Lupus Maris ("Ethnic and tragic ambience keys"), and Nisroth de Occulta Fraternitatis ("Traditional, classical and vile percussions"). Produced by Quim Monte at Edit Studios in the winter of 1993, the tracks incorporated musical embellishments from Sara Carreiras on Bisel flute; Nuno Flores on violin; timpani and gongs courtesy of the Sociedade Filarmónica Comércio e Indústria da Amadora; and additional vocalists in Antonieta Lopes, Sara Arega (who supplied "moans" on 'Opus Diabolicum'), and Arabic vocals from Abdul Sewtea.

MOONSPELL discography

Goat On Fire / Wolves From The Fog, Molon Lave MLR-SP-039 (Europe) (1994) 7-inch vinyl single

Under The Moonspell, Adipocere CD AR 021 (Europe) (1994)

WOLFHEART, Century Media CM 77097-2 (Europe), Century Media CM 7797-2 (USA) (1995)

IRRELIGIOUS, Century Media CM 77123-2 (Europe), Century Media CM 7823-2 (USA) (1996)

Opium, Century Media CM 77140-2 (Europe) (1996)

2econd Skin, Century Media CM 77189-2 (Europe) (1997)

SIN – PECADO, Century Media CM 77190-2 (Europe), Century Media CM 7890-2 (USA) (1998)

THE BUTTERFLY EFFECT, Century Media CM 77290-2 (Europe), Century Media CM 7990-2 (USA) (1999)

DARKNESS AND HOPE, Century Media CM 77390-2 (Europe), Century Media CM 8090-2 (USA) (2001)

THE ANTIDOTE, Century Media CM 77490-2 (Europe), Century Media CM 8190-2 (USA) (2003)

MEMORIAL, Steamhammer SPV 085-99822 (Europe), Steamhammer SPV 99822 (USA) (2006)

Now the frontrunners of the Portuguese metal scene, Moonspell were quick to accept an offer from the German label Century Media. The resulting album was April 1995's *Wolfheart*, produced by Grip Inc. guitarist Waldemar Sorychta, and it received much favourable press. Subsequent digipack variants of *Wolfheart* hosted an additional track, 'Atægina'.

Moonspell toured Europe supporting Tiamat and Morbid Angel in 1995 before recording a second album, *Irreligious*, which was released in July 1996. Female vocals were contributed by Brigit Zacher on the song 'Raven Claws' while Markus Freiwald scored a percussion credit on 'For A Taste Of Eternity'. Promoting *Irreligious*, Moonspell conducted two European tours as their stature grew – evolving from a guest slot with Samael to a much higher-profile jaunt with Type O Negative.

In 1997, the band released the *2econd Skin Live* double EP, including a Sorychta-produced cover of Depeche Mode's 'Sacred' and seven live tracks recorded on the 'Perverse Almost Religious' tour in 1997. The 1998 album *Sin-Pecado* displayed a more adventurous style than previous efforts, although the band's move away from metal led bassist Ares to depart. Moonspell persevered, putting in shows during 1997 supporting heavyweights such as Kiss and Manowar. UK gigs in September 1998 saw Moonspell packaged with Anathema and Therion before releasing *The Butterfly Effect* in 1999.

The band toured Germany in early 2000 supported by Kreator and Katatonia. Their 2001 album *Darkness And Hope* made Number 79 on the German charts, and (bravely) they took on a cover version of Ozzy Osbourne's classic 'Mr. Crowley'. The band then began a headline North American tour, supported by Italian act Lacuna Coil, on December 5th at the Trocadero in Philadelphia. Moonspell were back on a further European string of dates in March 2002, co-billed with label-mates Tiamat and Flowing Tears.

The band recorded a version of the jazz standard 'I'll See You In My Dreams' in early 2003 for inclusion on the soundtrack of a Portuguese horror movie. In March, Moonspell severed ties with bass player Sérgio Crestana (who had joined the band in 1997), drafting in Niclas Etelävuori of Finnish act Amorphis for the recording of a new album, *The Antidote*, in Helsinki with producer Hiili Hiilesmaa. Former Malevolence man Aires Pereira took over the bass position in June.

The Antidote was a first for Moonspell as the band collaborated with novelist José Luis Peixoto, who authored a book based upon the album. An English translation of this work was included on the record as a bonus multimedia track. The single 'Everything Invaded' entered the Portuguese charts at Number 9. Initial North American touring found them packaged with Type O Negative and Cradle Of Filth for shows in November before European co-headline gigs in December, on which the band topped a bill comprising Lacuna Coil, Passenger, and Poisonblack. The band got back on the road in the New Year supporting Opeth on their 'Lamentations Over America Tour 2004' commencing in Redmonton, Canada on January 20th.

Moonspell entered the studio in April to commence work on a new album, before dates in Chile, Mexico, and Brazil. In recognition of their services to their homeland, the band were invited to a formal reception at the Portugal Embassy in Santiago. Ribeiro guested on tracks for two fellow Portuguese acts, featuring on Thragedium's album *Isolationist* and on 'Devil's Lover' on The Temple's *Diesel Dog Sound*.

Ribeiro then issued a collection of poems, *As Feridas Essenciais* ('The Essential Wounds'), and translated into Portuguese a fictional biography of HP Lovecraft written by Hans Rodionoff. The singer also cut a guest appearance on Volstad's version of The Cure's 'Apart' for inclusion on a tribute album issued by Germany's Equinox label.

The band were then commissioned by choreographer Rui Lopes Graça to compose a score for a contemporary dance performance, premiering in January 2005 at the Gulbenkian main auditorium in Lisbon. Moonspell played as special guests to Cradle Of Filth, with support band

The Haunted, for an extensive European tour commencing February through to April 2005.

Working with producer Sorychta once again, the band entered Woodhouse Studios in Germany during September to cut tracks for a new album, *Memorial*. In November, they announced a new contract with SPV Records. In downtime, Fernando Ribeiro guested on the track 'Silent Cries' included on Assemblent's *Equilibrium* album.

In March 2006, live activity for the band included Russian shows in Moscow and St. Petersburg. Their status in their homeland was affirmed in early May when the *Memorial* album debuted at Number 1 on the Portuguese charts. Further live work included a gig in Casablanca, Morocco in June and festival appearances at the Belgian 'Graspop Metal Meeting' and the Abtsgmünd 'Summer Breeze' event in Germany.

A DVD titled *Lunar Still/13 Years Of Doom*, centred on a live concert in Katowice, Poland, was scheduled for a 2007 release via Century Media at the time of writing. Moonspell deserve much respect for bringing international attention to their country from metal fans.

NIGHTWISH
GENRE-DEFINING METAL PIONEERS

UNDOUBTEDLY THE FOREMOST exponents of the operatic metal genre, Nightwish accumulated a crop of Number 1 chart placings and homeland platinum discs – only to shock fans in 2005 by dismissing their striking singer Tarja Turunen. The band were originally conceived in the town of Kitee, Finland as a side project for Nattvindens Gråt keyboard player Tuomas Holopainen. Nattvindens Gråt had put out two albums for Germany's Solistitium label, 1995's *A Bard's Tale* and 1997's *Chaos Without Theory*. From the very outset, Holopainen drove the concept, writing music and lyrics.

The first incarnation of Nightwish consisted of Holopainen, guitarist Erno 'Emppu' Vuorinen, and singer Turunen, who had studied classical singing at the Sibelius Academy of Kuopio. They started life as a folk band, recording three acoustic-based songs between October and December 1996, collecting them as *Wishes In The Night*. However, they decided that a better vehicle for the singing power of Turunen was heavy metal.

Nightwish's inaugural demo was a strictly acoustic affair, but a second tape cut in April the following year introduced electric guitars and drums. The band drafted in a permanent drummer, Jukka Nevalainen. By May they had secured a two-album deal with the Finnish label Spinefarm. A debut single titled 'The Carpenter', split with Children Of Bodom and Thy Serpent, entered the Finnish charts at Number 8 in 1997.

Nightwish's debut album – effectively a set of demos, with some tracks lacking bass parts – was recorded at Kitee's Huvikeskus studio. Entitled *Angels Fall First*, the record was released that November, reaching Number 31 in the Finnish charts. The band's first live appearance was in Kitee on December 31st 1997. Momentum slowed, however, as Holopainen and Vuorinen were waylaid by their military draft and Turunen engaged herself in studies. During this period, Spinefarm extended the band's contract and a video was filmed for 'The Carpenter' in April 1998.

Recordings commenced at Caverock Studio with Tero Kinnunen for a second album, *Oceanborn*, which featured a guesting Tapio Wilska (of Darkwoods My Betrothed and Nattvindens Gråt) donating 'devil' and 'Pharaoh' vocals. Unexpectedly, a new single, 'Sacrament Of Wilderness', hit Number 1 in Finland.

Another single, 'Sleeping Sun', was recorded in mid 1999. It included a cover of 'Walking On The Air', originally on the soundtrack to the children's animated movie *The Snowman*. Such was the band's impact in Germany that 'Sleeping Sun' sold over 15,000 copies in its first month of release. Nightwish then partnered Rage for 26 gigs in Germany.

In early 2000, the band took an unexpected diversion by entering the Eurovision Song Contest with the track 'Sleepwalker' and finished in a respectable second place. They then repeated their earlier success with the *Wishmaster* album, which reached gold status just two hours after stores opened. The album easily took the Finnish Number 1 spot and remained there for three weeks. Co-produced by the band and Tero Kinnunen, the album's *tour de force*, 'The Kinslayer' with Ike Vil of Babylon Whores on guest vocals, took the band into controversial territory, with its story based on the 1999 US Columbine school massacre. *Wishmaster* also made significant headway in Europe, peaking at Number 21 in Germany and Number 66 in France. With interest in Nightwish rising rapidly, Spinefarm issued a limited-edition set, *Golden Wishes*, comprising the band's first three albums and a disc of rarities in picture-disc format.

Nightwish headlined a clutch of major festival events in Finland before touring Panama, Mexico, Brazil, Chile, and Argentina in July 2000. Returning to Europe, they put in appearances at the 'Wacken Open Air'

event in Germany and the Belgian 'Biebop' festival before a European headline trek. Canada was next on the agenda, with a brace of Montreal gigs in November. The year was capped with the filming and recording of a live album and DVD at Tampere on December 29th.

The band scored their fourth consecutive gold single in Finland during summer 2001 with 'Over The Hills And Far Away', a cover of the Gary Moore tune. The EP also hosted two new recordings and a remake of 'Astral Romance'. A German variant, released through the Drakkar label, added a further six live tracks. The single entered the charts at the top spot and remained on the listing for nearly a year, re-entering again in 2004. In October 2001, Vänskä was replaced by Marco Hietala, a founder member of Finnish metal act Tarot.

The *Century Child* album, released in May 2002, boosted Nightwish on the global scene. It debuted on the Finnish charts at Number 1 and soon achieved platinum status for 30,000 units sold. Singles from the record performed well and the band toured South America again. At this

NIGHTWISH discography

ANGELS FALL FIRST, Spinefarm SPI 47CD (Europe) (1997)
OCEANBORN, Spinefarm SPI 67CD (Europe) (1998)
WISHMASTER, Spinefarm SPI 87CD (Europe) (2000), Century
   Media CM 8001-2 (USA) (2001)
FROM WISHES TO ETERNITY – LIVE, Spinefarm SPI 100CD
   (Europe) (2001)
Over The Hills And Far Away, Spinefarm SPI 118CD (Europe)
   (2001)
CENTURY CHILD, Spinefarm SPI 149CD (Europe) (2002), Century
   Media CM 8189-2 (USA) (2003)
ONCE, Nuclear Blast NB 1291-2 (Europe), Roadrunner 618217
   (2004) (USA) **108 UK**
END OF AN ERA, Nuclear Blast NB 1679-0 (Europe) (2006)

commercial peak, Turunen announced that she was planning to take time out from the band. The other members maintained their work schedule with sessions and other projects. An October 2003 DVD, *End Of Innocence*, featured a bonus CD titled *Nightwish: Live At Summer Breeze 2002.*

The first signs of a 2004 release from Nightwish came with the announcement that they were to work with esteemed film director Antti Jokinen on a video for the 'Nemo' single. As expected, 'Nemo' was a huge success across Europe. So successful had the band become in their homeland that the Finnish post office printed a commemorative stamp, and the Pirkanmaan Uusi Panimo company brewed a Nightwish 'Megabueno Cerveza' beer. The band, having cut a video for the single 'I Wish I Had An Angel', lined up a North American tour for August 2004, supported by fellow Finnish band Lullacry.

The album, *Once*, sold over 80,000 copies in its first week on sale in Germany to debut at the top of the album charts there. Nightwish repeated the feat in Greece, Finland, and Norway and the album became Nuclear Blast's most successful record to date.

In September, Turunen entered Finnvox Studios in Helsinki with producer Esa Nieminen to record two traditional Christmas songs, 'En Etsi Valtaa, Loistoa' and 'Kun Joulu On' for her first solo single. A retrospective compilation album, *Tales From The Elvenpath*, landed at Number 7 on the German album charts.

A third single lifted from the album for Finnish release on November 24th, 'Kuolema Tekee Taiteilijan', included a live version of Megadeth's 'Symphony Of Destruction' recorded at the Nosturi in Helsinki in October. On the same day as the single release, which debuted at Number 1 in Finland, Spinefarm put out a special 'platinum' edition of the *Once* album, adding extra tracks and the 'Nemo' video.

Renewed European touring throughout February 2004 saw Norwegians Tristania as opening act. The same month, the band dominated the prestigious Finnish Emma-Gaala awards, held at the Kulttuuritalolla in Helsinki. Nightwish won the 'Metal Album Of The Year', 'Best Selling Album', 'Band Of The Year', and 'Export-Emma' categories, and the public voted them 'Best Finnish Artist'.

Immediately after the band's final show of 2005, at the Hartwall Arena in Helsinki, Nightwish fans were stunned to read an "open letter" on the official website, effectively sacking Turunen. Written by keyboard player Holopainen, the statement was harshly critical (and clearly suffered in translation): "To you, unfortunately, business, money and things that have nothing to do with those emotions have become much more important. You feel that you have sacrificed yourself and your musical career for Nightwish, rather than thinking what it has given to you. You have said yourself that you are merely a 'guest musician' in Nightwish. Now that

visit ends and we will continue Nightwish with a new female vocalist." Further accusations blamed Turunen for a "diva"-like attitude and for having apparently threatened to leave the band "at a day's notice".

Subsequently, Holopainen revealed that the personal problems were entrenched to such a degree that he and Turunen had "not spoken with each other for many years". The singer responded, saying simply that she was "devastated" and adding: "It has been very cruel the way the band handled this in public." She subsequently held a tearful press conference in Finland where she revealed that she had in fact resolved to leave Nightwish in December 2004.

A planned live DVD, *End Of An Era*, was apparently in jeopardy: Finnish newspapers reported that Turunen was refusing to sign the necessary contracts for its release unless agreements were made forbidding any comments by the band about Turunen or her husband-manager Marcelo Cabuli. This suggestion would reportedly impose a 250,000 fine (about $330,000) each time the terms of the contract were violated. *End Of An Era* was eventually released in June 2006.

Although still yet to announce the name of their new vocalist, Nightwish commenced new recordings on September 15th 2006. In November, as Turunen's solo album *Henkäys Ikuisuudesta* entered the Finnish charts at Number 7, gossip magazine *Katso* reported that Holopainen and manager Ewo Rytkönen had been in contact with Epica singer Simone Simons with a view to her replacing Turunen; however, this was denied by Epica who issued a statement saying that Simone Simons would not be leaving the band.

Nightwish's enormous fanbase were still waiting for news of the new singer as this book went to press. Whatever Nightwish do next, it is sure to be on a grand scale.

PARADISE LOST
ONE OF THE UNHOLY TRINITY OF GOTH-DOOM

ALONGSIDE ANATHEMA AND My Dying Bride, Paradise Lost are one of three groundbreaking acts from northern England discovered and fostered by the Peaceville label. The band from Halifax, replete with gothic overtones and a trademark bleak outlook on life, gradually diverted into more mainstream territory to increasing commercial success.

They started life as a death metal act in early 1988 with singer Nick Holmes, guitar players Gregor Mackintosh and Aaron Aedy, bassist Stephen Edmondson, and Matthew Archer on drums. Their debut live performance at Bradford's Frog And Toad pub was secured by their debut demo, a 1988 single-track rehearsal recording titled *Morbid Existence*. Proceeds from the three-track *Paradise Lost* demo financed two gigs in Holland. Further demo cassettes ensued: 1989's *Frozen Illusion* and *Pain Of Desolation.*

Signing with Peaceville, Paradise Lost laid down tracks throughout the winter of 1989 at Academy Studios in Bradford, label boss Paul Halmshaw manning the board. Kay Field contributed female vocals to the track 'Breeding Fear'. The eminence of *Lost Paradise* in the sea of international death metal was due to the unusually brooding, near-doom metal nature of the band's approach and the conviction of Holmes's narrative, especially his unorthodox lyrical delivery. This latter trait came to serve the band well, often a focal point of fans' obsession. The group's second release came in June with the 12-inch EP *In Dub*, hosting two radically remixed album tracks. The year closed with the issue of a live video, *Live Death*, filmed at the Bradford Queens Hall in November 1989.

Capitalising on this solid progress, Paradise Lost were rushed back into Academy Studios in November 1990, working with engineer Keith Appleton on a second album. March 1991's *Gothic* secured chart placings across Europe, doing especially well in Germany. The album once again

PARADISE LOST discography

LOST PARADISE, Peaceville VILE17CD (UK) (1990)

In Dub, Peaceville VILE19TCD (UK) (1990)

GOTHIC, Peaceville VILE26CD (UK) (1991)

SHADES OF GOD, Music For Nations CDMFN135 (UK), Metal Blade 3984-14001-2 (USA) (1992)

As I Die, Music For Nations CDKUT150 (UK) (1993)

ICON, Music For Nations CDMFN152 (UK), Metal Blade 3984-14021-2 (USA) (1993)

Seals The Sense, Music For Nations CDKUT157 (UK) (1994)

Gothic EP, Peaceville VILE41CD (UK) (1994)

The Last Time, Music For Nations CDKUT165 (UK) (1995) **60 UK**

DRACONIAN TIMES, Music For Nations CDMFN184 (UK) (1995), Relativity CRT 1537 (USA) (1996) **16 UK**

ONE SECOND, Music For Nations CDMFN222 (UK) (1997) **31 UK**

HOST, EMI Electrola 5205672 (Europe) (1999) **61 UK**

BELIEVE IN NOTHING, EMI Electrola 5307072 (Europe) (2001), Koch KOC-CD-8433 (USA) (2002)

SYMBOL OF LIFE, G.U.N. 74321 96178 2 (Europe), Koch KOC-CD-8434 (USA) (2002)

PARADISE LOST AT THE BBC, Strange Fruit SFRSCD 114 (UK) (2003)

PARADISE LOST, G.U.N. 82876 67189 2 (Europe), Abacus Recordings 19 (USA) (2005)

expanded beyond the traditional death metal format, employing the Raptured Symphony Orchestra and singer Sarah Marrion. *Gothic* catalysed a whole genre that followed in its wake, the album's authority spawning legions of imitators.

After live dates, Paradise Lost switched labels to Music For Nations and released the *Shades Of God* album in July 1992. Produced by Simon Effemy at Longhome Studios in Northampton, with keyboards from Robert John Godfrey of progressive outfit The Enid and more vocals from Sarah Marrion, the record pulled the band out of the underground and into the mainstream. Until now, Paradise Lost's triumphs had all been on mainland Europe: even the UK had not truly recognised the band. *Shades Of God* made their presence felt at home and across the world. Regular vinyl versions of the album came minus the track 'As I Die', which was chosen for single release in April 1993 backed by out-takes 'Rape Of Virtue' and a cover of Atomic Rooster's 'Death Walks Behind You'.

In 1993, Paradise Lost undertook their first tour of North America, supporting Morbid Angel and Kreator. That summer, the band commenced work on *Icon* at Jacobs Studios, retaining Effemy as producer. Female vocals were contributed by Denise Bernard while Andrew Holdsworth supplied keyboards. *Icon*, released in September 1993, hit the national German charts at Number 31. To close the year, the band put in openers in the UK to Sepultura.

At the start of 1994, the band and producer Effemy retreated to the confines of Academy Studios in January, assembling tracks for the *Seals The Sense* EP in February. In May, the group appeared at the Aerosmith-headlined 'Rock Am Ring' festival in Germany to over 80,000 people; their rise had been so swift that by mid 1994, Paradise Lost were outselling even Metallica in Germany. Their status was strengthened by the popularity of the *Harmony Breaks* concert video, recorded at the Longhorn in Stuttgart, Germany on September 5th 1993 and bolstered by four promo clips, which secured a Number 19 position in the German video charts. The *In Dub* songs, along with a previously unheard variant of 'The Painless', was put out in June by Peaceville as the *Gothic* EP.

By the end of 1994, Paradise Lost were already working on the follow-up to *Icon*, although the stability of the unit was broken when they parted company with drummer Matt Archer. By Christmas, ex-Marshall Law and Life man Lee Morris found himself on the drum stool. Fans had the first opportunity to sample the new band when the single 'The Last Time' emerged in May 1995 featuring a cover of The Sisters Of Mercy's 'Walk Away'. The group performed British warm-up dates around this release, under the guise of The Painless.

The album *Draconian Times* arrived in June, recorded by the band and Effemy at Great Linford Manor studios. A limited-edition digipack offered a second disc, *Live Tracks, Demos & B-Sides*, comprising five live recordings, plus demos and out-takes. The band toured hard promoting the new record, taking in new territories such as Australia, Japan, South America, and Mexico and putting in a headlining appearance at the Dynamo Festival in Holland for good measure. After the tour, *Draconian Times* could boast over one million worldwide sales. Relativity Records licensed the record for the USA, although the group did not tour there to promote it.

After a lengthy spell away from the public eye, Paradise Lost re-emerged in 1997 with a new look and a radically different style. The opening release of the year was the 'True Belief' single, hosting an interpretation of The Smiths' 'How Soon Is Now'. The album, July's *One Second*, retained heaviness but drew on more diverse artists in the gothic mould. Ironically, the album turned out to be Paradise Lost's most important release. *One Second* cracked the German and Swedish Top 10s and gave the band a boost everywhere ... except, it seemed, in the UK. Longstanding fans condemned the band's new image and the way they had discarded their doom/death metal roots, and the protest was felt in a rather lowly UK chart entry at Number 31. Gregor Mackintosh responded by stating that he was "bored" of guitar solos. Subsequent touring found the band concentrating on the European market, although British dates were slotted in during January 1998.

Now a significant force in Europe and enjoying headline festival positions, Paradise Lost took a step up to a major label by contracting with EMI Electrola in Germany for their next album, *Host*. The record was produced by Simon Lyon and delivered in May 1999. The band plunged headlong into electro-rock, completely shedding any vestiges of their extreme metal past. *Host* performed well across the continent, peaking at Number 4 in Germany – but only managing a humble 61 in the UK.

They returned with the John Fryer-produced *Believe In Nothing*, rectifying the sparse guitar quota of *Host* somewhat, in February 2001. Japanese versions, issued on the Toshiba EMI label, came with three extra tracks – 'Sway', 'Gone', and 'Waiting For God'.

The band toured Germany in March, where *Believe* had achieved another high chart placing, co-headlining with gothic veterans The Sisters Of Mercy. Paradise Lost then announced a new deal with the G.U.N. label in May 2002, setting to work with producer Rhys Fulber on a new record – provisionally entitled *Deus* but subsequently switched to *Symbol Of Life*. Early reports revealed that the band had demoed a cover of Bronski Beat's 'Small Town Boy' (one in a long line of gothic bands to have covered this track) and Dead Can Dance's 'Xavier'. *Symbol Of Life* became another hit in Germany, reinforced by headline dates throughout Europe in February 2003. Scandinavian dates had the band packaged alongside Within Temptation and Lithium. They announced North American tour dates for January 2003, billed as the '4 Absent Friends Tour', with Opeth and Tapping The Vein. UK shows in March also included Tapping The Vein and added Killing Miranda to the bill.

Following a run of September European headline shows, the band united with Amorphis for Scandinavian dates in October. Closing a nine-year tenure, Paradise Lost parted ways with drummer Lee Morris in March 2004: he soon returned to the studio to session for Marshall Law. The

band entered the studio with producer Fulber in April and announced Jeff Singer (Blaze and Kill II This) as their new sticksman the following month. Backing vocals came from Tapping The Vein singer Heather Thompson.

The band geared up toward a new album, billed simply *Paradise Lost* and issued through G.U.N. in February 2005 – but a succession of delays in major territories such as the UK and the USA greatly diluted its impact.

Live activity commenced in December 2004 with a string of European and Scandinavian shows. However, the band were forced to withdraw from Spain's 'Atarfe Vega Rock' festival when Mackintosh was hospitalised with a burst appendix in February 2005. Live dates in Europe saw the band gaining a valuable support slot to Judas Priest in April, but they withdrew from these due to concerns over Mackintosh's health. Subsequent headline European gigs saw Israeli act Orphaned Land in support.

A notable gig on September 17th saw Paradise Lost headline a festival in the Ukrainian capital of Kiev – without Mackintosh, who was recuperating in England after surgery. He also missed the final dates in Moscow, St. Petersburg, Bucharest, and Sofia to have a second operation.

In October 2006, Paradise Lost announced that they would soon be entering the studio with producer Rhys Fulber to begin recording a new album. A tentative worldwide release date was set for Spring 2007 through Century Media, and the fans wait with great eagerness for the new record.

RHAPSODY OF FIRE
POWER AND PRECISION COMBINED

THE EPIC METAL ACT RHAPSODY OF FIRE – for many years known simply as Rhapsody – hail from the Trieste and the Friuli-Venezia Giulia region of Italy. They started life in 1993 as Thundercross. Guitarist Luca Turilli's classical heritage (his father had been a famous concert cellist) combined with symphonic metal made the 1994 *Thundercross* demo, fronted by singer Cristiano Adacher, stand out from the crowd. Once Rhapsody's debut album had burst onto the European musical landscape, so many fans and budding musicians took notice of the group's grandiose approach – laden with pomp, lavish keyboard flurries, and unashamedly romantic fantasy content – that an entirely new genre was born.

Thundercross's *Land Of Immortals* demo included tracks that would evolve into Rhapsody numbers – 'Invernal Fury' becoming 'Rage Of The Winter' and 'Holy Wind' re-worked into 'Riding The Winds Of Eternity'. The cassette was shaped by Turilli, Adacher, bassist Andrea Furlan, keyboard player Alex Staropoli, and Daniele Carbonera on drums, and it

attracted the attention of German melodic rock guru Limb Schnoor. Signing to Schnoor's Limb Music Products, the band soon changed names to Rhapsody.

Now fronted by ex-Labyrinth and Athena vocalist Fabio Leone, they debuted with the seven-track *Eternal Glory* demo in 1995. Rhapsody's debut album, *Legendary Tales*, issued in October 1997, reaped massive plaudits for the band across the European metal community. However, bass player Andrea Furlan departed prior to its release. Despite Rhapsody's rising profile, Leone still stuck to his vocal position with Athena. *Legendary Tales* defined the Rhapsody sound from the outset, with keyboards to the fore, liberal showers of strings, and frequent flute and piano passages punctuating a set of songs wallowing in nostalgic, heraldic mythology. The album marked the start of a sprawling 'Emerald Sword' legend that would pan out over future albums.

Rhapsody's second album really put them on the map. October 1998's *Symphony Of Enchanted Lands*, for which ex-Sinesthesia bassist Alessandro Lotta joined the band, sold in excess of 100,000 copies in Europe alone. Collectors' appetites were satisfied by a 5,000-only run with an expanded booklet, a set of six postcards, six stickers, two dragon tattoos, an 'Emerald Sword' pendant, and a dragon-shaped metal badge. For live work, the band were joined by ex-Sieges Even drummer Alex Holzwarth and former Dream Child guitarist Dominique Leurquin.

Luca Turilli issued a successful solo album, *King Of The Nordic Twilight*, in 1999. Leone busied himself with an outside project, too, forming Vision Divine for a self-titled album in alliance with Labyrinth guitarist Olaf Thörsen in 2000. Meanwhile, Rhapsody committed a version of 'Guardians' to the 2000 Helloween tribute album *Keepers Of Jericho*.

Holzwarth united some of his ex-Sieges Even colleagues to found Looking Glass Self in 2000. The drummer sessioned on Edguy man Tobias Sammet's Avantasia album the same year. Rhapsody's third outing, the more guitar-orientated *Dawn Of Victory*, emerged in October. Limited digipack variants hosted an additional disc of alternative versions and videos. Sales of *Dawn Of Victory* surpassed those of its predecessor, ranking higher in Germany and also impacting in Sweden. Switches in the recording line-up saw the mysterious Thunderforce manning the drum stool, an individual whose anonymity was enforced for "contractual reasons". Meanwhile, Leone guested on the 2001 debut album from Argentinian symphonic metal band Beto Vasquez Infinity, who often performed Rhapsody's 'Land Of Immortals'.

Rhapsody re-emerged in November 2001 with the grandiose *Rain Of A Thousand Flames*. This extended EP included the track 'Queen Of The Dark Horizons', for which Rhapsody claimed direct inspiration from prog-rock pioneers Goblin's *Phenomena* soundtrack. The album also hosted 'The Wizard's Last Rhymes', a reconstructed rendition of Antonin Dvorak's *New World Symphony*.

The following month it was announced that bassist Lotta was going on to join Finnish prog-metal band Wingdom and had been replaced by Patrice Guers, a man boasting credits with the Patrick Rondat band and Consortium Project. Holzwarth then acted as a stand-in for the first nine shows of Kamelot's January 2002 European dates.

The fourth and concluding chapter of the 'Emerald Sword' saga, *Power Of The Dragonflame*, arrived in March 2002 with a darker, sinister production capped by the 20-minute monolith 'Gargoyles, Angels Of Darkness'. Once again the group utilised guest vocalists and choirs, embellishing this aspect of their sound to a greater degree with the inclusion of baroque singer Bridget Fogle. Rhapsody continued touring in Europe with an April schedule alongside Angel Dust and At Vance.

The band then revealed plans for two working projects, one titled *Rhapsody In Black*, the other a Tolkien-inspired *Lord Of The Rings* piece. However, by June, Rhapsody had scotched both ideas, apparently deeming *Rhapsody In Black* as not in keeping with the band's 'positive'

RHAPSODY discography

LEGENDARY TALES, Limb Music Products LMP 9710-001 (Europe / USA) (1997)

SYMPHONY OF ENCHANTED LANDS, Limb Music Products LMP 9810-007 (Europe / USA) (1998)

DAWN OF VICTORY, Limb Music Products LMP 0010-023 (Europe / USA) (2000)

RAIN OF A THOUSAND FLAMES, Limb Music Products LMP 0110-036 (Europe / USA) (2001)

POWER OF THE DRAGONFLAME, Limb Music Products LMP 0203-040 (Europe /USA) (2002)

The Dark Secret, Magic Circle Music SPV 69730 (Europe / USA) (2004)

SYMPHONY OF UNCHARTED LANDS II – THE DARK SECRET, Steamhammer SPV 085-69612 (Europe), Steamhammer SPV 69612 (USA) (2004)

The Magic Of The Wizard's Dream, Steamhammer SPV 076-99300 (Europe), Steamhammer SPV 99300 (USA) (2005)

LIVE IN CANADA 2005 – THE DARK SECRET, Magic Circle Music SPV 85588 (Europe / USA) (2006)

(as RHAPSODY OF FIRE)
TRIUMPH OR AGONY, Magic Circle Music SPV 97580 (Europe / USA) (2006)

image. During August, Blind Guardian pulled in the services of Holzwarth for Brazilian dates, as their regular drummer Thomas Stauch was suffering from a tendon infection. Holzwarth also donated his services to Greek electro-metal band Dol Ammad, appearing on their debut album, *Star Tales.*

Rhapsody's 2004 album, *Symphony Of Enchanted Lands II – The Dark Secret*, was recorded in four different studios across Europe. A narrative text was donated by none other than veteran actor Christopher Lee. His daughter Christina also contributed, marking the first time that father and daughter had worked together professionally. This portion of the album was produced by Joey DeMaio of Manowar. The Bohuslav Martinu Philharmonic Orchestra from the Czech Republic as well as a 50-piece choir were on hand to give the record an additional sense of the epic.

In November, Rhapsody were in the recording studio with Christopher Lee once again to re-record the song 'The Magic Of The Wizard's Dream'. The new version was produced in four different languages, English, German, French, and Italian, and featured a duet by Lee – a noted bass/baritone vocalist in his own right and fluent in no fewer than 12 languages – and Fabio Lione. A video for the song, filmed by director Neil Johnson, featured a 40-piece orchestra and a 20 piece choir.

Dates in North America witnessed a touring partnership with Manowar. In July, Christopher Lee narrated the track 'Unholy Warcry' live on stage for Rhapsody's appearance at the Manowar-headlined 'Earthshaker' festival in Germany in July 2005. The band then teamed up with Manowar and Holy Hell for US dates commencing on June 2nd 2005 in Cleveland, Ohio. A show in Quebec, Canada on June 13th was recorded for the album *Live In Canada 2005 – The Dark Secret*, released in January 2006.

Following copyright and trademark problems, the band announced in July 2006 that they had changed their name to Rhapsody Of Fire. An album, *Triumph Or Agony*, was released in September 2006. The name change appears not to have hindered their progress, which looks set to continue.

SYMPHONY X
SHRED-PROGGERS EXTRAORDINAIRE

NEW JERSEY ACT SYMPHONY X are an outrageously progressive metal band formed by the ex-Phantom's Opera duo of guitarist Michael Romeo – world renowned for his eight-finger tapping technique – and bassist Thomas Miller. Symphony X's main markets appear to be in Japan and continental Europe, especially France. The catalyst for the band was the positive media response to a Romeo solo demo, *The Dark Chapter*, while Symphony X's first product was the *Danse Macabre* demo.

Their self-produced *Symphony X* scored distribution across Europe through an arrangement with InsideOut Music and in the Far East through Japan's Zero Corporation. The musicians employed for this set included Romeo, Miller, sometime Phantom's Opera man Rod Tyler on vocals, keyboard player Michael Pinnella, and drummer Jason Rullo.

Shortly after the album arrived in stores, Tyler was replaced by Russell Allen. Just a few months earlier, Tyler had introduced singer Allen to bassist Miller. With that vacancy to fulfil, the group initiated contact and November 1995's *The Damnation Game* – produced by Eric Rachel and Steve Evetts – marked Allen's inaugural appearance. Symphony X's March 1997 album *The Divine Wings Of Tragedy* included a title track nearly 21 minutes long.

In addition to working on a new album for March 1998, *Twilight In Olympus* – the first to feature new drummer Tom Walling – Romeo also released his first solo album, *The Dark Chapter*, based on tracks originally laid down as a demo in the early 1990s, a demo that gained the guitarist a great deal of interest from industry movers such as Mike Varney of Shrapnel Records.

Bassist Thomas Miller departed after *Twilight In Olympus* and Andy DeLuca stood in for touring commitments until Mike LePond joined the band. Releases came thick and fast: a Symphony X compilation, *Prelude To The Millennium: Essentials Of Symphony*, was issued in 1998 and a new studio album, *V: The New Mythology Suite*, appeared in 2000. A lavish double live album, *Live On The Edge Of Forever*, arrived in 2001.

Although the band were announced for the 2002 'Bang Your Head' festival in Germany, they pulled out when frontman Allen was found to be suffering from intestinal bleeding and required emergency medical treatment. An extensive run of North American dates in November and December saw the band supporting Blind Guardian.

Symphony X promoted *The Odyssey* with headlining US shows throughout November, pulling in Canadian eccentrics The Devin Townsend Band as openers. Allen came to attention outside his main

SYMPHONY X discography

SYMPHONY X, InsideOut Music IOMCD 005 (Europe) (1994)

THE DAMNATION GAME, InsideOut Music IOMCD 004 (Europe) (1995)

THE DIVINE WINGS OF TRAGEDY, InsideOut Music IOMCD 009 (Europe) (1997)

TWILIGHT IN OLYMPUS, InsideOut Music IOMCD 021 (Europe) (1998)

V: THE NEW MYTHOLOGY SUITE, InsideOut Music IOMCD 066 (Europe), Metal Blade 3984-14344-2 (USA) (2000)

LIVE ON THE EDGE OF FOREVER, InsideOut Music IOMCD 091 (Europe), InsideOut Music America IOMACD 2030-2 (USA) (2001)

THE ODYSSEY, InsideOut Music IOMCD 109 (Europe), InsideOut Music America IOMACD 2044-2 (USA) (2002)

band when he portrayed the character Dream League Commander for a 2004 Genius outing, *In Search Of The Little Prince*. Romeo also guested on *The Burning* by Finnish power metal band Thunderstone, appearing on the track 'Drawn To The Flame'.

Live work in April 2004 found the band supporting Queensryche. Later that year, Allen recorded a duet album, *The Battle*, with Masterplan vocalist Jørn Lande and Last Tribe guitarist Magnus Karlsson.

Symphony X joined the Megadeth and Dream Theater-headlined 'Gigantour' festivals in summer 2005 and in July issued *Rarities And Demos* to fan-club members, including Romeo's 13-guitar interpretation of the 'Star Wars Suite'. Later that year, Romeo contributed guest solos to Eidolon recordings.

The band announced 2006 European festival appearances in June but were forced to cancel when LePond was diagnosed with Crohn's Disease, requiring surgery. This notwithstanding, they remain near the vanguard of the technical prog-metal movement.

THEATRE OF TRAGEDY
WELCOME TO THE OPERATING THEATRE

FOR MANY YEARS FRONTRUNNERS in the European gothic metal arena, Theatre Of Tragedy were led by the guttural death metal growls of Raymond István Rohonyi juxtaposed against the dynamic clarity of soprano Liv Kristine Espenæs. In more recent years, they have shed much of their gothic skin and successfully transported their maturing fanbase into more industrial landscapes.

The catalyst for the band – hailing from Røyneberg, Stavanger in Norway – was drummer Hein Frode Hansen, previously a member of Phobia, an act that included pre-Enslaved vocalist Grutle Kjellson and guitarist Ivar Bjørnson. Hansen, together with vocalist Raymond I. Rohonyi, guitar players Pål Bjåstad and Tommy Lindal, Painthead bassist Eirik T Saltrø, and 15-year-old keyboard player Lorentz Aspen assembled to create Suffering Grief in October 1993.

Despite Rohonyi's trademark death metal vocals, even at this early stage the band were endeavouring to branch out into more atmospheric material. Having constructed their first composition, 'Lament Of The Perishing Roses', the band operated as Le Reine Noir for a matter of days before settling on the title Theatre Of Tragedy in April 1994.

The same year, Theatre Of Tragedy added female vocalist Liv Kristine Espenæs and, unleashing a debut four-song demo in May, immediately scored a deal with the German Massacre label. December found the group in Unisound Studios with Edge Of Sanity's Dan Swanö.

The group debuted in July 1995 with a self-titled album, embellished by the mournful cello work of Anders Måreby. They hit the road with Atrocity but lost the services of Pål Bjåstad, enrolling Geir Flikkeid as replacement. Working at Commusication Studios in Frankenthal during July 1996, the band cut their second record, *Velvet Darkness They Fear*, with Peter Coleman. The Moscow-based Nedeltcho Boiadjiev string quartet play on four songs. The album, released in September, promptly sold over 40,000 copies in Germany. After completing the record, guitarist Tommy Lindal suffered a stroke, and he was replaced for the ensuing European tour.

Touring to promote the record saw further dates with Atrocity and inclusion on the 'Out Of The Dark' festival alongside Gorefest, Samael, and Moonspell in September 1996. The band undertook a further European tour in April 1997 with Heavenwood and Lake Of Tears to promote the mini-album *A Rose For The Dead*. The record contained a cover of Joy Division's 'Decades' and remixes by industrialists Das Ich of 'And When He Falleth' and 'Black As The Devil Painteth'. Another change in membership saw Flikkeid taking his leave.

THEATRE OF TRAGEDY discography

THEATRE OF TRAGEDY, Massacre MASSCD 063 (Europe) (1995)
VELVET DARKNESS THEY FEAR, Massacre MASCD 0107 (Europe) (1996), Century Media CM 7881-2 (USA) (1997)
A Rose For The Dead, Massacre MASCD 0130 (Europe) (1997)
AÉGIS, Massacre MASCD 0159 (Europe), Century Media CM 7933-2 (USA) (1998)
['MJU:ZIK] Nuclear Blast NB 568-2 (Europe), Nuclear Blast America 6568 (USA) (2000)
Inperspective, Massacre MASCD 0267 (Europe) (2000)
CLOSURE:LIVE, Massacre MASCD 0293 (Europe) (2001)
ASSEMBLY, Nuclear Blast NB 711-2 (Europe), Nuclear Blast America 6711 (USA) (2002)
STORM, AFM AFM 117-2 (Europe), Candlelight CD CDL 304 (USA) (2006)

Liv Kristine issued the *Deus Ex Machina* solo album during a lull before 1998's *Aégis*, which was stripped of guitar harshness and found the band venturing into fresh musical territory. In a conceptual work dedicated to mythological female beauty, Rohonyi tempered his vocal style considerably, only utilising his trademark malevolence for the song 'Venus', while Liv Kristine Espenæs made full use of her expansive and emotive range throughout. This near-flawless execution prompted many European critics to award *Aégis* perfect review scores. The musicians on the album included Elusive and New Breed guitarist Kristian Gundersen and second six-stringer Tommy Olsson, another member of Elusive. The band drafted in new guitarist Frank Claussen, previously with thrashers Malpractice, for this album – which broke the band, scoring chart success in both Germany and Holland. Digipack variants added a bonus track, 'Samantha'.

The band signed to major label East West for October 2000's *['mju:zik]* album, shedding guitarist Tommy Olsen and bassist Eirik T. Saltrø in the process. Guitarist Erik Andre Rydningen stepped in for recording, and the band constructed the album with producer Erik Ljunggren at two studios, Soundsuite in Marseille, France and Lydlab in Oslo, Norway.

Theatre Of Tragedy took on a whole new guise for *['mju:zik]*, jumping brazenly into techno-pop, a new direction that made inroads into the pop and darkwave club markets but froze out many longstanding fans. A subsequent date at the Polish 'Metal Mania' festival in Katowice was released as the *Closure:Live* collection. In January 2001, session guitarist Vegard K. Thorsen was granted permanent membership.

The band spent the latter half of 2001 in Finland at Karillo Studios in Porvoo and MD Studios in Helsinki to record *Assembly* with producer Hiili Hiilesmaa, also cutting a version of the Vanilla Fudge/Motown staple 'You Keep Me Hangin' On'. An EP entitled *Let You Down* was scheduled for Norway-only release in 2002.

In July 2003, Liv Kristine Espenæs married Atrocity's Alexander Krull. This union spilled over into a creative force with the announcement of a new band, Leaves' Eyes, with Liv Kristine Espenæs-Krull and her husband alongside members of Atrocity. Just days after this announcement, it was reported that the singer had been fired from Theatre Of Tragedy. The remaining band members vowed to carry on.

In late December, the band teased fans with photos from rehearsals placed on their website featuring an unidentified dark-haired singer who "may, or may not" be the new Theatre Of Tragedy vocalist. Cryptically, the only picture featuring the candidate showed her from behind. Theatre Of Tragedy officially announced Nell Sigland of fellow Norwegians The Crest as their new vocalist in a statement issued at the beginning of June

2004. Sigland's first show with the band was at a gig at Checkpoint Charlie on June 19th.

The band reported a European road alliance with Sirenia, Tiamat, and Pain to take them through late 2004 and into 2005. That September, announcing an intended return to their formative style, the band unveiled a new label deal with AFM, and by early October they were back in the studio with producer Rico Darum to cut a new album, *Storm*, which was released in March 2006. European shows that year saw Gothminister as support. The band's fans have remained loyal and the new line-up looks set to last the course.

TRISTANIA
WHERE GOTH-METAL AND GOTH-ROCK MEET

A FEMALE-FRONTED DARKWAVE band, Tristania are regarded as among the elite of their genre. The band were formed in Stavanger in Norway in late 1996 by keyboard player Einar Moen and guitarist Morten Veland, both previously with Uzi Suicide, and drummer Kenneth Olsson. Subsequently they added bassist Rune Østerhus along with guitarist and main composer Anders Høyvik Hidle. At this stage, they were all in their teens, with Hidle the youngest at 17. Tristania's first demos were crafted at Klepp Lydstudio in May 1997, with singer Vibeke Stene initially employed on a session basis, but with her skills proved during these recordings she was asked to join the band. Tristania subsequently developed their trademark sound with three distinctly different lead vocalists.

The Austrian Napalm label signed the band and issued the *Tristania* EP, actually a remixed version of the demo in new artwork. The Terje Refsnes-produced *Widow's Weeds* album emerged in March 1998, and the record (and the band) struck a positive chord with the rock media.

On the vocal front, the immense, soaring power of Stene soon put paid to any notions that she had gained her position just for visual effect – while Veland countered with trollish rumblings to root the proceedings firmly in the extreme metal camp. Østen Bergøy of Morendoes lent backing vocals to this and subsequent recordings. Another significant session contributor was violinist Pete Johansen, a studio veteran of Morgul and The Sins Of Thy Beloved.

Live promotion included support shows to Lacrimosa in Belgium and an appearance at the Austrian 'Mind Over Matter' festival. The same year, the band partnered Haggard and Solefald for their first European tour.

September 1999's *Beyond The Veil* featured guest backing vocals from Elusive's Jan Kenneth Barkved, Hilde T. Bommen, Jeanett Johannessen, and Vibeke's family members Maiken and Sissel. Both Østen Bergøy and Pete Johansen again donated their services. *Beyond The Veil* elevated the band to headlining status, and Tristania traversed Europe supported by The Sins Of Thy Beloved, Trail Of Tears, and Antichrisis. They put in a notable appearance at the German 'Wacken' festival and undertook

further touring with Tiamat and Anathema. As touring extended into 2000, Tristania put in their first shows in Mexico that August and a one-off US concert in November – an event that put the band on stage alongside porn stars and wrestlers.

Stene engaged in a side project, Green Carnation, with Emperor's Tchort and members of In The Woods..., featuring on the 2000 album *Journey To The End Of The Night*.

Veland left the band during May 2001, founding Sirenia for a 2002 debut album. His place was taken by two vocalists, Kjetil Ingebrethsen of Blindfolded and Østen Bergøy. Tristania made a significant impact with their third album, *World Of Glass*, recorded at Sound Suite Studio in France in spring 2001. For the first time, the band attempted a cover version, cutting 'The Modern End' by Siegmen. Guest session vocals for this recording came courtesy of Ronny Thorsen of Trail Of Tears and Scariot, Jan Kenneth Barkved, Damien Surian of Trail Of Tears, Hilde T. Bommen, Johanna Giraud, Emile Lesbros, and Sirenia's Sandrine Lachapelle, among others. Another extensive round of live dates ensued, opening with a European headline tour backed by Rotting Christ, Vintersorg, and Madder Mortem. Tristania toured Brazil, Argentina, Columbia, and Chile during January 2002 before headline gigs in Colombia and Mexico during August.

The band entered Toproom Studios in Oslo in April 2004 with producer Børge Finstad to commence work on a new studio album, *Ashes*. Having fulfilled their three-album contract with Napalm Records, Tristania at first self-financed these recordings before signing to new label SPV/Steamhammer in July. They scheduled a July appearance at the 'Mind Over Matter' festival in Austria but withdrew due to Ingebrethsen's illness. Tristania then hooked up with Therion and Trail Of Tears for a mammoth European tour throughout the autumn.

Promoting *Ashes* in January 2005, the group toured with guitarist Svein Terje Solvang, taking in their first Norwegian dates (an alliance with Gothminister on a government-sponsored cultural set of gigs). The same month, the band filmed a video at the old Tou Brewery in Stavanger for 'Equilibrium' with director Ralf Strathmann. Supports to Nightwish took them through February before South American dates with Kreator and Dark Tranquillity.

Tristania announced recording sessions set for March 2006 in Woodhouse Studios in Hagen, Germany to be produced by Grip Inc. guitarist Waldemar Sorychta. Headline shows set for September were cancelled to enable Vibeke Stene to finish her training as a teacher.

Kjetil Ingebrethsen left the band in April 2006, and the band announced that the new Tristania album would be titled *Illumination*. The future remains bright for the band.

TYPE O NEGATIVE
AMERICAN GOTH-METAL – BEFORE THE TERM WAS HIJACKED BY EMO

FORMED BY EX-CARNIVORE frontman Peter Steele, Type O Negative premiered as a quartet in 1988, going by the early names of Repulsion and Sub Zero. The gothic atmosphere and nihilistic, experimental bent of their distinct brand of metal enabled the band to find their own unique place in the rock field. Steele's deliberate approach was evident right from the first album, 1992's *The Origin Of The Feces (Not Live At Brighton Beach)*, which featured a blurred close-up of the vocalist-bassist's anus.

Brooklyn band Fallout launched Steele (aka Peter Ratajczyk) and Josh Silver (keyboards) onto the New York City scene. Fallout also included John Campos on second guitar and drummer Louie Beateaux (Agnostic Front, and later Carnivore). Pre-Fallout, both Steele and Silver had operated with Aggression. Fallout, assembled in 1979, issued the now

---

TRISTANIA discography

Tristania, Napalm NPR 036 (Europe / USA) (1997)
WIDOW'S WEEDS, Napalm NPR 041 (Europe / USA) (1998)
BEYOND THE VEIL, Napalm NPR 070 (Europe / USA) (1999)
WORLD OF GLASS, Napalm NPR 095 (Europe / USA) (2001)
ASHES, Steamhammer SPV 085-99202 (Europe), Steamhammer SPV 99202 (USA) (2005)
MIDWINTER TEARS, Napalm NPR 168 (Europe / USA) (2005)
ILLUMINATION, Steamhammer SPV 085-99880 (Europe), Steamhammer SPV 99880 (USA) (2007)

highly collectable *Rock Hard* 7-inch single in 1981: only 500 copies were pressed, through Silver Records. Gigs included a support to Twisted Sister, but in 1982 the band folded. While Steele and Beateaux formed Carnivore, Silver and Campos created Original Sin.

As frontman for Carnivore, Steele went under the stage name Petrus Steele, with Louie Beateaux opting for Lord Petrus T. The early gigs by Carnivore made quite an impact, with Steele often resorting to self-mutilation, carving crosses into his face. His talents in other areas were also much in demand: he is credited with penning the lyrics on the debut Agnostic Front album.

Following their self-titled debut album, released in 1985, Carnivore fractured as guitarist Keith Alexander left the fold in 1986 to create Primal Scream with ex-Hellicon vocalist Steve Alliano and former Black Virgin bassist Rob Graham. He was replaced by Marc Piovanetti for 1988's *Retaliation* album. Subsequently, Steele set about completely reinventing the band through Repulsion to Sub Zero, eventually evolving into Type O Negative. The band – Steele (vocals/bass), Kenny Hickey (guitar), Josh Silver (keyboards), and Sal Abruscato (drums) – debuted in 1991 with the Roadrunner-released *Slow, Deep And Hard*, recorded under the working title *None More Negative*.

The second album, *The Origin Of The Feces (Not Live At Brighton Beach)*, featured live audience catcalls of "You suck" and band-members' photographs obscured by excrement. However, 1993's *Bloody Kisses* tamed them a little, as they prepared to muscle in on the mainstream. The album's commercial success prompted the re-release of its predecessor in less offensive packaging. Steele earned himself a following from both female and gay male fans by appearing in the January 1996 issue of *Playgirl* magazine. This was followed by the release of *October Rust*.

Type O Negative were inactive during late 1997. Drummer Johnny Kelly, who had replaced Sal Abruscato in 1993 when Abruscato quit to join Life Of Agony, kept active by stepping into the breach for Pist.On drummer Jeff McManus, who had suffered a serious respiratory illness on his band's American tour.

In 1998, Steele shared lead vocals on the track 'Finale' with Kay Bjelland of Babes In Toyland as part of a sci-fi cartoon series soundtrack album, *Songs Of The Witchblade*. European dates in December 1999 saw the band packaged with Coal Chamber and Static-X. Touring in February 2000 featured Coal Chamber as support again. The amusingly titled 2000 compilation *The Least Worst Of* included three new songs – 'It's Never Enough', 'Stay Out Of My Dreams', and '12 Black Rainbows'.

TYPE O NEGATIVE discography

SLOW, DEEP AND HARD, Roadracer RO 9313-2 (Europe / USA) (1991)

THE ORIGIN OF THE FECES (NOT LIVE AT BRIGHTON BEACH), Roadrunner RR 9006-2 (Europe), Roadrunner RR 9174-2 (USA) (1992)

BLOODY KISSES, Roadrunner RR 9100-2 (Europe / USA) (1993)

OCTOBER RUST, Roadrunner RR 8874-2 (Europe / USA) (1996) **26 UK, 42 USA**

WORLD COMING DOWN, Roadrunner RR 8660-2 (Europe / USA) (1999) **49 UK**

THE LEAST WORST OF, Roadrunner RR 8510-2 (Europe / USA) (2000)

LIFE IS KILLING ME, Roadrunner RR 8438-2 (Europe), Roadrunner 618438 (USA) (2003) **39 USA**

DEAD AGAIN, Steamhammer catalogue number tba (Europe / USA) (2007)

Type O Negative re-emerged in 2002 with a version of the old Deep Purple warhorse 'Highway Star' as their contribution to the NASCAR *Crank It Up* album. Steele's presence was also felt on the 2002 *Fight* album by German metal queen Doro, the frontman duetting with Ms. Pesch on 'Descent'. Drummer Kelly sat in with Danzig on their November 2002 European gigs as well as playing gigs with his Led Zeppelin covers band Earl's Court.

Reports in early 2003 had the new Type O Negative album title as *The Dream Is Dead*, but this was later switched to *Life Is Killing Me*. Initial UK copies included a bonus CD of rare B-sides plus two previously unreleased tracks, 'Out Of The Fire (Kane's Theme)' and 'Haunted'. The band's US tour commenced in Worcester, Maine, on July 25th. A further bout of co-headlining US shows in November saw the band play with Cradle Of Filth, Moonspell, and Soilwork.

Meanwhile, Steele established a band with drummer Steve Tobin of Dust To Dust and guitarist Paul Bento. The Dust To Dust connection continued when Hickey and Kelly teamed up with that band's vocalist and bass player Rob Traynor in yet another spin-off band, Skynd (a name subsequently dropped in favour of Black Water Rising).

Type O Negative revealed plans for October US shows with Amorphis. The band had cut a cover of Santana's 'Evil Ways' for a tribute to the science fiction/fantasy writer Neil Gaiman, and they switched labels from Roadrunner to the German SPV operation. A European tour in December with Cradle Of Filth was announced and then postponed. October dates in the USA were also pulled when a management statement revealed that a medical examination of Steele had shown "undisclosed anomalies".

In December, Kelly hooked up with Eric Griffin from Murderdolls,

Mike Duda of W.A.S.P., and Mayuko Okai from The Dizzy Reed Band for a batch of 'Happenin' Harry' Midwest shows. Kelly temped with Danzig for February 2005 US touring. Silver became one of five high-profile writers contributing to Roadrunner's 25th anniversary album *Roadrunner United: The All-Star Sessions*, featuring on the track 'Roads' fronted by Opeth's Mikael Åkerfeldt.

As Type O Negative announced a further album for 2007, *Dead Again*, through Steamhammer/SPV, it was reported that Steele had landed a role in the horror movie *Tao Of M* portraying the vampire Viktor Baine. The movie, directed by James L. Bills and produced by Velvet Life Productions, also starred Stevie Blaze of Lillian Axe and members of Twisted Sister.

Kenny Hickey and drummer Johnny Kelly announced the Seventh Void project in May 2006, with Hickey, taking the lead vocal role, and Kelly working with Supermassi guitar player Matt Brown and bassist Ryan Jurhs. Former Pantera and Damageplan drummer Vinnie Paul Abbott, alongside longtime Pantera producer Sterling Winfield, mixed the debut recordings for an early 2007 release.

Peter Steele then put together a new version of Carnivore, featuring Life Of Agony guitarist Joey Zampela and the Metal Health Association duo of guitarist Paul Bento and drummer Steve Tobin, for a performance at Germany's 'Wacken Open Air' festival in August 2006. This was preceded by a warm-up show at Fontana's in New York City on July 28th, where the band were billed as The Bensonhoist Lesbian Choir. Further Carnivore US headlining dates followed in September.

That same month, Hickey and drummer Kelly joined the touring line-up of Danzig. These many side activities notwithstanding, Type O Negative continue to occupy a cherished place in the darker corners of America's metal scene.

WITHIN TEMPTATION
NIGHTWISH'S CLOSEST COMPETITORS?

GOTHIC DOOM METAL ACT Within Temptation have made serious headway into the European market with a series of adventurous releases. The band, founded in 1996 in Utrecht, Netherlands, are fronted by the striking Sharon Janny den Adel. Former Circle and Voyage guitarist Robert Westerholt convened the act with his girlfriend den Adel and former band colleagues Jeroen van Veen on bass and guitar player Michiel Papenhove. Initially, the former Ejaculate and Near Dark drummer Richard Willemse was involved, but Nemesis' Dennis Leeflang later occupied the drum stool and Westerholt's brother Martijn played keyboards.

This line-up recorded the *Enter* demo, which led to various record-company offers within months. Signing to the DSFA label, Within Temptation manoeuvred Ivar de Graaf onto the drum stool (Leeflang subsequently joined Time Machine and Sun Caged).

The *Enter* album was released in April 1997. An appearance by the band at the 'Dynamo' festival led to a two-week tour throughout Europe. However, by the close of the year de Graaf made his exit. His replacement was Ciro Palma, a former member of death metal combo Xenomorph. Within Temptation performed at 'Dynamo' again the following year, this

time on the main stage, and also at the 'Noorderslag' event. A mini-album, *The Dance*, was released to capitalise on this exposure.

In 1999, de Graaf returned to the band. For the Oscar Holleman-produced *Mother Earth* album, the band completely dispensed with the death metal vocal style with which they had begun, now relying solely on den Adel's majestic vocals. The move gained a whole new fanbase for the band. Meanwhile, den Adel guested for Ayreon and on After Forever's *Prison Of Desire* album. Guitar player Michiel Papenhove departed in mid 2001. Ruud Jolie of Brotherhood Foundation filled in before Jelle Bakker, a member of Frozen Sun, adopted the position permanently.

During November, Within Temptation announced a unique show at the Broerekerk Church in Zwolle, complete with full choir and opera singer. Fans received the news with such enthusiasm that a second show had to be added to satisfy demand. Martijn Westerholt left the band in 2001 and was replaced by ex-Voyage keyboard player Martijn Spierenburg.

Band members van Veen, de Graaf and Papenhove operated with the avant-garde rock outfit J.I.M. Generator. By mid 2002, de Graaf was also ensconced in the Dutch-Belgian doom 'supergroup' Les Faidits, having been replaced in Within Temptation by Ambeon and Paralysis drummer Stephen van Haestregt. Bakker founded the metal/hip-hop act Chen Mo.

Within Temptation signed to the German G.U.N. label in December. The first fruit of this relationship was a re-release of the *Mother Earth* album, certified platinum in Holland and gold in Belgium, with new cover art and four additional tracks. The group secured the opening slot to Paradise Lost's February 2003 European dates.

They made a major return in 2004, introducing their new album *The Silent Force* with a special one-off performance at the Bataclan venue in Paris on November 8th. The show was filmed and broadcast live in several theatres around Europe. *The Silent Force* debuted at Number 1 in Holland. February 2005 European shows saw the band supported by Autumn. As the new single 'Memories' entered the German charts at Number 17, the 2000 album *Mother Earth* went double platinum in Germany for sales of 200,000 copies.

A notable gig in March 2005 came with the band's inclusion at the 'Desert Rock' festival alongside The Darkness, Machine Head, and Sepultura at the Dubai Rugby Country Club in the United Arab Emirates. After signing to Roadrunner for the UK, Australia, and Japan, Within Temptation put in another unusual gig in July, headlining alongside After Forever on Java Island in Amsterdam to 10,000 fans. Summer festival slots and supports to Iron Maiden in Zurich and Paris followed. The Roadrunner re-release of *The Silent Force* for the UK, issued in August, included a bonus DVD.

On August 31st, the band's commercial success was recognised when they received the 'Best Selling Dutch Artist' award at the World Music Awards, held at the Kodak Theatre in Los Angeles, adding to previous accolades such as the Edison Award in the 'Best National Group' category, the TMF Award for 'Best National Rock Band', and the Dutch Music Export Award. They headlined at the UK 'Bloodstock' gig on September 3rd.

The band announced a forthcoming DVD, *The Silent Force Tour* – ultimately released in November 2006 – and revealed that den Adel was five months pregnant. Her baby daughter arrived on December 7th 2005, some eight weeks early.

The band put in an appearance at the Metallica and Korn-headlined 'Download' festival at Castle Donington, England on June 10th 2006. Sharon Den Adel duetted with Marco Hietala of Nightwish on 'No Compliance' on Delain's debut *Lucidity* album, the project of ex-Within Temptation keyboard player Martijn Westerholt.

As this book goes to press, opportunities for Within Temptation to consolidate their standing are many, but whatever their next moves, the band are almost certain to remain successful in today's modern metal climate.

WITHIN TEMPTATION discography

ENTER, DSFA 1007 (Europe) (1997)
The Dance, DSFA 1015 (Europe) (1998)
MOTHER EARTH, DSFA 1021 (Europe) (2001)
THE SILENT FORCE, G.U.N. 82876 64516 2 (Europe) (2004)

US
METAL

ONCE the New Wave Of British Heavy Metal had hit American shores, US bands were quick to respond. Stadium rock had always been huge but now looked rather tame in comparison to the fare that Iron Maiden, Judas Priest and Saxon were offering – and America metalled up in rapid-fire fashion. However, this coincided with the deluge of thrash metal, another arm of metal triggered by the NWOBHM. For a lengthy period, many non-speed-orientated bands struggled to grasp their share of the limelight or – like the "headbanging-est band in LA", Armored Saint, the edifying Metal Church and the sterling Vicious Rumors – were awkwardly placed into the thrash melée and suffered greatly for it.

Former Black Sabbath singer Ronnie James Dio played an important role. Having proved with the revitalised Sabbath that metal could hold a large audience, his solo vehicle Dio delivered hard-hitting, fantasy-infused metal that proved equally lucrative. The sense of depth that Dio bestowed upon the scene was mirrored by Manowar, Savatage and Virgin Steele. These prominent bands took the British formula and injected it with American individuality. In all probability, the very fact that they held an ingrained American psyche gave them a bombastic edge that many British bands would not have dared to contemplate – in particular, Manowar's completely over-the-top barbarian personae, Virgin Steele's classical epics, and Savatage's unique spin on Broadway metal that ultimately led to the foundation of Trans-Siberian Orchestra.

Behind them came Lizzy Borden, Malice, Jag Panzer, Crimson Glory, Omen, Damien, Hittman, Attacker, Tyrant, Brocas Helm, Manilla Road, Cirith Ungol, Savage Grace, Fates Warning, Lääz Rockit and others. Some would only realise their true status in later years, when the cause of "true metal" was resurrected in Germany, Italy and Greece. Many bands' survival was determined by their sheer dedication to the cause, as the media jumped from one bandwagon to the next, ignoring the rich vein of talent.

Europe was then a saviour to a second generation of purist US metal. Iced Earth and Nevermore were quickly taken to heart in Germany many years before they impacted upon home soil. Now it appears the circle is closing once again, as younger bands such as Cage, Cellador, New Eden, Icarus Witch and Benidictum re-explore inventive song structures, soloing and riffing.

ARMORED SAINT
MARCH OF THE SAINT

ARMORED SAINT, SELF-DESCRIBED as the "headbanging-est" band in East Los Angeles, were a riff-driven, traditional metal band unwittingly caught up in the melée of the Californian thrash boom. Officially formed in summer 1982, they immediately attracted attention for the quality of a five-track demo tape and the spirited, purist nature of the quintet's live show. Famously, singer John Bush was once under consideration for the vocal position with Metallica but turned the offer down. The band concept was initially suggested sometime in 1981 by third-grade school friends but only fully completed in mid 1982. The individuals concerned had all played in other bands but none had recorded: however, bassist Joey Vera had played with Mötley Crüe drummer Tommy Lee and Ozzy Osbourne guitarist Jake E. Lee during his formative years.

Vera, then a guitarist, and vocalist Bush first got together in their El Sereno school band, Rhapsody. A covers act including songs by the likes of Foreigner and Deep Purple in their act, Rhapsody also included guitarist David Avila, bassist Channing Estrada, keyboard player Mark Patton and drummer Martin Zuniga.

Vera and Bush stuck together to create their next school band, Royal Decree, in alliance with the Sandoval siblings, drummer Gonzo and guitarist Phil. Vera moved to bass after Bush made an attempt to play it but became bored with the instrument. On Royal Decree's demise, Bush and Vera hooked up with Sapphire, but shortly after, Bush was ousted by guitarist Brad Parker. The band underwent numerous line-up changes, but

toward the end of the band's career Vera found himself playing alongside Tommy Lee.

Vera joined ex-Dokken guitarist Greg Leon in his Invasion unit following Lee's departure to Mötley Crüe. During this time Gonzo, Sandoval and Vera were jamming in a garage, with latterday MX Machine and Motofury man Diego Negrete performing a brief stint on bass. This unnamed band, featuring Dave Prichard on second guitar, pulled Bush in on vocals, although they informed the frontman that the only reason for the invitation was because he owned an impressive PA system. This line-up began to formulate early Armored Saint material as well as covering Iron Maiden tunes: one song that didn't make it to an official release was titled 'You Suck My Anal Dry'.

Vera continued bass duties with The Greg Leon Invasion while a musician known only as Mike took his role in the garage band. In May 1982, Vera officially joined the newly titled Armored Saint: as legend has it, the band's demo tape was directly financed from compensation arising from injuries sustained by Vera in an automobile accident while he was in a car driven by Tommy Lee.

With the band building a strong local following, an attempt was made by the then-fledgling Metallica to poach Bush in 1982. After witnessing a show at The Woodstock in Anaheim, Metallica requested Bush's services, an offer he declined. Armored Saint's first commercial recorded appearance came with a contribution to Metal Blade's *Metal Massacre II* compilation album, the group supplying the Bill Metoyer-produced 'Lesson Well Learned'. Naturally, Metal Blade then stepped in with a deal for an EP, resulting in a three-track 12-inch single issued in August of the following year. The record, which rapidly sold over 15,000

ARMORED SAINT discography

Armored Saint, Metal Blade MBR 1009 (USA) (1983)
MARCH OF THE SAINT, Chrysalis CHR 1479 (UK), Chrysalis 41476 (USA) (1984) **138 USA**
DELIRIOUS NOMAD, Chrysalis CHR 1516 (UK), Chrysalis 41516 (USA) (1985) **108 USA**
RAISING FEAR, Chrysalis CHR 1610 (UK), Chrysalis 41601 (USA) (1987) **114 USA**
SAINTS WILL CONQUER, Roadrunner RR 9520-1 (Europe), Metal Blade 72301 (USA) (1988)
SYMBOL OF SALVATION, Metal Blade CDZORRO 20 (UK), Metal Blade 9 26577-2 (USA) (1991)
REVELATION, Metal Blade 3984-14288-2 (Europe / USA) (2000)
NOD TO THE OLD SCHOOL, Metal Blade 3984-14373-2 (Europe / USA) (2001)

copies, included 'Lesson Well Learned', 'False Alarm' and 'On The Way'.

Chrysalis stepped in to snap up the group, placing them in Ocean Way Studio with producer Michael James Jackson, fresh from his work on Kiss's *Creatures Of The Night* album, to deliver *March Of The Saint*. Most fans agree that while the material couldn't be faulted, the production left a good deal to be desired as it failed to capture the intensity of the group – and the artwork, reminiscent of a box of toy soldiers, seemed a little weak for such a powerful act. These distractions masked a potentially great record, with Sandoval and Prichard's tightly synched lead work and Bush's huge roar being standouts. *March Of The Saint* was released in 1984, scaling *Billboard* to attain Number 138. The band toured America opening for W.A.S.P. and Metallica soon afterwards: Metallica and the Saint now shared management at Q-Prime. Other live dates found the Saint supporting Quiet Riot and Whitesnake.

The group's second album, *Delirious Nomad*, surfaced a year later. Produced by Max Norman, the record found the band down to a quartet following the exit of guitarist Phil Sandoval during recording. *Delirious Nomad* gave them the state-of-the-art production values they needed and was an edifying slab of technical metal. The record, peaking at Number 108 on the US charts, drew international praise for its technical approach, but sales unfortunately did not match expectations. Fans seemed confused by the complexities of the record, the ditching of the beloved armour, and another album cover of little merit.

A third album, 1987's *Raising Fear*, was recorded over a six-month period at no fewer than four studio locations across California as a co-produced effort between the band and Chris Minto with Chrysalis Records (fans were unaware that the group's first demo proposals had been rejected by the label). With the experimentation of *Delirious Nomad* less than a success, the band fell back on older themes, even going so far as to include their knight motif once again on the album cover. To appease Chrysalis's yearning for a radio hit, they provided a less-than-inspiring rendition of Lynyrd Skynyrd's 'Saturday Night Special'. The band then teamed up with Grim Reaper and Helloween for the 'Hell On Wheels' North American tour to promote the album.

The record only hit Number 144 on the US album charts, this deflating result signalling the close of relations with Chrysalis. Returning to the Metal Blade stable, the band recorded a 1988 live album, *Saints Will Conquer*, at Cleveland's Agora Ballroom in October 1987. Once again, though, the group's choice of artwork was found wanting, the cover being far too similar to a famous Frank Frazetta Molly Hatchet classic.

For touring with King Diamond in America during 1988, Armored Saint drafted in former Odin guitarist Jeff Duncan. However, with no

major backing and Q-Prime Management also having severed ties, the Saint's demise was inevitable. Duncan quit, with his position taken by Alan Barlam, before he put together Bird Of Prey with his brother and ex-Odin colleague Shawn on drums, vocalist Kyle Michaels, later of Masi and the Geezer Butler Band, and Paul Puljiz, subsequently a member of Killing Kulture. Vera, meanwhile, joined Lizzy Borden for their 1989 album *Master Of Disguise*.

Tragically, Saint guitarist Dave Prichard died from leukemia in February 1990. For many years the guitarist had complained of constant headaches, and once diagnosed he survived only a few months. Shattered, the group disbanded, only coming together to celebrate their comrade's life with the video anthology *A Trip Thru' Red Times*.

However, in March 1991 the group released an album, *Symbol Of Salvation*, produced by Dave Jerden. The bulk of it had been composed by their fallen colleague, and it even featured Prichard's guitar parts on the track 'Tainted Past'. The album sold strongly in Europe and opened up new areas of appreciation for the group, the adversity which had engendered its construction resulting in the band's most powerful, but diverse, set of songs so far. Armored Saint now found themselves heralded as power metal pioneers and embarked on dates across the USA with Megadeth and Suicidal Tendencies.

Once these concerts were fulfilled, singer Bush became the focus of yet another major player. Having resisted overtures from Metallica in the past, he decided to take up an offer to become Anthrax's new vocalist in the wake of Joey Belladonna's departure in 1992. Initially, this union lifted Anthrax high into the charts, but the group's fortunes began to slide with each successive release.

With Bush gone, Armored Saint ceased to exist. Joey Vera released a solo album, *A Thousand Faces*, through Metal Blade, before hooking up with Fates Warning; he was also involved in the recording of new colleague Mark Zonder's side project Chroma Key in 1998.

The Saint – now with the Sandoval brothers, Vera, Bush and Duncan – took the opportunity to reform in 1999 as Bush's career with Anthrax seemed to be on the wane. The comeback album, *Revelation*, emerged in March 2000 and garnered heady praise from the European metal press, proving to be a return to former glories. Duncan also issued his solo band DC4's first outing the same year.

In 2001, a highly collectable compilation titled *Nod To The Old School* was issued, featuring a glut of early demo tracks, new songs 'Unstable' and 'Swagger', covers of Judas Priest's 'Never Satisfied' and Robin Trower's 'Day Of The Eagle', and live cuts. Tracks from the band's very first EP

Armored Saint

were also included. Road dates with Dio and Lynch Mob took the band across the USA throughout February and into March 2001.

In March 2002, Joey Vera, still maintaining his posts in both Armored Saint and Fates Warning, teamed up with Savatage guitarist Jack Frost in the side endeavour Seven Witches for European touring. The bassist also handled production chores for Engine's *Superholic* album.

The other Armored Saint personnel also maintained their workload, Jeff Duncan readying a Joey Vera-produced DC4 album release for Europe and Gonzo busying himself with his Monster G venture with Phil Sandoval. In late 2002, Gonzo and guitarist Phil Sandoval united with Jack Emrick and Ray Burke to reform their 1996 project Life After Death. Vera and Gonzo put in sessions on the 2003 album *Raise Your Fist To Metal* from Frost.

In February 2004, Vera temporarily enrolled in Anthrax as stand-in for the departed Frank Bello. That summer, Phil Sandoval and Gonzo activated the blues outfit Yo Diddley, putting in club shows in union with the Life After Death pairing of Ray Burke and singer Jack Emrick. Another project in 2004 was Forever Say Die, a one-off collaboration assembled to record a version of 'Sabbath Bloody Sabbath' for Cleopatra Records' Black Sabbath tribute album *Evil Lives: A True Metal Tribute To Black Sabbath*. The band was fronted by Happenin' Harry of The Haptones, with guitars courtesy of Jeff Duncan and the Spiders And Snakes rhythm section of bassist Joe Petro and drummer Tim Yasui completing the roster.

With John Bush ousted from Anthrax, the Armored Saint machine revved back into action in 2005, announcing a support gig to the Scorpions at the Dodge Theater in Phoenix, Arizona on July 30th before a welcome and long overdue return to European stages.

CIRITH UNGOL
KINGS OF THE DEAD

CIRITH UNGOL FROM VENTURA, CALIFORNIA, were lambasted for much of their early work but eventually attained cult status among the European metal masses. Taking their name from the lair of the spider Shelob in JRR Tolkien's *The Lord Of The Rings*, the band – based around former Titanic guitarists Jerry Fogle and Greg Lindstrom, plus drummer Robert Garven – were established in seventh grade as far back as 1969. The original incarnation of the band was fronted in 1975 by vocalist Neal Beattie. Titanic combined varying influences and gained a loyal cult following before morphing into Cirith Ungol in 1972. This move prompted a switch from pop to rock, the formative act performing covers by the likes of Hard Stuff, Thin Lizzy and Budgie.

Cirith Ungol demoed numerous original tracks from 1977 onwards but didn't record an album until 1980's *Frost And Fire*, self-financed and released on their own Liquid Flames label. These songs were recorded by the Fogle-Lindstrom-Garven axis together with frontman Tim Baker and bassist Michael 'Flint' Vujea.

Although *Frost And Fire* sported an amazing piece of fantasy cover artwork from Michael Whelan, the content of the record disappointed many critics. It even featured an instrumental titled 'Maybe That's Why', for which lyrics were printed in error. In spite of some exceptionally harsh reviews, particularly in the UK, Cirith Ungol sold substantial numbers of albums, the record being given a second lease of life courtesy of a 1981 re-release on Enigma. Cirith Ungol then parted company with Lindstrom in late 1982.

Many fans proclaimed the band's ensuing contribution to the first *Metal Massacre* compilation – the hyper-speed 'Death Of The Sun' – as rather listenable. Enigma picked up the band for a further album, and the highly rated *King Of The Dead* emerged during July 1984, licensed to Roadrunner in Europe. This record showed a vast improvement in the standard of songwriting and musicianship, even going as far as an adventurous rip through Bach's 'Toccata In D'. Baker perfected his style, alternating between a high shriek and guttural reverberations. *King Of The Dead* gained the band a host of new admirers and, although the group performed infrequently, gigs to promote the record generated exposure with pyrotechnics and Baker's entrance onstage in a coffin, borne aloft by robed roadies.

The group took their lyrical inspiration from the works of novelist Michael Moorcock on August 1986's *One Foot In Hell*, released on new label Metal Blade and produced by label boss Brian Slagel. The band bowed out in 1991 with the Ron Goudie-produced *Paradise Lost*, including a cover of Arthur Brown's 1960s hit 'Fire'. The group's personnel had shifted yet again, seeing Garven and Baker working alongside guitarist Jim Barraza and bassist Vernon Green. Studio contributors included Joe Malatesta on guitars and bassist Robert L. Warrenburg.

Despite the derision heaped upon their early albums, the band began to attain a cult status in mainland Europe during the 1990s (for example, Italian act Doomsword covered the Cirith Ungol track 'Nadsokor'). Their legacy took a bizarre twist in 1995 when a live single was issued, financed by none other than Deceased's King Fowley. Their appeal spread with the September 2001 retrospective *Servants Of Chaos*, a double CD compiling unreleased studio material plus rehearsal and live tapes. Jerry Fogle was not fated to experience this new wave of appreciation: he died in 1998 of liver failure.

In early 2003, Greg Lindstrom revealed his participation in the Falcon project, a union with Destiny's End, Obscure and Artisan guitarist Perry Grayson and Pale Divine drummer Darin McCloskey. The Falcon logo incorporated Cirith Ungol's famous kneeling skeletons motif.

In late 2005, German label Solemnity Music revealed that it planned to issue the first 'official' tribute to Cirith Ungol, titled *One Foot In Fire*. This collection included Lindstrom participating in Falcon's interpretation of 'Shelob's Lair'. Contributing bands included Italy's Rosae Crucis with 'Death Of The Sun', the Germany act Solemnity's version of 'What Does It Take', Dawn Of Winter – with members of Sacred Steel – delivering 'Doomed Planet', Italy's Battle Ram on 'Join The Legion', Greek outfit Holy Martyr with 'Frost And Fire', Emerald from Switzerland on 'Heaven Help Us', Polish band Monstrum with 'Fallen Idols', Italy's Assedium with 'Black

---

CIRITH UNGOL discography

FROST AND FIRE, Liquid Flames LF001 (USA) (1980)
KING OF THE DEAD, Roadrunner RR 9832 (Europe), Enigma E 1089 (USA) (1984)
ONE FOOT IN HELL, Roadrunner RR 9681 (Europe), Metal Blade 72143 (USA) (1986)
PARADISE LOST, Restless 7-72518-2 (USA) (1991)
SERVANTS OF CHAOS, Metal Blade 3984-14383-2 (Europe / USA) (2001)

Machine', a union between NWOBHM veterans Elixir and Polish group Crystal Viper on 'Chaos Rising', and Dutchmen Rotten delivering a Cirith Ungol medley.

CRIMSON GLORY
BEHIND THE MASKS

CRIMSON GLORY FROM SARASOTA, FLORIDA, first came to attention thanks to a simple gimmick – their use of silver face masks. Although they were technically proficient, the media soon decided that Crimson Glory's brand of epic metal – and Midnight's vocals – were too similar to the sound of their better known Seattle counterparts Queensrÿche for comfort. Fortunately, successive releases shed this stigma and the European metal market in particular soon welcomed the band.

The band started out in 1979 under the name Pierced Arrow, then later changed their name to Beowulf. Pierced Arrow consisted of singer Tony Wise, lead guitarist Bernado Hernandez, second guitarist Ben Jackson, bass player Jeff Lords and Dana St. James (aka Dana Burnell) on drums. Hernandez and Lords were replaced by Chris Campbell on guitar and John Colemorgan on bass in late 1981/early '82. Lords rejoined in 1983. Vocalist Mark Ormes and lead guitarist Jon Drenning joined that same year. Finally, the vocal talents of Midnight were added in. Unusually, the group didn't play a full-scale live show until five years after their original formation.

Crimson Glory debuted in 1986 on the PAR label with a self-titled first album produced by Dan Johnson and licensed to Roadrunner for European consumption, before a solitary British show opening for Anthrax and Metal Church at London's Hammersmith Odeon. February 1987 saw the band traversing mainland Europe in support of Celtic Frost and Anthrax.

Following 1988's *Transcendence*, laid down at Tampa's Morrisound with Jim Morris behind the board, the band's masks had now become 'half-masks', revealing more of their features. Unfortunately, at this critical juncture they were hit by line-up problems, with both Jackson and Burnell leaving the fold. Jackson joined Parish and recorded an album titled *Envision*, on which Burnell made a guest appearance.

The 1991 *Strange And Beautiful* album, co-produced by Mitch Goldfarb, saw the band ditching the facial disguises, dropping the black leather and Midnight's falsetto, and debuting new drummer Robi Jakhotia. A new deal was signed with Atlantic in the USA, and two singles, 'Song For Angels' and 'The Chant', were released.

With *Strange And Beautiful* the group changed tack in radical fashion, incorporating world elements as well as the inclusion of piano, saxophone, female backing vocals and a greater orientation towards keyboards. However, these embellishments didn't find widespread favour among fans: the band had jumped genres from metal to rock and, in doing so, sealed their fate.

Midnight quit the group after getting married, wishing to spend more time with his new bride, and left before an upcoming tour. David Van Landing, who had previously worked with Tony MacAlpine, was recruited for the shows. Dates in Japan were booked but subsequently cancelled when the group broke up, and Van Landing hooked up with The Michael Schenker Group. Meanwhile, Swedish metal band Morgana Lefay covered 'Lost Reflections' on their *Past, Present, Future* album in 1995.

Drenning, Lords and Jakhotia formed the Arizona-based Erotic Liquid Culture in 1996 and released an album of funk-metal through a Japanese label and in the UK via Quadra Records. However, the trio were back in the Crimson Glory ranks by the following year, in a revised line-up that featured Drenning, Lords, Jakhotia, guitarist Billy Martinez and new vocalist Wade Black (previously with Lucian Blacque), to record a new

album titled *Astronomica*. The album was finally released in 1999 and featured a line-up of Black, Jackson, Drenning, Lords and drummer Steve Wacholz (of Savatage repute). After the many delays the album was greeted with great appreciation, especially in Europe.

Midnight, meanwhile, was approached by the Swedish group Zoic for recording, but their finances were too tight and the deal fell through. However, the singer did unite with Atheist guitarist Rand Burkey to work on new material until the pair fell out publicly. Black decamped to Seven Witches in 2000; the following year it emerged that Black, Ben Jackson and Jesse Martillo had founded a new progressive rock act, Sector 9.

Jackson developed The Ben Jackson Group, performing vocals and guitar, with guitarist Mark Borgmeyer, bass player Danny Binz and drummer Rich Tabor. Recordings for a debut album titled *Here I Come* saw a guest spot from guitarist John Bajas and contributions from two Crimson Glory colleagues, vocalist Wade Black and bassist Jeff Lords.

Midnight's *M* album arrived in December 2001. Meanwhile, Black broke away from Seven Witches in mid 2002 and enlisted the services of former Nocturnus guitarist and bassist-vocalist Mike Davis plus Emo Mowery for a side project, Tiwanaku. Signals from the Crimson Glory camp in July 2003 pointed to a possible reunion of the original line-up but this did not transpire.

In December 2004, the Greek Black Lotus label announced that they had signed Midnight for a solo deal and an album project entitled *Sakada*. Crimson Glory's Ben Jackson played guitar, Scott Gibson handled guitar and bass and Phil Anderson played drums.

Crimson Glory's own plans for 2005 included a new studio album dubbed *Metatron, Lucifer And The Divine Chaos* plus a DVD titled *Phantoms Of The Opera* featuring an entire concert from 1989 and footage from the 'Transcendence' world tour. A retrospective 20th anniversary box set titled *Valley Of Shadows – Kingdoms Of Light* contained unheard tracks and demos. Wade Black joined Anaheim metal veterans Leatherwolf in July.

Having reunited with Midnight, the band announced the signature of a multi-album deal with Black Lotus in April. This campaign was set to open with a series of original album remasters, the group taking the opportunity to reissue the debut LP under the title of *Lost Reflections* with new artwork and previously hard-to-find bonus tracks 'Love Me – Kill Me' and 'Dream Dancer'. The second Crimson Glory album, re-dubbed *Transcendence: Renovatio*, came in for similar treatment with new album art and additional tracks. However, it seemed all their effort had been in vain when, in May 2006, an ailing Black Lotus Records postponed all releases. Fortunately, a new Crimson Glory studio album is due in 2007.

DIO
A MAN FOR ALL SEASONS

THE STATESMANLIKE RONNIE JAMES DIO is a man blessed with amazing vocal talent, combining an engagingly rich delivery and diction with breathtaking power. As such, he has remained at the very pinnacle of the rock community for three decades and counting. Dio has fronted some of the biggest names in the business, most notably Black Sabbath and Rainbow, both of whom many critics think enjoyed a renaissance while Dio was at the helm. Meanwhile, his solo band rapidly attained major headlining status, built on a quartet of strong records and stage shows renowned for theatrical devices such as mechanical dragons.

Throughout his highest-achieving years, Dio imbued his songs with medieval romanticism, including familiar – some might say overly familiar – motifs such as dragons and rainbows. This trademark lyrical content has been delivered with a majestic vocal range and tone that has made him one of the true rock greats. His lyrics in the 1990s, in particular on Black Sabbath's 1992 album *Dehumanizer*, saw a change of tack into sci-fi and more malevolent areas.

He was born of Italian descent as Ronald James Padovana in Portsmouth, New Hampshire, on July 10th, although the year itself is the subject of frequent conjecture, but reliable sources say his passport states 1940. The singer was raised in his early years in Cortland, New York. The first acts to feel the Dio touch were school outfits such as The Vegas Kings in 1957, where he performed on bass guitar, Ronnie & The Rumblers, and Ronnie & The Red Caps. These bands issued a stream of 7-inch singles. Once he had graduated from Cortland High School in 1960, Ronnie assembled The Prophets. In the autumn of 1967 a fresh project was forged, The Electric Elves (subsequently The Elves, then simply Elf), as Dio finally broke away from the rock'n'roll format and began his journey into the realms of hard rock. Somewhere in the mix of these formative acts, Padovana assumed the stage name Dio, less-than-humbly translating from Italian as 'god'.

Elf's adopted blues-flavoured rock won favour with Deep Purple's Roger Glover and Ian Paice at a showcase gig for Columbia Records in January 1972. The famous British musicians recognised Dio's talent and promptly secured a record deal for his band. Signed to Purple's own imprint, Purple Records, Elf – entered Studio One in Atlanta, Georgia, in April with Glover and Paice as producers to lay down an opening album, simply titled *Elf*. Once again with Glover as producer, their sophomore 1974 outing emerged as *Carolina County Ball*, titled *L.A. 59* for the US market. A third Elf album, *Trying To Burn The Sun*, was recorded before the close of the year.

Elf began their break into the big league by supporting Purple and issuing ever better albums. Dio's relationship with Purple guitarist Ritchie Blackmore eventually resulted in the singer's induction into the Man In Black's post-Purple act, Rainbow. Here, Ronnie first captured the appreciation of a global audience with the majestic *Ritchie Blackmore's Rainbow* in 1975, *Rainbow Rising* in 1976 and *Long Live Rock'n'Roll* in 1978. When Blackmore opted to pursue the radio route, Dio exited.

Ronnie James Dio: "After the Long Live Rock'n'Roll album, Rainbow was really being steered into a completely different direction. A direction I really didn't want to travel down. Ritchie wanted success with singles and on the radio. At first I was writing new songs in the familiar fantasy areas, which had served us very well, but then Ritchie tells me he wants to hear something simpler. I didn't quite get it at first, but then he made it clear he wanted love songs, relationships, more boy-girl type material. That just isn't me. I've never done that and never will, so I could see this was being engineered.

"It all came to a head when I was told Ritchie was leaving the band. When I questioned this I asked, 'OK, who else is leaving the band?' It seemed as though Ritchie and Cozy (Powell) were sticking together and the rest of us were out, so it was a less than subtle way of forcing us out. They finally admitted it. And that was it. I was given the elbow.

"Ritchie had decided in his own mind that the pop audience was for him, which was not what the rest of the band was into at all. Y'know, it was Ritchie's band, we all knew that, but there was a group of musicians there that had achieved quite a bit … well, a lot … and then Ritchie just decides to change his mind and play something else. I had in mind my own band: I was very keen on the band philosophy of pulling together and striving for a common aim. Ritchie went off and brought in some Russ Ballard songs. I can't imagine I would have been happy doing that kind of stuff."

Relocating from Rainbow's base in Connecticut to Los Angeles, Dio found himself in demand. His first project was set to be an all-star collaboration with Blood Sweat & Tears guitarist Al Kooper, the highly respected Doobie Brothers and Steely Dan guitarist Jeff 'Skunk' Baxter, and Little Feat drummer Richie Hayward. This progressive rock-inclined venture got through just one rehearsal before a chance meeting with Black Sabbath guitarist Tony Iommi brought Dio's involvement to a conclusion.

Replacing Ozzy Osbourne, Dio then stepped into a lucrative if fraught sojourn with the mighty Sabbath. This tenure included the titanic albums *Heaven And Hell* (1980) and *Mob Rules* (1981), both records indelibly stamped with Dio's staggering vision. He succeeded not only in breathing new life into Black Sabbath but also in placing them firmly in renaissance. Regrettably, during the mixing stages of the *Live Evil* album, the Dio-led version of Sabbath disintegrated in a vicious public airing of grievances and vilifications. Fortunately for Dio, the scale of success he had generated with Sabbath prompted Warner Bros to request a solo album clause in their contract, which he used to full effect.

Ronnie James Dio: "It had been a battle. With Heaven And Hell being the last album under contract for Warners, nobody from the label really cared. They certainly had not bothered to find out what we were up to in the studio when we were recording it. Their indifference gave us the attitude of 'we'll show the bastards!' and it did well to bond us together.

"When the album came out, Warners did not really get behind the record like they should have. Pretty soon, though, the word of mouth started to really push the record. As soon as they realised there was a big buzz on the album, the Warners machine kicked into gear and took over.

"I think that when the record came out the quality of the songs and the production really took people by surprise. Heaven And Hell was a true 'street' record, by which I mean it sold by word of mouth. What we heard from the feedback to the label and management was that people were listening to the tracks on the radio and at gigs through the PA and asking, 'Who the hell is that?' When they were told 'Black Sabbath' they couldn't quite believe it. We knew this was happening because we heard versions of the same story again and again."

Bob Daisley: "Ozzy was very bitter about Ronnie. It must have been a huge slap in the face for him because here was Ronnie, technically a much better singer than Ozzy, taking over his band and having this massive success. It wasn't nice for him. I mean, you can't say with singers whether someone is better than another, because you are dealing with matters of personal preference, but the cold fact was that Ronnie was technically superb. You just couldn't deny it. Ozzy might have been a better singer for Black Sabbath because his voice and character suited the band, and he certainly had stamped his trademark on there over many years, but Ronnie had just blown all of that away. At times Ozzy would get exceptionally low about just how big and how fast Black Sabbath had got without him. That is why

things got so bitter and personal because Ronnie was so good. Hence the dwarf and all the ridiculous comments in later years. Ozzy could verbally have a go at him for being short or having a big mouth, but he wouldn't dare start slagging Ronnie off for his vocal abilities. When you look back at all those things that were said, the bitterness really comes across. A lot of it is so over the top it was, I'm sure, designed to grab the headlines away from Dio."

Ronnie James Dio: "Jimmy Bain told us he had a couple of tapes, so he came over and we listened to cassettes of John Sykes and Vivian Campbell. Both were amazing players but Vivian stuck out a bit more. It was unique and even had a little bit of Chuck Berry in there, which I liked. The guy was flying by the seat of his pants, he pulled off some unexpected, quirky stuff, and I liked that attitude. Jimmy called him and we arranged a jam. Jimmy took it on himself to bring his bass and kind of made the assumption he was in too! Thank god, actually. Vivian was just great. Once we had a band we flew to Los Angeles to start writing and recording.

"For three weeks nobody even bothered to come down to the studio and check it out. It was kind of amusing and alarming at the same time. Eventually someone from the label called my manager, Wendy, and inquired: 'Is Ronnie in the studio recording an album?' Wendy says: 'Yes, and he's using your money to do it!' They say: 'Oh, we didn't know. Who's producing it?' This is when it gets interesting. Wendy replies: 'Why, Ronnie is of course'. Warner Bros just went 'Oh...'"

Assembling his new solo vehicle in October 1982, the singer, keeping his partnership with ex-Black Sabbath drummer Vinny Appice intact, initially requested the services of erstwhile Rainbow bassist Bob Daisley, although the four-stringer was still contracted with Dio's arch-rival Ozzy Osbourne. An auditioning process held in London eventually pulled in former Sweet Savage guitarist Vivian Campbell, suggested – along with Thin Lizzy's John Sykes – by another Rainbow colleague, bassist Jimmy Bain.

Dio's inaugural post-Black Sabbath album, the masterly *Holy Diver* of May 1983 – crafted at Sound City studios in Los Angeles – was a sharp statement of intent and an album of such magnitude that it succeeded in carrying many Black Sabbath fans along with it. Indeed, the self-produced LP was regarded by many as an example of how Black Sabbath might have evolved if Dio had stayed the course, compared to Sabbath's own follow-up, *Born Again*.

As well as delivering a world-class album, Dio aided their cause enormously with an electrifying performance at the Whitesnake-headlined Donington 'Monsters Of Rock' festival. Prior to this European date, the band had put in their first public performance on July 23rd 1983 at the Concert Barn in Antioch, California. Dio then burned up the road throughout July guesting for a flagging Aerosmith. Back on US soil, Dio took out Queensrÿche and Y&T in support for nationwide dates that winter. Support was so fervent for the band that sold-out concerts in San Jose and Santa Monica, California, on October 5th and 7th spilled over into double-headers as afternoon matinee performances were added to cope with ticket demand.

With UK fans putting *Holy Diver* into the upper reaches of the charts, a British tour with Waysted as guests was scheduled for November, extending into Scandinavian and European legs. Dio closed 1983 by hitting North American stages in December, bolstered by Y&T and Rough Cutt. Ronnie himself had handled all the keyboard work on the album sessions, but for this live work these duties were delegated to ex-Magic and Rough Cutt member Claude Schnell. In his previous outfit, Schnell had adopted the stage name of Claude Steel, but he reverted to his birth name for Dio.

These concerts, illustrating a pattern throughout Dio's career, paid equal homage to Dio's liaisons with Black Sabbath and Rainbow, as well

as featuring newer material. The dates also gave an indication of future extravagances with a stage set of mountains, based on the album cover. *Holy Diver*'s artwork, a chain-whip-wielding demon lashing out at a drowning priest, made a lasting impact, as did the sales figures: by the end of the year Dio had sold over a million copies of his debut in the USA.

During 1984, Ronnie added backing vocals to the Australian act Heaven's *Where Angels Fear To Tread* album, although for contractual reasons he was credited simply as Evil Eyes. Label, fans and band were keen for a quick-fire follow-up, and Dio delivered with *The Last In Line*, which if anything was even more ambitious than the debut, featuring epic historical subject matter. The subsequent world tour found the band backed by an Egyptian theme, echoing the album artwork.

The group commenced their second world tour sandwiched between an eclectic cast of artists at the 'Pinkpop' festival in Geleen, Holland on June 11th 1984. The summer months were allocated for nationwide US touring, firstly packaged with Whitesnake and Black'n'Blue, then headlining over Twisted Sister into August. Back in Europe, Dio played the AC/DC-topped German 'Monsters Of Rock' events before undertaking UK shows in September, backed up by Queensrÿche. Not only was this British run twice as long as the first trek, but Dio easily sold out a three-night stand at London's Hammersmith Odeon. Queensrÿche remained as running mates into Sweden, Norway, Finland, Denmark, Belgium, Holland and Germany. A second US campaign in November saw Dokken as warm-up band until the tour wrapped in January 1985.

Although 1985's *Sacred Heart* gave Dio another hit album, it was generally recognised that the songs were not up to the standard of its predecessors. This third Dio album was not the only project to occupy Ronnie James Dio, though: after an initial idea suggested by Jimmy Bain and Vivian Campbell, the singer put his full weight and enthusiasm behind the Hear 'n Aid benefit project for famine relief in Africa. The all-star cast Dio assembled on May 21st and 22nd at the A&M Studio in Hollywood, California, to record the hit single 'Stars' included Judas Priest's Rob Halford, Geoff Tate of Queensrÿche, Adrian Smith and Dave Murray of Iron Maiden, Dave Meniketti of Y&T, Blue Öyster Cult, Dokken, Neal Schon of Journey, Ted Nugent, Quiet Riot and Twisted Sister. It raised over $1 million and made a colossal impression on the global rock community.

A further successful tour ensued, kicking off with Dio's first live appearance in Japan at the 'Super Rock' festival flanking Foreigner and Sting on August 10th. From there Dio launched straight into a four-month slog of US concerts, backed by fellow management-stable act Rough Cutt. In December, Yngwie Malmsteen took over the role of opener; European concerts found Keel as guests. Deflecting media attention away from *Sacred Heart*'s shortcomings were the valuable tour props, consisting of an 18-foot mechanical dragon and a pair of duelling knights.

However, all was not well within the band. Increasingly disgruntled with the ongoing power struggle with Dio, Campbell quit in April 1986 to form a low-key act, Trinity, with bassist Davy Watson and drummer Pat Waller. He would not be out of the limelight long, though, and was to enjoy high-profile stints in Whitesnake, Riverdogs, Shadowking (with Foreigner vocalist Lou Gramm) and later Def Leppard. Campbell released his debut solo album, *Two Sides Of If*, in September 2005.

Craig Goldy, an associate of Dio's from his time in the Wendy Dio-managed Rough Cutt, was recruited from Driver. Since leaving Rough Cutt, the guitarist had been involved with Giuffria's successful first album and subsequent tour. Locked into some gruelling touring, the band were packaged with Accept for a US campaign in mid 1986, and they put forward the idea of a Dio live album to keep the momentum flowing. Dio's American record company, Warners, rejected the plan, so a compromise was reached with the stopgap mini-album *Intermission*, featuring mainly live tracks and a new studio cut, 'Time To Burn'.

The group's third global excursion closed in Japan and Australia in September 1986.

Dio appeared to be losing ground with the acquisition of Goldy and creatively treading water. The album *Dream Evil*, released in August 1987, heralded Schnell's admission as a full-time band member, the keyboard player appearing onstage for the first time rather than in the wings. Touring commenced with a showing at a Los Angeles 'Children Of The Night' charity event at Irvine Meadows Theatre on August 1st before a special guest appearance at the 'Monsters Of Rock' festivals across Europe, second on the rankings to Bon Jovi and reinforced by Metallica, Anthrax, W.A.S.P. and Cinderella – reminding one and all that Dio were very much still a force to be reckoned with.

Headline dates, supported in Spain by Helloween, with Warlock taking over for the rest of the continent, saw the singer battling not only with a dragon, whose hydraulics often failed to function, but also a huge mechanical spider. In Europe the band's bus was involved in a multi-vehicle pile-up, although thankfully nobody was injured. In December the group wound its way across the USA with Megadeth and Savatage in tow.

With the conclusion of the fourth world tour in March 1988, Dio effectively splintered. During July 1988 Bain joined Cinderella for their tour when Eric Brittingham had to attend to his newborn baby. Dio himself engaged in a brief outside endeavour, acting as producer for Ann Boleyn's Hellion, gaining credits for the track 'Run For Your Life' on the *Postcards From The Asylum* album. The singer would also find recognition from his hometown of Cortland, New York, that same year when a street between Central Avenue and East Court Street was officially renamed Dio Way on November 15th.

The exiled rhythm section of Bain and Appice would forge a new metal act, WWIII, for one over-the-top album fronted by Mandy Lion and with guitars from Tracy G. Following his Craig Goldy's Ritual album, Goldy founded Hard Luck with ex-Alien and Bone Angels singer Frank Starr, guitarist Tim Propeparcy, ex-Killerwatt and Bone Angels bassist Terry Nails and drummer Mark Bistany.

In July 1989, Dio announced a replacement for Goldy in the form of the 17-year-old British guitarist Rowan Robertson. Dio had deferred for quite some time before recruiting Robertson – then heading his own act, Shoot The Moon – because of the musician's youth.

Former Tytan and AC/DC drummer Simon Wright was added and, to complete the band, Dio brought in former Hotshot bassist Teddy Cook and former Yngwie Malmsteen keyboard player Jens Johansson, the latter drafted in after a parting of ways with Claude Schnell. Dio debuted his new band at Oliver's Pub in New York in July 1989.

Supporting the Tony Platt co-produced *Lock Up The Wolves*, Dio gained the valuable guest spot on Metallica's June 1990 European tour on a bill that also included Warrior Soul and Bonham, prior to British headline shows with openers Trouble. Further US gigs saw Dio heading up a billing comprising Yngwie Malmsteen and the Wendy Dio-managed Cold Sweat.

On August 28th 1990, Ronnie's erstwhile Black Sabbath cohort Geezer Butler appeared onstage as a guest at the Minneapolis Forum – a portent of what was to come. Fan support was seriously on the wane, as evidenced on this US tour by half-empty venues and cancelled shows due to slow ticket sales. On September 23rd, at the 18,000-capacity Costa Mesa Pacific Amphitheater – backed up by Stryper, Love/Hate and Cold Sweat – the venue held just under 4,000 fans.

Somewhat inevitably, 1991 saw Dio succumbing to the lure of a Black Sabbath reunion. With band members now free agents, Johansson found fresh employment with noted Finns Stratovarius. During Dio's Black Sabbath interlude, Wright joined UFO while Robertson formed the shortlived Freedom with Lynch Mob vocalist Oni Logan and Triangle drummer Jimmy Paxson. The guitarist was later found with his own act,

Violet's Demise, before joining V.A.S.T. for their *Music For The People* album. Teddy Cook joined China Rain before enlistment into the ranks of Great White in 1992 and subsequently Virgin Steele, Rondinelli and The Sign.

For Dio, the resulting Black Sabbath album *Dehumanizer* was a patchy affair, with few songs making the grade achieved by the illustrious early-1980s predecessors. The subsequent tour had both Dio and Black Sabbath back on track, both parties benefiting from healthier audiences – but, stalling at Number 44 on the US album charts, *Dehumanizer* was a far cry from the heady days of *Heaven And Hell*.

Predictably, it was to end on a sour note. Black Sabbath's management agreed to a brace of shows at Costa Mesa on November 14th and 15th as guests to Ozzy Osbourne. Playing second fiddle to Ozzy was anathema to Dio, who promptly announced that he would not undertake the shows, and the resulting stalemate forced his departure once more. Another ugly war of words erupted, including a fax to journalists from the Ozzy management camp detailing the paltry attendance figures Dio had mustered last time they played the venue. Sabbath went ahead with the shows using the talents of Judas Priest vocalist Rob Halford.

Ronnie James Dio: "Remember, I had given up my band to do Black Sabbath, so it kind of cheapened both achievements in my eyes. I had sacrificed Dio for Black Sabbath. I had an assurance that it was a band effort, so to admit to your fans that you would throw it all away just because Sharon Osbourne called and they're all jumping around like little kids again… . Ozzy claps his hands and Tony and Geezer jump. That's how it is. I felt it was a slap in the face to those fans who had bought the album, bought the tickets, and were expecting us to deliver more. Dehumanizer was about the best album we could make at that time. I loved it. I was very proud of that album and the tour was good, we were getting an excellent response, so to shoot it like a lame horse at the end was insulting. That's what I thought they were doing.

"When the whole Costa Mesa mess hit, the band was frantically trying to find singers to do it. That I do know. It was interesting being an observer on the outside of that picture. Anyhow, they sorted something out with Rob. He called Wendy and I and said, 'Listen, I've been asked to do these Black Sabbath shows but I really don't want to lose our friendship. If it is going to upset things between us I'll decline.' Now, Rob didn't need to do that, but he's a true gentleman so he did the right thing. I wouldn't say Rob needed our permission, but he wanted our blessing – not that he needed it – and he got it. It didn't matter to me at that stage who was going to do it, but I was glad it was Rob, and I thought some of the song choices were interesting too. I knew everything about what was going on. I would see Vinny in the mornings and I would say, 'Going to rehearsals?' and Vinny would say, 'Yeah, going to rehearse with Rob.' It was all out in the open."

Ronnie soon re-founded Dio, drawing both Appice and Bain into the fold. The errant bassist was soon forced out again, however, and the 1993 album *Strange Highways* found Dokken man Jeff Pilson on bass and Appice's ex-WWIII colleague guitarist Tracy G (real name Grijalva) in the band. The Japanese version of the album featured an exclusive cut, 'God Hates Heavy Metal'. Pilson had to opt out of touring as the reformed Dokken were getting into gear, and Larry Dennison took the bass slot. However, with Dokken's fortunes as tumultuous as ever, Pilson returned in November 1994. Bassist Jerry Best, previously with Lion and Freak Of Nature, joined Dio in August 1995 for a little over a month, but Pilson resumed the role. Unfortunately, *Strange Highways* failed to reverse the trend in downward sales and Dio lost his deal with both Warners and Mercury.

Support for Dio in Europe was as solid as ever, however, signalling a move to the German SPV label. For the 1996 album *Angry Machines* the singer utilised the talents of Tracy G once more. Employed on keyboards was ex-Keel man Scott Warren. Overall, the experimental *Angry Machines* took Dio into new, starker realms: the track 'Stay Out Of My Mind' would later resurface on Pilson's War And Peace 2001 album *The Light At The End Of The World*.

Dio, with Larry Dennison taking over on bass again, set about a mammoth world tour to revive the band's fortunes, co-headlining in America and Europe with Motörhead prior to American headliners with support from My Dying Bride. Following these dates, Warren hooked up with Warrant for their American tour and later sessioned for pop band Berlin as an aside to Dio.

Appice and G undertook negotiations with the UFO pairing of vocalist Phil Mogg and bassist Pete Way to create a new version of UFO: contractually, however, the new act could not be titled UFO minus guitarist Michael Schenker, and legalities put paid to this venture.

The Dio triumvirate of Ronnie James Dio, Tracy G and Jeff Pilson made a rare collective guest appearance in 1997, featuring on the *Dreamcastle – Free World* album released by Munetaka Higuchi, drummer of veteran Japanese heavy metal band Loudness. Released only in Japan, this guest involvement passed most fans by.

Dio delivered *Dio's Inferno The Last In Live*, the group's first real live representation, making for an accurate snapshot of a live set, with Dio tracks featured alongside Rainbow and Sabbath standards. Dio's 1997-98 tour hit problems, however, with Appice contracting pneumonia. Kingdom Come and Scorpions drummer James Kottak took over the reins until Appice regained fitness. In May 1998 Dio embarked upon a nationwide headline set of dates supported by Love/Hate, but just three dates into the trek, at San Francisco's Maritime Hall on the 22nd, Appice put in his last show, then rejoining Black Sabbath. By the time Dio hit Las Vegas the following day Simon Wright was the man behind the drum kit. In late June, Dio hooked up with Iron Maiden and Dirty Deeds for a round of arena dates.

Returning to Europe, the group executed an extensive European schedule, backed up by Black Symphony and Narnia. Pilson made a return for the South American leg of the tour, after which Dennison was back in position. Late 1998 found Dio opening for Motörhead in Scandinavia, backing up the release of the live album. Unable to make these dates, due to prior commitments, Dennison did not appear and in October the veteran ex-Ozzy Osbourne and Uriah Heep man Bob Daisley filled the gap.

During 1999, Craig Goldy made a return to the band in time for appearances at European festivals. Dio was then linked to speculations regarding a classic Rainbow reunion, apparently involving Ritchie Blackmore, drummer Cozy Powell and Jimmy Bain. Despite Dio himself stating that he would not be averse to such a move, the concept was crushed with the tragic death of Powell in a car crash.

The millennium was rounded off for Ronnie with the release of an album, *Holy Dio*, a worthy collection of name acts offering tributes including Yngwie Malmsteen, Hammerfall and Stratovarius. The year 2000 found Dio full steam ahead with the *Magica* album, a sci-fi concept record cut at Total Access in Redondo Beach that had many critics announcing a return to former glories. The album, originally set to be the first in a three-part trilogy, climaxed with an 18-minute spoken narration by Ronnie. Both Bain and Wright returned to their former positions. Dio went back out onto the road on a strong double billing in Europe with Deep Purple, these shows providing an opportunity to witness Dio with the headline act's bassist Roger Glover performing a track from their 1974 album *The Butterfly Ball*. Joining the band for these dates was former LA Guns and Beautiful Creatures bassist Chuck Garrick. The new four-stringer's stay

was fleeting and he was soon back in Los Angeles with Killowatt.

In 2001, ex-Dio men Tracy G and Larry Dennison would re-emerge with a new project, Driven. The band released their debut in September, featuring vocalist Tim Saxton and pedigree drummer Mike Terrana of Rage, Yngwie Malmsteen and Artension among others.

Dio, with Bain reinstated, headed up a muscular billing with Yngwie Malmsteen and Doro for a November North American tour prior to a guest slot in May opening for Alice Cooper in the UK. European shows, billed as the 'Monsters Of The Millennium' festivals, saw Ratt included on the bill. Dates in South Africa were also projected, although with Goldy unable to make these shows, former guitarist Rowan Robertson – then with his pop-rock band AM Radio – deputised for rehearsals. The gigs, planned for October, were shelved after the September 11th terrorist attacks. Robertson got back to work on his Violet's Demise project with erstwhile Lynch Mob frontman Oni Logan.

As 2002 broke, it emerged that erstwhile Lion, Bad Moon Rising and House Of Lords guitarist Doug Aldrich had taken Goldy's place in time for a new studio album, *Killing The Dragon*. The record, which debuted at Number 199 on the *Billboard* album charts, triggered a renewal of fortunes for the band as Dio geared up for a high-profile run of American arena dates with Scorpions and Deep Purple.

A lavish Bill Schacht-directed video for the single 'Push' included appearances from the Tenacious D duo of Jack Black and Kyle Gass, who had signalled their respect for the band with the inclusion of the track 'Dio' on their album *Tenacious D*. The video concept, in which a multitude of special effects were employed, involved Tenacious D jamming Black Sabbath's 'Heaven And Hell' as an intro. With interest in Dio at a renewed high, Spitfire Records reissued *Killing The Dragon* in September, containing two tracks, 'Fever Dreams' and 'Rainbow In The Dark', recorded live at the Ahoy in Rotterdam, Holland on the Dio/Deep Purple *Concerto* tour and featuring members of Purple.

Dio set out for a further round of successful North American headline dates throughout the winter supported by rising Swedish metal revivalists Hammerfall and the esteemed King's X. As 2003 dawned, Dio's debut DVD, *Evil Or Divine*, recorded at the Roseland Ballroom in New York City on December 13th 2002, was scheduled for April release. US dates

---

DIO discography

HOLY DIVER, Vertigo VERS 5 (UK) (1983) **13 UK, 56 USA**
THE LAST IN LINE, Vertigo VERL 16 (UK) (1984) **4 UK, 23 USA**
SACRED HEART, Vertigo 834 848-2 (UK) (1985) **4 UK, 29 USA**
Intermission, Vertigo VERB 40 (UK) (1986) **22 UK, 70 USA**
DREAM EVIL, Vertigo 832 530-2 (UK) (1987) **8 UK, 43 USA**
LOCK UP THE WOLVES, Vertigo 846 033-2 (UK) (1990) **28 UK, 61 USA**
STRANGE HIGHWAYS, Vertigo 518486-2 (UK) (1993) **142 USA**
ANGRY MACHINES, Steamhammer SPV 085-18292 (Europe), Mayhem 11104-2 (USA) (1996)
INFERNO: THE LAST IN LIVE, Steamhammer SPV 085-18842 (Europe), Mayhem 11115-2 (USA) (1998)
MAGICA, Spitfire 6-702114-5020-2 (2000)
KILLING THE DRAGON, Spitfire SPITCD 199 (2002) **194 UK, 199 USA**
MASTER OF THE MOON, Steamhammer SPV 085-69912 (Europe) (2004) **159 UK**
EVIL OR DIVINE: LIVE IN NEW YORK CITY, Spitfire SPITCD 253 (2005)
HOLY DIVER LIVE, Eagle Rock EAGCD324 (2006)

commencing in July saw the band co-headlining a strong package tour with Iron Maiden and Motörhead.

Doug Aldrich relinquished his position in April, switching his allegiance to Whitesnake, having joined that band for live work earlier in the year. A quick-fire replacement was announced, Warren DeMartini of Ratt, also a former Whitesnake player. However, this arrangement soon fell by the wayside and Dio reinstated Craig Goldy. Meanwhile, former Dio guitarist Tracy G was in the news with a multitude of musical projects, including a new solo album, a third Driven opus, the formation of his heavy blues group Curly Fester, a band with Vinnie Appice, and the acoustic all-instrumental The Nocturnal Garden.

Bizarrely, tales circulated in 2003 that Ronnie had severed his thumb in a gardening accident. Initially dismissed by many fans, it transpired that the reports were true. The singer cut off the end of his thumb when, surreally, a garden gnome which he had been trying to place on a hill fell over and crushed his hand against a rock. Some quick thinking and a dash to hospital saved the thumb.

Ronnie James Dio: "It was a killer garden gnome. I'm not joking, although I certainly wish I was. What happened was that I was in my yard trying to place this garden gnome on a slope. This is a seriously heavy piece of garden ornament, probably 60 pounds or so. Anyway, it fell over, I fell into the shrubbery and then began to slide down to the bottom of the hill. I was trying to stop myself with my feet but put my hand out at the wrong moment. You can understand this all happened in a split second. My hand landed on a rock, and the gnome landed on it, squashing my thumb between the rock and the gnome. Basically it was crushed and took the end of my thumb off. I just looked at my hand and the first thought that flashed into my mind was, 'How on earth am I going to make my devil horn sign now? That's my trademark!' I wasn't worried about the injury, more concerned with my career.

"I just picked up the end of the thumb, went back into the house, washed the nub of my thumb, then got myself down to the hospital. It was quite surreal because I had one hand with this crushed thumb, basically just red meat and miniscule bits of bone, and I was holding the end of the thumb in my other hand. It was quite fascinating. It's not too often you get to see inside your thumb.

"I got a shock when I arrived in the emergency room because a nurse took a look at it and said, 'No, I don't think we can save this.' I had to wait a while then for a doctor, all the time praying that he would come up with a different evaluation. Anyhow, he did, thankfully. He said he could sew it back on. 'Please do!' I said."

Conjecture circulating in January 2004 suggested that bassist Jimmy Bain and drummer Vinnie Appice were assembling a new band with erstwhile Quiet Riot guitarist Carlos Cavazo. By March, Bain was confirmed as having left the Dio ranks, superseded by a returning Jeff Pilson for recording. With the album complete, billed with the title *Master Of The Moon*, a sprawling set of global dates commencing in Moscow on July 16th was put in place with the Whitesnake and Ozzy Osbourne veteran Rudy Sarzo stepping in on bass. The four-stringer's tour was marred at the August 26th gig in Valencia, Spain when Dio's tour bus was broken into and two bass guitars were stolen.

Dio's August 2004 record *Master Of The Moon* was preceded by Universal's two-disc compilation *We Rock – Greatest Hits*. A line of Dio toy action figures was also in the works. A US tour allied with Anthrax and Fireball Ministry commenced in September. *Master Of The Moon* charted in Germany and Finland but, selling just over 3,300 units in the USA in its first week of sale, it failed to crack the *Billboard* charts.

In early 2005, Rudy Sarzo and Simon Wright were included on

Ronnie James Dio: "There is just too much going on in the world for me to be able to sing about dragons again. I mean, anyone, anywhere in the world can turn on the TV news and see the same horrific things as I see, because it really is a global phenomenon. I don't think we've ever really experienced so much terrorism, famine, murder and war as right now. It's actually pretty miserable, so not really the environment to write happy songs.

"With Magica I went straight back into the world of fantasy and that worked really well. Then with Killing The Dragon I took the band back towards the early Dio albums, to reflect that side of the band, but this time around I just went with how I felt. There was no theme or idea, really. It did turn out very dark, though, very heavy in every sense of the word."

Michael Schenker's covers album *Heavy Hitters*, featuring on a rendition of 'Blood Of The Sun'. Japanese gigs for Dio in May saw Spiritual Beggars as support act. Further tour work that year included many European festivals, a 15-date tour of Russia, Ukraine and Belarus in September, and a UK tour in October. A historical gig came on October 29th with a debut band appearance in Israel at the Hangar 11 venue in Tel Aviv.

Ronnie then scored his first acting role in a movie, reprising his association with Tenacious D comedian Jack Black in *Tenacious D In The Pick Of Destiny* based on the fictitious 'band'. Rare guest appearances included Dio featuring on the *Axes To Axes* debut solo album from Twisted Sister guitarist Eddie Ojeda and on Ian Gillan's anniversary album *Gillan's Inn*. Another album with strong Dio connections emerged with San Diego heavy metal band Benedictum's *Uncreation* opus: it was not only produced by ex-Dio bassist Jeff Pilson but also featured both Craig Goldy and Jimmy Bain as studio guests, as well as featuring a cover version of Black Sabbath's 'The Mob Rules'.

On the Dio front, homage was paid to the band's landmark 1983 debut album by Rock Candy Records in a lavish reissue on September 30th, which included additional audio commentary from Ronnie. To mark this event, the band proposed to perform *Holy Diver* in full, recording and filming these shows in Russia for future release. Craig Goldy injured his arm during these gigs and, although he soldiered on for further shows, he was forced into recuperation. Doug Aldrich replaced him and within days this position was made permanent.

Ronnie James Dio took both his own and Black Sabbath's fans by surprise in mid October with a casual remark during a BBC Radio 2 *Masters Of Rock* radio interview. He said: "Tony Iommi and I are going to write a couple of tracks together for a project that I think is called *Black Sabbath – The Dio Years*." Also revealed was Dio's inclusion as the sinister Dr. X character on Queensrÿche's *Operation Mindcrime II*.

In April 2006, Eagle Rock Entertainment released the Dio double concert recording and DVD *Holy Diver Live*, capturing the band running through the entire first solo opus. With further album projects and touring rolling out into the future, the age-defying Dio's energies and the staunch support from his fan base seem to have no bounds.

JAG PANZER
METAL OF TANK-LIKE POWER

ORIGINALLY A COVERS BAND and initially known as Purple Haze, Jag Panzer from Denver, Colorado, rose to enjoy cult status on the American metal scene and later in their career amplified this into major appreciation on the European mainland. Their early works could easily have remained as collector's curios, but such was the fervent appreciation of their music that demand for bootlegs led in turn to a full blown reformation and a highly

Denver metal titans Jag Panzer

productive renaissance. The band have delved into many styles in their career and undergone line-up tribulations, but they won through eventually, finally stabilising their line-up and reaping the rewards in the 1990s.

The band had been playing the local club circuit for around two years before, as legend has it, guitarist Mark Briody heard a copy of the *Monsters Of Rock* compilation album, commemorating the first ever festival at Donington in 1980. Briody was blown away by the likes of Saxon and Riot and promptly discovered NWOBHM bands such as Angel Witch. The fledgling band, then titled Tyrant, set about recording a demo of their first song 'Tower Of Darkness'. A further demo contained the tracks 'Battlezones' and 'The Crucifix', and thanks to a friend was passed to the Metal Blade and Azra labels in Los Angeles.

However, news arrived of the established Los Angeles metal band Tyrant. The band decided they liked the sound of the Jagdpanzer WW II German tank destroyer, but subtly reworked the name for an American audience as Jag Panzer. They opted to sign with Azra on the strength of a higher royalty offer and a colour cover for the debut offering, the *Tyrants* EP, which was first issued as *Jag Panzer* in 1983. The EP was issued in many collectable versions, including picture discs featuring a monster, a lady with chainsaw, a torture rack, and a promotional release with a gas mask disc. Just prior to the release, Jag Panzer relocated to Los Angeles in an effort to crack the big time. Initially, before the release of the EP, gigs were hard to come by – but as soon as *Jag Panzer* was issued the group pulled over 400 people to their first gig.

In 1984, Azra released Jag Panzer's first full album. *Ample Destruction* marked the recording debut of the newly recruited Joey Tafolla, who teamed up with existing guitarist Mark Briody in a formidable frontline. The band put in support slots with acts as diverse as Grim Reaper and Slade. In an effort to establish a new deal, they committed two new songs to tape, 'Shadow Thief' and 'Viper'.

Tafolla, taking drummer Reynold Carlson with him, quit for a solo career, eventually debuting with the 1987 album *Out Of The Sun* on Shrapnel Records before teaming up with Alice Cooper. Jag Panzer drafted guitarist Christian Lesegue as substitute. In 1986, vocalist The Tyrant (real name Harry Conklin) appeared fronting a black metal band, Satan's Host, under the even stranger pseudonym of Leviathan Thesiren, releasing the album *Metal From Hell*. Conklin reverted back to his real name to enjoy a fleeting tenure with New York cult rockers Riot. At his first Riot live

performance, Conklin unfortunately lost his voice and was dumped. He later assembled Titan Force, issuing two albums – 1989's *Titan Force* on the US Metal label and 1991's *Winner/Loser* for the German Shark label.

Jag Panzer regrouped, drawing in drummer Rikard Stjernquist. A succession of vocalists then flowed through the ranks, including Chris Cronk of Karian, Steve Montez, and Bob Parduba of Denver metal band Alloy Czar. With this line-up, Jag Panzer self-financed the recording of a new album's worth of material – *Chain Of Command* – which included a remake of Iron Butterfly's 1960s hit 'In A Gadda Da Vida'. On the live front the group guested for Helloween and Megadeth. A contract with a major label was offered for *Chain Of Command* but the band deemed it too restrictive and declined. Both Parduba and Lesegue left soon after.

Meanwhile, the *Ample Destruction* album was the subject of varying release formats, with the Canadian release on Banzai retitled *License To Kill* and with an extra track, 'Black Sunday'. The British release on Metalcore Records added 'Black Sunday' and also squeezed in 'Eyes Of The Night' and 'Fallen Angel'. The two latter tracks were recorded at a different session and featured drummer Reynold 'Butch' Carlson, who had replaced original skinsman Rick Hilyard back in 1984. With little official activity, interest in the band was sustained with the emergence in 1991 of an unofficial split album with Majesty and of the *Shadow Thief* bootleg in 1992.

The band cut a 1994 album, *Dissident Alliance*, with new singer Daniel Conca and guitarist Chris Kostka but unfortunately, despite the extra promotional push of a single, 'Jeffrey Behind The Gate', this record – released by Rising Sun in Europe and Pavement Music in America – was panned by critics. Nevertheless, the band managed to tour Europe for the first time as openers to Overkill before their two newest recruits made their exit. Conca later made his mark with Gothic Slam.

Jag Panzer made a return to the scene in 1996, tempted no doubt by the burgeoning interest in retro-trad metal in Europe and Japan. The band, re-enlisting Harry Conklin, demoed the more traditionally aligned tunes 'Future Shock', 'Ready To Strike' and 'Shadow Thief', promptly landing a deal with Century Media. The resulting album, *The Fourth Judgement*, issued in August 1997, was hailed as a renaissance for the band, and the European rock media in particular enthused over Jag Panzer's return to form. Notably, Joey Taffola contributed guitar solos to the record but was unable to tour. Eden's Chris Broderick took over the vacant guitar slot for European dates billed alongside Hammerfall and Gamma Ray.

September 1998's *The Age Of Mastery*, a collection of re-recorded archive tracks as requested by a poll of fans, confirmed the validity of the band's comeback. A nationwide American tour found Jag Panzer sharing stages with Iced Earth. The band undertook a headlining tour of Germany to close off 1998 supported by Angel Dust, Gladiators and GB Arts. Collectors were tempted by Jag Panzer's inclusion of a live version of 'Tyranny' on an *Ungebrochen Metal* compilation.

Although 1999 didn't deliver a new album, Jag Panzer did offer up their rendition of 'Children Of The Sea' to the *Holy Dio* Century Media tribute album and put in a sterling set at the 'Wacken Open Air' festival. As the year drew to a close, Century Media surprised fans by offering a download of Mark Briody and Harry Conklin's Christmas song 'Do You See What I See'.

Jag Panzer made a return with the May 2000 *Macbeth*-inspired *Thane To The Throne* opus. The ambitious album track 'The Prophecies (Fugue In D Minor)' included a Moscow string quartet. With *Thane To The Throne*, the band managed to elevate themselves above cult status, making serious headway on the sales front. The following year a diversion saw the ice-hockey-loving band reworking Judas Priest's 'You've Got Another Thing Comin'' into 'You've Got Another Cup Comin'', donated as a theme song to the Colorado Avalanches team. Jag Panzer's continued revival was bolstered by the arrival of the Jim Morris-produced *Mechanized Warfare* album in July 2001.

JAG PANZER discography

Jag Panzer, Azra 010 (USA) (1983) later retitled *Tyrants*

AMPLE DESTRUCTION, Iron Works IW 1001 (USA) (1984)

DISSIDENT ALLIANCE, Rising Sun 084-62292 (Europe) (1994)

THE FOURTH JUDGEMENT, Century Media CM 77172-2 (Europe), Century Media CM 7872-2 (USA) (1997)

THE AGE OF MASTERY, Century Media CM 77225-2 (Europe), Century Media CM 7925-2 (USA) (1998)

THANE TO THE THRONE, Century Media CM 77293-2 (Europe), Century Media CM 7993-2 (USA) (2000)

MECHANIZED WARFARE, Century Media CM 77369-2 (Europe), Century Media CM 8069-2 (USA) (2001)

DECADE OF THE NAIL-SPIKED BAT, Century Media CM 77493-2 (Europe), Century Media CM 8125-2 (USA) (2003)

CHAIN OF COMMAND, Century Media CM 77569-2 (Europe) (2004)

CASTING THE STONES, Century Media CM 77593-2 (Europe), Century Media CM 8293-2 (USA) (2004)

The Wreck Of The Edmund Fitzgerald, Century Media 8269EP (2005) limited edition 7-inch vinyl single 500 copies

Alongside In Flames, the band lent strong support to Iced Earth's April 2002 American tour. For these shows an exclusive DVD package, dubbed *The Era Of Kings And Conflict* – hosting feature videos and a bootleg live film of a show in Switzerland – was made available. Jag Panzer united with Helloween and Beyond The Embrace for a short burst of North American dates in October.

Jag Panzer fans had much to be thankful for in 2003 with the release of the two-disc *Decade Of The Nail Spiked Bat* collection through Century Media. The albums consisted of tracks from the *Jag Panzer* EP, *Ample Destruction* and *Dissident Alliance*, in brand new re-recorded form. The group had been endeavouring to re-release this old material for some time but, failing to reach a settlement with Joey Taffola, opted to re-record all the songs. This move satisfied fans and gave the earlier records even further rarity value.

In February 2004, Conklin, while retaining his ties to Jag Panzer, joined the ranks of Ballistic, this act also involving Broderick and Stjernquist. Although Gattis himself had recorded vocals for their 2003 debut, he was prevented from further singing due to severe headaches. Sad news came that same month when former Jag Panzer man Daniel Conca, singer during the *Dissident Alliance* era, died at just 39 years old.

In May 2004, Jag Panzer entered Tampa's Morrisound studios with producer Jim Morris to record a new album, *Casting The Stones*. The band headlined the January 2005 'Deep Freeze Winter Metal' festival in Westminster, Colorado. They also appeared at the Motörhead-headlined 'Monterrey Metal Fest' at the Auditorio Coca Cola in Monterrey, Mexico in May. To coincide with the band's appearance at the German 'Bang Your Head' festival, a 7-inch single limited to just 500 copies was issued, featuring a cover of Gordon Lightfoot's 'The Wreck Of The Edmund Fitzgerald'.

Chris Broderick scored guest session credits on Italian metal band Raising Fear's *Avalon* album. In May 2006 the guitarist temporarily joined the ranks of Seattle's Nevermore for US touring, substituting for Steve Smyth who had been diagnosed with end-stage kidney failure.

LEATHERWOLF
HOWLING METAL

BASED IN LOS ANGELES, power metal act Leatherwolf were founded in 1981 and, in their rise to signing with a major label, supported Poison, Great White and W.A.S.P. along the way. The band put themselves in the history books on May 28th 1982 when their gig at the Concert Factory in Los Angeles saw support from a fledgling Metallica.

Leatherwolf stood apart from the majority of metal bands for two reasons. One was their unashamed LA 'look', which was rare for a trad-metal act, the other a three-pronged guitar attack. The group originally released a self-titled mini-album in 1984 on the Tropical label, a subsidiary of Enigma, and this record was issued in Britain by the Heavy Metal label a year later with the addition of extra tracks, titled *Endangered Species*. Confusingly, Tropical Records also released an extended version of the mini-album with additional tracks, retaining the *Leatherwolf* title.

Leatherwolf's Matt Hurich deputised for Stryper bassist Tim Gaines when he mysteriously disappeared during the recording of the *To Hell With The Devil* album in 1986. However, Hurich soon lost his position in Stryper when Gaines returned, and later he also relinquished his post in Leatherwolf.

The 1987 self-titled album, produced by Kevin Beamish – noted for his softer AOR work – featured new bassist Paul Carmen, a veteran of Black Sheep. *Street Ready* in 1989 was produced by Beamish once more, recorded at Compass Point Studios in Nassau in the Bahamas and mixed by Michael Wagener. It was released in Britain to coincide with a support tour during March 1989 to Japanese outfit Vow Wow. Leatherwolf also

opened for Zed Yago in Germany. Unfortunately, label support fell away, leaving a sizeable contingent of European fans in dismay as the group splintered.

In 1992, members of Leatherwolf turned up in the melodic rock act Hail Mary. A new short-haired version of Leatherwolf returned in 1999 with a self-financed album, *Wide Open*, although by this stage Carey Howe was also operating with another band, 420Koma. The reception afforded *Wide Open* showed that Leatherwolf's fanbase had remained resilient during the hiatus. Despite this support, long-term vocalist Olivieri quit in August 2000.

Leatherwolf retired again, finally announcing a new frontman in Chris Adams during March 2002. However, by March 2004 Leatherwolf had recruited Racer X vocalist Jeff Martin, a multi-skilled individual who also claimed credits as a drummer for outfits such as UFO, Michael Schenker Group, George Lynch and Badlands. Leatherwolf uploaded new demo songs, 'Disconnect', 'Behind The Gun' and 'Burned', onto the internet for download in August.

With Martin out of contention, the band announced their search for a new singer in December, although it would not be until July 2005 that the band revealed that the Crimson Glory, Tiwanaku and Seven Witches veteran Wade Black had secured the position. By October they were in the recording studio with Warrior guitarist Joe Floyd as producer. Eric Halpern from Helstar laid down guest guitar solos and former Leatherwolf vocalist Michael Olivieri added both guitar and backing vocals. Jacob Hansen mixed the album, *World Asylum*, at Hansen Studios in Denmark.

In March 2006, the group signed over *World Asylum* to German label Massacre for a June release. That month Los Angeles shows found the Hail

Leatherwolf

Mary and Shotgun Messiah-credited Pat Guyton handling bass, while Paul Carmen returned for festival appearances in Germany. Guyton co-composed the *World Asylum* Japanese bonus track 'Tools Of Discipline'.

LIZZY BORDEN
AXE MEN

THIS THEATRICAL HEAVY metal band from Los Angeles were suitably named after an infamous murderess and fronted by the almost Afro-topped singer 'Lizzy Borden'. The band never truly broke out of cult appeal, with finances too limited to enable effective touring and early albums blighted by low-budget production, but the band eventually overcame these obstacles to gain respect, particularly in Europe. Although masked somewhat by their reliance on stage antics, Lizzy Borden did deliver some sophisticated, punishing heavy metal, peaking with the masterly *Visual Lies*.

They debuted in 1983 with an eight-track demo cassette. Signing to Metal Blade, the combo contributed the song 'Rod Of Iron' to *Metal Massacre Volume 4* and delivered the *Give 'Em The Axe* 12-inch EP in May 1984, following this with the full-length *Love You To Pieces* album in June 1985. At this juncture the band consisted of Borden alongside guitarists Gene Allen and Tony Matuzak, bassist Mike Davis and drummer Joey Scott Harges (Lizzy's brother). An earlier four-stringer, Steve Hochheiser, had opted out to join Détente.

Love You To Pieces was equally high on shock value (especially on cuts such as 'Flesheater') and metal content with 'Council For The Cauldron', 'Warfare', 'Psychopath' and the Jack The Ripper-themed 'Red Rum'. Unfortunately, the album suffered greatly from a below-par production, a disadvantage also shared by the band's next offering.

Lizzy Borden maintained the momentum with 1986's *Menace To Society*, their first to enter the *Billboard* charts, peaking at Number 195. Nationwide touring with Motörhead increased the band's standing. For the 1987 *Terror Rising* EP – which included a cover of Jefferson Airplane's psychedelic classic 'White Rabbit' – Bitch's infamous Betsy made an appearance on the track 'Don't Touch Me There', a song originally by The Tubes. Meanwhile, Armored Saint bassist Joey Vera featured on 'Catch Your Death' and 'Terror Rising'.

The ambitious double live album, *The Murderess Metal Roadshow*, released in April 1986 with Alex Nelson replacing Matuzak, included a rendition of Wings' cinematic epic 'Live And Let Die'. Two extra studio cuts were added to the concert tapes, 'Dead Serious' and '(Wake Up) Time To Die'. An accompanying video for *The Murderess Metal Roadshow*, filmed in Los Angeles, gave viewers a chance to see Lizzy's renowned coffin-smashing stunt as well as the somewhat surreal mugging of Santa Claus for 'Psychopath'.

The band's debut British appearance came in 1987 with a headline slot at London's Marquee club prior to a 'Reading Festival' appearance on a bill headlined by Alice Cooper. Meanwhile, ex-member Tony Matuzak formed New York Rocks.

The band added ex-Terriff guitarist Joe Holmes for the Max Norman-produced *Visual Lies* – probably their most polished effort in terms of overall sound and commerciality. Here, Lizzy Borden finally gained the muscular studio sound that had been so sorely lacking on their previous output, and reviews reflected this positive step forward. *Visual Lies* only hit Number 146 on *Billboard* but strengthened their fanbase considerably in Europe.

Guitarist Gene Allen quit to found a project with ex-Metal Church vocalist David Wayne in 1988. He later assumed the stage name KaBong, contributing to the Phoenix Down project of former Alice Cooper guitarist Kane Roberts.

By 1989, Lizzy Borden was essentially a solo vehicle for the man himself; he had split the group and assembled a new bunch of musicians to assist in the recording of *Master Of Disguise*, a semi-conceptual affair produced by Alex Woltman and Elliot Solomon and mixed by Terry Brown. Joining Lizzy on the record was drummer Joey Scott Harges, original bassist Mike Davis, Armored Saint bassist Joey Vera and more permanent four-stringer Bryan Perry, ex-King Kobra guitarist David Michael Phillips, New York axeman Ronnie Jude, and co-producer Solomon on keyboards. *Master Of Disguise* gave Lizzy Borden their highest chart placing on *Billboard* at Number 133. David Michael Phillips only stayed long enough to perform one concert with the band, at the Palace in Hollywood, before vacating. European touring in 1991 found the band in alliance with Welsh glam-metallers Tigertailz.

Former band member Joe Holmes put Terriff back together with a new line-up including sometime Lizzy Borden bassist Mike Davis. The band failed to last the course, however, and Holmes later found high-profile work with David Lee Roth and Ozzy Osbourne.

Without a deal, the band soldiered on through 1992, playing the American club circuit with a new member, Swedish bassist Marten Andersson. With metal out of favour, Lizzy Borden and Joey Scott Harges forged the punkier Diamond Dogs project, a union with guitarist Joe Steals and bassist Michael White. This band did not record or tour.

The resurrected band returned in 1999, performing a well-received set at the 'Bang Your Head' festival in southern Germany on a major bill headlined by W.A.S.P., Motörhead, Dio and Deep Purple. They put on a full blood-and-gore spectacle, although Lizzy was arrested at the airport on the way back to America, asked to explain why he was in possession of a blood-soaked axe.

Lizzy Borden then ensconced themselves in The Crypt studios in North Hollywood with producer Elliot Solomon to craft *Deal With The Devil*, a set of new compositions alongside two 1980s tracks, 'Lovin' You Is Murder' and 'We Only Come Out At Night'. Japanese versions, which included a raucous take on Alice Cooper's 'Generation Landslide', came with a bonus track titled 'We'll Burn The Sky'. The band now consisted of Borden, guitarist Alex Nelson, bass player Marten Andersson of Legacy and Takara, and long-term drummer Joey Scott Harges. Guest sessions came from Armored Saint's Joey Vera and erstwhile Borden bassist Davis.

The new-look Lizzy Borden put out *Deal With The Devil* in October

LIZZY BORDEN discography

Give 'Em The Axe, Metal Blade 71078 (USA) (1984)
LOVE YOU TO PIECES, Roadrunner RR 9771 (Europe), Metal Blade 72057 (USA) (1985)
THE MURDERESS METAL ROAD SHOW, Roadrunner RR 9702 (Europe), Metal Blade 72113 (USA) (1986)
MENACE TO SOCIETY, Roadrunner RR 9664 (Europe), Metal Blade 73224 (USA) (1986) **185 USA**
Terror Rising, Roadrunner RR 9621 (Europe), Metal Blade 73254 (USA) (1987) **188 USA**
VISUAL LIES, Roadrunner RR 9592 (Europe), Metal Blade 73232 (USA) (1987) **146 USA**
MASTER OF DISGUISE, Roadrunner RR 9454-2 (Europe), Metal Blade 7 73413-2 (USA) (1989) **133 USA**
DEAL WITH THE DEVIL, Metal Blade 3984-14343-2 (Europe / USA) (2000)

2000 and toured America in April 2001 as guests to Yngwie Malmsteen. They found themselves back in the media when at a gig in Charlotte, North Carolina, the band's guitar tech Ulrik Zander was shot three times attempting to foil a robbery. Fortunately Zander recovered and the tour went on. Mike Davis was found on the Los Angeles club circuit in 2000 as a member of Branom. In March 2003 he joined Rob Halford's solo band. Lizzy Borden soldiered on, drafting in former Diamond Dogs man Joe Steals as fill-in guitarist. In March 2004, Andersson joined the George Lynch band for road work in the USA.

Tragedy struck the band on May 17th 2004 when guitarist Alex Nelson was killed in a head-on car crash. Lizzy Borden then completely revamped themselves to become Starwood, comprising Borden, Steals, bassist Marten Andersson and drummer Joey Scott (Scott Harges). This 'new' unit cut the album *If It Ain't Broke, Break It!* for Metal Blade. Adopting a much more upbeat, radio-friendly approach and an image to match, Starwood employed reworked songs from the Diamond Dogs venture. Strangely, Starwood's biography and website made no reference to Lizzy Borden's history. By coincidence, as this transition was made, Metallic Archangel Records announced plans for a Lizzy Borden tribute album, *Baptized In Blood.*

Bizarrely, official Starwood press releases in October came with a unique postscript advising the media that no changes be made to the text "unless verified for truth and accuracy by Starwood's management", presumably a reference to the complete omission of Lizzy Borden history. Starwood lent support to UFO for a solo Californian gig in October. They were also set to join Vince Neil's proposed November UK tour dates before these gigs were pulled. This uncertainty severely damaged the band's prospects, with their greatest achievement a performance at the hairspray-sponsored 'Manic Panic' festival in Tokyo in November 2005.

March 2006 delivered word that the axe was set to rise again as Lizzy Borden, reverting to their original name and style, announced that they were seeking a new guitar player to replace the late Alex Nelson. Days later Ira Black, from Vicious Rumors, The SideFX and Heathen, took the position as the group announced US tour dates for May backing W.A.S.P.

MALICE
PRIESTALIKES WITH REAL TALENT

FORMED FIRMLY IN THE JUDAS PRIEST mould, Malice were a highly impressive Los Angeles-based metal band noted for strenuous live work.

Not only did they sound like Judas Priest by warrant of their heavy European-style guitar riffing, but vocalist James Neal – a practising Buddhist – sounded uncannily like Priest frontman Rob Halford. Guitarist Jay Reynolds, meanwhile, was a visual dead ringer for Priest guitarist K.K. Downing. Malice's insistence on wearing studded black leather only compounded the comparisons.

Bassist Mark Behn had previously played in Fire Eye and another local outfit, Kharma, which had included Pete Holmes (better known in later years for his role in Black'n'Blue). Guitarist Mick Zane had started out with the 1978 act Rude Awakening, fronted by Matt McCourt (later of Wild Dogs). Zane and McCourt alongside Wild Dogs guitarist Jeff Horton and Black'n'Blue man Holmes would share a later band, DMZ, in 1981. Reynolds was part of the same club scene, coincidentally appearing in two Matt McCourt-fronted acts: punk band The Violators and The Ravers.

It was Reynolds who provided the catalyst for Malice. Having returned to Portland from Hawaii, where the guitarist had worked with various acts, he soon forged The Ravers. When this band folded, he set to work assembling Malice: the first rehearsals also featured Neal, Deen Castronovo of Wild Dogs on drums, Matt McCourt on bass and the then 16-year-old Kip Doran of Evil Genius and The Enemy on guitar.

Despite making their initial appearance on Metal Blade's first *Metal Massacre* compilation as the only band to contribute two tracks (with 'Captive Of Light' and 'Kick You Down'), Malice were in fact at that stage still not a band – the members only decided on a permanent union after the sessions. Recruiting bassist Mark Behn and drummer Peter Laufmann, this formation of the group relocated to Los Angeles.

The buzz on Malice now rollercoastered, with the respected Dutch magazine *Aardschok* giving them a cover story a mere two months after their formation. The quintet's first gig came in November 1982 at the Los Angeles Troubadour club, headlining over Metallica and Pandemonium. A line-up change saw the introduction of new drummer Cliff Carruthers, previously with Snow and Assassin. The band's Michael Wagener-produced demo proved a tour de force, and Malice found themselves at the centre of a record-company bidding war. Atlantic snapped up the band in July 1984. The demo became half of Malice's first album, 1985's *In The Beginning...*, with the remaining tracks produced by Ashley Howe.

The second album, *License To Kill*, was produced by Max Norman. The record, surfacing during 1986, was another strong contender. Guests in the studio included Megadeth men Dave Mustaine and Dave Ellefson, and Black'n'Blue's Tommy Thayer and Jaime St. James.

Malice toured with W.A.S.P. on the West Coast and, despite making headway with a strong record, a European tour supporting thrashers Slayer proved to be a disastrous mismatch – as the headliners' fans showed their hostility openly with spitting and verbal abuse.

Strangely, Atlantic – known as a home for many metal artists – declined the option on a third album, and Malice folded in late 1987. Reynolds flirted very briefly with Megadeth – although his friend Jeff Young, to whom he entrusted this confidential information, and who had even tutored Reynolds on Megadeth riffs, put his own name forward and landed the coveted position.

MALICE discography

IN THE BEGINNING..., Atlantic 781 250-1 (UK), Atlantic 81250 (USA) (1985)
LICENSE TO KILL, Atlantic K 781 714 1 (UK), Atlantic 81714 (USA) (1987) **177 USA**
Crazy In The Night, Roadracer RO 9445-2 (Europe), Metal Blade 7 73414-2 (USA) (1989)

A third Malice release, *Crazy In The Night*, a four-track EP, was issued in 1989, although none of the tracks featured Neal, his place having been taken in the studio by two singers, 19-year-old Mark Weitz and Paul Sabu. The latter was a strange union bearing in mind Sabu's AOR history. The Neal-fronted version of Malice did, however, appear in a concert sequence in the movie *Vice Versa*.

Zane, Behn and Carruthers attempted to sustain Malice, but with no product forthcoming were obliged to split the band. In 1995, Zane and Behn returned to the fray with the Los Angeles-based Monster, releasing *Through The Eyes Of The World* on Long Island Records. Monster featured Behn's old Kharma bandmate Pete Holmes and the previously unknown vocalist Mark Isham. Ex-Malice guitarist Jay Reynolds resurfaced in early 2004 as a member of the revamped Metal Church.

MANILLA ROAD
OLD-SCHOOL METAL FOR THE MASSES

MANILLA ROAD ARE A CULT UNDERGROUND metal band from Wichita, Kansas, with a lengthy history. Dating back to 1976, the band's first product was the 1980 *Invasion* album on the custom imprint Roadster. Before this, the band – vocalist-guitarist Mark Shelton, formerly of Embryo and Apocalypse, guitar player Robert Park, bassist Scott Park and drummer Myles Sipe – had distributed a three-track demo cassette to local radio stations in 1979. Two songs from these sessions, 'Manilla Road' and 'Herman Hill' (the latter based on Wichita's Herman Hill Park riots) featured only on this tape.

Invasion did not yet place Manilla Road in heavy metal territory, instead portraying a band rooted in progressive rock, spearheaded by Shelton's distinctive nasal vocals over a complex array of loose, unorthodox arrangements. As further albums were recorded, the group became increasingly heavier with each title. *Metal*, incorporating the Robert E. Howard-inspired 'Queen Of The Black Coast', followed in 1982, although the group had recorded an album's worth of unreleased material during the interim, originally planned to be titled *The Dreams Of Eschaton*.

The first brace of albums only achieved limited distribution, but the inclusion of the song 'Flaming Metal System' on the Shrapnel label's 1983 *U.S. Metal Vol. III* compilation generated positive reviews in the American rock media. Mike Metz contributed keyboards to 1983's Mark Mazur-produced *Crystal Logic*: this third effort greatly furthered exposure to the band due to a licensing arrangement with French label Black Dragon. This highly specialised imprint had taken on a clutch of cult metal bands such as Liege Lord, Candlemass, Heir Apparent and Savage Grace, putting the Kansas outfit in esteemed company.

Manilla Road had adopted a doomier air on *Crystal Logic*, constructing

an album of epic proportions. Unfortunately, *Logic's* amateurish cover artwork, which misrepresented the quality of the songs on many of the group's early albums, dissuaded all except the most inquisitive of purchasers.

Drummer Rick Fisher lost his place to Randy 'Thrasher' Foxe before the Arthurian-themed *Open The Gates* album in 1985. The impressive jacket by Eric Larnoy led to increased sales, which was fortuitous as Manilla Road had evolved into a classy, riff-dominant metal band. Although Shelton was suffering from an illness during recording, this affliction only served to lend a menacing rasp to his vocals.

The Deluge in 1986 and the following year's quick-fire *Mystification*, rooted in the horror fiction of Edgar Allan Poe, continued the formula to great effect, despite *Mystification* being severely hampered by a hamfisted final master. Regardless, Manilla Road set out on tour, flanking labelmates Liege Lord. Tapes from these shows were later compiled for the 1988 live album *Roadkill*. Another studio album, *Out Of The Abyss*, was delivered that same year. Manilla Road turned up the heat for this eighth endeavour, accelerating in speed to near-thrash levels and exploring disquieting topics.

Strangely, 1990's *The Courts Of Chaos* saw two versions, one credited to Manilla Road, the other a cassette attributed solely to frontman Mark Shelton. The recording trio for this opus consisted of Shelton, bassist Scott Park and drummer Foxe. The record included a worthy cover version of Bloodrock's 'D.O.A.'.

Shelton, forging a studio union with Aaron Brown and Andrew Coss, took leave from the band schedule to put down tracks for a solo album, *The Circus Maximus*. He was dismayed to find the tracks released onto the market in 1992 under the Manilla Road name. Undaunted, Shelton's new combo gigged as Circus Maximus.

A best-of collection appeared in 1998, *Live By The Sword – The Very Best Of Manilla Road*, through Black Dragon in association with the Greek version of *Metal Hammer* magazine. The 14-track album clocked in at approximately 72 minutes in length and closed the first chapter of the band's career.

Manilla Road unexpectedly returned in 2001 with a new album, *Atlantis Rising*, on the German Iron Glory label and a performance at the German 'Bang Your Head' festival. The line-up stood at vocalist-guitarist Shelton, bassist Mark Anderson and drummer Scott Peters. Stamping Ground's Darby Pentecoast also lent backing vocals.

Renewed interest in the band prompted the issue in 2002 of the aborted *The Dreams Of Eschaton* sessions, given the title *Mark Of The Beast*. The Iron Glory label issued a new studio set in November, the album first given a working title of *Seven Trumpets* and finally named *Spiral Castle*.

Manilla Road

The band also reunited during 2003, returning to Europe the following year with shows in Italy, Greece and a headline position at the 'Keep It True' event at the Tauberfrankenhalle in Lauda-Königshofen, Germany alongside Satan, Helloween, Elixir, Paradox and Majesty. The new band consisted of Shelton, vocalist Bryan Patrick, bassist Harvey Patrick and drummer Cory 'HardCore' Christner.

In mid 2005, as Manilla Road launched a new album, *Gates Of Fire*, it was reported that Mark Shelton was contributing to the Dawnrider project assembled by Majesty mentor Tarek 'Metal Son' Maghary. In October, the band revealed they had signed to the Greek Black Lotus label for a new album.

MANOWAR
METAL FOR REAL MEN

Manowar stand at the pinnacle of true, unwavering heavy metal. Bedecked in barbarian battlewear and with equal emphasis placed on the band members' muscles as on the merit of their Ennio Morricone-style metal, Manowar's concept of what constitutes pure heavy metal has naturally polarised opinions. Manowar fans are slavish in their devotion and so loyal that the group's presence in the European charts is now commonplace.

Over a lengthy career the Auburn, New York, band have steadfastly refused to compromise and as a result have amassed what is probably the staunchest fanbase in the world. They hold the *Guinness Book Of World Records* honour of world's loudest band, with music captured at a mind-numbing 129.5 decibels and singer Eric Adams clocked at 136 decibels.

Bandleader Joey DeMaio, part Italian and part Cherokee, first stepped onstage with his bass at the age of 12 and had a stab at creating a metal band when he formed a power trio, David Feinstein's Thunder, with ex-Elf vocalist-guitarist David Feinstein and drummer Carl Canedy. This early band contributed a track, 'Slippin' And Slidin'', to a Buddy Holly tribute EP.

While with Thunder, DeMaio suffered an onstage accident that came close to putting his rock'n'roll dreams beyond reach. An explosion from a pyrotechnic device set the bassist's clothes ablaze, and burns to his hands put the musician into hospital for two months. It took a lengthy period of recuperation before DeMaio could play bass again. Feinstein and Canedy went on to form the power trio The Rods, while the recovered DeMaio worked with Ronnie James Dio in the final incarnation of Elf.

Manowar's inception can be pinpointed exactly to May 18th 1980. On this day, DeMaio was doing double duty as pyro operative and bass technician to Black Sabbath's Geezer Butler. The French act Shakin' Street was the support band for Sabbath's UK tour and, at Newcastle Upon Tyne's City Hall, DeMaio – on an introduction by Ronnie James Dio – struck up a strong alliance with their American guitarist, Ross 'The Boss' Friedman, a fellow New Yorker whose credentials included the punk-metal act The Dictators and New Yorkers Lyre. With so much in common, on their return to the States the pair jammed together and immediately set the wheels in motion for the ideal metal band, an idea that had been formulated backstage at that Black Sabbath show in Newcastle. Adding ex-Kids and Harlequin vocalist Eric Adams (previously occupied as a meat-cutter) and finally drummer Karl Kennedy, Manowar were born.

After recording a crude demo at Vision Studios in Auburn for a mere $250, which consisted of two songs, 'Battle Hymn' and 'Shellshock', and which was produced by Canedy, Manowar attracted the attention of EMI America. This union, brokered by producer Bob Currie, gave the quartet the opportunity to record a better-quality demo and led them to the Liberty imprint.

While recording their debut album, *Battle Hymns*, with Bob Currie behind the board and new drummer Donnie Hamzik in place, Manowar gained backing from Bill Aucoin at Aucoin Management, who had been greatly instrumental in putting Kiss on the map in the 1970s.

Recorded in Florida and launched in August 1982, *Battle Hymns* featured none other than the legendary Orson Welles appearing in a narrator's role on the track 'Dark Avenger'. Ambitiously – and successfully, it should be added – DeMaio rendered Rossini's 'William Tell Overture' into a bass solo titled 'William's Tale'. Triggered by the roar of motorbike engines, the huge aspirations and conviction of *Battle Hymns* were dampened by a less-than-flattering production. This sonic inadequacy thwarted Manowar's initial attempt to impress the world.

Nevertheless, the album's release prompted a wave of media coverage. Their image, all *Conan*-style animal skins and weaponry, and their belief in 'true heavy metal' – a form of music that the group passionately described as being the most glorious form of music in the world – and their lyrical sagas of glory, battle and barbarian triumph placed Manowar in a unique position.

They attempted to play an inaugural concert at 'Summers On The Beach' in Fort Lauderdale, Florida, in June 1982. However, once their soundcheck had brought plaster down from the ceiling and cracked the venue's windows, the manager politely asked the band not to perform that evening.

Unfortunately, the impetus gained wasn't enough to save them from being unceremoniously dropped from EMI America's roster – and losing Aucoin when a new deal wasn't immediately forthcoming. The loss of the EMI America deal prevented Manowar from making a planned appearance at the 'Reading Festival' in Britain during August 1982.

Hamzik was dispensed with in early 1983, and the band unveiled a new man behind the skins, Scott Columbus, at two gigs in New York (which were opened by Virgin Steele). The drummer had reportedly been discovered by a female fan of the band, beating aluminium in a local foundry. The shows marked their first live appearances in their home city, although the quartet had previously found promoters and venues willing enough to put on headlining gigs in Chicago, as well as a short tour in the south-east opening for Ted Nugent.

Taking monies owed to them by EMI America for breach of contract, Manowar retreated upstate with producer Jon Mathias and recorded a new album, *Into Glory Ride*, their first with Columbus. By summer 1983, they had contracted a new deal, naturally forgoing pen and paper in favour of a knife blade and their own blood when signing to Jonny Zazula's Megaforce label. In the UK, Manowar's album was licensed to Music For Nations, this label's enthusiasm playing an important part in the group's success. The *Into Glory Ride* album, heralded with the infamous "Death to false metal" legend, appeared around the same time as a second recording with Orson Welles – 'Defender' – materialised on a 12-inch single backed with 'Gloves Of Metal'. (Welles had recorded this piece at the same time as 'Dark Avenger', but the song had not made the *Battle Hymns* LP.) The record closed in bombastic style with the eight-and-a-half-minute stage favourite 'March For Revenge (By The Soldiers Of Death)'.

The band courted controversy when a British tour degenerated into a public bickering match between Manowar and their fellow Music For Nations band Mercyful Fate, whom they had taken out as support act. The Danes pulled out after just one date at St Albans City Hall, claiming that although they had contributed to the costs of the tour, they were being treated unfairly by the headliners when it came to set-up times and soundchecking. Manowar refuted these allegations and the Scandinavians were promptly ditched in favour of Birmingham band Crazy Angel.

During February 1984, Manowar issued *Hail To England*, a record titled in tribute to their British fans, among whom the band had quickly found dedicated support. Recorded in 12 days at Toronto's Phase One Studios and costing an estimated $20,000, the Jack Richardson-produced album included Joey DeMaio's legendary 'Black Arrows', a solo recorded

MANOWAR discography

BATTLE HYMNS, Liberty LBG 30349 (UK), Liberty LT-51125 (USA) (1982)

INTO GLORY RIDE, Music For Nations MFN 6 (UK), Megaforce MRI-666 (USA) (1983)

HAIL TO ENGLAND, Music For Nations MFN 19 (UK) (1984) **83 UK**

SIGN OF THE HAMMER, Ten DIX 10 (UK), Grand Slamm 14 (USA) (1984) **73 UK**

FIGHTING THE WORLD, Atlantic 781 693-1 (UK), Atco 790 563-1 (USA) (1987)

KINGS OF METAL, Atlantic K 781 930 2 (UK), Atlantic 81930-2 (USA) (1988)

THE TRIUMPH OF STEEL, Atlantic 7567 82423-2 (UK), Atlantic 82423-2 (USA) (1992)

LOUDER THAN HELL, Geffen 24925 (USA) (1996)

HELL ON WHEELS, Universal UMD 70062 (1997)

HELL ON STAGE – LIVE, Nuclear Blast NB 0379-2 (Europe), Metal Blade 3984-14254-2 (USA) (1999)

WARRIORS OF THE WORLD, Nuclear Blast NB 0715-2 (Europe), Metal Blade 3984-14414-2 (USA) (2002)

The Sons Of Odin, Metal Circle Music SPV 85590 (Europe / USA) (2006)

---

in one take on a piccolo bass, and the St. Mary's Cathedral choir gracing the title track. *Hail To England* hosted a clutch of tracks – 'Kill With Power', 'Blood Of My Enemies' and 'Bridge Of Death' – that would lodge themselves in the Manowar live set for decades to come.

In March 1984, the group finally debuted in Britain. It took just a brace of shows to secure label backing, and in June the quartet announced that they had signed to Virgin's Ten label and intended to record with Jack Richardson again for *Sign Of The Hammer*. The album was released in September, Grand Slamm handling the US licence, and was preceded by the aptly chest-beating anthem, the 'All Men Play On 10' single. This was, without a doubt, noted by spoof act Spinal Tap, who promptly designed amps that went up to 11. The volume levels were highlighted on the 'Spectacle Of Might' tour when the group was officially inducted into the *Guinness Book of World Records*.

Sign Of The Hammer showed signs of expansion into subject matter beyond the realms of fantasy, as 'Guyana (Cult Of The Damned)' tackled the Jonestown massacre, while 'Mountains' drew from the Vietnam conflict. To back up the release, Manowar announced further British and European dates for October the same year.

However, 1986 saw the band maintaining a low profile as they split from their record label. Following an Easter jaunt in Europe opening for Motörhead as part of the 'Easter Metal Blast' festivals, it was announced that Manowar had inked a deal with Jason Flom at Atlantic.

Pre-production for the next album was handled by Eddie Kramer, but for the final recording the band produced themselves. The resulting album, *Fighting The World*, released in March 1987, revealed that they had enjoyed access to the necessary studio time and budget with which to capture their enormous sound. However, the finished product was somewhat muted and, as many fans pointed out, too un-metallically clean for the tastes of the devoted fans, although this was tempered to some extent by epics such as 'Black Wind, Fire And Steel' and a reworked 'Defender'.

Delivered in 1988 through Atlantic, *Kings Of Metal* was a significant marker in the band's career by first brandishing the clarion call "Other bands play, Manowar kills". Again DeMaio demonstrated his extreme bass

expertise, transforming Rimsky-Korsakov's 'Flight Of The Bumblebee' into the rebranded 'Sting Of The Bumblebee'.

On the eve of the release of *Kings Of Metal*, Manowar were hit with the inconceivable as Ross The Boss quit, the guitarist quickly announcing a liaison with his ex-Dictators colleague Dick Manitoba in a new act, Wild Kingdom. He then put The Pack together in 1989, with vocalist Frank Vestry, bassist Ronnie G., keyboard player Larry Soc and drummer Rich Fazio, before recording an album with Heyday.

Manowar added Chicago resident Dave 'The Death Dealer' Shankle to the group almost immediately, having met the guitarist while recording the new album at Universal Studios. Their successive European tour gave them another first, employing a form of psychological warfare on their fans by eschewing the expected support band in favour of nerve-grating medieval Chinese music.

September 1989 brought the announcement that Scott Columbus had been forced to quit due to personal business away from the group, but he was back on the tubs for a European trek in December. However, Manowar ultimately replaced Scott with the enigmatic Rhino, whose first act as a member of the band was to torch his own drum kit after the outgoing Columbus presented him with a new set.

The band's standing in Europe was confirmed in 1992 when *The Triumph Of Steel* landed on the German national chart at Number 8. The new record had been hammered out at the band's new, custom-built New York studios – titled Haus Wanfried after composer Richard Wagner's residence.

By now, Manowar's legions of fans stretched across the entire continent, and the band could count on strong album sales across the Low Countries, France, the Mediterranean and Iberia. If anyone ever doubted their commitment to the cause, *The Triumph Of Steel*'s opener was a 28-minute *Iliad* homage called 'Achilles, Agony And Ecstasy In Eight Parts'.

They toured across Europe, including a debut Russian concert, throughout October and November, including British folk-metal band Skyclad in support. In Greece, Manowar played to over 15,000 fans at the Athens Stadium Of Peace And Friendship. Taking the opportunity to put their previous record-breaking feat beyond reach, in Hannover the band employed sound specialists to measure a new volume level generated by ten tons of PA at 129.5 decibels.

Karl Logan was drafted into the ranks during the summer of 1994 as Shankle opted out to create his own Dave Shankle Group. Switching to Geffen, the band scored again in Germany during 1996 with the *Louder Than Hell* opus, hosting a further epic in the nine-minute 'Today Is A Good Day To Die' and climbing to Number 7 in the charts. The Manowar faithful soon picked up on the fact that the track 'Brothers Of Metal' dated back to a 1986 demo. The single 'Courage' even gave the band unexpected radio airplay.

Manowar visited Brazil in November 1996 before touring Europe again during April 1997, culminating in a massive show at the Forest National in Brussels, a 7,000-capacity venue. The shows were filmed and recorded for a live album and video, and Universal picked up the double concert album *Hell On Wheels*.

The band's standing in Europe was now at an unprecedented high: fortune truly had favoured the brave. As a bonus, the group found themselves appealing to fans of the relatively new power metal movement.

Ignoring convention, as was their tradition, Manowar followed up the live *Hell On Wheels* with another blast of concert recordings with *Hell On Stage*. For this outing the band signed to the Nuclear Blast label, this partnership undoubtedly taking Manowar to even loftier heights. *Hell On Stage* exceeded all expectations in Germany, where it sold in excess of 40,000 copies on the first day of release. The DVD version would later break into the national Top 10. This triumph echoed across the Atlantic, where Metal Blade handled the album for the USA.

Manowar in all their glory

In 2001, German metal band Powergod covered 'Kill With Power' on their *Bleed For The Gods* album. Manowar themselves broke their silence in April 2002 with a new single, 'Warriors Of The World United', which hit Number 15 in Germany – the highest ever chart placing for a Nuclear Blast act – and sold over 80,000 copies in the process.

The band pleased their fanbase by announcing a North American 'Gods Of War' tour. Initial dates saw Havochate and Usurper as support, with Norwegian black metal act Immortal and American death metal band Catastrophic added for a second leg. Select supports also came from Chicago's Bludgeon, a thrash metal act signed to Manowar's own Magic Circle Music label.

Warriors Of The World was the most bombastic Manowar release to date, including a grandiose interpretation of the Puccini opera standard 'Nessun Dorma', a patriotic 'An American Trilogy', an amalgam of US Civil War anthems, and the band's 25th anniversary homage to none other than Elvis Presley. Japanese versions of *Warriors Of The World* came complete with an extra track, a live version of 'Kill With Power'.

The album prompted near-hysteria in Germany, with *Warriors Of The World* at one stage outselling Eminem's latest release and being tipped for Number 1. The record eventually bowed in at a highly respectable Number 2. The band put in an in-store performance with a difference at the Saturn record branch in Hamburg, forgoing the usual acoustic or playback norm and blasting the audience with a full PA-powered live set.

Another first for the band, and one which amply displayed their determination to deliver only true metal, was an appearance on the now-defunct UK TV show *Top Of The Pops* – Manowar naturally insisted on playing live. The resurgence of interest in the band would be confirmed when the band's 1992 album *The Triumph Of Steel* was certified gold in Germany for sales in excess of 250,000 copies.

They capitalised on their recent success by releasing a double A-side single of 'An American Trilogy' / 'The Fight For Freedom' on August 19th, the 25th anniversary of Elvis Presley's death. The single not only put the band back into the national charts in Germany but reinvigorated album sales, pushing *Warriors Of The World* back into the upper reaches of the album chart. An extensive tour of major German venues was scheduled for December.

A third single from *Warriors Of The World*, 'Call To Arms', added new studio tracks 'The Dawn Of Battle' and 'I Believe'. It too entered the national German singles charts, debuting at Number 44, pushing *Warriors Of The World* back into the album charts for a second time. Shortly afterward, the album landed a gold award in the territory for sales in excess of 150,000 copies. It was revealed that Joey DeMaio had taken on the management of the Italian symphonic metal band Rhapsody.

In August 2004, Manowar revealed that they had split from Nuclear Blast. Curiously, fans received a pleasant, though rather bizarre, surprise in November when it was learned that anyone buying more than $150 worth of merchandise from the band's official webstore was to receive a complimentary Manowar chocolate fudge ingot.

The band's return in 2005 was marked by US dates in North America in partnership with Rhapsody. The band then announced an appearance at the Rainer Hansel-promoted 'Earthshaker Fest' held in July at Geiselwind, Germany. Not only did they debut their new single, but also the event signalled the first Manowar Mega Fan Convention, organised by World Wide Web Warriors, the band's 230,000-strong fan club. The event

took on more epic proportions when it was announced that former band members Ross The Boss, David Shankle, Rhino and Donnie Hamzik had all been invited to perform. Actor Christopher Lee narrated the original parts recorded by Orson Welles for the songs 'Dark Avenger' and 'Defender' live on stage, and the group were backed by a 100-piece choir and full orchestra. Naturally, the monumental scale of the proceedings was captured on film for future release. As if that wasn't enough, one lucky Manowar fan won a custom-made chopper motorbike, presented onstage.

The band teamed up with Rhapsody and Holyhell for US dates, commencing on June 2nd in Cleveland, Ohio. The same two bands announced that they were to accompany Manowar on the 'Demons, Dragons And Warriors' tour in Europe in the spring of 2006, backed by a new single titled 'The Sons Of Odin'. However, Karl Logan sustained severe injuries to his left arm in a motorbike accident on January 24th, putting plans on hold.

As Manowar re-scheduled, former guitarist Ross The Boss was seen performing a set of "early Manowar" backed by tribute band Men Of War, at the 'Keep It True VI' festival on April 8th at the Tauberfrankenhalle in Lauda-Königshofen, Germany.

What does the future hold for Manowar? Certainly any hint at compromise will never be on the agenda. Their unbending determination has defeated all their detractors and, perhaps more impressively, an industry unable to comprehend the band's vision.

QUEENSRŸCHE
CONCEPTUAL METAL EXPERTISE

QUEENSRŸCHE DELIVER A MAJESTIC form of heavy metal laden with the awe-inspiring vocal abilities of Geoff Tate. After a brace of 'trial and error' albums, which hinted at great promise, the band broke the floodgates with the seminal concept album *Operation: Mindcrime* in 1988. This single work not only broke the band internationally, but also it set the standard for a legion of imitators. Although they sustained this dynamic with the subsequent *Empire*, they have struggled since then, seeming to eschew the grandiose style that so typified their heyday in favour of simpler and less commercially viable themes. This radical change in direction has provoked severe criticism from their fans and resulted in a downward spiral on the sales front. Finally, in 2006, it appears that the band has come full circle in an attempt at recapturing the glory years.

Long before Queensrÿche, guitarists Michael Wilton and Chris DeGarmo had been members of a Bellevue, Washington, heavy metal covers band, Joker, at Interlake High School. This act also included singer Paul Passarelli, later of glam band Lipstick. The roots of Queensrÿche began to grow with a 1981 outfit, The Mob, which soon recruited Tate. The frontman had been the vocalist with Myth, a Seattle metal band that had supported the likes of Culprit and Wild Dogs and, coincidentally, featured drummer Jimmy Parsons, another Lipstick member. Tate split from Myth in late 1982 as The Mob became Queensrych (without the more familiar spelling).

The budding musicians had all trodden the boards with fledgling Seattle metal bands: Tate had debuted with the late-1970s teen covers act Tyrant – led by Adam Bomb (aka Adam Brenner) – and then Babylon, before moving on to Myth. Guitarists DeGarmo and Wilton had stuck together through Joker and Crossfire, the latter including drummer Scott Rockenfield. DeGarmo had also served a term with Tempest.

Queensrych's June 1982 demo, recorded in drummer Scott Rockenfield's parents' basement, featured 'The Lady Wore Black', 'Queen Of The Reich', 'Blinded' and 'Nightrider'. This cassette soon created waves on the underground tape trading circuit, with many comparing the band to primetime British metal thanks to Geoff Tate's operatic style and the precise riffing of Wilton and DeGarmo.

A local record store, owned by the husband and wife team of Kim and Diana Harris, were impressed enough to press up the demo on their 206 record label. The subsequent EP, cut at Triad Studios in Redmond and released in May 1983, was self-titled but commonly known as *Queen Of The Reich*. In just a few months the EP rapidly sold out pressing after pressing as the mystique surrounding the act grew: eventually it shifted over 20,000 copies. Legions of power metal purists cite the EP's title track as possibly the greatest power metal track of all time. This was reinforced by Tate's high vocals, although his upper range would weaken with each successive album – much to fans' displeasure.

With a commercial release, Queensrÿche – having added an e and an umlaut to their name – undertook their first concert on June 29th 1983 opening for Zebra at Portland's Paramount Theater. The band were now garnering ecstatic worldwide press and were soon snapped up by EMI America. The major swiftly reissued the EP that August, which climbed to Number 81 on the US charts. On the tour front, the group went out on the road backing Dio in October before jumping on board a Twisted Sister tour.

The debut full-length album, *The Warning*, issued in September 1984, was produced by James Guthrie and recorded at three different locations, including the world-famous Abbey Road Studios in London. However, it proved to be an overambitious effort, marred by spreading good ideas too thinly. Notably, the album artwork was executed by Matt Bazemore, drummer for one of Tate's previous acts, Babylon. The band toured Japan that August as headliners before heading out across the USA for a series of dates with Dio and Kiss. As 1985 opened, the schedule was maintained with a run of headline gigs, segueing into further Kiss supports.

Justifying their early promise, Queensrÿche's second attempt, *Rage For Order*, was produced by Neil Kernon at MDH Studios in Bellevue and Le Mobile Remote Sound Studio and Mushroom Studios in Vancouver, Canada and was a major statement of intent. Where the band had been previously content to occupy traditional heavy metal territory, *Rage For Order* ushered in refined, near-progressive elements. The record jacket used a device – subsequently utilised on all the band's future outings – designed by this book's author for a proposed 12-inch picture disc that never appeared.

The first single from *Rage For Order*, 'Gonna Get Close To You', was a spirited and somewhat malevolent cover of the song by Canadian artist Dalbello. The original had appeared on her *Whomanfoursays* album of 1984; the singer also played the female interest in Queensryche's video for the track.

Rage For Order, which arrived in July 1986 and reached Number 47 in *Billboard*, saw an obvious maturing of lyrical and musical content. One aspect of the band's evolution did not meet with such a positive reception, however: Queensrÿche were to be vilified for their decision to wear flamboyant Ray Brown-designed stage costumes, eyeliner and even lipstick on the jacket photographs. Learning their lesson quickly, the band got back to basics with haste and set out on a mammoth American tour.

August 1986 saw the band guesting on AC/DC's mammoth arena shows; by September they were acting as warm-up for Ozzy Osbourne. Further road work to push *Rage For Order* in the UK and Europe saw a support stint to Dio lasting from early September into late October before they hit the UK with Bon Jovi and Europe in November. Following the tour dates, Queensrÿche ditched their previous management team, signing a new deal with the Q Prime organisation responsible for the careers of Def Leppard and Metallica.

Despite external appearances, rumours abounded that, behind the scenes, the band's financial affairs were shaky. According to new manager

Peter Mensch, Q Prime's first duty was to bankrupt the band, as they had allegedly run up an alleged $700,000 of touring debts.

With their next album – *Operation: Mindcrime* – Queensrÿche's career went stratospheric. Released in May 1988, the Peter Collins-produced record was a brave move for a band at the crossroads between success and failure. Undaunted, they pulled out all the stops, crafting a superb weave of metal, theatrics and a sinister plot line. Tate's vision involved a story centred on the characters of Nikki, a narcotics-addicted assassin, and Mary, a prostitute turned nun, both betrayed by an underground movement. Orchestration was arranged by Michael Kamen, noted for his sweeping movie scores.

Queensrÿche toured America in mid 1989, opening for Q Prime colleagues Def Leppard before performing British shows as headliners and then returning to the States supporting Metallica. The later shows utilised more theatrics to build the album scenario onstage, in particular bringing in Seattle-born Pamela Moore to sing the part of Sister Mary.

Operation: Mindcrime, in spite of the global adulation upon its release, had been a relatively slow seller, at first finding it tough even to equal sales of *Rage For Order*. The relentless grind of taking the music to the people on tour had paid off, however, and the record was set on a path of steady sales that would last for many years. This slow-burning enthusiasm for the band saw their next album, *Empire*, benefit from an underground fanbase: it broke the multi-platinum sales barrier with consummate ease. *Empire*, delivered in September 1990 and retaining Peter Collins as producer, supplied no fewer than three hit singles, with the ballad 'Silent Lucidity' hitting the US Top 10 and being nominated for a Grammy award.

The 'Building Empires' American tour saw Queensrÿche hit the road for nearly a year and a half. Kicking off in Europe, they took along Lynch Mob as support. Unfortunately, their concert on November 20th at Ichtegen's Sporthal Keiberg in Belgium was cut short when an audience member was stabbed. They also slotted in a showing at the Brazilian 'Rock In Rio' festival at the Meracana Soccer Stadium in Rio de Janeiro on January 23rd 1991, alongside Guns N'Roses, Judas Priest, Megadeth and Sepultura, prior to Japanese dates and shows in America commencing in April with Suicidal Tendencies in support. An appearance at the European run of 'Monsters Of Rock' festivals saw the band play beneath AC/DC and Metallica.

A high-profile date on October 12th found Queensrÿche once again rubbing shoulders with Metallica at the 'Day On The Green' festival in San Francisco. This concert provided the launch for a new trek across the USA in alliance with Warrior Soul. The 'Building Empires' journey came to a close on January 3rd 1992 with a special homecoming at the Spokane Coliseum. During this concert the group filmed a promo video for the track 'Anybody Listening?' A final gasp came when they performed 'Silent Lucidity' with Michael Kamen at the Grammy Awards on February 24th.

The musicians took time out from writing sessions to perform a special one-off set at the 'Rock The Environment' benefit concert, organised by Ann and Nancy Wilson of Heart. Taking place on June 6th 1992 at the Gorge Natural Bowl in George, Washington, the show saw Queensrÿche playing not only rarely-performed originals but also jams through The Beatles' 'Revolution' and The Rolling Stones' 'Gimme Shelter'.

Operation: Mindcrime was still being pulled along by the success of *Empire* and, with its songs featuring heavily in the live set, was fast becoming the band's all-time classic. Meanwhile, *Empire* racked up a monumental three million sales in the USA.

To keep the fire burning on *Mindcrime*, Queensrÿche recorded and videoed two shows at Madison, Milwaukee, and La Crosse, Wisconsin, which featured the album in its entirety and were subsequently released as *Operation: Livecrime*. The lull in Queensrÿche activity was broken by the release of the 1993 'Real World' single, a track recorded for the

QUEENSRYCHE discography

Queensryche, 206 R-101 (USA) (1983) **81 USA**
THE WARNING, EMI America 2402201 (1984) **61 USA**
RAGE FOR ORDER, EMI America 3105 (1986) **66 UK, 47 USA**
OPERATION: MINDCRIME, EMI America 48640 (1988)
  58 UK, 50 USA
EMPIRE, EMI Manhattan 92806 (1990) **13 UK, 7 USA**
OPERATION: LIVECRIME, EMI America 97048 (1991) **38 USA**
PROMISED LAND, EMI 30711 (1994) **13 UK, 3 USA**
HEAR IN THE NOW FRONTIER, EMI America 56141 (1997)
  46 UK, 19 USA
Q2K, Atlantic 83225 (1999) **46 USA**
LIVE EVOLUTION, Metal-Is MISDD 016 (2001) **143 USA**
TRIBE, Metal-Is MIS 018 (2003) **56 USA**
THE ART OF LIVE, Mayan MYN 024 (2004)
OPERATION: MINDCRIME II, Rhino 8122-73306-2 (Europe), Rhino
  R2 73306 (USA) (2006)

soundtrack to the Arnold Schwarzenegger movie *Last Action Hero*.

The band now enjoyed such a high standing that their next outing, October 1994's *Promised Land*, entered the US charts at a lofty Number 3. The record was co-produced at the musicians' own home studios, The Dungeon, Triad and Big Log, in collaboration with James Barton. Keeping the final process a local affair, Barton mixed *Promised Land* at Seattle's Bad Animals studios, owned by the Wilson sisters of Heart.

While *Promised Land* debuted impressively, the first rumblings of discontent began to seep through from fans and critics, who expected a continuation of its epic predecessors. Unfortunately, *Promised Land* was a more stripped-down, basic affair. Three attempts were made to crack the singles market, with 'I Am I', 'Bridge' and 'Disconnected', but all failed to hit home.

To market the record, the group took the unusual step of playing two one-off European concerts in October 1994, at the Astoria in London, England on the 20th and in Cologne, Germany the following day. A proper European tour was launched in February 1995. Alarmingly, however, Tate had forsaken any form of traditional metal uniform and now stalked the stages in sunglasses and 'stubbie' shorts. The band hit

Queensrÿche

Japan in March and then forged a union with Type O Negative for an exhaustive US expedition in April, running through into July.

This trend towards musical simplicity continued with *Hear In The Now Frontier*, put together at Sixteenth Avenue Sound, Nashville, Tennessee and Studio Litho, Seattle, and launched in May 1997. A wary yet still loyal fanbase put the album into the US charts at Number 19. This slump impacted hard, however, as the group found themselves searching for a new record label.

Undaunted, in July 1997 they commenced a long tour, this time in North America. There would be no consistent support band for this leg, Queensrÿche picking up local bands as they went along, but before the end of the month they were cancelling shows and cutting sets short due to Geoff Tate's ill health. In December, they travelled to South America with Megadeth and Whitesnake for shows in Brazil and Argentina. On the 13th, the band played the Ferro Carril Oeste Stadium in Buenos Aires – as it transpired, their final concert with the existing line-up.

It came as a shock to fans when DeGarmo announced that he was to quit in January 1998, as Queensrÿche had never experienced line-up problems before this point. The guitarist soon busied himself with Inflatable Soule frontman Peter Cornell (brother of Soundgarden's Chris) and was recruited in June 1998 into the solo band of Alice In Chains guitarist Jerry Cantrell. DeGarmo later demoed material with other ex-Alice In Chains men – bassist Mike Inez and drummer Sean Kinney. This band, together with Sponge and Crud singer Vinnie Dombroski, evolved into Spys 4 Darwin and they eventually released an album, *Microfish*.

Having found a new home with Atlantic, Queensrÿche offered up *Q2K* in September 1999. Unfortunately, the creative direction had not been reversed, and by now the reaction from the metal press was almost hostile. Geoff Tate's defiance – and remarks which many fans took to be at best disparaging of heavy metal – didn't help. *Q2K*, produced by Kelly Gray (a colleague of Tate's in Myth) only just scraped into the Top 50.

With Gray officially bowing in as new guitarist, the band toured America in October 1999 before continental European concerts with Canadian act The Tea Party to open 2000. Further solo shows in the USA included an unexpected cover of U2's 'Bullet The Blue Sky'. The band picked up momentum as part of a triple billing flanking Halford and Iron Maiden that August: obviously stung by the lacklustre reaction to *Q2K*, they placed renewed emphasis on archive material, resurrecting 'Queen Of The Reich' for the occasion. These concerts also fostered a rumour that Tate, Halford and Iron Maiden's Bruce Dickinson were to record a project billed as The Three Tremors. Regrettably, this never transpired.

Two tribute albums were released the same year before Queensrÿche signed to Sanctuary in 2001. The band recorded two shows on July 27th and 28th 2001 at Seattle's Moore Theater for their first release with the new partnership, a lavishly packaged double live CD, *Live Evolution*. Although the album rekindled some of the enthusiasm that media and fans had afforded to early works, there was a minor hiccup when the first 75,000 pressings came with incorrect track-listings and other misprints.

Drummer Scott Rockenfield revealed an outside venture with partner Paul Speer. Suitably titled Rockenfield/Speer, the duo released the album *Hell's Canyon*. Yet another Queensrÿche offshoot was Slaves To The System, which found both Rockenfield and Gray in league with Damon Johnson and Roman Glick of Brother Cane along with Scotty Heard of Sweaty Nipples. Rockenfield's new outfit debuted live in October at the Nashville New Music Conference.

Michael Wilton was not to be left out, emerging with his Soulbender project in league with My Sister's Machine vocalist and former Alice In Chains member Nick Pollock, guitarist Dave Groves and drummer Wes Hallam. Soulbender recorded a seven-track EP exclusively for industry promotion purposes.

Tate also hit the solo trail, announcing an album project originally billed as *Old World Order*. His recording band for this venture consisted of guitarists Jeff Carrell and Scott Moughton, bassist Cris Fox, keyboard player Howard Chillcott and Sadhappy drummer Evan Schiller.

In mid May 2002, Queensrÿche announced that Gray was no longer with the band, fuelling immediate speculation that Chris DeGarmo was set to make a return. This latest conjecture was soon officially denied by the band as wishful thinking. Tate, meanwhile, announced details of his debut solo tour, commencing on June 22nd at the Sky Church venue in Seattle. In promotion for his solo venture, Tate stunned longstanding fans when he reportedly admitted that he had never been a metalhead and cited electronic pop acts as his main inspiration. Scott Rockenfield struck out solo too, delivering an album called *The X Chapters*.

Queensrÿche, announcing a projected album title of *Tribe*, employed second guitarist Mike Stone, previously with the Peter Criss band, the Jonas Hansson Band and others, for their New Year's Eve headlining performance in Anchorage, Alaska. Much to fans' relief, they subsequently reinstated Chris DeGarmo. A full-strength Queensrÿche headed up a US progressive metal touring extravaganza in June, packaged with Dream Theater and Fates Warning. Strangely, however, an official press statement revealed that DeGarmo was not to accompany the band for European dates.

With *Tribe* signalling renewed support for the band, longstanding fans were intrigued by comments by Tate in November that the band was seriously considering recording an up-to-date version of *Operation: Mindcrime*. An in-concert DVD, *The Art Of Live*, released in March 2004, preceded North American gigs with Symphony X in support. Further tour dates saw the band touring Europe throughout the summer.

Finally bowing to fan pressure, Queensrÿche announced their intention to perform *Operation: Mindcrime* in its entirety on their autumn tour but also revealed that they intended to cut a sequel album for new label Rhino. The shows closed with 'Silent Lucidity' featuring orchestral string sections. In addition, Pamela Moore returned as the character Sister Mary and Michael Igor Delassandra – formerly an official composer for the Vatican – accompanied the band on keyboards and conducted a string section. In interviews, Tate made it clear that the prospect of working with DeGarmo once more was an option. However, Mike Stone occupied the second guitar position by the time the tour kicked off.

During the recording of *Operation: Mindcrime II* in January 2005, Tate confirmed that DeGarmo was not involved, but that he was welcome to return. By May it transpired that Snake River Conspiracy mainman Jason Slater was aiding the band on the production front. North American arena gigs commenced in June supporting Judas Priest: the set for these shows concentrated on early material. After this tour, Queensrÿche embarked on headline dates into October. However, three Mexican concerts were cancelled due to "recording deadlines".

It was revealed in December that the character of Dr X on *Operation: Mindcrime II* would be sung by none other than Ronnie James Dio. Pamela Moore also reprised her role. The record was slated for a March 2006 release. Tate revealed in January 2006 that he had been commissioned to oversee a movie script based on the story of the two albums. The band remain one of America's most powerful live draws.

RIOT
PIONEERS IN THEIR FIELD

RIOT COULD WELL LAY CLAIM TO BEING the defining cult rock outfit of North America. Despite being dogged by unrelenting business problems, they have released a succession of well-honed albums of impeccable quality. Strangely, Riot's trademark was a cuddly baby seal, which adorned many of their album covers.

As the years progressed, Riot's sound developed from high-quality hard rock – though always heavier in approach than their contemporaries – to a more technical metal direction that served the band well on the European market. Riot's stature in Japan, reinforced by tours in 1989, 1990, 1994 and 1996, has always been exalted.

The band was founded in 1975 by former People and Kon Tiki guitarist Mark Reale, bassist Phil Fiet and ex-Kon Tiki drummer Peter Bitelli. Vocalist Guy Speranza arrived shortly after and the band's first recordings came with a four-track tape laid down for inclusion on a proposed *New York Anthology* compilation album. The backers of this projected album journeyed to the French Midem music festival in order to get a deal; in their absence, the band decided on a tamer approach and brought in keyboard player Steve Costello. However, Reale and the rest were stunned to learn on the production company's return that there was enthusiasm only for the Riot tracks – and that the compilation idea had been shelved in favour of a full-blown Riot release.

With this in mind, the band ditched the keyboards, pulled in second guitarist Louie 'LA' Kouvaris, and set about recording their debut album for local company Fire Sign Records with producer Steve Loeb at Greene Street Recording Studio. Two tracks from the initial sessions, 'Angel With A Broken Wing' and 'Desperation', made it intact onto the album, *Rock City*, which was released in 1977 featuring guitarists Reale and Kouvaris, Bitelli, Speranza and new bass player Jimmy Iommi.

Riot then set about a succession of local New York gigs before venturing further afield, appearing at a festival in Florida headlined by Neil Young and undertaking a run of Ohio gigs opening for The Godz. Further dates in 1978 were brought about by an invitation to guest for Sammy Hagar on dates in Texas. For the first time, Riot were made aware of their growing fanbase, and learned that local DJ Joe Anthony had been plugging *Rock City* with a vengeance.

Returning to New York, however, Riot effectively stagnated. Disillusioned by the current music scene, the band members even contemplated adopting a new wave approach after one producer insisted that this was the way to go. In this climate of despair, Riot almost fragmented for good. The situation became so bad that Reale and Speranza teamed up with Fiet once more and a drummer named Freddie to create a new band. After a handful of gigs, a call came from a promoter that Riot were required to open shows for the Texan leg of AC/DC's 'Highway To Hell' tour alongside Molly Hatchet. Reale and Speranza were quick to resurrect the band, pulling in Fiet and former Rex drummer Sandy Slavin for a couple of week's worth of high-profile shows.

This high point was followed by another lengthy period in the doldrums at home in New York and, with the craze for disco and punk apparently taking over, Riot were on the verge of breaking up once more. A telephone call from England pulled them back from the brink: it seemed that tracks from their debut album were appearing in the heavy metal charts of the *Sounds* music paper there.

Kouvaris, disillusioned by the fact that his mellow songwriting contributions were being rejected, departed during the recording of 1979's *Narita*, his place being taken by former Riot roadie Rick Ventura. The album, named after the controversial airport built on the site of ancient burial grounds near Tokyo, garnered Riot much praise in Europe.

The band were then offered a support stint in England with Sammy Hagar, which they naturally accepted. The British arm of Ariola jumped in with an offer of the necessary funding, but just before the band's departure the Capitol label offered the band a worldwide deal – which Riot duly took up. The Sammy Hagar shows proved a huge success, and Riot threw in some club headliners in Britain to round things off.

The band then played third on the bill on the American 'Black'n'Blue' tour, which featured Blue Öyster Cult and Black Sabbath, before an appearance at the inaugural 'Monsters Of Rock' festival in Britain in 1980. Riot shared a bill with Touch, Saxon, Scorpions, Judas Priest and Rainbow.

Q Prime management guru Cliff Bernstein, convinced of the band's global potential and a longtime fan of Riot, began negotiations with the band's New York production company in order to manage the act, but no agreement was reached. By now, Fiet had had enough and left: in later years he played with Joan Jett and performed on the Billy Idol hit 'White Wedding'.

Capitol, meanwhile, had persuaded the band to pursue a more radio-friendly AOR direction, even indicating that make-up and a glitzier image was a distinct possibility, and recordings along these lines commenced. With feedback from the UK and Europe indicating a preference for harder-edged material, the band, now with bassist Cliff 'Kip' Leming, scrapped these initial tracks (with the exception of the song 'Swords And Tequila') and laid down a brash hard rock album.

Riot were pleased with the outcome, but Capitol, as Reale described it, "freaked". The label deemed the album commercially unviable: not only did they refuse to release it, but they also enforced their contractual ties with the band, refusing to let them leave. This action prompted one of the most famous backlashes against a record label in history, with fans picketing the company's offices in both the USA and the UK. Other artists on the same label came to Riot's aid with vocal support, and eventually Capitol relented. At a Brooklyn showcase, Elektra signed the band after witnessing just three numbers.

The new label bought the *Fire Down Under* tapes and Riot got back on the road, supporting Mahogany Rush, Triumph, Saxon and Grand Funk Railroad in the USA before returning to Britain in 1981, where they opened for Saxon on their 'Denim And Leather' tour. Riot had visited the UK earlier in the year, participating in the legendary 'Heavy Metal Holocaust' festival at Port Vale FC in Burslem, Staffordshire on the same bill as Motörhead, Ozzy Osbourne, Triumph, Vardis, and Frank Marino & Mahogany Rush. Proposed dates across Europe with Ozzy Osbourne and Saxon on the 'Heavy Metal Battles' tour were curtailed, however, when *Fire Down Under* entered the *Billboard* charts and Riot were recalled to support Rush on their 'Moving Pictures' tour of the USA.

Despite their chart album and a part in the most successful tour of the year, Riot were crushed when Speranza – battling with his religious convictions and the rock'n'roll lifestyle – announced his intention to leave the band midway through the dates. The singer agreed to finish the tour,

---

RIOT discography

ROCK CITY, Ariola ARL 5007 (1977)

NARITA, Capitol E-ST 12081 (1979)

FIRE DOWN UNDER, Elektra K 52315 (1981) **90 USA**

RESTLESS BREED, Elektra K 52398 (1982)

Riot Live, Elektra 0-67969 (1982)

BORN IN AMERICA, Grand Slamm SLAM 6 (1983) **175 USA**

THUNDERSTEEL, Epic 4609762 (1988) **150 USA**

THE PRIVILEGE OF POWER, CBS ZK45132 (1990)

NIGHTBREAKER, Rising Sun 084 62222 (Europe), Metal Blade 14239 (USA), (1994)

THE BRETHREN OF THE LONG HOUSE, Rising Sun SRCS 7852 (Europe) Metal Blade 14240 (USA) (1996)

INISHMORE, Metal Blade 3984-14150-2 (Europe), Metal Blade 14150 (USA) (1998)

SHINE ON, Metal Blade 14182 (1998)

LIVE IN JAPAN, Metal Blade 14241 (1999)

SONS OF SOCIETY, Metal Blade 14249 (1999)

THROUGH THE STORM, Metal Blade 14399 (2002)

ARMY OF ONE, Toshiba EMI TOCP-67977 (2006)

however, and after much persuasion also offered to record the next album – but on condition that the band's managers were not allowed to enter the studio. On hearing this, the management pulled the band off the Rush tour in North Carolina without notice.

With negotiations now frantic, Riot returned to New York, only to be told that they had to jump back on the Rush tour again. They missed one show in Atlanta, but resumed their position for the next day's gig in Tennessee. An elaborate although wholly transparent cover story was concocted by the band's management, stating that Speranza had been suddenly taken ill with food poisoning, contracted from a burrito.

The Rush tour ended with two sold-out New Jersey shows, and Speranza finally left the band. Riot held auditions and drafted in Rhett Forrester, previously with New York covers band Rachel, in time for the recording of *Restless Breed* in 1982 and subsequent touring with the Scorpions and Whitesnake in America.

Forrester proved to be an energetic frontman and gave Riot a new edge. However, he embraced rock'n'roll life to the full – and a batch of shows opening for Rainbow on their American 'Straight Between The Eyes' tour were cancelled when he simply vanished, turning up in hospital a week later with a mysterious illness.

The band got back into their swing supporting Kiss on their US 'Lick It Up' extravaganza, which also featured Vandenberg, and threw in a bunch of headliners on the West Coast. One bizarre date saw Riot opening for Ratt and Steeler. However, the strain was beginning to show, and the band left Elektra for the Canadian independent label Quality for the release of the patriotic *Born In America*, later reissued by Grand Slamm in the USA. Coming off the road in 1983, Reale and Slavin agreed that they were flogging a dead horse. Forrester opted out in 1984 to pursue a solo career, opening with *Out Of The Darkness* the same year.

Rick Ventura left Riot around the same time as Forrester, and was replaced by the 19-year-old Gerard T. Trevino. The band then parted company with both label and management, and Reale quickly decided to terminate the group in order to pursue a different musical path. Sandy Slavin joined forces once more with Fiet and ex-TKO guitarist Adam Brenner in Adam Bomb's band.

Mark Reale formed Narita (originally The Mark Reale Project), releasing a three-track demo in 1985, which featured the tracks 'The Feeling Is Gone', 'Liar' and 'Thundersteel'. Narita also featured members of S. A. Slayer, bassist Don Van Stavern and drummer Dave McClain (later of Machine Head and Sacred Reich). A series of auditions in Los Angeles

for a vocalist followed, but with no luck – and so S. A. Slayer frontman Steve Cooper was enrolled.

Narita then played live throughout the Midwest of America until Slavin convinced Reale that Riot still retained a sizeable fanbase and that a reunion tour would work in their favour. In 1983 Riot regrouped, now comprising Reale, Slavin and Van Stavern. Approaches were made to both Speranza and Forrester, but Speranza was uninterested and Forrester was involved with his solo work.

Riot finally re-emerged fronted by ex-Jag Panzer and Satan's Host vocalist Harry 'The Tyrant' Conklin, and a three-month touring schedule was set up. Disaster struck almost immediately, however, when four songs into the band's debut show (the first of two sold-out nights at the Los Angeles Troubadour), Conklin lost his voice. He bailed out to create Titan Force. After the cancellation of the tour, hasty auditions were held and a vocalist named Steffan travelled into the desert with Riot for a test gig at an obscure club. It was a dismal failure, prompting Reale to contact Forrester. This time Rhett took the bait, and a Reale-Forrester-Van Stavern-Slavin line-up commenced touring.

The old malaise was quick to set in, of course. The band, now located in Los Angeles, were effectively destitute. Although they were the subject of healthy record company interest, Mark Reale was living in his car – and they were dealt a further blow when Forrester departed once again.

A major rethink was required, and subsequently Reale journeyed back to New York to renew the acquaintance of his old management team. A new band was quickly assembled. Slavin, opting out, undertook studio work, including a guest appearance on Ted Nugent's 1986 *Little Miss Dangerous* album. He would later appear in Ace Frehley's live band. Reale and Van Stavern were joined by Steeler, Lion and Burning Starr drummer Mark Edwards and vocalist Tony Moore (real name Morvido).

The new Riot cut four demo tracks, which led to a deal with CBS. The 1988 comeback album, *Thundersteel*, recorded over a lengthy period of downtime at the management's recording studio, was issued on CBS in America and Epic in Europe. New man behind the drum kit was Bobby Jarzombek. A video was shot for 'Bloodstreets', and once more Riot got back on the road in America.

Former Rainbow and Deep Purple singer Joe Lynn Turner made a guest appearance on *The Privilege Of Power* alongside contributions from the Tower Of Power Horns and a slew of well-known New York session musicians. The return of Riot led to increased interest in Japan, with the *Rock City* and *Narita* albums being released there on CD. The Far East also received a new live album, culled from Riot's performances at the 1980 'Monsters Of Rock' festival and a 1981 London Hammersmith Odeon show.

New bassist Pete Perez, previously with Carrion, replaced Van Stavern in 1990. Line-up changes also struck the band in the mid-'90s, with former Stuttering John vocalist Mike DiMeo and guitarist Mike Flyntz drafted in. Riot now began to concentrate specifically on the European and Japanese markets.

In 1993, the band were due to play in continental Europe as part of a power metal package deal with Titan Force, but this was cancelled. A further set of shows with Metal Church was also pulled, leaving the band frustrated at being unable to perform in Europe. Tragedy struck the Riot family when, on January 22nd 1994, Rhett Forrester was murdered, gunned down while trying to prevent an armed robbery in Atlanta, Georgia.

The band regrouped for 1994's *Nightbreaker*, which featured a brand new version of 'Outlaw' and covers of Procol Harum's 'Whiter Shade Of Pale' and Deep Purple's 'Burn'. The album was released by various labels worldwide, and at least three different jacket designs were employed. The European version through Rising Sun Records was one of the more effective, with a shark on the cover. The Japanese version of the album featured a bonus cut, 'Black Mountain Woman'.

Riot

In 1995, a Japanese live album was compiled without the band's knowledge, made from recordings given to Sony Japan and taken from a camcorder microphone and a single DAT tape. Riot's next official release was 1996's conceptual *The Brethren Of The Long House*, based on the plight of the native Americans, featuring a cover version of Gary Moore and Phil Lynott's 'Out In The Fields'. Riot toured in Europe in May 1996 alongside thrashers Whiplash and British folk-metal band Skyclad.

Needless to say, Riot's latest album saw a new member, drummer John Macaluso (ex-Powermad and TNT) replacing Bobby Jarzombek, who had opted for a solo career with his project Spastic Ink, an outfit that, coincidentally, features Pete Perez. Jarzombek later returned to Riot and appeared on the *Inishmore* (1998) and *Sons Of Society* (1999) albums. By 2000, Jarzombek was a member of Judas Priest vocalist Rob Halford's solo band.

In 1998, Don Van Stavern re-emerged with the industrial outfit Pitbull Daycare. Macaluso also found time to perform drumming duties for Yngwie Malmsteen and A.R.K.. It was to be Mark Reale, however, who launched the highest-profile side venture, with the melodic rock outfit Westworld. Debuting for Roadrunner, the band – fronted by TNT vocalist Tony Harnell – featured Danger Danger bass player Bruno Ravel and former Blue Öyster Cult and Rainbow drummer John O'Reilly.

August of the same year saw Riot putting in a performance at the German 'Wacken Open Air' festival. Early 2000 found them headlining in Germany once again for a tour with support from Canada's Anvil, Agent Steel and Domine. In 2002, bassist Pete Perez was announced as the latest recruit into David Wayne's Reverend.

Riot made a return in August 2002, touting a brand new studio album for Metal Blade titled *Through The Storm*. This included two cover versions – UFO's 'Only You Can Rock Me' and an instrumental variation of The Beatles' 'Here Comes The Sun'. The line-up for this album was guitarists Mark Reale and Mike Flyntz, vocalist Mike DiMeo, bassist Pete Perez and former Black Sabbath and Rainbow skinsman Bobby Rondinelli on drums.

In early 2003, Flyntz teamed up with former Riot frontman Tony Moore, Blue Öyster Cult bass player Danny Miranda and the Rainbow and Meat Loaf credited drummer John Miceli, to found a new project billed as Faith And Fire. Riot themselves were back for action in the latter half of the year, recruiting Virgin Steele man Frank Gilchriest on the drums. On November 8th 2003, Guy Speranza died after a lengthy battle with pancreatic cancer.

In July 2004, vocalist Mike DiMeo joined The Lizards alongside drummer Bobby Rondinelli of Rainbow, Blue Öyster Cult and Black Sabbath. A one-off Riot gig at Don Hill's in New York on August 27th saw the Yngwie Malmsteen and Ark-credited Randy Coven assuming bass duties. Coven resumed this role for Riot's appearance at the February 2005 'Atarfe Vega Rock' festival in Granada, Spain. This show also found the band sporting a temporary new frontman as DiMeo was committed elsewhere with The Lizards: Mike Tirelli, a veteran of Holy Mother, Messiah's Kiss and Burning Starr, stepped into the role. Confusingly, DiMeo issued a press release stating that he was leaving Riot to prioritise The Lizards, but this was retracted. Nevertheless, Tirelli was still on board for gigs in Texas and the Italian 'Iron Fest' in Milan during June.

Katagory bassist Dustin Mitchell temp'd for Riot on their January 28th 2006 show in Salt Lake City, Utah, when regular four-stringer Pete Perez suffered an accident, putting him out of commission for the show. Mike Tirelli fronted the band for a series of European gigs in April. Riot's latest album, *Army Of One*, arrived in July and was picked up by Metal Heaven Records for Europe in October. Despite their second-tier status in commercial terms, Riot deserve recognition for their influential music. Many of today's biggest bands owe them a debt.

SAVATAGE
RESPECTED AND INDIVIDUAL METAL ACT

TAMPA, FLORIDA, ACT SAVATAGE gave their distinctive brand of metal to the world by way of two unique talents, the Bronx-born Oliva brothers – singer Jon, often hailed as 'The Mountain King', and guitarist Criss. Jon, born Jonathan Nicholas Oliva, was blessed with a thunderous roar embellished by a lyrical sense of the bizarre and fantastical, while Criss constructed riff patterns and solos of quirky complexity. The six-string prodigy was already turning heads as a teenager, winning a Tampa guitar contest with a blazing rendition of Eddie Van Halen's 'Eruption'. This double dose of individualism immediately set Savatage's early releases apart.

They gained a major label deal, but would always swim against the tide, releasing a succession of commendable but overlooked albums. The group found a ready audience but had difficulty breaking into the mainstream. Eventually their tenacity paid off when producer Paul O'Neill's more progressive style drew in an international audience.

The Oliva family relocated from New York via California to Dunedin, Florida, in 1976, where the seeds of Savatage were sown. With Jon on vocals and guitar, Criss on bass guitar and drummer Steve 'Dr. Killdrums' Wacholz, the teenagers paid their dues with shows at Tarpon Springs High School and the Florida clubs, performing cover sets by artists such as Deep Purple, Kiss and Black Sabbath.

Jon and Criss's first solid steps into the heavy metal arena came with a 1977 band called Alien. Criss, working with guitar player Rich Biganno, had also gigged with an outfit dubbed Tower, whilst Jon had previously acted as lead vocalist and drummer for Metropolis. Subsequently, Tony Ciulla took on bass duties and Joe Conn became the drummer. This early act issued a now rare 7-inch single, 'Let's Get Rowdy'/'Take Off With The Crowd', in 1978.

Adopting the title of the benevolent sorcerer in the movie *Wizards*, Alien became Avatar. The familiar story has Avatar undergoing a succession of line-up changes: passing through the ranks were ex-Paradox bassist Brian Lennon and many others, until Jon and Criss were joined by Steve Wacholz of Blaze, Warhead and Paradox on drums, with Jon switching to bass. Another Blaze and Paradox man, guitarist Pat Dubs, was involved, and bassist Andy Grelin was recruited.

Wacholz opted out to join Imagine, leaving Jon no option but to take command of the drums once again. Bob Boyer was briefly acquired as lead singer and Rich Pigano became rhythm guitarist. In 1981, Keith Collins, previously with Solar City, took on bass and Wacholz rejoined. One of the earliest shows Avatar performed was in a support slot for Shooting Star.

As the need for original material grew, Avatar contributed two tracks, 'Rock Me' and 'Minus Love', to a local compilation, *The Pirate Album*, assembled in 1983 by radio station 95 WYNF. Promotion for this LP saw Avatar performing in the local K-Mart parking lot. The band then released the now extremely rare *City Beneath The Surface* EP in 1982 through local imprint PAR Records. Only 1,000 copies were pressed, and a handful on yellow vinyl are more collectable still. Once Savatage became popular, the Avatar sessions were heavily bootlegged.

With the budget tight at just $3,000, the group laid down 15 tracks in just three days, recording over two days and mixing on the third. This set of tracks was spread over the next two releases – *Sirens* and *The Dungeons Are Calling*. The day before PAR were about to press *Sirens*, a hasty name change to Savatage took place. Label boss Dan Johnson had been served warning by a European band also entitled Avatar, who laid legal claim to the title, necessitating a quick rethink.

PAR's first issue of *Sirens* came in a blue jacket depicting a ship and a woman's face hidden in the clouds. This artwork had not been chosen by the band, and subsequent reissues through Combat and Relativity feature the now more familiar 'killer sewer children' design. Album credits described the band members' contributions as "Shrieks of terror", "Metalaxe", "Barbaric cannons" and "The bottom end".

Sirens pulled in laudatory reviews worldwide, particularly in Europe where a licence through UK label Music For Nations significantly raised the band's profile. The mini-album *The Dungeons Are Calling* arrived in 1984, and with artwork warning of the horrors of drug abuse, this set too found an eager global audience.

When Savatage opened for Atlantic Records signings Zebra at a Tampa Mahaffey Theatre showcase, Robert Zemsky and Zebra bassist Randy Jackson persuaded Atlantic A&R supremo Jason Flom to check out the band. Already intrigued by the group's rapid ascent, Flom arranged a further showcase in Brandon, Florida, and duly put Savatage into Morrisound Studios. With esteemed guitarist Rick Derringer producing them, Savatage committed further demos to tape. At this juncture, word of Savatage's prowess had circulated and the group were fending off bids from Elektra, Pasha, Geffen, Metal Blade and Megaforce – but it was Atlantic who swiftly contracted the band, installing Robert Zemsky as manager.

The band repaid the opportunity given to them by delivering a tour de force in the Max Norman-produced *Power Of The Night* in early 1985. This album, recorded at Bearsville Studios in New York during late 1984, and with both Oliva brothers and Keith Collins laying down bass in the studio, proved beyond all doubt that Savatage were a major force to be reckoned with.

Jon Oliva: "I'm proud to say it – we're a heavy metal band. It might be that radio hates that, or your mother hates it too, but I'm not apologising for it. You've got a bunch of guys who eat, sleep and drink in the heavy metal way. The difference is, we add a little twist to the mix because of my voice, the way we write and the way Criss plays his guitar. There's no formula here. You can't quite put your finger on it with us, and it's entertaining to see reviewers and journalists try."

The group embarked upon the 'Monsters Of The Universe' tour in July 1985 backed by Illusion and UK act Rogue Male, during which Collins was replaced by Johnny Lee Middleton of the Florida act Lefty. The band performed a one-off headliner at the London Marquee on July 1st 1986 prior to hitting US venues, again in support of Ted Nugent.

Unfortunately, Savatage then stalled, hitting a creative nadir with 1986's *Fight For The Rock*. Switching producers to Stefan Galfas, they journeyed to London to craft these tracks in late 1985 at Trident Studios, but the power and commitment displayed on previous releases was tempered by blatant commercialism and uninspired renditions of Free's 'Wishing Well' and Badfinger's 'Day After Day'. The decision of management and record label to steer the band into radio territory backfired horrendously, and the results were soundly panned by critics and fans alike. Jon Oliva took the strain badly, later admitting not only that he resorted to drink and drugs to get him through this bleak period, but also that he very nearly folded the group.

They endeavoured to tour, but the singer's downhill spiral forced the cancellation of many dates, with the band put on hold while Jon cleaned up. A one-off show did find the group headlining a festival in Oulu, Finland after the original bill-toppers, Metallica, withdrew due to the Chernobyl disaster. In the midst of this turmoil, Criss Oliva was offered larger paychecks by Ozzy Osbourne and Megadeth among others, but chose to remain loyal to Savatage.

Jon Oliva: "We got fooled and suckered with Fight For The Rock. It really damaged our career, because up to that point everything was coming our way. Unfortunately, we listened to the wrong people, and it was a hard lesson. Everything about that period, that record, was just very weird. When we started getting the reviews it was like confirmation, but we knew before we had even finished the damn thing that people were going to hate it. I'm not saying it's a terrible record, there are some really cool parts, but it was not what Savatage should have been doing – and boy, did our fans let us know. We even did a cover version, the Free track, just because one of the top label guys said it was his favourite song. We kissed ass, I admit it."

Thankfully, they returned in grandiose style with *Hall Of The Mountain King*, sparking a renaissance for the band. This was the first album produced by Paul O'Neill and marked the start of a relationship that remained solid until the present day. With *Hall Of The Mountain King*, Savatage spread their musical wings and even included a radical reworking of Grieg's *Peer Gynt* suite of the title. In the studio, Black Sabbath vocalist Ray Gillen complemented Jon Oliva on the chorus to the track 'Strange Wings'. *Hall Of The Mountain King* peaked at Number 116 on the US charts.

Expanding their format to handle the live practicalities of their vision, the band added former Heaven guitarist Chris Caffery for live work: this revised unit guested for Dio and Megadeth in North America from December 1987 until March 1988. Unfortunately, these dates were marred by physical altercations between Jon Oliva and Megadeth's Dave Mustaine. Savatage also put in a European date at the legendary 'Aardschok' festival in Holland. After these dates, Caffery joined Dirty Looks but later returned to Savatage, and by the recording of the *Gutter Ballet* album the guitarist had become a full-time member.

Cut in New York with Paul O'Neill, the demo sessions for this record went through the projected working album titles of *Temptation Revelation* and *Hounds Of Zaroff* until *Gutter Ballet* was chosen once the recording had commenced. The record arrived in December 1989 and reached Number 124 on the US charts.

Gutter Ballet's title track – influenced by Jon Oliva's experience of *The Phantom Of The Opera* stage show – hinted strongly at the concept works to come. However, more traditional Savatage music was to be heard, such as the horror noir of 'Hounds' and 'The Unholy', and Jon Oliva's autobiographical 'Thorazine Shuffle', which documented his pre-recording tenure in a Minnesota detox facility.

Touring in Europe and the UK saw the band partnered with King Diamond for the 'Rulin' Gutter' dates, commencing in February 1990. By March they were back in US territory, collaborating with Testament and Nuclear Assault for a sustained campaign between March and late summer.

July 1991's *Streets – A Rock Opera*, which featured the Metropolitan Opera Children's Choir, was an ambitious affair, taking up nine months of studio time and lyrically based on the fortunes of a fictional New York musician named DT Jesus who was embroiled in the world of street drugs. While many related the storyline to Jon Oliva's tribulations, in fact the draft concept had been written by Paul O'Neill in 1979 and was later fleshed out with songs such as 'Tonight He Grins Again', 'Agony And Ecstasy' and 'If I Go Away' by the Oliva siblings. A further track, 'Can You Hear Me Now', was put down as album sessions closed, with Jon Oliva on drums and Criss Oliva on bass.

Streets – A Rock Opera was originally intended to be a double album, but Atlantic baulked at the idea. As a compromise, the group whittled the track-listing down to 16 songs with a spoken narrative as a common thread. The label trimmed their ambitions further by removing the narration entirely, apart from the introduction to 'Jesus Saves', and excising the song 'Larry Elbows'. Although, in context, *Streets* was an important release and one that surpassed the sales of previous efforts, it was often overlooked due to its unfortunate timing – coming as it did so soon after the massive impact of Queensrÿche's *Operation: Mindcrime*.

Savatage toured heavily to push the album, opening operations in Europe that October backed by Vicious Rumors and into 1992 in the USA with Armored Saint prior to Japanese shows. This road work took a severe toll on Jon, who suffered from a severe illness. Losing his voice entirely, and even coughing up blood onstage, he reluctantly withdrew in order to recuperate. As a diversion from their priority act, Jon and Caffery issued an album from their side project, Doctor Butcher, a record that surprised many fans with its rawness.

Jon Oliva: "The problem is playing live for an hour and a half every night. It just beats your throat in night after night. Breathing in all that fog juice doesn't help either. The voice is like an old car: it's a grand thing but you just have to look after it a bit more.

"When I was younger I did everything possible to destroy my throat without actually knowing I was doing it. Nobody told me. I just thought you got up on stage and sang. I was the poster child for what not to do as a singer – smoking, drugs, drink, no sleep. I paid the price in a big way, because for a lot of years my voice was just fucked – totally fucked. I remember on the very last show of the Streets tour in North Carolina my throat just gave in. I was at the side of the stage just hacking up blood. I couldn't even talk for three weeks."

Chris Caffery: "After Streets was all done, both Jon and I were in a mess. Strange to look back on it, but we were both really low and it was very difficult to see what had been achieved. One day I phoned up Jon, and this is how the conversation went. He said: 'Hi Chris, what are you doing?' I said something like: 'Nothing, I'm just sitting here with a bottle of whiskey,' so Jon says: 'So am I; get down here and we can at least drink together.' That's what I did, I got back down to Florida and we spoke a lot, watched a lot of movies, a lot of sport, and out of that came the Doctor Butcher project. It was like a release for both of us. Just good fun. Then the record company heard what was going on and they suggested forming a band and everything, and we both thought the same thing. Wasn't this to get away from all that?"

In April 1993, Savatage issued *Edge Of Thorns*. The group pulled in new lead vocalist Zachary Stevens (aka Zak Trussell), previously with Boston band Wicked Witch, although Jon Oliva maintained an overseeing presence as main writer. *Edge Of Thorns* was Savatage's last album with drummer Steve Wacholz, with Jon Oliva sessioning on drums on 'He Carves His Stone' and 'Degrees Of Sanity'. The record, of which the Japanese issues added two extra tracks in 'Forever After' and 'Shotgun Innocence', collated many of the riffs and song ideas culled from the previous record's original concept.

Bereft of the core membership of Jon Oliva and Steve Wacholz, Savatage set out on tour, drafting in two new members – Wes Garren on rhythm guitar and keyboards and Andy James of Roxx Gang on drums. Gigs in Europe saw the band topping an impressive billing with Overkill and Non-Fiction in May and June, before US concerts supported by Galactic Cowboys.

The year was overshadowed by the death of Criss Oliva. Travelling home from the 'Livestock Festival' in Zephyrhills, Florida, on the night of October 17th, Criss's car was hit head-on by a truck that strayed into his lane. His wife, Dawn, eventually recovered, but the 30-year-old guitarist was killed outright. Jon Oliva resolved to pursue Savatage with renewed vigour following the death of his brother.

Chris Caffery: "When Criss was taken, everybody thought the band was over. It was a blow that seemed too big to recover from. Obviously the other guys were hurting far deeper than I was. After a time, I started to think about other options, but then I got word that

the fans all over the world were sending in all these letters begging for Savatage to carry on. It was a strange thing, because Criss has now become this legend. I think at the time everyone knew that what Criss was doing was exceptional and one-off, but it maybe might have taken a couple more records for him to get that legend status.

"Because Savatage has carried on, people are now always reminded about Criss and new people are discovering his music. With every new Savatage record, we get told that sales are up, but also so are the sales of all the early records. It happens every time. It's like the new fans discover Savatage, and then realise there are all these other records. They don't just buy one or two either, they get them all."

Phil Campbell (Motörhead): "One of the guitarists that really impressed me was Criss from Savatage. We've had hundreds of support bands and they range from great to good to fucking awful, of course, but it's rare you spot one guy who can really show you something different. I used to love watching Criss play. Always something new – and it was all from him, no gimmicks. He never put his guitar down. Criss was just bloody astounding."

Dave Mustaine (Megadeth): "Criss Oliva was on my list. We toured together and it was chaotic, but Criss stood out as a gifted natural. There's no way he would have jumped from Savatage, though, because of his brother, and I'm sure he was not too keen to get involved with Megadeth the way we were running the ship back then. I would have had him in the band in a heartbeat, though."

Handful Of Rain appeared in 1994 with keyboards and songwriting back in the hands of Jon Oliva and a line-up of Middleton, Wacholz, Stevens and former Testament guitarist Alex Skolnick. The album was again produced under the guidance of Paul O'Neill and included a tribute to Criss Oliva, 'Alone You Breathe'.

Skolnick was merely on loan from his own project, the funk-rock-flavoured Exhibit A, but did fulfil tour dates – appearing twice a night as Exhibit A were the support band. These shows witnessed the induction of new drummer Jeff Plate, another recruitment from Wicked Witch. The very last show of the world tour, on November 13th 1994 in Tokyo, was recorded for a live album.

After his departure, Skolnick joined Ozzy Osbourne's band, although his stay was fleeting – one secret gig at Nottingham's Rock City venue. Savatage, meanwhile, pulled in ex-CPR, Talas, Alice Cooper, Asia and Widowmaker guitarist Al Pitrelli, a man whose past credits were both an indicator of his versatility and the demand for his skills.

During 1995, Metal Blade issued promotional copies of a live Savatage album, *Live Devastation*. However, after an objection from the band this proposed release never saw the light of day. The *Dead Winter Dead* album, released in October 1995 through Edel, gave Savatage their biggest seller in Europe. The group now included Jon Oliva and Zak Stevens operating as joint lead vocalists and the returned guitarist Chris Caffery. Lyrically based on the Balkan wars, the record had a storyline mixing historical saga with the theme of Christmas. The festive element served the band well, with a single, 'Christmas Eve, Sarajevo 12-24', reaping major radio airplay. This success provided the catalyst for a second, parallel chapter of the Savatage family.

O'Neill and Savatage members Oliva, Pitrelli and Middleton were involved in the 1996 Christmas rock album *Christmas Eve And Other Stories* for Atlantic subsidiary Lava Records under the name of Trans-Siberian Orchestra. The album includes 'Christmas Eve (Sarajevo 12/24)' lifted directly from the *Dead Winter Dead* sessions. This outside venture evolved into a highly successful touring operation in its own right, and over a million albums of the debut album were sold.

As a reminder of Criss Oliva's talents, Savatage released the live *Ghost*

SAVATAGE discography

City Beneath The Surface, PAR 1002, (1982) 7-inch vinyl single; as Avatar

SIRENS, Music For Nations MFN 48 (UK), PAR 1050 (USA) (1983)

The Dungeons Are Calling, Music For Nations MFN42 (UK), Combat 6016 (USA) (1984)

POWER OF THE NIGHT, Atlantic 781 247-1 (UK), Atlantic 81247 (USA) (1985)

FIGHT FOR THE ROCK, Atlantic 781 634-1 (UK), Atlantic 81634 (USA) (1986) **158 USA**

HALL OF THE MOUNTAIN KING, Atlantic K 781 775 1 (UK), Atlantic 81775-2 (USA) (1987) **116 USA**

GUTTER BALLET, Atlantic K 782 008 2 (UK), Atlantic 82008-2 (USA) (1989) **124 USA**

STREETS – A ROCK OPERA, Atlantic 7567-82320-2 (1991)

EDGE OF THORNS, Atlantic 7567 82488-2 (1993)

HANDFUL OF RAIN, Atlantic 82660 (1994)

JAPAN LIVE '94, Zero Corporation XRCN 1257 (1994)

DEAD WINTER DEAD, Edel 0086252RAD (Europe), Atlantic 82850 (USA) (1995)

GHOST IN THE RUINS – A TRIBUTE TO CRISS OLIVA, Fresh Fruit SPV 085-12142 (Europe), Nuclear Blast America 6477 (USA) (1996)

THE WAKE OF MAGELLAN, Edel 0089832 (Europe), Atlantic 83100 (USA) (1998)

POETS AND MADMEN, Steamhammer SPV 088-72150 (Europe), Nuclear Blast America 6618 (USA) (2001)

In The Ruins – A Tribute To Criss Oliva, with recordings from 1987 to 1990. Although initially only issued in Japan, where it was titled *Final Bell*, the album was issued in Europe after it flooded onto the European market as an import.

Metal Blade's re-release of *The Dungeons Are Calling* in 1997 added an extra 'lost' track, 'Fighting For Your Love', as well as a live version of 'Sirens'. The same year's reissue of *Sirens* was rounded off with two further archive cuts, 'Lady In Disguise' and 'The Message'. Pitrelli made time during 1997 to contribute to the Flesh And Blood blues project band assembled by former Drive, She Said mainman Mark Mangold and Tyketto vocalist Danny Vaughn.

Savatage undertook a mammoth European tour during late 1997, supported by fellow Americans Vanderhoof, while Caffery found time in the schedule to record the Metalium band's first album, *Millennium Metal*. Savatage released a new studio album, *The Wake Of Magellan*, in April 1998. Impressively, their dedicated fans in Europe put this album into the German national charts at number 11.

By early 1999 Pitrelli was performing live work with Blue Öyster Cult. The following year he left for fresh, if predictably temporary, pastures in Megadeth. Savatage, newly signed to SPV in Europe and Nuclear Blast in America, spent the bulk of 2000 recording a new concept album, *Poets And Madmen*, although its proposed release date was put back numerous times due to work on the third Trans-Siberian Orchestra album. Meanwhile, a tribute album, *Return Of The Mountain King*, surfaced.

In November it was announced that Zachary Stevens had left the band. The holiday period was taken up with Trans-Siberian Orchestra dates, splitting the project into two to satisfy fan demand. The 'West' variant saw Caffrey alongside Savatage drummer Jeff Plate and erstwhile six-string colleague Alex Skolnick, while Johnny Lee Middleton anchored the 'East' version.

Florida native and ex-Diet Of Worms man Damond Jiniya became Savatage's new lead vocalist in March 2001, with second guitar in the hands of Jack Frost. Frost had been a member of Caffery's Metalium as well as spreading his talents over such acts as Seven Witches, Speeed and Bronx Casket Co.

Poets And Madmen finally arrived in April, its debut at Number 7 in the national German album charts providing ample proof of the patience of Savatage fans. Touring in America included Fates Warning as support act.

The band toured continental Europe with festival appearances at the Italian 'Gods Of Metal' event, Germany's 'Bang Your Head' show and the Dutch 'Dynamo' gig prior to supporting Judas Priest on their Spanish dates. These Iberian shows proved more memorable for guitarist Chris Caffrey than he would have liked, however, as he was struck down with severe food poisoning. Soldiering on with the tour, Caffrey was eventually hospitalised in Holland.

Headlining gigs in Brazil found local act Hanger as support. A run of American headlining shows beginning in San Francisco on September 5th rolled out with Seattle's Nevermore as opening act. However, in the light of the terrorist strikes on New York and Washington DC on the 11th, Savatage cancelled their projected European return dates. They were later rescheduled for early 2002, with Vicious Rumors and Blaze as opening acts.

Caffery then took time out to act as session guitarist for erstwhile 24-7 Spyz bassist Rick Skatore's new Block 16 debut album. Along with Jeff Plate, the guitarist also weighed in with Royal Hunt vocalist John West's Earthmaker project. Frost dived straight back into action with both Seven Witches and Bronx Casket Co. Meanwhile, it was reported that Zachary Stevens had re-emerged with a fresh venture entitled Circle II Circle. This project signed to the German AFM label for a debut record, *Watching In Silence*. The record included four songwriting collaborations each, shared between Stevens, Oliva and Caffery. Oliva and Stevens also duetted on the track 'Forgiven'.

In early April, fans were surprised, to say the least, at an official announcement that Jack Frost had been fired, with Savatage re-recruiting Al Pitrelli from the recently disintegrated Megadeth. However, before taking up this post, Pitrelli undertook live work with former Skid Row vocalist Sebastian Bach. In an odd twist of events, Jeff Waters of Canadian thrash veterans Annihilator joined Savatage for their summer 2002 European dates. Al Pitrelli, only recently re-inducted, was unable to make the tour due to "prior commitments": within 24 hours it was announced that Pitrelli had formed a new band with Megadeth's former guitarist Marty Friedman, bassist David Ellefson and drummer Jimmy DeGrasso.

The Green Parrot Pub in Largo, Florida, played host to the 'Criss Oliva 10th Anniversary Memorial Concert' on October 17th 2003, which witnessed the first time in eight years that bassist Johnny Lee Middleton and drummer Steve 'Doc' Wacholz had shared a stage with Jon Oliva and Caffery. The following month, Caffery signed a deal with Greece's Black Lotus Records for the release of his debut solo album, *Faces*. By December, Jon was out on the solo trail, billed as The Jon Oliva Project, gigging with guitarist Matt Laporte, bass player Kevin Rothney, keyboard player John Zahner and drummer Christopher Kinder. This band had only recently exited from former Savatage singer Zak Stevens' Circle II Circle project, under acrimonious circumstances.

In February 2004, Oliva's project had taken on the new title of Tage Mahal, with Wacholz guesting on the debut album *Tage Mahal*. Subsequently this venture evolved into Jon Oliva's Pain, due to the discovery of a longstanding European blues artist laying claim to the former name. One album track, 'People Say – Gimme Some Hell', involved Savatage song titles as its lyrical base, and sampled guitar parts by Criss Oliva and Steve Wacholz were featured too.

Damond Jiniya then announced the formation of The Neglected, a creative union with Diet Of Worms and Lover Of Sin guitarist and producer Juan Gonzalez. The duo's debut album, simply entitled *The Neglected*, was written and recorded in February at DOW Studios in Mango, Florida. September saw two Savatage-related projects on the road, as Jon Oliva's Pain and Chris Caffery's solo band united with ex-Judas Priest vocalist Tim 'Ripper' Owens's band Beyond Fear for US live dates. Drummer Jeff Plate joined Metal Church in February 2006, replacing mainstay Kirk Arrington, who was forced out due to diabetes.

Into 2006 it seemed as though Savatage were in hiatus as the second album from Jon Oliva's Pain, *Maniacal Renderings*, arrived in September and Chris Caffery busied himself with further solo recordings. For their dedication and musical dexterity alone, Savatage have earned the respect of thousands of metal fans. It's to be hoped that they continue to tread their distinctive musical path for many years to come.

Jon Oliva: "I'm blessed, I tell you. Twenty-three years is one heck of a career. To think of all the things I've been able to achieve, all those great records, the people I've met, the friends who have been through it all with me. It's just amazing – and what makes it even more incredible is that we're now here with my new record, Savatage enjoying a lot of respect, and Trans-Siberian Orchestra playing Madison Square Garden. Who would have thought it?

"It makes me laugh so hard, though, sometimes. When I think of all those idiots on radio who would never give Savatage a chance. I remember they used to laugh at us for even suggesting they try Savatage on radio. Now they're playing our records and they don't even know it. We got the last laugh, for sure.

"I just love what we're able to do now – the creativity of it all. We got stuck in this black hole for so many years of being just another heavy metal band when, given the chance, we really have proved ourselves. Our fans knew it, but the people who controlled the industry just said, 'Yeah, Savatage, heavy metal, whatever…' You asked our fans, though, they would tell you we were always more than that. I mean, Criss was always unique in his approach and with his gift; my voice was always just that little bit different; and our ambition on record was often a lot more than our early producers could cope with. Now that we have control, the scope of what we can achieve now is just limitless.

VICIOUS RUMORS
THRASHERS WITH FINESSE

A POWER THRASH METAL BAND of great repute, Vicious Rumors formed in Santa Rosa, California, in August 1979, co-founded by mainstay guitarist Geoff Thorpe. Their debut performance came in 1980 at one of the fabled 'Metal Monday' meetings at The Old Waldorf in San Francisco. Two years later the first recording arrived in the form of 'I Can Live Forever', a track included on the KMEL *New Oasis* compilation. The band were vocalist Mark Tate, guitarists Thorpe and Jim Cassero, bass player Jeff Barnacle and drummer Walt Perkins. In 1983, Jim Lange supplanted Perkins. At this formative stage, Vicious Rumors were heavily reliant on image, with co-ordinated black and blue stage costumes. The singer entered the stage held aloft in a coffin borne by monks.

The band was quickly taken under the wing of guitar guru and Shrapnel Records boss Mike Varney. Thorpe had met Varney through Varney's Rock Justice project. At the time of their meeting, Varney was in the process of putting the Shrapnel label together, a company that first made its name with the *US Metal* compilation albums, which highlighted the playing abilities of the guitarists in the bands featured.

New bassist Starr had been a founder member of Lääz Rockit, having renamed that act from their previous title of Depth Charge. Fired from Lääz Rockit in 1983, Starr created a power trio titled Black Leather with guitarist Rick Richards and drummer Jim Wells. In 1985, Starr formed part of the regrouped Vicious Rumors, completing a line-up of ex-Hawaii singer Gary St. Pierre, guitarist Thorpe and drummer Charles Emmil. During this period, Vain guitarist Jamie Scott (then under the name Chuck Mooney) made some recordings with Vicious Rumors. The drummer for their next period was Don Selzer.

Vicious Rumors made their first appearance for Shrapnel on *US Metal Volume III* with the track 'Ultimate Death'. Varney gave the group another shot with 'One Way Ticket', included on 1984's *US Metal Volume IV*. At the time, Thorpe had been looking for the perfect guitar partner and was getting nowhere. Former Black Leather man Rick Richards filled in for one gig, but then Varney introduced Thorpe to a guitarist from Delaware called Vinnie Moore, who swiftly joined up. Varney then put them in the studio to record a debut album for Shrapnel in 1985. *Soldiers Of The Night*, released in Europe through Roadrunner, featured St. Pierre on vocals, Moore and Thorpe on guitars, bassist Starr and drummer Larry Howe.

Moore, only a temporary member, quit to pursue his goal of solo stardom, and Vicious Rumors promptly picked up former Tyrant man Terry Montana as a replacement. Montana lasted a year, recording demos and touring for the first album, before the Alameda, California-raised Mark McGee came into the frame. Formerly the vocalist and rhythm guitarist of local act Overdrive, McGee had also spent time in the fading pomp rock outfit Starcastle.

McGee made his debut with Vicious Rumors on 1988's *Digital Dictator*, a record that also premiered ex-Ruffians and Villain vocalist Carl Albert in place of the departed Gary St. Pierre. Vicious Rumors hooked up Savatage manager Robert Zemsky and signed with major label Atlantic for an eponymous 1990 album, co-produced by Thorpe and Michael Rosen. The record title had originally been set to be *Immortal Battalion*.

The band then toured North America on a headlining club jaunt prior to European dates with Death Angel and Forbidden as well as a performance at the prestigious 'Dynamo' festival in Holland. Although media and fan response was enthusiastic, the band did not seem to be receiving the benefits that a major label like Atlantic could have delivered.

For 1991's *Welcome To The Ball*, again seeing Thorpe and Rosen in command of the board, the band toured Europe with Savatage and put in further headline club gigs in America. Japanese dates were followed by the live *Plug In And Hang On – Live In Tokyo* album.

The following year, the band were dealt two blows. Not only were

---

VICIOUS RUMORS discography

SOLDIERS OF THE NIGHT, Roadrunner RR 9734 (Europe), Shrapnel SH-1020 (USA) (1986)

DIGITAL DICTATOR, Roadrunner RR 9571 (Europe), Shrapnel SH-1033 (USA) (1988)

VICIOUS RUMORS, Atlantic 7567820752 (UK), Atlantic 82075 (USA) (1990)

WELCOME TO THE BALL, Atlantic 75682276121 (UK), Atlantic 82276 (USA) (1991)

PLUG IN AND HANG ON – LIVE IN TOKYO, Atlantic cnu (1992)

WORD OF MOUTH, Rising Sun SPV 084-62232 (Europe) (1994)

A TRIBUTE TO CARL ALBERT, Headless Butcher cnu (1995)

SOMETHING BURNING, Massacre MASSCD 091 (Europe) (1996)

CYBERCHRIST, Massacre MASSCD 0142 (Europe) (1998)

SADISTIC SYMPHONY, Perris 72 (USA) (2001)

WARBALL, Mascot M7206-2 (Europe) (2006)

they dropped by Atlantic but also Thorpe was found to be suffering from carpal tunnel syndrome and had to undergo surgery. For a while the band operated as a quartet without him. Howe filled his downtime by creating a side project, Bomb Threat, with Heathen members Lee Altus and Thaen Rasmussen alongside singer Jay of My Victim. Bomb Threat toured Californian clubs, playing a nostalgic set of NWOBHM covers.

By mid 1993, Thorpe was recovered enough to get out on the road again, but by November line-up problems beset the band, with Starr being fired and replaced by Tommy Sisco. The 1994 album *Word Of Mouth* included two bonus cuts for the Japanese market – covers of The Rolling Stones' 'Paint It Black' and Led Zeppelin's 'Communication Breakdown'. In Germany the album emerged through Rising Sun Productions, and limited edition digipacks there added two live tracks, 'Hellraiser' and 'The Quest'.

In April 1995, Vicious Rumors were rocked again when Albert was killed in an auto accident. McGee quit the band, eventually uniting with Greg Allman. In October 1995, with Thorpe assuming vocals, the band toured Europe once again, hitching a ride on the heavyweight Metal Church, Zodiac Mindwarp and Killers package.

Thorpe took over lead vocals in the studio for the 1996 album *Something Burning*, with the band bolstered by guitarist Steve Smyth. The following year, they drafted in vocalist Brian O'Connor. High-profile European dates saw them guesting for Accept. Back in America, further gigs were executed as openers to established artists such as Thin Lizzy, Rainbow and Blue Öyster Cult. The band played to their biggest audiences in 1998, billed as special guests to Germany's Blind Guardian on their European tour promoting the album *Cyberchrist*.

In 1999, Vicious Rumors announced that their new vocalist was ex-High Treason and Megaton Blonde man Morgan Thorn, while Smyth joined thrash veterans Testament. That same year, former guitarist Mark McGee established a new outfit, Luvplanet, joined later by his erstwhile Vicious Rumors colleague, bassist Tommy Sisco.

The band bounced back in 2001 with the *Sadistic Symphony* album. Vicious Rumors' new look consisted of Thorn, Thorpe, guitarist Ira Black, bassist Cornbread and drummer Atma Anur. Black's history traces back through Rexxen, the 1992 incarnation of Heathen, Uteris (featuring Tesla guitarist Tommy Skeoch), and Dogface with erstwhile Exodus man Steve Souza. Bassist Cornbread had played in Bizarro, the band founded by ex-Forbidden and Testament guitarist Glen Alvelais, while drummer Anur boasted numerous studio appearances with diverse acts such as David Bowie, Journey, Tony MacAlpine and Marty Friedman. Dave Starr and drummer Larry Howe both joined Chastain in 2001. Meanwhile, Ira Black delved into nostalgia by forming part of the reunion of 1980s thrash act Mercenary.

With the release of *Sadistic Symphony*, Vicious Rumors once again changed tack, re-employing Brian O'Connor on vocals. The band, with Dan Lawson on drums, hooked up with Savatage and Blaze for European dates commencing in Sweden during January 2002 but soon pulled out, citing friction with Blaze. Later they pulled off a major coup by landing the support slot to the mammoth Aerosmith and Kid Rock show at the Marysville Autowest Amphitheater on November 7th.

Guitarist Steve Smyth took time out in early 2003 to collaborate with ex-Ariah and Sweet Leaf bassist Steven Hoffman on a progressive venture dubbed The Esseness Project. Guitarist Geoff Thorpe also engaged in outside projects, guesting on the 'Lake Of Memory' single from The 7th Order.

Having signed to the Dutch Mascot label, Vicious Rumors set to work on a 2004 album, provisionally billed as *Immortal*. A DVD release was also announced. *Crushing The World – Part 1* included archive film featuring the late Carl Albert, footage from the 2002 European tour with Savatage, the band's appearances at the 'Wacken Open Air' and 'Bang Your Head' festivals, as well as three previously unheard tracks. The band then scheduled Italian dates for the summer of 2004 but pulled out due to Geoff Thorpe's illness.

The band were rejoined by drummer Howe in January 2005. More changes saw bassist Cornbread exiting in April, with Tommy Sisco as his replacement. A release party to celebrate the issue of *Crushing The World*, held at the Last Day Saloon in Santa Rosa, California, on May 21st, saw a reformation of the complete *Word Of Mouth* line-up – Brian O'Connor, Geoff Thorpe, Mark McGee, Larry Howe and Tommy Sisco.

That same summer, Ira Black announced a brand new band, The Side FX, in union with Rough Cutt veterans vocalist Paul Shortino and bassist Matt Thorn, plus the Yngwie Malmsteen-credited Patrik Johansson on drums.

On July 9th 2005, Vicious Rumors lined up at the Pound outdoor amphitheatre in San Francisco alongside Testament, Dreams Of Damnation, Lääz Rockit, Hirax, Agent Steel, Dekapitator, Mudface, Neil Turbin, Brocas Helm and Imagika for the 'Thrash Against Cancer' benefit. Later that year, guitarist Ira Black temporarily replaced Kurdt Vanderhoof in Metal Church for a three-week US tour.

Brian O'Connor closed an eight-year tenure as Vicious Rumors frontman in August. Within hours of this announcement, guitarist Ira Black also officially terminated his position, joining Emerald Triangle. The band reformed, with bassist Dave Starr and drummer Larry Howe rejoining guitarist Geoff Thorpe. Days later it was revealed that James Rivera of Helstar, Seven Witches and Flotsam And Jetsam would front the band. Another unexpected addition to the ranks was Brad Gillis, best known for his tour of duty with Ozzy Osbourne and as the mainstay of melodic rockers Night Ranger. For European gigs the group drafted in another high-profile guitarist, Anvil Chorus veteran Thaen Rasmussen, temporarily replacing Gillis. Ira Black enrolled himself into the ranks of Lizzy Borden in April 2006 and shortly afterward Larry Howe took up an offer, albeit fleeting, to join W.A.S.P.. Promoting the *Warball* album, Vicious Rumors toured Europe in November with Beyond Fear.

Despite the enduringly convoluted nature of the various Vicious Rumors line-ups over the years, it seems that their determined fan support will never allow this beast to be muted.

VIRGIN STEELE
TECHNICALLY LITERATE METALLERS

VIRGIN STEELE ARE ONE OF A NUMBER of new North American heavy metal bands who take their cue from British groups from the 1970s by performing a new form of pomp-edged metal. Although the band's early works were hampered by budget restrictions, their music increased in scope and daring breadth with each release. The seeds of the band were laid in Long Island, New York, when French-born guitarist Jack Starr relocated to America after a position in French rock outfit Trust early on in their career. Indeed, Starr claims to have played with the group for their first ever gig at the Olympia Theatre in Paris.

On returning to America, Starr had begun playing with drummer Joey Ayvazian in 1981 and that June the duo recruited vocalist-keyboard player David DeFeis (previously with Mountain Ash) after being impressed with his rendition of Deep Purple's 'Child In Time' at the audition. The band's first bassist was Kelly Nichols, although subsequently DeFeis drafted in bassist Joe O'Reilly. Nichols joined Angels In Vain and then relocated to Los Angeles, later to join Faster Pussycat and LA Guns.

The group's audio debut came in 1982 with the inclusion of 'Children Of The Storm' on the Shrapnel US Metal Vol. II compilation. Virgin Steele became the first signings to former Secret Records boss Martin Hooker's new metal label, Music For Nations. The band's debut album – originally intended to be a demo and costing a mere $1,000 – was released in Europe with the landmark catalogue number MFN 1 in 1983. It had originally appeared on the group's own label the previous December, Starr claiming that it had sold 5,000 copies in its first two and a half weeks. Among Virgin Steele's early high-profile shows were two dates in New York opening for Manowar, after which the group were quick to begin work on a second album at Sonic Sound Studios in Freeport, New York. *Guardians Of The Flame* was issued before the end of the year. UK editions sported a fantasy-themed album cover, while US variants came with a simpler sword design.

Mongol Horde Records put out the EP *Wait For The Night*, this set delivered in Europe with a revised track-listing as *A Cry In The Night*. A diversion during 1984 saw various members appearing anonymously on two thrash albums billed as Exorcist (with David DeFeis as Damian Rath), and Devil Childe, with Starr under the pseudonym Lucifer.

Virgin Steele then parted company with Starr due to the time-honoured musical differences: he went on to forge a reasonably successful career with his Burning Starr projects. Virgin Steele eventually replaced him with Edward Pursino, a high school friend of DeFeis.

After Starr had left the band, his former colleagues apparently discovered that he had copyrighted the band name. Eventually, the situation was resolved and the group was able to continue with the name. Later they returned with the *Noble Savage* album, released on their Canadian manager Zoran Busic's Cobra label. Busic, once the manager of Canadian prog-rock outfit Saga, also had a hand in various Canadian issues of early Virgin Steele product on the Maze label, often with alternative art and track lists. Notably, Maze licensed the *Guardians Of The Flame* album for Canada, which dropped three tracks and added the *Cry In The Night* and *Wait For The Night* EPs, under the new title *Burn The Sun*.

In 1986, DeFeis produced the second Burning Starr album, *No Turning Back*, and added keyboards. DeFeis also put in time with another Cobra act, female thrashers Original Sin, producing their debut album, *Sin Will Find You Out*, under the pseudonym of The Lion. Both Pursino and DeFeis contributed anonymously to the second album *Stay Ugly* from spoof thrash metal band Piledriver.

With enthusiasm at a high, Virgin Steele undertook two tours of Europe in 1987 supporting Manowar and then Black Sabbath before recording *Age Of Consent*. The album, released in late 1988, did not feature Joe O'Reilly: bass was supplied by DeFeis and Pursino.

In a lengthy period of downtime, Starr and DeFeis reunited briefly in 1990 with Smokestack Lightning in union with ex-Foghat bassist Craig McGregor. This blues-rock act's life was short; a later recruit was bassist Rob DeMartino, later of Rondinelli.

The lengthy hiatus saw a shift in the band. Sonically and lyrically, they moved away from their early US/NWOBHM hybrid sound and the relatively lightweight lyrical stance of the earlier material. The band embraced a much more epic, sweeping metal sound and began a long-standing lyrical exploration of themes of classic literature and ancient times – specifically Greece and Rome. The band had dabbled with historical themes with tracks such as 'The Burning Of Rome (Call For Pompeii)' on the *Age Of Consent* but it wasn't until the 1990s that the new sound and approach came to the fore.

Virgin Steele pulled in former Dio, Great White and Rondinelli bassist Teddy Cook for the *Life Among The Ruins* album, but the bass sessions were finished by Rob DeMartino. They promoted the album with a lengthy headlining jaunt in Europe, with July 1993 dates in Germany supported by Sahara.

DeFeis's next project was the epic concept *The Marriage Of Heaven And Hell*, released over two sprawling albums: *The Marriage Of Heaven And Hell: Part One* in 1995 and *The Marriage Of Heaven And Hell: Part Two* in 1996. During the recording, DeMartino left briefly to join Rainbow. Pursino took over bass duties and in 1995 a projected tour of Europe was cancelled when headline act Uriah Heep pulled out. The band regrouped with DeMartino for a headlining European schedule later in the year and drafted in a new drummer, Frank Gilchriest.

The reworked re-release of *Age Of Consent* in 1997 featured a revised track order and newly-recorded bonus tracks, among them a keyboard-driven reworking of Judas Priest's 'Desert Plains'. The band appeared on the bill of *Heavy Oder Was?* magazine's 'Bang Your Head' festival in Tübingen, Germany in September 1997.

In 1998, the line-up of DeFeis, Pursino, DeMartino and Gilchriest embraced the inevitable and produced their first full-length rock opera, titled *Invictus* after Defeis considered and rejected *A Season In Purgatory* and *Marriage Of Heaven And Hell Part III*. The lengthy album, released on the T&T label, tells the tale of heroes and epic battles and stands as the band's heaviest work to date.

The 1999 album *The House Of Atreus: Act I*, recorded at Media Recording in Bellmore, New York, was a bold concept based on Greek mythology. DeFeis toured this in Europe as an ambitious stage play. With the release in 2000 of the second part of the concept, *The House Of Atreus: Act II*, Virgin Steele took to the road in Europe at the start of the new year as guests of Hammerfall. DeFeis lent his talents to *Avantasia*, Edguy mainman Tobias Sammet's eponymous project album, the same year.

The House Of Atreus Act I & II was set to be the band's tour de force, involving a sprawling three-disc set clocking in at two hours and 45 minutes. The story is an interpretation of the Greek myth of King

---

VIRGIN STEELE discography

VIRGIN STEELE, Music For Nations MFN1 (UK), Virgin Steele CEP 0001 (USA) (1982)

GUARDIANS OF THE FLAME, Music For Nations MFN 5 (UK), Mongol Horde MONGOL 1 (USA) (1983)

A Cry In The Night, Music For Nations 12KUT 104 (UK) (1983)

Wait For The Night, Mongol Horde MONGOL 4 (USA) (1983)

NOBLE SAVAGE, Steamhammer SPV 85-7531 (Europe), Cobra CL 1005 (USA) (1985)

AGE OF CONSENT, Maze 1060 (USA) (1988)

LIFE AMONG THE RUINS, T&T TT 0006-2 (1993)

THE MARRIAGE OF HEAVEN AND HELL PART ONE, T&T 0012-2 (1994)

THE MARRIAGE OF HEAVEN AND HELL PART TWO, T&T TT 0019-2 (1995)

INVICTUS, T&T TT 034-2 (1998)

THE HOUSE OF ATREUS – ACT I: KINGDOM OF THE FEARLESS, T&T TT 0042-2 (1999)

Magick Fire Music, T&T TT 0050-3 (2000)

THE HOUSE OF ATREUS – ACT II: WINGS OF VENGEANCE, T&T 0051-2 (2000)

VISIONS OF EDEN, T&T 0065-2 (2006)

Agamemnon and his son Orestes in the years following the Trojan War. The band supplemented the project in 2000 with the release of the long EP, *Magick Fire Music*, which tied in to the concept with a few new songs and alternative versions.

Although Virgin Steele have not recorded a new studio album in almost six years, they have not been inactive. To mark their 20th anniversary in 2002 , the act planned a greatest hits package entitled *Hymns To Victory* and a further affair billed as *The Book Of Burning*. The latter consisted of re-recorded early material culled from both *Virgin Steele* and *Guardians Of The Flame*, plus eight unreleased bonus tracks.

During October it emerged that DeFeis was preparing two ambitious musical ventures for 2003, one based on the myths of ancient Sumeria. During December the band recorded and filmed their show at the Downtown in Farmingdale, Long Island, for a live album and DVD. The singer put in guest sessions on the 2003 solo album *Raise Your Fist To Metal* from erstwhile Metalium and Savatage guitarist Jack Frost, prior to involving himself in the production of another leviathan Virgin Steele release. Drummer Frank Gilchriest also made time to session for Riot, Gothic Knights and Holy Mother.

In May 2004, Virgin Steele's DeFeis, Pursino and bassist Josh Block united with former Exorcist drummer Geoff Fontaine and keyboard player Lynn Delmato under the billing Carnival Of Souls to perform a one-off covers gig in aid of the South Shore Music Foundation.

Dates in 2005 at Germany's 'Bang Your Head' and Finland's 'Nummirock' festivals in June were cancelled with a statement revealing that DeFeis was undergoing medical tests. As it transpired, Virgin Steele's solo European concert was the headlining slot at the November 5th 'Keep It True V' festival at Tauberfrankenhalle in Lauda-Königshofen, Germany alongside Jag Panzer, Raven and Ruffians.

The band's set on the March 10th 2006 at the 'Atarfe Vega Rock' festival in Atarfe, Granada, Spain was performed without drums. Frank Gilchriest had missed his flight, the official explanation citing the drummer's "confusion over flight arrangements".

The band's new album, *Visions Of Eden (The Lilith Project – A Barbaric Romantic Movie Of The Mind)* suitably clocking in at an epic 79 minutes, was released in September. Virgin Steele retain a loyal fanbase.

WARLORD
WARLIKE HEAVY METAL

DESPITE CLAIMING TO HAIL "from the North", Warlord purveyed bombastic heavy metal from the less-than-mysterious climes of Los Angeles. They put out a limited number of releases, but the band – founded by erstwhile Russian Roulette drummer Thunder Child (aka Mark Zonder) and guitarist Destroyer (William J. Tsamis) – soon attracted a cult following thanks to their theatrical stage show and grandiose musical approach.

Adding Sahara keyboard player Sentinel (Diane Arens Kornarens) and singer Damien King (Jack Rucker), they were picked up by Brian Slagel's Metal Blade label after he heard the demo track 'Winds Of Thor'. 'Lucifer's Hammer' was featured on *Metal Massacre II*, while 'Mrs. Victoria' appeared on the third volume.

Prior to this, Warlord released a six-track album titled *Deliver Us* in April 1983. It attracted ecstatic praise from the international metal community. With the recruitment of a new vocalist, Texan Rick Cunningham (dubbed Damien King II), and bassist Archangel (Dave Watry), the band returned to action with the 'Lost And Lonely Days' 12-inch in 1984. This was followed that October by the more ambitious orchestrated opus *And The Cannons Of Destruction Have Begun*. Cunningham was replaced on lead vocals by Rick Anderson (Damien

WARLORD discography

DELIVER US, Metal Blade MBR 1005 (USA) (1983)
AND THE CANNONS OF DESTRUCTION HAVE BEGUN..., Metal Blade 71112 (USA) (1984), Roadrunner RR 9806 (Europe) (1986)
Lost And Lonely Days, Metal Blade MBR 1023 (USA) (1984)
THY KINGDOM COME, Roadrunner RR 9637 (Europe), Metal Blade 72169 (USA) (1986)
RISING OUT OF THE ASHES, Atrheia ATRCD 0012 (2002)

King III) as the band delivered its final album, the compilation set *Thy Kingdom Come*, in December 1986. With Warlord's collapse, Zonder teamed up with progressive metal band Fates Warning.

A full decade later, 'Child Of The Damned' was covered by Sweden's Hammerfall for their groundbreaking retro-metal revival album *Glory To The Brave* in 1997. King reciprocated by guesting on Hammerfall's follow-up, *Legacy Of Kings*. The Hammerfall connection didn't end there – Warlord reformed with guitarist William J. Tsamis and drummer Mark Zonder in mid-2001, with Hammerfall vocalist Joacim Cans fronting the entire affair.

The long-awaited comeback album, *Rising Out Of The Ashes*, was delivered in July 2002. Taking on board Italian management, a new live band found Cans, Zonder and Tsamis joined by second guitarist Paolo Viani of Black Jester and Moonlight Circus, keyboard player Daniele Soravia of Moonlight Circus and Helreidh, and Sigma bassist Pasko. The band appeared at the German 'Wacken Open Air' festival as a co-headline act.

During 2005, it was revealed that Zonder had fired up a new band billed Templewithin, later renamed Slavior, in collaboration with Michael Schenker Group guitarist-keyboard player Wayne Findlay and the Masi and Hawk-credited vocalist David Fefolt. The Tribe Of Gypsies singer Gregg Analla was also involved in these sessions. Signing to Greece's Black Lotus Records, Slavior cut an eponymous debut album. However, the band were released from their contract before the album was released.

W.A.S.P.
SHOCK-ROCK TITANS

IN THE EARLY 1980S, LOS ANGELES was a hotbed of thriving rock talent, populated by literally thousands of acts who were all trying to force their attention on the major labels. Every band claimed street credibility, a fanbase and potential – but one of the few acts that could genuinely shock audiences was W.A.S.P.. Their theatrics deliberately took each show over the edge: six-foot-four vocalist-bassist Blackie Lawless acted the mock torture of a woman bound to a rack onstage, threw raw meat into the audience, sported a chainsaw codpiece bearing the legend "Fuck Like A Beast", and all with his buttocks proudly on display. However, W.A.S.P. later adopted a tamer approach in an effort to achieve mainstream appeal before stepping up to ambitious, conceptual heavy metal with successively darker works.

Staten Island, New York, native Blackie Lawless (real name Steve Duren, born September 4th 1956) first trod the boards with East Coast outfits The Underside and Black Rabbit before a stint in The New York Dolls during their post-Johnny Thunders days. At this juncture, Lawless was operating under the pseudonym of Blackie Gooseman. Relocating to California, he passed through a series of Los Angeles acts. The band Killer Kane cut the single 'Mr. Cool' with 'Gooseman' on guitar alongside frontman Arthur Kane (the ex-New York Dolls bassist), guitarist Andy Jay and drummer Jimi Image (aka Jimmy Moore). Lawless and Image then

evolved the band into Sister, with guitarist Randy Shatz and bassist Joey Palemo. Shatz was superseded by 19-year-old Chris Holmes, previously with Glendale's Buster Savage. This union also fragmented, and Lawless located guitarist Randy Piper backstage at a Kiss concert at the Los Angeles Forum in September 1978. Hailing from San Antonio, Piper had played with the Michael White-fronted LA Fox.

Lawless, Piper, Palemo and Image branded themselves Circus Circus and, for shows on the Los Angeles club circuit in 1979 and 1980, put on over-the-top stage shows that included Lawless setting fire to his thigh boots. Palemo was forced out when he was allegedly shot in the back. Lawless briefly joined the band London alongside future Mötley Crüe bassist Nikki Sixx for a short period. London live shows at this time included Lawless songs 'Sweet Dreams', 'Mr. Cool' and 'Harley Heart'.

Ditching London, Lawless set about forming a new act, once again with Randy Piper. A succession of bassists and drummers came and went, this proto-W.A.S.P. at one stage even including future Great White drummer Gary Holland. Eventually, drummer Tony Richards, raised in Phoenix, Arizona, and ex-Dante Fox, stabilised the percussion position. The band then drafted in Brooklyn native Rik Fox (real surname Sulima-Suligowski) on bass guitar, and shortly after the band switched names to W.A.S.P.. Fox has since claimed that this infamous band name was his invention.

Just as Kiss had supposedly derived their name from an acronym of Knights In Satan's Service, W.A.S.P. were rumoured to have a hidden meaning to their name, helped by Lawless's publicity, which hinted that the name was taken from We Are Sexual Perverts. The rumour was reinforced by Kiss guitarist Ace Frehley's involvement as producer of the band's first set of demos.

The band set about gigging on the LA club scene, stoking up a fearsome reputation. Before long Fox left, joining Ron Keel's Steeler and then founding Sin before enjoying a brief tenure with Arizona's Surgical Steel. Don Costa, previously with Dante Fox, took over the bass position.

Piper also quit, finding employment at McDonald's, and W.A.S.P. pulled in guitarist Chris Holmes, allegedly fresh from a jail sentence. The guitarist's advert had been spotted in the porn mag *Hustler*. However, a backstage altercation between Costa and Holmes after a show in Orange County at Radio City resulted in the bassist's departure: he joined Damien and then Ozzy Osbourne for a fleeting, if eventful, tenure.

Blackie assumed bass duties and in September 1982 W.A.S.P. made a lasting impression at The Troubadour by flinging raw meat into the audience. For this gig W.A.S.P. doubled their guitar arsenal, inviting Piper back into the fold.

The band were quickly pulled into the Capitol Records fold and gained an extra boost by signing to the heavyweight management team of Sanctuary Music, responsible for Iron Maiden – only to have their controversial first single, the Mike Varney-produced 'Animal (Fuck Like A Beast)' refused a release. The track eventually emerged through the independent label Music For Nations in Britain. The press garnered by Capitol's squeamish reaction to their new signings' first product only served to accelerate the group's rise. Thankfully, W.A.S.P.'s outrageous anthem happened to be a fine song with a hooky chorus that swiftly entrenched itself in rock clubs.

The debut album, produced by Mike Varney, provided ample evidence that behind the hype, the band, and particularly Lawless, were accomplished songwriters. With much of LA rock already slipping into mediocrity, W.A.S.P.'s opening gambit took many critics by surprise – it was high in muscular metal content and boasted a collection of high-quality tracks such as 'L.O.V.E. Machine', 'I Wanna Be Somebody', 'The Flame' and the pseudo-ballad 'Sleeping (In The Fire)'. Intriguingly, the 'School Daze' single hosted a B-side cover of The Rolling Stones' 'Paint It Black'.

By now, the band were sporting sci-fi warrior stage garb, with Piper having to carry various pipework on his back. At frenzied shows in America, fans took audience participation to the limit, throwing animal offal and pigs' heads onstage. W.A.S.P. hit Britain in September 1984 supported by English glam-rockers Wrathchild. These concerts saw them flanked by two enormous smoke-spewing skulls.

With many local councils objecting to the band's infamous torture rack, the band's female companion often found herself without a job, but Lawless still capped each show by decorating himself in 'blood' poured from a skull. Duly making their mark in the UK, W.A.S.P. engaged in a solid six months of touring North America in support of the undisputed grand masters of theatrical rock'n'roll – Kiss. The tour saw the appearance of former Roadmaster and B'zz drummer Stephen Riley in place of the ousted Tony Richards. Riley had been a recent recruitment into Keel when the W.A.S.P. job came up.

Maintaining their presence on the circuit, the band collaborated with Metallica and Armored Saint for dates in early 1985. By the close of their world tour, they could look back on US album sales of over half a million copies. The record only peaked at Number 74 but remained on the album charts for a lengthy duration.

Blackie Lawless: "The cold fact is that I won't take no from anybody when it comes to this band. There is no room for compromise when it comes to performing this style of music. With the first record, I just took all of my influences and made them even more extreme. It was like: how far can I really take this thing? But, at the end of the day, it has to be about escapism and entertainment. Nobody dies, y'know? It's all about the experience, and W.A.S.P. is about making that show as vivid, confrontational, as loud and as nasty as it can be. It's about manipulating the senses. If you come to a gig you'll not only be shocked, you'll be covered in blood, meat and all kinds of shit and going home knowing you've just experienced something unique. Hopefully we'll have put a smile on your face too."

The Spencer Proffer-produced *The Last Command* caught the band progressing into more refined territory in an attempt to break them on radio. The material ranged from blatant commerciality to crotch-level cuts such as 'Ballcrusher', 'Jack Action' and 'Sex Drive'. Strangely, the track 'Running Wild In The Streets', although credited to Blackie Lawless, was in fact written by Canadian band Kick Axe. It had first been submitted to Black Sabbath by Proffer and rejected before being given a second chance by W.A.S.P.. During studio sessions the band would also tackle Mountain's seminal 'Mississippi Queen' but chose not to include it. *The Last Command,*

W.A.S.P.

gaining another gold award in the USA, charted worldwide. Extensive touring, including an opening slot for Krokus in America, was bolstered by two radio hits – 'Wild Child' and the debauched 'Blind In Texas'.

Randy Piper then departed, the guitarist seeking a liaison with Alice Cooper, which failed to materialise. Lawless took over rhythm guitar and ex-King Kobra bassist Johnny Rod joined the team. The resulting self-produced album, *Inside The Electric Circus*, included covers of Uriah Heep's 'Easy Livin'' and Humble Pie's 'I Don't Need No Doctor'. However, W.A.S.P. were struggling to maintain songwriting quality. The band then lent support to Black Sabbath's ill-fated tour of North America alongside Anthrax in March 1986.

Although *Inside The Electric Circus* hit the stores with cover photography depicting a caged and naked Lawless covered in strategically-placed tiger stripes, there was a distinct tempering of the outrageous elements of the music that fans had by now come to expect. A new stage show, more Barnum than blood'n'bondage, had many wondering whether the glory gory days of yore were over. Nevertheless, W.A.S.P. still pulled in the crowds for the obligatory world tour, with Germans Warlock supporting in Britain. The absence of Blackie's notorious codpiece was more than made up for by a new groin-attached gadget that shot pyrotechnics over the audience. Blackie Lawless's nether regions had a lucky escape once when this device malfunctioned and exploded.

Even though W.A.S.P. had toned down their act, their infamy increased due to the influence of outside forces. By now the PMRC (Parental Music Resource Center), a moral rights campaign led by senator's wife Tipper Gore, was hounding heavy metal for its supposedly anti-social influence. W.A.S.P. were singled out by the PMRC as their prime target and held up as corruptors of the nation's youth.

W.A.S.P. were featured as the main protagonists in Gore's book, *Raising PG Kids In An X Rated Society*, in which Lawless's lyrics were printed without permission, and worse, altered. The band won the day and gained priceless publicity with Lawless's successful lawsuit against the PMRC for abuse of copyright.

Blackie Lawless: "The whole PMRC thing was beautifully timed, I have to say. I think they expected a bunch of dumb rock'n'rollers to take it and then plead for forgiveness. What they forget is that artists are generally cultured people and will give it back. It was actually too easy to respond, because all they offered was dogma and ignorance. Well, OK, you can wave that little book of yours at me, but have you read it? Do you really understand it?

"My whole upbringing was steeped in organised religion. I have Jewish blood. My father was a supervisor at the Sunday school, his brother is a preacher, my grandfather before him was a church deacon. I got a good schooling. They took on the wrong guy."

They fared less well, however, with their support band for their early-1987 American tour: new bad boys Slayer harangued the headliners in the press at every opportunity. The LA thrashers maintained that it was they, and not Lawless's crew, who were selling the majority of the tickets – and furthermore that W.A.S.P. were finding it difficult to follow them.

Regardless, a live album, *Live... In The Raw*, culled from the band's last three shows in San Bernardino, San Diego and Long Beach Arena on the 'Welcome To The Electric Circus' tour, kept up the pace but once again omitted 'Animal', the staple work of W.A.S.P.'s live set.

However, a studio track, 'Scream Until You Like It', written by former Hero guitarist Neil Citron for the soundtrack to the movie *Ghoulies II*, was included and kept the band in the charts. The promotional video even utilised the fiendish mini-monsters from the movie to good effect. A six-week tour of America ensued, although the band were still finding that the PMRC's pressure on local authorities denied them access to many cities.

W.A.S.P. were thrown into further controversy over the cover artwork for their 1988 single, a live version of the stage favourite 'Animal', which depicted a dog about to molest a woman. Even Lawless poured scorn on it, denying any involvement: he devoted serious effort during this period to making his views on free speech well known with a series of lectures and seminars. This was the background for the band's latest album *The Headless Children*, generally acknowledged as one of their finest works to date.

Piper reappeared with an outfit called Animal in June 1988, with Rich Lewis on vocals, Shredder on guitar, Burn on bass and Steve Solon on drums. Steve Riley quit W.A.S.P. and joined LA Guns, making way for former Quiet Riot drummer Frankie Banali. W.A.S.P. then launched *The Headless Children*, which reputedly came in at over three times its allotted budget at a whopping half a million dollars. The album showcased Lawless's scathing views on censorship and politics, backed by the finest metal the band had crafted to date. Keyboard parts, strangely in keeping with the overall menace of the record, were added by former Uriah Heep and Blackfoot veteran Ken Hensley.

The Headless Children, produced by Lawless and mixed by Michael Wagener, was an important road marker for W.A.S.P., attracting new fans and deftly manoeuvring the band out of the cartoonish territory that they had previously occupied. Stark lyrical themes were employed, other than on 'Mean Man' (with its chorus of "mean muthafuckin' man"), an ode to the lifestyle of guitarist Chris Holmes. Only one cover was thrown in, a rousing version of The Who's 'The Real Me', although the band also cut Jethro Tull's 'Locomotive Breath', which would appear as a single B-side.

The resulting tour did well, complete with a stage set based on the skull of the album cover and real-life horror-video footage, but the burnt-out Holmes, who had recently married Lita Ford, quit in Europe, curtailing the planned string of dates. This defection came at a critical point for W.A.S.P., with the momentum generated by *The Headless Children* lost. Many fans who had seen Holmes's drunken appearance in the movie *Decline And Fall Of Western Civilization Part II: The Metal Years* had noted this bleak portrait of a man facing his self-made abyss.

Holmes then forged the shortlived Psycho-Squad. With W.A.S.P. effectively on hold from late 1989, Rod and Banali opted out to create a new act billed as Geronimo with ex-Keel, Icon and King Kobra guitarist David Michael Phillips and singer Thomas Adam Kelly.

Blackie Lawless: "That album brought in a whole new set of fans for us. Headless Children got the respect from all those people who were always kind of intrigued by the W.A.S.P. concept but never quite got the theatrics. That record proved we were not just blood, beer 'n' beaver. Although it was as heavy as hell, it also had 'The Real Me' on there too, which was really important to me because that right there is where W.A.S.P. came from, my childhood obsession with The Who.

"The record was a real grower. First of all it sold very strongly in places like Germany, Sweden and the UK, then it began to filter through over the months and years by word of mouth. Marketing can only take you so far. It's the fans telling their friends that make the real difference, and Headless Children achieved that for us. I think it's probably our bestselling album so far, because the damn thing just keeps on selling year on year."

Although W.A.S.P.'s leader was giving no clues to his next move, rumours suggested that Lawless was in line to play the evil robot T-1000 in the Arnold Schwarzenegger movie *Terminator 2: Judgment Day*. Apparently this idea was scotched by the film's star, who deemed Lawless too tall.

Lawless persevered, retiring from public view in order to construct his next musical project. Mammoth sessions at Blackie's own Fort Apache

studios commenced in July 1990 and only came to a close in February 1992. Now billed as Blackie Lawless And W.A.S.P., he drew in session musicians, including Ken Hensley once again and ex-Balance and Meat Loaf guitarist Bob Kulick, for a full-blown concept album – *The Crimson Idol*, centred on the rock star character of Jonathon Steele. Initial drum tracks were laid down by Banali but were re-recorded by one-time Impellitteri drummer Stet Howland.

Described as a rock opera by Lawless, the album succeeded in drawing back many fans who had grown disillusioned after Holmes's departure. *The Crimson Idol* was notable for its employment of assistant engineer Ross Robinson, soon to make his name as an instrumental figure in nu-metal. Unfortunately for Lawless, while he had been piecing together his magnum opus the rest of the rock world had been engulfed by grunge, severely diminishing the appreciation shown towards *The Crimson Idol*.

Rod made a return and the band – now Lawless, Howland and guitarist Dan McCabe – reverted to its regular name, simply W.A.S.P.. Ex-Driver and Impellitteri keyboard player Philip Wolfe was added for live work. Touring, including a return visit to the Donington 'Monsters Of Rock' festival, saw the W.A.S.P. figurehead alongside Rod, Howland and guitarist Doug Blair, the latter having supplanted McCabe.

Having borne the costs of two hugely expensive endeavours in *The Headless Children* and *The Crimson Idol* – both successful artistic achievements but not lucrative enough to satisfy the accountants – Capitol let the band go. W.A.S.P. signed to British imprint Raw Power Records and delivered the stripped-down, supremely dark *Still Not Black Enough* in 1995. These sessions found Lawless handling the bulk of the instrumentation, aided by Bob Kulick and Banali. However, with no real band, *Still Not Black Enough* didn't reap the benefit of live promotion.

Doubtless inspired by the success of Marilyn Manson and the rejuvenated Alice Cooper, Lawless rolled W.A.S.P. out once more during 1997 with an album – *Kill, Fuck, Die* – that outgrossed all its predecessors. By far Lawless's most disturbing catalogue of songs, *Kill, Fuck, Die* was utterly uncompromising: many fans believed that it was W.A.S.P.'s response to the commercial highs enjoyed by Manson. *Kill* appeared in digipack format, ingeniously constructed so as to open a fridge door displaying stacked body parts. Many territories refused to print the original image.

Blackie Lawless: "Chris Holmes is a large part of why Kill, Fuck, Die turned out so insanely disturbing. The man really is the personification of madness. The whole thing was borderline criminal before, so throwing Chris into the mix just tipped it over the edge into the truly dangerous. It's by far the darkest, most malevolent record W.A.S.P. has ever made and it's been a huge risk. It was actually quite difficult to put together because, if you're going to make something this brutal, it has to be really pure. I know musicians who are in some of the nastiest, meanest bands around and they've been shocked by the intensity of this record. Commercially, this is not what we should be doing, but our souls were screaming out for this, and so artistically it is exactly what W.A.S.P. should be doing right now."

A much-trumpeted reconciliation between Lawless and Holmes fired up press enthusiasm. Stet Howland and new bassist Mike Duda completed the line-up and W.A.S.P. geared up for live campaigning with three Californian gigs in late September 1996. These shows were the last to feature the band as a full live entity, as from this point onwards W.A.S.P. employed an arsenal of effects and samples in their concerts, much to the chagrin of fans and the displeasure of critics. In January 1997, *Kill, Fuck, Die* was promoted on European stages.

A US tour was announced but then pulled as the group returned to

W.A.S.P. discography

Animal (Fuck Like A Beast), Music For Nations MFN 12 KUT 109 (UK) (1984)

W.A.S.P., Capitol EJ 2401951 (1984) **51 UK, 74 USA**

THE LAST COMMAND, Capitol WASP 2 (1985) **48 UK, 49 USA**

INSIDE THE ELECTRIC CIRCUS, Capitol EST 2025 (1986) **53 UK, 50 USA**

LIVE... IN THE RAW, Capitol EST 2040 (1987) **23 UK, 77 USA**

THE HEADLESS CHILDREN, Capitol EST 2087 (1989) **8 UK, 48 USA**

THE CRIMSON IDOL, Capitol PCSD 118 (1992) **21 UK**

STILL NOT BLACK ENOUGH, Raw Power RAWCD 103 (1995) **52 UK**

KILL, FUCK, DIE, Raw Power RAWCD 114 (1997) **94 UK**

DOUBLE LIVE ASSASSINS, CMC International 06076 86237-2 (USA) (1998)

HELLDORADO, Apocalypse SMACD 818 (UK), CMC International 06076 86269-2 (USA) (1999) **111 UK**

THE STING, Snapper SMACD 836 (UK), Snapper Music 118362 (USA) (2000)

UNHOLY TERROR, Metal-Is MISCD 005 (UK), Metal-Is 06076 85204-2 (USA) (2001)

DYING FOR THE WORLD, Metal-Is MISCD 022 (UK), Metal-Is 06078 52322 (USA) (2002)

THE NEON GOD: PART ONE – THE RISE, Noise NO 3782 (Europe), Sanctuary 85240 (USA) (2004)

THE NEON GOD: PART 2 – THE DEMISE, Noise NO 3802 (Europe), Sanctuary 85242 (USA) (2004)

DOMINATOR, Steamhammer catalogue number tba (Europe / USA) (2007)

Europe for a second round of shows in April. Finally hitting North America, W.A.S.P. partnered with Motörhead for a co-headlining jaunt commencing in June. This tour was marred by a major and very public fall-out between the two running mates. Although the bands were co-headliners, W.A.S.P. closed the shows each night after Motörhead refused to perform on stages plastered with feathers and fake blood. The British band ultimately walked off the tour midway through the schedule. W.A.S.P. fared better in Japan that September. A new studio album, *Helldorado*, was released in 1999.

The 2000 *Best Of The Best* compilation included two new cuts, 'Unreal' and a cover of Elton John's 'Saturday Night's Alright For Fighting'. A further album that year – *The Sting*, a live record – was initially broadcast over the internet.

Duda and Howland then formed part of the band Killing Machine, along with ex-Loudness and Obsession vocalist Mike Vescera, for a self-titled 2000 album.

As W.A.S.P. released 2001's *Unholy Terror*, it was revealed that for a short period Holmes had been out of the band, replaced by Tuff and Alcoholica guitarist Darrell Roberts. The pair soon switched positions once more, as Holmes reconvened with W.A.S.P. and Roberts returned to Tuff. Confusion reigned, however, when Roberts pulled out of a projected Tuff gig at the last minute – apparently rejoining W.A.S.P..

American touring to promote *Unholy Terror*, with Roberts installed as guitarist, ensued on August 22nd at the Boynton Beach Orbit in Florida. Support for the two-month trek came from Mushroomhead and Dog Fashion Disco.

W.A.S.P., with a re-recruited Banali on drums, geared up for a new

studio album for June 2002, titled *Dying For The World*. The album theme was reportedly created by Lawless – re-invigorated with patriotism following the 9/11 terrorist attacks – after receiving letters from tank commanders in the Gulf who had gone into battle blaring 'Wild Child' and 'Animal (Fuck Like A Beast)' over their sound systems. Japanese variants on the JVC Victor label added three exclusive tracks – 'Stone Cold Killers, 'Rubberman' and an acoustic take of 'Hallowed Ground'.

Lawless announced before any touring that live promotion for *Dying For The World* would not be extensive, as W.A.S.P. were already engaged in formulating a brand-new concept album. Nevertheless, live dates in North America throughout October and November saw support from Alabama Thunderpussy, Engine and Stephen Pearcy. These projected dates hit difficulties when Alabama Thunderpussy and Stephen Pearcy withdrew, replaced by Dirt, and were cancelled entirely in late September.

W.A.S.P. drummer Stet Howland announced the formation of a side venture dubbed The Howlin' Dogs, joining forces with vocalist-bassist Bryce Barnes of Blackfoot and Edwin Dare, Engine Joe guitarist Joe Monroe, and guitarist Steve Lutke of Tobasco Kat. Randy Piper's Animal project came back into the limelight, not only with a record deal but also a brand new line-up, featuring two of the classic-era W.A.S.P. personnel – guitarist Chris Holmes and drummer Tony Richards.

Meanwhile, Mike Duda put in guest sessions on the 2003 solo album *Raise Your Fist To Metal* from erstwhile Metalium and Savatage guitarist Jack Frost.

Renewed signs of W.A.S.P. activity in 2004 came with the announcement of European headline gigs commencing on May 3rd in Dublin, Ireland, supported by British power metal band Dragonforce and Finns Dyecrest. *The Neon God: Part One – The Rise* album, recorded at Lawless's Fort Apache Studios and co-produced by Bill Metoyer, was scheduled for a two-part release. The studio men were Darrell Roberts on guitar, bassist Duda and drummer Banali. Banali was making a return after recently leaving Quiet Riot. It was subsequently learned that both Lawless and Roberts had contributed bass and drums – the guitarist cutting drum tracks for 'What I'll Never Find' and 'X.T.C. Riders' while the guitarist added his percussive skills to 'Red Room Of The Rising Sun'. Meanwhile, Stet Howland joined the New York-based Carnival Of Souls and also toured Florida clubs with The Howlin' Dogs.

Howland made a return to the ranks just prior to the European tour. All progressed smoothly until a scheduled gig at Helsinki's Tavastia club, which was called off due to Lawless suffering from an "allergic reaction". US dates saw support slots going to Belladonna and Omen. In a surreal piece of negative press, it was reported that W.A.S.P. had pulled out of a sold-out gig in Montreal on August 8th due to the stage not being strong enough to carry Lawless's 1,000-pound metal skeleton microphone stand.

W.A.S.P. then cancelled their gig at Barrymore's Music Hall in Ottawa two days later, apparently due to more concerns over staging. The band's woes increased the following day when a concert at Club Infinity in Buffalo was also pulled, with fans informed that Lawless was ill with food poisoning. The drama continued into the following day as the Mr. Smalls Theatre date in Pittsburgh was curtailed, with sources stating that the singer was suffering from pneumonia this time.

In October, Duda featured in ex-Ratt bassist Stephen Pearcy's band for the shooting of a promo video for the track 'Drive With Me'. Later the same month, Banali made it clear in interviews that, although he had been uncredited, it was his drumming that featured on *The Neon God – Part 2: The Demise*.

In W.A.S.P. downtime, December found Duda hooked up with Eric Griffin of Murderdolls, Johnny Kelly of Type O Negative and Mayuko Okai from Dizzy Reed's band for a batch of 'Happenin' Harry' Midwest shows. Meanwhile, in April 2005 Stet Howland joined forces with Temple Of Brutality, a high-profile project convened by former Megadeth bassist Dave Ellefson, guitarist Peter Scheithauer, and Todd Barnes of 13-A on vocals.

W.A.S.P. were back in action on the live front in the summer of 2005, headlining gigs in Mexico, Argentina and Brazil. US shows found the band headlining the eclectic 'Metal Blast' tour packaged with Wednesday 13, Stephen Pearcy and LA Guns. W.A.S.P. promised a return to a full, over-the-top stage show and a set made up of archive songs. In mid May the Wednesday 13 group withdrew from the tour, citing "business-related" issues. Metal Church duly filled the vacancy.

It was reported in December that Darrell Roberts was conducting sessions for a solo album, working with bassist Danny O'Brien and drummer Jeremy Spencer. That same month, leading Spanish death metal band Avulsed covered 'I Wanna Be Somebody' on their EP *Reanimations*. Longstanding W.A.S.P. drummer Stet Howland closed a 16-year tenure by vacating his position in February 2006. The band duly recruited drummer Patrik Johansson – of the Yngwie Malmsteen band and The SideFX – as replacement for another round of US dates to test out new material in February and March, but then pulled in Vicious Rumors drummer Larry Howe.

Confusion followed, as shortly afterward guitarist Darrell Roberts took his leave, subsequently joining Five Finger Death Punch, and subsequently Howe revealed he was not in fact taking up the W.A.S.P. offer. Finally, the new band shaped up by acquiring guitarist Mark Zavon (of JRZ System, 40 Cycle Hum, Stephen Pearcy's shortlived Nitronic, and Hair Of The Dog) and drummer Mike Dupke (Eric Sardinas band). However, within days Zavon had lost his position and former member Doug Blair was re-installed on guitar. US shows in May saw the resurrected Lizzy Borden as support.

A set of European shows were announced but the band withdrew, due to concerns over Blackie's health. A management statement subsequently revealed that the singer had been diagnosed with an abnormality in one of the arteries leading to his heart. Despite the fragile state of both Blackie's constitution and the band, fans are betting on more W.A.S.P. action in the near future.

GERMAN METAL

FOR DECADES

Germany has been an international anchor in the storm for heavy metal bands. While fads and fashions swept across the globe, Germany seemed for the most part to be immune and provided a valuable body of support for groups who, during the lean years, found it tough going at home.

Just what makes Germany such a welcoming host for the metal genre is not hard to see. Rich in epic history, full of pride, and with an uncanny talent for manufacturing large, dangerous things out of metal, the nation has always loved the heavier and darker end of the musical spectrum. Throughout the 1990s, US and UK acts openly scoffed at the country's unwillingness to change with the times, but this resilience, and a dogged refusal to ditch the mullet and moustache, came to serve the metal genre well. It is hard to imagine just where bands such as Motörhead, Saxon and especially Manowar would be today without the loyalty offered by Deutschland.

Homegrown heavy metal was ushered in by the mightiest of German acts, the Scorpions, who are still at the top of the pack. It is remarkable that no other band has come remotely close to their trademark sound. However, once the Scorpions had broken onto the international arena it would be many years before other bands followed suit. (See Chapter 1: Heavy Metal for full Scorpions entry.)

Accept's rise to popularity was a slow one, the group's progress from their 1971 inception only boiling over with the blistering *Breaker* in 1981. The importance of this album cannot be underestimated. Accept had paid their dues with some dodgy earlier offerings, but *Breaker* showed that a German band could riff it up to match the NWOBHM phenomenon. If *Breaker* had got things stirring, it was the follow-up, *Restless And Wild*, that jabbed a stick into the nest and let a million anger-fuelled metal wanna-bees into the population. Simply put, *Restless And Wild* is a monster of a metal album that ranks for many among the Top 5 of all time.

A key figure in the scenario was Karl Walterbach at Noise Records. Although bands today are swift in their condemnation of Walterbach's alleged fiscal machinations, the influence of the Noise stable was huge. The Berlin-based imprint spewed out metal like a venting volcano. Bands such as Helloween, Running Wild, Rage, Mania, Deathrow, Grave Digger, Kreator, Tankard and Warrant – not to mention the Swiss outfits Coroner and Celtic Frost – all got their start here.

What set German metal apart was a strict non-reliance on the blues. These bands had been raised on 1970s Krautrock and the NWOBHM. Those influences, combined with a national aptitude and fondness for heavy industry, meant that Teutonic metal was as cold and unforgiving as it could get. Once the first wave of metal had entrenched itself into the mindset of European youth, a whole crop of bands such as Assassin, Warlock, Protector, Stormwitch, Holy Moses, Living Death and Angel Dust burst forth. In the rest of the world, the words Chinchilla and Custard convey the concepts of cuteness and fluffiness: in Germany they are heavy metal bands. Uniquely, labels such as Nuclear Blast, Massacre, Century Media and Steamhammer not only backed established bands but were (and remain) always hungry for new metal. As a result, the country sheltered and fostered metal bands against the grunge explosion. Even when they were unwanted in the UK and America, bands always found dedicated, enthusiastic audiences in Germany. Strangely, German acts, while finding keen appreciation in the UK, achieved almost no significant results in the USA beyond the underground.

Grunge did affect Germany but not to the same degree as the rock powerbases across the sea, but Germany then delivered the counter punch to grunge with 'true metal'. This phrase was adopted by the country's dedicated die-hards, at first in honour of their NWOBHM heroes and early-1980s US metal counterparts, as well as an expression of contempt towards grunge and the hair bands, but subsequently as a label for an entirely fresh wave of acts. These bands, such as Majesty, Brainstorm, Paragon, Human Fortress and Sacred Steel, took their inspiration from Blind Guardian, Virgin Steele, Manilla Road and Manowar, and rapidly gained a groundswell of support.

Today, Germany is still as much a metal stronghold as it ever was. The touring circuit is one of the healthiest in the world and the national charts are regularly punctuated by the hardest of music. Annual festival institutions such as the world famous 'Wacken Open Air' plus 'Full Force', 'Rock Hard' and 'Summer Breeze' top a vast touring network that bolsters metal on a global level.

ACCEPT
THE RELUCTANT METAL PIONEERS

AFTER THE SCORPIONS, SOLINGEN-BASED Accept easily outstrip all other German metal contenders. The group issued a succession of groundbreaking albums of highly distinctive material, given a unique edge by the vocals of Wuppertal native Udo Dirkschneider. This pug-featured, skinhead-cropped dictator of decibels gave Accept an undeniable lead in the international arena courtesy of probably the most abrasive vocal style yet heard.

The band's premier outings, *Restless And Wild*, *Balls To The Wall* and *Metal Heart*, are universally regarded as metal must-haves. Unfortunately, the group's assault on the world market revealed internal tensions that ultimately pulled them apart.

Accept's inaugural line-up, established as far back as 1971, consisted of Dirkschneider, guitarists Michael Wagener and Jan Komet, and drummer Birke Hoe. They were first called Band X on their formation in 1968, becoming Accept some three years later. Subsequent additions were bassist Dieter Rubach and drummer Frank Friedrich. In 1975 Komet made his exit; he made a briefly impact in later years with Bad Steve.

Accept began to take on its familiar guise during 1976 with the acquisition of teenage axe-slinger Wolf Hoffmann (pulled from the Wuppertal-based Baal), second guitarist Gerhard Wahl and ex-Pythagoras bassist Peter Baltes. Wagener's part in the story was far from over, though, as he would establish himself as a renowned heavy metal producer, scoring credits with major international artists.

Accept's head-start into the mainstream came by way of a third-place result in a Düsseldorf band competition. The prize was a record deal, which duly generated the 1979 debut album, simply billed *Accept*. The band underwent a further period of flux but settled on second guitarist Jörg Fischer and drummer Stefan Kaufmann. Both Fischer and Kaufmann had previously played in Frenzy and Fathers Of Intention.

Accept's formative albums were released in 1979 and 1980 but both, confusingly, were self-titled and published in a range of different covers (the second was also issued as *I'm A Rebel*). They only hinted at the glories to come, delivering rock with an anthemic, near-pop slant quite unlike the aggressive brand of metal with which the band would become synonymous. It was with the third album, *Breaker*, that Accept found their groove: the album soon gained notoriety for the "you asshole" lyrics to the track 'Son Of A Bitch'. This song would be cut in two versions – one with lyrics for the fans, one with tamer wording to please the radio censors.

By the release of *Breaker*, Dirkschneider had developed his vocals into an unmistakable ear-piercing siren wail, complemented by the hoariest of smoker's coughs. This primal roar became known as the Accept trademark, backed by another supreme asset in the distinctive lead playing of Hoffmann.

With only a dedicated hardcore of import buyers to rely on, Accept famously self-financed a 1981 British support tour to Judas Priest. This trek, seeing Dirkschneider ludicrously sporting silver glitter pants, instantly won over the critics despite a complete lack of record company promotion – so lacking that in most venues the band was billed as Attack. The tour saw other problems, with personality clashes leading to the departure of Fischer on the tour's completion.

During this period of transition, Accept recorded what is widely acknowledged to be one of the most outrageously over-the-top heavy metal albums ever made. Blessed with crushing guitars, Dirkschneider's banshee wail and classical influences, the fourth album *Restless And Wild* established a style template for the rest of the band's career.

Restless And Wild gained widespread underground kudos thanks to the circulation of thousands of pre-release bootleg cassettes traded by fans

many months before the official launch. Upon the record's eventual release, Hoffman soon located a replacement for Fischer from a local band. The new candidate, Herman Frank, enrolled in time to participate in a world tour. *Restless And Wild* gained an official release in Britain through Wolverhampton's Heavy Metal label, sporting a brand new jacket.

Just as the world seemed at their feet, the band faced internal disagreements that began to jeopardise Dirkschneider's position. Accept covertly auditioned possible replacements, putting Steeler vocalist Karl Holthaus through his paces on the recommendation of producer Dieter Dierks and others. Fortunately, the band settled their differences with Dirkschneider without the media getting wind of this.

Accept soon suffered further tensions within the ranks. According to reports in 1983, Dirkschneider was fleetingly replaced by Englishman Mark Kelser. However, Dirkschneider swiftly rejoined the ranks as Accept split with their German label Brain and contracted to major imprint Epic. The resulting album, *Balls To The Wall*, while a significant commercial success, raised questions due to the bizarre lyrical content of such cuts as 'London Leatherboys'. This, combined with the gay overtones of the cover photo, attracted much attention for *Balls To The Wall*. Still, the rumour-mongering only served to fuel the rising status of Accept, and the band hit the world stage in a forceful manner, including North American tours with Mötley Crüe, Kiss and Ozzy Osbourne. The group also put in a highly creditable performance at the 1984 'Monsters Of Rock' festival at Donington Park in Britain.

With this bout of touring fulfilled, the band excised Herman Frank from the equation. The ousted guitarist pursued roles in Hazzard, Sinner, Victory and Moon'Doc. With the latter outfit, Frank issued one album prior to joining Echopark with ex-Zeno vocalist Michael Flechsig and former Eloy bassist Klaus-Peter Matziol. Accept soldiered on, re-enlisting Jörg Fischer.

Balls To The Wall's successor was *Metal Heart*, ably produced by long-time Scorpions mentor Dieter Dierks and continuing the trend of experimentation while still retaining the band's trademark, bludgeoning heaviness. Accept's penchant for delivering pounding raw metal enhanced by left-field tactics even saw an ambitious segueing of Tchaikovsky and Beethoven's 'Für Elise' into the title track. *Metal Heart* continued the upward trend in Accept's popularity, which spread to the Far East, resulting in their first tour of Japan. This was later commemorated with the release of a live mini-album, *Kaizoku-Ban* (translated as *Bootleg*), issued in 1985.

The band quickly released a brand new studio album, *Russian Roulette*, the same year. This entered the German national charts at Number 10, and Accept again undertook a mammoth world tour, including British dates with hot US outfit Dokken and a homeland tour with UFO as support. Always keen to provoke controversy, Accept's show routine for these dates saw the band members goose-stepping on stage for their encores. Dirkschneider in particular cut a unique figure, decked out in military fatigues with a sidearm truncheon.

To the dismay of the fans, as Accept's previous attempts at replacing their singer had not been made public, Dirkschneider announced his displeasure with Accept's recent commercial leanings and left the band to form U.D.O.. In a bizarre twist, U.D.O.'s debut album, *Animal House*, consisted entirely of Accept songs reportedly demoed but deemed too heavy for a proposed successor to *Russian Roulette*. The first U.D.O. album was a winner, notching up sales of 60,000 in Germany alone.

The remaining Accept personnel bowed to label pressure and – surprisingly – revealed their new frontman to be Englishman Rob Armitage, known for his work with melodic rock act Baby Tuckoo. As fans and press speculated on just how Armitage's much smoother vocal style could possibly fit within the confines of Accept's material, his departure was announced prior to any tracks being committed to tape. Jörg Fischer also exited, subsequently forging Billionaires Boys Club.

ACCEPT discography

ACCEPT, Brain 0060.188 (Europe) (1979)

I'M A REBEL, Brain 0060.389 (Europe) (1980) also issued as *Accept*

BREAKER, Brain 0060.390 (Europe), Passport PB-6010 (USA) (1981)

RESTLESS AND WILD, Brain 0060.513 (Europe), Portrait BFR 39213 (USA) (1982) **98 UK**

BALLS TO THE WALL, Portrait PRT 25791 (UK), Portrait BFR 39241 (USA) (1984) **74 USA**

METAL HEART, Portrait PRT 26358 (UK), Portrait BFR 39974 (USA) (1985) **50 UK, 94 USA**

Kaizoku-Ban, Portrait PRT 54916 (UK), Portrait 5R-40261 (USA) (1985) **91 UK**

RUSSIAN ROULETTE, Portrait PRT 26893 (UK), Portrait BFR 40354 (USA) (1986) **80 UK, 114 USA**

EAT THE HEAT, Epic 465229-2 (UK), Epic EK 44368 (USA) (1989) **139 USA**

STAYING A LIFE, BMG ND74720 (Europe), Epic EK 46944 (USA) (1990)

OBJECTION OVERRULED, RCA 74321 12466-2 (Europe) (1993)

DEATH ROW, RCA 74321 23016-2 (Europe), Pavement Music 72445-15006-2 (USA) (1994)

PREDATOR, RCA 74321 33570-2 (Europe) (1996)

ALL AREAS – WORLDWIDE, G.U.N. 74321 53645-2 (Europe) (1997)

THE FINAL CHAPTER, CMC International 06076 86232-2 (USA) (1998) US release of *All Areas – Worlwide* live album

Opting for a re-think, the band settled on Minneapolis native and ex-Dare Force frontman David Reece, releasing *Eat The Heat* in 1989. Another American, Jim Stacey, filled in the guitar parts. The record was a far cry from former glories. They toured the USA in alliance with W.A.S.P. but found that, without Dirkschneider, album sales had waned. The tour was a disaster, with Baltes and Reece coming to blows and Kaufmann, afflicted with a muscular disease, replaced on the road by Fifth Angel's Ken Mary. News then emerged that the deeply wounded Accept had called it a day.

Wolf Hoffman retired from music to practise photography; Peter Baltes re-surfaced working alongside former Europe guitarist John Norum and ex-Dokken frontman Don Dokken for the latter's solo project; and Stefan Kaufmann renewed his interest in production, including handling the board on two U.D.O. albums, *Mean Machine* and *Faceless World*. David Reece, meanwhile, put together the more commercial Bangalore Choir, which released only one album before the singer returned to action with the heavier Sircle Of Science.

The legend of Accept soon began to blight Dirkschneider's solo career as fans longed for a return to the classic Hoffman-Dirkschneider axis. In 1990, Kaufmann produced tapes of Accept's 1985 Japanese dates for a thundering live album, *Staying A Life*. Strong sales demonstrated the unflagging worldwide interest in the band – and in 1993 the various members succumbed to the pressure and re-formed.

The reunion album, February 1993's *Objection Overruled*, witnessed a return to straight-down-the-line metal. Accept's world tour to promote the release saw the band playing in such far-flung territories as North America, Japan, South America, Russia, Bulgaria and, naturally, Western Europe. The band was to have added ex-Vengeance guitarist Arjen Lucassen for live work but this liaison never actually transpired, despite press announcements.

Stefan Schwarzmann was newly installed on drums in 1994. Buoyed up by their triumphant return, the band chose to record another studio album, October 1994's *Death Row*, but it lost the momentum as fans deemed them to have softened their approach and bowed to grunge. *Death Row* was not even issued in the UK.

A 1996 album, *Predator*, recorded in New York, saw Accept back to their full metal glory. Drums on this album were handled by Damn Yankees' Michael Cartellone and, in a radical change, Peter Baltes took over lead vocals for a number of tracks, prompting rumours of further dissension with Dirkschneider.

In the wake of the 'Predator' tour, confusion reigned as to the band's status. Accept seemed to have been put on ice. Dirkschneider, never one to rest on his laurels, was quick to issue a further solo album, *Solid*, in 1997.

With Accept's profile at their highest since the glory days of the mid 1980s, Norwegian black metal band Dimmu Borgir paid homage with a rip-roaring version of 'Metal Heart' on their 1998 mini-album *Godless Savage Garden*.

The band's third live album was released in 1997 as they announced that they were still very much a going concern. Udo issued a further U.D.O. album, entitled *Holy*, on his new label Nuclear Blast, which preceded this with an epic Accept tribute album that included homages from Hammerfall, Axxis, Grave Digger, Sinner and Sodom among others. Notably, Hammerfall's track 'Head Over Heels' featured a vocal duet with Herr Dirkschneider himself.

In 2000, Schwarzmann would add another act to his list of bands by joining Voice. The overwhelming success of the debut tribute album prompted Nuclear Blast to issue a quick-fire second volume in 2001. With such acts as Therion, Rough Silk, Witchery, Raise Hell, Agent Steel and Darkane all paying homage, the album – strangely – saw U.D.O. covering 'X.T.C.', a track culled from the only Udo Dirkschneider-less Accept album, 1989's *Eat The Heat*.

Ongoing demand for Accept product would be met in July of 2002 with the *Metal Blast From The Past* DVD. The release compiled previously unreleased tracks and a rare Japan bonus track 'Rich And Famous' alongside demo takes of five *Breaker* album cuts. Video material included a live gig from Osaka, a documentary of the group's debut Japanese tour, and footage from Accept's show in Sofia, Bulgaria in 1983.

Despite some vitriolic words between band members, fan demand proved unrelenting, and Accept reunited again in October 2004, headlining the 2005 'Rock Hard' and 'Wacken Open Air' events. A rash of gigs across Russia in April preceded these events. The band line-up initially involved Dirkschneider, Hoffman, Frank, Baltes and U.D.O. drummer Francesco Jovino, the latter supplanted by Accept veteran Stefan Schwarzmann just prior to the gigs. Accept's live campaign reached further, adding dates at the Sölvesborg 'Sweden Rock' event, the Italian 'Gods Of Metal' show and Finland's 'Tuska' festival, plus Japanese shows in July.

The group then went its separate ways once more and again engaged in verbal spats, Hoffman claiming that Dirkschneider was resistant to furthering the Accept cause. The guitarist duly joined ex-Skid Row singer Sebastian Bach for a one-off performance at the Mid-Hudson Civic Center in Poughkeepsie, New York, on November 26th. Naturally, a version of Accept's 'Balls To The Wall' was included. It was revealed later that year that Hoffman, together with Michael Schenker and Uli Jon Roth, was in the frame to conduct a German G3 tour of Europe in 2006. Former Accept drummer Stefan Schwarzmann joined Swiss veterans Krokus in 2006.

Accept stand proud as Germany's hardest-hitting heavy metal band. Although Dirkschneider's U.D.O. output is industrious, it would seem that an unwavering desire by fans to witness Accept just one more time will continue to draw the opposing forces back together.

BLIND GUARDIAN
MIDDLE-EARTH METAL

BLIND GUARDIAN ARE RENOWNED for massively complex, intricate metal epics, with much of their material focused on fantasy themes. While they are an extremely powerful heavy metal band with massive success in their native Germany, Blind Guardian's reputation means little in English-speaking countries.

The seeds of the band were sown with European, a formative outfit led by guitarist André Olbrich. In turn, this act evolved into Zero Fault and then Lucifer's Heritage, with the introduction of erstwhile Executor rhythm guitarist Hansi Kürsch. The two musicians had met at Krefeld's commercial college in 1984 and assembled the new band with Thomen Stauch behind the drum kit and Marcus Dörk of Redeemer on second guitar. In 1984 they expanded to a quintet, performing one concert with lead singer Thomas Kelleners before swiftly reverting to a four-piece. In later years Kelleners would front Heavenward.

In this guise the quartet issued the demo *Symphonies Of Doom* in December 1985, but tensions over the financing of the demo sessions (eventually part funded by Olbrich's grandmother) led to Stauch's departure. He went to Redeemer, and Hans-Peter Frey was installed as the new drummer.

In 1986, Christof Theissen superseded Dörk. Critically, at this juncture Lucifer's Heritage began to explore J.R.R. Tolkien Middle Earth themes on their next batch of new songs, released as the *Battalions Of Fear* demo. The band attempted to locate a lead singer for a period, with Kürsch unconvinced of his own talents, but the search was fruitless and Kürsch resolved to persevere with the vocal duties. Theissen soon lost his place and Marcus Dörk rejoined, as did Thomen Stauch.

The self-managed group evolved into Blind Guardian after they had signed to No Remorse Records and the label expressed concerns about the occult flavour of the existing name. Blind Guardian was picked over several other contenders including Battery (in relation to Metallica) and Raging Waters. They debuted with the release of the *Battalions Of Fear* album in 1988. The opening track from that record, 'Majesty', remains a live favourite to this day.

Produced by Kalle Trapp at Karo Studios in Münster, *Battalions Of Fear* served the group well, selling 10,000 copies. They supported it on tour with Grinder. The sophomore album, *Follow The Blind*, also produced by Trapp, saw them experimenting with orchestral passages and a strange choice of a cover song, The Beach Boys' 'Barbara Ann'. More predictably, the record included a cover of Demon's 'Don't Break The Circle'. Kai Hansen, latterly of Gamma Ray, guested on vocals and guitar on the tracks 'Hall Of The King' and 'Valhalla'.

Follow The Blind not only improved the group's standing in their native Germany but also led to interest in Japan and enabled them to negotiate a deal in that country. Oddly, despite the success of the records, Blind Guardian's live appearances were rather sporadic. Instead, the band remained content at improving their musical prowess in the studio, evolving from a speed metal outfit to one that combined many different metallic styles and arrangements, with lyrics often inspired by the work of Stephen King or J.R.R. Tolkien.

Tales From The Twilight World in 1990 was the first album to highlight the improved standards, and it promptly sold over 30,000 copies in Germany. It also became a big hit in Japan. The album followed a familiar pattern, with Kalle Trapp manning the desk and another guest showing from Kai Hansen.

In 1991 the band finally toured again, this time with Iced Earth. They appeared at the 'Rock Hard' festival the same year. By this time Blind Guardian had plans to produce their own demo material, and they began

building their own studio. They also split from No Remorse and signed to major label Virgin.

The resulting record was 1992's *Somewhere Far Beyond*, once more featuring the work of Trapp and Hansen and a concept album that featured further experimentation, with bagpipes making a debut on a Blind Guardian record. The CD version featured covers of Queen's 'Spread Your Wings' and Satan's 'Trial By Fire'. The album sold 130,000 copies in its first year and enabled Blind Guardian to tour once more with Iced Earth and to put in a second showing at the 'Rock Hard' festival.

In 1993, Blind Guardian visited Japan for the first time, recording the *Tokyo Tale* live album while there. On their return to Germany the quartet set to work on a new album and, breaking with tradition, wound up working at Sweet Silence in Denmark with producer Flemming Rasmussen. *Imaginations From The Other Side* took a massive eight months to complete and saw Pretty Maids' Ronnie Atkins guesting on backing vocals. The album sold more than 220,000 copies worldwide and succeed in opening up markets in southern Europe, South Korea and Thailand.

At this point the group engaged Manowar manager Tom Miller to handle their affairs as they toured Germany in 1995, with Seattle's Nevermore opening, and travelled to Japan and Thailand, playing in

Blind Guardian

Bangkok to an audience of over 7,000. The band rounded off the year headlining the December 'Christmas Metal Meeting' over an eclectic billing of Saxon, Yngwie Malmsteen, Rage, Skyclad and Love/Hate.

The Forgotten Tales, more or less a best-of package, also contained such delights as covers of the 1950s chestnut 'Mr. Sandman', The Beach Boys' 'Surfin' USA', Uriah Heep's 'The Wizard' and Mike Oldfield's 'To France'. Other highlights included an orchestral version of 'Theatre Of Pain' and a live rendition of 'The Bard Song – In The Forest' on which the crowd provide the vocals. This latter track is said to have been included to illustrate the bond between Blind Guardian and their fans, who regularly recite songs by heart. Blind Guardian also honoured Judas Priest by including their version of 'Beyond The Realms Of Death' on Century Media's Priest tribute album *Legends Of Metal*.

The quartet headlined the 1996 'Bang Your Head' festival in southern Germany on a bill including Glenmore, Tokyo Blade and Savage before starting work on a new album. Kürsch also found time to guest on Argentinian band Nepal's *Manifiesto* album.

The 1998 album *Nightfall In Middle Earth* was a first, recorded on a massive 120-channel mixing board. Tolkien themes abounded, and for touring purposes the band drafted in former Sieges Even bassist Oliver Holzwarth.

An intended side project blossomed into a major undertaking when Kürsch allied himself with guitarist Jon Schaffer from American metal band Iced Earth in 1999, creating the hugely popular Demons & Wizards. The self-titled album, sounding not too dissimilar to Blind Guardian, scored the duo a Number 1 record in Greece. Holzwarth would accompany Kürsch and Schaffer on tour with Demons & Wizards.

On the Blind Guardian front, an impressive fan campaign was launched in order to persuade the makers of the epic *Lord Of The Rings* movie trilogy to use the band's music on the soundtrack. Although it was highly publicised, this campaign failed, much to the vocal displeasure of their fans.

Blind Guardian announced a return to action in December 2001 with the epic 14-minute single 'And There Was Silence'. The CD single, the first ever released on the Century Media label, also included the rare outtake 'Harvest of Sorrow' recorded during the *Nightfall In Middle Earth* sessions. The accompanying album, *A Night At The Opera*, would reap an impressive tally of European chart placings, going Top 5 in Germany and grabbing the Number 1 position in Greece for two weeks. The band were announced as headliners of the 2002 'Bloodstock' festival, Blind Guardian's debut UK appearance, and they put in their first North American show at the 'ProgPower USA' festival in Atlanta, Georgia, during November. Although South American dates were also organised, scheduled shows in Argentina were pulled due to the country's financial crisis.

The band's status in Europe was such that they ambitiously revealed plans for a full-blown 'Blind Guardian' festival in Coburg, Germany in mid 2003. A supporting cast numbering artists such as A.O.K., Brainstorm, Freedom Call, Grave Digger, Mago De Oz, Metalium, Rage, Stormhammer, Tankard and White Skull was quickly confirmed. The group performed completely different sets over two nights, made up of tracks requested from their fans through their website.

With regular drummer Thomen Stauch suffering from a tendon infection, Blind Guardian pulled in the services of Rhapsody drummer Alex Holzwarth for Brazilian dates. For North American shows in November, the band hooked up with US band Symphony X. With Stauch suffering a recurrence of tendonitis, Holzwarth was back behind the kit for the European leg of the world tour.

Blind Guardian readied a DVD, *Imaginations Through The Looking Glass*, for issue in June with material mainly recorded at the June 2003 'Blind Guardian' festival. That September, guitarist Marcus Siepen broke his leg badly in a skateboarding accident, although the injury luckily fell in a period of downtime for the band.

During early 2005, drummer Thomen Stauch announced the formation of side project Coldseed in collaboration with Soilwork frontman Björn Strid, guitarists Thorsten Praest and Gonzalo Alfageme López, and the Blind Guardian and Sieges Even bassist Oliver Holzwarth. In early April, Stauch officially revealed he had severed ties with Blind Guardian. Soon afterwards, the drummer teamed up with vocalist-guitarist Jens Carlsson and lead guitarist Emil Norberg – both of Persuader – in a new project entitled Savage Circus. Initial demos, with Piet Sielck of Iron Savior on bass, were cut at Powerhouse Studios in Hamburg during August. Savage Circus signed to Sielck's label Dockyard 1 and commenced album recordings in February 2005 at Karo Studios. *Dreamland Manor* was scheduled for September.

Blind Guardian signed to Nuclear Blast in early April and revealed their new drummer in July as Frederik Ehmke from Schattentanz and Pink Floyd covers band Interstellar Overdrive. September 2006 European tour dates, with Sweden's Astral Doors in support, were announced a year in advance.

Blind Guardian's February 2006 single 'Fly' included a cover rendition of Iron Butterfly's seminal 'In-A-Gadda-Da-Vida'. Sensationally, the single hit the Number 1 position in Japan. The group revealed an album working title of *A Twist In The Myth*. September European tour dates would see Sweden's Astral Doors as openers whilst a lengthy US tour throughout November and December saw Leaves' Eyes in support.

DESTRUCTION
TWENTY YEARS OF THRASH

FORMED IN LÖRRACH DURING 1983 under their original title of Knight Of Demon, this German speed metal band went on to win much acclaim and healthy album sales – but at a critical juncture they flinched from their chosen path of furious thrash. Although damaging, the aberration was made good and Destruction enjoy hallowed status on the German metal scene to this day. Headed up by vocalist-bassist Schmier (aka Marcel Schirmer) alongside guitarist Mike Sifringer and drummer Thomas 'Tommy Sandman' Senmann, the band made their recording debut with the *Speed Kills* 1983 demo set, capitalising on this quickly with the *Bestial Invasion Of Hell* demo. This session featured the track 'Mad Butcher', which ignited a tape-trading frenzy, putting the Destruction name at the forefront of underground German thrash. Destruction opened proceedings with 1984's *Sentence Of Death* EP, a promotional photograph for which depicted the trio collapsed on the ground – no doubt weighed down by bullet-belts. The band's debut full-length album, *Infernal Overkill*, was released in 1985.

The 1986 *Eternal Devastation* album was produced by Manfred Neurer for Steamhammer Records. After that, Senmann quit the music business to become a policeman, and for tour duties Destruction drafted in Chris Witchhunter of Sodom. The succeeding *Mad Butcher* EP, released in 1987, featured a notable cover version of The Plasmatics' 'The Damned'. This release was the first to be bolstered by additional second guitarist Harold Wilkens and new drummer Oliver Kaiser. The band reaped sizable European sales with the EP and opened for Motörhead on their 1987 European tour, these dates including their first British show at the Brixton Academy. They maintained the momentum with their first shows in North America, including dates opening for Slayer.

Release From Agony, masterfully produced by Kalle Trapp and viewed by many as the group's finest moment, enabled Destruction to break into the worldwide market in 1988. They returned to Britain again in 1989 supporting Celtic Frost and promoting their live album *Live Without Sense*, recorded at shows in Austria, Spain and Portugal.

In 1990, the band spectacularly fired Schmier, asserting that the frontman's studio performances were below par. Schmier began negotiations with a view to joining Swiss act Paganini but ended up forming a totally new outfit, Headhunter. Schmier's place was filled by former Poltergeist vocalist André Grieder, and the resulting album, *Cracked Brain*, provided fans with more of the same gut-wrenching fare, only let down by an appalling cover of The Knack's 'My Sharona'. The band proved unstable without Schmier, and in early 1991 Artillery vocalist Flemming Ronsdorf joined. His tenure lasted barely two weeks.

Destruction then entered a disturbing phase of their career, later dubbed as 'Neo-Destruction'. Contracting to the Brain Butcher label, they re-debuted with a self-titled 1994 EP, this effort signalling a radical departure from their thrash heritage. The band consisted of Sifringer, Kaiser and bassist Christian Engler alongside the Ephemera's Party duo of vocalist Thomas Rosenmerkel and guitarist Michael Piranio. *Them Not Me*, a 1995 six-track EP, and a 1998 album, *The Least Successful Human Cannonball*, followed suit. As Destruction's fanbase evaporated and sales slid downward, this version of the group dissolved, Rosenmerkel and Piranio duly re-creating Ephemera's Party.

Schmier and Siffringer finally resolved their differences in 1999 and Destruction put in some triumphant return performances at European festivals. The band, with new drummer Sven Vormann onboard, signed to Nuclear Blast for the 2000 Peter Tägtgren-produced *All Hell Breaks Loose*. As a bridge between Destruction's history and their renewed position, the classic 'Mad Butcher', a fan favourite, was answered with a new cut, 'The Butcher Strikes Back'.

Sales were buoyant and the album attained Number 67 on the national German album charts. A brief burst of warm-up shows led into European festival performances. The band then hit the road as part of the 'Nuclear Blast Festival' roadshow alongside labelmates Hypocrisy, Kataklysm, Crematory and Raise Hell. A partnership with Canadians Kataklysm was forged with dates in the USA, which saw Dying Fetus as openers.

During April 2001 the group again entered Abyss Studios with Peter Tägtgren to record the follow-up album, *The Antichrist*. It ran into a slew of production problems when finished copies were found to have the track order compiled incorrectly, covers printed in red instead of full colour, and mysterious sound drop-outs on the 'hidden' track 'Curse The Gods', a re-worked version of the song that appeared originally on the *Eternal Devastation* album. Naturally, these initial mispressings were snapped up by collectors. The album was also seized by Swiss customs officials, although it was later released.

Destruction parted ways with drummer Vormann during October, replacing him with Berliner Marc Reign, a scene veteran of Orth and Gunjah. Meanwhile, Vormann founded Jesus Chrysler Superskunk, linking

up with ex-Destruction singer Thomas Rosenmerkel and erstwhile Hate Squad man Michael Gerstlauer.

Destruction initiated a nostalgic thrash metal mammoth tour of Germany with compatriots Sodom and Kreator, commencing in late December 2001 in Ludwigsburg and running into the new year. The band's successful live alliance with Kreator was furthered when the pairing revealed tour plans for dates in Brazil, Chile, Peru, Colombia and Venezuela throughout August and September. The thrash union then hit North America with Cephalic Carnage and December in tow. Solidifying their comeback, the band cut a rendition of 'Whiplash' for a Nuclear Blast Metallica tribute collection. However, the ongoing tour was jeopardised when Schmier broke bones in his hand. Although he played for two weeks with his hand in a cast, this only exacerbated the damage.

DESTRUCTION discography

Sentence To Death, Steamhammer SH 0020 (Europe), Metal Blade 72021 (USA) (1984)

INFERNAL OVERKILL, Steamhammer SH 0029 (Europe), Metal Blade MBR 1048 (USA) (1985)

ETERNAL DEVASTATION, Steamhammer SH 0046 (Europe), Metal Blade 72161 (USA) (1986)

Mad Butcher, Steamhammer SH 0062 (Europe), Steamhammer SHE4001 blood red vinyl 12-inch EP (USA) (1987)

RELEASE FROM AGONY, Steamhammer SH 0076 (Europe), Profile PCD-1255 (USA) (1988)

LIVE WITHOUT SENSE, Noise CDNUK 126 (UK), Noise 4807-2-U (USA) (1989)

CRACKED BRAIN, Noise CDNUK 136 (UK), Noise 4823-2-U (USA) (1990)

Destruction, Brain Butcher Compact UAM 0447 (Europe) (1994)

Them Not Me, Brain Butcher Compact BBC 0714 (Europe) (1996)

THE LEAST SUCCESSFUL HUMAN CANNONBALL, Brain Butcher Compact BBC 0715 (Europe) (1998)

ALL HELL BREAKS LOOSE, Nuclear Blast NB 0494-9 (Europe), Nuclear Blast America 6494 (USA) (2000)

THE ANTICHRIST, Nuclear Blast NB 0632-2 (Europe), Nuclear Blast America 6632 (USA) (2001)

ALIVE DEVASTATION, Nuclear Blast NB 1248-2 (Europe), Nuclear Blast America 1248 (USA) (2003)

METAL DISCHARGE, Nuclear Blast NB 1170-2 (Europe), Nuclear Blast America 1170 (USA) (2003)

INVENTOR OF EVIL, AFM AFM 096-2 (Europe), Candlelight CD CDL 194 (USA) (2005)

THRASH ANTHEMS, AFM catalogue number tba (Europe), Candlelight CD CDL 327 (USA) (2007)

The band announced their debut Japanese shows for May 2003 at the Shibuya Club Quattro in Tokyo, revealing that a special live record, *Alive Devastation*, would be issued by King Records to mark the event. In a display of genuine altruism, the first 10,000 copies of the band's September 2003 studio album *Metal Discharge* came complete with a bonus CD compilation of up-and-coming thrash acts.

With the start of Gulf War II, Destruction weighed in with their own political statement – making their position clear by issuing a downloadable cover of The Exploited's 'Fuck The USA'. On the live front, the band were confirmed as co-headliners for the 'X-Mass Festivals' European tour commencing in London on December 7th 2003, heading up a strong billing of Deicide, Amon Amarth, Nile, Graveworm, Dew-Scented, Misery Index and Disbelief. The band's own heaviness curtailed the projected Antwerp show of this leg of dates when large pieces of concrete started to rain down from the ceiling during a soundcheck.

Destruction's recording campaign continued and Japanese versions of the September 2003 album *Metal Discharge* came complete with four extra demo cuts. European limited-editions added a bonus disc incorporating the aforementioned 'Fuck The USA' and covers of Iron Maiden's 'Killers' and Metallica's 'Whiplash' as well as a previously unreleased 1999 take of 'Bestial Invasion' and demo cuts of 'The Butcher Strikes Back', 'Nailed To The Cross' and 'Metal Discharge'. The band embarked upon the 'Live Discharge – Latino' tour of Brazil in April 2004. They were joined onstage at the Blackmore bar in São Paulo by Andreas Kisser of Sepultura for 'Curse Of The Gods' and a rendition of Metallica's 'Whiplash'. Unfortunately, a projected date in Costa Rica was shelved when band members became ill.

Further trouble ensued following a May gig in Brescia, Italy as drummer Marc Reign was arrested by security people at Milan airport. Apparently, the musician's chrome bullet-belt triggered officials' suspicion and the band were detained until they could convince the authorities that the ammunition was blank and merely for show.

That same year the band had their classic cut 'Curse The Gods' chosen as a pioneering piece of music for a compilation assembled by Darkthrone drummer Fenriz, released through Peaceville and entitled *Fenriz Presents The Best Of Old School Black Metal*.

In January 2005, Destruction switched labels to AFM, managed by Andy Allendörfer of Squealer. That February, the band entered the studio with Peter Tägtgren of Hypocrisy and Pain acting as producer. They cut a new album, *Inventor Of Evil*. Former Iron Maiden singer Paul DiAnno guested on the track 'The Alliance Of Hellhoundz'. The record hosted a slew of guest participations, including Doro Pesch, Biff Byford of Saxon, Shagrath of Dimmu Borgir, Björn 'Speed' Strid of Soilwork, Messiah Marcolin of Candlemass, Mark Osegueda of Death Angel and Peter 'Peavy' Wagner from Rage.

Retro heavy metal band Powergod cut a cover of 'Total Desaster' for inclusion on their *Long Live The Loud – That's Metal Lesson II* album, released through Massacre in July 2005. Schmier showed his appreciation by guesting in the studio on this version. The frontman also put in a showing on Italian act Elvenking's *The Winter Wake*.

European dates in November had the band sharing stages with Swedish doom veterans Candlemass and Finland's Deathchain. The first leg of dates was opened by Belgians After All, with the latter half supported by German act Perzonal War. Destruction scored a fortuitous placing on the 'Metal Crusaders' North American tour, set to take place in May and June 2006 alongside Kataklysm, Graveworm, Vader, Speed Kill Hate and The Absence, replacing Nuclear Assault who had withdrawn due to an "urgent immediate family situation". Back on their true path, Destruction seem intent on purveying Teutonic thrash for many years to come.

GAMMA RAY
KAI HANSEN'S HI-TECH HELLOWEEN OFFSHOOT

GAMMA RAY'S ORIGINS LAY IN THE surprising decision by guitarist Kai Hansen to split from Helloween during 1988, just as the German group had begun to reach the peak of their success with their *Keeper Of The Seven Keys* concept albums. Hansen, a Helloween founder member and the band's focal point as lead singer, at first cited disillusionment with constant road work as the primary reason for his departure, but would swiftly bounce back with Gamma Ray. He took with him a valuable core of fans who held the early Helloween works in high esteem. A popular figure on the German metal scene, the ever-cheerful Hansen is known for his altruistic enthusiasm in fostering up-and-coming bands.

The new Hamburg-based act included Tyran Pace vocalist Ralf Scheepers, bassist Uwe Wessels and drummer Mathias Burchardt in their initial line-up. Gamma Ray's January 1990 Noise International debut album, *Heading For Tomorrow*, scored immediate success. The original intention was for Gamma Ray's debut to mark a radical musical departure from his previous act, as evidenced by pre-release tapes, but the product ultimately arrived in a style that would not challenge his existing fanbase. The title track was actually a re-work of the theme song by Hansen's pre-Helloween outfit Second Hell.

In Japan, the record company was so concerned that Hansen's Helloween faithful might not recognise the new band name that they obscured the logo with a decal simply stating "Kai Hansen". Impressively, *Heading For Tomorrow* reached Number 2 in the Japanese charts and sold in excess of 180,000 copies throughout Europe in its first year. Gamma Ray had been given a valuable kick-start by the single 'Space Eater', a catchy number backed by a promotional video clip featuring Tammo Vollmers on drums. The band stabilised by pulling in Dirk Schlächter on bass and filling the drum position with ex-Holy Moses drummer Uli Kusch.

An EP to coincide with September touring witnessed a re-recorded 'Heaven Can Wait', now with Kusch manning the drums. Also included was a brand new song, 'Who Do You Think You Are?', alongside three outtakes taken from the *Heading For Tomorrow* sessions, 'Mister Outlaw', 'Sail On' and 'The Lonesome Stranger'. A further Japanese EP marked the start of a quirky tradition for Gamma Ray in the Far East with a singalong karaoke version of 'Heading For Tomorrow'. Demand for the group in Japan triggered a tour supported by fellow German metallers Risk, also generating a 1991 concert video. Despite this burst of activity, Hansen still found time to produce the *This Is The News* demo for Megace.

September 1991's follow-up, *Sigh No More*, produced by Victory's Tommy Newton, solidified the band's standing but alienated some fans with its strong anti-Gulf War sentiments. This period would signal the onset of membership problems. In mid 1992, after a second round of Japanese dates, Kusch and Wessel both quit. The drummer, following a 1993 stint with punk band Die Skeptiker, eventually wound up in Helloween.

By early 1993 Gamma Ray had regrouped, recruiting a fresh rhythm section of bassist Jan Rubach and drummer Thomas Nack. A third opus, *Insanity And Genius*, appeared in July and succeeded in re-establishing the Gamma Ray format of high-octane, melodic speed metal. The preceding limited-edition single, 'Future Madhouse', featured a seven minute B-side cover of a Birth Control track, aptly titled 'Gamma Ray'. The band then drew together the bands Rage, Conception and Helicon for a package tour dubbed 'Melodic Metal Strikes Back!'. Live activity continued with European supports to Manowar. That same year, Scheepers guested on the FBI mini-album *Hell On Wheels*.

Although Gamma Ray's career path was on a strong upward curve, Scheepers departed in an effort to accelerate his prospects by auditioning for Judas Priest. Although Gamma Ray was a success, the singer was still holding down a day job at an electronics company in Stuttgart. This left Hansen to handle lead vocal duties in addition to supplying guitar. Kai made his frontman debut on May 1995's *Land Of The Free* album, which featured guest vocal parts from Hansen's ex-Helloween colleague Michael Kiske as well as Hansi Kürsch from Blind Guardian. Scheepers did not succeed in his ambitions to front Judas Priest and turned up fronting a brand new act, Primal Fear, including Sinner mainman Mat Sinner, with more than a few similarities to Birmingham's finest. Meanwhile, Thomas Nack was operating a side project, oddly billed as Twork, in allegiance with former Kingdom Come guitarist Heiko Radke.

Promoting *Land Of The Free*, Gamma Ray played Germany in June 1995 on a touring festival billed the 'Summer Metal Meetings', including Iced Earth, Grave Digger, Glenmore, Running Wild and Rage. The aptly-titled *Alive '95* record appeared the following year, featuring another noteworthy cover version in 'Heavy Metal Mania', originally recorded by NWOBHM act Holocaust. The group later recorded further Judas Priest covers – 'Victim Of Changes' and a Ralf Scheepers-fronted version of 'Exciter' – for two Priest tribute albums. In the autumn of 1996, the band split with both Rubach and Nack. The ousted duo reformulated their pre-Gamma Ray band Anesthesia. Gamma Ray switched Dirk Schlächter from guitar to bass and in February 1997 recruited guitarist Henjo Richter and drummer Dan Zimmermann.

An EP, *Valley Of The Kings*, was released in May, boasting the Judas Priest cover version 'Victim Of Changes'. The band hit back in weightier style during August 1997 with a brand new studio album, the highly rated *Somewhere Out In Space*, boasting a far more complex brand of metal. In keeping with their established tradition of cover versions, the album boasted a rendition of Uriah Heep's 'Return To Fantasy'. The band had also added Henjo Richter on guitars and keyboards and enthusiastically set about touring.

German dates included a headlining appearance at *Heavy Oder Was?* magazine's 'Bang Your Head' festival in Tübingen in southern Germany, before the a bout of European touring with Hammerfall and Jag Panzer. They then headed over to Japan in October for a particularly lengthy tour – certainly by Japanese standards. These shows were promoted by a metal first: a full-blown collection of vocal-less tracks entitled *The Karaoke Album*. Competitions in the Japanese rock media allowed winning contestants to sing with the band, karaoke style, during soundchecks. Hansen occupied himself outside his main act by renewing ties with Piet Sielck from some of his earliest bands, Gentry and Second Hell, to forge Iron Savior, also enlisting Zimmermann. Before long the band was engaged in the familiar album and touring cycle. Subsequently, Zimmermann joined the ranks of Freedom Call. Coincidentally, Iron Savior later enrolled Thomas Nack into the fold for the *Interlude* album.

Gamma Ray's 1999 *Powerplant* album, another muscular release, was clad in elaborate cover artwork from Derek Riggs, renowned for his Iron Maiden album jackets. More surprising was a cover of 'It's A Sin' by The Pet Shop Boys; the record hit Number 25 on the German charts.

As a career staging post, Gamma Ray then released a best-of album, *Blast From The Past*, with a twist. They invited their fans to draw up a list of their favourite tracks, which the band then duly re-recorded for the occasion. Extracurricular activity found both Hansen and Richter donating their skills to Edguy man Tobias Sammet's mammoth Avantasia project album of 2000. Strengthening the Edguy connection, both Hansen and Schlächter would be on hand in the studio to mix Taraxacum's conceptual *Spirit Of Freedom* opus, conceived by Edguy's Tobias Exxel.

Gamma Ray returned to the fore in 2001 with a new album, *No World Order*, peaking at Number 23 in Germany – giving the band its highest chart placing to date. Hansen relinquished his post in Iron Savior earlier in the year due to conflicting schedules between the two bands. On

Gamma Ray dates in Mexico, Megace's Jörg Schrör filled in temporarily for an injured Dirk Schlächter. Japanese issues of the 'Heaven Or Hell' single featured an exclusive cover version of Thin Lizzy's 'Angel Of Death'. Headline dates in Germany during October, topping a billing featuring Sonata Arctica and Australians Vanishing Point, saw Helloween's Martin Großkopf assisting his erstwhile bandmate Hansen by filling in for the still out-of-commission Schlächter.

Spreading their wings, Gamma Ray then announced their first ever North American show, billed as special guests to countrymen Blind Guardian at the annual Atlanta 'ProgPower' festival. Recognising past achievements, Sanctuary Records would weigh in with a heavyweight reissue schedule of the first six albums, all of which were bolstered by extra tracks. 1990's debut *Heading For Tomorrow* added 'Mr. Outlaw', 'Lonesome Stranger' and 'Sail On'; sophomore effort *Sigh No More's* bonus tracks would be 'Heroes', a pre-production version of 'Dream Healer', and 'Who Do You Think You Are?'; and 1993's *Insanity And Genius* came with an extended take on 'Gamma Ray', a cover of Judas Priest's 'Exciter', and a live version of 'Save Us'. As for more recent outings, 1995's *Land Of The Free* boasted the inclusion of Holocaust's 'Heavy Metal Mania', a pre-production rendition of 'As Time Goes By', and 'The Silence'; the 1997 album *Somewhere Out In Space* added 'Return To Fantasy', 'Miracle', and another Judas Priest cover in 'Victim Of Changes'; and lastly, 1999's *Powerplant* offered bonuses of 'A While In Dreamland', 'Rich And Famous (2000 Version)', and Rainbow's 'Long Live Rock'n'Roll'.

Gamma Ray scheduled tour dates in June as support to Motörhead, as well as an appearance at the August Moscow 'Long Live Rock'n'Roll' festival before headline shows across Eastern Europe. August found the band at the 'Soyorock 2002' festival in Kyung Gi Do, Korea, the 'Bloodfest' UK festival and the 'Spodek Mystic' event in Katowice, Poland.

The band's headline European dates, commencing in October, were dubbed the 'Skeletons In The Closet' tour, with a set compiled entirely from fan requests. A live album of the same title, recorded at shows in Barcelona's Razzmatazz and Strasbourg's La Laiterie, then arrived in stores. The support act for these dates was Paragon.

Gamma Ray scored a valuable guest slot with Iron Maiden for European gigs in October 2003. Hansen guested on the 2004 album from high profile Brazilian prog-metal band Angra before Gamma Ray commenced work on a new album, *Majestic*. Completed in May 2005, it was the last recording made at Hamburg's Hansen Studios.

European touring in September and October saw support from countrymen Powerwolf and Swedes Nocturnal Rites: keyboards for these shows were handled by Eero Kaukomies of Finnish Gamma Ray tribute

---

GAMMA RAY discography

HEADING FOR TOMORROW, Noise CDNUK 151 (UK) (1990)

SIGH NO MORE, Noise N 0178-2 (Europe) (1991)

INSANITY AND GENIUS, Noise N 0203-2 (Europe), Futurist 9086-11034-2 (USA) (1993)

LAND OF THE FREE, Noise N 0227-2 (Europe / USA) (1995)

ALIVE '95, Noise N 0265-2 (Europe / (USA) (1996)

SOMEWHERE OUT IN SPACE, Noise N 0283-2 (Europe), F.A.D. N 0283-2UX (USA) (1997)

POWER PLANT, Noise N 0310-2 (Europe), F.A.D. N 0310-2 (USA) (1999)

NO WORLD ORDER!, Metal-Is MISCD012 (UK) (2001)

SKELETONS IN THE CLOSET, Metal-Is MISDL023 (UK), Metal-Is 73017 (USA) (2003)

MAJESTIC, Mayan MYNCD044 (UK), Sanctuary 34109 (USA) (2005)

band Guardians Of Mankind. Kai Hansen made it clear in interviews during this period that he would be keen to pursue a full-blown Helloween reunion, as it seemed fans' enthusiasm for such a venture was gathering pace.

During a run of South American gigs, Hansen celebrated Angra's 14th anniversary by appearing with them on stage in São Paulo. Bad luck then hit the band when guitarist Henjo Richter fell down a stairwell, badly injuring his arm, while performing on a Baltic Sea cruise boat concert between Stockholm and Helsinki in mid January 2006. The tour continued, with Kasperi Heikkinen, also of Guardians Of Mankind, acting as substitute.

With Gamma Ray's output a familiar sight in the national German charts, a rock-solid core of diehard fans, and the prospect of a Helloween reunion on the horizon, it seems that the band's run is far from over.

GRAVE DIGGER
THRASH STALWARTS

GRAVE DIGGER ARE TRUE SURVIVORS of the early-1980s German thrash metal boom. While the band were lumped in with the emerging thrash acts of the day, mainly for convenience's sake by the rock media (particularly in the UK), they were a more sophisticated musical act. Once the thrash phenomenon had abated, Grave Digger – after a disastrous wayward period of confusion, during which they were billed as Digger – reinvented themselves as an epic, conceptually-orientated heavy metal band, and they found renewed commercial fortunes in the process.

Grave Digger formed in November 1980 in Gladbeck, and their hard-hitting debut album, *Heavy Metal Breakdown*, sold more than 40,000 copies in Europe. The band had initially made their recording debut with two tracks on the *Rock From Hell* compilation album.

The original line-up of the band consisted of vocalist-guitarist Peter Masson, bassist Chris Boltendahl and drummer Lutz Schmelzer, a trio that remained stable until 1982 when Schmelzer was replaced by Philip Seibel.

The following year the decision was taken for Masson to concentrate on guitar and allow Boltendahl to take over the microphone.

The band split in mid 1983, with Boltendahl joining Challenger, which featured Willi Lackmann on bass and Albert Eckardt on the drums. However, Noise offered them a deal – at a time when Grave Digger did not technically exist – so the band regrouped with previous members Boltendahl on lead vocals and Masson on guitar, joined by Lackmann and Eckardt in the new-look outfit, and they recorded *Heavy Metal Breakdown*. Keyboards were played on the LP by Dietmar Dillhardt.

Alongside Lackmann, one Rene T. Bone (real name René Teichgräber) is credited for playing bass on Grave Digger's second album, 1985's *Witch Hunter*, but a new bassist, C.F. Brank, had joined the band by the time Noise released the record. Indeed, bass duties were actually undertaken by both Boltendahl and Masson on the record as they had fired Teichmann during recording in March 1985.

Their third album, *War Games*, appeared in 1986 and was something of a disappointment to all concerned in terms of sales. Upon completion of European dates with Celtic Frost and Helloween, this led to the departure of Masson from the ranks. Opting for a more commercial direction, and pulling in new guitarist Uwe Lulis, the outfit adopted the new name of Digger and recorded an album titled (rather misleadingly in hindsight) *Stronger Than Ever*. Fans were horrified by both the musical content and the band's new motif – a metal duck. Needless to say, the record flopped and the group split.

In the wake of the Digger debacle, Brank hooked up with S.A.D.O. while Lulis and Boltendahl opted to stay together and formed Hawaii with drummer Jochen Börner and bassist Rainer Bandzus, although this project never got beyond the demo stage.

In 1991, Boltendahl opted to reform Grave Digger, the new line-up also including Uwe Lulis, bassist Tomi Göttlich (an ex-Asgard and Iron Angel man), and drummer Peter Breitenbach. This group released a four-track promo CD in 1992 and then 1993's *The Reaper*. However, prior to cutting the album, Breitenbach was out – joining Warhead – in favour of the well-travelled Jörg Michael, ex-Avenger, Mekong Delta, Rage and Headhunter.

Grave Digger recorded the six-track EP *Symphony Of Death* before Michael joined Running Wild and new drummer Frank Ulrich – a veteran of Mendacious Messiah, X Wild, Living Death and Vanize – teamed up with the Gladbeck crew. Ulrich's tenure with the band was to be relatively brief. Although he played on 1995's *Heart Of Darkness*, he experienced personal differences with his band-mates and was succeeded by former Capricorn and Wallop drummer Stefan Arnold. Ulrich joined X Wild for their third album, *Savage Land*. Grave Digger then played on a touring festival billed the 'Summer Metal Meetings' in June 1995, alongside Iced Earth, Gamma Ray, Glenmore, Running Wild and Rage.

Grave Digger's return to form came courtesy of the ambitious *Tunes Of War*. A conceptual piece based on Scottish history, the record would be liberal in its use of that tried and trusted heavy metal instrument – the bagpipes. The band also invited the German rock media on a trip through the ancient battlefields of Scotland. They toured Germany in 1997 with support from Sinner, the record having enjoyed several weeks in the loftier regions of the German national charts.

Grave Digger stuck to the historical theme for 1998's *Knights Of The Cross*, an album based on the exploits of the Knights Templar and providing further momentum to their revival. Japanese variants of the album saw bonus tracks in covers of Black Sabbath's 'Children Of The Grave' and Rainbow's 'Kill The King'. Despite this welcome reversal of fortunes, the man behind the revival, Tomi Göttlich, decamped and was superseded by ex-Running Wild, X Wild and Crossroads musician Jens Becker. Touring found the band on the road in Europe with Iron Savior and American act Imagika. Both Boltendahl and Lulis would both guest on Imagika's *And So It Burns* album.

The band's tenth studio album, the mediaeval-themed *Excalibur*, released in 1999, would once again find them with a strong presence in the national album charts, giving the band their highest ever placing in Germany at Number 21. This time they took journalists by bus from Germany to Stonehenge and Tintagel Castle in England for the pre-launch listening party.

Grave Digger toured Germany in January 2000 supported by Italians White Skull. Lulis departed toward the end of the year and was swiftly replaced by Manni Schmidt, previously with Rage. A limited digipack run of the *Grave Digger* record would include an exclusive track, 'Black Cat', while the Japanese release, in keeping with tradition, held another bonus cut – a cover of Iron Maiden's 'Running Free'. The band would delve into cover territory once more in late 2001, cutting a version of Led Zeppelin's 'No Quarter'. This resurfaced on Locomotive Music's 2002 Zeppelin tribute album *The Metal Zeppelin – The Music Remains The Same*. The band's set at the annual 'Wacken Open Air' in Germany would see the light of day as the 2002 live album *Tunes Of Wacken*.

With support from Brainstorm, they toured Europe to kick off 2002. However, following January dates in Germany and shows in southern Europe the band's projected Belgian and Dutch gigs for March were cancelled when Schmidt was incapacitated with a virus he had caught on the Iberian continent.

In March 2002, ex-members Uwe Lulis and Tomi Göttlich returned to the fore with the adventurous Rebellion, which adopted Shakespeare's *Macbeth* as the theme for their first album, *Shakespeare's MacBeth – A Tragedy In Steel*. Warhead frontman Björn Eilen played second guitar alongside drummer Randy Black from Canadian thrashers Annihilator and vocalist Michael Seifert from Osnabrück acts Black Destiny and Xiron. A first for Grave Digger came in November with the band's first gig in Moscow at the 4,500-capacity Luzhniki Small Sport Hall, co-headlining with Blaze.

The band then plunged deep into ancient German folklore with their 2003 studio album *Rheingold*, basing their by-now-expected fable-set-to-metal style on Richard Wagner's *Nibelungen* saga. The band united with Symphorce and Wizard for European shows in January 2004.

Back in recording mode, the group entered Principal Studios in Münster in September to record *The Last Supper*, announcing February 2005 tour dates with Astral Doors and Stormhammer as support acts. Grave Digger's latest album came hot on the heels of a blockbuster movie, Mel Gibson's *The Passion Of The Christ*. Putting a new spin on an old convention, the retrospective three-CD box set *Das Hörbuch* included not only the expected career retrospective in song form but also spoken passages from Chris Boltendahl. With Grave Digger's reputation now firmly entrenched, fans can look forward to the group's next (no doubt conceptual) offering.

HELLOWEEN
PUMPKIN POWER

A HAMBURG POWER METAL BAND of respected status, Helloween quickly developed a large and loyal fanbase built upon a series of strong album releases that culminated in the twin *Keeper Of The Seven Keys* album project. Stylistically, Helloween have trodden a path from speed metal, diverting through an ill-fated change of tack with the injection of oddball humour, through to a career revival to deliver consistent melodic metal. However, in spite of two decades of maturity, Helloween still show their speed metal teeth on occasion.

Frontman Kai Hansen (formatively a member of school outfit Ancient Call), bassist Marcus Großkopf and drummer Ingo Schwichtenberg had been playing together since the late 1970s in a band billed as Gentry, later renamed Second Hell. This unit featured singer-guitarist Peter Sielck, Hansen, Großkopf and Schwichtenberg – the last two joined in 1980. During 1982, the group morphed into Iron Fist. Sielck took his leave the same year, effectively putting the band on ice, and during this period of

Grave Digger

inactivity Hansen received an offer to join Powerfool, featuring guitarist Michael Weikath. As things turned out, Hansen lured Michael to his own band.

The group came to prominence upon their signing to Noise Records and changed their name to Helloween before contributing two tracks, 'Oernst Of Life' and 'Metal Invaders', to the four-way split *Death Metal* album in collaboration with Hellhammer, Running Wild and Dark Avenger in 1984. Their debut 1985 mini-album, *Helloween*, and the first full length LP, *Walls Of Jericho*, issued that same December, garnered Helloween media attention and critical favour. The mid 1980s saw a massive resurgence of interest in German rock bands, and Helloween – with their quirky pumpkin mascot – quickly established themselves at the top of the heap with successive strong releases.

Following the release of the 1986 *Judas* EP, Helloween set about changing their musical direction, intending to add more scope to their music with the recruitment of Ill Prophecy frontman Michael Kiske, who took over main vocal duties from Hansen. It is worth noting that Helloween subsequently re-worked two Ill Prophecy era tracks for their own use, 'A Little Time' and 'You'll Always Walk Alone'. The band peaked with an elaborate brace of concept albums, forming the *Keeper Of The Seven Keys* saga. The song 'Ride The Sky' appeared on Under One Flag's *Speed Kills II* compilation LP in 1986; Helloween also had a remixed version of 'Murderer', taken fron the *Helloween* mini-album, included on the *Metal Attack Vol. 1* compilation, released in April 1985.

The first *Keeper* album, produced by Victory's Tommy Newton, was a useful vehicle for gaining popularity for the band outside Europe. It went on to sell over half a million copies worldwide, shifting over 125,000 units in Germany alone. Released in North America by RCA, it peaked at Number 102 in the *Billboard* charts. This modest success enabled the band to appear as part of the 'Hell On Wheels' US tour flanking Grim Reaper and Armored Saint. RCA did not foster favour with the band, though, when they released the 13-minute track 'Halloween' as a savagely-edited four-minute single.

US dates were followed by the quintet's first tour of Japan prior to recording the *Keeper Of The Seven Keys Part II*. In 1988, Helloween appeared at the Castle Donington 'Monsters Of Rock' festival and toured as support to that event's headline act, Iron Maiden, throughout Europe before their own German headlining shows. In 1989, they again toured across America, sharing a bill with Anthrax and Exodus. A live mini-album, *Live In The UK*, charted in Britain but provided ardent fans with two more good reasons to shell out for product as the record was issued in Japan as *Keepers Live*, with different artwork, and in America as *I Want Out – Live*, again with completely different artwork.

However, Helloween's driving force, guitarist Kai Hansen, was having trouble with stardom, and in particular touring, and he left to form the studio project Gamma Ray with former Tyran Pace vocalist Ralf Scheepers. (Scheepers had toured with Helloween in 1986, taking over vocal duties from Hansen, who was having problems with his voice. Scheepers was asked to join the band full-time after the tour but declined the offer.) Ironically, in certain territories Gamma Ray overtook Helloween in popularity. Helloween persevered and Hansen was replaced by ex-Rampage guitarist Roland Grapow. Another shift in personnel saw the induction of drummer Riad 'Ritchie' Abdel-Nabi in 1993 after Schwichtenberg was dismissed on a Japanese tour for drug abuse. Abdel-Nabi left in December 1993 after Helloween had finished touring.

The band signed to Iron Maiden's management, Sanctuary Music, and, convinced that signing to a major label would further their career, began efforts to extricate themselves from their Noise deal. They signed to EMI and promptly landed themselves in a lengthy legal wrangle with Noise, who claimed that they were still under contract. During this period of inactivity the press speculated that Kiske was to join Iron Maiden.

Following all the delays, Helloween committed apparent commercial suicide by releasing the ludicrously-titled *Pink Bubbles Go Ape* in 1991. Intended to show that the band had a sense of humour, the Chris Tsangarides-produced album (with song titles such as 'Heavy Metal Hamsters') only served to alienate a large section of their fanbase. Indeed, worse was to come when Noise placed an injunction on the album, effectively stopping its release and any live work in Germany.

In 1993, EMI released the band's new album, *Chameleon*, a record that was certainly not up to the standards of the past and found the group seriously lacking in direction. With their commercial fortunes taking a nosedive, it came as no surprise when Helloween lost their record deal.

The band returned in the summer of 1994, signed to the Rawpower imprint, an offshoot of Castle Communications. As well as signing to a new label, the band had used the period away from the spotlight for a drastic rethink of both music and personnel. Kiske departed and in came former Holy Moses, Gamma Ray and Die Skeptiker member Uli Kusch and Pink Cream 69's Andy Deris. While Kiske released a 1996 solo album, *Instant Clarity*, featuring Kai Hansen, fate was less kind to Schwichtenberg who, suffering from depression and fighting a drug problem, committed suicide in 1995.

A 1994 Helloween album, *Master Of The Rings*, ploughed a much more traditional path, harking back to their Noise days. The album charted strongly in their home country and reached Number 1 in Japan. But the group was forced to take a break in early 1995 when Deris suffered a throat infection, forestalling any live work. Still, they returned in 1996 with the single, 'The Time Of The Oath', which included covers of Jean Michel Jarre's 'Magnetic Fields' and Judas Priest's 'Electric Eye', and an album of the same name, which found Tommy Hansen once more behind the board. Touring with Bruce Dickinson and Skin, Helloween were also to release concert recordings as *High Live* during 1996.

Their upward momentum finally paid dividends in 1998 with the *Better Than Raw* album, which sounded heavier than ever. The record rapidly racked up Japanese sales of over a quarter of a million. Pushing

HELLOWEEN discography

Helloween, Noise N 0021 (Europe) (1985)

WALLS OF JERICHO, Noise N 0032 (Europe), Combat MX 8093 (USA) (1985)

KEEPER OF THE SEVEN KEYS – PART 1, Noise N 0061 (Europe), RCA 6399-2-R (USA) (1987)

KEEPER OF THE SEVEN KEYS – PART II, Noise CDNUK 117 (UK), RCA 8529-2-R (USA) (1988)

LIVE IN THE UK, Noise/EMI CDEMC 3558 (UK) (1989)

I WANT OUT – LIVE, RCA 9709-2-R (USA) (1989) US version of *Live In The UK* album

PINK BUBBLES GO APE, Noise/EMI EMC 3588 (UK) (1991)

CHAMELEON, Noise/EMI 7 89368 2 (UK) (1993)

MASTER OF THE RINGS, Rawpower RAW CSC 7150-2 (UK), Castle Communicationc CASTLE 101-2 (USA) (1994)

THE TIME OF THE OATH, Rawpower RAW CD109 (UK) (1996)

HIGH LIVE, Rawpower RAW DF116 (UK) (1996)

BETTER THAN RAW, Rawpower RAW CD125 (UK) (1998)

METAL JUKEBOX, Rawpower RAW CD143 (UK) (1999)

THE DARK RIDE, Nuclear Blast NB 480-2 (Europe), Nuclear Blast America 6480 (USA) (2000)

RABBIT DON'T COME EASY, Nuclear Blast NB 1043-2 (Europe), Nuclear Blast America 1043 (USA) (2003)

KEEPER OF THE SEVEN KEYS – THE LEGACY, Steamhammer SPV 99132 2CD (Europe) (2005)

the album on the live front, Helloween played selective European dates as guests to Iron Maiden.

Großkopf made space to execute a side endeavour, Shockmachine, during 1999, with vocalist Olly Lugosi, X-13 guitarist Rolly Feldman, Helloween drummer Uli Kusch and guitarist Roland Grapow, and Rough Silk keyboard player Ferdy Doernberg. Kusch too pursued a solo project, Catch The Rainbow, a conglomeration of German rockers dedicated to paying homage to Rainbow. An album, *Catch The Rainbow: A Tribute To Rainbow*, arrived in 1999 featuring the entire Helloween cast alongside Gamma Ray, Primal Fear and Brainstorm personnel as guests.

The band's next outing took them away from the expected format: *Metal Jukebox* provided fans with an insight into the band members' favourite songs as they re-worked an eclectic range of tracks. The album saw Helloween tackling the Scorpions' 'He's A Woman – She's A Man', Jethro Tull's 'Locomotive Breath', Cream's 'White Room' and even Abba's 'Lay All Your Love On Me'.

Helloween shifted labels to the ever-expanding Nuclear Blast for their next effort, *The Dark Ride*, issued in 2000. Although it charted well across Europe, the making of the album apparently put the band members under a strain that publicly surfaced with significant ramifications some time later. Issued in Europe and Japan in 2000, *The Dark Ride* had to wait a full two years for a North American release.

Großkopf contributed to Edguy mainman Tobias Sammet's ambitious *Avantasia* album in 2000; the same year saw the issue of a worthy Helloween tribute album, *The Keepers Of Jericho*. It benefited from cover artwork by Uwe Karczewski, the man responsible for the sleeve artwork on the classic Helloween albums *Walls Of Jericho* and *Keeper Of The Seven Keys*, and included many of the European metal scene's rising stars, featuring reworks by acts such as Metalium, Heaven's Gate, Sonata Arctica and Italian bands Rhapsody, Dark Moor, Luca Turilli and Labyrinth.

In August 2001, the band suffered a severe blow when guitarist Roland Grapow and drummer Uli Kusch quit. The pair soon forged a fresh project with Symphony X vocalist Russell Allen. News also leaked out that the duo had assembled a project with the strange title of Mr. Torture (later scrapped), cutting demos produced by ex-Sabbat guitarist Andy Sneap and confirming their intention to work with ex-Helloween vocalist Kiske. Later still the Grapow-Kusch venture was renamed Masterplan in collaboration with the erstwhile Yngwie Malmsteen vocalist Jørn Lande. Grapow found time during this period to session on Swedish act Locomotive Breath's *Heavy Machinery* album.

In mid September it was announced that British drummer Mark Cross had joined the fold. He had a cosmopolitan range of credits across the rock field with Greek acts Scraptown, Magna Carta and Spitfire, occult metal band Nightfall, and more recently Kingdom Come and Metalium.

Gamma Ray guitarist Henjo Richter was also in the running, although apparently his services were offered on a temporary basis. By July, media attention was focused on Freedom Call guitarist Sascha Gerstner as Grapow's successor, and his recruitment was confirmed that August.

Andi Deris donated his services to the German Rock Stars October 2001 song 'Wings Of Freedom' in honour of the September 11th World Trade Center victims. Großkopf assisted his erstwhile Helloween colleague Kai Hansen by filling in for an injured Dirk Schlächter of Gamma Ray for October German gigs. A lavish retrospective set, *Treasure Chest*, was released in March 2002 through Metal-Is, complete with a bonus disc of rarities.

The international success of a 2000 tribute album, *The Keepers Of Jericho*, spawned a further collection for 2002. *The Keepers Of Jericho Part II*, issued by the Spanish Arise label, consisted of respectful homages from artists such as Iron Savior, Powergod, Axenstar, Dragonlord, Highlord and Freternia among many others.

For the new Helloween album in late 2002, Motörhead drummer Mikkey Dee stepped in as Mark Cross was suffering from the Epstein-Barr virus. By February 2003, reports emerged that ex-Running Wild and Accept skinsman Stefan Schwarzmann had taken the position.

In disturbing echoes of the disastrous *Pink Bubbles* era, a press statement alleged that the forthcoming album was to be titled *Rabbit Don't Come Easy*. Fans breathed a collective sigh of relief when the record emerged as a fine melodic metal album: drum duties were divided, with Cross performing on two album tracks and Dee on the remainder. Schwarzmann had cut drums for projected B-side recordings of Accept's 'Fast As A Shark', Queen's 'Sheer Heart Attack' and the original composition 'Far Away'. Forced out of Helloween, Cross made a recovery and set to work in Greece with his act Valanos, subsequently joining US act Winter's Bane. Besides his Helloween activities, Schwarzmann made time to deliver a guest appearance on a solo project by Feuerengel frontman Boris Delic, entitled Der Bote.

Helloween scheduled South American shows through September with stops in Brazil, Chile, Argentina, Venezuela, Colombia and Mexico before uniting with Jag Panzer and Beyond The Embrace for a short burst of North American dates in October. European headline gigs, with fellow German veterans Rage as guests, took the band through until the close of November. Rage had earlier cut their *Soundchaser* album at vocalist Andi Deris's Tenerife studios, the singer guesting on the track 'Wake The Nightmares'.

Helloween toured North America in 2004: Japanese dates later that month saw British band Dragonforce as support act before a run of dates in Indonesia. The band's headline set at the August 'Wacken Open Air' festival in Germany included a long-overdue reunion with original frontman Kai Hansen for two songs, 'How Many Tears' and 'Future World'. The same month, Helloween announced that they had signed a new deal with SPV.

February 2005 saw them amicably parting ways with drummer Stefan Schwarzmann. The new man behind the drums was the Glenmore, Rawhead Rexx and Blaze-credited Dani Löble. Helloween then surprised many with their intention to revisit the former glories of the *Keeper* saga. The first product to emerge from the new recordings, billed *Keeper Of The Seven Keys – The Legacy*, was a single, 'Mrs. God', released in Japan in early June. A DVD, *Hellish Videos: The Complete Video Collection*, arrived through Sanctuary in August. The new album included Candice Night of Blackmore's Night guesting on the track 'Light The Universe'.

A mammoth world tour allied with Primal Fear commenced in the Czech Republic in November and took in Slovakia, Poland and Finland with support from The Storyteller. They then passed through Norway,

Sweden, Germany, Holland, Belgium, France and Spain, into December, before resuming in 2006 with shows across Germany, Austria, Rumania, Croatia, Bulgaria, Turkey, Greece, Italy, Switzerland and the UK. Helloween then hit South America, with concerts in Mexico, Costa Rica and Brazil, during March.

Kai Hansen made it clear in interviews during this period that he would be keen to pursue a full-blown Helloween reunion. However, Michael Kiske, while not objecting to festival dates, issued a staunch rejection. Helloween fans – used to Kiske's now traditional broadsides against heavy metal – still held out hope of a reunion.

KREATOR
THE FINEST NON-US THRASH BAND EVER?

THIS ESSEN-BASED TRIO FORMED in 1982 as Tormentor with a line-up of vocalist-drummer Ventor (aka Jürgen Reil), guitarist Mille Petrozza and bassist Rob Fioretti, with their roots in the school band Tyrant. Having switched names to Kreator, the German outfit went on to become much favoured by European thrash fans in the mid 1980s, setting themselves apart from the pack with a series of albums that added an original and deliberately crude strain to the standard thrash sound. As such, Kreator soon became a major force on the European mainland, and their cult appeal and reputation also reaped rewards in North America.

Debuting with the caustic Horst Müller-produced *Endless Pain*, cut over a ten-day session at Berlin's Musiclab Studios and released in October 1985, Kreator toured Europe and North America. Keen to augment their live sound, they spent time searching for a second guitarist: Michael Wulf from Sodom joined for a brief period in 1986, and Kreator, promoting the classic *Pleasure To Kill* released that April, were found sharing a bill with fellow Germans Rage and Destruction, after which guitarist Jörg Tritze was added to the line-up. Despite being firmly entrenched in thrash territory, *Pleasure To Kill* had an uncompromising ferocity, honed by Harris Johns at the board, and the record inspired legions of latter-day death metal bands. That August, the *Flag Of Hate* EP arrived, an interim product that kicked off with a re-recorded, speeded up version of the 'Flag Of Hate' track from *Endless Pain*, scoring the band high praise.

In October 1987, Kreator toured Britain with Virus and Celtic Frost, and then flew to North America as support to DRI: a promo video for 'Toxic Trace' gained the band valuable MTV exposure and ensured sales of the band's third album, *Terrible Certainty*, crafted at Hannover's Horus Studios with producer Roy Rowland. This album set the tone for the subsequent *Out Of The Dark... Into The Light* and *Extreme Aggression*. The latter was produced by leading thrash knob-twiddler Randy Burns at the Los Angeles Music Grinder Studios and featured a cover of Raven's 'Lambs To The Slaughter'. The album was boosted by MTV rotation of the video for 'Betrayer', giving Kreator their biggest-selling record to date.

Just prior to their 1989 American tour alongside Suicidal Tendencies, Tritze was ousted in favour of Sodom's Frank Blackfire (aka Frank Gosdzik). This line-up recorded 1990's *Coma Of Souls* in Los Angeles, once again with Burns at the helm. A rather bizarre incident occurred later the same year when Kreator pulled out of their London Electric Ballroom show, complaining that they would have to play with a decibel meter in attendance. However, no such problems prevented the group from completing a successful South American tour in 1992, performing in Chile, Brazil and Argentina. Kreator were now pushing the *Renewal* album, laid down at Morrisound Studios in Tampa with legendary death metal producer Tom Morris.

Having left Noise after a relationship of nearly ten years, Kreator signed to G.U.N. in late 1994, with the first fruits of the new deal coming

in the form of 1995's *Cause For Conflict*. The group introduced a new line-up of Petrozza, Blackfire bassist Christian Giesler and ex-Whiplash drummer Joe Cangelosi. By the end of the year both Blackfire and Cangelosi had departed: the band filled the gap with former Coroner guitarist Tommy Vetterli (aka Tommy T. Baron) and Jürgen Reil returning to the drum position. A bad case of inflamed tendons saw Vetterli taking a back seat for some shows, for which Rags, Jimsonweed and Waltari man Sami Yli-Sirniö deputised. With the band once again gaining momentum, Noise rushed out the *Scenarios Of Violence* collection of live material and remixed archive cuts to satisfy demand.

In addition to a brace of new records in 1996 and 1997, Kreator contributed a version of Judas Priest's 'Grinder' to Century Media's *Legends Of Metal Volume II* tribute album in 1996. Touring in Germany to push *Outcast* in the winter of 1997 saw them headlining a billing over Dimmu Borgir, Richthofen and Brazilian death metallers Krisiun. The album saw a radical departure as the group indulged in almost gothic ambience and applied the brakes to their usual hectic delivery. Instead, Kreator's music now brooded rather than bludgeoned. The change generated praise from the media but consternation from a large body of fans. Nevertheless, the band continued the experiment with 1999's *Endorama*. The collections *Voices Of Transgression – A 90s Retrospective* and *1985-1992 Past Life Trauma* appeared in 1999 and 2000.

The band's status was recognised when a tribute album to Kreator emerged in 2000, *Raise The Flag Of Hate*. Contributors included Pazuzu, Angel Corpse, Acheron, Mystifier and Black Witchery.

Vetterli was replaced by Yli-Sirniö for the recording of the 2001 album *Violent Revolution*, a revisiting of their speed-orientated glory years produced by former Sabbat guitarist and respected console-tweaker Andy Sneap.

Promoting the return-to-form album, which landed in the German charts at Number 38, Kreator toured Europe with Cannibal Corpse before forming part of a nostalgic thrash metal tour of Europe with compatriots Sodom and Destruction: this commenced on December 26th in Ludwigsburg and ran through into the new year.

with Napalm Death, Undying and A Perfect Murder for gigs in February. With two decades of metal behind the band, who are basking in a thrash renaissance, there seems to be no force on earth capable of hindering their relentless drive.

METALIUM
AS METALLIC AS THE NAME IMPLIES

METALIUM ARE A HIGHLY SUCCESSFUL project band initiated by former Velvet Viper and Viva bassist Lars Ratz. At first the group consisted of a fully international cast of players – Savatage guitarist Chris Caffrey, second guitarist Matthias Lange, and the Beau Nasty, Artension and Yngwie Malmsteen-credited drummer Mike Terrana. Metalium's debut 1999 album, *Millennium Metal – Chapter One*, produced by Ratz, made a major impact on the European scene, delivering flawless power metal. The whole album hung on a tale of a 'metal hero' – the Metalian. As bonus tracks, the band cut versions of Deep Purple's 'Smoke On The Water' and Accept's 'Burning', the latter included on a limited edition digipack. Recorded for Armageddon Products, the record's global reach was aided by licences with Massacre in Europe, Pavement for North America, Avalon Marquee in Japan and Hellion Records in South American territories.

The band toured as support to Primal Fear and Sinergy in Europe during 1999, but not before Terrana had opted out to commence a lengthy tenure with Rage. The band pulled in British-born Mark Cross, whose credits stretched across Greek acts such as Scraptown, Magna Carta and Spitfire, as well as occult metal band Nightfall. While in the employ of Metalium, Cross sessioned on Kingdom Come's *Too* album. Matthias Lange put in a guest appearance on the Shockmachine 1999 self-titled debut album, performing on the Japanese bonus-cut cover version of Ozzy Osbourne's 'Steal Away (The Night)'. Metalium made inroads into the DVD market with the issue of *Metalian Attack – Part One*. Both Cross and Lange also operate on the German club circuit with Judas Priest tribute band Electric Eye, an all-star collective including X-13 and Shockmachine guitarist Rolly Feldman, Paragon bass player Big M and X-13 singer Jörg Wesenberg.

Metalium's second offering, 2000's *State Of Triumph – Chapter Two*, was given extra texture by the orchestral arrangements of Paul Morris and furthered their cause with another solid display of riffage. Ratz's Zed Yago colleague Jutta Weinhold provided some colour on the vocal front. Another offbeat cover version saw the record closing with an interpretation of John Miles's 'Music'. Japanese editions included the customary extra song with a take on the Kansas classic, 'Dust In The Wind'. A version of the Scorpions 'Another Piece Of Meat' was included on a tribute package, and the group covered a somewhat unexpected track with their beefed-up 'Thank You For The Music' – donated to a Nuclear Blast Abba tribute compilation.

American guitarist Jack Frost, known for his work with Seven Witches and The Bronx Casket Company, was involved in these sessions. For live work, Metalium emulated their album-cover hero and stalked the stages of Europe in full metal-muscle body armour. The shows were also notable for Ratz's fire-breathing. Unfortunately, in August 2001 Cross decamped, joining Helloween. Frost also took his leave, hooking up with Savatage.

Metalium appointed Michael Ehre of Murder One as substitute for Cross on the third album, February 2002's *Hero-Nation – Chapter Three*. Guests included the soprano Carolin Fortenbacher plus keyboard players Don Airey (a veteran of Ozzy Osbourne, Rainbow and Whitesnake among many others) and erstwhile Uriah Heep man Ken Hensley. For this outing, which hosted a hidden track, 'Heart Of The Tiger', the band generated love interest for their Metalian character by introducing his partner Metaliana, portrayed by former Fairy Mirror singer Saeko Kitamae.

Petrozza shared lead vocals with ex-At The Gates singer Thomas Lindberg for 'Dirty Coloured Knife' on the 2003 self-titled album by Israeli metal act Nail Within. Also in the works for Petrozza was a guest appearance on the new album *Divine Blasphemies* from fellow German thrashers Desaster.

Kreator's successful live alliance with Destruction continued as the pair revealed plans for dates in Brazil, Chile, Peru, Colombia and Venezuela throughout August and September. That same month the band headed up a two-month trek across North America, their first visit since 1996. They then topped a bill for the 'Hell Comes To Your Town' tour of Destruction, Cephalic Carnage and December. A live album and DVD, *Live Kreation*, produced by Andy Sneap and mixed in 5.1 Surround Sound, was scheduled for early 2003.

Kreator's live programme intensified, with September North American dates dubbed 'The Art Of Noise 2'. This run of shows saw the band allied with Nile, Vader, Amon Amarth and Goatwhore. Retiring to Backstage Studios in Derbyshire, England in spring 2004, the group set about recording a new album, *Enemy Of God*, with Sneap retained as producer. Arch Enemy guitarist Michael Amott recorded a guest solo for the song 'Murder Fantasies'. Some unusual promotion included Petrozza appearing on German TV on November 19th – as a guest on the children's programme *KinderKanal*, explaining the complexities of thrash metal to an audience of pre-school kids.

The album, scheduled for a January 2005 release, saw a limited edition version with a bonus DVD containing a making-of documentary and video clips. Impressively, *Enemy Of God* entered the national German charts at Number 19. Live promotion found Kreator teaming up with Dark Tranquillity, Ektomorf and Hatesphere for the 'Enemy Of God' tour, commencing in February 2005. US shows in April had the band packaged with Vader and The Autumn Offering. Californian thrashers Death Angel were originally scheduled to participate but were replaced by Pro-Pain. A notable gig in early June saw Kreator carving out a slice of rock history as the first foreign metal band to perform in Morocco. The band played at Casablanca in front of an estimated crowd of 20,000.

Kreator were back on North American soil in early 2006, packaged

METALIUM discography

MILLENNIUM METAL – CHAPTER ONE, Massacre MASCD 0191 (Europe) (1999)

STATE OF TRIUMPH – CHAPTER TWO, Massacre MASCD 0243 (Europe) (2000)

HERO NATION – CHAPTER THREE, Massacre MASCD 0311 (Europe) (2002)

AS ONE – CHAPTER FOUR, Armageddon Products AP 002-0 (Europe) (2004)

DEMONS OF INSANITY – CHAPTER FIVE, Armageddon Music AMG 017-0 (Europe), Crash Music 61144 (USA) (2005)

NOTHING TO UNDO – CHAPTER SIX, Armageddon Music catalogue number tba (Europe), Crash Music 61193 (USA) (2007)

Live promotion throughout the summer saw headline shows with support from Edenbridge. September found the band performing at an all-star metal benefit festival in aid of victims of the Elbe flooding. Guests included Jutta Weinhold of Zed Yago and Ken Hensley with his distinctive Hammond organ sound. The band then journeyed to Brazil in October for a run of dates, again supported by Edenbridge.

The 2003 album *In League As One – Chapter Four* found Don Airey guesting again. To promote the record, the band united with Freedom Call and Dark Age for the European 'Wacken Road Show 2004', commencing in late April. September gigs in Europe saw the band partnered with Saxon and Mercyful Fate. In side activity, Michael Ehre, Henning Basse and Lars Ratz were heavily involved in the career of Japanese singer Saeko and her debut album *Above Heaven Below Heaven*.

Metalium's fifth opus, *Demons Of Insanity – Chapter Five*, again embellished with the keyboard touches of Don Airey, was recorded at Jumpower Studios in Mallorca and Tornado Studios in Hamburg. Japanese versions of the album added a cover version of the Loudness classic 'Rock'n'Roll Crazy Night', re-billed as 'Heavy Metal Crazy Night'. The band partnered with Dream Evil for a further round of Japanese shows in February 2005. September dates at the UK 'Bloodstock' festival and the Jahnhalle in Nordenham were filmed for a DVD release titled *Metalian Attack – Part Two*.

Matthias Lange joined Sinner in May 2006 for the album *Masks Of Sanity*. In June, the Metalium rhythm section of bassist Lars Ratz and drummer Michael Ehré announced the Apolon side project, an eclectic union with Dark Fortress guitarist V Santura and Dutchman Joost van den Broek of After Forever on keyboards. Despite these diversions, chapter six in the Metalium power metal saga is almost certainly on the cards.

PRIMAL FEAR
THE EAGLE HAS LANDED

PRIMAL FEAR HAVE QUICKLY RISEN to become one of Germany's leading metal outfits with considerable sales and a loyal fanbase. The band was conceived by Mat Sinner, the leading force behind his own popular act Sinner. Fronted by ex-Gamma Ray vocalist Ralf Scheepers, they have made a significant impact on the global metal market, delivering a series of albums blessed with characteristically muscular riffs.

Before the formation of Primal Fear, Mat Sinner had carved a reputation with a consistent string of Sinner albums dating back to the mid 1980s, as well as scoring with a solo album and building a reputation as an in-demand producer. He had signed the Primal Fear project to the Japanese JVC Victor label before negotiating a deal with Nuclear Blast in

Germany. Meanwhile, Ralf Scheepers, who had quit Gamma Ray and come close to landing the job as vocalist for Judas Priest, was gigging with a covers band titled Just Priest. Mat Sinner already had a contract secured with Japanese label JVC, and Primal Fear was officially born when he pulled in Scheepers and Sinner colleague Tom Naumann for recording.

The debut 1998 album *Primal Fear* included drums from Prolopower's Klaus Sperling. Scheeper's former Gamma Ray guitar partner Kai Hansen also contributed to three tracks. With Germany's late-1990s appetite for traditional Metal and Scheepers' standing in the metal community, it was no great surprise that the debut album charted in its homeland. Although it featured a version of Deep Purple's 'Speed King', the album was heavily rooted in traditional heavy metal territory – a little too closely to Judas Priest for many fans. The band's use of a metal eagle trademark, just like *Screaming For Vengeance*, served only to entrench this impression.

In April 1998, Primal Fear toured Europe with Running Wild. The band also put in numerous festival appearances, including the Dutch 'Dynamo', where they hit the stage at three o'clock in the morning.

The second album, *Jaws Of Death*, again sported a metal eagle and was released in 1999, with a cover of Rainbow's 'Kill The King'. The band cut a take on Accept's 'Breaker' for a Nuclear Blast Accept tribute album. They toured Germany in 1999 supported by Metalium and Sinerg and extended their reach into ten European countries, as well as playing gigs in Brazil and double-headliners in Japan with Sinner.

Supporting the third album, *Nuclear Fire*, the band toured Germany in February 2001 – now with Scheepers sporting a shaved head, like Rob Halford – with support from Children Of Bodom and Sacred Steel. In Europe they gigged across a total of 12 nations. The album, another eagle-clad affair, gave the band further chart success, reaching Number 37 in the German national charts. Another showing at 'Wacken' ensued and the band put in their debut showing on British soil with an appearance at the Derby 'Bloodstock' festival. Two US festival appearances, marking their North American debut, figured on the band's itinerary.

Primal Fear then donated a rendition of Gary Moore's 'Out In The Fields' to the Phil Lynott tribute album *The Spirit Of The Black Rose*. In September, they issued a new single compiling their version of 'Out In The Fields', Accept's 'Breaker' and Rainbow's 'Kill The King'. Scheepers and Sinner donated their services to the German Rock Stars October 2001 song 'Wings Of Freedom' in honour of the September 11th World Trade Center victims. Meanwhile, drummer Klaus Sperling played with death metal band My Darkest Hate on their *Massive Brutality* album. This side act also numbered Azmodan vocalist René Pfeiffer and Sacred Steel personnel Jörg M. Knittel and Oliver Großhans.

Halford guitarist Mike Chlasciak contributed guitar solos to 'Controlled' and 'Fear' on 2002's *Black Sun*, a record that gave Primal Fear their fourth consecutive German chart entry, landing at Number 55. An extensive live schedule was announced, commencing with Russian shows in August before a lengthy European trek and South American action in Colombia, Mexico and Brazil. An extensive run of European dates saw the band paired with Rage.

Mat Sinner added guest vocals to US guitarist Rick Renstrom's solo album *Until The Bitter End*, featuring on the track 'Calling On Vengeance'. Primal Fear had their version of 'The Rover' included on the Locomotive Music Led Zeppelin tribute album *The Metal Zeppelin – The Music Remains The Same* and recorded 'Seek And Destroy' for a Nuclear Blast Metallica collection. During November, guitarist Henny Wolter bowed out for personal reasons. The band rapidly re-inducted original guitarist Tom Naumann in his stead. In early 2003, Naumann contributed a guest solo to the Rob Rock album *Eyes Of Eternity*.

The band then teamed up with Halford, Testament, Pain Museum, Carnal Forge, Amon Amarth and Immortal for the 'Metal Gods' 2003 North

American tour package in April, but these dates collapsed spectacularly. Annihilator and Rebellion drummer Randy Black took the place of Sperling for these gigs. In August it was revealed that Black had become a permanent member.

The band originally leaked a working title of *In Metal* for their next studio album but by September had switched this to *Devil's Ground*. A cover version of Black Sabbath's 'Die Young' appeared on both the limited European digipak version and the Japanese version. European shows were projected for March 2004 to coincide with an album launch, partnered with Brainstorm and Rob Rock's Rage Of Creation. Successive mainland gigs had the group proposed for a union with Iced Earth and Finns Thunderstone, but when the headliner act pulled out due to an injury to Jon Schaffer's back, Primal Fear endeavoured to plug some of the dates on their own. As it transpired, they leapt into the headlining position for the European 'Wacken Roadshow' tour above Freedom Call, Metalium and Dark Age. A second promo video was shot in April, for 'The Healer',

filmed in the Netherlands with director Maurice Swinkels. Gigs in June saw the band traversing Brazil, Argentina and Mexico.

Guitarist Naumann donated a guitar solo for the track 'Impaler' on the Paragon album *Revenge* in October, and in December it was revealed that songwriting sessions for a new Primal Fear album included collaborations with Ronny Milianowicz of Dionysus and Sinergy.

A benefit appearance with myriad Primal Fear connections saw the band performing at the March 4th 2005 'Rock For One World' event in Esslingen alongside Sinner's recently resurrected Shiva. Also included were: My Darkest Hate, featuring Sperling; Runamok, including Stormwitch and ex-Tyran Pace members; Bastards, a Motörhead cover band with Sperling and Chinchilla members; Who Knows, with former Tyran Pace members; and Kaminari.

Drummer Randy Black, retaining his Primal Fear ties, joined Skew Siskin in April. Primal Fear's *Seven Seals* album emerged in October, promoted by a series of dates in partnership with Helloween, commencing in the Czech Republic in November and taking in ten European countries before resuming in 2006 with shows across Germany, Austria, Rumania, Croatia, Bulgaria, Turkey, Greece, Italy, Switzerland and the UK. Sinner and Scheepers found time in November 2005 to appear live with Renato Tribuzy at two gigs at Sao Paulo's Credicard Hall in an all-star band alongside Bruce Dickinson, Roland Grapow, Angra's Kiko Loureiro and Roy Z.

The group entered 2006 by closing their longstanding business relationship with Nuclear Blast Records, bowing out with the compilation *Metal Is Forever*. Unexpectedly, Primal Fear signed to the Italian label Frontiers, better known until then for their work in the AOR field.

PRIMAL FEAR discography

PRIMAL FEAR, Nuclear Blast NB 302-2 (Europe), Nuclear Blast America 6302 (USA) (1998)

JAWS OF DEATH, Nuclear Blast NB 391-2 (Europe), Nuclear Blast America 6391 (USA) (1999)

NUCLEAR FIRE, Nuclear Blast NB 557-2 (Europe), Nuclear Blast America 6557 (USA) (2001)

BLACK SUN, Nuclear Blast NB 500-2 (Europe), Nuclear Blast America 6500 (USA) (2002)

DEVIL'S GROUND, Nuclear Blast NB 1225-2 (Europe), Nuclear Blast America 1225 (USA)(2004)

SEVEN SEALS, Nuclear Blast NB 1495-2 (Europe), Nuclear Blast America 1495 (USA) (2005)

METAL IS FOREVER – THE VERY BEST OF PRIMAL FEAR, Nuclear Blast NB 1739-2 (Europe), Nuclear Blast America 1739 (USA) (2006)

RAGE
TRUE BALLS-TO-THE-WALL METAL

RAGE ARE A STOIC, INDUSTRIOUS and enduring force on the German heavy metal landscape. Like so many other bands of their type, they first shot to attention with the mid-1980s thrash boom but adopted sleeker, pure metal leanings into the '90s and enjoyed a deserved renaissance with

a series of heavily orchestrated albums. Despite having been afflicted by a succession of membership trials, Rage have operated as a stable trio for many years.

They were formed with a line-up of Peter Wagner (aka 'Peavey'), the creative mentor and nowadays the only remaining original member, plus guitarists Jochen Schröder and Thomas Grüning, and drummer Jörg Michael. Peavey had chosen heavy metal over and above his apprenticed career path as a pathology assistant. The band were originally known as Avenger, based in Herne and releasing the *Prayers Of Steel* album and *Depraved To Black* EP on Wishbone Records before adopting the Rage name in 1986, following confusion with the English band Avenger.

Signing to Noise to release 1986's *Reign Of Fear*, crafted at Horus Sound Studios in Hannover with producer Ralf Hubert, Rage toured Germany on a bill with thrash brethren Kreator and Destruction in 1986. Shortly after the tour, Grüning left and his position was filled by the high-profile figure of ex-Warlock guitarist Rudy Graf for the quick-fire 1987 follow-up, the self-produced *Execution Guaranteed*. Michael also operated in the 'anonymous' avant-garde side project Mekong Delta during 1987.

That same year, both Graf and Michael were out, superseded by guitarist Manni Schmidt and drummer Chris Efthimiadis. Michael would become the permanent drummer for German guitar hero Axel Rudi Pell and rack up impressive credits with fellow Teutonic metal bands Headhunter, Grave Digger, Glenmore and Running Wild. The 1988 *Perfect Man* album enjoyed considerable critical success with the media and went on to sell over 30,000 copies in Europe alone. Part of this success was due to the inclusion of the anthemic bass-drum driven 'Don't Fear the Winter'. *Perfect Man*'s cover artwork debuted the razor-toothed robot character that would become synonymous with successive Rage releases. The band

then utilised producer Armin Sabol and the Skytrak Studios in Berlin to cut the *Secrets In A Weird World* album in spring 1989, and the following year they toured Germany with Running Wild.

They released *Reflections Of A Shadow* in 1991, embellished with the keyboards of Ulli Köllner, and the stopgap EP *Extended Power*. The 1992 album *Trapped!* featured a cover of the Accept classic 'Fast As A Shark', while Japanese issues added two bonus cuts, 'Innocent Guilty' and 'Marching Heroes – The Wooden Cross'. *Trapped!* marked a number of important changes for the band. It was recorded at two locations – Narhavaci Studios in Prague and Powerplay Studios, Berlin. The tracks benefited from a mix by renowned producer Tom Morris and extra textures provided by the Collegium Concertante Sextet of the Smetana Orchestra. The group toured Japan before joining Saxon and Motörhead in Europe on the 'Eagles And Bombers' tour.

Backed by a further EP, the Sven Conquest-produced *Beyond The Wall*, Rage undertook further touring in 1993 on a bill alongside Gamma Ray and Norwegians Conception as they geared up to unleash the album of their career, *The Missing Link*. In 1994 guitarist Schmidt left the band. His position was filled by Spiros Efthimiadis and ex-Pyracanda man Sven Fischer, and the ensuing collection, *Ten Years In Rage*, hosted new cuts alongside old favourites.

Rage split from Noise in 1994 in the wake of many of their contemporaries and contracted with G.U.N., an arm of major label BMG. After their debut for G.U.N., *Black In Mind* – produced by Ulli Pösselt at RA.SH. Studios in Gelsenkirchen, Rage played a series of 'Summer Metal Meetings' with Running Wild, Grave Digger, Gamma Ray, Glenmore and Iced Earth. The year ended on a high as the band joined the December 'Blind Guardian Christmas Party' tour, headed up by Blind Guardian and also boasting Love/Hate, Saxon, Skyclad and Yngwie Malmsteen.

RAGE discography

REIGN OF FEAR, Noise N 0038 (Europe) (1986)
EXECUTION GUARANTEED, Noise N 0073 (Europe) (1987)
PERFECT MAN, Noise N 0112-1 (Europe) (1988)
SECRETS IN A WEIRD WORLD, Noise N 0137-1 (Europe) (1989)
REFLECTIONS OF A SHADOW, Noise N0 160 (Europe) (1990)
Extended Power, Noise NO 0169-3 (Europe) (1991)
Beyond The Wall, Noise NO 202-3 (Europe) (1992)
TRAPPED!, Noise N 0189 (Europe) (1992)
THE MISSING LINK, Noise NO 217 (Europe) (1993)
TEN YEARS IN RAGE, Noise N 0219-2 (Europe) (1994)
BLACK IN MIND, G.U.N. GUN 062 (Europe) (1995)
LINGUA MORTIS, G.U.N. GUN 090 (Europe) (1996)
END OF ALL DAYS, G.U.N. GUN 101 (Europe) (1996)
XIII, G.U.N. GUN 156 (Europe) (1998)
GHOSTS, G.U.N. GUN 185 (Europe) (1999)
WELCOME TO THE OTHER SIDE, G.U.N. GUN 189 (Europe) (2001)
UNITY, Steamhammer SPV 085-72972 (Europe), Steamhammer
72972 (USA) (2002)
SOUNDCHASER, Steamhammer SPV 085-69362 (Europe),
Steamhammer 69362 (USA) (2003)
FROM THE CRADLE TO THE STAGE, Steamhammer SPV 088-
69662 (Europe), Steamhammer 69662 (USA) (2004)
SPEAK OF THE DEAD, Nuclear Blast NB 1483-2 (Europe), Nuclear
Blast America 1483 (USA) (2006)

In 1996, Rage released the *Lingua Mortis* album, on which they were joined by the Symphony Orchestra of Prague on some of their best cuts. This inventive approach put Rage back in the limelight, re-invigorating their career.

March 1998's *XIII*, laid down at Principal Studios in Senden and co-produced with Christian Wolff, continued with this successful orchestrated approach and hosted a rendition of The Rolling Stones' 'Paint It Black'. Asian variants boasted a further cover in Rush's 'Tom Sawyer'. Rage's grand experiment was now familiar to German metal fans, who duly put *XIII* into the charts at Number 21.

Unfortunately, Rage suffered a mass walkout in 1999 when both the Efthimiadis brothers and second guitarist Sven Fischer decamped, leaving Wagner to fly solo. Undaunted, he pulled in Russian guitar virtuoso Victor Smolski and quickly returned with the conceptual *Ghosts* album. In Germany this new incarnation of Rage debuted at the 'Wacken' festival and then set off on an extensive tour of Russia.

The year 2000 found Wagner guesting on the GB Arts album *The Lake*, while Smolski contributed lead solos to the Perzonal War *Newtimechaos* outing. Meanwhile, Manni Schmidt joined Grave Digger in December.

Peavey drafted former Yngwie Malmsteen and Metalium drummer Mike Terrana to cement a line-up that was to take Rage into a stable career path. Their 2001 album, *Welcome To The Other Side*, landed the group an unexpected bonus when the track 'Straight To Hell' was chosen for the soundtrack to the movie *Der Schuh Des Manitu*, which became one of the most commercially successful German-language films ever. The record, committed to tape at VPS Studio in Hamm, was entirely played and written by the Wagner-Smolski-Terrana line-up.

Terrana featured on the Driven album put together by ex-Dio guitarist Tracy G, and the drummer also re-grouped with Artension for a 2002 comeback album entitled *Sacred Pathways*, as well as performing on the *Shadow Zone* album from German guitar hero Axel Rudi Pell. A further collaboration saw the sticksman forging a jazz-fusion act, The Voodoo

Taboo Fusion Band, in collaboration with French guitarist Cyril Achard and bassist Ivan Rougny for the *Something's Cooking* album, issued through the Finnish Lion Music label.

The Japanese version of Rage's April 2002 album *Unity* boasted the traditional extra track in the form of 'Darkness Turns To Light'. The band embarked on a full-scale world tour, commencing in Seoul at the 'World Rock Festival' before continuing on to dates in Japan. They also scheduled a date in August at the 'Soyorock 2002' festival in Kyung Gi Do, Korea. An extensive September run of European concerts found them paired with Primal Fear.

On the recording front, the band made space to cut a live rendition of 'Motorbreath' for a Nuclear Blast Metallica tribute collection. Charlie Bauerfeind produced Rage's new album, *Soundchaser*, in 2003, recording at Helloween vocalist Andi Deris's Tenerife studios. Naturally, Deris lent guesting backing vocals. The Helloween connection continued with the promotion of the record as Rage were announced as the support act to the famed metal pumpkins' October European dates.

In early 2004, guitarist Victor Smolski recorded a guest appearance for the Der Bote solo project of Feuerengel frontman Boris Delic. He also convened a further solo album, comprising heavyweight reworkings of Bach classics, titled *Majesty & Passion*. Wagner and Mike Terrana helped out, as did former Scorpions guitar legend Uli Jon Roth.

Unfortunately, Smolski fell "seriously ill" following the group's performance at the Italian 'Gods Of Metal' festival in June. It transpired that he had been suffering from a testicular infection for some time and that during the concert in Bologna this organ burst, with serious consequences. With Smolski hospitalised, former guitarist Manni Schmidt was to step into the breach to cover for a show at the 'Helfenstein' festival in Geislingen. However, just days after this announcement, Rage cancelled the show.

November 2004 saw the issue of the band's 20th anniversary double live album, *From The Cradle To The Stage*. That same month Mike Terrana revealed plans for an "instrumental rock fusion" solo album, *Man Of The World*, comprising six studio tracks and four live songs recorded in Moscow at the 'Premier Drum Day Festival 2003'.

Smolski joined ex-Aria singer Valery Kipelov at a Moscow recording studio in late January 2005 for the recording of a solo album and live work. The guitarist also contributed guitar to Spanish thrash metal band Legen Beltza's conceptual 'War Of Wars', included on their album *Dimension Of Pain*.

As the band signed a new deal with Nuclear Blast, early 2005 saw the release of *Back In Time*, a Rage tribute album compiling no fewer than 28 Austrian heavy metal bands paying homage.

Peavey Wagner had a lucky escape in early May when he was injured by a car while he was riding a bicycle. After surgery to fix his arm, the singer was soon back in action, putting in a guest vocal appearance on Destruction's *Inventor Of Evil* album. Rage concerts in Europe announced for April 2006 had Freedom Call lined up as support. Now operating as a rock-solid trio, the band look set to rage hard well into the next decade and beyond.

RUNNING WILD
SPLICE THE MAINBRACE!

SWASHBUCKLING POWER METAL BAND Running Wild have carved out their own niche in the genre. The German band's earlier albums resolutely pursued pirate themes, across not only album covers but also the lyrical content. This was even reflected in their stage costumes before the band switched to Napoleonic military themes. Although much of the outside world scoffed at their efforts, the band found a ready audience in their

homeland. Led by Rock'n'Rolf (real name Rolf Kasparek), Running Wild have proved to be a mainstay of the German metal scene, with consistently high-profile albums and tours.

The band started out as Granite Heart, formed in 1976, switching to Running Wild in 1979 and making their first demo in 1981: this cassette featured 'Hallow The Hell', 'War Child' and 'King Of The Midnight Fire'. The band's first line-up as Granite Heart consisted of Rock'n'Rolf, guitarist Uwe Bendig, drummer Michael Hoffmann and bassist Jörg Schwarz. Schwarz was replaced by Carsten David in 1976. By the time of the 1981 Running Wild sessions, they were Rock'n'Rolf, Uwe Bendig on guitar, Matthias Kaufmann on bass with Wolfgang 'Hasche' Haggemann on the drums. When they came to record their second tape the following year, the suitably titled *Heavy Metal Like A Hammer Blow*, only Rolf and Hasche remained. Fresh blood was provided by guitarist Preacher (aka Gerald Warnecke) and bassist Stephan Boriss. Running Wild's third demo session secured a deal with Noise. The group's first two commercially available tracks, 'Iron Heads' and 'Bones To Ashes', were donated to a four-way split album titled *Death Metal* in 1984, sharing space with Helloween, Dark Avenger and Hellhammer. Their debut proper came with the album *Gates To Purgatory*.

On the release of 1985's *Branded And Exiled*, with new guitarist Majk Moti, Running Wild received an invitation to open for US glam-rockers Mötley Crüe on the 'German Theatre Of Pain' tour.

One of the first German power metal bands to tour North America, Running Wild undertook a lengthy club round with Celtic Frost and Voivod throughout June 1986. The group found US audiences generally lacking in appreciation and confused by their pirate garb. From this point, Running Wild, who churned out albums on a regular basis, devoted their energies almost entirely to Germany.

Following the release of 1987's popular *Under Jolly Roger*, drummer Hasche quit (and subsequently worked for the Rockfabrik club in Ludwigsburg). He was substituted by Stefan Schwarzmann. German gigs in April 1987 had British act Satan as openers. The band yielded to another blow shortly after when bassist Stephan Boriss departed to join U.D.O.. Before long, Schwarzmann followed into the same band. The live *Ready For Boarding* album saw winter 1988 shows, again with guests Satan.

The *Port Royal* album was promoted by an extensive run of European dates throughout January and February 1989 with support from Angel Dust. The rhythm section was re-established with bassist Jens Becker and English drummer Iain Finlay for 1990's *Death Or Glory*. Finlay's position was briefly substituted by Jörg Michael, this journeyman drummer boasting credits with Avenger, Rage, Mekong Delta, Laos, Headhunter,

Grave Digger and Axel Rudi Pell. A lengthy string of European dates in January and February 1990 found Rage, S.D.I. and Random supporting. Moti departed in early 1991 and was replaced by Axel Morgan. The *Blazon Stone* album marked another run of European touring, this time with Raven and Crossroads as guests throughout April and May 1991.

The *Pile Of Skulls* album of 1992 saw the addition of ex-U.D.O. bassist Thomas 'Bodo' Smuszynski and the return of drummer Stefan Schwarzmann. Recorded in Studio M in Hildesheim, *Pile Of Skulls* was the first Running Wild outing to benefit from Noise's co-operation with major label EMI. Meanwhile, Becker deputised for former touring partners Crossroads. The 'Pile Of Skulls' tour, with Jörg Michael back on drums, featured Universe as support in early 1993.

Running Wild then effectively split down the middle with Becker, Schwarzmann and Morgan creating the cheekily titled X Wild, an outfit that lasted for three albums. Becker was later to join Grave Digger.

Two years later, the group released their eighth album, *Black Hand Inn*, featuring the 15-minute epic 'Genesis', Running Wild's alternative view of the theory of evolution. Concert dates in Germany witnessed a summer 1994 co-headline alliance with Grave Digger. The following year yielded *Masquerade*, recorded with Gerhard 'Anyway' Wölfe at Horus Sound in Hannover. Upon its release, the group immediately played the 'Summer Metal Meetings' with the likes of Rage, Glenmore, Iced Earth and Grave Digger.

With the band inoperative for a period, new guitarist Thilo Hermann, previously with Holy Moses and Risk, joined Glenmore for live work but returned to Running Wild the following year. The band opened 1996 with another German tour, this time with Manchester's China Beach providing the opening honours. Schwarzmann continued his game of musical chairs by emerging once again as the man behind the kit for U.D.O. in 1997. The same year, Herrmann put together the side project Höllenhunde for the *Alptraum* album with Glenmore drummer Dany Löble. When Hollenhunde dissolved the same year, Herrmann resumed activities with Running Wild.

For 1997's *The Rivalry*, which saw Running Wild along with a clutch of label-mates switching to the G.U.N. ("Great Unlimited Noises") label, Rolf was joined by Smuszynski, Hermann and drummer Jörg Michael, the latter boasting credits with Avenger, Rage, Mekong Delta, Laos, Headhunter, Grave Digger and Axel Rudi Pell. With *The Rivalry*, Running Wild finally made a break from the predictable piracy themes and now had Rolf in full hussar costume. The band, with erstwhile Rage drummer Chris Efthimiadis now installed as Michael had committed himself fully to Stratovarius, toured with Primal Fear in April 1998.

1998 found Running Wild returning with the *Victory* album, on which Rolf was joined by Herrmann, Smuszynski and Angelo Sasso (the last a pseudonym for a non-metal drummer who did not wish to be associated with the genre).

For touring, Running Wild again pulled in drummer Chris Efthimiadis. The band now included new bass player Peter Pichl of the Jutta Weinhold

band (Thomas Smuszynski had joined covers band Bourbon) and would spend the latter half of 2001 recording a new album, *The Brotherhood*. In 2002 they inducted Angel Dust guitarist Bernd Aufermann. Rolf put in a cameo appearance in the video for a cover version of Twisted Sister's 'We're Not Gonna Take It' in September 2002 by the famous German spoof act The Donuts.

Running Wild guitarist Bernd Aufermann collaborated with Zak Stevens in early 2004 on songs destined for the second Circle II Circle album. Another collaboration saw bassist Peter Pichl uniting with The Rugged's José Juan Gallego and Juan Antonio Soria on 'The Reason Around'. Pichl was announced as joining Yargos, a progressive metal collaboration between guitarist Wieland Hofmeister, second guitarist Andreas Kienitz of Hydrotoxin and Human Fortress, Threshold singer Andrew McDermott and Moondog drummer Ossy Pfieffer. Additional vocals came courtesy of Anca Graterol.

With no respite, Running Wild set *Rogues En Vogue* as the title for a 2005 record. Limited editions of the album added two exclusive tracks, 'Cannonball Tongue' and 'Libertalia'. In August 2005 Remedy Records released a fitting double disc tribute album, *The Revivalry – A Tribute To Running Wild*.

SODOM
UNWAVERING THRASH STALWARTS

LAMBASTED OUTSIDE THEIR NATIVE Germany throughout much of their career, the stoic thrash outfit Sodom experienced a renaissance of appreciation in the 1990s for their brutal, almost primitive metal attack. They hail from Gelsenkirchen and debuted as a trio consisting of guitarist Angelripper (aka Thomas Such), drummer Witchhunter (Christian Dudeck) and vocalist Aggressor (Frank Testegen), who made the demo *Witching Metal* in 1983. The earliest Sodom incarnation, dating to 1982, had featured Bloody Monster (Rainer Focke) on drums.

In 1984, a second demo, *Victims Of Death*, included the original tracks boosted with the addition of four new songs. It began to receive a great deal of positive press, although Aggressor opted out. He was eventually replaced by Grave Violator (Josef 'Peppi' Dominic) and the new line-up debuted at the Black Metal Night in Frankfurt. After a further show with Destruction and Iron Angel, Steamhammer SPV Records signed the band and swiftly released a debut EP, *In The Sign Of Evil*.

Grave Violator left at the end of 1985 and the debut album, *Obsessed By Cruelty*, featured Destructor (Michael Wulf). An additional guitarist, Ahathoor (Uwe Christophers), recorded the track 'After The Deluge'. It's notable that two versions of *Obsessed By Cruelty* were issued in a short space of time: the original mix was pressed but then found to be unsatisfactory, and so the entire album was remixed at Hilpoltstein Studios in Nürnberg. A further variant came when the US licensee, Metal Blade Records, deleted 'After The Deluge', even though it was listed on the cover. Immediately after the record was released, Destructor quit to join

SODOM discography

In The Sign Of Evil, Steamhammer SPV 60-2120 (Europe) (1984)
OBSESSED BY CRUELTY, Steamhammer SPV 08-2121 (Europe) (1986)
Expurse Of Sodomy, Steamhammer SPV 50-21235 (Europe) (1987)
PERSECUTION MANIA, Steamhammer SPV 076-75092 (Europe) (1988)
MORTAL WAY OF LIVE, Steamhammer SPV 076-75762 (Europe) (1988)
AGENT ORANGE, Steamhammer SPV 076-75972 (Europe) (1989)
BETTER OFF DEAD, Steamhammer SPV 076-76262 (Europe) (1991)
The Law Is The Saw, Steamhammer SPV 055-76353 (Europe) (1991)
TAPPING THE VEIN, Steamhammer SPV 084-76542 (Europe) (1992)
GET WHAT YOU DESERVE, Steamhammer SPV 084-76762 (Europe) (1994)
MAROONED LIVE, Steamhammer SPV 084-76852 (Europe) (1994)
MASQUERADE IN BLOOD, Steamhammer SPV 085-76962 (Europe) (1995)
'TIL DEATH US DO UNITE, G.U.N. GUN 199 (Europe) (1997)
CODE RED, Drakkar DRCD 67384 2 (Europe) (1999)
M-16, Steamhammer SPV 085-72442 (Europe), Steamhammer SPV 72442 (USA) (2001)
ONE NIGHT IN BANGKOK, Steamhammer SPV 091-69392 (Europe), Steamhammer SPV 69392 (USA) (2003)
SODOM, Steamhammer SPV 085-69832 (Europe), Steamhammer SPV 69832 (USA) (2006)

Kreator. Uwe Christophers replaced him for live work. During a lull in 1986, Witchhunter travelled to Sweden to rehearse with Bathory for a proposed European tour with Celtic Frost and Destruction. The tour was shelved, however, and the drummer returned to Sodom.

Now with Blackfire (Frank Gosdzik) on guitar, the band toured Europe as co-headliners with Whiplash in 1987, promoting the Harris Johns-produced *Persecution Mania* album, but Blackfire quit the band on the eve of the *Agent Orange* tour with Sepultura in 1989, joining Kreator on an American tour. The band found a temporary replacement to fulfil the dates in Mekong Delta's Uwe Baltrusch. Still, the next album, *Agent Orange*, sold strongly, shifting in excess of 90,000 units in Europe.

In January 1990, Sodom recruited ex-Assassin guitarist Michael Hoffman, and the ensuing *Better Off Dead*, again produced by Harris Johns, included a cover of the Thin Lizzy classic 'Cold Sweat'. The *Tapping The Vein* album was released in 1992 with a new guitarist, Andy Brings. For the 1994 album *Get What You Deserve*, Sodom drafted in ex-Living Death, Violent Force and Sacred Chao drummer Atomic Steif.

Sodom released a live album, *Marooned Live*, in 1994 and a new studio album, *Masquerade In Blood*, the following year. Angelripper issued a solo album of drinking songs, *Ein Schöner Tag*, in 1995. Scoring a degree of success with this off-the-cuff recording, Angelripper unwittingly ignited a parallel solo career for himself as 'Onkel Tom'. Back with the main band, the man formed a new line-up with guitarist Bernemann (Bernd Kost) and drummer Bobby Schottkowski in order to record the adventurous *Til Death Do Us Unite* album for new label G.U.N..

Til Death Do Us Unite featured a drastically reworked version of Paul Simon's 'Hazy Shade Of Winter' (as made popular by The Bangles). The original version of the album sported a wonderful cover photograph, juxtaposing a pregnant woman, a skull and a male beer belly. Sadly, this image was banned after the first pressing.

Sodom continued their resurgence in 1999 with the Harris Johns-

Sodom

produced *Code Red* on a new label, Drakkar. This album saw them eschewing any form of experimentation, turning back the clock and delving into familiar lyrical territory. December shows in Germany, running from Christmas Day until New Year's Eve, saw the band packaged with Goddess Of Desire and Tankard. The group then formed part of a nostalgic thrash metal tour of Germany with compatriots Destruction and Kreator. *M-16*, released in 2001, was a concept album dealing with the Vietnam war that broke into the German charts at Number 88.

In June 2004, the group entered House of Audio studios in Karlsdorf with producer Achim Köhler for a new record. That same year their classic cut 'Burst Command Til War' was chosen as a pioneering piece of music for a compilation assembled by Darkthrone drummer Fenriz, released through Peaceville Records and entitled *Fenriz Presents... The Best Of Old-School Black Metal*.

February 2005 found Sodom touring South America. The band announced a one-off North American date at the Minneapolis 'Mayhem 2' festival in May; simultaneously, the Vinyl Maniacs label reissued *Agent Orange* and *In The Sign Of Evil* as limited-edition vinyl picture discs.

Tom Angelripper guested playing pedal steel guitar on Powergod's cover version of Tank's 'The War Drags Ever On' for inclusion on their *Long Live The Loud – That's Metal Lesson II* released through Massacre in July 2005.

Sodom's live schedule throughout mid 2005 included appearances at such events as 'A Summer Day In Hel'l in Rome, Italy, the Burgebrach 'Sternenfestival' in Germany, the Spanish 'Guernika Metalway' festival, the Dutch 'Bergen Hole In The Sky' festival, Germany's 'Hofheim Outer Limits Special' and the 'Baltic Metal Ferry 34.000 Tons Of Metal' event. The band also toured with Fatal Embrace and Vendetta for German dates in September 2005. They allied themselves with Finnish polka-metal exponents Finntroll for US touring in January 2006.

After two decades, Sodom stand proud as probably the only major-league German thrash exponents who never once deviated off course. This dogged adherence to formula has undoubtedly provided the bedrock for many, many more albums to come.

U.D.O.
METAL HEART

THE DIMINUTIVE UDO DIRKSCHNEIDER, a native of Wuppertal, was a founding member and lead vocalist of German metal legends Accept from their inception in 1971, but he sensationally quit the group at the height of their success in order to form U.D.O.. Dirkschneider's uniquely abrasive vocal style had without doubt played a major part in making Accept into world-class contenders. This metal ambassador cuts a distinctive figure, eschewing long hair and leather for a skinhead crop and combat fatigues. Rumours of splits in the Accept ranks had been filtering through for a number of years, and so Dirkschneider's break was hardly a surprise.

Viewed very much as Dirkschneider's solo project, despite constant protestations from the band he had assembled, U.D.O. debuted in 1987 with the hard-hitting and uncompromising Mark Dodson-produced *Animal House*. This was an album consisting entirely of rejected Accept tracks deemed "too heavy" for the act.

The initial U.D.O. line-up had two former Warlock men, guitarist Peter Szigeti and bassist Frank Rittel, plus drummer Thomas Franke. However, ex-Sinner guitarists Mathias Dieth and Andy Susemihl were later recruited in favour of Szigeti, who would go on to found Coracko and Stonewashed. Pre-Sinner, the highly rated Dieth had played guitar for Gravestone, recording three albums. With U.D.O. his guitar talents would come to the fore.

Touring revealed Susemihl's preference for lighter material: he in turn was superseded by Wolfgang Böhm of Darxon. In 1989 *Mean Machine*, once more produced by Dodson, served up more of the same fare despite being penned by the new roster. The band benefited from a completely new rhythm section of former Running Wild bassist Thomas Smuszynski and drummer Stefan Schwarzmann.

U.D.O. then went on to open for Ozzy Osbourne on his British tour of that year, but in 1990 the chain-smoking Dirkschneider suffered a massive heart attack that came close to claiming his life. The man himself put it down to working too hard: during the making of a new album, *Faceless World*, the band were without management, increasing the singer's workload.

Both *Faceless World* and the subsequent *Timebomb* album were produced by Accept drummer Stefan Kaufmann. Touring for *Timebomb* saw Susemihl back in the ranks, but sustained fan pressure on Accept's members to reform was unrelenting. In 1993 Dirkschneider could resist the lure of an Accept reformation no longer and teamed up with his old act, re-debuting with *Objection Overruled*. Smusynski and Schwarzmann duly rejoined Running Wild for their *Pile Of Skulls* album in 1994. Böhm created Universe with erstwhile Darxon and Axe Victims personnel, while Andy Susemihl founded Mr. Perfect for a 1993 album and issued a solo album, *Life Among The Roaches*.

Despite the new link with Accept, Dirkschneider still kept his group on the side and contributed a worthy cover of 'Metal Gods' to the Century Media Judas Priest tribute album in 1996, *A Tribute To Judas Priest: Delivering The Goods*. The line-up for this one-off track was Dirkschneider, Dieth, Schwarzmann, Michael Voss of Casanova and Demon Drive on bass, and Stefan Kaufmann on rhythm guitar. Media expectation was high and the interest was rewarded with a new U.D.O. album, aptly titled *Solid*.

With the record released through new label G.U.N. in 1997, a tour of Germany in the fall ensued, with Stefan Kaufmann and ex-Sin City and Bullet man Fitty Wienhold on bass, Jürgen Graf on guitar and a returning Stefan Schwarzmann on drums. Dirkschneider was once more involved with Accept as a further reunion occurred the same year on the back of a live album. October 1997 found U.D.O. on the road in Europe supported by Random, Blackshine and M-Force. The band were rewarded with strong sales in Eastern Europe and in the burgeoning metal market in Russia.

The 1998 U.D.O. album, *No Limits*, recorded at Roxx Studio in Pulheim and retaining the previous line-up, again saw strong sales and was noted for including a re-recording of the Accept classic 'I'm A Rebel'

WARLOCK / DORO
THE REIGN OF THE METAL QUEEN

THE BLONDE SIREN DORO PESCH has made a significant impact on the international metal scene fronting Warlock and as a solo artist. Once Warlock had attained a foothold it was only a matter of time before Doro was enticed out of the equation into a solo career. From a shaky start attempting to break into the US market, Doro has since concentrated on her homeland, where her title of metal queen has long been undisputed.

Her formative years saw Pesch joined by guitarist Rudy Graf and bassist Frank Rittel, together with Stallion drummer Thomas Franke; billed as Beast, this proto-act only issued a rehearsal demo tape. Pesch, who was with her first band named Snakebite, duly forged Warlock together with Graf and Rittel, debuting for the Belgian Mausoleum label with the 1984 album *Burning The Witches*.

The studio band backing Pesch on her February 1989 solo album debut, *Force Majeure*, consisted of Rainbow drummer Bobby Rondinelli, guitarist John Devin and bass player Tommy Henriksen. Keyboards were contributed by Dio's Claude Schnell. With interest in the USA, Doro relocated to New York at the instigation of Kiss's Gene Simmons. The ensuing *Doro* album of 1990 was produced with ex-Black'n'Blue guitarist Tommy Thayer, including a rendition of The Electric Prunes' 1967 song 'I Had Too Much To Dream Last Night'. *Doro* also featured a crop of Gene Simmons compositions, including a rework of the Kiss track 'Only You', which had originally appeared on the band's unsuccessful *(Music From) The Elder* album.

For 1991's *True At Heart* release, Pesch recorded in Nashville with producer Barry Beckett. This somewhat mellower album included session players including Giant guitarist Dann Huff, guitarist Michael Thompson, bassist Lee Sklar and drummer Eddie Bayers. Doro's touring line-up was augmented in 1992 by keyboard player Paul Morris, who had joined from New York's From The Fire. Following 1993's *Angels Never Die*, produced by Jack Ponti, Doro chose to issue her first live album, cut with a new touring band that included ex-World War III, Waysted and Britny Fox drummer Johnny Dee and ex-Mariah, Britny Fox, Waysted and Tyketto keyboard player Jimmy DiLella. Chart success in the USA eluded Pesch.

Fortunately, Doro's standing in Germany remained steadfast and was bolstered in 1995 with her experimental *Machine II Machine* album, the success of which saw a spin-off *Electric Club Mixes* album. In spite of a downward slide in popularity with each successive solo release in Britain and America, Doro remained a strong contender in Germany and from this point on would concentrate almost solely on her homeland.

The 1998 album *Love Me In Black* found the blonde chanteuse hitting her creative peak. Both brutal and melodic, the album, with a version of Heart's 'Barracuda', sparked renewed interest for Doro and was a huge seller across mainland Europe. Musicians on the recording were guitarists Jimmy Harry and Jürgen Engler, bassists Nick Douglas (aka Nick Mitchell of Deadly Blessing) and Andrew Goodsight, and drummer Damon Weber.

Her 2000 offering, entitled *Calling The Wild*, gave Doro a further hit album in Germany. High-profile studio participants included Lemmy of Motörhead, ex-Guns N'Roses guitarist Slash and then-Megadeth guitarist Al Pitrelli. The record, compiled with a different track listing for Europe and America, included a version of Billy Idol's 'White Wedding' and Motörhead's 'Love Me Forever'.

Doro toured North America in November 2000 on a highly successful package with Dio and Yngwie Malmsteen prior to a lengthy headlining jaunt in Germany early the following year. The dates were accompanied by a single release of 'White Wedding'. Another round of touring in the USA during April and May 2001 saw Doro sharing billing with Britny Fox. Drummer Johnny Dee had his endurance tested, performing with both bands.

and a version of the Supermax track 'Lovemachine'. Adding two Swiss members – guitarist Igor Gianola and drummer Lorenzo Milani – U.D.O. toured America with Saxon in late 2000.

A welcome and long overdue live album, *Live From Russia*, arrived in October 2001, with the U.D.O. band at this juncture comprising Dirkschneider, guitarists Kaufmann and Gianola, bass player Wienhold and drummer Milani. Another addition to U.D.O. fans' collections was Nuclear Blast's second Accept tribute album, which witnessed U.D.O. tackling 'X.T.C.', a track culled from the only Udo Dirkschneider-less Accept album, 1989's *Eat The Heat*.

U.D.O. returned in 2002 with the new studio album, *Man And Machine*, which included a duet with German metal queen Doro Pesch on 'Dancing With An Angel'. Japanese variants came with two extra tracks: live versions of 'Metal Eater' and 'Heart Of Gold'. Touring in Scandinavia during March found Vanize and Cyberyra as support. Earlier, Kaufmann had been responsible for producing the September 2001 Cyberyra album *Mindcontrol*, released through Dirkschneider's own Breaker label. Later gigs in mainland Europe throughout November saw Crystal Ball as opening act.

In 2003, Gianola was to be found as part of the Edge Of Forever side project, a 1980s-rock-styled venture with keyboard player Alessandro Del Vecchio, bassist Christian Grillo and Axe frontman Bob Harris.

U.D.O. fans were in for a treat in 2003: a live DVD titled *Nailed To The Metal* included a bonus live CD album *Metal Mayhem – The Missing Tracks*, comprising performances of Accept classics and Judas Priest's 'Metal Gods'. German gigs in May 2004, dubbed the 'Thunderball World Tour' after the new album of the same name, saw the band hooking up with Rebellion and Majesty. Subsequent dates found the tour extending through the Ukraine, Russia, Greece, Bulgaria and into Scandinavia. A mini DVD, *Thundervision*, was delayed when it was discovered that the first manufacturing run of 5,000 included not only band material but also some accounting financial software called Income Tax Pro. This first run had to be destroyed and a second batch produced.

Autumn gigs in Europe saw U.D.O. drummer Lorenzo Milani forced to sit out due to "personal problems". Francesco Jovino filled in for the tour and subsequently joined up full-time. Accept's summer 2005 reformation line-up consisted of Dirkschneider, guitarists Wolf Hoffman and Herman Frank, Peter Baltes on bass and Stefan Schwarzmann on drums. Meanwhile, U.D.O. set *Mission No. X* as their new album title for summer release via AFM. Schwarzmann joined the live band of fabled ex-Scorpions guitarist Uli Jon Roth for live dates later that year.

Dirkschneider then cut two duets with Russian acts, featuring on Anj's *100 Miles Straight Ahead* album on the track 'Pugachev' and with pop band Faktor-2 on the U.D.O. song 'Cry Soldier Cry'. The singer also guested on Finnish heavy metal band Lordi's *The Arockalypse*. U.D.O. announced a major live campaign for early 2006. Support on Scandinavian gigs came from Norwegians Memorized Dreams. If major heart attacks can't stop Udo in his tracks, it seems the only real obstacle barring future campaigns from U.D.O. is the unceasing clamour for an Accept reformation.

DORO/WARLOCK discography

WARLOCK:
BURNING THE WITCHES, Mausoleum SKULL 8325 (Europe) (1984)
HELLBOUND, Vertigo 824 660-1 (Europe) (1985)
TRUE AS STEEL, Vertigo 830 237-2 (Europe) (1986)
TRIUMPH AND AGONY, Vertigo VERH 50 (UK), Mercury 832 804-2 (USA) (1987)

DORO:
FORCE MAJEURE, Vertigo 838 016-2 (Europe) (1989)
DORO, Vertigo 846 194-2 (Europe), Mercury 846 194-2 (USA) (1990)
TRUE AT HEART, Vertigo 510 102-2 (Europe) (1991)
ANGELS NEVER DIE, Vertigo 514 309-2 (Europe) (1993)
DORO LIVE, Vertigo 518 680-2 (Europe) (1993)
MACHINE II MACHINE, Mercury 526 804-2 (Europe) (1995)
MACHINE II MACHINE: ELECTRIC CLUB REMIXES, Vertigo 528 724-2 (Europe) (1995)
LOVE ME IN BLACK, Warner Bros. 3984 23423-2 (1998)
CALLING THE WILD, Steamhammer SPV 085-72042 (Europe), Koch KOC-CD-8151 (USA) (2001)
FIGHT, Steamhammer SPV 085-74100 (Europe) (2002)
CLASSIC DIAMONDS, AFM AFM 085-2 (Europe), Locomotive 162 (USA) (2004)
WARRIOR SOUL, AFM AFM 141-2 (Europe), Locomotive 284 (USA) (2006)

Fans sought out an exclusive live version of 'Love Me In Black' that surfaced in 2001 on the WDHA radio compilation *The Tour Bus – Road Trip*. Another Doro rarity came courtesy of premier Spanish metal band Mago De Oz, whose May 2001 single 'La Danza Del Fuego' came with a version of Rainbow's 'Man On The Silver Mountain' featuring Doro on guest vocals. She also donated her services to the German All Stars October 2001 song 'Wings Of Freedom' in honour of the September 11th World Trade Center victims, was a guest duettist on U.D.O.'s 2002 album *Man And Machine*, and had a version of 'Babe, I'm Gonna Leave You' included on the Locomotive Music Led Zeppelin tribute album *The Metal Zeppelin – The Music Remains The Same*.

In May 2002, news arrived of a new Doro studio album, to be entitled *Fight*, the title song written in honour of the German female boxing champion Regina Halmich. The famous boxer had made her appreciation of Doro known earlier in her career by using Warlock's 'All We Are' as an entrance theme for her fights. Songwriters in collusion with Pesch for this outing included Gene Simmons once again, for 'Legends Never Die' (previously recorded by both Wendy O. Williams and King Kobra), Jean Beauvoir of Crown Of Thorns, and hit-maker Russ Ballard. Pesch adventurously pulled in Pete Steele of Type O Negative for the duet 'Descent'. The favour was returned to Jean Beauvoir on Crown Of Thorns' August 2002 album *Karma*, Doro duetting on the track 'Shed No Tears'.

Doro's band for the *Fight* album consisted of guitarist Joe Taylor, guitarist-keyboard player Oliver Palotai, bassist Nick Douglas and drummer Johnny Dee. *Fight* was promoted with an extensive run of headline gigs across mainland Europe in November. Before those shows, Doro hit the European festival trail, appearing at the Derby 'Rock & Blues' festival, Germany's 'Wacken Open Air', 'Metal Dayz' in Switzerland, the 'Pepsi Sziget' event in Hungary and 'Long Live Rock & Roll' in Moscow. She even turned up in the Azores for a gig, in September. The martial

theme was pursued further in October when the singer, a trained Thai boxer, was pitched in the ring against former porn star Gina Wild (aka Michaela Schaffrath) in a three-round bout televised for German station RTL's *Promi-Boxen 2002*.

The last three shows of Doro's December German tour were cancelled as the leading lady was involved in a car crash over the Christmas period. Fortunately she was unharmed and was back in action for headline German dates in April of 2003 with Rawhead Rexx as opening act.

The singer notably guested on two tracks, 'Believe In Your Self' and 'Key To Your Dreams', on Czech progressive metal band Seven's 2004 album *Sevens*. Doro then proved her staying power as she was voted Sexiest Woman Of The Year by the Czech rock magazine *Spark*.

She then announced plans for a joint tour of Europe throughout November and December partnered with Saxon, Dionysus and Circle II Circle. Her 20th anniversary show, held in Düsseldorf on December 13th, witnessed a unique set spanning her career and included former members of Warlock alongside friends such as Lemmy, Savatage's Jon Oliva, and ex-Iron Maiden singer Blaze Bayley. The industrious Doro was back on the road in April 2004, packaged alongside Blaze. With Blaze guitarist John Slater bowing out for "personal reasons", Doro guitarist Oliver Palotai stepped in as replacement, performing double duty each night.

Doro re-visited her creative relationship with boxing champion Regina Halmich by penning a new entrance theme song, to be aired at the world championship match at the DM Arena in Karlsruhe. A brand new EP, entitled *Let Love Rain On Me*, featured both Spanish ('Llueva En Mi Tu Amor') and French ('Pluie D'Amour') variants of the title track, a cover version of Judas Priest's 'Breaking The Law', an acoustic take on the track 'Rare Diamond', and the video for 'Unholy Love'. *Let Love Rain On Me* entered the German charts at Number 65, making it the most successful Doro EP ever and her first single in the German charts since 1993.

The EP preceded Doro's first record for AFM, *Classic Diamonds*. Friends donating their skills numbered ex-Iron Maiden man Blaze Bayley, U.D.O.'s Udo Dirkschneider and Gamma Ray's Kai Hansen. A further release was the *Mausoleum: 20th Anniversary Concert* album, including two archive Doro tracks alongside live material from erstwhile Warlock-era Mausoleum label-mates Killer and Ostrogoth, recorded at the Vosselaar Biebob venue in May 2002.

Alongside Saxon, Bonfire, Edguy, Crystal Ball and In Extremo, Doro was among acts participating in the January 27th 2005 'Rock For Asia' festival at the Saturn Arena in Ingolstadt, Germany to benefit the victims of the Indian Ocean tsunami.

Concerts scheduled for May were cancelled when it was learned that Doro had undergone surgery for endometriosis and the removal of a tumour. Fully recuperated, the singer soon resurfaced, putting in a guest vocal appearance on German thrash act Destruction's *Inventor Of Evil* album.

Doro cemented her ties further with German boxing champion Regina Halmich, performing her track 'She's Like Thunder' prior to Halmich's 50th professional fight on September 10th in front of 4,500 spectators at the DM Arena in Karlsruhe. The day proved victorious for Halmlich as she won a split decision over the previously unbeaten Spaniard Maria Jesus Rosa to successfully retain her WIBF flyweight title. A revised version of the track, re-billed 'We're Like Thunder' and featuring Halmich on vocals, was subsequently released.

Striking out into non-musical areas, Doro made her acting debut in the Swiss movie *Anuk – The Path Of The Warrior*, directed by Luke Gasser. European touring throughout April and May 2006 saw Doro supported by Finnish bands Sonata Arctica and Altaria. She remains a unique force in international metal.

SWEDISH
METAL

IT HAS taken Sweden some time to be recognised as a significant metal force in the world. Strangely, the country's obvious passion for heavy metal throughout the early to mid 1980s produced very few acts of note, with Heavy Load and 220 Volt notable exceptions. For the most part, Sweden seemed content to pour its resources into a succession of rock outfits, culminating in the group Europe, which imitated American bands.

However, two artists played a significant part in shaping the global metal spectrum – Candlemass and Yngwie Malmsteen. Although firmly rooted in the melodic rock tradition, Malmsteen's extreme abilities impacted upon just about every metal guitarist of the day. It proved a turning point for metal guitar when Shrapnel boss Mike Varney decided to export the young Malmsteen to California as part of a hastily re-assembled Steeler, then Alcatraz, and on to a fruitful solo career.

Candlemass's importance was just as weighty. The group were probably the first doom band to achieve much popularity since Black Sabbath, and the prolific doom movement today owes a great debt to them (see their full entry in Chapter 8: Doom Metal).

Once Sweden freed itself from the copyist yoke, talent simply poured into all realms of metal – thrash, doom, black and death, with Grave, The Crown, Unleashed, Dismember, Dissection and Entombed leading the way. Multiple innovations included the Gothenburg-centred NWOSDM (New Wave Of Swedish Death Metal), spearheaded by At The Gates, In Flames and Dark Tranquillity. This cauldron of talent was first stirred by the likes of Grotesque, Infestation, Desecrator and Megaslaughter. Throughout the 1990s, European labels snapped up a succession of high-quality acts such as Morgana Lefay, Amon Amarth and Nocturnal Rites. Sweden, courtesy of Bathory's Quorthon, also fired up Viking metal and, through Christofer Johnsson of Therion, operatic metal. Other individuals too, such as artist-producers Peter Tägtgren and Dan Swanö, have made an international mark.

The NWOSDM led into another seismic revolution of doom-death, highlighted by the awe-inspiring Katatonia and the progressive Opeth. Next in line came Hammerfall, an ad hoc collection of retro-metal aficionados who single-handedly sparked the power metal generation. As the death metal leaders engaged in international touring, many of them rapidly developed away from their early sound, struggling through a crop of adventurous albums and coming through with some highly melodic, if equally heavy, material. Nowadays, Sweden is recognised as a centre of excellence and forward thinking with an unceasing flow of talent such as Arch Enemy, Soilwork and Darkane.

220 VOLT
HIGH-POWERED METAL

220 VOLT WERE FORMED DURING April 1979 in Östersund and played refined, riff-based heavy metal high on melody. The musicians first assembled in 1976 in bizarre circumstances – on a round of miniature golf. When Mats Karlsson's ball went astray, it was retrieved by Thomas Drevin, who threw it back, injuring Karlsson's hand. This sparked a conversation revealing that both had interests beyond golf of a more metallic leaning.

Rehearsals took place at Vallaskolan School in Fröson, after they stole frontman Christer 'Frille' Åsell from another band and drew in drummer Pelle Hansson. Some weeks later the original bassist was superseded by Tommy Hellström. In April 1979, 220 Volt conducted their debut live gig at a school dance. Youth club dates and other school concerts followed, during which 14-year-old Mike 'Larsson' Krusenberg took over bass. In 1980, 220 Volt performed in Stockholm for the first time as part of a national youth club convention. Their local profile was raised considerably on June 4th 1980 with a show at the Östersund Gamla Teatern that was broadcast on radio. Peter Hermansson became their new drummer in early 1982.

220 Volt entered the studio in June 1982 to put down seven demo tracks. The results were positive, and in September Kjell Björk of Guntan's

Records sponsored a second session. This demo included the tracks 'Sauron', 'Prisoner Of War', 'White Powder', 'In The Night' and 'Stand By For Action'. Two tracks from this set were launched in November as an individually hand-numbered 7-inch single, 'Prisoner Of War' b/w 'Sauron', which sold out in a matter of weeks. Live promotion saw a valuable Östersund support to Heavy Load in December. At this same juncture, rock music in Sweden received a huge boost when Europe scored big in the charts and a national televised band contest. With major labels racing to track down the next sensation, 220 Volt were snapped up after a curious CBS financed a further demo.

Prior to recording the debut album for CBS – May 1983's *220 Volt* – vocalist Åsell departed to join Empire. His 220 Volt tenure had been truncated in the first attempts to record the debut, with the label insisting that his vocals were not up to par. Åsell later went on to join Inzight and eventually formed Daylight Dreamer. A swift replacement was found in Jocke Lundholm. Drevin also departed – eventually teaming up once more with Åsell in Empire – and was replaced by Peter Olander in 1984.

220 Volt's second album, with Thomas Witt behind the production board, was laid down over three weeks in November 1983 at Stockholm Studios. *Powergames*, issued in February 1984, came with cassette versions adding two tracks, 'Screaming For A Riot' and 'City Lights'.

CBS thought highly enough of the band to finance a continuous singles campaign, which enabled them to tour as support to Nazareth and

220 VOLT discography

Prisoner Of War, Guntans no catalogue number (Europe) (1982)
limited edition 7-inch vinyl single 500 copies
220 VOLT, Epic EPC 25449 (Europe) (1983)
POWERGAMES, CBS 25819 (Europe) (1984)
Heavy Christmas, CBS CBSA 4967 (Europe) (1984) 7-inch vinyl
single)
MIND OVER MUSCLE, CBS 26254 (Europe) (1985)
ELECTRIC MESSENGERS, Epic BFE 40099 (USA) (1985)
YOUNG AND WILD, CBS 4501201 (Europe) (1987)
EYE TO EYE, Epic EK45064 (Europe) (1988)
LETHAL ILLUSION, Empire ERCD 1035 (Europe) (1997)
VOLUME 1, Power Play (Europe) (2002) limited edition 1,000 copies
MADE IN JÄMTLAND, Swedmetal SM-01-CD (Europe) (2005)

German metal band Bullet. The band's third album, *Mind Over Muscle*, arrived in February 1985. For the North American market, the best songs of the first three albums were combined to form a new release, *Electric Messengers*, issued that June. On tour in the USA, 220 Volt supported AC/DC.

The Swedes' momentum was stalled when all of the band, with the exception of Olander, were required to do their national service, effectively putting the group on ice. In the downtime, Olander contributed to ex-Europe guitarist John Norum's solo album, *Total Control*.

220 Volt promoted the Max Norman-produced *Eye To Eye* in 1988, touring as part of the Swedish 'Monsters Of Rock' festivals alongside somewhat lighter outfits Treat and Electric Boys. The band ground to a halt in 1990 but reformed under the new title of Voltergeist, touting new vocalist Per Englund, previously a member of Blacksmith. Drummer Peter Hermansson later teamed up with guitarist John Norum's solo band, while Englund went on to Motherlode, Garbo and a Blacksmith reformation.

An album of previously unreleased 220 Volt material, *Lethal Illusion*, surfaced during 1997, fuelling anticipation of a reunion. Vocalist Christer Åsell, guitarists Mats Karlsson and Thomas Drevin, bass player Micke Larsson and drummer Peter Hermansson finally got back together for an appearance at the 'Sweden Rock' festival in 2002. The band soon set to work on a comeback album, *Volume 1*, including live tracks culled from 'Sweden Rock', and put in a 20th anniversary gig at Gamla Teatern on November 30th. *Volume 1*, restricted to a miserly 1,000 copies, sold out within two weeks. In October 2004, 220 Volt signed to Swedmetal Records for an early 2005 album release, *Made In Jämtland*.

AMON AMARTH
VIKING DEATH METAL

PURVEYORS OF HIGH-QUALITY, crushing death metal, Amon Amarth have a particular brand of aggression inspired by Norse mythology and the Viking sagas. Hailing from the Tumba suburb of Stockholm and named after Mount Doom of Mordor in J.R.R. Tolkien's *Lord Of The Rings* trilogy, the band can trace their roots back to 1991, when they named themselves Scum for a demo.

Once Scum folded, the musicians regrouped, originally adopting the name Nifelheim before discovering another Swedish act of that name. At this stage Amon Amarth involved frontman Johan Hegg, guitarists Olavi Mikkonen and Anders Hansson, erstwhile Eternal Oath bassist Ted Lundström, and Nico Kaukinen on drums. It was Lundström who suggested the name Amon Amarth.

The unit's first available recording was to have been 1993's *Thor Arise* demo, which featured a rendition of the Black Sabbath anthem 'Sabbath Bloody Sabbath'. However, this was withheld and it was a full year before a second demo, 1994's *The Arrival Of The Fimbul Winter*, made it onto the tape-trading scene, leading to a deal with Singapore label Pulverised.

Following the release of the melodic yet blistering mini-album *Sorrow Throughout The Nine Worlds*, produced by Hypocrisy's Peter Tägtgren at Abyss Studios, Kaukinen was replaced by Martin López in April 1996. This first release caused some degree of controversy when journalists pointed out that the flaming sun-cross on the cover art was unfortunately close to a recognised racist symbol. Amon Amarth had merely chosen the device because of its Viking origins but would have to deflect questioning about the symbol.

Frederik Andersson: "The first mini-CD, Sorrow Throughout The Nine Worlds, had a giant burning sun-cross on the cover, and a lot of people took it the wrong way and thought we were racists. We had to answer all sorts of questions for many years after that. To us it is just a Viking symbol and we like it a lot. But now, looking back, I guess it would've been smarter to use something else."

Fortunately, positive press resulting from the music contained on *Sorrow* scored the band a deal closer to home as the German branch of Metal Blade snapped up the band. Amon Amarth's sophomore release, February 1998's thundering *Once Sent From The Golden Hall*, was again produced by Tägtgren.

Hansson opted out just before a June 1998 European tour with Deicide, Six Feet Under and Brutal Truth, and was superseded by Johan Söderberg. New drummer Fredrik Andersson, also engaged with A Canorous Quintet and Allegiance, was inducted once these dates had concluded. Tägtgren tweaked faders again on September 1999's *The Avenger*.

Supported by Purgatory, the band undertook a tour of Germany in December 2000. A new, aptly titled album, *The Crusher*, featuring a re-recorded 'Risen From The Sea' from the band's debut demo, arrived in May 2001. Limited-edition digipacks hosted a cover of Possessed's 'Eyes Of Horror'. Fredrik Andersson launched a side venture, Curriculum Mortis, featuring Leo Pignon of A Canorous Quintet on guitar and Mattias Leinikka from Guidance Of Sin on vocals.

After gigs in Europe with co-headliners Marduk and Vader, a projected

Amon Amarth

AMON AMARTH discography

Sorrow Throughout The Nine Worlds, Pulverised ASH 001 MCD (Singapore) (1996)
ONCE SENT FROM THE GOLDEN HALL, Metal Blade 3984-14133-2 (Europe / USA) (1998)
THE AVENGER, Metal Blade 3984-14262-2 (Europe / USA) (1999)
THE CRUSHER, Metal Blade 3984-14360-2 (Europe / USA) (2001)
VERSUS THE WORLD, Metal Blade 3984-14410-2 (Europe / USA) (2002)
FATE OF NORNS, Metal Blade 3984-14498-2 (Europe / USA) (2004)
WITH ODEN ON OUR SIDE, Metal Blade 3984-14584-2 (Europe / USA) (2006)

US tour was cancelled in the wake of the terrorist attacks there. North American shows were scheduled again for January 2002, but Marduk withdrew, leaving Amon Amarth to persevere on their own before returning to hit Europe with Vomitory in April.

Frederik Andersson: "We were touring Europe in 2002 and had the worst bus driver ever. After having parked the 18-ton bus on an old bridge in Italy that had signs saying it was safe for five tons, he demolished a couple of cars and a piece of a balcony in Barcelona. Then he lost two wheels on the highway. We were sitting in the back top lounge when the bus started wobbling. The next thing, we looked out the window and saw these gigantic wheels rolling beside us in the damn freeway."

Following the band's appearance at the August 2002 'Wacken Open Air' festival in Germany, they went into the recording studio to cut a new album, *Versus The World*. Limited 'Viking' editions of this album came with a bonus CD comprising the band's initial demo recordings, the *Sorrow Throughout The Nine Worlds* tracks, plus a German-language version of 'Victorious March' entitled 'Siegreicher Marsch'.

The band was due to form part of the much-vaunted Halford-spearheaded 'Metal Gods 2003' North American tour, but this ambitious run of dates collapsed after just a handful of gigs. Nevertheless, the band's live schedule intensified with September North American dates dubbed 'The Art Of Noise 2'. This run of shows saw the band allied with Kreator, Vader, Nile and Goatwhore. The band were then confirmed as headliners for the 'X-Mass Festivals' European tour on a strong bill with Destruction, Deicide, Nile, Graveworm, Dew-Scented, Misery Index and Disbelief.

Andersson started up a fresh project in 2003: Laid To Rest was a death/thrash metal project featuring Kaput! and Orchards Of Odenwrath guitarist Zack Z. In 2004, Amon Amarth donated their rendition of 'Eyes Of Horror' to the *Seven Gates Of Horror* tribute album to Possessed.

The band announced the concept behind their 2004 studio album *Fate Of Norns* as referring to the three Norns or goddesses of fate – Urd, Skuld and Verdandi – who in Scandinavian mythology sit at the root of Yggdrasil, the world tree, weaving the fate of mankind. An incentive for fans to attend German pre-release shows in Bochum and Ludwigsburg in September came in the form of a taster album shared with Fragments Of Unbecoming, Disillusion and Impious. Initial limited-edition copies of the regular album came with a bonus DVD, *Live At Grand Rokk*, a 45-minute disc comprising three-camera video footage of Amon Amarth performing live in Reykjavik, Iceland on March 5th 2004.

The band united with Impious and German death metal crew Disillusion for October European-tour dates. Gigs were also announced alongside Cannibal Corpse, but Amon Amarth, claiming that the jaunt was

"economically impossible". Meanwhile, *Fate Of Norns* impacted hard on the European charts, hitting Number 31 in Germany and Number 56 in Austria. They toured Mexico in February 2005 with support from Evilheart and Men At Arms. European summer festivals were punctuated by a short European tour with Cataract and Impious.

In May 2006, the band entered Fascination Street studios in Örebro to commence work on a sixth album, *With Oden On Our Side*, accompanied by producer Jens Bogren. They teamed up with Wintersun and Tyr for a European tour, covering Germany, Italy, the Czech Republic, Hungary, Poland, France, the UK, Holland, Belgium, Sweden and Norway, beginning in early November.

ARCH ENEMY
SWEDISH SCENE-LEADERS

ARCH ENEMY, BASED IN HALMSTAD, are an extreme yet melodic death metal band featuring ex-members of Carnage, Carcass and Eucharist. They have attained a degree of commercial success, particularly in Japan. A high-profile switch in singers and an awe-inspiring live campaign transferred their European and Asian support to the USA, where they broke onto the *Billboard* charts in 2003 with *Anthems Of Rebellion*.

Original frontman Johan Liiva previously played with Carnage and Furbowl, while guitarist Mike Amott, best known for his role in Carcass, was also a Carnage member early on and, in addition to Arch Enemy, performed in Spiritual. Drummer Daniel Erlandsson occasionally played with In Flames and was previously with Eucharist.

The band's first album, 1996's *Black Earth*, produced by Fredrik Nordström at Studio Fredman and originally released through Wrong Again Records, was a mix of thrash and death metal and a genuinely groundbreaking release. The resulting word of mouth among the metal cognoscenti prompted huge worldwide sales and respect.

Black Earth was the work of Mike Amott rather than a full band collaboration: the guitarist composed all of the material and (in spite of jacket credits that gave Liiva bass credits) played guitar and bass. The record was met with considerable success in Japan, and a video for 'Bury Me An Angel' provided valuable global awareness. The band contributed a cover of 'Aces High' to the *Made In Tribute* Toy's Factory tribute to Iron Maiden.

Arch Enemy guitarist Christopher Amott, working with In Thy Dreams vocalist Jonas Nyrén and drummer Daniel Erlandsson, launched a side band, Armageddon, shortly afterwards, and their *Crossing The Rubicon* arrived in 1997.

For their second album, Arch Enemy pulled in Armageddon bass player Martin Bengtsson to allow Liiva to prioritise his vocals, while Peter Wildoer of Armageddon was recruited to the drum stool for recording sessions. Fredrik Nordström once again manned the board as Arch Enemy's second outing, April 1998's *Stigmata*, benefited from a label shift to Germany's Century Media. Japanese editions boasted an extra track, 'Damnation's Way'.

The band shifted shape again in 1999. Sharlee D'Angelo, an active member of Witchery and Mercyful Fate as well as citing credits with Sinergy and Dismember, assumed the role of bassist, while Erlandsson was again invited to handle drum duties. The band opened for Cradle Of Filth in 1999, a support slot gained by admitted nepotism – Erlandsson's older brother Adrian was Cradle's drummer. That March, the group undertook their first dates in South America, co-headlining with fellow Swedes Hammerfall, and performed at the famed 'Dynamo' festival in the Netherlands. In the autumn, the band hit Europe for a full-scale tour, sharing stages on a package bill with Dark Tranquillity, In Flames and Children Of Bodom. However, US tours would see Dick Lövgren, a

Arch Enemy, with Angela Gossow at front

seasoned campaigner with Armageddon, Cromlech, In Flames and Eucharist among many others, installed in the four-string position.

Japanese versions of the Nordström-produced *Burning Bridges*, issued in July 1999, hosted extra tracks including a cover version of Europe's 'Scream Of Anger' and a re-recorded version of 'Fields Of Desolation'. A live album, *Burning Japan Live 1999*, was issued in that country before fan pressure prompted an international release. Again the band recruited a temporary bassist for live action in 2000: he was Roger Nilson of Spiritual Beggars, The Quill and Firebird.

Arch Enemy transformed into a completely new beast for the next album, when the Amott siblings were joined by German journalist and

singer Angela Gossow, previously with Asmodina and Mistress. Gossow had been prolific on the local scene, heading up Asmodina for a November 1991 six-song demo, *Your Hidden Fear*, followed in February 1994 by *The Story Of The True Human Personality*, a further three-track promo in 1996, and the *Inferno* album in January 1997. Gossow then moved to death-rockers Mistress, who briefly operated as Devil In The Details, during which time Gossow opted out and returned to Arch Enemy.

Ensconcing themselves in the familiar surroundings of Studio Fredman, the new Arch Enemy worked with co-producer Nordström, mixing the final tracks for a new album, *Wages Of Sin*, in league with Andy Sneap. Any concerns over the incorporation of a woman into the formula were blown away within seconds of Gossow's introduction: the bile, spit and venom of her vocals easily outstripped her predecessor, while her schizophrenic, twisted-tongues approach, ranging from seductive whispers to trollish rumbles, gave Arch Enemy an entirely new character.

Wages Of Sin marked a further turning point, often overlooked in the magnitude of Gossow's arrival, in that the Amotts had shifted gear down to precision intimidation rather than the chaotic crunch that had previously driven all before it. The album, arriving in April 2001, saw a belated North American release but did come with a bonus track, 'Lament Of A Mortal Soul', a video clip for 'Ravenous', and a whole CD of rarities. This included an unreleased version of Judas Priest's 'Starbreaker', recorded in 1998, covers of Iron Maiden's 'Aces High' and Europe's 'Scream Of Anger', and a glut of other tracks originally found only on Japanese albums. The band then performed at the prestigious 2001 Japanese 'Beast Feast Festival' during August at the 30,000-capacity

ARCH ENEMY Discography

BLACK EARTH, Wrong Again WAR 011CD (Europe) (1996)
STIGMATA, Century Media CM 77212-2 (Europe), Century Media
  CM 7912-2 (USA) (1998)
BURNING BRIDGES, Century Media CM 77276-2 (Europe), Century
  Media CM 7976-2 (USA) (1999)
WAGES OF SIN, Century Media CM 77383-2 (Europe) (2001),
  Century Media CM 8083-2 (USA) (2002)
ANTHEMS OF REBELLION, Century Media CM 77483-2 (Europe),
  Century Media CM 8183-2 (USA) (2003)
DOOMSDAY MACHINE, Century Media CM 77583-2 (Europe),
  Century Media CM 8283-2 (USA) (2005)

Yokohama Arena alongside Slayer, V.O.D., Static X and Sepultura among others.

The ousted Liiva announced the formation of a new endeavour in late 2001, billed as Nonexist, with Matte Modin of Defleshed and Andromeda's Johan Reinholdz, and this band issued the *Deus Deceptor* album. However, by early 2002 he had made a re-appearance in Hearse alongside former Furbowl members drummer Max Thornell and guitarist Mattias Ljung for a debut album, *Dominion Reptilian*.

Arch Enemy toured Japan again during March 2002 and put in debut British shows as support to Opeth in May. They were then confirmed as one of the headline attractions at the mammoth 'Beast Fest' event in Tokyo in December 2002, preceded by UK headline dates with support coming from Corporation 187 and the Hungarian band Without Face. Michael Amott laid down a guest solo on recording sessions by The Haunted in November.

As 2003 broke, Arch Enemy put in January headline dates in Sweden, once again supported by Corporation 187. In April, for a BBC radio session, the band recorded new versions of 'Beneath The Skin', 'Young Man, Old Soul', and 'Mantra', as well as a cover version of Bachman Turner Overdrive's 1970s hit 'Not Fragile'.

Sharlee D'Angelo joined a new side venture in early 2003 dubbed Firegod. This saw the bassist uniting with an esteemed cast: Mercyful Fate and King Diamond guitarist Mike Wead, the King Diamond, Dream Evil and Notre Dame-credited guitarist Snowy Shaw, and drummer Simon Johansson of Memory Garden and Abstrakt Algebra.

Promoting a new studio album, *Anthems Of Rebellion*, saw a first for the band when they headlined the 'Busan International Rock Festival' at Daedepo Beach in Korea on August 8th. The group then allied with Hate Eternal, Evergrey and The Black Dahlia Murder for a short but intensive run of US dates in mid August before pairing up with Nevermore for co-headlined European gigs throughout September and October. The closing shows of this trek were pulled, however, when Arch Enemy were dealt the unique blow of a bug infestation on their tour bus.

Maintaining the band's road presence, a lengthy string of US Jägermeister-sponsored dates commenced on October 9th and ran through until mid December alongside Slayer and Hatebreed. *Anthems Of Rebellion*, breaking the charts across Europe, went on to be Century Media's fastest-selling record to date. In the USA, the record took just three months to sell over 25,000 copies. UK dates in December allied the band with Akercocke.

The band's profile rose higher in 2004 as they lent support to Iron Maiden's Canada, New York City and Japanese gigs. European headline dates in February and March saw Zyklon and Stampin' Ground in support. Gigs in Osnabrück, Essen and Antwerp were pulled when Gossow lost her voice. US gigs in April had the band scheduled as heavyweight support to Machine Head, although they missed the first show in Philadelphia on the 25th due to an apparent delay in processing Gossow's work visa. As it transpired, the group then pulled out of the entire tour, and headliners Machine Head issued a sarcastic press statement claiming the band had withdrawn "because singer Angela 'Gossard' broke a fingernail which had recently been through a vigorous French manicure".

Returning to Japan as headliners, Arch Enemy put in a short burst of dates in June. Meanwhile, Daniel Erlandsson debuted his new act, Revengia, in mid 2004, issuing *A Decade In The Dark*. Michael Amott took time out to record a guitar solo for the song 'Murder Fantasies' on the latest Kreator album. Amott's parallel act, Spiritual Beggars, entered Studio Fredman in July with producer Nordström to cut a new album. Sharlee D'Angelo played bass on these tracks.

Partners for the November 'Headbanger's Ball III' US tour were Cradle Of Filth, Bleeding Through and Himsa. That same month, a US issue of *Dead Eyes See No Future* appeared, while December saw the band on the road in Europe, forming up the 'Hammered At Xmas' tour in alliance with The Haunted and Dark Tranquillity. A London show was filmed for DVD. A 2005 compilation inclusion of note was the track 'We Will Rise' featured on the *Code Red* album, an exclusive collection given to US soldiers on duty in the Middle East.

In mid 2005, Greek guitarist Gus G. (aka Kostas Karamitroudis) of Nightrage, Mystic Prophecy, Dream Evil and Firewind joined Arch Enemy as the group's touring guitarist for the US 'Ozzfest' dates after Christopher Amott bowed out in order to "fully concentrate on his studies". *Doomsday Machine* arrived in stores worldwide during July. Japanese variants on the Toy's Factory label added the traditional bonus tracks – live versions of 'Heart Of Darkness' and 'Bridge Of Destiny'. In the USA, the album sold just under 12,000 copies in its first week of release to debut at Number 87 on the *Billboard* charts.

New guitarist Fredrik Åkesson was inducted: he was a veteran of acts such as One Cent, Krux, Tiamat and Southpaw. Arch Enemy's September and October European headline dates, taking in the UK, France, Belgium, Holland, Germany, Norway, Sweden and Denmark, saw strong support from Trivium. The two bands stuck together for Japanese gigs in October. However, the UK dates were re-scheduled for December when co-headliners Dark Tranquillity withdrew. Strapping Young Lad duly joined forces for the tour. Meanwhile, the band engaged in touring throughout November in the USA, sharing stages with All That Remains, Mnemic and A Perfect Murder.

Arch Enemy, Chimaira, Nevermore, God Forbid and Hate Eternal announced US shows for April 2006. That same month, Gossow featured as guest singer on the all-female Greek black metal band Astarte's *Demonized* album. Arch Enemy's Mexican debut came in May with shows in Monterrey and Mexico City. The band put in a significant appearance at the Metallica and Korn-headlined 'Download' festival in Castle Donington, England on June 10th. The importance of Arch Enemy lies not so much in their effortlessly melodic death metal – although that in itself is worthy of our respect – but also in the fact that the band have proved that a new approach can still work in the metal field.

AT THE GATES
MELODIC DEATH METAL PIONEERS

AT THE GATES ARE RECOGNISED as the instigators of the Gothenburg NWOSDM – or New Wave Of Swedish Death Metal – and play aggressive, technical thrash metal, but with added melody and a touch of the avant-garde. The quintet were initially known as Grotesque, forged by ex-Oral guitarist Alf Svensson, who was billed under a stage name of The Haunting. Vocals were handled by Goatspell (aka Tomas Lindberg) with Necrolord (aka 'Bullen' Kristian Wahlin) on guitars. The group's original rhythm section consisted of bassist Nuctemeron, with the Sorhin and Arckanum-credited Shamaatae (aka Johan S. Lager) on drums. Subsequently Offensor (aka Tomas Eriksson) manned the drums.

Recordings issued under the Grotesque name included the demos *Ripped From The Cross*, a three-song rehearsal session in 1988, and *The Black Gate Is Closed*, laid down on April 5th 1989. The Dolores label issued the *Incantation* mini-album in 1990, pressed in lilac or black vinyl editions. That same year the band folded. Tomas Lindberg and Alf Svensson, joining forces with identical twins Anders and Jonas Björler on guitar and bass respectively, plus drummer Adrian Erlandsson, duly created At The Gates.

Their first product was the mini-album *Gardens Of Grief*, appearing on Dolores Records in May 1991. The song 'At The Gates' was dedicated to the late Mayhem singer Dead (Per Yngve Ohlin), who had committed suicide that April.

Svensson's involvement with At The Gates was brief; he soon departed, going on to form the extraordinary Oxiplegatz, releasing *Fairy Tales (Selatyriaf)* in 1994 and *Worlds And Worlds* in 1996.

The first At The Gates full-length album was *The Red In The Sky Is Ours*, delivered in July 1992, an ultra-heavyweight affair, featuring guest violinist Jesper Jarold. They then toured Europe opening for My Dying Bride. Their second album, 1993's *With Fear I Kiss The Burning Darkness*, was produced by noted death metal studio man Tomas Skogsberg and again received solid reviews. Dismember's Matti Kärki notably provided some additional growls for good measure. The band appeared at the 'MTV/Peaceville' show at Nottingham's Rock City alongside label-mates Anathema and My Dying Bride, before once more touring Europe with Anathema and opening act Cradle Of Filth in January 1994.

Terminal Spirit Disease was produced by Fredrik Nordström and included a selection of live tracks culled from the previous three releases alongside new studio material, the first to feature new guitarist Martin Larsson, and embellished by cellist Peter Andersson and violinist Ylva Wåhlstedt. To back up the release, the band hit the road with Anathema, My Dying Bride and fellow Swedes Séance. That same year a shortlived but significant At The Gates-connected project emerged, Terror: this was a union of Anders and Jonas Björler and drummer Adrian Erlandsson with the soon-to-be-notorious Dissection frontman Jon Nödtveidt. Terror issued a solitary demo prior to collapse.

At The Gates then switched labels to Earache, and the first product of this liaison was the *Slaughter Of The Soul* album, which featured a version of Australian act Slaughterlord's track 'Legion' as a Japanese bonus track. King Diamond guitarist Andy La Rocque guested on 'Cold'. Clocking in at

---

AT THE GATES discography

Gardens Of Grief, Dolores DOL 005 (Europe) (1991)
THE RED IN THE SKY IS OURS, Deaf DEAF10CD (UK), Grind Core International 89810-2 (USA) (1992)
WITH FEAR I KISS THE BURNING DARKNESS, Deaf DEAF14CD (UK), Fierce 9086-11060-2 (USA) (1993)
TERMINAL SPIRIT DISEASE, Peaceville VILE47CD (UK), Futurist 9086-11061-2 (USA) (1994)
Gardens Of Grief, Peaceville Collectors CC 7 (UK) (1994) 7-inch yellow vinyl single
SLAUGHTER OF THE SOUL, Earache MOSH143CD (UK / USA) (1995)
SUICIDAL FINAL ART, Peaceville CDVILED86 (UK / USA) (2001)

---

an all-too-brief 34 minutes, the Nordström-produced *Slaughter* was close to death metal perfection. At The Gates contributed a rendition of 'Captor Of Sin' to the Slayer tribute album *Slatanic Slaughter*.

Despite *Slaughter Of The Soul* proving to be their highest-selling effort, the band split in late 1996. Various members of the band created The Haunted, fronted by former Face Down singer Marco Aro. Adrian Erlandsson founded H.E.A.L. and joined Cradle Of Filth in 1999.

Lindberg became vocalist for The Great Deceiver, releasing the 2000 album *Jet Black Art*, and many other projects, including Disincarnate, the band assembled by former Death, Testament and Cancer guitarist James

The legendary and much-missed At The Gates

Murphy. By mid 2000 Lindberg was fronting Lock Up, the side project of Napalm Death men Shane Embury and Jesse Pintado with Dimmu Borgir drummer Nick Barker.

Slaughter Of The Soul, recognised as a genre classic, was reissued in 2002 with a glut of extra tracks including the Slaughterlord 'Legion' Japanese bonus cut, two working demos, an outtake from the album sessions titled 'The Dying', the cover of Slayer's 'Captor Of Sin', and a rendition of No Security's 'Bister Verklighet'. A 2004 tribute album, Slaughterous Souls – A Tribute to At The Gates, was released in September through Drowned Scream Records.

DARK TRANQUILLITY
EVER-EVOLVING DEATH METALLERS

DARK TRANQUILLITY ARE A SWEDISH act who have generated a buoyant international fanbase with their unique strain of dark music. The band began life in the characteristic Gothenburg death metal style but have diversified with frightening speed with each successive release to carve out their own niche in the metal world. Later releases employed electronica, stark piano-led pieces, orchestration, female vocals and a heady, often wholly unexpected juxtaposition of sounds.

Dark Tranquillity date back to December 1989, starting life under the rather bizarre moniker of Septic Broiler. In this guise the band – lead vocalist Anders Fridén, guitarists Niklas Sundin and Mikael Stanne, Martin Henriksson on bass and drummer Anders Jivarp – released a 1990 demo entitled Enfeeble Earth. Only 100 copies of this cassette were made, co-produced by the band with Dragan Tanascovic and Stefan Lindgren.

Switching names to Dark Tranquillity, they booked three days at Studio Soundscape studios in Gothenburg in March 1991 to lay down tracks for the Trail Of Life Decayed demo, 800 copies of which were distributed. Two now-rare 7-inch singles followed in 1992: the Trail Of Life Decayed EP, limited to 1,000 copies, was released by a Mexican label, Guttural. Dedicated fans soon spotted that the B-side, listed as 'A Void Of Tranquillity', was in fact 'Vernal Awakening'. Only 500 pressings were made of the EP A Moonclad Reflection, which initially bore the Slaughter Records logo before a second run became the debut release from the Exhumed Productions label. Both recordings were re-released in Poland the following year on Carnage Records.

Dark Tranquillity

Dark Tranquillity's first album, August 1993's Skydancer – again with Tanascovic and Lindgren behind the desk – was issued through the Finnish Spinefarm label and featured guest vocals from Anna-Kajsa Avehall. Skydancer garnered global releases in Japan, through Toy's Factory, and in Russia, where Fono Records handled CDs and Counter Attack produced cassettes.

In the wake of this release, Fridén left for a lucrative career fronting In Flames and was replaced by Stanne, who had coincidentally also performed with In Flames as vocalist on their Lunar Strain debut album. Stanne first made his mark on Dark Tranquillity's 1995 EP, Of Chaos And Eternal Night. The band also employed second guitarist Fredrik Johansson. Between these sessions, Dark Tranquillity contributed a version of 'My Friend Of Misery' to the Metallica tribute album Metal Militia, released by Black Sun Records in 1994.

A second album, The Gallery, was produced by Fredrik Nordström at Studio Fredman and issued through French label Osmose in November 1995. Now regarded as a pillar of the Gothenburg sound, The Gallery blended massive riffage with classic lead soloing and philosophical subject matter. Stanne's performance in particular, which ranged from subterranean roars to a clean style, came in for much praise: his female accompaniment came courtesy of Eva-Marie Larsson. International versions of The Gallery were beefed up with extra tracks, Japan adding 'My Friend Of Misery' while Korean variants saw a rendition of Sacred Reich's 'Sacred Reich'. In addition, a limited-edition 10-inch vinyl box boasted the Sacred Reich track and a take on Kreator's 'Bringer Of Torture'. In side activity, Stanne contributed guest vocals to Denial's debut EP Rape Of The Century.

A stopgap EP then arrived: Enter Suicidal Angels was released in November 1996. Including three tracks cut for the next album, The Mind's I, the EP added a somewhat unsuccessful techno amalgam of previous Dark Tranquillity tracks, bundled into one entity and given the title 'Archetype'.

A more significant moment in the band's history came when Stanne and Sundin created a trad-metal side project with former Ceremonial Oath drummer Jesper Strömblad and Crystal Age guitarist Oscar Dronjac entitled Hammerfall. Although the original intention had been to form a non-serious hobby band, Hammerfall subsequently signed to Nuclear Blast and – amazingly – shifted over 100,000 copies of their debut album, *Glory To The Brave*, in Germany alone. Unfortunately for Stanne, this came after he had dropped out of the band to concentrate on Dark Tranquillity.

The Mind's I came out in April 1997, punctuated by acoustic guitar passages and the female voices of Sara Svensson. Once again it demonstrated the band's ability to balance technical finesse with unrelenting, oppressive metal. Former singer Anders Fridén guested on the song 'Hedon'. In November, Dark Tranquillity headlined Osmose's 'World Domination' tour over Enslaved, Bewitched, Swordmaster, Demoniac and Dellamorte.

In early 1999, second guitarist Fredrik Johansson bowed out. Dark Tranquillity duly shifted bassist Martin Henriksson over to guitar and inducted Martin Brändström on keyboards. The band, switching to Century Media, re-emerged with the album *Projector* in June, the final set to feature Johansson. Here the group took a leap forward, with the death metal growls stripped away and replaced by cleaner tones, increased female vocal content from Johanna Andersson, keyboard washes, piano, and a neo-gothic feel.

Dark Tranquillity toured Japan in September 1999. The band performed to their biggest audience the same year as part of the Italian 'Gods Of Metal' festival headlined by Iron Maiden. The same year, Dutch band Ethereal Spawn covered 'Punish My Heaven' on their debut album.

The vacant bass role was filled by Luciferion's Michael Nicklasson in time for the recording of July 2000's *The Haven*, on which the band reacted to criticism levelled at *Projector* by reintroducing the death metal vocals – but also increasing the keyboard content. During September, they toured Europe with In Flames and Finnish outfits Sentenced and To/Die/For. This was followed by a short burst of Mexican dates.

The band toured Japan for the second time in April 2001, co-headlining with Finnish act Children Of Bodom, and played at the 'Wacken Open Air' festival in Germany. Brändström was lent out to Tiamat frontman Johan Edlund's Lucyfire endeavour for live work, before Dark Tranquillity's first show in Istanbul, Turkey in October, supported by Dishearten and Affliction. Drummer Jivarp injured his wrist on the eve of this jaunt and Lefay's Robin Engström stepped into the breach at short notice.

In early 2002, Brändström loaned out his services again, this time for Tiamat. Dark Tranquillity's momentum quickened with the *Damage Done* album that August, reaping worthy media praise and sales. The record broke into the national German and Swedish album charts. Buoyed up by this success, the band organised an extensive run of European dates with co-headliners Sinergy for November and December. The band then teamed up with Nile, Napalm Death, Strapping Young Lad and The Berzerker for North American dates in January and February 2003.

They entered the DVD era in style with *Live Damage*, which consisted of live footage from a Kraków TV performance recorded in October 2002, fan video recordings taken in Athens, Essen and Paris the same year, and promo clips for 'Monochromatic Stains' and 'ThereIn'. The band then celebrated their 15th anniversary with a two-CD retrospective compilation, *Exposures – In Retrospect And Denial*. This collected archive material from the *Trail Of Life Decayed* demo and the EP *A Moonclad Reflection* along with live and bonus songs and the unreleased songs 'Static', 'No One' and 'In Sight'.

During 2004, Sundin donated guitar parts to Japanese avant-garde metal act Sigh's *Gallows Gallery*. Dark Tranquillity, wrapping up a new album, performed at the fourth annual 'Busan Rock Festival' in South Korea during August 2004, putting in a small club gig at Seoul's Live Hall venue just beforehand under the pseudonym of Damage Done. Shortly afterward, they filmed a video for the track 'Lost to Apathy' with director

Roger Johansson. An EP, billed *Lost To Apathy*, emerged in November and charted in Sweden at Number 47.

Live dates found the band on the road in Europe during December, forming up the 'Hammered At Xmas' tour in alliance with The Haunted and Arch Enemy. US dates in January 2005 with Soilwork and Hypocrisy followed before the band teamed up with German thrash veterans Kreator for the Enemy Of God tour in February. Brändström joined Tiamat for European dates. Spectacularly, the new album *Character* entered the national Swedish charts at Number 3.

Dark Tranquillity's early albums, 1995's *The Gallery* and 1997's *The Mind's I*, were set for re-release, both adding a wealth of rare bonus material. The former included covers of Kreator's 'Bringer Of Torture', Sacred Reich's 'Sacred Reich', Iron Maiden's '22 Acacia Avenue', Mercyful Fate's 'Lady In Black' and Metallica's 'My Friend Of Misery'. 'Lost To Apathy' was featured on the *Code Red* album given to US soldiers in the Middle East.

The band announced South American gigs for June, taking in Chile, Guatemala, Mexico, Colombia, Argentina and Brazil. They revealed plans for September and October European dates, taking in the UK, France, Belgium, Holland, Germany, Norway, Sweden and Denmark, where they intended to give strong support to Arch Enemy with backing from Trivium – but then pulled out of these gigs.

Sundin unveiled a project with vocalist-bassist Jonatan Nordenstam and The Provenance pairing of guitarist Joakim Rosén and drummer Joel Lindell, billed Laethora. The new band's debut album, *March Of The Parasite,* was completed in August. A brief burst of German dates saw the band supported by Hatesphere and Chimaira.

Dark Tranquillity's 2006 season of live campaigning opened up in the USA during February alongside Opeth and The Devin Townsend Band. They remain at the forefront of the Swedish metal scene.

DISMEMBER
GRISLY DEATH METAL FRENZY

A STOCKHOLM-BASED BRUTAL death metal act, Dismember have held to a single path, untroubled by any notions of softening their approach or experimenting with their sound. They formed in 1988 as a trio of vocalist-bassist Robert Sennebäck, guitarist David Blomqvist and drummer Fred Estby. This initial line-up lasted just over a year but did release two demos, 1988's *Dismembered* and 1989's *Last Blasphemies*. The first of these tapes included 'Substantially Dead', exclusive to these sessions, while the remaining material later resurfaced, reworked by Carnage.

The original Dismember folded in late 1989 with Estby joining Carnage and Blomqvist opting for Entombed. However, shortly before the recording of the first Carnage album, *Dark Recollections*, which included Dismember demo tracks in re-recorded form, Blomqvist jumped ship and rejoined the band.

Carnage dissolved when guitarist Mike Amott quit to join the pioneering British grindcore act Carcass, leaving Estby, Blomqvist and General Surgery man Matti Kärki (who switched from bass to vocals) to resurrect Dismember. Still as a trio, the new line-up released the Tomas Skogsberg-produced *Reborn In Blasphemy* demo, with Nicke Andersson of Entombed handling guitar solos.

The group then invited Sennebäck, a member of Unleashed, to resume his position in the band as rhythm guitarist. Dismember also augmented their sound with the addition of the Carbonized and General Surgery-credited Richard Cabeza on bass. Having signed to Germany's Nuclear Blast label, a home for many Swedish acts of this style, the band provided two demo tracks to the label's *Death Is Just The Beginning* compilation.

DISMEMBER discography

LIKE AN EVER FLOWING STREAM, Nuclear Blast NB 047-2 (Europe), Nuclear Blast America 6018 (USA) (1991)

Pieces, Nuclear Blast NB 060-2 (Europe), Nuclear Blast America 6021 (USA) (1992)

INDECENT AND OBSCENE, Nuclear Blast NB 077-2 (Europe), Nuclear Blast America 6088 (USA) (1993)

Casket Garden, Nuclear Blast NB 130-2 (1995)

MASSIVE KILLING CAPACITY, Nuclear Blast NB 123-2 (Europe), Nuclear Blast America 6123 (USA) (1995)

Misanthropic, Nuclear Blast NB 0254-2 (Europe), Nuclear Blast America 6254 (USA) (1997)

DEATH METAL, Nuclear Blast NB 0250-2 (Europe), Nuclear Blast America 6250 (USA) (1997)

HATE CAMPAIGN, Nuclear Blast NB 0419-2 (Europe), Nuclear Blast America 6419 (USA) (2000)

WHERE IRONCROSSES GROW, Karmageddon Media KARMA 025 (Europe), Candlelight CD CDL 91 (USA) (2004)

COMPLETE DEMOS, Regain RR CD068 (Europe), Candlelight CD CDL 228 (USA) (2005)

THE GOD THAT NEVER WAS, Regain RR CD083 (Europe), Candlelight CD CDL 255 (USA) (2006)

Dismember then garnered huge media attention in 1991 with their debut album, *Like An Ever Flowing Stream*. Recorded by Skogsberg at Sunlight Studios in March 1991, the album again featured a guesting Andersson, who also designed the band's logo.

The band played pure old-school death metal with no hint of the modern Gothenburg style being played on the other side of Sweden. *Like An Ever Flowing Stream* scored solid reviews, but the album was confiscated by British and Australian customs for being "indecent and obscene" (this legal term was used by the band for the title of their 1993 album), and the international metal fanbase began to pay more attention as a result. Her Majesty's customs had objected to song titles such as 'Skin Her Alive' and 'Brutal Orgy Of Flesh', and legal proceedings held in Great Yarmouth led government officials to brand Dismember's lyrical content as "hideous, frightful and repulsive to the senses [and] liable to inspire a sense of violence in the listener". Naturally, the court case shot Dismember's name to the forefront of the current wave of death metal.

The band toured Europe opening for Morbid Angel in June 1991, but these dates were curtailed due to disagreements between the two acts. Further live shows included appearances at the 'Rock Hard' festivals alongside Death, Pestilence and Napalm Death.

The band's notoriety was reinforced by the 1992 mini-album *Pieces*, the cover of which depicted the band members' severed heads, and had Richard Cabeza going by the title Richard Daemon. *Pieces* prefaced more live shows in Europe with Obituary and Napalm Death. A second full album, *Indecent And Obscene*, released in December 1993, gave fans more of the same formula that had so outraged the authorities. The band preceded the record's release with a bout of touring in America in 1993 alongside Suffocation and Deicide before hooking up with Morbid Angel once more for a European tour. With its artwork displaying the band's bloodied logo in an eviscerated chest cavity, *Indecent And Obscene* matched the brutality of its visuals with a collection of starkly lethal death metal tunes.

Following a lay-off period in which Cabeza worked on the Damnation project's *Divine Darkness* demo, Dismember returned to the fray in early 1995 as part of Nuclear Blast-organised festivals alongside label-mates Meshuggah, Hypocrisy and Benediction. An EP, *Casket Garden*, was released as a taster for the new album. *Massive Killing Capacity* arrived in August 1995 and gave Dismember their first German chart album. The record focused more intently on groove, reining back the speed somewhat and provoking a degree of criticism from the die-hards.

The June 1997 *Misanthropic* EP included Dismember's rendition of Autopsy's 'Pagan Saviour'. A full album, *Death Metal*, produced by Estby at Sunlight Studios arrived in August. By now, the group had made it clear that, in a climate coloured by many previously extreme bands exploring more subdued musical options, Dismember would remain steadfast. A song on the album, 'Trendkiller', spelled this out even more clearly.

In 1998, the band enrolled the Celeborn and Tiamat-credited Magnus Sahlgren on guitar. This unit cut the 2000 *Hate Campaign* album at Das Boot Studios. By this juncture, Cabeza had been replaced by Sharlee D'Angelo (aka Charles Petter Andreason). Cabeza, who had been briefly linked to Norway's Satyricon, worked alongside Matti Kärki plus Entombed's Uffe Cederlund and Peter Stjärnvind for their Murder Squad project, Pavement Records issuing the 2001 debut *Unsane, Insane And Mentally Deranged*.

Yet another Dismember offshoot arrived in 2001: Born Of Fire were founded by Cabeza alongside guitarist 'Mr. Dim' and the Loud Pipes duo of Peter Stjärnvind and Fredrik Lindgren. They bowed in with the 7-inch single 'Chosen By The Gods' on Primitive Art. Cabeza then teamed up with premier black metal act Dark Funeral for North American touring in spring 2002. European dates in November were announced with Dismember heading up a package bill comprising Septic Flesh, Sinister and Thyrfing. Embarking on a mammoth string of European shows throughout October and November 2002, Dismember formed part of a deadly union for the 'Generation Armageddon' festival. Joining the band were Norway's Blood Red Throne, Greece's Septic Flesh, Ireland's Primordial, Belgium's Ancient Rites, and fellow Swedish heavyweights Impious.

By January 2003, Dismember had signed to Hammerheart (later Karmageddon Media) and were scheduling a new album with the title of *Where Ironcrosses Grow* for a September release (later pushed back to early 2004). Meantime, Magnus Sahlgren had been replaced by Martin Persson in 2003. The album was recorded at Sami Studios in Stockholm during December and saw both David Blomqvist and Cabeza handling bass. A concert DVD emerged, *Live Blasphemies*, a two-disc set comprising the band's performance from a May 27th 2003 date at Klubben in Stockholm and a second disc of documentary and home video footage. Dutch dates in May saw Callenish Circle and Flesh Made Sin as support.

With Cabeza now residing in Dallas, Texas, Dismember announced the addition of bassist Johan Bergebäck of Necrophobic and Morpheus to the group in September 2004. A short burst of Benelux dates that same month saw them united with Callenish Circle, Occult and Hearse. Further shows had the band allied with Australians Psycroptic, fellow Swedes Anata and Slovakian act Sanatorium for a European tour commencing on November 3rd in Nürnberg, Germany. They opened 2005 with a tour of Finland backed by Bonegrinder and Omnium Gatherum.

Regain Records picked up the Dismember back catalogue for 2005 reissue, each release being expanded with extra tracks. The first of these, the digipack *Pieces* EP in June, boasted an additional ten live tracks recorded in Stockholm during 1993. The *Complete Demos* release collected *Dismembered* from 1988, *Last Blasphemies* from 1989 and 1990's *Reborn In Blasphemy*.

Dismember parted ways with bassist Johan Bergebäck in August, replacing him with Tobias Christiansson. The band's seventh album, *The God That Never Was*, was once again produced by Estby at Sami Studios in Stockholm. They then teamed up with Vital Remains, Grave, Demiricous and Withered for a North American tour beginning in late

Dismember: no longer 'indecent and obscene'

The late Dissection frontman Jon Nödtveidt

September. European shows announced for November, dubbed the 'Masters Of Death' tour, had the band lined up with a supremely heavyweight Scandinavian cast of Grave, Entombed and Unleashed. They then united once more with Entombed, Grave and The Absence for a US West Coast tour in December. Solid output and unwavering adherence to a formula seems to have positioned Dismember perfectly to capitalise on a further wave of old school death metal appreciation.

DISSECTION
COMMITTED BUT CONTROVERSIAL

IF EVER A BAND DESERVED the description "blackened death" it would be Strömstad's Satanic masters Dissection. This truly blasphemous band date back to 1989, instigated by vocalist-guitarist Jon Nödveidt and bassist Peter Palmdahl. Before Dissection, Nödveidt, Palmdahl and drummer Ole Öhman had operated with proto-thrash metal band Siren's Yell, releasing a 1988 demo.

Dissection's first offering was the rehearsal demo *Severing Into Shreds*, cut in April 1990. Their live entrance was made that October, acting as support to Entombed. For their next try-out, *The Grief Prophecy*, containing three tracks recorded on December 14th 1990, the band were temporarily boosted to a quartet with the introduction of rhythm guitarist Mäbe (aka Mattias Johansson), another erstwhile Siren's Yell member, employed at the time with Nosferatu. The cassette featured artwork from respected scene figure Necrolord (aka Kristian Wåhlin), which led to the artist's work appearing on all Dissection products except one. Notably, the artwork for a second April 1991 edition of this tape was rendered by Dead (aka Per Yngve Ohlin), the Morbid and Mayhem frontman.

In January 1991, second guitarist John Zwetsloot was recruited, and in September a limited edition three-track EP, *Into Infinite Obscurity*, followed on the French Corpsegrinder label. To promote the album and the accompanying shows, the group printed up T-shirts, the first to bear the infamous flaming trident cross logo. The live set for these early shows saw the original songs bulked out by covers of Possessed's 'Séance', Death's 'Evil Dead' and Mayhem's 'Freezing Moon'. Mayhem had begun to figure ever stronger in Dissection's career path: both Nödtveidt and Öhman guested with Mayhem at a concert that December held in Askim, Norway, and it was known that the Dissection frontman had been initiated into what was known as the Norwegian Black Circle. Nödtveidt demoed with another act billed as Satanized, performing a November 1991 gig with this band, which consisted of vocalist Per Alexandersson of Nifelheim, second guitarist Johan Norman and Decameron drummer Tobias Kjellgren.

A further crop of Dissection demos – *The Somberlain*, laid down in March 1992, and a 1993 set which featured a cover of 'Elizabeth Bathori', originally by Hungarian band Tormentor – led to a deal with No Fashion. Nödtveidt, going under the pseudonym of Rietas, was also operating his side project The Black at this stage.

The debut Dissection album, *The Somberlain*, was constructed at Hellspawn/Unisound studios in March 1993, overseen by producer Dan Swanö, frontman of Edge Of Sanity among many other acts. For such an extreme concept, Dissection's inaugural album surprised many with its sophistication. Although it was undoubtedly heavy, *The Somberlain* was balanced by its dexterous musicianship, notably Zwetsloot's classical persuasions, its acoustic passages, and a keen priority on melody. Dissection pointedly dedicated their first offering to the murdered Mayhem singer Euronymous.

While assembling *The Somberlain* throughout 1993, the group relocated to Gothenburg, sharing rehearsal facilities with At The Gates. Meanwhile, Nödveidt's extracurricular act The Black released their debut record *The Priest Of Satan* as *The Somberlain* arrived in stores in December 1993.

Yet another outside indulgence for Nödtveidt was the highly experimental Ophthalamia, a fantasy-fuelled metal exercise arranged by It (aka Tony Särkkä) of Abruptum. Nödtveidt appeared under the name Shadow on the 1994 album *A Journey In Darkness*.

Internal friction resulted in the exit of Zwetsloot, with the final concert of this line-up on April 14th 1994 in Oslo. Johan Norman, previously with Decameron, Satanized and Sacramentum, was drawn into the fold as a quick-fire replacement. Zwetsloot then forged Cardinal Sin, issuing the *Spiteful Intents* EP, and later figured briefly in the original line-up of The Haunted.

Dissection signed to Nuclear Blast that November, but not before releasing two tracks on a compilation album for Wrong Again Records, namely 'Elizabeth Bathori' and 'Where Dead Angels Lie'. The Swedes also contributed a cover of Slayer's 'The Antichrist' to the Black Sun Records compilation *Slatanic Slaughter*. That same year a shortlived but significant Dissection-connected project emerged titled Terror – a union between Nödtveidt and the At The Gates triumvirate of guitarist Anders Björler, bass player Jonas Björler and drummer Adrian Erlandsson. Terror issued a solitary demo and collapsed.

Dissection ensconced themselves in the familiar surroundings of the Hellspawn/Unisound studios in March 1995 for *Storm Of The Light's Bane*. Once the album had been completed, the band hit the UK for the first time, putting in three concerts with Cradle Of Filth. Music was not the sole priority, however, as that summer Nödveidt and Norman established an occult denomination known as the Misanthropic Luciferian Order.

On October 10th, supporting Morbid Angel at Gothenburg's Kåren venue, the band debuted a new drummer, Tobias Kjellgren, previously of

Satanized, Swordmaster and Decameron. The departing Öhman temporarily teamed up with Swordmaster and then joined Ophthalamia.

Storm Of The Light's Bane arrived in November 1995. Framed by two instrumentals – the opening 'At The Fathomless Depths' and a piano finale 'No Dreams Breed in Breathless Sleep' performed by Alexandra Balogh, then girlfriend of Abruptum's Tony Särkkä – the record pursued a more direct black/thrash approach than its predecessor. The record's clear Satanic aesthetic was tempered by swathes of reverb, supremely melodic riffs and more immediate songwriting, enabling Dissection to widen their support.

They toured Europe with label-mates Dismember in December, this trek encompassing Germany, Austria, the Czech Republic, Switzerland and Sweden. After touring in the UK in February 1996 with At The Gates, the band hit the west coast of North America alongside At The Gates and Morbid Angel. Dissection's return shows in Europe throughout April were played with with Satyricon and Gorgoroth.

The 1997 'Gods Of Darkness' dates placed Dissection into an unholy mix alongside Cradle Of Filth, Dimmu Borgir and In Flames. Operations were concluded with an appearance at the 'Wacken Open Air' event, captured on tape, and a headline spot at the Nuclear Blast festivals. This exhausting regime had affected the group's stability, however – Palmdahl opted out and the outdoor appearances witnessed a new line-up featuring Jon's brother Emil on bass. Another defection saw Johan Norman withdrawing into anonymity, allegedly under fear of the Misanthropic Luciferian Order.

During a down period in the band's activity, Jon created an anonymous ambient side project with Midvinter's Damien titled De Infernali in 1997: they released the album *Symphonia De Infernali*. Ole Öhman also engaged in side work, enrolling in Ophthalamia in 1997 under the nom de guerre of Bone.

In December, Dissection's future was thrown into doubt when Nödveidt was arrested on suspicion of the murder of a 37-year-old Algerian homosexual, Josef Ben Maddaour, some months earlier. The victim had been slain in Keillers Park in Gothenburg. Found guilty of being an accessory to a murder and in possession of an illegal firearm, Nödveidt would ultimately be incarcerated for eight years, commencing his punishment at the maximum security prison in Kumla before being sent to Tidaholm jail.

While Nödtveidt bided his time, composing new material and deepening his esoteric studies, Dissection fans were kept interested with the Necropolis release *The Past Is Alive*, which collected the early demos and singles as well as two tracks from Satanized.

Despite Dissection being inoperative, Nödtveidt's influence on the scene could still be felt from jail, as he contributed lyrics to Diabolicum's 2001 album *The Dark Blood Rising (The Hatecrowned Retaliation)*. The ousted Palmdahl joined Runemagick for *The Supreme Force Of Eternity*. The bassist also appeared on the 1998 album from Deathwitch, *Ultimate Death*.

During July 2002, reports indicated that the former Emperor and Thorns drummer Bård 'Faust' Eithun would be behind the kit for Dissection's planned comeback release in 2003. Purely as a PR exercise, let alone a creative union, this proposed arrangement stoked controversy as it paired two convicted felons: Eithun had been jailed for a similar crime. Before either man was released, Dissection re-established their credentials with the issue of a live album, *Live Legacy*, recorded in 1997 at the German 'Wacken Open Air' festival.

Before the close of 2003, Eithun backed out of Dissection, apparently due to a conflict over "the demands of Dissection's Satanic concept".

The band, recording new material in July before Nödtveidt's release on September 6th, announced UK tour dates for December 2004 with Watain as support. Alongside Nödtveidt in this new line-up were Aborym and Bloodline guitarist Set Teitan, bassist Brice Leclercq of Nightrage, and

DISSECTION discography

Into Infinite Obscurity, Corpse Grinder CGR 003 (Europe) (1991) 7-inch vinyl EP
THE SOMBERLAIN, No Fashion NFR 006 (Europe) (1993)
STORM OF THE LIGHT'S BANE, Nuclear Blast NB 129-2 (Europe), Nuclear Blast America 6129 (USA) (1995)
Where Dead Angels Lie, Nuclear Blast NB 167-2 (Europe), Nuclear Blast America 6167 (USA) (1996)
THE PAST IS ALIVE (THE EARLY MISCHIEF), Necropolis NR017 (USA) (1998)
LIVE LEGACY, Nuclear Blast NB 650-2 (Europe), Nuclear Blast America 6650 (USA) (2003)
Maha Kali, Escapi Music AUD 008X (Europe / USA) (2004)
Starless Aeon, The End TE071 (USA) (2006)
REINKAOS, Black Horizon BHM001 (Europe), The End TE067 (USA) (2006)

the Infernal, Dawn and Dark Funeral-credited Tomas 'Alzazmon' Asklund on drums.

The public response to the comeback was enthusiastic, with the band's Stockholm gig moved from the Klubben venue to the Lilla Arenan due to high ticket demand. A new single, entitled 'Maha Kali', described by the band as "a hymn to the wrathful black Hindu goddess of Mahapralaya, the great dissolution of cosmos, Jai Maha Kali", was made available solely at concert dates and through the band's website. The single entered the national Swedish charts at Number 50.

On November 17th, Dissection were joined by Tormentor, Aborym and the newly re-appointed Mayhem singer Attila Csihar for renditions of two old-school black metal classics, 'Elizabeth Bathori' by Tormentor and 'Freezing Moon' by Mayhem, during the band's appearance at Kultiplex in Budapest, Hungary.

Dissection's appearance at the 2005 'Metalist' festival in Israel was cancelled when event headliner Megadeth's mainman Dave Mustaine refused to play with Satanic bands. Jon Nödtveidt reacted by branding Mustaine a "coward", adding: "You do not dare to face true opponents in faith?! You think this will stop us?! We are Satanists, yes, truly enemies of yours! For we are the antithesis to cowards like you!"

Leclercq exited abruptly in early June just before Dissection's appearance at the 'Undead Festival' in Hungary. Undaunted, the band performed as a trio with the bass provided by a backing track. Subsequently, Haakon Nikolas Forwald (aka Kshatriya or Savant M and General K) of Myrkskog and Disiplin (and a member of the Misanthropic Luciferian Order) was installed on bass.

Gigs across South America were scheduled for September, but shows in Chile and Venezuela were cancelled, the band blaming the promoter for not honouring his contractual commitments. Returning to Sweden, they utilised Black Syndicate Studios in Stockholm to record a new album with Nödtveidt's brother Emil (aka The Deathstars' Nightmare Industries) and Skinny Kangur as producers.

Dissection suffered the loss of Forwald in November, a press statement revealing that the bassist had vacated his position "in order to focus on his esoteric and exoteric work in Norway". Rejecting rumours of a band split, Jon Nödtveidt stated: "We are now heading into a new phase, a darker phase." The following month a title of *Reinkaos* was announced, and appropriately the comeback album was released on Walpurgisnacht: April 30th 2006.

The End Records unveiled an expanded reissue campaign of remasters for June. *The Somberlain* added *The Grief Prophecy* and *Into*

Infinite Obscurity material of 1990 and 1991, plus live tracks and rehearsal sessions, while *Storm Of The Light's Bane* was enhanced with a second disc, comprising the 1996 *Where Dead Angels Lie* EP, previously unheard 1994 demos, and a completely different album mix.

In August 2006, Nödtveidt closed Dissection's career in a manner befitting his philosophies: he committed suicide. Band members released a statement claiming "he was more focused, happier and stronger than ever" and "he chose to end his life by his own hands. As a true Satanist he led his life in the way he wanted and ended it when he felt that he had fulfilled his self-created destiny".

Nödtveidt, 31 years old, was found dead at his apartment in Hässelby, a suburb of Stockholm, on August 16th. Newspapers reported that he had surrounded himself with candles and had a copy of Anton LaVey's *Satanic Bible* open before him when he shot himself. Shortly beforehand he had told friends he was "going to Transylvania". Subsequently, Dissection guitarist Set Teitan reportedly commented on an online forum that the book Nödtveidt had open in front of him was "a Satanic grimoire" and not LaVey's work, because "he despised LaVey and [the] 'Church Of Satan'."

ENTOMBED
CRUSHING METAL PIONEERS

STOCKHOLM'S ENTOMBED ARE ONE of the elite death metal bands, with their 1993 album *Wolverine Blues* generally acknowledged as a masterpiece of the genre. They were originally known as Nihilist, under which name they recorded the *Premature Autopsy*, *Only Shreds Remain* and *Drowned* demos. Vocalist Lars-Göran Petrov and guitarist Uffe Cederlund were credited as "session members" on the first demo, but Cederlund did not feature on the second. Both men had previously made their mark with Morbid, the band that featured the pre-Mayhem Per 'Dead' Ohlin. With bassist Johnny Hedlund forming Unleashed, Nihilist folded – only to reunite a matter of days later as Entombed.

Now with David Blomqvist on bass, the band visited Stockholm's Sunlight Studios on September 23rd 1989 to record the *But Life Goes On* demo. A contract was secured with leading British label Earache, and Entombed retained Sunlight producer Tomas Skogsberg's services for their first album that December, with Cederlund and Nicke Andersson sharing bass duties.

Following the release of *Left Hand Path* in June 1990, which included reworked versions of many earlier Nihilist songs, Entombed recruited a permanent bass player in former Conspiracy, Carbonized and Monastery man Lars Rosenberg. The band also included guitarist Alex Hellid. The year 1991 proved to be an eventful one for the band: vocalist Lars-Göran Petrov was fired after personal clashes with the other members and was temporarily replaced by Orvar Säfström of Nirvana 2002, who was then superseded by Johnny Dordevic. The second album, *Clandestine*, released in November 1991, credited Dordevic with lead vocals, although it was later reported that Andersson had recorded these. However, the 'Crawl' single, issued in April 1991, was recorded with Säfström. Another EP, *Stranger Aeons* – released in August 1992 – also credited Dordevic when in fact Andersson had performed the vocals.

In the autumn, the band toured America alongside fellow Swedes Unleashed and headliners Morbid Angel, although Dordevic left in September 1992 on the eve of the 'Gods Of Grind' tour. He was replaced by the reinstated Lars-Göran Petrov. In his sabbatical from Entombed, Petrov had recorded with both Comecon and Morbid.

The landmark *Wolverine Blues* arrived in late 1993, signalling a radical shift away from the tried and trusted death metal into wholly unexplored areas of extreme groove-loaded music – which would become known as death'n'roll. Long-standing fans were sharply divided in their opinions,

ENTOMBED discography

LEFT HAND PATH, Earache MOSH021CD (UK), Combat/Earache 88561-2021-2 (USA) (1990)

CLANDESTINE, Earache MOSH037CD (UK), Relativity/Earache 88561-1095-2 (USA) (1991)

Hollowman, Earache MOSH094CD (UK), Relativity/Earache CK 57504 (USA) (1993)

State Of Emergency, King Kong KK 004 (Europe) (1993) split 7-inch EP with Teddy Bear and Doll Squad

WOLVERINE BLUES, Earache MOSH082CD (UK), Colombia/Earache CK 57593 (USA) (1993)

Out Of Hand, Earache MOSH114CD (UK) (1994)

Night Of The Vampire, Earache 7MOSH132 (UK) (1995) split 7-inch vinyl single with New Bomb Turks

WRECKAGE, Pony Canyon PCCY 01207 (Japan) (1997)

ENTOMBED, Earache MOSH125CD (UK) (1997)

DCLXVI – TO RIDE, SHOOT STRAIGHT AND SPEAK THE TRUTH, Music For Nations CDMFN 216 (UK) (1997) **75 UK**

MONKEY PUSS – LIVE IN LONDON, Earache MOSH213CD (UK) (1998)

SAME DIFFERENCE, Music For Nations CDMFN 244 (UK) (1998)

Black Juju, Man's Ruin MR 119 (USA) (1999)

UPRISING, Music For Nations CDMFN 257 (UK) (2000)

MORNING STAR, Music For Nations CDMFN 265 (UK) (2001), Koch KOC-CD-8357 (USA) (2002)

SONS OF SATAN – PRAISE THE LORD, Music For Nations CDMFN 293 (UK) (2002)

INFERNO, Music For Nations CDMFN 295 (UK), Koch KOC-CD-8864 (USA) (2003)

UNREAL ESTATE, Threeman Recordings TRECD 015 (Europe), Candlelight CD CDL 174 (USA) (2004)

When In Sodom, Threeman Recordings TRECDEP 022 (Europe), Candlelight CD CDL 321 (USA) (2006)

but with *Wolverine Blues* the group had successfully avoided the artistic bankruptcy choking many other bands of their genre. The record came in two cover variations, one with artwork depicting Marvel Comics' Wolverine cartoon character. This design, unsanctioned by the band, resulted in acrimony between Earache and their new US corporate partners Columbia. As a marketing ploy, the gamble worked, bringing many new fans into the world of Entombed.

In 1994, they toured Europe as guests to Napalm Death: the general opinion was that Entombed consistently stole the show from the flagging headliners. Subsequent North American dates were marred by the band having to play as a trio in Canada, minus Lars-Göran Petrov, who had lost his passport when Entombed's tour van was stolen in Cleveland. Entombed persevered with a show in Toronto, Ontario, with guitarist Cederlund as lead vocalist. Further chaos came when, for the second show in Montreal, Cederlund lost his voice completely, prompting the band to invite audience members to participate.

In 1994, the band released the 'Out Of Hand' 7-inch single, which saw them covering tracks by diverse influences such as Kiss and Repulsion. Midway through 1995, bassist Rosenberg opted to join Therion, having filled in on a temporary basis for live work. Entombed added ex-Grave bassist Jörgen Sandström in his place and parted company with Earache in 1996 to sign with major label EastWest. However, despite recording an album, the band found themselves embroiled in record company politics and it was shelved. Luckily, a deal was hastily negotiated between

EastWest and the leading independent Music For Nations, and *DCLXVI – To Ride, Shoot Straight And Speak The Truth* was released in 1997. Digipack versions of the album came with a free *Family Favourites* EP, which saw Entombed ripping through Black Sabbath's 'Under The Sun', Venom's 'Bursting Out', King Crimson's '21st Century Schizoid Man' and MC5's 'Kick Out The Jams'. *To Ride* impacted impressively on the Swedish album charts, making Number 7.

Outside Entombed, Nicke Andersson – in the guise of Nicke Royale – dabbled with The Hellacopters with Dick Hakansson (aka Dregan) from Backyard Babies. The Hellacopters' first album was released in late 1996 and received such acclaim – with the band even being asked to support Kiss on their Scandinavian dates – that Andersson felt obliged to quit Entombed to concentrate fully on his new band. In 1996, Cederlund and Andersson released the *Seven Deadly Sins* album together with Konkhra's vocalist Anders Lundemark under the band name of Daemon. Cederlund contributed lead solos to two tracks on the album.

April 1997 found Entombed back on European soil, heading up the 'Full Of Hate Easter' festivals alongside Obituary, Death, Samael, Neurosis, Crowbar, Killing Culture and Strapping Young Lad. The band toured the UK as headliners in September and October 1997 supported by Neurosis and Breech. Cederlund also played in a punk band titled Haystack together with Backyard Babies bassist Johan Blomqvist: the band released a 1998 album, *Slave Me*.

Entombed, now with Merciless and Face Down drummer Peter 'Flinta' Stjärnwind, put in an American tour to kick off 1998. A new album, *Same Difference*, was greeted in November 1998 by indifferent reviews and only

scraped onto the Swedish charts at Number 52. The somewhat mellow *Same Difference* had been recorded at Polar Studios in Stockholm with Daniel Rey as producer. The following year, both Petrov and Hellid made their presence felt as guests on the *Wasting The Dawn* album from Finnish vampire rockers The 69 Eyes.

Opting for a complete rethink after the artistic failure of *Same Difference*, Entombed went back to basics. Relieving some of the pressure, the group put out a mini-album titled *Black Juju* in November 1999 through the US stoner label Man's Ruin. It consisted entirely of cover versions, including Captain Beyond's 'Mesmerization Eclipse', Alice Cooper's 'Black Juju', Hey On Glue's 'Sentimental Funeral', Twisted Sister's 'Tear It Loose', Jerry's Kids' 'Lost', Bob Dylan's 'The Ballad Of Hollis Brown', and 'Satan', originally by The Dwarves.

The 2000 album *Uprising* cost a miserly £4,000 (because it was deliberately underproduced by engineer Nico Elgstrand at Das Boot Studios) and harked back to past glories. Not only was the old logo revived but also the album cover was in fact the artwork from their original *But Life Goes On* demo. As if that weren't enough, Entombed reworked the title track from *Left Hand Path*, re-titling it 'Say It In Slugs'. Dismember's Fred Estby laid down drums on two tracks, 'Year In Year Out' and 'Returning To Madness'. US editions of *Uprising*, released on Sanctuary's Metal-Is imprint, added three extra tracks. With the band's star in the ascendant again, former label Earache issued a set of live tapes from a 1992 London Astoria show for the *Monkey Puss – Live In London* album.

The year 2000 saw Cederlund and Stjärnvind in collusion with Dismember's Matti Kärki and Richard Cabeza for the Murder Squad album

Entombed

Unsane, Insane And Mentally Damaged. Another Entombed offshoot, the thrash band Born Of Fire, featured Stjärnvind and Cabeza with Dimman and ex-Unleashed bassist Fredrik Lindgren. Sandström also engaged publicly with his new act, a gothic-electro death metal band called The Project Hate.

The band performed an about-turn with their next album, September 2001's *Morning Star*, delving back into prime death metal territory and considerably boosting their album sales – as evidenced by a respectable Number 41 entry on the Swedish charts.

Entombed stretched their creativity in February and March 2002 with a series of ambitious concerts at the Royal Opera Hall in Stockholm. Billed as The Unreal Estate, the band played a 45-minute Entombed set complemented by a ten-year-old actor and a ballet troupe. Recordings from these shows surfaced during 2004 as the *Unreal Estate* album.

Bassist Jörgen Sandstrom – moving to guitar – and drummer Peter Stjärnvind then announced the formation of a side venture entitled Krux, featuring prominent players such as Leif Edling of Candlemass, guitarist Michael Amott of Arch Enemy and vocalist Tomas Person. Krux signed to Mascot Records for their debut, although a line-up change saw erstwhile Yngwie Malmsteen and Abstrakt Algebra frontman Mats Levén assuming the role of lead vocalist. Uffe Cederlund then embarked on another high-profile side concern, entitled Washoe, with the Misery Loves Company trio of vocalist Patrik Wirén, bass player Patrik Thorngren and drummer Olle Dahlstedt. The title of this band was subsequently switched to Alpha Safari.

Music For Nations released a compilation of Entombed archive cover versions and B-sides in 2002, *Sons Of Satan – Praise The Lord*. In December, Cederlund revealed plans for renewed live action with his pre-Entombed band Haystack.

The band's May 2003 album, *Inferno*, was produced by Pelle Gunnerfeldt and accelerated the renewed appreciation for the band, hitting Number 21 on the domestic charts. Vinyl versions surfaced on the group's own Threeman imprint and boasted an extra track, 'When Humanity Is Gone'.

September and October European shows had Nine and Disfear as support before Entombed formed a union with King Diamond for US touring throughout October and November. Canadian gigs planned for Toronto and Montreal were cancelled as drummer Peter Stjärnvind was found to be suffering from "two pus-filled boils in his throat area". Returning home for the December *Close-Up* Made Us Do It tour in Scandinavia alongside Disfear and Raised Fist, Cederlund doubled up duties as guitarist for Disfear.

In January 2004, Entombed parted ways with Sandström and drafted in Nico 'Moosebeach' Elgstrand, formerly of Albatross and Terra Firma. Sandström maintained his ties with both The Project Hate and Krux as well as joining Stockholm-based death metal band Vicious Art. He also featured on a 2004 album from The Mighty Nimbus, playing on a cover of the Saint Vitus track 'Born Too Late'. Primitive Art then released a split single by Entombed and The Coffinshakers, both acts covering Lee Hazlewood songs: Entombed donated a version of 'Some Velvet Morning'. Lars-Göran Petrov recorded a guest appearance for the E-Type electropop album *Loud Pipes Save Lives*.

North American dates were announced for March but then retracted as the band were unable to secure a work visa for Nico Elgstrand in time. The revised band undertook a batch of Australian gigs in April, with support coming from Daysend. US versions of *Inferno*, released in August through Candlelight, added a bonus disc of extra material dubbed *Averno*, comprising two previously unreleased songs from the *Inferno* sessions and 'When Humanity's Gone' from the *Inferno* vinyl release.

The band headed up a billing with Crowbar, Pro-Pain, and The Mighty Nimbus for US dates in February 2005. A notable gig came in July at the 'Peace And Love' festival in Borlänge, Sweden when erstwhile drummer Nicke Andersson joined the band onstage as fill-in guitarist for Cederlund – who was on the road with Disfear. However, in early September the band put out an official statement that Cederlund was "no longer in the band". Entombed persevered, drafting in Alpha Safari and ex-Misery Loves Company session drummer Olle Dahlstedt to replace Stjärnvind. In early November, the band revealed *Serpent Saints* as the title of a new album, set for 2007 release through Threeman. They entered Studioland in Upplands Väsby in mid December.

During late 2005, Nicke Andersson and Jörgen Sandström concocted the deliberately retro-styled death metal combo Death Breath, joined by guitarist Robert Persson of Thunder Express. The first Entombed product of 2006 was the EP *When In Sodom*, issued in June. The band are now rightly regarded as pioneers in their field.

GRAVE
BRUTAL METAL VETERANS

VISBY'S GRAVE ARE ONE OF THE founders of the Swedish death metal scene. They released their first demo, *Sick Disgust Eternal*, in August 1988 after a name change from Corpse. The trio responsible for these tracks were Jörgen Sandström on lead vocals, guitar and bass, Ola Lindgren on guitar and drummer Jensâ Paulsson. The band had been formed at high school on the island of Gotland, and were first named Rising Power in honour of the AC/DC song of the same name on the *Flick Of The Switch* album. They then became Destroyer and Anguish in quick succession, before adopting Corpse for the *Black Dawn* demo in 1986. The name-change to Grave came with the *Sick Disgust Eternal* sessions. Sandström, Lindgren and Paulsson, together with bass player Jonas Edwardsson, also cut the *Painful Death* demo credited to Putrefaction in 1989. These tracks were adopted into the Grave catalogue.

Two further demos, February 1989's *Sexual Mutilation* and August 1989's *Anatomia Corporis Humanum*, recorded at Yellowhouse Studio, gained the band enviable cult status. *Anatomia* was also issued as a four-track EP by the German MBR Records.

The band were snapped up by another German label, Century Media, who put out the full-length *Into The Grave* in August 1991. The album was recorded at Stockholm's Sunlight Studios with producer Tomas Skogsberg – and Grave would use this studio and producer throughout their career. The album received laudatory reviews, with fans entranced by the bludgeoning riffing and oppressively mutated bass, as well as the subterranean roar of Sandström. The band toured Europe as guests to

Grave

GRAVE discography

Anatomia Corporis Humani, M.B.R. cnu (Europe) (1989)
GRAVE / DEVIATED INSTINCT / DEVOLUTION, Prophecy PRO-006CD (Europe) (1991) split album with Deviated Instinct and Devolution
INTO THE GRAVE, Century Media CM 84 9721 (Europe), Century Media CM 7721-2 (USA)(1992)
YOU'LL NEVER SEE..., Century Media CM 84 9733 (Europe), Century Media CM 7733-2 (USA) (1992)
...And Here I Die... Satisfied, Century Media CM 77062-2 (Europe), Century Media CM 7762-2 (USA) (1994)
SOULLESS, Century Media CM 77070-2 (Europe), Century Media CM 7770-2 (USA) (1994)
HATING LIFE, Century Media CM 77106-2 (Europe), Century Media CM 7806-2 (USA) (1996)
EXTREMELY ROTTEN LIVE, Century Media CM 77162-2 (Europe), Century Media CM 7862-2 (USA) (1997)
BACK FROM THE GRAVE, Century Media CM 77411-2 (Europe), Century Media CM 8111-2 (USA) (2002)
FIENDISH REGRESSION, Century Media CM 77511-2 (Europe), Century Media CM 8211-2 (USA) (2004)
AS RAPTURES COME, Century Media CM 77611-2 (Europe), Century Media CM 8311-2 (USA) (2007)

Florida thrashers Malevolent Creation in September before dates opening for countrymen Entombed.

In 1992, bassist Jonas Torndal quit and frontman Sandström took over four-string duties. The second album, *You'll Never See*, was recorded in June. A January 1994 EP, *...And Here I Die... Satisfied*, included a re-worked version of the early Corpse track 'Black Dawn'.

Following June 1994's *Soulless*, Grave toured North America as headliners before hooking up with the Cannibal Corpse and Samael tour as support. Further dates saw the band putting in an appearance at the 'Full Of Hate' festivals and opening for Morbid Angel. After this bout of activity, Sandström joined Entombed in 1995. Grave persevered as a duo, with Lindgren now responsible for vocals on the 1996 Skogsberg-produced *Hating Life*, again laid down at Sunlight Studios. A double concert recording, *Extremely Rotten Live*, arrived in April 1997.

Grave, now centred upon vocalist-guitarist Ola Lindgren, Jensâ Paulsson and bassist-turned-guitarist Jonas Torndal, who had previously vacated his post in 1992, reconvened in September 2001. The new man on bass was the Therion-credited Fredrik Isaksson. This unit set to work on *Back From The Grave*, the first editions of which came with a bonus disc of tracks from the *Sick Disgust Eternal*, *Sexual Mutilation* and *Anatomia Corporis Humani* demos.

Subsequent European live dates witnessed the introduction of Coercion drummer Pelle Ekegren into the fold, regular skinsman Jensâ Paulsson being temporarily out of action. By February, Paulsson was out of the picture for good, as Grave inducted Kaamos, General Surgery and Repugnant man Cristofer Barkensjö as a permanent replacement.

A projected run of European dates throughout March and April 2003 were to have Defleshed in support, but these shows were cancelled. There was no let-up on the live front for the summer, though, with Grave teaming up with Immolation, Crematorium and Goatwhore for US shows in June – the band's first North American dates in over seven years. Grave then played on the gargantuan 'Bonded By Metal Over Europe' tour in October alongside Exodus, Nuclear Assault, Agent Steel, Behemoth, Mortician, Carnal Forge, Occult and Callenish Circle.

They parted ways with Barkensjö in early 2004, as he opted out to prioritise his other act, Kaamos. The band replaced him with the Coercion-credited Pelle Ekegren for a new album in April, produced at Abyss Studios by Tommy and Peter Tägtgren, titled *Fiendish Regression*. The album included a cover version of Saint Vitus's doom classic 'Burial At Sea' and a re-recording of an archive song, 'Autopsied' from 1989.

December 2004 tours saw Grave in union with Rotting Christ before playing with God Dethroned for Low Countries shows in January 2005. A further run across Europe with Third Moon and Swiss act Disparaged preceded gigs in Finland in March, with support from Chaosbreed and Scent Of Flesh. More European dates followed.

Sandström announced the formation of a retro death metal band titled Death Breath in collaboration with his erstwhile Entombed colleague and Hellacopters frontman Nicke Andersson. Thunder Express guitarist Robert Persson joined them.

Grave announced European tour dates for January 2006 alongside a heavyweight cast of Hurtlocker, Aborted, Dew-Scented, Vesania and Cryptopsy. A new album, *As Rapture Comes*, was released in July 2006 and the band teamed up with Vital Remains, Dismember, Demiricous and Withered for a North American tour beginning in late September. This signalled a clear rejuvenation for the band as European shows announced for November, dubbed the 'Masters Of Death', had them lined up with a supremely heavyweight Scandinavian cast of Dismember, Entombed and Unleashed. The seemingly tireless group then united once more with Dismember, Entombed and The Absence for a US West Coast tour in December. Grave have earned much respect from the Swedish music scene.

HAMMERFALL
A MOST UNEXPECTED SUCCESS STORY OF RECENT TIMES

FOUNDED IN 1993, GOTHENBURG'S Hammerfall made a startling impact with their 1997 debut album *Glory To The Brave*, with its traditional heavy metal and a rousing cover of Warlord's 'Child Of The Damned'. The album crashed straight into the German national charts, rapidly selling over 100,000 copies and surprising even the band's record company. This completely turned the continent's metal scene on its head, triggering the onset of legions of power metal bands from all over the globe.

The band was begun purely as an extracurricular activity by members of various Swedish death metal bands. Drummer Jesper Strömblad and guitarist Oscar Dronjac created Hammerfall as a leisure pursuit away from what were then their full-time acts, Dronjac's Crystal Age and Strömblad's In Flames. The founding line-up was completed by Dark Tranquillity vocalist Mikael Stanne, In Flames bassist Johan Larsson, and Dark Tranquillity guitarist Niklas Sundin.

Hammerfall made an auspicious debut in 1994, covering Pretty Maids' 'Red Hot And Heavy' at 'Rockslaget', a local band competition. With Hammerfall reaching the semi-finals by 1996, Stanne bowed out due to tour commitments with Dark Tranquillity. Luciferon and Highlander vocalist singer Joacim Cans was drafted in – and Sundin bowed out, replaced by Glenn Ljungström of In Flames and Dimension Zero.

Hammerfall now found themselves the subject of recording contract offers, and the band members were forced into the decision to stay or concentrate on their main bands. Ljungström was superseded by Stefan Elmgren and bassist Larsson returned to None. His position was taken by Billionaires Boys Club and Keegan man Magnus Rosén. Drummer Patrik Räfling was introduced in 1997. Hammerfall admitted that a sixth member, Jesper Strömblad, also laid down drums and assisted in the writing process.

The Swedes then signed to an independent Dutch label, Vic Records, on the back of a live tape. The budget was minimal, but the tapes made

HAMMERFALL discography

GLORY TO THE BRAVE, Nuclear Blast NB 0265-2 (Europe),
Nuclear Blast America 6265 (USA) (1997)

Glory To The Brave, Nuclear Blast NB 0299-2 (Europe) (1997)

Heeding The Call, Nuclear Blast NB 0333-2 (Europe) (1998)

LEGACY OF KINGS, Nuclear Blast NB 0335-2 (Europe), Nuclear
Blast America 6335 (USA) (1998)

I Want Out, Nuclear Blast NB 0414-2 (Europe), Nuclear Blast
America 6414 (USA) (1999)

RENEGADE, Nuclear Blast NB 0511-2 (Europe), Nuclear Blast
America 6511 (USA) (2000)

Renegade, Nuclear Blast NB 0530-2 (Europe) (2000)

Always Will Be, Nuclear Blast NB 0610-2 (Europe) (2001)

Hearts On Fire, Nuclear Blast NB 1030-2 (Europe) (2002)

CRIMSON THUNDER, Nuclear Blast NB 1031-2 (Europe), Nuclear
Blast America 1031 (USA) (2002)

ONE CRIMSON NIGHT, Nuclear Blast NB 1196-2 (Europe), Nuclear
Blast America 1196 (USA) (2003)

Blood Bound, Nuclear Blast NB 1355-2 (Europe) (2005)

CHAPTER V: UNBENT, UNBOWED, UNBROKEN, Nuclear Blast
NB 1375-2 (Europe), Nuclear Blast America 1375 (USA) (2005)

Natural High, Nuclear Blast NB 1730-2 (Europe) (2006)

THRESHOLD, Nuclear Blast NB 1752-2 (Europe), Nuclear Blast
America 1752 (USA) (2006)

it to Markus Staiger, head of Nuclear Blast. His enthusiasm for Hammerfall saw the entire project eventually bought out by his label. Needless to say, original Vic variants of the debut Hammerfall album are now highly prized.

The rock media were quick to take the band to their hearts and the group's debut album, *Glory To The Brave*, scooped the Album Of The Month award in Germany's biggest metal magazine, *Rock Hard*, and maximum marks in *Metal Hammer*. It included the band's homage to Warlord with their interpretation of 'Child Of The Damned' and the power ballad 'I Believe', co-penned by Peter Stålfors (Pure X bassist and later of Dream Evil). *Glory To The Brave* was a no-frills, speed-inclined power metal album, loaded with fantasy lyrical content, singalong anthems, hooky riffs and guitar solos. With not an ounce of pretension in sight, personified by their warrior mascot Hector, featured on the record's jacket, the album captivated a metal generation and peaked at Number 34 in June 1997.

Nuclear Blast released a limited-edition vinyl version of the album in razor-saw shape, restricted to a mere 500 copies. The single release of 'Glory To The Brave' mistakenly included a rough-mix live version of 'The Metal Age' instead of the planned 'I Believe'. The band was furious and vented their anger in the press. The original single is now a rarity: from the second pressing the necessary correction was made.

To support the record, Hammerfall toured in Germany with Tank and Raven, consistently stealing the headliner's crowds. Further touring ensued as guests to Gamma Ray and Jag Panzer in September 1997. The band kept up their traditional metal on these dates by including the Stormwitch song 'Ravenlord' in their set and were honoured to be joined by former Stormwitch vocalist Andy Muck during their set at the 'Bang Your Head II' festival in southern Germany.

A second single, 'Heeding The Call', was issued in August and featured a take on Picture's 'Eternal Dreamer' alongside three live tracks. The sophomore album *Legacy Of Kings*, arriving in September and once more utilising the writing services of Strömblad, also fared well, hitting Number 15 in both Germany and Sweden. Still intent on honouring their 1980s heroes, the band included 'Back To Back', originally by Danish

outfit Pretty Maids. They stuck to the winning formula for this second album, bolstering the content with a more solid production.

In Europe, Hammerfall took to the festival scene with gusto, appearing at the Dutch 'Dynamo' event, Germany's 'Rock Hard' and 'With Full Force' festivals, Italy's 'Monsters Of Rock' and Austria's 'Mind Over Matter', as well as the Karlshamm outdoor gig in their homeland.

During 1999, Hammerfall made a significant change to the line-up, pulling in the esteemed Anders Johansson as their new drummer. Johansson's prior experience included terms with Yngwie Malmsteen, Keegan and Silver Mountain. He's also iassued two solo albums, *Shu-Tka* in 1993 and *Red Shift* in 1997. The world tour took Hammerfall on a global expedition that included their debut American, Japanese and South American shows. However, the band suffered a major tragedy in 1999 when tour manager Lelle Hildebrandt disappeared, presumed murdered.

A significant single release came in August 1999. 'I Want Out' was headed up by a Helloween cover version, enhanced by studio guests Udo Dirkschneider and Gamma Ray guitarist Kai Hansen. The record also featured a take on Rainbow's 'Man On The Silver Mountain' with Running Wild drummer AC and Hansen once again. A new original, 'At The End Of The Rainbow', included a guest spot for Warlord guitarist William J. Tsamis. This single charted in both Germany and Sweden.

Hammerfall recorded their third album, October 2000's *Renegade*, with producer Michael Wagener in America. The launch party, held in Gothenburg during September, saw the band joined onstage by AC, Motörhead drummer Mikkey Dee, and Dirkschneider. The evening rounded off with a rendition of Judas Priest's seminal 'Breaking The Law', with the band members swapping instruments.

Hammerfall bounced back in spectacular fashion, debuting at Number 1 in Sweden with *Renegade* and charting high in Germany. The 'Renegade' single also cracked the charts open and offered fans a cover of Heavy Load's 'Run With The Devil', doubly honouring the original by drafting the Wahlquist brothers in for backing vocals. Touring in Europe saw the band headlining with guests Virgin Steele and Freedom Call.

During the summer of 2001, they offered up a rendition of Twisted Sister's 'We're Gonna Make It' to the tribute album *Twisted And Strange*. News also emerged that Cans was forming a pivotal part of the Warlord resurrection project, acting as frontman alongside original members Thunderchild and Destroyer.

Elmgren formed the melodic metal band Full Strike in the latter half of 2001 with erstwhile Lost Horizon singer Niclas Johnsson, ex-Crawley bassist Chris Savage Goldsmith and Freak Kitchen drummer Björn Fryklund. Releasing May 2002's *We Will Rise* through the Spitfire label, the band recruited a new drummer in former Hammerfall compatriot Patrik Räfling, with Lost Horizon's Fredrik Olsson augmenting the band for live work. Hammerfall bassist Magnus Rosén wasn't idle either, forging Execution, a band fronted by Renato Tribuzy of Brazilian power metal band Thoten.

Hammerfall themselves worked on their new album, *Crimson Thunder*, throughout the spring and early summer. Recorded at Helloween vocalist Andi Deris's studio in Tenerife, the record was produced by Charlie Bauerfiend. A cover version of Chastain's 'Angel Of Mercy' was laid down, and after the sessions Johansson made time to session on Christian metal band Narnia's 2002 album *The Great Fall*. Japanese versions of *Crimson Thunder*, issued by the JVC Victor label, added three extra tracks: 'Crazy Nights' and live versions of 'Renegade' and 'Hammerfall'.

The band's momentum was halted by a vicious attack on Cans just before a video shoot for the single 'Hearts On Fire'. Cans was assaulted at a bar in the group's hometown of Gothenburg on August 10th when a black metal fan attacked him with a beer glass, and he sustained an injury

around his right eye that required 25 stitches. On a more positive note, 'Hearts On Fire' debuted at Number 11 in Sweden.

In October, *Crimson Thunder* gave Hammerfall their highest chart position in Germany to date, debuting at Number 13, and also performed commendably in Sweden, reaching Number 3. Various limited editions appeared, including a version packaged with a free comic book and an additional track, a cover of Yngwie Malmsteen's 'Rising Force', as well as a 1,000-copies-only issue packaged with two 3-inch CDs with renditions of 'Crazy Nights' by Loudness and Kiss's 'Detroit Rock City'.

Hammerfall supported Dio on the rock veteran's November North American dates. A sustained bout of touring throughout Europe in January and February found Masterplan as special guests. The opening acts were fellow Swedes Nostradameus for the first leg of the tour before Dream Evil took over this position. The band, in union with Nocturnal Rites, lined up co-headline dates in Japan for March 2003 before gigs across Chile, Brazil, Argentina and Mexico in May. An interesting diversion saw them participating as celebrity contestants in the popular Swedish TV game show *Fångarna*.

The band suffered a casualty – both personally and financially – when on August 10th guitarist Oscar Dronjak was involved in a motorcycle crash, fracturing his left arm. Hammerfall's summer dates, including Sweden's 'Malmöfestivalen' event and the UK 'Bloodstock' festival, were postponed as a result. Rosén took time out from Hammerfall to lay down bass on Masterplan vocalist Jørn Lande's masterly solo album, *Out To Every Nation*.

The band's October 2003 live album, *One Crimson Night*, soon found them back in the charts, but another reminder of their touring past was less welcome. According to reports in the Swedish newspaper *Aftonbladet*, an individual had stolen over $30,000 of US tour receipts and merchandise money. In addition, Cans claimed that this person, hired by the band, stole "drums, the amplifiers, and all the other rental equipment".

Cans announced a solo album under his own surname, confirming that he was working with Dionysus and ex-Sinergy drummer Ronny Milianowicz for these recordings. Indeed, the pair had been working together on an epic concept piece entitled *The Conspiracy* for the preceding four years. A guest was the Halford and Painmuseum guitarist 'Metal' Mike Chlasciak and Hammerfall's own Stefan Elmgren. The singer also contributed lyrics to the track 'Bringer Of War' on the 2004 Dionysus album *Anima Mundi*.

Dronjak and Cans closed the year performing at an epic anniversary bash at the renowned Rockfabrik Rock club in Ludwigsburg, Germany. The duo performed Hammerfall songs 'At The End Of The Rainbow', 'Hearts On Fire' and 'Hammerfall' with Godiva's Mitch Koontz and Primal Fear's Tom Naumann as backing musicians.

Anders Johansson joined Stratovarius alongside his brother Jens in January 2004 but quit within a week to concentrate on Hammerfall. Meanwhile, Cans' solo project was confirmed for an appearance at the 'Sweden Rock' festival, his Hammerfall colleague Elmgren joining him for the occasion.

To mark the release of Cans' *Beyond The Gates* album, the singer held a launch party on May 8th at the Metallterrassen Club in Gothenburg. Cans was DJ for the evening while a band dubbed the Metal Monarchs, featuring Dronjak, provided the live entertainment.

Hammerfall reconvened with producer Charlie Bauerfiend in September to craft a new album, *Chapter V: Unbent, Unbowed, Unbroken*, for March 2005 release, and crafted a hi-tech video for the track 'Blood Bound' with director Roger Johansson. Venom frontman Conrad 'Cronos' Lant was a special guest on the album. Meanwhile, Rosén put in time laying down bass on the AOR studio project *Heartbreak Radio*.

Rosén then announced the issue of a solo album entitled *Arose* and dates in South America during October, utilising Destiny drummer Birger Löfman. These gigs were a not-for-profit operation, with Rosén donating all proceeds to homeless children. (On the previous Hammerfall South American tour, he had donated his proceeds to the funding of a year's education for a member of the public.)

The 'Bound Blood' single then entered the Swedish charts at an impressive Number 5. European and Scandinavian gigs in April, dubbed the 'Icebreaker' tour, featured Firewind, Thunderstone and Lordi in support. Veteran Danish act Pretty Maids opened for them at Gothenburg's Scandinavium venue on April 30th. The same month, Hammerfall reaped enormous domestic exposure by covering the Schlager tune 'Vindarna Viskar Mitt Namn' live on Swedish television. Elmgren made time to guest on Nocturnal Rites' album *Grand Illusion.*

The band then played gigs in Japan, South America and the US before a lengthy European tour in October through to early December with Stratovarius. Rosén extended his musical reach beyond the realms of metal by collaborating with the Gothenburg Symphonic Orchestra under the 'Respekt' banner for 15 shows at the Concert Hall in Gothenburg in September 2006. Rosén and Johansson featured on the 2006 *Planet Alliance* album mentored by guitarist Magnus Karlsson of Last Tribe and Cloudscape vocalist Mike Andersson.

In January 2006, Hammerfall gave their backing to the national Swedish women's curling team by filming a video for their 2002 track 'Hearts On Fire', used by the athletes as their theme tune during the Winter Olympics held in Turin. The song was re-released as a single to coincide with the games, with exposure given a boost when the team won the gold medal.

Johansson involved himself with Geff, the hard rock band of singer Göran Edman, noted for a wealth of credits with the Yngwie Malmsteen band and others, together with guitarist Ralf Jedestedt and former Silver Mountain and Snake Charmer bass player Pär Stadin.

Hammerfall spent the early months of 2006 crafting a further slab of heroic metal. They continued the successful sporting theme by shooting a video in June to coincide with the 19th European Athletics Championships, held in Gothenburg in August. Band members shot footage alongside Swedish athletes Robert Kronberg (110m hurdles), Alhaji Jeng (pole vault), Johan Wissman (200 metres), and Kajsa Bergqvist (holder of the high jump world-record).

That same month, Hammerfall's ties to the sports world were strengthened further when 'Glorious', celebrating the 2006 World Cup soccer tournament, hit the Swedish charts at number 7. Co-composed by Joacim Cans and featuring Oscar Dronjak alongside a multitude of other metal musicians, the song was credited to Mikeyla Feat. The Metal Forces and was fronted by 19-year-old female rocker Mikeyla.

The group debuted their new single 'The Fire Burns Forever' on August 5th at their headlining show at the 'Gates Of Metal' festival in Hultsfred, Sweden. The hammer rose again for another strike as new album *Threshold* emerged in October. Followers of pure heavy metal can be reassured that their chosen music will always have an outlet while Hammerfall are leading the scene.

THE HAUNTED
NEO-THRASH PIONEERS

THE HAUNTED STRADDLE THE BORDER between death and thrash metal and have strong links with the elite pioneers of the Gothenburg death metal scene. They have been largely responsible for breathing new life into the once-moribund thrash genre.

The band were founded by former Orchriste, Seance and Satanic Slaughter guitarist Patrik Jensen and former At The Gates drummer Adrian Erlandsson. The exact starting point of the band can be pinpointed to July 27th 1996: within half an hour of melodic death metal legends At The

Gates deciding to split, Erlandsson was on the telephone to Jensen, inviting him to explore the possibilities of a new band. Jensen and Erlandsson jammed the next day, working on tracks originally intended for Séance, then invited another ex-At The Gates man, Jonas Björler, into the fold a week later to cover bass. The Haunted also drafted in former Dissection and Cardinal Sin man John Zwetsloot, but he only lasted a matter of months before erstwhile Infestation, At The Gates and Terror guitarist Anders Björler, twin brother of Jonas, took over second guitar.

The band then attempted to lure in a lead vocalist: discussions were held with Toxine (aka Tony Kampner) of Satanic Slaughter and Witchery, and Rogga of Merciless. Ultimately it was Peter Dolving of Mary Beats Jane who landed the job.

During 1997, Erlandsson created the side project Hyperhug, and in due course he decamped from The Haunted to concentrate on this act full time. The Haunted attempted to fill the drum position with Dissection and Ophthalamia man Ole Öhman, but when Hyperhug's singer damaged his hearing, curtailing that group, Erlandsson rejoined his former colleagues.

The band didn't need to hunt for a deal. At The Gates owed still owed money to Earache, so the new band simply took over the contract obligations to record their eponymous debut album, made with co-producer Fredrik Nordström at Gothenburg's Fredman Studio in June 1998. To promote this release, The Haunted undertook touring in Europe with Napalm Death, but projected Japanese dates were cancelled. In November 1998, Dolving, frustrated with a lack of progress on the live front, quit to found Zen Monkey. His replacement, Face Down's Marco Aro, was located in March 1999, and this new line-up then toured the European festival circuit.

The band were offered the support slot to Testament's American dates the same year, but in mid-rehearsal for these shows Erlandsson quit to join Cradle Of Filth. The tour went ahead with Per Møller Jensen of Konkhra and Invocator.

They bounced back in commanding style with *The Haunted Made Me Do It* in October 2000, produced by Berno Paulsson. In 2001 it was announced that Mike Wead, of Mercyful Fate and King Diamond, had joined the band, supplanting Anders Björler, who had opted out to pursue university studies. However, a subsequent American tour alongside Catastrophic and Martyr A.D. saw The Crown guitarist Marcus Sunesson temporarily taking the vacancy.

The Haunted also prepared tracks, recorded in Japan at the Akasaka Blitz in Tokyo in 2000 and mixed by Konkhra's Anders Lundemark, for a live album, *Live Rounds In Tokyo*, first issued in the Far East by Toy's Factory in May 2001. This set of recordings would eventually surface as a bonus disc packaged with a re-released *The Haunted Made Me Do It* in December. Anders Björler returned to the band shortly before they entered the studio to record a third album, *One Kill Wonder*. Arch Enemy guitarist Michael Amott laid down a guest solo during these sessions.

The *One Kill Wonder* album arrived in stores in February 2003. Significantly, the record gave the band its first national chart placing, reaching Number 23 on the Swedish charts. The title track dominated all three major US metal radio charts – the CMJ Loud Rock Chart, the CMJ Loud Rock Spins Chart and the FMQB Metal Detector chart – for a four-week run at Number 1.

The Haunted announced South African shows for March 2003. European touring featured the band packaged with Mastodon and Hatesphere in April before they jumped the Atlantic for US gigs throughout the summer headlining over Kataklysm, Shai Hulud and Skinless. This took place as awareness of the band was building due to positive reviews for *One Kill Wonder*. Despite this upward momentum, during October The Haunted parted ways with Aro, replacing him with the group's original frontman Peter Dolving.

The band then held a competition among its fans to find a new album title, the winner coming up with *Subliminal Messages Of Suicide Promotion*, although this title was not used. Touring in spring 2004 found the band – with Dolving nursing four fractured ribs – traversing the UK as support to Funeral For A Friend. The band, having cut a new album at Studio Fredman in Gothenburg with co-producers Patrik J. Sten – the drummer with Passenger – and Fredrik Nordström, signed to Century Media in June.

They were chosen alongside Mercenary, Mnemic, Hatesphere, Raunchy, Melted, Blindfault and Stomped for the 'Nordic Threat' show for the Popkomm 2004 music convention in Berlin on September 29th. US touring in October saw the band playing with Damageplan and Shadows Fall: the *rEVOLVEr* album, preceded by a video for the track 'All Against All', entered the Swedish charts at Number 18. High-profile tours followed.

To aid victims of the December 2004 Indian Ocean tsunami, The Haunted participated in a special single with Heaven Shall Burn and Napalm Death, donating the track 'Smut King'. These singles, restricted to just 1,000 hand-numbered copies, were sold only at Napalm Death's Bochum and London shows in January 2005. That same month, Per Møller Jensen recorded the *Music For Tough Guys* demo with Slow Death Factory, featuring Illdisposed's Morten Gilsted, vocalist Martin Rosendahl of Strangler, Zahrim and Iniquity and Corpus Mortale's Roar Christofferson on bass.

The Haunted acted as special guests to the Moonspell and Cradle Of Filth European tour in March. However, guitarist Jensen left the tour shortly after the Lisbon date in order to attend to family matters, leaving the band to carry on as a quartet. US gigs in May were scheduled with Devildriver, Machine Head and It Dies Today, but they withdrew from these dates, citing Jensen's desire to spend time with his sick father in Sweden. That month, The Haunted filmed a video for the track 'No Compromise' with director Roger Johansson.

The group got back onto the US touring circuit in major fashion, appearing on the second stage at the Black Sabbath and Iron Maiden-headlined 'Ozzfest' before further US dates alongside Meshuggah, God

---

THE HAUNTED discography

THE HAUNTED, Earache MOSH197CD (UK) (1999)
THE HAUNTED MADE ME DO IT, Earache MOSH241CD (UK) (2000)
LIVE ROUNDS IN TOKYO, Toy's Factory TFCK-87284 (Japan) (2002)
ONE KILL WONDER, Earache MOSH265CD (UK) (2003)
rEVOLVEr, Century Media CM 77488-2 (Europe), Century Media CM 8188-2 (USA) (2004)
THE DEAD EYE, Century Media CM 77588-2 (Europe), Century Media CM 8288-2 (USA) (2006)

Forbid and Mnemic. The Haunted then toured Europe with Manntis and God Forbid in November.

The band's shows in 2006 included the Japanese 'Extreme The Dojo Vol. 15' dates with Nile and Exodus in late February before Australian headliners in March. The group scheduled recording sessions at Antfarm Studios in Århus, Denmark in May with producer Tue Madsen, and they geared up for further global campaigning with the release of *The Dead Eye* in October. A slower, more considered album than previous releases, it nonetheless reinforced the band's status on the scene.

HEAVY LOAD
HEAVY BY NAME

A HIGHLY INFLUENTIAL AND SUCCESSFUL Stockholm metal outfit, Heavy Load saw regular chart placings in their home country with a series of strong self-financed albums. Although Sweden is now recognised as a metal stronghold, during Heavy Load's career domestic bands were thin on the ground and made negligible headway outside the country. Their resolve gave impetus to many acts that followed in their wake. They dated back to 1976, when Ragne Wahlquist, on lead vocals and guitar, and his brother Styrbjörn on drums teamed up with bassist Michael 'Bachler' Backlund. Heavy gigging ensued, and the following year Backlund was replaced by Dan Molén.

Heavy Load scored their first album release in 1978, when Stockholm record store Heavy Sound released *Full Speed At High Level*, recorded at Mill Recording Studio in July, and the trio undertook a headline tour of Sweden to promote its release. Their brand of metal was both riff-orientated and melodious: visually, they addressed every heavy metal cliché in the book, with each album cover depicting a Viking warrior in battle mode.

By 1979, the touring schedule had taken its toll on Molén, who quit. Heavy Load added bassist Eero Koivisto and rhythm guitarist Leif 'Lillen' Liljegren, to become a quartet. However, within months both new members had left, going on to form Red Baron in 1985. Liljegren also turned up as a member of melodic rockers Treat.

During the summer of 1979, the band found replacements in bassist Torbjörn Ragnesjö and ex-High Brow guitarist Eddy Malm. Heavy Load's next release was the September 1981 mini-album *Metal Conquest*, cut at Decibel Studios that July. This gained the band many honours, beating several international acts to grab the highest airplay position on the HMH metal radio station playlist and making the national charts. Naturally, the album sleeve featured Vikings at war. This success was reinforced by an extensive headline tour, which included live radio broadcasts from Malmö and Stockholm.

A further album, *Death Or Glory*, arrived in October 1982, earning

HEAVY LOAD discography

FULL SPEED AT HIGH LEVEL, Heavy Sound HSLP 03 (Europe)
(1978)
Metal Conquest, Thunderload TMP 811 (Europe) (1981)
DEATH OR GLORY, Thunderload TLP 822 (Europe) (1982)
Take Me Away / Trespasser, Thunderload TSP 823 (Europe)
(1982) 7-inch vinyl single free with *Death Or Glory*
STRONGER THAN EVIL, Thunderload TLP 834 (Europe) (1983)
Free, Thunderload TSP 835 (Europe) (1982)
Monsters Of The Night, WEA 248983-7 (Europe) (1985)

another national chart placing, at Number 47. The first editions of this record came with a free 7-inch single, 'Take Me Away'/'Trespasser'. *Death Or Glory*'s artwork now saw an axe-wielding Viking pitched against a polar bear.

Heavy Load began 1983 by releasing a concert video and recording *Stronger Than Evil*, sporting a Viking atop a pile of recently slaughtered foes, for issue in October. Thin Lizzy frontman Phil Lynott, who was in Sweden promoting his solo album at the time, appeared on the track 'Free'. At this point, Heavy Load extended their touring into Europe as album sales strengthened, although gigs were curtailed in mid 1984 when Ragnesjö departed. It was 1985 by the time they added new bassist Andreas Fritz.

Having been self-financed since inception, the band now sought a record deal and signed with WEA. A single, 'Monsters Of The Night', was released, backed up by further Swedish dates, but a projected album never materialised, and Malm left to pursue a solo project. As a result, Heavy Load were put on ice: the Wahlquist brothers concentrated on building a recording studio that later would be used by Candlemass and others.

In 1986, Heavy Load recruited guitarist Patrik Karlsson to work on a new album, although further delays were caused when Fritz left to work with ex-member Malm. Ex-Damned and UFO bassist Paul Gray joined the band, but business considerations at the recording studio always hindered any new release. However, a new Heavy Load album apparently remains a possibility. The Wahlquist brothers resurrected their Thunderload label to release Christian metal band Veni Domine's *Material Sanctuary* in 1995.

The band's legacy was still strong in 2000, as evidenced by Swedish metal kings Hammerfall cutting a version of 'Run With The Devil' for a bonus track on their chart single 'Renegade'. Italian power metal band Noble Savage covered 'Dreaming' on their *Killing For The Glory* album in 2005.

HYPOCRISY
APOCALYPTIC HYBRID METAL

HYPOCRISY WERE FORMED IN LUDVIKA, Stockholm in October 1991 by guitarist Peter Tägtgren, who has built up a considerable and highly-esteemed catalogue of work with other projects such as the industrial solo concept Pain, Lockup, The Abyss and Bloodbath. He was an in-demand producer for many years, operating from his Abyss Studio and racking up recognition on the other side of the glass with acts such as Children Of Bodom, Therion, Immortal, Celtic Frost, Dark Funeral, Destruction and Dimmu Borgir.

Hypocrisy are rooted in a band initially known as Seditious. Long before this venture, both Tägtgren and drummer Lars Szöke were members of Conquest, an act dating back as far as 1984. Hypocrisy were established when Tägtgren returned from North America, where he had

put in stints with Malevolent Creation and Meltdown.

Seditious recorded the 1991 demo *Rest In Pain*, but this was not distributed as Tägtgren was unsatisfied with his vocal performance. A second attempt to re-cut the same tracks, adding 'Nightmare' and 'Left To Rot', emerged as Hypocrisy's first product.

Their opening line-up was Tägtgren, bassist Mikael Hedlund, Epitaph guitarist Jonas Österberg and erstwhile Votary vocalist Masse Broberg. The band soon secured a deal with Nuclear Blast and issued the brutal debut album *Penetralia* in October 1992. Stylistically, Hypocrisy pursued Florida-style death metal, laden with ripping guitar chaos and uncompromisingly blasphemous subject matter. The same year, Österberg and Szöke released the *Tranquility* album by their other act, Epitaph. The following year, US label Relapse put out the *Pleasure Of Molestation* EP, whose four tracks were then re-recorded for the next album. By this stage Hypocrisy were down to a quartet, with Tägtgren handling guitars.

For their second album, *Osculum Obscenum*, released by Nuclear Blast in October 1993, they covered Venom's seminal 'Black Metal'. Tour dates included shows with Deicide and Cannibal Corpse. While on tour, vocalist Broberg was reported to have suffered a breakdown, requiring Tägtgren to take over lead vocals. Subsequently, Broberg hooked up with Dark Funeral, taking on the stage name of Emperor Magus Caligula.

Hypocrisy decided to carry on as a trio of Tägtgren, Hedlund and Szöke, releasing the *Inferior Devoties* mini-album, which included a cover of Slayer's 'Black Magic'. This track also appeared on the Slayer tribute compilation album *Slatanic Slaughter Volume One*.

In 1995, the band toured Mexico and Portugal promoting *The Fourth Dimension*. This record had been laid down in March 1994 at Park Studios in Stockholm, with the band exploring new directions away from the satanic lyrical content and replacing the buzzsaw riffage with more melancholic chord patterns. It was also the first Hypocrisy album with prominent keyboards. Japanese versions added the *Inferior Devoties* material.

In 1995, the band released the *Maximum Abduction* chicken-shaped (yes, chicken-shaped) mini-album, which included a cover of Kiss's 'Strange Ways'. The following year, Tägtgren was the stand-in guitarist for Marduk on their European tour and also worked on a solo project, Pain. As it transpired, Pain would later outstrip Hypocrisy in popularity. Tägtgren, Hedlund and Szöke also pursued a side project, entitled The Abyss, all swapping instruments for the occasion; this band released two albums, *The Other Side* and *Summon The Beast*.

The alien-themed *Abducted* album, recorded at Abyss Studio, arrived in February 1996. A notable Hypocrisy release was the 'Roswell 47' 7-inch split single with Meshuggah. For concerts, the group expanded with second guitarist Mathias Kamijo, known for his roles in Pain, The Abyss and Abemal. Kamijo regularly reprised this role on future tours.

Hypocrisy's fifth album, October 1997's *The Final Chapter*, included a cover version of 'Evil Invaders' by Canadian thrashers Razor. As *The Final*

Peter Tägtgren of Hypocrisy

HYPOCRISY discography

PENETRALIA, Nuclear Blast NB 0067-2 (Europe), Nuclear Blast America 6067 (USA) (1992)

Pleasure Of Molestation, Relapse cnu (USA) (1993)

OSCULUM OBSCENUM, Nuclear Blast NB 0080-2 (Europe), Nuclear Blast America 6080 (USA) (1993)

Inferior Devoties, Nuclear Blast NB 0098-2 (Europe), Nuclear Blast America 6098 (USA) (1994)

THE FOURTH DIMENSION, Nuclear Blast NB 0112-2 (Europe), Nuclear Blast America 6112 (USA) (1994)

Carved Up, Relapse RR-030 (USA) (1995) 7-inch vinyl single

ABDUCTED, Nuclear Blast NB 0133-2 (Europe), Nuclear Blast America 6133 (USA) (1996)

Maximum Abduction, Nuclear Blast NB 0145-2 (Europe) (1996) (Shaped CD EP)

THE FINAL CHAPTER, Nuclear Blast NB 0283-2 (Europe), Nuclear Blast America 6283 (USA) (1997)

HYPOCRISY DESTROYS WACKEN, Nuclear Blast NB 0376-2 (Europe), Nuclear Blast America 6376 (USA) (1999)

HYPOCRISY, Nuclear Blast NB 0388-2 (Europe), Nuclear Blast America 6388 (USA) (1999)

INTO THE ABYSS, Nuclear Blast NB 0529-2 (Europe), Nuclear Blast America 6529 (USA) (2000)

10 YEARS OF CHAOS AND CONFUSION, Nuclear Blast NB 0630-2 (Europe), Nuclear Blast America 6630 (USA) (2001)

CATCH 22, Nuclear Blast NB 0710-2 (Europe), Nuclear Blast America 6710 (USA) (2002)

THE ARRIVAL, Nuclear Blast NB 1230-2 (Europe), Nuclear Blast America 1230 (USA) (2004)

VIRUS, Nuclear Blast NB 1141-2 (Europe), Nuclear Blast America 1141 (USA) (2005)

Chapter saw the light of day, Tägtgren announced that this would be Hypocrisy's final fling, as he wished to concentrate on the increasingly fruitful Pain. However, reaction from fans to this announcement, combined with good reviews of *The Final Chapter*, persuaded Tägtgren to change his mind and grant Hypocrisy a reprieve.

The band issued the live albumm *Hypocrisy Destroys Wacken*, in March 1999, recorded as a quartet with Kamijo on second guitar, and this was followed in June by another acclaimed studio album, given a provisional name of *Cloned* but eventually simply titled *Hypocrisy*. This tour de force, which benefited enormously from increased songwriting input from both Hedlund and Szöke, transported the band's trademark rawness to new vistas of sound, generating their most atmospheric outing to date. After summer festival shows, a European campaign in September featured running mates The Kovenant, Gardenian, Dismal Euphony and Disbelief.

Tägtgren also involved himself in the commercially successful Lockup with Napalm Death bassist Shane Embury and guitarist Jesse Pintado, plus Dimmu Borgir drummer Nick Barker. Although the *Pleasures Pave Sewers* Lockup album sold well in Germany, Tägtgren backed out of the project before live work ensued.

The year 2000 found Tägtgren busier than ever with a further Pain album, *Rebirth*, which garnered a healthy and lengthy placing in the national Swedish album charts, as well as a fresh Hypocrisy effort, the retro-flavoured *Into The Abyss*, released in August.

The band, now installing a new second live guitarist in Scattered Corpses member Andreas Holma and promoting the *Catch 22* album, were part of the European 'No Mercy' festival in March and April 2002 with Vader, Catastrophic, Destroyer 666, Immortal, Disbelief, Malevolent Creation and Obscenity.

Hypocrisy cut a new album for 2004 release entitled *The Arrival*. The recording didn't run smoothly, however, and upon completion the whole album was remastered and remixed. Fan demand persuaded the band to re-record 'The Abyss' for this record: the song had originally only appeared as a bonus track on *The Fourth Dimension*. Silenoz of Dimmu Borgir was co-credited on the track 'New World' and a switch in drummers found the Immortal, Pain and Grimfist-credited Horgh (aka Reidar Horghagen) taking over from Szöke in January 2004.

Tägtgren donated a guest vocal to the 2004 Kataklysm album *Serenity In Fire*, appearing on 'For All Our Sins'. He also contributed his services to *Within The Mind*, assembled by guitarist James Murphy in honour of the late Death mentor Chuck Schuldiner, and joined the Dan Swanö-mentored Bloodbath.

Hypocrisy then toured North America in league with Exhumed, Cannibal Corpse and Vile before a run of South American gigs. They then played the 2004 European 'No Mercy' festivals with Spawn Of Possession, Cannibal Corpse, Kataklysm, Carpathian Forest, Vomitory, Prejudice and Exhumed. Horgh relinquished his Grimfist position in June in order to prioritise Hypocrisy.

The band performed an unusual concert dubbed the '34,000 Ton Metal Cruise' on September 25th, performing aboard the Münchenbryggeriet car ferry in Stockholm alongside Tankard, Amon Amarth, Skyclad, Tad Morose, Stormwarrior and Wolf. US dates for January 2005 had the band packaged with Dark Tranquillity and Soilwork. In February, Tägtgren worked in the studio as producer for German thrash metal veterans Destruction. That August, he ensconced himself in Horus Sound Studios in Hannover, producing the *Monotheist* comeback album for Celtic Frost, and then engaged in promotion for Hypocrisy's *Virus* record, launched in September. He then got back to work on a new record for Pain.

Virus had the band pursuing a more technical direction and featured new guitarist Andreas Holma, a man with a jazz background. Notably, Gary Holt of Exodus guested on the track 'Scrutinized'. European gigs that November, allied with Exodus, saw support from Keep Of Kalessin while 2006 saw the band teaming up with Nile, Soilent Green, Raging Speedhorn, With Passion and Polish act Decapitated for a North American tour commencing in early January.

The band then joined the *Metal Hammer*-sponsored European 'Neckbreaker's Ball' tour in April. Guitarist Andreas Holma quit in September; the band claimed this was because the musician was "not motivated any more". Hypocrisy utilised the services of Darkane's Klas Ideberg as a session guitarist for their North American 'Machines At War' tour before US shows commencing on October 26th 2006 with headliners Fear Factory, Suffocation and Decapitated. The band remain among the finest exemplars of their genre.

IN FLAMES
RED-HOT METAL

IN FLAMES ARE A HIGH-RANKING Gothenburg band, founded in late 1990 and widely recognised as one of the key practitioners of the melodic death metal genre. As the band have broadened their appeal, a dilution in aggression has alienated older fans, but each successive album has strengthened their overall position with increased sales.

The quintet assumed the name In Flames in 1993 after guitarist Ander Iwers (later of Tiamat) backed out of the founding quartet, leaving ex-Ceremonial Oath guitarist Jesper Strömblad, bassist Johan Larsson and second guitarist Glenn Ljungström. Their three-track August 1993 demo, featuring 'In Flames', 'Upon An Oaken Throne' and 'Clad In Shadows', secured a deal with Wrong Again Records.

The band's line-up for the debut album *Lunar Strain*, recorded by engineer Fredrik Nordström at Studio Fredman and released in August 1994, consisted of the original trio plus sessioning friends such as Iwers, guitarist Carl Näslund, Ceremonial Oath guitarist Oscar Dronjak, female singer Jennica Johansson on 'Everlost (Part II)', violinist Ylva Wåhlstedt on the instrumental 'Hårgalåten', and the Dark Tranquillity duo of vocalist Mikael Stanne and drummer Anders Jivarp.

By the time of 1995's five-track *Subterranean* mini-album, In Flames had added Eucharist drummer Daniel Erlandsson, although Jivarp contributed. Session vocals were handled by Henke Forss of Dawn and Funeral Feast. However, on the album's release the band found a new frontman in ex-Ceremonial Oath and Dark Tranquillity singer Anders Fridén, and further shifts saw Erlandsson losing his place to Björn Gelotte.

Following these two critically acclaimed releases, In Flames contributed a cover version of 'Eye Of The Beholder' for the Metallica tribute album *Metal Militia Volume 1* compiled by Black Sun Records. As the band had no lead vocalist at this juncture, Ancient Slumber frontman Robert Dahne lent his lungs for this recording.

In Flames tried out various vocalists in an attempt to gain some degree of stability. Demo tracks at this juncture witnessed the inclusion of Marduk's Jocke Göthberg on 'Dead Eternity' and Deranged's Per Gyllenbäck (also the label boss at Wrong Again) on 'The Inborn Lifeless', later to evolve into the following album's 'Dead God In Me'.

The band eventually re-enlisted Fridén in time to record *The Jester Race*, released in February 1996, the album that pushed them to the forefront. They had stepped upwards to the major Nuclear Blast label, and the studio sessions, conducted once again by Nordström, found Oscar Dronjak adding vocals to 'Dead Eternity', Kaspar Dahlqvist of Treasureland donating keyboards to 'Wayfaerer', and Dark Tranquillity's Fredrik Johansson laying down lead guitar on 'December Flower'. Japanese variants of *The Jester Race*, clad in different artwork to the European tank design, added two exclusive tracks with demos of 'Dead Eternity' and 'The Inborn Lifeless'.

Backed up by numerous positive reviews, In Flames set out on the spring 'Out Of The Darkness' package in Germany with Dimmu Borgir, Cradle Of Filth and Dissection. In 1997, the Japanese Iron Maiden tribute album, *Made In Flames*, arrived through the Toy's Factory label, with In Flames contributing a version of 'Murders In The Rue Morgue'.

Strömblad entered the national German charts in late 1997, although not with In Flames. The guitarist was the unofficial sixth member of trad-metal outfit Hammerfall, assembled by his colleague Dronjak.

With the band now on hold, they took the opportunity to realign their line-up, dispensing with Ljungström and Larsson. Two new players, guitarist Niklas Engelin and bassist Peter Iwers of Chameleon, were quickly slotted in after October 1997's *Whoracle*, which included a version of Depeche Mode's 'Everything Counts'. This record was preceded by a picture-disc EP, *Black-Ash Inheritance*. *Whoracle* was the first In Flames product to register on the charts, reaching Number 78 in Germany.

Mid 1998 saw the band supporting Dimmu Borgir, hitting the continental festivals in earnest and undertaking their debut appearances in Japan. That same year, Daniel Svensson of Sacrilege and Dimension Zero took command of the drums, giving In Flames the solid line-up it had been sorely lacking for so long.

The opening gambit of the new-look In Flames, *Colony*, hit stores in

Melodic death metal scene-leaders In Flames

May 1999 across Europe as well as charts in Germany, Sweden and Finland. Produced by Nordström, who gained extra credits for Hammond organ, slide guitar and "some other hippie stuff", *Colony* also found Europe guitarist Kee Marcello (Kjell Lövbom) donating his soloing skills to the track 'Coerced Coexistence'.

Iwers stood down temporarily to devote time to his newborn daughter, and Dick Lövgren of Armageddon and Arch Enemy filled in as substitute. After a season on the European festival circuit and shows in the USA and Japan, In Flames closed 1999 with a December 18th concert in London with Cradle Of Filth and Arch Enemy.

Clayman took the band into the higher reaches of the European charts in July 2000. Although this record maintained the same team of musicians and producer as its predecessor, it gave the first hints of a change in direction, with the old abrasive edges undergoing refinement. *Clayman* hosted the song 'Only For The Weak', a track which would go on to establish itself as the band's anthem. A limited edition release, packaged in a 3D cover, was bolstered by the inclusion of an extra song, 'World Of Promises', a radical adaptation of melodic rockers Treat's original.

In Flames toured North America in 2000 with Earth Crisis and Skinlab before UK dates in November supporting Slipknot, which certainly placed the band in front of fresh audiences. After playing with the more traditional fare of Iced Earth and Jag Panzer in April 2002, they were then announced as part of the billing of the Slayer-topped American 'Extreme Steel' festivals.

In Flames set to work on a new studio record, *Reroute To Remain*, produced by Daniel Bergstrand and set for September release. The band's 1994 rendition of 'Eye Of The Beholder' resurfaced again on a Nuclear Blast Metallica tribute collection.

Reroute To Remain gave the band a Number 5 placing in the Swedish charts, and a month's worth of North American dates commenced in San Francisco backed up by Sentenced, Killswitch Engage and Lacuna Coil. October headliners in Germany were supported by Pain and Soilwork.

Fridén embroiled himself in yet another side venture by fronting Passenger, a late 2002 band incorporating his erstwhile In Flames colleague and Gardenian guitarist Niclas Engelin, Headplate bassist Håkan Skoger and ex-Transport League drummer Patrik J. Sten.

In Flames then toured America with fabled industrialists Ministry and math-metal act Mudvayne. An EP, *Trigger*, included a cover of the Genesis song 'Land Of Confusion'. The title track of the EP found its way onto the *Freddy Vs. Jason* movie soundtrack. Toward the close of 2003, Gelotte and Strömblad formed All Ends in collaboration with "musical artist" Tinna Karlsdotter and her sister Emma Gelotte.

The band, re-signing to Nuclear Blast, set *Soundtrack To Your Escape* as the title of a 2004 album produced by Bergstrand and ex-Misery Loves Co. man Örjan Örnkloo. A single, 'The Quiet Place', was promoted with a video shot by director Patric Ullaeus and landed at Number 2 in the Swedish charts. *Soundtrack To Your Escape* sold 10,659 copies during its first week of US release to debut at Number 145 on the *Billboard* charts. It also made the Top 5 in Sweden. Meanwhile, Regain Records reissued *Lunar Strain* and *Subterranean*, both with rare and demo tracks. European dates in April saw Devildriver as support act.

As Nielsen SoundScan reports showed that *Soundtrack To Your Escape* was selling around 3,000 units a week in the USA, the UK's *Metal Hammer* magazine presented In Flames with their Best Underground Act award in June. After Australian dates in September with Chimaira, the band played two special shows the same month at the Los Angeles Roxy and New York's CBGBs for a live album. They performed two sets each night, the first comprising the entire *Soundtrack To Your Escape* album before they closed the night with back-catalogue tracks. Returning to Sweden, Gelotte and Strömblad swiftly set to work on new material. The band closed the year with a special performance on December 27th at the

Carling Apollo in London alongside Lacuna Coil, Caliban and Chimaira. As part of the show, In Flames performed a cover of Pantera's 'Fucking Hostile' as a tribute to guitarist 'Dimebag' Darrell Abbott.

The band then grabbed a high-profile support slot to Judas Priest's February 2005 European dates. Throughout the spring, the band were ensconced in Dug-Out Studios in Uppsala crafting a new album, which was given a working title of *Crawl Through Knives* but was subsequently switched to *Come Clarity*. The album crashed into the Number 1 position on both the Swedish and Finnish album charts. Impressively, it sold 24,000 copies in the United States in its first week of release to debut at Number 58 on the *Billboard* chart.

The group opened for Mötley Crüe on their two Finnish dates in early June. Their lavish DVD *Used And Abused – In Live We Trust* topped the Swedish charts upon its release in July. In Flames, Trivium, Devildriver and Pennsylvania's Zao pooled their talents for a January 2006 US tour. European shows throughout April and May witnessed veteran Brazilian thrashers Sepultura and Frenchmen Dagoba as opening acts. The band put in a significant appearance at the Guns N'Roses-headlined 'Download' festival at Castle Donington, England on June 11th. The group were then engaged on a gigantic roving festival bill with the US 'Sounds Of The Underground' tour throughout the summer. In Flames remain one of the few death metal bands to have made serious inroads into the mainstream, and their reputation precedes them.

KATATONIA
GOTHIC EXPERTISE

KATATONIA ARE CELEBRATED propagators of ambitious and supremely melodic doomdeath metal with heavy gothic elements.The Avesta-based band started life in 1987 as a duo, guitarist Sombreius Blakkheim (aka Anders Nyström) and vocalist-drummer Lord Seth (real name Jonas Renkse). They worked with Edge Of Sanity frontman Dan Swanö as

producer at Gorysound Studios over three days in July 1992 to record the demo *Jhva Elohim Meth*. Five hundred copies of this tape were manufactured, 300 on blue cassettes, 100 on red, and 100 transparent.

The *Jhva Elohim Meth* material was later released on CD as *Jhva Elohim Meth – The Revival* by Dutch label Vic, the only change being a subtle renaming of the intro track from the original 'Prologue: Midwinter Intergates' to 'Midwinter Gates'. This time, Swanö featured among the band credits on keyboards under the pseudonym Day Disyhrah.

Having signed to No Fashion, Katatonia added former Tears Of Luna bassist Israphael Wing (real name Guillaume Le Huche). Their opening album, *Dance Of December Souls*, was recorded at Unisound Studios with Swanö. Over just five days in April 1993, they re-recorded their original demo tracks and cut fresh songs to form the album.

Despite being a debut album, *Dance Of December Souls* staggered many with its maturity. Resolutely doom-orientated, the record hung on its bleak, almost hollow production. From the opening siren laments of 'Seven Dreaming Souls' and the first track 'Gateways Of Bereavement', eschewing a chorus in favour of a mantric "Let me die!", Katatonia showed their scorn for convention, which was apparent from the outset. The band's black/death metal origins were apparent on the blasphemous 'Without God' while their ability to tackle epic subject matter was illustrated by the monumental 'Velvet Thorns (Of Drynwhyl)' and 'Tomb Of Insomnia'. The album rose to a finale with the oblique 'Dancing December', a composition whose entire lyric consisted of one word repeated at a whisper.

In addition to this material, the band contributed two tracks ('Black Erotica' and 'Love Of The Swan') to the Wrong Again compilation album *W.A.R.* in 1995. The same year, Katatonia released the *For Funerals To Come* EP through Italian label Avantgarde, containing songs put down on tape in a day-long session at Unisound the previous September. Further recordings included a split 10-inch EP through Hammerheart with Irish act Primordial the following year.

Le Huche opted out in 1994, resurfacing as a member of progressive

KATATONIA discography

JHVA ELOHIM METH... THE REVIVAL, Vic VIC 1 (Europe) (1994)

DANCE OF THE DECEMBER SOULS, No Fashion NFR 005 (Europe) (1995)

For Funerals To Come, Avantgarde Music AV009 (Europe) (1995)

Scarlet Heavens, Misanthropy AMAZON 010 (UK) (1996) split 10-inch vinyl EP with Primordial

BRAVE MURDER DAY, Avantgarde Music AV022 (Europe) (1996), Century Media CM 7887-2 (USA) (1997)

Sounds Of Decay, Avantgarde Music AV024 (Europe) (1997)

Saw You Drown, Avantgarde Music AV 028 (Europe) (1998)

DISCOURAGED ONES, Avantgarde Music AV029 (Europe), Century Media CM 7903-2 (USA) (1998)

TONIGHT'S DECISION, Peaceville CDVILE76 (UK / USA) (1999)

LAST FAIR DEAL GONE DOWN, Peaceville CDVILED89 (UK / USA) (2001)

Teargas, Peaceville CDVILES98 (UK) (2001)

Tonight's Music, Peaceville CDVILES113 (UK) (2001)

VIVA EMPTINESS, Peaceville CDVILEF103 (UK / USA) (2003)

THE BLACK SESSIONS, Peaceville CDVILEB129 (UK / USA) (2005)

My Twin, Peaceville CDVILES138 (UK) (2006)

THE GREAT COLD DISTANCE, Peaceville CDVILEF128 (UK / USA) (2006)

Deliberation, Peaceville CDVILES140 (UK) (2006)

metal band Mindwatch, later known as Eyekon. Coincidentally, another Mindwatch man, Mikael Oretoft, took over the bass in 1996. Unknown to the outside world, Katatonia had actually folded during this period, but soon re-assembled.

Blakkheim, having relinquished a position with In Grey, had worked up a side project titled Bewitched, releasing the *Diabolical Desecration* album on Osmose in 1996. Seth was working on his October Tide project with Fulmination guitarist Fredrik Norrman – who was then inducted into Katatonia.

Avantgarde issued the acclaimed, hypnotic *Brave Murder Day* in 1996, again recorded at Unisound by Swanö. Opeth's Mikael Åkerfeldt featured as studio guest on distorted vocals as a foil to Renske's cleanly-delivered lamentations. Katatonia performed a short British tour in late 1996 with support acts In The Woods... and Voice Of Destruction. An EP, *Sounds Of Decay*, also with contributions from Åkerfeldt, was delivered in December 1997.

The *Saw You Drown* EP was released in January 1998, limited to 1,500 hand-numbered copies. *Discouraged Ones* followed in April, a self-produced record crafted at Sunlight Studios with engineers Fred Estby of Dismember and Tomas Skogsberg. Once again, Åkerfeldt was in evidence for backing vocals.

Discouraged Ones, a balance between the doomdeath of yore and a courageous leap into the unknown, shocked fans with its complete overhaul of the Katatonia sound. Forsaking speed and aggression, the band had discovered that utter despair and cold bleakness was just as effective. As songs became simpler, stripped down to standard rock formats, the impact of the message became harder still. Needless to say, the band lost fans due to this change of path but gathered in many more newer admirers.

At this juncture, Blakkheim and Seth were also playing in a death metal project titled Diabolical Masquerade, and they forged old-school death metal act Bloodbath with longstanding allies Swanö and Åkerfeldt, both of whom appeared on Katatonia's masterly *Tonight's Decision* in August 1999. This collection, the band's first for Peaceville, featured a cover version of Jeff Buckley's 'Nightmares By The Sea'. *Tonight's Decision* was a progression from *Discouraged Ones*, with the audibility of Renkse's introspective lyrics now attracting the previously suspicious media.

The 2001 *Teargas* EP, with two exclusive tracks, was another strong release, marking the incorporation of two new band members, ex-Dellamorte bassist Mattias Norrman and Subdive and Wicked drummer Daniel Liljekvist. By this stage, the band had rid themselves totally of their formative death metal skin and were plunging headlong into deeply disturbing yet melodic songs, gaining wider acceptance and recognition for their efforts across the globe. A further full-length album, *Last Fair Deal Gone Down*, was released in 2001.

Katatonia took on the services of Swanö to mix their sixth full-length album for early 2003 through Peaceville. The band united with Finntroll for European touring throughout April and May. The emergence of 2003's *Viva Emptiness*, a tapestry of morosely compelling dirges, put Katatonia firmly into the major league bracket with unanimous praise. German gigs to promote the album in April saw Before The Dawn and Dark Suns as support.

A 2004 release, *Brave Yester Days*, compiled tracks from EPs alongside rarities and the unreleased 'Untrue'. With Katatonia's status rising rapidly, Black Lodge Records reissued their early *Dance Of December Souls* album but sparked some criticism from the band, who issued the statement: "We do not support this reissue and take complete distance from its existence." Apparently the record's new artwork and logo, designed to be in keeping with more recent Katatonia albums, led the band to believe that the recordings were being passed off to look like new material. Meanwhile, Peaceville compiled *The Black Sessions*, a set of post-1998 recordings comprising singles, B-sides, cover songs and selected tracks from *Discouraged Ones* through *Viva Emptiness*, plus an unreleased recording.

Leading up to the band's appearance at the October 'Barlo' festival in Holland, Katatonia united with Amaran for a run of Scandinavian and European gigs. The group then engaged in songwriting for a new album. In early 2005 the *Saw You Drown* EP from 1998 was licensed to Infinite Vinyl for a limited edition release of 1,000 hand-numbered copies.

In June, Katatonia entered Fascination Street Studios in Örebro to craft *The Great Cold Distance*, released in March 2006. Their debut Russian performances came in September with gigs in Moscow and St. Petersburg. European road work in April and May 2006 saw Novembre as support band. The band put in a small run of Turkish concerts in September, and Katatonia, Moonspell and Daylight Dies teamed up for a North American tour commencing in October.

OPETH
SUPERBLY TECHNICAL MUSICOLOGISTS

ALTHOUGH THEY WERE REGARDED at first as just another project from Edge Of Sanity mentor Dan Swanö, Opeth have become a true force for change in the international arena with their neo-progressive masterpieces of modern metal. Starting life in Sörskogen influenced by raw black metal, Opeth have steadily matured into more profound soundscapes with each release.

Vocalist-guitarist Mikael Åkerfeldt and drummer Anders Nordin, both ex-Eruption, had known each other since the age of five. Established during 1987, Eruption – comprising Åkerfeldt, Nordin, guitarist Nick Döring and bassist Jocke Horney (swiftly replaced by Stephan Claesberg) – mainly pursued covers by the likes of Death, Black Sabbath and Bathory. Singer David Isberg's previous band were Opeth, centred in the Täby suburb of Stockholm and taking their name from the Opet moon city

---

OPETH discography

ORCHID, Candlelight CANDLE 010 (UK) (1995), Century Media CM 7845-2 (USA) (1997)

MORNINGRISE, Candlelight CANDLE 015 (UK) (1996), Century Media CM 7849-2 (USA) (1997)

MY ARMS, YOUR HEARSE, Candlelight CANDLE 025 (UK), Century Media CM 7894-2 (USA) (1998)

STILL LIFE, Peaceville CDVILE78 (UK / USA) (1999)

BLACKWATER PARK, Music For Nations CDMFN 264 (UK), Koch KOC-CD-8237 (USA) (2001)

DELIVERANCE, Music For Nations CDMFN 291 (UK), Koch KOC-CD-8437 (USA) (2002)

DAMNATION, Music For Nations CDMFN 294 (UK), Koch KOC-CD-8652 (USA) (2003)

GHOST REVERIES, Roadrunner RR 8123-2 (UK / USA) (2005) **62 UK**

---

described by author Wilbur Smith. They floundered when Isberg attempted to introduce Åkerfeldt into the ranks, and the main members split off to create Crowley, issuing a 1991 demo, *The Gate*. Meanwhile, Åkerfeldt and Isberg combined to re-form the act – subtly retitled Opeth. The duo's inaugural compositions were 'Requiem Of Lost Souls' and 'Mystique Of The Baphomet', subsequently re-worked into 'Mark Of The Damned' and 'Forest Of October' respectively.

Eruption colleagues Döring and Nordin were invited to enroll, and then second guitarist Andreas Dimeo was recruited for Opeth's debut gig – comprising just two songs – supporting Therion, Excruciate and Authorise in February 1991. Dimeo and Döring decamped shortly after. The former Crimson Cat duo of Kim Pettersson and Johan DeFarfalla plugged the gap for a second show in Gothenburg. The new pair also drifted off, although Pettersson stayed loyal for a 1991 concert with Asphyx and Desultory; more significantly, Isberg left for pastures new in Liars In Wait.

Just three gigs into their career, Opeth were starting to pen moodier material such as the prototype 'Poise Into Celeano', later to mutate into the album track 'Advent'. Åkerfeldt took the lead vocal role as he rebuilt the band with ex-Sylt I Krysset (it means Jam On The Cross) guitarist Peter Lindgren and bassist Stephan Guteklint. Opeth never officially cut any demos, although a two-track 1994 cassette was leaked comprising 'Forest Of October' and 'In The Mist She Was Standing'.

After a deal with the British Candlelight label, the debut album *Orchid* was cut at Dan Swanö's Unisound studio in March 1994 with previous member DeFarfalla on session bass, with Guteklint journeying on to join Mindwatch. A double vinyl edition pressed by Dutch label Displeased added an extra track, 'Into The Forest Of Winter'.

Orchid's presentation, with the album cover simply bearing the flower of the same name, was deceptive. Once past the packaging, fans revelled in a labyrinth of sound, discordant song structures, and an apparently chaotic structure. Guitar tones ranged from crunching death metal to lilting acoustics; the bass had an uncharacteristic prominence; percussion was more in keeping with freeform jazz – and vocals took on many tongues, from blackened howls via gut-wrenching shrieks to ethereal, pure tones. So confusing was this album that in the mastering process some tracks were misplaced, with the closing segment of 'Requiem' mistakenly tacked onto the beginning of 'The Apostle In Triumph'.

Gigs followed in spring 1995, including a London Astoria show alongside Ved Buens Ende, Hecate Enthroned and Impaled Nazarene. Opeth's second album, *Morningrise*, once again produced by Dan Swanö and released in June 1996, was an exercise in oppressive malaise, a quintet of morose, lumbering songs imbued with near-impenetrable poetic detail. The album left reviewers either perplexed or in awe, while existing fans lapped up the 20-minute 'Black Rose Immortal'. Detractors labelled the band's progressive rock persuasions as boring.

Morningrise was promoted with a support slot to Morbid Angel in the UK and to Cradle Of Filth in Europe. After these dates, both Nordin and DeFarfalla made their exit. Persevering, Åkerfelt pulled in a new Uruguayan rhythm section of bassist Martin Méndez and ex-Amon Amarth drummer Martin López, both members of Requiem Aeternum. This latest incarnation of Opeth cut the *My Arms, Your Hearse* album, although Mikael Åkerfeldt played the bass parts, described as a "third observation", during August and September 1997. The band chose a new location to have their art "absorbed by the electronic devices", utilising Fredman Studios and employing the production team of Fredrik Nordström and Anders Fridén. Heavier than previous outings, the album benefited from a brighter sound: the criticism aimed at Opeth's meandering approach to songwriting saw the tracks reduced in length.

My Arms, Your Hearse was delivered to the public in August 1998, and further UK live action saw supports to Cradle Of Filth in December 1997, after which the band signed to new label Peaceville. This union resulted in the self-produced album *Still Life*, hammered out at both Fredman Studios and Maestro Musik during April and May 1999 and ushered out in October.

Meanwhile, a diversion was afforded by Steel, an impromptu traditional 1980s-style heavy metal liaison between Åkerfeldt and singer Dan Swanö with the Opeth-credited Peter Lindgren and drummer Anders Nordin. Never intended as a serious venture, Steel nevertheless attracted the attention of Near Dark Productions, who issued two tracks on a 1998 7-inch picture disc single titled 'Heavy Metal Machine'. Åkerfeldt also teamed up with Swanö, Katatonia's Blakkheim (Andres Nyström) and Jonas Renkse to create the old school death metal band Bloodbath in 2000.

Returning to Fredman Studios, Opeth changed labels to Music For Nations for *Blackwater Park* in March 2001. These sessions were produced by the band in alliance with Porcupine Tree frontman Steven Wilson. A limited double CD emerged the following year, restricted to just 1,000 copies, and hosted two extra songs – 'Still Day Beneath The Sun' and 'Patterns In The Ivy II' – plus the video for 'Harvest'.

Opeth toured the UK in May 2002 supported by Arch Enemy. Later that year they revealed that they were planning not one but two new Nordström-produced albums, a 'heavy' album to be mixed by Andy Sneap and a 'mellow' record mixed by Steven Wilson. The original concept was to unveil both works simultaneously, but label pressure resulted in *Deliverance* arriving in November 2002 and *Damnation* the following April. As it transpired, Wilson ended up manning the board for both collections. The band announced North American tour dates for January 2003, billed as the '4 Absent Friends' tour, with Paradise Lost and Tapping The Vein. Subsequent dates in May had the band packaged with Lacuna Coil and Beyond The Embrace. Dedicated fans were forced to move fast to pick up a 7-inch single through the Robotic Empire label. Opeth's first single release, 'Still Day Beneath The Sun', was limited to 1,092 black vinyl and just 150 grey vinyl copies.

The status of *Deliverance* was confirmed in February when Opeth received a Swedish Grammy award for the record in the Best Hard Rock category. The band united with Porcupine Tree for summer North American co-headlining dates, drafting in Spiritual Beggars' organ player Per Wiberg for these shows. October Scandinavian dates had Norwegians Extol as support.

In November, Åkerfeldt was confirmed as a session guest on the 2004 Ayreon concept album *The Human Equation*. Less fortunate news for Opeth came when gigs in Chile and Jordan were pulled, the latter due to a "stress related breakdown" by drummer López and the withdrawal of crew members because of terrorist attacks in the Middle East.

Opeth got back on schedule with their 'Lamentations Over America Tour 2004', commencing in Edmonton, Canada on January 20th. These shows saw the band partnered with Devildriver and Portugal's Moonspell. However, the band pulled out of the Edmonton gig as Martin López was still in Sweden. Further reports suggested the drummer was undergoing treatment for panic attacks. Persevering, Opeth gave an abbreviated five-song performance in Calgary with a drum technician acting as stand-in. Strapping Young Lad and Dark Angel drummer Gene Hoglan stepped in as stopgap for the January 23rd Vancouver stop, performing on two tracks 'The Drapery Falls' and 'Demon Of The Fall'. Earlier that evening, Opeth had played a truncated acoustic set including a take on Deep Purple's 'Soldier Of Fortune'. López returned for the band's Seattle date.

With Music For Nations acquired by the Zomba group in summer 2004, Opeth found themselves without a label. Announcing in April 2005 that touring keyboard player Per Wiberg had been enrolled as a permanent member of the band, Opeth entered Fascination Street Studios in Örebro during May to craft a new album, *Ghost Reveries*, for Roadrunner. Åkerfeldt was included on the Roadrunner United 25th anniversary album *The All-Stars Sessions*, featuring on the track 'Roads' penned by Type O Negative's Josh Silver.

With López temporarily forced out as the drummer underwent treatment for a blood disorder, Opeth re-enlisted Hoglan to fill in for live work. The summer of 2005 found the group participating in the US 'Sounds Of The Underground' tour, a collaboration between independent labels Ferret Music, Prosthetic, Trustkill and Metal Blade. The billing for these shows saw the band sharing stages with unlikely acts such as Clutch, Poison The Well, From Autumn To Ashes, Unearth, Norma Jean, Chimaira, Strapping Young Lad, Every Time I Die, Devildriver, High On Fire, Throwdown, A Life Once Lost, All That Remains and Gwar.

Ghost Reveries gave Opeth numerous international chart positions in important territories such as the UK and Australia. In the USA the record sold 15,000 copies in its first week of sale to debut impressively at Number 64 on the *Billboard* charts. Elsewhere, *Ghost Reveries* made its presence felt in the national charts across Canada, Finland, Denmark, France, Norway, Holland, Italy and Germany. Most impressive of all was a Number 9 score in Sweden.

European touring in September saw support again from Christian metal band Extol. For these shows, with López still undergoing treatment, Opeth pulled in the much-travelled drummer Martin Axenrot of Bloodbath, Witchery, Nifelheim, Blasphemous, Morgue, Coven, Triumphator, N.C.O. and Satanic Slaughter. Opeth returned to the USA in October, a first leg of dates supported by Pelican and Fireball Ministry, with Nevermore and Into Eternity supporting on the second leg.

Entering the BBC studios in Maida Vale, London, the band cut extra tracks for use on an expanded reissue of *Ghost Reveries* – 'When', 'The Grand Conjuration' and a cover of Deep Purple's 'Soldier Of Fortune'. European gigs in November and December were supported by Sweden's Burst. The band's 2006 live campaign opened up in the USA during February alongside Dark Tranquillity and Devin Townsend. During these dates, the group engaged in special concerts dubbed 'Chronology MCMXCIV-MMV – A Live Observation By Opeth'. Held in New York, Chicago and Los Angeles, these seated shows encompassed a chronological set of material, some never before performed live, from each of their albums.

The band put in a significant appearance at the Metallica and Korn-headlined 'Download' festival in Castle Donington, England on June 10th. South and Central American shows, taking in Mexico, Chile, Argentina and Brazil, were announced for September and October. Opeth remain at the very top of their game.

SOILWORK
MELODIC BUT HEAVY DEATH ACT

AT FIRST, THE TRADEMARK OF HELSINGBORG act Soilwork was a heady mixture of thrash and death metal, but later releases, marked by the key *A Predator's Portrait* album, have seen the band promoted to the forefront of the melodic death metal movement.

They formed as a school combo in 1995, Inferior Breed. As Soilwork, they opened proceedings with the 1997 demo *In Dreams We Fall Into The Eternal Lake*. The band at this point involved frontman Björn Strid, going under the name of Speed, guitarist Peter Vicious (aka Peter Wichers), second guitarist Ludvig Svartz and drummer Jimmy Persson. A bassist, Carl-Gustav Döös, had decamped beforehand, as had a guitarist, Mattias Nilsson (he would resurface with Kayser).

A copy of *In Dreams* was given to Arch Enemy guitarist Mike Amott who, obviously impressed, passed it onto various labels, and there were a number of offers. The May 1998 album *Steel Bath Suicide*, released through French label Listenable, was produced by Fredrik Nordström at Fredman Studios. The band now incorporated Ola Flink on bass and Carlos Del Olmo Holmberg on keyboards. Japanese versions were augmented with 'Disintegrated Skies' and a cover of Deep Purple's 'Burn'. Soilwork then toured in Europe backing Naglfar, Darkane and Krisiun.

Listenable kept the band on for a further round of death/thrash metal in October 1999's *The Chainheart Machine*, again a Nordström-produced effort. The Jaffa Quartet – a violin section of Ullik Johansson, Julia Petersson, Amanda Ingvaldsson, Fanny Petersson, Alva Ingvaldsson and Katalin Tibell – were employed on the album, as was new drummer Henry Ranta and a new guitarist, Ola Frenning, to replace the departed Svartz. The European touring circuit felt the force of Soilwork again when the band supported Cannibal Corpse, Defleshed and Marduk prior to their first live engagement in Japan with Dark Tranquillity.

They signed to Nuclear Blast for the album *A Predator's Portrait*, launched in February 2001. This was where the band hit the crossroads of their career, not fully embracing experimentation but adopting more melody and, significantly, dropping Björn Strid's previous death metal growls for a cleaner approach. Nordström maintained his position as producer, Eskil Simonsson provided samples, and studio guests included Mattias IA Eklundh of Freak Kitchen and Opeth's Mikael Åkerfeldt. In the Far East, *A Predator's Portrait* had an extra cut, 'Asylum Dance'.

The band returned to the studio in October 2001 with new keyboard man Sven Karlsson, of Evergrey, and producer Devin Townsend, a Canadian who made a strong impression on the band. Soilwork's burgeoning reputation was heightened by the delivery of the March 2002 album, *Natural Born Chaos*. Strid's vocal parts were now almost wholly clean, and Karlsson's keyboard atmospherics figured prominently, including the use of Hammond organ on 'Black Star Deceiver'. Townsend's lush production breathed new life into the band, who adopted his techniques for future outings.

The band toured America during the summer with Hypocrisy and Killswitch Engage, one notable gig being at the San Jose Cactus Club where Chuck Billy of Testament lent backing vocals to the track 'Follow The Hollow'. Soilwork joined In Flames and Pain for touring in mainland Europe during October.

With gaps in their schedule, members of the band, with Darkane personnel and Construcdead drummer Erik Thyselius, also operated Terror 2000. Bassist Ola Flink was active with Hatelight, issuing the *Word Ammunition* and *Ricochet* demos in 2002 and 2003 respectively.

The band entered Helsingborg's Queenstreet studios with Nordström during December to cut their fifth album. Backing vocals for these sessions came courtesy of Hatelight's Jens Broman. *Figure Number Five*,

SOILWORK discography

STEEL BATH SUICIDE, Listenable POSH 012 (Europe / USA) (1998)

THE CHAINHEART MACHINE, Listenable POSH 017 (Europe) (1999), Century Media CM 7966-2 (USA) (2000)

A PREDATOR'S PORTRAIT, Nuclear Blast NB 0582-2 (Europe), Nuclear Blast America 6582 (USA) (2001)

NATURAL BORN CHAOS, Nuclear Blast NB 0581-2 (Europe), Nuclear Blast America 6581 (USA) (2002)

FIGURE NUMBER FIVE, Nuclear Blast NB 1108-2 (Europe), Nuclear Blast America 1108 (USA) (2003)

The Early Chapters, Listenable POSH 054 (Europe) (2004)

STABBING THE DRAMA, Nuclear Blast NB 1377-2 (Europe), Nuclear Blast America 1377 (USA) (2005)

issued by Nuclear Blast in April, was the recipient of huge acclaim in the metal world, and touring in North America saw the band hooking up with In Flames, Chimaira and Unearth for a month-long trek. They lost drummer Ranta beforehand, replacing him with Richard Evensand, a veteran of Ebony Tears, Dog Faced Gods and Sorcerer. The new recruit debuted with the band at the Gelsenkirchen, Germany 'Rock Hard' festival.

The band put in a showing at the Arch Enemy-headlined 'Busan International Rock Festival' at Daedepo Beach in Korea on August 8th before uniting with Children Of Bodom for a Japanese tour in September. A further bout of US shows saw the band partnered with Cradle Of Filth and New York's Type O Negative. Evensand joined Chimaira during December. Soilwork pulled in Dirk Verbeuren from French neo-thrashers Scarve on drums and undertook a headline tour of the UK in February 2004 supported by fellow countrymen The Forsaken. The band then partnered with Anthrax and Killswitch Engage for Australian and Japanese dates in April 2004. Verbeuren stepped in as substitute drummer for Belgian gore band Aborted's live dates.

After festival appearances, the band entered Studio Kuling in Örebro during September to work with producer Daniel Bergstrand on their sixth album, *Stabbing The Drama*, for early 2005 issue. European digipacks and Japanese copies added the track 'Wherever Thorns May Grow', the Japanese release also boosted with an additional song, 'Killed By Ignition'. US dates for January 2005 had the band packaged with Dark Tranquillity and Hypocrisy.

Soilwork's profile rose significantly as *Stabbing The Drama* entered the Swedish album charts at Number 14 in late February, and the album provided first-time chart entries for the band in Austria, Finland and France. The title track featured on the soundtrack to the *Rainbow Six: Lockdown* game issued by 3volution Productions.

The following month, Strid revealed a new side project, Coldseed, in collaboration with Blind Guardian drummer Thomen Stauch, guitarists Thorsten Praest and Gonzalo Alfageme López and the Blind Guardian and Sieges Even bassist Oli Holzwarth. Strid also put in a guest vocal appearance on German thrash act Destruction's *Inventor Of Evil* album.

Throughout the summer of 2005, the band joined the cast of acts on the US 'Ozzfest' tour alongside Black Sabbath, Iron Maiden and Velvet Revolver. Scandinavian, UK and European dates in October saw Construcdead as support. November 8th marked the start of another US tour, the band forming up a bill comprising Fear Factory, Darkane and Strapping Young Lad. Guitarist Peter Wichers announced his departure in mid December.

In early 2006, Björn Strid involved himself in a studio collaboration with bassist Steve DiGiorgio of Sadus, Testament and Death, Glen Alvelais

Soilwork, the new voice of Swedish metal

from Forbidden, Testament and LD/50, and Jeremy Colson of the Steve Vai band, among others.

A temporary replacement guitarist was installed in April 2006, the new man being Daniel Antonsson of Dimension Zero and Pathos. Soilwork joined the *Metal Hammer*-sponsored European 'Neckbreaker's Ball' 2006 tour, also featuring Hypocrisy, Scar Symmetry and One Man Army And The Undead Quartet. The band were due to put in a significant appearance at the Guns N'Roses-headlined 'Download' festival in Castle Donington, England on June 11th but were forced to pull out after guitarist Ola Frenning suffered a vascular spasm.

That same month, word arrived that Peter Wichers was working on his debut solo album in collaboration with Sanctuary and Nevermore singer Warrel Dane. Despite the gravity of this high-profile union, Soilwork announced further touring plans to push another album project. Their fans await the next move.

TIAMAT
AVANT-GARDE METALWORKS

TIAMAT ARE A GOTHIC METAL combo from Täby, masterminded by Johan Edlund, and have evolved with each successive release. Less tastefully known in their formative years as Treblinka – during which time vocalist Edlund pursued his gruesome side project General Surgery – the Swedish quartet adopted the title of the Sumerian goddess of chaos and mythical planet Tiamat. They have developed from a generic death metal act to a more substantial outfit, offering aggression with adventurous progressive elements. This makeover gave Tiamat access to the underground European darkwave club scene.

As Treblinka, the band consisted of vocalist-guitarist Edlund (Lucifer Hellslaughter), bassist Klas Wistedt, guitarist Stefan Lagergren (Emetic) and drummer Andreas Holmberg (Najse Auschwitzer). This unit released the 1988 demo *Crawling In Vomits* and a follow-up tape, *The Sign Of The Pentagram*, in 1989. The *Severe Abomination* EP also emerged that year on Mould In Hell Records. A later incarnation of Treblinka included Nicke Andersson of Entombed.

The group issued the September 1990 debut album *Sumerian Cry* through C.M.F.T. Productions. They were firmly entrenched in black metal, evidenced by an album cover brandishing pentagrams and inverted crosses, harsh riffing driven by blastbeats, and the musicians caked in corpsepaint and studded with nails. Once the tracks were completed, a decision was made to switch from the controversial name Treblinka to a more palatable Tiamat, debuting live under their new banner on April 6th 1990 in Stockholm.

Sumerian Cry was, in truth, a fairly basic affair, marred by some amateurish drumming and ill-conceived attempts at experimentation, such as a clumsy 'Evilized'. Nonetheless, the album succeeded in getting the Tiamat brand onto the European metal scene. But from this point onwards the band was rocked by constant re-shuffling of personnel. For the Tomas Skogsberg-engineered 'A Winter Shadow' single, released in December 1990 by CBR Records, the line-up was credited as Hellslaughter, guitarist A.D. Lord (aka Thomas Petersson), bass player Jörgen Thullberg (Juck The Ripper) and drummer Oakbeach (Niklas Ekstrand).

Signing with Century Media, Tiamat toured Europe in 1991 with label mates Unleashed, and then with Death for German concerts in February. September 1991's *The Astral Sleep* saw both Lagergren and Holmberg depart: the record was recorded by Edlund, Petersson, Thullberg and drummer Lars Sköld with Jonas Malmsten on keyboards. The album was conceived at Woodhouse Studios in Dortmund, with production delegated to Grip Inc. guitarist Waldemar Sorychta. Europe again felt the force of the Tiamat experience in October as the group, together with Paradise, hit

Belgium, Holland, Denmark, Sweden, Germany, Poland, Slovakia, Slovenia, Hungary and Italy. The campaign carried on into the new year, another circuit of the continent conducted alongside Samael and Unleashed. In April, they hopped onboard a brutal package comprising Cannibal Corpse, Death and Carcass.

The band's 1992 line-up for the third effort, *Clouds*, issued that September, consisted of Edlund, Petersson, ex-Sorceror bassist Johnny Hagel, keyboard player Kenneth Roos and drummer Niklas Ekstrand. *The Sleeping Beauty – Live In Israel* was recorded in Tel Aviv on June 3rd 1993 prior to touring Germany again with Morgoth and Tankard. Later shows found the band touring alongside Morgoth, Unleashed and, into 1994, Voodoo Cult and Crematory. Petersson and Roos took their leave, requiring Edlund to carry on with a new formation that included bassist Johnny Hagel.

September 1994's *Wildhoney* found the band expanding into fresh vistas of sound. In the studio, Birgit Zacher lent her vocals, keyboards were contributed by Sorychta, and the group's confidence resulted in no fewer than four instrumentals, 'Wildhoney', '25th Floor', 'Kaleidoscope' and 'Planets'. The single choice was 'Gaia', included on a six-track EP of that name released in 1995 and including a cover of Pink Floyd's 'When You're In'. Predictably, the line-up changed yet again with Ekstrand and Petersson discharging themselves and drummer Sköld welcomed back into the fold. Former Celeborn guitarist Magnus Sahlgren sessioned on *Wildhoney* and was kept on for tour work. Sahlgren subsequently joined Dismember and Lake Of Tears.

The band toured as support to Type O Negative in Europe during 1994 and again in 1995 with an exhaustive round of dates flanking Sentenced. They successfully headlined the 1995 'Dynamo' festival in Holland and scored a sizeable coup with a tour of the USA, Europe and

---

TIAMAT discography

SUMERIAN CRY, C.M.F.T. Productions CMFT 6 (UK) (1990)

A Winter Shadow, CBR CBR-S-125 (Europe) (1990)

THE ASTRAL SLEEP, Century Media 84 9722-2 (Europe), Century Media CM 7722-2 (USA) (1991)

CLOUDS, Century Media 84 9736-2 (Europe), Century Media CM 7736-2 (USA) (1992)

THE SLEEPING BEAUTY – LIVE IN ISRAEL, Century Media CM 77065-2 (Europe), Century Media CM 7765-2 (USA) (1994)

WILDHONEY, Century Media CM 77080-2 (Europe), Century Media CM 7780-2 (USA) (1994)

Gaia, Century Media CM 77089-2 (Europe) (1994)

THE MUSICAL HISTORY OF TIAMAT, Century Media LC 6975 (Europe) (1995)

Cold Seed, Century Media CM 77167-2 (Europe) (1997)

A DEEPER KIND OF SLUMBER, Century Media CM 77180-2 (Europe), Century Media CM 7880-2 (USA) (1997)

Brighter Than The Sun, Century Media CM 77279-3 (Europe) (1999)

SKELETON SKELETRON, Century Media CM 77280-2 (Europe), Century Media CM 7980-2 (USA) (1999)

For Her Pleasure, Century Media CM 77281-3 (Europe) (1999)

JUDAS CHRIST, Century Media CM 77380-2 (Europe), Century Media CM 8080-2 (USA) (2002)

Vote For Love, Century Media CM 77379-3 (Europe) (2003)

Cain, Century Media CM 77479-3 (Europe) (2003)

PREY, Century Media CM 77480-2 (Europe), Century Media CM 8180-2 (USA) (2003)

Britain in support to the mighty Black Sabbath. The same year a limited-edition album, *The Musical History Of Tiamat*, was released.

April 1997's *A Deeper Kind Of Slumber* heralded another shift in Tiamat's musical landscape as Edlund, now employing a near-Gregorian vocal timbre, ventured into uncompromising progressive-rock territory. Members of German band The Inchtabokatables enhanced the proceedings with string arrangements. Collectors were appeased when Century Media issued *A Deeper Kind Of Slumber* in two sets of cover art, one for Europe and another for the USA. Naturally the ebb and flow of band members continued unabated, with Cemetary's Anders Iwers enrolling in a straight swap as Johnny Hagel joined Cemetary. The ex-Tiamat man was later found in Sundown before pursuing his own Cinnamon Spiral and Lithium projects. Meanwhile, further internal manoeuvres in Tiamat saw Iwers shifting to bass when Petersson rejoined. Once dates with The Gathering had been fulfilled in September, Iwers deputised for Italian act Lacuna Coil after both their guitarists pulled out of an October 1997 tour at short notice.

Tiamat returned with the August 1999 *Skeleton Skeletron*. An earlier EP, *Brighter Than The Sun*, had included a rendition of the Rolling Stones staple 'Sympathy For The Devil'. European dates in November saw the band supported by Anathema, but Petersson bailed out yet again. The band, with a yo-yoing Petersson, got to grips with a November European package tour alongside running mates Anathema and Tristania.

Edlund struck out on a no-frills gothic diversion with his 2001 solo project Lucyfire. Scoring a deal with SPV, Lucyfire issued the commended *This Dollar Saved My Life At Whitehorse*. Edlund, billing himself Notorious PIG for the endeavour, assembled a live band for an appearance at the 'Mera Luna' festival in Hildesheim, Germany. The same year, the leading German gothic-rock act Love Like Blood covered 'Whatever That Hurts' for their covers album *Chronology Of A Love Affair*.

A February 2002 Tiamat album, the Lars H. Nissen-produced *Judas Christ*, which garnered the band chart success in Sweden, came with American variants adding the bonus cut 'Cold Last Supper' plus a video clip of 'Vote For Love'. Peter Tägtgren of Hypocrisy and Pain guested on the track 'Spine'. *Judas Christ* triggered European gigs opened up by Moonspell and Flowing Tears in March.

European summer festival appearances throughout July and August included the German 'Zillo' and 'Summer Breeze' events as well as Spain's 'Rock Machina' festival, the Czech 'Brutal Assault' open air gig and the Viennese 'Metalfest'. Tiamat then toured mainland Europe with the equally adventurous Pain. Regular guitarist Thomas Petersson was unable to participate, replaced temporarily by Southfork's Henrik Bergqvist, while Dark Tranquillity's Martin Brändström handled keyboards.

A new Edlund-produced Tiamat album, *Prey*, delivered in October 2003, was preceded by the single 'Cain': this release included a cover version of W.A.S.P.'s 'Sleeping (In The Fire)'. Former Tiamat touring keyboard player P.A. Danielsson was killed in a car accident in Italy on November 26th 2004, at 35 years old.

The band reported a European tour with Sirenia, Theatre Of Tragedy and Pain to take them through late 2004 and into 2005. For these concerts they would be joined by Talisman guitarist Fredrik 'Kulle' Åkesson, replacing regular guitarist Thomas Petersson (detained by "parental duties"), and Brändström. Tiamat concerts took place in Greece in February 2005. They made festival appearances in 2006 and released a DVD, *The Church Of Tiamat*, in May. Like all their releases, it was eagerly received.

UNLEASHED
UNCOMPROMISING VIOLENCE

THIS KUNGSÄNGEN-BASED DEATH metal band enhance their material with ancestral themes and Viking mythology. Featuring ex-Nihilist guitarist Johnny Hedlund, Unleashed recorded two 1990 demos – *The Utter Dark* in March and September's *… Revenge*, which soon sold out, leading to a deal with Germany's Century Media label. The group featured Hedlund alongside erstwhile Dismember frontman Robert Sennebäck, guitarist Fredrik Lindgren and Anders Schultz on drums. However, Sennebäck rejoined Dismember shortly afterwards, leaving Hedlund to take over vocals.

Two now-rare 7-inch singles – October 1990's *…Revenge* EP and the 1991 EP *And The Laughter Has Died* – were issued before the group debuted with the *Where No Life Dwells* album in May 1991. Produced by Grip Inc. guitarist Waldemar Sorychta, the album was recorded at Woodhouse Studios in Dortmund, Germany that April. Unleashed toured Europe and North America during the year as support to Morbid Angel.

Returning in May 1992 with *Shadows In The Deep*, again with Sorychta as producer and featuring a cover of Venom's 'Countess Bathory', Unleashed again toured hard, including a European headline outing with support acts Tiamat and Samael before American shows with Cannibal Corpse.

Unknown to the band, the group's music – and in particular the album track 'Onward Into Countless Battles' – was an influence on the most unexpected of major acts, Nirvana. Many years later, drummer Dave Grohl admitted that Nirvana had reworked the song to their own ends but felt that it was too close to the Unleashed original to pass off.

The group's third album, October 1993's *Across The Open Sea*, found them delving deep into Scandinavian history, although the record is also notable for a cover of Judas Priest's 'Breaking The Law'. They cut a live album during 1993, although the recordings were initially released as a bootleg – prior to the band responding by issuing the *Live in Vienna '93* album the following year. They released an album, entitled *Victory*, in February 1995, and a double live collection, *Eastern Blood – Hail To Poland*, in November 1996. Lindgren was replaced by Fredrik Folkare for June 1997's *Warrior*.

In October 2002 the band, and in particular Hedlund, had to contend with rumours that they pursued Nazi politics. Apparently Dave Grohl of The Foo Fighters had considered Hedlund for inclusion on his extreme metal Probot project until he was advised of the singer's supposed fascist

---

UNLEASHED discography

And The Laughter Has Died..., Century Media CM7 020 (Europe) (1991) limited edition 2,000 copies

WHERE NO LIFE DWELLS, Century Media 84 9718-2 (Europe), Century Media CM 7718-2 (USA) (1991)

SHADOWS IN THE DEEP, Century Media 84 9732-2 (Europe), Century Media CM 7732-2 (USA) (1992)

ACROSS THE OPEN SEA, Century Media CM 77055-2 (Europe), Century Media CM 7705-2 (USA) (1993)

LIVE IN VIENNA '93, Century Media CM 77056-2 (Europe), Century Media CM 7756-2 (USA) (1993)

VICTORY, Century Media CM 77090-2 (Europe), Century Media CM 7790-2 (USA) (1995)

EASTERN BLOOD – HAIL TO POLAND, Century Media CM 77118-2 (Europe), Century Media CM 7818-2 (USA) (1996)

WARRIOR, Century Media CM 77124-2 (Europe), Century Media CM 7824-2 (USA) (1997)

HELL'S UNLEASHED, Century Media CM 77424-2 (Europe), Century Media CM 8124-2 (USA) (2002)

SWORN ALLEGIANCE, Century Media CM 77524-2 (Europe), Century Media CM 8224-2 (USA) (2004)

MIDVINTERBLOT, Steamhammer SPV 97952 (Europe), Steamhammer 97952 (USA) (2006)

leanings. Hedlund was quick to deny the claims, branding them as false and stating: "Unleashed praises nature, beast and man. Man... regardless of background, place of birth or colour of the skin."

Unleashed returned in August 2002 with *Hell's Unleashed*. They followed up in July 2004 with *Sworn Allegiance*, recorded and mixed by Fredrik Folkare at Chrome Studios and mastered by Peter In de Betou of Tailor Maid Productions. They toured with In Battle and Yattering for a European outing commencing in late November. Anders Schultz featured as backing vocalist on The Project Hate's 2005 album *Armageddon March Eternal (Symphonies Of Slit Wrists)*. Unleashed filmed their July 1st performances at the 'With Full Force' festival in Leipzig and August 'Up From The Ground' festival in Gemünden, Germany for DVD release. During November, Fredrik Folkare took time out to engineer album sessions for Necrophobic.

Unleashed

The band announced a touring partnership as part of the December 2005 'X-Mass' festivals in Europe ranked alongside the recently resurrected UK thrashers Onslaught, Exodus, Kataklysm, Occult, Behemoth, and Primordial.

To perform at the 'Metalmania' festival in Katowice, Poland in March 2006 the group drafted in Incardine drummer Jonas Tyskhagen as a temporary replacement for Anders Schultz, who had suffered a lung collapse. They announced in July that they had signed with the German SPV Steamhammer label for a new studio album, *Midvinterblot*. European shows announced for November, dubbed the 'Masters Of Death', had the band lined up with a supremely heavyweight Scandinavian cast of Dismember, Entombed and Grave. Their future seems assured.

WITCHERY
TOXIC METAL MASTERY

LINKÖPING METAL ACT WITCHERY were formed during 1997 from the ashes of Séance and Satanic Slaughter. They set themselves apart from the crowd by blending elements of black, death and retro-thrash metal, an amalgamation that saw the band rapidly attaining solid international sales. Musically, Witchery are unafraid to show their influences, as is evident from the frequent 1980s cover versions that litter their catalogue.

Both vocalist Toxine (aka Tony Kampner) and drummer Mique (aka Micke Pettersson) had been members of Total Death. Mique had also been involved in Morgue alongside guitarist Richard Corpse (aka Rille Rimfält). Toxine cut his teeth on the music scene with the punk act Passiva Mongoloider as far back as 1979.

Witchery came together when Satanic Slaughter vocalist Ztephan Dark fired his entire band days before a scheduled album recording. Undaunted, the quartet – Toxine, Corpse, Mique and second guitarist Patrik Jensen – stuck together to found Witchery, enlisting Mercyful Fate and Illwill bassist Sharlee D'Angelo (aka Charles Petter Andreason). D'Angelo's commitments to Mercyful Fate meant that the recording of the debut Witchery album was delayed until January 1998, sessions being conducted at Blue Hill Studios in Linköping. Necropolis Records in the USA took the band on to issue *Restless & Dead* in 1998. They put in their debut show that April in Copenhagen, minus Richard Corpse, who was too ill to perform.

The March 1999 mini-album *Witchburner*, assembled at Los Angered Studio in Gothenburg with King Diamond guitarist Andy LaRocque taking the production reins, contained originals plus covers including Accept's 'Restless And Wild', Black Sabbath's 'Neon Knights', W.A.S.P.'s 'I Wanna Be Somebody' and Judas Priest's 'Riding On The Wind'. Witchery put in a showing at the renowned German 'Wacken' festival in 1999.

The band returned in September with the unsavoury *Dead, Hot And Ready*, recorded at Blue Hill Studios. Engaging in their first real touring, they took to European stages in January 2000 alongside Moonspell and Kreator, following up with a one-off US appearance at the New Jersey

---

WITCHERY discography

RESTLESS AND DEAD, Necropolis NR 029 (USA) (1998)
Witchburner, Necropolis NR 034 (USA) (1999)
DEAD, HOT AND READY, Necropolis NR 041 (USA) (1999)
SYMPHONY FOR THE DEVIL, Music For Nations CDMFN 273 (UK), Necropolis NR 066 (USA) (2001)
DON'T FEAR THE REAPER, Century Media CM 77505-2 (Europe), Century Media CM 8205-2 (USA) (2006)

'March Metal Meltdown' festival. The remainder of the year found members prioritising other bands: guitarist Patrik Jensen was operational with The Haunted, while Toxine and Corpse busied themselves with Infernal, and Mique has a side project entitled Rhoca Gil.

For the 2001 album *Symphony For The Devil*, cut in February at Berno Studios in Malmö, Witchery employed veteran drummer Martin 'Axe' Axenrot, who had seen service as Demon Pounding Devastator in Morgue, Coven, Satanic Slaughter, Nifelheim, Blasphemous and Triumphator. Mercyful Fate's Hank Shermann provided guest guitar on 'Hearse Of The Pharaohs', prompting reviewers to remark upon its similarities to Mercyful Fate's own 'Curse Of The Pharaohs'.

Witchery cut versions of King Diamond's 'The Shrine' and the Scorpions' 'China White' for tribute albums. Once their other commitments had been fulfilled, the band entered Berno Studios in Malmö during August 2004 to craft a new album, *Don't Fear The Reaper*, finally released in 2006. Shermann appeared again and 'Crossfixation' featured a guest appearance by ex-Crown member Marcus Sunesson. The record also saw a remake of Satanic Slaughter's 'Immortal Death'. In August 2005, Martin Axenrot temporarily joined Opeth for European touring, covering for regular drummer Martin López who was forced out due to medical concerns.

FINNISH METAL

OVER the past ten years or so, Finland – a country with little rock heritage other than Hanoi Rocks – has become awash with metal bands. And many of them are of such high quality that they have made serious inroads into the global market.

During the 1980s, Finland played host to festivals but produced very few homegrown artists, with the notable exception of Tarot and Airdash. As the '90s drew in, the extreme metal waves that were sweeping neighbours Sweden and Norway seemed to awaken a slumbering giant, and within a very short space of time Finland was teeming with bands. The black and death metal generation rose rapidly, with bands such as Barathrum, Beherit, Ajatarra, Sethian, and Thy Serpent, and they brought with it a national persuasion towards the gothic, something at which the Finns excelled.

The taste in Finland for high-quality metal has made the country's singles and album chart a haven for the harder end of the spectrum. It is commonplace for exceptionally heavy bands – Lullacry, To/Die/For, Sentenced, Amorphis, Children Of Bodom, and others – to feature prominently on radio and television. For example, Nightwish (see chapter 10) totally dominated the charts when 'Over The Hills And Far Away, a cover of a minor UK hit by Gary Moore, remained on the listings for close to a year.

The biggest acts to come out of Finland have spearheaded entirely new movements – Stratovarius with their symphonic, progressive metal; Amorphis with a strong folk leaning (placing the traditional kantele instrument onto the world stage); Impaled Nazarene's filthy punk-metal; and Nightwish's grandiose operatic riffage. In their wake came other genuine leaders, such as the eccentric 'oompah-metal' delivered by Finntroll.

All this came to the fore recently when the 'monster metal' band Lordi swept the 2006 Eurovision Song Contest with 'Hard Rock Hallelujah'. For once this really did seem to be a case of truth being stranger than fiction.

AMORPHIS
PROG-DEATH EXPERTS

ONE OF FINLAND'S PREMIER ACTS, Amorphis derived their name from the word 'amorphous', meaning without shape or form. They have ploughed their own distinct furrow by combining death metal with elements of 1970s-inspired progressive rock and even psychedelia. Based in Helsinki, Amorphis were formed in 1990 by erstwhile Violent Solution and Abhorrence guitarist Tomi Koivusaari.

Abhorrence were assembled during 1989 by Koivusaari, the Disaster-credited singer Jukka 'Shrike' Kolehmainen, second guitarist Kalle Mattsson, bassist Jussi Ahlroth, and drummer Kimmo Heikkinen. With this line-up they recorded the *Vulgar Necrolatry* demo in February 1990. The group bulldozed their way onto the local club scene, even putting in a solitary Norwegian gig with Antidote's Mikael Arnkil on drums, before issuing a self-titled 7-inch EP on the Seraphic Decay label. Although they received no revenue from this release, its presence did arouse interest from other record companies. However, Abhorrence didn't know this and they went their separate ways in 1990.

Alongside Koivusaari, the founding Amorphis line-up consisted of guitarist Esa Holopainen, bass player Olli-Pekka Laine, and drummer and keyboard player Jan Rechberger. Abhorrence singer Jukka Kolehmainen was offered the lead-vocal position but declined. The band recorded a demo, *Disment Of Soul*, the same year for a January 1991 release.

They were picked up by American label Relapse almost by accident – the record company made an offer to Abhorrence, not realising that the group had folded. The newly established Amorphis recorded six tracks in May 1991 at TTT Studios in Helsinki with Timo Tolkki of Stratovarius behind the mixing board. These was intended for a split album with Incantation but never appeared. However, 'Vulgar Necrolatry' and 'Misery Path' made it onto a limited-edition 7-inch single in June 1992.

The first Amorphis album, *The Karellian Isthmus* – taking its title from a historic Finnish battleground – was co-produced by the band and Tomas Skogsberg at Stockholm's Sunlight Studios in May 1992. It received creditable media response and strong sales upon its release that November, prompting Relapse to release previous tracks as the *Privilege Of Evil* mini-album in 1993. At this juncture, Amorphis were still entrenched in classic death metal territory, content to let guitars buzz with expressive riffage over near-epic tunes. Importantly, the European licence for *The Karellian Isthmus* was taken up by Germany's Nuclear Blast, who marketed the album aggressively.

The next Amorphis album, *Tales From A Thousand Lakes* – once again cut with Skogsberg – was delivered in September 1994. It was loosely based on the Finnish national myth of Kalevala. From this point on, narrative and "clean" singing were provided by Kyyria's Ville Tuomi. The album featured a cover of The Doors' 'Light My Fire' and included the first appearance of new keyboard player Kasper Mårtenson. *Tales From A Thousand Lakes* received an ecstatic reception from fans, its content quickly being exalted across the metal underground as the very pinnacle of atmospheric death metal. The group toured North America in 1994 alongside Entombed and then played in Europe with Tiamat. With interest in the band gathering pace, the album's standout track 'Black Winter Day' headed up an EP, bolstered by album out-takes, in January 1995.

Drummer Rechberger was replaced by ex-Stone man Pekka Kasari in 1995. Further line-up changes occurred for the *Elegy* album, adding vocalist Pasi Koskinen and replacing Mårtenson with keyboard player Kim Rantala. Retaining the successful formula, the band employed both Sunlight Studios and Skogsberg but opted to engage engineer Pete Coleman for a final mixdown at Parr Street Studios in Liverpool, England. *Elegy* plundered native folklore for inspiration – this time the 1840-compiled Kanteletar body of 7,000 verses – and gave Amorphis their first chart entry in May 1996 when it entered the German listings at Number 67. Reviews were positive, with fans accepting the smoother, refined vocal tones of Koskinen and the group's determination to push boundaries,

including the alarming interpolation of a traditional polka refrain in 'Cares'. The song 'My Kantele' was lifted for a spin-off EP release in May 1997 to maintain momentum, alongside renditions of Hawkwind's 'Levitation' – the British space-rock godfathers were an increasing influence – plus Kingston Wall's 'And I Hear You Call'.

Amorphis returned in February 1999 with the 'Divinity' single and a new album, *Tuonela*, which hit the German charts at Number 46. A transitional staging post, this Simon Effemy-produced record took an enormous leap from metal into chilled retro-progressive rock, with a 1970s vibe solidified by Hammond organ, sitar, flute overlays on 'Rusty Moon', and Sakari Kukko's saxophone. Indeed, Tomi Koivussaari's death-metal growl on 'Greed' was the last apperance of these harsh tones. Line-up shuffles followed and a retrospective compilation, *Story: 10th Anniversary*, was put out in May 2000 for fans who had recently discovered the band and their rich back catalogue.

The April 2001 album *Am Universum*, which debuted at Number 3 on the Finnish charts, provided a homeland Number 1 single, 'Alone'. Amorphis retained their studio partnership with Effemy, committing *Am Universum* to tape at Finnvox Studios in Helsinki. Sakari Kukko's saxophone stretched across the entire body of work this time: guitars were downplayed while the emphasis on keyboards was heightened. Japanese editions closed with an exclusive track, 'Too Much To See'. Touring in America with support act Opeth commenced with an appearance at the New Jersey 'Metalfest' before Canadian gigs and a short run of headline dates in the USA. During April 2002, drummer Pekka Kasari announced his retirement from the band: his replacement was none other than ex-Amorphis man Jan Rechberger. The band contributed a new recording, a cover of the 1976 Finnish pop hit 'Kuusamo', for the soundtrack to the Finnish movie *Menolippu Mombasaan* in late 2002.

Amorphis revealed in March 2003 that they had signed a new record deal with major label EMI. The first product of this union was the *Far From The Sun* album, preceded by the 'Day Of Your Beliefs' single in April. Naturally the band's experimental bent was evident – this time they even drafted in the Sveaborg Boys' Choir. Koskinen and bassist Niclas Etelävuori then found time to forge a side project in league with H.I.M. drummer Mika 'Kaasu' Karppinen. H.I.M. and Amorphis members also formed a grindcore band, To Separate The Flesh From The Bones.

Amorphis united with British goth-rock veterans Paradise Lost for Scandinavian dates in October. However, regular drummer Rechberger was forced out due to personal circumstances, his place taken by Atte

Sarkima from Verenpisara, also a member of black metal combo Ajattara (as Malakias III) and a seasoned campaigner of 1980s hair band Christine, Havana Black, and prog merchants Five Fifteen.

In spring 2004, as the band entered CCPC Studios in Helsinki to demo new material, *Far From The Sun* finally secured a North and South American release – a full year after its European issue. The US Nuclear Blast version added five bonus tracks, including an acoustic version of the title track, while Japanese variants added 'Darkrooms'.

The band revealed tour plans for an October run of North American shows with Type O Negative. However, in a move that shocked many fans, longtime singer Pasi Koskinen quit, performing his last gig with the band on August 21st at the 'Kontu Rock' festival. Vocal duties for the North American trek were delegated to Charon and ex-Poisonblack frontman Juha-Pekka Leppäluoto. In the event, the US dates were pulled when a Type O Negative management statement in mid-September revealed that a medical examination of frontman Pete Steele had resulted in the discovery of "undisclosed anomalies".

In November, it was revealed that Amorphis guitarists Esa Holopainen and Tomi Koivusaari, bassist Niclas Etelävuori, and keyboard player Santeri Kallio had all donated their services to a country/blues covers album, *Welcome To Carcass Cuntry*, assembled by Carcass frontman Jeff Walker.

In January 2005, the band inducted new singer Tomi Joutsen. US Amorphis dates scheduled for March had the band partnered with Into Eternity, Single Bullet Theory, and Beyond The Embrace. The group re-signed with Nuclear Blast shortly afterwards, entering Sonic Pump Studios in Helsinki on July 1st to craft a new album. The first single, 'House Of Sleep', topped the Finnish charts in January 2006. The album, *Eclipse*, was released in Europe in February and in the USA in March. And so the future looks bright for Amorphis, one of Finland's most interesting metal bands.

BARATHRUM
AS BLACK AS IT GETS

KUOPIO BLACK METAL BAND BARATHRUM have entrenched themselves in the rawest, coldest corner of the black metal arena, and in doing so they have managed to preserve the complete anonymity of many of their earlier members. In keeping with the volatile nature of the genre, Barathrum's line-up has been fluid, but the band have still adhered to a long-term strategy. This was revealed after more than a decade's worth of albums were found to spell out the words 'Heil Sova' (this refers to mainman Janne 'Demonos' Sova) with the first letter of each title.

The band started life as Darkfeast and with a series of demos. *Darkfeast* and *Hail Satan!* were both issued in 1990. They changed their name to Barathrum in the summer of 1991, releasing the *From Black Flames To Witchcraft* rehearsal tape followed by the *Witchmaster* demo in 1991, produced by Holocausto (aka Juha Kullpi) of Beherit. The *Battlecry*

AMORPHIS discography

Amorphis, Relapse RR-016 (USA) (1992)

THE KARELIAN ISTHMUS, Nuclear Blast NB 072-2 (Europe), Relapse RR 6045-2 (USA) (1992)

Privilege Of Evil, Relapse RR 6024-2 (USA) (1993)

TALES FROM THE THOUSAND LAKES, Nuclear Blast NB 097-2 (Europe), Relapse RR 6901-2 (USA) (1994)

Black Winter Day, Nuclear Blast NB 0117-2 (Europe), Relapse RR 6918-2 (USA) (1995)

ELEGY, Nuclear Blast NB 0141-2 (Europe) (1996)

My Kantele, Nuclear Blast NB 0270-2 (Europe) (1997)

TUONELA, Nuclear Blast NB 0382-2 (Europe) (1999)

AM UNIVERSUM, Nuclear Blast NB 0535-2 (Europe) (2001)

FAR FROM THE SUN, EMI 07243 583923 2 6 (Europe) (2003), Nuclear Blast America 1330 (USA) (2004)

ECLIPSE, Nuclear Blast NB 1596-2 (Europe), Nuclear Blast America 1596 (USA) (2006)

demo was recorded in March 1992 with a line-up of Demonos Sova (vocals/bass), Niko Ikonen (guitar), and Ilu Jantti (drums). Three further studio sessions were recorded in 1993.

After several further reshuffles, Barathrum signed to the German Nazgûl's Eyrie label, which issued the *Hailstorm* and *Eerie* albums in 1995. In May 1996, a rehearsal demo, *Bride Of Lucifer*, was released. The *Infernal* album followed in 1997. Sova also busied himself as a member of Wizzard, the project of Teemu Kautonen aka Hexenmeister (Darkwoods My Betrothed, Nattvindens Gråt).

With the collapse of Nazgûl's Eyrie, Barathrum toured Finland on a bill with Babylon Whores, Wizzard, and Horna during late 1997. Frozen Lands Productions issued the 7-inch 'Jetblack' single, limited to the obligatory 666 copies, while a demo session entitled *Devilry* soon secured a new deal with renowned Finnish label Spinefarm for June 1998's *Legions Of Perkele*. *Okkult* was released in 2000.

The official Barathrum line-up in 2002 stood at Demonos Sova on vocals and bass, guitarists Anathemalignant and Pelcepoop, second bassist Nuklear Tormentörr, third bassist G'Thaur, and Abyssir (aka Janne Parviainen of Sinergy, Jimsonweed, Waltari and Zwanziger) on the drums. The next stage in Barathrum's strategy, *Venomous*, emerged in December 2002 backed by a limited-edition single 'Black Flames And Blood' with a B-side cover of Manowar's 'Kill With Power'.

The Barathrum camp suffered a tragedy with the death on March 16th 2003 of ex-member Teemu Raimoranta, aka Somnium, also a member of

Finntroll, Impaled Nazarene, and Thy Serpent. (See Finntroll entry in this chapter.) Alongside Finntroll, Impaled Nazarene, Children Of Bodom and Ensiferum, Barathrum took part in a memorial concert to honour Raimoranta at Helsinki's Nosturi venue on March 25th.

For further live dates, the Sinergy and To/Die/For-credited Tommi Lillman deputised for German concerts in spring 2003, although Abyssir returned in May. In keeping with their grand game plan, Barathrum were reportedly working on a swansong album entitled *Antikristus Neutronstar* later that year. The title was switched to *Anno Aspera: 2003 Years After Bastard's Birth* for the record's January 2005 release through Spinefarm.

Anathemalignant decamped in 2004, and Barathrum recruited guitarist Daimos666 (aka Aki Järvinen or Zildja'h Daimos) of Shadows Of Sunset. Drummer Janne Parviainen joined Ensiferum in September 2005. Despite the many line-up shuffles, the band seem dedicated to their path.

CHILDREN OF BODOM
THE FINNS MOST LIKELY TO

A POWERFUL METAL ACT FROM the town of Espoo, Children Of Bodom are named after Finland's Lake Bodom, the scene of an unsolved attack in 1960 that left three teenagers dead. The children had died from multiple stab wounds, and the sole survivor, Nils Gustafsson, was famously declared insane and institutionalised after he blamed the attack on the Grim Reaper. This character would feature prominently on all of the group's output.

Applying power metal precision to the thrash metal recipe, Children Of Bodom have built a significant global fanbase. Old-school persuasions, keyboard layers, chugging riffs, and pounding double-bass-drums are overlaid by Laiho's exceptional talents, his fluid lead solos being a distinguishing factor in the band's success.

Founder member and vocalist Alexi 'Wildchild' Laiho made his name as part of Thy Serpent, creating Children Of Bodom in 1993 with drummer Jaska Raatikainen. Initially, the group called themselves Inearthed, issuing a batch of melodic death metal demos commencing with *Implosion Of Heaven*, recorded at Munkkiniemen Studios in August 1994 and released that December.

Inearthed followed this with *Ubiquitous Absence Of Remission* in July 1995, recorded at Astia Studios. (Melodies from the track 'Translucent Image', which featured female guest vocals from Nina Keitel, resurfaced in Sinergy's 'Beware The Heavens' at a later date.) Once again composed and performed by Laiho and Raatikainen, the tape also mentioned bassist Samuli Miettinen (who wrote the song lyrics but did not perform on the

Demonos Sova of Barathrum

demo) and rhythm guitarist Alexander Kuoppala (who joined after the tape was recorded but is listed as a band member). A third demo, *Shining*, was committed to tape at Astia Studios in February 1996 utilising keyboard player Jani Pera Pirisjoki. A line-up change found bassist Miettinen superseded by Henkka Seppälä.

As Inearthed, the group scored a label deal in Belgium, but a better offer convinced the band to go with the highly respected Finnish label Spinefarm. At this stage the group, now with Janne Warman on keyboards, switched their name to Children Of Bodom and recorded the *Something Wild* debut, produced by Anssi Kippo, Alex Laiho, and Jaska Raatikainen. The album was issued in Finland in February 1997 and picked up for European licence by Nuclear Blast shortly after emerging on the continent in April 1998 and then through Toy's Factory in Japan. Adding a degree of colour to the mix, the group employed movie narrative from *Ben-Hur* as an intro to 'The Nail'. The opening section of 'Deadnight Warrior' was taken from the film *It*, and Mozart's Symphony No. 25 was reworked for 'Red Light in My Eyes, Part 2'.

The group recorded an additional track, 'Children Of Bodom', which – when released as a single alongside tracks from Cryhavoc and Wizzard – scored the unexpected achievement of hitting the Number 1 spot on the charts. The band supported Norwegian black metal combo Dimmu Borgir on their 1997 Finnish dates and in February the following year hooked up with Hypocrisy, Covenant, and Benediction for mainland European gigs. For these shows, a friend of the band, Erna Siikavirta, substituted for Warman, who was unable to extricate himself from his educational commitments.

With album sales on a sharp rise, Children Of Bodom were back on the road in Europe during September, performing as part of a bill with Dismember, Agathodaimon, Raise Hell, and Night In Gales. Once again Warman had to sit it out, and Kimberley Goss (of Avernus, Dimmu Borgir, and Therion) filled in. A one-off concert in St. Petersburg, Russia with Impaled Nazarene resulted in Laiho opting to join his fellow Finns when Children Of Bodom's schedule allowed. He subsequently performed with them in February 1999 on their tour of North America and Mexico.

Children Of Bodom scored another domestic Number 1 single with 'Downfall' in early 1999. The single also contained a cover of Stone's 'No Commands'. The *Hatebreeder* album saw the band break into the German charts for the first time, peaking at Number 75. The introductory narrative for the opening song 'Warheart' was lifted from Milos Forman's *Amadeus* movie, and the keyboard introduction to 'Black Widow' brazenly borrowed from 1980s TV series *Miami Vice*.

Touring began with dates in Japan during the summer (concert recordings from Club Citta, Tokyo later surfaced as *Tokyo Warhearts – Live In Japan*), followed by a Nuclear Blast European venture with In Flames, Dark Tranquillity, and Arch Enemy. This time, Pimeys was finally in place behind the keyboards. In downtime, Warman, under the name of Warmen, cut a solo album titled *Unknown Soldier*.

In May 2000, another partnership with Impaled Nazarene led to Greek gigs in Thessaloniki and Athens, with Laiho performing double guitar duty each night. The ensuing album, *Follow The Reaper* was cut at Abyss Studios in Sweden with Hypocrisy's Peter Tägtgren and Lars Szöke as producer and engineer, and was issued in Japan with a bonus track, an interpretation of Ozzy Osbourne's 'Shot In The Dark'. Fans were quick to spot the band's oddball habit of planting the unexpected, with the bridge section of 'Bodom After Midnight' a homage to *The Rock* movie, while speeches in 'Taste Of My Scythe' came transplanted from *The Exorcist III*.

As a precursor of what was to come, the band's 'Hate Me!' single of October 2000, featuring a cover version of W.A.S.P.'s 'Hellion', swiftly went platinum in Finland by selling over 10,000 copies. Raatikainen deputised for Sinergy toward the close of the year before Children Of Bodom supported Primal Fear for a European tour across Germany,

Austria, Italy, Spain, and France in February 2001. Their *Follow The Reaper* album quickly shifted over 50,000 copies in Europe, reaching the Top 5 in Finland. In October, the band featured on the Spinefarm compilation *Metal Rocks* with an exclusive cover version of Iron Maiden's 'Aces High'.

Children Of Bodom broke their silence in mid 2002, unveiling plans for an August single, the new 'You're Better Off Dead!' coupled with a cover of The Ramones' 'Somebody Put Something In My Drink'. The single was swiftly certified gold. By October, the band had flagged up *Hate Crew Deathroll* as a projected title for their next Anssi Kippo-produced album. The record, released in January 2003, crashed into the Finnish charts at Number 1, soon numbering over 15,000 domestic sales and attaining gold status.

Children Of Bodom's live dates in Japan with Halford were announced for February 2003. Rhythm guitarist Kuoppala left the ranks following the band's appearance at the July Helsinki 'Tuska' festival. The band announced that Sinergy and ex-Stone man Roope Latvala had joined as session guitarist for the remainder of their world tour, debuting this new line-up in Moscow on August 16th. They were back in the Far East for a further run of Japanese shows that September, partnered with Soilwork. The same month, *Hate Crew Deathroll* was released in the USA

CHILDREN OF BODOM discography

SOMETHING WILD, Spinefarm SPI 49CD (Europe) (1997), Nuclear Blast America 6308 (USA) (1998)

HATEBREEDER, Spinefarm SPI 69CD (Europe), Nuclear Blast America 6387 (USA) (1999)

TOKYO WARHEARTS – LIVE IN JAPAN 1999, Nuclear Blast NB 0440-2 (Europe) (1999)

FOLLOW THE REAPER, Spinefarm SPI 99CD (Europe), Nuclear Blast America 6560 (USA) (2000)

HATE CREW DEATHROLL, Spinefarm SPI 165CD (Europe), Century Media CM 8164-2 (USA) (2003)

Trashed, Lost And Strungout, Spinefarm SPI 207EP (Europe) (2004), Century Media CM 8182-2 (USA) (2005)

ARE YOU DEAD YET?, Spinefarm SPI 230CD (Europe) (2005)

CHAOS RIDDEN YEARS – STOCKHOLM KNOCKOUT LIVE, Spinefarm SPI 299CD (Europe) (2006)

on the Century Media label. In the interim, Laiho gained co-production credits on Griffin's album *No Holds Barred*. In Japan, the Toy's Factory label revealed an exclusive compilation album, *Bestbreeder From 1997 To 2000*.

Children Of Bodom then united with Dimmu Borgir, Nevermore, and Hypocrisy for US dates in November. During a gap in the band's schedule, Laiho reunited with his ex-Sinergy comrade Tommi Lillman, founding Kylähullut ('Village Idiot') alongside lead singer Vesku Jokinen of Finnish punk band Klamydia. The band issued the *Keisarinleikkaus* EP in May 2004.

An extensive North American trek throughout April and May of 2004 had the band partnered with Iced Earth and Swedish progressive metal band Evergrey. The EP *Trashed, Lost & Strungout* included covers of Alice Cooper's 'Bed Of Nails' and Andrew W.K.'s 'She Is Beautiful'. The record, backed by a video for the title track directed by Patric Ullaeus, debuted on the Finnish charts at Number 1. Meanwhile, Latvala guested on Soulgrind's *The Origins Of The Paganblood*.

The band toured Brazil in August. October shows across the USA had the band partnered with Lamb Of God, Fear Factory, and Throwdown. On January 5th 2005, Laiho and Latvala gathered with Finland's metal community at Helsinki's Rock'n'Roll Station to pay homage to the recently murdered Pantera/Damageplan guitarist 'Dimebag' Darrell Abbott by forming a one-off Pantera tribute band, Dimen Neemen ('In Dime's Name').

In early 2005, the Back On Black label reissued the albums *Something Wild*, *Hatebreeder* and *Follow The Reaper* on limited-edition vinyl picture discs. Children Of Bodom's new studio album title was revealed as *Are You Dead Yet?*. Unfortunately, the similarity to Carnal Forge's recent *Aren't You Dead Yet?* drew immediate comparisons.

Children Of Bodom's single 'In Your Face', issued in August 2005, included a surprising cover version of Britney Spears' 'Oops I Did It Again'. *Are You Dead Yet?* was released in September: a limited-edition vinyl picture disc, restricted to just 2,000 copies, was pressed by Universal in Germany. In keeping with the band's leftfield choice of cover songs, Japanese variants of the record added a rendition of 'Talk Dirty To Me' by Poison. *Are You Dead Yet?* debuted at Number 1 in Finland and in Japan at Number 17, where it sold 21,000 copies in its first week of release.

US tour dates commenced in November with Trivium and Amon Amarth. The group then hooked up with Ektomorf and One Man Army And The Undead Quartet for European and Scandinavian gigs. North American gigging witnessed a union with Bullet For My Valentine and Chimaira in March 2006. After a high-profile slot on the European leg of the 'Unholy Alliance' tour with Slayer, a live album and separate DVD, *Chaos Ridden Years – Stockholm Knockout Live*, were released in October 2006. Children Of Bodom teamed up with Amon Amarth, Sanctity, and Gojira for further North American touring in December and seem sure to take the next step up in 2007.

FINNTROLL
WHERE METAL MEETS MENTAL

FINNTROLL ARE A UNIQUE PROPOSITION in extreme metal, basing their lyrics on the 'trollish' myths of Scandinavia and backing them up with polka and shanty-inspired 'schlager-death' metal. The band took their cue from the likes of 'humppa' pioneers Eläkeläiset (humppa is a variety of polka) and were formed in Helsinki by Katla (aka Jan Jämsen) and Thy Serpent and Barathrum guitarist Teemu Raimoranta (Somnium). Employing a drum machine, they cut the January 1998 demo *Rivfader*.

According to legend, the Finntroll concept came to Katla and Somnium in March 1997 upon waking from a drunken stupor induced by a marathon drinking binge. It was not only the act's revolutionary clash of tradition and amplification that set them apart: Finntroll also chose to

sing in Swedish, apparently because this language better evoked the trollish spirit.

Later recruits were Rapture and ex-Barathrum drummer Samu Ruotsalainen (B. Dominator), Ahti and Moonsorrow's Henri Urponpoika Sorvali (Trollhorn) on keyboards, bassist Sami Uusitalo (Tundra), and live guitarist Ørmy (Samuli Ponsimaa). Guitarist Somnium was also a member of Impaled Nazarene.

The November 1999 *Midnattens Widunder* album ('Monsters Of Midnight') was probably the band's harshest. It was recorded at Walltone Studios with Tuomo Valtonen as producer and was an exploratory affair, juxtaposing raw black metal and medieval Finnish music. The bizarre formula worked and triggered much curiosity.

Samuli Ponsimaa adopted the revised stage name of Skrymer, and in 2001 the band welcomed Jonne Järrela of Shaman on vocals and guitar for touring in Scandinavia and Germany. The band had by this point established such a reputation that their second album, *Jaktens Tid* ('Hunting Season'), delivered in May 2001, even made it into the Finnish album charts, at Number 20. *Jaktens Tid* featured a cover of 'Varg Timmen' by Hedningarna, with *joik* singing (a Sami vocal style) from Jonne Järvelä and banjo from Hanky Bannister. Tapio Wilska donated "Latin mumblings". The record credits listed 13 songs, but in reality *Jaktens Tid* closed with a hidden track, 'Försvinn Du Som Lyser'. Century Media picked up the band for an American release of the record in September.

For gigs in Moscow alongside Impaled Nazarene, the band were forced to participate minus the services of vocalist Katla, who was suffering from a "tumour" on his vocal cords. He was replaced for the Russian shows by Tapio Wilska, a veteran of Sethian, Darkwoods My Betrothed, Nattvindens Grat, and Wizzard, and bowed out permanently in June 2002 after surgery.

After the band's October headlining tour of Europe over Borknagar, Susperia, Suidakra, and Windir, Wilska debuted on the experimental acoustic album *Visor om Slutet* ('Songs For The End'). These tracks were laid down over just seven days in an isolated Hästholmen log cabin deep in the forest outside Helsinki. The band united with Katatonia for European touring throughout April and May.

Raimoranta died on March 16th 2003 at the age of just 25 after sustaining fatal injuries from a fall from Helsinki's Pitkäsilta bridge onto river ice below. Initial reports suggested an accident, although later eyewitness statements verified that the musician took his own life. Alongside Impaled Nazarene, Children Of Bodom, Barathrum, and Ensiferum, Finntroll took part in a memorial concert to honour Raimoranta at Helsinki's Nosturi venue on March 25th.

Tundra busied himself in a side venture, the doom band The Mist And The Morning Dew, with singer Veera Muhli of Unholy, The Seventh Planet's guitarist Mikael Karlbom and drummer Henri Tuomi, Shape Of Despair's guitarist Jarno Salomaa, and violinist Jaakko Lemmetty of Shaman.

FINNTROLL discography

MIDNATTENS WIDUNDER, Spikefarm NAULA 003 (Europe), (1999)

JAKTENS TID, Spikefarm NAULA 014 (Europe), Century Media CM 8077-2 (USA) (2001)

VISOR OM SLUTET, Spikefarm NAULA 033 (Europe), (2003)

Trollhammaren, Century Media 74762-3 (Europe), (2004)

NATTFÖDD, Spikefarm NAULA 034 (Europe), Century Media CM 8177-2 (USA) (2004)

Finntroll issued the *Trollhammaren* (Trollhammer) EP in March and then a new album, *Nattfödd* ('Nightborn'), in April 2004, produced by keyboard player Trollhorn. It was Finntroll's most expansive and eccentric work to date. Primarily a collection of drinking songs, the record involved accordions, sea shanties, the bashing of anvils, monastic choirs, didgeridoo, seagulls, a horse whinny, an ominous raven squawk, and an owl.

A European headline tour in April had Ensiferum and The Wake as support. Swedish Spinetour shows in September featured a bill with Norther and The Wake. To close out the year, the band were announced as one of the main attractions at the 'X-Mass Fest' with Napalm Death,

Marduk, Vader, The Black Dahlia Murder, and Belphegor. Throughout March and April 2005, the group undertook European touring with Graveworm and Amoral. Aleksi Virta of Imperanon played keyboards.

Finntroll allied with Sodom for US touring in January 2006. However, on January 29th the group informed Wilska that he had been fired due to "personal differences and lack of discussion", and the band withdrew from the European 'No Mercy' tour as a result. By early April, it was reported that Twilight Moon frontman Mathias Lillmåns (aka Vreth) had taken over the role.

The new group entered Sonic Pump Studios in Helsinki on September 25th to record fresh material for an early 2007 release. They

Finntroll – a treat for the ladies

supported veteran German thrashers Sodom on European dates in December. Concerts projected for May 2007, the 'Earthshaker Roadshock 2007' tour in union with Marduk, were announced as this book went to press,. Despite their outlandish approach, Finntroll's future seems assured.

IMPALED NAZARENE
UNRELENTINGLY BLASPHEMOUS FINNS

DATING BACK TO NOVEMBER 1990, Impaled Nazarene have created a unique niche for themselves in the extreme metal scene. The Oulu-based band have graduated from ugly black-grind to lean more towards punk with each successive release and have landed themselves in hot water with various authorities.

The band's inaugural line-up consisted of the Luttinen brothers Mika on vocals and Kimmo on drums, guitarists Ari Holappa and Mika Pääkkö, plus bass player Anti Pihkala. Mike and Kimmo had been members of Mutilation. The first song recorded by Impaled Nazarene was 'Condemned To Hell', although early live sets also included Mutilation numbers 'The Crucified' and 'Morbid Fate'.

The band's presence was first felt in February 1991 when the debut demo emerged, *Shemhamforash*. The tape, which sported cover versions of Deicide's 'Crucifixation' and Extreme Noise Terror's 'Conned Thru Life', was laid down by Eero Vuolukka on a primitive 2-track recorder (and saw the departure of Pihkala in favour of Harri Halonen). It was the first audio product to witness Impaled Nazarene's trademark combination of the occult and sexual perversion. Songs such as 'Disgust Suite' and 'Worms In Rectum' were the first in a long line of increasingly eccentric compositions.

In April 1991, Impaled Nazarene put in their first live gig, as support to Beherit in Kempele. Further shows ensued as openers to Sentenced. The second demo, *Taog Eht Fo Htao Eht* ('The Oath Of The Goat', backwards), recorded at Tico Tico Studios in Keme by Ahti Kortelainen, followed in August. This 10-track tape was promoted with a festival appearance at the Oulu 'Days Of Darkness' event alongside Amorphis. As an interesting diversion, Mikka Luttinen issued some less-than-savoury demos bearing the titles *Glumph* and *Never Mind Burzum … Here's Anus Cunt* from his Anus Cunt project.

A 7-inch single, 'Goat Perversion', was released by the Italian

Impaled Nazarene

Nosferatu label in February 1992, after which both Holappa and Halonen decamped. Although listing four tracks, the EP bore a fifth (uncredited) song – a cover of 'The Black Vomit' by cult Brazilian band Sarcofago. Undeterred by the loss of two key players, Impaled Nazarene gigged for a while as a trio. New recruit 'The Fuck You Man' (Sentenced's Taneli Jarva) was drafted in for a second single for French label Osmose, pairing 'Sadogoat' with a cover of Johnny Cash's 'Ghost Riders'. However, that same month, Pääkkö broke ranks and Jarno Anttila deputised on guitar. This soon turned into a full-time tenure.

Retaining Kortelainen as producer, the band recorded an album in February 1993, *Tol Cormpt Norz Norz Norz* (which approximately translates as 'And Its Number Was 666' in the ancient Enochian language), released on Osmose Productions. Initial copies included an extra 13 tracks from the earlier demos. Credits for the album – apparently "recorded faraway in pain and mistery XXVII Anno Satanas" – went to Mikaakim (Mika Luttinen) and Kimmoomik (Kimmo Luttinen) with Jarno Anttila and Taneli Jarva only given session status. Musically, *Tol Cormpt Norz Norz Norz* purveyed the very harshest of blackened grindcore, with the barked vocals making lyrics totally unintelligible. Sales were strong enough to break into the Finnish Top 40.

Impaled Nazarene's third single, 'Satanic Masowhore', was backed with their earlier cover version of Extreme Noise Terror's 'Conned Thru Life'. In July, the band re-entered Tico Tico to record their second album, *Ugra-Karma*. Released in December and proclaiming the band's support for "nuclear energy and the destruction of the environment", the album came in a cover with a serene Madame Koslovsky painting depicting an Indian goddess, which would come back to haunt the band in later years.

The band toured Europe with Ancient Rites in January 1994 before recording their third album, *Suomi Finland Perkele*, switching from the earlier title of *Hail To Finland*. Issued in October with three different-coloured jacket designs, the record's supposedly right-wing lyrics were controversial: the title of the album means 'Finland For The Finnish'. Instructions were issued by French authorities to withdraw the album from FNAC stores. However, sales were not unduly harmed as misinformation led to the band's previous album, *Ugra-Karma*, being removed from the racks instead. Controversy doubled when attention was drawn to the song 'Total War – Winter War', which was "dedicated to those glorious who died by red scum". Embroiled in the resulting press frenzy, Impaled Nazarene toured Europe during April 1995 with American band Absu and Australia's Sadistik Exekution.

Impaled Nazarene were set to utilise Tico Tico once again in August on a planned EP with the working title *Hamnasnas*. However, following a fight between bass player Taneli Jarva and founder member Kimmo Luttinen, the recording was cancelled and the drummer left. Reima Kellokoski took over the Impaled Nazarene drum stool for October tour dates in Europe with Ministry Of Terror and Krabathor. The group also put in their first British show, headlining a Halloween event at London's Astoria.

In February 1996, the band returned to Tico Tico to record the *Latex Cult* album, released in April 1996, and the *Motörpenis* EP. Immediately following the recordings, Jarva left and was replaced by ex-Belial and Obfuscation bassist Jani Lehtosaari. Both Jarva and Kimmo Luttinen, having put their differences behind them, founded The Black League in 1998.

The *Motörpenis* mini-album featured covers of tracks from Finnish punk acts Faffbey and Terveet Kadet as well as Gang Green's 'Alkohol'. Pushing *Latex Cult*, the band set out in April 1996 on their lengthiest trek around Europe so far, as part of the 'No Mercy' festival with Cannibal Corpse, Immolation, Rotting Christ, Krabathor, and Grave.

Recovering after these dates, they laid down an exclusive track, 'I Am The Killer Of Trolls', in October 1996 at Tico Tico, for the compilation

IMPALED NAZARENE discography

Goat Perversion, Nosferatu cnu (Europe) (1992)

Sadogoat, Osmose Productions OPEP 001 (Europe) (1993)

TOL CORMPT NORZ NORZ NORZ, Osmose Productions OPCD 010 (Europe), JL America 3815-41081-2 (USA) (1993)

UGRA KARMA, Osmose Productions OPCD 018 (Europe / USA) (1993)

Satanic Masowhore, Osmose Productions OPEP 003 (Europe) (1993)

SUOMI FINLAND PERKELE, Osmose Productions OPCD 026 (Europe / USA) (1994)

LATEX CULT, Osmose Productions OPCD 038 (Europe / USA) (1996)

Motörpenis, Osmose Productions OPMCD 039 (Europe / USA) (1996)

RAPTURE, Osmose Productions OPCD 069 (Europe / USA) (1998)

NIHIL, Spinefarm SPI 101CD (Europe) (2000)

Impaled Nazarene Vs. Driller Killer, Solardisk SOLDB 004 (Europe) (2000) split EP with Driller Killer

DECADE OF DECADENCE, Osmose Productions OPCD 108 (Europe / USA) (2000)

ABSENCE OF WAR DOES NOT MEAN PEACE, Osmose Productions OPCD 123 (Europe / USA) (2001)

ALL THAT YOU FEAR, Osmose Productions OPCD 152 (Europe / USA) (2003)

DEATH COMES IN 26 CAREFULLY SELECTED PIECES, Osmose Productions OPCD 172 (Europe / USA) (2005)

PRO PATRIA FINLANDIA, Osmose Productions OPCD 178 (Europe / USA) (2006)

---

album *World Domination II.* They rounded off 1996 with a further bout of European touring with Angel Corpse and Gehennah.

The band found themselves back in trouble in 1997 when the Hare Krishna movement objected to the use of their artwork on the earlier *Ugra-Karma* album. Eventually this was resolved outside the courts, resulting in a reissue of the record in 1999 with new cover art. In a relatively quiet year for the band outside their legal woes, Impaled Nazarene put down instrumental demos in preparation for their next outing.

During the summer of 1998, the group were again on the road, marketing the *Rapture* album issued that April, and they played international shows at the Milwaukee 'Metalfes', gigs in Canada, and a series of dates in Mexico. Film from the band's 'Tuska' festival appearance was used for a video for the song 'Penis And Circes'. In September 1998 the band drafted in guitarist Alexi Laiho (Thy Serpent, Children Of Bodom, Sinergy), an alliance cemented at a one-off concert in St. Petersburg, Russia that paired Impaled Nazarene and Children Of Bodom. However, Laiho's commitments kept him out of the line-up for a further round of European shows, this time with Driller Killer and Ritual Carnage. Laiho did perform with the band in February 1999 on their second visit to North America and Mexico, but cut short his commitment, returning to Finland. Nevertheless, Impaled Nazarene undertook their first Japanese shows as a quartet.

The band were soon back in Europe as part of the 'No Mercy III' festival with Peccatum, Limbonic Art, The Crown, Emperor, and Morbid Angel. Still as a four-piece, the band put in shows in Australia and New Zealand, the latter dates supported by Malevolence. Surprisingly, the group suffered its first concert cancellation as a result of local community pressure when a concert in Wollongong, Australia was called off.

In New Zealand, Mika Luttinen and Jarno Anttila were lucky to survive a car crash on the way to an Auckland concert. Upon their return to Finland in August, the band took to Astia Studios in Lappeenranta to record another album. They also recorded two non-album tracks for a split 7-inch picture disc EP with Driller Killer for Lehtosaari's Solardisk imprint.

The new album, *Nihil*, surfaced in February 2000. A brace of Finnish gigs with Finntroll and Throne Of Chaos witnessed a brief re-acquaintance with Alexi Laiho, after which the group appeared at the chaotic New Jersey 'March Metal Meltdown'. Tomi Ullgren of Shape Of Despair and Thy Serpent was enlisted on guitar for the 'Assault The Weak' tour of France. This trek was highlighted as authorities refused permission for the band to sell any Satanically-themed merchandise, and Impaled Nazarene were convinced that they were being tailed by French "secret police". In May, another partnership with Children Of Bodom led to Greek gigs in Thessaloniki and Athens, with Laiho performing double duty each night. The *Decade Of Decadence* ten-year anniversary collection was cut at Astia in August and delivered in November.

The band's status was now such that several bootleg singles and albums, most notably *Live In The Name Of Satan*, seeped onto the market. In the autumn of 2000 it was announced that both Laiho and Lehtosaari had fled the fold, with new members guitarist Teemu Raimoranta (aka Somnium) of Finntroll and bass player Mikael Arnkil, known as the drummer for Antidote and Abhorrence. A concert at the Nosturi venue in Helsinki in December 2000 featured Tomi Ullgren on guitar and Raimoranta temporarily on bass, as Arnkil had not yet learned the set.

In March 2001, the band renewed their business relationship with Osmose, re-signing for a further two albums. Czech gigs in April debuted Mikael Arnkil on bass, but with Jarno Anttila unable to attend, Tomi Ullgren deputised. Major Finnish festival appearances, at Tuska and Koria in July, were preceded by a 'Down By The Laituri' gig at Turku notable for a one-off reappearance of corpsepaint.

In September 2001, the band issued the *Absence Of War Does Not Mean Peace* album, promoted by a video for the track 'Hardboiled And Still Hellbound', enhanced by the presence of porn actress Rakel Liekki. Successive live work involved shows at the London 'X-Mass' festival, in Italy and, as a union with Finntroll, in Moscow in March 2002. In July, a memorable performance at the 'With Full Force' event in Leipzig, Germany caught Impaled Nazarene hitting the stage at 4:35am.

Teemu 'Somnium' Raimoranta died in tragic circumstances on March 16th 2003 after a fall from Helsinki's Pitkäsilta bridge onto ice. At the time, official reports stated that Raimoranta had met his death accidentally, although later eyewitness statements verified that the musician took his own life. Alongside Finntroll, Children Of Bodom, Barathrum, and Ensiferum, Impaled Nazarene took part in a memorial concert to honour Raimoranta at Helsinki's Nosturi venue on March 25th. Persevering, the band brought in Antidote guitarist Tuomo Louhio for the album *All That You Fear*, released in November 2003.

The band planned with their engineer Tapio Pennanen to record three Italian gigs in September 2004 for a live album. Unfortunately, the band arrived in Milan to find that their equipment had not arrived, forcing them to use the support band's gear. Shows in Catania and Ascoli could not provide adequate digital recording equipment. Undaunted, they resolved to record a subsequent show in Stockholm but only captured three songs on tape due to a mid-show power cut.

Their bad luck carried on into Russia in October when, just before a concert in Moscow, Mika Luttinen claimed he was drugged. After he passed out and was revived, Mika and the band performed the show. They announced that they would record a December gig at the Tavastia club in Helsinki for the live *Death Comes In 26 Carefully Selected Pieces*, successfully released in May 2005.

European shows for January 2005 found the band playing with Yyrkoon and Phazm. In June, they confirmed a re-signing with Osmose for two more albums, and entered Sonic Pump studios with producer Tapio Pennanen on November 21st to begin recording *Pro Patria Finlandia,* released in March 2006. The group then embarked on European dates throughout April and May 2006 with Switzerland's Dark Rise, then Italians Resurrecturis, and finally Master and Zuul FX. Swedish death metal act Zonaria were later added to the bill. As long as the metal-buying public's appetite for Impaled Nazarene's particularly twisted metal theatrics endures, it seems that the band will go from strength to strength.

LORDI
A GENUINE MONSTER METAL BAND

Hailing from the Lapland capital of Rovaniemi, Lordi hide their identities behind elaborate creature costumes, refusing to be seen in public without them. The band prompted mild curiosity with their first two albums but then achieved overnight international fame through the unlikeliest of means available to a heavy metal band – winning the 2006 Eurovision Song Contest.

Early band-members included bassists Magnum and Kalma (Pekka Tarvanen), plus Enary (Erna Siikavirta), a session player for Children Of Bodom, on keyboards. Frontman Mr. Lordi is in fact Tomi Putaansuu, while drummer Kita is better known as Sampsa Astala of Ain't Fake. Putaansuu formed the concept of Lordi at just 18 years old and drew

LORDI discography
GET HEAVY, Drakkar 21981112 (Europe) (2003)
THE MONSTERICAN DREAM, Drakkar 76619632 (Europe) (2004)
Hard Rock Hallelujah, RCA 82876 806762 (Europe) (2006) **59 UK**
THE AROCKALYPSE, Sony BMG 82876789852 (Europe) (2006)

upon his two other vocations: instigator of the official Kiss fan club in Finland, and a parallel career in movie special-effects make-up.

Lordi's January 2003 album, *Get Heavy,* was released through the German Drakkar label and preceded by the Number 1 Finnish single 'Would You Love A Monsterman?'. The album came complete with a 12-page comic book and was produced by TT Oksala at Finnvox Studios in Helsinki. The second album, April 2004's *The Monsterican Dream,* was produced by Hiili Hiilesmaa. Limited-edition variants of this record had a DVD of the 18-rated short movie *Lordi's The Kin.* The band now consisted of guitarist Amen (Jussi Sydänmaa), bassist Ox (Samer el Nahhal), keyboard player Awa (Leena Peisa), and drummer Kita, and they were openers to Hammerfall's April 2005 European dates.

The Arockalypse album for Drakkar featured former Accept frontman Udo Dirkschneider, ex-Kiss guitarist Bruce Kulick, and Twisted Sister's frontman Dee Snider and guitarist Jay Jay French.

In March 2006, coinciding with the release of *The Arockalypse,* Lordi became the official Finnish entrant for the Eurovision Song Contest after winning the national heats with 'Hard Rock Hallelujah', scoring 42.2 per

Lordi, the unlikely winners of the 2006 Eurovision Song Contest

cent of the total vote, which outstripped their nearest rival, Tomi Metsäkedon, by a significant margin. In a first for metal, Lordi then won the 51st Contest, held at the Olympic Stadium in Athens, Greece.

The Arockalypse duly shot to the top of the Finnish charts. In celebration, the mayor of the band's hometown, Rovaniemi, declared a new city square would be named for the band. On their return to Finland, Lordi played a celebratory concert in Helsinki's central market square to over 90,000 people, the largest public gathering ever seen in the city. In addition, over a million Finns (a quarter of the entire population) watched the event on television. *The Arockalypse* gathered new pace to climb to the top of the Swedish charts and bounced its way onto chart listings across much of Europe. You couldn't make up a story like that.

SENTENCED
MUCH-MISSED DEATH METAL ACT

SENTENCED WERE A MUHOS-BASED death metal band who leaned more towards the NWOBHM and thrash sound until their later works shifted to a doom-death direction. The band's classic British influences were evident: a 1994 EP even covered Iron Maiden's 'The Trooper'. Muhos had a population of less than 10,000, and prior to the arrival of Sentenced the town's only contribution to the international world of entertainment had been the 1975 Miss Universe winner, Armi Kuusela. Sentenced were formed in 1989 by guitarists Miika Tenkalu and Sami Lopakka. Vesa Ranta soon replaced original drummer Tuure Heikkilä. The band were originally called Deformity before a change in musical direction from thrash to death metal. In this incarnation the band cut the demo *When Death Joins Us*. They then added former Impaled Nazarene bassist Taneli Jarva to the line-up.

Thanks to a second demo, June 1991's *Rotting Ways To Misery*, the band scored a deal with the French Thrash label for the Ahti Kortelainen-produced debut album *Shadows Of The Past*, issued that November. A no-frills death metal assault, *Shadows* featured Tenkalu on vocals.

The band included the track 'Desperationed Future' on a free split EP for *Thrash Your Brain* fanzine – the misspelled *Cronology Of Death* – alongside Bluuurgh…, Xenophobia, and Sweden's Carbonized. They then cut a further demo, *Journey To Pohjola*, in March 1992. These efforts led to a deal with Spinefarm and June 1993's *North From Here*, the first record on which Jarva took over vocals, and it found the band adding more melody to their work. Their next product was a two-track demo in 1994, comprising 'Glow Of 1000 Suns' and 'Amok Runs', devised as a tool to gain a new label deal.

An October 1993 EP, *The Trooper*, recorded at Tico Tico studios in Kemi for new label Century Media, kept the faithful happy until the arrival of *Amok* in January 1995. This album sold over 35,000 units worldwide, with Japanese copies enhanced by two extra songs, 'Dreamlands' and 'Obsession'.

Sentenced toured Europe with Tiamat and Samael as Century Media re-released their first brace of albums to a wider audience. Ever eager to experiment, the band included a version of Billy Idol's 1980s classic 'White Wedding' on the September 1995 EP *Love And Death*.

Jarva toured and recorded as bassist for Impaled Nazarene when the band's schedule allowed – featuring on their 1992 *Sadogoat* EP and the follow-up album *Tol Cormpt Norz Norz Norz* – but departed after Sentenced recorded the *Love & Death* EP. Jarva's place was filled by Niko Karppinen of Legenda and Maple Cross on a session basis, while former Breed man Ville Laihiala took over as singer for the 1996 Waldemar Sorychta-produced *Down* album. Backing vocals came courtesy of Vorph of Samael with female accompaniment from Birgit Zacher.

The band's new vocalist brought a further new dimension to the

Sentenced sound: Laihiala opted for a clean vocal style more suited to the recent doomier outings. Global touring had Sentenced hitting their stride with dates in Europe, North America, and Japan. Sentenced also formed part of the bill for the December 1996 'Dark Winter Nights' festival alongside Depressive Age, Lacrimosa, The Gathering, and Dreams Of Sanity. Touring in Europe during March 1997, the band played alongside Therion, My Dying Bride, Orphanage, and Dark for the 'Out Of The Dark III' festivals.

June 1998's *Frozen*, which found bassist Sami Kukkohovi of Breed and Mythos added to the roster, was once again produced by Sorychta. As ever, Japanese copies hosted an extra song, 'No Tomorrow'. A 'gold' digipack edition added four cover versions, namely W.A.S.P.'s 'I Wanna Be Somebody', Radiohead's 'Creep', Faith No More's 'Digging The Grave', and The Animals' 'House Of The Rising Sun'.

The January 2000 *Crimson* album, also crafted at Tico Toco, reached

Sentenced

Number 1 in the Finnish album charts. Later the same year the album was reissued on picture-disc LP. In February 2001, Century Media repackaged the *Amok* and *Love & Death* records on a single CD.

Sentenced bounced back in style in May 2002 with the Hiili Hiilesmaa-produced album *The Cold White Light*, and their 'No One There' single made Number 2 in Finland. Shortly afterwards, the album hit the top spot in its first week of release, gaining gold status for 15,000 sales. The musical transformation of Sentenced was now complete, a journey that had brought them to an album focused on groove, atmosphere, and melancholic balladry.

A month's worth of North American dates commenced in San Francisco on September 16th, backing up headliners In Flames with support from Killswitch Engage and Dark Tranquillity. The band then unveiled an extensive European tour schedule for October with Lacuna Coil.

In September 2003, Sentenced recorded their first ever Finnish-language song, 'Routasydän', for use as a theme song for their hometown Oulu's ice hockey team. However, this diversion backfired on the band in spectacular fashion when a local newspaper alleged that the lyric "Sisu, veri ja kunnia" ("courage, blood, and honour") displayed Nazi sympathies – because it was similar to an oath sworn by the Hitlerjugend organisation. Sentenced vehemently denied these assertions, but the Oulu team pulled the song from their events nonetheless. The band had the last word, though, performing the song in front of a crowd of over 30,000 people when the team won the Finnish championship in April 2004.

Early 2004 found Laihiala engaged in his side project, Poisonblack, as well as finding the time to add a guest vocal to the *Sweet And Deceitful* album from glam-rock outfit Negative – which topped the Finnish charts. Summer dates included performances at 'Rock The Nations' in Istanbul, 'Athens Open Air', 'Gates Of Metal' in Sweden, and 'Summer Breeze' in Germany. The band then selected Hiili Hiilesmaa as producer to craft a new studio album during November.

In early February 2005, Lopakka announced: "The title of the new album is *The Funeral Album*, and with it we, Sentenced, are coming to the end of our road. This album will be our last one. The decision is mutual, thoroughly thought over, and final. Metaphorically speaking, this is a mass suicide of five."

Sami Lopakka: "It's very strange. For a lot of our records we've been told we are writing about suicide all the time, and how dangerous it can be for young kids to be listening to this and maybe doing something dreadful. We gave up trying to explain it in the end. Our songs were really about things ending, like a relationship or something, but now here we are – it really is all ending. We're not coming back, because that would be a step backwards – and we're not going to piss all over what we've achieved with some cheap reunion. It's quite amusing. Now Sentenced is committing suicide, and we are all quite positive and happy about it."

A preceding single, 'Ever-Frost', released only in Finland, duly entered the domestic charts at Number 1. Sentenced announced their performance at the August 2005 'Wacken Open Air' festival in Germany as their final live appearance. *The Funeral Album* topped the Finnish album charts (and Japanese variants added bonus live tracks in 'Brief Is The Light' and 'Nepenthe').

Sentenced then added their actual final live show, held on October 1st 2005 at Club Teatria in Oulu, which was recorded and filmed. With tickets selling out in less than an hour, the band added a further show for September 30th. Recordings of the band's final show, titled *Buried Alive*, were released in Europe in November 2006, available in various CD and DVD packages. A US release followed in January 2007 as a suitably lavish send-off to Finland's almost-favourite metal sons.

SINERGY
KIMBERLY GOSS'S UNIQUE METAL PROJECT

THIS POWER METAL BAND WAS founded by lead vocalist Kimberly Goss, a keyboard player and vocalist with acts such as Chicago doom act Avernus, Norway's Ancient, Dimmu Borgir, and Therion. Goss was born in Los Angeles in February 1978 and owes her distinctive looks to her American mother (an accomplished jazz singer) and her Korean father.

Goss played in Avernus while just 15 years old, and two years later she made her way to Oslo, fascinated by the tide of extreme metal emanating from Norway. Here she swiftly joined Ancient, appearing on the June 1996 album *The Cainian Chronicle*. Hooking up with Therion, she put in concert work to support *Theli*.

Sinergy were first mooted in August 1997 when Goss, then on tour in Europe with Dimmu Borgir, discussed the proposal with guitarist Jesper Strömblad of In Flames. Goss toured with Children Of Bodom in 1998, substituting temporarily for Janne Warman. However, schedules held off the new band and the plan remained on the backburner until Goss relocated to Sweden.

Sharlee D'Angelo (Charles Andreason), a veteran of Mercyful Fate, Witchery and Arch Enemy, played bass in the new band; the original drummer was Ronny Milianowicz of Saturnine and Falcon; and guitars came courtesy of Thy Serpent, Impaled Nazarene and Children Of Bodom man Alexi Laiho. Completed by Goss and Strömblad, the quintet recorded at Studio Fredman during October 1998, and in June 1999 the Fredrik Nordström-produced *Beware The Heavens* scored strong European sales. Laiho had injected into the title track some melodies from the pre-Children Of Bodom track 'Translucent Image', which featured on Inearthed's 1995 demo *Ubiquitous Absence Of Remission*. Fans also picked up on 'The Warrior Princess', an obvious homage to the Lucy Lawless TV character.

While waiting for *Beware The Heavens*, Goss moved to Finland, recruiting a new band. They cut their teeth on stage in Japan with Children Of Bodom and In Flames shortly after the album's release. Goss and Laiho were joined for this expedition by Waltari guitarist Roope Latvala, Tarot bassist Marco Hietala, and To/Die/For drummer Tommi Lillmann. Strömblad also contributed on guitar.

Sinergy retained this line-up for the second album, *To Hell And Back*, recorded at Astia Studios: joining Goss once again were Roope Latvala, Marco Hietala, and Tommi Lillmann. The album, released in June 2000, included a twisted cover of the Blondie hit 'Hanging On The Telephone', and Japanese copies added the exclusive track 'Invincible', a cover of the

Sinergy

SINERGY discography

BEWARE THE HEAVENS, Nuclear Blast NB 0338-2 (Europe), Nuclear Blast America 6338 (USA) (1999)
TO HELL AND BACK, Nuclear Blast NB 0503-2 (Europe), Nuclear Blast America 6503 (USA) (2000)
SUICIDE BY MY SIDE, Nuclear Blast NB 0697-2 (Europe), Nuclear Blast America 6697 (USA) ((2002)

1980s Pat Benatar hit. Another unexpected take on a pop classic came with the band's interpretation of Abba's 'Gimme Gimme Gimme (A Man After Midnight)', donated to a Nuclear Blast tribute collection. Both Goss and Latvala took time out to session on the 2000 debut *Unknown Soldier* album by Warmen.

As Laiho's commitments to the increasingly successful Children Of Bodom took precedence, for live work Sinergy pulled in second guitarist Peter Huss. This combination toured to promote *To Hell And Back* supporting Nightwish. After recording the third album, *Suicide By My Side*, drummer Tommi Lillman parted ways with the band, in August 2001. He was replaced by Mats Karlsson, a veteran of Tears Of Sahara, and then Janne Parviainen, a campaigner with Waltari, Zwanziger, Jimsonweed, and Barathrum (as Abyssir).

Suicide By My Side, launched in February 2002, hit Number 11 on the Finnish charts and displayed a far more aggressive edge to Goss's vocals. The Toy's Factory label in Japan issued the album, adding a cover rendition of Iron Maiden's 'Number Of The Beast'. Goss and Laiho were married the same month.

Sinergy's line-up tribulations continued into 2002: in May, bassist Marco Hietala was temporarily replaced by session musician Lauri Porra of Tunnelvision and Warmen. Japanese dates in June with Brazilians Angra were preceded by guitarists Laiho and Latvala conducting three guitar clinics in Japan for the ESP brand. The following month, bass player Melanie Sisneros, previously with New Eden and Raven Mad, was added to the line-up. Sisneros is also famed for her role as Stephanie Harris in the renowned tribute band The Iron Maidens. However, by October Sisneros was out of the picture and Lauri Porra took over the bass once again. In 2003, Sisneros joined Crescent Shield, the band assembled by erstwhile Onward singer Michael Grant.

Sinergy then returned to the studio to assemble their fourth album, *Sins Of Our Past*. It was compiled at various stages throughout 2004, with bass and drums laid down at Finnvox Studios and the remaining tracks at Beyond Abilities, the studio of Janne Warman from Children Of Bodom. Lauri Porra joined Stratovarius as their new bassist in June; Parviainen enrolled himself into the ranks of Ensiferum in September 2005. As this book went to press, it was expected that *Sins Of Our Past* would be released through Nuclear Blast in 2007. Sinergy's considerable fanbase is sure to support it whenever it arrives.

SONATA ARCTICA
ICE-COLD METAL LANDSCAPES

KEMI-BASED SYMPHONIC METAL BAND Sonata Arctica have made a great impression on the European metal scene with their grandiose sense of style. Uniquely for a metal band, they employ two keyboard players live for an extra dose of pomposity. The band were founded in 1995 playing poppier music under the original name of Tricky Beans. After demoing under that name, they changed to Sonata Arctica and made rapid progress.

The three Tricky Beans demo sessions were *Friend Till The End* (1996), *Agre Pamppers* (1996), and *Peacemaker* (1997). Line-up shuffles during 1997 forced a subtle name shift to Tricky Means, and a further promo recording, *FullMoon* (1999), was perfectly timed to exploit the symphonic metal phenomenon sweeping Europe.

The Spinefarm label showed interest during the switch to Sonata Arctica and the band debuted with the 1999 'UnOpened' single. The first album, *Ecliptica*, produced by Ahti Kortelainen and recorded at Tico Tico studios, was issued in September 1999. It immediately made an impression, with reviewers acknowledging the mature songwriting and the blazing lead guitar work of Jani Liimatainen while lambasting the band for their cringeworthy lyrics. Japanese copies added the extra song 'Mary-Lou'.

With Sonata Arctica in ascendancy, frontman Tony Kakko opted to enroll another keyboard player in order to concentrate on his lead vocal role. Kenziner's Mikko Härkin took on the role as the band gained a

SONATA ARCTICA discography

ECLIPTICA, Spinefarm SPI 91CD (Europe) (1999)
Successor, Spinefarm SPI 106CD (Europe) (2000)
SILENCE, Spinefarm SPI 111CD (Europe), Century Media CM 8063-2 (USA) (2001)
Orientation, Avalon Marquee MICP-10256 (Japan) (2001)
SONGS OF SILENCE – LIVE IN TOKYO, Avalon Marquee MICP-10290 (Japan) (2002)
WINTERHEART'S GUILD, Spinefarm SPI 172CD (Europe), Century Media CM 8215-2 (USA) (2003)
Takatalvi, Avalon Marquee MICP-10403 (Japan) (2003)
Don't Say A Word, Nuclear Blast NB 1348-2 (Europe) (2004)
RECKONING NIGHT, Nuclear Blast NB 1315-2 (Europe), Nuclear Blast America 1315 (USA) (2004)
FOR THE SAKE OF REVENGE, Nuclear Blast NB 1619-2 (Europe), Nuclear Blast America 1618 (USA) (2006)

valuable support slot on the Stratovarius and Rhapsody tour of Europe.

In the summer of 2000, bass player Janne Kivilahti bowed out and the band drafted Marko Paasikoski, a founding member and guitarist of Tricky Beans. The *Silence* album, reprising the Kortelainen and Tico Tico formula, arrived in June 2001. The band stuck rigidly to their blueprint, appeasing fans with another dose of precise, overwrought metal. A show on September 4th in Tokyo was captured on tape for a live album, *Songs Of Silence – Live In Tokyo*, released in July 2002. The band toured Europe with Gamma Ray. Meanwhile, vocalist Kakko guested on the Nightwish single 'Over The Hills And Far Away'.

Sonata Arctica's 'Last Drop Falls' single included a version of Iron Maiden's 'Die With Your Boots On'. This and an adventurous rendition of Bette Midler's 'Wind Beneath My Wings' made an appearance on the Japanese *Orientation* EP. The band then cut a cover of 'Fade To Black' for a Nuclear Blast Metallica tribute collection.

Keyboard player Mikko Härkin announced his departure in September 2002, and the position was filled by erstwhile Silent Voices and Requiem man Henrik Klingenberg. Stratovarius musician Jens Johansson guested on keyboards. Naturally, Japanese fans received an extra song, this time 'The Rest Of The Sun Belongs To Me'. The band opened 2003 in fine style with the 'Victoria's Secret' single, which entered the Finnish singles chart at Number 2 before gaining the top spot the following week.

Outside activity found Liimatainen donating guitar solos to Human Temple's debut 2004 album, *Insomnia*. Meanwhile, Sonata Arctica set *Reckoning Night* as the title of their fourth record. Two cover versions, Vanishing Point's 'Two Minds One Soul' and Depeche Mode's 'World In My Eyes', were laid down in the same sessions. The band's lead single for *Reckoning Night* was 'Don't Say A Word', which topped the Finnish charts in August. The album debuted at Number 2 in October. The band then toured across Europe throughout November as support to Nightwish but cancelled gigs in Madrid, Spain and in Montpellier, France when Kakko came down with a fever. 'Shamandalie' entered the Finnish singles charts at Number 3 in December.

A Japanese-only compilation, *The End Of This Chapter*, was released in August 2005. The band were back on Finnish territory in November for headlining gigs. Kakko also found time to contribute guest vocals to the 2006 Eternal Tears Of Sorrow album *Before The Bleeding Sun*.

The first Sonata Arctica product of 2006 was the live CD and DVD *For The Sake Of Revenge*. Spinefarm released the compilation album *The Collection* in November 2006, featuring re-recorded versions of 'My Land' and 'Replica'. The latter was issued as a single, hitting Number 1 on the Finnish charts – a sign that the band's success looks set to continue, in their homeland as well as elsewhere.

STRATOVARIUS
EXPERT POWER METALLERS

THE CREATIVE CORE OF STRATOVARIUS, led by former Road Block and Thunder guitarist Timo Tolkki, was formed as far back as 1979. The band's grandiose, elaborately polished work has brought enormous international rewards for the Finns and has inspired a whole new genre of music – symphonic metal.

The first incarnation of the Helsinki-based group included Staffan Stråhlman on guitar, John Vihervä on bass, and vocalist-drummer Tuomo Lassila, a trio that had previously operated under the name of Black Water. Road Block bassist Jyrki Lentonen was introduced in 1984. The following year a disgruntled Stråhlman bowed out just a week before a concert in Aalborg, Denmark. Turning to Tolkki, the band asked him to learn the set, and after a successful show the guitarist joined the band. The group then decided that Tolkki might be better suited to the vocal

STRATOVARIUS discography

FRIGHT NIGHT, CBS cnu (Europe) (1989)
STRATOVARIUS II, Blue Light BLR 335CD (Europe) (1992)
TWILIGHT TIME, Shark 033 (Europe) (1992)
DREAMSPACE, Noise T&T 008-2 (Europe) (1994)
FOURTH DIMENSION, Noise T&T 0014-2 (Europe) (1995)
EPISODE, Noise T&T 0014-2 (Europe) (1996)
VISIONS, Noise T&T 0031-2 (Europe) (1997)
LIVE! VISIONS OF EUROPE, Noise T&T 0038-2 (Europe) (1998)
DESTINY, Noise T&T 0040-2 (Europe)(1998)
THE CHOSEN ONES, Noise T&T 0045-2 (Europe) (1999)
INFINITE, Nuclear Blast NB 0464-2 (Europe), Nuclear Blast America 6464 (USA) (2000)
INTERMISSION, Nuclear Blast NB 0586-2 (Europe), Nuclear Blast America 6586 (USA) (2001)
ELEMENTS PT. I, Nuclear Blast NB 1037-2 (Europe), Nuclear Blast America 1037 (USA) (2003)
ELEMENTS PT. 2, Nuclear Blast NB 1176-2 (Europe), Nuclear Blast America 1176 (USA) (2003)
STRATOVARIUS, Mayan MYN 040 (Europe), Santuary 34108 (USA) (2005)

role, and in this formation Stratovarius recorded their first demo in 1987, consisting of 'Future Shock', 'Fright Night', and 'Night Screamer'.

A showcase at the Tavastia Club in Helsinki led to a deal with CBS. First came the singles 'Future Shock' and 'Black Night', then the May 1989 debut, *Fright Night*, a straightahead heavy metal album that, despite studio keyboard parts by Antti Ikonen, had few of the neo-classical elements present on later works. Live work across Finland in 1989 included a slot at the 'Giants Of Rock' festival in Hämeenlinna before bassist Jyrki Lentonen left the band. Dropped from CBS, who had rejected demos for the proposed next album, the band signed to the tiny Finnish Blue Light Records, who released their second album, *Stratovarius II*, in 1991. These sessions were totally self-funded.

Written entirely by Tolkki, the sophomore effort demonstrated some early examples of his evolving neo-classical style. Lyrically, the band worked predominantly within the refined horror genre. Although bass player Jari Behm appeared in the line-up photos for *Stratovarius II*, in fact all bass parts were performed by Tolkki. He also handled lead vocals and all the guitar parts, with Antti Ikonen on keyboards and Tuomo Lassila on drums. *Stratovarius II* was released by Blue Light in two versions, the first with cover art depicting a pair of feet, the second simply bearing a band photo.

In October 1992, things started to pick up for the band, with the album reissued in Europe by Shark Records. Imported versions began to flood Japan, the album impacting to such an extent there that it became the highest-selling foreign album of 1993. That July, the giant JVC/Victor label licensed the record for official release. Both versions had new cover art – the now familiar 'outer-space' scene – and a new title, *Twilight Time*. Original Finnish pressings of the second album with a simple photo of the four members on the front have become rare collectables.

Noise Records were quick to move in and signed the Finns for 1994's *Dreamspace*. The album marked the debut of yet another bassist, Jari Kainulainen – previously a member of late-1980s hair-rock bands Heat and Christine – who joined the group before the recording. Tuomo Lassila suffered a severe stress injury in both his hands, effectively putting him out of action. To complete the record, Stratovarius enlisted Sami Kuoppamäki from the Finnish prog act Kingston Wall.

Released in February 1994, *Dreamspace* gave the musicians their first

Stratovarius

chance to tour Japan that June. As another Stratovarius album was prepared, Tolkki released a solo album, *Classical Variations And Themes*, through Shark. At this point, Tolkki decided to concentrate solely on guitar playing, necessitating the recruitment of Lappajärvi native Timo Kotipelto, an ex-member of Filthy Asses. Issued worldwide in March 1995, *Fourth Dimension* doubled the sales of *Dreamspace* as the music was taken to stages in Germany, Switzerland, The Netherlands, Finland, Greece, and Japan.

Following a European tour with label-mates Enola Gay, keyboard player Antti Ikonen and drummer Tuomo Lassila both quit. With the drummer's defection, Stratovarius now found themselves in the rare position of having no original band members left. In order to record the *Episode* album, at Finnvox Studios in Helsinki, ex-Yngwie Malmsteen and Dio keyboard player Jens Johansson and drummer Jörg Michael were added. Michael's credits read like a who's who of German metal: he'd played with Rage, Mekong Delta, Headhunter, Laos, Grave Digger, Axel Rudi Pell, and Running Wild, among others. *Episode* took the Stratovarius sound into new vistas, with Tolkki's vision of symphonic metal realised with a 40-piece choir and a 20-strong string section.

A proposed tour in 1996 with Virgin Steele to coincide with the album's release was cancelled after the American band's vocalist, David DeFeis, was injured in a car accident. In the autumn, Stratovarius hit the road with Rage before preparing to lay down a new album, again enlisting Johansson and Michael. The highly polished *Visions* arrived in April 1997, hitting Number 4 in Finland and considerably raising international appreciation for the band. A mammoth tour of Europe ensued, after which Stratovarius hit Brazil and Argentina. A March 1998 live album followed, *Visions Of Europe*, recorded at concerts in Milan and Athens. They spent the summer months on the European festival circuit.

October 1998's *Destiny* gave Stratovarius a prestigious Number 1 in their homeland as well as their debut chart entry in Germany, and the record opened up an even wider international market to the band. The lead single 'S.O.S.' scored Number 3 on the Finnish charts. Stratovarius then undertook a headline tour of Finland before travelling to Japan for shows to close the year. The band played dates in 1999 in Germany, Belgium, Holland, Spain, Italy, Austria, Turkey, Denmark, Brazil, Argentina, Chile, and Portugal. As they switched labels to Nuclear Blast, Noise issued a parting-shot best-of, *The Chosen Ones*, including tracks only available previously in Japan.

Destiny was still selling strongly into 2000 when *Infinite*, another Finnish chart-topper, was delivered. More dates followed, with a run of 82 shows broken only when Kotipelto burnt his hand in a pyrotechnic explosion at the 'Wacken' festival, forcing a re-scheduling of South American gigs.

The band announced a break in 2001, predicting a new studio album for 2003. Kotipelto recorded his debut solo album, *Waiting For The Dawn*, a conceptual piece rooted in Egyptian mythology that was a much harder-edged affair than expected. Meanwhile, Johansson left his mark on four tracks as guest contributor to Sonata Arctica's February 2003 album, *Winterheart's Guild*.

In the interim, Nuclear Blast issued the *Intermission* collection, which combined foreign rarities with covers of Judas Priest's 'Bloodstone' and Rainbow's 'I Surrender' and 'Kill The King', the latter with lead vocals by Tolkki.

Stratovarius broke their silence in late November 2002 with the single 'Eagleheart'. The album, *Elements Part I*, was released in January 2003, Japanese variants on the JVC/Victor label hosting the traditional extra track, 'Into Deep Blue', while variants released in France included a French-language version of 'Papillon'. A limited edition of *Elements Part I* housed in a 3D design box hosted a second disc comprising 'Run Away' and demo recordings of 'Soul Of A Vagabond' and 'Find Your Own Voice'. Collectors also sought a mail-order-only release with a second disc featuring the entire album in demo form.

Reception to the album was cool, with many fans believing that Stratovarius had overreached themselves – losing the art of good songwriting in a march towards complexity and excessive soloing, particularly on the ten-minute *Neverending Story*-inspired 'Fantasia'. Nonetheless, the album debuted on the Finnish charts at Number 2.

Stratovarius announced Far Eastern dates in Japan, Taiwan, and Hong Kong during June, but these dates were curtailed when the Finnish foreign office advised the band of the threat from the SARS virus. In October, *Elements Part 2* was released.

They switched labels to Sanctuary with a bizarre press release claiming that the three-album deal was to be signed in elk's blood. The band did in fact make their mark on the contract with the unfortunate animal's blood, in a deal purportedly worth over $3.5 million – apparently the biggest ever for a Finnish artist.

This rapid ascendancy was halted in spectacular fashion. The band's fans were dismayed to learn from a post by guitarist Timo Tolkki on the Stratovarius message board that the band was "in a severe crisis". Intriguingly, Tolkki suggested that, although he was in discussion with individuals, he was "95 per cent sure that three band members have to leave". In late December, it was revealed that Stratovarius had trimmed down to a trio of Tolkki, Kainulainen, and Johansson; rumours of the induction of a new female singer proved to be true when Aurora K's Katriina Wiiala stepped into the fold. This latest recruit not only boasted a three-octave vocal range – she had also been crowned Finnish gymnastics champion, not once but twice. Official induction photographs of Wiiala smeared with blood caused consternation for longstanding fans, more familiar with a far more refined approach. However, the surreal nature of the band's transformation had only just begun.

Anders Johansson – the Yngwie Malmsteen, Blue Murder, and Hammerfall-credited brother of Jens – was set to man the drums for an album with the provisional working title of *Popkiller*. However, as Stratovarius endured a huge backlash in the media regarding its new line-up, Anders quit within a week of joining. Rumours sparked by Tolkki's admission that he wanted a female percussionist focused on Simona Bressi (aka Jill Ward) from the Los Angeles-based Ballistik and the Black Sabbath covers band Mistress Of Reality. Bressi swiftly denied the speculation.

Tolkki's reshaping of the band had ramifications behind the scenes as the guitarist revealed that Sanctuary had asked for the return of a 1m advance (about $1.3m), claiming that this was based on a contract with the previous line-up. The label also issued a statement maintaining that the ex-members were still under contract. These restrictions extended deeper, as the previous version of Stratovarius was legally obliged to make a live appearance on February 28th 2004 at the 'Piorno Rock' festival in Spain.

Matters in the Stratovarius camp became increasingly strange when, after the official website administrator publicly distanced himself from the guitarist, Tolkki posted a "statement" claiming that he had heard voices in his head, going on to describe it as "Kabbalah, Kabbalah, Kabbalah. I believe it was the voice of Jesus Christ". Accompanying the verbiage was a picture of Tolkki smeared with blood.

Despite all of this, the 'Piorno Rock' festival performance went ahead, the band's last with its classic line-up. Local reports suggested that Tolkki, brandishing a bottle of vodka onstage, was obviously drunk. Incredibly, the show included a moment when Jens Johansson, in full audience view, urinated on Tolkki during the opening notes of 'Forever'.

Matters got much worse for the guitarist the following day. While taking a walk in Granada's central plaza he was assaulted by an unknown attacker, punched in the face, and stabbed twice in the arm with what was believed to be a box-cutter knife. He was admitted to emergency care in the local hospital but released that same night. Tolkki later commented: "I do not want to end up like John Lennon. I don't know if I want to continue Stratovarius any more." However, the guitarist did manage to record some new material during this period, travelling to Dortmund in late March to rehearse with drummer Jörg Michael and then recording at Soundtrack Studios in Pitäjänmäki in early April, before these sessions were curtailed.

The culmination of this extraordinary set of events was Tolkki's hospitalisation on April 10th, the guitarist entering the Mehiläinen private hospital in Helsinki to treat what his webmaster described as "suicidal feelings and chronic depression". Upon his release in early May, Tolkki – revealing that he had released Wiiala from her contract – issued a statement about the band's status, declaring "Stratovarius is Timo Kotipelto, Jens Johansson, Jörg Michael, Jari Kainulainen, and Timo Tolkki. If this line-up is not possible, then there cannot be any band called Stratovarius."

Reconciling their differences, the band – including Kotipelto – stuck to their obligations to perform at European festivals. Michael then joined veteran British hard rockers Saxon for their *Lionheart* album. The drummer also found time to guest on Italian symphonic power metal band Kaledon's *The Way Of The Light*. Making a surprise appearance, Jens Johansson joined Nightwish for a cover of Megadeth's 'Symphony Of Destruction' at B.B. King's Blues Club in New York City on August 22nd.

Steelborn Records collated a Stratovarius tribute album in 2004, entitled *Within Infinity – Tribute to Stratovarius*. Meanwhile, Kotipelto performed several classic heavy metal covers with female vocalist Maija Vilkkumaa and Finland's Heavy Lilja Orchestra on August 26th at the Manala bar in Helsinki. Songs included Deep Purple's 'Highway Star' and Black Sabbath's 'Heaven And Hell' before encoring on a medley of 'Paranoid'/'Smoke On The Water'.

With a turbulent year behind them, Tolkki, Michael, Kotipelto, Kainulainen, and Johansson met in Helsinki during early December to discuss prospects for the band's future. As 2005 dawned, the group released an official statement declaring that "after much talk, soul-searching and reflection" the quintet would forge ahead with a new album, *Stratovarius*.

Unfortunately, by February the Stratovarius camp was once more deep in controversy. A song intended for the new record entitled 'Hitler' (subsequently re-branded 'Götterdämmerung [Zenith Of Power]') included an introduction of a genuine Hitler speech and was deemed objectionable by Sanctuary. Tolkki announced that he had submitted the anti-Hitler song to the German Interior Ministry for clearance.

With recordings for the album complete, a video for its first single, 'Maniac Dance', was shot in mid April by director Antti Jokinen. Despite the album being given a September release date, leaked tracks were available on the internet as early as May. Japanese editions added an extra DVD featuring *Stratovarius Rockumentary* and a live version of 'Break The Ice'.

Sustaining his career behind the mixing board, Tolkki gained production credits for the Italian band Vision Divine's album *The Perfect Machine*. In June, Stratovarius parted ways with bassist Jari Kainulainen, a longstanding member with over a decade's service to his credit. Kainulainen duly reactivated his side venture, Mess. The Kotipelto and Sinergy-credited bassist Lauri Porra soon stepped in as substitute. Johansson made time to guest on Nocturnal Rites' album *Grand Illusion*.

Stratovarius landed at Number 4 on the Finnish charts. A lengthy European tour in October 2005 through to early December had the band sharing stages with Hammerfall, taking in Finland, Norway, Belgium, Germany, Holland, France, the UK, Spain, Switzerland, Italy, Slovenia, Austria, and Hungary. November shows saw Shakra as support, and Stratovarius's future seems assured.

TAROT
CARDS ON THE TABLE

IN AN AGE WHEN SCANDINAVIAN rock was polarised between melodic pop-rock and ersatz thrash metal, Kuopio's Tarot bravely

TAROT discography

SPELL OF IRON, Flamingo FGL 4010 (Europe) (1986)
FOLLOW ME INTO MADNESS, Flamingo FGL 4026 (Europe)
   (1988)
TO LIVE FOREVER, Bluelight BLR 3316-2 (Europe) (1993)
TO LIVE AGAIN, Zero Corporation XRCN 1199 (Japan) (1995)
STIGMATA, Bluelight BLR 3321-2 (Europe) (1995)
FOR THE GLORY OF NOTHING, Bluelight BHR 3347-2 (Europe)
   (1998)
SHINING BLACK, Bluelight BHR 3363 2 (Europe) (2003)
SUFFER OUR PLEASURES, Spinefarm SPI 176CD (Europe) (2003),
   Metal Blade 3984-14488-2 (USA) (2004)
CROWS FLY BACK, King Foo Entertainment KFCD-011 (Finland)
   (2006), Nuclear Blast NB 1763-2 (Europe) (2007)

ploughed their own furrow of heavy, melodic classic metal. The band achieved considerable commercial success in their homeland long before the start of the country's metal export drive. Many of the bands that followed in their wake were directly inspired by Tarot's dedication to volume, riffage, extravagant stage shows, and a refusal to pander to trends.

The group were initially named Purgatory, conceived during the early 1980s by the teenage Hietala brothers, guitarist Zachary and frontman Marco, alongside guitarist Mako H and drummer Pecu Cinnari. The band went through numerous incarnations before stabilising.

First came the 'Wings Of Darkness' and 'Love's Not Made For My Kind' singles, followed by the self-produced debut album *The Spell Of Iron*, which arrived through Flamingo Music in late 1986. In a novel marketing ploy, initial copies of the album came with a one-sided bonus 7-inch boasting a drum solo entitled 'Aaaargh! What's Goin' On Here?!' blasted out by Cinnari.

For the April 1988 album *Follow Me Into Madness*, Tarot replaced Mako H with keyboard player Janne Tolsa. The record was released in two different covers, one clad in a skulls design while a second depicted a grasping claw about to encircle an unsuspecting (and scantily-clad) female. Strangely for such a well-known act, Tarot then faded from view. Frontman Marco Hietala was apparently in line as one of the frontrunners to replace Bruce Dickinson in Iron Maiden.

However, the band bounced back in February 1993, finding renewed success with their *To Live Forever* album, which included a cover of Black Sabbath's 'Children Of The Grave'. The Japanese market soon picked up on the band and a live album, recorded at the Tavastia Club in Helsinki, was issued in the Far East by Zero Corporation during 1994, titled *To Live Again*. A new studio album, *Stigmata*, arrived in April 1995 and was followed in June by the *As One* EP, which included a cover of Jethro Tull's 'Locomotive Breath'.

After another break, Tarot returned in 1998 with a new studio album, *For The Glory Of Nothing*, through the Blastic Heaven label. These recordings showed Tarot edging into progressive realms. Another album emerged that year in the shape of the compilation *Shining Black*. Initially a Japan-only release, the album would be repackaged with additional material and issued worldwide in March 2003.

Marco Hietala later joined the high-profile Kimberley Goss-led power metal band Sinergy, performing on their 1999 debut *Beware The Heavens*. He also performed with Conquest and covers band Metal Gods. During October 2001, Hietala supplanted bassist Sami Vänskä in Finland's leading metal band, Nightwish. With Nightwish taking time out during 2003, Hietala regrouped with Tarot for a new album, *Suffer Our Pleasures*. A preliminary single, 'Undead Son', was backed by a metallic take on 'Mama' by Genesis.

The album arrived at Number 10 in the national Finnish album charts on its release. The major label Universal picked up the album for territories outside Finland while Metal Blade licensed it for US release in March 2004.

Hietala aided Charon with backing vocals on their September 2003 album *Dead Man Walking*. Keyboard player Tolsa joined the reformed line-up of Eternal Tears Of Sorrow in late 2004. Tarot then conducted new album recordings in early 2006, with Hietala taking time out of his Nightwish schedule to participate. He also found time to contribute guest vocals to the 2006 Eternal Tears Of Sorrow album *Before The Bleeding Sun*.

In March 2006, Bluelight Records reissued the Tarot back catalogue, adding bonus tracks in the form of demos and live recordings to each album. The band announced in 2006 that long-time backing vocalist Tommi 'Tuple' Salmela was now a permanent member.

Tarot's May 2006 single, 'You', which entered the charts at Number 1, was backed by a cover of Blue Öyster Cult's 'Veteran Of The Psychic Wars'. The new album, *Crows Fly Black*, released in Finland during October 2006 through KingFoo Entertainment, charted at Number 5. *Crows* was scheduled to be released elsewhere in Europe during January 2007. With so much activity to look forward to, the omens for Tarot are good.

TO/DIE/FOR
MODERN SOUNDS EXPERTLY PLAYED

KOUVOLA-BASED TO/DIE/FOR are an intensely melodic yet heavy modern metal act. They formed as Mary-Ann during 1993 with Marko Kangaskolkka on bass. This unit issued an eponymous album in 1997, after which singer Jarno 'Jape' Perätalo and drummer Tonmi Lillman were

joined by guitarists Juppe 'J.P.' Sutela and Andy. Lillman then backed out for a period and Mary-Ann enrolled bass player Miikka 'Sepe' Kuisma, keyboard player Juska Salminen, and drummer Jaani Peuhu. The band issued a further batch of recordings on the 1998 self-financed EP 'Deeper Sin', featuring a cover version of The Pet Shop Boys' 'It's A Sin'.

Scouted by Ewo Rytkönen, the group signed to Spinefarm in July 1999 under the new name of To/Die/For. By this juncture, former Malpractice guitarist Joonas 'Jope' Koto had enrolled and Lillman had also returned. Erstwhile member Salminen subsequently joined H.I.M. and reunited with Miikka Kuisma in 2000 with New Dawn Foundation.

The March 2000 debut *All Eternity* and the follow-up EP *In The Heat Of The Night*, featuring a cover of the eponymous hit by disco artist Sandra, saw Koto joined by singer Jape Perätalo, second guitarist J.P. Sutela, bassist Miikka Kuisma, and drummer Tommi Lillman. Tommi was also employed on the second Sinergy album, *To Hell And Back*, in 2000. The *All Eternity* album was licensed to Pony Canyon for Japan, with the addition of the rendition of 'It's A Sin', and Nuclear Blast for Germany. In autumn 2000, the band undertook a European tour with In Flames, Dark Tranquillity, and Sentenced.

To/Die/For's second album, May 2001's *Epilogue*, found Marko Kangaskolkka assuming bass duties after Kuisma quit during recording,

TO/DIE/FOR discography

ALL ETERNITY, Spinefarm SPI 90CD (Europe) (2000)
EPILOGUE, Spinefarm SPI 114CD (Europe), Nuclear Blast America 6615 (USA) (2001)
JADED, Spinefarm SPI 181CD (Europe) (2003)
IV, Spinefarm SPI 222CD (Europe) (2005)
WOUNDS WIDE OPEN, Spinefarm SPI 260CD (Europe) (2006)

with Lullacry frontwoman Tanya Kemppainen and Sinergy's Marco Hietala guesting in the studio. *Epilogue* bolstered the band's standing, and the public outside metal circles became aware of the band as the single 'Hollow Heart' struck Number 1 on the Finnish charts. Naturally, global editions were boosted by additional music: the Japanese version added 'Victim Of Love' while a Russian variant included To/Die/For's take on the Scorpions' 'When Passion Rules The Game'. Sutela exited in summer 2001, but the undeterred band toured Finland alongside Nightwish and in Europe with Lacrimosa before hitting Russia and Mexico in early 2002.

The band were joined by guitarist Mika Ahtiainen for the recording of a new album, *Jaded*, produced by TT Oksala. Japanese copies were augmented by a number of extra songs. Sinergy and Nightwish bassist-vocalist Marco Hietala were tapped for a guest-vocal role on the record, which included a cover version of Cutting Crew's '(I Just) Died In Your Arms'. Tommi Lillman deputised for black metal band Barathrum during the summer of 2003.

To/Die/For lost the services of singer Perätalo in August and temporarily enrolled For My Pain and Reflexion singer Juha Kylmänen to fulfil dates in Mexico that October. This signalled the start of major friction that would eventually split the band, with Kangaskolkka, Lillman, and Koto searching for a new singer.

Perätalo soon returned with a new act, Tiaga, that had further To/Die/For connections as it included guitarists Juppe Sutela and Mika Ahtiainen, and keyboard player Juska Salminen (and even the band's former drum tech, Santtu Lonka). The line-up was completed by Jarkko 'Josey' Strandman from New Dawn Foundation on bass. Confusingly, reports in February 2004 suggested that Spinefarm had insisted on contracting Perätalo's new band on condition that the To/Die/For name was used. This outfit toured Mexico in April. The move incensed the Kangaskolkka-Lillman-Koto trio and confused fans, but the revised Tiaga had legally taken the name.

Entering Sonic Image Studios in Kouvola, To/Die/For set about recording a new album. In October, it was reported that guitarist Joonas Koto, bassist Marko Kangaskolkka, and drummer Tonmi Lillman had recorded an album, *Sign Of Demise*, under their new band name, HateFrame.

To/Die/For's 2005 album, succinctly entitled *IV*, included a cover of U2's 'New Year's Day' and gained the group a valuable foothold on the German darkwave circuit. With the band's music flying headlong into gothic realms, older fans departed, but *IV* certainly generated fresh appreciation.

Guitarist Sutela exited in June citing "personal reasons". He was immediately replaced by Antti 'Antza' Talala of Eternal Tears Of Sorrow, Fleshtone, and Soulrelic. To/Die/For announced a lengthy tour of Mexico throughout November and December. Talala bowed out of Soulrelic that same month in order to prioritise To/Die/For. Meanwhile, it was revealed that Juska Salminen would be taking an indefinite break from performing and recording activities with the band for health reasons.

As 2006 opened, To/Die/For fractured once again, losing the services of guitarist Mika Ahtiainen. The group nevertheless ensconced themselves in the studio in March to undertake recordings for a fifth album. *Wounds Wide Open* was recorded by Samu Oittinen at Fantom Studios and by Jari-Jukka Nippala at Sonic Image. The final product was mixed by Peter Tägtgren at Abyss Studios in Sweden. In May, it was announced that the band's former guitarist Joonas 'Jope' Koto had rejoined the ranks as a replacement for Ahtiainen.

A single, 'Like Never Before', included a cover of Ozzy Osbourne's '(I Just) Want You', and this was followed by *Wounds Wide Open* in October. To/Die/For teamed up with Sinamore, Das Scheit, and Indigo Child for a European tour beginning in November. Their path to further success looked set as this book went to press.

JAPANESE
METAL

JAPAN has always provided a bedrock of support for US and European bands, very often showing appreciation and fanatical support in excess. In troubled times, many a Western band has given thanks both to the moral encouragement and financial sustenance that dedicated Japanese fans have offered them.

In the main, Japanese bands conform to the national stereotype. They work prodigiously, producing albums at a frightening rate. Famously, the Japanese soak up Western culture, with heavy metal being no exception, but they have found it difficult to elevate their homegrown bands onto the international stage.

With metal's rise during the 1980s, a few bands took a chance on breaking out: of these it was Loudness and Bow Wow who took the furthest strides. Loudness achieved a great deal of respect, mainly due to the extraordinary talents of guitarist Akira Takasaki, but even an ill-fated switch to an American singer could not ultimately generate the necessary sales. They retired back to Japan, re-recruited their original singer, and seemed content to remain superstars at home. Recently, they have attempted a second assault on the American market.

Bow Wow's plans were even more daring. Not only did they relocate to the UK, but also they changed their name to suit from Bow Wow to Vow Wow. Again blessed with a bona fide guitar hero, Kyoji Yamamoto, the group put in some sterling work before returning to Japan and reverting to Bow Wow, and they continue to enjoy exalted status at home to this day.

Other bands who made worthy forays into the West included Earthshaker, EZO, and Anthem. This incited interest in bands such as 44 Magnum, Casbah, X, Hurry Scuary, Saber Tiger, and Outrage.

Critics pointed towards a "lack of feeling" in the music, perhaps betraying a lack of blues foundation. While Japanese guitar gurus could match and outstrip their Western counterparts, it often seemed that their technicality masked a dearth of true passion. Somehow, it seemed that the Japanese had been able to emulate – and expand upon – the heavy metal formula, but somehow failed to recognise the gut instinct and individuality that was the very heart and soul of it.

However, in the main, Japanese bands rely on the domestic market, while developing cult underground appreciation in Europe and the USA. Perhaps the most infamous exponents of this practice are black metal outfit Sabbat, a band whose catalogue of singles and albums is so vast it baffles even their official webmaster. The legacy of the NWOBHM is keenly felt in Japan, too, where detail-obsessed acts such as Gorgon and the bizarre Metalucifer not only cover their favourite songs but go to great lengths to emulate their heroes. On the grindcore front, Japan very often takes this extreme art form to the absolute limit.

Recent Japanese bands who make an impression worldwide vary across a wide range, from doomsters Church Of Misery and Eternal Elysium, through black metal act Sigh, to the symphonic metal of Concerto Moon. The East, it seems, remains an enigma.

ANTHEM
APPROPRIATELY-NAMED HM WARRIORS

HEAVY METAL ACT ANTHEM were founded in Tokyo during 1981 as a quartet of singer Toshihito Maeda, guitarist Akifumi Koyanagi, bass player Naoto 'Ski' Shibata, and drummer Takamasa Ohuchi. Koyanagi left in November 1983 to be replaced by Hiroya Fukada. In December 1984, vocalist Toshihito Maeda left and Anthem drafted in Eizo Sakamoto for their debut eponymous album, issued in July 1985 by Nexus and licensed to Europe through Roadrunner. This set was followed by the *Ready To Ride* EP that December.

Tightrope followed in April 1986, gaining the band a good degree of international acclaim through the European issue on the French Black Dragon label, as did *Bound To Break* during March 1987. Again Anthem scored overseas distribution when Restless picked up the album for US territories.

Anthem switched their vocalist to Yukio Morikawa following the live album and its accompanying video *The Show Carries On* in September 1987. This collection of tracks, captured in Los Angeles that June, was spruced up in the studio by noted English producer Chris Tsangarides. Anthem maintained a stable line-up for May 1988's *Gypsy Ways* and the May 1989 set *Hunting Time*, the latter seeing Yoshitaka Mikuni credited with the keyboard role. Both records were put out in the UK by Music For Nations.

The March 1990 album *No Smoke Without Fire* featured former Hurry Scuary guitarist Hideaki Nakama. King Records compiled the first Anthem compilation, *Best 1981-1990*. The March 1992 album *Domestic Booty* saw Akio Shimizu assuming guitar duties. Bassist Naoto Shibata joined Loudness the same year.

Anthem returned in 2000 with the *Heavy Metal Anthem* album, which reworked older numbers with vocals from former Rainbow, Michael Schenker Group and Alcatrazz vocalist Graham Bonnet. The

Anthem

record included three Rainbow tracks. Essentially put together by Shibata, it featured Akio Shimizu and Kazumasa Saitoh on guitar, Hirotsugu Homma of Loudness, Takamasa Ohuchi on drums, and keyboard player Yoshitaka Mikuni.

When they issued *Seven Hills* in August 2001 the band was down to a quartet of Sakamoto, Shimizu, Shibata and Homma. Eizo Sakamoto released a solo album, the oddly titled *Shout Drunker*, in February 2002, and this triggered a succession of further solo outpourings.

ANTHEM discography

ANTHEM, Nexus K28P-566 (Japan), Roadrunner RR 9729 (Europe) (1985)

TIGHT ROPE, Nexus K28P-628 (Japan), Black Dragon BD 019 (Europe) (1986)

BOUND TO BREAK, Nexus K28P-655 (Japan), Medusa 72202-1 (USA) (1987)

THE SHOW CARRIES ON!, Nexus K32Y-2100 (Japan) (1987)

GYPSY WAYS, Nexus K32Y-2130 (Japan), Music For Nations MFN 103 (UK) (1988)

HUNTING TIME, Nexus KICS-2138 (Japan), Music For Nations MFN 104 (UK) (1989)

NO SMOKE WITHOUT FIRE, Nexus KICS-2139 (Japan), Music For Nations MFN 101 (UK) (1990)

DOMESTIC BOOTY, Nexus KICS-2870 (Japan) (1992)

LAST ANTHEM, Nexus KICS-235 (Japan) (1992)

HEAVY METAL ANTHEM, JVC Victor VICP-60992 (Japan) (2000)

SEVEN HILLS, JVC Victor VICP-61464 (Japan) (2001)

OVERLOAD, JVC Victor VICP-62023 (Japan) (2002)

LIVE MELT DOWN, JVC Victor VICP-62308 (Japan) (2003)

ETERNAL WARRIOR, JVC Victor VICP-62775 (Japan) (2004)

THE SHOW CARRIES ON! – COMPLETE VERSION, King KICS-1170 (Japan) (2005)

PROLOGUE LIVE BOXX, JVC Victor VICP-63112 (Japan) (2005) limited edition 5,000 copies

IMMORTAL, JVC Victor VICP-63550 (Japan) (2005)

Anthem released the *Overload* album in 2002 with Sakamoto on vocals.

Chris Tsangarides was then employed by King to remaster the Anthem back catalogue, and these CDs were issued in 2004 with additional tracks. A new album, *Eternal Warrior,* was also released in 2004. Anthem issued the highly collectable *Prologue Live Boxx* in 2005, a three-CD boxed set restricted to 5,000 copies. Anthem's latest offering, *Immortal,* was released in August 2006, and the band were continuing their momentum as this book went to press.

CASBAH
ROCK THE CASBAH?

ALTHOUGH NOW LONG DEFUNCT, the Funabashi, Chiba thrash metal band Casbah made a great impression upon the Japanese metal scene. The band originally went under the title of Explosion. After a name change in October 1983, they featured on two compilation albums – *Heavy Metal Forum 3* on Explosion Records and *Devil Must Be Driven Out With Devil* on Hold Up. Casbah then released a live single in May 1985 featuring 'Fear 'n Destruction' and 'Kill You All'. The single's slogan, "Bang your heads to hell", aptly summed up the band's devotion to undiluted thrash.

At this stage, Casbah consisted of distinctively deep-voiced frontman Taka Hatori, guitarist Nariaki Kida, bassist Kouichi Mitani,

CASBAH discography

Casbah Live, Explosion cnu (Japan) (1985)
Russian Roulette, Music Visions NPR-001 (Japan) (1986) 7-inch vinyl single
BOLD STATEMENT, Roadrunner cnu (Japan) (1996)
DINOSAURS, Roadrunner RRCA 1003 (Japan) (1997)
Barefooted On Earth EP #1, Roadrunner RRCA 9004 (Japan) (1999)
Barefooted On Earth EP #2, Roadrunner RRCA 9005 (Japan) (1999)
RUSSIAN ROULETTE – NO POSERS ALLOWED: 1985-1994, Bang The Head cnu (Japan) (2005)
INFINITE PAIN – OFFICIAL BOOTLEG 1985-2006, Bang The Head cnu (Japan) (2006)

and drummer Takashi Usui. Unusually for such a heavyweight act, Casbah also paid great attention to their visuals, and were often decked out in "Attack Metal" costumes and garish make-up. As their sound moved into the hardcore arena, the standard denim and leather uniform took over.

The self-financed 'Russian Roulette' single appeared in 1986, which

Casbah

saw Kida replaced by Ryo Murayama. A demo session, *Infinite Pain*, arrived in 1987. Casbah continued demoing, putting out *Believe Or Bleed* in 1989, *The Cloning* in 1991, and *Swan Song* in 1992.

The band put in a noteworthy live gig at the New York CBGBs club during 1992 but then underwent line-up changes. Yet another demo session, *March Of The Final Decade*, was laid down in 1994. They signed to Roadrunner in 1996, issuing the *Bold Statement* album the following year. A collection of re-recorded archive material, *Dinosaurs*, arrived in 1998. Casbah vocalist Hatori also deputised live for Outrage.

Subsequently, Casbah's rhythm section changed to bass player Takatoshi Kodaira and drummer Suguru Kobayashi. Kobayashi joined Solitude in late 2001. In 2005, all the band's demo material was collected together on the compilation album *Russian Roulette – No Posers Allowed*. Casbah retain a cult fanbase to this day.

EZO
KABUKI KAMIKAZE

A SAPPORO-BASED GLAM 'KABUKI' heavy metal band, EZO's striking visuals meant they couldn't fail to force their attentions onto the US public. Originally entitled Fratvacker, under which title they released the *Minagoroshi* demo, they became Flatbacker, releasing two domestic albums (*Senso* in October 1985 and *Esa* in February the following year). The band then self-financed a relocation to the USA. The line-up was vocalist Masaki Yamada, guitarist Shoyo Iida, bass player Taro Takahashi, and Hirotsugu Homma on drums. Prior to Flatbacker, 'Hiro' Homma had played with Killer and with Wizard.

Their image involved towering hairdos, outlandish theatrical masks, and full facial make-up, but fortunately the band had the musical talent to back it up. EZO took their new name from the historical name for their homeland island of Hokkaido. They launched a full-scale attack on North America in 1984, and the band, now resident in New Jersey, were snapped up by Geffen. The debut Western album, January 1987's *E-Z-O*, was produced by none other than Kiss mainman Gene Simmons, with songwriting contributions from Black'n'Blue singer Jamie St. James. Upon the album's release, EZO toured America as support to Great White and then Guns N' Roses. *E-Z-O* impacted on the US *Billboard* chart, peaking at 150.

The May 1989 *Fire, Fire* album, produced by Stefan Galfas, featured the highly respected Grim Reaper vocalist Steve Grimmett on backing vocals. Road work in the USA included supports to Dirty Looks, Helloween, Skid Row, and Tuff. *Fire, Fire* failed to ignite, however, and the group were dropped by Geffen. Rumour had it that EZO was to spearhead a new Japanese media concern, Amuse America, but no product was forthcoming, and in July 1990 EZO called it a day.

Lead vocalist Masaki Yamada joined veteran Japanese rockers Loudness in 1992 and Homma followed him two years later. Yamada featured on a succession of Loudness albums from 1992 to 1999 before the classic line-up of that band reformed. Notably, the album *Once And For All* included a re-work of EZO's most popular tune, 'House Of 1000 Pleasures'.

EZO discography

EZO, Victor VDR1343 (Japan), Geffen GHS 24143 (USA) (1987)
  150 USA
FIRE, FIRE, Victor VDR1596 (Japan), Geffen GHS 24230 (USA)
  (1989)

Homma featured on the 2000 Anthem album *Heavy Metal Anthem*. The drummer had also worked on the 1991 Cycle Sluts From Hell album as a session musician. During 2002 Yamada and Homma reunited to found Snake Bites. The EZO legacy remains intact.

LOUDNESS
RESPECT IS DUE – THEY ALMOST CRACKED IT

LOUDNESS, LED BY THE EXTRAORDINARY guitar talent of Akira Takasaki, are the best known of the Japanese heavy metal bands. They issued a run of highly respected albums during the 1980s, with 1985's *Thunder In The East* in particular being regarded as a true classic of the genre. Since dropping their global strategy, Loudness retired to their homeland, where they still occupy an exalted position and regularly deliver high quality metal for the domestic audience.

The band were originally created as a pop act, Lazy, during 1978, where Takasaki went under the stage name of Suzy. But a shift to heavier material prompted a name-change to Loudness in May 1981. The musicians included Takasaki, his fellow Lazy colleague, drummer Munetaka Higuchi, ex-Zephyr bass player Masayoshi Yamashita, and singer Minoru Niihara – the latter enticed away from his role as frontman for Earthshaker.

Wasting no time, Loudness soon put together their debut album offering that August. *The Birthday Eve* was issued as a bilingual Anglo-Japanese effort through Columbia's Denon subsidiary in November 1981. A showcase debut concert, held at the Asakusa International Theater, attracted a sold-out audience of 2,700 fans. Although the album was only released in Japan, word of *The Birthday Eve*'s quality filtered through to the international metal underground.

Their next record, *Devil Soldier*, released in July 1982, propelled Loudness to major status in Japan. However, its reliance on intricate and distinctly Japanese rhythms and tempo changes made it a bewildering listen for most Western ears. January 1983's *The Law Of Devil's Land*, engineered by Daniel McClendon, reverted to the melodic accessibility of the debut and was promoted by a short burst of concert dates in the USA in July 1983 and in Europe the following month.

In the wake of the band's global success, Takasaki recorded a solo album, *Tusk Of Jaguar*, for a 1982 release. Only available in Japan, it sold strongly abroad on import as word of Takasaki's blistering guitar prowess spread. For this record Takasaki utilised his Loudness band-mates: vocalist Minoru Niihara, bassist Masayoshi Yamashita, and drummer Munetaka Higuchi.

Drummer Higuchi also engaged in a swathe of extracurricular endeavours. As well as delivering his solo opus, *Destruction*, he worked alongside singer Hamada Mari on her first brace of albums as The Higuchi Project Team and scored production credits for local act Make-Up. Meanwhile, Takasaki, Yamashita, and Higuchi all sessioned on the first two albums by Honjoh Misako.

Loudness then re-entered the fray with 1984's *Disillusion* album, recorded in the UK in September 1983 with engineer Julian Mendelsohn and distributed by the enterprising Music For Nations label in the UK and Roadrunner for Europe. A double live album, *Live-Loud-Alive*, capitalised on this progress.

The Loudness brand now warranted effective worldwide distribution and the band signed with Atlantic for the USA and Boudisque for Europe. Now perfectly placed, they wisely used this opportunity to launch their tour de force, January 1985's *Thunder In The East*. Produced in Los Angeles the previous August by Max Norman (the esteemed studio man responsible for metal landmarks by

Ozzy Osbourne among many others), *Thunder In The East* muscled its way onto the US *Billboard* charts, peaking at Number 74 and remaining lodged there for 19 weeks. In Japan, the album entered the Top 5.

Keen to tear up the road in the USA, Loudness played support to Mötley Crüe's nationwide tour. This trek made them the first Japanese act ever to perform at the prestigious Madison Square Garden venue in New York City, where they appeared on August 14th 1985.

The winning Norman formula was retained for the follow-up, *Lightning Strikes*, cut in December 1985 and surfacing in March 1986. The Japanese edition had a different title, *Shadows Of War*, giving collectors enough reason to purchase both. *Lightning Strikes* climbed to Number 64 on the *Billboard* chart, and Loudness hooked up with Saxon for UK tour dates to promote the record.

The *Hurricane Eyes* album of August 1987, co-produced by Eddie Kramer and Andy Johns, witnessed the first attempt by their US label to smooth out any perceived cultural differences. This meant that former Angel keyboard player Gregg Giuffria added a few deft touches, while backing vocals came from the Giuffria band's David Glen Eisley and Todd Howarth of Frehley's Comet. The experiment failed, and *Hurricane Eyes* barely scraped into the US Top 200.

May 1988's *Jealousy* mini-album, only released in Japan, involved studio guests Paul Raymond (ex-UFO and Michael Schenker Group) and Frank Dimino (ex-Angel) supplying backing vocals. Yamashita subsequently returned the favour to Raymond on his Paul Raymond Project album.

The group had staked their claim outside Japan but struggled to expand their support beyond the diehards. Niihara's vocal style was thought by many to sound too Japanese to appeal to foreign radio programmers, and Loudness underwent a drastic facelift in December 1988 when the band dumped him. The frontman went on to Ded Chaplain and then Sly with drummer Munetaka Higuchi for four albums.

In his place, Loudness drafted in American vocalist Mike Vescera (ex-Obsession). This revised line-up, renewing ties with former producer Max Norman, bowed in during 1989 with *Soldier Of Fortune*. Keyboards were delegated to Dio man Claude Schnell. A combination of archive tracks and new material, *On The Prowl*, came out in

February 1991, and an EP, *Slap In The Face*, followed that October. The results were kinder to the Western ear but, while US objectives were being pursued, Loudness's change of policy had triggered a downturn in enthusiasm for recent albums back in Japan. Vescera opted out, going on to work with Yngwie Malmsteen, Roland Grapow, and MVP. Another casualty was founding member Masayoshi Yamashita, who took his leave.

By 1992, Akira Takasaki had had enough of the machinations of Atlantic and brought Loudness back to being an all-Japanese band, with Masaki Yamada – previously of Ezo – now handling vocals, and Taiji Sawada, from the successful X and D.T.R., installed on bass guitar. This unit cut the self-produced and decidedly heavyweight *Loudness* album for Warners. The record triumphed, hitting Number 2 in Japan in June 1992. The band gigged across Japan in January 1993, but both Sawada and Higuchi decided to leave shortly afterwards.

With grunge biting hard, even in Japan, Takasaki adopted an unconventional approach for 1994's *Heavy Metal Hippies*. Yamada's Ezo drumming colleague Hirotsugu Homma was requisitioned for recording. Musically, this collection of tracks, engineered by Chris Tsangarides and with Takasaki also adding bass guitar, veered between aggressive, stripped-down thrash and languid sub-grunge, and it was critically dismissed by much of the core fanbase.

The new-look Loudness was debuted at a December 1994 show at Club Citta in Tokyo when Anthem veteran Naoto Shibata marched on stage with his new comrades. A full tour took place in April 1995, spawning another concert recording, October's *Loud'n'Raw*, which included a cover version of Deep Purple's 'Speed King'.

Ex-bassist Sawada came back to the fore in 1995 with the high-profile Kings project in collaboration with Shuichi Aoki of Night Hawks on vocals and guitar, Seikima II guitarist Luke Takamura, and 44 Magnum drummer Satoshi 'Joe' Miyawaki. During 1996, Akira Takasaki issued another solo album, *Respirator*, which found him enjoying the company in the studio of the Mr. Big duo of guitarist Paul Gilbert and drummer Pat Torpey.

For the 1997 album *Ghetto Machine*, released on the Rooms label, Takasaki relocated Loudness to California to record at the famous Berkeley Fantasy Studios. Songwriting and lyrics were aided by Stefan Galfas, known for his work on Ezo's *Fire, Fire* album. Ex-Loudness drummer Munetaka Higuchi issued his *Dreamcastle – Free World* solo set the same year in collaboration with Dokken's Jeff Pilson and an international guest cast. On a roll, Loudness laid down the quick-fire *Dragon* in San Francisco, promoting it with shows across Britain, Holland, Belgium, and Germany in May 1999. Paying homage, the Swedish symphonic death metal act Therion covered 'Crazy Nights' on their *Crowning Of Atlantis* album. Loudness released the *Engine* album in 1999.

Shibata and Homma both contributed to the 2000 Graham Bonnet-fronted Anthem album *Heavy Metal Anthem*, and ex-Loudness frontman Minoru Niihara was fronting X.Y.Z. that same year. However, Niihara and Takasaki buried their differences for 20th anniversary Loudness gigs and a reformation album, March 2001's *Spiritual Canoe*. With Loudness fever at a new high, a DVD, *The Soldier's Just Came Back*, satiated fans, and the group partnered with Canadian thrashers Annihilator for Japanese concerts that September.

During November 2001, a Loudness tribute album arrived in Japan entitled *Rock'n'Roll Crazy Nights*, released consecutively with a brand new Loudness album, *Pandemonium*. Contributors to *Crazy Nights* included Fulltrap, Cloud Nine, Pulling Teeth, Suns Owl, Tommy Heart of Fair Warning on 'Crazy Nights', and Akira Takasaki himself lending a hand to Dev Large's take of 'How Many More Times'. *Pandemonium* live dates were captured for posterity on the *20th Anniversary*

Loudness

LOUDNESS discography

THE BIRTHDAY EVE, Columbia AF-7085 (Japan) (1981)

DEVIL SOLDIER, Columbia AF-7085 (Japan), Roadrunner RR 9896 (Europe) (1982)

THE LAW OF DEVIL'S LAND, Columbia AF-7174 (Japan), Roadrunner RR 9896 (Europe) (1983)

LIVE-LOUD-ALIVE: LOUDNESS IN TOKYO, Columbia AZ-7173/4 (Japan) (1983)

DISILLUSION, Columbia AF-7246 (Japan) (1984)

DISILLUSION (ENGLISH VERSION), Columbia COCA-12143 (Japan), Music For Nations MFN 22 (UK) (1984)

THUNDER IN THE EAST, Columbia COCA-12143 (Japan), Music For Nations MFN 38 (UK) (1985)

SHADOWS OF WAR, Warner Bros. WPCL-249 (Japan) (1986)

LIGHTNING STRIKES, Warner Bros. WPCL-250 (Japan), Atco 790 512-1 (UK / USA) (1986)

'81-'86 LIVE, Warner Bros. WPCL-251/2 (Japan) (1986)

HURRICANE EYES, Warner Bros. WPCL-255 (Japan), Atco 790 619-1 (UK / USA) (1987)

Jealousy, Warner Bros. WPCL-257 (Japan) (1988)

SOLDIER OF FORTUNE, Warner Bros. WPCL-258 (Japan), Atco 7 91283-2 (UK / USA) (1989)

ON THE PROWL, Warner Bros. WPCL-191 (Japan), Atco 7 91637 (UK / USA) (1991)

LOUDEST, Warner Bros. WPCL-556/557 (Japan) (1991)

LOUDNESS, Warner Bros. WPCL-657 (Japan) (1992)

ONCE AND FOR ALL, Warner Bros. WPC6-8037 (Japan) (1994)

HEAVY METAL HIPPIES, Warner Bros. WPC6-8078 (Japan) (1994)

LOUD'N'RAW, Warner Bros. WPC6-8126 (Japan) (1995)

GHETTO MACHINE, Rooms BMCR-7017 (Japan) (1997)

DRAGON, Rooms BMCR-7027 (Japan) (1998)

ENGINE, Rooms BMCR-7035 (Japan), Dream Catcher CRIDE 23 (UK) (1999)

SPIRITUAL CANOE, Columbia COCP-31280 (Japan) (2001)

THE SOLDIER'S JUST CAME BACK (LIVE BEST), Columbia COCP-31421 (Japan) (2001)

PANDEMONIUM, Columbia COCP-31683 (Japan) (2001)

BIOSPHERE, Tokuma Japan Communications TKCA-72403 (Japan) (2002)

LOUDNESS LIVE 2002, Tokuma Japan Communications TKCA-72551 (Japan) (2003)

TERROR, Tokuma Japan Communications TKCA-72627 (Japan) (2003)

ROCK SHOCKS, Tokuma Japan Communications TKCA-72768 (Japan) (2004)

RACING, Tokuma Japan Communications TMCA-72853 (Japan), Drakkar DRAKKAR 087 (Europe) (2004)

The Battleship Musashi, Tokuma Japan Communications TKCA-72891 (Japan) (2005)

Pandemonium Tour DVD, released in February 2002. With a work ethic now fully established, Loudness put out *Biosphere* in September, again backed up by a concert DVD, *Live Biosphere*.

On January 7th 2004, the band released *Terror*, their 18th studio album, and played the gigantic Osaka and Tokyo 'Sonic Mania' festivals with Evanescence and Korn. Naturally, a further DVD, *Live Terror 2004*, ensued.

The October 2004 collection *Rockshocks*, released through Tokuma Japan Communications, was a compilation of re-recorded archive tracks chosen by fans. The following month, a brand new Japanese-language album, *Racing*, was issued by the same label. Loudness released the live DVD *Rock-Shocking The Nation* in March 2005, with the English-language version of *Racing* following in April.

Japanese versions of German metal band Metalium's fifth album, *Demons Of Insanity – Chapter Five*, added a cover version of Loudness's classic 'Rock'n'Roll Crazy Nights' re-billed as 'Heavy Metal Crazy Nights'. Another German heavy metal band, Powergod, cut a cover version of 'Heavy Chains' for inclusion on their *Long Live The Loud – That's Metal Lesson II* album in July 2005. This recording saw Minoru Niihara adding vocals with Rod Gonzales of Die Ärzte on lead guitar. German label Drakkar picked up the *Racing* album for European licence in September.

In a surprise move, Loudness launched a second attack on Western markets and scheduled US dates for 2006, their first appearance on the American continent in many years. Minoru Niihara announced the release of a new solo album, *Ashes To Glory*, issued in February in Japan through Tokuma Japan Communications. Self-produced by Niihara and Wyn Davis, the record featured Dokken and Dio bassist Jeff Pilson plus drummer Vinny Appice of Dio and Black Sabbath.

Footage from the Loudness US dates was released as the *Loudness Liveshocks* DVD in August, and Akira Takasaki issued a solo album, *Nenriki*, in September 2006. With a promise of a further studio album on the horizon, it seems that the band's ambitions are far from fulfilled.

VOW WOW (aka Bow Wow)
WHERE EAST MET WEST

TOKYO'S BOW WOW WERE FORMED IN 1975. They gained prestige not only in their homeland but also throughout Europe during the 1980s under the revised name of Vow Wow, before reverting back to Bow Wow to prioritise their career in their homeland.

The group first performed live in July 1976 with an impromptu gig on a flatbed truck outside a film studio in Tokyo before debuting with the *Bow Wow* album in December 1976 for the Invitation label. Their line-up consisted of vocalist-guitarist Kyoji Yamamoto, vocalist-guitarist Mitsuhiro Saito, bass player Kenji Sano, and drummer Toshihiro Niimi. Niimi had earlier been a member of pop band Dot Dolls. Yamamoto proved himself early on as an accomplished guitarist, developing a tapping technique long before Eddie Van Halen.

High-scale exposure was afforded when Bow Wow opened for Kiss on their 1977 Japanese tour, promoting the second album *Signal Fire*, and for Aerosmith the year after. The third studio album, *Charge*, arrived in December 1977, with the *Guarantee* set following in December 1978. A concert recording released in June 1978, *Super Live*, included Bow Wow's take on Eddy Cochran's 'Summertime Blues'. Kyoji Yamamoto issued his debut solo effort *Horizons* in 1980, an industrious year for him as Bow Wow issued three albums within 12 months – *Glorious Road* in February, *Telephone* in September, and *X Bomber Suite*, an animated movie soundtrack, in November. *Hard Dog* was issued in April 1981.

Spreading their wings internationally, Bow Wow played the Reading Festival in Britain and the world-famous Montreux Jazz Festival in Switzerland in 1982. To capitalise, Roadrunner released the *Asian Volcano* album across Europe. Releases of *Warning From Stardust* appeared in September 1982 on the VAP label (a UK release through Heavy Metal Worldwide followed in April 1983) and *Holy*

BOW WOW / VOW WOW Discography

As BOW WOW:

BOW WOW, Invitation VIH-6009 (Japan) (1976)
SIGNAL FIRE, Invitation VIH-6005 (Japan) (1977)
CHARGE, Invitation VIH-6013 (Japan) (1977)
SUPER LIVE, Invitation VIH-6022 (Japan) (1978)
GUARANTEE, Invitation VIH-6035 (Japan) (1978)
THE BOW WOW, Invitation VIH-6049 (Japan) (1979)
GLORIOUS ROAD, SMS SM25-5040 (Japan) (1980)
TELEPHONE, SMS SM28-5059 (Japan) (1980)
X BOMBER SUITE, SMS SM25-5066 (Japan) (1980)
HARD DOG, SMS SM28-5073 (Japan) (1981)
ASIAN VOLCANO, VAP 30027-28 (Japan), Roadrunner cnu (Europe) (1982)
WARNING FROM STARDUST, VAP 30041-28 (Japan) (1982), Heavy Metal Worldwide HMILP 5 (UK) (1983)
HOLY EXPEDITION, VAP 30113-25 (Japan), Heavy Metal Worldwide HMILP 14 (UK) (1983)

As VOW WOW:

BEAT OF METAL MOTION, EastWorld WTP-80196 (Japan), Roadrunner RR 9827 (Europe) (1984)
CYCLONE, EastWorld WTP-90331 (Japan), East Rock ERLP50 (UK) (1985)

VOW WOW III, EastWorld WTP-90381 (Japan) (1986)
LIVE, EastWorld WTP-90422 (Japan) (1986), Passport PBL 102 (UK) (1987)
HARD ROCK NIGHT, EastWorld CA32-1274 (Japan) (1986)
SHOCKWAVES, Capitol ST-12541 (USA) (1987)
V, EastWorld CA32-1551 (Japan), Arista 258 678 (UK) (1987)
VOW WOW, Heavy Metal Worldwide HMILP 109 (UK) (1988)
VIBE, EastWorld CT32-5321 (Japan) (1989)
HELTER SKELTER, Arista 259 691 (UK) (1989) European version of Japanese *Vibe* album
MOUNTAIN TOP, Toshiba/EMI TOCT-5656 (Japan) (1990)

As BOW WOW:

Bow Wow #0, Oo Records OOCO-3 (Japan) (1995)
BOW WOW #1, Oo Records OOCO-5 (Japan) (1995)
LED BY THE SUN, Oo Records OOCO-20 (Japan) (1996)
Still On Fire, Tears Music TMAC-001 (Japan) (1998)
BACK, EastWest AMCY-2750 (Japan) (1998)
ANCIENT DREAMS, Wildland MARS-8888 (Japan) (1999)
LIVE EXPLOSION 1999, Wildland MARS-8889 (Japan) (1999)
BEYOND, Wildland MARS-8890 (Japan) (2000)
ANOTHER PLACE, Wildland MARS-8891 (Japan) (2001)
WHAT'S GOING ON?, Wildland MARS-8892 (Japan) (2002)
SUPER LIVE 2004, Wildland MARS-8894 (Japan) (2005)
ERA, Wildland MARS-8895 (Japan) (2005)

Expedition was issued through Roadrunner in Europe and Heavy Metal Worldwide in the UK in July 1983. Both records drew significant media praise, initiating considerable fan support in the West. A further Yamamoto solo album, *Electric Circus*, found his reputation growing as interest in Japanese metal began to spread.

Bow Wow morphed into Vow Wow – to avoid confusion with Malcolm McLaren's pop act Bow Wow Wow – and original vocalist Mitsuhiro Saito lost his position. The band were brought back up to strength by former Noiz vocalist Genki Hitomi, plus Sense Of Wonder and Moondancer keyboard player Rei Atsumi, for June 1984's *Beat Of Metal Motion* album.

During their period as Vow Wow, the band released seven albums: *Beat Of Metal Motion* was followed by June 1985's *Cyclone* and January 1986's Tony Platt-produced *Vow Wow III*. Then came July 1986's *Live* (repackaged in Japan with additional material under the title *Hard Rock Night*) and September 1987's *V*, recorded in Ibiza with producer Kit Woolven. Asia and Uriah Heep bassist John Wetton featured on the 'Don't Leave Me Now' single. Next was 1989's *Helter Skelter* – hosting the obvious Beatles cover version and retitled *Vibe* in Japan with a different track listing – plus April 1990's *Mountain Top*. This final outing under the Vow Wow name was produced by Brian Christian and Stan Katayama under the supervision of Bob Ezrin.

The 1988 Heavy Metal Records *Vow Wow* cash-in compilation was actually made up of tracks recorded as Bow Wow. The band relocated to London in 1986, and in down-time, various band-members contributed to Tom Galley's *Phenomena II* concept album. Bassist Kenji Sano departed to make way for the surprise inclusion of ex-Whitesnake and Gary Moore bassist Neil Murray. The band's February and March 1987 British dates witnessed Murray standing a good foot taller than his band-mates.

UK headline dates took place in March 1989, the London Astoria gig on the 15th generating the video *Live In The UK*, prior to German concerts in May backing Warlock. Murray quit in 1990 after the *Helter Skelter* album, and he went on to join Black Sabbath. Vow Wow then folded.

Yamamoto created Wild Flag, while Atsumi joined Revolution Of Red Warriors. Yamamoto then decided to concentrate on the Japanese market almost exclusively and reverted to the previous name of Bow Wow for the August 1995 mini-album *Bow Wow #0*. Two months later, the full-length album *Bow Wow #1* arrived in Japanese stores. The group now featured a much revised line-up, with Yamamoto joined by vocalist Tetsuya Horie, second guitarist Hiroshi Yaegashi, bassist Shotaro Mitsuzono, and drummer Eiji Mitsuzono. The band, back with Saito and with Toshihiro Niimi on drums, put out *Led By The Sun (Bow Wow #2)* in July 1996.

A further change saw the trio of Saito, Yamamoto, and Niimi reforming yet again during 1998, testing the waters with an April live mini-album, *Still On Fire*, through Tears Music in Japan. The subsequent *Back* compilation, released by EastWest, included three new songs.

Bow Wow's energies were renewed and more releases ensued. *Ancient Dreams*, issued in July 1999 on the Mars label, was recorded by singer Kyoji Yamamoto, guitarist Mitsuhiro Saito, bass player Daisuke Kitsuwa, and Toshihiro Niimi on drums. For live work, the band re-recruited Kenji Sano, and this line-up was captured on the concert album *Live Explosion 1999* issued that December. Successive releases in Japan included *Beyond* in December 2000, *Another Place* in July 2001, *What's Going On?* in February 2002, the live *Super Live 2004* in October 2005, and *Era* in November 2005. All of which seems to indicate that Bow Wow are still a viable project.

SOUTH AND CENTRAL AMERICAN METAL

SOUTH

America and Central America have always provided support for heavy metal but, until the internet age, this was territorially restricted due to political barriers and language (many major 1970s and '80s rock artists sang in Spanish and Portuguese). Some countries in the region suffered under dictatorships and military juntas, and for many years the performing of heavy metal across South America was highly restricted.

High-ranking Western acts always fared well on the South American festival circuit and also found enthusiastic recognition in Mexico. Sales of records by Black Sabbath, Deep Purple, Judas Priest, Baron Rojo, and Iron Maiden inspired waves of domestic bands that achieved high status but remained unknown to the outside world.

Courtesy of Angra, Soulfly, and Krisiun, Brazil is now a recognised world leader, but Sepultura's success really put the country on the metal map, opening the doors to other bands. Brazil greatly benefited from pioneering acts such as Dorsal Atlantica, Volcano, Karisma, Harppia, Viper, Hangar, Thoten, and Patrulha Do Espaco, and Belo Horizonte's Cogumelo label gave a start to many Brazilian metal acts.

Bands such as Riff (led by the late scene hero Pappo), Kamikaze, V8, Hermertica, Horcas, and Rata Blanca paved the way in Argentina. With the advent of power, death, and black metal, the "Nueva Ola De Metal Argentino" evolved and the country went on to produce hundreds of bands.

Mexico is also supplying the world with a variety of interesting acts, such as The Legion Of Hetheria and Elfonia. Its tradition lies in bands such as Cristal Y Acero, Luzbel, and the highly industrious and staunchly traditionalist thrash act Transmetal.

ANGRA
METALLIC PROG

RANKING ALONGSIDE SEPULTURA AS Brazil's biggest metal export, São Paulo's Angra – for many years fronted by erstwhile Viper vocalist André Matos – perform complex progressive rock with a definite metal touch. At first this complexity caused the European media to dub the band the "metal Yes".

Angra were named after an ancient fire goddess, Angra Mainyu, and convened in 1991 when Matos was joined by the ex-Spitfire duo of guitarist Rafael Bittencourt and drummer Marco Antunes, plus former Firefox bassist Luís Mariutti and second guitar player Kiko Loureiro. With Viper already a well known band in Brazil, thanks to the Matos-fronted *Soldiers Of Sunrise* and *Theatre Of Fate* albums, a great degree of attention was focused on the new combo.

Angra debuted with the grandiose, eight-song *Reaching Horizons* demo, recorded at Guidon Studios in São Paulo during July 1992. Later that year, the debut Angra sessions were issued in Europe as one of the first releases by the fledgling Limb Music Products label (LMP) in Germany. Fortunately for the band, LMP went on to become one of Europe's premier power metal labels. Four of the six songs from the debut EP made the subsequent *Angels Cry* album, recorded for another German label, Rising Sun Productions, and the two remaining tracks surfaced as bonus cuts on various licensed versions of future albums and EPs.

Angels Cry, which boasted an adventurous cover version of Kate Bush's 'Wuthering Heights' and an even more daring penchant for metal-samba, was recorded at Gamma Ray guitarist Kai Hansen's studios in Hamburg, Germany. Hansen and his Gamma Ray colleague Dirk Schlächter contributed solos, as did Heaven's Gate man Sascha Paeth. Studio drums were supplied by Alex Holzwarth of Sieges Even, except for 'Wuthering Heights', which featured Thomas Nack of Gamma Ray. Shortly before the recording, Antunes made way for new drummer Ricardo Confessori.

Angels Cry was issued in Brazil in 1993 and was a runaway success, shifting a spectacular 100,000 copies in Japan alone. The videos for 'Time' and 'Carry On' enjoyed heavy rotation on Brazilian MTV for many months, and Angra dominated polls in the leading Brazilian *Rock Brigade* magazine, scooping awards for Best New Band, Best Album, Best Singer, Best Album Cover, and Best Keyboard Player. In Japan, a special EP was released in 1994, *Evil Warning*, consisting of remixed versions of 'Evil Warning', 'Angels Cry', 'Carry On', and 'Wuthering Heights'. It was licensed to Europe through Dream Circle (and CNR Music for France).

The following year was similarly successful for Angra, who opened for AC/DC and formed part of the billing of the inaugural Brazilian 'Monsters Of Rock' festival, sharing the stage with Kiss, Black Sabbath, and Slayer. Brazilian touring was equally rewarding: the band sold out the enormous São Paulo Aeroanta venue for two consecutive nights. In May 1995, the band hit the road in Europe.

They capitalised on their achievements with 1996's *Holy Land*, an ambitious concept involving choirs and orchestration, once more produced by Sascha Paeth and Charlie Bauerfiend. Although the bulk of the record was recorded in Germany in the summer of 1995 across three studios (in Hamburg, Hannover and Wolfsburg), they returned to Djembe Studios in São Paulo that autumn to add a range of embellishments involving traditional instrumentation, such as congas, djembe, timbales, claves, and repinique, all scored by Tuto Ferraz. Operatic vocals came courtesy of soprano Celeste Gattai, with a choir from the Farrambamba Vocal Group. The band even managed to squeeze Ben Bishcoff and his didgeridoo into the mix for good measure.

Despite this arsenal of potential diversions, *Holy Land* – centred on the ten-minute epic 'Carolina IV' – actually ratcheted up the metal content compared to the debut. The tranquil introduction, choirs, and birdsong proved to be a deceptive opener for a record so loaded with speed, power, and aggression, prompting reviewers worldwide to laud the album as perhaps the pinnacle of the prog-metal genre so far.

Holy Land saw increased sales on mainland Europe and in Brazil. The Japanese JVC Victor release included the traditional Japanese bonus track, in this case 'Queen Of The Night'. A mini-album of the same year, *Freedom Call* – recorded At Be Bop Studios and Grooveria Eletro-Acústica Studios in São Paulo that May – included a cover of Judas Priest's

'Painkiller'. The concert recording *Holy Live*, recorded at the Aquaboulevard-Salle Provençale venue in Paris on November 15th 1996, took the band into 1997.

Fireworks in 1998 was produced by veteran studio hand Chris Tsangarides and landed on the French charts at an impressive Number 41. The ethnic content had been scaled back as Angra delivered a back-to-basics approach.

A lengthy world tour opened up with Brazilian headline shows before the band's debut Japanese shows and then an appearance at the Buenos Aires 'Monsters Of Rock' festival. In 1999, North America woke up to the Angra phenomenon when Century Media released the band's back catalogue.

In 2000, Angra bowed in for European shows with Italian act Time Machine in support: at a Milan gig, Lucretia Records – Angra's Italian distributor – gave out 1,000 free CDs with two tracks by each band. Co-headlining dates with Stratovarius followed. Also in 1998 came the issue of *The Holy Box*, a lavish limited-edition set released by Lucretia including exclusive acoustic tracks.

After seven years of stability, the band split in two in mid 2000, with Matos, Mariutti, and Confessori all bailing out. Matos reportedly began work in Germany on a solo project, Virgo. Later announcements reported that the entire trio were working with guitar player Hugo Mariutti and Blezqi Zatsaz keyboard player Fabio Riberio under a new band name, Shaman. In this enforced hiatus, Loureiro took time out to produce the debut album of his countrymen Thoten.

As 2001 began, it emerged that Loureiro and Bittencourt were endeavouring to persevere as Angra, drafting in former Mitrium, Opium, and Symbols vocalist Eduardo Falaschi, and drummer Aquiles Priester from the Paul DiAnno band. A latter recruit was keyboard player Gunther Werno, who had credits with Norwegian act Conception. Meanwhile, Angra bassist Felipe Andreoli joined Karma in 2001.

Angra's resurrection album, *Rebirth*, won over fans in consummate style, and by February 2002 the album had shifted over 100,000 copies. European headline dates commenced in Nancy, France on February 26th. A mini-album, *Hunters And Prey*, arrived in May 2002, including acoustic takes plus a cover version of 'Mama' by Genesis. Live dates found the band in Japan in June and appearances at the 'Rock Machine' festival in Spain, 'Wacken Open Air' in Germany, and the 'ProgPower' festival in Atlanta, Georgia. They also claimed the honour of being the very first South American metal band to play Taiwan, performing at a show in Taipei on June 14th.

Loureiro sessioned on the 2002 Blezqi Zatsaz album *The Tide Turns*, paradoxically the project of Shaman keyboard player Fabio Riberio. Angra had their version of 'Kashmir' included on the Locomotive Music Led Zeppelin tribute album *The Metal Zeppelin – The Music Remains The Same*. Falaschi came to attention outside his main band, portraying the Sultan Oddyfer character for Daniele Liverani's Genius album *In Search Of The Little Prince* in 2004. Fellow Sao Paulo act Tropa De Shock's 2004 album *Survivors* included a Rafael Bittencourt solo on the track 'The Love Of Angels', while Loureiro donated his talents to Atlantida's *Painted Reality* opus. Loureiro and Andreoli also guested on the Avantgard demo *The Sound Of Reason*.

Angra commenced the recording of a new album at Mosh Studios in São Paulo in January 2004. Pink Cream 69's Dennis Ward manned the board, and guest vocalists included Gamma Ray's Kai Hansen, Edenbridge's Sabine Edelsbacher, and Blind Guardian's Hansi Kürsch. Shortly after these sessions, Loureiro recorded his debut solo album, *No Gravity*, for Replica Records, produced once again by Dennis Ward at House Of Audio Studios in Germany during April and May. Studio guests included Rage and Artension drummer Mike Terrana, and Andreoli.

By July, Angra had wrapped up *Temple Of Shadows*, revealing that the record was a conceptual piece based around a character known as The

ANGRA discography

ANGELS CRY, Rising Sun 35897 (Europe) (1993)
HOLY LAND, Rising Sun 34601-422 (Europe) (1996)
Freedom Call, Rising Sun 35885-3 (Europe) (1996)
HOLY LIVE, Lucretia LU 97017-2 (Europe) (1997)
FIREWORKS, Steamhammer SPV 085-18482 (Europe), Century Media CM 7969-2 (USA) (1998)
REBIRTH, Steamhammer SPV 085-72782 (Europe), Steamhammer 72782 (USA) (2001)
Hunters And Prey, Steamhammer SPV 076-74302 CDE (Europe), Steamhammer 74302 (USA) (2002)
REBIRTH WORLD TOUR – LIVE IN SÃO PAULO, Lucretia ATRCD 0014 (Europe) (2003)
TEMPLE OF SHADOWS, Steamhammer SPV 085-99162 (Europe), Steamhammer 99162 (USA) (2004)
AURORA CONSURGEONS, Steamhammer SPV 085-99172 (Europe), Steamhammer 97972 (USA) (2006)

Shadow Hunter and describing it as "a saga of a crusader knight that ends up disputing the expansionist ideals of the Catholic Church in the 11th century". The record sold over 20,000 copies in its first week on sale in Japan.

The band then headlined shows in Southern Europe throughout Spain, Italy, and France in February 2005. They made their debut in the UK at the Mean Fiddler in London, supported by Dragonforce, before uniting with leading Finnish act Nightwish for Japanese dates in March.

In November, Loureiro appeared live with Renato Tribuzy at two gigs at São Paulo's Credicard Hall in an all-star band including Masterplan guitarist Roland Grapow, Primal Fear's Mat Sinner and Ralph Scheepers, Iron Maiden's Bruce Dickinson, and Roy Z. That same month, Angra celebrated their 14th anniversary with a gig in São Paulo and were joined onstage by Kai Hansen.

In early 2006, it was revealed that Fabio Laguna and ex-Angra singer André Matos had recorded guest sessions for the Eyes Of Shiva album *Deep*. Meanwhile, Aquiles Priester sessioned on Paul DiAnno's *The Living Dead* album and Eduardo Falaschi worked up his Almah solo project. Concurrently, three Angra players announced their participation in an instrumental project album under the title Freakeys. Drummer Aquiles Priester, bass player Felipe Andreoli, and keyboard player Fábio Laguna established an alliance with guitarist Eduardo Martinez of Hangar and Leviaethan.

In June 2006, Priester laid down drum tracks in Germany for a new Angra album, *Aurora Consurgens*, under the supervision of producer Dennis Ward. The band then utilised Way Musique Studios and LCM Studios in São Paulo to finish the album, which arrived in October. Their unique position on their domestic music scene should enable them to take the next step with ease.

DR. SIN
ACCOMPLISHED BRAZILIANS

THIS RENOWNED BRAZILIAN HEAVY metal outfit centres on the talents of ex-A Chave Do Sol and Supla guitarist Eduardo Ardanuy with the Busic brothers, bassist Andria and drummer Ivan. The Busics had journeyed through acts such as Platina in 1985, Cherokee in 1987, and Wander Taffo in 1988, and featured on the 1991 Taffo album *Rosa Branca*.

Dr. Sin's eponymous debut album, recorded for Warner Music in America with the noted producer Stefan Galfas at the helm, arrived in

DR. SIN discography

DR. SIN, Warner Bros. 993622-1 (Brazil) (1993)
BRUTAL, Warner Bros. cnu (1995)
INSINITY, Warner Bros. cnu (1997)
Live In Brazil, Warner Bros. cnu (1998)
ALIVE, Warner Bros. cnu (1999)
DR. SIN II, Warner Bros. cnu (2000)
SHADOWS OF LIGHT, Metal Mayhem Music cnu (2001)
LISTEN TO THE DOCTORS, Trinity C cnu (2005)

1993, followed by *Brutal* in 1995, also laid down in the USA, this time with producer Johnny Montagnese. The band supported a whole stream of visiting acts, including L7, Nirvana, Black Sabbath, AC/DC, Gillan, and Kiss.

They were quick to carve out a reputation as one of the most accomplished Brazilian bands, opening shows for artists such as Dream Theater, Scorpions, and Dio in 1997. They expanded to a quartet with the guest introduction of ex-Obsession, Loudness, and Yngwie Malmsteen singer Mike Vescera, and the American newcomer produced their third album, *Insinity*.

The following year saw the band guesting for Yngwie Malmsteen, and they landed the honour of having their live set, *Alive*, included as a double package with the Swedish star's own *Live In Brazil*. Other gigs included dates with Quiet Riot. *Insinity* was granted a Japanese release through the Pony Canyon label with a completely revised track listing.

The *Brutal* album was reissued in Japan during 1996, retitled *Silent Scream*. Ardanuy took time out to undertake the Tritone project in collusion with Frank Solari and Sergio Buss, and in 2000 Vescera renewed his relationship with the band, drafted in as a full-time member for the *Dr. Sin II* album (retitled *Shadows Of Light* for an American release in 2001).

Andria Busic joined Angra and then progressive metal band Karma, but decamped in August 2001. Ardanuy added guest sessions to the 2002 Blezqi Zatsaz project album, *The Tide Turns*, for Shaman keyboard player Fabio Riberio. He also featured on Mike Vescera's MVP album *The Altar*.

Dr. Sin conceived a unique approach for their December 2005 album, *Listen To The Doctors*. It consisted entirely of cover versions of famous tracks that included the word doctor, such as 'Calling Dr. Love' by Kiss, 'Rock'n'Roll Doctor' by Black Sabbath, 'Doctor Doctor' by UFO, 'I Don't Need No Doctor' by Humble Pie, 'Dr. Rock' by Motörhead, 'Dr. Feelgood' by Mötley Crüe, 'Just What The Doctor Ordered' by Ted Nugent, and others. Despite this slightly novel approach, the band have judged their fanbase perfectly and should move from strength to strength in the coming months and years.

KRISIUN
BREATHTAKING DEATH METAL PRECISION

THE BRAZILIAN DEATH METAL band Krisiun (Latin for 'seers of abomination') come from Ijuí, Rio Grande de Sul and are a family affair, consisting of three brothers: vocalist-bassist Alex Camargo (who uses his mother's maiden name), guitarist Moyses Kolesne, and drummer Max Kolesne. The band first recorded in 1991, for the *Evil Age* demo, and *The Plague* followed in September 1992. During this phase they operated as a quartet, with Altemir Souza on second guitar. Maurício Nogueira then briefly occupied this post before moving on to Torture Squad and In Hell.

A further session, the Tchelo Martins-produced *Curse Of The Evil One*, was split with Violent Hate and appeared in January the following year, and a release in October, laid down at Anonimato Record Studios in São

Paulo, was a shared EP with Germany's Harmony Dies for Rottenness Records. This led to the *Unmerciful Order* album on Dynamo Records in March 1994 (on which the trio are all credited with the surname Kolesne).

Krisiun debuted in Europe with August 1995's *Black Force Domain*. The tracks were cut at Army Studios in São Paulo, with production credits going to Sergio Sakamoto. Germany's G.U.N. label reissued *Black Force Domain* in 1997. German dates in the winter of 1997 saw the band opening on a bill comprising Richthofen, Dimmu Borgir, and headliners Kreator.

Apocalyptic Revelation emerged in August 1998 – the first Krisiun recording outside Brazil, made at Musiclab Studios in Germany – with Simon Fuhrmann in control of the board. The band made a significant impact on European shores in 1998 on tour with Napalm Death, Cradle Of Filth, and Borknagar before embarking on a series of headline dates with support act Soilwork. February 1999 saw them on their inaugural North American tour alongside Incantation and Angel Corpse.

The band switched to Century Media Records, reissuing *Black Force Domain* again, adding bonus tracks in the form of cover versions of Sodom's 'Nuclear Winter' and a vastly accelerated take on Kreator's 'Total Death'. Their March 2000 album *Conquerors Of Armageddon* was produced by Morbid Angel's Eric Rutan at Stage One Studio in Büchne, Germany. Limited-edition variants added a bonus cut, 'Seas Of Slime'.

The band toured with Satyricon, Immortal, and Angel Corpse in America. Angel Corpse disintegrated mid-tour, with the departure of mainman Pete Helmkamp, so Krisiun obligingly loaned them Camargo so that they could complete the dates. There was no let-up for Krisiun, who then engaged in European touring on a package with Old Man's Child, Gorgoroth, and Soul Reaper.

The Tchelo Martin-produced *Ageless Venomous* arrived in 2001, prompting a full scale global tour for the band, who performed in Europe, North America, South America, Russia, and Japan. By now they had risen to headline status for the 'Thrash 'Em All' festivals in Poland and Russia, topping a bill of Vader, Lux Occulta, and Behemoth. November 2001 had the band on the road in the UK and Ireland for seven shows with Cannibal Corpse and Kreator, this union transferring to Europe before hooking up with Marduk, Dark Funeral, Nile, and Vomitory to participate in the hugely

KRISIUN discography

Krisiun / Harmony Dies, Rottenness cnu (1993) split EP with Harmony Dies

Curse Of The Evil One, Rock Machine cnu (1993) split EP with Violent Hatred

UNMERCIFUL ORDER, Dynamo cnu (1994)

BLACK FORCE DOMAIN, G.U.N. GUN 147 (Europe) (1995)

APOCALYPTIC REVELATION, G.U.N. GUN 163 (Europe) (1998)

CONQUERORS OF ARMAGEDDON, Century Media CM 77259-2 (Europe), Century Media CM 7959-2 (USA) (2000)

AGELESS VENOMOUS, Century Media CM 77367-2 (Europe), Century Media CM 8067-2 (USA) (2001)

WORKS OF CARNAGE, Century Media CM 77467-2 (Europe), Century Media CM 8167-2 (USA) (2003)

BLOODSHED, Century Media CM 77567-2 (Europe), Century Media CM 8267-2 (USA) (2004)

ASSASSINATION, Century Media CM 77667-2 (Europe), Century Media CM 7959-2 (USA) (2006)

successful, sold-out 'X-Mass' festivals. News arrived in 2002 that former Krisiun guitarist Altemir Souza had been killed in a motorbike accident.

The band co-headlined a run of dates with Vader across mainland Europe from late August 2002, supported by Decapitated and Prejudice. *Works Of Carnage*, including a rendition of Venom's 'In League With Satan' and produced by Obliveon guitarist Pierre Rémillard, arrived in October 2003, and the band announced touring plans for the USA in November with Hate Eternal, Deicide, and Cattle Decapitation.

They resumed live work in 2004, playing support to Morbid Angel's extensive European dates. Further European shows that November, the 'Clash Of Demigods' tour, featured Krisiun with Behemoth, Ragnarok, and Incantation. The *Bloodshed* album, released in October, consisted of eight new recordings alongside tracks from the rare *Unmerciful Order* album of 1994.

Krisiun toured with Hate Eternal, Incantation, Into Eternity, and All Shall Perish for US gigs in June, after which the band entered Bühne's Stage One Studios with erstwhile Holy Moses guitar player Andy Classen as producer to craft a new album, *Assassination*. European dates were announced for August, including Prague's 'Brutal Assault' festival, Germany's 'Party San Open Air' event, and the 'Mountains Of Death' festival in Switzerland.

Assassination arrived in February 2006. Krisiun then scheduled April 2006 US tour dates with Morbid Angel, Canadians Despised Icon, and Behemoth. US dates for September and October saw the band hooking up with Six Feet Under, Decapitated, and Abysmal Dawn, while live work in December across Europe saw them hooking up with Six Feet Under, Gorefest, Cataract, and Darzamat for the 'X-Mass' festivals. They remain one of the hardest-hitting bands to emerge from the continent.

RATA BLANCA
METAL RODENTS

A REVERED NAME ON THE SOUTH AMERICAN metal circuit, Rata Blanca from Argentina are led by former V8 guitarist Walter Giardino and have inspired countless other bands in their wake. They enjoy major status across the Latin American world and Iberia, and have recently made strong inroads into Spanish-speaking areas of the United States, where they perform regularly.

Rata Blanca ('White Rat') recorded a 1985 demo commissioned by Giardino in 1985, originally intended as a vehicle to establish ties with the UK market. The tape was recorded with vocalist Rodolfo Cava, bass player Yulie Ruth, and drummer Gustavo Rowek. However, Giardino was so inspired by the final result that the planned relocation to Britain was put on hold. Some two years after their inception, the band made their live debut at the Buenos Aires Luz Y Fuerza theatre on August 15th 1987.

Rata Blanca convened as a full band for an eponymous debut album in 1988. Joining Giardino was lead vocalist Saúl Blanch, second guitarist Sergio Berdichevsky, bassist Guillermo Sánchez, and drummer Gustavo Rowek. The album was released through major label Polygram Discos. It included the singles 'El Sueño De La Gitana' and 'Chico Callejero' and was a huge success. Despite this huge leap forward, Blanch bowed out and Rata Blanca entered their second stage with the induction of singer Adrián Barilari and keyboard player Hugo Bistolfi.

The band's second album was released in 1990, *Magos, Espadas Y Rosas* ('Wizards, Swords, And Roses'), was promoted by support slots with Ian Gillan. The album generated high praise and surpassed the million sales mark worldwide. Their third album appeared the following year: *Guerrero Del Arco Iris* was named in honour of Greenpeace's Rainbow Warrior ship and the band debuted it live in front of over 30,000 fans at a single concert at Velez Sarsfield Stadium (still holding the record as the biggest ever gig for a local band).

The group undertook live work across all of South America, Mexico, and even Los Angeles, performing at the famous Whisky A Go-Go club. Back in Buenos Aires, the band recorded over three nights at the Opera Theatre with a full chamber orchestra for a groundbreaking live album. Live dates further afield had them trekking across Portugal and Spain, the first Argentine band to do so, recording their fourth album there, *El Libro Oculto* ('The Secret Book').

With the close of the world tour, Bistolfi and Barilari decided to leave. The erstwhile Rata Blanca duo founded Alianza, issuing three albums – *Sueños Del Mundo* in 1993, *Alianza* in 1997, and *Huellas* in 1999. Rata Blanca persevered, pulling in Mario Ian, previously with Hellion and Alakran, on vocals, and Javier Retamozo on keyboards.

A fifth album, the exceptionally heavy *Entre El Cielo Y El Infierno* ('Between Heaven And Hell'), was recorded in the midst of a 1994 world tour. The band performed at the Brazilian 'Monsters Of Rock' festival in São Paolo, sharing the stage with international heavyweights Ozzy Osbourne, Alice Cooper, and Megadeth before an audience of 100,000. That live album recorded in 1992, *En Vivo En Buenos Aires*, was finally issued in Argentina.

With popularity waning in the band's homeland, Mario Ian made his exit in 1996, and Gabriel Marian was appointed as frontman for the *Rata*

RATA BLANCA discography

RATA BLANCA, PolyGram Discos S.A. 836596 (1988)

MAGOS, ESPADAS Y ROSAS, PolyGram Discos S.A. cnu (1990)

GUERRERO DEL ARCO IRIS, PolyGram Discos S.A. 27560 (1991)

EL LIBRO OCULTO, Ariola 74321 163982 (1993)

ENTRE EL CIELO Y EL INFIERNO, Ariola cnu (1994)

EN VIVO EN BUENOS AIRES, PolyGram Discos S.A. 3154629 (1996)

RATA BLANCA VII, Ariola 691051 (1997)

GRANDES CANCIONES, Tocka Discos cnu (2000)

EL CAMINO DEL FUEGO, Delanuca 4510120 (2002)

PODER VIVO, Delanuca 4526329 (2003)

LA LLAVE DE LA PUERTA SECRETA, EMI 0724347753824 (2005)

Blanca VII album. The band were in a fractious state by now: it was public knowledge that other band members were keen to decamp but had been persuaded to stay on for the sessions. The album received little promotion, and in April 1998 Giardino signalled the end of the band.

Gustavo Rowek and Sergio Berdichevsky assembled a fresh heavy metal act, Nativo, going on to release two albums – *Consumo* in 1999 and *Futuro* in 2001. Giardino too founded a new endeavour, Temple. He toured Argentina during 1999 and then put together a new band with former Rata Blanca singer Adrián Barilari as guest singer. Eventually, Guillermo Sánchez came in on bass and, resuming the name Rata Blanca, the band played in Bolivia. After they returned to Argentina, Hugo Bistolfi returned to the fold.

In 2001, a gathering of South American metal talent paid homage with the tribute album *La Leyenda Continúa*. Artists such as Azeroth, Beto Vasquez Infinity, Humanimal, and Rosacruz were included. Both Adrián Barilari and Walter Giardino made a special appearance, uniting with members of premier league Finnish bands Nightwish and Stratovarius – guitarist Emppu Vuorinen, bassist Sami Vänskä, keyboard player Jens Johansson, and drummer Jukka Nevalainen – on the track 'La Leyenda Del Hada Y El Mago'.

The new Rata Blanca, with Fernando Scacella on drums, toured South America and Mexico to enthusiastic response. A 2000 compilation, *Grandes Canciones*, was backed by further gigs, including shows in Spain. A new studio album, *El Camino Del Fuego*, was delivered in June 2002. Singer Adrián Barilari, billed simply as Barilari, released a debut solo album in mid 2003.

Coinciding with Black Sabbath's return to the live stage for the summer 2004 'Ozzfest', the Argentine label Blackstar issued a tribute album, *Sabbath Crosses: Tribute To Black Sabbath*, and the collection featured a take on 'No Stranger To Love' from Rata Blanca, featuring ex-Deep Purple and Black Sabbath vocalist Glenn Hughes on vocals. Barilari donated a Spanish-language version of 'Heaven And Hell'.

Promoting the 2005 album *La Llave De La Puerta Secreta* ('The Key To The Secret Door'), Rata Blanca put in another high-profile hometown gig in September, opening for Whitesnake and Judas Priest. Argentinian first editions of *La Llave* were highly prized as they were cased in a custom-built box with a metal key to unlock the CD. The band's fans appreciate this level of quality and will no doubt continue to support them into the future.

SEPULTURA
KINGS OF SOUTH AMERICA?

THE UNDISPUTED LEADING BRAZILIAN band on the international metal scene, Sepultura (meaning 'sepulchre' or 'grave') were created in Belo Horizonte in 1983, with their earliest albums timed perfectly to benefit from the thrash explosion of that decade. Although the act's first albums were far from sensational, the musicians looked the part and their professed influences of British punk and American metal stood them in good stead until the breakthrough *Arise* album.

Sepultura took on stereotypical death metal noms de guerre for the early part of their career: singer-rhythm guitarist Max Cavalera was known as Max Possessed, guitarist Jairo Guedez as Tormentor, Max's drumming brother Igor as Igor Skull Crusher, and Paulo Xisto Pinto Junior as Destructor.

Having played their first concert in 1984 at the Barroliche Club in Belo Horizonte – during which Igor Cavalera's 'drum kit' consisted of a single snare drum, floor tom, and one cymbal – the band were on their way. Paulo Junior was inducted for a gig at the Santa Teresa Ideal Clube in March 1985, and the world first learned of Sepultura later that year when

they released a split album, *Bestial Devastation*, through a local record store, Cogumelo Records, shared with local outfit Overdose.

These songs were committed to an 8-track recorder at JG Studios in Belo Horizonte that August, self-produced by the band with engineer João Guimarães at the board. Opening with a lycanthropic slurred growl billed as 'The Curse', Sepultura's debut would have proven remarkable if it had been launched in Europe or Scandinavia. Hellishly raw, as dictated by the band's youth and inexperience, *Bestial Devastation* offered primal death metal with, arguably, the world's very first example of the now-famed blastbeat drum technique, on 'Antichrist'. Despite the studio restrictions, the neutering of Max's guttural rasp with echo, and the guitars being completely out of tune, *Bestial Devastation* has stood the test of time.

Reported domestic sales of some 15,000 copies were deemed a success and both bands were offered an extension on their contract. A full-length album, *Morbid Visions*, arrived in 1985. Eduardo Santos and Zé 'Heavy' Luiz now guided the teens in the confines of Estudio Vice Versa, Belo Horizonte. Given seven days in which to work, Sepultura drew from both death metal and thrash metal; again, the production values were haphazard and the band's influences plain, making the whole album contrived yet honest. However, its ferocity could not be denied. Still very much an underground act, Sepultura had their inaugural US release courtesy of New Renaissance Records, the imprint owned by Hellion singer Ann Boleyn, which issued *Morbid Visions* the following year.

Jairo Guedez was superseded after *Morbid Visions* by erstwhile Pestilence man Andreas Kisser. After impressing at an audition by jamming on Kreator and Destruction songs, the new guitarist first stepped onstage with the band in May 1987 in Caruaru, Pernambuco. Kisser had risen through the ranks of local amateur metal bands such as Sphinx, an outfit that took on covers by acts such as Slayer and Judas Priest before injecting original material and renaming themselves Pestilence.

Jairo initially announced that he no longer had any interest in metal but emerged in 1989 as a member of thrashers The Mist on their *Phantasmagoria* album. This band had other Sepultura connections, too, with vocalist Vladimir Korg – previously with Chakal – credited for the lyrics to Sepultura's 'To The Wall', and bassist Marcelo Diaz was a Sepultura roadie.

Utilising JG Studios once again in August 1987, Sepultura together with engineer Tasro Senra crafted the *Schizophrenia* album. The title was apt, as the band laid down a deluge of riffage, culminating in the titanic 'From The Past Comes The Storm', with multiple tempo changes and a volley of riffs. Violinist Paolo Gordo and keyboard player Henrique of Poliso Alto added a little colour to the thrash barrage. Shark Records took on the German licence.

The US-based journalists Borivoj Krgin and Don Kaye were enthusiastic supporters and arranged meetings between Max Cavalera and record labels in New York. According to Krgin, Cavalera disguised himself as a Pan-Am employee in order to make the flight from Brazil. He arrived in North America armed with a bag full of *Schizophrenia* cassettes. After numerous rejections, Monte Connor at Roadrunner took a chance on the band.

Beneath The Remains in 1989 signalled the band's first move away from the standard thrash template. Laid down in nine overnight sessions in December 1988 at Nas Nuvens Studio in Rio de Janeiro, the end result was mixed in Florida by Scott Burns. Importantly, the band's international exposure had affected their overall sound: this was particularly noticeable in the lyrical department, which often had been received with hilarity due to the band's poor command of English.

The lyrics to 'Stronger Than Hate' were contributed by Atheist's Kelly Shaefer, who alongside Obituary's John Tardy plus Scott Latour and Francis Howard of Incubus also donated backing vocals. As an entrance onto the global scene – Roadrunner were now distributing the band's

product in the USA – *Beneath The Remains* was a mighty statement of intent, a caustic thrashfest viewed by many as the creative pinnacle of their career to date.

The band's first international live work came in September 1989, opening for Sodom in Vienna, Austria before tackling gigs in the USA and Mexico, headlining the East Coast with Faith Or Fear as openers. Their biggest concert to date was held on June 4th 1990 in front of 26,000 fans at the Dutch 'Dynamo' festival. It was here that they met Sacred Reich manager Gloria Bujnowski, who took over their management.

By 1991, Sepultura had become national heroes in Brazil, putting in a worthy performance at the 'Rock In Rio' festival at the Maracana Stadium in front of 50,000 people and sharing the stage with Guns N'Roses, Judas Priest, and Megadeth. To commemorate this occasion, the unprecedented decision was taken to rush-release a limited edition 'rough mix' version of their forthcoming album *Arise* (which has since become a highly collectable item). The band then played a free outdoor concert in São Paulo in Charles Muller Square, drawing over 40,000 fans. Tragically, an audience member was murdered, and this event made the band a target for the Brazilian authorities.

Arise was released in March 1991 and it took Sepultura into new realms. The cover artwork was by sci-fi artist Michael Whelan, depicting the mutated deity Yog-Sothoth. Another new inclusion on the visual front was the now world-famous bone 'S' logo, executed by old friend Bozó (aka Pedro Amorim), singer of Overdose. For the recording, the band had travelled to Tampa, Florida, to record at the fabled Morrisound studios with producer Scott Burns. Singles drawn from the album included 'Third World Chaos', 'Under Siege (Regnum Irae)', and 'Dead Embryonic Cells'.

UK headline shows in June saw Sacred Reich as a strong support act and, spreading their reach, the group put in shows in Australia and Indonesia, playing to over 100,000 fans at just two concerts. With interest rising in Europe, Germany's Shark label repackaged *Morbid Visions* as a split album with Metal Conquest. Roadrunner reissued *Schizophrenia*, remastering the entire set and adding a newly-recorded version of 'Troops Of Doom' for good measure.

On March 1st 1992 the band – complete with Andreas Kisser sporting retaining rods in his broken arm – put in a pre-European tour 'secret' gig, billed as Third World Posse, at the small Amersham Arms pub in London. The band also figured on the landmark Black Sabbath reunion gigs at Costa Mesa, California, on November 14th and 15th.

Chaos AD in 1993 saw Sepultura stripping down their sound to punk basics, gearing down into proto-groove metal. The band's lyrical stance now became more openly political, including a collaboration with Jello Biafra of the Dead Kennedys on the sub-two-minute speed-fest 'Biotech Is Godzilla', and faithfully covering New Model Army's 'The Hunt'. Other poignant statements included 'Kaiowas', an acoustic lament for a native tribe who committed mass suicide, and 'Manifest', concerning a police massacre at the Pavilhao Nove prison in São Paulo. Versions of *Chaos AD* also came with a bonus track, 'Polícia', originally by Titãs.

America was now coming under Sepultura's spell, and *Chaos AD*, helped by the singles 'Territory' (with a promotional video shot in Israel), 'Refuse/Resist', and 'Slave New World', broke into the *Billboard* charts. UK shows in December saw Halifax's Paradise Lost as opening act, and the tour took Sepultura as far as Russia.

In 1994, Max Cavalera and Fudge Tunnel's Alex Newport formed Nailbomb as a side project. The resulting album, *Point Blank*, saw participation from Kisser, Igor Cavalera, and Fear Factory's Dino Cazares. Demos for the next Sepultura album, *Roots*, were recorded by Newport.

The band took the pioneering step of recording tracks deep in the Brazilian jungle with the Xavante Indians. The resulting album, issued in February 1996 and produced by Ross Robinson, took the band into completely new areas of operation, as they offered the rock world an album of unrelenting metal infused with their own cultural heritage. *Roots*, closing with an unlisted 13-minute epic 'Canyon Jam', proved to be their biggest seller to date, even entering the Top 5 in Britain. Sepultura channelled their ferocity away from fast riffing and into heavy, slab-like chords in songs such as 'Dictatorshit' and 'Endangered Species', and the street anthem 'Roots Bloody Roots' was punctuated by native drumming passages. A remarkable, groundbreaking claymation video for

SEPULTURA discography

BESTIAL DEVASTATION, Cogumelo COG 001 (1985) split album
with Overdose
MORBID VISIONS, Cogumelo COG 002 (Brazil), New Renaissance
NRCD 43 (USA) (1986)
SCHIZOPHRENIA, Cogumelo COG 009 (Brazil), RC RCD 9511
(USA) (1987)
BENEATH THE REMAINS, Roadrunner RO 9511-1 (Europe), RC
RCD 9511 (USA) (1989)
ARISE, Roadracer RO 9328-2 (Europe), RC RCD 9328 (USA) (1990)
40 UK
CHAOS A.D., Roadrunner RR 8859-2 (Europe / USA) (1993)
11 UK, 32 USA
ROOTS, Roadrunner RR 8900-2 (Europe / USA) (1995)
4 UK, 27 USA
BLOOD-ROOTED, Roadrunner RR 8821-2 (Europe / USA) (1997)
AGAINST, Roadrunner RR 8700-2 (Europe / USA) (1998) **40 UK**
NATION, Roadrunner RR 8560-2 (Europe / USA) (2001)
UNDER A PALE GREY SKY, Roadrunner RR 8436-2 (Europe / USA)
(2002)
Revulosongs, Sepultura 828765321525 (Brazil) (2003)
REVULOSONGS, JVC Victor VICP-62084 (Japan) (2003)
ROORBACK, Steamhammer SPV 092-74830 (Europe),
Steamhammer 74830 (USA) (2003)
LIVE IN SÃO PAULO, Steamhammer 087-99522 (Europe),
Steamhammer 99522 (USA) (2005)
DANTE XXI, Steamhammer SPV 087-99812 (Europe), Steamhammer
99812 (USA) (2006)

'Ratamahatta' is a music-TV staple to this day. The digipack option was boosted by 'Chaos B.C.', a cover of Black Sabbath's 'Symptom Of The Universe', and a live take of 'Kaiowas'. Another elaborate wooden box package included a video, necklace, and candles.

With *Roots* having carved out a position as one of the most important metal releases in recent years, the band were at the top of their game. However, in late 1996 fans and media were shocked to learn of Max Cavalera's sudden departure. Media speculation about the reasons behind this split was rife, fuelled by many personal grievances from band members. Whatever the truth of any allegations, the divisions within the band were so strong they even forced two brothers, the Cavaleras, into opposite camps. Max Cavalera fronted Sepultura for the last time on December 16th 1996 at the London Brixton Academy.

Cavalera returned to the fore in quick fashion, touting new combo Soulfly, not only taking producer Ross Robinson and manager Gloria Bujnowski with him but also retaining his Roadrunner deal and recruiting former Sepultura roadie Marcello D. Rapp on bass guitar.

The 1997 filler album *Blood-Rooted* gave fans more than the usual interim product before Sepultura could regroup and before Max announced Soulfly. It included a barrage of live tracks, the song 'Mine' with Faith No More's Mike Patton on vocals, and 'Lookaway' with Korn's Jonathan Davis as well as Patton again. Other rare cuts included the band's covers of Celtic Frost's 'Procreation (Of The Wicked)', the Dead Kennedys' 'Drug Me', Bob Marley's 'War', and Sabbath's 'Symptom Of The Universe'. Another release of interest that same year was the re-mastered *Beneath The Remains*, adding a cover version of 'A Hora E A Vez Do Cabelo Nascer' by Os Mutantes.

With the media's attention focused on Cavalera's successful new Soulfly venture for a lengthy period, the spotlight returned to Sepultura

only when it was announced that Cavalera's position had finally been filled. The new recruit was the towering figure of Derrick Green, formerly of Alpha Jerk, Overfiend, and Outface.

The Howard Benson-produced *Against* continued Sepultura's tradition of tribal themes with the inclusion of the Japanese Kodo drummers on 'Kamaitachi'. A reworking of the track, retitled 'Diary Of A Drug Fiend', with vocals from Faith No More's Mike Patton, was removed from the album at the last minute after fears of a sales backlash due to its lyrical content. The album did include a rare appearance outside Metallica for Jason Newsted, appearing as guitarist and guest vocalist on 'Hatred Aside'. The band tested the waters with American shows, billed as Troops Of Doom. Sepultura then got to grips with promoting *Against* with a US support slot to Slayer.

The single from the album, 'Choke', featured versions of the Bad Brains tracks 'Gene Machine' and 'Don't Bother Me'. The band also contributed a track to the 1999 Bad Brains tribute album *Never Give In.* Meanwhile, Green turned up as a guest on Integrity 2000's self-titled album the same year. In April 2000, Swedish label Black Sun released a Sepultura tribute, *Sepulchral Feast*, which included artists such as Sacramentum, Swordmaster, Deathwitch, Gardenian, Children Of Bodom, Lord Belial, Defleshed, The Crown, and Impious.

The band returned in 2001 with the Steve Evetts-produced *Nation* album. Recorded in Brazil, the record had diverse guest performances from Jello Biafra on 'Politricks', reggae artist Dr. Israel, the Finnish cello quartet Apocalyptica on 'Valtio', and Hatebreed's Jamey Jasta. Unfortunately for Sepultura, the curiosity value was beginning to wear thin and sales of *Nation* were far from encouraging.

March 2002 brought the news that drummer Igor Cavalera was pursuing a side venture with Biohazard guitarist Billy Graziadei and Brazilian DJ Patife. Other outside activities found Cavalera and guitarist Andreas Kisser credited with material for a soundtrack album entitled *No Coracao Dos Deuses*. Originally cut in 1999, the recordings were made available in Europe by Mascot. The material included a guest appearance from Patton on 'Procura O Cara'. Meanwhile, Max Cavalera's last concert with Sepultura was slated for a September 2002 release under the title *Under A Pale Grey Sky*.

The band's Brazilian dates in the summer were topped off by a landmark performance at São José Dos Campos in front of a 10,000 capacity crowd. Billy Graziadei joined the band onstage for renditions of Motörhead's 'Iron Fist' and the Titãs track 'Polícia'. Another mammoth gig in São Paulo, on June 29th, featured more than a dozen high-ranking Brazilian acts – including Korzus, Necromancia, and Claustrofobia – paying homage to Sepultura by performing over 50 of their songs. Back in the spotlight, ex-Sepultura man Jairo Guedez announced his return to the fray as bassist with a new act entitled Eminence.

The band returned with an exclusive Brazilian EP of cover versions. Among the tracks were Hellhammer's 'Messiah', Public Enemy's 'Black Steel In The Hour Of Chaos' with guesting rappers Sabotage and DJ Ze Gonzales, Jane's Addiction's 'Mountain Song', Debo's 'Mongoloid', Exodus' thrash classic 'Piranha', and 'Bullet The Blue Sky' by U2. The video for the last track scooped the Brazilian MTV award for Best Direction Of Photography. In September, Kisser took time out to perform live on the Brazilian club circuit with a new blues-based solo venture. The band then took a further diversion by contributing music to the Brazilian movie *Lisbela E O Prisioneiro* with the Ze Ramalhos cover 'Dança Das Borboletas'.

Sepultura scheduled *Roorback* as the title for a 2003 album, recorded in São Paulo with producer Steve Evetts. The band opened a co-headline US tour with Canadians Voivod in San Francisco, California, on April 18th. Unfortunately, *Roorback* underperformed in stores and sales appeared to be on a downward spiral. With both Sepultura and Soulfly now struggling, industry conjecture began to strongly suggest that a reunion was inevitable.

A collaboration between Mike Patton and Sepultura, 'The Waste', was included on the soundtrack to the horror movie *Freddy Vs. Jason* in August, the track having been recorded during 1998's *Against* sessions. Sepultura then united with British rock stalwarts Deep Purple and The Hellacopters for four major 'Kaiser Music Festival' Brazilian shows in September.

Andreas Kisser cut a cover version of John Lennon's anthem 'Give Peace A Chance' for inclusion on a Brazilian tribute album titled *De Uma Chance A Paz* in January 2004. Later that year, Igor Cavalera performed double duty for Sepultura's autumn Brazilian gigs, and under the pseudonym of El Covero, Cavalera also performed with the tour's support band Massacration. Massacration then performed a set of Death and Control Denied covers in tribute to Chuck Schuldiner at the September 18th Bonded By Blood Thrash Fest in São Paulo. The event, headlined by Exodus, saw a strong billing of Korzus, Andralls, Torture Squad, and Mad Dragzter. Kisser also found time to donate a guitar solo to 'A Farewell To Kings' for the Magna Carta 2005 Rush tribute album, *Subdivisions*.

In recognition of the band's status in their homeland, a São Paulo event on September 25th, 'Sepulfest', was naturally headlined by Sepultura with a strong support cast consisting of Ratos De Porão, Nacão Zumbi, Claustrofobia, and Massacration. Sepultura returned to Europe in November and December, lending support to Motörhead.

A new album, cut at Trauma Studios in São Paulo and titled *Dante XXI*, was a conceptual piece based upon Dante's *Divine Comedy*. During the sessions, the group also laid down cover versions of Judas Priest's 'Screaming For Vengeance' and Sick Of It All's 'Scratching The Surface'.

Kisser contracted a deal with Holland's Mascot label to release his first solo album, *Hubris 1 & 2*, recorded at A Voz Do Brasil studios in São Paulo. A notable stop on Sepultura's 2005 tour schedule came on March 25th when the band, alongside The Darkness and Machine Head, performed in Dubai in the United Arab Emirates, marking the first such occasion for a Western metal band in the Gulf. Support came from local bands Nervecell and Juliana Down.

On April 3rd, the band filmed a hometown São Paulo gig for commercial DVD release. Highlights included the group performing 'Troops Of Doom' with Jairo Guedez and both 'Reza' and 'Biotech Is Godzilla' with Ratos De Porão's João Gordo. A brief round of Mexican dates featured the Viper veteran Guilherme Martin stepping in as temporary drummer when Igor was unable to attend.

The following month saw a special anniversary reissue of *Roots*, complete with a bonus disc of demos, remixes, and alternative versions. Meanwhile, Igor Cavalera collaborated with Brooklyn "death rapper" Necro, guesting on the album *Circle Of Tyrants*. Sepultura put out the CD/DVD package *Live In São Paulo* through SPV in November. On December 15th, Kisser joined the Roadrunner United conglomerate at the New York Nokia Theater for an all-star metal evening. Sepultura tracks played in the set included 'Refuse/Resist' and 'Roots Bloody Roots' fronted by Machine Head's Rob Flynn alongside Anthrax guitarist Scott Ian, ex-Fear Factory guitarist Dino Cazares, and Slipknot drummer Joey Jordison.

Founder member Igor Cavalera, having just become a father to a baby boy, announced his temporary withdrawal on January 13th 2006 in order to attend to his family life. Roy Mayorga (Thorn, Crisis, Soulfly) stepped in to cover the Sepultura drum duties. That same month, Kisser guested on a cover version of Slayer's 'War Ensemble' by Silent Civilian.

Promoting *Dante XXI*, the band opened for In Flames at European shows throughout April and May. In mid June, Igor Cavalera officially announced his departure, citing "artistic incompatibility" with his bandmates and stating his belief that "the group's current formation no longer lives up to my expectations as a musician and a person". Fans were intrigued by a previous public comment from Soulfly's Max Cavalera, who

indicated that a Sepultura reunion was unfeasible without his brother's involvement. Pointedly, Roadrunner announced a September compilation, *The Best Of Sepultura*, that only included material featuring Max. Meanwhile, Igor announced plans to forge a fresh band, Necro, and informed the media in Brazil that because the Cavalera siblings were no longer involved with the band in its current formation, the Sepultura name could only legally be used until the close of the *Dante XXI* touring cycle. All indicators appeared to be pointing towards a reunion of the classic line-up.

Despite this gathering momentum, in October the band were scheduled to unite with Stratovarius, Nevermore, Black Label Society, Saxon, After Forever, Primal Fear, and Gotthard for the 'Live n'Louder' festivals across Mexico, Argentina, and Brazil. Fans are agog for the next move.

TRANSMETAL
LATINO EXTREMITY

MEXICO CITY'S TRANSMETAL CENTRE on the Partida brothers – guitarist Juan, bassist Lorenzo, and drummer Javier – and are among the biggest Mexican metal acts. Founded in January 1987, they have stuck to their thrash/speed metal stance over 20 Spanish-language albums. Although they are a major concert draw in Mexico, the band's appeal is almost solely limited to Latin America. They have performed in the United States, El Salvador, Colombia, Ecuador, Peru, and Bolivia.

On their formation, Transmetal were fronted by vocalist Alberto Pimentel, who featured on the 1988 debut *Muerto En La Cruz*, produced by Dark Angel's Eric Meyer, and the follow-up EP *Desear Un Funeral*. In 1990, Pimentel departed to found Leprossy. Alejandro González of Illusion

---

TRANSMETAL discography

MUERTO EN LA CRUZ, Denver DCD 3058 (1988)
Desear Un Funeral, Denver (1989)
SEPELIO EN EL MAR, Denver DCD 3039 (1989)
ZONA MUERTA, Denver DCD 3061 (1990)
AMANECER EN EL MAUSELEO, Denver DCD 3060 (1992)
BURIAL AT SEA, Grindcore International 89804-2 (1992)
EN CONCIERTO VOL. 1, Denver DCD 3062 (1992)
EN CONCIERTO VOL. 2, Denver DCD 3063 (1992)
EL INFIERNO DE DANTE, Denver DCD 3045 (1993)
DANTE'S INFERNO, Denver DCD 3046 (1993) English version
CRÓNICAS DE DOLOR, Denver DCD 3049 (1994)
VELOZ Y DEVASTADOR METAL, Denver DCD 3095 (1995)
MÉXICO BÁRBARO, Denver DSD 6005 (1996)
EL LLAMADO DE LA HEMBRA, Denver DSD 6110 (1996)
LAS ALAS DEL EMPERADOR, Denver DSD 6025 (1998)
XIII ANOS EN VIVO PRIMERA PARTE, Denver DSD 6078 (1999)
XIII ANOS EN VIVO SEGUNDA PARTE, Denver DSD 6079 (1999)
DE BAJO DE LOS CIELOS PURPURA, Denver DSD 6106 (2000)
TRISTEZA DE LUCIFER, Denver DSD 6186 (2001)
EL AMOR SUPREMO, Denver DSD 6258 (2002)
LO PODRIDO CORONA LA INMENSIDAD, Denver DSD 6277 (2003)
17 YEARS DOWN IN HELL, Denver DSD-6307 (2004)
TEMPLE DE ACERO, Denver DSD 6305 (2005)
EL DESPERTAR DE LA ADVERSIDAD, Denver cnu (2006)

(and subsequently frontman for Arkhe) filled the vacancy before Juan Carlos Camarena took the role of second guitarist. The band featured on the high-profile 'New Titans Over Mexico' tour in 1991 with Sepultura, Sacred Reich, and Napalm Death. In May 1992, they appeared as part of the 'Mexican Mosh' festival alongside Sick Of It All, Deicide, and Nuclear Assault.

In 1992 the latest two recruits departed, and Pimental resumed activities with the band on a stand-in basis. A successful Mexican tour during October found them headlining over Mortuary and Inquisidor before a further slot at the March 1993 'Mexican Mosh' festival, this time sharing honours with Overkill, Kreator, and Monstrosity, among others.

The following year, Transmetal represented Mexico at the June 1994 'Monstruos De Rock' gathering in Spain, together with fellow native acts Angels De Infierno and Rata Blanca. Pimentel opted out yet again to form another version of Leprosy (spelt with one S on this occasion) with Ramses guitarist Julio Marquez and ex-Inquisidor drummer Felipe Chacon.

The band took on board the esteemed former Luzbel and Huizar frontman Arturo Huizar as their lead vocalist, but by February 1998 two members of Panic – vocalist Mauricio Torres and guitarist Eric Towers (aka Ernesto Torres) – joined the band for the album Las Alas Del Emperador. Transmetal's show at the Adolph Lopez Mateos de Tlalnepantla Arena in Mexico City in July 1999 was recorded and subsequently put out as two separate live discs, XIII Años... En Vivo - Primera Parte and XIII Años... En Vivo - Segunda Parte. Meanwhile, Lorenzo Partida and ex-Transmetal vocalist Alejandro González created the side project Ultratumba.

Transmetal took a novel approach of recording tracks for two albums at once, Tristeza De Lucifer and De Bajo De Los Cielos Púrpura, at sessions in Hammond, Indiana, with producer Mike Sheffield. On the release of Tristeza during 2001, the group toured South America. Shows in Ecuador, in Bogota, Manizales, and Calí in Colombia, in Arequipa in Peru, and in La Paz and Santa Cruz in Bolivia were all firsts for a Mexican metal band. De Bajo De Los Cielos Púrpura arrived in July 2000, prompting a 30-date run of shows across the USA. The same year, Muerto En La Cruz was reissued on CD with four extra tracks. The band's legacy was honoured in 2001 with the delivery of no fewer than two tribute albums: Milicia Infernal... Tributo A Transmetal and the live Milicia Infernal... Tributo A Transmetal (En Vivo), both on the Denver label. Bands paying homage included Luzbel, Panic, Disgorge, Ricter, Allusion, Ultratumba, Domain, Ira, A.N.I.M.A.L., Leprycorn, and Mechanical Chaos.

Transmetal returned in September 2002 with the experimental El Amor Supremo, their first album to incorporate keyboards. It was recorded at Studio 880 in San Pablo, California, with production duties going to the Death, Testament, and Konkhra-credited guitarist James Murphy. The band's December 2003 album, Lo Podrido Corona La Inmensidad, featured keyboard contributions from Erick Fuentes Quintana and a guest guitar solo on the track 'Creador De La Amargura' from Murphy.

In 2004 the band tackled an album of cover versions, including Scorpions' 'The Zoo', Candlemass's 'At The Gallows End', Celtic Frost's 'Return To The Eve' and 'Dethroned Emperor', Accept's 'Balls To The Wall', AC/DC's 'Back In Black' and 'Let Me Put My Love Into You', Sodom's 'Remember The Fallen', Black Sabbath's 'Evil Woman', Death's 'Evil Death', Uriah Heep's 'Free And Easy', and Twisted Sister's 'The Kids Are Back'.

A notable compilation issued in June of the same year, 17 Years Down In Hell, re-worked the tracks from the previous two albums, El Amor Supremo and Lo Podrido Corona La Inmensidad, in English language. An uncredited track, a newly recorded version of 'Aborrecer Al Forence', had Mauricio Torres on vocals. The new studio album, El Despertar De La Adversidad, arrived in February 2006, on which they capitalised with a run of Mexican shows, gigs in Honduras, El Salvador, Guatemala, and spot US dates. The band were back in the recording studio before the end of the year, and their fans were awaiting the results as this book went to press.

VIPER
FAST AS A SNAKE

VIPER WERE A HEAVILY EUROPEAN-INFLUENCED speed metal act created in São Paulo during 1985 by teenage brothers Yves and Pit Passarell (guitar and bass respectively). They announced their presence with the four-song Killara Sword demo, which soon snagged a deal with the domestic Rock Brigade label. The band also included the equally youthful vocalist André Matos, second guitar player Felipe Machado, and drummer Cassio Audi. Promoting the debut Soldiers Of Sunrise album in 1987, they supported Motörhead, before pulling in former Warkings guitarist Rodrigo Alves for gigs that year and into 1988. Alves later departed to reform Warkings and perform in Merlin and Blasfemia before going solo.

For 1989's Theatre Of Fate, Viper switched drummers, bringing in Sergio Facci. However, Guilherme Martin played drums on tour before the position was finally settled with the arrival of Renato Graccia. At this juncture, Matos split away from the band, apparently over a conflict of interest in stylistic direction. The vocalist founded the immensely successful progressive metal act Angra. Pit Passarell took over the vocals as Viper trimmed down to a quartet.

By now, Viper's reputation had spread internationally, with Theatre Of Fate licensed to Japan in 1991 and in Europe through Germany's Massacre label the following year. Viper scored a Brazilian radio hit in 1992 with 'Rebel Maniac'.

Evolution in 1992 and the follow-up EP Vipera Sapiens were released in Europe under the billing of Viper Brazil, due to the presence of a German outfit with a prior claim to the name. The 1994 Live – Maniacs In Japan album included a cover version of Queen's 'We Will Rock You' alongside a take of The Ramones' 'I Wanna Be Sedated'. Coma Rage, released in 1995, saw strong hardcore elements introduced into the band's sound. However, they then took a major diversion with 1996's Tem Pra Todo Mundo, including violin, trombones, saxophone, cello, and trumpet.

Yves Passarell played live with former vocalist André Matos in 2001 as Matos debuted his post-Angra outfit, Shaman. Alves resurfaced in 2004 with a new combo, Rygel, an assemblage of scene veterans including Paulo Sérgio of Push, Karol Silvestre (formerly of Harvest Moon), and Danilo Lopes of Ceremonya (and, previously, Eterna).

Viper returned to live action in mid 2005 with a line-up of vocalist Ricardo Bocci, guitarists Felipe Machado and Val Santos, bassist Pit Passarell, and Guilherme Martin on drums. This formation cut the demo Do It All Again, fresh material enhanced by a reworking of their early favourite, 'Knights Of Destruction'. The band have successfully wrested themselves away from the Matos legacy and remain a major force on the Brazilian scene.

VIPER discography

SOLDIERS OF SUNRISE, Rock Brigade RBR 0060 (Brazil) (1987)
THEATRE OF FATE, Massacre MASSCD 002 (Europe) (1989)
EVOLUTION, Massacre MASSCD 009 (Europe) (1992)
Viperia Sapiens, JVC Victor VICP-2072 (Japan) (1993)
LIVE – MANIACS IN JAPAN, Eldorado 478012 (1994)
COMA RAGE, Roadrunner RR 8964-2 (Europe / USA) (1995)
TEM PRA TODO MUNDI, Castle Brasil cnu (Brazil) (1996)

EUROPEAN METAL

THE EUROPEAN

metal scene was overshadowed for many years by a succession of high-profile bands from the UK and the USA, but it was the thrash metal movement that first placed a global focus on Europe – and, in particular, on Germany. Prior to thrash, successful metal in Europe had been confined to Trust from France and Baron Rojo from Spain.

The Iberian appreciation of metal has always been healthy, with acts such as Ramp and Tarantula from Portugal and Spanish bands Baron Rojo, Obus, Mago De Oz, Panzer, and Muro all performing well. However, only Baron Rojo attempted English lyrics: the other acts were more or less limited to the Hispanic countries because they used only Spanish lyrics.

France enjoyed a robust metal scene in the 1980s, with Killer, Nightmare, Vulcain, and Sortilege, but language limitations severely stifled any attempts to break beyond the home country. The Netherlands managed to create a presence, first with traditional rock such as Vandenberg and Picture, and then techno-thrash with Asphyx and Pestilence. Nowadays, Holland's forte is female-fronted gothic metal.

Greece and Italy have always held metal in high esteem, with international bands regularly charting high in Greece. In fact, it is the only country in the world where Judas Priest have claimed a Number 1 album. Domestic bands lean towards symphonic and 'true' metal. Italy too, despite a staunch bastion of black and death acts, follows suit in this tendency towards the epic.

Eastern Europe is thriving with metal. The former East Germany teemed with bands and, with the surge in popularity of the extreme end of the spectrum, the Czech Republic, Poland, Hungary, Rumania, and Bulgaria developed a reputation for producing some of the very sickest death metal and grindcore.

Continental Europe now easily outstrips the USA for the enthusiasm and weight of numbers of its fans. This is illustrated by the fanaticism displayed at famous events such as Germany's 'Wacken Open Air' festival – a must-experience event for any self-respecting purchaser of this book – and at the 'Rock Am Ring', 'Rock Im Park', and 'Rock Hard' festivals, as well as the longstanding Dutch 'Dynamo' event, the same country's 'Aardschok Dag', and Italy's 'Gods Of Metal'.

ASPHYX
EUROPEAN DEATH METAL PIONEERS

ASPHYX WERE A LEADING FORCE ON THE European death metal scene, forging a path for a swathe of bands to follow. They date back to 1987, when the band was formed in Oldenzaal, Netherlands, by drummer Bob Bagchus, with Tonny Brookhuis on guitar and Chuck (aka Christian Colli) handling vocals and bass. The fledgling band took their cue from international pioneers, at first performing cover versions such as Death's 'Infernal Death', Celtic Frost's 'Nocturnal Fear', and Mayhem's 'Necrolust'. They soon got to grips with composing original material, swiftly cutting the *Carnage Remains* rehearsal demo and then the *Enter The Domain* tape, recorded December 1987.

They replaced Colli briefly with Benno Kremers and then Theo Loomans the following year, and expanded from a trio to a quartet in March 1989 with the introduction of second guitarist Eric Daniels. Their second tape, *Crush The Cenotaph*, was issued in July, gaining the band favour across the international underground and selling over 5,000 copies in the process. Meanwhile, maintaining their roots, Bagchus and Loomans set up the Hellhammer tribute band Evoker. A third effort, 1989's two-track 7-inch 'Mutilating Process', gained distribution through Nuclear Blast subdivision Gore Records. Brookhuis left the band after these sessions. In 1990, Asphyx's fame was such that a gig in Hardenberg saw Paradise Lost as support act.

Frontman Martin van Drunen split from Dutch techno-thrashers Pestilence in late 1990, due to personality clashes within the band. Shortly after his departure, he hooked up with Asphyx, replacing Loomans. The revised band went into the studio to record a projected debut album for the UK-based CMFT Productions, planned to be titled *Embrace The Death*. However, due to the record company's financial problems, these tapes never saw a commercial release, but unofficial tapes soon circulated among the metal underground, bolstering the band's standing.

Asphyx's second attempt at a debut album, *The Rack*, was released in April 1991, recorded on a minimal budget in a deliberate attempt to achieve a primitive sound. Worldwide sales approaching 30,000 copies were boosted by a European tour alongside Entombed, proving that they had chosen the right path.

Crush The Cenotaph, issued during June 1992, was a mini-album produced by Waldemar Sorychta containing reworkings of pre-van Drunen material and live tracks. Another album, *Last One On Earth*, laid down at Harrows Studios, arrived that October. Live work included an extensive European tour with Benediction and Bolt Thrower. (Van Drunen joined the latter in 1994. He also made time outside the Asphyx camp to guest as vocalist for Swedish death metal band Comecon, appearing on their 1993 album *Converging Conspiracies*.)

A revised line-up emerged, consisting of new vocalist-bassist Ron van Pol, guitarist Eric Daniels, and drummer Sander van Hoof, and they recorded an eponymous album in July 1994, crafted at Stage One Studio in Bühne, Germany with Andy Classen of Holy Moses at the board. Further ructions hit the Asphyx line-up in 1995 as Daniels briefly joined

Soulburn invariably included such Asphyx classics as 'Abomination Echoes', 'Vermin', and 'The Sickening Dwell' in their live set, and once rehearsals got underway for a further album, the band members realised that the new material was sounding very like Asphyx – and duly reverted to their former name. A 2000 album, *On The Wings Of Inferno*, recorded at Harrow Production Studios in Losser, found Asphyx back to their more familiar name as a mark of respect to Loomans. However, after its release, Asphyx announced their retirement.

Martin van Drunen resurfaced in mid 2002 with his new act, Death By Dawn, on the European live circuit. Early 2005 saw him and erstwhile Pestilence bassist Jeroen Paul Thesseling collaborating with King Locust guitarist Niels Drieënhuizen in a new band, Projekt Tabun. The trio entered Studio Het Lab in Schaarsbergen to put down initial recordings before van Drunen pulled out, citing "personal reasons".

With demand for Asphyx product still unsatiated, From Beyond Productions released a limited-edition vinyl variant of *Embrace The Death* in June 2005. The reissue added liner notes from drummer Bagchus and new artwork. Asphyx, it seems, will retain a loyal fanbase for years to come.

ATROCITY
FROM DEATH METAL TO THE CHARTS

ATROCITY BEGAN LIFE AS A RAUCOUS death metal band, but a drastic change in musical style launched them into the national German charts with their 1980s covers album, *Werk 80*. Founded in Ludwigsburg, Germany in 1985 as Instigator, the band's line-up consisted of erstwhile Ripper vocalist Alex Krull, guitarists Mathias Röderer and Frank Knodel, bassist René Tometschek, and Gernot Winkler on drums. Renamed Atrocity, the band issued the October 1988 five-track demo *Instigators*. The band signed to Nuclear Blast and, enlisting Belching Beet drummer Michael Schwarz, released the *Blue Blood* EP in 1989. The cover artwork presented problems, as Atrocity's original intention to depict Lady Diana and Prince Charles splattered in blood was vetoed by the printing company. Undaunted, the band photocopied the jackets by hand.

The follow-up came with the Scott Burns-produced *Hallucinations* album, recorded in Florida the following year and clad in distinctive H.R. Giger-painted artwork. For these sessions, Atrocity realigned their personnel, inducting guitarist Richard Scharf and bassist Oliver Klasen. The departing Tometschek subsequently formed Mighty Decibel, who released an EP, *Relieve The Distress*.

Atrocity toured Europe as support to Carcass in 1990, Sodom in 1991, and Deicide in 1992. That year, the *Todessehnsucht* album was delivered for Roadrunner, with the band branching out into grand orchestral arrangements. Without the consent of the band, Roadrunner issued the record in North America under the translated title *Longing For Death*. The 1993 European 'Todessehnsucht Über Deutschland' headline tour saw Dark Millennium as support. Proposed US dates with Death were cancelled.

In 1994, the band drafted Markus Knapp to substitute for Klasen and signed to Massacre for the *Blut* album. In keeping with the vampire theme of the project, Krull and band-mates travelled to Transylvania to imbibe some creative energies. Although the production of *Blut* was criticised by the group, the promotion – including video clips shot for 'Calling The Rain' and 'Miss Directed' – was of high quality. They supported Obituary on a British tour, following a cancellation by Eyehategod, and put in shows alongside Pitchshifter, Crematory, and Hate Squad. In early 1995, the band replaced Scharf and Markus Knapp with, respectively, guitarist Torsten Bauer (previously with Enslaved, Battle Angel, Stradiveri, and Thrash Massacre) and bassist Chris Lukhamp (Scarab, White Krauts, Corpus Christi).

Not content to rest on their laurels, Atrocity experimented bravely for

Eternal Solstice; original vocalist Theo Loomans returned to contribute bass and vocals to the *God Cries* album of May 1996. The *Embrace The Death* sessions finally found a release in 1996 through Century Media, with extra tracks from the *Mutilating Process* 7-inch single.

Despite the constant line-up changes, Asphyx continued to build on their popularity in the death metal market with consistent album sales. The band by now consisted of Daniels, Bagchus, and erstwhile Pentacle vocalist-bassist Wannes Gubbels, and they changed names to Soulburn for 1998's *Feeding On Angels* album. Loomans was killed the same year: the musician had been in his car, hit by a train while stationary across rail tracks, and an open verdict was recorded.

ASPHYX discography

Mutilating Process, Nuclear Blast cnu (Europe) (1990)

THE RACK, Century Media 84 9716-2 (Europe), Century Media CM 7716-2 (USA) (1991)

Crush The Cenotaph, Century Media 79 9723-2 (Europe), Century Media CM 7723-2 (USA) (1992)

LAST ONE ON EARTH, Century Media 84 9734-2 (Europe), Century Media CM 7734-2 (USA) (1992)

ASPHYX, Century Media 77063-2 (Europe), Century Media CM 7763-2 (USA) (1994)

GOD CRIES, Century Media 77117-2 (Europe), Century Media CM 7817-2 (USA) (1996)

EMBRACE THE DEATH, Century Media 77141-2 (Europe) (1996)

ON THE WINGS OF INFERNO, Century Media 77263-2 (Europe) (2000)

ATROCITY discography

Blue Blood, Nuclear Blast NB 23 (Europe) (1989)
HALLUCINATIONS, Nuclear Blast NB 038 (Europe) (1990)
TODESSEHNSUCHT, Roadrunner RR 9128-2 (Europe) (1992)
BLUT, Massacre MAS CD 0033 (Europe) (1994)
DIE LIEBE, Swan Lake MAS CD 069 (Europe) (1995)
CALLING THE RAIN, Swan Lake MAS CD071 (Europe) (1995)
WILLENSKRAFT, Massacre MAS CD099 (Europe) (1996)
WERK 80, Massacre MAS CD0138 (Europe) (1997)
GEMINI, Motor Music 549 315-2 (Europe) (2000)
ATLANTIS, Napalm NPR 143 (Europe) (2004)

their two 1995 releases: *Calling The Rain* was graced with an ethnic lead vocal from Alex's sister Yasmin, while *Die Liebe* was a joint project with electronic band Das Ich.

To promote the *Willenskraft* album, the band toured Germany on a package tour with strong support from In Flames, Heavenwood, and Totenmond. Strangely, they began to attract media attention for their supposedly far-right political imagery, but Atrocity made their feelings clear on this issue at the 'Wacken Open Air' festival in 1996 by symbolically destroyed a giant swastika during 'Willenskraft', encouraged by applause from thousands of fans. Meanwhile, drummer Michael Schwarz busied himself in a variety of extracurricular bands, including mincecore act Belching Beet, crustcore merchants Accion Mutante, and gothic veterans Umbra Et Imago.

Experimenting further still, the 1997 single 'Shout' was Atrocity's interpretation of Tears For Fears' hit song, and included a version of D.A.F.'s 'Verschwende Deine Jugend'. 'Shout' proved to be a taster for *Werk 80*, a collection of cover versions by pop artists such as O.M.D., David Bowie, Duran Duran, Frankie Goes To Hollywood, Human League, and Soft Cell. The album's impact was sustained with a later Festivals Edition, which added three extra tracks – a cover of D.A.F.'s 'Das Letzte Mal', 'Die Deutschmaschine', and 'Verschwende Deine Jugend'. The band's tenacity finally paid rewards when they achieved their first chart hit – *Werk 80* entered the German chart at Number 33, doubtless helped along by a tasteful advertising campaign featuring the two models chosen for the single and album artwork. The momentum was maintained by the 33-track retrospective *Non Plus Ultra*, compiling the band's newer hits plus videos and archive and rare material.

The band delved into covers once more during 2000, releasing a version of Simon & Garfunkel's 'The Sound Of Silence' as a single. The accompanying album, *Gemini*, was issued in two different versions. Variants with a red sleeve included the wartime marching song 'Lili Marlene' in English, while the blue-covered versions offered the track in German.

In September 2002, Atrocity hooked up with In Extremo for a short run of dates in Mexico. During the recording of tracks for a new studio album slated for 2003, the group – bringing in former From Thy Ashes and Teabag guitarist Sebastian Schult – contributed a cover of The Sisters Of Mercy's 'More' for a tribute album.

Guitarist Thorsten Bauer rejoined in April 2003 before sessioning on the Erben Der Schöpfung Twilight album *Twilight*, produced by Krull with Martin Schmidt on session drums. In July, Krull married his long-term girlfriend, Theatre Of Tragedy singer Liv Kristine Espenæs. This marital union spilled over into a creative force with the announcement of a brand new band, Leaves' Eyes, which had the pair founding a fresh venture with members of Atrocity.

The 2004 Atrocity album *Atlantis*, recorded at Mastersound Studio in Fellbach, Germany under the production guidance of Krull, emerged in

April. A single, 'Cold Black Days', preceded it. The group were engaged in a search for a new drummer in early October when Martin Schmidt announced his intention to leave. Extensive tour dates saw Atrocity hooking up with Leaves' Eyes, Battlelore, and Elis for October gigs throughout Europe and Scandinavia before a further mainland trek in November, once again with Leaves' Eyes, Battlelore, and Norwegian band Sirenia.

As 2005 opened, Atrocity announced that they had acquired the services of drummer Moritz Neuner. Heavily in demand on the underground metal scene, Neuner had prior credits with acts such as Graveworm, Abigor, Dornenreich, and Korova. In October, the band performed on the 'International Extreme Music Festival' in collaboration with Byzantine, Nightrage, Epoch Of Unlight, Hell Within, Leaves' Eyes, and Lilitu. Throughout 2006, the band worked on new recordings for *Werk 80 II*, aiming to repeat their successful 1997 experiment. Few bands of the extreme metal genre can boast such an unusual career path.

BARÓN ROJO
UNDERRATED IBERIAN METALLERS

GLOBALLY, BARÓN ROJO IS PROBABLY the best known of all Spanish heavy metal bands, if only because they have been the only one to gain any major recognition outside their native country. During the mid 1980s, even the UK took note of the band, thanks to a cover feature in *Kerrang!* and a series of tours and Reading Festival appearances. In Spain and South America, Barón Rojo maintain a loyal following to this day.

Before forming Barón Rojo (it means 'Red Baron'), the De Castro brothers – guitarists Carlos and Armando – had played with Coz, and Uruguayan drummer Hermes Calabria had been with Siglo. Meanwhile, bassist José Luis Campuzano (aka Sherpa) had been in Modulos, releasing a self-titled 1979 album, and had issued a string of singles and albums throughout the 1970s credited to Sherpa.

Signing to the Chapa Discos label, Barón Rojo issued their debut album, *Larga Vida Al Rock And Roll*, in 1981, featuring both Sherpa and Carlos de Castro as lead vocalists. It was produced by the noted rock DJ, Vicente Mariscal Romero. The band soon became successful in their own country.

The successor, *Volumen Brutal*, was recorded at Ian Gillan's Kingsway Studios in the UK and featured Gillan band-member Colin Towns guesting on keyboards. King Crimson's Mel Collins contributed saxophone to 'Son Como Hormigas'. The record sold over 100,000 copies in Spain and led to a deal in Britain with Kamaflage.

The band then supported Hawkwind on their British tour in 1982, for which *Volumen Brutal* was re-recorded with English lyrics for British consumption. They later put in two consecutive nights at London's Marquee club, where they were joined onstage by Gary Moore keyboard player John Sloman, guitarist Paul Samson, and ex-Yardbirds drummer Jim McCarty. Another jam session at the London Greyhound included ex-UFO guitarist Michael Schenker. Striking up a creative friendship, Sherpa collaborated with Schenker on his Group's *Built To Destroy* album, co-writing the song 'Red Sky'.

Maintaining their UK connection, Barón Rojo and Mariscal Romero travelled back to London to cut the next album, *Metalmorfosis*. Recorded only in the Spanish language this time, the first 1,000 pressings of the album came packaged with a free 7-inch single, 'Invulnerable' / 'Herencia Letal'. In the band's homeland, the record produced two major hit singles: 'Casi Me Mato' and 'El Malo'. Barón Rojo rounded out their live promotion by co-headlining the Belgian 'Heavy Sound' festival alongside Gary Moore.

Two back-to-back shows in Madrid in February 1984 in front of 24,000 fans were captured on the Chris Tsangarides-produced live album

Barón Al Rojo Vivo. Unusually for a live record, the band bravely included five brand new songs: 'Campo De Concentración', 'El Mundo Puede Ser Diferente', 'Mensajeros De La Destrucción', 'Atacó El Hombre Blanco', and the instrumental 'Buenos Aires'. Once more they played the 'Heavy Sound' festival as a headline act in 1984 before launching into a fully sold-out tour of South America.

The self-produced *En Un Lugar De La Marcha* album, released in the autumn of 1985, achieved gold sales status in Spain and scored well across South America. At this juncture, their success began to stifle further progress. The major label EMI wished to sign the band but their existing label refused to release them; a period of enforced inactivity was broken only by an unpopular live affair, assembled by Chapa Discos in 1986, *Siempre Estáis Allí.* Record sales took a progressive downward curve for 1987's *Tierra De Nadie*, 1988's *No Va Más*, and the 1990 effort *Obstinato.*

Ultimately, this decline in popularity forced the exit of both José Luis Campuzano and Hermes Calabria, and fans were dismayed to see both parties entering into litigation over ownership of the band name. The De Castro siblings won the case and duly assembled a beefed-up version of the band, inducting new blood: Maxi González on vocals, Pepe Bao on bass guitar, and José Antonio del Nogal (aka Ramakhan) on the drums. This unit did not last, however, and the band's 1992 album, *De Safio* – which included a cover version of AC/DC's 'Girls Got Rhythm' – saw the De Castros working alongside Panzer and Saratoga bassist Niko del Hierro, retaining Ramakhan on drums.

Barón Rojo's relentless touring, along with worthy sales of a 1995 retrospective album, *Larga Vida Al Barón*, attracted renewed attention. The line-up changed again in 1997 as a fresh rhythm section of bassist Ángel Arias and drummer José Martos made their presence felt on the *Arma Secreta* album. Some two years later, the band issued *Cueste Lo Que Cueste* through Ariola Records, a set of archive tracks along with five new songs and a re-recording of the classic 'Resistiré' with their new drummer Valeriano Rodríguez. A new studio album, *20+*, was released in 2001.

The band contracted to a new label, Zero, for *Báron En Aqualung*, a double live album recorded at the Divino Aqualung in Madrid on October 5th 2001. For their next studio outing, 2003's *Perversiones*, Barón Rojo used two whole discs to pay tribute to their musical heroes with an ambitious set of cover versions. The Michael Schenker Group's 'Assault

Attack', Black Sabbath's 'Neon Knights', Rainbow's 'Spotlight Kid', and Jimi Hendrix's 'Spanish Castle Magic' all featured, among others.

The band's July 24th 2004 gig at the Pavello Olimpic de Badalona in Barcelona, as support to Judas Priest, saw Schenker onstage for a version of his own 'Assault Attack'. That same year, Sherpa and Calabria, uniting with erstwhile Sangre Azul guitarist Juanjo Melero, formed a new act, Sherpa, debuting with the *Guerrero En El Desierto* album.

Barón Rojo supported Judas Priest on their April 2005 Spanish dates. The group's 25th anniversary in 2006 was celebrated with a triptych of significant releases: the retrospective double CD and DVD set *Las Aventuras Del Barón*, an Argentinean tribute album, *El Barón Vuela Sobre Argentina*, and the recording of a brand new studio album at Oasis studios in Madrid. The band continue to fly the flag for their native country.

BENEDICTION
PIONEERING UK DEATH METAL BAND

THIS ACT FROM BIRMINGHAM, ENGLAND were formed in February 1989, and are more noted in their home country for having supplied vocalist Mark 'Barney' Greenway to Napalm Death than their own musical achievements. Outside Britain, Benediction – affectionately known in their home city as 'The Bennies' – have gathered a sizeable following through a series of ever-improving albums and constant touring.

The group evolved from an earlier band, Stillborn, and debuted with *The Dreams You Dread* demo in June 1989, which secured them a deal with Nuclear Blast – a stable base for the band to the present day. The first line-up was Greenway, guitarists Peter Rewinski and Darren Brookes, bassist Paul Adams, and Ian Treacy on the drums. Their first audio release was a split 7-inch single, 'Confess All Goodness', shared with Austrian goremongers Pungent Stench. From the outset it was clear that the group were intent on breaking down the stereotypes of the genre, effortlessly amalgamating thrash and death metal and capping their mid-paced, bass-heavy rumblings with Greenway's effective if thoroughly indecipherable roar.

Following the release of September 1990's *Subconscious Terror*, co-produced by the band and Napalm Death's Mick Harris, Dave Ingram stepped in for Greenway on vocals and contributed to live activity during the year, which included British supports to Paradise Lost and Autopsy.

The band undertook a further British tour opening for Bolt Thrower before recording a follow-up album at Silverbirch Studios in Birmingham. The was the Paul Johnston-produced *The Grand Leveller*, which had Bolt Thrower's Karl Willetts guesting on 'Jumping At Shadows' and closed with a rendition of Celtic Frost's 'Return To The Eve'. Before the record came out, the band undertook further headlining dates throughout 12 countries, reinforced by British and German dates on its release. Shows in 1991 included gigs with labelmates Dismember and Massacra.

The group endured another line-up change when bassist Paul Adams departed in late 1991. Early the following year, Benediction hit the road once more with Bolt Thrower and Asphyx: the 'World Violation' tour crossed Europe, the USA, Canada, and even Israel. In October, Benediction released the *Dark Is The Season* EP, which featured a reworking of the old Anvil chestnut 'Forged In Fire' with former singer Barney Greenway on vocals. They endured another line-up change when bassist Paul Adams departed, recruiting ex-Cerebral Fix man Frank Healy.

The April 1993 album *Transcend The Rubicon* opened up more new ground as the band tackled a one-take studio jam of The Accused's 'At The Wrong Side Of The Grave' and reworked the songs 'Artefacted Irreligion' and 'Spit Forth The Dead' from the *Subconscious Terror* sessions. They then topped the bill on a European tour with Atheist and Cemetery in support, travelling to Ireland, Portugal, and Mexico.

Backed by an interim EP *The Grotesque/Ashen Epitaph*, they

supported Bolt Thrower on their American club tour, but found themselves the headliners on latter dates as the Thrower were obliged to withdraw. Benediction also appeared at the Milwaukee 'Metalfest' alongside fellow heavyweights Biohazard and Slayer. Such travelling cost the group the services of drummer Ian Treacy, and the skinsman was superseded by 18-year-old Neil Hutton in time for the Nuclear Blast New

Year festivals in January 1995. *The Dreams You Dread* arrived in June, promoted by a European trek with Death. That year, Neil Hutton and David Ingram formed the side project Warlord UK, releasing the *Maximum Carnage* album on Nuclear Blast in 1996. The album included covers of Amebix and Slayer songs.

Frontman Dave Ingram lent a helping hand to Bolt Thrower for a batch of live dates during 1997, when their vocalist Martin van Drunen bailed out without warning. However, this helping hand turned out to be permanent – and Benediction promptly pulled in Dave Hunt to fill the vacated vocal position. The band's March 1998 album *Grind Bastard* – the first with erstwhile Sabbat guitarist Andy Sneap in control of the faders – included covers of Judas Priest's 'Electric Eye' and Twisted Sister's 'Destroyer'. Digipack variants hosted another cover, 'We Are The League' by the Anti-Nowhere League. Once again the group toured with Death (Chuck Schuldiner's last live expedition) before uniting with Norwegian black metal combo Immortal.

Benediction return with September 2001's *Organised Chaos*, once again produced by Andy Sneap. Road work saw the band in familiar company, co-headlining a January 2002 European expedition with Bolt Thrower and Fleshcrawl. Once these commitments had been fulfilled, drummer Neil Hutton bowed out to join Stampin' Ground. In September 2004, the band headed up the 'Thunderstorm Over Europe' tour with Godhate and Nominon. They provided an interpretation of Slayer's 'Necrophiliac' for the Blackend tribute album *Slatanic Slaughter*.

In early 2005, the band announced the high-profile addition to the ranks of drummer Nick Barker (Cradle Of Filth, Lock-Up, Dimmu Borgir). He made his live debut with them at Austria's 'Devil Days' festival on June 10th. Initial recordings laid down by the new formation included a cover

BENEDICTION discography

Confess All Goodness, Nuclear Blast NB 031 (Europe) (1990) split 7-inch vinyl single with Pungent Stench

SUBCONSCIOUS TERROR, Nuclear Blast NB 033-2 (Europe) (1990)

THE GRAND LEVELLER, Nuclear Blast NB 048-2 (Europe), Nuclear Blast America 6017 (USA) (1991)

Dark Is The Season, Nuclear Blast NB 059-2 (Europe), Nuclear Blast America 6019 (USA) (1992)

TRANSCEND THE RUBICON, Nuclear Blast NB 073-2 (Europe), Nuclear Blast America 6058 (USA) (1993)

The Grotesque / Ashen Epitaph, Nuclear Blast NB 088-2 (Europe), Nuclear Blast America 6899 (USA) (1994)

THE DREAMS YOU DREAD, Nuclear Blast NB 0120-2 (Europe), Nuclear Blast America 6873 (USA) (1995)

GRIND BASTARD, Nuclear Blast NB 0246-2 (Europe), Nuclear Blast America 6246 (USA) (1998)

ORGANISED CHAOS, Nuclear Blast NB 0522-2 (Europe), Nuclear Blast America 6522 (USA) (2001)

of Sacrilege's 'Lifeline' that included Bolt Thrower vocalist Willetts and guitarist Barry Thompson. Nuclear Blast again handled the 2006 Benediction album, *Killing Music*. In April, the band revealed they had laid down studio cover versions of 'Seeing Through My Eyes' by Broken Bones, 'Into The Void' by Black Sabbath, and 'Banned From The Pubs' by Peter & The Test Tube Babies. The schedule was interrupted yet again in early May as the band announced a temporary suspension of activities due to Nick Barker breaking his foot in what was described as "an incident in Estonia". The saga continues.

BOLT THROWER
WAR GAMES AHOY!

FOUNDED IN BIRMINGHAM, ENGLAND in September 1986, Bolt Thrower gained notoriety on the local metal scene with their unique, war-themed heaviness – and while they were never the most technically proficient of outfits, the band cannily carved out their own niche. At their earliest point, Bolt Thrower featured vocalist Alan West, guitarist Barry Thomson, bassist Gavin Ward, and drummer Andy Whale. Their name was taken from a siege device in a Games Workshop fantasy role playing game, *Warhammer*. Famously, the initial idea for the band was conceived in a pub toilet in Coventry by Ward and Thompson. Their first product came in the form of an April 1987 demo session, *In Battle There Is No Law*. With Ward switching to guitar, Bolt Thrower drafted in Alex Tweedy to cover on bass.

Following a September 1987 demo, *Concessions In Pain*, the fledgling band still had Ward as temporary bassist because new man Tweedy had failed to commit, and they acquired bassist Jo-Anne Bench. The second demo resulted in a four song BBC Radio One session on the John Peel show, recorded in January 1988. This led to a deal with Vinyl Solution Records, but not before West's departure.

The band brought in vocalist Karl Willetts, the official Bolt Thrower van driver, to record a debut album at Loco Studios in Wales in 1988. This was the Andrew Fryer-produced *In Battle There Is No Law*. The band submitted a separately recorded version of the album track 'Drowned In Torment' to a fanzine-only split EP, alongside Instigators, H.D.Q., and Culture Shock. Although support for the band was rising on the metal underground, they felt Vinyl Solution's hardcore ethic was restrictive and switched labels to Nottingham's underground label Earache. A notable gig that July saw them supporting Death Angel and Warfare at London's Astoria. They scored a further John Peel session, cutting more tracks for Radio One in November.

The group's first album for Earache, October 1989's *Realm Of Chaos: Slaves To Darkness*, was recorded at Slaughterhouse Studios and sold in excess of 50,000 copies worldwide, with expansive gatefold artwork from Games Workshop that carried on the theme of fantasy RPGs. The world of gaming also infused the lyrical content of *Realm Of Chaos*, with 'Plague Bearer' and 'World Eater' borrowing heavily from gaming titles. *Realm Of Chaos* was the first record to introduce Bolt Thrower to an international audience: critics were polarised between jaw-dropping appreciation (especially for the super-low bottom end, with guitars dragged right down to A) or horror at its unashamed lack of sophistication. Meanwhile, Vinyl Solution reissued the debut album on CD with different artwork to the original.

After the Earache-organised 'Grindcrusher' tour of 1989 with Carcass, Morbid Angel, and Napalm Death, and the contribution a track to the compilation album of the same name, the band played dates in The Netherlands throughout February 1990 with Autopsy and Pestilence, on the 'Bloodbrothers' tour. A third John Peel session was recorded in July 1990.

The release of the next studio album in September proved fortuitous:

BOLT THROWER discography

IN BATTLE THERE IS NO LAW, Vinyl Solution SOL 11 (UK) (1988)
REALM OF CHAOS: SLAVES TO DARKNESS, Earache MOSH13CD (UK), Relativity/Earache 88561-2034-2 (USA) (1989)
WARMASTER, Earache MOSH29CD (UK), Combat/Earache 88561-2028-2 (USA) (1990)
THE PEEL SESSIONS 1988-90, Strange Fruit DEI 8118-2 (UK) (1991)
Cenotaph, Earache MOSH 33 (UK) (1991)
THE IVth CRUSADE, Earache MOSH70CD (UK), Relativity/Earache 88561-1157-2 (USA) (1993)
Spearhead, Earache MOSH73CD (UK) (1993)
FOR VICTORY, Earache MOSH120CD (UK) (1994)
WHO DARES WINS, Earache MOSH208CD (UK) (1998)
MERCENARY, Metal Blade 3984-14147-2 (Europe / USA) (1998)
HONOUR – VALOUR – PRIDE, Metal Blade 3984-14386-2 (Europe / USA) (2001)
THOSE ONCE LOYAL, Metal Blade 3984-14506-2 (Europe / USA) (2005)

Warmaster was also crafted at Slaughterhouse, with noted producer Colin Richardson now in control, and was cut just before the studio burned down. For this offering, Bolt Thrower curtailed the speed somewhat, retaining a degree of clarity by tuning down merely to C-sharp. Even with this fine tuning, *Warmaster* was still a monstrously ugly death metal album.

The *Cenotaph* EP arrived in January 1991. The band again toured Europe, this time as part of the 'War Mass' package with support from US outfit Nocturnus and Sweden's Unleashed. That October, the group conducted a tour of the USA together with Believer and Toronto thrashers Sacrifice before engaging in further European shows, where they were supported by Benediction and Asphyx. In 1991, the three combined John Peel sessions saw commercial release on CD format.

The band drew back from their grind influences and changed tack towards a doom-edged feel for October 1992's *The IVth Crusade*, again with Richardson. Retaining the militaristic stance, they went for a more classical feel, adapting a medieval Eugène Delacroix painting for the cover. European dates to open up 1993 witnessed a strong union with Poles Vader and Swedes Grave. This activity was backed by an EP release comprising a remixed 'Spearhead' alongside new material. Unfortunately, Bolt Thrower's first Australian tour in 1993, supported by Armoured Angel, ended in disarray, resulting at one stage with the musicians being stuck without a flight home.

Eventually making it back to Britain, the band were off for another American club tour in July 1994 with fellow Brummies Benediction in support, but failed to complete the schedule. The album of that year, *...For Victory*, enjoyed strong sales. Richardson took production honours again, and once more the band's imagery took a further leap in history as the cover depicted marines yomping across the tundra of the Falkland Islands. Initial copies came with a free bonus live disc recorded in Manchester during 1992.

Ex-Pestilence, Asphyx, and Submission vocalist Martin van Drunen joined the band in 1994, replacing the departed Willets, and drummer Martin Kearn was added in the line-up shuffle. Taking their metal to the European masses, the band undertook the 1995 'No Guts, No Glory' tour with Brutality and Cemetary. They hit the continent again the following year, making an anti-industry statement on the 'Fuck Price Politics' expedition with Sentenced, Expression Of Power, and The Varukers.

Severing connections with Earache in early 1997 and signing to

American label Metal Blade, the band saw van Drunen quit unexpectedly on the eve of European festivals; he was suffering from a disease that made his hair fall out. Bolt Thrower killed time by throwing in a few live gigs with Benediction's Dave Ingram as a guest.

As the band went into the studio in late 1997 it was announced that 19-year-old Alex Thomas had succeeded skinsman Kearns and that Willets had rejoined. With this line-up, the band cut the 1998 album *Mercenary* for their new label Metal Blade. This offering, despite the lengthy hiatus between recordings, re-established Bolt Thrower's fanbase – and gave the group a place in the German album charts. Although Willetts had performed on the album, it was a reinstated Dave Ingram, recently out of Benediction, who took up the vocals for live work (with Crowbar and Totenmond). Confusingly, Thomas then left and the drummer he had replaced in the first instance returned in time for Bolt Thrower's second showing at the major German 'Full Force' festival.

The band toured Europe in January 2001, supported by Fleshcrawl and Heaven Shall Burn, to push a new album, *Honour, Valour, Pride*. Further road work saw the band in familiar company, co-headlining a January 2002 European expedition with Benediction backed up by Fleshcrawl. Van Drunen resurfaced in mid 2002, debuting his new act Death By Dawn on the European live circuit. Bolt Thrower were then confirmed as one of the headline acts at the October 'Westfalen' festival in Dortmund, Germany. They were also finalised for the running order of the *Rock Hard* magazine festival at the Gelsenkirchen Amphitheatre for June 2003 but withdrew at short notice to allow Ingram to be present at the birth of his first child.

Bolt Thrower finally announced the departure of Ingram, apparently due to the singer "suffering with health and personal problems", in August 2004. The singer later revealed that he had been suffering from mental difficulties, but once recovered, he founded a new band, Full Scale Hatred, which subsequently evolved into Downlord.

In November, original vocalist Karl Willetts returned to the band, soon re-entering the studio to craft a new album. Willetts also re-recorded the vocal lines on the 2001 *Honour, Valour, Pride* album produced by former Marshall Law bassist Andy Faulkner. Digipack variants hosted an exclusive track, 'Covert Ascension'.

Early 2005 found van Drunen and erstwhile Pestilence bassist Jeroen Paul Thesseling collaborating with King Locust guitarist Niels Drieënhuizen in a new band, Projekt Tabun. The trio entered Studio Het Lab in Schaarsbergen to put down initial recordings, although van Drunen later pulled out of this project for "personal reasons". Back on the Bolt Thrower front, vocalist Karl Willetts and guitarist Barry Thompson guested on a cover of Sacrilege's 'Lifeline' recorded by fellow Brummies Benediction.

In May, the band entered Sable Rose Studios, again with Andy Faulkner as producer, to craft a new album for Metal Blade. *Those Once Loyal* emerged in November and gave them their highest charting record in Germany, debuting at Number 76. To coincide, former label Earache reissued *Realm Of Chaos*, remastered and clad in new artwork. European headline shows in January and February 2006 witnessed strong backing from Malevolent Creation, Nightrage, and Necrophagist. Gigs for April across Europe were originally scheduled with Gorefest as support, but these plans were changed and Kataklysm, God Dethroned, and Downlord took over the opening roles. Bolt Thrower are now a highly respected metal band, proving that quality endures.

CANCER
UK EXTREMISTS

SPEED METAL BAND CANCER were formed in Telford, England during 1988 at the Tontine public house in Ironbridge by singer-guitarist John Walker, bassist Ian Buchanan, and Carl Stokes on drums. A two-track demo, *No Fuckin' Cover*, was recorded at the legendary Pits studio, owned by Starfighters vocalist Steve Burton. The two songs – 'The Growth Has Begun' and 'Burning Casket (My Testimony)' – were produced by Stevie Young, cousin of AC/DC guitarist Angus Young, and 'Big' Mick Hughes, Metallica's live sound engineer. Their first gig took place in nearby Birmingham, opening for Bomb Disneyland.

A second demo in 1989 led to an unofficial green-vinyl live album, *Bloodbath In The Acid*, recorded at Wrexham Memorial Hall and released by Headache. Having been granted a deal by Vinyl Solution, Cancer cut their 1990 debut album, *To The Gory End*, at Loco studios in Usk in a mere four days. The finished product was given extra sheen courtesy of a mixdown at Morrisound Studios in Florida by death metal alchemist Scott Burns. During this final phase, Obituary's John Tardy was drafted in to supply backing vocals to the song 'Die Die'. The cover art, featuring a head sliced by a machete, betrayed the band's brutally unsophisticated approach.

Erstwhile Agent Steel and Obituary guitarist James Murphy was enlisted to record the sophomore album, *Death Shall Rise*, produced by Burns and recorded and mixed at Morrisound in Tampa, Florida. Deicide's Glen Benton contributed vocals to the lead track, 'Hung, Drawn And Quartered'. Released in April 1991, the album caused a great deal of

controversy in Germany, where it was banned by the state body for censorship of "works dangerous to youth" on the grounds that the cover would incite youngsters to inflict violence upon one another. Restless Records handled the album for North America.

UK gigs saw a headline run throughout May supported by Unleashed and Desecrator. The band then played the 1991 Milwaukee 'Metalfest' and supported Deicide and Obituary. By December 1991, Murphy had quit the band to form Disincarnate, later joining Testament and Danes Konkhra. The year 1993 was another busy one for the band, inducting new guitarist Barry Savage, releasing *The Sins Of Mankind*, produced by Simon Efemy at The Windings in Wrexham, and performing a European tour with openers Cerebral Fix.

A setback occurred when Carl Stokes was involved in an accident when his motorbike hit a van. He suffered multiple injuries, necessitating the enlistment of Monolith's Nick Barker on a temporary basis for live work. Barker later made his name with Cradle Of Filth and Dimmu Borgir. The group toured Britain and America with Deicide, and two live tracks recorded at the Milwaukee 'Metalfest' surfaced on the Restless compilation *Live Death* released in 1994.

That year, the band stepped up a level, signing to major label East West. The next album was recorded at Great Linford Studios in Milton Keynes with Simon Efemy at the helm once again, with the finished tracks mixed at Pink Floyd's Britannia Row Studios. If longstanding fans found the caustic cover of Deep Purple's 'Space Truckin'' too much to stomach, they could console themselves with the fact that Stokes had used a real human thigh bone for percussion on 'Temple Song'. Following the release of the new album, *Black Faith*, the quartet toured Britain with support act Meshuggah.

During 1997, Carl Stokes was involved with Nothing But Contempt, the shortlived act assembled by vocalist Barney Greenway in his period away from Napalm Death. This included Greenway, Stokes, Napalm Death guitarist Danny Herrera, and Sacrificial Altar and Asatru guitarist Rob Engvikson. Nothing But Contempt folded when Greenway rejoined Napalm Death. Stokes also filled in for Telford hardcore band Assert in 2000 before founding a new metal project, Remission, with Walker.

Guitarist Savage joined the high-profile grindcore act Lockup in early 2002 as touring guitarist. Cancer made a return during 2003 with a line-up consisting of Walker, Stokes, Asatru guitarist Rob Engvikson, and bassist Adders. Reunion gigs were backed by a new EP, *Corporation$*, including a cover of the Celtic Frost classic 'Dethroned Emperor'. Following European tour dates, the band parted ways with Engvikson, in September 2004, enlisting Dave Leitch of Pulverized as replacement.

Cancer's 2005 album, *Spirit In Flames*, recorded over a three-week period at Philia Studios in Henley-on-Thames, emerged on Copro Records in June. However, in February 2006 Carl Stokes issued a statement: "Due to the lack of commitment to the band from John Walker, Cancer is no more." The drummer also revealed plans for a new band, Hail Of Fire, featuring ex-Cancer members guitarists Dave Leitch and Barry Savage, bassist Ian Buchanan, and newcomer Rob Lucas on vocals.

CANCER discography

TO THE GORY END, Vinyl Solution SOL 022 (UK), Silent Scream SSCD-8002 (USA) (1990)
DEATH SHALL RISE, Vinyl Solution SOL 028 (UK), Restless 7 72587-2 (USA) (1991)
THE SINS OF MANKIND, Vinyl Solution SOL 035 (UK), Restless 7 72734-2 (USA) (1993)
BLACK FAITH, East West 0630 10752-2 (1995)
Corporation$, Copro COP033CD (UK) (2004)
SPIRIT IN FLAMES, Copro COP044CD (UK) (2005)

Not playing games: Bolt Thrower

CARCASS
LEGENDS ON TWO COUNTS

ORIGINATORS OF THE GORE-DEATH GENRE, Carcass were a Liverpool-based extreme metal band formed in 1985. The impact of the British band has been such that not only are Carcass cover versions a near staple requirement for many budding death metal combos, but also their song titles have been adopted for band names. Masterminded by ex-Napalm Death man Bill Steer and ex-Electro Hippies vocalist-bassist Jeff Walker, Carcass's 1988 debut album, *Reek Of Putrefaction*, triggered

immediate controversy – its cover depicted a collage of human and animal flesh – and spawned a legion of imitators.

Steer had first made his presence felt with Disattack, releasing *A Bomb Drops…*, a hardcore/punk "dis-core"-styled six-song demo in March 1986. Disattack consisted of Steer, vocalist Pek, bassist Paul, and drummer Middie. The guitarist was an active promoter of extreme music, being co-publisher, alongside Middie and Pek, of the fanzine *Phoenix From The Crypt*. Walker came on board, initially as bassist, and Ken Owen took over on drums as the transition to Carcass was implemented. Steer and Walker first honed an act playing Judas Priest cover versions as a bedroom band, but this soon gave way to something far more sinister. The group's recordings started in 1987 with a 13-track demo cassette entitled *Flesh Ripping Sonic Torment*. The vocals for this session were provided by Sanjiv (the band never learned his surname), who exited soon afterwards. With Walker adopting the vocal role, a further five tracks were released on cassette in 1988 as *Symphonies Of Sickness*. This set secured a recording contract with Nottingham's Earache Records.

With *Reek Of Putrefaction*, Carcass scored a notable first, claiming that the whole point of the repulsive cover art was to get it banned. Lyrically, they raised the standard of grossness by looting medical textbooks for inspiration. *Reek Of Putrefaction* led fans to discover words such as 'uterogestation', 'mucopurulence', 'pyosisified' and 'detruncation' – but Carcass went beyond mere shock value, making a more subtle point: behind the slabs of raw meat were a set of earnest vegetarians.

Radio One DJ John Peel, known for his adventurous tastes in music, pulled Carcass into the BBC studios on December 13th 1988 to record a session for his show. Produced by Dale Griffin, these four tracks aired in January 1989 and were followed up by *The Peel Sessions* EP that same year. The band credited themselves as W.G. Thorax Embalmer (Steer), J. Offalmangler (Walker), and K. Grumegargler (Owen).

Steer left Napalm Death to concentrate fully on Carcass just before the recording of 1989's *Symphonies Of Sickness*. That same year the Mexican label Distorted Harmony issued a three-track live EP, *Live St. George's Hall, Bradford 15.11.89*, consisting of concert recordings from the Bradford venue as well as London University. It resembled a low-budget bootleg, but the 7-inch was authorised by the band, although it was heavily bootlegged in later years. Also on the live front, the group participated in Earache's now legendary 'Grindcrusher' tour of Europe, shoulder to shoulder with labelmates Bolt Thrower, Morbid Angel, and Napalm Death.

The band added Swedish guitarist Mike Amott, previously with Carnage, in March 1990, to thicken their live sound. The same year, German shows saw Atrocity as support act, while Dutch gigs featured Acrostichon as openers.

As the grind wave peaked, November 1991's *Necroticism – Descanting The Insalubrious* album, recorded at Amazon Studios in Simonswood with producer Colin Richardson, rapidly sold in excess of 100,000 copies. The combination of Richardson at the board, Amott on second guitar, and a greater proficiency from the founding members took Carcass to new heights of creativity and technical proficiency.

CARCASS discography

REEK OF PUTREFACTION, Earache MOSH 6 (UK) (1988)
SYMPHONIES OF SICKNESS, Earache MOSH 18 (UK) (1989)
The Peel Sessions, Strange Fruit SFPS 073 (UK) (1989)
Live At St. George's Hall, Bradford 15.11.89, Distorted Harmony cnu (Mexico) (1989)
NECROTICISM – DESCANTING THE INSALUBRIOUS, Earache MOSH42CD (UK) (1992)
Tools Of The Trade, Earache MOSH49CD (UK) (1992)
HEARTWORK, Earache MOSH97CD (UK), Columbia CK 57525 (USA) (1994) **54 UK**
WAKE UP AND SMELL THE CARCASS, Earache MOSH161CD (UK) (1996)
SWANSONG, Earache MOSH160CD (UK) (1996) **58 UK**

Touring to promote the album and the June 1992 *Tools Of The Trade* EP included last-minute support dates alongside French thrashers Loudblast on Death's British tour (after Pestilence pulled out). This was followed by Earache's epic 'Gods Of Grind' tour, featuring Carcass, Cathedral, Entombed, and Confessor.

Amott departed after October 1993's *Heartwork*, returning to Sweden to form the highly-rated retro outfit Spiritual Beggars and the death metal act Arch Enemy. Carcass, meanwhile, had endeavoured to mature in order to rid themselves of the death metal tag and progress musically. *Heartwork* was laid down that summer at Parr Street Studios with Richardson and displayed a greater degree of musicianship than its predecessors, with classic heavy metal influences very much on display, especially in the guitar solos. The album benefited from a cover with a photograph of an HR Giger sculpture, *Preserve Life*, in contrast to the expected gore graphics.

Carcass then recruited the American ex-Venom guitarist Mike Hickey for live work. The band toured Britain in December 1993 alongside Headswim as guests to rap-metallers Body Count before a mammoth European and American tour. Sales of *Heartwork* were strong – over 50,000 in the USA alone – and towards the end of the American dates the band were signed to major label Columbia. In June, Hickey was replaced (later turning up in Cathedral and Cronos) by erstwhile Devoid guitarist Carlo Regadas. In late 1995, Walker opted to tour with Year Zero on a temporary basis while Carcass waited for Columbia to release the new album. However, the label dropped the band during November, resulting in the departure of Steer.

Although Carcass regrouped and re-signed the already recorded album to their previous label, Earache, Steer's former colleagues carried on under the new banner of Blackstar, adding ex-Cathedral and Year Zero guitarist Mark Griffiths.

Ken Owen suffered a brain haemorrhage in his sleep in February 1999. This put the drummer into a coma for ten months and required surgery in March 2000. Owen only left hospital in February 2001.

Steer re-emerged in 1999 fronting Blacksmith. By the following year, he had created Firebird with Cathedral's Leo Smee and Spiritual Beggars' Ludwig Witt. The Carcass name was kept in the public eye in 2001 with the issue of *Requiems Of Revulsion* by Deathvomit Records: this was a tribute collection witnessing homage by acts such as Regurgitate, Pig Destroyer, Disgorge, General Surgery, Dead Infection, Avulsed, Impaled, Vulgar Pigeons, Nasum, Cattle Decapitation, Rotten Sound, Haemorrhage, and Engorged.

Earache reissued the first two Carcass albums, *Reek Of Putrefaction* and *Symphonies Of Sickness*, in late 2002, restored with the banned cover art. Both albums had been unavailable in the original covers since 1992. Walker made a return to action in 2004, producing an album for Liverpool's Diamanthian. In October, he provided guest vocals on the Napalm Death album *The Code Is Red... Long Live The Code*, featuring on the track 'Pledge Yourself To You'.

Walker surprised many in October 2005 when he revealed that he had recorded a solo album of country and blues covers of work by artists such as Skeeter Davis, Hank Williams, Johnny Cash, Connie Smith, and John Denver. Conducted, of course, with an extreme metal twist, the record, *Welcome To Carcass Cuntry*, featured Carcass colleagues Steer and Owen plus a host of guest contributors, including H.I.M. frontman Ville Valo, ex-Faith No More bassist Bill Gould, and the Amorphis collective of guitarists Esa Holopainen and Tomi Koivusaari, bassist Niclas Etelävuori, and keyboard player Santeri Kallio.

Repaying the favour, Walker guested on the debut album by the Amorphis/H.I.M. side project To Separate The Flesh From The Bones, *Utopia Sadistica*. He also contributed to the *No End In Sight* album from This Is Menace, a collaboration by Pitchshifter bassist Mark Clayden and drummer Jason Bowld. January 2006 found Walker joining the infamous 'Mexican' death metal band Brujeria for South American dates. Carcass are still revered today as legends – and quite rightly so.

CORONER
SWISS METAL PRECISION

ZÜRICH METAL BAND CORONER achieved European success with a distinct brand of experimental avant-garde metal in the tradition of Celtic Frost, which they developed into post-thrash executed with the finest detailed precision – in true Swiss style. They were formed in 1984 with a line-up of vocalist-bassist Ron Royce (aka Ron Broder), guitarist Oliver Amberg (later to join Celtic Frost), and drummer Marquis Marky (Markus Edelmann). The personnel shifted with Amberg's departure and the recruitment of replacement Tommy T. Baron (Thomas Vetterli). In the first stages of their career the band hardly toured, adding to their mystique.

Tom G. Warrior, mainstay of Celtic Frost, contributed vocals and lyrics to the band's October 1985 demo, *Death Cult*. Only 250 hand-numbered copies were manufactured, prominently displaying Warrior's credits on the front cover. Guitarist Baron and drummer Marky then joined Celtic Frost's US 'Tragic Serenades' tour as road crew. From then on, Coroner were continually blighted by comparisons to Celtic Frost, which were not discouraged when Noise (Frost's label) signed the Swiss trio.

Coroner's first album, *R.I.P.*, had production overseen by Harris Johns at Music Lab studios in Berlin in March 1987. It received good reviews and went on to sell over 50,000 units in Europe. The band's distinct lack of gigs came about more by circumstance than planning: for example, a proposed European tour supporting Billy Milano's M.O.D. was cancelled by the headliners when protesters threatened to sabotage the tour.

Coroner

> **CORONER discography**
>
> **R.I.P.**, Noise N 0075 (Europe), Wintrop Music WK 45186 (USA) (1987)
> **PUNISHMENT FOR DECADENCE**, Noise NUK 119 (UK), Wintrop Music WK 44269 (USA) (1988)
> **NO MORE COLOR**, Noise NUK 138 (UK) (1989)
> **MENTAL VORTEX**, Noise N 0177-1 (Europe) (1991)
> **GRIN**, Noise N 0210-2 (Europe) (1993)
> **CORONER**, Noise N 0212-2 (Europe), Noise N 0212-2-UX (USA) (1995)

The second album, 1988's *Punishment For Decadence*, was produced by Guy Bidmead and featured a cover of Jimi Hendrix's classic 'Purple Haze'. Once more the band were unable to tour properly to promote the album, with a planned American jaunt with Sabbat and Rage cancelled at the last minute, and British dates were postponed when the band were incarcerated by British customs for lack of work permits. They did, however, manage to snatch a few support shows with Sacred Reich later in the year.

Coroner's third album, *No More Color*, appeared in 1989, produced by Pete Hinton, and the band finally toured Europe in 1990 with strong support from cult Texans Watchtower.

In January 1992 Noise issued *Mental Vortex*, which closed with an ambitious cover of The Beatles' 'I Want You (She's So Heavy)'. The record had been crafted the previous summer at Berlin's Sky Trax Studios by Tom Morris, with a final mix conducted at his Morrisound studio in Tampa, Florida.

The group's final effort, the contract-fulfilling *Grin*, was self-produced at Greenwood Studios in Switzerland with Mekong Delta's Peter Haas on drums, and arrived in September 1993. That year, Coroner supported Canadians Annihilator on a British tour and, although they were still utilising the services of Marky and Royce, the band had effectively become a solo vehicle for Baron by 1995. They bowed out with a farewell European tour in January and February 1996, giving fans a keepsake, the free cassette *The Unknown Unreleased Tracks (1985-1995)*. Baron, now using his real name of Tommy Vetterli, formed the shortlived Clockwork with Peter Haas, toured with French pop singer Stephen Eicher, and then teamed up with German thrash pioneers Kreator in the late 1990s.

Marky briefly worked with Dwell and turned up again in 1999 as part of Tom Warrior's (by then Thomas Fischer's) Apollyon Sun. Marky had reverted to his real name of Markus Edelmann. In 2004, Vetterli produced Pure Inc.'s debut album, and in June 2005 the three Coroner musicians apparently met with a view to discuss a proposed reunion, but opted not to pursue the idea.

NAPALM DEATH
ENEMIES OF THE MUSIC BUSINESS?

WEST MIDLANDS BAND NAPALM DEATH not only defined the grindcore genre but took it to its absolute limits. Founded in 1981 in Meriden, Birmingham under the original title of Civil Defence by vocalist Nic 'Nic Scab' Bullen and drummer Miles 'Rats' Ratledge, the band adopted the Napalm Death name after seeing the *Apocalypse Now* movie. Guitarist Daryl 'Sid' Fideski and bassist Graham Robertson joined, but Fideski opted out and Robertson switched to guitar as Finbar Quinn enrolled on bass. The first product was the 1982 demo *Punk Is A Rotting Corpse*.

Early gigs were supports to bands such as The Subhumans, The Apostles, and Chaos UK. This version of Napalm Death contributed a track to the *Bullshit Detector Volume 3* album, after submitting a tape to the organisers, the anarcho-punk act Crass, but then went into stasis. They were relatively inactive throughout 1984, undertaking only one concert that year, as a benefit for the miners' union.

They regrouped in May 1985 with Bullen on vocals, Justin Broadrick of Final on guitar, P-Nut on bass, and Rats on the drums. Before long, Napalm Death became a trio when P-Nut exited and Bullen took command of bass guitar. Following a demo titled *Hatred Surge*, Rats was ejected. The drummer subsequently forged Witch Hunt with another ex-Napalm man, Finbar Quinn. Meanwhile, the band started to veer more towards thrash metal with the arrival of drummer Mick Harris, who put in his first live showing on January 18th 1986 for a support to Amebix. Not only did his joining signal a radical shift in musical direction, but also Harris lays claim to the invention of the term 'grindcore'. From that point on, Napalm Death would lead the field.

Digby Pearson, the owner of the Nottingham-based Earache label, signed the group and in 1986 half of the songs which would become the debut album, *Scum*, were committed to tape. After these sessions, Jim Whitely was added on bass to allow Bullen to concentrate on singing. Whitely also contributed to Doom's first recordings for the *A Vile Peace* compilation.

When guitarist Broadrick departed following initial demos – he went on to Head Of David and later formed the seminal Godflesh – the band asked Warhammer and Unseen Terror man Shane Embury to replace him, but the invitation was declined. Frank Healy of Sacrilege was inducted, but his tenure was brief, and he was superseded by guitarist Bill Steer (of *Phoenix Militia* fanzine) and vocalist Lee Dorrian. Dorrian had never been in a band before, having just lost the offer of a job as bassist with Icons Of Filth when they broke up. As frontman for Napalm Death, Dorrian debuted at the Hand And Heart pub in Coventry with Anti-Sect and Heresy. This gig saw Frank Healy of Sacrilege standing in as guitarist for a temporarily absent Steer.

It was in this incarnation that the band laid down the remaining songs for *Scum* at Rich Bitch Studios in Selly Oak during May 1987. The album rocked the metal world to its core as the most ferocious record of the genre so far. Napalm Death's caustic delivery – exemplified by 'You Suffer', a song lasting less than one second – immediately divided critics.

Importantly, *Scum* strongly emphasised the new blastbeat drumming style. Although Mick Harris was not technically the first to employ it – the credit goes to D.R.I.'s drummer Eric Brecht – Napalm Death brought the new style to public attention and made it a cornerstone of their material.

Whitely quit shortly after the album release, replaced in August 1987 for a series of dates supporting D.R.I. by Shane Embury, who later joined on a full-time basis. The band contributed tracks to two compilation albums, *North Atlantic Noize Attack* and *Pathological*, and cut two John Peel sessions, on September 13th 1987 and March 8th 1988. Peel's championing of the band resulted in increased demand for *Scum*; the resulting cashflow gave considerable impetus to the Earache label. Typically, though, just as Peel had proven a staunch supporter, another Radio One DJ, Steve Wright, represented the other end of the spectrum, using Napalm Death songs as a punishment in his afternoon quiz show.

With the exception of Dorrian, all members of the band had ongoing side projects at the time of *Scum*. Steer had formed the brutal Carcass and secured a deal for them with Earache; bassist Embury was drumming for Unseen Terror; and Harris worked with Doom, Extreme Noise Terror, and Unseen Terror.

The band's second album, *From Enslavement To Obliteration* – recorded at Birdsong Studios in Worcester – held a staggering 54 tracks, many merely seconds long, and was delivered in 1988. Initial copies came with a five-track 7-inch EP. The BBC TV documentary series *Arena* featured the band in a heavy metal special, bringing Napalm Death into Britain's living rooms.

Such was the band's reputation at this early stage that in July 1989 they undertook their first successful tour of Japan. These dates, conducted with hardcore combo S.O.B., marked the advent of Dorrian's label Rise Above with the issue of the *Live* EP, a collection of tracks recorded in Copenhagen, Roskilde, and London. Only 2,500 copies of this 7-inch single were pressed. A further collaboration with S.O.B. was the now-rare 7-inch flexidisc split single on the Sound Of Burial label. Earache then put out a record-breaking 7-inch single, packaged with the *Grindcrusher* compilation album, featuring 'You Suffer' and Electro Hippies' 'Mega Armageddon Death Part. 3', which clocked in at just over a second.

On the live front, the group participated in the Earache-organised 'Grindcrusher' tour of Europe that winter with Bolt Thrower, Morbid

NAPALM DEATH discography

SCUM, Earache MOSH 3 (UK) (1987)
FROM ENSLAVEMENT TO OBLITERATION, Earache MOSH 8 (UK) (1988)
The Curse, Earache MOSH 8 BONUS (UK) (1988) free single with *From Enslavement To Obliteration* album
Mentally Murdered, Earache MOSH14 CD (UK) (1989)
Napalm Death / S.O.B., Sounds Of Burial (1989) split 7-inch flexidisc with S.O.B.
Live, Rise Above RISE 001 (UK) (1989) limited edition 2,500 copies
HARMONY CORRUPTION, Earache MOSH19CD (UK) (1990) **67 UK**
Suffer The Children, Earache MOSH24CD (UK) (1990)
Mass Appeal Madness, Earache MOSH46CD (UK) (1991)
DEATH BY MANIPULATION, Earache MOSH51CDL (UK) (1992)
UTOPIA BANISHED, Earache MOSH53CD (UK), Relativity/Earache 88561-1127-2 (USA) (1992) **58 UK**
World Keeps Turning, Earache MOSH 65CD (UK) (1992)
THE PEEL SESSIONS, Strange Fruit SFRCD 120 (UK) (1993)
Nazi Punks Fuck Off, Earache MOSH92CD (UK) (1994)

FEAR EMPTINESS DESPAIR, Earache MOSH109CD (UK), Columbia CK 64361 (USA) (1994)
Greed Killing, Earache MOSH 146 (UK) (1995)
DIATRIBES, Earache MOSH141CD (UK) (1996)
In Tongues We Speak, Earache MOSH168 (U) (1997) split EP with Coalesce
INSIDE THE TORN APART, Earache MOSH171CD (UK) (1997)
Breed To Breathe, Earache MOSH158CD (UK) (1998)
WORDS FROM THE EXIT WOUND, Earache MOSH212CD (UK) (1998)
BOOTLEGGED IN JAPAN, Earache MOSH209CD (UK) (1999)
Leaders Not Followers, Dreamcatcher CRIDE 19M (UK) (1999)
ENEMY OF THE MUSIC BUSINESS, Dreamcatcher CRIDE 33 (UK), Spitfire SPT-15164-2 (USA) (2000)
ORDER OF THE LEECH, Spitfire SPT-15172-2 (UK / USA) (2002)
NOISE FOR MUSIC'S SAKE, Earache MOSH266CD (UK / USA) (2003)
LEADERS NOT FOLLOWERS: PART 2, Century Media 77487-2 (Europe), Century Media CM 8187-2 (USA) (2004)
THE CODE IS RED... LONG LIVE THE CODE, Century Media CM 77587-2 (Europe), Century Media CM 8287-2 (USA) (2005)
SMEAR CAMPAIGN, Century Media 77687-2 (Europe), Century Media CM 8387-2 (USA) (2006)

Angel, and Carcass. They then restructured themselves to become an Anglo-American outfit, as Dorrian departed to form the successful Cathedral and former Benediction man Mark Greenway stepped into his shoes. Better known as 'Barney', the new Napalm Death frontman possessed a primal roar perfectly suited to the band's now supremely focused ferocity. Steer had also quit, concentrating on Carcass, and his position was filled by an American, ex-Terrorizer guitarist Jesse Pintado. The band soon added a second guitarist in former Righteous Pigs man Mitch Harris, and the group set to work once more.

Initial copies of July 1990's *Harmony Corruption*, cut at Tampa's Morrisound Studios with producer Scott Burns, came with a free live album, recorded at London's ICA, notably including Justin Broadrick guesting on the Godflesh cover 'Avalanche Master Song'. Deicide's Glen Benton and Obituary's John Tardy were studio guests on the studio track 'Unfit Earth'.

Harmony Corruption, probably the band's most traditional album, gave Napalm Death their first UK chart entry, at Number 67. Early 1991 saw the American leg of the 'Grindcrusher' tour, where they appeared alongside Nocturnus and Godflesh. An interim EP, *Mass Appeal Madness*, recorded at the Violent Noise Experience Club in March, bridged the gap between albums.

Before a US tour in summer 1991, drummer Harris quit to form his industrial project, Scorn, reuniting with Nic Bullen for this venture. He generated some unexpected press when he was arrested in a case of mistaken identity after a jeweller's robbery in Derby. Harris's replacement was the American musician Danny Herrera, who joined in time for dates with Sick Of It All, Sepultura, and Sacred Reich, as well as the band's first shows in Russia.

Utopia Banished in 1992 was laid down in Wrexham with Colin Richardson and had the band eschewing the technicality of their predecessor and immersing themselves deep in ugly grind once again. Band members illustrated this return to brutality by printing on the cover that Greenway had supplied 'Vocular Armageddon', Pintado 'Dissonant Distorted Delirium No. 1', Harris 'Dissonant Distorted Delirium No. 2', Embury 'Sub-End Vexation', and Herrera 'Hyper Cans'.

The band undertook extensive tours in Europe with Obituary and Dismember and in America alongside Carcass, Cathedral, and Brutal Truth. Further shows followed in Holland, opening for Faith No More before inaugural South African shows. Returning from the political turmoil of South Africa, they released a version of the Dead Kennedys' classic 'Nazi Punks Fuck Off' as a single, donating all proceeds to the anti-racism campaign. The single went on to sell over 10,000 copies, and they rounded off the year with a headline Canadian tour.

May 1994 saw the release of *Fear, Emptiness, Despair*, self-produced with engineer Pete Coleman, and a British tour with label-mates Entombed. The initial reaction to the album was lukewarm, with media attention mainly focused on Entombed rather than Napalm Death. The band fared better in North America, touring alongside Obituary and Machine Head, and scored a notable success with the inclusion of the track 'Plague Rages' on the soundtrack to the film *Mortal Kombat*, which broke into the American *Billboard* Top 5. Further evidence of a return to form came with the well-received *Greed Killing* mini-album.

The full-length Colin Richardson-produced *Diatribes* was recorded at Framework Studios in Birmingham, England and was issued in North America in January 1996 with a bonus split CD, *Cursed To Tour*, shared with tour partners At The Gates.

In 1996, Embury teamed up with Dan Lilker of Brutal Truth to record the Malformed Earthborn album *Defiance Of The Ugly By The Merely Repulsive*. Embury also formed an alliance with Sick Of It All vocalist Lou Koller in Blood From The Soul for the *To Spite The Gland That Breeds* album. April that year found Napalm Death conducting UK headline dates with support from Crowbar and Swedes Face Down.

In early 1997, it was announced that Greenway had departed, one of the reasons being the vocalist's well-known fear of flying. The band quickly announced their new frontman as Phil Vane of Extreme Noise Terror and, in a surreal turn of events, within days Extreme Noise Terror put out a press statement naming their new vocalist for the *Damage 381* album – Barney Greenway. The ex-Napalm Death man also founded a fresh act, Nothing But Contempt, a shortlived act that included Greenway, Cancer and Assert drummer Carl Stokes, and Herrera and Sacrificial Altar guitarist Rob Engvikson.

Vane made his mark on a split EP with Coalesce, *In Tongues We Speak*, but on its release it became apparent that Greenway and Napalm Death had patched up their differences and were back together. Recording then began for the *Inside The Torn Apart* album.

Napalm Death conducted a lengthy European tour as support to Machine Head during April and May 1997. *Inside The Torn Apart*, produced by Richardson in June, benefited from a boisterous mix by former Sabbat guitarist Andy Sneap. In an attempt to keep themselves in the press, the band issued a split EP with German act Fatality, who had won a competition to cover a Napalm Death track on the release.

The band then toured South America to wind up the year, but only after Embury had suffered a head injury requiring stitches after moshing at an Entombed gig in Nottingham. While they were on tour, the band's video for 'Breed To Breathe' came under severe criticism from several European TV stations, and editing was required. The video featured live material shot at the New York CBGBs club interspersed with documentary footage of various scenes of brutality.

In addition to his work in Napalm Death, Greenway was becoming known for his alternative career as a journalist. Having contributed to a number of titles, including *Raw* and Germany's *Rock Hard*, he was to be found penning a computer-games column in *Kerrang!*.

Words From The Exit Wound, once more overseen by Richardson and out in October 1998, was an uncharacteristically lacklustre effort, delivered as a parting shot for Earache. The band signed to new label Dream Catcher during 1999 following a festival appearance at 'Wacken'. The Simon Efemy-produced *Leaders Not Followers* EP followed that October.

Both Embury and Pintado made a mark later the same year with the their Lockup project, a new band created with Peter Tägtgren of Hypocrisy and Dimmu Borgir drummer Nick Barker. The resulting album, *Pleasures Pave Sewers*, proved extremely successful, charting in Germany. Embury and Harris embroiled themselves in a further side project, Little Giant Drug, with vocalist-guitarist Simon Orme and drummer Simon Hornblower, for the 2000 album *Prismcast*.

Napalm Death toured Europe in early 2000 with guests Konkhra. Later European gigs found Harris performing onstage sitting down: he had broken his foot falling downstairs in a video shoot. A set of UK dates in April 2001 saw the band supported by Defenestration.

Later that year, Lockup cut a second album, *Hate Breeds Suffering*, released in 2002 with Tomas Lindberg taking Tägtgren's position. The bassist had his past endeavours with the youthful Warhammer resurrected when a vintage track appeared on the *Britannia Infernus* compilation. Napalm Death returned with their first full-length post-Earache album, *Enemy Of The Music Business*, in September 2000. This effort, helmed again by Simon Efemy, contained some of the band's most biting lyrical matter, which successive interviews made clear were directed at the band's former label.

Napalm Death toured Britain in November 2001 with support from Bristol's Onedice. European dates into January 2002 where upset when Embury was hospitalised for a time with influenza. An unfazed Napalm Death completed the shows as a four-piece.

As the band busied themselves with a live DVD and live album, *Punishment In Capitals*, released in 2003, as well as the recording of a new studio opus, *Order Of The Leech*, word arrived in mid 2002 that Embury was recording a grindcore solo-project album with erstwhile Fear Factory drummer Raymond Herrera and Dorrian. It was also revealed that Napalm Death had recorded two Septic Death cover versions – 'Terror Rain' and 'Thaw' – for exclusive use on the vinyl version of the album.

December UK gigs were supported by The Great Deceiver. The band played in January and February 2003 alongside Nile, Strapping Young Lad, The Berzerker, and Dark Tranquillity. Embury made time to guest on Nasum's *Helvete* album early that year. The Nasum connection was strengthened with the announcement of a split EP shared with the Swedish veterans: Nasum covered the Napalm Death track 'Unchallenged Hate' and Napalm replied with Nasum's 'The Masked Face'.

Earache then issued a two-disc retrospective, *Noise For Music's Sake*. The collection hosted a number of rarities and unreleased recordings, including a 1987 live take of 'Deceiver' with Mitch Dickinson of Unseen Terror on guitar and a 1986 live version of 'Traitor' from the Mermaid in Birmingham, captured on Embury's tape recorder before he joined the band. On top of a myriad other activities, Embury officially joined 'Mexican' extreme metal band Brujeria in July 2003.

Following German dates in August, the band revisited their successful *Leaders Not Followers* EP with a full-blown album. *Leaders Not Followers Part 2* consisted of covers of Cryptic Slaughter's 'Lowlife' and many others. Notably, the album featured an appearance on two songs by Jim Whitely, the original bass player from *Scum*.

August brought news of the formation of a grind supergroup, Venomous Concept (punning Poison Idea), which consisted of Embury, Mick Harris, Melvins and Fantomas guitarist Buzz Osbourne, and former Brutal Truth singer Kevin Sharp. The unit subsequently strengthened the Napalm Death connection when drummer Herrera took over the drum position. Meanwhile, Napalm Death undertook a round of European gigs throughout November, albeit without Pintado, absent because of health issues. The band headlined the January 2004 'Extreme The Dojo VII' tour of Japan alongside Nasum, a reformed Anal Cunt, and Pig Destroyer.

In May 2004, the band, with Pintado back on board, signed a worldwide deal with Century Media for the issue of *Leaders Not Followers: Part 2*. Pintado made time to guest on the EP *Welcome To Reality* from Los Angeles punk-grind band Resistant Culture.

In August, Attila Csihar, the Mayhem, Tormentor, and Aborym scene veteran, revealed plans for an extreme metal supergroup, Born To Murder This World, with Embury, Mick 'Irrumator' Kenney of Anaal Nathrakh, Necrobutcher of Mayhem, and drummer Nick Barker.

In September, the band entered Foel Studios in North Wales to lay down material for a new album, *The Code Is Red... Long Live The Code*, which was released in April 2005. Former Carcass frontman Jeff Walker contributed guest vocals to the track 'Pledge Yourself To You', Jello Biafra of the Dead Kennedys made his presence felt on 'The Great And The Good', while Hatebreed's Jamey Jasta featured on 'Instruments Of Persuasion'. US tours for October saw the band set to flank Kataklysm and Goatwhore, and to close the year they were announced as one of the main attractions at the annual 'X-Mass Fest' dates with Marduk, Finntroll, Vader, The Black Dahlia Murder, and Belphegor.

To aid victims of the December 2004 tsunami, Napalm Death participated in the issue of a special single with The Haunted and Heaven Shall Burn. They donated a new song, 'The Great And The Good', featuring Biafra. The single, restricted to just 1,000 hand-numbered copies, was for sale only at Napalm Death's Bochum and London shows in January 2005. Billed as part of the Anaal Nathrakh line-up, Embury cut a BBC radio session at Maida Vale Studios on March 18th.

On April 16th, Napalm Death conducted their first concert in Indonesia, performing at Ancol Beach, Jakarta with local grind band Tengkorak as support. Oddly, bearing in mind the band's social politics, the event, which saw record crowds, was sponsored by the Gudang Garam tobacco company. Upon their return home, the band filmed a video for 'Silence Is Deafening' with director Roger Johansson.

European tour dates in the summer had the band supported by Most Precious Blood and Diecast. To celebrate Japanese dates, Shane Embury teamed up with Gargamel Toys to produce the Garga-Death toy, a five-inch figure limited to just 150 units and made available only at gigs. September found Embury involved in Insidious Disease, a side project initiated by Old Man's Child guitarist Jardar (aka Jon Øyvind Andersen), with guitarist Silenoz (Sven Atle Kopperud) and drummer Tony Laureano of Dimmu Borgir.

Brazilian gigs in late October saw support from Acao Direta and Claustrofobia before the band engaged with the 'European Persistence' tour in December, ranked alongside Agnostic Front, Hatebreed, The Red Chord, Born From Pain, Bleed The Sky, and Full Blown Chaos. Greenway made studio time to session on German hardcore band Maroon's *When Worlds Collide* album.

The band were back on North American soil in early 2006 with Kreator, Undying, and A Perfect Murder for gigs in February. In late May, they entered Foel Studios in Wales to cut a new album, with Anneke van Giersbergen from Dutch band The Gathering contributing vocal parts. The band's summer schedule was centred on a run of festival appearances. Sad news came on August 27th with the death of former band member Jesse Pintado. The guitarist died from liver failure at the Erasmus MC hospital in Holland.

Napalm Death hit the USA in September alongside Hatebreed, Exodus, The Black Dahlia Murder, Despised Icon, and First Blood. That same month, Embury collaborated with Mistress and Anaal Nathrakh's Mick Kenney to announce the formation of a new label, Feto Records. This imprint served as an outlet for Kenney's Exploder, Mistress, and Professor Fate projects and Embury's *Live In Japan* opus from Lockup.

The band then launched into live work with A Life Once Lost, Dead To Fall, Impaled, Arsis, and Animosity throughout November and December as part of the 'Death By Decibels' US tour. Napalm Death are now among the UK's longest-serving extreme metal acts, and all metal fans owe them a considerable debt.

PESTILENCE
LEGENDARY EURODEATH PIONEERS

PESTILENCE WERE A POPULAR Technical death metal outfit who enjoyed considerable album sales in Europe in spite of an ever-fluctuating line-up. During the late 1980s and early '90s the Enschede-based Pestilence reigned as the leading Dutch death metal band, releasing a quartet of influential records.

The band were conceived in spring 1986, originally as a trio of guitarist Randy Meinhard, drummer Marco Foddis, and vocalist-guitarist Patrick Mameli. This three-piece released their first 1987 demo, *Dysentery*, but later the group added vocalist-bassist Martin van Drunen, who assumed vocal duties from Mameli, and they cut another demo, *The Penance*. The debut album, 1988's *Malleus Maleficarum*, was produced by Kalle Trapp for Roadrunner.

They then underwent a major line-up reshuffle. Foddis left for a short period in late 1988 to form Sacrosanct with Meinhard but returned in time to play on the *Consuming Impulse* album. Meinhard, replaced by former Theriac man Patrick Uterwijk, joined Sacrosanct and later Submission. Van

Drunen concentrated purely on vocals from this point. The band played dates in Holland throughout February 1990 with Autopsy and Bolt Thrower on the 'Bloodbrothers' tour.

Van Drunen quit after December 1989's *Consuming Impulse* to join Asphyx, Submission, and later Bolt Thrower. For *Testimony Of The Ancients*, arriving in September 1991 and recorded at Morrisound Recording in Tampa, Florida, by Scott Burns, Pestilence employed the services of keyboard player Kent Smith and Cynic bassist Tony Choy.

The band's last album, May 1993's *Spheres*, was co-produced by Mameli and Steve Fontano. They employed the services of Dutchman Jeroen Thesseling as a permanent bassist in late 1993 but, following European dates with Cynic, the band folded.

Van Drunen resurfaced in mid 2002 with his new act, Death By Dawn, and played the European live circuit. Mameli made studio time in early 2004 to donate his services to the Death tribute album *Within The Mind*, assembled by James Murphy. Meanwhile, Jeroen Paul Thesseling embarked upon an entirely different form of music by forming his own flamenco troupe.

Early 2005 found van Drunen and Thesseling collaborating with King Locust guitarist Niels Drieënhuizen in a new band, Projekt Tabun. The trio entered Studio Het Lab in Schaarsbergen to put down initial recordings, but van Drunen later pulled out of this project for "personal reasons". In 2006, Thesseling announced the formation of Ensemble Salazhar.

PUNGENT STENCH
AUSTRIAN TASTELESSNESS EXTRAORDINAIRE

VIENNA'S PUNGENT STENCH INCLUDE erstwhile Carnage personnel: vocalist-guitarist Martin Shirenc ('Don Cochino'), bass player Jacek Perkowski ('Pitbull Jack'), and drummer Alex Wank ('Rector Stench'). They deal in deliberately sick song content and imagery designed to

---

PESTILENCE discography

MALLEUS MALIFICARUM, Roadrunner RR 9519-2 (Europe), RC RCD 9519 (USA) (1988)

CONSUMING IMPULSE, Roadracer RO 9421-2 (Europe), RC RCD 9421 (USA) (1989)

TESTIMONY OF THE ANCIENTS, Roadracer RO 9285-2 (Europe), RC RCD 9285 (USA) (1991)

SPHERES, Roadrunner RR 9081-2 (Europe / USA) (1993)

---

shock, although their controversial work did foster local appreciation, and with each record they find fresh ways to disgust the listener.

They began life as a death-grind band but gradually introduced groove into the music as their profile rose. The band debuted with the April 1st 1988 demo *Mucus Secretion*, and a split EP with Disharmonic Orchestra followed in 1989. The group toured with Master and Abomination during 1990 in order to promote their debut album, *For God Your Soul... For Me Your Flesh*, issued in 'splatter' vinyl. The cover was distastefully adorned with severed limbs. The same year, Nuclear Blast issued the split 7-inch single 'Blood, Pus And Gastric Juice', shared with Benediction.

In October 1991, copies of the *Been Caught Buttering* album were confiscated by British customs because of the cover photograph of a cadaver's surgically bisected head. The band basked in the resulting publicity, and the album was eventually cleared as the photograph had previously been on display in various art galleries. To celebrate, the band manufactured a picture-disc version.

Naturally, they capitalised fully on the controversy and toured hard. Dates included gigs in Israel and American shows alongside Brutal Truth and Incantation. The band even made it as far as New Zealand, a tradition they maintained for many years to come.

April 1993's *Dirty Rhymes And Psychotronic Beats* EP was noted for its covers of The Mentors' notorious 'Four 'F' Club' and Warp Spasm's 'Why Can The Bodies Fly'. European headline dates in April through to June 1994 promoting the *Club Mondo Bizarre – For Members Only* album saw the band supported by Macabre and Brutal Truth. In now traditional style, the record's original pornographic pastiche cover art was banned in Germany.

A spate of extracurricular activity found drummer Wank forming the industrial group Spine, while Shirenc created Hollenthon and subsequently forged Kreuzweg Ost with Silenius of Summoning.

Following Pungent Stench's lengthy absence from the scene, Nuclear Blast issued the comeback album *Masters Of Moral – Servants Of Sin* during November 2001. Live dates that year saw the incorporation on bass of Mario Klausner (Scent Of Paradise, Belphegor, Pathetic). The band's 'Holy Inquisition' 2002 tour commenced in Warsaw during September and made its way through the Low Countries, Russia, and the Ukraine before gigs in their native Austria supported by Cadaverous Condition. As 2003

broke, the band travelled as far as Australia and New Zealand for gigs in January, these latter shows supported by Kiwis Malevolence.

A short burst of dates in February, the 'Rotting With Your Christ' tour, found the band on North American soil with Incantation, Beyond The Embrace, and Rune. The year was rounded out by European headline gigs in November with support from London gore metal outfit Gorerotted. In early 2004, Klausner announced his departure in order to concentrate fully on his own band, Collapse 7. Klausner was replaced in February by Fabio Testi.

Pungent Stench's new album, *Ampeauty*, appeared in September 2004, released through Nuclear Blast and with Martin Shirenc on bass. Testi was removed from the equation in December 2004, and Klausner briefly returned, before departing again, citing family reasons. A new bass payer, El Gore, was recruited.

The band toured New Zealand again in March 2005 with support from local acts Backyard Burial, Meatyard, 8 Foot Sativa, and Ulcerate. British shows were followed by festival appearances at events such as the 'Grind Your Mother Fest' in Italy, 'Obscene Extreme' in the Czech Republic, and 'Metallic Noise' in Germany. Another round of European gigs took the band through until the end of the year. European shows in January 2006 had Eisregen as support.

The band launched into a North American tour in May but withdrew in mid trek as Alex Wank announced that "under these extreme chaotic and fucked-up conditions, we just can't continue this so-called tour", although the group did perform prior engagements at New York City's CBGBs on May 26th and the Maryland 'Deathfest' event on May 28th. They remain among their country's best-known metal exports.

SINISTER
DEATH METAL REBORN

PREMIER DUTCH DEATH METAL ACT Sinister hail from Schiedam and have enjoyed two peaks of popularity: first as pioneers of their genre, and latterly as a revitalised, female-fronted force, spearheading the return of death metal in mainland Europe.

The band formed in April 1988 as a trio of frontman Mike van Mastrigt, guitarist Ron van de Polder, and drummer Aad Kloosterwaard, adding bassist Corzas in January 1989. This line-up recorded the *Perpetual Damnation* demo on March 17th 1990, taping four originals and an unlisted cover of Slayer's 'Praise Of Death'. Sales of the tape were strong, with over 1,800 sold in 18 months, and Sinister toured as support to Entombed and Disharmonic Orchestra. Seraphic Decay Records delivered a three-track 7-inch EP in August 1991. Swiss label Witchhunt Records, an imprint noted for picking out influential bands, weighed in with a 7-inch single, 'Putrefying Remains', in September, and the following year Sicktone put together two tracks as a split 7-inch single with Dutch/Swedish alliance Monastery (notably consisting of Sinister's Ron van de Polder and Aad Kloosterwaard in collaboration with Entombed's Lars Rosenberg).

Corzas left in May 1991 and bass duties were handed over to Sempiternal Deathreign's Frank Faase. Another line-up shuffle saw van de Polder moving to bass as the band added second guitarist André Tolhuis (aka André Tolhuizen, ex-Vulture). Their second demo, 1991's *Sacramental Carnage*, secured enough interest to land a deal with Nuclear Blast. That September, Sinister toured as support to Atrocity. More touring opened up 1992 as they gained a valuable support slot to Morgoth.

The debut album, *Cross The Styx*, was produced at Mainstreet Studio Fautspach in Germany by Atrocity singer Alexander Krull, and introduced a thrash-infused death metal approach that was far ahead of its time, winning many plaudits. The band toured to promote the album by opening for Deicide, Entombed, Cannibal Corpse, and Atrocity among others.

An equally savage second album, *Diabolical Summoning*, was

recorded at TNT Studios in Gelsenkirchen in March 1993 and produced by Colin Richardson, with a third album, *Hate*, appearing in 1995. By this juncture, Sinister were down to a trio of Van Mastrigt, Kloosterwaard, and Bart van Wallenberg (handling both guitar and bass). Promoting *Hate*, the band put in European headline dates in February 1996 together with Creepmime, Avulsed, and Darkseed. A stopgap 1996 EP, *Bastard Saints*, marked the introduction of the Severe Torture-credited bassist Michel Alderliefsten. The EP created consternation with a shift towards American nu-metal influences – the songs were arranged in a much simpler fashion and, controversially, two archive cuts, 'Cross The Styx' and 'Epoch Of Denial', were completely refashioned in a similar stripped-down style.

Sinister reformed as Kloosterwaard and van Wallenberg brought in new singer Eric de Windt from Severe Torture and bass player Alex Paul to record 1998's *Aggressive Measures*, co-produced by Vincent Dijkers. In side operations, van Mastrigt and Kloosterwaard founded Houwitser in 1997 for the *Death... But Not Buried* album, released in 1998.

Vocalist Eric de Windt decamped in August 1999, after which Joost Silvrants of grindcore outfit Inhume and Drowning In Tears took care of the vocal role – until Sinister surprised many by adopting a female lead singer, Rachel Heyzer of Occult. Heyzer, a woman in possession of a mighty roar that would shame most male death metal vocalists, made her debut with the Hans Pieters-produced *Creative Killings*. Sinister switched from Nuclear Blast to the Hammerheart label, licensed in America to the Martyr Music Group, for the November 2001 release. The album included a cover of Possessed's 'Storm In Your Mind'. Meanwhile, Kloosterwaard occupied the drum stool for death act Thanatos, but vacated this position in August 2001.

By early 2002, van Wallenberg had left, replaced by God Dethroned guitarist Pascal Grevinga for touring purposes. The band then supported Nile's October European tour. Further European dates for November were announced with Septic Flesh, Dismember, and Thyrfing. The band had their efforts rewarded by re-signing to the Nuclear Blast label for a new studio album, *Savage Or Grace*.

Former Sinister singer Mike van Mastrigt resurfaced in late 2002 in a new band, Death Squad, working with ex-Radiathor guitarist Walter Tjwa, second guitarist J.G., and drummer Michel.

In August 2003, Sinister ousted guitarist Pascal Grevinga and bassist Alex Paul. Guitar player Ron van de Polder, who had been involved in the songwriting process for *Cross The Styx* and *Savage Or Grace*, stepped in as a replacement as the new-look trio set to work on a fresh album, *Heaven Termination*. This renewed burst of activity also manifested itself in a side project, Infinited Hate, comprising the full Sinister triumvirate of Heyzer, Van de Polder, and Kloosterwaard. The first Infinited Hate album, *Revel In Bloodshed*, was released in 2003, and the follow-up, *Heaven Termination*, appeared two years later.

In 2004, Sinister donated their rendition of 'Storm In My Mind' to the *Seven Gates Of Horror* tribute album assembled by the Karmageddon Media label in homage to Possessed.

After 16 years of delivering extreme metal, Sinister folded in April 2004. However, word arrived in March 2005 that the band – now with Kloosterwaard handling vocals, Paul Beltman (ex-Judgement Day) on drums, and Alex Paul on bass and guitar – had reformed yet again. Bas van den Boogard, also ex-Judgement Day, was subsequently added on bass. The band entered Stage One studio in Germany to cut a new album, *Afterburner*, in December for April 2006 release through Nuclear Blast.

TRUST
GALLIC RIFFMASTERS

BY FAR THE MOST SUCCESSFUL FRENCH heavy metal band of all time, Nanterre-based Trust produced some excellent albums chock full of aggression and lyrics that were not afraid to explore social and political themes. Founded by singer Bernie Bonvoisin (previously drummer with Taxi and Killerdrink) and guitarist Nono (aka Norbert Krief), the band even made it to UK shores, touring nationwide as headliners. Despite this, Trust had a stormy career, dogged by line-up changes that were allegedly the result of frontman Bonvoisin's dictatorial methods.

The band's first stage performance, with Christian Cheffeu on drums, came on September 9th 1977 as support to Bang at the Golf Drouot in Paris. They went through numerous band members in their formative stages, including drummer Omar Ben El Mabrouk and second guitarist 'Moho' (Mohammed Shemlok).

The group's initial roster, which cut tracks for a 1977 demo, *Prends Pas Ton Flingue*, consisted of Bonvoisin, Nono, bassist Raymond Manna, and drummer Jean-Émile 'Jeannot' Hanela. Two of these tracks were issued as a 7-inch single, released that October by Pathé-Marconi. Another switch in drummers found Sherwin Rosman taking the role, while Mann was substituted by ex-Volcania man 'Vivi' (Yves Brusco). Trust famously provided the opening honours for AC/DC on October 24th 1978 at Le Stadium in Paris, with Bonvoisin forging a famous friendship with the rock legends' singer Bon Scott.

They released their first album on CBS in May 1979, *L'Élite*, recorded in London with producer Hervé Muller and including a cover of AC/DC's

'Ride On'. Initially this album was self-titled *Trust* but later became known as *L'Élite* to avoid confusion with the band's fourth album, which was also self-titled at first. A French tour to promote the album, which included a concert at the Fleury-Merogis prison, saw many town authorities drafting in extra police, fearing that Trust's political message would incite rioting. The group was an immediate hit, scoring platinum sales and boasting a sell-out crowd of 10,000 for a headline show at the Pavillon de Paris on January 12th 1980.

With the exception of the core pairing of Bonvoisin and Nono, the band was unable to cement a solid line-up of players, a curse that would dog them throughout their lifespan. At one stage, guitarist Jack Starr was offered a position but declined, opting to relocate to New York, where he founded Virgin Steele. For May 1980's *Répression*, co-produced by the band with Dennis Weinreich and again recorded in London, Manna was ousted in favour of Yves Brusco, and Kevin Morris handled drums. Subsequently, ex-Pat Travers band and Streetwalker drummer Nicko McBrain joined the fold as Trust re-introduced second guitarist Moho.

Répression is generally regarded as the band's best album, with its much-admired opener 'Antisocial'. It covered a wide range of controversial topics, with Bonvoisin spitting out venomous lyrics in his mother tongue, aimed at police and politicians alike. The band's profile in France was kept at boiling point as Bonvoisin's acerbic and cutting lyrics gave the media plentiful scope with which to either vilify or praise the band. Social injustice was the singer's main target, with 'Mr. Comédie' attacking Iran's Ayatollah Khomeini, then enjoying exile in France, 'Darquier' dealing with Nazi quisling Louis Darquier de Pellepoix, 'Les Brutes' directed at the Czech security forces for their ill-treatment of protesters in Prague, and 'H & D' ('Hôpital & Débiles') exposing the Soviet Lubyanka prison.

Répression's main point of controversy in France came with Bonvoisin's apparently enthusiastic support for the late French criminal Jacques Mesrine, although the subject meant little if anything to foreign record buyers. Indeed, it has often been acknowledged that Trust sounded more subdued when Bonvoisin was forced to translate the band's songs into English, with the help of Sham 69's Jimmy Pursey, in order to make an entry into the international market.

In 1981, the French quintet crossed the Channel in order to push the English-language version of *Répression*, opening for Iron Maiden on the East Londoners' 'Killers' British tour that February, before returning for a successful headline run. *Savage* in 1982 was in fact a renamed English version of the October 1981 *Marche Ou Crève* album, produced by Tony Platt in Stockholm. Pointedly, the track 'Les Brutes' – featuring a line chastising the current British Prime Minister, Margaret Thatcher – was omitted from the English version.

After a ten-date tour of Germany supporting Iron Maiden to promote *Marche Ou Crève*, drummer McBrain was informed that Trust could no longer afford to pay him. Fortuitously, with Clive Burr leaving the Iron Maiden drum stool, McBrain was offered that position, where he has remained ever since.

The live formation of Trust added Thibault Abrial as second guitarist, and he in turn was superseded by Shakin' Street's Eric Levy. By the time they recorded 1983's Andy Johns-produced *Trust IV* album (also known as *Idéal*), which ambitiously included a full symphony orchestra, Farid Medjane was manning the drums. Concerts naturally ushered in yet another version of the band, this time featuring Benjamin Raffaeli as rhythm guitarist. In a bizarre swap, Clive Burr joined the fold alongside new bassist Frederique Guillemt to record *Man's Trap*, in fact an English-language version of *Idéal*. Burr's tenure was fleeting, however, with the Englishman decamping for the ill-fated Gogmagog before terms with Elixir and Praying Mantis. He would be replaced by Thierry Dutru and then Farid Medjane.

At this point, the group had apparently given up any idea of international recognition and opted instead to concentrate solely on the French market. But a change in domestic politics had seen their audience dwindle: the arrival of left-wing president François Mitterrand had made a significant impact.

A poor reception to their 1984 *Rock'n'Roll* album led to a split, with Bonvoisin subsequently recording a couple of solo albums for Polygram and Nono working with legendary French crooner Johnny Hallyday. Meanwhile, New York thrash giants Anthrax covered 'Antisocial' on their 1988 *State Of Euphoria* album, prompting renewed curiosity from the English-speaking world. Bonvoisin subsequently joined Anthrax singer Joey Belladonna for a live rendition of 'Antisocial', included on the US act's 'Make Me Laugh' single. That same year, the reformed Trust put in two major shows opening for Iron Maiden and performed at the 'Monsters Of Rock' festival, which spawned a live album, *Live – Paris By Night*. A studio offering, *...En Attendant...*, was released before the year was out.

In 1990, guitarist Nono teamed up with ex-Speed Queen vocalist Stevie to form Touch. Other former Trust men, Thibault Abrial and Farid Medjane, subsequently formed Furioso with erstwhile Sortilège vocalist Christian Augustin and former Satans Jokers drummer Renaud Hantson.

Bonvoisin returned to his solo career after Epic released during 1992 a greatest hits-style live album, *Répression Dans L'Hexagone*, recorded in 1980 and boasting two AC/DC tributes, 'Live Wire' and 'Problem Child'. The singer subsequently released his third solo album for Polygram in 1993, but Epic persuaded him and Nono to reunite for a 1996 Trust record, *Europe Et Haines*. The new musicians on these recordings were bassist David Jacob and drummer Nirox John.

Impressively, the band's latest offering quickly sold over 100,000 copies but – somewhat predictably – they changed shape soon afterwards, as live work saw Hervé Koster recruited to play drums. Another hiatus ensued, broken by the delivery in April 2000 of *Ni Dieu Ni Maître*. However, Bonvoisin issued legal proceedings to withdraw the album from stores, claiming that he was not satisfied with the finished product. The band remain something of a domestic legend.

Polish metal overlords Vader

VADER
DARK LORDS OF THE RIFF

THE INTENSE DEATH METAL BAND VADER broke out of Olsztyn, Poland with an unrelenting album schedule and a seemingly inexhaustible appetite for global touring. This approach has elevated them to the very top of the Polish metal league, and they remain notable for their victory over difficult early circumstances in the pre-perestroika era.

Vader came together in 1986, initially operating very much in the traditional thrash metal mould. That same year, they generated two demos, *Tyrani Piekie?*, actually a tape of a live radio broadcast, and December's *Live In Decay*. The band at this point consisted of lead vocalist Czarny (aka Robert Czarneta), guitarists Peter (Piotr Wiwczarek) and Vika (Zbigniew Wróblewski), bassist Astaroth (Robert Struczewski), and Belial (Grzegorz Jackowski) on drums. Czarneta and Wróblewski decamped to found Raxas.

The band released a further demo tape, *Necrolust*, working with engineer W?adys?aw Iljaszewicz at Studio PR in Olsztyn in March 1989. They were now down to a trio, Peter being joined by bassist Jackie (aka Jacek Kalisz) and the Slashing Death-credited drummer Krzysztof 'Docent' / 'Doc' Raczkowski. The tape gained them a deal with Carnage Records. A deal was struck subsequently to distribute the July 1990 demo *Morbid Reich*, sessions co-produced by Mariusz Kmiolek at Pro-Studios in Olsztyn. This tape went down in metal history for selling over 10,000 copies.

The band had inducted ex-Impurity and Dies Irae guitarist Jaroslaw 'China' Labieniec and bassist Shambo (aka Leszek Rakowski) before travelling to the UK to cut their debut record, *The Ultimate Incantation*, laid down at Rhythm Studios with Paul Johnson manning the board. On the record's release in November 1992, the band toured Europe with Bolt Thrower and Grave. Further dates in America followed, with Deicide, Suffocation, and Dismember.

The Darkest Age – Live '93, which included a cover of Slayer's 'Hell Awaits', was recorded in front of a home crowd in Krakow. The 1994 *Sothis* EP witnessed another cover, Black Sabbath's anthemic 'Black Sabbath', as well as a complete rework of the band's 1989 track 'The Wrath'.

June 1995 found Vader out on the road in Europe once more, touring alongside Cradle Of Filth, Malevolent Creation, Oppressor, Dissection, and Solstice to promote the *De Profundis* album, which had been released domestically through Croon Records and was subsequently reissued rapidly through Conquest Music and Impact.

The band undertook a full European tour in spring 1996 as guests to Cannibal Corpse. Docent then united with Cezar of Christ Agony to found a black metal side venture, Moon, and appeared on the first Moon album, *Daemon's Heart* released in 1997, before relinquishing the role to concentrate on Vader.

Keen to display their influences, the band closed 1996 with an album of cover versions. *Future Of The Past* collected renditions of Sodom's 'Outbreak Of Evil', Kreator's 'Flag Of Hate', Terrorizer's 'Storm Of Stress' and 'Fear Of Napalm', Possessed's 'Death Metal', Dark Angel's 'Merciless Death', Celtic Frost's 'Dethroned Emperor', Slayer's 'Silent Scream', Anti-Nowhere League's 'We Are The League', Depeche Mode's 'I Feel You', and Black Sabbath's 'Black Sabbath'. Vader's ascendancy into the world rankings was now assured, with *Future Of The Past* granted releases in Europe, the USA, and Japan.

During 1997 the band were joined by another Dies Irae man, guitarist Mauser (aka Maurycy Stefanowicz) as Labieniec opted out to found Nyia. That October, Impact put out the next Vader instalment, *Black To The Blind*. Diligent fans soon noticed that the lyric sheet included an absent track, 'Anamnesis', apparently excised from the final running order by mistake. In August, they hit Japan, and a concert at the Tokyo Club Quattro on the 31st was captured on tape for a live album. 'Anamnesis' finally received a public airing on the November 1998 mini-album *Kingdom*.

Wiwczarek produced the debut album by fellow Poles Decapitated during 2000 as Vader themselves worked on the high-ranking *Litany* opus, released via Metal Blade that May. Japanese editions boasted a brace of extra songs, 'Red Dunes' and 'Lord of Desert'. Vader themselves headlined the European 'No Mercy' festivals alongside Americans Vital Remains, Brazilians Rebaelliun, and Germany's Fleshcrawl.

Mauser reactivated Dies Irae in 2000, drafting in his Vader colleague Docent on drums, Sceptic guitarist Hiro, and frontman Novy of Devilyn.

This new version of Dies Irae entered the studio in June 2000 with producer Szymon Czech for their debut album, *Immolated*.

Vader attacked a further batch of covers with April 2001's *Reign Forever World*, paying homage to Destruction's 'Total Desaster', Judas Priest's 'Rapid Fire', and Mayhem's 'Freezing Moon'.

September 2001 saw Vader on the lookout for a new bassist as the previous occupant, Shambo, had departed. They found their man with Simon (aka Konrad Karchut), an ex-member of Hunter. The band were part of the gargantuan European 'No Mercy' touring package in March and April 2002 with Immortal, Catastrophic, Destroyer 666, Hypocrisy, Disbelief, Malevolent Creation, and Obscenity.

That June, the *Revelations* album arrived; it was recorded at Red Studio, Gdańsk with Wiwczarek acting as producer. Studio guests included Nergal of Behemoth vocalising on 'Whispers' and Ureck of Lux Occulta featured as session keyboard performer on 'Torch Of War' and 'Revelation Of Black Moses'. Loosely conceptual, the album's artwork tied together lyrical observations on the 9/11 twin towers disaster. Digipacks hosted an additional track, 'Sons Of Fire'.

The band toured Japan as headliners in October before a run of dates across mainland Europe from late August, supported by Krisiun, Decapitated, and Prejudice. North American shows, commencing on November 6th, had the Poles topping a strong death metal package of Immolation, Cephalic Carnage, Origin, and December. Vader issued a CD single version of Thin Lizzy's 'Angel Of Death' in 2002, restricted to the obligatory 666 copies.

Wiwczarek aided the prog-metal act Ceti on their 2003 album *Shadow Of The Angel*, adding guest vocals to 'Falcon's Flight'. The band parted ways with bassist Simon, replacing him in June with the Behemoth and Devilyn-credited Novy (aka Marcin Norwak) and appearing at the gargantuan 'Woodstock 2003' festival in Poland, playing not only in front of national TV cameras but also before a huge crowd of 400,000 rock fans.

VADER discography

THE ULTIMATE INCANTATION, Earache MOSH59CD (UK), Relativity/Earache 88561-1158-2 (USA) (1993)

Sothis, Massive MASS 001 MCD (Europe) (1994)

THE DARKEST AGE – LIVE '93, Arctic Serenades SERE 007 (Europe) (1994)

DE PROFUNDIS, System Shock IR-C-067 (Europe) (1995)

FUTURE OF THE PAST, System Shock IR-C-092 (Europe) (1996)

BLACK TO THE BLIND, System Shock IR-C-104 (Europe) (1997), Pavement Music 76962-32277-2 (USA) (1998)

REBORN IN CHAOS, Hammerheart cnu (Europe) (1997), Pavement Music 76962-32292-2 (USA) (1998)

Kingdom, Metal Mind Productions MMP CD 0057 (Europe), Pavement Music 76962-32295-2 (USA) (1998)

LIVE IN JAPAN, System Shock IR-C-132 (Europe), Pavement Music 76962 32302-2 (USA) (1998)

LITANY, Metal Blade 3984-14297-2 (Europe / USA) (2000)

Reign Forever World, Metal Blade 3984-14365-2 (Europe / USA) (2001)

REVELATIONS, Metal Blade 3984-14411-2 (Europe / USA) (2002)

Blood, Metal Blade 3984-14461-2 (Europe / USA) (2003)

THE BEAST, Metal Blade 3984-14485-2 (Europe / USA) (2004)

The Art Of War, Regain RR074CD (Europe) (2005), Candlelight CD CDL 251 (USA) (2006)

IMPRESSIONS IN BLOOD, Regain RR098CD (Europe) (2005), Candlelight CD CDL 314 (USA) (2006)

The band's already demanding live schedule intensified further with September 2003 Polish gigs alongside running-mates Decapitated, Frontside, and Vesania, before North American dates, 'The Art Of Noise 2'. This run of shows saw the band allied with Kreator, Nile, Amon Amarth, and Goatwhore, and took them through October.

A September-released EP, *Blood*, featured two new studio songs, 'We Wait' and 'Shape-shifting', alongside cuts from the *Revelations* sessions that had only surfaced previously as part of foreign versions of the album, digipacks, and on EPs. Frontman Wiwczarek readied a solo project, Panzer X, for the studio in September, cutting the EP *Steel First*. Novy, retaining his Vader ties, joined Spinal Cord as bassist in November 2003.

The band planned to work again with producer Piotr Lukaszewski in February 2004 for a new studio album, *The Beast*, but Doc met with an accident in the studio, seriously injuring his hand and leg. Cancelling the sessions, they rebooked studio time at the PR Studios in Gdańsk for a later date, pulling in Daray (aka Darek Brzozowski) from Polish black metal band Vesania as a session musician.

The band then toured in Slovakia and the Czech Republic with Hypnos before a European tour with Malevolent Creation, Naglfar, and Blood Red Throne in June. They played a massive 160-date-plus world tour to keep them active throughout the year, including a prestigious opening slot to Slipknot and Metallica on May 31st to over 50,000 fans at the Silesian Stadium in Chorzów. Also in 2004, Vader donated their rendition of 'Death Metal' to the *Seven Gates Of Horror* tribute album assembled by the Dutch Karmageddon Media label in homage to Possessed.

A run of European gigs was interrupted in late August when, en route to Falkenstein, near Leipzig, the band's tour bus was involved in an accident. Although the bus was seriously damaged, its occupants managed to escape unharmed. US touring plans for October them set to flank Napalm Death, Kataklysm, and Goatwhore. However, the band pulled out of these shows as Wiwczarek required an operation to treat "a minor spinal injury" sustained on tour in Scandinavia.

To close the year, the band were announced as one of the main attractions at 2004's 'X-Mass Fest' festival with Napalm Death, Marduk, Finntroll, The Black Dahlia Murder, and Belphegor. In March 2005, Vader parted ways with longtime drummer Doc, drafting Daray as substitute. Frontman Wiwczarek explained: "Doc tried pretty hard to 'fight' against his weaknesses, which were troubles for all of us."

US shows in April 2005 had the band packaged with Kreator, Pro-Pain, and The Autumn Offering. They broke this exhaustive touring schedule to enter Hertz Studios in Bialystok in early July, recording the EP *The Art Of War*, their first product for new label Regain. Orchestral introductions for these sessions were conducted by Siegmar from Vesania.

European gigs in June saw Lost Soul as support act, and a Polish tour of September, 'Blitzkrieg III', saw support from Greek veterans Rotting Christ, fellow Poles Lost Soul again, and French extreme metal band Anorexia Nervosa. Tragedy hit in August with the announcement of the death of Docent. The musician was just 35 years old and had a history of alcohol-related problems.

Renewed road work in the USA continued in late 2005, with November shows with Suffocation, Cephalic Carnage, and Aborted. The group headlined a memorial show for Docent at the Proxima Club in Warsaw on December 11th, supported by a local cast of Ceti, Hate, Dead Infection, Lost Soul, Corruption, Azarath, Chainsaw, and Virgin Snatch.

The band were included on the 'Metal Crusaders' North American tour, taking place in May and June 2006 alongside Kataklysm, Graveworm, Speed Kill Hate, Destruction, and The Absence. Nightrage and Bloodthorn were confirmed as support acts for the Scandinavian leg of the world tour, taking in Denmark, Norway, Sweden, and Finland, in November. They remain one of the most reliable metal acts on the scene.

NEO-METAL

BY THE

1990s, heavy metal had enjoyed three commercial peaks, first with the NWOBHM, then with the thrash metal wave, and then the massive 1980s popularity of the hair-rock generation. However, in 1991 grunge delivered an almighty blow that shook metal to its core.

While high-profile rock bands withered and died in the wake of Nirvana and their plaid-shirted ilk, the metal underground hunkered down and got on with business away from the spotlight. With the US touring circuit temporarily dried up for most metal bands, they refocused their sights on Europe. Germany in particular shrugged off grunge as an aberration and continued to support metal, throwing a lifeline to acts such as Saxon, Iron Maiden, and Motörhead.

Pantera were the first and most important band to rise to the surface once grunge had collapsed in the wake of Kurt Cobain's death in 1994 (and inevitably grunge itself had died). The Texan outfit had just undergone a staggering musical transformation, producing an entirely new strain of metal. The overblown clichés that had sustained the genre throughout the 1980s were now replaced by a stripped-down, hardcore attitude. Once Pantera hit Number 1 in the USA, neo-metal had well and truly proved that metal had found a new way to reach the masses. Another important act was Fight, Rob Halford's solo act, although his attempts to capitalise on the new sound were met by an unconvinced audience.

Thankfully, neo-metal was a diverse and eclectic pool of talent. Bands that carved out a career during this period included industrialists Fear Factory and Clawfinger, the pioneering (and too often neglected) Stuck Mojo, the million-selling Biohazard, the perennially popular Machine Head, and the cerebrally challenging Strapping Young Lad. None of these utilised metal's traditional lyrical fare of fantasy and fornication – all were street smart, employing a heavier sound and gearing their music towards the youth market. The advent of neo-metal across the USA and the UK also called an end to the stereotypical metal uniform: long hair, leathers, and patch-festooned denims were out; buzzcropped skulls and shorts were in.

Unfortunately, neo-metal paved the way for nu-metal, a dumbed-down and – thankfully – shortlived exercise. Whereas neo-metallers Machine Head, Pantera and the rest had chosen to strip metal down to its raw, primal element, the nu-metal bands appeared devoid of technical aptitude and ambition. Famously, guitar solos hit the dust. However, once this hollow white elephant imploded, real metal charged back in fine style.

BIOHAZARD
THE NEW YORK HARDCORE

BIOHAZARD WERE FORMED IN BROOKLYN, New York City, in 1987 as a trio of vocalist-bassist Evan Seinfeld, guitarist Bobby Hambel, and drummer Anthony Meo. Guitarist Billy Graziadei joined shortly after. Drummer Danny Schuler replaced Meo in 1988 after the band's first demo. A second demo was issued in 1989: both tapes were self-titled. Biohazard re-sculpted metal music at a time when the scene was stale, with their prescient sense of timing rapidly transferring into significant album sales. Besides fronting Biohazard, Seinfeld has built a career in the adult movie industry, billed as Spyder Jones and working exclusively with his wife, the porn star Tera Patrick. His parallel porn and mainstream TV career served him well once Biohazard's star began to dim.

Early Biohazard shows included opening for Exodus at L'Amours club. Their first demo caused a stir with some journalists, who alleged that the lyrics displayed fascist and white supremacist views. This was strenuously denied by the band; both Seinfeld and drummer Danny Schuler are Jewish.

An eponymous album arrived on the Maze label in 1990, followed by *Urban Discipline*, produced by Wharton Tiers at Fun City Studios and released in October 1992 by Roadrunner. Digipak versions added live versions of 'Shades Of Grey' and 'Punishment'. Biohazard were yet to break out of Brooklyn, with the band members still holding down day jobs. Graziadei was a truck driver, Seinfeld delivered building materials, and Schuler worked in a stockroom.

Urban Discipline's timing was fortuitous, the album not only breaking Biohazard internationally but influencing a new generation of up-and-coming bands with its blend of hip-hop and hardcore. The radio hit 'Slam' was given a new lease of life by rap act Onyx: the Onyx-Biohazard duo reunited to cut the title track for the seminal *Judgment Night* movie soundtrack, which sold over two million units in the USA. *Urban Discipline*, spurred on by major MTV rotation for the video of 'Punishment' and support slots to Kyuss, House Of Pain, Fishbone, and Sick Of It All, eventually broke one million sales.

Now with worldwide status, Biohazard switched labels to the Warners corporation. *State Of The World Address* in 1994 broke the American Top 50 and racked up a million sales. A single, 'How It Is', featured Sen Dog of Cypress Hill. Prior to their appearance at the Kiss-headlined Donington 'Monsters Of Rock' festival in front of 45,000 people, Biohazard put in a secret warm-up show at London's Garage venue with Fear Factory.

Biohazard parted company with guitarist Bobby Hambel in 1995 after touring to promote the *State Of The World Address* album. The new album, *Mata Leão* ('To Kill The Lion'), was recorded as a trio. They replaced Hambel in 1996 with ex-Helmet and Rest In Pieces guitarist Rob Echeverria. The band's focus was reportedly distracted by internal struggles, drug dependency, and alcohol abuse – but despite it all they

BIOHAZARD discography

BIOHAZARD, Maze MCD 1067 (USA) (1990)

URBAN DISCIPLINE, Roadrunner RR 9112-2 (Europe / USA) (1992)

STATE OF THE WORLD ADDRESS, Warner Music 9362-45595-2 (Europe), Warner Bros. 9362-45595-2 (USA) (1994) **72 UK, 48 USA**

MATA LEÃO, Warner Music 9362-46208-2 (USA), Warner Bros. 9362-46208-2 (USA) (1996) **72 UK, 170 USA**

NO HOLDS BARRED – LIVE IN EUROPE, Roadrunner RR 8803-2 (Europe / USA) (1997)

NEW WORLD DISORDER, Mercury 546 032-2 (Europe / USA) (1999) **187 USA**

TALES FROM THE B-SIDE, Renegade cnu (UK), Orchard 801120 (USA) (2001)

UNCIVILIZATION, Steamhammer SPV 085-72392 (Europe), Sanctuary 06076-84519-2 (USA) (2001)

KILL OR BE KILLED, Steamhammer SPV 085-74782 (Europe), Sanctuary 06076-84563-2 (USA) (2002)

MEANS TO AN END, Steamhammer SPV 085-69882 (Europe), Steamhammer 69882 (USA) (2005)

remained a stable unit. However, *Leão*, released in 1996, did not match the sales of *State Of The World Address*.

The band re-signed to Roadrunner when *Leão* failed to live up to Warners' expectations. The *No Holds Barred* live album – released in 1997 – kept up the pace, including a version of Black Sabbath's 'After Forever'. Their April 1997 British tour saw support from My Own Victim and Consume, and Seinfeld put in a guest appearance on Italian hardcore act Crackdown's 1998 debut *Rise Up*.

The band signed to Mercury and released the *New World Disorder* album in 1999 but were dropped after one album. Echeverria left in 2000 and was replaced by former Outline and All Means Necessary guitarist Leo Curley before a compilation album, *Tales From The B-Side*, was released independently by the band in 2001.

Biohazard signed to SPV/Steamhammer for Europe and Sanctuary for the rest of the world for a 2001 album, *Uncivilization*, recorded at their own Rat Piss Studios in downtown Brooklyn. Guests included the Sepultura duo of Derrick Green and Andreas Kisser on 'Trap', their band-mate Igor Cavalera on 'Gone', Cypress Hill's Sen Dog on 'Last Man Standing', Pantera's Phil Anselmo on 'H.H.F.K.', and Type O Negative main-man Peter Steele on 'Cross The Line'. Roger Miret of Agnostic Front and the Skarhead duo of Danny Diablo and Puerto Rican Mike appeared on 'Unified' while Hatebreed's Jamey Jasta and members of Slipknot contributed to 'Domination'.

The band's European and UK tour, with support principally from Tattoo, was delayed by the September 11th US terrorist attacks but was rescheduled later the same month.

Biohazard then scheduled an American set of headliners beginning on November 7th at Los Foufounes Electriques in Montreal. Clutch and Candiria were added to the bill on the 15th in New York.

March 2002 brought the news that Graziadei was pursuing a side venture with Sepultura drummer Igor Cavalera and Brazilian DJ Patife. Rumours were persistent throughout May that Leo Curley had lost his position in the band. Nucleus guitarist Carmine Vincent, a former Biohazard roadie, was then confirmed as his replacement.

European festival dates, including the 'Bulldog Bash' in the UK, were cancelled when new guitarist Carmine Vincent underwent major surgery. The band then revealed an impressive package tour of Europe, the

'Eastpak Resistance' dates, during November and December of 2002, with Biohazard topping a bill of Agnostic Front, Hatebreed, Discipline, All Boro Kings, and Born From Pain. Guitarist Scott Roberts of Cro-Mags acted as stand-in. Schuler guested on demo tracks for Among Thieves in September.

After releasing *Kill Or Be Killed* in 2003, Biohazard were set to get back onto the touring circuit in North America in January 2003 with Kittie, Brand New Sin, and Eighteen Visions. The group announced Scott Roberts, of Among Thieves and The Spudmonsters, as their permanent live guitarist. However, these shows were curtailed when Seinfeld came down with a mystery illness.

With Biohazard out of action, Schuler and Graziadei engaged themselves as a mixing team for Life Of Agony's comeback live album. Before long the band were back in action, putting in Japanese headline dates in May followed by the 'Jailhouse Rock' North American tour in June. These shows had Biohazard headlining over Hatebreed, Agnostic Front, Throwdown, and Full Blown Chaos.

Biohazard undertook recordings for a new album, *Means To An End*, in late 2004. However, due to a "studio disaster", the record was apparently lost, forcing the band to re-record it. The album finally emerged in August 2005 with the announcement that it would be Biohazard's last record. On December 15th, Seinfeld and Graziadei joined the Roadrunner United conglomerate at the New York Nokia Theater. The gig opened with Biohazard's 'Punishment' performed by Seinfeld, Graziadei, Sepultura's Andreas Kisser, ex-Fear Factory man Dino Cazares, and Slipknot's Joey Jordison.

In February 2006, Seinfeld filmed a VH1 television series, *Supergroup*, a reality show also starring Ted Nugent, Scott Ian of Anthrax, vocalist Sebastian Bach, and Jason Bonham of Bonham, UFO, and Foreigner. Meanwhile, founding Biohazard guitarist Bobby Hambel re-emerged, breaking a ten-year hiatus from the music scene, to record a new solo record. Biohazard may be gone but the impact they left on the metal scene is permanent.

CLAWFINGER
RAP-METAL PIONEERS

CLAWFINGER ARE A RAP-METAL ACT FORMED in 1988 by singer Zak Tell and keyboard player Jocke Skog, two disillusioned orderlies from Sweden's Rosenlund hospital. The two guitarists, Bård Torstensen and Erlend Ottem, had played in another local outfit, Theo. The Stockholm

Clawfinger

CLAWFINGER discography

DEAF DUMB BLIND, EastWest 4509-93321-2 (UK) (1993), Metal
 Blade 3984-14073-2 (USA) (1994)
USE YOUR BRAIN, EastWest 4509-99631-2 (UK) (1995)
CLAWFINGER, WEA 3984-20177-2 (Europe) (1997)
A WHOLE LOT OF NOTHING, Supersonic 080 (Europe) (2001)
ZEROS AND HEROES, Supersonic 132 (Europe) (2003)
HATE YOURSELF WITH STYLE, Nuclear Blast NB 1550-2
 (Europe), Nuclear Blast America 1550 (USA) (2005)

DAMAGEPLAN discography

NEW FOUND POWER, Elektra 7559-62939-2 (Europe / USA) (2004)
38 USA

band's original three-track demo, consisting of 'Waste Of Time', 'Nigger', and 'Profit Preacher', quickly secured them local radio airplay and attracted the attention of the MVG label.

Clawfinger's first single, 1993's 'Nigger', caused something of a stir, mainly for its title. In fact it was an anti-racism statement that became a huge hit in their home country and brought them to the attention of the masses throughout Europe. Major support slots with Anthrax and Alice In Chains followed the addition of bassist André Skaug and drummer Richard Netterman. Recognition for their efforts came with the Swedish Grammy Awards in 1994, where they scored awards in the Best Hard Rock Band and Best Video categories.

Their debut album, *Deaf Dumb Blind*, was released in April 1993 and sold around 400,000 copies. MVG, with links to EastWest Records throughout Europe, were only too happy to put the band back in the studio for *Use Your Brain*. This album, surfacing in 1995, benefited from a harder-hitting production and a heavier edge to the guitars. The same year, the band donated a remix of Die Krupps' 'To The Hilt' to the *Rings Of Steel* album.

A self-titled album emerged in September 1997, charting high in Germany and backed by three singles, 'Biggest And The Best', 'Don't Wake Me Up', and 'Two Sides'. Clawfinger added Ottar Vigerstol on drums for live work in 1998, and UK gigs in September saw fellow Swedes Psycore as opening act.

Japanese editions of the album *A Whole Lot Of Nothing*, released in August 2001, bore an extra track, a version of Pink Floyd's seminal 'Shine On You Crazy Diamond'. Although the band had adopted a far more complex approach, fans lapped it up, putting Clawfinger back into charts across Europe. Switching tack again, the band opted for a raw, stripped-down stance on May 2003's *Zeros And Heroes*. Guitarist Erlend Ottem left the band (and the music business) in October when he shifted to a career as a software specialist.

Clawfinger commenced work on a new album with drummer Henka Johansson, *Hate Yourself With Style*, in May 2005, signing to Germany's Nuclear Blast. Released in November, the album's initial copies came with a bonus DVD of the band's performance at the 'Greenfield' festival in Interlaken, Switzerland, filmed that June. The band continue along their path with apparently unstoppable enthusiasm.

DAMAGEPLAN
PROMISING POST-PANTERA OUTFIT CUT TRAGICALLY SHORT

FORMED DURING JANUARY 2003 IN TEXAS, the post-Pantera outfit of guitarist Darrell 'Dimebag' Abbott and his brother, drummer Vinnie Paul, went under the working name of New Found Power for many months. The brothers finally decided upon the name Damageplan that October. The group, fronted by Patrick Lachman – known as guitarist for Halford,

Dr. Mastermind, State Of The Art, and Diesel Machine – also featured bass guitarist Shawn Matthews of the Jerry Cantrell band. But Matthews left before the name change, and Hawaii native Bob 'Zilla' Kakaha, a man with dubious credentials with 1980s rapper Vanilla Ice, took up the role.

Studio guests for the February 2004 debut album *New Found Power* included Slipknot's Corey Taylor, donating vocals to the track 'Fuck You', and Zakk Wylde, lending his distinctive skills to 'Soulbleed' and 'Reborn'. A promotional video for the track 'Breathing New Life' preceded the album launch as the band conducted a lightning four-date tour of Japan.

New Found Power shifted just under 45,000 copies in its first week of US sales to land at Number 38 in the *Billboard* charts. Meanwhile, the band's collaboration with Jerry Cantrell, the non-album cut 'Ashes To Ashes', featured on the soundtrack to the *Punisher* movie. In a diversion from Damageplan activities, Dimebag and Vinnie guested with Sammy Hagar at his March 9th show at the Palms Casino in Las Vegas, the duo featuring on The Troggs' 'Wild Thing' and The Kinks' 'You Really Got Me'.

Damageplan launched an extensive range of US dates partnered with Drowning Pool, Hatebreed, and Unearth throughout the spring. The band also appeared at the major German 'Rock Am Ring' event and the Metallica-headlined Castle Donington 'Download' festival in the UK. A brief burst of Canadian dates in June saw them hook up with Slayer and Otep. Live work continued in North America as they stepped onto another nationwide trek, and October dates allied them with Shadows Fall and The Haunted.

Damageplan were set to round off their schedule with a series of headline gigs. However, on December 8th tragedy struck the band. Just as they started their set with the song 'New Found Power' at the Alrosa Villa club in Columbus, Ohio, 23-year-old Nathan Gale climbed onto the stage and shot Dimebag a number of times at close range with a Beretta 9mm semi-automatic handgun, killing the guitarist. The assailant also killed the band's technician Jeff Thompson, a club employee named Erin Halk, and fan Nathan Bray. Chris Paluska, the band's tour manager, and John Brooks, a drum technician, were injured. After taking a hostage, the killer was himself shot dead by Columbus police officer James Niggemeyer.

Dimebag was buried in a Kiss coffin, donated at his family's request by Gene Simmons, and it was filled with memorabilia from friends, including a Charvel guitar given for the occasion by Eddie Van Halen. Black Label Society played at the service and Jerry Cantrell and Mike Inez from Alice In Chains, along with Pat Lachman, played a short acoustic set.

The impact on the international metal scene was profound, with Dimebag's murder even making it onto Britain's BBC Evening News. Pundits labelled the killing "metal's 9/11" and profound questions were asked about the issues of onstage security. Dimebag's murder has been the biggest incident in heavy metal's history for decades, and his fans are still deep in mourning as this book goes to press. RIP.

FEAR FACTORY
PIONEERS OF CYBERMETAL

FEAR FACTORY WERE FOUNDED in Los Angeles in 1989 as Ulceration before changing their name in October 1990. They combine industrial sounds with death metal and first came to attention with two tracks on the *LA Death Metal* compilation produced by Faith No More bassist Bill Gould.

The tracks led the band to a deal with Roadrunner and the debut Colin Richardson-produced album, *Soul Of A New Machine,* released in 1992.

The band consisted of singer Burton C. Bell, guitarist Dino Cazares, drummer Raymond Herrera, and bassist Andy Romero, who was replaced by Dave Gibney in 1990. Bassist Andrew Shives, later of Cool For August, joined the band in 1991, but did not play on *New Machine* (Cazares played bass on the album). Shives was then replaced by Christian Olde Wolbers, a native of Belgium and a lead guitarist at the time. He had been spotted by Biohazard's Evan Seinfeld playing upright bass in a Belgian club, and Seinfeld recommended Olde Wolbers for the Fear Factory bass position.

The band undertook a European tour opening for Brutal Truth prior to American dates with Sick Of It All and Biohazard. To capitalise on this progress and the warm reception afforded the debut album, Canadian industrial band Frontline Assembly remixed tracks for the 1993 mini-album *Fear Is The Mind Killer.* Live dates were rounded off by support slots to Sepultura.

The second album, 1995's *Demanufacture,* was recorded in Chicago and at New York's Bearsville studios. Supporting the album, Fear Factory acted as openers on Ozzy Osbourne's November 1995 'Retirement Sucks' UK dates. In downtime, Bell recorded vocals for Black Sabbath bassist Geezer Butler's G//Z/R album, *Plastic Planet.* Herrera sessioned for Phobia, appearing on the *Return To Desolation* EP. The *Remanufacture* album, featuring electronica and hardcore techno remixes of tracks from *Demanufacture,* was released in 1997.

Obsolete, released in 1998, included a cameo appearance from electro pioneer Gary Numan: the band had been covering Numan's Tubeway Army track 'Cars' as a live encore for some time. Fear Factory then toured America as openers for Slayer, Rob Zombie, and Monster Magnet. European shows in December found them headlining with labelmates Spineshank as support.

Burton C. Bell contributed guest vocals to British act Apartment 26's debut album – the connection being that the band are led by Biff, son of Geezer Butler. Bell also worked with Kill II This and Static-X, while Cazares guested on guitar with German techno-metal act Atari Teenage Riot. Cazares and Herrera also moonlighted with Brujeria with Bill Gould.

Meanwhile, Olde Wolbers founded a successful alternative career as a hip-hop producer and programmer, naming himself The Edgemaster and scoring high-profile credits with the likes of Snoop Dogg and Ice Cube.

The 2001 *Digimortal* album was issued in Japan with four extra tracks, 'Full Metal Contact', 'Dead Man Walking', 'Strain Vs. Resistance', and 'Repentance'. Fear Factory returned in January 2002 with the DVD/CD package *Digital Connectivity*: as well as live and video footage, it included eight audio tracks. Their 'Evolution Through Revolution' American tour in May 2002 was supported by Dry Kill Logic and others.

Fans were shocked in early March 2002 when the band announced a split: apparently artistic differences between Bell and Cazares were the main cause. As a parting shot, Roadrunner released a previously-unreleased 1991 album, *Concrete,* produced by Ross Robinson.

Subsequent rumours suggested that Bell was embarking on a stoner-rock project with his colleague Herrera, Olde Wolbers, and keyboard player John Bechdel. However, Fear Factory reformed more or less immediately without Cazares, who was now involved in Asesino with Static-X bassist Tony Campos.

Archetype was released in April 2004. The band explained that Olde Wolbers had played both guitar and bass in the studio, and that live bass would be played by Byron Stroud of Strapping Young Lad. Tour plans for February 2004 put Fear Factory in partnership with Korn and Static-X for a run of Australian dates, after which the band joined Slipknot and Chimaira for the fourth instalment of the 'Jägermeister Music' US tour.

In May 2005, the band began work with producer Toby Wright to cut a new album, *Transgression,* including cover versions of Killing Joke's 'Millennium' and Godflesh's 'Anthem'. Billy Gould contributed to 'Echo of My Scream' and 'Super Nova' while Mark Morton of Lamb Of God scored a co-composition credit on 'New Promise'. After extensive touring, Olde Wolbers worked as co-producer on album material for Danish band Mnemic before temporarily joining Korn for three concerts in Europe.

Fear Factory united with Suffocation, Hypocrisy, and Decapitated for US shows in November 2006. At the time of writing they seem to have recovered from Cazares' departure, but only time will tell if they can regain the commercial peak they enjoyed with *Digimortal.*

FEAR FACTORY discography

SOUL OF A NEW MACHINE, Roadrunner RR 9160-2 (Europe), Roadrunner RRD 9160 (USA) (1992)

Fear Is The Mindkiller, Roadrunner RR 9082-2 (Europe) (1993)

DEMANUFACTURE, Roadrunner RR 8956-2 (Europe / USA) (1995) **27 UK**

REMANUFACTURE: CLONING TECHNOLOGY, Roadrunner RR 8834-2 (Europe / USA) (1997) **22 UK**

Revolution, Roadrunner RR 2232-5 (Europe) (1998)

OBSOLETE, Roadrunner RR 8752-2 (Europe / USA) (1998) **20 UK**

Cars, Roadrunner RR 2189-3 (Europe) (1999) **57 UK**

DIGIMORTAL, Roadrunner RR 8561-2 (Europe / USA) (2001) **32 USA**

CONCRETE, Roadrunner RR 8439-2 (Europe / USA) (2002)

HATEFILES, Roadrunner RR 8398-2 (Europe / USA) (2003)

ARCHETYPE, Roadrunner RR 8311-2 (Europe), Liquid 8 LIQ12189 (USA) (2004) **30 USA**

Bite The Hand That Bleeds – And Related Archetypal Imagery, Liquid 8 LIQ12250 (USA) (2004)

TRANSGRESSION, Roadrunner RR 8131-2 (Europe), Calvin 037 (USA) (2005) **45 USA**

FIGHT
ROB HALFORD'S EXTRACURRICULAR PROJECT

FIGHT WERE CREATED BY JUDAS PRIEST vocalist Rob Halford in 1991 when he bowed out of that band after their hugely successful *Painkiller* world tour, taking drummer Scott Travis with him. Although at first he had the blessing of Priest for this out-of-the-blue project, a bitter verbal conflict ensued.

Longstanding fans were somewhat bemused by the shift in Halford's traditional leather-and-studs image to a look that clearly mimicked that of Pantera vocalist Phil Anselmo. On March 3rd 1992, Halford joined Pantera on stage at Irvine Meadows in California, where they performed Judas Priest tracks 'Grinder' and 'Metal Gods'. This in turn led to the two parties collaborating on a Halford-composed song, 'Light Comes Out Of Black'. Recorded in Dallas, the track was included on the soundtrack to the movie *Buffy The Vampire Slayer* in July.

Halford then recruited guitarist Brian Tilse and bass player Jay Jay (aka John Brown), with Guitar Institute of Technology graduate Russ Parrish of War And Peace on second guitar. Jay Jay, who divided his energies with Satanic Industries Ltd., had met Rob in his capacity as a tattooist at HTC Precision Piercing in Phoenix, inking much of Halford's body art. This line-up of Fight cut demos at Vintage Sound Studio in Phoenix, scoring a deal with Epic Records, and debuted live in Halford's home-town of Phoenix, Arizona, at the Mason Jar in August 1993.

The eagerly-awaited debut album, September 1993's *War Of Words*, was light years removed from Judas Priest: Halford had toned down his vocal range and was using down-tuned guitars on much simpler songs. The tracks had been recorded at Wisseloord Studios in Hilversum, Holland with production credits shared between Halford and Attie Bauw. Many critics panned the release as a second-rate Pantera copy, but Halford still managed to take many Priest fans with him. The singer's reputation put *War Of Words* into the US charts at Number 83, while Bauw received Grammy nominations for Producer Of The Year and Best Engineered Album.

Touring began in Frankfurt on October 19th with The Organization in support. However, English dates at Nottingham Rock City and London's Astoria 2 were marred by paltry attendance figures, with many Priest fans feeling almost betrayed by Halford's endeavours. The vocalist reacted with vitriolic statements about the British media. In the States, Halford enjoyed a better response, engaging in a series of club headliners with guests Cathedral.

International tours with Voivod, Anthrax, and Metallica followed before line-up changes and the January 1994 mini-album *Mutations*, consisting of remixes and live tracks, including a raucous rendition of Judas Priest's 'Freewheel Burning'. Halford was busying himself outside Fight with his EMAS Management organisation. Taking on Australian thrashers Allegiance, he secured a deal for the young act with major label Polygram for their *D.E.S.T.I.T.U.T.I.O.N.* album. As 1994 came to a close, Rob forged a one-off studio band billed as The Bullring Brummies, consisting of the Black Sabbath rhythm section of bassist Geezer Butler and drummer Bill Ward, Wino of The Obsessed, and harmonica player Jimmy Wood, to cut a version of Black Sabbath's 'The Wizard' for the *Nativity In Black* tribute album. Fight rounded out 1994 with a radio promo single, 'Christmas Ride', a unique, seasonal track that included festive greetings from Rob.

April 1995's *A Small Deadly Space*, which debuted at a lowly Number 120 in the USA, featured former Coup De Grace guitarist Mark Chaussee in the group. The band once again opted to work with producer Bauw for this album (which closed with a hidden track, 'Psycho Suicide').

Tours followed, but Fight's days were numbered. After a brief period working with Black Sabbath guitarist Tony Iommi in 1996, the singer formed a new band named Halford. This act initially consisted of two Fight personnel, Brian Tilse and Jay Jay. Together with Vent drummer Don Juan, they delivered a one-off show at the Phoenix Mason Jar on December 20th in aid of the Child Crisis Center's Children Of The Desert charity.

Halford then embarked upon a truly radical path. The band renamed themselves Gimp and then Two, emerging with an industrial rock album, *Voyeurs*, produced by Trent Reznor of Nine Inch Nails. Many of Halford's fans were left scratching their heads in bemusement – and even more so when Rob apparently denounced metal as dead and buried.

Much to the relief of his fans, the singer renamed his band Halford and relaunched his career in 2000 with the suitably titled *Resurrection* album, a remarkable statement of metal intent that charted internationally.

Rob signed to Iron Maiden manager Rod Smallwood's Sanctuary organisation for management and label, and saw his profile rise sharply with a guest slot to Iron Maiden's American dates.

Inevitably, Rob rejoined Judas Priest in 2004. In December, while promoting the Priest comeback album *Angel Of Retribution*, he voiced the possibility of a live Fight DVD and the prospect of the band reuniting to record new material.

On June 1st 2006, Rob announced the formation of the Metal God Entertainment label to reissue his Halford and Fight material, including DVD concert footage of Fight. That October, Metal God Entertainment unveiled plans for the DVD *Fight, War Of Words – The Film*, containing footage filmed throughout 1992 and 1993. In November, the archive set *K5 The War Of Words Demos* was released. And so the Fight story seems far from over.

GWAR
MONSTROUS, SEMEN-SQUIRTING METAL FREAKS, ANYONE?

GWAR BURST ONTO THE METAL scene with some of the most outrageous stage costumes ever used by a rock band (or anyone else). Offering a heady brew of sci-fi and an unhealthy sexual fixation, GWAR succeeded in shocking the establishment from the outset, and their high-quality theatrics soon drew in legions of supporters. Band-members took to the stage adorned in exaggerated fantasy costumes, wielding oversize weaponry and spraying their audiences with (thankfully) fake bodily fluids.

They claimed a lineage of millions of years as a group of rebel space pirates, the Scumdogs Of The Universe. Supposedly banished to Earth, GWAR claimed responsibility for the extinction of the dinosaurs, the emergence of mankind, and the destruction of Atlantis. For these heinous deeds they were imprisoned in Antarctica until their escape in time for a debut album, *Hell-O* in 1988.

The outlandish costumes hid the alter egos of vocalist Dave Brockie (Oderus Urungus), guitarist Mike Derks (Balsac The Jaws Of Death), guitarist Zack Blair (Flattus Maximus), and bassist Casey Orr (Beefcake The Mighty). By this juncture GWAR, who were formed in 1985, had undergone a series of line-up combinations.

Needless to say, the band's origins lay not in Antarctica but at Commonwealth University in Richmond, Virginia. Pre-GWAR, Brockie had been a member of the hardcore trio Death Piggy, which had released three singles in the 1980s – 'Love War', 'Death Rules The Fairway', and 'R45'. In 1985, Brockie and Death Piggy drummer Sean Sumner teamed up with director Hunter Jackson, who was planning a movie entitled *Scumdogs Of The Universe*. The costumes for the intended movie provided the catalyst for the first GWAR incarnation. This version also featured guitarist John Cobbett, later to make his mark with an eclectic range of acts including The Lord Weird Slough Feg. For a while, both Brockie and Sumner divided their duties between Death Piggy and GWAR, but the drummer was imprisoned for attempted murder.

GWAR's debut came in 1988 with the Mark Kramer-produced *Hell-O* for Shimmy Disc Records. *Hell-O*'s bizarre concept hung on basic punk-metal and a mind-boggling patchwork of scatology, political satire, automobile-eating, and even a twisted affection for deceased pets in 'I'm In Love (With A Dead Dog)'. Things would only get more surreal with each album.

Metal Blade picked up the band for their second dose, 1990's *Scumdogs Of The Universe*, triggering a business relationship that would deliver a whole decade's worth of metal. Produced mainly by Ron Goudie, the record benefited hugely from its position as GWAR's opening gambit for much of the world, the previous effort having enjoyed very

little exposure beyond the underground. Fans of the band Ministry soon learned that Hypo Luxa and Hermes Pan, credited with production of the track 'Horror Of Yog', were in fact Al Jourgensen and Paul Barker.

Scumdogs Of The Universe witnessed a significant change in the band structure. Only Brockie, Rowell, and Bishop remained, with a fresh cast comprising guitarist Michael Derks as Balsac The Jaws of Death and Brad Roberts on drums (Jizmak Da Gusha), with studio vocals donated by Danielle Stampe (Slymenstra Hymen), Chuck Varga (Sexecutioner), and Don Drakulich (Sleazy P. Martini).

America Must Be Destroyed in 1992 included session musicians Tim Harris of Eek A Mouse and Kepone, and Rosebud Brian Fechino on guitars. The catalyst for the record's anti-authority stance was Brockie's conviction in North Carolina for public display of his prosthetic penis.

GWAR tours featured Barry Ward (Rich Kids On LSD) as on-stage guitarist. During 1993, the band introduced Rigor Mortis's Peter Lee on guitar and the following year drafted in Casey Orr on bass. Orr's prior experience included terms with Texan thrash metal band Warlock. Further albums – *This Toilet Earth* (1994) and *Ragnarök* (1995) – kept the GWAR brand in the public eye.

In 1995, they released *You Have The Right To Remain Silent* under further assumed names, billing themselves X-Cops. This side project credited themselves as Sheriff 'Tub' Tucker ("vocals + shotgun"), Sgt. Al Depantsia (guitar + Colt .22), Lt. Louis Scrapinetti (guitar + Beretta 9mm), Patrolman Cobb Knobbler (bass + .357 magnum), and Cadet Billy Club (drums + Uzi 9mm), with guests Mountain Bike Officer Biff Buff (vocals + police issue .45), Sgt. Zypygski (vocals + taser), and Dectective Philip

McRevis ('samples + snub nose .38'). Touring to promote the album without revealing their identities as the GWAR characters proved a struggle. The following year original GWAR drummer Sean Sumner took his own life. Meanwhile, another former GWAR drummer, Jim Thompson, founded Bio Ritmo for a Spanish-language metal album. GWAR, backed by X-Cops, toured Europe throughout March and April 1996.

They returned in March 1997 with their sixth offering, the experimental *Carnival Of Chaos*. Peter Lee as Flattus Maximus bowed out with this album, suffering from the after-effects of a gunshot wound.

The expletive-ridden *We Kill Everything* arrived in April 1999. Balsac The Jaws Of Death featured as lead vocalist for the first time on the track 'Escape From The Mooselodge', actually a remake of an earlier cut, 'The Needle'. The band also re-assembled 1989's 'Cardinal Syn Theme', renaming it 'A Short History Of The End Of The World'. Notably, *We Kill Everything* marked the final appearance of Michael Bishop (temporarily acting as Beefcake The Mighty), Danielle Stamp, Hunter Jackson, and keyboard player Dave Musel. In another change, Tim Harris played the character of Flattus Maximus.

The band's 2000 album, *Slaves Going Single*, was only issued to Total Slavery fan-club members, and only 1,000 copies were pressed of this collection of out-takes. The live *You're All Worthless And Weak* was initially released as a fan club 2,000-copies-only album, but appeared commercially in 2002. It was recorded at Washington DC's 9:30 Club on Halloween 1999. For their 2000 American dates, GWAR re-recruited Sexecutioner and Sleazy P. Martini. The dates were supported by Amen and Lamb Of God.

GWAR discography

HELL-O!, Shimmy Disc SDE 8910/CD (Europe), Shimmy Disc 010 (USA) (1988)

SCUMDOGS OF THE UNIVERSE, Master MASCD 001 (Europe), Metal Blade 9 26243-2 (USA) (1990)

AMERICA MUST BE DESTROYED, Metal Blade CDZORRO 37 (UK), Metal Blade 9 26807-2 (USA) (1991) **177 USA**

The Road Behind, Metal Blade 9 45101-2 (USA) (1992)

THIS TOILET EARTH, Metal Blade CDZORRO 63 (UK), Metal Blade/Priority P2 53889 (USA) (1994)

RAGNAROK, Metal Blade 3984-17001-2 (Europe), Metal Blade/Priority P2 50527 (USA) (1995)

CARNIVAL OF CHAOS, Metal Blade 3984-14125-2 (Europe / USA) (1997)

WE KILL EVERYTHING, Metal Blade 3984-14237-2 (Europe / USA) (1999)

SLAVES GOING SINGLE, Slavepit cnu (USA) (2000)

YOU'RE ALL WORTHLESS AND WEAK, Slavepit cnu (USA) (2000)

VIOLENCE HAS ARRIVED, Metal Blade 3984-14374-2 (Europe / USA) (2001)

LET THERE BE GWAR, Slavepit SP004 (USA) (2004)

WAR PARTY, DRT Entertainment RTE 00426 (Europe / USA) (2004)

LIVE FROM MT. FUJI, DRT Entertainment RTE 00431 (Europe / USA) (2005)

BEYOND HELL, DRT Entertainment RTE 00441 (Europe / USA) (2006)

The following year, Brockie emerged with his DBX (Dave Brockie Experience) album *Diarrhea Of A Madman*. Also featured in DBX were GWAR men guitarist Mike Derks and drummer Dave Roberts (Jizmak Da Jusha). Having first revealed the identity of the band to the media in order to avoid the previous calamity with their X-Cops venture, DBX toured America. Also on the billing for these shows was RAWG – actually the full complement of GWAR without costumes.

GWAR promoted their 2001 album *Violence Has Arrived* – with cover artwork from famed Warhammer artist Adrian Smith – by undertaking another bout of North American touring, billed as 'Blood Drive 2002' with God Forbid and Soilent Green. These dates were without the recently departed Slymenstra Hymen. The tour was hit when members of Soilent Green suffered a car accident. Goatwhore took up the newly vacant position. Oderus Ungerus claimed production credits on the 2002 *In The Face Of The Enemy* from Nashville extreme Metal band Disarray.

The band underwent a major line-up shuffle in September, with Orr and Blair both stepping down to concentrate on another act, The Burden Brothers. GWAR duly inducted a new Beefcake in Todd 'T' Evans of Lazy American Workers and Cory Smoot for the role of Flattus. October headline dates in the USA saw Cattle Decapitation and Bloodlet in support.

The band set out on the 'War Party' tour across the USA again in April 2004, selling an album of early demo material at these shows, *Let There Be GWAR*. They switched labels from longstanding partner Metal Blade to DRT Entertainment. Working once again with producer Glen Robinson, they cut *War Party* at Wreckroom Studios in Richmond, Virginia. A national headlining tour, 'Mock The Vote', was supported by Dying Fetus and All That Remains.

GWAR opened 2005 with US dates supported by All That Remains and Alabama Thunderpussy. That May, DRT Entertainment issued a new live album, *Live From Mt. Fuji*. Flattus Maximus took time out of his schedule to act as producer for Municipal Waste's *Hazardous Mutation* album.

The summer of 2005 found the group participating in the US 'Sounds

Of The Underground' tour before dates with Devildriver, A Dozen Furies, and Mensrea. The 'Sounds' tour slot happened again in 2006. In June came the release of a 20-year retrospective DVD, *Blood Bath And Beyond!* Hosted by Oderus Urungus and Sleazy P. Martini, the disc incorporated rare and unreleased material alongside short films, lost demo cuts, and scarce bootleg footage accumulated over the years.

A new GWAR album, *Beyond Hell*, produced by Devin Townsend, was released in August 2006 and featured a cover version of Alice Cooper's 'School's Out'. Nothing, it seems, will stop the progress of this band.

MACHINE HEAD
MODERN METALLERS WITH FULL MARKS FOR PERSEVERANCE

METAL ACT MACHINE HEAD WERE FOUNDED in Oakland, California, by sometime Vio-lence man Robb Flynn in 1992. Before Vio-lence, Flynn had a lengthy spell with Forbidden when they were known as Forbidden Evil, and he is credited with writing much of the material on the Forbidden debut album *Forbidden Evil*. Relative latecomers in the thrash explosion, the Bay Area's Vio-lence, formed in early 1985, nevertheless managed to scramble to a major deal offered by MCA Mechanic during 1988. Original guitarist Troy Fua was superseded by Flynn in January 1987. In this incarnation, the group put out the albums *Eternal Nightmare* in 1988 and *Oppressing The Masses* in 1990. Following the release of the now scarce *Torture Tactics* EP, Flynn exited and Vio-lence managed only one further album without him, 1993's *Nothing To Gain*.

Flynn was keen to form a new band and pulled in guitarist Logan Mader and bass player Adam Duce. Drummer Chris Kontos had been in Attitude Adjustment and an active member of Grinch and Verbal Abuse. An early incarnation of the band featured former Possessed drummer Walter Ryan.

Considerably upping the aggression compared to Flynn's earlier work, the very first Machine Head song was 'Death Church'. The band soon snagged a deal with Roadrunner and debuted live with an American tour, opening for Napalm Death and Obituary. The debut Machine Head album, August 1994's *Burn My Eyes* was recorded at Fantasy Studios in Berkeley, California with producer Colin Richardson, and it made an immediate international impact thanks to its revolutionary blend of traditional thrash metal, groove-oriented hardcore, and modern breakdowns. Embroiled in controversy from the outset, the infamous "Let freedom ring with a shotgun blast!" line from 'Davidian' soon had that track removed from radio airplay. Impressively, the debut muscled its way onto the UK charts at Number 25, signalling the start of steadfast appreciation in that country.

Following the release of *Burn My Eyes*, Machine Head toured North America as part of the 'Divine Intourvention' shows alongside Biohazard and headliners Slayer. Gigs in August saw the band packaged with Obituary and Napalm Death. They continued as guests on Slayer's November 1994 British tour, re-releasing *Burn My Eyes* in digipack format with a bonus track, a cover of Poison Idea's 'Alan's On Fire'. UK headline dates throughout May 1995 saw Mary Beats Jane as support. The group also put in a high-profile appearance at the 1995 Donington festival.

Flynn then engaged with Metallica's Jason Newsted, Sepultura's Andreas Kisser, and Exodus man Tom Hunting on their oddball metal venture Sexoturica, performing live but not featuring on the resulting album. This same illustrious quartet worked up another one-off project, Quarteto Da Pinga, recording in August 1995.

Chris Kontos joined Konkhra in 1996. Machine Head duly auditioned such figures as Tommy Buckley from Soilent Green and future Downset

MACHINE HEAD discography

BURN MY EYES, Roadrunner RR 9016-2 (Europe / USA) (1994) **25 UK**
THE MORE THINGS CHANGE..., Roadrunner RR 8860-2 (Europe / USA) (1997) **16 UK, 138 USA**
THE BURNING RED, Roadrunner RR 8651-2 (Europe / USA) (1999) **13 UK, 88 USA**
YEAR OF THE DRAGON – TOUR DIARY: JAPAN, Roadrunner RRCY-19021 (Japan) (1999)
SUPERCHARGER, Roadrunner RR 1239-2 (Europe / USA) (2001) **34 UK, 115 USA**
HELLALIVE, Roadrunner RR 8437-2 (Europe / USA) (2003) **143 UK**
THROUGH THE ASHES OF EMPIRES, Roadrunner RR 8363-2 (Europe / USA) (2003) **77 UK, 88 USA**

and Bloodsimple drummer Chris Hamilton. Discussions were also held with future Ill Nino drummer Dave Chavarri and Ozzy Osbourne sticks-man Deen Castronovo. The band in fact re-recruited Walter Ryan to fill in on European and Australian gigs while Will Carroll deputised in the USA. Dave McClain, a veteran of Murdercar, Catalepsy, San Antonio Slayer, and Sacred Reich, finally joined in December 1995.

The second album, *The More Things Change...*, again produced by Richardson, witnessed a break away from the band's thrash roots. A limited edition digipack offered three extra cuts, 'My Misery', a take on Discharge's 'The Possibility Of Life's Destruction', and 'Colors', originally by Ice-T. The album emerged in March 1997, breaking into the US charts at Number 138 and making it to Number 16 in the UK. The band toured Britain in April supported by veteran grindcore band Napalm Death and newcomers Skinlab. Further dates saw the band guesting for Pantera in Europe and Megadeth in North America. Flynn found time to add guest vocals to the Earth Crisis album *Breed The Killers*.

The band's line-up troubles were far from over, as early 1998 witnessed the bitter departure of Mader to Soulfly. His replacement was Ahrue Luster, a veteran of such acts as Man Made God, Horde Of Torment, and Pestilence. As the group anticipated the recording of a third album, *The Burning Red*, Flynn revealed that a song tentatively pencilled in for inclusion on that record, 'Devil With The King's Card', had been written about "a certain person who recently left the band". *The Burning Red* was released in August 1999, somewhat obliquely sporting a rendition of the Police hit 'Message In A Bottle', and was crafted at Indigo Ranch in Malibu, California, with Ross Robinson at the board. Again a limited edition added extra tracks: 'Alcoholocaust' and an interpretation of Bad Brains' 'House Of Suffering'. The band's strengthening reputation put the record into the US chart at Number 88 and in the UK at Number 13.

Rumours surfaced in late 2000 that McClain had jumped ship to join Systematic, although this proved to be unfounded, and Machine Head released a new album in October 2001, *Supercharger*. This set veered into a less refined 'mallcore' direction, evidenced by an input of rap vocals, and was unappreciated by the faithful. Naturally, Roadrunner released an expanded *Supercharger*, bolstered with extra songs: the Black Sabbath cover 'Hole In The Sky', out-take 'Ten Fold', and live recordings of 'The Blood, The Sweat, The Tears' and 'Desire To Fire'.

A single, 'Crashing Around You', included live versions of 'Silver' and 'Ten Ton Hammer' recorded in Sweden and produced by Candlemass bassist Leif Edling, and was set for release, but in the wake of the September US terrorist attacks, its release, video, and marketing campaign were cancelled. An alternative idea – to release 'Deafening Silence' as a single – was later scrapped: the plan was to go ahead and release the originally intended 'Crashing Around You' single in the USA in January 2002. However, as sales of *Supercharger* had been poor, Roadrunner decided not to release a single in America at all. 'Crashing Around You' was nonetheless released as a single by Roadrunner in Europe.

Machine Head put in a 'secret' San Francisco gig billed as Ten Ton Hammer in November. Bizarrely, the group dressed up in Mötley Crüe stage gear and performed 'Shout At The Devil' and 'Live Wire'.

In early 2002, a Californian court ruled that the band had the full rights to use the name Machine Head. They had faced legal action from a US sound design company, Dewey Global Holding, Inc., which claimed rights to the title dating back to 1991.

Machine Head announced a clutch of headline European festival dates for the summer of 2002 including the Finnish 'Tuska' and 'Ilosaari' events, Germany's 'Full Force' and Belgium's 'Graspop'. These gigs were scheduled to promote the band's first live album, *Hellalive* (not released until March 2003), recorded mainly at London's Brixton Academy on December 8th 2001. However, as the band confirmed a further Ten Ton Hammer gig in the UK, it was revealed that guitarist Luster had left the fold. Flynn's erstwhile Vio-lence colleague Phil Demmel plugged the gap. The incestuous relationship between Machine Head and Vio-lence was cemented further at the Milwaukee 'Metalfest' event when Machine Head bassist Duce filled in for a honeymooning Deen Dell during Vio-lence's five-song set. Flynn was reportedly approached to audition for the position of vocalist with Drowning Pool, left vacant by the death of Dave Williams – an offer he declined.

Machine Head undertook a novel experiment in early 2003, asking forum members on the band's official website to vote for songs they would like the band to cover. After voting had whittled the tracks down to Metallica's 'Battery', Faith No More's 'Jizzlobber', and 'Toxic Waltz' by Exodus, these three were recorded for internet download. Meanwhile, the recording of a new album, produced by Flynn and Andy Sneap and billed as *Through The Ashes Of Empires*, commenced in the summer. A limited two-disc version of the album added demo tracks and video footage. The new record was released by Roadrunner in Europe, but the band severed ties with the company for North America. November gigs in Europe saw British act Kill II This in support.

Despite *Through The Ashes Of Empires* being slammed in certain sectors of the UK rock press, the album gave the band a new lease of life

Machine Head

in mainland Europe. Germany in particular proved a strong market, as the album – entering the national Media Control charts at Number 24 – gave Machine Head their biggest-selling record to date. The band's summer 2004 live schedule included a number of major European festival performances, including both Scottish and English 'Download' events and Germany's 'Rock Am Ring'.

Machine Head re-signed to Roadrunner in North America to issue *Through The Ashes Of Empires* in April 2004, the record selling over 11,000 copies in the first week to land at Number 88 on the *Billboard* charts. The initial pressing came with bonus tracks.

The band set out on an extensive US spring tour with Arch Enemy, God Forbid, and 36 Crazyfists. Arch Enemy pulled out after just one date, and the God Forbid and 36 Crazyfists vocalists were afflicted by vocal problems, probably streptococcal pharyngitis. In early May, it was Flynn's turn: his strained throat forced the cancellation for the band's Columbus, Ohio, performance.

Machine Head then toured with Chimaira and Trivium for the August 'RoadRage' 2004 dates in North America. The August 8th Philadelphia show was noteworthy as the band celebrated the tenth anniversary of *Burn My Eyes* by performing the record in its entirety along with a clutch of covers. Chimaira's Mark Hunter guested on vocals. There was a batch of Australian gigs in early October followed by an extensive run of European, UK, and Scandinavian shows partnered with Caliban and God Forbid. A show in Rome, Italy was cancelled after their tour bus broke down on its way through the Swiss Alps. A single, 'Days Turn Blue To Gray', was launched to coincide with British dates. Once again, the band performed the entire *Burn My Eyes* album on November 26th at the Academy in Manchester, while the band's London Brixton Academy performance on December 5th was filmed for the *Elegies* DVD, released in October 2005.

A notable stop on the 2005 tour schedule came on March 25th when the band, alongside The Darkness and Sepultura, performed at the 'Desert Rock Festival 2005' in Dubai in the United Arab Emirates, marking the first such occasion for a Western metal band in the Gulf. Support came from local bands Nervecell and Juliana Down. US gigs in May saw a burst of shows allied with Lamb Of God and then headliners with support from Devildriver, The Haunted, and It Dies Today. The band were forced to cancel gigs in Winston-Salem and Charlotte with Flynn suffering from a "severe viral throat infection".

Flynn was one of five high-profile 'team captains' contributing to the Roadrunner United 25th anniversary album *The All-Stars Sessions*, featuring on the tracks 'The Dagger', with vocals from Howard Jones of Killswitch Engage, and 'The Rich Man', with vocals from Corey Taylor of Slipknot. On December 15th, Flynn and Duce joined the Roadrunner United conglomerate at the New York Nokia Theater.

The band then played their part in honouring Metallica, contributing their rendition of 'Battery' to the album *Remastered*, a complete remake of *Master Of Puppets* in joint celebration of the 20th anniversary of the classic album's release and the 25th anniversary of UK rock magazine *Kerrang!* in April 2006. That August, the band entered Sharkbite Studios in Oakland and revealed *The Blackening* as the title of their new album. With their profile at its highest in years, Machine Head are sure to find success with the new record.

PANTERA
TEXAN METAL PIONEERS

THE INFLUENTIAL ARLINGTON-BASED metal band Pantera adopted an aggressive new direction that made them one of the major artists in the metal field, enjoying platinum sales and a Number 1 US album. While the

---

PANTERA discography

METAL MAGIC, Metal Magic MMR 1283 (USA) (1983)
PROJECTS IN THE JUNGLE, Metal Magic MMR 1984 (USA) (1984)
I AM THE NIGHT, Metal Magic MMR 1985 (USA) (1985)
POWER METAL, Metal Magic MMR 1988 (USA) (1988)
COWBOYS FROM HELL, Atco 7567-91372-2 (UK), Atco 7 91372-2 (USA) (1990)
VULGAR DISPLAY OF POWER, Atco 7567-91758-2 (UK), Atco 7 91758-2 (USA) (1992) **64 UK, 44 USA**
FAR BEYOND DRIVEN, EastWest 7567-92302-2 (UK), EastWest America 92302-2 (USA) (1994) **3 UK, 1 USA**
THE GREAT SOUTHERN TRENDKILL, EastWest 7559-61908-2 (UK), EastWest America 61908-2 (USA) (1996) **17 UK, 4 USA**
OFFICIAL LIVE: 101 PROOF, EastWest 7559-62068-2 (UK), EastWest America 62068-2 (USA) (1997) **54 UK, 15 USA**
REINVENTING THE STEEL, EastWest 7559-62451-2 (UK), EastWest America 62451-2 (USA) (2000) **4 USA**

---

mainstream discovered Pantera in 1990 thanks to the *Cowboys From Hell* album, the group had been operational for many years. Their former musical stance and image was wildly different to that portrayed from 1990 onwards – and initially their record company attempted to bury these past excesses, to no avail.

Pantera (Spanish for panther) started life in 1981 on the Texan club scene, performing covers of Van Halen and Kiss songs. Darrell was inspired to pick up the guitar after he'd seen Ace Frehley: he proudly sported an Ace Frehley tattoo and Kiss-emblazoned guitars. Founded at high school, the first Pantera line-up consisted of singer Donnie Hart, guitarists Darrell and Glaze, bassist Tommy Bradford and drummer Vinnie Paul. By 1982 Hart had exited, with Glaze switching from guitar to vocals, and Bradford had been superseded by Rex Brown.

Pantera quickly became cult favourites on the underground metal scene – although fans were constantly bemused by the band's undoubted quality compared with a series of amateur album covers and their apparent inability to break into the big time outside Texas, Oklahoma, and Louisiana.

Nevertheless, Pantera soon became adopted sons on their home turf, supporting the likes of Stryper, Dokken, and Quiet Riot when promoting their debut album *Metal Magic* in 1983, produced at Pantego Studios by The Eld'n (in reality Jerry, father of Darrell and Vinnie and a respected country artist and songwriter). Glaze changed his surname to Lee for 1984's *Projects In The Jungle*, a record again produced by The Eld'n, which saw Pantera drifting away from their more melodic influences.

I Am The Night, emerging in 1985, boosted the band's profile, scoring maximum marks in much of the world's metal press and finding the band in a heavier mood. Pantera were still suffering from poor distribution, with some fans forced to pay extortionate import prices for the album. Consequently the record struggled to sell 25,000 copies.

Soon after the release of *I Am The Night*, Lee split from the band to form Lord Tracy (originally Traci Lords) and Pantera retreated into the shadows. A series of vocalists followed, including Matt L'Amour, who later joined the band Diamond, and David Peacock. These liaisons were shortlived, however, and Pantera eventually re-emerged fronted by Louisiana native and ex-Samhain and Razorwhite singer Phil Anselmo. (Future Crowbar man Matt Thomas and Fall From Grace's Wil Buras had also been in Razorwhite.)

Despite finding a frontman, Pantera still had problems. Their new record label, Gold Mountain, had been tipped off about the band's prowess by Keel guitarist Marc Ferrari, and met Pantera when Keel had played in Dallas with Loudness during 1985. They tried to manoeuvre the band into commercial territory. Undaunted and unconvinced, Pantera recorded their heaviest album to date, *Power Metal*, and negotiated for its release on their own Metal Magic label. Ferrari guested on the album, with Pantera returning the favour by recording Ferrari's composition 'Proud To Be Loud'. Despite the hardness of *Power Metal*, it was nothing compared to what was to come.

The band drew back from the limelight and came close to splintering. Darrell had auditioned for the vacant guitar position in Megadeth and was reportedly offered the post. However, he insisted that Vinnie Paul be part of the package, and Megadeth, who already had a drummer in Nick Menza, backed off, recruiting Marty Friedman instead.

Legend has it that Atco A&R rep Mark Ross discovered Pantera almost by chance, stranded in Texas due to the ravages of Hurricane Hugo. Having caught the band live and noted their significant fanbase, Ross instigated negotiations. The musicians placed their faith in new management, too, contracting with Walter O'Brien at Concrete Inc. in New York. Upon their re-emergence, Pantera surprised many with a new look (Anselmo now sporting shorn hair and a patchwork of tattoos) and a radical change in direction. *Cowboys From Hell*, delivered in July 1990, offered bludgeoning hardcore riffs and a solid intensity to the new songs that buried any comparisons to their more melodic predecessors.

The intensity of tracks such as 'Primal Concrete Sledge' and 'Cemetery Gates' made a keen impression on extreme music fans eager to find a replacement for the waning thrash metal movement. In particular, Diamond Darrell, as he was then still known, had single-handedly re-invented the art of metal guitar playing. His unorthodox yet highly rhythmic stacking of non-conformist notes and liberal use of 'pinch' harmonics engaged a whole new generation of budding six-stringers. *Cowboys From Hell* was a transitional album, with Anselmo retaining at least some of his former vocal stylings, but it projected the band's new focus so strongly that there could be no turning back. MTV took to the group too, giving regular rotation to videos for 'Cowboys From Hell', 'Cemetery Gates', and 'Psycho Holiday'. This 're-debut' album put Pantera into a whole new league.

The 'Cowboys From Hell' tour opened in North America with a bill that saw the Texans sharing the stage with Exodus and Suicidal Tendencies. Later dates had Pantera alongside Mind Over Four and Prong. In the midst of Canadian dates, Judas Priest vocalist Rob Halford joined the band onstage for versions of Priest's 'Grinder' and 'Metal Gods', a union that aided Pantera later the same year as they performed their first European shows opening for the British metal gods. (It's interesting to note that Priest frontman Halford seemingly metamorphosed into an Anselmo clone – both vocally and image-wise – for his subsequent Fight project.) Road work was topped by an appearance at the Tushino Air Field in Moscow on September 28th 1991, featuring on a bill alongside AC/DC, Metallica, and The Black Crowes in front of a crowd of over half a million people.

Two and a half years on the road convinced Pantera to pursue their new-found direction with even more vigour, and February 1992's *Vulgar Display Of Power* silenced all critics as it broke the band worldwide, charting at home at Number 44 and in Britain at 64. These initial entries were deceptive, however: once the Pantera machine started to roll onward, *Vulgar Display*'s sales would prove strong for many years to come. The band renewed their association with Halford, backing him on a promo single, 'Light Comes Out Of Black', featured on the soundtrack to the *Buffy The Vampire Slayer* movie.

While a succession of singles blazed across radio and MTV – 'Walk', 'This Love', and 'Mouth For War' – a gruelling schedule of concerts across the globe found the act sharing stages with Megadeth on their 'Countdown To Extinction' dates, White Zombie, Sacred Reich, Skid Row,

and Soundgarden. Pantera hit Japan for the first time in July 1992, and played the Iron Maiden and Black Sabbath-headlined 'Monsters Of Rock' festival in Italy on September 12th. Soon after that, Darrell changed his nickname from Diamond to Dimebag.

Remarkably for a record of such ferocity, *Far Beyond Driven* – launched in March 1994 with a cover of Black Sabbath's 'Planet Caravan' – topped the American *Billboard* album charts. Pantera were quick to fling themselves headlong into touring with Crowbar. Dates in Argentina had Animal and Lethal as openers, and in Brazil Dr. Sin were the guests. July saw a strengthening of the package as Pantera were now topping a bill of Sepultura and Biohazard before a June 4th Castle Donington 'Monsters Of Rock' performance.

The Donington show, headlined by Aerosmith, was slightly marred by an ugly incident the night before at Nottingham's Rock City club, where both Darrell and Vinnie were involved in altercations with journalists Morät of *Kerrang!* and Paul Rees of *Raw*, the latter due to the drummer having once been portrayed by the magazine in cartoon form as Obelix, Asterix The Gaul's rotund partner.

The May 1994 single '5 Minutes Alone' came backed with a B-side cover of Poison Idea's 'The Badge', originally cut for the band's contribution to the *Crow* movie soundtrack. Back on the road, UK dates that September saw support coming from Downset. By the close of the global trek the band had put in some 90 dates.

The year 1995 began with more live work, but by March Pantera had landed themselves in trouble when, at a Canadian gig in Montreal, a radio DJ perceived some of Anselmo's onstage raps as racist in nature. Anselmo was forced into issuing a public retraction, claiming that his drunken remarks were off-the-cuff and ill-advised.

The same year saw the release of *Nola* by Anselmo's side project Down. The frontman had recorded a batch of brutal songs in Pantera downtime with Pepper Keenan from Corrosion Of Conformity, Crowbar's Kirk Windstein and Todd Strange, and Eyehategod's Jimmy Bower. Although merely assembled as a jam session between friends, Down's debut gained cult status. It signalled a stream of extracurricular projects by the singer.

Pantera bounced back in April 1996 with *The Great Southern Trendkill*. The music for this was recorded with Terry Date at Chasin Jason Studios in Texas, while Anselmo put his vocals down at Nothing Studios in New Orleans. Additional "screams" came courtesy of Anal Cunt's notorious mentor Seth Putnam. A more introspective, moodier affair than

Pantera (Dimebag far right)

its predecessors, the record caught some flak from some reviewers but garnered no such qualms from hardened fans. Worryingly, on July 13th 1996 – an hour after a homecoming Texas gig – Anselmo overdosed on heroin, although he was successfully resuscitated. Taking the metal to the masses once again, Pantera launched into a US tour in August 1996 backed up by White Zombie and Deftones.

As the live campaign rolled into 1997, the band invited Clutch and Soilent Green along for the ride. That year *Cowboys From Hell*, *Vulgar Display Of Power*, and *Far Beyond Driven* each attained platinum status in the USA for one million sales. That July, the concert album *Official Live: 101 Proof*, hosting two studio cuts 'Where You Come From' and 'I Can't Hide', arrived in stores, hitting Number 15 in the USA. However, rumoured dissent within the band was seized upon by the media, and Pantera took a lengthy spell away from the limelight.

Anselmo, billing himself as Anton Crowley, turned up as guitarist with the reformed Necrophagia for their 1999 *Holocausto De La Morte* album. Pantera's audio output that year was restricted to a raucous rendition of Ted Nugent's 'Cat Scratch Fever', included on the *Detroit Rock City* movie soundtrack. Another cover appeared the following year, a take on Black Sabbath's 'Electric Funeral' on the tribute collection *Nativity In Black*. The year 2000 found Anselmo involved in the black metal project Eibon, recording a song for the Moonfog 2000 compilation with Satyricon's Satyr Wongraven, Darkthrone's Fenriz, Maniac of Mayhem, and Necrophagia's Killjoy.

Pantera's *Reinventing The Steel* hit home in March 2000. Two singles were spun off – 'Goddamn Electric' and the Grammy-nominated 'Revolution Is My Name' – and the album fared well, impacting on the *Billboard* charts at Number 4. 'Goddamn Electric' included a guest guitar solo dropped in by Kerry King of Slayer, recorded onto a portable tape machine backstage at a Dallas 'Ozzfest' stop. Unfortunately, the theme of brotherhood and longevity intended by 'We'll Grind That Axe For A Long Time' would later ring false.

Pantera's 2000 European tour found Satyricon as openers, but American dates were curtailed when Anselmo broke two ribs at an early gig. Another of Anselmo's 'Anton Crowley' side projects, the black metal act Viking Crown, issued the *Innocence From Hell* album the same year. A left-field diversion, Rebel Meets Rebel, found Vinnie, Dimebag, and Brown working with country musician David Allan Coe.

After a batch of American headliners winding up in Anchorage, Alaska, the band struck out to Seoul in Korea prior to Australasian gigs in May supported by Corrosion Of Conformity and Australian act Segression. They then assembled the 'Extreme Steel' package for a further American leg bolstered by Morbid Angel, Slayer, Static-X, and Skrape. European 'Tattoo The Planet' dates with Slayer, Biohazard, Vision Of Disorder, and Static X were far from trouble-free. Following the September 11th US terrorist attacks, Pantera pulled out of the tour, leaving Slayer as headliners.

Toward the close of the year, Anselmo took his passion for side ventures into overdrive, adding further bands to his list of projects. Southern Isolation, which featured his girlfriend, Stephanie Opal, as lead vocalist, featured Anselmo as guitarist. The band was rounded out by Ross Karpelman and Kevin Bond of Christ Inversion and Sid Montz on drums. A self-titled four-track EP was issued in October 2001 on the Baphomet label.

Vinnie and Dimebag's ongoing affiliation with David Coe Allen morphed into a southern rock-styled venture, Gasoline. Darrell had also been in discussions with erstwhile Alice In Chains guitarist Jerry Cantrell, Nickelback frontman Chad Kroeger, and Default frontman Dallas Smith about a proposed band.

Anselmo's Down project resurfaced in 2002 with a new album, *Down II: A Bustle In Your Hedgerow*. Another of the singer's endeavours, Superjoint Ritual, released *Use Once And Destroy*, this band made up of bassist Hank Williams III, Eyehategod guitarist Jimmy Bower on guitar, ex-Crowbar guitarist Kevin Bond, and drummer Joseph Fazzio of Stressball.

During mid December it was revealed that Dimebag had teamed up with Kid Rock and Kroeger to record a cover version of Elton John's 1970s hit 'Saturday Night's Alright (For Fighting)'.

After many months of uncertainty, Pantera officially split in 2003, when Vinnie and Dimebag accepted that Anselmo would not be returning to the band. In January, Dimebag and Vinnie united with guitarist Patrick Lachman (Diesel Machine and ex-Halford) and erstwhile Jerry Cantrell guitarist Sean Matthews for a band billed as New Found Power. By October, Matthews was out of the project, which had taken on the new name of Damageplan. The debut album, *New Found Power*, shifted just under 45,000 copies in its first week of US sales to land at Number 38 in the *Billboard* charts.

Throughout 2004, Anselmo (promoting Superjoint Ritual) and the Damageplan members played out a very public verbal sparring match. Despite the bitter words between the camps, fans still hoped for a Pantera reunion in the future. Tragically, those hopes were dashed when the Pantera family was struck the heaviest of blows. Dimebag was murdered at the hands of a disturbed fan on December 8th. (See Damageplan entry for more details.)

On January 5th 2005, Finland's metal community gathered at Helsinki's Rock'n'Roll Station to pay homage, forming a one-off Pantera tribute band Dimen Neemen ('In Dime's Name'). Musicians included Children Of Bodom's Alexi Laiho and Roope Latvala, Atte Sarkima of Ajattara and Verenpisara, Tony Jelencovich from Transport League, Petteri Hirvanen and Nicke of Monsterball, Toni, Pete, Kride, and Jukkis of Norther, and Nico, Euge, and OJ from Godsplague, among many others.

Anselmo had virtually retired from public view in the wake of Dimebag's murder, apart from a video message that he released to the public on the internet. But he did return as a guest guitarist at Eyehategod's August 15th 2005 gig at New York's CBGBs club in New York City. Meanwhile, previously unheard guitar solos by Dime were included on Nickelback's album *All The Right Reasons* in the track 'Side Of A Bullet' after Vinnie donated unused guitar solos from *Vulgar Display Of Power* and *Far Beyond Driven*. Vinnie himself announced the formation of Big Vin Records in November, with the first release the Rebel Meets Rebel project. The war of words between the drummer and singer continued.

Anselmo marked his return to the public eye with a March 10th 2006 concert for VH1 Classic's *Decades Rock Live!* tribute to Heart at the Trump Taj Mahal in Atlantic City, performing with a reunited Alice In Chains.

During August 2006 it was revealed that for a brand new project Vinnie Paul had teamed up with Mudvayne vocalist Chad Gray and guitarist Greg Tribbett, plus Nothingface's guitarist Tom Maxwell and bass player Jerry Montano. In October, having commenced recording for their debut, they named themselves Hell Yeah. The tragic story of Pantera is now closed, but their legacy will remain strong for as long as heavy metal has fans.

SOULFLY
MODERN METAL PERSONIFIED

SOULFLY CENTRE UPON THE larger-than-life character of ex-Sepultura frontman Max Cavalera, a striking figure adorned with heavy tattoos and tangled dreadlocks who once prompted the tag of "the Bob Marley of heavy metal". The imagery surrounding the band, with each album branded with Rastafarian motifs and colours, only served to strengthen this view.

The singer bowed out from Sepultura at their peak, in the wake of their successful *Roots* album, performing with the band for the last time on December 16th 1996 at London's Brixton Academy. He departed in acrimonious circumstances, not even speaking to his drummer brother

Igor for many years. Joining Cavalera's new venture was former Thorn and Crisis drummer Roy Mayorga, Chico Science man Jackson Bandeira on guitar, and former Sepultura lighting technician Marcello Dias Rapp on bass.

The semi-extreme, semi-nu-metal Soulfly embraced the recent tribal and world experimentation of Sepultura's groundbreaking *Chaos AD* and *Roots* albums but took the concept forward, as Cavalera soon recognised the limitations of a set cast of players, instead heading a fluid unit with flavours ranging from metal through to reggae. As his band name implied, Cavalera poured out an increasingly impassioned baring of his soul with each successive album.

Retaining his deal with Roadrunner and his alliances with Sepultura producer Ross Robinson and wife-manager Gloria Bujnowski, Cavalera launched *Soulfly* in May 1998. Guest sessions abounded, with the opening track, 'Eye For An Eye', featuring a vocal spot from Fear Factory's Burton C. Bell, 'Bleed' hosting Limp Bizkit's DJ Lethal and Fred Durst, and Chino Moreno of Deftones making his presence felt on 'First Commandment'. Fear Factory's Christian Olde Wolbers supplied bass on 'No'. The album peaked at Number 79 on the *Billboard* charts. Returning the favour to Moreno, the Soulfly mentor guested on the Deftones' 1997 album *Around The Fur*, poignantly heading up the song 'Headup', written about the unsolved murder of Cavalera's stepson Dana Wells.

Soulfly were announced as part of the prestigious 'Ozzfest' 1998 European touring package, but Bandeira was forced to bow out due to touring commitments with his previous act. Stepping into the breach was American musician Logan Mader who had just quit Machine Head amid a bitter war of words. A subsequent tour edition of *Soulfly* was enhanced by three bonus tracks, 'Cangaceiro' and, acknowledging the seminal British punk band, two Discharge cover versions, 'Ain't No Feeble Bastard' and 'The Possibility Of Life's Destruction'. With momentum still quickening, a 1999 double-disc version of *Soulfly*, packaged in new artwork, boasted a separate disc of remixes and live tracks.

As Soulfly limbered up for the 'Ozzfest' with a batch of American dates, Mader's position within the band was made permanent. However, the guitarist was out by the end of the year due to friction between Cavalera and the guitarist over his side project, Mystriss. The final straw apparently came when Mader neglected to turn up for a soundcheck at a support gig to Black Sabbath. He was replaced by Mike Doling, previously with esteemed American punk act Snot. Both Cavalera and Doling contributed to the *Strait Up* album, a tribute to late Snot frontman Lynn Strait who was killed in December 1999.

In 2000, Soulfly announced that Mayorga had decamped. Former Lääz Rockit and Pro-Pain man Dave Chavarri filled in on the drum stool for the next two months (after which he created Ill Nino). Ex-Fleshold drummer Joe Nunez enrolled and Soulfly, still with bass player Rapp, headlined the second stage at the 'Ozzfest'.

Mader and Mayorga founded Pale Demons (later Medication) alongside ex-Ozzy Osbourne and Suicidal Tendencies bassist Robert Trujillo and Ugly Kid Joe singer Whitfield Crane. Mayorga was then announced as the new drummer for Ozzy Osbourne, joining the recalled Trujillo.

Soulfly's September 2000 album *Primitive*, recorded at the Saltmine in Mesa, Arizona, boasted an array of guests including Slayer's Tom Araya, Slipknot's Corey Taylor, Deftones' Chino Moreno, and Will Haven's Grady Avenell. Rapper Cutthroat Logic also appeared, as did Sean Lennon on 'Son Song'. The record fared well, peaking at Number 32 on the US charts, and the band toured Russia and Europe (including Britain) in late 2000 with support act Glassjaw. Digipack editions of the album added remixes and live cuts from the 1998 Danish Roskilde festival.

In October 2001, Soulfly made another switch in drummers with Nunez making his exit for the Chicago-based Stripping The Pistol. The band persevered, demoing new material with Sacred Reich man Greg Hall on the drum stool, although former member Mayorga was hotly tipped.

Mayorga did finally succumb, announcing his re-recruitment in November.

With a new album imminent, simply titled *3*, Soulfly announced a run of American dates in January 2002 in a co-headlining package with Static-X and support from Soil and Onesidezero. The band's third album, hitting Number 46 on the charts in North America, also came in a limited-edition European version featuring covers of Pailhead's 'I Will Destroy', Black Sabbath's 'Under The Sun', and the Sacred Reich track 'One Nation', with guest appearances from the Sacred Reich personnel Greg Hall and guitarist Wiley Arnett. The rest of the year was taken up with high-profile touring, continuing into 2003 before reports in September that Cavalera had suffered a mass exodus of band members. Doling, Rapp, and Mayorga all defected to form Abloom with Onesidezero members Jason Radford and Levon Sultanian. Their stand-ins for live work were guitarist Marc Rizzo, bassist Bobby Burns of Primer 55, and drummer Joe Nunez. Shortly after this announcement, it was reported that former Megadeth bassist Dave Ellefson had already contributed to four tracks on the new Soulfly record, *Prophecy*. As questions arose about the stability of the band, Cavalera signalled that this revolving cast of band members would be a continuing trend.

Initial versions of *Prophecy*, delivered in March 2004, came with a bonus disc of live material recorded at the 2001 'Hultsfred Festival' in Sweden. An expansive body of work, *Prophecy* drew in a diverse range of influences. Cavalera had travelled to Serbia to record with traditional musicians and local act Eyesburn, and the record employed flute and sheepskin bagpipes as well as pro-Christian lyrics. Alongside the expected

SOULFLY discography

SOULFLY, Roadrunner RR 8748-2 (Europe / USA) (1998) **79 USA**
PRIMITIVE, Roadrunner RR 8565-2 (Europe / USA) (2000) **32 USA**
3, Roadrunner RR 8455-2 (Europe / USA) (2002) **61 UK, 46 USA**
PROPHECY, Roadrunner RR 8304-2 (Europe / USA) (2004) **82 USA**
DARK AGES, Roadrunner RR 8191-2 (Europe / USA) (2005)
　　　　155 USA

metal content, hardcore fused comfortably with Caribbean rhythms alongside a faithful take on Helmet's 'In The Meanwhile'.

Tours in 2004 included a headline slot at the August 14th 'Window Rock Fest II' in Arizona, the largest metal festival on Native American soil – the proceeds of which went to the development of a skateboarding park for Navajo youth. But this turned into a disaster when the band failed to show up for the event, apparently because of inclement weather. Winter shows were pulled, with an official press release stating that Cavalera needed time to recuperate from a leg injury.

Soulfly subsequently announced co-headline US dates with Morbid Angel for February 2005, and with God Forbid and Death By Stereo for shows in March. April dates in Moscow, Novgorod, Kaliningrad, and St. Petersburg saw Hostile Breed as support. European gigs subsequently had the band supporting Black Sabbath.

The band's 2005 album *Dark Ages* included a guest vocal from S.O.D.'s Billy Milano, his contribution apparently recorded via cellphone. Eyesburn vocalist Kojot featured on the song 'Inner Spirit'. A debut single, 'Carved Inside', was promoted by a video filmed in a medieval castle on the Danube river in Serbia.

August saw Soulfly touring the USA, although due to a family emergency bassist Bobby Burns was forced to miss shows in Tempe, Arizona, and Long Beach, California. David Ellefson stepped in as substitute. Meanwhile, *Dark Ages* sold just under 8,000 copies in its first week to debut at Number 155 on the US *Billboard* album chart. Gigs throughout October and November saw support from Throwdown, Bloodsimple, and Incite (the last of these an Arizona band fronted by Ritchie Cavalera, stepson of Cavalera).

Somewhat incestuously, Roy Mayorga joined the ranks of Sepultura in January 2006. Welsh ragga-metal band Skindred lined up to support Soulfly on UK and European dates throughout February and March 2006. A short US West Coast tour had Manntis, A Perfect Murder, and Incite as openers. The band also put in an appearance at the 'Download' festival at Castle Donington on June 9th.

The media march to drive Max Cavalera and Sepultura back together gathered pace throughout the year. In July, Cavalera went on record to say that a reunion would be "cool" and that he had spoken to his brother Igor (who had left Sepultura the previous month) for the first time in many years.

On August 17th 2006, Igor and Max Cavalera were reunited for the first time in ten years, at the 10th annual 'D-Low Memorial Festival' at the Marquee Theatre in Tempe, Arizona. Igor joined headliners Soulfly on stage for renditions of Sepultura classics 'Attitude' and 'Roots Bloody Roots'.

Soulfly gigs in the USA during September 2006 had Wicked Wisdom as support. Bassist Bobby Burns suffered a mild stroke on September 14th, and ex-Megadeth bassist Dave Ellefson stepped into the breach until September 26th, before Anthrax, Nuclear Assault, and Brutal Truth veteran Danny Lilker was recruited to close out the dates. Soulfly's career has been stratospheric, and they will inevitably take second place to any reformed Sepultura with Igor and Max, but the impact they have made on the modern metal scene should not be underestimated.

STRAPPING YOUNG LAD
THE FINEST CANADIAN METAL BAND EVER?

STRAPPING YOUNG LAD FROM VANCOUVER are the adventurous, stereotype-defying act created by ex-Wildhearts guitarist Devin Townsend. Before SYL, Townsend had made a mark with the likes of Steve Vai – on whose *Sex & Religion* album he appeared – industrial experimentalists Frontline Assembly, and Metallica bassist Jason Newsted's side project IR8. As SYL's stature grew, Townsend's reputation at the studio board rose in parallel, and his uncanny ability to engineer monolithic slabs of crystal-clear audio provided him with a side career as an in-demand producer. His chameleon-like nature has given him two distinctly separate platforms from which to vent his artistry – as Strapping Young Lad and also on a series of solo albums.

Townsend initially worked with guitarist Ash Blue, who later formed Unit:187 and Fuel Injected 45. Strapping Young Lad's April 1995 debut – the disjointed, expletive-infested, and grating *Heavy As A Really Heavy Thing* – made an immediate impression, simply for its unadulterated heaviness. Although Townsend's opening gambit utterly confounded critics, it unequivocally achieved its mentor's objectives. Essentially a solo undertaking, the album featured session guitarist Jed Simon, keyboard player Chris Meyers, and no fewer than three drummers: Adrian White, Chris Bayes, and Greg Price. European versions hosted a bonus cut, a hypercharged rendition of Judas Priest's 'Exciter'.

January 1997's Daniel Bergstrand-produced album *City*, with drums contributed by Dark Angel and Death alumnus Gene Hoglan, made a significant impact thanks to the quality of the material. Besides Townsend, Hoglan, and Simon, Strapping Young Lad were now rounded out by bassist Byron Stroud. *City*, including the Cop Shoot Cop cover 'Room 429', effectively channelled the unrestrained aggression of its predecessor into a more familiar song-based vehicle. Townsend found a valuable creative foil in Hoglan, with the drummer's near-superhuman abilities giving the band greater expression into ever more extreme territory. It also introduced Townsend's supreme skills for casting keyboards into a deluging audio wave – now a recognised Strapping Young Lad trademark. The absoluteness of *City* was personified with 'Oh My Fucking God', a song with such a huge crescendo that fans' assertions that it was the heaviest song ever recorded seemed entirely plausible.

The band, plus Unit:187 keyboard player John Morgan, then formed part of the 'Full Of Hate' European tour alongside Obituary, Entombed, and Crowbar before successful American shows with Testament and Stuck Mojo. As a solo artist, Townsend debuted in 1997 with *Ocean Machine – Biomech*; he also gained credits as co-producer of Atlanta heavyweights Stuck Mojo's album *Pigwalk*.

In August 1997, an Australian SYL tour spawned the live album *No Sleep 'Till Bedtime*. Two new studio tracks, 'Japan' and 'Centipede', were included as a bonus. During November the same year Townsend voluntarily entered a mental institution in order to restore some balance to his chaotic lifestyle. Strapping Young Lad then added keyboard player Matteo Caratozzolo, while Stroud and Simon operated the toilet humour-fuelled side project Zimmer's Hole.

Strapping Young Lad was put on hold while Townsend immersed himself in sessions for his next solo album, November 1998's *Infinity*. The track 'Cristeen' was written by Ginger of The Wildhearts, who also put in a studio session. Hoglan contributed drums while Christian Olde Wolbers of Fear Factory supplied bass, Chris Valag provided additional vocals, and Andy Codrington played saxophone. Although the music created a stir, so too did the album cover – a photograph of a gleefully naked Townsend.

On his June 2000 *Physicist* album, Townsend experimented with conflicting soundscapes and industrial-styled collages. Simon, Stroud, and the ever-reliable Hoglan were employed for these sessions before Townsend leapt back into the public eye in 2001 with a typical whirlwind of activity. Not only was he working on his own *Terria* solo project with Hoglan and Mirv's Craig McFarland but he was also deeply involved in Hoglan's Just Cause, as well as producing records for Frygirl and Zimmer's Hole.

Strapping Young Lad provided two live tracks – 'S.Y.L.' and 'Detox', recorded at the Hollywood Roxy in September 2001 – as part of Century Media's tenth anniversary DVD. Townsend then acted as producer for Swedish act Soilwork during October 2001 before taking the reins for Reno metalcore act December's *The Lament Configuration*. Taking his solo band out on the road, he hooked up with Kill II This and Godflesh for a tour of Britain during December 2001.

Townsend put his efforts into three projects in 2002: a new SYL album, plus two solo efforts, with provisional working titles *Project EKO* and *Relationships*. He also co-produced Lamb Of God's second album, *As The Palaces Burn*. Activity on the live front found Townsend employing a new solo band of Evenlight guitarist Brian Waddell, bassist Mike Young, keyboard player Dave Young, and the Static In Stereo and Bif Naked drummer Scotty McCargar.

Chris Valagao was pulled in as keyboard player for Strapping Young Lad but then swiftly backed out, citing commitments to Zimmer's Hole as well as movie work. He was replaced by Will Campagne. Simon and Hoglan unveiled a new Vancouver-based thrash band, Tenet, in August 2002, with ex-Grip Inc. bassist Stuart Carruthers and former Sacrifice and current Interzone frontman Rob Urbinati. With Tenet signed to the German Virusworx label, Townsend was slated to produce their debut offering. Jed Simon apparently found space in his schedule to join the reformed thrashers Dark Angel, taking Jim Durkin's place for West Coast and European gigs. Although this was officially announced, within days Simon had scotched the proposed union.

The group's third studio album, the more coherent, riff-structured *SYL*, arrived in February 2003. With a novel touch, Devin had included notes in the lyric sheet indicating where he expected fans to sing during concerts. Backed by a video for 'Relentless', the band joined an impressive extreme metal cast for North American dates during January and February alongside Nile, Napalm Death, The Berzerker, and Dark Tranquillity. Later US shows in May featured the band paired with Meshuggah.

A heavyweight doom metal project involving Townsend, dubbed Tree Of The Sun and incorporating Dale Crover of the Melvins and erstwhile Kyuss bassist Scott Reeder, was rumoured to be on its way, billed as The Devin Townsend Band. Townsend then aired a new solo record, *Accelerated Evolution*, to unanimous praise among the global rock media. Guitarist Brian Waddell, bassist Mike Young, keyboard player Dave Young, and God Awakens Petrified drummer Ryan Van Poederooyen all worked on this album. Early editions came with a bonus disc of *Project EKO* material.

Strapping Young Lad activity then resumed, the band latching on to the 'Superjoint Ritual' tour commencing on August 15th in Little Rock, Arkansas. The band subsequently united with Cathedral and Samael for North American dates in September, labelled the 'Redemption' tour. October found them headlining in Canada with familiar road partners The Devin

Townsend band and Zimmer's Hole. Byron Stroud joined Californian cybermetallers Fear Factory in December, retaining his place in SYL.

Hoglan stepped in as temporary substitute for Opeth's Vancouver date in January 2004 as the Swedish act's regular drummer, Martin Lopez, was recovering from panic attacks. Amid all this activity, Strapping Young Lad announced that they had re-signed to Century Media for further product and had recorded a set at the Commodore Ballroom in Vancouver for a DVD, *For Those Aboot To Rock*. The band entered studios in Vancouver to craft a new studio album, *Alien*, for release in March 2005. A press releases stated that an unlikely cover of Tom Jones's 1960s hit 'What's New Pussycat?' would be among the tracks laid down, but it was excised from the track-listing just before manufacture. Hoglan laid down the drums at Armoury Studios in just three days before vocals and guitar were cut at Greenhouse Studios, with the recordings finalised at Townsend's studio in Maple Ridge.

Strapping Young Lad headlined US and Canadian dates throughout April and May 2005, backed up by The Agony Scene, Misery Signals, and Reflux. Bassist Byron Stroud hooked back up with Fear Factory for participation in the US 'Gigantour'.

European headline dates in June were supported by End Of Days and Cephalic Carnage. The summer of 2005 found Strapping Young Lad rejoined by keyboard player Will Campagna and participating in the US 'Sounds Of The Underground' tour, a collaboration between independent labels Ferret Music, Prosthetic Records, Trustkill Records, and Metal Blade Records. The shows saw the band sharing stages with Clutch, Opeth, Poison The Well, and other acts. After July 14th, Jon Miller of Devildriver took over the bass position as Stroud had been contracted out to Fear Factory. Hoglan was also subbing for another band, Opeth, who used his services while regular drummer Martin Lopez underwent treatment for a blood disorder.

The band contributed a rendition of 'Zodiac' to a Melvins tribute album, *We Reach: The Music Of The Melvins*, through Fractured

Strapping Young Lad

Transmitter Records. They also featured in a studio collaboration with Fear Factory and Mastodon on a take of 'Joan Of Arc' for the same compilation and had their track 'Love?' track featured on the soundtrack to the 'Rainbow Six Lockdown' game issued by 3volution Productions. 'Love?' gave the band a degree of extra exposure when it was included on the soundtrack to movie *The Cave*, released in August. Once off the road, Townsend scheduled time in his studio to cut a new Devin Townsend Band album, *Synchestra*, for release in January 2006.

There was little respite, with a date on October 28th in Lawrence, Kansas, marking the start of another Strapping Young Lad US tour, this time with Fear Factory, Darkane, and It Dies Today. Swedish act Soilwork replaced It Dies Today on the bill from November 8th. Strapping Young Lad then hooked up with Arch Enemy and Throwdown for UK shows in December.

The band's album *The New Black* featured a bevy of guests including Bif Naked on 'Fucker', Gwar's Oderus Urungus on 'Far Beyond Metal', and Cam Kroetsch of The Almighty Punchdrunk on 'You Suck'. They put in an appearance at the Tool and Deftones-headlined 'Download' festival at Castle Donington in England on June 9th. As *The New Black* arrived on Century Media in July, the 'Ozzfest' loomed for the 2006 summer season. With Stroud absent due to Fear Factory commitments, bassist James MacDonough (Iced Earth, Megadeth, Nevermore) took over for touring in August. Gene Hoglan stated in November 2006 that SYL were on an "extended hiatus", but the band's legions of fans will certainly be waiting for them when they return.

STUCK MOJO
VETERAN RAP AND RIFF-MONGERS

A HARDCORE RAP-METAL BAND with loud guitars, muscles, and record sales to match, Stuck Mojo were Century Media's biggest-selling act in America until 2004. The Kennesaw, Georgia-based band were first assembled in 1989 by guitarist Rich Ward, bassist Dwayne Fowler, and drummer Richard Farmer, later inducting singer Andrew Freund. Ward – who had a day job in pizza delivery – noticed that one of the restaurant's chefs, Bonz, liked to play loud hip-hop in the workplace. The pair soon saw a future blending rap vocals with metal guitars, and Freund was replaced by Bonz. Stuck Mojo rapidly built a fanbase in Georgia and over the next two years took their music onto stages in Chicago, Tampa, Charlotte, Columbia, and Tallahassee. A three-song demo was recorded with producer Jozef Nuyens in Nashville, Tennessee, resulting in a deal brokered with Borivoj Krgin at Century Media.

Stuck Mojo, now with Brent Payne handling drums, arrived in spectacular fashion during March 1995 with the Jozef Nuyens-produced *Snappin' Necks* album. Tours of Europe and a ten-week stint opening for Machine Head in North America followed. To maintain the momentum, the *Violated* EP emerged in Europe during early 1996, featuring a new rhythm section of bassist Corey Lowery and drummer Frank 'Bud' Fontseré. That April, the band embarked upon the 'Crossover 2000' tour in Europe, closing with an appearance at the Dutch 'Dynamo' festival. Their status on the touring circuit was recognised when MTV Europe gave Stuck Mojo their Best Live Band award.

The second full-length album, *Pigwalk*, released in 1996 and produced by Devin Townsend and Daniel Bergstrand, pushed record sales higher still. Dates in 1997 came in support to Testament, Life Of Agony, and Type O Negative.

Stuck Mojo's breakthrough came with March 1998's *Rising* album. Produced by Andy Sneap, it racked up an impressive 50,000 sales in North America. The band's wrestling affiliations were proudly displayed on the cover, which sported the World Championship Wrestling's US

STUCK MOJO discography

SNAPPIN' NECKS, Century Media CM 77088-2 (Europe), Century Media CM 7788-2 (USA) (1995)
PIGWALK, Century Media CM 77133-2 (Europe), Century Media CM 7833-2 (USA) (1996)
Violated, Century Media cnu (Europe / USA) (1996)
RISING, Century Media CM 77188-2 (Europe), Century Media CM 7888-2 (USA) (1998)
HVY 1, Century Media CM 77288-2 (Europe), Century Media CM 7988-2 (USA) (1999)
DECLARATION OF A HEADHUNTER, Century Media CM 77291-2 (Europe), Century Media CM 7991-2 (USA) (2001)
VIOLATE THIS, Century Media CM 77375-2 (Europe), Century Media CM 8075-2 (USA) (2001)

Heavyweight Championship belt buckle. A video for the title track featured cameos from wrestling stars The Flock, 'Diamond' Dallas Page, and Raven. *Rising* was promoted by European shows in June 1998, which included a return to the 'Dynamo' festival before North American concerts with Pantera and shows with Sevendust and Clutch.

A six-month US tour in 1999 found Belt Fed bassist Dan Dryden, a Minnesota native, substituting for Corey Lowery, who had opted out to join Life Of Agony. The bassist subsequently founded Stereomud for two albums, uniting with the drummer Dan Richardson (Crumbsuckers, Pro-Pain, Life Of Agony) and ex-Life Of Agony guitarist Joey Z.

Stuck Mojo continued upwards with positive reaction to later albums such as September 1999's *HVY 1* (a concert recording taped at the Masquerade in Atlanta) and 2000's *Declaration Of A Headhunter*, but rumours spread in 2001 of their break-up, despite recently adding new guitarist Ryan Mallam to the line-up. *Violate This* was issued in August, a collection of demos and rarities including covers of Mötley Crüe's 'Shout At The Devil' and Iron Maiden's 'Wrathchild', the latter with Devin Townsend on guest vocals.

Ward and Fontseré moonlighted as melodic rock act Sickspeed, and Dryden (as Shawn 'Sports' Popp), Ward (Duke LaRue), and Fontseré (KK LaFlame) provided the backing band for WWF wrestler Chris Jericho's 1980s-style metal act Fozzy.

Stuck Mojo reunited at the Masquerade Club in Atlanta, Georgia, for their traditional New Year's Eve get-together in 2002. With Lowery committed to his Stereomud schedule, Keith Watson of Sickspeed played bass. A DVD, *Inside the Monster: The Evilution Of Stuck Mojo Vol. I*, was released early in 2005. Meanwhile, Rich Ward launched a solo project, releasing demos credited simply to The Duke. Ward's venture soon secured a deal with Spitfire for the album *My Kung Fu Is Good*.

Ward announced plans to reform Stuck Mojo in October 2004 to record a new album. The reunited band – Bonz, Ward, Fontseré, and bass player Sean Delson – toured Europe in February 2005. US dates followed in June. The band parted ways with Fontseré in September 2005, announcing Eric Sanders as replacement. Touring in the UK in October and November saw support from Fourwaykill, Forever Never, Panic Cell, and Died Smiling.

In February 2006, Stuck Mojo began recording their new album, *Southern Born Killers*, at Backstage Studios in Derbyshire, England with producer Andy Sneap. Following the recordings, Saunders was replaced by former Dead Gospel drummer Rodney Beaubouef, and the band announced a spring US tour. In October, it was revealed that Lord Nelson was the new Stuck Mojo frontman. They retain a loyal fanbase – and the Andy Sneap connection looks set to serve them well in the future.

NWOAHM

THE NWOAHM

('New Wave Of American Heavy Metal') is a disputed term. The argument polarises two opposing views: was there in fact a genuine resurgence in retro-heavy metal in the USA; or was this a term coined by an industry attempting to foist its latest fad on the fans? Once Pantera, Machine Head, and Biohazard had made their mark, a fresh audience was ushered in, who wanted the same degree of aggression but laced with more finesse.

The NWOAHM suffered from lack of focus. However, among the plethora of hardcore, metalcore, emocore, and desperately ageing nu-metal, there was a very real movement gathering pace. Fans latched onto the proudly retro riffing of Avenged Sevenfold, Mastodon, Unearth, All That Remains, and Trivium, and these groups quickly attained major status. Breakdowns had been replaced by well-engineered riffs; where once there was an annoying turntable scratch, the space was filled by the long-overdue return of the guitar solo. The NWOAHM also stood apart from the flood of core bands thanks to its reliance on the metal tradition, as opposed to punk roots.

Spearheading the NWOAHM was a cadre quickly dubbed "the big six" – Zakk Wylde's Black Label Society, Chimaira, Shadows Fall, Lamb Of God, God Forbid, and Killswitch Engage. Wylde's mob had been lumped in by circumstance (their sound was more akin to that of Black Sabbath) but it was Shadows Fall who stole a march on the competition, taking the music industry by surprise with massive album sales.

Strangely, despite the obvious popularity of this fresh crop of bands, the term NWOAHM remained fragile, with purists comparing it with the glorious NWOBHM era. Many praised the new outfits' appreciation of riffs and solos but also observed a lack of respect for other primary elements – vocal excellence and melody. Most of the young NWOAHM bands had grown up through the death metal era, and this rawness was evident. Such a marriage of European-style riffing and throaty vocals alienated audiences outside the USA to some degree. But with grunge and nu-metal consigned to the dust, perhaps the NWOAHM paves the way for an even greater metallic monster lurking just beyond the horizon.

3 INCHES OF BLOOD
SANGUINE ATTEMPT AT VINTAGE METAL

VANCOUVER-BASED 3 INCHES OF BLOOD are an anomaly. In a modern scene awash with emocore, they have an honest appreciation of retro metal – a love apparently shared by their fans. At first, critics perceived their devotion as an attempt at humour, but the band members quickly made it clear that their craft was executed in earnest.

The original line-up featured vocalist Jamie Hooper, guitarists Bobby Froese, Sunny Dhak, and Jay Watts, bass player Rich Trawick, and drummer Geoff Trawick. Watts departed before the debut self-titled April 2001 EP release, which featured a guesting Cam Pipes on vocals. Subsequently, Pipes was asked to join as a full-time member, and from this point 3 Inches Of Blood operated with dual vocalists: the clean vocals of Cam Pipes and the screams of Jamie Hooper. (Pipes had played bass for Allfather in 1998.) 3 Inches Of Blood then had the exclusive track 'Headwaters Of The Rivers Of Blood' included on the 2001 *West Coast Canadian Metal Feast* compilation.

The band released their debut album, *Battlecry Under A Winter Sun*, through the Teenage Rampage label in March 2002. The roughly-hewn record's gung-ho approach harked back to the NWOBHM glory years. An exclusive European single, 'Destroy The Orcs', was issued by Death O'Clock Records to coincide with October UK tour dates supporting The Darkness. December US dates saw 3 Inches Of Blood performing as the opening act to The Black Dahlia Murder and Himsa. They then signed a deal with Roadrunner for a Neal Kernon-produced album, *Advance And Vanquish*, released in October 2004. Before the album was recorded, brothers Rich and Geoff Trawick were replaced by former Trial bass player Brian Redman and Goatsblood drummer Matt Wood.

Shane Clark of Ten Miles Wide and The Almighty Punchdrunk and Justin Hagberg from war metal band Allfather joined them before a US winter tour supporting Metal Church. Bobby Froese and Sunny Dhak left the band in July 2004 after the recording of the *Advance And Vanquish* album. Initially, guitarists Justin Hagberg and Kevin Keegan were brought in as replacements, but Keegan was soon superseded by Shane Clark. The band were soon back on the road once again, acting as support to Norwegian black metal act Satyricon in the USA.

3 Inches Of Blood joined the 'Roadrunner Road Rage' US tour with Trivium, The Agony Scene, and Still Remains in March 2005. The following month saw the band acting as openers to Motörhead and Corrosion Of Conformity's Canadian dates. In May and June, they teamed up again with Trivium and Still Remains for the European leg of the 'Roadrunner Road Rage' trek. However, in mid July drummer Matt Wood opted out, swiftly replaced by Catharsis, Summers End, and Walls Of Jericho man Alexei Rodriguez.

---

3 INCHES OF BLOOD discography

3 Inches Of Blood, 3 Inches Of Blood no catalogue number (Canada) (2001)
BATTLECRY UNDER A WINTER SUN, Teenage Rampage TRCD-001 (Canada) (2002), Death O'Clock TOC 001D (UK) (2003)
Ride Darkhorse Ride, Death O'Clock TIC 001SD (UK) (2003)
Destroy The Orcs, Death O'Clock TIC 002SD (UK) (2003)
ADVANCE AND VANQUISH, Roadrunner RR 8274-2 (Europe / USA) (2004)

Further US touring in August witnessed an alliance with Chimaira, All That Remains, and Six Feet Under before they headlined the 'Critical Strike' tour in a union with Diecast and If Hope Dies. In an ever busy touring schedule, October saw 3 Inches Of Blood joining up with Crisis, Watch Them Die, and headliners Exodus on the North American 'World AbomiNations' tour before closing 2005 with dates in Europe supporting Himsa.

Working with Joey Jordison of Slipknot as producer and Jack Endino as engineer, the band cut demos in Seattle during April 2006. In November, they entered Vancouver's Armoury Studios with producer Joey Jordison and engineer Dan Turner to begin recording a new album for 2007 release. In such esteemed company, their star seems sure to rise.

AVENGED SEVENFOLD
OUTSPOKEN METAL NEWBIES

AVENGED SEVENFOLD, SOMETIMES abbreviated to A7X, morphed from their hardcore punk roots in Orange County, California, to an act unafraid to preach their love of heavy metal. Their success put them at the spearhead of the NWOAHM movement. The band's current line-up is vocalist M. Shadows (real name Matthew Sanders), guitarists Zacky Vengeance (Zachary Baker), and Synyster Gates (Brian Elwin Haner Jr., son of country music guitarist Brian Haner), bassist Johnny Christ (Jonathan Lewis Seward), and drummer The Rev (aka The Reverend Tholomew Plague, real name James Owen Sullivan).

The Huntington Beach band, who took their title from the Cain & Abel bible story, were founded at high school. Originally formed in the summer of 1999 by M. Shadows, the first Avenged Sevenfold line-up featured Shadows, Vengeance from punk band MPA, bass player Matt (surname unknown), and drummer The Reverend Tholomew Plague. With this line-up, the band recorded a three-song demo in 1999. Bassist Matt left the band to return to college and was replaced by Justin Sane (who would play on the debut album).

The band provided tracks for various compilation albums before cutting the January 2001 *Warmness On The Soul* EP, featuring songs from the then-unreleased debut album, a video for the title song, shot in March 2001, and a new song, 'To End The Rapture (Heavy Metal Version)', recorded with guitarist Synyster Gates, who had joined the band in early 2001. The EP was released in August 2001 for Goodlife Recordings.

The full-length debut album, *Sounding The Seventh Trumpet*, produced by Donnell Cameron and including re-worked material from the EP, was originally recorded in November 2000 for Goodlife Recordings, but the label decided to put the release on hold in order to give it some serious promotion. The record eventually surfaced after the *Warmness* EP, repackaged with an additional song, 'To End The Rapture (Heavy Metal Version)' from the EP and released in the USA by Hopeless Records in March 2002. At this juncture, the band's members were all still in their teens. In due course Dameon Ash took up the bass position before being replaced later in the same year by Johnny Christ.

The band issued *Waking The Fallen* in August 2003, again through Hopeless Records. The record included a re-recorded version of 'Second Heartbeat', which had originally appeared on the *Hopelessly Devoted To You, Vol. 4* compilation. Summer exposure came when the band played with Poison The Well, Rancid, Dropkick Murphys, The Used, Sum 41, Andrew W.K., and Less Than Jake on the 'Vans Warped' festival. Road work followed through into September as they played the 'Take Action!' tour alongside The Dillinger Escape Plan, Eighteen Visions, and Poison The Well.

Such was Avenged Sevenfold's momentum that, although a deal with major label Warners was announced in October, they continued on with

---

AVENGED SEVENFOLD discography
Warmness On The Soul, Goodlife Recordings GL071CD (Europe) (2001)
SOUNDING THE SEVENTH TRUMPET, Goodlife Recordings GL073CD (Europe) (2001), Hopeless HR 660-2 (USA) (2002)
WAKING THE FALLEN, Hopeless HR 671-2 (USA) (2003)
CITY OF EVIL, Warner Bros. 9362-48613-2 (2005) **63 UK, 30 USA**

concerts into November, hooking up with Mushroomhead, The Unseen, Suicide Machines, Western Waste, and The Agony Scene. A hectic year was capped with the filming of a video for 'Unholy Confessions' with director Thomas Mignone, and December East Coast shows alongside From Autumn To Ashes.

The band opened 2004 with their inaugural journey to the UK, in February, with The Bronx and Lostprophets. Although the band generated print, it probably wasn't in the way they had hoped: an aftershow brawl in London resulted in the arrest of drummer The Reverend Tholomew Plague, now more commonly known as The Rev. Their woes continued when a gig in Leeds was cancelled when M. Shadows was afflicted with food poisoning.

Back on North American soil, another round of headline touring led to more 'Vans Warped' gigs. This time, the band shared stages with Bad Religion, Good Charlotte, Break The Silence, Underminded, Rancid, From Autumn To Ashes, The Casualties, Atmosphere, The Vandals, Tiger Army, and Rise Against.

Promoting June 2005's *City Of Evil*, Avenged Sevenfold joined the 'Vans Warped' festival yet again. The album sold an impressive 32,000 units in its first week on US sale, peaking at Number 30 on the *Billboard* charts. US and Canadian headline dates running through October to December saw supports from Death By Stereo, Saosin, and Bullets And Octane.

January 2006 US shows had CKY as openers, and touring continued in April and May, partnered with Coheed And Cambria and support acts Head Automatica and Eighteen Visions. The band scored a notable coup in June, opening up for Metallica's European stadium shows, including an appearance at the 'Download' festival in Castle Donington, England on June 10th. Their rise appears to be inexorable.

THE BLACK DAHLIA MURDER
NWOAHM PERSONIFIED

DETROIT METALCORE ACT The Black Dahlia Murder take their name from the murder of 22-year-old actress Elizabeth Short, known as The Black Dahlia. On January 15th 1947, her body, severed in two at the waist, was discovered in a vacant lot on South Norton Avenue in the Leimert Park neighbourhood of Los Angeles. The brutality of the crime turned the murder into one of history's most infamous unsolved cases.

Formed in Detroit, Michigan, in 2001, the original line-up of The Black Dahlia Murder consisted of vocalist Trevor Strnad, guitarists Brian Eschbach and Jon Deering, bassist Mark Ratay, and drummer Cory Grady. Ratay quit on the eve of the band's first show, for which Mike Schepman filled in on bass, and a permanent replacement for Ratay was found in Sean Gauvreau. With this line-up, the group issued the 2001 demo *What A Horrible Night To Have A Curse*.

An EP, *A Cold Blooded Epitaph*, followed in May 2002 through Lovelost Records, by which time David Lock had taken over the bass. Another personnel change before the close of the year saw John Kempainen replace Deering, who went on to form hardcore outfit Let It

Die. The band then signed to Metal Blade and released their debut full-length album, *Unhallowed*, in June 2003. Along with Soilent Green and Lickgoldensky, the band planned a summer tour of the USA, to commence on July 30th 2003 in Fort Lauderdale, Florida. However, they were forced to pull out due to "personal reasons", later revealed to be the sudden exit of bassist David Lock. Following these shows, the band – with Set Ablaze's Joe Boccuto on bass – allied with Hate Eternal, Evergrey, and headliners Arch Enemy for a short but intensive run of US 'Anthems Of Rebellion' dates in August and September. With Strnad also absent, Anthony Ezzi of New Jersey's Arson filled in as lead vocalist.

By October, both Strnad and Lock had rejoined the band. Touring throughout March 2004 had the band hooked up with Entombed, but the Swedes subsequently cancelled. Nevertheless, the Americans did strike up a touring union with label-mates As I Lay Dying for shows alongside Every Time I Die and Scarlet later that same month. However, drummer Cory Grady was ousted in June "due to personal and professional conflicts" and was succeeded by Zach Gibson of death metallers Gutrot and Mutiliated. Grady subsequently joined Premonitions Of War.

Renewed touring in mid summer saw the band hooked up with Cannibal Corpse and Severed Savior, preceding a run of headliners backed by Cattle Decapitation and Goatwhore. To close the year, they played the 'X-Mass Fest' European tour with Napalm Death, Marduk, Vader, Finntroll, and Belphegor. The band then scheduled US tour dates for April and May 2005 with Nile, Behemoth, and headliners King Diamond. Going into September, they headed up shows backed by

THE BLACK DAHLIA MURDER discography

A Cold Blooded Epitaph, Lovelost LL01 (USA) (2002)
UNHALLOWED, Metal Blade 3984-14442-2 (Europe /USA) (2003)
MIASMA, Metal Blade 3984-14536-2 (Europe /USA) (2005)

Between The Buried And Me, Cephalic Carnage, and Into The Moat. A new album was recorded in March 2005 at Planet Red Studio in Richmond, Virginia, with former Scarlet drummer Andreas Magnusson at the production helm. Entitled *Miasma*, the album was released by Metal Blade in July of the same year.

Drummer Gibson took his leave in late October in acrimonious circumstances, departing in order to rejoin Gutrot with a stinging attack on his ex-band mates. It was revealed that bassist Lock too had taken his leave, and the band fired back a retort, claiming: "Both are gone because they couldn't actually play our material." A run of November Canadian dates, backed by The End and A Life Once Lost, was duly cancelled. Dates in Korea and Japan saw the installation of a new temporary rhythm section consisting of Today I Wait bassist Bart Williams and the renowned Tony Laureano on drums.

The Black Dahlia Murder teamed up with Belgian hardcore act Liar for a European tour during January and February 2006. However, new touring drummer Pierre Langlois of Canadian bands Frozen Shadows and

The Black Dahlia Murder

Tenebrae was denied entry to the USA, forcing the band to miss gigs in Minneapolis and Chicago on February 22nd and 23rd. In the interim, former Chimaira skinsman Kevin Talley stepped in. The band's relentless live campaign continued unabated into 2006 as they forged a union in North America throughout March with Throwdown, The Agony Scene, and The Red Chord.

With bassist Williams and drummer Langlois now confirmed as permanent members, the group subsequently engaged in a gigantic touring festival, the 'Sounds Of The Underground', throughout the summer, commencing in Cleveland, Ohio, on July 8th. The group hit the US touring circuit again in September and October, forming a strong bill for the 'Monsters Of Mayhem' tour alongside Hatebreed, Exodus, Napalm Death, Despised Icon, and First Blood. Their future now seems assured.

BLACK LABEL SOCIETY
OZZY AXEMAN'S SHRED VEHICLE

BLACK LABEL SOCIETY ARE THE trio founded by Zakk Wylde, the Ozzy Osbourne and Allman Brothers guitarist, following his more Southern-flavoured band Pride And Glory. Before achieving global notoriety with Ozzy, Wylde paid his dues with New Jersey club acts Stonehenge and Zyris. (He was born Jeffrey Philip Weilandt but legally changed his name to Zachary Phillip Wylde after he joined the Osbourne band. In Zyris, Wylde had gone by the stage name Zakari Wyland.)

Wylde has generated a huge cult appeal for his work with Ozzy, which he started with the 1988 *No Rest For The Wicked* album, and is regarded as having come the closest of all Ozzy's esteemed axemen to filling the void left by the late, great Randy Rhoads. Wylde developed a larger-than-life character to suit his adopted pseudonym: a bearded, beer-swilling caveman image with a self-proclaimed aversion to personal hygiene, matching this with a band image akin to a biker club.

Wylde spent time rehearsing with Guns N' Roses, but songs written during this period were used for the debut Black Label Society album. Originally the band was intended to be titled Hell's Kitchen, and album artwork was even commissioned to match. The debut album was *Sonic Brew*, featuring drummer Phil Ondich and crafted with producers Ron and Howard Albert. It emerged in Japan during October 1998 but was not made officially available in the USA until May of the following year. This later US edition came with an extra track, 'Lost My Better Half'.

Wylde was recalled for duty for live work with Ozzy in 1998, fulfilling Japanese dates, but struck out on his own again shortly after. He made it onto celluloid in 2000 in the movie *Metal God* as guitarist for actor Mark Wahlberg's fictitious band Steel Dragon. This poorly-received movie was eventually released in August 2001 with a new title, *Rock Star*.

Black Label Society toured America in 2000 with Crowbar and Sixty Watt Shamen, but the initial dates were marred when Ondich fell ill, necessitating Crowbar's drummer Craig Nunenmacher stepping into the breach for some shows. 'Ozzfest' dates found Frey Theiler temporarily filling in on bass. A new Black Label Society album, *Stronger Than Death*, was released in May 2000.

The year 2001 brought renewed fortunes for Wylde when it emerged that the guitarist was back in the Ozzy camp recording the *Down To Earth* album. Black Label Society, meanwhile, formed part of the 'Ozzfest' festival promoting the live/acoustic album *Alcohol Fuelled Brewtality*. By June, bassist Steve 'S.O.B.' Gibb had parted ways with the act and Mike Inez, sometime of Ozzy's band and a former Alice In Chains man, stepped in.

The band returned in March 2002 with *1919 Eternal*, a title amended from the intended *Deathcore WarMachine Eternal* following the US terrorist attacks of September 11th 2001. This outing was promoted with yet more 'Ozzfest' shows, this time on a European leg. It was suggested

that the tracks on *1919 Eternal* were in fact originally slated for Ozzy's *Down To Earth* album (apparently, when Ozzy heard the demo he said that the songs sounded "too Black Label").

Ozzy bassist Robert Trujillo would step up to the mark for these shows, doubling bass duties with Black Label Society and Ozzy. Troubles hit the European leg of 'Ozzfest' as Wylde reportedly fell ill, citing mental and physical exhaustion, necessitating a rapid return to America. The shows in Zurich, Copenhagen, Stockholm, Helsinki, St. Petersburg, and Moscow were all cancelled. Back in action, Wylde took his place alongside Ozzy Osbourne and Black Label Society for the North American leg of the tour. A run of September headliners, supported by Brand New Sin, ensued throughout September.

BLS commenced work on a new studio album, *The Blessed Hellride*, during November. During January 2003, Ozzy greatly enhanced the CD's profile by recording guest vocals for the track 'Stillborn'. Japanese variants added the exclusive bonus track 'F.U.N.'. Promotion for the album, released in April and scoring commendably on the US *Billboard* charts, commenced with a rash of US dates in March prior to Japanese, Australian, and New Zealand shows. Trujillo played bass for these gigs. A matter of days after this liaison was confirmed, Trujillo was confirmed as the new Metallica bass man.

In parallel to the album, a live DVD hit stores: *Broozed, Boozed & Broken-Boned: Live With The Detroit Chapter* was recorded at Harpo's Concert Theater in Detroit, Michigan, on September 14th 2002. April 2003 found the band, with Inez installed on bass, on the road in North America once again, billed alongside Meldrum and Nashville Pussy.

Changing the mood somewhat, BLS began recording an acoustic, piano-based album, *Hangover Music Vol. VI*, during December. Recorded at Paramount Studios in Los Angeles and produced by Wylde in collaboration with Barry Conley, it was issued in April 2004 and included a vocal-piano interpretation of Procol Harum's 1967 hit 'A Whiter Shade Of Pale', and 'Layne', Wylde's tribute to the late Alice In Chains frontman Layne Staley. Cameo spots came from Inez, former Pride And Glory and White Lion bassist James Lomenzo, and Rob Zombie's drummer John Tempesta.

Black Label Society were once again confirmed for the 'Ozzfest' in 2004, with Black Sabbath as the headline act. Bass for these shows was delegated to Lomenzo. Former bassist Steve Gibb (aka S.O.B.) joined New Orleans heavyweights Crowbar as their new guitarist in March. *Hangover*

BLACK LABEL SOCIETY discography

SONIC BREW, Spitfire SPITCD004 (UK), Spitfire SPT 15004-2 (USA) (1999)

STRONGER THAN DEATH, Spitfire SPITCD046 (UK), Spitfire SPT 15046-2 (USA) (2000)

ALCOHOL FUELED BREWTALITY, Spitfire SPITCD112 (UK), Spitfire SPT 15112-2 (USA) (2001)

1919 ETERNAL, Spitfire SPITCD176 (UK), Spitfire SPT 15176-2 (USA) (2002)

THE BLESSED HELLRIDE, Spitfire SPITCD091 (UK), Spitfire SPT 15091-2 (USA) (2003) **50 USA**

HANGOVER MUSIC VOL. VI, Spitfire SPITCD081 (UK), Spitfire SPT 15081-2 (USA) (2004) **40 USA**

MAFIA, Artemis/Rykodisc RCD 17309 (Europe), Artemis ATM-CD-51610 (USA) (2005) **15 USA**

KINGS OF DAMNATION – '98-'04, Spitfire SPITCD255 (UK), Spitfire SPT 15255-2 (USA) (2005)

SHOT TO HELL, Roadrunner RR 8048-2 (Europe / USA) (2006) **69 UK, 21 USA**

Music Vol. VI sold over 24,000 copies in its first week of American sales, landing at Number 40 on the *Billboard* charts.

In December 2004 BLS switched labels to Artemis and announced a new album, *Mafia*. An unlisted and untitled track 15 on the album was a cover version of 'I Never Dreamed', originally by Lynyrd Skynyrd. A lead single, 'Suicide Messiah', went to radio in January 2005 with the album following in March. Meanwhile, Wylde guested on Derek Sherinian's 2004 opus *Mythology*, donating his distinctive guitar tones, penning lyrics, and providing vocals for 'The River Run'.

In early 2005, the collectors' market recognised Wylde's status as KnuckleBonz Inc produced a limited-edition figurine of the guitarist. The $99 Zakk Wylde Guitar Hero figure, each hand numbered and mounted on a wooden base, came wearing his signature black-and-white 'Bullseye' Gibson Les Paul. North American tour dates throughout March and April saw Meldrum as support.

Damageplan drummer Vinnie Paul joined BLS at the WAAF Indoor Beach Party on April 9th at the Tsongas Arena in Lowell, Massachusetts. Paul stepped up once more on April 17th for the song 'Suicide Messiah' during their performances at the House of Blues in Orlando, Florida, and, naturally, in Pantera's hometown of Dallas, Texas. Black Label Society later shot an Eric Zimmerman-directed video for 'In This River', a tribute to the slain Dimebag, which featured Wylde sailing down a river seated at a grand piano.

European gigs throughout May and June had Meldrum as opening act, but a concert at Bradford, England on June 2nd was cancelled, with an official statement explaining that Wylde was in need of "a day off to preserve his voice for the rest of the tour". The band's June 15th gig in Copenhagen, Denmark was also cancelled because, according to the band, "the promoter of the show was not able to meet the show's contract rider requirements". Further problems culminated with the pulling of a June 15th show scheduled at the Petofi Hall in Budapest, Hungary, reportedly due to "logistical problems".

More optimistically, the band were set to film for a DVD release their June 17th gig at the Paris Elysée Montmartre and the show at the Carling Academy 2 in Manchester the following day. Unfortunately, the Manchester show too was cancelled when a local biker gang, the 'Sons Of Hell', reportedly used physical violence to prevent fans and crew members from wearing the Black Label Society logo, claiming it was too close to their own skull motif.

Further Black Label Society product came in the form of Spitfire's double compilation *Kings Of Damnation – Era '98-'04*. Notable inclusions were previously unreleased acoustic versions of 'Spoke In The Wheel' and 'Bridge To Cross', plus "slightly amped" renditions of 'Stillborn' and 'The Blessed Hellride'.

The band parted ways with bassist Lomenzo in September, re-drafting former member John 'JD' DeServio in his stead. Five weeks of shows kicking off on October 14th in St. Petersburg, Florida, saw Brand New Sin as support. As 2006 was ushered in, it was reported that Wylde was set to participate in the recording of a new Ozzy Osbourne album. In March, the band worked with producer Michael Beinhorn on a new album, *Shot To Hell*, and revealed that they had switched labels to Roadrunner.

With the 'Ozzfest' looming for the 2006 summer season, the group shared the festival stages with Ozzy yet again. A new Black Label Society live DVD, *The European Invasion – Doom Troopin'*, was released in August. The *Shot To Hell* album was released the following month, selling around 32,000 units in its first week of sales in the USA to debut at Number 21 on the *Billboard* charts. And so the Wylde saga continues.

BYZANTINE
METALLERS WITH AN ORIGINAL MESSAGE…

THIS METALCORE COMBO FROM Charleston, West Virginia, are distinctive for their use of environmental issues and Appalachian history as lyrical subject matter. The group's rise coincided with the burgeoning New Wave of American Heavy Metal.

Byzantine formed in the spring of 2000 in Chapmanville as a trio of

BYZANTINE discography

BYZANTINE (2000-2001 Demos), Caustic Eye Productions CAUS002 (USA) (2002)
Broadmoor, Caustic Eye Productions S003 (USA) (2003)
THE FUNDAMENTAL COMPONENT, Prosthetic 10011-2 (Europe / USA) (2004)
...AND THEY SHALL TAKE UP SERPENTS, Prosthetic 10024-2 (Europe / USA) (2005)

singer Chris Ojeda, guitarist Tony Rohrbough, and bassist Chris Adams. Both Ojeda and Adams had worked with Morgantown-based thrash metal band New Family. Opening live shows saw Byzantine employing a drum machine, capitalising on an inaugural four-song demo toward the close of 2000, with a seven-track effort the following year. These recordings were later released in a very limited CD, known as *Byzantine (2000-2001 Demos)*, with a pressing of just 100 in August 2002 by West Virginia independent label Caustic Eye Productions. A further version with enhanced sound quality and limited to 150 copies was issued in January 2003.

In the winter of 2002, with Charleston native Matt Wolfe now on drums, Byzantine entered the Broadmoor Studios in Huntington, West Virginia, to cut a third demo session. This was then set to surface as the band's debut album, through the DK Entertainment label, but did not materialise, so in March 2003 Caustic Eye once again obliged by producing a CD from these sessions, the *Broadmoor* EP, with a limited run of just over 300 copies. It attracted the interest of Lamb Of God drummer Chris Adler, who invited the band out as support on an East Coast tour. This eventually led to Byzantine securing a deal with Los Angeles-based Prosthetic Records.

A debut album, *The Fundamental Component*, arrived in February 2004, promoted by gigs opening for Prong on a two-week run in late July. The record scored good reviews, with fans impressed by the blend of Southern style, unorthodox tempos, and vicious guitar work. Live campaigning saw further dates with Lamb Of God and Shadows Fall. The band also performed on the main stage of 2004's New England 'Hardcore And Metal Festival' in Worcester, Massachusetts. Byzantine teamed up with Beyond The Embrace and Children Of Tragedy for the 'Sofa King Metal' tour commencing on September 24th at the Sound Factory in Charleston, West Virginia.

The band's second album was *...And They Shall Take Up Serpents* as the released in July 2005 through Prosthetic. Bassist Chris Adams had left before they went into the studio to make the record, so guitarist Tony Rohrbough played all the bass parts, and Michael 'Skip' Cromer was recruited as a replacement for Adams soon after the album was finished. Byzantine headlined a UK tour in May with support from D-Rail and Indica, and North American touring in June found them forming an alliance with Eyehategod and Canadians Buried Inside.

Extended touring beginning in October 2006, dubbed the Under The Underground dates, had Byzantine sharing stages with Halo Of Locusts and The Dream Is Dead. They parted ways with lead guitarist Rohrbough, hiring Eric Seevers of Liecus as tour fill-in.

With Rohrbough back on board, the band announced their 2006 season of live campaigning, with US dates in March with Agnostic Front, Still Remains, and headliners Shadows Fall. These shows were backed by a Donnie Searls-directed video for 'Jeremiad'. In mid April, Byzantine entered 101 Productions Studios to cut a version of 'Shoplift' for an Eyehategod tribute album, *For The Sick: A Tribute To Eyehategod*, on the Season Of Mist label (at the time of writing due in February 2007). Gigs in May with Kittie followed.

In December 2006, the band started work on a new album with producer Aaron Fisher. They were set to support God Forbid on The Chains Of Humanity US tour in February 2007 and seem well placed to reinforce the success they have enjoyed to date.

CHIMAIRA
EXPERT RIFFAGE WITH VARIED INFLUENCES

CLEVELAND'S CHIMAIRA WERE CREATED by guitarist Jason Hager, previously a member of Ascension, during 1998. The line-up evolved to include former Skipline vocalist Mark Hunter, second guitarist Rob Arnold, bassist Jim LaMarca, drummer Andols Herrick, and Chris Spicuzza on electronics, and they debuted in January 2000 with the self-financed *This Present Darkness* EP. The band's sense of humour came into play with this record – it featured 69 tracks, but only eight involved audio, including the spoof 'Satan's Wizards'. Chimaira signed to Roadrunner for their 2001 opus *Pass Out Of Existence*. That same year, Hager opted out and was replaced by former Ascension guitarist Matt DeVries.

The band donated a version of The Cure's 'Fascination Street' to the Too Damn Hype tribute compilation *Disintegrated*. They were also responsible for a take on the Accept classic 'Balls To The Wall' for another compilation. Hunter and LaMarca announced a side venture with vocalist-guitarist Ed Gandolf and drummer Drew Scalero, billed as High Point, in August 2002. Herrick stood in for Ascension shows during September before the recording of Chimaira's new album, *The Impossibility Of Reason*, produced by Sw1tched frontman Ben Schigel. Japanese variants came with an extra track, a cover of Björk's 'Army Of Me'.

North American touring throughout April and May 2003 saw the band packaged alongside Lamb Of God, Eighteen Visions, and Atreyu. A further round of dates saw the band hooking up with headliners In Flames, Soilwork, and Unearth for a month-long trek. The Soilwork connection was strengthened in December when the group parted ways with Herrick, bringing in Soilwork skinsman Rickard Evensand. The live schedule continued into 2004 with February shows aligning Chimaira with Stampin' Ground and Every Time I Die, after which the band joined Slipknot and Fear Factory for the fourth instalment of the 'Jägermeister Music' US tour. Their next trek was a month's co-headline tour across Europe in June with label-mates Killswitch Engage, Shadows Fall, and God Forbid.

The group was unable to continue with Evensand due to visa complications. They drafted in a new drummer, ex-Deity, Dying Fetus, Suffocation, M.O.D. and Misery Index man Kevin Talley, and forged an alliance with Machine Head and Trivium for the August 'Road Rage' 2004 dates in North America. The band then put in Australian dates in September with In Flames. On December 18th, DeVries hooked up with his erstwhile Ascension colleagues for a reunion show at Peabody's Down Under in Cleveland.

CHIMAIRA discography

This Present Darkness, East Coast Empire ECE16 (USA) (2000)
PASS OUT OF EXISTENCE, Roadrunner RR 8477-2 (Europe / USA) (2001)
THE IMPOSSIBILITY OF REASON, Roadrunner RR 8397-2 (Europe / USA) (2003)
CHIMAIRA, Roadrunner RR 8262-2 (Europe / USA) (2005)
   62 UK, 74 USA
RESURRECTION, Nuclear Blast catalogue number tba (Europe), Ferret Music catalogue number tba (USA) (2007)

The band closed the year with a special performance on December 27th at the Carling Apollo in London alongside Lacuna Coil, Caliban, and In Flames. April 2005 gigs in the USA had Chimaira allied with Trivium. The same month, former Chimaira guitarist/co-founder Hager re-emerged in a new Cleveland-based band, Years Of Fire.

The summer of 2005 found Chimaira participating in the US 'Sounds Of The Underground' tour, a collaboration between independent labels Ferret Music, Prosthetic Records, Trustkill, and Metal Blade. The mammoth billing for these shows saw the band sharing stages with Clutch, Opeth, Poison The Well, From Autumn To Ashes, Unearth, Norma Jean, Every Time I Die, Strapping Young Lad, Throwdown, High On Fire, Devildriver, All That Remains, A Life Once Lost, and GWAR. Further gigs had the band playing with Six Feet Under, All That Remains, and 3 Inches Of Blood.

The band's self-titled 2005 album was recorded at Spider Studios in Ohio with producer Ben Schigel. The record saw release in the UK as a limited-edition 'black box', adding bonus material including two album outtakes, 'Clayden' and 'Malignant', plus seven live tracks recorded on the 2003 European 'Road Rage' tour. First-week US sales of over 14,000 copies saw *Chimaira* land at Number 74 on the *Billboard* charts.

The band had their 'Eyes Of A Criminal' featured on the soundtrack to the *Rainbow Six Lockdown* game issued by 3volution Productions. Hunter was included on the Roadrunner United 25th anniversary album *The All-Star Sessions*, featuring on the track 'The Enemy' penned by ex-Fear Factory guitarist Dino Cazares.

The band joined the Danzig-headlined 'Blackest Of The Black' US dates in September accompanied by Mortiis, Behemoth, Himsa, and The Agony Scene. A brief burst of dates in Germany saw them supporting Hatesphere and Dark Tranquillity. In January 2006, the *Chimaira* album was given an expanded re-release, adding seven live tracks and two previously unreleased studio songs. That same month, the group welcomed original drummer Herrick back into the fold.

North American gigging witnessed a union with Through The Eyes Of The Dead and Children Of Bodom in March. The band played their part in honouring Metallica, contributing their rendition of 'Disposable Heroes' to *Remastered*, a remake of *Master Of Puppets* organised by *Kerrang!* magazine in April 2006.

Chimaira teamed up with Arch Enemy, Nevermore, Hate Eternal, and God Forbid for US shows in April before crossing the Atlantic to join the European edition of the 'Sounds Of The Underground' tour the following month.

In mid October, Sabbat guitarist Andy Sneap recorded the drum tracks for a new Chimaira album, *Resurrection*, in Cleveland, Ohio, with drummer Andols Herrick. The remaining material was cut with producer Jason Suecof at Audiohammer Studios in Sanford, Florida, before the album returned to Sneap for a final mix. An accompanying DVD chronicling the making of the record was directed by Tom Bell. Chimaira are now, like their mythical namesake, something of a legend.

GOD FORBID
PROMISING NWOAHM FORERUNNERS

GOD FORBID WERE FORMED in New Brunswick, New Jersey, by drummer Corey Pierce and ex-Feint 13 guitarist Dallas Coyle, and they issued early product on the independent 9 Volt Records label. They had evolved from Manifest Destiny to Insalubrious before settling on God Forbid. During May 1997, Pierce and Coyle were joined by vocalist Bryon Davis and in September the same year by erstwhile Womb bassist John 'Beeker' Outcalt. (Guitarist Doc Coyle, Dallas's brother, deputised on a temporary basis for As Darkness Falls in 1998.) 9 Volt issued the *Out Of Misery* EP in September 1998 and the band's debut full-length album, *Reject The Sickness*, in 1999.

God Forbid

The band were signed to Century Media just after the New Jersey 'Metalfest' appearance in support of the highly-praised *Determination* album, released in April 2001. They toured with Amen, Shadows Fall, Nevermore, Opeth, and Children Of Bodom. Touring in Britain, they were supported by Labrat and Co-Exist.

In September 2001, the band's *Out Of Misery* EP was re-released to capitalise on their new status, adding bonus live tracks including a take on Sepultura's 'Propaganda', recorded at New York's CBGBs club. They toured the States in alliance with Hatebreed, Converge, and Poison The Well, and then announced more dates with headliners GWAR and Soilent Green. Further shows were scheduled with Shadows Fall and Killswitch Engage but the band withdrew to focus their efforts on songwriting.

In 2003, the band cut a rendition of the Guns N' Roses track 'Out Ta Get Me' with producer Chris Pearce for use on a Law Of Inertia Records tribute album. The long-out-of-print debut album *Reject The Sickness* was reissued through the band's own PR Records label. They got back into tour mode in August, headlining US dates over Atreyu, Darkest Hour, and Underoath, and were on the road again in October for the five-week 'Headbanger's Ball' dates alongside Killswitch Engage, Shadows Fall, Unearth, and Lamb Of God. The band gave themselves no respite, hopping onto the 'Mushroomhead' tour into November. They resumed live activity in 2004, headlining February US dates with Walls Of Jericho, Blood Has Been Shed, and Full Blown Chaos, and released a new album, *Gone Forever*, in February.

GOD FORBID discography

Out Of Misery, 9 Volt 9V 004 (USA) (1998)
REJECT THE SICKNESS, 9 Volt 9V 008 (USA) (1999)
DETERMINATION, Century Media CM 77366-2 (Europe), Century Media CM 8066-2 (USA) (2001)
OUT OF MISERY, We Put Out 80002 (USA) (2001)
Better Days, Century Media CM 8150-2 (USA) (2004)
GONE FOREVER, Century Media CM 77466-2 (Europe), Century Media CM 8166-2 (USA) (2004)
IV: CONSTITUTION OF TREASON, Century Media CM 77566-2 (Europe), Century Media CM 8266-2 (USA) (2005) **119 USA**
To The Fallen Hero, Century Media CM 8328-2 (2006)

They engaged in a month's co-headline tour in June 2004 with labelmates Killswitch Engage, Chimaira, and Shadows Fall. This was followed by an appearance on the 'Ozzfest' headlined by Black Sabbath, Judas Priest, and Slayer. September headline gigs, supported by A Life Once Lost, Norma Jean, and The Red Chord, were filmed by director Zach Merck for a video.

The band allied with Soulfly and Death By Stereo for North American shows in March 2005, and UK headline shows then extended into April and May with headline dates supported by Caliban, It Dies Today, and Full Blown Chaos. A notable compilation appearance came with the track 'Soul Engraved' on *Code Red*, given to US soldiers in the Middle East.

Just a day after they completed touring, God Forbid commenced work on a new album, *IV: Constitution Of Treason*, in May, utilising the services of Jason Suecof at Audiohammer Studios in Florida and Eric Rachel at Trax East in New Jersey. Gigs in July had the band partnered with Full Blown Chaos and Himsa. *IV: Constitution Of Treason*, released in September 2005, sold over 8,300 copies in its first week to debut at Number 119 on the US *Billboard* charts.

The band announced further US dates alongside Meshuggah, The Haunted, and Mnemic throughout October, which were immediately followed by more dates with The Haunted in Europe the following month. They opened 2006 with US dates throughout January supporting Anthrax, followed by headlining dates with Manntis, Cannae, and Sworn Enemy. March had the band scheduled for The 'Crusade III: Ascend Above The Ashes' concerts in the UK and Ireland alongside Trivium and Bloodsimple, and they put in a significant appearance at the Guns N' Roses-headlined 'Download' festival at Castle Donington in the England on June 11th.

God Forbid headed up the UK and European 'Hell On Earth' tour in September and October on a bill that included Heaven Shall Burn, Cataract, Maroon, Purified In Blood, Narziss, and A Perfect Murder. The band remain one of a select few who seem certain to take the next step upwards during 2007.

HATEBREED
HARDCORE AND METAL IN PERFECT HARMONY

HATEBREED ARE A HARDCORE-influenced metal band founded during 1993 in New Haven, Connecticut. The band eventually stabilised as vocalist Jamey Jasta (aka Jamie Shanahan), guitarists Lou 'Boulder' Richards and Sean Martin, bassist Chris Beattie, and drummer Rigg Ross, and they built a live reputation with supports to the likes of Entombed, Deftones, Napalm Death, and Slayer. Their initial demo recordings, *Hate Stricken Creation*, were utilised for a split 7-inch single shared with Neglect; a further split 7-inch, also in 1995, was released with Integrity. A further demo, *Under The Knife*, which was released as an EP in 1996, scored the band recognition, especially for the popular track 'Kill And Addict'. In 1995, Pin Drop Records included the cut 'Mark My Words' on a four-way split 7-inch EP, *Together As One*, with Holdstrong, Brothers's Keepers, and Cross Current.

The band released the 1997 Victory Records album *Satisfaction Is The Death Of Desire*, playing dates with Despair. The Smorgasboard label weighed in shortly afterwards, releasing the *Under The Knife* sessions as a mini-album that December. In 1998, Matt McIntosh and Jamie 'Pushbutton' McVey were replaced by guitarist Sean Martin and drummer Rigg Ross (real name Cliff Ross). However, Ross was fired in June 2001 and replaced by Matt Byrne, who had been in an earlier version of Hatebreed. The band were signed as support to Slayer's autumn 'God Hates Us All' American tour but withdrew shortly before the dates to concentrate on a new album. Frontman Jasta contributed guest vocals to 'Domination' on the 2001 Biohazard album *Uncivilization*.

Slayer guitarist Kerry King guested on 'Final Prayer For The Human Race' on the March 2002 Hatebreed album *Perseverance*. The record debuted on the *Billboard* charts at Number 50, selling over 28,000 copies in its first week of sale and eventually topping the 200,000 mark. The album's success and the band's touring profile also regenerated interest in *Satisfaction Is The Death Of Desire*, which clocked up over 150,000 sales. The band embarked on a series of North American dates, although the Montreal and Quebec shows were cancelled at short notice when Jasta had to undergo emergency dental treatment. The band parted company with guitarist Lou 'Boulder' Richards following a show at the Palladium in Worcester, Massachusetts, on April 20th. They announced that they would continue as a four-piece.

Promoting their October 2003 Zeus-produced album *The Rise Of Brutality*, the band united with Madball, Hate Eternal, Terror, and Cephalic Carnage for the North American 'Rise Of Brutality' tour in September. US Jägermeister-sponsored dates saw them hooked up with Slayer and Arch Enemy. *The Rise Of Brutality* entered the *Billboard* charts at a respectable number 30, shifting over 32,000 units in its first week of sale.

Hatebreed signed up for the US 'Headbangers Ball' tour alongside Damageplan, Drowning Pool, and Unearth in March 2004 but withdrew from the first batch of dates in the wake of the death from cancer of their manager Steve Richards. Touring resumed, although a glitch in the schedule came in early May when they missed a Vancouver show after being refused entry to Canada by border guards.

The band were then confirmed for the US 'Ozzfest' for the summer, sharing the second stage with co-headline act Slipknot and fellow supports Unearth, Lamb Of God, Every Time I Die, Atreyu, Lacuna Coil, and Bleeding Through. They cancelled shows in Bulgaria, Turkey, Greece, and Norway because of more dental surgery for two of the band members and scheduled 'Off-fest' dates with Slayer and headliners Judas Priest along the way. Jasta donated guest vocals to the Icepick track 'Born To Crush You', on the *UFC Ultimate Beatdowns Vol. 1* compilation through Nitrus Records. Both Jasta and guitarist Martin donated their skills as studio guests to MC Necro's album *The Pre-Fix For Death*.

Hatebreed returned to Europe in October, acting as openers to Slipknot and Slayer. The band put in a sustained campaign in North America to round out the year, uniting with Terror, Full Blown Chaos, and No Warning. That same month, their track 'Live For This' was nominated in the Best Metal Performance category for the 47th annual Grammy Awards.

The group scheduled US gigs with Agnostic Front, Diecast, Love Is

Red, and The Autumn Offering for the second leg of the 'Heavyweights Of Hardcore' tour in January 2005. In June, Jasta announced a new musical union, Kingdom Of Sorrow, with Down and Crowbar's Kirk Windstein. Hatebreed gigs with Agnostic Front in South America followed before the 'Persistence' European tour and the '10 Years Of Brutality' tour. On December 15th, Jasta was host and performer for the 'Roadrunner United' conglomerate at the New York Nokia Theater for an all-star metal evening. A previously unreleased track, 'To The Threshold', was included on the Roadrunner compilation *MTV Headbanger's Ball – The Revenge*.

Hatebreed expanded to a quintet during March 2006, pulling in From The Depths guitarist Frank Novinec. In April, they toured Australia with Disturbed, 10 Years, and Korn, after which they announced a new deal with Roadrunner. The band put in a significant appearance at the 'Download' festival in Castle Donington, England on June 11th. 'Ozzfest' loomed again for summer 2006, with the group sharing stages with Ozzy Osbourne, System Of A Down, Black Label Society, Lacuna Coil, Disturbed, and a supporting cast.

The new Hatebreed album, *Supremacy*, sold 27,000 copies in the USA in its first week of release in August to debut at Number 31 on the *Billboard* charts. Pushing their new release, the group hit the US touring circuit in September, heading up a strong billing of Napalm Death, Exodus, The Black Dahlia Murder, Despised Icon, and First Blood. Former guitarist Lou 'Boulder' Richards, who had appeared on the group's 1997 *Satisfaction Is The Death Of Desire* and 2002's *Perseverance* albums, died on September 13th, aged 36.

Hatebreed teamed up with Unearth and Full Blown Chaos for a European tour in November, hitting Germany, Denmark, Holland, Italy, France, Switzerland, Austria, the UK, and Belgium. US gigs the following month had Sick Of It All as guests. Jasta, who presents Headbanger's Ball on MTV2 in the USA, also owns Stillborn Records and has become a well-known industry figure. His band look set to dominate their particular niche for some time to come.

KILLSWITCH ENGAGE
WHERE METALCORE MEETS MELODY

KILLSWITCH ENGAGE HAVE RISEN TO the forefront of the New Wave of American Heavy Metal. They were created in 1998 by erstwhile Overcast man Mike D'Antonio and Aftershock personnel Joel Stoetzel (guitar) and Adam Dutkiewicz (drums). Shortly afterwards, Corrin frontman Jesse Leach (aka Jesse David) joined, and Killswitch Engage were complete, apparently taking their title from an episode of the TV series *The X Files*. The act debuted live as openers to In Flames and released their first (self-titled) album for Ferret Music in July 2000, which led in turn to a deal with Roadrunner. After that signing, the band recruited former Aftershock drummer Tom Gomes, and Dutkiewicz switched to guitar.

Roadrunner released the *Alive Or Just Breathing* album in 2002 and Killswitch Engage joined headliners Kittie for a North American tour in the summer. Vocalist Jesse Leach announced his departure in mid June, and Blood Has Been Shed frontman Howard Jones landed the job.

The band formed part of the 2003 'Ozzfest', after which Gomes opted out and was replaced by Blood Has Been Shed drummer Justin Foley. His live debut was on the *Headbanger's Ball* tour. The band were back on the road in October for the five-week 'Headbanger's Ball' tour alongside Lamb Of God, Shadows Fall, Unearth, and God Forbid. Guitarist Dutkiewicz also made time for Burn Your Wishes, a band consisting of Unearth guitarist Ken Susi, The Acacia Strain bass player Karrie Whitfield, and Pictures Of Gabriel drummer Paul DeBenedictis. Burn Your Wishes released a split EP with Quebec City's The Award through Milk And Cookies Records.

Killswitch Engage

Subsequently, Dutkiewicz produced the 2004 All That Remains album *This Darkened Heart*.

D'Antonio was operational on the club covers circuit in early 2004 in Late Night Crüe, a Mötley Crüe tribute band featuring vocalist Brian Fair of Shadows Fall, Unearth guitarists Ken Susi and Buz McGrath, and Seemless drummer Derek Kerswill. Killswitch Engage partnered thrash veterans Anthrax and Swedish band Soilwork for Australian and Japanese dates in April 2004, promoting their third record, *The End Of Heartache*, issued through Roadrunner. The album debuted at Number 40 in the UK and Number 39 in Australia. It sold over 37,000 copies in its first week on sale in the USA, entering the charts at Number 21. Surreally, part of the album's promotion included a snippet of the track 'The Element Of One' in a TV Pop Tarts commercial.

Touring in the latter half of the year had the band as direct support to Slayer's US Jägermusic dates and headlining August gigs with From Autumn To Ashes, Eighteen Visions, and 36 Crazyfists. They hooked up with Slayer again for another Jägermeister tour alongside Mastodon, and in December 'The End Of Heartache' was nominated in the Best Metal Performance category for the 47th annual Grammy Awards. To mark this achievement, and a quarter of a million US sales for *The End Of Heartache*, Roadrunner issued a special edition of the record with a bonus CD hosting live tracks, videos, and previously unreleased cuts 'My Life For Yours' and 'Irreversal', the latter featuring original singer Leach and Phil Labonte of All That Remains on vocals.

Canadian gigs in January 2005 had the band supporting Slipknot, although Jones was forced to sit out the band's performance in Toronto

KILLSWITCH ENGAGE discography

KILLSWITCH ENGAGE, Ferret Music F 22 (USA) (2000)
ALIVE OR JUST BREATHING, Roadrunner RR 8457-2 (Europe / USA) (2002)
THE END OF HEARTACHE, Roadrunner RR 8373-2 (Europe / USA) (2004) 40 UK, 21 USA
A DAYLIGHT DIES, Roadrunner RR 8058-2 (Europe / USA) (2006) 64 UK, 32 USA

on January 9th after losing his voice. Trevor Phipps from support act Unearth with two fans plucked from the audience filled the gap. These US shows were followed by a brief burst of UK headliners. The group then teamed up with The Used and My Chemical Romance for the 'Taste Of Chaos' US tour in February 2005. Halfway through this trek, Dutkiewicz missed a few shows thanks to an ongoing back injury. Back with a full roster, Killswitch filmed a gig at the Palladium in Worcester, Massachusetts, on July 25th with director Lex Halaby for the DVD (Set This) World Ablaze. The track 'Irreversal' was included on the soundtrack of The Cave in August.

Leach donated his vocals to the Roadrunner United 25th anniversary album The All-Star Sessions, featuring on the track 'Blood And Flames' composed by Matthew Heafy of Trivium. Dutkiewicz's recurring back problem sidelined him from Australian gigs in October as the guitarist underwent corrective surgery; the tour pitched the band alongside The Used, Story Of The Year, Funeral For A Friend, and Rise Against. On December 15th, Jones, Stroetzel, Foley, D'Antonio, and Leach joined the Roadrunner United conglomerate at the New York Nokia Theater.

The group recorded an exclusive cover version of Dio's 'Holy Diver' for inclusion on UK magazine Kerrang!'s 25th anniversary issue cover-mounted CD, High Voltage, issued in May 2006. Arriving the same month, the WWE: Wreckless Intent compilation featured the previously unreleased Killswitch Engage track 'This Fire Burns'.

October saw the band join forces with Lamb Of God and Unearth for an Australian tour. They teamed up with All That Remains, Hatebreed, Bury Your Dead, and 2 Cents for a number of US dates in November. A new album, As Daylight Dies, released the same month, sold just under 60,000 copies in the USA during its first week of release to debut at Number 32 on the Billboard chart. Critics praised its expansive sound and, as this book went to press, the album looks set to take its creators to the next stage with ease.

KITTIE
GIRLS JUST WANNA HAVE FUN?

THE ALL-FEMALE ACT KITTIE, from London, Ontario, were conceived by drummer Mercedes Lander and South African-born guitarist Fallon Bowman in a school gymnasium in 1996. Kittie learned their craft by covering songs by artists such as Nirvana and Silverchair, but the band's first guitarist soon decamped, making space for Morgan Lander, sister of Mercedes, to take on vocals and guitar.

They cut a demo in 1998, Sexizhell, a tape that soon had the industry taking note thanks to song titles such as 'Get Off (You Can Eat A Dick)' and 'Just A Bunch Of Fucked Up Kids'. Further sessions resulted in the 1999 Kittie demos. Original bass player Tanya Candler bailed out to create punk band The Candy Darlings, and Kittie pulled in Talena Atfield as substitute. The Garth Richardson-produced Spit arrived in 2000 on the Artemis label with a doctored band photo on the cover in which Atfield's image replaced that of Candler.

Kittie's rise was dramatic, aided by a succession of high-profile support gigs to Slipknot, Sevendust, and Pantera, and the band graced the second stage of the 'Ozzfest'. Rumours circulated that they had cut a version of Pink Floyd's 'Run Like Hell' for a tribute album and, although the recording never emerged, the band often included the track in their live show.

They opened 2001 as part of the 'SnoCore' shows across America, during which two new tracks, 'A Mouthful Of Poison' and 'Pain', were road-tested. Recognition from the Canadian music industry escaped the band, however: although they were nominated for a Juno award, Kittie walked away empty-handed. Bowman left the band in mid-2001.

Their second album got underway in August with Richardson once again at the helm. Launched in November, Oracle sold over 30,000 copies in its first week in America, landing a Number 57 chart placing. After inaugural UK shows in February 2002 supported by Shadows Fall, it was reported that Atfield had broken ranks: Jennifer J. Arroyo of Spine supplanted her on bass. Ex-guitarist Bowman resurfaced in May with a solo endeavour, Amphibious Assault.

The band took on a North American tour throughout the summer, headlining a bill over Shadows Fall, Poison The Well, Killswitch Engage, and Hotwire. Another round of US shows had them topping a bill consisting of Unloco, Clockwise, and Acacia. A seven-track EP Safe was launched to coincide with these gigs. Dates with Biohazard, Brand New Sin, and Eighteen Visions and a place on the 'Kiss Of Infamy' tour followed.

In April 2004, the band revealed that they had inducted new guitarist Lisa Marx, previously a member of Seattle hardcore band To See You Broken. Promoting the new album Until The End, Kittie got back on the road in July for US dates with Candiria, 36 Crazyfists, Thine Eyes Bleed, and Twelve Tribes. However, they cancelled shows in Cleveland and Cincinnati after drummer Mercedes Lander was hospitalised "due to severe dehydration and exhaustion". The entire tour was subsequently postponed as Lander returned to Canada for examinations to determine the nature of her illness. They were back on the road in September, backed by Otep and Crisis.

With the band on hold in early 2005, awaiting a renewal of the contractual option from Artemis, guitarist Marx left in February, and bassist Arroyo exited shortly afterward. They cut new demo tracks in July, recording at Mole Studios in London, Ontario. Morgan Lander put in a guest vocal on the Kataklysm album In the Arms Of Devastation. Aside from music, the Lander sisters launched their Poisonedblack line of clothing in September.

On September 29th at a gig at Call The Office in London, Ontario, Kittie revealed two new members: guitarist Tara McLeod, formerly with Ontario band Sherry, and bassist Trish Doan of Her. In early November, they signed with Rock Ridge Music for a download-only digital EP titled Never Again, released in February 2006. The band teamed up with

KITTIE discography

SPIT, Artemis ATM 497630 2 (Europe), Artemis ATM-CD-51002 (USA) (2000) 79 USA
Paperdoll, Artemis ATM-CD-51066 (USA) (2000)
ORACLE, Artemis ATM 504810 2 (Europe), Artemis ATM-CD-51088 (USA) (2001) 57 USA
Safe, Artemis ATM-CD-51155 (USA) (2002)
UNTIL THE END, Artemis/Rykodisc RCD 17017 (Europe), Artemis ATM-CD-51538 (USA) (2004)
FUNERAL FOR YESTERDAY, X Of Infamy catalogue number tba (2007)

Evergreen Terrace and Calico System for US dates in April 2006. That summer, the foursome lined up a mammoth touring schedule, the 'Never Again' tour, and pulled in a swathe of regional support acts.

In July 2006, the band entered Retromedia Studio in Red Bank, New Jersey, with producer Jack Ponti to begin recording a new album, *Funeral For Yesterday*, for a February 2007 release through the band's own Kiss Of Infamy label. It is to be hoped that they will continue with their previous successes: few all-female acts manage to sustain a career in rock music, but Kittie may be a notable exception to this apparent rule.

LAMB OF GOD
METALCORE SCENE-LEADERS

Metalcore outfit Lamb Of God, from Richmond, Virginia, consist of singer Randy Blythe, guitarist Mark Morton, bassist John Campbell, and drummer Chris Adler. They spent their formative months billed as Burn The Priest, but following the release of an eponymous album, a split 7-inch single, and a split EP with Agents Of Satan, the band switched their name to Lamb Of God, adding guitarist Will Adler, who replaced guitarist Abe Spear in 1999. The newly named group signed to Prosthetic for September 2000's *American Gospel*, produced by Steve Austin of Today Is The Day. The record closed with 'O.D.H.G.A.B.F.E. ' ('Officer Dick Head Gets a Black Fucking Eye'), and the band were categorised as part of the New Wave of American Heavy Metal.

Lamb Of God teamed up with Shadows Fall, Scissorfight, Darkest Hour, From Autumn To Ashes, and Unearth for a series of American East Coast dates in May 2002. They scheduled the recording of a second album, *As The Palaces Burn*, for November 2002, bringing in the highly respected Devin Townsend as co-producer. Former Megadeth guitarist Chris Poland guested on the album.

North American touring throughout April and May 2003 saw the band play alongside Chimaira, Eighteen Visions, and Atreyu. They were back on the road in October for 'Headbanger's Ball' dates alongside Killswitch Engage, Shadows Fall, Unearth, and God Forbid. The year closed with frontman Randy Blythe guesting on the 'F.U.B.A.R.' track on Canadian act Bloodshoteye's *Without Any Remorse*.

The band signed to major label Epic for the Machine-produced *Ashes Of The Wake*, featuring guest appearances by Poland and ex-Testament axeman Alex Skolnick. The album sold just over 35,000 copies during the first week of its sale in the USA, debuting at Number 27 on the *Billboard* charts.

The band stepped up for the 2004 'Ozzfest', sharing the second stage with headline act Slipknot and fellow supports. In the midst of these shows, *As The Palaces Burn* passed the 100,000 sales mark. October shows across the USA had the band partnered with Children Of Bodom, Fear Factory, and Throwdown. UK gigs in December were supported by Throwdown and As I Lay Dying.

The band opened 2005 with a run of arena shows from March through May, the 'Subliminal Verses' tour, with Shadows Fall and Slipknot. However, they were barred from performing at the Los Angeles Forum on the tour due to an objection by the venue owners, the Faithful Central Bible Church, over the band's present and former names. Lamb Of God also put in numerous headline 'Off-fest' dates.

To coincide with this live activity, the band released a live DVD, *Killadelphia*, directed by Doug Spangenberg and filmed during their two performances at Philadelphia's Trocadero in October 2004. Epic Records engaged producer Colin Richardson to remix and remaster the 1998 *Burn The Priest* album for a 2005 reissue, and Morton made his presence felt on Fear Factory's *Transgression* album, gaining a co-composition credit on 'New Promises'.

LAMB OF GOD discography

NEW AMERICAN GOSPEL, Prosthetic/Metal Blade 3984-14345-2 (Europe / USA) (2000)
AS THE PALACES BURN, Prosthetic 10008-2 (Europe / USA) (2003)
ASHES OF THE WAKE, Epic 517933-2 (Europe), Epic 90702 (2004) **27 USA**
KILLADELPHIA, Epic 762862 (Europe), Epic 75765 (USA) (2005)
SACRAMENT, Epic 757652 (Europe), Epic 83385 (2006) **8 USA**

European dates in June 2005 had the band unified with Unearth, Every Time I Die, and Caliban. The following month, *Killadelphia* was certified gold by industry organisation the RIAA for US sales in excess of 50,000 copies. A subsequent CD version of *Killadelphia* offered additional material not included on the DVD. UK and European gigs in December saw support from Devildriver and The Agony Scene.

In side activity, Chris Adler played with Machinations Of Dementia, a technical metal project masterminded by guitarist Ron Jarzombek of Watchtower and Spastic Ink alongside Cannibal Corpse bassist Alex Webster. Adler bowed out of this project in December 2005 due to other commitments.

Early 2006 found the band in the recording studio with producer Machine working on *Sacrament*. Summer 2006 US dates, the 'Unholy Alliance – Preaching To The Perverted' tour, had the group packaged with Slayer, plus Mastodon, Thine Eyes Bleed, and Children Of Bodom as support. In August, *Sacrament* sold 63,000 copies in the United States in its first week of release to debut at Number 8 on the national *Billboard* album chart.

They joined up with the Megadeth-headlined 'Gigantour' North American festivals in early September, sharing billing with Opeth, Arch Enemy, Overkill, Into Eternity, Sanctity, and The Smashup. Gigs in October included the Tokyo 'Loud Park '06' festival followed by a run of Australian shows alongside Killswitch Engage and Unearth in October. Pundits foresee a continued run of success for Lamb Of God in 2007 and beyond.

MASTODON
AWE-INSPIRING METAL BEAST

THE GENRE-DEFYING MASTODON consist of two erstwhile Lethargy and Today Is The Day members, vocalist-guitarist Bill Kelliher and drummer Brann Dailor, along with ex-Social Infestation personnel bassist Troy Sanders and guitarist Brent Hines. Kelliher and Dailor relocated from Rochester, New York, to Atlanta, Georgia, in order to build the new band in January 2000. Just weeks afterwards, the four musicians met at a High On Fire concert held in Hines's basement and by June had crafted a nine-track demo. These recordings featured original singer Eric Saner, who left the band for personal reasons shortly after. Initially, the band took on a grind/death metal stance but then expanded their horizons to incorporate modern thrash and sludge influences. The demo was promoted by a hectic tour supporting the likes of Cannibal Corpse, Queens Of The Stone Age, and Morbid Angel.

The combination of the demo (a picture disc EP called *Slick Leg*) and live work led to a deal with Relapse. In spring 2001, they played with Eyehategod, Keelhaul, and Burnt By The Sun for Eastern US dates, followed by gigs with The Fucking Champs and appearances at events such as the Milwaukee 'Metalfest'. A further EP, *Lifeblood*, was issued in August. The band's debut album, June 2002's *Remission* – recorded at Zero Return Studios in Atlanta with producer Matt Bayles – drew exceptional praise on the metal underground. They toured Japan

MASTODON discography

Slick Leg, Reptilian REP 059 (USA) (2000) 7-inch vinyl picture disc EP
Lifesblood, Relapse RR 6506-2 (USA) (2001)
REMISSION, Relapse RR 6523-2 (Europe / USA) (2002)
LEVIATHAN, Relapse RR 6622-2 (Europe / USA) (2004) **139 USA**
CALL OF THE MASTODON, Relapse RR 6515-2 (Europe / USA) (2006) **139 USA**
BLOOD MOUNTAIN, Relapse 9362-44364-2 (Europe / USA) (2006) **46 UK**

in November 2002 with Swedish thrashers Darkane and stoners High On Fire.

European gigs in April 2003 saw the band lined up with The Haunted and Hatesphere. They undertook the North American 'Contamination' tour in May 2003 alongside Denver's Cephalic Carnage, Santa Barbara's Uphill Battle, and Philadelphia's Dysrhythmia. That August saw the band hooking up with Clutch for further US shows. They continued to drive forward into January 2004, touring alongside Nebula and Clutch. A limited 7-inch through the Belgian Delboy label saw the band covering Thin Lizzy's 'Emerald' on a split release shared with American Heritage.

The 2004 album *Leviathan*, recorded at both Robert Lang Studios and Litho Studios in Seattle with producer Bayles, was a conceptual offering based in part on Herman Melville's classic novel *Moby Dick*. In the first week it went on sale in the USA, the record sold just over 8,000 copies, debuting at Number 139 on the *Billboard* charts.

US gigs in July had the band playing at the New Jersey 'Hellfest' before touring with Fear Factory and Sworn Enemy for a run of shows including the 'Pigstock' and 'DFW Metalfest'. Chad Rullman directed a Moby Dick-themed video for the track 'Iron Tusk'. Many more high-profile tours followed before the band signed to major label Warner Bros in April 2005.

Mastodon contributed a rendition of 'The Bit' to a Melvins tribute album, *We Reach: The Music Of The Melvins*, through Fractured Transmitter Records. They also featured in a studio collaboration with Fear Factory and Strapping Young Lad to craft a take of 'Joan Of Arc' for the same compilation. 'Blood And Thunder' gave the band extra exposure when it was included on the soundtrack to *The Cave*, released in August 2005.

Mastodon then played on the Black Sabbath and Iron Maiden-headlined 'Ozzfest', interspersing these weekend events with 'Off Fest' dates with Iron Maiden and Rob Zombie. Relapse Records issued a special 'Festival' edition of *Leviathan* in August, with new artwork and the addition of videos for 'Iron Tusk' and 'Blood And Thunder'. A retrospective collection of early recordings was remastered by original producer Matt Washburn and entitled *Call Of The Mastodon*, and there was an archive DVD, too, titled *The Workhorse Chronicles: The Early Years 2000-2005*. UK concerts in December saw support from High On Fire and Atlanta's Withered.

The band played their part in honouring Metallica, contributing their rendition of 'Orion' to *Remastered*, a remake of *Master Of Puppets* organised by *Kerrang!* magazine in April 2006. Summer US dates, the 'Unholy Alliance – Preaching To The Perverted' tour, saw the group packaged with headliners Slayer, plus Thine Eyes Bleed, Lamb Of God, and Children Of Bodom as support.

A new Mastodon album, *Blood Mountain*, was delivered in September. Japanese variants hosted a customary additional track, a live recording of 'Crystal Skull'. They are perhaps the most exciting metal band to emerge in recent years, and hopes are high for their continued progress.

SHADOWS FALL
POPULAR METAL NEWCOMERS

MASSACHUSETTS METAL BAND Shadows Fall are named after an underground comic series. The original line-up featured vocalist Damien McPherson, guitarists Jonathon Donais and Matthew Bachand, temporary bassist Mark Laliberte, and drummer David Germain. With this line-up the band recorded the 1996 six-song demo *Mourning A Dead World*. After just three shows, McPherson bailed out. Donais and Bachand then shared vocal duties until June 1997 when the band recruited Phil Labonte. In July 1997, a permanent bass player was found in Paul Romanko. A two-song 7-inch single, *To Ashes*, was released in 1997 on Ellington Records before the *Somber Eyes In The Sky* album arrived in 1998.

Support gigs with Six Feet Under, Overcast, and Shai Hulud followed. Other notable outings included slots at the Cleveland 'World Series Of Metal', the Milwaukee 'Metalfest', and one of the 'Vans Warped' tour dates. During autumn 1998, the band opted to let Labonte go, fearing that his vocal style placed the band too far into the death metal camp. Undaunted, Labonte soon re-emerged with his new act, All That Remains, signing to Metal Blade for the *Behind Silence And Solitude* album. The new frontman was Brian Fair, recently disengaged from a collapsing Overcast.

The revised line-up cut their teeth at the Milwaukee 'Metalfest' once again and Century Media signed the band in late 1999. After topping the bill at the New England 'Metal And Hardcore' festival in 2000, the band hit a run of bad luck when a projected tour with Candira and Madball was cancelled as Madball broke up. Further dates were planned with Opeth and Amorphis, but the band pulled out in order to concentrate on recording *Of One Blood*. They did manage to play later gigs with Amen and God Forbid. Then Germain left, due to musical differences, playing his swansong gig with the band at L'Amours club in Brooklyn on May 4th 2000.

They issued an exclusive Japanese EP, *Deadworld*, for JVC Records on August 22nd 2001 to coincide with their appearance at the Yokohama 'Beast Feast' festival alongside 29 other metal acts including Pantera, Slayer, Machine Head, and Sepultura. The band had put in American club dates as a warm-up to this event.

Shadows Fall temporarily enlisted the percussive talents of Derek Kerswill, a longtime friend of the band, and he featured on two new studio songs for the EP – the title track and 'Stepping Outside The Circle'.

Shadows Fall

SHADOWS FALL discography

To Ashes, Ellington cnu (USA) (1997) 7-inch vinyl single
SOMBER EYES IN THE SKY, Lifeless LR 01 (USA) (1998)
OF ONE BLOOD, Century Media CM 77284-2 (Europe), Century
   Media CM 7981-2 (USA) (2000)
FEAR WILL DRAG YOU DOWN, Century Media CM 77321-2
   (Europe), Century Media CM 7321-2 (USA) (2002)
THE ART OF BALANCE, Century Media CM 77428-2 (Europe),
   Century Media CM 8128-2 (USA) (2002)
THE WAR WITHIN, Century Media CM 77528-2 (Europe), Century
   Media CM 8228-2 (USA) (2004) **20 USA**
FALLOUT FROM THE WAR, Century Media CM 77728-2 (Europe),
   Century Media CM 8428-2 (USA) (2006) **83 USA**
THREADS OF LIFE, Roadrunner catalogue number tba (Europe),
   Atlantic catalogue number tba (USA) (2007)

Other cuts included two laid down for the Boston radio station WERS and a live version of 'Of One Blood' recorded at New York's legendary CBGBs club.

During December, the band recruited drummer Jason Bittner, previously a member of cult hardcore act Stigmata and Crisis, and then acted as openers for Kittie's European 2002 tour. The *Of One Blood* and *Deadworld* EPs were combined for European release, as *Fear Will Drag You Down*. A new album, *The Art Of Balance*, issued in September 2002 and including a cover of Pink Floyd's 'Welcome To The Machine', was cut with producer Zeuss.

Shadows Fall once again joined headliners Kittie and a support package of Poison The Well, Killswitch Engage, and Hotwire for a North American tour in late summer. Meanwhile, the band had two tracks included on the Century Media tenth anniversary DVD, 'The First Noble Truth' and a live 'The Mystery Of One Spirit'. During the summer of 2003, they played the second stage at the 'Ozzfest'.

The band then formed part of the 'Take Action' tour of North America, designed to raise awareness of and funding for the youth suicide prevention body The National Hopeline Network. The group were back on the road in October for 'Headbanger's Ball' dates alongside Killswitch Engage, Lamb Of God, Unearth, and God Forbid. Fair was operational on the club circuit in early 2004 in Late Night Crüe, a Mötley Crüe tribute band with Unearth guitarists Ken Susi and Buz McGrath, bassist Mike D'Antonio from Killswitch Engage, and Kerswill.

Shadows Fall scheduled time at Planet Z Studios in April to commence work on a new album and to compile a DVD with the working title of *The Art Of Touring: Drunk And Shitty In Every City*. Both Bachand and Bittner made time to session on the Death tribute album *Within The Mind – In Homage To The Musical Legacy Of Chuck Schuldiner*. Summer 2004 was taken up with more tours, but the year was overshadowed by the death of a fan at a concert on July 29th in St. Petersburg, Florida.

The new album, *The War Within* – again produced by Zeuss – was scheduled for September, duly selling 39,250 copies in the United States in the first seven days of its release and debuting at Number 20. The first pressing was limited to 150,000 embossed digipack copies, packaged with a DVD featuring a video for 'Stepping Outside The Circle' from *The Art of Balance*, two live videos, guitar lessons with Bachand and Donais, a drum lesson with Bittner, and a Century Media sampler.

The new album passed the 100,000 sales mark in June. A video *for The War Within* track 'The Power Of I And I' was directed by Dale Resteghini. The band put in a one-off support to Judas Priest at the Mohegan Sun Arena in Connecticut on August 29th and then headed up

dates backed by All That Remains, Candiria, and Full Blown Chaos. Live work continued in North America as they stepped straight onto another nationwide trek, this time with Damageplan and The Haunted. In October, they saw their 'Destroyer Of Senses' used in the Eidos video game *Backyard Wrestling 2: There Goes The Neighborhood*. UK shows were projected with Fear Factory but Shadows Fall had to pull out following a family bereavement.

In early November, Transient – the space-rock project of Brian Fair, ex-Arise guitarist Tim Hayes, and ex-Overcast guitarist Scott McCooe – issued a three-song demo. The same month, *The War Within*, driven by the radio single 'What Drives The Weak', passed 100,000 sales in the USA.

Shadows Fall played San Juan, Puerto Rico in January 2005, filming a video for 'Inspiration On Demand' with director Zach Merck while on the island. They then put in a date in Seoul, South Korea and headed up the 'Extreme The Dojo Volume 12' Japanese tour in early February with support from As I Lay Dying and Everytime I Die. Australian gigs saw guest slots going to As I Lay Dying and Parkway Drive. The band then embarked on a major run of US arena shows, the 'Subliminal Verses' tour, in union with Lamb Of God and headliners Slipknot, from March through May. These dates were immediately followed by shows with Cephalic Carnage, Terror, and Zao.

During summer 2005, the band played at the Black Sabbath-headlined 'Ozzfest' on the main stage. Meanwhile, the track 'Inspiration On Demand' gave them exposure when it was included on the soundtrack to the movie *The Cave*. Next, they went into the studio to record material for what would become their final Century Media release, as in December the band had signed a North American deal with Atlantic and subsequently contracted with Roadrunner for all territories outside the USA.

In mid January 2006, Bittner filled in for Anthrax's Charlie Benante for the last two dates on their US tour while Benante awaited the birth of his first child. The 48th Grammy Awards were held on February 8th and saw Shadows Fall's 'What Drives the Weak' nominated for Best Metal Performance. US dates in March had them sharing stages with Agnostic Front, Still Remains, and Byzantine. The *WWE: Wreckless Intent* compilation album, issued in May, boasted the previously unreleased Shadows Fall track 'Fury Of The Storm', a song composed for wrestler Rob Van Dam.

The band's final Century Media offering, *Fallout From The War*, arrived in June 2004. It contained material originally written during sessions for *The War Within* and was billed as a companion piece to that album, along with new versions of 'This Is My Own' and 'Deadworld' and three cover songs previously only available as bonus tracks on Japanese and European releases – 'Mark Of The Squealer' by Leeway, a take on Only Living Witness's 'December', and 'Teasin', Pleasin'' by Dangerous Toys, with their original frontman Jason McMaster as guest.

Touring in July through August saw Shadows Fall as part of the 'Strhess Tour 2006' alongside Poison The Well, It Dies Today, Himsa, Darkest Hour, Bury Your Dead, Suffocation, Throwdown, and Still Remains. The band entered Studio 606 in Northridge, California, with producer Nick Raskulinecz during September to begin recording a new album, titled *Threads Of Life*, for a 2007 release. Can Shadows Fall consolidate their progress so far? Watch this space.

TRIVIUM
NEW HOPE FOR OLD METAL?

TRIVIUM ARE A METALCORE/THRASH METAL act from Altamonte Springs, Florida, created in 2000 by guitarist Matt Heafy and drummer Travis Smith so that they could enter a high-school Battle Of The Bands contest. Heafy's colleagues spotted his talents when he sang his version of The Offspring's 'Self Esteem'. The name Trivium – a Latin word meaning the intersection between grammar, rhetoric, and logic – was chosen as it implied an open-mindedness towards various musical styles. Fortunately for the band, Trivium's approach coincided perfectly with the metalcore boom.

An early round of line-up changes saw the addition of Brent Young on rhythm guitar and Heafy taking over vocals. The following year, Richie Brown of black metal outfit Mindscar filled in as bassist for live work, but subsequently Young switched instruments to cover this position.

The year 2002 proved a pivotal one for the group as they claimed top honours at that school contest and supported Pessimist and Pissing Razors. Heafy also won the local Orlando Metal Awards as best guitarist. A self financed mini-album had Jason Suecof of Capharnaum acting as producer, and the band found themselves hailed as frontrunners in the New Wave of American Heavy Metal. They signed to Lifeforce for *Ember To Inferno*, cut at Audiohammer Studios in Sanford, Florida, and added Corey Beaulieu as second guitarist in September 2003.

The group re-entered Audiohammer in May 2004 to commence pre-production for their Roadrunner debut album, with producer Suecof. The band acted as support to Iced Earth and Beyond The Embrace for summer shows in the USA, and then forged an alliance with Machine Head and Chimaira for the August 'Road Rage 2004' dates in North America.

The band entered Tampa's Morrisound studios on September 13th with Suecof for their sophomore album, *Ascendancy*. Mastering was conducted by Andy Sneap in the UK. In November, the group added former Metal Militia bassist Paolo Gregoletto to the ranks. The album was released in March 2005 and sold just under 7,000 copies upon its release, opening at Number 151 on the US *Billboard* charts. The band had 'Like Light To The Flies' featured on the soundtrack to the *Rainbow Six Lockdown* game issued by 3volution Productions.

They opened 2005 with US headlining dates, heading up a package with All That Remains, It Dies Today, and The Acacia Strain. Gigs into February found them partnered with Danzig and Kataklysm. They then joined the Roadrunner 'Road Rage' tour with 3 Inches Of Blood, The Agony Scene, and Still Remains in March prior to April gigs alongside Chimaira. This tour extended into UK dates during May. Initially announced as an opening act on the Slipknot/Shadows Fall US arena tour

Trivium

TRIVIUM discography

EMBER TO INFERNO, Lifeforce LFR 040-2 (Europe) (2003)
ASCENDANCY, Roadrunner RR 8251-2 (Europe / USA) (2005)
  151 USA
THE CRUSADE, Roadrunner RR 8059-2 (Europe / USA) (2006)
  7 UK, 151 USA

of spring 2005, the band were forced to drop from the bill due to "union-enforced time constraints".

Heafy was one of five high-profile writers contributing to the Roadrunner United 25th anniversary album *The All-Star Sessions*, featuring on the tracks 'The Dawn Of A Golden Age' with lead vocals from Dani Davey of Cradle Of Filth, 'Superheroes' with vocals from Michale Graves of the Misfits, and 'Blood And Flames' sung by ex-Killswitch Engage man Jesse Leach. Heafy himself vocalised on 'The End', penned by ex-Fear Factory guitarist Dino Cazares.

The Trivium track 'Pull Harder On The Strings Of Your Martyr' gave them a degree of extra exposure when it was included on the soundtrack to the Bruce Hunt-directed movie *The Cave*, released in August. To coincide with European and Japanese dates, a tour edition of *Ascendancy* was issued, adding a bonus disc featuring two previously unreleased tracks and three videos. On December 15th, Heafy, Smith, and Beaulieu joined the Roadrunner United conglomerate at the New York Nokia Theater. Trivium included the track 'Washing Me Away In The Tides' on the *Underworld: Evolution* movie soundtrack.

In Flames, Trivium, and Devildriver pooled their talents for a January 2006 US tour. March had the band scheduled for 'The Crusade III: Ascend Above The Ashes' concerts in the UK and Ireland alongside God Forbid and Bloodsimple. They played their part in honouring Metallica, contributing their rendition of 'Master Of Puppets' to the album *Remastered*, a remake of *Master Of Puppets* organised by magazine *Kerrang!* in April 2006.

The band put in a significant appearance at the Metallica and Korn-headlined 'Download' festival at Castle Donington in the UK on June 10th. They subsequently engaged in the US 'Sounds Of The Underground' tour alongside the likes of As I Lay Dying, Killswitch Engage, In Flames, Cannibal Corpse, GWAR, Behemoth, The Black Dahlia Murder, and Through The Eyes Of The Dead.

Trivium's first headline US trek took place through late September into early November, supported by The Sword, Protest The Hero, Seemless, Sanctity, and Cellador. The band's new album *The Crusade*, recorded at Audiohammer Studios with producer Suecof, arrived in October and was officially certified silver status upon release in the UK, with sales in excess of 60,000 copies and hitting Number 7 on the charts. In the USA, *The Crusade* sold over 31,000 on release and debuted at Number 25 on the *Billboard* top 200.

The band scored a notable coup by supporting Iron Maiden for their massive series of arena dates throughout Europe in November. This alone would seem to justify the hype that has accompanied them since their rise to prominence: respect, it appears, is due.

UNEARTH
METALCORE FORERUNNERS

MASSACHUSETTS ACT UNEARTH, established in Winthrop during 1998, made their first impression on the metalcore scene with the 1999 EP *The Fall Of Man*. Their arrival placed them as part of the New Wave of American Heavy Metal. The original line-up was Trevor Phipps (vocals),

Buz McGrath (guitar), Ken Susi (guitar), Chris 'Rover' Rybicki (bass), and Mike Rudberg (drums). Signing to Eulogy Records, the band delivered the album *The Stings Of Conscience* in 2001 followed by the *Endless* EP in September 2002.

Bassist Rybicki was replaced by John 'Slo' Maggard during the production of the *Endless* EP, and drummer Mike Rudberg gave way to Mike Justain of The Red Chord as the band signed to Metal Blade in October 2003 and recorded *The Oncoming Storm* at Zing Studios in Westfield, Massachusetts, with Killswitch Engage guitarist Adam Dutkiewicz as producer. They took part in the 'Headbangers Ball' US tour with Killswitch Engage, Shadows Fall, and Lamb Of God later that same month.

Guitarist Ken Susi made time to fire up Burn Your Wishes with Dutkiewicz on guitar, The Acacia Strain bass player Karrie Whitfield, and Pictures Of Gabriel man Paul DeBenedictis on drums. Burn Your Wishes released a split EP with Quebec City's The Award through Milk And Cookies Records. Susi and fellow guitarist Buz McGrath were also operational on the club circuit in early 2004 as Late Night Crüe, a Mötley Crüe tribute band with vocalist Brian Fair of Shadows Fall, bassist Mike D'Antonio from Killswitch Engage, and Seemless drummer Derek Kerswill.

Unearth stepped up a few gears on the touring front in summer 2004, joining the Damageplan, Drowning Pool, and Hatebreed co-headlined 'Headbanger's Ball' tour in March and April followed by the 'Ozzfest', where they shared the second stage alongside Slipknot, Atreyu, Lamb Of God, Every Time I Die, Hatebreed, Lacuna Coil, and Bleeding Through. A run of Canadian gigs in June saw the band acting as openers to Burnt By The Sun.

In July, *The Oncoming Storm* album shifted 13,285 copies in its first week of release to enter the US *Billboard* charts at Number 105. European 'Eastpak Resistance' shows in November saw the band hooking up with Walls Of Jericho, 7 Seconds, Slapshot, The Bones, Sick Of It All, and others.

They opened 2005 with a round of US headline dates with Atreyu. Meanwhile, Metal Blade reissued *The Oncoming Storm*, adding the newly-recorded songs 'One Step Away' and 'The Charm'. The summer of 2005 found the group participating in the US 'Sounds Of The Underground' tour, a collaboration between independent labels Ferret Music, Prosthetic Records, Trustkill, and Metal Blade. After extensive touring, Susi found time to produce an EP, *Still Monologue*, for Cincinnati, Ohio, metalcore band A Present Day Nightmare.

A retrospective release, *Our Days Of Eulogy*, was released in November. It featured live tracks recorded at The Downtown in Long Island, New York, during 2004, along with the cuts from the *Above The Fall Of Man* and *Endless* EPs. Susi produced Burn In Silence's *Angel Maker* album in December.

Unearth then utilised Studio X in Seattle with producer Terry Date in March 2006 to cut a new album. Crossing the Atlantic, the band played alongside Chimaira, Madball, Terror, All That Remains, and Manntis on the European edition of the 'Sounds Of The Underground' tour. The 'Ozzfest' followed in the summer.

A new Unearth album, *III: In The Eyes Of Fire*, came out in August 2006, selling over 22,000 copies upon and landing at Number 35 in the US album charts. Unearth are set to support Slayer on their North American tour in January and February 2007, and with such heavyweight allies they look set to rise even further.

UNEARTH discography

Above The Fall Of Man, Endless Fight EFR-1602 (USA) (1999)
THE STINGS OF CONSCIENCE, Eulogy EUL025 (USA) (2001)
Endless, Eulogy EUL039-2 (USA) (2002)
THE ONCOMING STORM, Metal Blade 3984-14479-2 (Europe / USA) (2004) **105 USA**
III: IN THE EYES OF FIRE, Metal Blade 3984-14574-2 (Europe / USA) (2006) **196 USA, 35 USA**

Unearth

INNOVATORS

INNOVATION

INNOVATION in heavy metal is rampant. While there are vast legions of bands content to plough a familiar furrow in order to appease traditionalists, in more recent times the expansion of the genre has seen metal reaching into new territories. Whereas the NWOBHM and thrash metal movements had, in the main, simply engendered more of the same music, the advent of black and death metal provided the means for musicians to explore new areas.

One of the very few thrash-style acts to push out any boundaries were the visionary Celtic Frost. Their early albums employed an arsenal of experimentation – before the undignified bellyflop that was *Cold Lake*. Another thrash act to test the limits was Watchtower, who were a long way ahead of their time, even if they failed to transfer this adventurous streak into sales.

Black metal soon looked beyond the fiery pits of hell, with Bathory's first investigation of ancestral Scandinavian themes inspiring Viking metal, folk metal, medieval folk, and neo-folk. Bands initially seeking Satan turned their attention to Thor, Loki, and the Norse pantheon of gods, trolls, and beasts to fuse a completely fresh musical style. This historically-focused output naturally prompted the use of traditional and medieval instrumentation, giving rise to groundbreaking acts such as Finntroll and Amorphis.

It was British band Skyclad who first brought folk and metal together in a serious fashion. Frontman Martin Walkyier's vision of melding metal and ancient British and Pagan themes lent itself easily to jigs and reels, and before long imitators such as In Extremo and Subway To Sally had fired up another brand new genre – and sadly left Skyclad in the dust.

By coincidence, circumstance forced black metal into another new vista of sound – that of dark ambience. Although Burzum's Varg Vikernes had been steering towards this direction anyway, his imprisonment for murder by necessity limited his access to instruments, giving rise to minimalist electro-folk. From his prison cell, Varg inspired a thousand bedroom-based devotees to do the same. Meanwhile, Norwegian act Ulver stamped their authority on the black metal scene before twisting off into extreme unpredictability.

Sweden's Therion proved to be one of the most bombastic artists of their day. As the gothic metal genre took flight, they multiplied the number of vocalists, choirs, and orchestral players to such a degree that their records involved hundreds of performers.

Suddenly it seemed that all borders had been broken down, and that all styles – from the opera and orchestration of Nightwish to the tribal percussion and rap of Soulfly – could be made to fit within the metal spectrum. Even avant-garde jazz crept into the metal arena courtesy of Meshuggah and Ephel Duath. Nowadays, it is commonplace to find albums littered with all manner of effects, samples, and unexpected twists. All this diversity shows that the future of metal is as assured as it is creative.

BAL-SAGOTH
BATTLECORE EXTRAORDINAIRE

BAL-SAGOTH ARE A SUPREMELY dark, neo-pagan battle metal band from Yorkshire with a predilection for lengthy song titles. They were named after fantasy novelist Robert E. Howard's story *The Gods Of Bal-Sagoth* and conceived by Anglo-Canadian vocalist Byron Roberts as early as 1989, firstly as Dusk. It wasn't until July 1993 that the Maudling brothers, guitarist Christopher and drummer Jonny, took the concept into a band format. Bassist Jason Porter and keyboard player Vincent Crabtree were recruited in September of the same year, bringing Bal-Sagoth up to full strength, and by the close of '93 they had cut an inaugural demo. Of the four songs included in that December session, 'By The Blaze Of The Fire Jewels' was subsequently re-worked as 'Shadows 'Neath The Black Pyramid', and parts of 'A Shadow On The Mist' would be used in future tracks.

The band duly signed a three-album deal with the London-based Cacophonous label, but delays held back the issue of the tantalising debut album, *A Black Moon Broods Over Lemuria*, until May 1995. Cradle Of Filth guitarist Gian Pyres notably donated a lead guitar solo to 'The Ravening'. The record, opening with a lavish intro 'Hatheg Kla' after H.P. Lovecraft's *The Other Gods*, immediately provoked gushing reviews from the extreme metal press, which had rarely encountered such a labyrinth of genius built on death and black metal. *Black Moon's* subject matter covered eclectic characters such as Skulthur the serpent king, the ebon fiends from Z'Xulth, and Lord Angsaar. For all its complexity, this was only the beginning.

Crabtree departed and was replaced by Leon Forrest. Bal-Sagoth were scheduled to put in their first live performances supporting labelmates Cradle Of Filth, but Roberts sustained an injury while stage-diving at a Cannibal Corpse concert, and this scotched the plans. In April 1995, the band finally embarked on the live trail with a gig at the Dublin Castle in London.

Upon the album's eventual release, the band played support dates to Portuguese gothic metal act Moonspell during July, before a tour of the

UK and Ireland planned with label-mates Primordial and Sigh in September. However, they pulled out of these shows due to disagreements with the promoter. Notwithstanding this setback, the band's star was already in the ascendant in mainland Europe, and they headlined the Belgian 'Ragnarok' festival in November. The following month, Porter was ousted with the recruitment of Alistair MacLatchy, a former acquaintance of Byron's in Dusk.

Starfire Burning Upon The Ice-Veiled Throne Of Ultima Thule arrived in 1996. Having piqued so much curiosity with their debut, the band saw this second album shooting them further up the rankings. They supported their music by a wealth of lyrical matter that was so dense that only a portion of it was actually sung on the record: the remainder was used within the accompanying booklet as a guide for the listener. The band toured Europe for the first time on a bill with Dark Funeral and Ancient in February 1997. They supported Emperor at the London Astoria and Sinister in Belgium before completing a second round of European shows, again with Emperor and Nocturnal Breed, in October of the same year.

As 1998 broke, Forrest announced his exit for a career in the police. Jonny Maudling shifted over to keyboards to plug the gap, and Dave Mackintosh took the drum stool. During July, MacLatchy broke ranks too and Mark Greenwell took over on bass. The third album, *Battle Magic*,

recorded at Academy Studios in Bradford, had been recorded between October and December 1997, before the arrival of new drummer Dave Mackintosh in May 1998. Jonny Maudling played both drums and keyboards on the album. Another epic, the new record succeeded in amplifying the band's already audacious sense of purpose. By this point, Bal-Sagoth had stepped out on their own unique path with such bravado that no other group could even remotely compare.

Jonny Maudling found himself on loan to My Dying Bride for European touring during 1999 while the band signed to Nuclear Blast for the release of a new album, *The Power Cosmic*, in October. Strangely, only Russian variants on the Irond label included the essential lyric sheets.

The fifth album, *Atlantis Ascendant*, was highlighted by the patriotic stage favourite 'Draconis Albionensis', and Bal-Sagoth promoted the record by supporting black metal Swedes Marduk at the London Dome in December 2001. In November 2003, Mackintosh joined London-based power metal band Dragonforce. Having spent the spring of 2004 recording a new studio album, the band announced his replacement as Dan Mullins, a veteran of such acts as Epitaph, The Raven Theory, Thine, The Axis Of Perdition, and (as Mr Storm Monolith) Sermon Of Hypocisy. Mullins played his first show with the band at Germany's 'Wacken Open Air' festival in August. Bal-Sagoth made a return in March 2006 with the album *The Chthonic Chronicles*. They continue to plough their own remarkable furrow.

CELTIC FROST
PIONEERS OF AVANT-GARDE METAL

A HIGHLY INFLUENTIAL METAL ACT from Zürich, Switzerland, Celtic Frost pushed the musical boundaries of the genre to the limit, fusing aggression with classical and avant-garde leanings to create a unique style. A world-class reputation was ensured by the group's obsessive attention to detail and meticulous planning, with their intended career path fully planned even before their first record hit the shelves. At their peak, the band looked set to rival America's big-name speed metal outfits for world domination – but then they crashed spectacularly to earth after one of the most disastrous changes of style ever witnessed.

BAL SAGOTH discography

A BLACK MOON BROODS OVER LEMURIA, Cacophonous NIHIL 4CD (UK) (1995)

STARFIRE BURNING OVER THE ICE-VEILED THRONE OF ULTIMA THULE, Cacophonous NIHIL 18CD (UK) (1996)

BATTLE MAGIC, Cacophonous NIHIL 29CD (UK) (1998)

THE POWER COSMIC, Nuclear Blast NB 0421-2 (Europe), Nuclear Blast Anerica 6421 (USA) (1999)

ATLANTIS ASCENDANT, Nuclear Blast NB 0584-2 (Europe), Nuclear Blast America 6584 (USA) (2001)

THE CHTHONIC CHRONICLES, Nuclear Blast NB 01048 (Europe), Candlelight CD CDL 302 (USA) (2006)

Frontman and renowned 'death grunter' Tom G. Warrior (aka Thomas Gabriel Fischer) and bassist Martin Eric Ain were members of Hellhammer, generally acknowledged to have been one of the worst (and most influential) bands ever. Tom started out musically in Grave Hill, who were heavily influenced by NWOBHM bands such as Diamond Head and Venom.

Hellhammer were originally known as Hammerhead. Initially, bass was handled by the 14-year-old Michael Baum, who handed these duties to Fischer, then wishing to be known as Satanic Slaughter. Baum then journeyed to Los Angeles to found AOR act Sierra before enrolling in Tribe Of Gypsies.

Hellhammer's debut 1982 rehearsal demo saw them apparently inspired by NWOBHM band Raven – Fischer, bassist Steve Patton (aka Savage Damage; previously vocalist in Grave Hill), and drummer Pete Stratton all adopted the stage surname of 'Warrior'. In August, Hellhammer drafted in former Moorhead drummer Jörg Neubart (aka Bloodhunter) to replace Stratton. Neubart subsequently became Bruce Day.

Day left Hellhammer briefly in October 1985, and the band recruited Stephen Priestly (aka Evoked Damnator) from Schizo (or 'Shizo' as some early biographies had it), but he only lasted three weeks before Day returned (now using the name Denial Fiend).

The band recorded their first studio demo, the nine-track *Death Fiend*, in July 1983, but distribution of this cassette, through Prowlin' Death Promotions, was very limited. The band were still very much in their embryonic stages, with songs full of copycat NWOBHM riffs and juvenile lyrics, such as the opening line "She's got my joystick right in her mouth" from the song 'Bloody Pussies'. The band had committed a total of 17 tracks to tape, which surfaced first on *Death Fiend* and then on the infamous *Triumph Of Death*. After this demo, bassist Steve Warrior (Savage Damage) was fired. The band tried out a couple of new bass players before recruiting Schizo bassist Martin Ain (aka Slayed Necros).

Once *Triumph Of Death* made it out of the tape-trading underground and into the mainstream, it provoked extreme opinions. Primitively made, the recording offered an ugly wall of sound, with choking, doom-styled riffs matched in intensity by stampeding bass and tortured vocals. Hellhammer's image, lifted straight from fantasy board games, saw the trio in bullet belts, leather, and spikes. Ambitiously, the cassette cover bore the printed challenge: "Venom are killing music … Hellhammer are killing Venom."

While leading French magazine *Enfer* hailed it as a classic, the UK's *Metal Forces* editor Bernard Doe labelled it the most appalling thing he had ever heard. However, Hellhammer were later recognised as one of the roots of the black metal genre. Although the band-members have admitted that their knowledge of music was basic – to say the least – when the Hellhammer recordings were made, they evidently possessed an artistic vision that would shape the metal scene for many years.

Martin Ain left Hellhammer a day before the *Satanic Rites* demo was recorded in the first week of December. As a result, Tom Warrior played both guitar and bass on that. The demo secured the band a deal with Noise, and Ain returned. The Berlin-based label released the Horst Müller-engineered *Apocalyptic Raids* EP in March 1984. The cover failed to specify which speed the vinyl should be played at – and sounded just as strange at 33rpm as it did at 45. The label ordered a first pressing of only 1,200 copies, which soon flew out of stores (and this inaugural pressing was the only official version to include a lyric sheet). Subsequent pressings came with varying colours and tones on the cover artwork, making for unintentional collectability. Metal Blade released the EP in America with two extra tracks.

Hellhammer then split, and Tom Warrior and Martin Ain regrouped in May 1984 to become Celtic Frost. They were named after a combination of song titles and lyrics on a Cirith Ungol album cover and consisted of Warrior, Ain, and drummer Isaac Darso. Darso's tenure lasted precisely

one rehearsal before Schizo's Stephen Priestly was brought in as a session drummer for recording. At this stage, Celtic Frost were still working on songs by NWOBHM favourites such as Angel Witch and Aragorn.

With Hellhammer's reputation preceding them – and magazine reviews polarised at either end of the spectrum – Celtic Frost retained their previous deal with Noise by submitting a master plan detailing the names of all their future releases. The policy called for an initial demo to be titled *A Thousand Deaths*, but the label soon persuaded the band that they should record a full album instead.

Celtic Frost's first product, June 1984's *Morbid Tales* mini-album, featured additional vocals from Horst Müller and Hertha Ohling and a contribution from violinist Oswald Spengler. As soon as the sessions were completed, Priestly decamped. The band set about negotiations with American drummer Jeff Cardelli of Seattle act Lipstick, but eventually they hired another American, ex-Crown drummer Reed St. Mark (real name Reid Cruickshank).

As with Hellhammer, reviews of *Morbid Tales* ranged from excellent to dire. European editions consisted of six tracks, while a US version, through Metal Blade, added two extra tracks, 'Morbid Tales' and 'Return To The Eve'. The controversy stoked by the opposing views served the band well. At this juncture, Celtic Frost were still wearing the monochrome stage make-up that would be called 'corpsepaint' by later generations of black metal bands. Another EP, 1985's *The Emperors Return* – issued in regular format and as a limited-run picture disc – generated equally opposed reviews and even received condemnation from the band themselves. By now, however, Celtic Frost were being acknowledged as leaders in their field. The band's first live performances came with a run of shows opening for German bands Beast and Mass in Germany and Austria, although planned shows in Italy with Astaroth were shelved.

During the recording of the next album, *To Mega Therion*, Ain left to pursue a "more advanced, experimental heavy metal solo project", according to the band's official biography. So the band pulled in Dominic Steiner from glam-rock act Junk Food. The album surfaced in October 1985 and saw the band utilising timpanis, French horns courtesy of Wolf Bender, operatic vocals from Claudia-Maria Mokri, and sound effects from Horst Müller and Urs Sprenger. It was the first Celtic Frost record to feature cover artwork from the renowned Swiss artist H.R. Giger, who here depicted Christ's outstretched arms being used as a catapult by a serpentine devil.

Friction between band members resulted in Steiner's dismissal as soon as *To Mega Therion* was concluded. Their debut show outside Europe was at the November 30th 1985 'World War III' festival in Montreal alongside Voivod, Possessed, Destruction, and Nasty Savage. Martin Eric Ain was enticed back for this event. Meanwhile, Warrior worked as producer for fellow Swiss metal band Coroner, a gesture they repaid by becoming Celtic Frost's road crew.

February 1986 saw Celtic Frost back on the live circuit, touring Europe on a bill with Helloween and Grave Digger. They played a headline slot at the Belgian 'Metalysee' festival, a debut UK show at London's Hammersmith Palais with Grave Digger and Helloween in support, and dates in North America with Running Wild and Voivod.

With the band's status rising sharply, the 1986 *Tragic Serenades* EP was issued to keep fans happy between albums. It consisted of remixed tracks from *Into Mega Therion*.

The group's third full-length album, *Into The Pandemonium*, was released in November 1987. It was another bizarre offering, including a cover of Wall Of Voodoo's 'Mexican Radio' and the rap cut 'One In Their Pride'. Before the recording, New York-based guitarist Ritchie Desmond was briefly linked with the band, but, having travelled to Switzerland to work with the group, he soon returned home, citing "too many conflicting attitudes". Warrior countered that Desmond had brought uninvited family members along to the audition and looked nothing like his submitted photograph. Desmond later fronted Sabbat for their final *Mourning Has Broken* album and the subsequent disastrous tour.

During a break in recording, the band played a series of European gigs with Anthrax, Crimson Glory, and even Metallica. The final sessions witnessed a further expansion in Celtic Frost's aural dynamics with the employment of a swathe of session contributors. Claudia-Maria Mokri once again featured as an additional vocalist, and other singers included Thomas Berter, Marchain Regee Rotschy, and Manü Moan. Classical instruments were recorded by violinists Malgorzata Blaiejewska Woller and Eva Cieslinski, cellist Wulf Ebert, French horn player Anton Schreiber, and Jürgen Paul Mann on viola. Additional guitar work was provided by Andreas Dobler.

For live dates to promote *Into The Pandemonium*, the band added second guitarist Ron Marks, and they toured Britain in winter 1987 with support from Kreator, moving on to North America on a bill with Exodus and Anthrax. The band were dogged throughout the tour's duration by legal wrangles with Noise. Disillusioned, Marks quit and was replaced by former Junk Food guitarist Oliver Amberg. Upon their return to Europe, they hit further problems when Martin Ain decided to abandon the music business entirely. Warrior quickly drafted in Curt Victor Bryant.

Celtic Frost were now in a state of flux, besieged by business and financial problems. Even a potentially lucrative offer from director Ken Russell to lay down the soundtrack to the movie *The Lair Of The White Worm* had to be declined, simply because the group was in such disarray. The final blow to the classic line-up came when Reed St. Mark left to join Mindfunk. His position was filled by the returning Stephen Priestly.

This was the line-up for the disastrous *Cold Lake* album. Produced by Tony Platt at Hansa Studios and Sky Trak Studios in Berlin, the record severely damaged the band's career in Europe. Indeed, its negative impact was of such magnitude that the term *Cold Lake* became entrenched in metal folklore, used thereafter to describe any particularly poor album.

Issued in September 1988, the record found the band ditching their former pretensions and adopting a new glam-rock image, much to the horror of their following. Tom dropped the 'Warrior' from his stage name and became plain Thomas Gabriel Fischer, even sporting an LA Guns T-shirt in official press photos.

Fans were quick to spot that Celtic Frost were now crediting Michelle Villanueva as "wardrobe and styling artist". (She was Fischer's 17-year-old American girlfriend and soon-to-be bride; the pair would separate in 2000 and divorce in 2004.) It was rumoured in the European media that the band had, in a *Spinal Tap*-style move, appointed Tom's girlfriend as manager and that the new look was her masterplan for Celtic Frost's step into the big league. The band themselves maintained that overtly commercial tracks like 'Teaze Me' were merely parodies of glam rock, but fans were outraged and the rock press universally attacked the album. A single, 'Cherry Orchards', was announced but shelved. A European tour commenced in late February with UK shows supported by Destruction, but it fared badly, with audiences deserting in droves. Despite these setbacks in Europe, in America *Cold Lake* made serious sales headway, and a US tour was judged a success.

In late 1989, the badly bruised Celtic Frost announced a return to their former style and regrouped with Ron Marks. Martin Eric Ain was also persuaded to put down guest bass tracks and contribute lyrics. The Roli Mossiman-produced *Vanity/Nemesis* album was regarded by many as the band's best to date, but the legacy of *Cold Lake* haunted the quartet to such a degree that sales suffered.

They only managed minimal touring to back up the release of the record, including a British tour backed by thrashers Slammer. Earlier German dates had been cancelled due to the band's perilous business state, but they did play two Dutch shows and the entire UK leg. By now,

Warrior was spotted playing a guitar emblazoned with his wife's name, Michelle. She had by now become a backing singer for the band.

Celtic Frost performed their last concert on May 29th 1990 at the Derby Assembly Rooms in England. New management hooked up a deal with major label BMG in North America, but this was shelved at the last minute, leaving the band high and dry. Warrior almost took the band into an even more radical direction when he mooted the idea of working with ex-Time guitarist Jesse Johnson on a funk-metal project. Priestly went on to play drums for French act Treponem Pal's 1991 *Aggravation* album.

Following a 1992 demo featuring the tracks 'Honour Thy Father', 'Seeds Of Rapture', 'Icons Alive', and Oh Father', the band searched in vain for a new deal. Initial tapes were laid down with Priestly on drums, but sessions in Texas saw Reed St. Mark back behind the kit and Renée Hernz on bass. Nothing came of this latest venture, and Celtic Frost effectively split, with Marks relocating to America to form Stepchild and then Subsonic.

In 1992, Noise released a Celtic Frost epitaph, *Parched With Thirst Am I And Dying*, a collection of rare and unreleased studio outtakes. Subsequently, Martin Ain produced the debut album from doom band Sadness, in 1995, while Warrior was found fronting a new venture, Apollyon Sun, in 1996.

Rumours came in 2001 of a full-blown Celtic Frost reunion with Tom G. Warrior (now under the name Tom Gabriel Fischer), Martin Eric Ain, and Reed St. Mark, along with Fischer's songwriting partner and Apollyon Sun co-founder Erol Unala. At first these were vehemently denied but later confirmed. By November 2002, a projected album title, *Probe*, had emerged, and in April 2003 a demo track, 'Ground', was posted online. The Celtic Frost camp also disseminated a revised and apparently spurious album title, *Dark Matter Manifest*. Meanwhile, Martin Eric Ain contributed vocals to Los Angeles based Hatesex's industrial take on the Slayer track 'Black Magic'.

In June 2004, Fischer announced plans for a solo album for 2005 release, although Celtic Frost persevered by composing new material with drummer Franco Sesa. The band's classic 'Dawn Of Megiddo' appeared on *Fenriz Presents The Best Of Old School Black Metal*.

With drummer Sesa, Celtic Frost revealed that a new set of demos had been completed in May 2005, and they entered Horus Sound Studios in

Hannover in August to record the album. Peter Tägtgren was selected as producer.

For tour work, the band drafted in guitarist Anders Odden (Satyricon, Cadaver, Mayhem). Live campaigning for 2006 included scheduled appearances at Sölvesborg's 'Sweden Rock' festival in June, Helsinki's 'Tuska' festival in July, and Germany's 'Wacken' and Norway's 'Hole In The Sky' events in August. However, the band's June 3rd 'Rock Hard' festival appearance in Gelsenkirchen was cancelled, with Martin Eric Ain announcing from the stage that Fischer had been rushed to hospital with acute kidney problems (subsequently diagnosed as a kidney stone).

The new album, *Monotheist*, was released in May 2006, and according to Nielsen SoundScan it sold just under 2,500 copies in its first week on sale in North America. In the band's homeland of Switzerland the record entered the charts at Number 41. They filmed a promotional video for the track 'A Dying God Coming Into Human Flesh', directed by Jessie Fischer (no relation to the Celtic Frost frontman) in Zürich, and then took on a 46-date North American tour, kicking off on September 12th, backed by Sahg and 1349.

Japanese dates were scheduled for January 2007 on the 'Extreme The Dojo Vol. 16' tour alongside Satyricon and Naglfar. Celtic Frost also announced a co-headlining European tour with Kreator commencing in March. Their comeback has been astounding, and it is to be hoped that they maintain their success for many years to come.

FAITH NO MORE
THE GREATEST ROCK BAND THAT EVER EXISTED?

SAN FRANCISCO BAND FAITH NO MORE were founded in 1982, and they pushed the boundaries of rock in all directions with a diverse set of influences, anticipating the nu-metal wave and creating a unique sound in the process. Funk, pop, and hardcore punk elements were all on display, but with more than enough riffage to keep metal fans happy. The band gained respect and kudos during their two-decade run, but major commercial success always eluded them, although they came close on a number of occasions.

Guitarist 'Big Sick' Jim Martin had journeyed through the Californian music scene, making appearances in many bands across widely differing musical styles. Along with drummer Mike Bordin, the guitarist first stepped into the limelight with Ez-Street, an act that included in its ranks future Metallica bassist Cliff Burton. Ez-Street pursued the commonly trodden path of Rolling Stones and Led Zeppelin covers, with the line-up completed by vocalist Kevin Costa and rhythm guitarist Danny Magalhaes.

This first incarnation folded when Burton quit for Trauma and Bordin followed suit, teaming up with Sharp Young Men. That band, in which Bordin received his nickname 'Puffy' due to his outrageous Afro, included bassist Bill Gould, previously a member of The Animated, an act that featured keyboard player Chuck Moseley.

Martin busied himself with numerous side projects, appearing in many 'battle of the bands' contests, including the three-guitar crossover of Vicious Hatred, a blues act with a horn section called Pigs Of Death, and Agents Of Misfortune, in which he teamed up again with Burton. Meanwhile, Ez-Street evolved into Recluse before a nebulous version of Faith No More kicked into gear during 1985 when Sharp Young Men recruited guitarist Mark Bowen, keyboard player Roddy Bottum, Bordin, and Gould.

Billed as Faith No Man, the group were headed by Mike 'The Man' Morris alongside Roddy Bottum, Mike Bordin, and Bill Gould. When the other three decided to oust Morris, they decided that the simplest way was to leave en masse, swiftly re-billing themselves as Faith No More.

Courtney Love was in an early line-up of the band – she would later be propelled to world stardom as the leader of Hole and, more significantly, the widow of Nirvana's Kurt Cobain. However, she was swiftly fired, lasting only four gigs. It was also clear that Bowen wasn't working out and so, on Burton's recommendation, Martin was hired – as was Chuck Moseley, leaving Haircuts That Kill to become FNM's vocalist.

Faith No More's self-financed debut, first issued in 1985 through Mordam Records in the USA and licensed to De Konkurrent in Europe, was recorded at Prairie Sun Studios in Cotati, California. A subsequent club tour provoked enough interest for a deal to be signed with ex-Quiet Riot manager Warren Enter and from there to Warner Bros subsidiary Slash Records. The resulting album, *Introduce Yourself,* was released in April 1987, produced by the Los Lobos duo of Steve Berlin and Matt Wallace. It more than justified Warners' faith in the band, and the accompanying single, 'We Care A Lot', quickly became a big club and MTV hit. The band toured America as support to the Red Hot Chili Peppers in late 1987. Despite healthy sales and press, the band, in a foretaste of what was to come, reportedly tore itself apart – resulting in the departure of Moseley, first to Bad Brains (which he left before recording anything) and then his own act, Cement.

Moseley's place was taken during 1988 by Mike Patton. The new frontman, whose remarkable vocal range gave new focus to the band, relinquished his studies at Humboldt State University to take part. His four demos with Mr. Bungle prior to Faith No More – *The Raging Wrath Of The Easter Bunny* (1986), *Bowel Of Chiley* (1987), *Goddammit I Love America* (1988), and *OU818* (1989) – were ample evidence that the band had taken on one of the most extraordinary vocalists in the rock field. Patton remained in Mr Bungle alongside FNM, an unusual move but one that seemed to work well for both bands.

The seminal third album *The Real Thing,* released in June 1989, broke Faith No More out of the underground and into global chart success with a string of hit singles and well-received live shows. A diverse collection, the album was high on guitar crunch and proudly wore the band's metal influences with a rendition of Black Sabbath's 'War Pigs'. Importantly, Faith No More broke into the rock club circuit, their brand of heavy danceability giving them a strong presence at the grass roots level. This progression, hammered home by a platinum sales award for one million sales in the USA plus a prestigious Grammy award, could not hide the fact that internal disputes were constantly wracking the band as various members publicly voiced their dislike for one another. Nevertheless, Faith No More toured relentlessly.

An interim record, *Live At The Brixton Academy,* arrived in February 1991 accompanied by a video of the same concert, *You Fat Bastards!.* As

---

FAITH NO MORE discography

WE CARE A LOT, Konkurrent MDR 1 (Europe), Mordam MDR 1 (USA) (1985)

INTRODUCE YOURSELF, Slash SLAP 21 (UK), Slash 1-25559 (USA) (1987)

THE REAL THING, Slash 828 154-2 (UK), Slash 9 25878-2 (USA) (1989) **11 UK, 30 USA**

LIVE AT THE BRIXTON ACADEMY, Slash 828 238-2 (UK) (1991) **20 UK**

ANGEL DUST, Slash 828 401-2 (UK), Slash 9 26785-2 (USA) (1992) **2 UK, 10 USA**

KING FOR A DAY – FOOL FOR A LIFETIME, Slash 828 560-2 (UK), Slash 9 45723-2 (USA) (1995) **5 UK, 31 USA**

ALBUM OF THE YEAR, Slash 828 901-2 (UK), Slash 9 46629-2 (USA) (1997) **7 UK, 41 USA**

well as the live material, the album had two new studio tracks, 'The Grade' and 'The Cowboy Song'.

Post-world tour, Patton returned to Mr. Bungle, which had been temporarily put on hold, to record a self-titled album, as well as finding time to guest for John Zorn's Naked City. He was back with Faith No More when they re-assembled at Brilliant Studios in San Francisco to record the 1992 *Angel Dust* album. A schizophrenic, unpredictable but excellent record, *Angel Dust* juxtaposed pop-rock with daring experimentation – the band even tackled a piano waltz on 'RV' and a cover of John Barry's 'Midnight Cowboy' movie theme. Elsewhere, they got truly obnoxious with the likes of 'Jizzlobber' and 'Be Aggressive'. The record gave the band another hit, just missing out on a UK Number 1 and nearly hitting the million mark in North America, solidifying their reputation. All of the spin-off singles charted in Britain, and they provided fans with some interesting asides, such as a cover of the Dead Kennedys' 'Let's Lynch The Landlord' (a B-side to 'A Small Victory'). A re-released format of the same A-side later in the year saw the track remixed by Killing Joke bass player Youth.

Faith No More had their biggest British hit in 1993 with their slightly sarcastic cover of The Commodores' smooth ballad 'Easy', which peaked at Number 3. Not included on the original album, 'Easy' was hastily tacked on to subsequent pressings, giving *Angel Dust* a new lease of life. The same year, a collaboration with Boo Ya Tribe put the band back in the charts with 'Another Body Murdered' from the soundtrack to the movie *Judgement Day*. They maintained a high profile as guests on the Metallica and Guns N' Roses stadium tour in America and put in an appearance at the British 'Phoenix Festival'. This succession of prominent songs fostered an album with longevity, and *Angel Dust* outsold its predecessor in many territories.

By December 1993 the obvious disagreements within the band saw the ousting of Martin, who had been more than vocal in his lack of affection for *Angel Dust*. The guitarist claimed he had quit, while the other band-members took an opposing view. Mr. Bungle guitarist Trey Spruance took his place.

While recording the new album *King For A Day... Fool For A Lifetime* at Bearsville Studios in New York with Andy Wallace, it was reported that Bottum would not be taking part as he was involved in a battle against drug addiction. This fifth outing, issued in March 1995, proved a diverse album, as expected, ranging from the gung-ho metal of 'Cuckoo For Caca' and the hardcore of 'Digging The Grave' to the country & western twang of 'Take This Bottle'.

King For A Day hit Number 5 in the UK and Number 2 in Australia but suffered from a media backlash, with reviews often unjustly vicious. The band's touring schedule lasted a matter of months, with Spruance soon ejected in favour of former guitar tech and Duh guitarist Dean Menta, following the release of the album.

Amid rumours of an impending split, Faith No More were put on ice as the individual members pursued solo ventures. Patton worked with Mr. Bungle once again, while Bottum created Imperial Teen, releasing the *Seasick* album on London Records. Bordin leapt back into the limelight as drummer for Ozzy Osbourne and the Black Sabbath reformation, while Gould busied himself with production, including a stint in Moscow with Russian punks Naive. Patton also worked with Brazilian thrashers Sepultura, co-composing the track 'Mine' on their 1997 album *Blood-Rooted*.

Faith No More returned in June 1997 with the modestly-titled *Album Of The Year*, along with a new guitarist, Jon Hudson (previously with Systems Collapse). Japanese variants boasted two additional tracks, 'The Big Kahuna' and 'Light Up And Let Go'. Although it wasn't a huge seller, the record, co-produced by Gould and Roli Mosimann, provoked deserved praise and the band completed a well-attended American theatre tour. *Album Of The Year* only managed to attain a Number 41 placing on the US *Billboard* charts but did hit Number 1 in Australia and New Zealand. Jim Martin returned to the fray at the same juncture with his debut solo offering, *Milk And Blood*, which featured a re-working of Faith No More's 'Surprise! You're Dead'.

The band finally announced their collapse on April 20th 1998. They had been confirmed as support to Aerosmith on their European tour but frictions within the band proved too tortuous to endure.

Bordin continued his duties with Ozzy Osbourne, while Gould involved himself in production for acts such as Finland's CMX and German group Rammstein. Mike Patton founded Fantomas with noted Slayer and Grip Inc. drummer Dave Lombardo, Melvins guitarist Buzz Osbourne, and Mr. Bungle bassist Trevor Dunn. Renewing ties with Sepultura, Patton contributed to 'The Waste' on the Brazilians' *Tribus* EP. Bottum pressed on with a second Imperial Teen album. Gould, in collusion with Fear Factory's Dino Cazares and Raymond Herrera, founded the Kool Arrow record label during 2000. All three anonymously operated the 'Mexican' death metal band Brujeria.

During late 2002, Mike Bordin, as part of Ozzy Osbourne's band, became part of the ongoing dispute between Osbourne and his erstwhile rhythm section of bassist Bob Daisley and drummer Lee Kerslake. The March 2002 reissues of Ozzy's debut *Blizzard Of Ozz* and its follow-up *Diary Of A Madman* albums, both figuring heavily in the publicly played-out legal dispute, included re-recorded drum tracks laid down by the ex-Faith No More man.

Meanwhile, Patton added to his list of activities by contributing guest lead vocals to The Dillinger Escape Plan's mini-album *Irony Is A Dead Scene*. The singer revealed that some years earlier he had been approached to replace the deceased Michael Hutchence as frontman for INXS, but had turned down the offer. Of all the erstwhile Faith No More members, Patton has been the most industrious, spreading his talents across a vast canvas of endeavours – including his Ipecac label, releases with Fantomas, Tomahawk, and Peeping Tom, involvement with Team Sleep, Weird Little Boy, Maldorors, Merzbow, Melt Banana, Hemophiliac, Björk, and many, many more. The singer also cut a brace of solo works for the Composer Series of John Zorn's Tzadik imprint: *Adult Themes For Voice* (1996) and *Pranzo Oltranzista* (1997). None of these undertakings has resulted in significant commercial success on the scale of Faith No More, yet Patton's artful approach has given him respected cult status and a dedicated audience that awaits his every move.

Jim Martin resurfaced, cutting a film soundtrack album in union with sitar player Anand Bhatt for a new album, *Conflict*, while August 2003 brought news that guitarist Jon Hudson had formed a studio alliance with vocalist Whitfield Crane (Ugly Kid Joe, Life Of Agony, Medication). Gould contributed bass to the 2005 Fear Factory album *Transgression*, featuring on the tracks 'Echo of My Scream' and 'Super Nova'. Faith No More's enormous influence lies in their invitation for metal musicians to explore a range of musical territories, making the modern scene much more interesting as a result. They will never be forgotten.

KYUSS
STONER-ROCK GODS

CALIFORNIA'S KYUSS WERE THE FIRST in a line of doom metal-influenced acts to introduce a trancelike, slightly psychedelic 'desert' groove to their sound. Their amalgam of grunge attitude, 1960s garage-rock, '70s riffage, and B-movie imagery, allied to doom metal roots, almost single-handedly led to the invention of the phrase 'stoner rock'. Kyuss achieved this by tuning their guitars down and summoning up a subterranean, organic sound designed to impact equally upon both the brain and the stomach. Although they were never truly successful during their lifespan, the band's legacy has weighed heavily on the stoner scene.

The original Sons Of Kyuss line-up, formed in Palm Desert in 1989, included vocalist John Garcia, guitarist Josh Homme, bassist Chris Cockrell, and drummer Brant Bjork. After a self-titled EP released in 1990, Cockrell was replaced by Nick Oliveri and the band shortened their name to Kyuss.

Both Reeder and Hernandez had cut their teeth with school punk

band Dead Issue, an outfit that included vocalist-guitarist Herb Lineau and guitarist Mario Lalli. With Lineau's departure, Dead Issue evolved into Across The River. Reeder then decamped, and Hernandez and Mario added Larry Lalli on bass and Gary Arce on guitar to form Englenook in 1987. This band then shifted into Yawning Man. The Lalli brothers later created Fatso Jetson, and Hernandez and Reeder reunited in Kyuss, taking the name from a Dungeons And Dragons game character. At first the band performed purely for friends across the southern California desert, but their reputation soon spread further.

Kyuss debuted with 1991's *Wretch* on Dali Records, a basic punk rock album that went unnoticed. The band transformed their sound for the breakthrough, *Blues For The Red Sun*, produced by Chris Goss Of Masters Of Reality. Heavy on instrumentals, the record included future classics such as 'Thumb', the staccato 'Thong Song', the trance-inducing 'Mondo Generator', and 'Green Machine', a track hedonistic enough to boast a bass solo. Such was the influence of the album that later generations of stoner acts took these titles as band names.

Nick Oliveri left in 1993 and was replaced by ex-The Obsessed bassist Scott Reeder. Oliveri later joined The Dwarves, where he was known as Rex Everything. With the fragmentation of the Dali-Chameleon label, Kyuss were snapped up by Elektra for 1994's *Welcome To Sky Valley*. This album saw the inclusion of 'N.O.', an archive Across The River track with a guest guitar slot from co-writer Mario Lalli. It also came with the instructions "Listen without distraction" and – ingeniously – had its tracks divided into suites without pauses to discourage skipping. Although sales failed to match expectations, *Welcome To Sky Valley* is widely regarded now as a seminal rock release. The single 'Demon Cleaner' came with three album outtakes, 'Day One (To Dave & Chris)', 'El Rodeo', and 'Hurricane'. After the band toured to promote the album, Bjork left and was replaced by drummer Alfredo Hernandez.

The next album, *...And The Circus Leaves Town*, was released in July 1995, and again had reviewers in raptures. It included the track 'Catamaran', originally an early Yawning Man composition. A Germany-only single, 'One Inch Man', hosted the exclusive non-album tracks 'Flip The Phase', 'Mudfly', and 'A Day Early And A Dollar Extra'. The 'Gardenia' single also had a previously unavailable song in the eight-minute epic 'UN Sandpiper'. The Man's Ruin label put out a purple vinyl 7-inch single the same year, an uncredited cover of Black Sabbath's 'Into The Void' paired with 'Fatso Forgetso'. However, Kyuss were unable to make further headway and folded in October 1995.

Garcia put together Slo Burn with members of local act Wolf following the band's break-up. Although great things were anticipated from Slo Burn, the group issued just one EP, *Amusing The Amazing*, played on the 1997 'Ozzfest', and then folded. The singer also tried some other ventures, such as 13 and a proposed union with members of Chicago doom veterans Trouble, neither of which amounted to much.

Homme toured as a member of Screaming Trees for nearly two years. The guitarist also cut demos billed as Gamma Ray, which later evolved into Queens Of The Stone Age, a very successful major-league act. Queens Of The Stone Age also included former Kyuss drummer Alfredo Hernandez (1998-1999) and former Kyuss bassist Nick Oliveri (1998-2004).

Drummer Brant Bjork teamed up with Fatso Jetson as rhythm guitarist on a brace of split 7-inch singles before opting out to concentrate on his priority act Fu Manchu in late 1997 for their *The Action Is Go* album. Garcia was found fronting Karma To Burn in 1997, although his employment with the West Virginians lasted a mere 12 gigs. Both Bjork and Homme laid down the Desert Sessions album *Volume I & II* during 1998. More Desert Sessions albums followed into the next decade. In ensuing years, Garcia created Unida and Hermano (both formed in 1998, with Unida also featuring Scott Reeder). Bjork formed Brant Bjork & The Bros, and Oliveri – who left QOTSA in acrimonious circumstances in early 2004 – focused on his side project, Mondo Generator, later billed as Nick Oliveri And The Mondo Generator.

Man's Ruin Records released a split Kyuss/Queens Of The Stone Age album in 1997 featuring three tracks from each band, and Elektra released a compilation album, *Muchas Gracias: The Best Of Kyuss*, in 2000, which included rare B-sides and live material.

In 2002, Scott Reeder auditioned for Metallica to replace the departed Jason Newsted. In September 2005, Reeder joined California stoners Butcher after producing the band's debut album, *Auricle*, earlier that year. In 2006, Reeder released a solo album titled *TunnelVision Brilliance* through the Liquor And Poker Music label. The legacy of the brilliant Kyuss is twofold. First, there is the stoner sound that they pioneered, and second, the success of the remarkable Queens Of The Stone Age. The world of rock and metal would be a very different place without their lasting influence.

MESHUGGAH
COMPLEX BUT BRUTAL PROG-DEATH RIFFAGE

AN EXPERIMENTAL THRASH/DEATH metal band named after the Yiddish word for crazy, Meshuggah appeared in Umeå, Sweden during 1987 from the roots of Metallien. Metallien were formed in 1985 by guitarist Fredrik Thordendal, and when they broke up, Thordendal set up Meshuggah. The original line-up was vocalist Jens Kidman, guitarists Fredrik Thordendal and Johan Sjögren, bassist Jörgen Lindmark, and drummer Per Sjögren.

After a while, vocalist Kidman departed and formed a new band, Calipash, with guitarist Torbjörn Granström, bassist Peter Nordin, and drummer Niklas Lundgren. Granström then left Calipash, and with the original Meshuggah now defunct, Calipash recruited Thordendal as a replacement. Shortly after this, in 1987, the band dropped the Calipash name and reclaimed Meshuggah. The original 1987 line-up known as Meshuggah – the band that evolved into the outfit we know today – was vocalist-guitarist Jens Kidman, guitarist Fredrik Thordendal, bassist Peter Nordin, and drummer Niklas Lundgren.

Their first commercial offering was an independent 12-inch EP, *Psykisk Testbild*, released through local record store Garageland in 1989. Only 1,000 copies were pressed, and it was the only Meshuggah release to feature Niklas Lundgren on drums before he was supplanted by Tomas Haake. In 1989, the band recorded a six-song demo, *Ejaculation Of Salvation*, before briefly employing the services of Hollow guitar player Marcus Bigren the following year.

German label Nuclear Blast signed them for a debut album, *Contradictions Collapse*, in 1991. An out-and-out thrash-fest from start to finish, the record's hi-tech metal attracted exemplary reviews. However, it was soon swallowed up in the plethora of Swedish death/thrash releases and dropped off the radar. Sometime after this release, Kidman moved to vocals and Mårten Hagström took over his guitar duties.

In 1993, Thordendal joined the XXX Atomic Toejam duo alongside his former Memorandum colleague Petter Marklund to record the limited-edition EP *A Gathering Of The Tribes For The First/Last Human Be-In*, released on Cold Meat Industry. As for Meshuggah, progress was stalled when the quartet were beset by a catalogue of injuries: Thordendal, a carpenter by trade, cut the top off one of his fingers, and drummer Tomas Haake trapped his hand in a lathe.

The self-produced transitional EP *None*, recorded at Tonteknik Recordings in Umeå, followed in November 1994. July 1995 marked the airing of the new-sounding Meshuggah with the groundbreaking *Destroy Erase Improve*, laid down at Soundfront Studios in Uppsala with Daniel Bergstrand at the board. The title told the full story: the band had stripped down their metal to its bare essentials before rebuilding it in a totally abstract form.

When Meshuggah toured Europe in 1995 supporting Machine Head, Hagström stepped in for the headliners' frontman Rob Flynn after the American suffered a hand injury. Having lost bassist Peter Nordin to a severe ear infection, Meshuggah played as a quartet with Thordendal performing the guitar parts – including solos – on a bass. At other times, Hagström played guitar through a pitch-shifter to emulate a bass sound.

The 1995 EP *Selfcaged*, released by Nuclear Blast in both Europe and America, had a different track-listing for each territory. The same year, Thordendal donated a guitar solo to the Blender release *Back To Planet Softcore*. The guitarist also figured on three tracks on the 1996 Mats/Morgen album *Trends And Other Diseases*. Live work for Meshuggah in 1995 was rounded off with a batch of autumn dates shared with Clawfinger in Scandinavia and Germany, again completed without a bassist. Gustaf Hielm of Charta 77 was enrolled to fulfil four-string duties to finish the tour before a month-long set of shows with Hypocrisy.

Thordendal then assembled a side project, Fredrik Thordendal's Special Defects, recording an album in 1997, *Sol Niger Within*. Meshuggah's own 1997 release, the mini-album *The True Human Design*, included a remix of 'Future Breed Machine' featuring Clawfinger's Jocke Skog, and one new track, 'Sane'.

The November 1998 outing *Chaosphere* cemented the Meshuggah line-up of vocalist Kidman, guitarists Thordendal and Hagström, bass player Hielm, and drummer Haake. This album was stripped of any

Meshuggah

MESHUGGAH discography

Psykisk Testbild, Garageland BF 634 (Europe) (1989) limited
edition 12-inch vinyl EP 1,000 copies
CONTRADICTIONS COLLAPSE, Nuclear Blast NB 0049-2 (Europe),
Nuclear Blast America 6049 (USA) (1991)
None, Nuclear Blast NB 0102-2 (Europe), Nuclear Blast America
6102 (USA) (1994)
DESTROY ERASE IMPROVE, Nuclear Blast NB 0121-2 (Europe),
Nuclear Blast America 6121 (USA) (1995)
Selfcaged, Nuclear Blast NB 0132-2 (Europe), Nuclear Blast
America 6132 (USA) (1995)
The Human Design, Nuclear Blast NB 0268-2 (Europe), Nuclear
Blast America 6268 (USA) (1997)
CHAOSPHERE, Nuclear Blast NB 0366-2 (Europe), Nuclear Blast
America 6336 (USA) (1998)
RARE TRAX, Nuclear Blast NB 0605-2 (Europe), Nuclear Blast
America 6605 (USA) (2001)
NOTHING, Nuclear Blast NB 0542-2 (Europe), Nuclear Blast
America 6542 (USA) (2002) **165 USA**
I, Fractured Transmitter FTRCD 001 (Europe / USA) (2004)
CATCH THIRTYTHREE, Nuclear Blast NB 1311-2 (Europe),
Nuclear Blast America 1311 (USA) (2005) **170 USA**

remaining thrash vestiges, a full-blown math-metal smorgasbord of near-impenetrable time changes, atonality, and dissonant riffing. While fans revelled in these labyrinthine meanderings, critics struggled to dissect and analyse the record, hailing Haake's unconventional use of 23/16 rhythms, Kidman's mechanical staccato bark, and Thordendal's liberal use of avant-garde jazz.

Fans were quick to jump on the fact that promo copies of *Chaosphere* hosted the track 'Unanything', although it was absent from the regular release. Initial concerts to push the album saw the band on the road in the USA before a Scandinavian leg with Entombed. The band toured America in 1999 supporting Slayer and found that their unique slant on metal had gained them kudos outside the mainstream metal press, as many musicians' and instrument-based publications began picking up on the band. European shows that June had the band lined up with Austrian hardcore merchants Stahlhammer and legendary US act S.O.D..

The 2001 release *Rare Trax* was compiled to place the three songs from the band's 1989 *Psykisk Testbild* 12-inch EP on CD for the first time, alongside later demos and studio and live video footage. Hielm left the band in July.

Meshuggah received an enviable opportunity in 2001 when they were invited to open for the September US tour leg of platinum-selling band Tool. The highly anticipated *Nothing* album, released in September 2002, sold a respectable 6,500 copies in North America in its first week of release as Meshuggah became the first band in the history of Nuclear Blast to break into the *Billboard* Top 200, landing at Number 165. *Nothing* marked the debut of custom Nevborn and Ibanez eight-string guitars for Thordendal and Hagström, with two extra low-tuned strings enabling the pair to explore the lowest registers. The inhuman, regimented atmosphere of the record was reinforced by the programmed percussion. Meshuggah scored another first for Nuclear Blast with *Nothing*, attracting the first review in the esteemed *Rolling Stone* magazine for the label. The band's relationship with Tool was strengthened as Meshuggah united with the avant-garde American rockers for a further string of shows, taking them up to December. The band paired up with Strapping Young Lad for US dates in May 2003.

Scheduled appearances for early July at the 'Quartfestivalen' in Kristiansand, Norway and the 'Arvikafestivalen' in Arvika, Sweden were cancelled; apparently Hagström had been struck with an unspecified affliction, while Haake was suffering from carpal tunnel syndrome. Meanwhile, vocalist Kidman took time out to guest on the track 'The Dream Is Over' featured on the Mushroomhead album *XIII*. In November, Thordendal contributed a guitar solo to 'Asphyxiate' on the *Irradiant* album from French nu-thrash act Scarve.

Meshuggah adopted the In Flames-credited Dick Lövgren as stage bass guitarist in February 2004. The band entered the studio to record an EP, consisting of a solitary 20-minute track, *I*, for Fractured Transmitter Records, the label formed by Mushroomhead vocalist Jason Mann. That same month, they announced their next album for Nuclear Blast, *Catch Thirtythree* – yet another single-song session. Released in June, the album sold just under 7,000 copies in its first week of US sales to debut on the *Billboard* charts at Number 170.

European dates in June 2005 saw Scarve as opening act. The band then announced a return to the USA alongside God Forbid, The Haunted, and Mnemic as part of the 'Fury Of The Fall' world tour in October. Despite the incredible complexity of their music, Meshuggah have a strong following: proof – if any were required – that modern heavy metal fans are prepared to invest considerable effort into their idols. Respect is due all around.

SKYCLAD
FOLK-METAL GENIUS

SKYCLAD WERE FORMED IN 1990 by vocalist Martin Walkyier, following his break from the successful Nottingham, England thrash act Sabbat. Alongside the riffage of guitarist Andy Sneap, the singer was a major factor in Sabbat's popularity, and with Skyclad he was able to push his unique inspirations to the fore. The band contain diverse elements such as traditional metal riffing, electric folk violin, and the distinctive pagan lyrical stance and imagery of the man himself.

The band, based in Newcastle, were formed with ex-Satan and Pariah guitarist Steve Ramsey. Skyclad's initial demo for Noise Records featured Walkyier, Ramsey, and a drum machine. Soon after the band signed a deal, former Satan bassist Graeme English (aka 'Bean') and drummer Keith Baxter were added. They were followed, after recording and tour dates, by ex-D.A.M. guitarist Dave Pugh and violinist Fritha Jenkins.

The group's debut album, October 1991's *The Wayward Sons Of Mother Earth*, illustrated Walkyier's original approach to metal, combining his lyrical twists with the classic metal riff signatures of Ramsey. Mike Evans played violin on the debut album as a session musician. Expectations among the European metal-buying public were high, and Skyclad did not disappoint. A particularly significant track was 'The Widdershins Jig', an open appreciation of traditional folk and a first in the realms of metal. The Walkyier-less Sabbat quickly floundered and disintegrated, while Skyclad took the Sabbat concept several strides forward, supplanting occult lore with pagan history and ancient British mythology woven with Walkyier's elaborate sarcasm and witty twists. They toured Europe alongside Gamma Ray, Thunderhead, Candlemass, and Overkill.

In late 1991, Ramsey suffered a fractured skull in a fall and the band were forced to cancel a string of British dates. Their second album, *A Burnt Offering For The Bone Idol*, was delivered in March 1992, and they toured the UK in February with Overkill and Lawnmower Death. June saw further gigs, with Paradise Lost. The same month, Skyclad appeared at the 'Dynamo Open Air' festival in Eindhoven, Netherlands, jamming with ex-Thin Lizzy guitarist Brian Robertson on 'Emerald'. Irish dates followed in

September, leading up to the release of the EP *Tracks From The Wilderness*, which included live recordings from the 'Dynamo' set. The year was rounded off with support gigs to Manowar in Europe in October and November and a run of UK shows in December.

The band pushed forward with June 1993's *Jonah's Ark* album, Japanese versions of which added the six songs from the *Tracks In The Wilderness* EP. Jenkins had become pregnant earlier that year and was forced to bow out. Drafting in new violinist Cath Howell, the group put in UK shows supported by Forgodsake in June. Frustratingly, although a video for 'Thinking Allowed?' saw airplay, valuable support tours with bands such as Dio, Paradise Lost, and Sepultura fell through, with the band claiming lack of financial support from their record label. These frustrations coloured Skyclad's history from this point, despite the band maintaining strong support in mainland Europe, shifting over 50,000 albums with each release.

Walkyier and Jenkins guested on Forgodsake's *Blasthead* album in 1994. Meanwhile, Skyclad contributed a rendition of 'Prime Evil' to the Venom tribute album *In The Name Of Satan*. Their next offering, *Prince Of The Poverty Line*, was issued early in 1994, with initial limited-edition copies including an extra track, 'Brothers Beneath The Skin'. By now, the group's finances were in a perilous state, as hinted by the album title, but this misfortune was channelled into the band's 'bedraggled troubadour' look. For further live work, ex-Velvet Viper guitarist Dave Moore joined the band on a temporary basis. The band played a successful European tour the same year on the back of *Prince Of The Poverty Line*, with dates supporting Chicago's Trouble, their first German headline date on May 4th at the Stuttgart Röhre, support slots with Swedish axe god Yngwie Malmsteen, and shows in Germany with Freak Of Nature. Festival dates included 'Dynamo Open Air' and Germany's 'Wacken' events. At the conclusion of the tour, violinist Howells left to concentrate on studying and was replaced by Georgina Biddle. Graeme English took time out to session on Blitzkrieg's *Unholy Trinity* album.

After 1995's *The Silent Whales Of Lunar Sea*, Skyclad were beset by problems. Ramsey collapsed in the studio and had hospital treatment for a heart complaint (he was subsequently fitted with a pacemaker), and recording equipment was stolen from the studio. But the album was completed, and the new Skyclad debuted in early 1995 with gigs in Greece. But they hit more line-up problems in April as both Pugh and Baxter quit, the latter for UK punk revivalists 3 Colours Red. The band found session musicians for live performances in two ex-Inner Sanctum members, guitarist Dave Ray and drummer Jed Dawkins. In this incarnation, Skyclad toured Europe extensively, including a date at the 'Dynamo' festival in June and support gigs to Black Sabbath in the UK. The year ended on a high as the band joined Blind Guardian's 'Christmas Party' tour in December, alongside Love/Hate, Saxon, Rage, and Yngwie Malmsteen.

The *Irrational Anthems* album was released in February 1996, featured session drummer Paul Smith, and was promoted by a video for 'Inequality Street'. Highlights included a solo violin instrumental, 'The Spiral Starecase', and a radical reworking of Khachaturian's 'Sabre Dance'. German touring in May came with Riot and thrashers Whiplash.

Skyclad's second 1996 album, *Oui Avant-Garde A Chance* (pronounced 'We Haven't Got A Chance') included accordion player Les Smith, Subway To Sally musicians Eric Hecht on bagpipes, Frau Schmidt on violin, and Bodenski. There were covers of Dexy's Midnight Runners' 'Come On Eileen' and New Model Army's 'Master Race', and the band described the set as "experimental". *Oui Avant-Garde A Chance* was committed to tape at Parr Street Studios in Liverpool and Jacobs Studios in Surrey. With no permanent drummer, percussion on the record was shared between Paul A.T. Kinson and Paul Smith. The project was originally planned as an acoustic EP but evolved into a full-blown album. In support, the band, with drummer Paul A.T. Kinson behind the drum kit, played headline UK shows that September. December saw them back on German soil with support act Subway To Sally. However, the last few dates of this trek were cancelled when Walkyier came down with a severe throat infection.

SKYCLAD discography

THE WAYWARD SONS OF MOTHER EARTH, Noise N 0163-2 (Europe), Noise 4839-2-U (USA) (1991)

A BURNT OFFERING FOR THE BONE IDOL, Noise N 0186-2 (Europe / USA) (1992)

Tracks From The Wilderness, Noise N 0194-3 (Europe / USA) (1992)

JONAH'S ARK, Noise N 0209-2 (Europe / USA) (1993)

PRINCE OF THE POVERTY LINE, Noise N 0239-2 (Europe) (1994)

THE SILENT WHALES OF LUNAR SEA, Noise N 0228-2 (Europe / USA) (1995)

IRRATIONAL ANTHEMS, Massacre MASCD 084 (Europe) (1996)

OUI AVANT-GARDE À CHANCE, Massacre MASCD 0104 (Europe) (1996)

THE ANSWER MACHINE?, Massacre MASCD 0128 (Europe) (1997)

Outrageous Fourtunes, Massacre MASCD 0150 (Europe) (1998)

VINTAGE WHINE, Massacre MASCD 0178 (Europe) (1999)

FOLKÉMON, Nuclear Blast NB 0502-2 (Europe) (2000)

Swords Of A Thousand Men, Demolition DEMCDS 001B (UK) (2001)

ANOTHER FINE MESS, Demolition DEMCD 112 (UK) (2001)

NO DAYLIGHTS NOR HEELTAPS, Demolition DEMCD 115 (UK) (2002)

LIVE AT THE DYNAMO, Burning Airlines PILOT 139 (UK) (2002)

A SEMBLANCE OF NORMALITY, Demolition DEMCD 142 (UK) (2004)

Jig-A-Jig, Skyclad cnu (UK) (2006)

The group severed ties with manager Eric Cook and were back in the studio the following year to come up with the heavily folk-influenced album *The Answer Machine?*, released in September 1997. Their new second guitarist was Kevin Ridley, formerly the frontman of Screen Idols, The Shotgun Brides, and Forgodsake, as well as many credits as a producer. He did not play on the new album but did join the band to fill in on guitar and backing vocals for an acoustic in-store promotional tour in Germany during September 1997. Yasmin Krull of Atrocity contributed guest vocals to 'The Thread Of Evermore'.

That autumn, the group augmented their sound with Nick Acons of Seven Little Sisters on guitar and fiddle, John Leonard on accordion, mandolin, bagpipes, flute, and keyboards, and drummer Mitch Oldham. However, this union was fleeting. The *Outrageous Fourtunes* EP, limited to 1,000 copies, was released in 1998.

During 1998, both Walkyier and Biddle guested on the *Manifiesto* album from Brazilian band Nepal. In March, Skyclad launched another European tour, this time taking out Mindfeed and Across The Border as openers. These shows meant double duty for Ramsey, who also acted as Mindfeed's guitarist. Once these concerts were over, the band embarked on the first of their 'Irish Pub' tours of Germany in April, with Jay Graham on drums. This unique concept gained the band some favourable press, particularly in more mainstream areas of the European media. Wishing to break out of the confines of the traditional metal venues, Skyclad took things back to basics with a run of packed pub concerts, bringing in a whole new set of fans in the process. A double appearance at the 'Wacken' festival in August preceded a second round of 'Irish Pub' dates to close the year in December.

February 1999 saw the band back to the fore with a much harder release, *Vintage Whine,* featuring guitarist Kevin Ridley and drummer Jay Graham (both now permanent Skyclad members), and they put in no fewer than five German tours during the year on top of many prestigious festival performances. April dates had Italian newcomers Lacuna Coil as openers. In July, the band openly voiced dissatisfaction with their Massacre label onstage at the 'Ziegenrück Open Air' festival. An appearance at 'Wacken' was blighted when Ramsey, beaten up by overzealous backstage security, suffered a head injury.

The band signed to Nuclear Blast later that year for the October 2000 *Folkémon* album. Limited digipack versions included a cover of Tenpole Tudor's 'Swords Of A Thousand Men' while the Japanese edition boasted the exclusive 'Loco-Commotion' instrumental, featuring a guitar solo from Tygers Of Pan Tang's Fred Purser.

Paying homage, Suidakra covered 'The One Piece Puzzle' on their 2000 album *The Arcanum*. The same year found Walkyier guesting on Cradle Of Filth's version of the Sabbat classic 'For Those Who Died'. Live action on the continent in November saw a brief burst of dates with Spanish act Tierra Santa in November.

As 2001 broke, rumours spread that Walkyier had quit the band. However, they were scheduled to perform at the Derby 'Bloodstock' festival during May. The show was also set to feature a one-off set by Return To The Sabbat, a Sabbat reformation of sorts with Andy Sneap's role filled by ex-Talion guitarist Pete Wadeson. By April, the band had confirmed that Walkyier had left and that Bloodstock would mark their farewell show. Skyclad themselves resolved to carry on with Kevin Ridley taking over on lead vocals. The new band debuted with shows in Europe as openers to Fish.

As fans waited to see if Skyclad could survive without Walkyier, it became apparent that the band had every intention of persevering. They established their own label, Demolition, for the release of a live album *Another Fine Mess*. This first official live release featured material from the band's 1995 'Dynamo' festival appearance. Meanwhile, former label Massacre weighed in with another collector's item – a compilation CD,

Poetic Wisdom, distributed free with the July issue of the Greek *Metal Hammer* magazine.

The traditional round of touring in Germany continued unabated, although Graham decamped to Return To The Sabbat. His replacement was former Axis and Sticky Fingers drummer Aaron Walton. In October, Skyclad released a single of 'Swords Of A Thousand Men', roping in Eddie Tenpole as session guest. The single also included a reworked version of live favourite 'The Widdershins Jig'.

Another Skyclad cover arrived with Italian folk/speed metal act Elvenking, who committed 'Penny Dreadful' to their *Heathenreel* debut album. The connection with Elvenking was strengthened when Walkyier performed Skyclad songs with them at the Italian 'Metal.It' festival in March 2002. Meanwhile, the band issued the acoustic *No Daylights Nor Heeltaps* album, featuring acoustic re-workings of Skyclad songs, with Kevin Ridley on vocals. Released through the band's website some two months before its May street date, copies ordered over the net came with a bonus disc featuring 'No Deposit, No Return', 'A Great Blow For A Day Job', 'No Strings Attached', 'Building A Ruin', and 'Loco-Commotion'.

A new studio album, *A Semblance Of Normality*, appeared early in 2003. Martin Walkyier spent time with his new venture, The Clan Destined, an ambitious pagan collective involving Immortal bassist Iscariah. The singer also guested on 'Blood And Sand' on Bradford band Bloodstream's debut album, *Black Storm Harvest.*

It was reported in September that Skyclad were collaborating on a new album with none other than the Royal Philharmonic Orchestra. The group hooked up with The Quireboys for a short round of December gigs, the 'Demolition Xmas Ball'. A free CD with two new tracks from each band was given to gig-goers.

Ex-member Jay Graham was in the news during 2004, sessioning for Black Sabbath guitarist Tony Iommi and joining Helvis in June for their *Onset Of Winter Brings Death (The Crops Have Failed)* recordings.

Skyclad's co-headlining gig at the 'Burgfolk Festival' in Mülheim/Ruhr, Germany on July 24th was filmed as part of a DVD release. A new studio album, *A Semblance Of Normality*, was mixed and mastered at the Damage Inc. Studio in Italy by Dario Mollo of Voodoo Hill and The Cage, set for September issue through Demolition.

Skyclad then performed an unusual concert, the '34,000 Ton Metal Cruise', on September 25th, performing on board the Münchenbryggeriet car ferry in Stockholm, Sweden alongside Tankard, Amon Amarth, Hypocrisy, Tad Morose, Stormwarrior, and Wolf. In July 2005, the band celebrated their 15th anniversary with an electric and acoustic set at the 'Dong Open Air' festival in Neukirchen-Vluyn, Germany. They headlined the UK 'Dominion – Autumn Assault' festival in Hull during October over a cast of Human Fortress, Intense, Infobia, Pain Control, Warchild, Deliverance, Conquest Of Steel, Humanity, Evile, and Pitiful Reign. However, European concerts were cancelled when Ramsey sustained a shoulder injury in an accident.

The *Jig-A-Jig* EP, an independent release only available through the band's website and at concerts, preceded a new studio album. With The Clan Destined fragmenting in acrimonious circumstances, Walkyier broke a lengthy silence in April announcing that he was permanently withdrawing from making music. As this book went to press, fans were awaiting further developments.

THERION
EPIC METALLIC TALENT

Cited by many as one the most adventurous metal bands on the current scene, Christofer Johnsson's Therion present a sound swathed in huge, operatic choirs and Oriental orchestral arrangements. The band have also

Montezuma Recordings Studio as a trio to self-produce *Beyond Sanctorium* in 1992. CD versions added an extra track, 'Tyrants Of The Damned'.

For the *Symphony Masses: Ho Drakon Ho Megas* album, released through local imprint Megarock in April 1993, only Johnsson remained, having added ex-Conspiracy guitarist Magnus Barthelsson, the Hexenhaus-credited bassist Andreas Wahl, and Carbonized drummer Piotr Wawrzeniuk. Revisiting the Montezuma Recordings studio, the band co-produced the album with the aid of engineer Rex Gisslén. With a whole new cast, Johnsson enjoyed a good deal of experimentation, layering the traditional death metal elements with sumptuous keyboards – and even the audacity of a bass solo. Lyrically, the Therion frontman's well-documented occult persuasions came to the fore, with passages of Aramaic and Hebrew interlaced with the expected grunts and growls.

Wahl and Wawrzeniuk, guitarist Johan Lundell, and Entombed bassist Lars Rosenberg formed a 1993 side project, Serpent. The industrious Wahl also operated another side band, Concrete Sleep. Barthelsson subsequently formed industrial band Grain.

In a surreal move, Christofer Johnsson became embroiled in the machinations of the burgeoning Scandinavian black metal scene when a girl, claiming to be an emissary of Burzum's Varg 'Count Grishnackh' Vikernes, unsuccessfully tried to burn down his house. When apprehended, she apparently informed the authorities that Johnsson was "not a true Satanist". Johnsson left Sweden for a time to ally himself temporarily with Swiss death metal band Messiah, touring with them and participating in sessions for their 1994 album *Underground*.

Having signed to Nuclear Blast, the band released a single, 'The Beauty In Black', which had promising sales. April 1995's Harris Johns-produced album, *Lepaca Kliffoth*, was recorded by the core of Johnsson, bassist Fredrik Isaksson, and Carbonized drummer Piotr Wawrzeniuk. It featured a cover of Celtic Frost's 'Sorrows Of The Moon' and included contributions from baritone Hans Groning and vocalist Claudia Maria Mohri, who had appeared on Celtic Frost's *Into The Pandemonium* album.

Lepaca Kliffoth introduced ambient passages for the first time, marking a step into a new realm of sound. The band gigged across Germany partnered with Canadian thrashers Annihilator and toured South America during 1995, when bassist Lars Rosenberg, also of Carbonized, opted to leave Entombed and join Therion on a permanent basis. In November, they added ex-Unanimated guitarist Jonas Mellberg. Wawrzeniuk and Rosenberg released the debut Serpent album, *In The Garden Of The Serpent*, to round off 1995.

As 1996 began, Therion contributed a track to a Japanese Iron Maiden covers album on the Toys Factory label and entered a new stage of their career in August with *Theli*, an ambitious amalgam of metal and Middle Eastern influences overlaid with choral vocals. The record, recorded at Impulse Studio in Hamburg, marked a pivotal point in the band's career as Johnsson relinquished his vocal role and Therion began to rely more on orchestrated choirs. Participants included Edge Of Sanity's Dan Swanö, soprano soloists Anja Krenz and Constanze Arens, tenor Stephan Gade, bass baritone Axel Pätz, pianist Jan Peter Genkel, and keyboard player Gottfried Koch, as well as the full complement of the North German Radio Choir.

With the release of *Theli*, the band undertook an extensive tour of Germany, supporting Amorphis. For these shows, they introduced Avernus keyboard player Kimberley Goss, with former Necrophobic keyboard player Tobias Sidegård as session musician. Although the album had been hugely expensive to produce – requiring the biggest budget so far granted by Nuclear Blast – the initial response was positive, and within a month *Theli* had doubled the sales of its predecessor. An eight-minute edited version of the mournful track 'The Siren Of The Woods' was released as a single, snapped up by fans as it contained an exclusive track,

employed some of the most esteemed female vocalists in the metal world over the course of their labyrinthine career, including Sarah Jezebel Diva, Claudia Maria Mokri, Kimberley Goss, Martina Hornbacher Astner, and Marika Schonberg.

Therion started life as an accomplished if relatively run-of-the-mill death metal band from the Stockholm suburb of Upplands Väsby. They managed to be as adventurous as possible with each successive record, increasing their status in Europe along the way. The roots of the band lay in the Swedish band Blitzkrieg, formed in 1987, which featured bassist-vocalist Christofer Johnsson, guitarist Peter Hansson, and drummer Oskar Forss. The group reformed in 1988 as Megatherion (named after the Celtic Frost album of the same title), with Johnsson on vocals and guitar, guitarist Hansson, ex-Crematory bassist Johan Hansson, and drummer Mika Tovalainen. Shortly afterwards, the band replaced their rhythm section with former Dismember bassist Erik Gustafsson and the return of drummer Oskar Forss, and shortened their name to Therion. Parallel to his Therion activities, Johnsson was also holding down membership of the grind act Carbonized, recording three albums with them: *For The Security* (1991), *Disharmonization* (1993), and *Screaming Machines* (1996).

The first Therion demos surfaced in April 1989: *Paroxysmal Holocaust*, recorded with the temporary services of vocalist Matti Kärki, now of Dismember, and *Beyond The Darkest Veils Of Inner Wickedness*, with Johnsson back on vocals. This line-up, minus Kärki, recorded Therion's first mini-album, *Time Shall Tell*, at Sunlight Studios in Stockholm with producer Tomas Skogsberg. The record was initially released as a limited edition of 1,000 for sale through a local record store, House Of Kicks, but more pressings were subsequently issued.

Bassist Erik Gustaffson left following the 1991 *Of Darkness...* album, again recorded using the Skogsberg/Sunlight Studios combination. The new record was issued through British label Deaf Records, a subsidiary of Peaceville. While it was regarded as a commendable slice of death metal, the album gave little hint of what was to come.

Therion switched to another UK label, Active Records, and worked in

THERION discography

Time Shall Tell, House Of Kicks HOK LP 001 (Europe) (1990)

OF DARKNESS..., Deaf DEAF 6 (UK) (1991)

BEYOND SANCTORUM, Active CDATV23 (UK) (1992)

SYMPHONY MASSES – HO DRAKON HO MEGAS, Megarock MRR 002 (Europe), Pavement Music 76962-32205-2 (USA) (1993)

LEPACA KLIFFOTH, Nuclear Blast NB 0127-2 (Europe), Nuclear Blast America 6127 (USA) (1995)

THELI, Nuclear Blast NB 0179-2 (Europe), Nuclear Blast America 6179 (USA) (1996)

A'RAB ZARAQ LUCID DREAMING, Nuclear Blast NB 0249-2 (Europe), Nuclear Blast America 6249 (USA)(1997)

VOVIN, Nuclear Blast NB 0317-2 (Europe), Nuclear Blast America 6317 (USA) (1998)

Crowning Of Atlantis, Nuclear Blast NB 0398-2 (Europe), Nuclear Blast America 6398 (USA) (1999)

DEGGIAL, Nuclear Blast NB 0442-2 (Europe), Nuclear Blast America 6442 (USA) (2000)

BELLS OF DOOM, Therion Fan Club cnu (2001)

SECRETS OF THE RUNES, Nuclear Blast NB 0625-2 (Europe), Nuclear Blast America 6625 (USA) (2001)

LIVE IN MIDGÅRD, Nuclear Blast NB 1033-2 (Europe), Nuclear Blast America 1033 (USA) (2002)

LEMURIA, Nuclear Blast NB 1253-2 (Europe), Nuclear Blast America 1253 (USA) (2004)

SIRIUS B, Nuclear Blast NB 1265-2 (Europe), Nuclear Blast America 1265 (USA) (2004)

CELEBRATORS OF THE BECOMING, Nuclear Blast NB 1677 (Europe), Nuclear Blast America 1677 (USA) (2006)

GOTHIC KABBALAH , Nuclear Blast NB 1780-2 (Europe), Nuclear Blast America 1780 (USA) (2007)

'Babylon', composed by Lars Rosenberg. The song was being considered for recording by Entombed, but the bassist included it here to lay first claim to it.

Further dates saw the band with returned bass player Wahl and two professional classical singers as part of the 'Out Of The Dark' festival alongside My Dying Bride and Sentenced. Demand for them was such that a third European tour alongside Crematory and Lake Of Tears was undertaken, the first to feature the Cradle Of Filth-credited Sarah Jezebel Deva on vocals.

The May 1997 album *A'arab Zaraq Lucid Dreaming*, originally planned as an EP, featured versions of Running Wild's 'Under Jolly Roger' (fronted by singer Tobbe Sidegård with Hypocrisy's Peter Tägtgren on guitar), Judas Priest's 'Here Come The Tears', Scorpions' 'Fly To The Rainbow' (with vocals from drummer Wawrzeniuk), and Iron Maiden's 'Children Of The Damned'. The main part of the work, commencing with *Theli* out-takes 'Into Remembrance' and 'Black Fairy' sung by Dan Swanö, hinged on an oratorio consisting of six segments of music commissioned for a Per Albinsson-directed movie, *The Golden Embrace*. This amalgamation of sources put Therion into the German album charts for the first time.

For touring purposes, the band morphed into a duo of Johnsson and Wawrzeniuk joined by soprano vocalists Joanna Holmgren and Sandra Camenisch and session players – guitarist Tobias Sidegård, bassist Andreas Wahl, and Tommy Eriksson on drums. To commemorate the band's 10th anniversary, they released a limited two-disc edition of *A'arab Zaraq Lucid Dreaming* with extensive liner notes from Johnsson. The first disc included Therion's version of Iron Maiden's 'Children Of The Damned'. The album also featured a slightly altered track-listing and sequence. Touring in Europe during March of 1997, the band played with My Dying Bride, Sentenced, Orphanage, and Dark for the 'Out Of The Dark III' festivals.

The equally ambitious *Vovin*, issued in May 1998, featured lead vocals from former Dreams Of Sanity singer Martina Hornacher Astner. For the first time, the band relied upon the services of a full orchestra in the studio. Session bass player Jan Kazda and drummer Wolf Simons were taken on for the rhythm section. Ralf Scheepers of Primal Fear appeared on 'The Wild Hunt', and the producers – Grip Inc. guitarist Waldemar Sorychta and Siggi Bemm – both supplied guitar. *Vovin* took the band to new heights of success, selling over 150,000 copies in Europe alone. Therion's line-up to promote *Vovin* with co-headlining dates in Europe alongside Moonspell consisted of Johnsson, Tommy Eriksson (this time on guitar), Kim Blomqvist on bass, and Sami Karppinen on drums. Singers were Sara Jezebel Deva (soprano), Martina Hornbacher, and a girl called Cynthia. UK gigs in September saw Therion packaged with Anathema and Moonspell.

The band indulged in yet more covers with the June 1999 release *Crowning Of Atlantis*, with a guesting Scheepers making his presence felt on a version of 'Crazy Nights' by Japanese metal band Loudness. They also recorded takes of Manowar's 'Thor (The Powerhead)' and Accept's 'Seawinds', the latter featuring Sarah Jezebel Deva. Sorychta donated lead guitar once more. Drums were played by Wolf Simons, except for the title track, which featured Sami Karppinen. Once again Martina Hornbacher Astner made her presence felt on the album and in videos for 'Wine of Aluquah', 'Rise Of Sodom And Gomorrah', and 'Birth Of Venus Illegitima'. Falling pregnant, but still managing to tour with the band in 1999, she later departed to create a new act, Alas, with Morbid Angel's Erik Rutan.

Therion maintained their standing and scored impressive European chart returns with January 2000's *Deggial*. Lavishly orchestrated at the band's own Woodhouse Studios, the album had guitar and bass from the recently-recruited brothers Johan and Kristian Niemann, overlaid by a wealth of instrumentation including violin, viola, cello, contrabass, oboe, flute, tuba, sousaphone, French horn, flugelhorn, and trumpet, as well as no fewer than eight operatic solo vocalists. From the metal world, Blind Guardian's Hansi Kürsch guested as singer on 'Flesh Of The Gods'. Nuclear Blast invested heavily in the album, even issuing digipacks with an expensive velvet overlay. These limited-edition versions hosted an exclusive rendition of Carl Orff's 'O Fortuna'.

Road work for Therion in 2001 saw the band bolstered by Luciferase singer Risto Hämäläinen, Shadowseeds vocalist Petra Aho, the Lion's Share-credited Anders Engberg, and Silent Rites singer Suvi Virtanen, as well as the voices of Jari-Petri Heino, Johanna Mårlöv, and Maria Ottosson. Tour support in Europe was supplied by Evergrey and My Insanity before a round of Latin American dates was undertaken. The new drummer was Richard Evensand, a seasoned campaigner with experience with Dog Faced Gods, Ebony Tears, Soilwork, Southpaw, and Demonoid among many others.

Members of the band's fan club were treated in 2001 to the rarities album *Bells Of Doom*, compiling archive tracks from as far back as the early Blitzkrieg days. In keeping with their left-field character, Therion contributed a version of 'Summer Night City' to a 2001 death metal Abba tribute album. The track also turned up on the October album *Secrets Of The Runes* alongside a further cover of the 1976 Scorpions track 'Crying Days'. Operatic female vocals were delivered by Marika Schonberg. That album advanced distribution methods into previously uncharted territory when it was presented as a package with author Thomas Karlsson's *Uthark* treatise on Professor Sigurd Agrell's rune theories.

Former Therion bassist Fredrik Isaksson became part of the

reconvened Grave during September 2001. The band then parted ways with drummer Sami Karppinen during March 2002 before cutting a rendition of 'Fight Fire With Fire' for a Nuclear Blast Metallica tribute collection. In September, Therion's first official concert album, *Live In Midgard*, arrived as a double CD set recorded in Colombia, Hungary, and Germany. October found the Niemann brothers and Sami Karppinen on drums performing as part of Tiamat bassist Johnny Hagel's Lithium project. Johan Niemann busied himself as part of the melodic metal act Tears Of Anger.

In keeping with their grandiose reputation, Therion issued not one but two albums in May 2004 – *Sirius B* and *Lemuria*. Christofer Johnsson's vision required no fewer than 171 people to be involved in the recordings. As well as the traditional guitar, bass, and drums, there were balalaikas, domras, mandolins, a full symphonic orchestra, grand piano, harpsichord, opera soloists, and a 32-strong choir. The band also used an organ recorded at Copenhagen's oldest church and added Hammond organ and mellotron before reaching the final mixing stage. New members installed for live work included drummer Petter Karlsson (aka Petter Khraft) of Master Massive, Argento, and Kajarr, and soprano vocalist Karin Fjellander. The group rehearsed with the Yngwie Malmsteen-credited vocalist Mats Levén. A tour with Tristania and Trail Of Tears then took in Poland, Germany, Czech Republic, Belgium, France, Holland, Austria, Slovenia, Hungary, Italy, Switzerland, the UK, and Spain.

Therion's 2005 live campaign included many European festival slots before North American headline dates in September, with selected shows seeing support from Beyond The Embrace. Nuclear Blast combined *A'arab Zaraq Lucid Dreaming* and *The Crowning Of Atlantis* for the compilation *Atlantis Lucid Dreaming*.

In March 2006, Christofer Johnsson announced that he would retire from singing lead vocals and relinquished his role in his side project Demonoid, stating that his last performance in the role would be at the UK 'ProgPower' festival. Therion issued the mammoth *Celebrators Of Becoming* set in June, a four-DVD and two-CD package featuring over ten hours of video footage and two hours of live audio.

In a surprise move, it was announced in October that multi-instrumentalist Snowy Shaw (aka Tommy Helgesson), best known as drummer for Mercyful Fate, King Diamond, and Dream Evil, would be sharing the lead vocals on the new Therion album, *Gothic Kabbalah*, with Mats Levén and two female singers, Katarina Lilja and Hannah Holgersson.

In anticipation of the 2007 release of *Gothic Kabbalah*, the band announced concerts with Grave Digger and Sabaton for a headlining European tour beginning on January 17th in Essen, Germany. Singer Lori Lewis from Minneapolis, Minnesota, act Aesma Daeva was drafted into the touring line-up. Therion remain among the most visionary acts of the metal genre.

ULVER
FOLK AND METAL COMBINED

AT FIRST, ULVER WERE A SATANIC BLACK metal act who stood out from the pack thanks to their use of flute and acoustic instruments alongside the genre's familiar screams and grating guitars. The Norwegian band, who took their name from the local word for wolves, adopted neo-noir musical mutations that saw them draw rapidly away from stereotypes,

Ulver

ULVER discography

Ulver, Nekromantic Gallery Productions NGP 002 (Europe) (1994) split 7-inch vinyl single with Mysticum

BERGTATT – ET EVENTYR 15 CAPITLER, Head Not Found HNF 005 (Europe) (1994)

KVELDSSANGER, Head Not Found HNF 014 (Europe) (1996)

NATTENS MADRIGAL: AATTE HYMNE TIL ULVEN I MANDEN, Century Media 77158-2 (Europe) (1996), Century Black 7858-2 (USA) (1997)

THEMES FROM WILLIAM BLAKE'S THE MARRIAGE OF HEAVEN AND HELL, Jester TRICK 001 (Europe) (1998)

Metamorphosis, Jester TRICK 006 (Europe) (1999)

PERDITION CITY: MUSIC TO AN INTERIOR FILM, Jester TRICK 007 (Europe) (2000)

Silence Teaches You How To Sing, Jester TRICK 012 (Europe) (2001) limited edition 2,000 copies

Silencing The Singing, Jester TRICK 016 (Europe) (2001) limited edition 3,000 copies

LYCKANTROPEN THEMES: ORIGINAL SOUNDTRACK FOR THE SHORT FILM BY STEVE ERICSSON, Jester TRICK 024 (Europe), The End TE031 (USA) (2002)

Vargnatt Promo 1993, Infinite Vinyl IVS 002 (2003) limited edition 10-inch white vinyl 1,000 hand-numbered copies

1993-2003: 1st DECADE IN THE MACHINES, Jester TRICK 025 (Europe) (2003)

A Quick Fix Of Melancholy, Jester TRICK 026 (Europe), The End TE039 (USA) (2003)

TEACHINGS IN SILENCE, Jester TRICK 029 (Europe) (2003)

SVIDD NEGER – ORIGINAL MOTION PICTURE SOUNDTRACK, Jester TRICK 030 (Europe) (2003)

BLOOD INSIDE, Jester TRICK 033 (Europe), The End TE058 (USA) (2005)

---

pursuing ever more radical musical landscapes to such an extent that their later works are almost jazz-like.

Ulver's Oslo-based frontman Garm named himself after the Norse dog guardian of hell, although his real name is Kristoffer Rygg. He is also a member of two other black metal institutions, Arcturus and Borknagar. Ulver were created in 1992 by 15-year-old Rygg and Satyricon drummer Carl-Michael Eide (aka Exhurtum, Czral, or Aggressor), and they issued a November 1993 demo *Vargnatt* ('Wolf's Night'). Guitars were handled by A. Reza and Grellmund, while Håvard Jørgensen took on acoustic guitars and keyboards. Robin Malmberg of Mysticum sessioned on bass. Rehearsal sessions appeared that year on the tape-trading market and included Ulver's rendition of Celtic Frost's 'Babylon Fell'.

Eide left for Ved Buens Ende during 1993 and subsequently became an industrious figure on the black metal scene, contributing to Aura Noir, Cadaver Inc., Virus, and Inferno. Skoll (Hugh Steven James Mingay) of Fimbulwinter, Arcturus, and Ved Buens Ende was installed on bass in 1994. The drum position was taken by AiwarikiaR (Erik Olivier Lancelot) of Valhall. The Necromantic Gallery label released a split EP, *Ulverytternes Kamp*, in collaboration with Mysticum.

The debut album, *Bergtatt – Et Eeventyr I 5 Capitler* (which translates as 'Mountain Taken – A Fairy Tale In Five Chapters'), was delivered in November 1994 through the Head Not Found label. The record included Aismal (Torbjørn Pedersen) on guitars and keyboards, and it related the legend of abductions into the mountain netherworlds by fairytale creatures. Studio accompaniment came from the Ved Buens Ende-credited

Lill Kathrine Stensrud on vocals and flute alongside pianist Sverd (Steinar Johnsen). So strong was this release, juxtaposing the harshest of black metal with authentic folk, that many cite it as the most accomplished musical work to come out of the early Norwegian scene.

Ulver followed in 1996 with *Kveldssanger* ('Twilight Songs'), co-produced by Kristian Romsøe and recorded at Endless Lydstudio in Christiania. This was a drastic about-turn, a mesmerising, mainly acoustic affair overlaid with subtle orchestral landscapes. Although all elements of black metal had been dispensed with, the sheer quality of *Kveldssanger* effectively muted any potential backlash.

March 1996's *Nattens Madrigal – Aatte Hymne Til Ulven I Manden*, ('Madrigal Of The Night – Eight Hymns To The Wolf In Man') was released by Century Media and marked the return of Skoll and Aismal to the band, who temporarily returned to Satanic black metal, woven around lyrical themes based on lycanthropy. Tore Ylwizaker was then added to the group as permanent pianist. Rhythm guitarist Grellmund took his own life on New Year's Eve 1997.

In December 1998, Garm put out the ambitious conceptual piece, *Themes From William Blake's The Marriage Of Heaven And Hell*, on his own Jester imprint. With metal now completely absent from Ulver's palette, this sprawling work used song 'plate' titles not as individual identifiers but merely as reference points, and took the listener on a journey through electronic distortion and even trip-hop. Remarkably, despite such a huge musical change, Ulver appeared to carry their black metal/folk fanbase with them. The album featured regular contributors, including guitarist Håvard Jørgensen and drummer Erik Olivier Lancelot, along with bassist Hugh Stephen James Mingay, Emperor's Samoth (Tomas Thormodsæter Haugen) and Ihsahn (Vegard Sverre Tveitan), as well as Darkthrone mentor Fenriz (Gylve Nagell). The album appeared to close with the track 'A Song Of Liberty', although a 20-minute period of silence ensued before the real finale arrived in the form of 'Chorus'.

An interim ambient techno outing, the *Metamorphosis* EP, arrived in September 1999. Other Ulver contributions featured on the 1999 Emperor album *IX Equilibrium*, where they offered a radically remixed version of 'Sworn', while Hagalaz's Runedance came in for a similar treatment with a re-constructed 'Jaxtaposition' mix of 'The Falcon Flies' on the *Urd – That Which Was* EP.

Ulver's March 2000 album *Perdition City: Music To An Interior Film* proved to be far removed from the raw black metal of the band's roots as Garm delivered an electronic film soundscape imbued with organic jazz and blues passages. Bassist Øystein Moe of Tritonus appeared alongside saxophonist Rolf Erik Nyström and no fewer than three drummers – Ivar H. Johansen, Kåre J. Pedersen of Euroboys, and Faust (Bård G. Eithun) of Thorns and Emperor. The recording of the album, which bore the instruction "Headphones and darkness recommended", was partly funded by the Norsk Kassettavgiftsfond, the Norwegian Ministry of cultural affairs. Under the pseudonym of 'Trickster G', Garm guested on the Zyklon 2001 album *World Ov Worms*, the side project of Samoth and Emperor colleague Trym Torson (Kai Johnny Mosaker) alongside Myrkskog's Destructhor (Thor Anders Myhren).

In 2001, Ulver's unpredictability stretched into a brace of self-described "improv-glitch" EPs: September's *Silence Teaches You How To Sing* (a solitary 24-minute track of chaotic noise) and December's equally compelling *Silencing The Singing*. Both were restricted to limited runs and were subsequently collated on the *Teachings In Silence* album.

By February 2002, Garm was working with Dutch experimental rock act The Gathering. The next installment in the Ulver saga came with the *Lyckantropen Themes* album, a totally instrumental, supremely minimalist soundtrack to a short film by Steve Ericsson. In April 2003, a compilation of sorts appeared with *1993-2003: 1st Decade In The Machines*, consisting of remixes of Ulver compositions by artists such as Merzbow, Upland,

Information, Jazzkammer, and The Third Eye Foundation. New music came along in October with a string-orientated exercise in aural malevolence, the EP *A Quick Fix Of Melancholy*. A second film soundtrack emerged before the close of 2003, *Svidd Neger*. The film (a study of human violence) and Garm's music bore an equally dark aura.

During late 2004, Ulver contributed 'Strange Ways' to a Kiss tribute album, assembled by Kiss Army Norway and Voices Music Entertainment. The band committed to tape a 15-minute work in collaboration with Stephen O'Malley of Sunn O))) and Julian Cope of The Teardrop Explodes. Garm guested on Solefald album recordings in early 2005. That May, it was revealed that he had activated heavy rock project Sindrome, cutting a debut album, *A Killer View*.

Ulver's June 2005 album *Blood Inside* came in an array of packaging. A limited run of 2,000 CDs were encased in a red velvet box, while vinyl variants issued through Profound Lore Creations were pressed in no fewer than six different vinyl colours. Naturally, *Blood Inside* confounded fans and critics as the band once again employed analogue instrumentation, but in such twisted form that the songs were structureless. Ulver are, perhaps, the most experimental band in this book.

VOIVOD
LEGENDARY EXPERIMENTAL METALLERS

THE JONQUIÈRE, QUÉBEC-BASED act Voivod were an avant-garde thrash metal band who mixed punk, metal, and science fiction in a unique combination that won them many fans during the mid-1980s thrash boom. The Canadian band's early work provoked scorn from a large contingent of the metal fraternity, but their musical growth and ability to convey their ambitions came to fruition with the landmark *Nothingface* album – often rated by progressive metal aficionados as a groundbreaking set.

The French-speaking Voivod consisted of frontman Snake (Denis Bélanger), guitarist Piggy (Denis D'Amour), bassist Blacky (Jean-Yves Thériault), and drummer Away (Michel Langevin). Unusually, the band's concept was based on nuclear physics graduate Langevin's self-invented science fiction character, the Voivod Korgull – a post-apocalyptic vampire warrior. The musicians first assembled in late 1980 but only constructed a solid band around November 1982. Jean Fortin, later of Deaf Dealer, briefly occupied the bass position before Blacky learned the instrument. The nicknames were chosen in reference to the members' personal traits – Piggy due to his endomorphic stature, Snake because of his elongated visage, Blacky thanks to his mood swings, and Away because he often missed rehearsals.

Early Voivod gigs included numerous cover versions from the likes of Judas Priest, Motörhead, and Venom. The group released a number of live recordings in 1983, including the June 25th *Anachronism* cassette, which featured cover versions of Judas Priest's 'Rapid Fire', Motörhead's 'Ace Of Spades', 'Stone Dead Forever', and 'No Class', as well as Venom's 'Black Metal', 'Welcome To Hell', and 'Witching Hour'. The cassette credited the players as Snake on "throat, scream, insults, mike torture and weapon operator", Piggy "burning metal-axe, electro-motive force and tremolition", Blacky "blower bass, pyromania and shit", and Away "thunder and death machine, horror and visions".

The band's first forays into the recording studio resulted in the 1984 *To The Death* demo. They officially debuted in 1984 with 'Condemned To The Gallows', culled from the *To The Death* sessions, on Metal Blade's *Metal Massacre V* compilation.

With their debut *War And Pain* album out on Metal Blade in the USA and Roadrunner in Europe, Voivod immediately set themselves apart from the thrash bandwagon. Financed by a loan of $2,000 from the band-members' parents, *War And Pain* and its extremities intrigued the curious

while prompting lovers of conventional metal to run for the hills. The sessions were recorded on an 8-track recorder over an eight-day period at Le Terroir studio in Québec in June 1984. With the 'production' – which could only be described as abysmal – and the Korgull the Exterminator cover character, many found the sludge-thrash brutality of the album, spread over sides 'Iron' and 'Blower', far too primitive to stomach. However, *War And Pain* did find a keen audience in the metal stronghold of Germany, which generated a healthy portion of the album's 70,000 sales. In December 1984, the band recorded a live demo and released it as the *Morgöth Invasion* cassette. On April 4th 1985, they performed outside Canada for the first time, supporting Cro-Mags and Venom at New York City's Ritz.

Voivod's suitably titled *Rrröööaarrr!!!*, laid down at L'Autre studios in Montréal between October and November 1985 and released the following year, was their first for German label Noise, licensed to Combat for the USA. An extensive US tour was undertaken to promote the album, partnered with fellow experimentalists Celtic Frost and the somewhat mismatched Running Wild, throughout June 1986. The band then hooked up with Possessed and Deathrow for European gigs in November, adding punks English Dogs for the closing London Electric Ballroom date. Maintaining a close link with their fans, the band put out the Iron Gang fan-club *No Speed Limit Week-End* cassette, a live demo recorded in October 1986.

Their next album was recorded at Musiclab Studios in Berlin with producer Harris Johns in October and November 1986. *Killing Technology* was taken out on the road in North America in April and May 1987, backing German thrashers Kreator, with the two bands uniting again for European gigs in November. Unfortunately, their slot on the Megadeth-headlined UK 'Christmas On Earth' festival in Leeds on December 13th was stopped when customs officers confiscated the band's gear. Voivod turned up for the show but could only sit and watch the other bands perform. The faithful Iron Gang fan club was rewarded again, this time with two exclusive tapes of shows recorded in Montreal (*Spectrum*) and Brussels (*Live In Bruxelles*).

The group cut the *Dimension Hatröss* album, closing with a tongue-in-cheek *Batman* theme, again at Musiclab Studios in Berlin with Harris Johns, released in June 1988. Dominated by dissonant chords, unexpected time signatures, and Piggy's liberal use of unconventional minor chords, *Dimension Hatröss* alienated critics but drew in more adventurous metal fans. Progress was temporarily stalled when the band were forced to pull

Voivod

out of their *Dimension Hatröss* world tour because Piggy was diagnosed with a malignant brain tumour. When surgeons warned that surgery would probably curtail his guitar abilities, he declined the operation and threw his energies into the band. The group then forged an alliance with Vio-Lence for North American concerts to close the year. Naturally enough a further live cassette, *A Flawless Structure?*, was recorded at the Spectrum in Montréal during December.

Voivod's tenacity and reluctance to compromise was rewarded with a major label deal through MCA Records' subsidiary Mechanic, for 1989's Glen Robinson-produced *Nothingface*, which featured the band's take on Pink Floyd's 'Astronomy Domine'. Thematically, the Voivod character was now no longer content to wage war, but was struggling with multiple psychological issues. Evidence of this lyrical shift came in 'Pre-Ignition' and 'Missing Sequences', which related directly to the band's roots and a fear of Alzheimer's disease, with their friends and family living in the shadow of the Jonquière aluminium factory. Again embarking on US dates, Voivod took out Soundgarden and Faith No More as support acts. *Nothingface* was nominated for a Canadian Juno music industry award. The band then toured homeland arenas as guests to Rush.

Staying with MCA, *Angel Rat* arrived in 1991, after which Blacky was replaced by Pierre St Jean. Gigs across the USA in September 1993 had Voivod heading another adventurous bill alongside Damn The Machine and Clutch. A new album, *The Outer Limits*, was released in 1993.

Snake backed out for 1995's Mark S. Berry-produced *Negatron*, forcing Piggy and Away to re-think the band's future. *Negatron*, which included guest participation from industrial godfather Jim G. Thirlwell and ex-Liquid Indian vocalist-bassist Eric Forrest, was issued in December in Canada through Hypnotic and Mausoleum in Europe. The European version featured extra tracks 'Vortex' and 'Erosion'.

Continuing as a trio, the band released 1997's *Phobos*, co-produced by the band and Rob Sanzo at Signal To Noise in Toronto, and including a cover version of King Crimson's '21st Century Schizoid Man'. While touring to promote the album, Forrest was severely injured in a road accident in Germany during 1998. The vocalist was in a coma and suffered severe spinal injuries. His recuperation took many months.

As Voivod went into hiatus, the *Kronik* compilation emerged on Hypnotic, including four live tracks. The band's Montréal show in late 1999 reunited Voivod with Snake for one gig. That October, the band partnered with Neurosis for gigs in Europe. The August 2000 live album *Voivod Lives*, recorded in 1996 at the Dutch 'Dynamo Festival' and the renowned New York CBGBs club, included a cover of Venom's 'In League With Satan', a staple of the band's live set. Digipack versions were boosted by the inclusion of two studio cuts, 'The Prow' and 'Forlorn'. Forrest then left the band to form a new Montréal-based project, E-Force.

The seven-year break was brought to a close in 2001 when Piggy and Away opted to reunite with original singer Snake. Erstwhile Metallica bassist Jason Newsted co-produced the subsequent recordings and also played bass. Newsted had first worked with Away and Piggy when he recorded rehearsal tapes with the pair and vocalist Sophia Ramos in 1998 at his own Chophouse Studio under the project name Tarrat. The renewed line-up debuted on December 30th at the Foufounes Electrique venue in Montréal, performing a set of Sex Pistols covers.

During early 2002, the Virginian heavy metal band Deceased covered 'Blower' on their *Zombie Hymns* album. Piggy D'Amour was announced as a guest on the 2002 album *Black Light District* from premier Dutch avant-garde rockers The Gathering. Confirming reports, the classic Voivod line-up of vocalist Snake, guitarist Piggy, drummer Away, and bassist Blacky came out in public for an autograph-signing session in Montréal on June 2nd. They then formed part of a three-day 'Weekend Extreme' festival celebrating 20 years of Québec metal.

With Vincent Peake of Groovy Aardvark on bass, Voivod then opened

VOIVOD discography

WAR AND PAIN, Roadrunner RR 9825 (Europe), Metal Blade 71104 (USA) (1984)

RRROOOAAARRR!!!, Noise N 0040 (Europe), Combat/Noise 88561-8103-2 (USA) (1986)

Thrashing Rage, Noise N 0050 (Europe), Combat/Noise 88561-8124-1 (USA) (1986) 12-inch vinyl picture disc

KILLING TECHNOLOGY, Noise N 0058 (Europe), Combat/Noise 88561-8147-2 (USA) (1987)

DIMENSION HÄTROSS, Noise N 0106-1 (Europe) (1988)

NOTHINGFACE, MCA DMCG 6070 (UK), MCA/Mechanic MCA-6326 (USA) (1989)

ANGEL RAT, MCA MCD 10293 (1991)

THE OUTER LIMITS, MCA MCD 10701 (1993)

NEGATRON, Hypnotic HYP 001CD (Europe), Petrock Music 60019 (USA) (1995)

PHOBOS, Hypnotic HYPCD 1057 (Europe) (1997)

KRONIK, Hypnotic HYP 1065 (Europe) (1998)

VOIVOD LIVES, Century Media CM 77282-2 (Europe), Metal Blade 3984-14338-2 (USA) (2000)

VOIVOD, Chophouse 44012-2 (2003)

KATORZ, Nuclear Blast NB 1654-2 (Europe), The End TE074 (USA) (2006)

for rock legend Dio at two Québec dates in July. However, Newsted was confirmed as bass player for the 2003 *Voivod* album, and the erstwhile Metallica subsequently became a full member of the band. With anticipation running high for the next chapter in Voivod's career, over-eager fans were duped by reported album demos leaked onto the internet in December. The four tracks were in fact culled from a 1995 demo by the British group Collapse.

In a curious turn of events, Newsted teamed up with the Ozzy Osbourne band in March, just days after the former occupant of that position – Robert Trujillo – had taken Newsted's place in Metallica. Newsted stuck to his Voivod commitments, though, as the band was announced as support act to Ozzy's June Canadian dates. The Newsted version of Voivod debuted live on April 4th 2003 at the Bourbon Street Bar And Grill in Concord, California, under their previous name of Tarrat. Following a run of high-profile US 'Ozzfest' shows, Voivod were confirmed as the opening act on Ozzy's September European tour. These gigs were cancelled, however, when the headliner was forced out to undergo foot surgery.

Metal Blade issued a 20th Anniversary Ultimate Deluxe edition of *War And Pain* in April 2004. Bonus tracks included live recordings from the band's debut June 1983 show, the *Metal Massacre V* sessions, the *Morgoth Invasion* live demo, and film footage. The band's pioneering status was further recognised when acts such as E-Force, Delirium Tremens, Incinerator, Nominon, Mausoleum, Chemikiller, Deceased, and Order From Chaos participated in a tribute album to early Voivod, issued through France's Nihilistic Holocaust label.

Away allied himself with an unlikely collaborator, donating his skills to rapper MC Necro's album *The Pre-Fix For Death*. The drummer also worked on a book of his distinctive Voivod artwork. Away and Piggy participated in the 30th anniversary show of the 1970s Montréal outfit Aut'chose in April 2005; both Voivod musicians were members of this act. Aut'chose issued the album *Chansons D'epouvante*, featuring Piggy and Away, that May.

It was reported in August that Piggy was suffering from advanced colon cancer. Voivod made an official announcement, stating: "Our good friend and guitar hero Denis D'Amour is very ill." The guitarist died on August 26th 2005 at just 45 years old, and his funeral was held in Jonquière, Québec on September 1st.

Voivod's next album, *Katorz*, was completed despite Piggy's death. Just hours before he died, the guitarist gave his band-mates access to his computer in order to retrieve guitar tracks, and the group re-entered the studios in late September to finish the record. Piggy's legacy was furthered with his other band, Aut'chose, the guitarist having worked up numerous tracks before his death.

A unique, alternative mix of the Voivod song 'The X-Stream' was included on The End Records' compilation album *Alternate Endings: A Diverse Sound Collective Featuring A Distinguished Ensemble* in March 2006. The *Katorz* album was released in July 2006 by The End Records in North America and through Nuclear Blast in Europe. A fitting tribute to Piggy, the album was well-received by fans, who will keep the Voivod name alive for years to come.

WATCHTOWER
PROG-METAL PIONEERS

WATCHTOWER PROVIDED AN INTRIGUING twist on the standard metal formula upon their arrival on the scene, and this Austin, Texas, band were renowned for their inventiveness and complexity. They pre-empted the progressive metal generation and directly influenced many leading bands of the genre.

Formed by drummer Rick Colaluca and bassist Doug Keyser in 1981, the original incarnation of Watchtower also included vocalist Jason McMaster and guitarist Billy White. McMaster had paid his dues as vocalist-bassist with Fallen Angel. The group debuted with an out-of-place track on a hardcore compilation record, *A Texas Hardcore Compilation: Cottage Cheese From The Lips Of Death*. They also recorded a proposed debut album for Rainforest Records, but the label went bust and the recordings became widely sought on the tape-trading scene.

McMaster's voice, a distinctive high-altitude siren, was highly regarded: in 1986 the man turned down offers from Pantera and (to replace Don Doty) Dark Angel. The singer guested on fellow Austin thrashers Assalant's 1987 demo *The Damage Is Done*.

McMaster then recorded Watchtower's debut album, the 1985 outing *Energetic Dissasembly*. Originally a self-financed offering put out on the Zombo imprint, the record came in a run of 3,000 LPs and 1,500 cassettes. This highly involved chunk of metal, with surgically tight riffs writhing around unorthodox compositions, soon made international waves with exemplary reviews. Importantly, Watchtower defied convention by featuring the Keyser-Colaluca rhythm section as high in the mix as the guitars.

The singer stuck with the band for five months, until his other band, Dangerous Toys, was picked up by Columbia, whereupon he quit. Keyser, meanwhile, auditioned for Metallica after the loss of Cliff Burton – reportedly making it as far as the final placings. In 1986, the bassist was briefly recruited by Marty Friedman for Cacophony, and a couple of years later by Yngwie Malmsteen when the guitarist passed through Austin.

WATCHTOWER discography

ENERGETIC DISASSEMBLY, Zombo WT 001 (USA) (1985)
CONTROL AND RESISTANCE, Noise N 0140-2 (Europe) (1989)
DEMONSTRATIONS IN CHAOS, Monster cnu (USA) (2002)

McMaster was eventually replaced by ex-Militia and Assalant singer Mike Soliz. The man's tenure was short, however, and after an April 1987 demo – *Instruments Of Random Murder* – former Hades frontman Alan Tecchio took the position. Tecchio had been tipped off about the vacancy by McMaster, who urged his fellow singer to put in a call to Keyser.

Billy White left Watchtower in autumn 1986 after a West Coast tour and hooked up with the pre-Riot Bobby Jarzombek and Pete Perez in the shortlived Chimera. White also recorded with Will Sexton's Will And The Kill for their self-titled 1988 MCA album. The guitarist then joined Don Dokken's solo group and formed The Billy White Trio in the mid 1990s.

In late 1986, Watchtower recruited guitarist Ron Jarzombek, who had previously played with San Antonio Slayer, before recording a second album, *Control And Resistance*, at Sky Trak Studios in Berlin during 1989. Post-S.A. Slayer, Jarzombek had also recorded with studio project The Happy Kitties with his brother Bobby on drums. A mostly instrumental demo was recorded with Jason McMaster guesting on 'Hammer At The Ready' and Mike Grotheus of Winterkat on 'In Mind'. *Control And Resistance* was just as good as its predecessor and benefited from wider distribution, with Watchtower drawing in new fans, many of them dumbfounded by the group's jazz-fusion-metal amalgam.

Watchtower guested for Coroner on a 1990 European tour. The band were known at one point for playing a live metallic rendition of Michael Jackson's 'Billie Jean'. Tecchio bailed out to join Non Fiction in June. Jarzombek was then put out of action for multiple hand operations, which left the guitarist unable to play for a few years. With interest in the group remaining high, German label Institute of Art Records re-released *Energetic Disassembly* in 1993.

Tecchio rejoined his original act, Hades, while post-Dangerous Toys, McMaster appeared on albums from Broken Teeth and Godzilla Motor Company. Doug Keyser and Rick Colaluca then turned up in the ranks of Retarded Elf. During mid 2002, the Monster label issued a collection of archive Watchtower demos, rehearsal tapes, and live recordings as *Demonstrations In Chaos*. 'Meltdown' – from the 1984 compilation *Cottage Cheese From The Lips Of Death* – was also included. Apparently, McMaster later enrolled into the black metal band Hell Pig, a collaboration with Slipknot drummer and Murderdolls guitarist Joey Jordison, and Killjoy of Necrophagia, Eibon, Viking Crow, and Enoch, among others. Jarzombek, McMaster, and Keyser all pursued separate projects of their own and with other artists. Although Watchtower never became one of metal's biggest names, their fans are confident that the legacy will endure.

Watchtower